May 31–June 4, 2015
Melbourne, Victoria, Australia

Association for
Computing Machinery

Advancing Computing as a Science & Profession

PODS'15

Proceedings of the 33rd ACM Symposium on
Principles of Database Systems

Sponsored by:

ACM SIGMOD

Supported by:

Microsoft, Oracle, Facebook, Google, IBM, SAP, Tableau, Twitter, Intel, RMIT University, NEC, Morgan & Claypool, and Elsevier

Association for
Computing Machinery

Advancing Computing as a Science & Profession

The Association for Computing Machinery
2 Penn Plaza, Suite 701
New York, New York 10121-0701

ISBN: 978-1-4503-2757-2 (Digital)

ISBN: 978-1-4503-3865-3 (Print)

Additional copies may be ordered prepaid from:

ACM Order Department
PO Box 30777
New York, NY 10087-0777, USA

Phone: 1-800-342-6626 (USA and Canada)
+1-212-626-0500 (Global)
Fax: +1-212-944-1318
E-mail: acmhelp@acm.org
Hours of Operation: 8:30 am – 4:30 pm ET

Printed in the USA

PODS 2015 General and Program Chairs' Welcome Message

It is our great pleasure to welcome you to the 34th ACM SIGMOD-SIGACT-SIGAI Symposium on Principles of Database Systems (PODS 2015), held in Melbourne, Victoria, Australia, on May 31 – June 4, 2015, in conjunction with the 2015 ACM SIGMOD International Conference on Management of Data. Since the first edition of the symposium in 1982, the PODS papers are distinguished by a rigorous approach to widely diverse problems in data management, often bringing to bear techniques from a variety of different areas, including computational logic, finite model theory, computational complexity, algorithm design and analysis, programming languages, and artificial intelligence. The PODS Symposia study data management challenges in a variety of application contexts, including more recently probabilistic data, streaming data, graph data, information retrieval, ontology and semantic web, and data-driven processes and systems. PODS has a tradition of being the premier international conference on the theoretical and foundational aspects of data management, and the interested reader is referred to the PODS web pages at http://www.sigmod.org/the-pods-pages/ for information on the history of this conference series.

This year's symposium continues this tradition, but in addition the PODS Executive Committee decided to broaden the scope of PODS, and to explicitly invite for submission papers providing original, substantial contributions in one or more of the following categories:

a) deep theoretical exploration of topical areas central to data management;
b) new formal frameworks that aim at providing the basis for deeper theoretical investigation of important emerging issues in data management; and
c) validation of theoretical approaches from the lens of practical applicability in data management.

This volume contains the proceedings of PODS 2015, which include an abstract for the keynote address by Michael I. Johnson (University of California, Berkeley), papers based on two invited tutorials by Todd J. Green (LogicBlox, USA) and Graham Cormode (University of Warwick, UK), and 25 contributions that were selected by the Program Committee for presentation at the symposium.

This year, PODS experimented for the first time with two submission cycles, where the first cycle allowed also for papers to be revised and resubmitted. For the first cycle, 29 papers were submitted, 4 of which were directly selected for inclusion in the proceedings, and 7 were invited for a resubmission after a revision. The quality of most of the revised papers increased substantially with respect to the first submission, and 6 of those in the end were selected for the proceedings. For the second cycle, 51 papers were submitted, 15 of which were selected, resulting in 25 papers selected overall from a total number of 80 submissions. Most of the 25 accepted papers are extended abstracts. While all submissions have been reviewed by at least four Program Committee members, they have not been formally referred. It is expected that much of the research described in these papers will be published in a more polished and detailed form in scientific journals.

With respect to the three categories mentioned above, of the 80 submissions (resp., 25 accepted papers), 47 (resp., 19) were classified by the authors in category (a), 28 (resp., 5) in category (b), and only 6 (resp., 3) in category (c). The categories are non-exclusive, and classification was not mandatory; indeed, several papers were classified in more than one category, and for 13 (resp., 3) submissions, no category was specified.

An important task for the Program Committee has been the selection of the PODS 2015 Best Paper Award. The committee selected the paper

> "*Parallel-Correctness and Transferability for Conjunctive Queries*"
> by Tom J. Ameloot, Gaetano Geck, Bas Ketsman, Frank Neven and Thomas Schwentick

On behalf of the committee, we would like to extend our sincere congratulations to the authors. Since 2008, PODS assigns the ACM PODS Alberto O. Mendelzon Test-of-Time Award to a paper or a small number of papers published in the PODS proceedings ten years prior that had the most impact over the intervening decade. This year's committee, consisting of Dan Suciu (chair), Foto Afrati, and Frank Neven, selected the following two papers. Our warmest congratulations to their authors!

"*XPath Satisfiability in the Presence of DTDs*"
by Michael Benedikt, Wenfei Fan, and Floris Geerts

"*Views and Queries: Determinacy and Rewriting*"
by Luc Segoufin and Victor Vianu.

We thank all authors who submitted papers to the symposium. We would also like to thank all members of the Program Committee and all external referees for the enormous amount of work they have done. The two submission cycles, with the revision round for the first cycle, placed an extra burden on all of them. The program committee did not meet in person, but carried out extensive discussions during the electronic program committe meeting, relying on the EasyChair System.

We thank Maurizio Lenzerini and Richard Hull, the former two PODS General Chairs, for their unfailing support. Our thanks go also to the members of the PODS Executive Committee, who advised in the selection of the Program Committee, and who gave important advise on policy issues in all phases of the conference organization. We are particularly grateful to Martin Grohe, the previous PODS PC chair, for his help and advise. Special thanks go to Marco Montali, the Proceedings and Publicity Chair of PODS 2015, and to Wim Martens, for maintaining the PODS Web pages. We are also grateful to the SIGMOD 2015 General Chair, Timos Sellis, for his excellent coordination of the overall SIGMOD/PODS 2015 conference, and his collaboration and support in all the issues requiring coordination between SIGMOD and PODS. Finally, we thank all our sponsors, in particular the ACM Special Interest Groups on Management of Data, on Algorithms and Computation Theory, and on Artificial Intelligence, for their invaluable support.

Tova Milo
PODS 2015 General Chair

Diego Calvanese
PODS 2015 Program Chair

Table of Contents

Erratum

PODS 2015 Organization

General Chair: Tova Milo (Tel Aviv University, Israel)

Program Chair: Diego Calvanese (Free University of Bozen-Bolzano, Italy)

Proceedings & Publicity Chair: Marco Montali (Free University of Bozen-Bolzano, Italy)

Program Committee Members:

Peyman Afshani (Aarhus University, Denmark)
Edith Cohen (Microsoft Research, USA)
Minos Garofalakis (Technical University of Crete, Greece)
Lukasz Golab (University of Waterloo, Canada)
Gianluigi Greco (University of Calabria, Italy)
Benny Kimelfeld (LogicBlox, USA)
Leonid Libkin (University of Edinburgh, UK)
Carsten Lutz (University of Bremen, Germany)
Ioana Manolescu (INRIA Saclay Ile-de-France, France)
Yakov Nekrich (University of Waterloo, Canada)
Dan Olteanu (University of Oxford, UK)
Jeff M. Phillips (University of Utah, USA)
Reinhard Pichler (Technical University Vienna, Austria)
Riccardo Rosati (Sapienza University of Rome, Italy)
Mantas Simkus (Technical University Vienna, Austria)
Cristina Sirangelo (ENS Cachan, France)
Jianwen Su (University of California Santa Barbara, USA)
Yannis Theodoridis (University of Pyraeus, Greece)
Stijn Vansummeren (University Libre De Bruxelles, Belgium)
Rossano Venturini (University of Pisa, Italy)
Limsoon Wong (National University of Singapore, Singapore)

Additional reviewers:

Amir Abboud
Mario Alviano
Mohammad Amiri
Alexandr Andoni
Myrto Arapinis
Arvind Arasu
David Balduzzi
Luca Becchetti
Andrea Cali
Karthekeyan Chandrasekaran
Giuseppe De Giacomo
Daniel Deutch
David Dominguez-Sal
Christos Doulkeridis
Cynthia Dwork
David Eppstein
Andrea Farruggia
Rainer Gemulla
Mina Ghashami
André Hernich
Xiaocheng Hu
Zengfeng Huang
T. S. Jayram
Hossein Jowhari
Shivaram Kalyanakrishnan
Michael Kapralov

Additional reviewers (continued):

Eamonn Keogh
Michal Kratky
Martin Lackner
Domenico Lembo
Maurizio Lenzerini
Ninghui Li
Zhenming Liu
Ashwin Machanavajjhala
Andrew McGregor
Gerome Miklau
Gonzalo Navarro
Frank Neven
Magdalena Ortiz
Rasmus Pagh
Nikos Pelekis
Jorge Perez
Andreas Pieris
Christopher Ré
Stefan Rmmele
Raef Raef
Ilya Razenshteyn
Dana Ron
Emanuel Sallinger
Swaminathan Sankararaman
Vadim Savenkov
Francesco Scarcello
Sebastian Skritek
Christian Sohler
Uri Stemmer
Xiaoming Sun
Yutian Sun
Yan Tang
Yufei Tao
Balder ten Cate
Abhradeep Guha Thakurta
Ari Trachtenberg
Suresh Venkatasubramanian
Stratis Viglas
David Woodruff
Ke Yi
Haifeng Yu
Qin Zhang

Alberto O. Mendelzon Test-of-Time Award Committee:

Foto Afrati (National Technical Universtity of Athens, Greece)
Frank Neven (Hasselt University, Belgium)
Dan Suciu (chair) (University of Washington, USA)

PODS 2015 Sponsor & Supporters

Sponsor:

ACM SIGMOD

Platinum
pporters:

Microsoft

ORACLE

Gold
pporters:

facebook

Google

IBM

SAP

tableau SOFTWARE

Silver
pporters:

intel

RMIT UNIVERSITY

Other
upporters:

NEC Laboratories America
Relentless passion for innovation

Platinum Publisher:

MORGAN & CLAYPOOL PUBLISHERS

Gold Publisher:

ELSEVIER

Computational Thinking, Inferential Thinking and "Big Data"

Michael I. Jordan
University of California, Berkeley
jordan@cs.berkeley.edu

ABSTRACT

The phenomenon of "Big Data" is creating a need for research perspectives that blend computational thinking (with its focus on, e.g., abstractions, algorithms and scalability) with inferential thinking (with its focus on, e.g., underlying populations, sampling patterns, error bars and predictions). Database researchers and statistical machine learning researchers are centrally involved in the creation of this blend, and research that incorporates perspectives from both databases and machine learning will be of particular value in the bigger picture. This is true both for methodology and for theory. I present highlights of several research initiatives that draw jointly on database and statistical foundations, including work on concurrency control and distributed inference, subsampling, time/data tradeoffs and inference/privacy tradeoffs.

Categories and Subject Descriptors

H.2 [**Database Management**]; G.3 [**Probability and Statistics**]

Keywords

Big Data, computational thinking, inferential thinking, statistical machine learning

1. BIO

Michael I. Jordan is the Pehong Chen Distinguished Professor in the Department of Electrical Engineering and Computer Science and the Department of Statistics at the University of California, Berkeley. He received his Masters in Mathematics from Arizona State University, and earned his PhD in Cognitive Science in 1985 from the University of California, San Diego. He was a professor at MIT from 1988 to 1998. His research interests bridge the computational, statistical, cognitive and biological sciences. Prof. Jordan is a member of the National Academy of Sciences, a member of the National Academy of Engineering and a member of the American Academy of Arts and Sciences. He is a Fellow of the American Association for the Advancement of Science. He has been named a Neyman Lecturer and a Medallion Lecturer by the Institute of Mathematical Statistics. He received the David E. Rumelhart Prize in 2015 and the ACM/AAAI Allen Newell Award in 2009. He is a Fellow of the AAAI, ACM, ASA, CSS, IEEE, IMS, ISBA and SIAM.

2. REFERENCES

[1] J. C. Duchi, M. I. Jordan, and M. J. Wainwright. Privacy aware learning. *Journal of the ACM*, 61(6):38, 2014.

[2] M. I. Jordan. On statistics, computation and scalability. *Bernoulli*, 19(4):1378–1390, 2013.

[3] A. Kleiner, A. Talwalkar, P. Sarkar, and M. I. Jordan. A scalable bootstrap for massive data. *Journal of the Royal Statistical Society, Series B (Statistical Methodology)*, 76(4):795–816, 2014.

[4] X. Pan, J. E. Gonzalez, S. Jegelka, T. Broderick, and M. I. Jordan. Optimistic concurrency control for distributed unsupervised learning. In *Advances in Neural Information Processing Systems 26 (NIPS 2013)*, pages 1403–1411. Curran Associates, Inc., 2013.

PODS'15, May 31–June 4, 2015, Melbourne, Victoria, Australia.

DOI: http://dx.doi.org/10.1145/2745754.2745782.

Dichotomies in the Complexity of Preferred Repairs

Ronald Fagin
IBM Research – Almaden
fagin@us.ibm.com

Benny Kimelfeld
Technion, Israel
& LogicBlox, Inc.
bennyk@cs.technion.ac.il

Phokion G. Kolaitis
UC Santa Cruz
& IBM Research – Almaden
kolaitis@cs.ucsc.edu

ABSTRACT

The framework of database repairs provides a principled approach to managing inconsistencies in databases. Informally, a repair of an inconsistence database is a consistent database that differs from the inconsistent one in a "minimal way." A fundamental problem in this framework is the repair-checking problem: given two instances, is the second a repair of the first? Here, all repairs are taken into account, and they are treated on a par with each other. There are situations, however, in which it is natural and desired to prefer one repair over another; for example, one data source is regarded to be more reliable than another, or timestamp information implies that a more recent fact should be preferred over an earlier one. Motivated by these considerations, Staworko, Chomicki and Marcinkowski introduced the framework of preferred repairs. The main characteristic of this framework is that it uses a priority relation between conflicting facts of an inconsistent database to define notions of preferred repairs. In this paper we focus on the globally-optimal repairs, in the case where the constraints are functional dependencies. Intuitively, a globally-optimal repair is a repair that cannot be improved by exchanging facts with preferred facts. In this setting, it is known that there is a fixed schema (i.e., signature and functional dependencies) where globally-optimal repair-checking is coNP-complete.

Our main result is a dichotomy in complexity: for each fixed relational signature and each fixed set of functional dependencies, the globally-optimal repair-checking problem either is solvable in polynomial time or is coNP-complete. Specifically, the problem is solvable in polynomial time if for each relation symbol in the signature, the functional dependencies are equivalent to either a single functional dependency or to a set of two key constraints; in all other cases, the globally-optimal repair-checking problem is coNP-complete. We also show that there is a polynomial-time algorithm for distinguishing between the tractable and the intractable cases. The setup of preferred repairs assumes that preferences are only between conflicting facts. In the last part of the paper, we investigate the effect of this assumption on the complexity of globally-optimal repair checking. With this assumption relaxed, we give another dichotomy theorem and another polynomial-time distinguishing algorithm. Interestingly, the two dichotomies turn out to have quite different conditions for distinguishing tractability from intractability.

PODS'15, May 31–June 4, 2015, Melbourne, Victoria, Australia.

http://dx.doi.org/10.1145/2745754.2745762.

Categories and Subject Descriptors

H.2 [**Database Management**]: Miscellaneous

General Terms

Theory, Algorithms

Keywords

Inconsistent databases; database repairs; repair checking; preferred repairs; dichotomy in complexity

1. INTRODUCTION

Managing inconsistency in databases is a long-standing problem. An inconsistent database is a database that fails to satisfy one or more integrity constraints assumed to hold. Inconsistent databases arise for different reasons and in different applications; for example, they may arise if integrity constraints are not properly enforced or when integrating data distributed over different sources. Arenas, Bertossi and Chomicki [3] introduced a principled approach to the management of inconsistency by formulating the notions of a *repair* of an inconsistent database and of the *consistent answers* of a query. Informally, a *repair* of an inconsistent database I is a consistent database J that differs from I in a "minimal" way. The standard definition of minimality refers to the *symmetric difference*, and in the case of functional dependencies this means that J is a *subset repair* (i.e., J is a subinstance of I) that is not properly contained in any consistent subinstance of I. The *consistent answers* of a query q on an inconsistent database I are given by the intersection $\bigcap\{q(J) : J \text{ is a repair of } I\}$. Thus, the inconsistencies in the database are handled at query time by considering all repairs and returning the tuples that are guaranteed to be in the result of the query on every repair.

The *repair checking* problem (i.e., given instances I and J, is J a repair of I?) and the *consistent query answering* problem (i.e., compute the consistent answers of a query q on a given instance I) are the two main algorithmic problems in the framework of database repairs. Since the publication of [3], these two problems have been extensively studied for different types of repairs and for different types of constraints. Depending on the type of repairs and the type of constraints, these problems may vary from solvable in polynomial time (e.g., the repair-checking problem for subset repairs and functional dependencies) to undecidable (e.g., the consistent query answering problem for conjunctive queries, symmetric-difference repairs, and tuple-generating dependencies [15]); see [4] for an overview of results.

In the above framework, all repairs of a given database instance are taken into account, and they are treated on a par with each other. This often results in having a large number of repairs, which, in turn, may lead to some of the high complexity results for the consistent query answering problem. There are situations, however, in which it is natural to prefer one repair over another; for example, this is the case if one source is regarded to be more reliable than another or if available timestamp information implies that a more recent fact should be preferred over an earlier fact. Motivated by these considerations, Staworko, Chomicki and Marcinkowski [14] introduced the framework of *preferred* repairs. The main characteristic of this framework is that it uses a *priority* relation between conflicting facts of an inconsistent database to define a notion of *preferred* repairs. Specifically, a *globally-optimal* repair is, intuitively, a repair that cannot be improved by exchanging facts with preferred facts. (The formal definition is in Section 2.4.)

Fagin et al. [7] have built on the concept of preferred repairs (in conjunction with the framework of *document spanners* [6]) to devise a language for declaring *inconsistency cleaning* in text information-extraction systems. They have shown there that preferred repairs capture ad-hoc cleaning operations and strategies of some prominent existing systems for text analytics [2, 5].

Unfortunately, the notion of globally-optimal repairs may incur high computational complexity; in particular, Staworko et al. [14] showed that there is a fixed schema with functional dependencies, where globally-optimal repair checking is coNP-complete. For this reason, in addition to globally-optimal repairs, they considered alternative notions of preferred repairs, namely, *Pareto-optimal* repairs and *completion-optimal* repairs, where repair checking is solvable in polynomial time.

In this paper, we aim to characterize the class of schemas for which the problem of globally-optimal repair checking is indeed intractable. We investigate in depth the computational complexity of globally-optimal repair checking when the constraints are functional dependencies. Our main result is a *dichotomy* theorem: for each fixed relational signature and each fixed set of functional dependencies, the globally-optimal repair-checking problem either is solvable in polynomial time or is coNP-complete. Specifically, we show that the problem is solvable in polynomial time if for each relation symbol R in the signature, the functional dependencies on R are equivalent to either a single functional dependency or to a set of two key constraints; in all other cases, the problem is coNP-complete. We also give a polynomial-time algorithm for distinguishing between the tractable and the intractable cases.

It should be pointed out that, to this day, only a few dichotomy theorems for database repairs have been obtained. Moreover, conjectures involving the existence of dichotomy theorems for database repairs have resisted resolution, in spite of concerted efforts by different groups of researchers. Consider, for example, the consistent query answering problem for boolean conjunctive queries under key constraints. It was conjectured in [1] that for each conjunctive query and for each set of key constraints, this problem is either solvable in polynomial time or coNP-complete. While some dichotomy theorems for special cases of conjunctive queries and key constraints have been obtained (e.g., [11, 12]), the dichotomy question for the general problem remains open to date. An explanation as to why establishing dichotomy theorems for database repairs may be a challenging task was provided by Fontaine [9], who showed that a dichotomy theorem for unions of conjunctive queries and GAV constraints implies a dichotomy theorem for the *constraint satisfaction* problem, thus resolving the celebrated Feder-Vardi conjecture [8].

We now outline the strategy we developed to establish the dichotomy theorem for the globally-optimal repair-checking problem. As is often the case with other dichotomy theorems, one first identifies certain polynomial-time solvable cases, and then the challenge is to establish that all other cases are hard, which means that they are coNP-complete in our case. The hardness side of our dichotomy theorem is established in two separate steps. The first step is to show that the globally-optimal repair-checking problem is coNP-complete for six different concrete schemas, where a *schema* is a relational signature and a set of functional dependencies. The second step is to show that for every arbitrary schema that does not fall in one of the polynomial-time cases, there is a delicate polynomial-time reduction that, intuitively, preserves consistency and inconsistency from one of the six concrete hard schemas to the schema at hand.

As mentioned earlier, globally-optimal repairs use a priority relation that imposes preferences between conflicting facts. In the last part of the paper, we relax this assumption by considering globally-optimal repairs based on *cross-conflict* priority relations, i.e., priority relations that impose preferences between facts that need not necessarily conflict (for example, one may prefer using facts from one source over another source, even if the facts are not conflicting). We establish a dichotomy theorem for globally-optimal repair checking under cross-conflict priority relations. Specifically, we show that if all functional dependencies are single key constraints or if all functional dependencies are of the form $\emptyset \rightarrow B$, for some attribute B, then the globally-optimal repair-checking problem is solvable in polynomial time; in all other cases, the globally-optimal repair-checking problem is coNP-complete. Again, we show that there is a polynomial-time algorithm for distinguishing between the tractable and the intractable cases.

The dichotomy theorems established in this paper yield a complete classification of the computational complexity of the globally-optimal repair-checking problem, when the constraints are functional dependencies. As the other semantics of preferred repairs (namely, Pareto and completion) admit polynomial-time repair checking [14], our theorems complete the picture for the complexity of preferred-repair checking. Moreover, we believe that the tools developed in this paper may be deployed to establish other complexity classifications in the study of preferred repairs. In particular, they may pave the road towards the classification of the computational complexity of the other major algorithmic problem for repairs, namely, that of consistent query answering, in the framework of preferred repairs.

2. PRELIMINARIES AND BASIC NOTIONS

In this section, we describe the formal setup for this paper, including the framework of preferred repairs.

2.1 Relational Signatures

A *relational signature* or, simply, a *signature* $\mathcal{R}$ is a finite set $\{R_1, \dots, R_n\}$ of *relation symbols* each with a designated positive integer as its *arity*, denoted $\text{arity}(R_i)$. We assume an infinite set Const of constants that are used as values in database instances. More formally, an *instance* I over a signature $\mathcal{R} = \{R_1, \dots, R_n\}$ consists of finite relations $R_i^I \subseteq \mathsf{Const}^{\text{arity}(R_i)}$, where $R_i \in \mathcal{R}$. We write $[\![R_i]\!]$ to denote the set $\{1, \dots, \text{arity}(R_i)\}$, and we refer to the members of $[\![R_i]\!]$ as *attributes* or *indices* of R_i. If I is an instance over $\mathcal{R}$ and $\mathbf{t}$ is a tuple in R_i^I, then we say that $R_i(\mathbf{t})$ is a *fact of* I. Every instance I can be identified with the set of its facts. Thus, $J \subseteq I$ means that $R_i^J \subseteq R_i^I$, for every $R_i \in \mathcal{R}$; in this case, we say that J is *subinstance* of I.

EXAMPLE 2.1. We now introduce our running example. The signature $\mathcal{R}$ consists of a ternary relation symbol

$$\textit{BookLoc}(\text{isbn}, \text{genre}, \text{lib})$$

that specifies in which libraries book copies can be found, and a binary relation symbol

$$\textit{LibLoc}(\text{lib}, \text{loc})$$

that describes library locations. Our formalism does not include the attributes names (e.g., "isbn"), but rather refers to them by positions in tuples (e.g., "isbn" is attribute 1 in *BookLoc*). Figure 1 depicts an instance I over $\mathcal{R}$. To ease following our running example, the subscript of the symbol that represents each fact is encoding the content of that fact. For example, in g_{1f1} the first "1" stands for "b1," "f" stands for "fiction," and the second "1" stands for "lib1." The reader can easily observe, without referring to Figure 1, that the facts g_{1f1} and f_{1d3} agree on the first attribute (isbn) but not on the second (genre). Such observations will be useful later on in the paper. □

2.2 FDs, Schemas and Instances

Let $\mathcal{R}$ be a signature. A *functional dependency* (*fd*) over $\mathcal{R}$ is an expression of the form $R : A \to B$, where R is a relation symbol of $\mathcal{R}$, and A and B are subsets of $[\![R]\!]$. A *schema* $\mathbf{S}$ is a pair $(\mathcal{R}, \Delta)$, where $\mathcal{R}$ is signature and Δ is a set of fds over $\mathcal{R}$. Let $\mathbf{S} = (\mathcal{R}, \Delta)$ be a schema, let I be an instance over $\mathcal{R}$, and let δ be an fd $R : A \to B$ in Δ. A pair $\{f_1, f_2\}$ of facts in I is a *δ-conflict* if f_1 and f_2 agree on (that is, have the same values for) all the attributes in A, but disagree on at least one attribute in B. We say that I *satisfies* δ, denoted $I \models \delta$, if I contains no δ-conflict. We say that fact f_1 *conflicts with* a fact f_2, or that f_1 and f_2 are *conflicting facts*, if $\{f_1, f_2\}$ is a δ-conflict for some $\delta \in \Delta$. We say that I *satisfies* Δ, denoted $I \models \Delta$, if I satisfies every fd in Δ (that is, I does not contain conflicting facts); in that case, we also say that I is a *consistent instance* (*w.r.t.* $\mathbf{S}$).

We now introduce some terminology, which will be used in the sequel. Let $(\mathcal{R}, \Delta)$ be a schema. If R is a relation symbol in $\mathcal{R}$, then we write $\Delta_{|R}$ to denote the subset of Δ that consists of all fds $R' : A \to B$ such that $R' = R$. If A is a singleton $\{a\}$, then we may write $R : a \to B$, instead of $R : A \to B$. Similarly, if $B = \{b\}$, then we may write $R : A \to b$, and if $A = \{a\}$ and $B = \{b\}$, then we may write $R : a \to b$. Moreover, if R is clear from the context, then we may omit R from $R : A \to B$ and write just $A \to B$. We will often consider the following special cases of fds.

- The fd $R : A \to B$ is *trivial* if $B \subseteq A$. Note that a trivial fd is satisfied by every instance.
- The fd $R : A \to B$ is a *key constraint* if $B = [\![R]\!]$. We may sometimes refer to a key constraint as simply a *key*.

Let $\mathbf{S} = (\mathcal{R}, \Delta)$ be a schema. The *closure* Δ^+ of Δ is the set of all fds that are logically implied by Δ. Note that Δ^+ contains every fd in Δ and every trivial fd. As an example, if $\mathcal{R}$ contains a ternary relation symbol R and Δ consists of the fds $R : 1 \to 2$ and $R : 2 \to 3$, then Δ^+ contains, among others, the fds $R : 1 \to 3$, $R : \{1, 2\} \to 3$, and $R : 3 \to 3$. Let R be a relation symbol of $\mathcal{R}$, and let A be a subset of $[\![R]\!]$. The *closure of A under Δ and R*, denoted $[\![R.A^{\Delta}]\!]$, is the set of all indices i such that $R : A \to i$ is in Δ^+. Note that for every set B of indices, the fd $R : A \to B$ is in Δ^+ if and only if $B \subseteq [\![R.A^{\Delta}]\!]$.

Two sets Δ_1 and Δ_2 of fds over a signature $\mathcal{R}$ are *equivalent* if $\Delta_1^+ = \Delta_2^+$. In other words, Δ_1 and Δ_2 are equivalent if the schemas $(\mathcal{R}, \Delta_1)$ and $(\mathcal{R}, \Delta_2)$ have the same set of consistent instances.

EXAMPLE 2.2. We expand on our running example. Consider the schema $\mathbf{S} = (\mathcal{R}, \Delta)$, where $\mathcal{R}$ was defined in Example 2.1 and Δ consists of the following fds:

$$\delta_1 \stackrel{\text{def}}{=} \textit{BookLoc} : 1 \to 2$$

$$\delta_2 \stackrel{\text{def}}{=} \textit{LibLoc} : 1 \to 2$$

$$\delta_3 \stackrel{\text{def}}{=} \textit{LibLoc} : 2 \to 1$$

In words, δ_1 states that in *BookLoc* a book's isbn determines its genre (i.e., two tuples with the same isbn must agree on the genre), δ_2 states that in *LibLoc* a library determines the location, and δ_3 states that every location has one library. The instance I of Figure 1 violates Δ; for example, $\{g_{\mathsf{1f1}}, f_{\mathsf{1d3}}\}$ is a δ_1-conflict, $\{d_{\mathsf{1e}}, e_{\mathsf{1b}}\}$ is a δ_2-conflict, and $\{d_{\mathsf{1a}}, g_{\mathsf{2a}}\}$ is a δ_3-conflict. Note also that δ_2 and δ_3 are key constraints. Moreover, we have that $\Delta_{|\textit{BookLoc}} = \{1 \to 2\}$ and $\Delta_{|\textit{LibLoc}} = \{1 \to 2, 2 \to 1\}$. An example of an fd in Δ^+ that is not in Δ is $\textit{BookLoc} : \{1, 3\} \to \{1, 2\}$. Finally, note that $[\![\textit{BookLoc}.\{1\}^{\Delta}]\!] = \{1, 2\}$ and $[\![\textit{BookLoc}.\{1, 3\}^{\Delta}]\!] = \{1, 2, 3\}$. □

2.3 Prioritizing Instances

Let $\mathcal{R}$ be a signature. Assume that I is an instance over $\mathcal{R}$, and $\succ$ is a binary relation on the facts of I. A *cycle* in $\succ$ is a sequence $f_1, \dots, f_k$ of facts in I such that $f_i \succ f_{i+1}$ holds for all $i = 1, \dots, k-1$, and $f_k \succ f_1$. We say that $\succ$ is *acyclic* if there are no cycles in $\succ$. In particular, we cannot have $f \succ f$ if $\succ$ is acyclic. A *prioritizing instance* over $\mathcal{R}$ is a pair $(I, \succ)$, where I is an instance over $\mathcal{R}$ and $\succ$ is an acyclic binary relation on the facts of I. We say that the relation $\succ$ is a *priority* on I. Thus, the statement $f \succ g$ should be interpreted as "the fact f has higher priority than the fact g."

Let $\mathbf{S} = (\mathcal{R}, \Delta)$ be a schema. An *inconsistent prioritizing instance* over $\mathbf{S}$ is a prioritizing instance $(I, \succ)$ over $\mathcal{R}$ such that I is inconsistent w.r.t.$\mathbf{S}$, and such that if f and g are facts of I with $f \succ g$, then f and g are conflicting facts. This

	BookLoc		
	isbn	genre	lib
g_{1f1}	b1	fiction	lib1
g_{1f2}	b1	fiction	lib2
f_{1d3}	b1	drama	lib3
f_{2p1}	b2	poetry	lib1
h_{3h2}	b3	horror	lib2

	LibLoc	
	lib	loc
d_{1a}	lib1	almaden
d_{1e}	lib1	edenvale
g_{2a}	lib2	almaden
f_{2b}	lib2	bascom
f_{3a}	lib3	almaden
f_{3c}	lib3	cambrian
e_{1b}	lib1	bascom
e_{3b}	lib3	bascom

Figure 1: Inconsistent database of the running example

requirement implies that, whenever $f \succ g$, it is necessarily the case that f and g are in the same relation of I, since all constraints in Δ are functional dependencies (hence, f and g violate Δ only if they belong to the same relation).

EXAMPLE 2.3. Recall the schema $\mathbf{S}$ of our running example. Consider the prioritizing instance $(I, \succ)$ consisting of the instance I of Figure 1 and the priority relation $\succ$ that is defined as follows:

- $g_y \succ f_x$ for all conflicting f_x and g_y;
- $e_y \succ d_x$ for all conflicting d_x and e_y.

As an example, $g_{1f1} \succ f_{1d3}$ and $e_{1b} \succ d_{1a}$.

Observe that $\succ$ is acyclic, as is required. □

2.4 Preferred Repairs

Let $\mathbf{S} = (\mathcal{R}, \Delta)$ be a schema, and let I be an inconsistent instance w.r.t. $\mathbf{S}$. Following Arenas et al. [3], we define a *repair* of I to be a maximal consistent subinstance J of I. That is, we cannot add any fact in I to J without violating consistency. Now let $(I, \succ)$ be an inconsistent prioritizing instance over $\mathbf{S}$. The priority relation $\succ$ that gives preferences among the tuples of I can be extended to a priority relation that gives preferences among the consistent subinstances of I. Staworko et al. [14] considered three such extensions, each of which gives a different notion of *preferred* repairs, namely, the notion of a *globally optimal* repair, a *Pareto-optimal* repair, and a *completion-optimal* repair. As mentioned in the Introduction, the repair-checking problem for the last two notions is in PTIME, while the repair-checking problem for globally-optimal repairs can be coNP-complete. Here, we give the precise definition of the notion of a *globally-optimal* repair, which is the focus of this paper. We also define the notion of a *Pareto-optimal* repair that we will use later in the paper.

DEFINITION 2.4. Let $(I, \succ)$ be an inconsistent prioritizing instance over a schema $\mathbf{S} = (\mathcal{R}, \Delta)$. Let J and J' be two consistent subinstances of I. We say that J is a *global improvement* of J' if $J \neq J'$, and for every fact $f' \in J' \setminus J$ there exists a fact $f \in J \setminus J'$ such that $f \succ f'$. We say that J is a *Pareto improvement* of J' is there exists a fact $f \in J \setminus J'$, such that $f \succ f'$ for all facts $f' \in J' \setminus J$. We say that J is a *globally-optimal* repair of I if J does not have a global improvement. Similarly, J is a *Pareto-optimal* repair of I if J does not have a Pareto improvement. □

Note that every globally-optimal repair is Pareto-optimal; as we shall see shortly, the converse is not true. It is easy to see that every globally-optimal or Pareto-optimal repair is indeed a repair, as defined earlier.

One can also show that a consistent subinstance J is a globally-optimal repair of I if and only if no non-empty subset X of J can be replaced with a subset Y of $I \setminus J$, so that the subinstance $(J \setminus X) \cup Y$ is consistent and for every fact f' in X, there is a fact f in Y such that $f \succ f'$.

EXAMPLE 2.5. Let $(I, \succ)$ be the prioritizing instance of our running example. Consider the following subinstances of I.

- $J_1 \stackrel{\text{def}}{=} \{g_{1f1}, g_{1f2}, f_{2p1}, h_{3h2}, d_{1e}, f_{2b}, f_{3a}\}$
- $J_2 \stackrel{\text{def}}{=} \{g_{1f1}, g_{1f2}, f_{2p1}, h_{3h2}, d_{1e}, g_{2a}, e_{3b}\}$
- $J_3 \stackrel{\text{def}}{=} \{g_{1f1}, g_{1f2}, f_{2p1}, h_{3h2}, d_{1e}, f_{2b}, f_{3a}\}$
- $J_4 \stackrel{\text{def}}{=} \{g_{1f1}, g_{1f2}, f_{2p1}, h_{3h2}, e_{1b}, g_{2a}, f_{3c}\}$

Each J_i is consistent, and, in fact, a repair. Observe that $J_1 \setminus J_2 = \{f_{2b}, f_{3a}\}$ and $J_2 \setminus J_1 = \{g_{2a}, e_{3b}\}$; since $g_{2a} \succ f_{2b}$ and $g_{2a} \succ f_{3a}$, we get that J_2 is a Pareto (and global) improvement of J_1. The reader can verify that, as a matter of fact, J_2 is a globally-optimal (hence, Pareto-optimal) repair of I. The reader can also verify that J_3 does not have any Pareto improvement; in particular, J_4 is not a Pareto improvement of J_3 since $J_3 \setminus J_4 = \{d_{1e}, f_{2b}, f_{3a}\}$ and $J_4 \setminus J_3 = \{e_{1b}, g_{2a}, f_{3c}\}$, and no fact f in $J_4 \setminus J_3$ satisfies all of $f \succ d_{1e}$, $f \succ f_{2b}$ and $f \succ f_{3a}$. But J_4 is a global improvement of J_3, since $e_{1b} \succ d_{1e}$, $g_{2a} \succ f_{2b}$, and $g_{2a} \succ f_{3a}$. Hence, although J_3 is a Pareto-optimal repair, it is not a globally-optimal repair. □

3. MAIN RESULT

Our main result is about the complexity of preferred repair checking; this is the problem of deciding, given a subinstance of an inconsistent prioritized instance, whether the subinstance is a prioritized (i.e., Pareto-optimal or globally-optimal) repair. Staworko et al. [14] observed that, for every schema, this problem admits a polynomial-time solution under the Pareto semantics, and is in coNP under the global semantics. They also proved that for a specific schema with four fds, globally-optimal repair checking is coNP-complete. Our main result yields a complete classification of the complexity of globally-optimal repair checking.

THEOREM 3.1. *Let $\mathbf{S} = (\mathcal{R}, \Delta)$ be a schema. Globally-optimal repair checking can be solved in polynomial time if for every relation symbol $R \in \mathcal{R}$ at least one of the following holds.*

1. *$\Delta_{|R}$ is equivalent to a single fd.*
2. *$\Delta_{|R}$ is equivalent to a set of two key constraints.*

In every other case, globally-optimal repair checking is coNP-complete.

In the next two sections we discuss the proof of this theorem. In Section 6 we will show that one can test in polynomial time whether a given schema belongs to the tractable or the hard the side of the theorem. Before that, we give a few examples of applying the theorem.

EXAMPLE 3.2. In our running example, $\Delta_{|BookLoc}$ consists of a single fd, and $\Delta_{|LibLoc}$ is a pair of key constraints; hence, globally-optimal repair checking is solvable in polynomial time for this schema. □

EXAMPLE 3.3. Consider the schema $\mathbf{S} = (\mathcal{R}, \Delta)$ with $\mathcal{R}$ consisting of two ternary relation symbols R and S and a quaternary relation symbol T, and Δ consisting of the following fds.

$$R : 1 \to 2 \quad T : 1 \to \{2,3,4\} \quad T : \{2,3\} \to 1$$

The schema **S** satisfies the condition of Theorem 3.1, for the following reasons:

- $\Delta_{|R}$ consists of a single fd;
- $\Delta_{|S}$ is empty, and hence, is equivalent to a single (trivial) fd such as $S : \emptyset \to \emptyset$;
- although $\Delta_{|T}$ is neither a single fd nor a pair of keys, it is equivalent to $\{T : 1 \to \{1,2,3,4\}, T : \{2,3\} \to \{1,2,3,4\}\}$, which is a pair of keys.

Therefore, globally-optimal repair checking is solvable in polynomial time for **S**. □

EXAMPLE 3.4. Each of the following six schemas violates the condition of Theorem 3.1, and so, is such that the globally-optimal repair-checking problem is coNP-complete. These schemas have the form $\mathbf{S}^i = (\mathcal{R}^i, \Delta^i)$ for $i = 1, \ldots, 6$, where $\mathcal{R}^i$ consists of a single ternary relation symbol R^i. The Δ^i are defined as follows.

1. $\Delta^1 = \{\{1,2\} \to 3, \{1,3\} \to 2, \{2,3\} \to 1\}$
2. $\Delta^2 = \{1 \to 2, 2 \to 1\}$
3. $\Delta^3 = \{\{1,2\} \to 3, 3 \to 2\}$
4. $\Delta^4 = \{1 \to 2, 2 \to 3\}$
5. $\Delta^5 = \{1 \to 3, 2 \to 3\}$
6. $\Delta^6 = \{\emptyset \to 1, 2 \to 3\}$

As we will show in Section 5, these specific schemas play an important role in the proof of the hardness part of Theorem 3.1. □

3.1 Proof Strategy

A straightforward observation is that, to prove Theorem 3.1, it suffices to consider schemas with a single relation, since each of the constraints we consider is an fd, hence applied to a single relation, and preferences are applied to conflicting facts, hence facts from the same relation. (In Section 7 we study the impact of avoiding the restriction of priorities to conflicting facts.) Formally, we have the following proposition.

PROPOSITION 3.5. *Let $\mathbf{S} = (\mathcal{R}, \Delta)$ be a schema. The following are equivalent.*

1. *Globally-optimal repair checking is solvable in polynomial time for* **S**.
2. *For every relation symbol $R \in \mathcal{R}$, globally-optimal repair checking is solvable in polynomial time for the schema $\{\{R\}, \Delta_{|R}\}$.*

Moreover, the following are equivalent as well.

1. *Globally-optimal repair checking is coNP-complete for the schema* **S**.
2. *For at least one relation symbol $R \in \mathcal{R}$, globally-optimal repair checking is coNP-complete for the schema $\mathbf{S}_R = \{\{R\}, \Delta_{|R}\}$.*

Hence, our proof (discussed in the next two sections) is restricted to schemas with a single relation symbol.

4. ALGORITHMS FOR THE TRACTABLE SCHEMAS

In this section, we fix a schema $\mathbf{S} = (\mathcal{R}, \Delta)$, such that $\mathcal{R}$ consists of a single relation symbol R. We will prove that globally-optimal repair checking is solvable in polynomial time if Δ (which is the same as $\Delta_{|R}$) satisfies one of the two conditions of Theorem 3.1. We begin with the first condition.

4.1 Single FD

The case of a single FD seems, on the face of it, to have been resolved by Staworko et al. [14]. Specifically, their Proposition 10 (iii) states that global and completion optimality coincide in the case of a single FD, and their Corollary 4 states that completion optimality can be tested in polynomial time. Hence, by combining these two results it follows that in the case of a single FD, global optimality can be tested in polynomial time. Unfortunately, Proposition 10 (iii) in [14] is incorrect, as we have established in private communication with the authors of [14]. In this section we give a proof of the polynomial-time upper bound for the case of a single FD .

We assume that Δ is the singleton $\{A \to B\}$. Consider the input $(I, \succ)$ and J for globally-optimal repair checking. Since J is a repair, by definition J is a maximal consistent subset of I, and so $J \cup \{f\}$ is inconsistent for every fact $f \in I \setminus J$. Two facts f and g in I are said to *agree* on A (respectively, B) if f and g have the same value in every position in A (respectively, B).

Let f and g be two facts in I, such that

1. $f \in J$,
2. f and g agree on A, and
3. f and g disagree in B.

Note that $g \notin J$ since we assume that J is consistent. We denote by $J[f \leftrightarrow g]$ the instance that is obtained from J by removing all the facts in I that agree with f on A and B, and adding to J all the facts that agree with g on A and B.

EXAMPLE 4.1. Continuing with our running example, we now restrict our attention to *BookLoc* and ignore *LibLoc*. So now we have a single fd, namely $1 \to 2$. Consider the subinstances $J = \{g_{1f1}, g_{1f2}, f_{2p1}\}$ and $J' = \{f_{1d3}, f_{2p1}\}$ (of the instance I in Figure 1). Observe that g_{1f1} and f_{1d3} agree on the first attribute (isbn) but disagree on the second (genre). Then $J[g_{1f1} \leftrightarrow f_{1d3}] = J'$ and $J'[f_{1d3} \leftrightarrow g_{1f1}] = J$. In particular, observe that $J[g_{1f1} \leftrightarrow f_{1d3}]$ misses both g_{1f1} and g_{1f2}, and that $J'[f_{1d3} \leftrightarrow g_{1f1}]$ includes both g_{1f1} and g_{1f2}. □

The following are straightforward observations.

Algorithm GRepCheck1FD(I, J)

```
for all conflicting facts f ∈ J and g ∈ I \ J do
    if J[f ↔ g] is a global improvement of J then
        return false
    end if
end for
return true
```

Figure 2: Globally-optimal repair checking in the case where the schema consists of a single relation symbol R and a single fd $A \to B$

1. $J[f \leftrightarrow g]$ is consistent (that is, $A \to B$ is satisfied).
2. Whether $J[f \leftrightarrow g]$ is a global improvement of J can be tested in polynomial time.

Consequently, to show that J is not a globally-optimal repair, it is sufficient to find some f and g as above, such that $J[f \leftrightarrow g]$ is a global improvement of J. The next lemma shows that this procedure is also necessary to show that J is not a globally-optimal repair.

LEMMA 4.2. *If J has a global improvement, then there are facts f and g (as defined above) such that $J[f \leftrightarrow g]$ is a global improvement of J.*

PROOF. Suppose that J' is a global improvement of J. Let f be a fact in $J \setminus J'$. Note that such f indeed exists, since we assumed J cannot be extended without violating Δ. Let $g \in J'$ be a fact such that $g \succ f$. Then f and g are as defined above, that is, f and g agree on A but disagree on B. So, it remains to prove that $J[f \leftrightarrow g]$ is a global improvement of J. In other words, we need to show that if $\hat{f}$ is a fact in J that agrees with f on A (hence, on B), then there is a fact $\hat{g}$ in I that agrees with g on A and B (hence, $\hat{g} \in J[f \leftrightarrow g]$), such that $\hat{g} \succ \hat{f}$. So, let $\hat{f}$ be such a fact. Since $\hat{f}$ disagrees with g on B, it must be the case that $\hat{f}$ is not in J' (since J' contains g, and J' is consistent). Therefore, $J' \setminus J$ contains a fact g' such that $g' \succ \hat{f}$. Let $\hat{g}$ be such a fact g'. Then $\hat{g}$ and $\hat{f}$ agree on A, and so $\hat{g}$ and g agree on A. And since J' contains both g and $\hat{g}$, we have that g and $\hat{g}$ agree on B. It follows that $\hat{g}$ is as claimed. □

Consequently, we conclude that the simple (and obviously polynomial-time) algorithm GRepCheck1FD of Figure 2 solves globally-optimal repair checking in the case of this section.

4.2 Two Key Constraints

We now consider the case where Δ is equivalent to two key constraints, which we shall refer to as simply "two keys." For presentation sake, we give the algorithm for the specific case where R is binary and $\Delta = \{1 \to 2, 2 \to 1\}$. The generalization to the general case of two keys will be straightforward, as we shall discuss. For the inputs $(I, \succ)$ and J, the idea is as follows. To improve J, we try to replace a fact $R(a_1, a_2)$ in J with a preferred fact in $I \setminus J$, say $R(a_1', a_2)$; if we succeed (i.e., the resulting instance is consistent), then the replacement results in a Pareto (and in particular global) improvement, and we are done. Otherwise, $R(a_1', a_2)$ conflicts with a fact

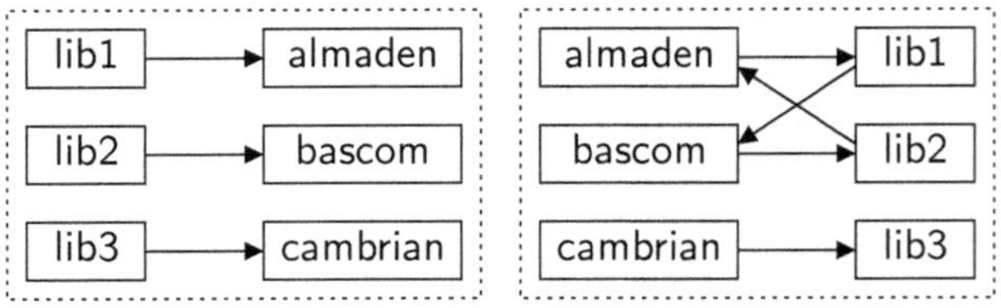

Figure 3: The graphs G_J^{12} (left) and G_J^{21} (right)

$R(a_1', a_2')$ in J. ($R(a_1', a_2)$ cannot conflict with a fact that has a_2 as the second attribute, since only $R(a_1, a_2)$ has this property in J.) So, we also need to replace $R(a_1', a_2')$ with a preferred fact $R(a_1'', a_2')$. We continue with this process and, assuming that J does not have a Pareto improvement (which can be tested in polynomial time), we eventually succeed (find a global improvement) in this process if we close a cycle (that is, each fact we remove is improved by a fact we added). Next, we formalize this idea.

Consider the given inputs $(I, \succ)$ and J. For $i = 1, 2$, denote by $[J]_i$ the set of constants that occur in the ith component of J. Denote by G_J^{12} the bipartite directed graph that has $[J]_1$ on its left side, $[J]_2$ on its right side, and the following edges:

- $a_1 \to a_2$ for every $R(a_1, a_2) \in J$;
- $a_1' \leftarrow a_2$ for every $R(a_1', a_2) \in I \setminus J$ such that $R(a_1', a_2) \succ R(a_1, a_2)$ for some $R(a_1, a_2) \in J$.

Similarly, denote by G_J^{21} the bipartite directed graph that has $[J]_2$ on its left side, $[J]_1$ on its right side (that is, we swap between the two sides of G^{12}), and the following edges:

- $a_2 \to a_1$ for every $R(a_1, a_2) \in J$;
- $a_2' \leftarrow a_1$ for every $R(a_1, a_2') \in I \setminus J$ such that $R(a_1, a_2') \succ R(a_1, a_2)$ for some $R(a_1, a_2) \in J$.

EXAMPLE 4.3. Continuing with our running example, we now restrict to *LibLoc* and ignore *BookLoc*. So now we have the fds $1 \to 2$ and $2 \to 1$. Consider the subinstance $J = \{d_{1a}, f_{2b}, f_{3c}\}$ (of the instance I in Figure 1). Figure 3 depicts the graphs G_J^{12} and G_J^{21}. Observe that G_J^{12} does not have right-to-left edges (since no relevant priorities exist), and G_J^{21} has two such edges. The edge from lib2 to almaden is due to $g_{2a} \succ f_{2b}$, and the edge from lib1 to bascom is due to $e_{1b} \succ d_{1a}$. □

Our algorithm is due to the following characterization of (not) being a globally-optimal repair.

LEMMA 4.4. *Assume that J is a consistent subinstance. Then J has a global improvement if and only if at least one of the following conditions is true:*

1. *J has a Pareto improvement;*
2. *G_J^{12} has a cycle;*
3. *G_J^{21} has a cycle.*

PROOF. We prove each direction separately.

The "if" direction. Since a Pareto improvement is also a global one, we get that if the first condition is true then

J has a global improvement. So, suppose that the second condition is true, that is, G_J^{12} has a cycle. Let $a_1^1 \to a_2^1 \to a_1^2 \to \cdots \to a_1^n$ be a simple cycle in G_J^{12}, where each a_1^i is in $[J]_1$, each a_2^i is in $[J]_2$, and $a_1^1 = a_1^n$. Let F be the set of facts $R(a_1^i, a_2^i)$ for $i = 1, \dots, n-1$, and let F' be the set of facts $R(a_1^{i+1}, a_2^i)$ for $i = 1, \dots, n-1$. We will prove that $(J \setminus F) \cup F'$ is a global improvement of J.

Observe that $(J \setminus F) \cup F'$ satisfies Δ, since both J and F' satisfy Δ, and $(J \setminus F)$ and F' do not share any left component or any right component. From the definition of G_J^{12} it follows that F' is a subset of $I \setminus J$. It also follows from the definition of G_J^{12} that each $R(a_1^{i+1}, a_2^i)$ is a fact in I, and there exists some fact $R(a_1', a_2^i) \in J$ such that $R(a_1^{i+1}, a_2^i) \succ R(a_1', a_2^i)$; but then, since also $R(a_1^i, a_2^i) \in J$ and J satisfies $2 \to 1$, it follows that a_1' is necessarily a_1^i. We conclude that every fact $f \in F$ has a fact $f' \in F'$ such that $f' \succ f$. Hence, $(J \setminus F) \cup F'$ is a global improvement of J, as claimed.

The proof that the third condition implies that J has a global improvement is symmetric to that of the second condition.

The "only if" direction. We assume that J has a global improvement, and we need to prove that at least one of the three conditions holds true. So assume that J does not have a Pareto improvement; we will prove that at least one of G_J^{12} and G_J^{21} has a cycle.

Suppose that $(J \setminus F) \cup F'$ is a global improvement of J. Then F is necessarily nonempty, since otherwise $(J \setminus F) \cup F'$ is a Pareto improvement of J. Let $R(a_1^1, a_2^1)$ be a fact in F. Then there exists a fact $f_1' \in F'$ such that $f_1' \succ R(a_1^1, a_2^1)$, so f_1' conflicts with $R(a_1^1, a_2^1)$. We first consider the case where $f_1' = R(a_1^2, a_2^1)$ for some a_1^2. We will construct an infinite path in G_J^{12}, starting with $a_1^1 \to a_2^1 \to a_1^2$, where the edges alternate between corresponding to facts in F and facts in F'. If J does not contain any fact with a_1^2 in its first component, then $(J \setminus \{R(a_1^1, a_2^1)\}) \cup \{f_1'\}$ is a Pareto improvement of J, in contradiction to our assumption. So, let $R(a_1^2, a_2^2) \in J$ be such a fact. Then $R(a_1^2, a_2^2)$ cannot be in $J \setminus F$, since it conflicts with a member of F'; hence, $R(a_1^2, a_2^2)$ is in F. We claim that $f_1' \not\succ R(a_1^2, a_2^2)$. Indeed, otherwise we could obtain a Pareto improvement of J by removing $R(a_1^1, a_2^1)$ and $R(a_1^2, a_2^2)$ and adding $f_1' = R(a_1^2, a_2^1)$. Since $R(a_1^2, a_2^2)$ is in F, it follows that F' contains a fact f_2' such that $f_2' \succ R(a_1^2, a_2^2)$. From what we showed earlier, we know that $f_2' \neq f_1'$. Observe that f_2' conflicts with $R(a_1^2, a_2^2)$, but it cannot have a_1^2 as its first component, since it would then conflict with f_1'; hence, f_2' conflicts with $R(a_1^2, a_2^2)$ on the second component, and so is of the form $R(a_1^3, a_2^2)$. So we add $a_1^2 \to a_2^2 \to a_1^3$ to our path. We can then continue to do so indefinitely. In particular, G_J^{12} contains a cycle since G_J^{12} is finite.

When we consider the case where f_1' is of the form $R(a_1^1, a_2^2)$ for some a_2^2, we similarly get to the conclusion that G_J^{21} contains cycle. This concludes our proof. □

As we said above, the proof extends straightforwardly to the case where Δ is a set of two keys on a relation. In particular, suppose that $\Delta = \{A_1 \to [\![R]\!], A_2 \to [\![R]\!]\}$. We assume that $A_1 \not\subseteq A_2$ and $A_2 \not\subseteq A_1$, since otherwise one of the fds can be removed (and then we are in the previous case). For a fact f over R, we denote by $f[A_i]$, where $i \in \{1, 2\}$, the tuple that is obtained from f by taking the components in the positions of A_i in some predefined order. Moreover, in the graph G_J^{12} we now have the following edges:

- $f[A_1] \to f[A_2]$ for every fact $f \in J$;
- $f'[A_1] \leftarrow f'[A_2]$ for every fact $f' \in I \setminus J$ such that $f[A_2] = f'[A_2]$ for some $f \in J$ such that $f' \succ f$.

We similarly extend the definition of G_J^{21}. Observe that in every edge of G_J^{12} and G_J^{21}, the two endpoints agree on all the attributes of $A_1 \cap A_2$.

Consequently, the algorithm GRepCheck2Keys of Figure 4 solves globally-optimal repair checking in the case of this section. This algorithm terminates in polynomial time, since both having a Pareto improvement and graph acyclicity can be tested in polynomial time.

Algorithm GRepCheck2Keys(I, J)

```
if J has a Pareto improvement then
    return false
end if
if both G_J^12 and G_J^21 are acyclic then
    return true
else
    return false
end if
```

Figure 4: Globally-optimal repair checking in the case where the schema consists of a single relation symbol R and the key constraints $A_1 \to [\![R]\!]$ and $A_2 \to [\![R]\!]$

5. PROOF STRATEGY FOR HARDNESS

In this section, we describe our proof of the hardness side of Theorem 3.1, namely, if the condition is violated then globally-optimal repair checking is coNP-complete.

5.1 General Strategy

Our proof strategy consists of two steps, similarly to the proof for the dichotomy of the complexity in deletion propagation by Kimelfeld [10].

In the first step, we consider several specific schemas, and prove that globally-optimal repair checking is coNP-complete for these schemas. The specific schemas we consider are precisely those of Example 3.4.

LEMMA 5.1. *For each of the six schemas $\mathbf{S}^1, \dots, \mathbf{S}^6$ of Example 3.4, globally-optimal repair checking is coNP-complete.*

Next, we consider an arbitrary schema $\mathbf{S}$ that violates the condition of Theorem 3.1 and define a reduction from globally-optimal repair checking for one of the schemas of Example 3.4 to globally-optimal repair checking for $\mathbf{S}$. The specific choice of the schema $\mathbf{S}^i$ from Example 3.4 depends on a case analysis that we describe later in this section. All of our reductions follow a general pattern that we describe next.

Suppose that we want to reduce globally-optimal repair checking in $\mathbf{S}^i$ (which is one of the six schemas in Example 3.4) to globally-optimal repair checking in $\mathbf{S}$ (which is an arbitrary schema that violates the condition of Theorem 3.1). Recall that $\mathbf{S}^i$ consists of a single relation symbol

R^i. Also recall from Proposition 3.5 that we can assume that $\mathbf{S}$ consists of a single relation symbol, say R. We begin with the input $(I^i, \succ^i)$ and J^i for globally-optimal repair checking under $\mathbf{S}^i$, and construct an input $(I, \succ)$ and J for $\mathbf{S}$. The construction is done by defining a function Π that takes as input fact f^i from I^i and constructs, in constant time, a fact $\Pi(f^i)$ over $\mathbf{S}$. For a subinstance K^i of I^i we define $\Pi(K^i) = \{\Pi(f^i) \mid f^i \in K^i\}$. Hence, $\Pi(K^i)$ is an instance over $\{R\}$. Every reduction uses a different definition of Π, and in each reduction we prove that Π has the following key properties.

1. Π is injective over the facts of I^i; that is, for all facts f^i and g^i of I^i, if $\Pi(f^i) = \Pi(g^i)$ then $f^i = g^i$. It thus follows that Π is injective on the subinstances of I^i; that is, for all instances $K^i, L^i \subseteq I^i$, if $\Pi(K^i) = \Pi(L^i)$ then $K^i = L^i$.
2. Π preserves consistency and inconsistency; that is, for every instance K^i over $\mathcal{R}^i$ it holds that K^i satisfies Δ^i if and only if $\Pi(K^i)$ satisfies Δ.

With Properties 1 and 2 shown, the definition of the input for globally-optimal repair checking over $\mathbf{S}$ is straightforward:

- $I \overset{\text{def}}{=} \Pi(I^i)$.
- $\succ \overset{\text{def}}{=} \{(\Pi(f^i), \Pi(g^i)) \mid f^i, g^i \in I^i \ \wedge \ f^i \succ^i g^i\}$.
- $J \overset{\text{def}}{=} \Pi(J^i)$.

The construction is correct due to the following.

1. A repair $K^i \subseteq I^i$ is a global improvement of J^i for $(I^i, \succ^i)$ if and only if $\Pi(K^i)$ is a global improvement of J for $(I, \succ)$.
2. J^i is a globally-optimal repair of $(I^i, \succ^i)$ if and only if J is a globally-optimal repair of $(I, \succ)$.

In summary, for each reduction it suffices to define Π and prove that the two key properties are satisfied.

5.2 Case Branching

In this section, we fix a schema $\mathbf{S} = (\mathcal{R}, \Delta)$ that violates the condition of Theorem 3.1 (that is, Δ is equivalent to neither a single fd nor two keys). We assume that $\mathcal{R}$ consists of a single relation symbol R. We will describe the different cases that our proof of hardness considers. We begin with the first case.

Case 1: Three or more keys. In this case, $\Delta = \{A_1 \to [\![R]\!], \dots, A_k \to [\![R]\!]\}$ for $k \geq 3$, and $A_i \not\subseteq A_j$ for all $i \neq j$ (otherwise one of the fds can be removed). Here we show a reduction from globally-optimal repair checking for the schema $\mathbf{S}^1$ of Example 3.4.

For the remaining cases, we need some notation. Let $A \subseteq [\![R]\!]$ be a set of indices. We say that A is a *nontrivial determiner* if $A \subsetneq [\![R.A^\Delta]\!]$, and a *non-redundant determiner* if there is no set $B \subsetneq A$ such that $([\![R.A^\Delta]\!] \setminus A) \subseteq [\![R.B^\Delta]\!]$. In words, A is a non-redundant determiner if the set of attributes not in A that A determines is not already determined by any proper subset of A. Observe that a non-redundant determiner is necessarily nontrivial, but a nontrivial determiner is not necessarily non-redundant. We say that A is a *minimal determiner* if A is a nontrivial determiner and A does not strictly contain any nontrivial determiner. Observe that a minimal determiner is also non-redundant, but a non-redundant determiner is not necessarily minimal.

Suppose that $\mathbf{S}$ is not in Case 1 (in addition to violating the conditions of Theorem 3.1). We fix a minimal determiner $A \subseteq [\![R]\!]$, such that A is not a key. Note that such A exists since we assume that Δ is not equivalent to any set of key constraints. Observe that A may be the empty set. Since Δ is not equivalent to any single fd, there is at least one non-redundant determiner that is different from A; we select such a non-redundant determiner B that is minimal w.r.t. set containment. Observe that B can be a key, and B may contain A.

We will use the following notation:

- $A^+ \overset{\text{def}}{=} [\![R.A^\Delta]\!]$ and $\hat{A} \overset{\text{def}}{=} A^+ \setminus A$
- $B^+ \overset{\text{def}}{=} [\![R.B^\Delta]\!]$ and $\hat{B} \overset{\text{def}}{=} B^+ \setminus B$

Cases 2–7: Not all keys. The cases we consider here are the following.

- **Case 2:** $A^+ = B^+$
- **Case 3:** $B^+ \not\subseteq A^+$, $A \cap \hat{B} \neq \emptyset$ and $\hat{A} \cap B \neq \emptyset$
- **Case 4:** $B^+ \not\subseteq A^+$, $A \cap \hat{B} \neq \emptyset$ and $\hat{A} \cap B = \emptyset$
- **Case 5:** $B^+ \not\subseteq A^+$, $A \cap \hat{B} = \emptyset$, and $\hat{B} \subseteq \hat{A}$
- **Case 6:** $B^+ \not\subseteq A^+$, $A \cap \hat{B} = \emptyset$, and $\hat{B} \not\subseteq \hat{A}$
- **Case 7:** $A^+ \not\subseteq B^+$

Note that Cases 2–6 cover all the subcases of $B^+ \not\subseteq A^+$. Hence, together with Cases 1 and 7 we cover all the possible cases. In Cases 2–6 we show reductions from globally-optimal repair checking for the schemas $\mathbf{S}^i$ of Example 3.4 for $i = 2, \dots, 6$, respectively. For Case 7 we show symmetry to the case of $B^+ \not\subseteq A^+$. Observe that some argument is required for this symmetry, since A and B are not defined in a symmetric manner.

5.3 End-to-End Case

In this section, we illustrate our proof strategy by giving the complete proof for one of the cases above, namely Case 1. We begin by showing coNP-hardness for the schema $\mathbf{S}^1$. Recall that $\mathbf{S}^1 = (\mathcal{R}^1, \Delta^1)$, where $\mathcal{R}^1$ consists of a single ternary relation symbol R^1, and $\Delta^1 = \{\{1,2\} \to 3, \{1,3\} \to 2, \{2,3\} \to 1\}$.

LEMMA 5.2. *The problem of globally-optimal repair checking is coNP-hard for the schema* $\mathbf{S}^1$.

PROOF. We will show a reduction from the undirected Hamiltonian Cycle problem, which is the following. Given an undirected graph $G = (V, E)$ with $V = \{v_0, \dots, v_{n-1}\}$, where the v_i's are distinct, determine whether there is a permutation π over the set $\{0, \dots, n-1\}$ such that there is an edge between $v_{\pi(i)}$ and $v_{\pi(i+1)}$ for all $i = 0, \dots, n-1$, where addition (i.e., $+1$) is taken modulo n. So, let $G = (V, E)$ be a given graph with $V = \{v_0, \dots, v_{n-1}\}$. We will construct inputs $(I, \succ)$ and J for globally-optimal repair checking. Our construction is illustrated in Figure 5 for the special case

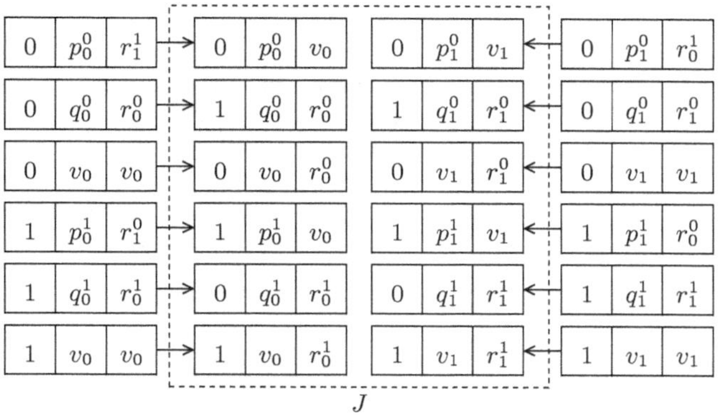

Figure 5: Illustration of the reduction from Hamiltonian Cycle to globally-optimal repair checking for $\mathbf{S}^1$, when $G = (V, E)$ where $V = \{v_0, v_1\}$ and E consists of the edge $\{v_0, v_1\}$

where G consists of two nodes v_0 and v_1 that are connected by an edge. The facts are represented as tuples without mentioning the relation symbol R^1.

The instance I has the following facts for every index $i \in \{0, \dots, n-1\}$ and for every node $v_j \in V$: $R^1(i, p^i_j, v_j)$, $R^1(i-1, q^i_j, r^i_j)$, $R^1(i, v_j, r^i_j)$, $R^1(i, q^i_j, r^i_j)$, and $R^1(i, v_j, v_j)$. As before, throughout this proof, the sum $i+1$ is interpreted modulo n (i.e., it refers to the number $(i+1) \mod n$), and similarly for the difference $i-1$. Each symbol p^i_j, q^i_j and r^i_j is assumed to be a fresh constant.

In addition, I has the fact $R^1(i, p^i_j, r^{i+1}_k)$ for every index $i \in \{0, \dots, n-1\}$ and edge $\{v_j, v_k\} \in E$.

The priority $\succ$ is defined as follows for every index i, node v_j and edge $\{v_j, v_k\}$.

- $R^1(i, p^i_j, r^{i+1}_k) \succ R^1(i, p^i_j, v_j)$
- $R^1(i, q^i_j, r^i_j) \succ R^1(i-1, q^i_j, r^i_j)$
- $R^1(i, v_j, v_j) \succ R^1(i, v_j, r^i_j)$

Finally, the instance J consists of the following facts for every index $i \in \{0, \dots, n-1\}$ and node $v_j \in V$:

- $R^1(i, p^i_j, v_j)$
- $R^1(i-1, q^i_j, r^i_j)$
- $R^1(i, v_j, r^i_j)$

The reader can verify that the input we have defined is legal; that is, $\succ$ is acyclic and gives preferences only between conflicting facts, and J is consistent. It is now left to prove that there is a global improvement J' of J if and only if G has a Hamiltonian cycle.

The "if" direction. Suppose that G has a Hamiltonian cycle π (which is a permutation over $\{0, \dots, n-1\}$). We construct from π a global improvement J' by starting with J, and replacing:

- every $R^1(i, p^i_j, v_j)$ with $R^1(i, p^i_j, r^{i+1}_k)$ where $j = \pi(i)$ and $k = \pi(i+1)$;
- every $R^1(i-1, q^i_j, r^i_j)$ with $R^1(i, q^i_j, r^i_j)$ where $j = \pi(i)$;
- every $R^1(i, v_j, r^i_j)$ with $R^1(i, v_j, v_j)$ where $j = \pi(i)$.

The construction is such that every fact in $J \setminus J'$ is improved by some fact in $J' \setminus J$. It remains to prove that J' is consistent.

We have already claimed that J is consistent. The reader can easily verify that the facts in $J' \setminus J$ are consistent among themselves. So, it remains to show that every fact $f \in J \setminus J'$ is consistent with every fact $f' \in J' \setminus J$. We do so via a case by case analysis.

Suppose first that $f = R^1(i, p^i_j, v_j)$. If f' agrees with f on the attributes 1 and 2, then f' is necessarily the fact $R^1(i, p^i_j, r^{i+1}_k)$ that replaced f (hence, a contradiction). If f' agrees with f on the attributes 1 and 3, then f' is necessarily $R^1(i, v_j, v_j)$ where $j = \pi(i)$; but in that case, f has been replaced with $R^1(i, p^i_j, r^{i+1}_k)$. Finally, it is clear that f does not agree with f' on the second and third attributes.

Suppose now that $f = R^1(i-1, q^i_j, r^i_j)$. Then it is clear that f' does not agree with f on the attributes 1 and 2. If f' agrees with f on the attributes 1 and 3, then f' is necessarily of the form $R^1(i', p^{i'}_{j'}, r^{i'+1}_{k'})$ where $i' = i-1$, $j' = \pi(i')$ and $k' = \pi(i'+1)$; but this means that $j = k' = \pi(i)$, and then f has been removed in the construction of J'. Finally, if f' agrees with f on the attributes 2 and 3, then f' is necessarily $R^1(i, q^i_j, r^i_j)$ where $j = \pi(i)$, which replaced f.

Finally, suppose that $f = R^1(i, v_j, r^i_j)$. If f' agrees with f on attributes 1 and 2, then f' is necessarily the fact $R^1(i, v_j, v_j)$, which replaced f. If f' agrees with f on attributes 1 and 3, then f' is necessarily $R^1(i, q^i_j, r^i_j)$ where $j = \pi(i)$; but then $j = \pi(i)$ implies that f has been replaced in our construction. Finally, it is clear that f' cannot agree with f on the attributes 2 and 3.

We conclude that J' is indeed a global improvement of J, as claimed.

The "only if" direction. We now assume that J' is a global improvement of J, and we will construct a Hamiltonian cycle π in G.

Let $i \in \{0, \dots, n-1\}$ be given. We will first prove that if J' contains a fact of the form $R^1(i, v_j, v_j)$, then it must also contain a fact of the form $R^1(i', v_{j'}, v_{j'})$ where $i' = i+1$ and $v_{j'}$ is a neighbor of v_j. So, suppose that J' contains $R^1(i, v_j, v_j)$. Then $J \setminus J'$ must contain the conflicting $R^1(i, p^i_j, v_j)$ (since J contains $R^1(i, p^i_j, v_j)$ by construction, and $R^1(i, p^i_j, v_j)$ cannot be in J' since it conflicts with $R^1(i, v_j, v_j)$, which is in J'). Consequently, $J' \setminus J$ must contain $R^1(i, p^i_j, r^{i+1}_{j'})$ for some neighbor $v_{j'}$ of v_j. Therefore, $J \setminus J'$ must contain the conflicting $R^1(i'-1, q^{i'}_{j'}, r^{i'}_{j'})$ where $i' = i+1$. Hence, $J' \setminus J$ must contain $R^1(i', q^{i'}_{j'}, r^{i'}_{j'})$. Thus, $J \setminus J'$ must contain the conflicting $R^1(i', v_{j'}, r^{i'}_{j'})$, implying that $J' \setminus J$ must contain $R^1(i', v_{j'}, v_{j'})$, as claimed.

The arguments of the previous paragraph also show that if $J' \setminus J$ is nonempty, then J' must include at least one $R^1(i, v_j, v_j)$. (Thus, for each of the three types of facts in $I \setminus J$, namely those of the form $R^1(i, q^i_j, r^i_j)$, $R^1(i, v_j, v_j)$, and $R^1(i, p^i_j, r^{i+1}_k)$ where $\{v_j, v_k\} \in E$, we see that by starting at some point in the middle of the previous paragraph, we end up concluding at the end of the paragraph that J' must include at least one fact of the form $R^1(i, v_j, v_j)$.) Therefore, J' contains a fact $R^1(i, v_j, v_j)$ for every $i = 0, \dots, n-1$. Moreover, due to the constraint $\{2, 3\} \to 1$ we get that every v_j occurs in $R^1(i, v_j, v_j)$ with at most one i. Therefore, since we have n indices and n nodes, we get that for every index i there is a unique fact $R^1(i, v_{j_i}, v_{j_i})$ in J'. As explained above, there is an edge between v_{j_i} and $v_{j_{i+1}}$ for all i, and consequently, the permutation π defined by $\pi(i) = j_i$ for $i = 0, \dots, n-1$ is a Hamiltonian cycle. □

Recall in the case we consider, $\mathbf{S} = (\mathcal{R}, \Delta)$, $\mathcal{R} = \{R\}$ and $\Delta = \{A_1 \to [\![R]\!], \dots, A_k \to [\![R]\!]\}$ where $k \geq 3$, and for all $i \neq j$ we have $A_i \not\subseteq A_j$. We now define the function Π that maps facts over R^1 into facts over R. For clarity, we denote A_1 by $A_{1,2}$, we denote A_2 by $A_{2,3}$, and we denote A_3 by $A_{1,3}$.

For a fact $f = R^1(c_1, c_2, c_3)$, the fact $\Pi(f)$ is the fact $R(d_1, \dots, d_k)$, where for all $i = 1, \dots, k$ the value d_i is defined as in the following equation. Each of the first two lines in this equation is quantified universally over (i.e., repeated for) all series $\langle a, b, c\rangle$ among the series $\langle 1,2,3\rangle$, $\langle 1,3,2\rangle$ and $\langle 2,3,1\rangle$.

$$d_i = \begin{cases} \langle c_a, c_b\rangle & \text{if } i \in A_{\{a,b\}} \setminus (A_{\{a,c\}} \cup A_{\{b,c\}}); \\ c_b & \text{if } i \in (A_{\{a,b\}} \cap A_{\{b,c\}}) \setminus A_{a,c}; \\ \diamond & \text{if } i \in A_{\{1,2\}} \cap A_{\{1,3\}} \cap A_{\{2,3\}}; \\ \langle c_1, c_2, c_3\rangle & \text{otherwise.} \end{cases}$$

We need to prove that Π has the two key properties, and we prove so in the following two lemmas.

Lemma 5.3. *Π is injective.*

Proof. To prove that Π is injective, it suffices to prove that for $f = R^1(c_1, c_2, c_3)$, each c_i occurs in $\Pi(f)$ at least once, and in a position that depends only on i (hence, we can restore f from $\Pi(f)$). We will show that for c_1, and by symmetry we will conclude the same for c_2 and c_3. Since $A_{\{2,3\}}$ is a minimal key, there is at least one index $i \in A_{\{1,2\}}$ that is not in $A_{\{2,3\}}$. For such i, the value in $\Pi(f)$ is either $\langle c_1, c_2\rangle$ or c_1 (depending on whether or not i is in $A_{\{1,3\}}$). In any case, c_1 occurs in a specific position within the ith attribute, as claimed. □

Lemma 5.4. *Π preserves consistency and inconsistency.*

Proof. Let $f = R^1(c_1, c_2, c_3)$ and $f' = R^1(c'_1, c'_2, c'_3)$ be two facts. We will show that f and f' are consistent w.r.t. $\mathbf{S}^1$ if and only if $\Pi(f)$ and $\Pi(f')$ are consistent w.r.t. $\mathbf{S}$.

The "if" direction. Suppose that $\Pi(f)$ and $\Pi(f')$ are consistent w.r.t. $\mathbf{S}$. We will show that $\{f, f'\}$ satisfies the fd $\{1,2\} \to 3$. By symmetry, we also cover the other two fds. Suppose that $c_1 = c'_1$ and $c_2 = c'_2$. We must show $c_3 = c'_3$. For that, it suffices to prove that $\Pi(f)$ and $\Pi(f')$ agree on $A_{\{1,2\}}$. But, from the definition of Π it follows none of the attributes in $A_{\{1,2\}}$ mentions c_3 and c'_3 in f and f', respectively. It thus follows that f and f' agree on $A_{\{1,2\}}$, since $c_1 = c'_1$ and $c_2 = c'_2$.

The "only if" direction. Suppose that f and f' are consistent w.r.t. $\mathbf{S}^1$. We need to show that $\Pi(f)$ and $\Pi(f')$ are consistent w.r.t. $\mathbf{S}$. Recall that Δ is equivalent to a set of key constraints. So, we assume that Δ is, in fact, a set of key constraints. Let $R : A \to [\![R]\!]$ be a key constraint in Δ, and suppose that $\Pi(f)$ and $\Pi(f')$ agree on A. We need to show that $\Pi(f) = \Pi(f')$. If A contains attributes i that, in the definition of Π at least two of c_1, c_2 and c_3 are mentioned on the left hand sides, then f and f' must be the same due to the key constraints of $\mathbf{S}^1$. The only remaining case is where the left hand sides in the attributes i in A contain only c_b and $\diamond$ for some $b \in \{1,2,3\}$. This means that A is a subset of $A_{\{a,b\}} \cap A_{\{b,c\}}$ for corresponding a and c, and hence a strict subset of $A_{\{a,b\}}$ (and $A_{\{b,c\}}$), because $A_{\{a,b\}}$ and $A_{\{b,c\}}$ are different and minimal. However, this contradicts the fact that $A_{\{a,b\}}$ is minimal (since $A_{\{a,b\}}$ strictly contains the key A). □

This completes Case 1, where we have established the following result.

Lemma 5.5. *Let $\mathbf{S} = (\mathcal{R}, \Delta)$ be a schema such that Δ is equivalent to a set of three or more keys, but not fewer. Then globally-optimal repair checking is coNP-complete over $\mathbf{S}$.*

6. DISTINGUISHING HARD SCHEMAS FROM TRACTABLE SCHEMAS

In this section, we investigate the problem of determining, given a schema $\mathbf{S}$, whether preferred repair checking is solvable in polynomial time or is coNP-complete; that is, whether $\mathbf{S}$ belongs to the tractable or the hard side of the dichotomy of Theorem 3.1. (Of course, this problem is of interest only under the assumption that P $\neq$ NP). We prove the following.

Theorem 6.1. *Whether a schema $\mathbf{S}$ belongs to the tractable or the hard side of Theorem 3.1 can be decided in polynomial time in the size of $\mathbf{S}$.*

In the remainder of this section, we prove Theorem 6.1. Given Theorem 3.1, we can consider every relation symbol R separately, and test for every R whether $\Delta_{|R}$ is equivalent to a single fd or two keys.

Lemma 6.2. *Let $\mathbf{S} = (\mathcal{R}, \Delta)$ be a schema that consists of a single relation symbol R. The following hold.*

1. *If Δ is equivalent to a nontrivial fd $A \to B$, then at least one fd in Δ has A as the left hand side.*
2. *If Δ is equivalent to a set $\{A_1 \to B_1, A_2 \to B_2\}$ of nontrivial fds where $A_1 \not\subseteq A_2$ and $A_2 \not\subseteq A_1$, then Δ has at least one fd with A_1 as the left hand side, and at least one fd with A_2 as the left hand side.*

We also need the following well-known theorem.

Theorem 6.3. [13] *Given a schema $\mathbf{S} = (\mathcal{R}, \Delta)$ and an fd δ over $\mathbf{S}$, it can be tested in polynomial time whether δ is implied by Δ (that is, Δ is equivalent to $\Delta \cup \{\delta\}$).*

With Lemma 6.2 and Theorem 6.3, we can now devise the following polynomial-time algorithm for deciding whether $\Delta_{|R}$ is equivalent to a single fd. For each left hand side A in $\Delta_{|R}$, use Theorem 6.3 to find the set B of all the indices b such that $A \to \{b\}$ is implied by Δ. Then, test whether every fd in $\Delta_{|R}$ is implied by $A \to B$. Part 1 of Lemma 6.2 implies that the test succeeds for some A, if and only if $\Delta_{|R}$ is equivalent to a single fd (with A as the left hand side).

To decide whether $\Delta_{|R}$ is equivalent to two key constraints, we consider two cases. In the case where one key is implied by the other (i.e., one key contains the other), we test whether $\Delta_{|R}$ is implied by a single key constraint similarly to the previous paragraph. Otherwise, we can use Part 2 of Lemma 6.2. Specifically, we consider every two left hand sides A_1 and A_2 in $\Delta_{|R}$, verify (using Theorem 6.3) that every index is functionally dependent on each of A_1 and A_2 (i.e., both are keys), and test whether every fd in $\Delta_{|R}$ is implied by $\{A_1 \rightarrow [\![R]\!], A_2 \rightarrow [\![R]\!]\}$.

7. CROSS-CONFLICT PRIORITIES

In this section, we relax the assumption that priorities are allowed only between conflicting facts, and consider the impact of this relaxation on the computational complexity of globally-optimal repair checking. Formally, the definition of a prioritizing instance $(I, \succ)$ is the same as the original definition in Section 2.3, except that $f \succ g$ can hold even if f and g are not in conflict. To distinguish from the ordinary case, we call such $(I, \succ)$ a *cross-conflict-prioritizing* instance, or *ccp-instance* for short. The remaining definitions, including global/Pareto improvement and globally/Pareto-optimal repairs, do not change.

Observe that the complexity of globally-optimal repair checking can only go higher (or remain unchanged), since now we allow inputs that were previously illegal. It is a straightforward observation that Pareto-optimal repair checking remains polynomial-time solvable for every schema. How does the relaxation affect globally-optimal repair checking? We answer this question in the remainder of this section. To present our main result, we need to introduce some notation.

7.1 Dichotomy for CCP-Instances

Let $\mathbf{S} = (\mathcal{R}, \Delta)$ be a schema, and let R be a relation symbol in $\mathcal{R}$. The fd $R : A \rightarrow B$ is a *constant-attribute constraint* if $A = \emptyset$. Note that such an fd states that all the tuples of R have the same values in each of the attributes of B. We say that Δ is a *primary-key assignment* if for every relation symbol $R \in \mathcal{R}$ the set $\Delta_{|R}$ (i.e., the restriction of Δ to the fds over R) is equivalent to a single key constraint, that is, a set of the form $\{A \rightarrow [\![R]\!]\}$. We say that Δ is a *constant-attribute assignment* if for every relation symbol $R \in \mathcal{R}$ the set $\Delta_{|R}$ is equivalent to a constant-attribute constraint, that is, a set of the form $\{\emptyset \rightarrow B\}$. Note that, as a special case, if Δ is empty then Δ is both a primary-key assignment and a constant-attribute assignment. Our main result for this section is the following.

THEOREM 7.1. *For a schema $\mathbf{S} = (\mathcal{R}, \Delta)$, the following hold.*

1. *If Δ is either a primary-key assignment or a constant-attribute assignment, then global optimality is solvable in polynomial time over ccp-instances.*
2. *Otherwise, global optimality is* coNP*-complete over ccp-instances.*

As an example, recall that under the schema $\mathbf{S}$ of Example 3.3, (ordinary) globally-optimal repair checking is solvable in polynomial time. For ccp-instances over $\mathbf{S}$, globally-optimal repair checking is coNP-complete, since $\Delta_{|R}$ is not equivalent to any single key constraint (nor is $\Delta_{|S}$) and is not equivalent to any constant-attribute asignment (nor is $\Delta_{|T}$). As another example, suppose that in Example 3.3 we replace Δ with $\{R : 1 \rightarrow 2, 3, S : \emptyset \rightarrow 1\}$. Then globally-optimal repair checking would still be coNP-complete, since Δ is neither a primary-key assignment nor a constant-attribute assignment. But if we replace Δ with $\{R : 1 \rightarrow 2, 3, S : \{1, 2\} \rightarrow 3\}$, then globally-optimal repair checking is solvable in polynomial time since Δ is now a primary-key assignment. (In particular, recall that we can always add a trivial constraint for the relation symbol T.)

In what follows, we discuss the proof of Theorem 7.1.

7.2 Algorithms for Tractable Schemas

We now prove the tractability part of Theorem 7.1 by presenting two polynomial-time algorithms for globally-optimal repair checking, one for the case where Δ is a primary-key assignment and one for the case where it is a constant-attribute assignment. In the case of a primary-key assignment, we again reduce globally-optimal repair checking to graph acyclicity, but the graph construction is different from that of Section 4.2. In the case of a constant-attribute assignment, we show that we can actually enumerate all the repairs in polynomial time (and in particular, there are only polynomially many repairs); once we do so, we can check whether any of the repairs improves upon the given J.

7.2.1 Primary-Key Assignment

We will now show that when Δ is a primary-key assignment for $\mathcal{R}$, then globally-optimal repair checking is testable in polynomial time over ccp-instances. Let $\mathbf{S} = (\mathcal{R}, \Delta)$ be such a schema, and let $(I, \succ)$ and J be input for globally-optimal repair checking. We assume that J is a repair (i.e., J is a maximal consistent subinstance of I), since the problem is straightforward otherwise. The idea in the algorithm is as follows. To improve J, we need to add a fact $g_1 \in I \setminus J$ to J, but then g_1 conflicts with some fact $f_1 \in J$. So, we need to remove f_1 from J; but for that, we need to add to J a fact $g_2 \in I \setminus J$ such that $g_2 \succ f_1$. Then again, g_2 conflicts with some $f_2 \in J$, and so on. We succeed in this process (i.e., produce an improvement of J) if we close a cycle (that is, we add g_i or f_i that we already encountered in this process). Next, we formalize this idea.

We define the graph $G_{J,I\setminus J}$ over the facts of I, as follows. The graph $G_{J,I\setminus J}$ is a directed bipartite graph that has J on one side, and $I \setminus J$ on the other side. There is an edge $f \rightarrow g$ from $f \in J$ to $g \in I \setminus J$ if f conflicts with g, and there is an edge $g \rightarrow f$ if $g \succ f$.

EXAMPLE 7.2. Suppose that $\mathcal{R} = \{R\}$ where R is a binary relation symbol, and $\Delta = \{R : 1 \rightarrow 2\}$. Suppose that I is the instance such that

$$R^I = \{(0,1), (0,2), (0,c), (1,a), (1,b), (1,3)\}.$$

Moreover, suppose the following.

- $R(1,3) \succ R(0,2) \succ R(0,1)$.
- $R(0,c) \succ R(1,b) \succ R(1,c)$.

Finally, let J be the repair that consists of the facts $R(0,2)$ and $R(1,b)$. Figure 6 depicts the graph $G_{J,I\setminus J}$. The thickness of the weights can be ignored for now; those will be discussed later. □

LEMMA 7.3. *J has a global improvement if and only if $G_{J,I\setminus J}$ has a cycle.*

PROOF. We prove each direction separately.

The "if" direction:
We assume that $G_{J,I\setminus J}$ has a cycle. Then $G_{J,I\setminus J}$ has a simple cycle. Consider such a simple cycle $f_1 \rightarrow g_1 \rightarrow \cdots \rightarrow$

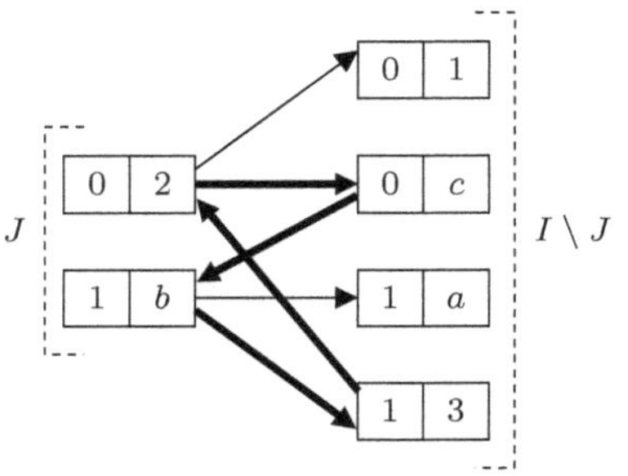

Figure 6: The graph $G_{J,I\setminus J}$ for Example 7.2

$g_k \to f_{k+1}$, where each f_i belongs to J, each g_i belongs to $I \setminus J$, and $f_{k+1} = f_1$. Define the following.

$$J' \stackrel{\text{def}}{=} (J \setminus \{f_1, \dots, f_k\}) \cup \{g_1, \dots, g_k\}$$

We claim that J' is a global improvement of J. To prove that, we first need to show that J' is consistent. Suppose, by way of contradiction, that J' has a Δ-conflict. Since J is consistent, such a conflict must be of the form $\{f_j, g_i\}$ or $\{g_i, g_j\}$ for $i \neq j$. Suppose that the conflict is $\{f_j, g_i\}$. From the construction of $G_{J,I\setminus J}$ we know that $\{f_i, g_i\}$ is a conflict; hence, $\{f_i, f_j\}$ is also a conflict (because all the fds are primary key constraints), which contradicts the fact that J is consistent. So now, suppose that the conflict is $\{g_i, g_j\}$. Since both $\{f_i, g_i\}$ and $\{f_j, g_j\}$ are conflicts, we get that $\{f_i, f_j\}$ is a conflict (again due to the fact that the fds are primary key constraints), and again we get a contradiction. We conclude that J' is consistent.

It remains to show that J' is a global improvement of J. For that, we need to show that for each f_i there is a g_j such that $g_j \succ f_i$. So, as g_j we select g_{i-1} if $i > 1$, and g_k if $i = 1$. From the constriction of $G_{J,I\setminus J}$ it follows that, indeed, we have $g_j \succ f_i$, as claimed.

The "only if" direction:
Now we assume that J has a global improvement J', and we need to show a cycle in $G_{J,I\setminus J}$. We do so by simply repeating the argument at the beginning of this section, and obtain a path $f_1 \to g_1 \to \cdots \to g_k \to f_{k+1}$ that is long enough to contain a cycle (since $G_{J,I\setminus J}$ is a finite graph). □

As a consequence, we get the following proposition.

PROPOSITION 7.4. *For a schema $\mathbf{S} = (\mathcal{R}, \Delta)$ where Δ is a primary-key assignment, globally-optimal repair checking is solvable in polynomial time over ccp-instances.*

7.2.2 *Constant-Attribute Assignment*

We will now show that when Δ is a constant-attribute assignment for $\mathcal{R}$, then globally-optimal repair checking is testable in polynomial time. Let $\mathbf{S} = (\mathcal{R}, \Delta)$ be a schema such that Δ is a constant-attribute assignment for $\mathcal{R}$. Let $(I, \succ)$ and J be input for globally-optimal repair checking. Consider a relation symbol R of Δ. A *consistent partition* of R^I is a maximal subset of R^I that agrees on (i.e., has the same value in each attribute in) $[\![R.\emptyset^{\Delta}]\!]$. An easy observation is that a subinstance K of I is a repair of I if and only if K consists of one consistent partition from each R^I. Therefore, we can simply enumerate all such K in polynomial time and test (in polynomial time) whether any of them is a global improvement of J. Observe that the degree of the polynomial is bounded by the number of relations in $\mathcal{R}$. As a consequence, we get the following proposition.

PROPOSITION 7.5. *For a schema $\mathbf{S} = (\mathcal{R}, \Delta)$ where Δ is a constant-attribute assignment, globally-optimal repair checking is solvable in polynomial time over ccp-instances.*

7.3 Proof Strategy for Hardness

The hardness part of Theorem 7.1 is proved in a pattern similar to that of the proof of the hardness part of Theorem 3.1. In particular, we prove coNP-hardness for a set of specific schemas, and then build reductions (by means of the function Π) from these specific schemas to the rest of the schemas. The specific schemas in this case are $\mathbf{S}^x = (\mathcal{R}^x, \Delta^x)$ for $x = \mathsf{a}, \mathsf{b}, \mathsf{c}, \mathsf{d}$, where:

- $\mathcal{R}^{\mathsf{a}}$ consists of two binary relation symbols R and S, and $\Delta^{\mathsf{a}} = \{R : 1 \to 2,\ S : \emptyset \to 1\}$;
- $\mathcal{R}^{\mathsf{b}}$ consists of a single relation symbol, which is ternary, and $\Delta^{\mathsf{b}} = \{1 \to 2\}$.
- $\mathcal{R}^{\mathsf{c}}$ consists of a single relation symbol, which is ternary, and $\Delta^{\mathsf{c}} = \{1 \to 2, \emptyset \to 3\}$.
- $\mathcal{R}^{\mathsf{d}}$ consists of a single relation symbol, which is binary, and $\Delta^{\mathsf{d}} = \{1 \to 2, 2 \to 1\}$.

7.4 Distinguishing Between the Cases

By repeating the arguments of Section 6, we get the following theorem, stating that we can test in polynomial time whether a schema belongs to one of the other side of the dichotomy of Theorem 7.1.

THEOREM 7.6. *Whether a schema* **S** *belongs to the tractable or the hard side of Theorem 7.1 can be decided in polynomial time in the size of* **S**.

8. CONCLUDING REMARKS

Globally-optimal repair checking is the problem of deciding, given an inconsistent database I and a subinstance J of I, whether J is a globally-optimal repair of I. When the constraints are given by a set Σ of functional dependencies, we gave a complete characterization, in terms of Σ, of the computational complexity of the globally optimal repair-checking problem. In fact, we proved a dichotomy theorem, stating that that this problem is either solvable in polynomial time or is coNP-complete, and we gave a polynomial-time algorithm that decides, given Σ, which of these two cases holds. We believe that our work (including the tools we developed) will pave the road towards other complexity classifications in the study of preferred repairs. One important such direction is the computational complexity of the preferred consistent query-answering problem. Another interesting direction to pursue is to determine the number of globally-optimal repairs, and in particular, to characterize when precisely one such repair exists. The latter is an important problem because the existence of precisely one repair implies that the constraints and priorities define an unambiguous *cleaning* of inconsistencies.

Acknowledgments

We are grateful to Slawek Staworko for helpful discussions on this paper. Phokion Kolaitis is partially supported by NSF Grant IIS-1217869.

9. REFERENCES

[1] F. N. Afrati and P. G. Kolaitis. Repair checking in inconsistent databases: algorithms and complexity. In *ICDT*, pages 31–41, 2009.

[2] D. E. Appelt and B. Onyshkevych. The common pattern specification language. In *Proceedings of the TIPSTER Text Program: Phase III*, pages 23–30, Baltimore, Maryland, USA, 1998.

[3] M. Arenas, L. E. Bertossi, and J. Chomicki. Consistent query answers in inconsistent databases. In *PODS*, pages 68–79. ACM Press, 1999.

[4] L. E. Bertossi. *Database Repairing and Consistent Query Answering*. Synthesis Lectures on Data Management. Morgan & Claypool Publishers, 2011.

[5] L. Chiticariu, R. Krishnamurthy, Y. Li, S. Raghavan, F. Reiss, and S. Vaithyanathan. SystemT: An algebraic approach to declarative information extraction. In *ACL*, pages 128–137, 2010.

[6] R. Fagin, B. Kimelfeld, F. Reiss, and S. Vansummeren. Spanners: a formal framework for information extraction. In *PODS*, pages 37–48, 2013.

[7] R. Fagin, B. Kimelfeld, F. Reiss, and S. Vansummeren. Cleaning inconsistencies in information extraction via prioritized repairs. In *PODS*. ACM, 2014.

[8] T. Feder and M. Y. Vardi. The computational structure of monotone monadic SNP and constraint satisfaction: A study through datalog and group theory. *SIAM J. Comput.*, 28(1):57–104, 1998.

[9] G. Fontaine. Why is it hard to obtain a dichotomy for consistent query answering? In *LICS*, pages 550–559, 2013.

[10] B. Kimelfeld. A dichotomy in the complexity of deletion propagation with functional dependencies. In *PODS*, pages 191–202, 2012.

[11] P. G. Kolaitis and E. Pema. A dichotomy in the complexity of consistent query answering for queries with two atoms. *Inf. Process. Lett.*, 112(3):77–85, 2012.

[12] P. Koutris and D. Suciu. A dichotomy on the complexity of consistent query answering for atoms with simple keys. In *ICDT*, pages 165–176, 2014.

[13] D. Maier, A. O. Mendelzon, and Y. Sagiv. Testing implications of data dependencies. *ACM Trans. Database Syst.*, 4(4):455–469, 1979.

[14] S. Staworko, J. Chomicki, and J. Marcinkowski. Prioritized repairing and consistent query answering in relational databases. *Ann. Math. Artif. Intell.*, 64(2-3):209–246, 2012.

[15] B. ten Cate, G. Fontaine, and P. G. Kolaitis. On the data complexity of consistent query answering. In *ICDT*, pages 22–33, 2012.

The Data Complexity of Consistent Query Answering for Self-Join-Free Conjunctive Queries Under Primary Key Constraints

Paraschos Koutris
University of Washington, Seattle, USA
pkoutris@cs.washington.edu

Jef Wijsen
Université de Mons, Mons, Belgium
jef.wijsen@umons.ac.be

ABSTRACT

A relational database is said to be uncertain if primary key constraints can possibly be violated. A repair (or possible world) of an uncertain database is obtained by selecting a maximal number of tuples without ever selecting two distinct tuples with the same primary key value. For any Boolean query q, CERTAINTY(q) is the problem that takes an uncertain database $\mathbf{db}$ as input, and asks whether q is true in every repair of $\mathbf{db}$. The complexity of this problem has been particularly studied for q ranging over the class of self-join-free Boolean conjunctive queries. A research challenge is to determine, given q, whether CERTAINTY(q) belongs to complexity classes $\mathbf{FO}$, $\mathbf{P}$, or $\mathbf{coNP}$-complete. In this paper, we combine existing techniques for studying the above complexity classification task. We show that for any self-join-free Boolean conjunctive query q, it can be decided whether or not CERTAINTY(q) is in $\mathbf{FO}$. Further, for any self-join-free Boolean conjunctive query q, CERTAINTY(q) is either in $\mathbf{P}$ or $\mathbf{coNP}$-complete, and the complexity dichotomy is effective. This settles a research question that has been open for ten years.

Categories and Subject Descriptors

H.2.3 [**Database Management**]: Languages—*query languages*; H.2.4 [**Database Management**]: Systems—*relational databases*

Keywords

Conjunctive queries; consistent query answering; primary keys

1. INTRODUCTION

Primary key violations provide an elementary means for capturing uncertainty in the relational data model. A *block* is a maximal set of tuples of the same relation that agree on the primary key of the relation. Tuples in the same block are mutually exclusive: exactly one tuple is true, but we are uncertain about which one. We will refer to databases as "uncertain databases" to stress that they can violate primary key constraints.

A *repair* (or possible world) of an uncertain database is obtained by selecting exactly one tuple from each block. In general, the number of repairs of an uncertain database can be exponential in its size. For instance, if an uncertain database contains n blocks with two tuples each, then it contains $2n$ tuples and has 2^n repairs.

PODS'15, May 31–June 4, 2015, Melbourne, Victoria, Australia.

ACM 978-1-4503-2757-2/15/05 ...$15.00.
http://dx.doi.org/10.1145/2745754.2745769 .

There are two natural semantics for answering Boolean queries q on an uncertain database. Under the *possibility semantics*, the question is whether the query evaluates to true on some repair. Under the *certainty semantics*, which is adopted in this paper, the question is whether the query evaluates to true on every repair. The certainty semantics adheres to the paradigm of *consistent query answering* [1, 4], which introduces the notion of database repairs with respect to general integrity constraints. In this work, repairing is exclusively with respect to primary key constraints, one per relation.

For any Boolean query q, the decision problem CERTAINTY(q) is the following.

PROBLEM:	CERTAINTY(q)
INPUT:	uncertain database $\mathbf{db}$
QUESTION:	Does every repair of $\mathbf{db}$ satisfy q?

Three comments are in place. First, the Boolean query q is not part of the input. Every Boolean query q gives thus rise to a new problem. Since the input to CERTAINTY(q) is an uncertain database, we consider the *data complexity* of the problem. Second, we will assume that every relation name in q or $\mathbf{db}$ has a fixed known arity and primary key. The primary key constraints are thus implicitly present in all problems. Third, all the complexity results obtained in this paper can be carried over to non-Boolean queries; the restriction to Boolean queries eases the technical treatment, but is not fundamental.

The complexity of CERTAINTY(q) has gained considerable research attention in recent years, especially for q ranging over the set of self-join-free conjunctive queries. A challenging question is to distinguish queries q for which the problem CERTAINTY(q) is tractable from queries for which the problem is intractable. Further, if CERTAINTY(q) is tractable, one may ask whether it is first-order expressible. We will refer to these questions as the *complexity classification task of* CERTAINTY(q).

In the past decade, a variety of tools and techniques have been used in the complexity classification task of CERTAINTY(q) for self-join-free conjunctive queries q. In their pioneering work, Fuxman and Miller [7] introduced the notion of *join graph* (not to be confused with the classical notion of join tree). Later on, Wijsen [16] introduced the notion of *attack graph*. Kolaitis and Pema [8] applied Minty's algorithm [14] to the task. Koutris and Suciu [9] introduced the notion of *query graph* and the distinction between consistent and possibly inconsistent relations. All these techniques have limited applicability: join graphs seem too rudimentary to obtain general complexity dichotomies; attack graphs enable to characterize first-order expressibility of CERTAINTY(q), but only for acyclic (in the sense of [3]) queries q; Minty's algorithm has been used to establish a **P**-**coNP**-complete dichotomy in the complexity of CERTAINTY(q), but only for queries q with exactly two atoms; the framework of Koutris and Suciu has also resulted in a **P**-**coNP**-complete dichotomy, but only when all primary keys consist of a single attribute. On top of the limited applicability of each individual technique, there is the difficulty that complexity classifications expressed in terms of different techniques cannot be easily compared.

In this paper, we make significant progress in the complexity classification task of CERTAINTY(q) for q ranging over the set of self-join-free conjunctive queries, by establishing the following results:

- Given a self-join-free Boolean conjunctive query q, it is decidable whether CERTAINTY(q) is in **FO**. In [16], this was only shown under the assumption that queries are acyclic (in the sense of [3]).
- Given a self-join-free Boolean conjunctive query q, if CERTAINTY(q) is not in **FO**, then it is **L**-hard. In previous works [16, 18], Hanf locality was used to show first-order inexpressibility, resulting in involved proofs. The current paper takes a complexity-theoretic approach to first-order inexpressibility, which results in an easier proof of a stronger result.
- For every self-join-free Boolean conjunctive query q, CERTAINTY(q) is either in **P** or **coNP**-complete, and the dichotomy is effective. In [9], this was only shown under the assumption that all primary keys are simple (i.e., consist of a single attribute).

Furthermore, given a self-join-free Boolean conjunctive query q, it can be decided in polynomial time in the size of q whether CERTAINTY(q) is in **FO**, in $\mathbf{P} \setminus \mathbf{FO}$, or **coNP**-complete. Our results solve a problem that has been open since 2005 [7].

Organization. This paper is organized as follows. Section 2 discusses related work. Section 3 introduces our data and query model. Section 4 defines attack graphs for Boolean conjunctive queries, extending an older notion of attack graph [18] that was defined exclusively for acyclic Boolean conjunctive queries. The section also states the main result of the paper, Theorem 1. Section 5 establishes an effective procedure that takes in a self-join-free Boolean conjunctive query q, and decides whether CERTAINTY(q) is in **FO**. Section 6 shows that for every self-join-free Boolean conjunctive query q, CERTAINTY(q) is either in **P** or **coNP**-complete. Section 7 concludes the paper.

2. RELATED WORK

Consistent query answering (CQA) goes back to the seminal work by Arenas, Bertossi, and Chomicki [1]. Fuxman and Miller [7] were the first ones to focus on CQA under the restrictions that consistency is only with respect to primary keys and that queries are self-join-free conjunctive. The term CERTAINTY(q) was coined in [16]. A recent and comprehensive survey on CERTAINTY(q) is [20].

Little is known about CERTAINTY(q) beyond self-join-free conjunctive queries. An interesting recent result by Fontaine [6] goes as follows. Let UCQ be the class of Boolean first-order queries that can be expressed as disjunctions of Boolean conjunctive queries (possibly with constants and self-joins). A daring conjecture is that for every query q in UCQ, CERTAINTY(q) is either in **P** or **coNP**-complete. Fontaine showed that this conjecture implies Bulatov's dichotomy theorem for conservative CSP [5], the proof of which is highly involved (the full paper contains 66 pages).

The counting variant of CERTAINTY(q), denoted ♯CERTAINTY(q), asks to determine the exact number of repairs that satisfy some Boolean query q. In [12], it was shown that for every self-join-free Boolean conjunctive query q, the counting problem ♯CERTAINTY(q) is either in **FP** or ♯**P**-complete. For conjunctive queries q with self-joins, the complexity of ♯CERTAINTY(q) has been established under the restriction that all primary keys consist of a single attribute [13].

3. PRELIMINARIES

We assume disjoint sets of *variables* and *constants*. If $\vec{x}$ is a sequence containing variables and constants, then $\mathsf{vars}(\vec{x})$ denotes the set of variables that occur in $\vec{x}$. A *valuation* over a set U of variables is a total mapping θ from U to the set of constants. At several places, it is implicitly understood that such a valuation θ is extended to be the identity on constants and on variables not in U. If $V \subseteq U$, then $\theta[V]$ denotes the restriction of θ to V.

If θ is a valuation over a set U of variables, x is a variable, and a is a constant, then $\theta_{[x \mapsto a]}$ is the valuation over $U \cup \{x\}$ such that $\theta_{[x \mapsto a]}(x) = a$ and for every variable y such that $y \neq x$, $\theta_{[x \mapsto a]}(y) = \theta(y)$. Notice that $x \in U$ is allowed.

Atoms and key-equal facts. Each *relation name* R of arity n, $n \geq 1$, has a unique *primary key* which is a set $\{1, 2, \ldots, k\}$ where $1 \leq k \leq n$. We say that R has *signature* $[n, k]$ if R has arity n and primary key $\{1, 2, \ldots, k\}$. We say that R is *simple-key* if $k = 1$. Elements of the primary key are called *primary-key positions*, while $k+1, k+2, \ldots, n$ are *non-primary-key positions*. For all positive integers n, k such that $1 \leq k \leq n$, we assume denumerably many relation names with signature $[n, k]$.

If R is a relation name with signature $[n, k]$, then $R(s_1, \ldots, s_n)$ is called an R-*atom* (or simply atom), where each s_i is either a constant or a variable ($1 \leq i \leq n$). Such an atom is commonly written as $R(\underline{\vec{x}}, \vec{y})$ where the primary key value $\vec{x} = s_1, \ldots, s_k$ is underlined and $\vec{y} = s_{k+1}, \ldots, s_n$. An R-*fact* (or simply fact) is an R-atom in which no variable occurs. Two facts $R_1(\underline{\vec{a}_1}, \vec{b}_1)$, $R_2(\underline{\vec{a}_2}, \vec{b}_2)$ are *key-equal* if $R_1 = R_2$ and $\vec{a}_1 = \vec{a}_2$. An R-atom or an R-fact is *simple-key* if R is simple-key.

We will use letters F, G, H for atoms. For an atom $F = R(\underline{\vec{x}}, \vec{y})$, we denote by $\mathsf{key}(F)$ the set of variables that occur in $\vec{x}$, and by $\mathsf{vars}(F)$ the set of variables that occur in F, that is, $\mathsf{key}(F) = \mathsf{vars}(\vec{x})$ and $\mathsf{vars}(F) = \mathsf{vars}(\vec{x}) \cup \mathsf{vars}(\vec{y})$.

Uncertain databases, blocks, and repairs. A *database schema* is a finite set of relation names. All constructs that follow are defined relative to a fixed database schema.

An *uncertain database* is a finite set $\mathbf{db}$ of facts using only the relation names of the schema. We refer to databases as "uncertain databases" to stress that such databases can violate primary key constraints.

We write $\mathsf{adom}(\mathbf{db})$ for the active domain of $\mathbf{db}$ (i.e., the set of constants that occur in $\mathbf{db}$). A *block* of $\mathbf{db}$ is a maximal set of key-equal facts of $\mathbf{db}$. The term R-block refers to a block of R-facts, i.e., facts with relation name R. If A is a fact of $\mathbf{db}$, then $\mathsf{block}(A, \mathbf{db})$ denotes the block of $\mathbf{db}$ that contains A. An uncertain database $\mathbf{db}$ is *consistent* if no two distinct facts are key-equal (i.e., if every block of $\mathbf{db}$ is a singleton). A *repair* of $\mathbf{db}$ is a maximal (with respect to set containment) consistent subset of $\mathbf{db}$. We write $\mathsf{rset}(\mathbf{db})$ for the set of repairs of $\mathbf{db}$.

Boolean conjunctive queries. A *Boolean query* is a mapping q that associates a Boolean (true or false) to each uncertain database, such that q is closed under isomorphism [11]. We write $\mathbf{db} \models q$ to denote that q associates true to $\mathbf{db}$, in which case $\mathbf{db}$ is said to *satisfy* q. A *Boolean first-order query* is a Boolean query that can be defined in first-order logic (with equality and constants, but without other built-in predicates). A *Boolean conjunctive query* is a finite set $q = \{R_1(\underline{\vec{x}_1}, \vec{y}_1), \ldots, R_n(\underline{\vec{x}_n}, \vec{y}_n)\}$ of atoms. We denote by $\mathsf{vars}(q)$ the set of variables that occur in q. The set q represents the first-order sentence

$$\exists u_1 \cdots \exists u_k \left(R_1(\underline{\vec{x}_1}, \vec{y}_1) \wedge \cdots \wedge R_n(\underline{\vec{x}_n}, \vec{y}_n)\right),$$

where $\{u_1, \ldots, u_k\} = \mathsf{vars}(q)$. This query q is satisfied by uncertain database $\mathbf{db}$ if there exists a valuation θ over $\mathsf{vars}(q)$ such that for each $i \in \{1, \ldots, n\}$, $R_i(\underline{\vec{a}}, \vec{b}) \in \mathbf{db}$ with $\vec{a} = \theta(\vec{x}_i)$ and $\vec{b} = \theta(\vec{y}_i)$.

We say that a Boolean conjunctive query q has a *self-join* if some relation name occurs more than once in q. If q has no self-join, then it is called *self-join-free*. By a little abuse of notation, we may confuse atoms with their relation names in a self-join-free Boolean conjunctive query q. That is, if we use a relation name R at places where an atom is expected, then we mean the (unique) R-atom of q.

If q is a Boolean conjunctive query, $\vec{x} = \langle x_1, \ldots, x_\ell\rangle$ is a sequence of distinct variables that occur in q, and $\vec{a} = \langle a_1, \ldots, a_\ell\rangle$ is a sequence of constants, then $q_{[\vec{x}\mapsto\vec{a}]}$ denotes the query obtained from q by replacing all occurrences of x_i with a_i, for all $1 \leq i \leq \ell$.

Typed uncertain databases. For every variable x, we assume an infinite set of constants, denoted $\mathsf{type}(x)$, such that $x \neq y$ implies $\mathsf{type}(x) \cap \mathsf{type}(y) = \emptyset$. Let q be a self-join-free Boolean conjunctive query, and let $\mathbf{db}$ be an uncertain database. We say that $\mathbf{db}$ is *typed relative to* q if for every atom $R(x_1, \ldots, x_n)$ in q, for every $i \in \{1, \ldots, n\}$, if x_i is a variable, then for every fact $R(a_1, \ldots, a_n)$ in $\mathbf{db}$, $a_i \in \mathsf{type}(x_i)$ and the constant a_i does not occur in q. Significantly, since q is self-join-free, the assumption that uncertain databases are typed is without loss of generality.

Purified uncertain databases. Let q be a Boolean conjunctive query, and let $\mathbf{db}$ be an uncertain database. We say that a fact $A \in \mathbf{db}$ is *relevant for q in* $\mathbf{db}$ if for some valuation θ over $\mathsf{vars}(q)$, $A \in \theta(q) \subseteq \mathbf{db}$. We say that $\mathbf{db}$ is *purified relative to q* if every fact $A \in \mathbf{db}$ is relevant for q in $\mathbf{db}$.

Frugal repairs. For every uncertain database $\mathbf{db}$, Boolean conjunctive query q, and $X \subseteq \mathsf{vars}(q)$, we define a preorder $\preceq_q^X$ on $\mathsf{rset}(\mathbf{db})$, as follows. For every two repairs $\mathbf{r}_1, \mathbf{r}_2$, we define $\mathbf{r}_1 \preceq_q^X \mathbf{r}_2$ if for every valuation θ over X, $\mathbf{r}_1 \models \theta(q)$ implies $\mathbf{r}_2 \models \theta(q)$. Here, $\theta(q)$ is the query obtained from q by replacing all occurrences of each $x \in X$ with $\theta(x)$; variables not in X remain unaffected (i.e., θ is understood to be the identity on variables not in X). Clearly, $\preceq_q^X$ is a preorder (i.e., it is reflexive and transitive), and its minimal elements are called $\preceq_q^X$*-frugal repairs.*[1]

Functional dependencies. Let q be a Boolean conjunctive query. A *functional dependency for* q is an expression $X \rightarrow Y$ where $X, Y \subseteq \mathsf{vars}(q)$. We say that an uncertain database $\mathbf{db}$ *satisfies* $X \rightarrow Y$ *for* q, denoted $\mathbf{db} \Vdash_q X \rightarrow Y$, if for all valuations θ, μ over $\mathsf{vars}(q)$ such that $\theta(q), \mu(q) \subseteq \mathbf{db}$, if $\theta[X] = \mu[X]$, then $\theta[Y] = \mu[Y]$.

Example 1. The relation R shown next does not satisfy the standard functional dependency $2 \rightarrow 3$, because its tuples agree on the second position, but disagree on the third position. Nevertheless, for $q = \exists y \exists z R(\underline{a}, y, z)$, we have $R \Vdash_q y \rightarrow z$. The second tuple of R is not relevant for the query, because a and d are distinct constants; the relation R' is purified relative to q.

R	$\underline{1}$	2	3
	a	b	c
	d	b	f

R'	$\underline{1}$	2	3
	a	b	c

Consistent query answering. For every Boolean conjunctive query q, the decision problem $\mathsf{CERTAINTY}(q)$ takes as input an uncertain database $\mathbf{db}$, and asks whether q is satisfied by every repair of $\mathbf{db}$. It is straightforward that for every Boolean first-order query q, $\mathsf{CERTAINTY}(q)$ is in **coNP**.

The following two lemmas are useful in the study of the complexity of $\mathsf{CERTAINTY}(q)$.

LEMMA 1 ([19]). *Let q be a Boolean conjunctive query. Let $\mathbf{db}$ be an uncertain database. It is possible to compute in polynomial time an uncertain database $\mathbf{db}'$ that is purified relative to q such that every repair of $\mathbf{db}$ satisfies q if and only if every repair of $\mathbf{db}'$ satisfies q.*

LEMMA 2. *Let q be a Boolean conjunctive query, and $X \subseteq \mathsf{vars}(q)$. Let $\mathbf{db}$ be an uncertain database. Then, every repair of $\mathbf{db}$ satisfies q if and only if every $\preceq_q^X$-frugal repair of $\mathbf{db}$ satisfies q.*

4. ATTACK GRAPHS

Attack graphs were introduced in [16] for studying first-order expressibility of $\mathsf{CERTAINTY}(q)$ for acyclic (in the sense of [3]) self-join-free conjunctive queries q. Here, we extend the notion of attack graph to all (cyclic or acyclic) self-join-free conjunctive queries.

Let q be a self-join-free Boolean conjunctive query. We define $\mathcal{K}(q)$ as the following set of functional dependencies:

$$\mathcal{K}(q) := \{\mathsf{key}(F) \rightarrow \mathsf{vars}(F) \mid F \in q\}.$$

For every atom $F \in q$, we define $F^{+,q}$ as the following set of variables:

$$F^{+,q} := \{x \in \mathsf{vars}(q) \mid \mathcal{K}(q \setminus \{F\}) \models \mathsf{key}(F) \rightarrow x\}.$$

The *attack graph of* q is a directed graph whose vertices are the atoms of q. There is a directed edge from F to G ($F \neq G$) if there exists a sequence

$$F_0, F_1, \ldots, F_n \tag{1}$$

of (not necessarily distinct) atoms of q such that

- $F_0 = F$ and $F_n = G$; and
- for all $i \in \{0, \ldots, n-1\}$, $\mathsf{vars}(F_i) \cap \mathsf{vars}(F_{i+1}) \nsubseteq F^{+,q}$.

A directed edge from F to G in the attack graph of q is also called an *attack from F to G*, denoted by $F \overset{q}{\rightsquigarrow} G$. The sequence (1) is called a *witness* for the attack $F \overset{q}{\rightsquigarrow} G$. We will often add variables to a witness: if we write $F_0 \overset{z_1}{\frown} F_1 \overset{z_2}{\frown} F_2 \ldots \overset{z_n}{\frown} F_n$, then it is understood that for $i \in \{1, \ldots, n\}$, $z_i \in \mathsf{vars}(F_{i-1}) \cap \mathsf{vars}(F_i)$ and $z_i \notin {F_0}^{+,q}$. If $F \overset{q}{\rightsquigarrow} G$, then we also say that F *attacks* G (or that G is attacked by F).

An attack from F to G is called *weak* if $\mathcal{K}(q) \models \mathsf{key}(F) \rightarrow \mathsf{key}(G)$; otherwise it is *strong*. A directed cycle in the attack graph of q is called *weak* if all attacks in the cycle are weak; otherwise the cycle is called *strong*.

[1] $\mathbf{r}_1$ is minimal if for all $\mathbf{r}_2$, if $\mathbf{r}_2 \preceq_q^X \mathbf{r}_1$ then $\mathbf{r}_1 \preceq_q^X \mathbf{r}_2$.

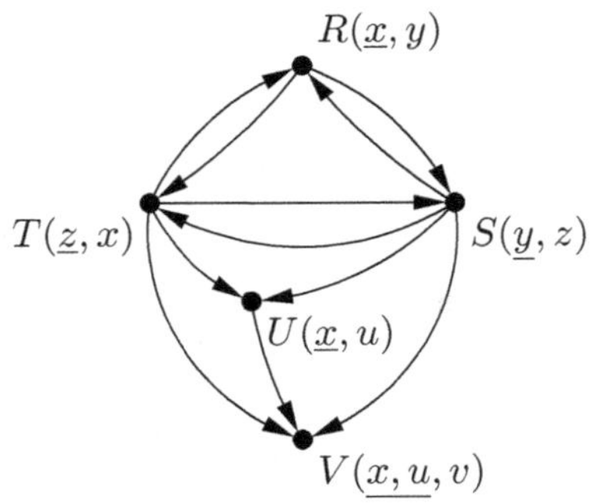

Figure 1: Attack graph of the query in Example 2.

Example 2. Consider $q = \{R(\underline{x}, y), S(\underline{y}, z), T(\underline{z}, x), U(\underline{x}, u), V(\underline{x, u}, v)\}$. By a little abuse of notation, we denote each atom by its relation name (e.g., R is used to denote the atom $R(\underline{x}, y)$). We have $R^{+,q} = \{x, u, v\}$. A witness for $R \overset{q}{\rightsquigarrow} T$ is $R \overset{y}{\frown} S \overset{z}{\frown} T$. The complete attack graph is shown in Fig. 1. All attacks are weak.

The above notion of attack graph is purely syntactic. Semantically, an attack from an R-atom to an S-atom in the attack graph of q means that there exists an uncertain database $\mathbf{db}$ such that every repair of $\mathbf{db}$ satisfies q, and such that two key-equal R-facts join exclusively with two S-facts that are not key-equal. For the query of Example 2, such a database could be $\mathbf{db} = \{R(\underline{1}, a), R(\underline{1}, b), S(\underline{a}, \alpha), S(\underline{b}, \beta), \dots\}$, in which the two R-facts are key-equal, $R(\underline{1}, a)$ joins exclusively with $S(\underline{a}, \alpha)$, and $R(\underline{1}, b)$ joins exclusively with $S(\underline{b}, \beta)$, and the two S-facts are not key-equal. Therefore, the attack graph of Fig. 1 contains a directed edge from the R-atom to the S-atom.

Equipped with the notion of attack graph, we can now present our threefold solution to the complexity classification task of CERTAINTY(q) for q ranging over the class of self-join-free Boolean conjunctive queries.

THEOREM 1. *Let q be a self-join-free Boolean conjunctive query.*

1. *If the attack graph of q is acyclic, then* CERTAINTY(q) *is in* $\mathbf{FO}$.
2. *If the attack graph of q is cyclic but contains no strong cycle, then* CERTAINTY(q) *is in* $\mathbf{P}$ *and is* $\mathbf{L}$*-hard.*
3. *If the attack graph of q contains a strong cycle, then* CERTAINTY(q) *is* $\mathbf{coNP}$*-complete.*

Furthermore, it can be decided in polynomial time in the size of q which of the above three cases applies.

The following lemma establishes that the three if-conditions in Theorem 1 can be decided in polynomial time.

LEMMA 3. *Given a self-join-free Boolean conjunctive query q, the following questions can be answered in polynomial time in the size of q:*

1. *Does the attack graph of q contain a strong cycle?*
2. *Does the attack graph of q contain a weak cycle?*

The rest of the paper completes the proof of Theorem 1. We first present some properties of attack graphs that will be useful in subsequent sections.

LEMMA 4. *Let q be a self-join-free Boolean conjunctive query. If $F \overset{q}{\rightsquigarrow} G$ and $G \overset{q}{\rightsquigarrow} H$, then either $F \overset{q}{\rightsquigarrow} H$ or $G \overset{q}{\rightsquigarrow} F$ (or both).*

LEMMA 5. *Let q be a self-join-free Boolean conjunctive query.*

1. *If the attack graph of q contains a cycle, then it contains a cycle of size two.*
2. *If the attack graph of q contains a strong cycle, then it contains a strong cycle of size two.*

LEMMA 6. *Let q be a self-join-free Boolean conjunctive query. Let $x \in \mathsf{vars}(q)$ and let a be an arbitrary constant.*

1. *If the attack graph of q is acyclic, then the attack graph of $q_{[x \mapsto a]}$ is acyclic.*
2. *If the attack graph of q contains no strong cycle, then the attack graph of $q_{[x \mapsto a]}$ contains no strong cycle.*

We conclude this section with two definitions. The following definition is taken from [2] and applies to directed graphs.

Definition 1. A directed graph is *strongly connected* if there is a directed path from any vertex to any other. The maximal strongly connected subgraphs of a graph are vertex-disjoint and are called its *strong components*. If S_1 and S_2 are strong components such that an edge leads from a vertex in S_1 to a vertex in S_2, then S_1 is a *predecessor* of S_2 and S_2 is a *successor* of S_1. A strong component is called *initial* if it has no predecessor.

Example 3. In the attack graph of Fig. 1, the atoms $R(\underline{x}, y)$, $S(\underline{y}, z)$, and $T(\underline{z}, x)$ together form an initial strong component.

So far we have defined an attack from an atom to another atom. The following definition introduces attacks from an atom to a variable of the query.

Definition 2. Let q be a self-join-free Boolean conjunctive query. Let R be a relation name with signature $[1, 1]$ such that R does not occur in q. For $F \in q$ and $z \in \mathsf{vars}(q)$, we say that F *attacks* z, denoted $F \overset{q}{\rightsquigarrow} z$, if $F \overset{q'}{\rightsquigarrow} R(\underline{z})$ where $q' = q \cup \{R(\underline{z})\}$.

Example 4. Clearly, if $F_0 \overset{z_1}{\frown} F_1 \dots \overset{z_n}{\frown} F_n$ is a witness for $F_0 \overset{q}{\rightsquigarrow} F_n$, then $F_0 \overset{q}{\rightsquigarrow} z_i$ for every $i \in \{1, \dots, n\}$. Notice also that if $q = \{R(\underline{x}, y)\}$, then the attack graph of q contains no edge, yet $R \overset{q}{\rightsquigarrow} y$.

5. FIRST-ORDER EXPRESSIBILITY

In this section, we prove the first item in the statement of Theorem 1, as well as the $\mathbf{L}$-hard lower complexity bound stated in the second item. Taken together, this leads to the following characterization of first-order expressibility of CERTAINTY(q).

THEOREM 2. *Let q be a self-join-free Boolean conjunctive query. Then the following are equivalent:*

1. CERTAINTY(q) *is in* $\mathbf{FO}$;
2. *the attack graph of q is acyclic.*

That is, acyclicity of the attack graph of q is both a necessary and sufficient condition for first-order expressibility of CERTAINTY(q). In Section 5.1, we show the contrapositive of the implication $1 \implies 2$. In Section 5.2, we show the implication $2 \implies 1$.

5.1 Necessary Condition

Let $q_0 = \{R_0(\underline{x}, y), S_0(\underline{y}, x)\}$. In [17], it was shown that CERTAINTY(q_0) is not in **FO**. The following lemma shows a stronger result.

LEMMA 7. *Let $q_0 = \{R_0(\underline{x}, y), S_0(\underline{y}, x)\}$. Then* CERTAINTY$(q_0)$ *is* **L***-hard.*

LEMMA 8. *Let q be a self-join-free Boolean conjunctive query. If the attack graph of q is cyclic, then* CERTAINTY(q) *is* **L***-hard (and hence not in* **FO***).*

PROOF. (*Outline.*) The proof shows that if the attack graph of q is cyclic, then there exists a first-order many-one reduction from CERTAINTY(q_0) to CERTAINTY(q). The desired result then follows from Lemma 7. The detailed proof is available in [10]. □

5.2 Sufficient Condition

In this section, we show that CERTAINTY(q) is in **FO** if the attack graph of q is acyclic.

LEMMA 9. *Let q be a self-join-free Boolean conjunctive query. Let F be an atom of q such that in the attack graph of q, the indegree of F is zero. Let $k = |\mathsf{key}(F)|$ and let $\vec{x} = (x_1, \ldots, x_k)$ be a sequence containing (exactly once) each variable of* $\mathsf{key}(F)$*. Then the following are equivalent for every uncertain database* **db***:*

1. *q is true in every repair of* **db***;*
2. *for some $\vec{a} \in (\mathsf{adom}(\mathbf{db}))^k$, it is the case that $q_{[\vec{x} \mapsto \vec{a}]}$ is true in every repair of* **db***.*

Lemma 9 immediately leads to the following result.

LEMMA 10. *Let q be a self-join-free Boolean conjunctive query. If the attack graph of q is acyclic, then* CERTAINTY(q) *is in* **FO***.*

PROOF. Assume that the attack graph of q is acyclic. The proof runs by induction on $|q|$. If $|q| = 0$, then CERTAINTY(q) is obviously in **FO**.

Let **db** be an instance of CERTAINTY(q). Since the attack graph of q is acyclic, we can assume an atom $R(\underline{\vec{x}}, \vec{y})$ that is not attacked in the attack graph of q. By Lemma 9, the following are equivalent:

1. q is true in every repair of **db**.
2. For some fact $R(\underline{\vec{a}}, \vec{b}) \in \mathbf{db}$, there exists of a valuation θ over $\mathsf{vars}(\vec{x})$ such that $\theta(\vec{x}) = \vec{a}$ and such that for all key-equal facts $R(\underline{\vec{a}}, \vec{b}')$ in **db**, the valuation θ can be extended to a valuation θ^+ over $\mathsf{vars}(\vec{x}) \cup \mathsf{vars}(\vec{y})$ such that $\theta^+(\vec{y}) = \vec{b}$ and $\theta^+(q')$ is true in every repair of **db**, where $q' = q \setminus \{R(\underline{\vec{x}}, \vec{y})\}$.

From Lemma 6, it follows that the attack graph of $\theta^+(q')$ is acyclic, and hence CERTAINTY$(\theta^+(q'))$ is in **FO** by the induction hypothesis. It is then clear that the latter condition 2 can be checked in **FO**. □

For a self-join-free Boolean conjunctive query q, the problem CERTAINTY(q) can be equivalently defined as the set containing every uncertain database **db** such that every repair of **db** satisfies q. If CERTAINTY(q) is in **FO**, then the set CERTAINTY(q) is definable in first-order logic (by definition of the complexity class **FO**). If CERTAINTY(q) is in **FO**, then its first-order definition is commonly called *first-order rewriting*. Such a first-order rewriting is actually an implementation, in first-order logic, of the algorithm in the proof of Lemma 10. This is illustrated next.

Example 5. Let $q = \{R(\underline{x}, y), S(\underline{y}, b)\}$, where b is a constant. The attack graph of q contains a single directed edge, from the R-atom to the S-atom. The first-order definition of CERTAINTY(q) is as follows:

$$\exists x \exists y (R(\underline{x}, y) \wedge \\ \quad \forall y \left(R(\underline{x}, y) \rightarrow \left(S(\underline{y}, b) \wedge \forall z \left(S(\underline{y}, z) \rightarrow z = b\right)\right)\right)).$$

6. POLYNOMIAL-TIME TRACTABILITY

In this section, we prove the **coNP**-hard lower complexity bound stated in the third item of Theorem 1, as well as the **P** upper complexity bound stated in the second item of Theorem 1. Those complexity bounds are recalled in the following two theorems.

THEOREM 3. *Let q be a self-join-free Boolean conjunctive query. If the attack graph of q contains a strong cycle, then* CERTAINTY(q) *is* **coNP***-hard.*

THEOREM 4. *Let q be a self-join-free Boolean conjunctive query. If the attack graph of q contains no strong cycle, then* CERTAINTY(q) *is in* **P***.*

The proof of Theorem 3 is available in [10], and differs little from the proof of Theorem 2 in [19]. In the remainder of this section, we elaborate on the proof of Theorem 4.

A very high-level outline of the proof of Theorem 4 is as follows. Let q be a self-join-free Boolean conjunctive query such that the attack graph of q contains no strong cycle. The proof will run by induction on syntax. If the attack graph of q contains an atom F without incoming attacks, then Lemma 9 tells us that the answer to CERTAINTY(q) can be obtained in polynomial time from the answers to a polynomial number of problems CERTAINTY(q'), all of which are in polynomial time by induction hypothesis. The more difficult case is if all atoms have incoming attacks in the attack graph of q. We will show that in this case, CERTAINTY(q) can be reduced in polynomial time to some problem CERTAINTY(q'') which is in polynomial time by induction hypothesis. The query q'' is obtained from q by a technique called *"dissolution of Markov cycles."*

Road map. The detailed proof of Theorem 4 is technically involved. We start by introducing in Section 6.1 an extension of the data model that allows some syntactic simplifications, expressed in Section 6.2. In Section 6.3, we introduce the notion of *Markov cycle*, and show how the "dissolution" of Markov cycles is helpful in the proof of Theorem 4, which is given in Section 6.4. The dissolution of Markov cycles is explained in detail in Section 6.5.

6.1 Relations Known to Be Consistent

We conservatively extend our data model. We first distinguish between two kinds of relation names: those that can be inconsistent, and those that cannot.

Relations known to be consistent. Every relation name has a unique and fixed *mode*, which is an element in $\{i, c\}$. It will come in handy to think of i and c as inconsistent and consistent respectively. We often write R^c to denote that R is a relation name with mode c. If q is a self-join-free Boolean conjunctive query, then $[\![q]\!]$ denotes the subset of q containing each atom whose relation name has mode c. The *inconsistency count* of q, denoted $\mathsf{incnt}(q)$, is the number of relation names with mode i in q. Modes carry over to atoms and facts: the mode of an atom $R(\underline{\vec{x}}, \vec{y})$ or a fact $R(\underline{\vec{a}}, \vec{b})$ is the mode of R.

The intended semantics is that if a relation name R has mode c, then the set of R-facts of an uncertain database will always be consistent.

Certain query answering with consistent and inconsistent relations. The problem CERTAINTY(q) now takes as input an uncertain database $\mathbf{db}$ such that for every relation name R in q, if R has mode c, then the set of R-facts of $\mathbf{db}$ is consistent. The problem is to determine whether every repair of $\mathbf{db}$ satisfies q.

All constructs and results shown in previous sections assumed that all relation names had mode i. Nevertheless, Proposition 1 (which has an easy proof) indicates that in the tractability study of CERTAINTY(q), relation names with mode c can be simulated by means exclusively of relation names with mode i. Therefore, having relation names with mode c will be convenient, but is not fundamental.

PROPOSITION 1. *Let q be a self-join free Boolean conjunctive query. Let $R^c(\underline{\vec{x}}, \vec{y})$ be an atom with mode c in q. Let R_1 and R_2 be two relation names, both with mode i and with the same signature as R, such that neither R_1 nor R_2 occurs in q. Let $q' = (q \setminus \{R^c(\underline{\vec{x}}, \vec{y})\}) \cup \{R_1(\underline{\vec{x}}, \vec{y}), R_2(\underline{\vec{x}}, \vec{y})\}$. Then* CERTAINTY($q$) *and* CERTAINTY($q'$) *are equivalent under first-order reductions.*

If relation names with mode c are allowed for syntactic convenience, the definition of $F^{+,q}$ needs slight change:

$$F^{+,q} := \{x \in \mathsf{vars}(q) \mid \mathcal{K}((q \setminus F) \cup [\![q]\!]) \models \mathsf{key}(F) \rightarrow x\}.$$

Modulo this redefinition, the notion of attack graph remains unchanged.

Proposition 1 explains how to replace atoms with mode c. Conversely, the following lemma states that in pursuing a proof for Theorem 4, there are cases where a self-join-free Boolean conjunctive query can be extended with atoms of mode c.

LEMMA 11. *Let q be a self-join-free Boolean conjunctive query. Let $x, z \in \mathsf{vars}(q)$ such that $\mathcal{K}(q) \models x \rightarrow z$ and for every $F \in q$, if $\mathcal{K}(q) \models x \rightarrow \mathsf{key}(F)$, then $F \overset{q}{\not\rightsquigarrow} x$ and $F \overset{q}{\not\rightsquigarrow} z$. Let $q' = q \cup \{T^c(\underline{x}, z)\}$, where T is a fresh relation name with mode c. Then,*

1. *there exists a polynomial-time many-one reduction from* CERTAINTY(q) *to* CERTAINTY(q')*; and*
2. *if the attack graph of q contains no strong cycle, then the attack graph of q' contains no strong cycle either.*

Saturated queries. Given a self-join-free Boolean conjunctive query, the reduction of Lemma 11 can be repeated until it can no longer be applied. The query so obtained will be called *saturated*.

Definition 3. Let q be a self-join-free Boolean conjunctive query. We say that q is *saturated* if whenever $x, z \in \mathsf{vars}(q)$ such that $\mathcal{K}(q) \models x \rightarrow z$ and $\mathcal{K}([\![q]\!]) \not\models x \rightarrow z$, then there exists an atom $F \in q$ with $\mathcal{K}(q) \models x \rightarrow \mathsf{key}(F)$ such that $F \overset{q}{\rightsquigarrow} x$ or $F \overset{q}{\rightsquigarrow} z$.

Example 6. Let $q = \{R(\underline{x}, y), S_1(\underline{y}, z), S_2(\underline{y}, z), T^c(\underline{x, z}, w), U(\underline{w}, x)\}$. We have $\mathcal{K}(q) \models y \rightarrow z$ and $\mathcal{K}([\![q]\!]) \not\models y \rightarrow z$. The set $\{F \in q \mid \mathcal{K}(q) \models y \rightarrow \mathsf{key}(F)\}$ equals $\{S_1, S_2\}$. We have neither $S_1 \overset{q}{\rightsquigarrow} y$ nor $S_1 \overset{q}{\rightsquigarrow} z$. Likewise, neither $S_2 \overset{q}{\rightsquigarrow} y$ nor $S_2 \overset{q}{\rightsquigarrow} z$. Hence, q is not saturated. By Lemma 11, there exists a polynomial-time many-one reduction from CERTAINTY(q) to CERTAINTY(q') with $q' = q \cup \{S^c(\underline{y}, z)\}$, where S is a fresh relation name with mode c. It can be verified that the query q' is saturated.

6.2 Syntactic Simplifications

The following lemma shows that any proof of Theorem 4 can assume some syntactic simplifications without loss of generality.

LEMMA 12. *Let q be a self-join-free Boolean conjunctive query. There exists a polynomial-time many-one reduction from* CERTAINTY(q) *to* CERTAINTY(q') *for some self-join-free Boolean conjunctive query q' with the following properties:*

- $\mathsf{incnt}(q') \leq \mathsf{incnt}(q)$*;*
- *no atom in q' contains two occurrences of the same variable;*
- *constants occur in q' exclusively at the primary-key position of simple-key atoms;*
- *every atom with mode i in q' is simple-key;*
- *q' is saturated; and*
- *if the the attack graph of q contains no strong cycle, then the attack graph of q' contains no strong cycle either.*

6.3 Dissolving Markov Cycles

The following definition introduces Markov graphs.

Definition 4. Let q be a self-join-free Boolean conjunctive query such that every atom with mode i in q is simple-key. For every $x \in \mathsf{vars}(q)$, we define

$$\mathsf{C}_q(x) := \{F \in q \mid F \text{ has mode } i \text{ and } \mathsf{key}(F) = \{x\}\}.$$

Notice that $\mathsf{C}_q(x)$ can be empty.

The *Markov graph* of q is a directed graph whose vertex set is $\mathsf{vars}(q)$. There is a directed edge from x to y, denoted $x \overset{q,\mathsf{M}}{\longrightarrow} y$, if $x \neq y$ and $\mathcal{K}(\mathsf{C}_q(x) \cup [\![q]\!]) \models x \rightarrow y$. If the query q is clear from the context, then $x \overset{q,\mathsf{M}}{\longrightarrow} y$ can be shortened into $x \overset{\mathsf{M}}{\longrightarrow} y$. We write $x \overset{q,\mathsf{M}*}{\longrightarrow} y$ (or $x \overset{\mathsf{M}*}{\longrightarrow} y$ if q is clear from the context) if the Markov graph of q contains a directed path from x to y.[2] Notice that for every $x \in \mathsf{vars}(q)$, $x \overset{q,\mathsf{M}*}{\longrightarrow} x$.

An elementary directed cycle $\mathcal{C}$ in the Markov graph of q is said to be *premier* if there exists a variable $x \in \mathsf{vars}(q)$ such that

1. $\{x\} = \mathsf{key}(F_0)$ for some atom F_0 with mode i that belongs to an initial strong component of the attack graph of q; and
2. for some y in $\mathcal{C}$, we have $x \overset{q,\mathsf{M}*}{\longrightarrow} y$ and $\mathcal{K}(q) \models y \rightarrow x$.

The term *Markov edge* is used for an edge in the Markov graph; likewise for *Markov path* and *Markov cycle*.

Example 7. Let $q = \{R(\underline{x}, y, v), S(\underline{y}, x), V_1^c(\underline{v}, w), W(\underline{w}, v)$ $V_2^c(\underline{w}, y)\}$. All atoms in q are simple-key. Then, $[\![q]\!] = \{V_1^c(\underline{v}, w),$ $V_2^c(\underline{w}, y)\}$.

We have $\mathsf{C}_q(x) = \{R(\underline{x}, v, y)\}$. Since $\mathcal{K}(\mathsf{C}_q(x) \cup [\![q]\!]) \models x \rightarrow \{y, v, w\}$, the Markov graph of q contains directed edges from x to each of y, v, and w.

We have $\mathsf{C}_q(v) = \emptyset$. Since $\mathcal{K}(\mathsf{C}_q(v) \cup [\![q]\!]) \models v \rightarrow \{y, w\}$, the Markov graph of q contains directed edges from v to both y and w. The complete Markov graph of q is shown in Fig. 2 (right).

The attack graph of q is shown in Fig. 2 (left). The two atoms $R(\underline{x}, y, v)$ and $S(\underline{y}, x)$ together constitute an initial strong component of the attack graph. It is then straightforward that each cycle in the Markov graph of q that contains x or y, must be premier. Further, the cycle v, w, v in the Markov graph of q is also premier, because there is a Markov path from x to v, and $\mathcal{K}(q) \models v \rightarrow x$.

[2]The term Markov refers to the intuition that in a Markov path, each variable functionally determines the next variable in the path, independently of preceding variables.

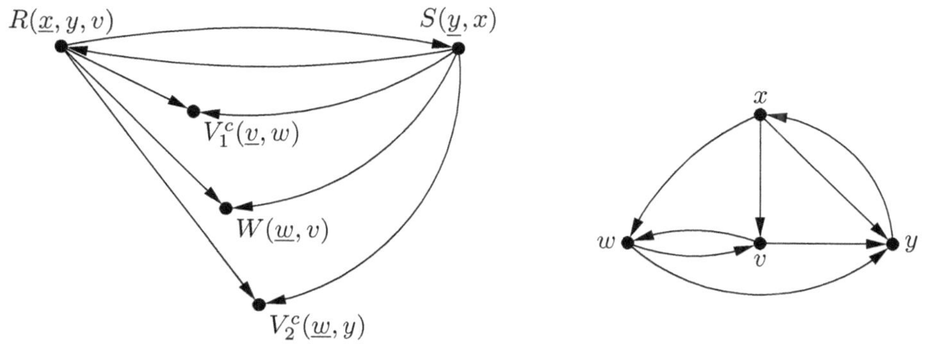

Figure 2: Attack graph (left) and Markov graph (right) of the query $\{R(\underline{x}, y, v)$, $S(\underline{y}, x)$, $V_1^c(\underline{v}, w)$, $W(\underline{w}, v)$ $V_2^c(\underline{w}, y)\}$.

Let q be like in Definition 4 and assume that the Markov graph of q contains an elementary directed cycle $\mathcal{C}$. Lemma 13 states that $\mathsf{CERTAINTY}(q)$ can be reduced in polynomial time to $\mathsf{CERTAINTY}(q^*)$, where q^* is obtained from q by "dissolving" the Markov cycle $\mathcal{C}$ as defined in Definition 5. Moreover, we will show (Lemma 14) that if $\mathcal{C}$ is premier and the attack graph of q contains no strong cycle, then the attack graph of q^* will contain no strong cycle either. The reduction that "dissolves" Markov cycles will be the central idea in our polynomial-time algorithm for $\mathsf{CERTAINTY}(q)$ when the attack graph of q contains no strong cycle.

Definition 5. Let q be a self-join-free Boolean conjunctive query such that every atom with mode i in q is simple-key. Let $\mathcal{C}$ be an elementary directed cycle of length $k \geq 2$ in the Markov graph of q. Then, $\mathsf{dissolve}(\mathcal{C}, q)$ denotes the self-join-free Boolean conjunctive query defined next. Let $x_0, \ldots, x_{k-1}$ be the variables in $\mathcal{C}$, and let $q_0 = \bigcup_{i=0}^{k-1} \mathsf{C}_q(x_i)$. Let $\vec{y}$ be a sequence of variables containing exactly once each variable of $\mathsf{vars}(q_0) \setminus \{x_0, \ldots, x_{k-1}\}$. Let $q_1 = \{T(\underline{u}, x_0, \ldots, x_{k-1}, \vec{y})\} \cup \{U_i^c(\underline{x_i}, u)\}_{i=0}^{k-1}$, where u is a fresh variable, T is a fresh relation name with mode i, and $U_1, \ldots, U_{k-1}$ are fresh relation names with mode c. Then, we define

$$\mathsf{dissolve}(\mathcal{C}, q) := (q \setminus q_0) \cup q_1 .$$

Notice that $\mathsf{dissolve}(\mathcal{C}, q)$ is unique up to a renaming of the variable u and the relation names in q_1.

Example 8. Let q be the query of Fig. 2. Let $\mathcal{C}$ be the cycle x, w, y, x in the Markov graph of q. Using the notation of Definition 5, we have

$$\begin{aligned} q_0 &= \{R(\underline{x}, y, v), S(\underline{y}, x), W(\underline{w}, v)\}, \\ q_1 &= \{T(\underline{u}, x, w, y, v), U_1^c(\underline{x}, u), U_2^c(\underline{w}, u), U_3^c(\underline{y}, u)\}. \end{aligned}$$

Hence, $\mathsf{dissolve}(\mathcal{C}, q) = \{V_1^c(\underline{v}, w)$, $V_2^c(\underline{w}, y)$, $T(\underline{u}, x, w, y, v)$, $U_1^c(\underline{x}, u)$, $U_2^c(\underline{w}, u)$, $U_3^c(\underline{y}, u)\}$.

LEMMA 13. *Let q be a self-join-free Boolean conjunctive query such that every atom with mode i in q is simple-key. Let $\mathcal{C}$ be an elementary directed cycle in the Markov graph of q, and let $q^* = \mathsf{dissolve}(\mathcal{C}, q)$. Then, there exists a polynomial-time many-one reduction from $\mathsf{CERTAINTY}(q)$ to $\mathsf{CERTAINTY}(q^*)$.*

The reduction of Lemma 13 will be explained in Section 6.5. To use the reduction in a proof of Theorem 4, two more results are needed:

- First, we need to show that the "dissolution" of Markov cycles can be done while keeping the attack graph free of strong cycles (this is Lemma 14). This turns out to be true only for Markov cycles that are premier (as defined in Definition 4).
- Second, we need to show the existence of premier Markov cycles that can be "dissolved" (this is Lemma 15).

LEMMA 14. *Let q be a self-join-free Boolean conjunctive query such that every atom with mode i in q is simple-key. Let $\mathcal{C}$ be an elementary directed cycle in the Markov graph of q such that $\mathcal{C}$ is premier, and let $q^* = \mathsf{dissolve}(\mathcal{C}, q)$. If the attack graph of q contains no strong cycle, then the attack graph of q^* contains no strong cycle either.*

LEMMA 15. *Let q be a self-join-free Boolean conjunctive query such that*

- *for every atom $F \in q$, if F has mode i, then F is simple-key and $\mathsf{key}(F) \neq \emptyset$;*
- *q is saturated;*
- *the attack graph of q contains no strong cycle; and*
- *the attack graph of q contains an initial strong component with two or more atoms.*

Then, the Markov graph of q contains an elementary directed cycle that is premier and such that for every y in $\mathcal{C}$, $\mathsf{C}_q(y) \neq \emptyset$.

The condition $\mathsf{C}_q(y) \neq \emptyset$, for every y in $\mathcal{C}$, guarantees that $\mathsf{dissolve}(\mathcal{C}, q)$ will contain strictly less atoms of mode i than q. This condition will be used in the proof of Theorem 4 which runs by induction on the number of atoms with mode i. The following example shows that Lemma 15 is no longer true if q is not saturated.

Example 9. Continuing Example 6. The query q of Example 6 is not saturated, but satisfies all other conditions in the statement of Lemma 15. In particular, the attack graph of q contains a weak cycle $R \overset{q}{\rightsquigarrow} U \overset{q}{\rightsquigarrow} R$, which is part of an initial strong component. The Markov graph of q consists of a single path $w \xrightarrow{q,\mathsf{M}} x \xrightarrow{q,\mathsf{M}} y \xrightarrow{q,\mathsf{M}} z$, and hence is acyclic.

The query q' of Example 6 is saturated, and we have $x \xrightarrow{q',\mathsf{M}} w \xrightarrow{q',\mathsf{M}} x$, a Markov cycle which can be shown to be premier.

6.4 The Proof of Theorem 4

PROOF OF THEOREM 4. Assume that the attack graph of q contains no strong cycle. The proof runs by induction on increasing

$\mathsf{incnt}(q)$. The desired result is obvious if $\mathsf{incnt}(q) = 0$. Assume that $\mathsf{incnt}(q) > 0$ in the remainder of the proof. Let $\mathbf{db}$ be an uncertain database that is input to $\mathsf{CERTAINTY}(q)$.

First, we reduce in polynomial time $\mathsf{CERTAINTY}(q)$ to $\mathsf{CERTAINTY}(q')$ with q' like in Lemma 12. We now distinguish two cases.

Case q' contains an atom F with mode i that has zero indegree in the attack graph of q. We can assume either $F = R(\underline{x}, \vec{y})$ or $F = R(\underline{a}, \vec{y})$, where $\vec{y}$ is a sequence of distinct variables. In the remainder, we treat the case $F = R(\underline{x}, \vec{y})$ (the case $F = R(\underline{a}, \vec{y})$ is even simpler).

Let $q'' = q' \setminus \{R(\underline{x}, \vec{y})\}$. By Lemma 9, every repair of $\mathbf{db}$ satisfies q' if and only if $\mathbf{db}$ includes an R-block $\mathbf{b}$ (there are only polynomially many such blocks) such for every $R(\underline{a}, \vec{b}) \in \mathbf{b}$, every repair of $\mathbf{db}$ satisfies $q''_{[x,\vec{y} \mapsto a,\vec{b}]}$. By Lemma 6, the attack graph of $q''_{[x,\vec{y} \mapsto a,\vec{b}]}$ contains no strong cycle. From $\mathsf{incnt}(q''_{[x,\vec{y} \mapsto a,\vec{b}]}) = \mathsf{incnt}(q') - 1 < \mathsf{incnt}(q)$, it follows that $\mathsf{CERTAINTY}(q''_{[x,\vec{y} \mapsto a,\vec{b}]})$ is in $\mathbf{P}$ by the induction hypothesis. It follows that $\mathsf{CERTAINTY}(q)$ is in $\mathbf{P}$ as well.

Case every atom F with mode i in q' has an incoming attack in the attack graph of q'. It will be the case that no constant occurs in an atom of mode i in q'.

Then, the attack graph of q' must contain an initial strong component with two or more atoms. By Lemma 15, the Markov graph of q' contains an elementary directed cycle $\mathcal{C}$ that is premier and such that for every y in $\mathcal{C}$, $\mathsf{C}_{q'}(y) \neq \emptyset$. By Lemma 13, we can reduce in polynomial time $\mathsf{CERTAINTY}(q')$ to $\mathsf{CERTAINTY}(q^*)$ where $q^* = \mathsf{dissolve}(\mathcal{C}, q')$. Since the attack graph of q' contains no strong cycle, it follows by Lemma 14 that the attack graph of q^* contains no strong cycle either.

Let $k \geq 2$ be the size of $\mathcal{C}$. It is easy to verify that $\mathsf{incnt}(q^*) \leq (\mathsf{incnt}(q') - k) + 1 < \mathsf{incnt}(q')$. By the induction hypothesis, $\mathsf{CERTAINTY}(q^*)$ is in $\mathbf{P}$. Since there exists a polynomial-time reduction from $\mathsf{CERTAINTY}(q)$ to $\mathsf{CERTAINTY}(q^*)$, we conclude that $\mathsf{CERTAINTY}(q)$ is in $\mathbf{P}$ as well. □

6.5 The Reduction of Lemma 13

This section first describes the reduction of Lemma 13, and then proves the lemma.

Relevance of subsets of repairs. In Section 3, we distinguished database facts that are relevant for a query from those that are not. This notion is extended next.

Definition 6. Let q be a self-join-free Boolean conjunctive query, and let $\mathbf{db}$ be an uncertain database. A consistent subset $\mathbf{s}$ of $\mathbf{db}$ is said to be *grelevant for q in* $\mathbf{db}$ (generalized relevant) if it can be extended into a repair $\mathbf{r}$ of $\mathbf{db}$ such that some fact of $\mathbf{s}$ is relevant for q in $\mathbf{r}$.

It can be seen that $A \in \mathbf{db}$ is relevant for q in $\mathbf{db}$ if and only if $\{A\}$ is grelevant for q in $\mathbf{db}$. Therefore, "grelevant" is a notion that generalises "relevant."

LEMMA 16. *Let q be a self-join-free Boolean conjunctive query, and let $\mathbf{db}$ be an uncertain database. Let $\mathbf{s}$ be a consistent subset of $\mathbf{db}$ that is not grelevant for q in $\mathbf{db}$. Let $\mathbf{db}_0 = \bigcup\{\mathsf{block}(A, \mathbf{db}) \mid A \in \mathbf{s}\}$. Then, the following are equivalent:*

1. *every repair of $\mathbf{db}$ satisfies q;*

2. *every repair of $\mathbf{db} \setminus \mathbf{db}_0$ satisfies q.*

PROOF. $\boxed{1 \Longrightarrow 2}$ By contraposition. Let $\mathbf{r}$ be a repair of $\mathbf{db} \setminus \mathbf{db}_0$ that falsifies q. Then, $\mathbf{r} \cup \mathbf{s}$ is a repair of $\mathbf{db}$. If $\mathbf{r} \cup \mathbf{s} \models q$, then it must be the case that $\mathbf{s}$ is grelevant for q in $\mathbf{db}$, a contradiction. We conclude by contradiction that $\mathbf{r} \cup \mathbf{s} \not\models q$. $\boxed{2 \Longrightarrow 1}$ Trivial. □

Introductory example. The following example illustrates the main ideas behind the reduction of Lemma 13.

Example 10. Let q be a self-join-free Boolean conjunctive query. Assume that q includes $q_0 = \{R(\underline{x}, y), S(\underline{y}, z), V(\underline{z}, x)\}$. Then, the Markov graph of q contains a cycle $x \xrightarrow{\mathsf{M}} y \xrightarrow{\mathsf{M}} z \xrightarrow{\mathsf{M}} x$. Let $\mathbf{db}$ be an uncertain database that is purified relative to q. Let $\mathbf{db}_0$ be the subset of $\mathbf{db}$ containing all R-facts, S-facts, and V-facts of $\mathbf{db}$. Assume that the following three tables represent all facts of $\mathbf{db}_0$ (for convenience, we use variables as attribute names, and we blur the distinction between a relation name R and a table representing a set of R-facts).

R: $\underline{x}$	y	S: $\underline{y}$	z	V: $\underline{z}$	x	
1	a	a	α	α	1	$\mathbf{db}_{01}$
		a	κ	κ	1	$\mathbf{db}_{01}$
2	b	b	β	β	2	$\mathbf{db}_{02}$
2	c	c	γ	γ	2	$\mathbf{db}_{02}$
3	d	d	δ	δ	3	$\mathbf{db}_{03}$
3	e	e	ϵ	ϵ	3	$\mathbf{db}_{03}$
4	e	e	δ	δ	4	$\mathbf{db}_{03}$
4	f	f	ϕ	ϕ	4	$\mathbf{db}_{03}$

As indicated, we can partition $\mathbf{db}_0$ into three subsets $\mathbf{db}_{01}$, $\mathbf{db}_{02}$, and $\mathbf{db}_{03}$ whose active domains have, pairwise, no constants in common. Consider each of these three subsets in turn.

1. $\mathbf{db}_{01}$ has two repairs, both satisfying q_0. For every repair $\mathbf{r}$ of $\mathbf{db}$, either $\mathbf{r} \models q_{0[x,y,z \mapsto 1,a,\alpha]}$ or $\mathbf{r} \models q_{0[x,y,z \mapsto 1,a,\kappa]}$.

2. $\mathbf{db}_{02}$ has two repairs, both satisfying q_0. For every repair $\mathbf{r}$ of $\mathbf{db}$, either $\mathbf{r} \models q_{0[x,y,z \mapsto 2,b,\beta]}$ or $\mathbf{r} \models q_{0[x,y,z \mapsto 2,c,\gamma]}$.

3. $\mathbf{db}_{03}$ has 16 repairs, and for $\mathbf{s} := \{R(\underline{3}, d), S(\underline{d}, \delta), V(\underline{\delta}, 4), R(\underline{4}, e), S(\underline{e}, \epsilon), V(\underline{\epsilon}, 3), S(\underline{f}, \phi), V(\underline{\phi}, 4)\}$, we have that $\mathbf{s}$ is a repair of $\mathbf{db}_{03}$ that falsifies q_0. It can be seen that $\mathbf{s}$ is not grelevant for q in $\mathbf{db}$. Then, by Lemma 16, every repair of $\mathbf{db}$ satisfies q if and only if every repair of $\mathbf{db} \setminus \mathbf{db}_{03}$ satisfies q. That is, $\mathbf{db}_{03}$ can henceforth be ignored.

The following table T summarizes our findings. In the first column (named with a fresh variable u), the values 01 and 02 refer to $\mathbf{db}_{01}$ and $\mathbf{db}_{02}$ respectively. The table includes two blocks (separated by a dashed line for clarity). The first block indicates that for every repair $\mathbf{r}$ of $\mathbf{db}$, either $\mathbf{r} \models q_{0[x,y,z \mapsto 1,a,\alpha]}$ or $\mathbf{r} \models q_{0[x,y,z \mapsto 1,a,\kappa]}$. Likewise for the second block.

T: $\underline{u}$	x	y	z
01	1	a	α
01	1	a	κ
02	2	b	β
02	2	c	γ

The table U_x shown below is the projection of T on attributes x and u. This table must be consistent, because by construction, the active domains of $\mathbf{db}_{01}$ and $\mathbf{db}_{02}$ are disjoint. Likewise for U_y

and U_z.

U_x

$\underline{x}$	u
1	01
2	02

U_y

$\underline{y}$	u
a	01
b	02
c	02

U_z

$\underline{z}$	u
α	01
κ	01
β	02
γ	02

Let $\mathbf{db}'$ be the database that extends $\mathbf{db}$ with all the facts shown in the tables T, U_x, U_y, and U_z.[3] Let $q^* = (q \setminus q_0) \cup \{T(\underline{u}, x, y, z), U_x^c(\underline{x}, u), U_y^c(\underline{y}, u), U_z^c(\underline{z}, u)\}$. From our construction, it follows that every repair of $\mathbf{db}$ satisfies q if and only if every repair of $\mathbf{db}'$ satisfies q^*.

Gblocks and gpurification. The following definition strengthens the notion of purification introduced earlier in Section 3.

Definition 7. Let q be a self-join-free Boolean conjunctive query such that all atoms with mode i in q are simple-key. Let $\mathbf{db}$ be an uncertain database that is purified and typed relative to q. A *gblock* (generalized block) of $\mathbf{db}$ relative to q is a maximal (with respect to $\subseteq$) subset $\mathbf{g}$ of $\mathbf{db}$ such that all facts in $\mathbf{g}$ have mode i and agree on their primary-key position (but may disagree on their relation name). Notice that a gblock has at most polynomially many repairs (in the size of $\mathbf{db}$).[4] We say that $\mathbf{db}$ is *gpurified relative to* q if for every gblock $\mathbf{g}$ of $\mathbf{db}$, every repair of $\mathbf{g}$ is grelevant for q in $\mathbf{db}$.

Clearly, every gblock is the union of one or more blocks. Two facts of the same gblock have the same primary-key value, but can have distinct relation names.

Example 11. Let $q = \{R(\underline{x}, y), S(\underline{x}, y)\}$. Let $\mathbf{db} = \{R(\underline{a}, 1), R(\underline{a}, 2), S(\underline{a}, 1), S(\underline{a}, 2)\}$. Then, $\mathbf{db}$ is purified and typed relative to q. All facts of $\mathbf{db}$ together constitute a gblock. The uncertain database $\mathbf{db}$ is not gpurified, since $\mathbf{s} = \{R(\underline{a}, 1), S(\underline{a}, 2)\}$ is a repair of the gblock, and also a repair of $\mathbf{db}$. However, neither $R(\underline{a}, 1)$ nor $S(\underline{a}, 2)$ is relevant for q in $\mathbf{s}$.

Example 12. Let $q = \{R_1(\underline{x}, y), R_2(\underline{x}, z), S(\underline{y, z})\}$, where the signature of S is $[2, 2]$. Let $\mathbf{db}$ be the uncertain database containing the following facts.

R_1

$\underline{x}$	y
a	1
a	2

R_2

$\underline{x}$	z
a	3
a	4

S

$\underline{y}$	$\underline{z}$
1	3
2	4

Then, $\mathbf{db}$ is purified and typed relative to q. All R_1-facts and R_2-facts together constitute a gblock. A repair of this gblock is $\mathbf{s} = \{R_1(\underline{a}, 1), R_2(\underline{a}, 4)\}$. The uncertain database $\mathbf{db}$ is not gpurified. Indeed, the only repair of $\mathbf{db}$ that extends $\mathbf{s}$ is $\{R_1(\underline{a}, 1), R_2(\underline{a}, 4), S(\underline{1, 3}), S(\underline{2, 4})\}$ (call it $\mathbf{r}$). Neither $R_1(\underline{a}, 1)$ nor $R_2(\underline{a}, 4)$ is relevant for q in $\mathbf{r}$.

The following lemma is similar to Lemma 1 and has an easy proof.

LEMMA 17. *Let q be a self-join-free Boolean conjunctive query such that all atoms with mode i in q are simple-key. Let $\mathbf{db}$ be an uncertain database that is purified and typed relative to q. It is possible to compute in polynomial time an uncertain database $\mathbf{db}'$ that is gpurified relative to q such that every repair of $\mathbf{db}$ satisfies q if and only if every repair of $\mathbf{db}'$ satisfies q.*

[3]Facts of $\mathbf{db}_0$ can be omitted from $\mathbf{db}'$, but that is not important.

[4]Indeed, since $\mathbf{db}$ is purified relative to q, every gblock of $\mathbf{db}$ contains at most $|q|$ distinct relation names, and hence has at most $|\mathbf{db}|^{|q|}$ distinct repairs.

Specification of the reduction of Lemma 13. Let q and $\mathcal{C}$ be as in the statement of Lemma 13. Assume that the elementary directed cycle $\mathcal{C}$ in the Markov graph of q is $x_0 \xrightarrow{\mathsf{M}} x_1 \cdots \xrightarrow{\mathsf{M}} x_{k-1} \xrightarrow{\mathsf{M}} x_0$. In what follows, let $\mathsf{dissolve}(\mathcal{C}, q)$ be as in Definition 5, with q_0, q_1, $\vec{y}$, u, T, and $U_0, \ldots, U_{k-1}$ as defined there. Moreover, we write $\oplus$ for addition modulo k, and $\ominus$ for subtraction modulo k. For every $i \in \{0, \ldots, k-1\}$, we define X_i as follows:

$$X_i := \mathsf{vars}(\mathsf{C}_q(x_i)).$$

The reduction of Lemma 13 will be described under the following simplifying assumptions which can be made without loss of generality:

- every uncertain database $\mathbf{db}$ that is input to $\mathsf{CERTAINTY}(q)$ is typed, purified, and gpurified relative to q. This assumption is without loss of generality as argued in Section 3, and by Lemmas 1 and 17; and
- for every $i \in \{0, \ldots, k-1\}$, no atom of $\mathsf{C}_q(x_i)$ contains constants or double occurrences of the same variable. This assumption is without loss of generality by Lemma 12.

Under these notations and assumptions, we describe the reduction of Lemma 13. Let $\mathbf{db}$ be an uncertain database that is input to $\mathsf{CERTAINTY}(q)$. Define a directed k-partite graph, denoted $\mathcal{G}(\mathbf{db})$, as follows:

1. the vertex set of $\mathcal{G}(\mathbf{db})$ is $\bigcup_{i=0}^{k-1} \mathsf{type}(x_i)$; and
2. there is a directed edge from $a \in \mathsf{type}(x_i)$ to $b \in \mathsf{type}(x_{i\oplus 1})$ if for some valuation θ over $\mathsf{vars}(q)$, we have that $\theta(q) \subseteq \mathbf{db}$ and $\theta(x_i) = a$ and $\theta(x_{i\oplus 1}) = b$. In this case, we say that $\theta[X_i]$ *realizes* the edge (a, b), where $\theta[X_i]$ denotes the restriction of θ on X_i.

Notice that distinct valuations can realize the same edge of $\mathcal{G}(\mathbf{db})$ (but if $\mathbf{db}$ is consistent, then every edge in $\mathcal{G}(\mathbf{db})$ is realized at most once).

Example 13. Let $q = \{R_1(\underline{x_0}, y_1), R_2(\underline{x_0}, y_2), S^c(\underline{y_1, y_2}, x_1), R_3(\underline{x_0}, y_3), V(\underline{x_1}, x_0)\}$. Then we have $x_0 \xrightarrow{\mathsf{M}} x_1$ and $X_0 = \{x_0, y_1, y_2, y_3\}$. Assume an uncertain database $\mathbf{db}$ containing, among others, the following facts.

R_1

$\underline{x_0}$	y_1
a	c_1

R_2

$\underline{x_0}$	y_2
a	c_2
a	c_3

S

$\underline{y_1}$	$\underline{y_2}$	x_1
c_1	c_2	1
c_1	c_3	1

R_3

$\underline{x_0}$	y_3
a	β
a	γ

The graph $\mathcal{G}(\mathbf{db})$ contains a directed edge $(a, 1)$, which is realized by $\{x_0 \mapsto a, y_1 \mapsto c_1, y_2 \mapsto c_2, y_3 \mapsto \beta\}$. The edge $(a, 1)$ is also realized by $\{x_0 \mapsto a, y_1 \mapsto c_1, y_2 \mapsto c_3, y_3 \mapsto \gamma\}$.

Let $[\![\mathbf{db}]\!]$ be the subset of $\mathbf{db}$ that contains all facts with mode c. Significantly, the edges in $\mathcal{G}(\mathbf{db})$ outgoing from some constant $a \in \mathsf{type}(x_j)$ (for some $j \in \{0, \ldots, k-1\}$) are fully determined by $[\![\mathbf{db}]\!]$ and the gblock of $\mathbf{db}$ containing all facts whose relation name is in $\mathsf{C}_q(x_j)$ and whose primary-key position contains the constant a (call this gblock $\mathbf{g}_a$). Since $\mathbf{db}$ is gpurified, for every repair $\mathbf{s}$ of $\mathbf{g}_a$, there exists a unique constant $b \in \mathsf{type}(x_{j\oplus 1})$ such that

$$\mathbf{s} \cup [\![\mathbf{db}]\!] \models (\mathsf{C}_q(x_j) \cup [\![q]\!])_{[x_j, x_{j\oplus 1} \mapsto a, b]},$$

in which case $\mathcal{G}(\mathbf{db})$ will contain a directed edge from a to b. Uniqueness of b follows from $\mathcal{K}(\mathsf{C}_q(x_j) \cup [\![q]\!]) \models x_j \rightarrow x_{j\oplus 1}$ and [18, Lemma 4.3].

Since $\mathbf{db}$ is gpurified, $\mathcal{G}(\mathbf{db})$ is a vertex-disjoint union of strong components such that no edge leads from one strong component to another strong component (i.e., all strong components are initial).[5] In what follows, let D be a strong component of $\mathcal{G}(\mathbf{db})$. Since $\mathcal{G}(\mathbf{db})$ is k-partite, the length of any cycle in $\mathcal{G}(\mathbf{db})$ must be a multiple of k, i.e., must be in $\{k, 2k, 3k, \dots\}$. Let $\mathbf{db}_D$ be the subset of $\mathbf{db}$ that contains $R(\underline{a}, \vec{b})$ whenever R is of mode i and the constant a is a vertex in D (and $\vec{b}$ is any sequence of constants). Obviously, every block of $\mathbf{db}$ is either included in $\mathbf{db}_D$ or disjoint with $\mathbf{db}_D$.

Clearly, D must contain a cycle. Among the cycles in D of length exactly k, we now distinguish the cycles that *support* q from those that do not, as defined next. Let such cycle in D be

$$a_0, a_1, \dots, a_{k-1}, a_0 \qquad (2)$$

where for $i \in \{0, \dots, k-1\}$, $a_i \in \mathsf{type}(x_i)$. For $i \in \{0, \dots, k-1\}$, let Δ_i be the set of all valuations over X_i that realize $(a_i, a_{i\oplus 1})$. We say that the cycle (2) *supports* q if for for all $i, j \in \{0, \dots, k-1\}$, for all $\mu_i \in \Delta_i$ and $\mu_j \in \Delta_j$, it is the case that μ_i and μ_j agree on all variables in $X_i \cap X_j$. Notice that $X_i \cap X_j$ can be empty. The cycle (2) may not support q, because μ_i and μ_j can disagree on variables in $X_i \cap X_j \cap \mathsf{vars}(\vec{y})$, as illustrated next.

Example 14. Let $q = \{R(\underline{x_0}, x_1, y),\ S(\underline{x_1}, x_0, y)\}$. We have $x_0 \xrightarrow{\mathsf{M}} x_1 \xrightarrow{\mathsf{M}} x_0$. Let $\mathbf{db}$ be the uncertain database containing the following facts.

R	$\underline{x_0}$	x_1	y
	a	1	α
	a	1	β

S	$\underline{x_1}$	x_0	y
	1	a	α
	1	a	β

The edge set of $\mathcal{G}(\mathbf{db})$ is $\{(a, 1), (1, a)\}$. Both $(a, 1)$ and $(1, a)$ are realized by the valuations $\{x_0 \mapsto a,\ x_1 \mapsto 1,\ y \mapsto \alpha\}$ and $\{x_0 \mapsto a,\ x_1 \mapsto 1,\ y \mapsto \beta\}$, which disagree on y. Hence, the cycle $a, 1, a$ does not support q.

On the other hand, we can assume without loss of generality that μ_i and μ_j agree on all variables in $X_i \cap X_j \cap \{x_0, \dots, x_{k-1}\}$. In particular, if $x_i \in X_j$, then $\mu_j(x_i) = \mu_i(x_i) = a_i$. To see why this is the case, assume that $x_i \in X_j$, where $i, j \in \{0, \dots, k-1\}$ and $i \neq j$. Then, it must be that $x_j \xrightarrow{\mathsf{M}} x_i$. Two cases can occur:

- if $j = i \ominus 1$, then μ_j realizes the edge $(a_{i\ominus 1}, a_i)$ and $\mu_j(x_i) = a_i$; and
- if $j \neq i \ominus 1$, then $x_j \xrightarrow{\mathsf{M}} x_i \xrightarrow{\mathsf{M}} x_{i\oplus 1} \cdots \xrightarrow{\mathsf{M}} x_{j\ominus 1} \xrightarrow{\mathsf{M}} x_j$ is a shorter Markov cycle.

The second case can be avoided by picking $\mathcal{C}$ to be the shorter cycle, as illustrated by Example 15. It can be seen that such choice of $\mathcal{C}$ is without loss of generality. In particular, in Lemma 15, if $\mathcal{C}$ was premier, then the shorter cycle will also be premier.

Example 15. Let $q = \{R(\underline{x_0}, x_1),\ S(\underline{x_1}, x_2, x_0),\ V(\underline{x_2}, x_0)\}$. Then, $x_0 \xrightarrow{\mathsf{M}} x_1 \xrightarrow{\mathsf{M}} x_2 \xrightarrow{\mathsf{M}} x_0$. We have $X_0 = \{x_0, x_1\}$, $X_1 = \{x_1, x_2, x_0\}$, and $X_2 = \{x_2, x_0\}$. Assume an uncertain database $\mathbf{db}$ with the following facts.

R	$\underline{x_0}$	x_1
	a	1
	b	1

S	$\underline{x_1}$	x_2	x_0
	1	β	a
	1	β	b

V	$\underline{x_2}$	x_0
	β	a
	β	b

[5] Strong components are defined by Definition 1.

The graph $\mathcal{G}(\mathbf{db})$ contains an elementary directed cycle $a, 1, \beta, a$. The edge $(a, 1)$ is realized by $\mu_0 = \{x_0 \mapsto a,\ x_1 \mapsto 1\}$. The edge $(1, \beta)$ is realized, among others, by $\mu_1 = \{x_1 \mapsto 1, x_2 \mapsto \beta, x_0 \mapsto b\}$. Notice that μ_0 and μ_1 disagree on x_0. Although it is easy to deal with this situation where two valuations disagree on a variable in the Markov cycle, it is even easier to avoid this situation by working with the shorter Markov cycle $x_0 \xrightarrow{\mathsf{M}} x_1 \xrightarrow{\mathsf{M}} x_0$.

We now distinguish two cases.

Case D contains either an elementary directed cycle of size k that does not support q, or an elementary directed cycle of size strictly greater than k. We show in the next paragraph how to construct a repair $\mathbf{s}$ of $\mathbf{db}_D$ such that $\mathbf{s}$ is not grelevant for q in $\mathbf{db}$. Then, by Lemma 16, every repair of $\mathbf{db}$ satisfies q if and only if every repair of $\mathbf{db} \setminus \mathbf{db}_D$ satisfies q. In this case, the reduction deletes from $\mathbf{db}$ all facts of $\mathbf{db}_D$.

The construction of $\mathbf{s}$ proceeds as follows. Pick an elementary cycle in D that has size strictly greater than k, or that has size k but does not support q. The cycle picked will henceforth be denoted by $\mathcal{E}$. Construct a maximal sequence

$$(V_0, E_0), b_1, (V_1, E_1), b_2, (V_2, E_2), \dots, b_n, (V_n, E_n)$$

where

1. V_0 is the set of vertices in $\mathcal{E}$, and E_0 is the set of directed edges in $\mathcal{E}$; and
2. for every $i \in \{1, \dots, n\}$,
   (a) $b_i \notin V_{i-1}$ and for some $c \in V_{i-1}$, (b_i, c) is a directed edge in $\mathcal{G}(\mathbf{db})$; and
   (b) $V_i = V_{i-1} \cup \{b_i\}$ and $E_i = E_{i-1} \cup \{(b_i, c)\}$.

The resulting graph (V_n, E_n) is such that V_n is equal to the vertex set of D, and E_n contains exactly one outgoing edge for each vertex in V_n. The graph (V_n, E_n) contains no directed cycle other than $\mathcal{E}$. To construct $\mathbf{s}$, for each $j \in \{0, \dots, k-1\}$, for each vertex $a \in V_n \cap \mathsf{type}(x_j)$, select some valuation μ that realizes the edge in E_n outgoing from a, and add $\mu(\mathsf{C}_q(x_j))$ to $\mathbf{s}$. If $\mathcal{E}$ has size k, then the valuations μ should be selected such that for some vertices a, b in $\mathcal{E}$, the valuations chosen for a and b disagree on some variable of $\mathsf{vars}(\vec{y})$. It is not hard to see that the set $\mathbf{s}$ so obtained is a repair of $\mathbf{db}_D$ that is not grelevant for q in $\mathbf{db}$.

We illustrate the above construction by two examples.

Example 16. In Example 14, one can choose $\mathbf{s} = \{R(\underline{a}, 1, \alpha), S(\underline{1}, a, \beta)\}$. The treatment of a directed cycle of size strictly greater than k is illustrated by $\mathbf{db}_{03}$ in Example 10.

Example 17. Let $q = \{R(\underline{x_0}, y_1, y_2), V(\underline{x_1}, y_2), S_1^c(\underline{y_1}, \underline{y_2}, x_1), S_2^c(\underline{y_2}, x_0)\}$. We have $x_0 \xrightarrow{\mathsf{M}} x_1 \xrightarrow{\mathsf{M}} x_0$, $X_0 = \{x_0, y_1, y_2\}$, and $X_1 = \{x_1, y_2\}$. Let $\mathbf{db}$ be an uncertain database with the following facts.

R	$\underline{x_0}$	y_1	y_2
	a	1	2
	a	3	4
	a	1	6

V	$\underline{x_1}$	y_2
	γ	2
	γ	4
	β	6

S_1^c	$\underline{y_1}$	$\underline{y_2}$	x_1
	1	2	γ
	3	4	γ
	1	6	β

S_2^c	$\underline{y_2}$	x_0
	2	a
	4	a
	6	a

The following table lists the edges in $\mathcal{G}(\mathbf{db})$, by type, along with the valuations that realize each edge.

Edges in $\mathsf{type}(x_0) \times \mathsf{type}(x_1)$

Edge	Realized by
(a, γ)	$\{x_0 \mapsto a, y_1 \mapsto 1, y_2 \mapsto 2\} = \mu_1$
	$\{x_0 \mapsto a, y_1 \mapsto 3, y_2 \mapsto 4\} = \mu_2$
(a, β)	$\{x_0 \mapsto a, y_1 \mapsto 1, y_2 \mapsto 6\} = \mu_3$

Edges in $\mathsf{type}(x_1) \times \mathsf{type}(x_0)$

Edge	Realized by
(γ, a)	$\{x_1 \mapsto \gamma, y_2 \mapsto 2\} = \mu_4$
	$\{x_1 \mapsto \gamma, y_2 \mapsto 4\} = \mu_5$
(β, a)	$\{x_1 \mapsto \beta, y_2 \mapsto 6\} = \mu_6$

Then, $\mathcal{G}(\mathbf{db})$ contains two elementary cycles, a, γ, a and a, β, a, both of length 2. The cycle a, β, a supports q. The cycle a, γ, a does not support q, because μ_1 and μ_5 disagree on y_2. Therefore, the edges (a, γ) and (γ, a), along with μ_1 and μ_5, will be used in the construction of a consistent set $\mathbf{s}$ that is not grelevant for q in $\mathbf{db}$. For the remaining vertex β, we add the edge (β, a), which is only realized by μ_6. Then, $\mathbf{s}$ contains the R-fact $R(\underline{a}, 1, 2)$ (because of μ_1), and the V-facts $V(\underline{\gamma}, 4)$ and $V(\underline{\beta}, 6)$ (because of μ_5 and μ_6 respectively). In this example, there is only one repair that contains $\mathbf{s}$, and this repair falsifies q.

Case every elementary directed cycle in D has length k and supports q. In this case, we will encode each cycle of D as a set of T-facts, as follows. Consider any cycle of the form (2) in D, and take the cross product

$$\Delta_0 \times \Delta_2 \times \cdots \times \Delta_{k-1}, \tag{3}$$

which is of polynomial size (in the size of $\mathbf{db}$). Since we are in the case where any cycle of the form (2) supports q, for every tuple $(\mu_0, \mu_1, \ldots, \mu_{k-1})$ in the cross product (3), the set $\mu := \bigcup_{i=0}^{k-1} \mu_i$ is a well defined valuation over $\{x_0, \ldots, x_{k-1}\} \cup \mathsf{vars}(\vec{y})$. In this case, for each such tuple, the reduction adds the following $k+1$ facts:

$$\begin{array}{l} T(\underline{D}, a_0, \ldots, a_{k-1}, \mu(\vec{y})) \\ U_0^c(\underline{a_0}, D) \\ \quad\vdots \\ U_{k-1}^c(\underline{a_{k-1}}, D) \end{array}$$

in which D is used as a constant. Recall that $a_i = \mu(x_i)$ for $i \in \{0, \ldots, k-1\}$. Notice that if the sequence $\vec{y}$ is empty, then the reduction will add exactly one T-fact for every cycle of the form (2). Otherwise, the reduction may add multiple T-facts for the same cycle, as illustrated next.

Example 18. Let $q = \{R(\underline{x_0}, x_1, y), S(\underline{x_1}, x_0)\}$. Then we have $x_0 \xrightarrow{\mathsf{M}} x_1 \xrightarrow{\mathsf{M}} x_0$ with $X_0 = \{x_0, x_1, y\}$ and $X_1 = \{x_0, x_1\}$. Let $\mathbf{db}$ be the uncertain database containing the following facts.

R	$\underline{x_0}$	x_1	y
	a	1	α
	a	1	β

S	$\underline{x_1}$	x_0
	1	a

The edge set of $\mathcal{G}(\mathbf{db})$ is $\{(a, 1), (1, a)\}$. The edge $(a, 1)$ is realized by both $\{x_0 \mapsto a, x_1 \mapsto 1, y \mapsto \alpha\}$ and $\{x_0 \mapsto a, x_1 \mapsto 1, y \mapsto \beta\}$. The edge $(1, a)$ is realized only by $\{x_0 \mapsto a, x_1 \mapsto 1\}$. The cycle $a, 1, a$ in $\mathcal{G}(\mathbf{db})$ supports q. The reduction will add the following T-facts (for some identifier D):

T	$\underline{u}$	x_0	x_1	y
	D	a	1	α
	D	a	1	β

Example 19. Take the query q of Example 17, with the following uncertain database $\mathbf{db}$.

R	$\underline{x_0}$	y_1	y_2
	a	1	2
	a	1	6
	a	3	6

V	$\underline{x_1}$	y_2
	γ	2
	β	6

S_1^c	$\underline{y_1}$	$\underline{y_2}$	x_1
	1	2	γ
	1	6	β
	3	6	β

S_2^c	$\underline{y_2}$	x_0
	2	a
	6	a

Then, $\mathcal{G}(\mathbf{db})$ contains two elementary cycles, a, γ, a and a, β, a, both of length 2 and both supporting q. The reduction will add the following T-facts (for some identifier D):

T	$\underline{u}$	x_0	x_1	y_1	y_2
	D	a	γ	1	2
	D	a	β	1	6
	D	a	β	3	6

Each relation U_i^c encodes that every constant in the set $\mathsf{type}(x_i) \cap \mathsf{adom}(\mathbf{db})$ occurs in a unique strong component of $\mathcal{G}(\mathbf{db})$. The meaning of the T-facts is as follows. Let $V = \{x_0, \ldots, x_{k-1}\} \cup \mathsf{vars}(\vec{y})$. Let Θ_D be the set of all valuations over V such that

$$T(\underline{D}, \mu(x_1), \ldots, \mu(x_{k-1}), \mu(\vec{y}))$$

has been added by the reduction. Then the following hold (recall $q_0 = \bigcup_{i=0}^{k-1} \mathsf{C}_q(x_i)$):

- for every repair $\mathbf{r}$ of $\mathbf{db}$, there exists $\mu \in \Theta_D$ such that $\mathbf{r} \models \mu(q_0)$; and
- for every $\mu \in \Theta_D$, there exists a repair $\mathbf{r}$ of $\mathbf{db}$ such that
    1. $\mathbf{r} \models \mu(q_0)$; and
    2. for each $\mu' \in \Theta_D$, if $\mu' \neq \mu$, then $\mathbf{r} \not\models \mu'(q_0)$.

The cycles in D can be found in polynomial time by solving reachability problems, as explained in [19, Theorem 4] and [9]. The crux is that the number of cycles in $\mathcal{G}(\mathbf{db})$ of length exactly k is polynomially bounded. Any longer cycle consists of an elementary path $a_0, a_1, \ldots, a_{k-1}, a_0'$ of length k ($a_0 \neq a_0'$), concatenated with an elementary path from a_0' to a_0 that contains no vertex in $\{a_1, \ldots, a_{k-1}\}$. Notice incidentally that the reduction needs to know the existence (or not) of cycles of size strictly greater than k in any strong component D, but the vertices on such cycle need not be remembered.

It can now be seen that, in general, the above reduction results in a database $\mathbf{db}'$ that is as in the following lemma.

LEMMA 18. *Let q and $\mathcal{C}$ be as in the statement of Lemma 13. Let $q^* = \mathsf{dissolve}(q, \mathcal{C})$, and let the variable u be as in Definition 5. Let $\mathbf{db}$ be an uncertain database that is input to $\mathsf{CERTAINTY}(q)$. We can compute in polynomial time an uncertain database $\mathbf{db}'$ that is a legal input to $\mathsf{CERTAINTY}(q^*)$ such that the following hold:*

1. *for every repair $\mathbf{r}$ of $\mathbf{db}$, there exists a repair $\mathbf{r}'$ of $\mathbf{db}'$ such that for every valuation θ over $\mathsf{vars}(q^*)$, if $\theta(q^*) \subseteq \mathbf{r}'$, then $\theta(q) \subseteq \mathbf{r}$; and*
2. *for every repair $\mathbf{r}'$ of $\mathbf{db}'$, there exists a repair $\mathbf{r}$ of $\mathbf{db}$ such that for every valuation θ over $\mathsf{vars}(q)$, if $\theta(q) \subseteq \mathbf{r}$, then there exists a constant D such that $\theta_{[u \mapsto D]}(q^*) \subseteq \mathbf{r}'$.*

We can now prove Lemma 13.

PROOF OF LEMMA 13. Let $\mathbf{db}$ be an uncertain database that is input to $\mathsf{CERTAINTY}(q)$. By Lemma 18, we can compute in polynomial time an uncertain database $\mathbf{db}'$ that is a legal input to $\mathsf{CERTAINTY}(q^*)$ such that $\mathbf{db}'$ satisfies conditions 1 and 2 in the statement of Lemma 18. It suffices to show that the following are equivalent.

1. Every repair of $\mathbf{db}$ satisfies q.
2. Every repair of $\mathbf{db}'$ satisfies q^*.

$\boxed{1 \Longrightarrow 2}$ Proof by contraposition. Assume a repair $\mathbf{r}'$ of $\mathbf{db}'$ such that $\mathbf{r}' \not\models q^*$. By item 2 in the statement of Lemma 18, we can assume a repair $\mathbf{r}$ of $\mathbf{db}$ such that for every valuation θ over $\mathsf{vars}(q)$, if $\theta(q) \subseteq \mathbf{r}$, then there exists a constant D such that $\theta_{[u \mapsto D]}(q^*) \subseteq \mathbf{r}'$. Obviously, if $\mathbf{r} \models q$, then $\mathbf{r}' \models q^*$, a contradiction. We conclude by contradiction that $\mathbf{r} \not\models q$. $\boxed{2 \Longrightarrow 1}$ Proof by contraposition. Assume a repair $\mathbf{r}$ of $\mathbf{db}$ such that $\mathbf{r} \not\models q$. By item 1 in the statement of Lemma 18, we can assume a repair $\mathbf{r}'$ of $\mathbf{db}'$ such that for every valuation θ over $\mathsf{vars}(q^*)$, if $\theta(q^*) \subseteq \mathbf{r}'$, then $\theta(q) \subseteq \mathbf{r}$. Obviously, $\mathbf{r}' \not\models q^*$. $\square$

7. CONCLUSION

This paper settles a long-standing open question in consistent query answering, by providing a solution to the complexity classification task of $\mathsf{CERTAINTY}(q)$ for q ranging over the class of self-join-free Boolean conjunctive queries. In particular, we showed that, given q, there exists a procedure that looks at the structure of the attack graph of q and decides whether $\mathsf{CERTAINTY}(q)$ is in $\mathbf{FO}$, in $\mathbf{P} \setminus \mathbf{FO}$, or $\mathbf{coNP}$-complete.

The exciting question that still remains open is whether our results can be extended beyond self-join-free conjunctive queries, to conjunctive queries with self-joins and unions of conjunctive queries.

Acknowledgments

This work is supported in part by the NSF through NSF grant NSF IIS-1115188.

8. REFERENCES

[1] M. Arenas, L. E. Bertossi, and J. Chomicki. Consistent query answers in inconsistent databases. In *PODS*, pages 68–79. ACM Press, 1999.

[2] B. Aspvall, M. F. Plass, and R. E. Tarjan. A linear-time algorithm for testing the truth of certain quantified boolean formulas. *Inf. Process. Lett.*, 8(3):121–123, 1979.

[3] C. Beeri, R. Fagin, D. Maier, and M. Yannakakis. On the desirability of acyclic database schemes. *J. ACM*, 30(3):479–513, 1983.

[4] L. E. Bertossi. *Database Repairing and Consistent Query Answering*. Synthesis Lectures on Data Management. Morgan & Claypool Publishers, 2011.

[5] A. A. Bulatov. Complexity of conservative constraint satisfaction problems. *ACM Trans. Comput. Log.*, 12(4):24, 2011.

[6] G. Fontaine. Why is it hard to obtain a dichotomy for consistent query answering? In *LICS*, pages 550–559. IEEE Computer Society, 2013.

[7] A. Fuxman and R. J. Miller. First-order query rewriting for inconsistent databases. In T. Eiter and L. Libkin, editors, *ICDT*, volume 3363 of *Lecture Notes in Computer Science*, pages 337–351. Springer, 2005.

[8] P. G. Kolaitis and E. Pema. A dichotomy in the complexity of consistent query answering for queries with two atoms. *Inf. Process. Lett.*, 112(3):77–85, 2012.

[9] P. Koutris and D. Suciu. A dichotomy on the complexity of consistent query answering for atoms with simple keys. In Schweikardt et al. [15], pages 165–176.

[10] P. Koutris and J. Wijsen. A trichotomy in the data complexity of certain query answering for conjunctive queries. *CoRR*, abs/1501.07864, 2015.

[11] L. Libkin. *Elements of Finite Model Theory*. Springer, 2004.

[12] D. Maslowski and J. Wijsen. A dichotomy in the complexity of counting database repairs. *J. Comput. Syst. Sci.*, 79(6):958–983, 2013.

[13] D. Maslowski and J. Wijsen. Counting database repairs that satisfy conjunctive queries with self-joins. In Schweikardt et al. [15], pages 155–164.

[14] G. J. Minty. On maximal independent sets of vertices in claw-free graphs. *J. Comb. Theory, Ser. B*, 28(3):284–304, 1980.

[15] N. Schweikardt, V. Christophides, and V. Leroy, editors. *Proc. 17th International Conference on Database Theory (ICDT), Athens, Greece, March 24-28, 2014.* OpenProceedings.org, 2014.

[16] J. Wijsen. On the first-order expressibility of computing certain answers to conjunctive queries over uncertain databases. In J. Paredaens and D. V. Gucht, editors, *PODS*, pages 179–190. ACM, 2010.

[17] J. Wijsen. A remark on the complexity of consistent conjunctive query answering under primary key violations. *Inf. Process. Lett.*, 110(21):950–955, 2010.

[18] J. Wijsen. Certain conjunctive query answering in first-order logic. *ACM Trans. Database Syst.*, 37(2):9, 2012.

[19] J. Wijsen. Charting the tractability frontier of certain conjunctive query answering. In R. Hull and W. Fan, editors, *PODS*, pages 189–200. ACM, 2013.

[20] J. Wijsen. A survey of the data complexity of consistent query answering under key constraints. In C. Beierle and C. Meghini, editors, *Foundations of Information and Knowledge Systems - 8th International Symposium, FoIKS 2014, Bordeaux, France, March 3-7, 2014. Proceedings*, volume 8367 of *Lecture Notes in Computer Science*, pages 62–78. Springer, 2014.

APPENDIX

A. PROOF OF LEMMA 9

We first show two helping lemmas.

LEMMA 19. *Let q be a self-join-free Boolean conjunctive query. Let $X \subseteq \mathsf{vars}(q)$ and let $G \in q$ be an R-atom such for every $x \in X$, $G \overset{q}{\not\rightsquigarrow} x$. Let $\mathbf{r}$ be a repair of some database such that $\mathbf{r} \models q$. Let $A \in \mathbf{r}$ be an R-fact that is relevant for q in $\mathbf{r}$. Let B be key-equal to A and $\mathbf{r}_B = (\mathbf{r} \setminus \{A\}) \cup \{B\}$. Then, for every valuation ζ over X, if $\mathbf{r}_B \models \zeta(q)$, then $\mathbf{r} \models \zeta(q)$.*

PROOF. Let ζ be a valuation over X such that $\mathbf{r}_B \models \zeta(q)$. We can assume a valuation ζ^+ over $\mathsf{vars}(q)$ such that $\zeta^+[X] = \zeta[X]$ and $\zeta^+(q) \subseteq \mathbf{r}_B$. Thus, ζ^+ extends ζ to $\mathsf{vars}(q)$. We need to show $\mathbf{r} \models \zeta(q)$, which is obvious if $B \notin \zeta^+(q)$. Assume next $B \in \zeta^+(q)$. Since A is relevant for q in $\mathbf{r}$, we can assume a valuation μ over $\mathsf{vars}(q)$ such that $A \in \mu(q) \subseteq \mathbf{r}$. Let $q' = q \setminus \{G\}$. Let $\mathbf{r}' = \mathbf{r}_B \setminus \{B\} = \mathbf{r} \setminus \{A\}$. Since q' contains no R-atom (no self-join), $\zeta^+(q') \subseteq \mathbf{r}'$ and $\mu(q') \subseteq \mathbf{r}'$. Moreover, $\zeta^+[\mathsf{key}(G)] = \mu[\mathsf{key}(G)]$, because A and B are key-equal.

From $\mathcal{K}(q') \models \mathsf{key}(G) \rightarrow G^{+,q}$ and [18, Lemma 4.3], it follows $\zeta^+[G^{+,q}] = \mu[G^{+,q}]$.

Let τ be the complete edge-labeled undirected graph whose vertices are the atoms of q; an edge between H and H' is labeled by $\mathsf{vars}(H) \cap \mathsf{vars}(H')$.

Let τ' be the graph obtained from τ by cutting every edge whose label is included in $G^{+,q}$. Let q_G be the subset of q containing all atoms that are in τ''s strong component that contains G. Let $q_X = q \setminus q_G$.

Let κ be the valuation over $\mathsf{vars}(q)$ such that for every $x \in \mathsf{vars}(q)$,

$$\kappa(x) = \begin{cases} \mu(x) & \text{if } x \in \mathsf{vars}(q_G) \\ \zeta^+(x) & \text{if } x \in \mathsf{vars}(q_X) \end{cases}$$

We show that κ is well defined. Assume $x \in \mathsf{vars}(q_X) \cap \mathsf{vars}(q_G)$. Then, there exist atoms $F' \in q_X$ and $G' \in q_G$ such that $x \in \mathsf{vars}(F') \cap \mathsf{vars}(G')$. Since F' and G' belong to distinct strong components of τ', it follows $\mathsf{vars}(F') \cap \mathsf{vars}(G') \subseteq G^{+,q}$. Consequently, $x \in G^{+,q}$. Since $\zeta^+[G^{+,q}] = \mu[G^{+,q}]$, it follows that $\mu(x) = \zeta^+(x)$.

Obviously, $\kappa(q) \subseteq \mathbf{r}$. Finally, we show that for every $u \in X$, $\kappa(u) = \zeta(u)$. This is obvious if $u \in X \cap G^{+,q}$. Assume next that $u \in X \setminus G^{+,q}$. Since $G \overset{q}{\not\rightsquigarrow} u$ by the assumption in the statement of Lemma 19, it must be the case $u \in \mathsf{vars}(q_X)$, hence $\kappa(u) = \zeta^+(u) = \zeta(u)$. It follows $\mathbf{r} \models \zeta(q)$. This concludes the proof. □

The following helping lemma extends [18, Lemma B.1].

LEMMA 20. *Let q be a self-join-free Boolean conjunctive query. Let $F \in q$ such that F has zero indegree in the attack graph of q. Let $\mathbf{r}$ be a repair of some database. Let $A \in \mathbf{r}$ such that A is relevant for q in $\mathbf{r}$.[6] Let B be key-equal to A and $\mathbf{r}_B = (\mathbf{r} \setminus \{A\}) \cup \{B\}$. Then, for every valuation ζ over $\mathsf{key}(F)$, if $\mathbf{r}_B \models \zeta(q)$, then $\mathbf{r} \models \zeta(q)$.*

PROOF. The proof is obvious if A has the same relation name as F. Assume next that relation names in A and F are distinct. We can assume some atom $G \in q \setminus \{F\}$ such that A has the same relation name as G. Since $G \overset{q}{\not\rightsquigarrow} F$, we have that for each $x \in \mathsf{key}(F)$, $G \overset{q}{\not\rightsquigarrow} x$. The desired result then follows by Lemma 19. □

Assume that a query q contains an R-atom that has no incoming attack in the attack graph of q. Paraphrasing Lemma 20, if one replaces, in a repair $\mathbf{r}$, some relevant fact A with another fact B that belongs to the same block as A, then every R-fact of $\mathbf{r}$ that was not relevant in $\mathbf{r}$, will remain non-relevant in $(\mathbf{r} \setminus \{A\}) \cup \{B\}$. Notice, however, that the fact B may be non-relevant in the new repair $(\mathbf{r} \setminus \{A\}) \cup \{B\}$. The proof of Lemma 9 can now be given.

PROOF OF LEMMA 9. Let $X = \mathsf{key}(F)$. Let $\mathbf{db}$ be an uncertain database. Let $\mathbf{r}$ be a repair of $\mathbf{db}$ that is $\preceq_q^X$-frugal. Let $\mathbf{s}$ be any repair of $\mathbf{db}$. Construct a maximal sequence

$$(\mathbf{r}_0, \mathbf{s}_0), (\mathbf{r}_1, \mathbf{s}_1), \ldots, (\mathbf{r}_n, \mathbf{s}_n) \tag{4}$$

where

1. $\mathbf{r}_0 = \mathbf{r}$ and $\mathbf{s}_0 = \mathbf{s}$;
2. for every $i \in \{1, \ldots, n\}$, one of the following holds:
   (a) $\mathbf{r}_i = \mathbf{r}_{i-1}$ and $\mathbf{s}_i = (\mathbf{s}_{i-1} \setminus \{A\}) \cup \{B\}$ for distinct, key-equal facts A, B such that $A \in \mathbf{s}_{i-1}$, $B \in \mathbf{r}_{i-1}$, and A is relevant for q in $\mathbf{s}_{i-1}$; or
   (b) $\mathbf{s}_i = \mathbf{s}_{i-1}$ and $\mathbf{r}_i = (\mathbf{r}_{i-1} \setminus \{A\}) \cup \{B\}$ for distinct, key-equal facts A, B such that $A \in \mathbf{r}_{i-1}$, $B \in \mathbf{s}_{i-1}$, and A is relevant for q in $\mathbf{r}_{i-1}$.

That is, the construction repeatedly replaces a fact that is relevant in one repair with its distinct, key-equal fact in the other repair. The sequence (4) is finite, since the total number of distinct relevant facts distinguishes at each step. For the last element $(\mathbf{r}_n, \mathbf{s}_n)$, it holds that the set of facts that are relevant for q in $\mathbf{r}_n$ is equal the set of facts that are relevant for q in $\mathbf{s}_n$. It follows that for every valuation θ over X,

$$\mathbf{r}_n \models \theta(q) \iff \mathbf{s}_n \models \theta(q). \tag{5}$$

By Lemma 20, for every valuation θ over X,

$$\mathbf{r}_n \models \theta(q) \implies \mathbf{r} \models \theta(q), \tag{6}$$

$$\mathbf{s}_n \models \theta(q) \implies \mathbf{s} \models \theta(q). \tag{7}$$

From (6) and since $\mathbf{r}$ is $\preceq_q^X$-frugal, it follows that for every valuation θ over X,

$$\mathbf{r}_n \models \theta(q) \iff \mathbf{r} \models \theta(q). \tag{8}$$

From (8), (5), and (7), it follows that for every valuation θ over X,

$$\mathbf{r} \models \theta(q) \implies \mathbf{s} \models \theta(q).$$

Since $\mathbf{s}$ is an arbitrary repair, the desired result follows. □

[6]Recall from Section 3 that $A \in \mathbf{r}$ is *relevant* for q in $\mathbf{r}$ if $A \in \theta(q) \subseteq \mathbf{r}$ for some valuation θ over $\mathsf{vars}(q)$.

High-Level Why-Not Explanations using Ontologies

Balder ten Cate
LogicBlox and UCSC
balder.tencate@gmail.com

Cristina Civili
Sapienza Univ. of Rome
civili@dis.uniroma1.it

Evgeny Sherkhonov
Univ. of Amsterdam
e.sherkhonov@uva.nl

Wang-Chiew Tan
UCSC
tan@cs.ucsc.edu

ABSTRACT

We propose a novel foundational framework for *why-not explanations*, that is, explanations for why a tuple is missing from a query result. Our why-not explanations leverage concepts from an ontology to provide high-level and meaningful reasons for why a tuple is missing from the result of a query.

A key algorithmic problem in our framework is that of *computing a most-general explanation* for a why-not question, relative to an ontology, which can either be provided by the user, or it may be automatically derived from the data and/or schema. We study the complexity of this problem and associated problems, and present concrete algorithms for computing why-not explanations. In the case where an external ontology is provided, we first show that the problem of deciding the existence of an explanation to a why-not question is NP-complete in general. However, the problem is solvable in polynomial time for queries of bounded arity, provided that the ontology is specified in a suitable language, such as a member of the DL-Lite family of description logics, which allows for efficient concept subsumption checking. Furthermore, we show that a most-general explanation can be computed in polynomial time in this case. In addition, we propose a method for deriving a suitable (virtual) ontology from a database and/or a schema, and we present an algorithm for computing a most-general explanation to a why-not question, relative to such ontologies. This algorithm runs in polynomial-time in the case when concepts are defined in a selection-free language, or if the underlying schema is fixed. Finally, we also study the problem of computing *short* most-general explanations, and we briefly discuss alternative definitions of what it means to be an explanation, and to be most general.

Categories and Subject Descriptors

H.2 [**Database Management**]

General Terms

Theory, Algorithms

Keywords

Databases; Why-Not Explanations; Provenance; Ontologies

PODS'15, May 31–June 4, 2015, Melbourne, Victoria, Australia.

ACM 978-1-4503-2757-2/15/05 ...$15.00.
http://dx.doi.org/10.1145/2745754.2745765.

1. INTRODUCTION AND RESULTS

An increasing number of databases are derived, extracted, or curated from disparate data sources. Consequently, it becomes more and more important to provide data consumers with mechanisms that will allow them to gain an understanding of data that they are confronted with. An essential functionality towards this goal is the capability to provide meaningful explanations about why data is present or missing form the result of a query. Explanations help data consumers gauge how much trust one can place on the result. Perhaps more importantly, they provide useful information for debugging the query or data that led to incorrect results.

This is particularly the case in scenarios where complex data analysis tasks are specified through large collections of nested views (i.e., views that may be defined in terms of other views). For example, schemas with nested view definitions and integrity constraints capture the core of LogiQL [18, 21, 19] (where view definitions may, in general, involve not only relational operations, but also aggregation, machine learning and mathematical optimization tasks). LogiQL is a language developed and used at LogicBlox [2] for developing data-intensive "self service" applications involving complex data analytics workflows. Similar recent industrial systems include Datomic[1] and Google's Yedalog [16]. In each of these systems, nested view definitions (or, Datalog programs) are used to specify complex workflows to drive data-analytics tasks. Explanations for unexpected query results (such as an unexpected tuple or a missing tuple) are very useful in such settings, since the source of an error can be particularly hard to track.

There has been considerable research on the topic of deriving explanations for why a tuple belongs to the output of a query. Early systems were developed in [3, 28] to provide explanations for answers to logic programs in the context of a deductive database. The presence of a tuple in the output is explained by enumerating all possible derivations, that is, instantiations of the logic rules that derive the answer tuple. In [28], the system also explains missing answers, by providing a partially instantiated rule, based on the missing tuple, and leaving the user to figure out how the rest of the rule would have to be instantiated. In the last decade or so, there has been significant efforts to characterize different notions of provenance (or lineage) of query answers (see, e.g., [15, 20]) which can also be applied to understand why an answer is in the query result.

There have also been extensive studies on the *why-not problem* (e.g., more recent studies include [6, 14, 23, 22, 25, 29]). The why-not problem is the problem of explaining why an answer is missing from the output. Since [28], the *why-not problem* was also studied in [22, 23] in the context of debugging results of data extracted via select-project-join queries, and, subsequently, a larger class of queries that also includes union and aggregation opera-

[1]`www.datomic.com`

tors. Unlike [28] which is geared towards providing explanations for answers and missing answers, the goal in [23] is to propose modifications to underlying database I, yielding another database I' based on the provenance of the missing tuple, constraints, and trust specification at hand, so that the missing tuple appears in the result of the same query q over the updated database I'. In contrast to the *data-centric* approach of updating the database to derive the missing answer, another line of research [8, 14, 29] follows a *query-centric* approach whereby the query q at hand is modified to q' (without modifying the underlying database) so that the missing answer appears in the output of $q'(I)$.

A new take on why-not questions: In this paper, we develop a novel foundational framework for why-not explanations that is principally different from prior approaches. Our approach is neither data-centric nor query-centric. Instead, we derive high-level explanations via an ontology that is either provided, or is derived from the data or schema. Our immediate goal is not to compute repairs of the underlying database or query so that the missing answer would appear in the result. Rather, as in [28], our primary goal is to provide understandable explanations for why an answer is missing from the query result. As we will illustrate, explanations that are based on an ontology have the potential to be high-level and provide meaningful insight to why a tuple is missing from the result. This is because an ontology abstracts a domain in terms of concepts and relationships amongst concepts. Hence, explanations that are based on concepts and relationships from an ontology will embody such high-level abstractions. As we shall describe, our work considers two cases. The first is when an ontology is provided externally, in which case explanations will embody external knowledge about the domain. The second is when an ontology is not provided. For the latter, we allow an ontology to be derived from the schema, and hence explanations will embody knowledge about the domain through concepts and relationships that are defined over the schema.

Formally, an explanation for why a tuple $\overline{a}$ is not among the results of a query $q(I)$, in our framework, is a tuple of concepts from the ontology whose extension includes the missing tuple $\overline{a}$ and, at the same time, does not include any tuples from $q(I)$. For example, a query may ask for all products that each store has in stock, in the form of (product ID, store ID) pairs, from the database of a large retail company. A user may then ask why is the pair *(P0034, S012)* not among the result of the query. Suppose *P0034* refers to a bluetooth headset product and *S012* refers to a particular store in San Francisco. If *P0034* is an instance of a concept *bluetooth headsets* and *S012* is an instance of a concept *stores in San Francisco*, and suppose that no pair (x, y), where x is an instance of *bluetooth headset* and y is an instance of *stores in San Francisco*, belongs to the query result. Then the pair of concepts (*bluetooth headset, stores in San Francisco*) is an explanation for the given why-not question. Intuitively, it signifies the fact that "*none of the stores in San Francisco has any bluetooth headsets on stock*".

There may be multiple explanations for a given why-not question. In the above example, this would be the case if, for instance, *S012* belongs also to a more general concept *stores in California*, and that none of the stores in California have bluetooth headsets on stock. Our goal is to compute a *most-general explanation*, that is, an explanation that is not strictly subsumed by any other explanation. We study the complexity of computing a most-general explanation to a why-not question. Formally, we define a *why-not instance* (or, *why-not question*) to be a quintuple $(\mathbf{S}, I, q, Ans, \overline{a})$ where $\mathbf{S}$ is a *schema*, which may include integrity constraints; I is an instance of $\mathbf{S}$; q is a query over $\mathbf{S}$; $Ans = q(I)$; and $\overline{a} \notin q(I)$.

As mentioned earlier, a particular scenario where why-not questions easily arise is when querying schemas that include a large collection of views, and where each view may be nested, that is, defined in terms of other views. Our framework captures this setting, since view definitions can be expressed by means of constraints.

Our framework supports a very general notion of an ontology, which we call $\mathbf{S}$-*ontologies*. For a given relational schema $\mathbf{S}$, an $\mathbf{S}$-ontology is a triple $(\mathcal{C}, \sqsubseteq, ext)$ which defines the set of concepts, the subsumption relationship between concepts, and respectively, the extension of each concept w.r.t. an instance of the schema $\mathbf{S}$. We use this general notion of an $\mathbf{S}$-ontology to formalize the key notions of *explanations* and *most-general explanations*, and we show that $\mathbf{S}$-ontologies capture two different types of ontologies.

The first type of ontologies we consider are those that are defined externally, provided that there is a way to associate the concepts in the externally defined ontology to the instance at hand. For example, the ontology may be represented in the form of a Ontology-Based Data Access (OBDA) specification [26]. More precisely, an OBDA specification consists of a set of concepts and subsumption relation specified by means of a description logic terminology, and a set of *mapping assertions* that relates the concepts to a relational database schema at hand. Every OBDA specification induces a corresponding $\mathbf{S}$-ontology. If the concepts and subsumption relation are defined by a TBox in a tractable description logic such as $DL\text{-}Lite_{\mathcal{R}}$, and the mapping assertions are Global-As-View (GAV) assertions, the induced $\mathbf{S}$-ontology can in fact be computed from the OBDA specification in polynomial time. We then present an algorithm for computing all most-general explanations to a why-not question, given an external $\mathbf{S}$-ontology. The algorithm runs in polynomial time when the arity of the query is bounded, and it executes in exponential time in general. We show that the exponential running time is unavoidable, unless P=NP, because the problem of deciding whether or not there exists an explanation to a why-not question given an external $\mathbf{S}$-ontology is NP-complete in general.

The second type of ontologies that we consider are ontologies that are derived either (a) from a schema $\mathbf{S}$, or (b) from an instance of the schema. In both cases, the concepts of the ontology are defined through concept expressions in a suitable language $L_{\mathbf{S}}$ that we develop. Specifically, our concepts are obtained from the relations in the schema, through selections, projections, and intersection. The difference between the two cases lies in the way the subsumption relation $\sqsubseteq$ is defined. In the former, a concept C is considered to be subsumed in another concept C' if the extension of C is contained in the extension of C' over all instances of the schema. For the latter, subsumption is considered to hold if the extension of C is contained in the extension of C' with respect to the given instance of the schema. The $\mathbf{S}$-ontology induced by a schema $\mathbf{S}$, or instance I, denoted $\mathcal{O}_{\mathbf{S}}$ or $\mathcal{O}_I$, respectively, is typically infinite, and is not intended to be materialized. Instead, we present an algorithm for directly computing a most-general explanation with respect to $\mathcal{O}_I$. The algorithm runs in exponential time in general. However, if the schema is of bounded arity, the algorithm runs in polynomial time. As for computing most-general explanations with respect to $\mathcal{O}_{\mathbf{S}}$, we identify restrictions on the integrity constraints under which the problem is decidable, and we present complexity upper bounds for these cases.

More related work: The use of ontologies to facilitate access to databases is not new. A prominent example is OBDA, where queries are either posed directly against an ontology, or an ontology is used to enrich a data schema against which queries are posed with additional relations (namely, the concepts from the ontology) [9, 26]. Answers are computed based on an open-world assumption and using the mapping assertions and ontology provided by the OBDA specification. As we described above, we make use of OBDA specifications as a means to specify an external ontology and with a database instance through mapping assertions. However, unlike in OBDA, we consider queries posed against a database instance under the traditional closed-world semantics, and the ontology is used only to derive why-not explanations.

The problems of providing why explanations and why-not explanations have also been investigated in the context of OBDA in [11] and [13], respectively. The why-not explanations of [13] follow the *data-centric* approach to why-not provenance as we discussed earlier where their goal is to modify the assertions that describe the extensions of concepts in the ontology so that the missing tuple will appear in the query result.

There has also been prior work on extracting ontologies from data. For example, in [24], the authors considered heuristics to automatically generate an ontology from a relational database by defining project-join queries over the data. Other examples on ontology extraction from data include publishing relational data as RDF graphs or statements (e.g., D2RQ [10], Triplify [5]). We emphasize that our goal is not to extract and materialize ontologies, but rather, to use an ontology that is derived from data to compute why-not explanations.

Outline: After the preliminaries, in Section 3 we present our framework for why-not explanations. In Section 4 we discuss in detail the two ways of obtaining an **S**-ontology. In Section 5 we present our main algorithmic results. Finally, in Section 6, we study variatations of our framework, including the problem of producing *short* most-general explanations, and alternative notions of *explanation*, and of what it means to be *most general*.

2. PRELIMINARIES

A *schema* is a pair $(\mathbf{S}, \Sigma)$, where $\mathbf{S}$ is a set $\{R_1, \ldots, R_n\}$ of relation names, where each relation name has an associated arity, and Σ is a set of first-order sentences over $\mathbf{S}$, which we will refer as *integrity constraints*. Abusing the notation, we will write $\mathbf{S}$ for the schema $(\mathbf{S}, \Sigma)$. A *fact* is an expression of the form $R(b_1, \ldots, b_k)$ where $R \in \mathbf{S}$ is a relation of arity k, and for $1 \leq i \leq k$, we have $b_i \in \mathbf{Const}$, where $\mathbf{Const}$ is a countably infinite set of constants. We assume a dense linear order $<$ on $\mathbf{Const}$. An *attribute* A of an k-ary relation name $R \in \mathbf{S}$ is a number i such that $1 \leq i \leq k$. For a fact $R(\overline{b})$ where $\overline{b} = b_1, \ldots, b_k$, we sometimes write $\pi_{A_1,\ldots,A_k}(\overline{b})$ to mean the tuple consisting of the A_1th, ..., A_kth constants in the tuple $\overline{b}$, that is, the value $(b_{A_1}, \ldots, b_{A_k})$. An *atom over* $\mathbf{S}$ is an expression $R(x_1, \ldots, x_n)$, where $R \in \mathbf{S}$ and every $x_i, i \in \{1, \ldots, n\}$ is a variable or a constant.

A *database instance*, or simply an *instance*, I over $\mathbf{S}$ is a set of facts over $\mathbf{S}$ satisfying the integrity constraints Σ. Equivalently, an instance I is a map that assigns to each k-ary relation name $R \in \mathbf{S}$ a finite set of k-tuples over $\mathbf{Const}$ such that the integrity constraints are satisfied. By R^I we denote the set of these tuples. We write $\text{Inst}(\mathbf{S})$ to denote the set of all database instances over $\mathbf{S}$, and $\text{adom}(I)$ to denote the active domain of I, i.e., the set of all constants occurring in facts of I.

Queries A *conjunctive query* (CQ) over $\mathbf{S}$ is a query of the form $\exists \overline{y}.\varphi(\overline{x}, \overline{y})$ where φ is a conjunction of atoms over $\mathbf{S}$. Given an instance I and a CQ q, we write $q(I)$ to denote the set of answers of q over I. In this paper we allow conjunctive queries containing comparisons to constants, that is, comparisons of the form $x \,\mathsf{op}\, c$, where $\mathsf{op} \in \{=, <, >, \leq, \geq\}$ and $c \in \mathbf{Const}$. We show that all upper bounds hold for the case of CQs with such comparisons, and all lower bounds hold without the use of comparisons (unless explicitly specified otherwise). We do *not* allow comparisons between variables.

Integrity constraints In this paper we consider different classes of integrity constraints, including functional dependencies and inclusion dependencies. We also consider UCQ-view definitions and nested UCQ-view definitions, which can be expressed using integrity constraints as well.

A *functional dependency* (FD) on a relation $R \in \mathbf{S}$ is an expression of the form $R : X \rightarrow Y$ where X and Y are subsets of the set of attributes of R. We say that an instance I over $\mathbf{S}$ satisfies the FD if for every $\overline{a}_1$ and $\overline{a}_2$ from R^I if $\pi_A(\overline{a}_1) = \pi_A(\overline{a}_2)$ for every $A \in X$, then $\pi_B(\overline{a}_1) = \pi_B(\overline{a}_2)$ for every $B \in Y$.

An *inclusion dependency* (ID) is an expression of the form

$$R[A_1, \ldots, A_n] \subseteq S[B_1, \ldots, B_n]$$

where $R, S \in \mathbf{S}$, each A_i and B_j is an attribute of R and S respectively. We say that an instance I over $\mathbf{S}$ satisfies the ID if

$$\{\pi_{A_1,\ldots,A_n}(\overline{a}) \mid \overline{a} \in R^I\} \subseteq \{\pi_{B_1,\ldots,B_n}(\overline{b}) \mid \overline{b} \in S^I\}.$$

Note that functional and integrity constraints can equivalently be written as first-order sentences [1].

View Definitions To simplify presentation, we treat view defintions as a special case of integrity constraints.

A set of integrity constraints Σ over $\mathbf{S}$ is said to be a *collection of UCQ-view definitions* if there exists a partition $\mathbf{S} = \mathbf{D} \cup \mathbf{V}$ such that for every $P \in \mathbf{V}$, Σ contains exactly one first-order sentence of the form:

$$P(\overline{x}) \leftrightarrow \vee_{i=1}^{k} \varphi_i(\overline{x}), \qquad (*)$$

where each φ_i is a conjunctive query (with comparisons to constants) over $\mathbf{D}$.

Similarly, a set of integrity constraints Σ over $\mathbf{S}$ is said to be a *collection of nested UCQ-view definitions* if there exists a partition $\mathbf{S} = \mathbf{D} \cup \mathbf{V}$ such that for every $P \in \mathbf{V}$, Σ contains exactly one first-order sentence of the form (*), where each φ_i is now allowed to be a conjunctive query over $\mathbf{D} \cup \mathbf{V}$, but subject to the following acyclicity condition. Let us say that $P \in \mathbf{V}$ *depends on* $R \in \mathbf{V}$, if R occurs in the view definition of P, that is, in the sentence of Σ that is of the form (*) for P. We require that the "depends on" relation is acyclic. If, in the view definition of every $P \in \mathbf{V}$, each disjunct φ_i contains at most one atom over $\mathbf{V}$, then we say that Σ is a collection of *linearly* nested UCQ-view definitions.

Note that a collection of nested UCQ-view definitions (in the absence of comparisons) can be equivalently viewed as a non-recursive Datalog program and vice versa [7]. In particular, a collection of linearly nested UCQ-view definitions corresponds to a linear non-recursive Datalog program.

Example 2.1. As an example of a schema, consider $\mathbf{S} = \mathbf{D} \cup \mathbf{V}$ with the integrity constraints in Figure 1. An instance I of the schema $\mathbf{S}$ is given in Figure 2. □

3. WHY-NOT EXPLANATIONS

Next, we introduce our ontology-based framework for explaining why a tuple is not in the output of a query. Our framework is based on a general notion of an ontology. As we shall describe in Section 4, the ontology that is used may be an external ontology (for example, an existing ontology specified in a description logic), or it may be an ontology that is derived from a schema. Both are a special case of our general definition of an **S**-ontology.

Definition 3.1 (**S**-ontology). *An* **S**-ontology *over a relational schema* $\mathbf{S}$ *is a triple* $\mathcal{O} = (\mathcal{C}, \sqsubseteq, ext)$*, where*

Data schema $\mathbf{D}$:

{Cities(name, population, country, continent),
Train-Connections(city_from, city_to)}

View schema $\mathbf{V}$:

{BigCity(name), EuropeanCountry(name),
Reachable(city_from, city_to)}

UCQ-view definitions:

BigCity(x)	$\leftrightarrow$	Cities(x,y,z,w) $\wedge$ $y \geq 5000000$
EuropeanCountry(z)	$\leftrightarrow$	Cities(x,y,z,w) $\wedge$ w = Europe
Reachable(x,y)	$\leftrightarrow$	Train-Connections(x,y) $\vee$ (Train-Connections(x,z) $\wedge$ Train-Connections (z,y))

Functional and inclusion dependencies:

country	$\rightarrow$	continent
BigCity[name]	$\subseteq$	Train-Connections[city_from]
Train-Connections[city_from]	$\subseteq$	Cities[name]
Train-Connections[city_to]	$\subseteq$	Cities[name]

Figure 1: Example of a schema S.

Cities

name	population	country	continent
Amsterdam	779,808	Netherlands	Europe
Berlin	3,502,000	Germany	Europe
Rome	2,753,000	Italy	Europe
New York	8,337,000	USA	N.America
San Francisco	837,442	USA	N.America
Santa Cruz	59,946	USA	N.America
Tokyo	13,185, 000	Japan	Asia
Kyoto	1,400,000	Japan	Asia

Train-Connections

city_from	city_to
Amsterdam	Berlin
Berlin	Rome
Berlin	Amsterdam
New York	San Francisco
San Francisco	Santa Cruz
Tokyo	Kyoto

BigCity

name
New York
Tokyo

EuropeanCountry

name
Netherlands
Germany
Italy

Reachable

city_from	city_to
Amsterdam	Berlin
Berlin	Rome
Berlin	Amsterdam
New York	San Francisco
San Francisco	Santa Cruz
Tokyo	Kyoto
Amsterdam	Rome
Amsterdam	Amsterdam
Berlin	Berlin
New York	Santa Cruz

Figure 2: Example of an instance I of S.

- $\mathcal{C}$ *is a possibly infinite set, whose elements are called* concepts,
- $\sqsubseteq$ *is a pre-order (i.e., a reflexive and transitive binary relation) on* $\mathcal{C}$, *called the* subsumption relation, *and*
- $ext : \mathcal{C} \times \text{Inst}(\mathbf{S}) \rightarrow \wp(\mathbf{Const})$ *is a polynomial-time computable function that will be used to identify instances of a concept in a given database instance* ($\wp(\mathbf{Const})$ *denotes the powerset of* $\mathbf{Const}$).

More precisely, we assume that ext *is specified by a Turing machine that, given* $C \in \mathcal{C}$, $I \in \text{Inst}(\mathbf{S})$ *and* $c \in \mathbf{Const}$, *decides in polynomial time if* $c \in ext(C, I)$.

A database instance $I \in \text{Inst}(\mathbf{S})$ *is* consistent *with* $\mathcal{O}$ *if, for all* $C_1, C_2 \in \mathcal{C}$ *with* $C_1 \sqsubseteq C_2$, *we have* $ext(C_1, I) \subseteq ext(C_2, I)$.

An example of an S-ontology $\mathcal{O} = (\mathcal{C}, \sqsubseteq, ext)$ is shown in Figure 3, where the concept subsumption relation $\sqsubseteq$ is depicted by means of a Hasse diagram. Note that, in this example, $ext(C, I)$ is independent of the database instance I (and, as a consequence, every S-instance is consistent with $\mathcal{O}$). In general, this is not the case (for example, the extension of a concept may be determined through mapping assertions, cf. Section 4.1).

We define our notion of an ontology-based explanation next.

Definition 3.2 (Explanation). *Let* $\mathcal{O} = (\mathcal{C}, \sqsubseteq, ext)$ *be an* $\mathbf{S}$*-ontology,* I *an* $\mathbf{S}$*-instance consistent with* $\mathcal{O}$. *Let* q *be an* m*-ary query over* $\mathbf{S}$, *and* $\overline{a} = (a_1, \ldots, a_m)$ *a tuple of constants such that* $\overline{a} \notin q(I)$. *Then a tuple of concepts* $(C_1, \ldots, C_m)$ *from* $\mathcal{C}^m$ *is called an* explanation *for* $\overline{a} \notin q(I)$ *with respect to* $\mathcal{O}$ *(or an* explanation *in short) if:*

- *for every* $1 \leq i \leq m$, $a_i \in ext(C_i, I)$, *and*
- $(ext(C_1, I) \times \ldots \times ext(C_m, I)) \cap q(I) = \emptyset$.

In other words, an explanation is a tuple of concepts whose extension includes the missing tuple $\overline{a}$ (and thus explains $\overline{a}$) but, at the same time, it does not include any tuple in $q(I)$ (and thus does not explain any tuple in $q(I)$). Intuitively, the tuple of concepts is an explanation that is orthogonal to existing tuples in $q(I)$ but relevant for the missing tuple $\overline{a}$, and thus forms an explanation for why $\overline{a}$ is not in $q(I)$. There can be multiple explanations in general and the "best" explanations are the ones that are the most general.

Definition 3.3 (Most-general explanation). *Let* $\mathcal{O} = (\mathcal{C}, \sqsubseteq, ext)$ *be an* $\mathbf{S}$*-ontology, and let* $E = (C_1, \ldots, C_m)$ *and* $E' = (C'_1, \ldots, C'_m)$ *be two tuples of concepts from* $\mathcal{C}^m$.

- *We say that* E *is* less general *than* E' *with respect to* $\mathcal{O}$, *denoted as* $E \leq_{\mathcal{O}} E'$, *if* $C_i \sqsubseteq C'_i$ *for every* i, $1 \leq i \leq m$.
- *We say that* E *is* strictly less general *than* E' *with respect to* $\mathcal{O}$, *denoted as* $E <_{\mathcal{O}} E'$, *if* $E \leq_{\mathcal{O}} E'$, *and* $E' \not\leq_{\mathcal{O}} E$.
- *We say that* E *is a* most-general explanation *for* $\overline{a} \notin q(I)$ *if* E *is an explanation for* $\overline{a} \notin q(I)$, *and there is no explanation* E' *for* $\overline{a} \notin q(I)$ *such that* $E' >_{\mathcal{O}} E$.

As we will formally define in Section 5, a *why-not problem* asks the question: "why is the tuple $(a_1, \ldots, a_m)$ not in the output of a query q over an instance I of schema $\mathbf{S}$?" The following example illustrates the notions of explanations and most-general explanations in the context of a why-not problem.

Example 3.4. Consider the instance $I_{\mathbf{D}}$ of the relational schema $\mathbf{S}$ = {Cities(name, population, country, continent), Train-Connections(city_from, city_to)} shown in Figure 2.

Suppose q is the query $\exists z$. Train-Connections(x, z) $\wedge$ Train-Connections(z, y). That is, the query asks for all pairs of cities that are connected via a city. Then $q(I)$ returns tuples {⟨Amsterdam, Rome⟩, ⟨Amsterdam, Amsterdam⟩, ⟨Berlin, Berlin⟩, ⟨New York, Santa Cruz⟩}. A user may ask why is the tuple ⟨Amsterdam, New York⟩ not in the result of $q(I)$ (i.e., why is ⟨Amsterdam, New York⟩ $\notin q(I)$?). Based on the $\mathbf{S}$-ontology defined in Figure 3, we can derive the following explanations for ⟨Amsterdam, New York⟩ $\notin q(I)$:

E_1 = ⟨Dutch-City, East-Coast-City⟩
E_2 = ⟨Dutch-City, US-City⟩
E_3 = ⟨European-City, East-Coast-City⟩
E_4 = ⟨European-City, US-City⟩

E_1 is the simplest explanation, i.e., the one we can build by looking at the lower level of the hierarchy in our $\mathbf{S}$-ontology. Each subsequent explanation is more general than at least one of the prior explanations w.r.t. to the $\mathbf{S}$-ontology. In particular, we have $E_4 >_{\mathcal{O}} E_2 >_{\mathcal{O}} E_1$, and $E_4 >_{\mathcal{O}} E_3 >_{\mathcal{O}} E_1$. Thus, the most-general explanation for why ⟨Amsterdam, New York⟩ $\notin q(I)$ with respect to our $\mathbf{S}$-ontology is E_4, which intuitively informs that the reason is because Amsterdam is a city in Europe while New York is a city in the US (and hence, they are not connected by train). Note that all the other possible combinations of concepts are not explanations because they intersect with $q(I)$. □

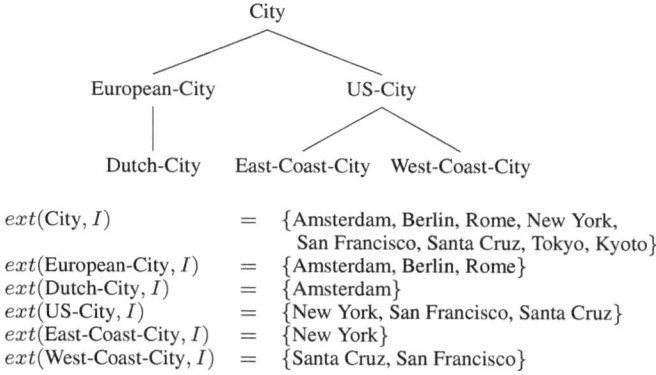

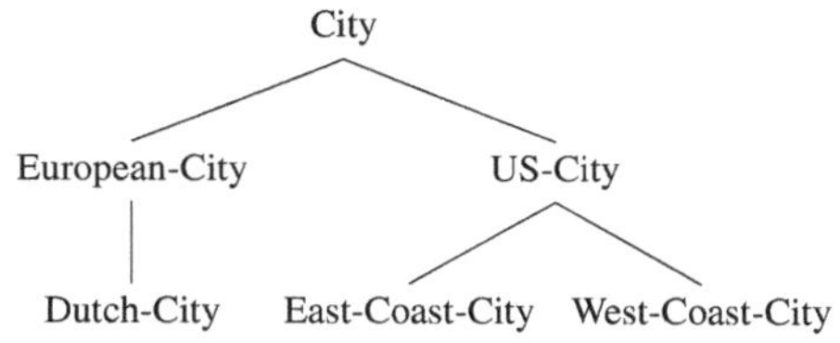

$$
\begin{array}{lcl}
ext(\text{City}, I) & = & \{\text{Amsterdam, Berlin, Rome, New York,} \\
 & & \quad \text{San Francisco, Santa Cruz, Tokyo, Kyoto}\} \\
ext(\text{European-City}, I) & = & \{\text{Amsterdam, Berlin, Rome}\} \\
ext(\text{Dutch-City}, I) & = & \{\text{Amsterdam}\} \\
ext(\text{US-City}, I) & = & \{\text{New York, San Francisco, Santa Cruz}\} \\
ext(\text{East-Coast-City}, I) & = & \{\text{New York}\} \\
ext(\text{West-Coast-City}, I) & = & \{\text{Santa Cruz, San Francisco}\}
\end{array}
$$

Figure 3: Example ontology.

As we will see in Example 4.9, there may be more than one most-general explanations in general.

Generalizing the above example, we can informally define the problem of explaining why-not questions via ontologies as follows: *given an instance I of schema $\mathbf{S}$, a query q over $\mathbf{S}$, an $\mathbf{S}$-ontology $\mathcal{O}$ (consistent with I) and a tuple $\overline{a} \notin q(I)$, compute a most-general explanation for $\overline{a} \notin q(I)$, if one exists, w.r.t. $\mathcal{O}$.* As we shall describe in Section 5, in addition to the above problem of computing one most-general explanation, we will also investigate the corresponding decision problem that asks whether or not an explanation for a why-not problem exists, and whether or not a given tuple of concepts is a most-general explanation for a why-not problem. In our framework, the $\mathbf{S}$-ontology $\mathcal{O}$ may be given explicitly as part of the input, or it may be derived from a given database instance or a given schema. We will introduce the different scenarios by which an ontology may be obtained in the next section, before we describe our algorithms for computing most-general explanations in Section 5.

4. OBTAINING ONTOLOGIES

In this section we discuss two approaches by which $\mathbf{S}$-ontologies may be obtained. The first approach allows one to leverage an external ontology, provided that there is a way to relate a concept in the ontology to a database instance. In this case, the set $\mathcal{C}$ of concepts is specified through a description logic such as $\mathcal{ALC}$ or *DL-Lite*; $\sqsubseteq$ is a partial order on the concepts defined in the ontology, and the function *ext* may be given through *mapping assertions*. The second approach considers an $\mathbf{S}$-ontology that is derived from a specific database instance, or from a schema. This approach is useful as it allows one to define an ontology to be used for explaining why-not questions in the absence of an external ontology.

In either case, we study the complexity of deriving such $\mathbf{S}$-ontologies based on the language on which concepts are defined, the subsumption between concepts, and the function ext, which is defined according to the semantics of the concept language.

4.1 Leveraging an external ontology

We first consider the case where we are given an external ontology that models the domain of the database instance, and a relationship between the ontology and the instance. We will illustrate in particular how *description logic ontologies* are captured as a special case of our framework.

In what follows, our exposition borrows notions from the Ontology-Based Data Access (OBDA) framework. Specifically, we will make crucial use of the notion of an *OBDA specification* [17], which consists of a description logic ontology, a relational schema, and a collection of mapping assertions. To keep the exposition simple, we restrict our discussion to one particular description logic, called *DL-Lite*$_{\mathcal{R}}$, which is a representative member of the *DL-Lite* family of description logics [12]. *DL-Lite*$_{\mathcal{R}}$ is the basis for the OWL 2 QL[2] profile of OWL 2, which is a standard ontology language for Semantic Web adopted by W3C. As the other languages in the *DL-Lite* family, *DL-Lite*$_{\mathcal{R}}$ exhibits a good trade off between expressivity and complexity bounds for important reasoning tasks such as subsumption checking, instance checking and query answering.

TBox and Mapping Assertions. In the description logic literature, an ontology is typically formalized as a TBox (Terminology Box), which consists of finitely many *TBox axioms*, where each TBox axiom expresses a relationship between concepts. Alongside TBoxes, ABoxes (Assertion Boxes) are sometimes used to describe the extension of concepts. To simplify the presentation, we do not consider ABoxes here.

Definition 4.1 (*DL-Lite*$_{\mathcal{R}}$). *Fix a finite set Φ_C of* "atomic concepts" *and a finite set Φ_R of* "atomic roles".

- *The* concept expressions *and* role expressions *of DL-Lite*$_{\mathcal{R}}$ *are defined as follows:*

Basic concept expression:	$B ::= A \mid \exists R$
Basic role expression:	$R ::= P \mid P^{-}$
Concept expressions:	$C ::= B \mid \neg B$
Role expressions	$E ::= R \mid \neg R$

  *where $A \in \Phi_C$ and $P \in \Phi_R$. Formally, a (Φ_C, Φ_R)-*interpretation *$\mathcal{I}$ is a map that assigns to every atomic concept in Φ_C a unary relation over* $\mathbf{Const}$ *and to every atomic role in Φ_R a binary relation over* $\mathbf{Const}$. *The map $\mathcal{I}$ naturally extends to arbitrary concept expressions and role expressions:*

$$
\begin{array}{ll}
\mathcal{I}(P^{-}) = \{(x,y) \mid (y,x) \in \mathcal{I}(P)\} & \mathcal{I}(\exists P) = \pi_1(\mathcal{I}(P)) \\
\mathcal{I}(\neg P) = \mathbf{Const}^2 \setminus \mathcal{I}(P) & \mathcal{I}(\neg A) = \mathbf{Const} \setminus \mathcal{I}(A)
\end{array}
$$

  Observe that $\mathcal{I}(\exists P^{-}) = \pi_2(\mathcal{I}(P))$.

- *A* TBox (Terminology Box) *is a finite set of* TBox axioms *where each TBox axiom is an inclusion assertion of the form $B \sqsubseteq C$ or $R \sqsubseteq E$, where B is a basic concept expression, C is a concept expression, R is a basic role expression and E is a role expression. An (Φ_C, Φ_R)-interpretation $\mathcal{I}$* satisfies *a TBox if for each axiom $X \sqsubseteq Y$, it holds $\mathcal{I}(X) \subseteq \mathcal{I}(Y)$.*

- *For concept expressions C_1, C_2 and a TBox $\mathcal{T}$, we say that C_1* is subsumed by C_2 relative to $\mathcal{T}$ *(notation: $\mathcal{T} \models C_1 \sqsubseteq C_2$) if, for all interpretations $\mathcal{I}$ satisfying $\mathcal{T}$, we have that $\mathcal{I}(C_1) \subseteq \mathcal{I}(C_2)$.*

An example of a *DL-Lite*$_{\mathcal{R}}$ TBox is given at the top of Figure 4. For convenience, we have listed next to each TBox axiom, its equivalent semantics in first-order notation.

Next we describe what mapping assertions are. Given an ontology and a relational schema, we can specify mapping assertions to relate the ontology language to the relational schema, which is similar to how mappings are used in OBDA [26]. In general, mapping assertions are first order sentences over the schema $\mathbf{S} \cup \Phi_C \cup \Phi_R$ that express relationships between the symbols in $\mathbf{S}$ and those in Φ_C and Φ_R. Among the different schema mapping languages that can be used, we restrict our attention, for simplicity, to the class of *Global-As-View (GAV) mapping assertions* (*GAV mapping assertions or GAV constraints* or *GAV source-to-target tgds*).

[2]`http://www.w3.org/TR/owl2-profiles/#OWL_2_QL`

DL-Lite TBox axiom	(first-order translation)
EU-City $\sqsubseteq$ City	$\forall x$ EU-City$(x) \rightarrow$ City(x)
Dutch-City $\sqsubseteq$ EU-City	$\forall x$ Dutch-City$(x) \rightarrow$ EU-City(x)
N.A.-City $\sqsubseteq$ City	$\forall x$ N.A.-City$(x) \rightarrow$ City(x)
EU-City $\sqsubseteq \neg$ N.A.-City	$\forall x$ EU-City$(x) \rightarrow \neg$N.A.-City(x)
US-City $\sqsubseteq$ N.A.-City	$\forall x$ US-City$(x) \rightarrow$ N.A.-City(x)
City $\sqsubseteq \exists$ hasCountry	$\forall x$ City$(x) \rightarrow \exists y$ hasCountry(x, y)
Country $\sqsubseteq \exists$ hasContinent	$\forall x$ Country$(x) \rightarrow \exists y$ hasContinent(x, y)
$\exists$hasCountry$^-$ $\sqsubseteq$ Country	$\forall x$ $(\exists y$ hasCountry$(y, x)) \rightarrow$ Country(x)
$\exists$hasContinent$^-$ $\sqsubseteq$ Continent	$\forall x$ $(\exists y$ hasContinent$(y, x)) \rightarrow$ Continent(x)
$\exists$connected $\sqsubseteq$ City	$\forall x$ $(\exists y$ connected$(x, y)) \rightarrow$ City(x)
$\exists$connected$^-$ $\sqsubseteq$ City	$\forall x$ $(\exists y$ connected$(y, x)) \rightarrow$ City(x)

GAV mapping assertions (universal quantifiers omitted for readability):

Cities$(x, z, w,$ "Europe")	$\rightarrow$	EU-City(x)
Cities$(x, z,$ "Netherlands"$, w)$	$\rightarrow$	Dutch-City(x)
Cities$(x, z, w,$ "N.America")	$\rightarrow$	N.A.-City(x)
Cities$(x, z,$ "USA"$, w)$	$\rightarrow$	US-City(x)
Cities(x, y, z, w)	$\rightarrow$	Continent(w)
Cities(x, k, y, w)	$\rightarrow$	hasCountry(x,y)
Cities(x, k, w, y)	$\rightarrow$	hasContinent(x,y)
Train-Connection(x, y), Cities(x, x_1, x_2, x_3), Cities(y, y_1, y_2, y_3)	$\rightarrow$	connected(x,y)

Figure 4: Example DL-Lite ontology with mapping assertions.

Definition 4.2 (GAV mapping assertions). *A GAV mapping assertion over* $(\mathbf{S}, (\Phi_C \cup \Phi_R))$ *is a first-order sentence* ψ *of the form*

$$\forall \vec{x}\ (\varphi_1(\vec{x_1}), \cdots, \varphi_n(\vec{x_n})) \rightarrow \psi(\vec{x})$$

where $\vec{x} \subseteq \vec{x_1} \cup \ldots \cup \vec{x_n}$, $\varphi_1, \ldots, \varphi_n$ *are atoms over* $\mathbf{S}$ *and* ψ *is an atomic formula of the form* $A(x_i)$ *(for* $A \in \Phi_C$*) or* $P(x_i, x_j)$ *(for* $P \in \Phi_R$*). Let* I *be an* $\mathbf{S}$*-instance and* $\mathcal{I}$ *an* (Φ_C, Φ_R)*-interpretation. We say that the pair* $(I, \mathcal{I})$ satisfies *the GAV mapping assertion (notation:* $(I, \mathcal{I}) \models \psi$*) if it holds that for any tuple of elements* $\bar{a}$ *from adom(I), with* $\bar{a} = \bigcup_{1 \le k \le n} \bar{a_k}$*, if* $I \models \varphi_1(\bar{a_1}), \ldots, \varphi_n(\bar{a_n})$*, then* $a_i \in \mathcal{I}(A)$*, with* $a_i \in \bar{a}$ *(if* $\psi = A(x_i)$*) or* $(a_i, a_j) \in \mathcal{I}(P)$*, with* $a_i, a_j \in \bar{a}$ *(if* $\psi = P(x_i, x_j)$*).*

Intuitively, a GAV mapping assertion associates a conjunctive query over $\mathbf{S}$ to an element (concept or atomic role) of the ontology. A set of GAV mapping assertions associates, in general, a union of conjunctive queries to an element of the ontology. Examples of GAV mapping assertions are given at the bottom of Figure 4.

OBDA induced ontologies

Definition 4.3 (OBDA specification). *Let* $\mathcal{T}$ *be a TBox,* $\mathbf{S}$ *a relational schema, and* $\mathcal{M}$ *a set of mapping assertions from* $\mathbf{S}$ *to the concepts of* $\mathcal{T}$*. We call the triple* $\mathcal{B} = (\mathcal{T}, \mathbf{S}, \mathcal{M})$ *an* OBDA specification.

An (Φ_C, Φ_R)*-interpretation* $\mathcal{I}$ *is said to be a* solution *for an* $\mathbf{S}$*-instance* I *with respect to the OBDA specification* $\mathcal{B}$ *if the pair* $(I, \mathcal{I})$ *satisfies all mapping assertions in* $\mathcal{M}$ *and* $\mathcal{I}$ *satisfies* $\mathcal{T}$*.*

Note that our notion of an OBDA specification is a special case of the one given in [17], where we do not consider view inclusion dependencies. Also, as mentioned earlier, our OBDA specifications in this paper assume that $\mathcal{T}$ is a *DL-Lite*$_\mathcal{R}$ TBox and $\mathcal{M}$ is a set of GAV mappings. These restrictions allow us to achieve good complexity bounds for explaining why-not questions with ontologies. In particular, it is not hard to see that, for the OBDA specifications we consider, every $\mathbf{S}$-instance I has a solution.

Theorem 4.1. *([12, 26]) Let* $\mathcal{T}$ *be a DL-Lite*$_\mathcal{R}$ *TBox.*

1. *There is a* PTIME*-algorithm for deciding subsumption. That is, given* $\mathcal{T}$ *and two concepts* C_1, C_2*, decide if* $\mathcal{T} \models C_1 \sqsubseteq C_2$*.*
2. *There is an algorithm that, given an OBDA specification* $\mathcal{B}$*, an instance* I *over* $\mathbf{S}$ *and a concept* C*, computes* $certain(C, I, \mathcal{B}) = \bigcap\{\mathcal{I}(C) \mid \mathcal{I}$ *is a solution for* I *w.r.t.* $\mathcal{B}\}$*. For a fixed OBDA specification, the algorithm runs in* PTIME *(*AC^0 *in data complexity).*

Every OBDA specification induces an $\mathbf{S}$-ontology as follows.

Definition 4.4. *Every OBDA specification* $\mathcal{B} = (\mathcal{T}, \mathbf{S}, \mathcal{M})$ *where* $\mathcal{T}$ *is a DL-Lite*$_\mathcal{R}$ *TBox and* $\mathcal{M}$ *is a set of GAV mappings gives rise to an* $\mathbf{S}$*-ontology where:*

- $\mathcal{C}_{\mathcal{O}_\mathcal{B}}$ *is the set of all basic concept expressions occurring in* $\mathcal{T}$*;*
- $\sqsubseteq_{\mathcal{O}_\mathcal{B}} = \{(C_1, C_2) \mid \mathcal{T} \models C_1 \sqsubseteq C_2\}$
- $ext_{\mathcal{O}_\mathcal{B}}$ *is the polynomial-time computable function given by* $ext_{\mathcal{O}_\mathcal{B}}(C, I) = \bigcap\{\mathcal{I}(C) \mid \mathcal{I}$ *is a solution for* I *w.r.t.* $\mathcal{B}\}$

Note that the fact that $ext_{\mathcal{O}_\mathcal{B}}$ is the polynomial-time computable follows from Theorem 4.1.

We remarked earlier that, for the ODBA specifications $\mathcal{B}$ that we consider, it holds that every input instance has a solution. It follows that every input instance I is consistent with the corresponding $\mathbf{S}$-ontology $\mathcal{O}_\mathcal{B}$.

Theorem 4.2. *The* $\mathbf{S}$*-ontology* $\mathcal{O}_\mathcal{B} = (\mathcal{C}_{\mathcal{O}_\mathcal{B}}, \sqsubseteq_{\mathcal{O}_\mathcal{B}}, ext_{\mathcal{O}_\mathcal{B}})$ *can be computed from a given OBDA specification* $\mathcal{B} = (\mathcal{T}, \mathbf{S}, \mathcal{M})$ *in* PTIME *if* $\mathcal{T}$ *is a DL-Lite*$_\mathcal{R}$ *TBox and* $\mathcal{M}$ *is a set of GAV mappings.*

We are now ready to illustrate an example where a why-not question is explained via an external ontology.

Example 4.5. Consider the OBDA specification $\mathcal{B} = (\mathcal{T}, \mathbf{S}, \mathcal{M})$ where $\mathcal{T}$ is the TBox consisting of the *DL-Lite*$_\mathcal{R}$ axioms given in Figure 4, $\mathbf{S}$ is the schema from Example 3.4, and $\mathcal{M}$ is the set of mapping assertions given in Figure 4. These together induce an $\mathbf{S}$-ontology $\mathcal{O}_\mathcal{B} = (\mathcal{C}_{\mathcal{O}_\mathcal{B}}, \sqsubseteq_{\mathcal{O}_\mathcal{B}}, ext_{\mathcal{O}_\mathcal{B}})$. The set $\mathcal{C}_{\mathcal{O}_\mathcal{B}}$ consists of the following basic concept expressions:

City, EU-City, N.A.-City, Dutch-City,
US-City, Country, Continent,
$\exists$ hasCountry, $\exists$ hasCountry$^-$, $\exists$ hasContinent,
$\exists$ hasContinent$^-$, $\exists$ connected, $\exists$ connected$^-$.

The set $\sqsubseteq_{\mathcal{O}_\mathcal{B}}$ includes the pairs of concepts of the TBox $\mathcal{T}$ given in Figure 4. We use the mappings to compute the extension of each concept in $\mathcal{C}_{\mathcal{O}_\mathcal{B}}$ using the instance I on the left of Figure 2. We list a few extensions here:

$ext_{\mathcal{O}_\mathcal{B}}$(City, I)	=	{Amsterdam, Berlin, Rome, New York, San Francisco, Santa Cruz, Tokyo, Kyoto}
$ext_{\mathcal{O}_\mathcal{B}}$(EU-City, I)	=	{Amsterdam, Berlin, Rome}
$ext_{\mathcal{O}_\mathcal{B}}$(N.A.-City, I)	=	{New York, San Francisco, Santa Cruz}
$ext_{\mathcal{O}_\mathcal{B}}$($\exists$hasCountry$^-$, I)	=	{Netherlands, Germany, Italy, USA, Japan}
$ext_{\mathcal{O}_\mathcal{B}}$($\exists$connected, I)	=	{Amsterdam, Berlin, New York}

Now consider the query $q(x, y) = \exists z$. Train-Connections(x, z) $\wedge$ Train-Connections(z, y), and $q(I)$ as in Example 3.4. As before, we would like to explain why is $\langle$Amsterdam, New York$\rangle \notin q(I)$. This time, we use the induced $\mathbf{S}$-ontology $\mathcal{O}_\mathcal{B}$ described above to derive explanations for $\langle$Amsterdam, New York$\rangle \notin q(I)$:

E_1	= $\langle$EU-City, N.A.-City$\rangle$	E_2	= $\langle$Dutch-City,N.A.-City$\rangle$
E_3	= $\langle$EU-City, US-City$\rangle$	E_4	= $\langle$Dutch-City,US-City$\rangle$

Among the four explanations above, E_1 is the most general. $\square$

4.2 Ontologies derived from a schema

We now move to the second approach where an ontology is derived from an instance or a schema. The ability to derive an ontology through an instance or a schema is useful in the context where an external ontology is unavailable. To this purpose we first introduce a simple but suitable concept language that can be defined over the schema $\mathbf{S}$.

Specifically, our concept language, denoted as $L_{\mathbf{S}}$, makes use of two relational algebra operations, projection (π) and selection (σ). We first introduce and motivate the language. We will then describe our complexity results for testing whether one concept is subsumed by another, and for obtaining an ontology from a given instance or a schema. We will make use of these results later on in Section 5.2 and Section 5.3.

Definition 4.6 (The Concept Language $L_{\mathbf{S}}$). *Let $\mathbf{S}$ be a schema. A concept in $L_{\mathbf{S}}$ is an expression C defined by the following grammar.*

$$D ::= R \mid \sigma_{A_1 \text{op}\, c_1, \ldots, A_n \text{op}\, c_n}(R)$$
$$C := \top \mid \{c\} \mid \pi_A(D) \mid C \sqcap C$$

*In the above, R is a predicate name from $\mathbf{S}$, $A, A_1, \ldots, A_n$ are attributes in R, not necessarily distinct, $c, c_1, \ldots, c_n \in$ **Const**, and each occurrence of* op *is a comparison operator belonging to $\{=, <, >, \leq, \geq\}$. For $\mathbf{C} = \{C_1, \ldots, C_k\}$ a finite set of concepts, we denote by $\sqcap\mathbf{C}$ the conjunction $C_1 \sqcap \ldots \sqcap C_k$. If $\mathbf{C}$ is empty, we take $\sqcap\mathbf{C}$ to be $\top$.*

*Given a finite set of constants $\mathcal{K} \subset$ **Const**, we define $L_{\mathbf{S}}[\mathcal{K}]$ as the concept language $L_{\mathbf{S}}$ whose concept expressions only use constants from $\mathcal{K}$. By* selection-free $L_{\mathbf{S}}$, *we mean the language $L_{\mathbf{S}}$ where σ is not allowed. Similarly, by* intersection-free $L_{\mathbf{S}}$, *we mean the language $L_{\mathbf{S}}$ where $\sqcap$ is not allowed, and by $L_{\mathbf{S}}^{\min}$, we mean the minimal concept language $L_{\mathbf{S}}$ where both σ and $\sqcap$ are not allowed.*

Observe that the $L_{\mathbf{S}}$ grammar defines a concept in the form $C_1 \sqcap \ldots \sqcap C_n$ where each C_i is $\top$ or $\{c\}$ or $\pi_A(R)$ or $\pi_A(\sigma_{A_1 \text{op}\, c_1, \ldots, A_n \text{op}\, c_n}(R))$. A concept of the form $\{c\}$ is called a *nominal*. A nominal $\{c\}$ is the "most specific" concept for the constant c. Given a tuple $\overline{a}$ that is not in the output, the corresponding tuple of nominal concepts forms a default, albeit trivial, explanation for why not $\overline{a}$.

As our next example illustrates, even though our concept language $L_{\mathbf{S}}$ appears simple, it is able to naturally capture many intuitive concepts over the domain of the database.

Example 4.7. We refer back to our schema $\mathbf{S}$ in Figure 1. Suppose we do not have access to an external ontology such as the one given in Example 3.4. We show that even so, we can still construct meaningful concepts directly from the database schema using the concept language described above. We list a few semantic concepts that can be specified with $L_{\mathbf{S}}$ in Figure 5, where we also show the corresponding SELECT-FROM-WHERE style expressions and intuitive meaning. □

Example 4.7 shows that, even though $L_{\mathbf{S}}$ is a simple language where concepts are essentially intersections of unary projections of relations and nominals, it is already sufficiently expressive to capture natural concepts that can be used to build meaningful explanations. It is worth noting that, for minor extensions of the language $L_{\mathbf{S}}$, such as with $\neq$-comparisons and disjunction, the notion of a most-general explanation becomes trivial, in the sense that, for each why-not question, there is a most-general explanation that essentially enumerates all tuples in the query answer.

By using $L_{\mathbf{S}}$, we are able to define an ontology whose atomic concepts are derived from the schema itself. This approach allows us to provide explanations using a vocabulary that is already familiar to the user. We believe that this leads to intuitive and useful why-not explanations.

If we view each expression $\pi_A(D)$ as an atomic concept, then the language $L_{\mathbf{S}}$ corresponds to a very simple concept language, whose concepts are built from atomic concepts and nominals using only intersection. In this sense, $L_{\mathbf{S}}$ can be considered to be a fragment of *DL-Lite*$_{core,\sqcap}$ with nominals (also known as *DL-Lite*$_{horn}$ [4]), i.e., the description logic obtained by enriching *DL-Lite*$_{core}$ (the simplest language in the DL-Lite family) with conjunction.

The precise semantics of $L_{\mathbf{S}}$ is as follows. Given a concept C that is defined in $L_{\mathbf{S}}$ and an instance I over $\mathbf{S}$, the extension of C in I, denoted by $[\![C]\!]^I$, is inductively defined below. Intuitively, the extension of C in I is the result of evaluating the query associated with C over I.

$$\begin{array}{ll}
[\![R]\!]^I & = R^I \\
[\![\sigma_{A_1 \text{op}_1 c_1, \ldots, A_n \text{op}_n c_n}(R)]\!]^I & = \{\bar{b} \in R^I \mid \pi_{A_i}(\bar{b}) \text{op}_i c_i, 1 \leq i \leq n\} \\
[\![\top]\!]^I & = \mathbf{Const} \\
[\![\{c\}]\!]^I & = \{c\} \\
[\![\pi_A(D)]\!]^I & = \pi_A([\![D]\!]^I) \\
[\![C_1 \sqcap C_2]\!]^I & = [\![C_1]\!]^I \cap [\![C_2]\!]^I
\end{array}$$

The notion of when one concept is subsumed by another is defined according to the extensions of the concepts. There are two notions, corresponding to concept subsumption w.r.t. an instance or subsumption w.r.t. a schema. More precisely, given two concepts C_1, C_2,

- we say that C_2 *subsumes* C_1 *w.r.t. an instance* I (notation: $C_1 \sqsubseteq_I C_2$) if $[\![C_1]\!]^I \subseteq [\![C_2]\!]^I$.
- we say that C_2 *subsumes* C_1 *w.r.t. a schema* $\mathbf{S}$ (notation: $C_1 \sqsubseteq_{\mathbf{S}} C_2$), if for every instance I of $\mathbf{S}$, we have that $C_1 \sqsubseteq_I C_2$.

We are now ready to define the two types of ontologies, which are based on the two notions of concept subsumption described above, that can be derived from an instance or a schema.

Definition 4.8 (Ontologies derived from a schema). *Let $\mathbf{S}$ be a schema, and let I be an instance of $\mathbf{S}$. Then the ontologies derived from $\mathbf{S}$ and I are defined respectively as*

- $\mathcal{O}_{\mathbf{S}} = (L_{\mathbf{S}}, \sqsubseteq_{\mathbf{S}}, ext)$ *and*
- $\mathcal{O}_I = (L_{\mathbf{S}}, \sqsubseteq_I, ext)$,

where ext is the function given by $ext(C, I') = [\![C]\!]^{I'}$ for all instances I' over $\mathbf{S}$. By $\mathcal{O}_{\mathbf{S}}[\mathcal{K}]$ we denote the ontology $(L_{\mathbf{S}}[\mathcal{K}], \sqsubseteq_{\mathbf{S}}, ext)$, and by $\mathcal{O}_I[\mathcal{K}]$ we denote the ontology $(L_{\mathbf{S}}[\mathcal{K}], \sqsubseteq_I, ext)$.

It is easy to verify that the subsumption relations $\sqsubseteq_{\mathbf{S}}$ and $\sqsubseteq_I$ are indeed pre-orders (i.e., reflexive, and transitive relations), and that, for every fixed schemas $\mathbf{S}$, the function $[\![C]\!]^{I'}$ is polynomial-time computable. Hence, the above definition is well-defined even though the ontologies obtained in this way are typically infinite. From the definition, it is easy to verify that if $C_1 \sqsubseteq_{\mathbf{S}} C_2$, then $C_1 \sqsubseteq_I C_2$.

The following result about deciding $\sqsubseteq_I$ is immediate, as one can always execute the queries that are associated with the concepts and then test for subsumption, which can be done in polynomial time.

Proposition 4.1. *The problem of deciding, given an instance I of a schema $\mathbf{S}$ and given two $L_{\mathbf{S}}$ concept expressions C_1, C_2, whether $C_1 \sqsubseteq_I C_2$, is in* PTIME.

On the other hand, the complexity of deciding $\sqsubseteq_{\mathbf{S}}$ depends on the type of integrity constraints that are used in the specification of $\mathbf{S}$. Table 1 provides a summary of relevant complexity results.

Theorem 4.3. *Let $\mathcal{W}$ be one of the different classes of schemas with integrity constraints listed in Table 1. The complexity of the problem to decide, given a schema $\mathbf{S}$ in $\mathcal{W}$ and two $L_{\mathbf{S}}$ concept*

$L_{\mathbf{S}}$ **concept expression**	**SELECT-FROM-WHERE formulation**	**Intuitive meaning**
$\pi_{\text{name}}(\text{Cities})$	name from Cities	City
$\pi_{\text{name}}(\sigma_{\text{continent=``Europe''}}(\text{Cities}))$	name from Cities where continent="Europe"	European City
$\pi_{\text{name}}(\sigma_{\text{continent=``N.America''}}(\text{Cities}))$	name from Cities where continent="N.America"	N.American City
$\pi_{\text{name}}(\sigma_{\text{population}>1000000}(\text{Cities}))$	name from Cities where population>1000000	Large City
$\pi_1(\text{BigCity})$	name from BigCity	name of BigCity
$\{\text{``Santa Cruz''}\}$	"Santa Cruz"	Santa Cruz
$\pi_{\text{name}}(\sigma_{\text{population}<1000000}(\text{Cities}))\sqcap$ $\pi_{\text{city\_to}}(\sigma_{\text{city\_from=Amsterdam}}(\text{Reachable}))$	name from Cities where population<1000000 AND city_from from Reachable where city_to=Amsterdam	Small City that is reachable from Amsterdam.

Figure 5: Example of concepts specified in $L_{\mathbf{S}}$.

Constraints	Complexity of subsumption for $L_{\mathbf{S}}$
UCQ-view def. (no comparisons)	NP-complete
UCQ-view def.	Π_2^P-complete
linearly nested UCQ-view def.	Π_2^P-complete
nested UCQ-view def.	CONEXPTIME-complete
FDs	in PTIME
IDs	? (in PTIME for selection-free $L_{\mathbf{S}}$)
IDs + FDs	Undecidable

All stated lower bounds already hold for $L_{\mathbf{S}}^{\min}$ concept expressions.

Table 1: Complexity of concept subsumption.

expressions C_1, C_2, whether $C_1 \sqsubseteq_{\mathbf{S}} C_2$, is as indicated in the second column of the corresponding row in Table 1.

For example, given two concepts C_1, C_2, and a schema $(\mathbf{S}, \Sigma)$ where Σ is a collection of nested UCQ-view definitions, the complexity of deciding $C_1 \sqsubseteq_{\mathbf{S}} C_2$ is CONEXPTIME-complete. The lower bound already holds for concepts specified in $L_{\mathbf{S}}^{\min}$. We conclude this section with an analysis of the number of distinct concepts that can be formulated in a given concept language and an example that illustrates explanations that can be computed from such derived ontologies.

Proposition 4.2. *Given a schema $\mathbf{S}$ and a finite set of constants $\mathcal{K} \subset$ **Const**, the number of unique concepts (modulo logical equivalence)*

- *in $L_{\mathbf{S}}^{\min}[\mathcal{K}]$ is polynomial in the size of $\mathbf{S}$ and $\mathcal{K}$,*
- *in selection-free or intersection-free $L_{\mathbf{S}}[\mathcal{K}]$ is single exponential in the size of $\mathbf{S}$ and $\mathcal{K}$.*
- *in $L_{\mathbf{S}}[\mathcal{K}]$ is double exponential in the size of $\mathbf{S}$ and $\mathcal{K}$.*

Example 4.9. Let $\mathbf{S}$ and I be the schema and instance from Figure 1 and Figure 2. Suppose the concept language $L_{\mathbf{S}}$ is used to define among others the concepts from Figure 5. The following concept subsumptions can be derived from $\mathbf{S}$. Note that subsumption $\sqsubseteq_{\mathbf{S}}$ implies $\sqsubseteq_I$.

$$\begin{array}{lll}
\pi_{\text{name}}(\sigma_{\text{continent=``Europe''}}(\text{Cities})) & \sqsubseteq_{\mathbf{S}} & \pi_{\text{name}}(\text{Cities}) \\
\pi_{\text{name}}(\sigma_{\text{population}>7000000}(\text{Cities})) & \sqsubseteq_{\mathbf{S}} & \pi_{\text{name}}(\text{BigCity}) \\
\pi_{\text{name}}(\text{BigCity}) & \sqsubseteq_{\mathbf{S}} & \pi_{\text{name}}(\text{Cities}) \\
\pi_{\text{name}}(\text{BigCity}) & \sqsubseteq_{\mathbf{S}} & \pi_{\text{city_from}}(\text{Train-Connections})
\end{array}$$

The first and second subsumptions follow from definitions. The third one holds because according to Π, a BigCity is a city with population more than 5 million. The fourth subsumption follows from the inclusion dependency that each BigCity must have a train departing from it. There are subsumptions that hold in $\mathcal{O}_I$ but not in $\mathcal{O}_{\mathbf{S}}$. For instance,

$$\pi_{\text{city\_to}}(\sigma_{\text{city\_from=Amsterdam}}(\text{Reachable})) \sqsubseteq_I \pi_{\text{city\_to}}(\sigma_{\text{city\_from=Berlin}}(\text{Reachable})),$$

holds w.r.t. $\mathcal{O}_I$, where I is the instance given in Figure 2, but does not hold w.r.t $\mathcal{O}_{\mathbf{S}}$, since one can construct an instance where not all cities that are reachable from Amsterdam are reachable from Berlin.

We now give examples of most-general explanations w.r.t. $\mathcal{O}_{\mathbf{S}}$ and $\mathcal{O}_I$. As before, let $q(x, y) = \exists z.$ Train-Connections$(x, z) \wedge$ Train-Connections(z, y) be a query with $q(I) = \{\langle\text{Amsterdam, Rome}\rangle, \langle\text{Amsterdam, Amsterdam}\rangle, \langle\text{Berlin, Berlin}\rangle, \langle\text{New York, Santa Cruz}\rangle\}$. We would like to explain why $\langle\text{Amsterdam, New York}\rangle \notin q(I)$ using the derived ontologies $\mathcal{O}_{\mathbf{S}}$ and $\mathcal{O}_I$. Note that if E is an explanation w.r.t. $\mathcal{O}_{\mathbf{S}}$, then it is also an explanation w.r.t. $\mathcal{O}_I$ and vice versa. Some possible explanations are:

$$\begin{array}{rl}
E_1 = & \langle \pi_{\text{name}}(\sigma_{\text{continent=Europe}}(\text{Cities})), \\
& \quad \pi_{\text{city_from}}(\sigma_{\text{city_to = San Francisco}}(\text{Train-Connections}))\rangle \\
E_2 = & \langle \pi_{\text{name}}(\sigma_{\text{continent=Europe}}(\text{Cities})), \\
& \quad \pi_{\text{name}}(\sigma_{\text{continent=N.America}}(\text{Cities}))\rangle \\
E_3 = & \langle \pi_{\text{city_to}}(\sigma_{\text{city_from = Berlin}}(\text{Reachable})), \\
& \quad \pi_{\text{city_from}}(\sigma_{\text{city_to = Santa Cruz}}(\text{Reachable}))\rangle \\
E_4 = & \langle \{\text{Amsterdam}\}, \pi_{\text{name}}(\sigma_{\text{population}>7000000}(\text{Cities}))\rangle \\
E_5 = & \langle \pi_{\text{name}}(\sigma_{\text{country=Netherlands}}(\text{Cities})), \\
& \quad \pi_{\text{name}}(\text{BigCity}) \sqcap \pi_{\text{name}}(\sigma_{\text{continent=N.America}}(\text{Cities}))\rangle \\
E_6 = & \langle \{\text{Amsterdam}\}, \{\text{New York}\}\rangle \\
E_7 = & \langle \pi_{\text{name}}(\sigma_{\text{continent=Europe}}(\text{Cities})), \pi_{\text{name}}(\text{BigCity})\}\rangle \\
E_8 = & \langle \pi_{\text{name}}(\sigma_{\text{continent=Europe}}(\text{Cities})), \\
& \quad \pi_{\text{name}}(\sigma_{\text{population}>7000000}(\text{Cities}))\}\rangle
\end{array}$$

For example, E_1 states the reason is that Amsterdam is a European city and New York is a city that has a train connection to San Francisco, and there is no train connection between such cities via a city. The trivial explanation E_6 is less general than any other explanation w.r.t $\mathcal{O}_{\mathbf{S}}$ (and $\mathcal{O}_I$ too). It can be verified that E_2 and E_7 are most-general explanations w.r.t both $\mathcal{O}_{\mathbf{S}}$ and $\mathcal{O}_I$. In particular, $E_2 >_{\mathcal{O}_I} E_5$ and $E_2 \geq_{\mathcal{O}_I} E_3$, but $E_2 \not>_{\mathcal{O}_{\mathbf{S}}} E_5$ and $E_2 \not>_{\mathcal{O}_{\mathbf{S}}} E_3$ since there might be an instance of $\mathbf{S}$ where Netherlands is not in Europe or where Berlin is reachable from a non-european city. □

In general, if E is an explanation w.r.t. $\mathcal{O}_I$ then E is also an explanation w.r.t. $\mathcal{O}_{\mathbf{S}}$, and vice versa. The following proposition also describes the relationship between most-general explanations w.r.t $\mathcal{O}_{\mathbf{S}}$ and $\mathcal{O}_I$.

Proposition 4.3. *Let $\mathbf{S}$ be a schema, and let I be an instance of $\mathbf{S}$.*

(i) Every explanation w.r.t. $\mathcal{O}_{\mathbf{S}}$ is an explanation w.r.t. $\mathcal{O}_I$ and vice versa.

(ii) A most-general explanation w.r.t $\mathcal{O}_{\mathbf{S}}$ is not necessarily a most-general explanation w.r.t. $\mathcal{O}_I$, and likewise vice versa.

Proof. The statement (i) follows from Definition 3.2 and the definition of ext for $\mathcal{O}_{\mathbf{S}}$ and $\mathcal{O}_I$. That is, ext is the same on the input instance I for both $\mathcal{O}_{\mathbf{S}}$ and $\mathcal{O}_I$, and the conditions of Definition 3.2 use only the value of ext on I. Going back to Example 4.9, E_1 is a most-general explanation w.r.t. $\mathcal{O}_{\mathbf{S}}$, but it is not a most-general explanation w.r.t. $\mathcal{O}_I$ (since E_3 is a strictly more general explanation than E_1 w.r.t. $\mathcal{O}_I$). Thus, the first direction of (ii) holds. For the other direction of (ii), consider E_8 which is a most-general explanation w.r.t. $\mathcal{O}_I$. But it holds that $E_7 >_{\mathcal{O}_\mathbf{S}} E_8$ and E_7 is an explanation. Note that E_7 and E_8 are equivalent w.r.t. $\mathcal{O}_I$. □

5. ALGORITHMS FOR COMPUTING MOST-GENERAL EXPLANATIONS

Next, we formally introduce the ontology-based why-not problem, which was informally described in Section 3, and we define algorithms for computing most-general explanations. We start by defining the notion of a why-not instance (or why-not question).

Definition 5.1 (Why-not instance). *Let* $\mathbf{S}$ *be a schema,* I *an instance of* $\mathbf{S}$*,* q *an* m*-ary query over* I *and* $\overline{a} = (a_1, \ldots, a_m)$ *a tuple of constants such that* $\overline{a} \notin q(I)$*. We call the quintuple* $(\mathbf{S}, I, q, Ans, \overline{a})$*, where* $Ans = q(I)$*, a* why-not instance *or a* why-not question.

In a why-not instance, the answer set *Ans* of q over I is assumed to have been computed already. This corresponds closely to the scenario under which why-not questions are posed where the user requests explanations for why a certain tuple is missing in the output of a query, which is computed a priori. Note that since *Ans*=$q(I)$ is part of a why-not instance, the complexity of evaluating q over I does not affect the complexity analysis of the problems we study in this paper. In addition, observe that although a query q is part of a why-not instance, the query is not directly used in our derivation of explanations for why-not questions with ontologies. However, the general setup accomodates the possibility to consider q directly in the derivation of explanations and this is part of our future work.

We will study the following algorithmic problems concerning most-general explanations for a why-not instance.

Definition 5.2. *The* EXISTENCE-OF-EXPLANATION *problem is the following decision problem: given a why-not instance* $(\mathbf{S}, I, q, Ans, \overline{a})$ *and an* $\mathbf{S}$*-ontology* $\mathcal{O}$ *consistent with* I*, does there exist an explanation for* $\overline{a} \notin Ans$ *w.r.t.* $\mathcal{O}$*?*

Definition 5.3. *The* CHECK-MGE *problem is the following decision problem: given a why-not instance* $(\mathbf{S}, I, q, Ans, \overline{a})$*, an* $\mathbf{S}$*-ontology* $\mathcal{O}$ *consistent with* I*, and a tuple of concepts* $(C_1, \ldots, C_n)$*, is the given tuple of concepts a most-general explanation w.r.t.* $\mathcal{O}$ *for* $\overline{a} \notin Ans$*?*

Definition 5.4. *The* COMPUTE-ONE-MGE *problem is the following computational problem: given a why-not instance* $(\mathbf{S}, I, q, Ans, \overline{a})$ *and an* $\mathbf{S}$*-ontology* $\mathcal{O}$ *consistent with* I*, find a most-general explanation w.r.t.* $\mathcal{O}$ *for* $\overline{a} \notin Ans$*, if one exists.*

Note that deciding the existence of an explanation w.r.t. a finite $\mathbf{S}$-ontology is equivalent to deciding existence of a most-general explanation w.r.t. the same $\mathbf{S}$-ontology.

Thus, our approach to the why-not problem makes use of $\mathbf{S}$-ontologies. In particular, our notion of a "best explanation" is a *most-general explanation*, which is defined with respect to an $\mathbf{S}$-ontology. We study the problem in three flavors: one in which the $\mathbf{S}$-ontology is obtained from an external source, and thus it is part of the input, and two in which the $\mathbf{S}$-ontology is not part of the input, and is derived, respectively, from the schema $\mathbf{S}$, or from the instance I.

5.1 External Ontology

We start by studying the case of computing ontology-based why-not explanations w.r.t. an external $\mathbf{S}$-ontology. We first study the complexity of deciding whether or not there exists an explanation w.r.t. an external $\mathbf{S}$-ontology.

Theorem 5.1.

1. *The problem* CHECK-MGE *is solvable in* PTIME.
2. *The problem* EXISTENCE-OF-EXPLANATION *is* NP*-complete. It remains* NP*-complete even for bounded schema arity.*

Intuitively, to check if a tuple of concepts is a most-general explanation, we can first check in PTIME if it is an explanation. Then, for each concept in the explanation, we can check in PTIME if it is subsumed by some other concept in $\mathcal{O}$ such that by replacing it with this more general concept, the tuple of concepts remains an explanation. The membership in NP is due to the fact that we can guess a tuple of concepts of polynomial size and verify in PTIME that it is an explanation. The lower bound is by a reduction from the SET COVER problem. Our reduction uses a query of unbounded arity and a schema of bounded arity. As we will show in Theorem 5.2, the problem is in PTIME if the arity of the query is fixed.

In light of the above result, we define an algorithm, called the EXHAUSTIVE SEARCH ALGORITHM, which is an EXPTIME algorithm for solving the COMPUTE-ONE-MGE problem.

Algorithm 1: EXHAUSTIVE SEARCH ALGORITHM

Input: a why-not instance $(\mathbf{S}, I, q, Ans, \overline{a})$, where $\overline{a} = (a_1, \ldots, a_m)$, a finite $\mathbf{S}$-ontology $\mathcal{O} = (\mathcal{C}, \sqsubseteq, ext)$
Output: the set of most-general explanations for $\overline{a} \notin Ans$ wrt $\mathcal{O}$

```
1 Let C(a_i) = {C ∈ C | a_i ∈ ext(C, I)} for all i, 1 ≤ i ≤ m
2 Let X = {(C_1, ..., C_m) | C_i ∈ C(a_i) and (ext(C_1, I) × ... × ext(C_m, I)) ∩ Ans = ∅}
3 foreach pair of explanations E_1, E_2 ∈ X, E_1 ≠ E_2 do
4     if E_1 >_O E_2 then
5         remove E_2 from X
6 return X
```

This algorithm first generates the set of all possible explanations, and then iteratively reduces the set by removing the tuples of concepts that are less general than some tuple of concepts in the set. In the end, only most-general explanations are returned. At first, in line 1, for each element of the tuple $\overline{a} = (a_1, \ldots, a_m)$, we build the set $\mathcal{C}(a_i)$ containing all the concepts in $\mathcal{C}$ whose extension contains a_i. Then, in line 2, we build the set of all possible explanations by picking a concept in $\mathcal{C}(a_i)$ for each position in $\overline{a}$, and by discarding the ones that have a non empty intersection with the answer set Ans. Finally, in lines 3-5, we remove from the set those explanations that have a strictly more general explanation in the set.

We now show that EXHAUSTIVE SEARCH ALGORITHM is correct (i.e. it outputs the set of all most-general explanations for the given why-not instance w.r.t. to the given $\mathbf{S}$-ontology), and runs in exponential time in the size of the input.

Theorem 5.2. *Let the why-not instance* $(\mathbf{S}, I, q, Ans, \overline{a})$ *and the* $\mathbf{S}$*-ontology* $\mathcal{O}$ *be an input to* EXHAUSTIVE SEARCH ALGORITHM *and let* $\mathcal{X}$ *be the corresponding output. The following hold:*

1. $\mathcal{X}$ *is the set of all most-general explanations for* $\overline{a} \notin Ans$ *(modulo equivalence);*
2. EXHAUSTIVE SEARCH ALGORITHM *runs in* EXPTIME *in the size of the input (in* PTIME *if we fix the arity of the input query).*

Theorem 5.2, together with Theorem 4.2, yields the following corollary (recall that, by construction of $\mathcal{O}_\mathcal{B}$, it holds that every input instance I is consistent with $\mathcal{O}_\mathcal{B}$).

Corollary 5.5. *There is an algorithm that takes as input a why-not instance* $(\mathbf{S}, I, q, Ans, \overline{a})$ *and an OBDA specification* $\mathcal{B} = (\mathcal{T}, \mathbf{S}, \mathcal{M})$*, where* $\mathcal{T}$ *is a DL-Lite*$_{\mathcal{R}}$ *TBox and* $\mathcal{M}$ *is a set of GAV mappings, and computes all the most-general explanations for* $\overline{a} \notin Ans$ *w.r.t. the* $\mathbf{S}$*-ontology* $\mathcal{O}_{\mathcal{B}}$ *in* EXPTIME *in the size of the input (in* PTIME *if the arity of the* q *is fixed)*.

5.2 Ontologies from an instance

We now study the why-not problem w.r.t. an $\mathbf{S}$-ontology O_I that is derived from an instance. First, note that the presence of nominals in the concept language guarantees a trivial answer for the EXISTENCE-OF-EXPLANATION W.R.T. $\mathcal{O}_I$ problem. An explanation always exists, namely the explanation with nominals corresponding to the constants of the tuple $\overline{a}$. In fact, a *most-general explanation* always exists, as follows from the results below.

Definition 5.6. *The* COMPUTE-ONE-MGE W.R.T. $\mathcal{O}_I$ *is the following computational problem: given a why-not instance* $(\mathbf{S}, I, q, Ans, \overline{a})$*, find a most-general explanation w.r.t.* $\mathcal{O}_I$ *for* $\overline{a} \notin Ans$*, where* $\mathcal{O}_I$ *is the* $\mathbf{S}$*-ontology that is derived from* I*, as defined in Section 4.2.*

First, we state an important proposition, that underlies the correctness of the algorithms that we will present. The following proposition shows that, when we search for explanations w.r.t. $\mathcal{O}_I$, we can always restrict our attention to a particular finite restriction of this ontology.

Proposition 5.1. *Let* $(\mathbf{S}, I, q, Ans, \overline{a})$ *be a why-not instance. If* E *is an explanation for* $\overline{a} \notin Ans$ *w.r.t.* $\mathcal{O}_I$ *(resp.* $\mathcal{O}_{\mathbf{S}}$*), then there exists an explanation* E' *for* $\overline{a} \notin Ans$ *such that* $E <_{\mathcal{O}_I[\mathcal{K}]} E'$ *(resp.* $E <_{\mathcal{O}_{\mathbf{S}}[\mathcal{K}]} E'$*), where* $\mathcal{K} = \text{adom}(I) \cup \{a_1, \ldots, a_m\}$ *and each constant in* E' *belongs to* $\mathcal{K}$*.*

In our proof, we iteratively reduce the number of constants occurring in the explanation. That is, for every explanation E with concepts containing constants outside of $\text{adom}(I) \cup \{a_1, \ldots, a_m\}$, we produce a new explanation E' which is more general than E and which contains less constants outside of $\text{adom}(I) \cup \{a_1, \ldots, a_m\}$.

Notice that since, in principle, it is possible to materialize the ontology $\mathcal{O}_I[\mathcal{K}]$ (i.e., to explicitly compute all the concepts $\mathcal{C}$ in the ontology, the subsumption relation $\sqsubseteq_I$, and the extension ext), the EXHAUSTIVE SEARCH ALGORITHM, together with Proposition 5.1, give us a method for solving COMPUTE-ONE-MGE W.R.T. $\mathcal{O}_I$. In particular, given a schema, EXHAUSTIVE SEARCH ALGORITHM solves COMPUTE-ONE-MGE W.R.T. $\mathcal{O}_I$ in 2EXPTIME (in EXPTIME if the arity of q is fixed). This is because to find a most-general explanation w.r.t $\mathcal{O}_I$, it is sufficient to restrict to the concept language $L_{\mathbf{S}}[\mathcal{K}]$ and its fragments, where $\mathcal{K} = \text{adom}(I) \cup \{a_1, \ldots, a_m\}$. Then COMPUTE-ONE-MGE W.R.T. $\mathcal{O}_I$ is solvable in 2EXPTIME follows from the fact that the $\mathbf{S}$-ontology $\mathcal{O}_I[\mathcal{K}]$ is computable in at most 2EXPTIME.

We now present a more effective algorithm for solving COMPUTE-ONE-MGE W.R.T. $\mathcal{O}_I$. (See Algorithm 2.) We start by introducing the notion of a *least upper bound* of a set of constants X w.r.t. an instance I, denoted by $\mathsf{lub}_I(X)$. This, intuitively, corresponds to the most-specific concept whose extension contains all constants of X. We first consider the case in which $\mathsf{lub}_I(X)$ is expressed using selection-free $L_{\mathbf{S}}$ concepts. The following lemma states two important properties of $\mathsf{lub}_I(X)$ that are crucial for the correctness of Algorithm 2.

Lemma 5.1. *Given an instance* I *of schema* $\mathbf{S}$ *and a set of constants* X*, we can compute in polynomial time a selection-free* $L_{\mathbf{S}}$ *concept, denoted* $\mathsf{lub}_I(X)$*, that is the smallest concept whose extension contains all the elements in* X *definable in the language. In particular, the following hold:*

1. $X \subseteq ext(\mathsf{lub}_I(X), I)$,
2. *there is no concept* C' *in selection-free* $L_{\mathbf{S}}$ *such that* $C' \sqsubset_I \mathsf{lub}_I(X)$ *and* $X \subseteq ext(C', I)$.

We are now ready to introduce the algorithm. We will start with a high-level description of the idea behind it. The algorithm navigates through the search space of possible explanations using an incremental search strategy and makes use of the above defined notion of lub. We start with an explanation that has, in each position, the lub of the constant (i.e., nominal) that occurs in that position. Then, we try to construct a more general explanation by expanding the set of constants considered by each lub.

Notice that INCREMENTAL SEARCH ALGORITHM produces explanations which are tuples of conjunctions of concepts. Therefore it produces an explanation whose concepts are concept expressions in the language $L_{\mathbf{S}}$ or selection-free $L_{\mathbf{S}}$. We will study the behavior of the algorithm in each of these cases separately.

Algorithm 2: INCREMENTAL SEARCH ALGORITHM

```
Input: a why-not instance (S, I, q, Ans, ā)
Output: a most-general explanation for ā ∉ Ans wrt O_I
Let K = adom(I) ∪ {a_1, ..., a_m}
Let X = (X_1, ..., X_m) s.t. each X_j = {a_j}.  // support set
Let E = (C_1, ..., C_m) s.t. each C_j = lub_I(X_j).  // first candidate explanation
foreach 1 ≤ j ≤ m do
    foreach b ∈ adom(I) \ ext(E_j, I) do
        X'_j = X_j ∪ {b}
        Let C'_j = lub_I(X'_j)  // a more general concept in position j
        Let E' := (C_1, ..., C'_j, ... C_m)  // a more general explanation
        if E' ∩ Ans = ∅ then
            E := E'
            X := (X_1, ..., X'_j, ... X_m)
return E
```

First, we focus on the case in which INCREMENTAL SEARCH ALGORITHM produces most-general explanations using selection-free $L_{\mathbf{S}}$ concepts. We show that the algorithm is correct, i.e., that it outputs an explanation for $\overline{a} \notin Ans$ w.r.t. $\mathcal{O}_I$, and that it runs in polynomial time with selection-free $L_{\mathbf{S}}$.

Theorem 5.3 (Correctness and running time of INCREMENTAL SEARCH ALGORITHM). *Let the why-not instance* $(\mathbf{S}, I, q, Ans, \overline{a})$ *be an input to* INCREMENTAL SEARCH ALGORITHM *and* E *the corresponding output. The following holds:*

1. E *is a most-general explanation for* $\overline{a} \notin Ans$ *w.r.t.* $\mathcal{O}_I = (\mathcal{C}, \sqsubseteq_I, ext)$*, where* $\mathcal{C}$ *is selection-free* $L_{\mathbf{S}}$*;*
2. INCREMENTAL SEARCH ALGORITHM *runs in* PTIME *in the size of the input.*

Now we extend our analysis of INCREMENTAL SEARCH ALGORITHM to the general case in which it works with $L_{\mathbf{S}}$. First, we state an analogue of Lemma 5.1 for $L_{\mathbf{S}}$.

Lemma 5.2. *Given an instance* I *of* $\mathbf{S}$ *and a set of constants* X*, we can compute in exponential time a* $L_{\mathbf{S}}$ *concept, denoted* $\mathsf{lub}_I^{\sigma}(X)$*, that is the smallest concept whose extension contains all the elements in* X *definable in the language. Such concept is polynomial-time computable for bounded schema arity. In particular, the following hold:*

1. $X \subseteq ext(\mathsf{lub}_I^{\sigma}(X), I)$,

2. *there is no concept C' in $L_{\mathbf{S}}$ such that $C' \sqsubset_I \mathsf{lub}_I^{\sigma}(X)$ and $X \subseteq ext(C', I)$.*

By INCREMENTAL SEARCH ALGORITHM WITH SELECTIONS we will refer to the algorithm obtained from INCREMENTAL SEARCH ALGORITHM by replacing $\mathsf{lub}_I(X)$ with $\mathsf{lub}_I^{\sigma}(X)$ in line 3 and line 7.

The following Theorem shows that INCREMENTAL SEARCH ALGORITHM WITH SELECTIONS is correct, i.e., that it outputs an explanation for $\overline{a} \notin Ans$ w.r.t. the S-ontology $\mathcal{O}_I$, and that it runs in exponential time (in polynomial time for bounded schema arity).

Theorem 5.4 (Correctness and running time of INCREMENTAL SEARCH ALGORITHM WITH SELECTIONS). *Let the why-not instance $(\mathbf{S}, I, q, Ans, \overline{a})$ be an input to* INCREMENTAL SEARCH ALGORITHM WITH SELECTIONS *and E the corresponding output. The following hold:*

1. *E is a most-general explanation for $\overline{a} \notin Ans$ w.r.t. $\mathcal{O}_I = (\mathcal{C}, \sqsubseteq_I, ext)$, where $\mathcal{C}$ is $L_{\mathbf{S}}$;*
2. INCREMENTAL SEARCH ALGORITHM *runs in* EXPTIME *in the size of the input (in* PTIME *for bounded schema arity).*

We close this section with the study of the following problem.

Definition 5.7. *The* CHECK-MGE W.R.T. $\mathcal{O}_I$ *problem is the following decision problem: given a why-not instance $(\mathbf{S}, I, q, Ans, \overline{a})$ and a tuple of concepts $E = (C_1, \ldots, C_n)$, is E a most-general explanation w.r.t. $\mathcal{O}_I$ for $\overline{a} \notin Ans$?*

Our next proposition states the running time of our algorithm for the CHECK-MGE W.R.T. $\mathcal{O}_I$ for various fragments of our concept language. The algorithm operates very similarly to lines 4-11 of INCREMENTAL SEARCH ALGORITHM. Given a tuple of concepts, we check whether that tuple of concepts can be extended to a more general tuple of concepts through ideas similar to lines 4-11 of INCREMENTAL SEARCH ALGORITHM. If the answer is "no", then we return "yes". Otherwise, we return "no".

Proposition 5.2. *There is an algorithm that solves* CHECK-MGE W.R.T. $\mathcal{O}_I$ *in:*

- PTIME *for selection-free $L_{\mathbf{S}}$, or for $L_{\mathbf{S}}$ with bounded schema arity;*
- EXPTIME *for $L_{\mathbf{S}}$ in the general case.*

5.3 Ontologies from Schema

We now study the case of solving the why-not problem w.r.t. to an S-ontology $\mathcal{O}_{\mathbf{S}}$ that is derived from a schema. As in the previous case, the presence of nominals in the concept language guarantees that the trivial explanation always exists. Therefore we do not consider the decision problem EXISTENCE-OF-EXPLANATION W.R.T. $\mathcal{O}_{\mathbf{S}}$.

Definition 5.8 (COMPUTE-ONE-MGE W.R.T. $\mathcal{O}_{\mathbf{S}}$). *The* COMPUTE-ONE-MGE W.R.T. $\mathcal{O}_{\mathbf{S}}$ *is the following computational problem: given a why-not instance $(\mathbf{S}, I, q, Ans, \overline{a})$, find a most-general explanation w.r.t. $\mathcal{O}_{\mathbf{S}}$ for $\overline{a} \notin Ans$, where $\mathcal{O}_{\mathbf{S}}$ is the* S*-ontology that is derived from* S*, as defined in Section 4.2.*

The complexity of COMPUTE-ONE-MGE W.R.T. $\mathcal{O}_{\mathbf{S}}$ depends on the complexity of subsumption checking for $L_{\mathbf{S}}$. As seen in Table 1, subsumption checking with respect to arbitrary integrity constraints is undecidable. Therefore, for the general case in which no restriction is imposed on the integrity constraints, COMPUTE-ONE-MGE W.R.T. $\mathcal{O}_{\mathbf{S}}$ is unlikely to be decidable. The restrictions on the integrity constraints of S allow for the definition of several variants of the problem that, under some restrictions, are decidable.

We restrict now to the cases in which we are able to materialize the S-ontology $\mathcal{O}_{\mathbf{S}}[\mathcal{K}]$, with $\mathcal{K} = \text{adom}(I) \cup \{a_1, \ldots, a_m\}$. EXHAUSTIVE SEARCH ALGORITHM gives us a method for solving COMPUTE-ONE-MGE W.R.T. $\mathcal{O}_{\mathbf{S}}$. The following proposition gives us a double exponential upper bound for COMPUTE-ONE-MGE W.R.T. $\mathcal{O}_{\mathbf{S}}$ in the general case, and a polynomial case under specific assumptions (cf. Table 1).

Proposition 5.3. *There is an algorithm that solves* COMPUTE-ONE-MGE W.R.T. $\mathcal{O}_{\mathbf{S}}$

- *in* 2EXPTIME *for $L_{\mathbf{S}}$, provided that the input schema* S *is from a class for which concept subsumption can be checked in* EXPTIME,
- *in* EXPTIME *for selection-free $L_{\mathbf{S}}$, and projection-free $L_{\mathbf{S}}$, provided that the input schema* S *is from a class for which concept subsumption can be checked in* EXPTIME,
- *in* PTIME *for $L_{\mathbf{S}}^{\min}$, if the arity of q is fixed and provided that the input schema* S *is from a class for which concept subsumption can be checked in* PTIME.

We end with the definition of CHECK-MGE W.R.T. $\mathcal{O}_{\mathbf{S}}$.

Definition 5.9. *The* CHECK-MGE W.R.T. $\mathcal{O}_{\mathbf{S}}$ *problem is the following decision problem: given a why-not instance $(\mathbf{S}, I, q, Ans, \overline{a})$ and a tuple of concepts $E = (C_1, \ldots, C_n)$, is E a most-general explanation w.r.t. $\mathcal{O}_{\mathbf{S}}$ for $\overline{a} \notin Ans$?*

As for COMPUTE-ONE-MGE W.R.T. $\mathcal{O}_{\mathbf{S}}$, the undecidability of concept subsumption in the general case suggests that it is unlikely for CHECK-MGE W.R.T. $\mathcal{O}_{\mathbf{S}}$ to be decidable without imposing any restriction on Π and Σ. However, also this problem allows for the characterization of several decidable variants.

In particular, since CHECK-MGE is solvable in PTIME (see Theorem 5.1), by materializing $\mathcal{O}_{\mathbf{S}}[\mathcal{K}]$ we can derive some upper bounds for CHECK-MGE W.R.T. $\mathcal{O}_{\mathbf{S}}$ too.

Proposition 5.4. *There is an algorithm that solves* CHECK-MGE W.R.T. $\mathcal{O}_{\mathbf{S}}$

- *in* 2EXPTIME *for $L_{\mathbf{S}}$ concepts, provided that the input schema* S *is from a class for which concept subsumption can be checked in* EXPTIME,
- *in* EXPTIME *for selection-free $L_{\mathbf{S}}$, and projection-free $L_{\mathbf{S}}$, provided that the input schema* S *is from a class for which concept subsumption can be checked in* EXPTIME,
- *in* PTIME *for $L_{\mathbf{S}}^{\min}$, provided that the input schema* S *is from a class for which concept subsumption can be checked in* PTIME.

The proof is analogous to the one for Proposition 5.3.

We expect that the upper bounds for COMPUTE-ONE-MGE W.R.T. $\mathcal{O}_{\mathbf{S}}$ and CHECK-MGE W.R.T. $\mathcal{O}_{\mathbf{S}}$ can be improved. Pinpointing the complexity of these problems is left for future work.

6. VARIATIONS OF THE FRAMEWORK

We consider several refinements and variations to our framework involving finding short explanations, and providing alternative definitions of *explanations* and of what it means to be *most general*.

Producing a Short Explanation. A most-general explanation that is *short* may be more helpful to the user. To simplify our discussion, we restrict our attention to ontologies that are derived from an instance and show that the problem of finding a most-general explanation of minimal length is NP-hard in general, where the *length* of an explanation $E = (C_1, \ldots, C_k)$ is measured by the total number of symbols needed to write out $C_1, \ldots, C_k$.

Proposition 6.1. *Given a why-not instance* $(\mathbf{S}, I, q, Ans, \overline{a})$*, the problem of finding a most-general explanation to* $\overline{a} \notin Ans$ *of minimal length is* NP*-hard.*

Given that computing a shortest most-general explanation is intractable in general, we may consider the task of shortening a given most-general explanation. The INCREMENTAL SEARCH ALGORITHM produces concepts that may contain superfluous conjuncts. It is thus natural to ask whether the algorithm can be modified to produce a most-general explanation of a shorter length. This question can be formalized in at least two ways.

Let I be an instance of a schema $\mathbf{S}$, and let $C = \sqcap\{C_1, \ldots, C_n\}$ be any $L_\mathbf{S}$ concept expression. We may assume that each C_i is intersection-free. We say that C is *irredundant* if there is a no strict subset $X \subsetneq \{C_1, \ldots, C_n\}$ such that $C \equiv_{\mathcal{O}_I} \sqcap X$. We say that an explanation (with respect to $\mathcal{O}_I$) is irredundant if it consists of irredundant concept expressions. We say that explanations E_1 and E_2 are *equivalent* w.r.t. an ontology $\mathcal{O}$, denoted as $E_1 \equiv_\mathcal{O} E_2$, if $E_1 \leq_\mathcal{O} E_2$ and $E_2 \leq_\mathcal{O} E_1$.

Proposition 6.2. *There is a polynomial-time algorithm that takes as input an instance* I *of a schema* $\mathbf{S}$*, as well as an* $L_\mathbf{S}$ *concept expression* C*, and produces an irredundant concept expression* C' *such that* $C \equiv_{\mathcal{O}_I} C'$*.*

Hence, by combining Proposition 6.2 with INCREMENTAL SEARCH ALGORITHM, we can compute an irredundant most-general explanation w.r.t. $\mathcal{O}_I$ in polynomial time.

We say that an explanation $E = (C_1, \ldots, C_k)$ is *minimized* w.r.t. $\mathcal{O}_I$ if there does not exist an explanation $E' = (C_1, \ldots, C_k)$ such that $E \equiv_{\mathcal{O}_I} E'$ and E' is shorter than E. Every minimized explanation is irredundant, but the converse may not be true. For instance, let O be an ontology with three atomic concepts C_1, C_2, C_3 such that $C_1 \sqsubseteq_O C_2 \sqcap C_3$ and $C_2 \sqcap C_3 \sqsubseteq_O C_1$. Then the concept $C_2 \sqcap C_3$ is irredundant with respect to O. However, C_1 is an equivalent concept of strictly shorter length.

Proposition 6.3. *Given a why-not instance* $(\mathbf{S}, I, q, Ans, \overline{a})$ *and an explanation* E *to why* $\overline{a} \notin Ans$*, the problem of finding a minimized explanation equivalent to* E *is* NP*-hard.*

Cardinality based preference. We have currently defined a *most-general explanation* to be an explanation E such that there is no explanation E' with $E' >_\mathcal{O} E$. A natural alternative is to define "most general" in terms of the cardinality of the extensions of the concepts in an explanation. Formally, let $\mathcal{O} = (\mathcal{C}, \sqsubseteq, ext)$ be an $\mathbf{S}$-ontology, and I an instance. We define the *degree of generality* of an explanation $E = (C_1, \ldots, C_m)$ with respect to $\mathcal{O}$ and I to be the (possibly infinite) sum $|ext(C_1, I)| + \cdots + |ext(C_m, I)|$. For two explanations, E_1, E_2, we write $E_1 >^{card}_{\mathcal{O},I} E_2$, if E_1 has a strictly higher degree of generality than E_2 with respect to $\mathcal{O}$ and I. We say that an explanation E is $>^{card}$-maximal (with respect to $\mathcal{O}$ and I) if there is no explanation E' such that $E' >^{card}_{\mathcal{O},I} E$.

Proposition 6.4. *Assuming P≠NP, there is no* PTIME *algorithm that takes as input a why-not instance* $(\mathbf{S}, I, q, Ans, \overline{a})$ *and an* $\mathbf{S}$*-ontology* $\mathcal{O}$*, and produces a* $>^{card}$*-maximal explanation for* $\overline{a} \notin Ans$*. This holds even for unary queries.*

In particular, this shows (assuming P≠NP) that computing $>^{card}$-maximal explanations is harder than computing most-general explanations. The proof of Proposition 6.4 goes by reduction from a suitable variant of SET COVER. Our reduction is in fact an L-reduction, which implies that there is no PTIME constant-factor approximation algorithm for the problem of finding a $>^{card}$-maximal explanation.

Strong explanations. We now examine an alternative notion of an explanation that is essentially independent to the instance of a why-not question. Recall that the second condition of our current definition of an explanation $E = (C_1, \ldots, C_m)$ requires that $ext(C_1, I) \times \cdots \times ext(C_1, I)$ does not intersect with Ans, where I is the given instance. We could replace this condition by a stronger condition, namely that $ext(C_1, I') \times \cdots \times ext(C_1, I')$ does not intersect with $q(I')$, for *any* instance I' of the given schema that is consistent with the ontology $\mathcal{O}$. If this holds, we say that E is a *strong explanation*.

A strong explanation is also an explanation but not necessarily the other way round. When a strong explanation E for $\overline{a} \notin Ans$ exists, then, intuitively, the reason why $\overline{a}$ does not belong to Ans, is essentially independent from the specific instance I, and has to do with the ontology $\mathcal{O}$ and the query q. In the case where the ontology $\mathcal{O}$ is derived from a schema $\mathbf{S}$, a strong explanation may help one discover possible errors in the integrity constraints of $\mathbf{S}$, or in the query q. We leave the study of strong why-not explanations for future work.

7. CONCLUSION

We have presented a new framework for why-not explanations, which leverages concepts from an ontology to provide high-level and meaningful reasons for why a tuple is missing from the result of a query. Our focus in this paper was on developing a principled framework, and on identifying the key algorithmic problems. The exact complexity of some problems raised in this paper remains open. In addition, there are several directions for future work.

Recall that, in general, there may be multiple most-general explanations for $\overline{a} \notin q(I)$. While we have presented a polynomial time algorithm for computing a most-general explanation to a why-not question w.r.t. $\mathcal{O}_I$ for the case of selection-free $L_\mathbf{S}$, the most-general explanation that is returned by the algorithm may not always be the most helpful explanation. In future work, we plan to investigate whether there is a polynomial delay algorithm for enumerating all most-general explanations for such ontologies.

Although we only looked at *why-not explanations*, it will be natural to consider *why explanations* in the context of an ontology, and in particular, understand whether the notion of most-general explanations, suitably adapted, applies in this setting. In addition, Roy and Suciu [27] recently initiated the study of what one could call "why so high" and "why so low" explanations for numerical queries (such as aggregate queries). Again, it would be interesting to see if our approach can help in identifying high-level such explanations.

We have focused on providing why-not explanations to missing tuples of queries that are posed against a database schema. However, our framework for answering the why-not question is general and could, in principle, be applied also to queries posed against the ontology in an OBDA setting.

Finally, we plan to explore ways whereby our high-level explanations can be used to complement and enhance existing data-centric and/or query-centric approaches. We illustrate this with an example. Suppose a certain publication X is missing from the answers to query over some publication database. A most-general explanation may be that X was published by Springer (supposing all Springer publications are missing from the answers to the query). This explanation provides insight on potential high-level issues that may exist in the database and/or query. For example, it may be that all Springer publications are missing from the database (perhaps due to errors in the integration/curation process) or the query has inadvertently omitted the retrieval of all Springer publications. This is in contrast with existing data-centric (resp. query-centric) approaches, which only suggest fixes to the database instance (resp. query) so that the specific publication X appears in the query result.

Acknowledgements We thank Vince Bárány, Bertram Ludäscher and Dan Olteanu for motivating discussion during early stages of the research. Ten Cate is partially supported by NSF grant IIS-1217869. Civili is partially supported by the EU under FP7 project Optique (grant n. FP7-318338). Sherkhonov is supported by the Netherlands Organization for Scientific Research (NWO) under project number 612.001.012 (DEX). Tan is partially supported by NSF grant IIS-1450560.

8. REFERENCES

[1] S. Abiteboul, R. Hull, and V. Vianu. *Foundations of databases*, volume 8. Addison-Wesley, 1995.

[2] M. Aref, B. ten Cate, T. J. Green, B. Kimelfeld, D. Olteanu, E. Pasalic, T. L. Veldhuizen, and G. Washburn. Design and implementation of the logicblox system. In *SIGMOD '15*, 2015.

[3] T. Arora, R. Ramakrishnan, W. G. Roth, P. Seshadri, and D. Srivastava. Explaining program execution in deductive systems. In *DOOD*, pages 101–119, 1993.

[4] A. Artale, D. Calvanese, R. Kontchakov, and M. Zakharyaschev. The DL-Lite family and relations. *J. Artif. Intell. Res. (JAIR)*, 36:1–69, 2009.

[5] S. Auer, S. Dietzold, J. Lehmann, S. Hellmann, and D. Aumueller. Triplify: Light-weight linked data publication from relational databases. In *WWW*, pages 621–630, 2009.

[6] A. Baid, W. Wu, C. Sun, A. Doan, and J. F. Naughton. On debugging non-answers in keyword search systems. In *EDBT*, 2015.

[7] M. Benedikt and G. Gottlob. The impact of virtual views on containment. *PVLDB*, 3(1):297–308, 2010.

[8] N. Bidoit, M. Herschel, and K. Tzompanaki. Query-based why-not provenance with nedexplain. In *EDBT*, pages 145–156, 2014.

[9] M. Bienvenu, B. ten Cate, C. Lutz, and F. Wolter. Ontology-based data access: A study through disjunctive datalog, CSP, and MMSNP. In *PODS*, pages 213–224, 2013.

[10] C. Bizer and A. Seaborne. D2rq - treating non-rdf databases as virtual rdf graphs. In *ISWC2004 (posters)*, 2004.

[11] A. Borgida, D. Calvanese, and M. Rodriguez-Muro. Explanation in the DL-Lite family of description logics. In *On the Move to Meaningful Internet Systems*, pages 1440–1457, 2008.

[12] D. Calvanese, G. De Giacomo, D. Lembo, M. Lenzerini, and R. Rosati. Tractable reasoning and efficient query answering in description logics: The dl-lite family. *J. of Automated reasoning*, 39(3):385–429, 2007.

[13] D. Calvanese, M. Ortiz, M. Simkus, and G. Stefanoni. Reasoning about explanations for negative query answers in DL-Lite. *J. Artif. Intell. Res.*, 48:635–669, 2013.

[14] A. Chapman and H. V. Jagadish. Why not? In *SIGMOD*, pages 523–534, 2009.

[15] J. Cheney, L. Chiticariu, and W. C. Tan. Provenance in databases: Why, how, and where. *Foundations and Trends in Databases*, 1(4):379–474, 2009.

[16] B. Chin, D. von Dincklage, V. Ercegovak, P. Hawkins, M. S. Miller, F. Och, C. Olston, and F. Pereira. Yedalog: Exploring knowledge at scale. In *SNAPL*, 2015. To appear.

[17] F. Di Pinto, D. Lembo, M. Lenzerini, R. Mancini, A. Poggi, R. Rosati, M. Ruzzi, and D. F. Savo. Optimizing query rewriting in ontology-based data access. In *EDBT*, pages 561–572, 2013.

[18] T. J. Green. Logiql: a declarative language for enterprise applications. In *PODS '15*, 2015.

[19] T. J. Green, M. Aref, and G. Karvounarakis. Logicblox, platform and language: A tutorial. In *Proceedings of the Second International Conference on Datalog in Academia and Industry*, pages 1–8, 2012.

[20] T. J. Green, G. Karvounarakis, and V. Tannen. Provenance semirings. In *PODS*, pages 31–40, 2007.

[21] T. Halpin and S. Rugaber. *LogiQL: A Query Language for Smart Databases*. CRC Press, 2014.

[22] M. Herschel, M. A. Hernández, and W. C. Tan. Artemis: A system for analyzing missing answers. *PVLDB*, 2(2):1550–1553, 2009.

[23] J. Huang, T. Chen, A. Doan, and J. F. Naughton. On the provenance of non-answers to queries over extracted data. *PVLDB*, 1(1):736–747, 2008.

[24] L. Lubyte and S. Tessaris. Automatic extraction of ontologies wrapping relational data sources. In *DEXA*, pages 128–142, 2009.

[25] A. Meliou, W. Gatterbauer, K. F. Moore, and D. Suciu. The complexity of causality and responsibility for query answers and non-answers. *PVLDB*, 4(1):34–45, 2010.

[26] A. Poggi, D. Lembo, D. Calvanese, G. De Giacomo, M. Lenzerini, and R. Rosati. Linking data to ontologies. *J. on Data Semantics X*, pages 133–173, 2008.

[27] S. Roy and D. Suciu. A formal approach to finding explanations for database queries. In *Proceedings of the 2014 ACM SIGMOD International Conference on Management of Data*, SIGMOD '14, pages 1579–1590, New York, NY, USA, 2014. ACM.

[28] O. Shmueli and S. Tsur. Logical diagnosis of ldl programs. In *Int'l Conf. on Logic Programming*, 1990.

[29] Q. T. Tran and C. Chan. How to conquer why-not questions. In *SIGMOD*, pages 15–26, 2010.

The ACM PODS Alberto O. Mendelzon Test-of-Time Award 2015

In 2007, the PODS Executive Committee decided to establish a Test-of-Time Award, named after the late Alberto O. Mendelzon, in recognition of his scientific legacy, and his service and dedication to the database community.

Mendelzon was an international leader in database theory, whose pioneering and fundamental work has inspired and influenced both database theoreticians and practitioners, and continues to be applied in a variety of advanced settings. He served the database community in many ways; in particular, he served as the General Chair of the PODS conference, and was instrumental in bringing together the PODS and SIGMOD conferences. He also was an outstanding educator, who guided the research of numerous doctoral students and postdoctoral fellows. The Award is to be awarded each year to a paper or a small number of papers published in the PODS proceedings ten years prior, that had the most impact (in terms of research, methodology, or transfer of practice) over the intervening decade. The decision was approved by SIGMOD and ACM. The funds for the Award were contributed by IBM Toronto.

The PODS Executive Chair has appointed us to serve as the Award Committee for 2015. After careful consideration and soliciting external assessments, we have decided to select the following two papers as the award winners for 2015:

XPath Satisfiability in the Presence of DTDs
Michael Benedikt, Wenfei Fan, and Floris Geerts

Views and Queries: Determinacy and Rewriting
Luc Segoufin and Victor Vianu.

The first paper studies the satisfiability problem for XPath queries under schema constraints. The satisfiability problem is a classical problem associated with query languages, and the query languages considered in this paper represent tree pattern languages of universal interest. The paper considers an exhaustive combination of query languages and schema formalism, establishing tight complexity bounds for the satisfiability problem. The conference paper, and its full version published in the Journal of the ACM three years later, contain a treasure trove of complexity results and proof techniques, most of which are state of the art today. The proofs are technically sophisticated, yet a pleasure to read. The paper has a large number of citations, has influenced many researchers, and it is considered today the standard reference for complexity results on the satisfiability problem for XPath expressions.

Prior to the second paper there had been considerable research activity on rewriting queries using views, which is a fundamental problem in databases. But all prior work had been confined to algorithms for finding such rewritings. This paper marks a complete conceptual shift in looking at the problem, focusing attention for the first time on the question of when rewritings exist, regardless of whether one can find them. The paper introduces the right conceptual framework for studying one of the most important problems in database theory, by defining formally the notion of determinacy. It also establishes several key theoretical results, demonstrating both the elegance and the depth of the notion of determinacy, and pointing to the general direction of how determinacy should be studied in the future. Today, the notion of determinacy, as defined by this paper, has been widely adopted by the theoretical database community, and has motivated several follow-up studies, ranging from work on the problem of decidability of FO rewritability to decidability results for restricted classes of queries.

Foto Afrati
NTU Athens, Greece

Frank Neven
Hasselt University, Belgium

Dan Suciu
University of Washington, USA

The Alberto O. Mendelzon Test-of-Time Award Committee for 2015

Parallel-Correctness and Transferability for Conjunctive Queries

Tom J. Ameloot[*]
Hasselt University & transnational University of Limburg
tom.ameloot@uhasselt.be

Gaetano Geck
TU Dortmund University
gaetano.geck@tu-dortmund.de

Bas Ketsman[†]
Hasselt University & transnational University of Limburg
bas.ketsman@uhasselt.be

Frank Neven
Hasselt University & transnational University of Limburg
frank.neven@uhasselt.be

Thomas Schwentick
TU Dortmund University
thomas.schwentick@udo.edu

ABSTRACT

A dominant cost for query evaluation in modern massively distributed systems is the number of communication rounds. For this reason, there is a growing interest in single-round multiway join algorithms where data is first reshuffled over many servers and then evaluated in a parallel but communication-free way. The reshuffling itself is specified as a distribution policy. We introduce a correctness condition, called *parallel-correctness*, for the evaluation of queries w.r.t. a distribution policy. We study the complexity of parallel-correctness for conjunctive queries as well as transferability of parallel-correctness between queries. We also investigate the complexity of transferability for certain families of distribution policies, including, for instance, the Hypercube distribution.

Categories and Subject Descriptors

H.2 [**Database Management**]: Languages; H.2 [**Database Management**]: Systems—*Distributed databases*

Keywords

Distributed databases; Parallel query evaluation; One-round evaluation; Distribution policies

1. INTRODUCTION

In traditional database systems, the complexity of query processing for large datasets is mainly determined by the number of IO requests to external memory. A factor dominating complexity in modern massively distributed database systems, however, is the number of communication steps [6]. Motivated by recent in-memory systems like Spark [12] and Shark [14], Koutris and Suciu introduced the massively parallel communication model (MPC) [11] where computation proceeds in a sequence of parallel steps each followed by global synchronization of all servers. In this model, evaluation of conjunctive queries [5, 11] and skyline queries [2] has been considered.

Of particular interest in the MPC model are the queries that can be evaluated in one round of communication. Recently, Beame, Koutris and Suciu [6] proved a matching upper and lower bound for the amount of communication needed to compute a full conjunctive query without self-joins in one communication round. The upper bound is provided by a randomized algorithm called Hypercube which uses a technique that can be traced back to Ganguli, Silberschatz, and Tsur [9] and is described in the context of map-reduce by Afrati and Ullman [3]. The Hypercube algorithm evaluates a conjunctive query $\mathcal{Q}$ by first reshuffling the data over many servers and then evaluating $\mathcal{Q}$ at each server in a parallel but communication-free manner. The reshuffling is specified by a distribution policy (hereafter, called Hypercube distribution) and is based on the structure of $\mathcal{Q}$. In particular, the Hypercube distribution partitions the space of all complete valuations of $\mathcal{Q}$ over the computing servers in an instance independent way through hashing of domain values. A property of Hypercube distributions is that for any instance I, the central execution of $\mathcal{Q}(I)$ always equals the union of the evaluations of $\mathcal{Q}$ at every computing node (or server).[1]

In this paper, we introduce a general framework for reasoning about one-round evaluation algorithms under *arbitrary* distribution policies.[2] Distribution policies (formally

[*]Postdoctoral Fellow of the Research Foundation - Flanders (FWO).

[†]PhD Fellow of the Research Foundation - Flanders (FWO).

PODS'15, May 31–June 4, 2015, Melbourne, Victoria, Australia.

ACM 978-1-4503-2757-2/15/05 ...$15.00.
http://dx.doi.org/10.1145/2745754.2745759.

[1]We emphasize that, for a query $\mathcal{Q}$, there is no single Hypercube distribution but rather a family of distributions as the concrete instantiation depends on choices regarding the address space of servers.

[2]Our aim is to study one-round evaluation algorithms, not to *advocate* them. We plan further investigation that also takes multi-round algorithms into account. Furthermore,

defined in Section 2) are functions mapping input facts to sets of nodes (servers) in the network. We introduce the following correctness property for queries and distribution policies: a query $\mathcal{Q}$ is *parallel-correct* for a given distribution policy $\boldsymbol{P}$, when for any instance I, the evaluation of $\mathcal{Q}(I)$ equals the union of the evaluation of $\mathcal{Q}$ over the distribution of I under policy $\boldsymbol{P}$. We focus on conjunctive queries and study the complexity of deciding parallel-correctness. We show that the latter problem is equivalent to testing whether the facts in every *minimal* valuation of the conjunctive query are mapped to a same node in the network by the distribution policy. For various representations of distributions policies, we then show that testing parallel-correctness is in Π_2^P. We provide a matching lower bound via a reduction from the Π_2^P-complete Π_2-QBF-problem.

One-round evaluation algorithms, like Hypercube, redistribute data for the evaluation of every query. For scenarios where queries are executed in sequence, it makes sense to study cases where the same data distribution can be used to evaluate multiple queries. We formalize this as *parallel-correctness transfer* between queries. In particular, parallel-correctness *transfers* from $\mathcal{Q}$ to $\mathcal{Q}'$ when $\mathcal{Q}'$ is parallel-correct under every distribution policy for which $\mathcal{Q}$ is parallel-correct. We characterize transferability for conjunctive queries by a (value-based) containment condition for minimal valuations of $\mathcal{Q}'$ and $\mathcal{Q}$, and use this characterization to obtain a Π_3^P upper bound for transferability. Again, we obtain a matching lower bound, this time via a reduction from the Π_3^P-complete Π_3-QBF-problem. We obtain a (presumably) better complexity, NP-completeness, in the case that $\mathcal{Q}$ is *strongly minimal*, i.e., when all its valuations are minimal. Examples of strongly minimal CQs include the full conjunctive queries and those without self-joins. At the heart of the upper bound proof lies the insight that the above mentioned value-based inclusion w.r.t. minimal valuations reduces to a syntactic inclusion of $\mathcal{Q}'$ in $\mathcal{Q}$ modulo a variable renaming when $\mathcal{Q}$ is strongly minimal. We obtain that deciding strong minimality is NP-complete as well.

Finally, we study parallel-correctness transfer from $\mathcal{Q}$ to $\mathcal{Q}'$ w.r.t. a specific family $\mathcal{F}$ of distribution policies rather than the set of *all* distribution policies. We show that it is NP-complete to decide whether $\mathcal{Q}'$ is parallel-correct for a given family $\mathcal{F}$ if this family has the following two properties: it is $\mathcal{Q}$-generous (for each, not only for minimal, valuation of $\mathcal{Q}$, its facts occur at some node) and $\mathcal{Q}$-scattered (for every instance some distribution has, at every node, only facts from one valuation). It is easy to see that the family of Hypercube distributions for a given CQ $\mathcal{Q}$ satisfies these properties, which implies that deciding transferability for Hypercube distributions is NP-complete, as well.

We complete our framework by sketching a declarative specification formalism for distribution policies, illustrated with the specification of Hypercube distributions.

Outline. We introduce the necessary definitions in Section 2. We study parallel-correctness in Section 3 and transferability in Section 4. We examine families of distribution policies including the Hypercube distribution in Section 5. We conclude in Section 6. We give at least sketches of most proofs but defer some proof details to the full version of this paper.

our emphasis is on *reasoning* about queries and distribution policies, not on the development of good distribution policies.

2. DEFINITIONS

Queries and instances.

We assume an infinite set **dom** of data values that can be represented by strings over some fixed alphabet. A *database schema* $\mathcal{D}$ is a finite set of relation names R where every R has arity $ar(R)$. We call $R(\mathbf{t})$ a *fact* when R is a relation name and $\mathbf{t}$ a tuple in **dom**. We say that a fact $R(d_1, \dots, d_k)$ is *over* a database schema $\mathcal{D}$ if $R \in \mathcal{D}$ and $ar(R) = k$. By $facts(\mathcal{D})$, we denote the set of possible facts over schema $\mathcal{D}$. A *(database) instance* I over $\mathcal{D}$ is a finite set of facts over $\mathcal{D}$. By $adom(I)$ we denote the set of data values occurring in I. A *query $\mathcal{Q}$ over input schema $\mathcal{D}_1$ and output schema $\mathcal{D}_2$* is a generic mapping from instances over $\mathcal{D}_1$ to instances over $\mathcal{D}_2$. Genericity means that for every permutation π of **dom** and every instance I, $\mathcal{Q}(\pi(I)) = \pi(\mathcal{Q}(I))$.

Conjunctive queries.

Let **var** be the universe of variables, disjoint from **dom**. An *atom* is of the form $R(\mathbf{x})$, where R is a relation name and $\mathbf{x}$ is a tuple of variables in **var**. We say that $R(x_1, \dots, x_k)$ is an atom *over* schema $\mathcal{D}$ if $R \in \mathcal{D}$ and $k = ar(R)$.

A *conjunctive query* $\mathcal{Q}$ (CQ) over input schema $\mathcal{D}$ is an expression of the form

$$T(\mathbf{x}) \leftarrow R_1(\mathbf{y}_1), \dots, R_n(\mathbf{y}_n),$$

where every $R_i(\mathbf{y}_i)$ is an atom over $\mathcal{D}$, and $T(\mathbf{x})$ is an atom for which $T \notin \mathcal{D}$. Additionally, for safety, we require that every variable in $\mathbf{x}$ occurs in some $\mathbf{y}_i$. We refer to the *head atom* $T(\mathbf{x})$ by $head_{\mathcal{Q}}$, and denote the set of body atoms $R_i(\mathbf{y}_i)$ by $body_{\mathcal{Q}}$.

A conjunctive query is called *full* if all variables of the body also occur in the head. We say that a CQ is *without self-joins* when all of its atoms have a distinct relation name.

We denote by $vars(\mathcal{Q})$ the set of all variables occurring in $\mathcal{Q}$. A *valuation* for a conjunctive query is a total function $V : vars(\mathcal{Q}) \to \mathbf{dom}$ that maps each variable of $\mathcal{Q}$ to a data value. We say that V *requires* or *needs* the facts $V(body_{\mathcal{Q}})$ for $\mathcal{Q}$. A valuation V is said to be *satisfying* for $\mathcal{Q}$ on instance I, when all the facts required by V for $\mathcal{Q}$ are in I. In that case, V *derives* the fact $V(head_{\mathcal{Q}})$. The result of $\mathcal{Q}$ on instance I, denoted $\mathcal{Q}(I)$, is defined as the set of facts that can be derived by satisfying valuations for $\mathcal{Q}$ on I. We note that, as we do not allow negation, all conjunctive queries are monotone.

We frequently compare different valuations for a query $\mathcal{Q}$ with respect to their required sets of facts. For two valuations V_1, V_2 for a CQ $\mathcal{Q}$, we write $V_1 \leq_Q V_2$ if $V_1(head_{\mathcal{Q}}) = V_2(head_{\mathcal{Q}})$ and $V_1(body_{\mathcal{Q}}) \subseteq V_2(body_{\mathcal{Q}})$. We write $V_1 <_Q V_2$ if furthermore $V_1(body_{\mathcal{Q}}) \subsetneq V_2(body_{\mathcal{Q}})$ holds.

A *substitution* is a mapping from variables to variables, which is generalized to tuples, atoms and conjunctive queries in the natural fashion [1].[3] We denote the composition of functions in the usual way, i.e., $(f \circ g)(x) \stackrel{\text{def}}{=} f(g(x))$.

The following notion is fundamental for the development in the rest of the paper:

[3]As we only consider CQs without constants, substitutions do not map variables to constants.

Definition 1. A *simplification* of a conjunctive query $\mathcal{Q}$ is a substitution $\theta : vars(\mathcal{Q}) \to vars(\mathcal{Q})$ for which $head_{\theta(\mathcal{Q})} = head_{\mathcal{Q}}$ and $body_{\theta(\mathcal{Q})} \subseteq body_{\mathcal{Q}}$.

A simplification is thus a homomorphism from $\mathcal{Q}$ to $\mathcal{Q}$ and by the homomorphism theorem [1] (and the trivial embedding from $\theta(\mathcal{Q})$ to $\mathcal{Q}$), $\mathcal{Q}$ and $\theta(\mathcal{Q})$ are equivalent. Of course, the identity substitution is always a simplification.

EXAMPLE 2.1. *We give a few examples to illustrate simplifications. Consider the query*

$$T(x) \leftarrow R(x,x), R(x,y), R(x,z).$$

Then $\theta_1 = \{x \mapsto x, y \mapsto y, z \mapsto y\}$ *as well as* $\theta_2 = \{x \mapsto x, y \mapsto x, z \mapsto x\}$ *are simplifications. For the query*

$$T(x) \leftarrow R(x,y), R(y,y), R(z,z), R(u,u),$$

possible simplifications are $\theta_3 = \{x \mapsto x, y \mapsto y, z \mapsto y, u \mapsto z\}$ *and* $\theta_4 = \{x \mapsto x, y \mapsto y, z \mapsto y, u \mapsto y\}$. *For the query* $T(x) \leftarrow R(x,y), R(y,z)$ *there are no simplifications besides the identity.* □

The notion of simplification is closely related to foldings as defined by Chandra and Merlin [7]. In particular, a *folding* of a conjunctive query $\mathcal{Q}$ is a simplification θ that is idempotent. That is, $\theta^2 = \theta$. Intuitively, the idempotence means that when θ gives a new name to a variable then it sticks to it. Notice that in Example 2.1 simplifications θ_1, θ_2, θ_4 are foldings but θ_3 is not as $\theta_3(u) = z \neq y = \theta_3(\theta_3(u))$.

Networks, data distribution, and policies.

A *network* $\mathcal{N}$ is a nonempty finite set of values from **dom**, which we call *(computing) nodes*.

A *distribution policy* $\boldsymbol{P}$ for a database schema $\mathcal{D}$ and a network $\mathcal{N}$ is a total function mapping facts from $facts(\mathcal{D})$ to sets of nodes.[4] For an instance I over $\mathcal{D}$, let $dist_{\boldsymbol{P},I}$ denote the function that maps each $\kappa \in \mathcal{N}$ to $\{\boldsymbol{f} \in I \mid \kappa \in \boldsymbol{P}(\boldsymbol{f})\}$, that is, the set of facts assigned to it by $\boldsymbol{P}$. We sometimes refer to $dist_{\boldsymbol{P},I}(\kappa)$ as a *data chunk*.

In this paper, we do not always explicitly give names to schemas and networks but tacitly assume they are understood from the queries and the distribution policies under consideration, respectively.

We do *not* always expect that distribution policies $\boldsymbol{P}$ are given as part of the input by exhaustive enumeration of all pairs $(\kappa, \boldsymbol{f})$, for which $\kappa \in \boldsymbol{P}(\boldsymbol{f})$. We also consider mechanisms, where instead the distribution policy is implicitly represented by a given "black box" procedure. While there are many possible ways to represent distribution policies, either as functions or as relations belonging to various complexity classes, in this paper, we only consider one such class. In particular, we define the class $\mathcal{P}_{\text{nrel}}$ where each distribution $\boldsymbol{P}$ is represented by a NP-testable relation, that on input $(\kappa, \boldsymbol{f})$ yields "true" if and only if $\kappa \in \boldsymbol{P}(\boldsymbol{f})$. We will discuss declarative ways to specify distribution policies in a non-black-box fashion in Section 5.

The definition of a distribution policy is borrowed from Ameloot et al. [4] (but already surfaces in the work of Zinn et al. [15]), where distribution policies are used to define the class of policy-aware transducer networks.

[4] Notice that our formalization allows to 'skip' facts by mapping them to the empty set of nodes. This is, for instance, the case for a Hypercube distribution (cf. Section 5), which skips facts that are not essential to evaluate the query at hand.

3. PARALLEL-CORRECTNESS

In this section, we introduce and study the notion of parallel-correctness, which is central to this paper.

Definition 2. A query $\mathcal{Q}$ is *parallel-correct on instance I under distribution policy $\boldsymbol{P}$*, if $\mathcal{Q}(I) = \bigcup_{\kappa \in \mathcal{N}} \mathcal{Q}(dist_{\boldsymbol{P},I}(\kappa))$.

That is, the centralized execution of $\mathcal{Q}$ on I is the same as taking the union of the results obtained by executing $\mathcal{Q}$ at every computing node. Next, we lift parallel-correctness to all instances.

Definition 3. A query $\mathcal{Q}$ is *parallel-correct under distribution policy $\boldsymbol{P}$*, if $\mathcal{Q}$ is parallel-correct on all input instances under $\boldsymbol{P}$.

Of course, when a query $\mathcal{Q}$ is parallel-correct under $\boldsymbol{P}$, there is a direct one-round evaluation algorithm for every instance. Indeed, the algorithm first distributes (reshuffles) the data over the computing nodes according to $\boldsymbol{P}$ and then evaluates Q in a subsequent parallel step at every computing node. Notice that as $\boldsymbol{P}$ is defined on the granularity of a fact, the reshuffling does not depend on the current distribution of the data and can be done in parallel as well.

While Definitions 2 and 3 are in terms of general queries, in the rest of this section, we only consider conjunctive queries. It is easy to see that a CQ $\mathcal{Q}$ is parallel-correct under distribution policy $\boldsymbol{P}$ if for each valuation for $\mathcal{Q}$ the required facts meet at some node, i.e., if the following condition holds:

(C0) for every valuation V for $\mathcal{Q}$,

$$\bigcap_{\boldsymbol{f} \in V(body_{\mathcal{Q}})} \boldsymbol{P}(\boldsymbol{f}) \neq \emptyset.$$

Even though (C0) is sufficient for parallel-correctness, it is not necessary (c.f., Example 3.2). It turns out that for a semantical characterization only valuations have to be considered that are minimal in the following sense.

Definition 4. Let $\mathcal{Q}$ be a CQ. A valuation V for $\mathcal{Q}$ is *minimal* for $\mathcal{Q}$ if there exists no valuation V' for $\mathcal{Q}$ such that $V' <_{\mathcal{Q}} V$.

The next lemma now states the targeted characterization:

LEMMA 3.1. *A CQ $\mathcal{Q}$ is parallel-correct under distribution policy $\boldsymbol{P}$ if and only if the following holds:*

(C1) for every minimal valuation V for $\mathcal{Q}$,

$$\bigcap_{\boldsymbol{f} \in V(body_{\mathcal{Q}})} \boldsymbol{P}(\boldsymbol{f}) \neq \emptyset.$$

PROOF (SKETCH). (if) Assume (C1) holds. Because of monotonicity, we only need to show that, for every instance I, $\mathcal{Q}(I) \subseteq \bigcup_{\kappa \in \mathcal{N}} \mathcal{Q}(dist_{\boldsymbol{P},I}(\kappa))$. To this end, let $\boldsymbol{f}$ be a fact that is derived by some valuation V for $\mathcal{Q}$ over I. Then, there is also a minimal valuation V' that is satisfying on I and which derives $\boldsymbol{f}$. Because of condition (C1), there is a node κ where all facts required for V' meet. Hence, $\boldsymbol{f} \in \bigcup_{\kappa \in \mathcal{N}} \mathcal{Q}(dist_{\boldsymbol{P},I}(\kappa))$.

(only-if) Proof by contraposition. Suppose that there is a minimal valuation V' for $\mathcal{Q}$ for which the required facts do not meet under $\boldsymbol{P}$. Consider $V'(body_{\mathcal{Q}})$ as input instance. Then, by definition of minimality, there is no valuation that agrees on the head-variables and is satisfied on one of the chunks of $V'(body_{\mathcal{Q}})$ under $\boldsymbol{P}$. So, $\mathcal{Q}$ is not parallel-correct. □

EXAMPLE 3.2. *For a simple example of a minimal valuation and a non-minimal valuation, consider the CQ $\mathcal{Q}$,*

$$T(x,z) \leftarrow R(x,y), R(y,z), R(x,x).$$

Both $V = \{x \mapsto a, y \mapsto b, z \mapsto a\}$ and $V' = \{x \mapsto a, y \mapsto a, z \mapsto a\}$ are valuations for $\mathcal{Q}$. Notice that both valuations agree on the head-variables of $\mathcal{Q}$, but they require different sets of facts. In particular, for V to be satisfying on I, instance I must contain the facts $R(a,b), R(b,a)$, and $R(a,a)$, while V' only requires I to contain $R(a,a)$. This observation implies that V is not minimal for $\mathcal{Q}$. Further, as V' requires only one fact for $\mathcal{Q}$, V' must be minimal for $\mathcal{Q}$.

We next argue that (C0) is not a necessary condition for parallel-correctness. Indeed, take $\mathcal{N} = \{1,2\}$ and $\boldsymbol{P}$ as the distribution policy mapping every fact except $R(a,b)$ onto node 1 and every fact except $R(b,a)$ onto node 2. Consider the valuations V and $W = \{x \mapsto b, y \mapsto a, z \mapsto b\}$. Then, $R(a,b)$ and $R(b,a)$ do not meet under $\boldsymbol{P}$, thus violating condition (C0). It remains to argue that $\mathcal{Q}$ is parallel-correct under $\boldsymbol{P}$. For every minimal valuation U, either $\bigcap_{\boldsymbol{f} \in U(body_{\mathcal{Q}})} \boldsymbol{P}(\boldsymbol{f}) \neq \emptyset$ or U requires both $R(a,b)$ and $R(b,a)$. In the latter case U is either valuation V or W as defined above, which are not minimal. Thus, by Lemma 3.1, query $\mathcal{Q}$ is parallel-correct under $\boldsymbol{P}$. □

Unfortunately, condition (C1) is complexity-wise more involved than (C0) as minimality of V needs to be tested. The lower bound in Theorem 3.6 below indicates that this can, in a sense, not be avoided.

Towards an upper bound for the complexity of parallel-correctness, we first discuss how minimality of a valuation can be tested. Obviously, this notion is related to the (classical) notion of minimality for conjunctive queries, as we will make precise next. First, recall that a CQ $\mathcal{Q}$ is *minimal* if there is no equivalent CQ with strictly less atoms.

LEMMA 3.3. *Let $\mathcal{Q}$ be a conjunctive query. For every injective valuation V for $\mathcal{Q}$, it holds that V is minimal if and only if $\mathcal{Q}$ is minimal.*

PROOF. In the following let $\mathcal{Q}$ be a CQ. We show that there is a non-minimal injective valuation V for $\mathcal{Q}$ if and only if $\mathcal{Q}$ is not minimal.

(if) Suppose that $\mathcal{Q}$ is not minimal. Then, by [7] there is a folding h for $\mathcal{Q}$, where $body_{h(\mathcal{Q})} \subsetneq body_{\mathcal{Q}}$ and $head_{h(\mathcal{Q})} = head_{\mathcal{Q}}$. Let V be an arbitrary injective valuation for $\mathcal{Q}$. Injectivity implies that $|V(body_{\mathcal{Q}})| = |body_{\mathcal{Q}}|$, that is the number of facts in $V(body_{\mathcal{Q}})$ equals the number of atoms in $body_{\mathcal{Q}}$.

Since $h(\mathcal{Q})$ only has variables that also appear in $\mathcal{Q}$, V is a valuation for $h(\mathcal{Q})$ as well. However, thanks to $body_{h(\mathcal{Q})} \subsetneq body_{\mathcal{Q}}$, $h(body_{\mathcal{Q}})$ has fewer atoms than $body_{\mathcal{Q}}$, therefore $(V \circ h)(body_{\mathcal{Q}})$ has fewer facts than $V(body_{\mathcal{Q}})$. Thus, $(V \circ h)$ is a counterexample for the minimality of V, since $(V \circ h)(body_{\mathcal{Q}}) = V(body_{h(\mathcal{Q})}) \subseteq V(body_{\mathcal{Q}})$ and $(V \circ h)(head_{\mathcal{Q}}) = V(head_{h(\mathcal{Q})}) = V(head_{\mathcal{Q}})$.

(only-if) Suppose there is an injective valuation V for $\mathcal{Q}$ and a valuation V' for $\mathcal{Q}$, such that $V' <_{\mathcal{Q}} V$. Then, $h \stackrel{\text{def}}{=} (V^{-1} \circ V')$ is a homomorphism from $\mathcal{Q}$ to itself, as $body_{h(\mathcal{Q})} = V^{-1}(V'(body_{\mathcal{Q}})) \subsetneq V^{-1}(V(body_{\mathcal{Q}})) = body_{\mathcal{Q}}$, $head_{h(\mathcal{Q})} = V^{-1}(V'(head_{\mathcal{Q}})) = V^{-1}(V(head_{\mathcal{Q}})) = head_{\mathcal{Q}}$. Therefore $h(\mathcal{Q})$ is equivalent to $\mathcal{Q}$, thanks to the homomorphism theorem (see, e.g., [1]). □

Lemma 3.3 immediately yields the following complexity result.

PROPOSITION 3.4. *Deciding whether a valuation V for a CQ $\mathcal{Q}$ is minimal is* coNP*-complete.*

PROOF (SKETCH). Lemma 3.3 allows a reduction from minimality of CQs to minimality of valuations. Therefore, coNP-hardness follows from the coNP-hardness of minimality for CQs, which follows from [10]. The upper bound is immediate from the definition of minimality of valuations and from the fact that, for given $V_1, V_2, \mathcal{Q}$, it can be tested in polynomial time whether $V_1 <_{\mathcal{Q}} V_2$ holds. □

Now, we are ready to settle the complexity of parallel-correctness for general conjunctive queries for a large class of distributions. We study two settings, $\mathcal{P}_{\text{fin}}$, where distribution policies are explicitly enumerated as part of the input, and $\mathcal{P}_{\text{nrel}}$, where the distribution policy is given by a black box procedure which answers questions of the form "$\kappa \in \boldsymbol{P}(\boldsymbol{f})$?" in NP. In the latter case, the distribution is not part of the (normal) input and therefore does not contribute to the input size. Instead, the input has an additional parameter n which bounds the length of addresses in the considered networks.

By $\mathbf{dom}_n$ we denote the set of all elements of $\mathbf{dom}$ that can be encoded by strings of length at most n. For a distribution policy $\boldsymbol{P}$ (coming with a network $\mathcal{N}$) and a number n, we denote by $\boldsymbol{P}_n$ the distribution policy that is obtained from $\boldsymbol{P}$ by (1) only distributing facts over $\mathbf{dom}_n$ and (2) only distributing facts to nodes whose addresses are of length at most n.

We study the following algorithmic problems for explicitly given database instances:

PCI($\mathcal{P}_{\text{fin}}$):
Input: CQ $\mathcal{Q}$, instance I, and $\boldsymbol{P} \in \mathcal{P}_{\text{fin}}$
Question: Is $\mathcal{Q}$ parallel-correct on I under $\boldsymbol{P}$?

PCI($\mathcal{P}_{\text{nrel}}$):
Input: CQ $\mathcal{Q}$, instance I, a natural number n in unary representation
Black box input: $\boldsymbol{P} \in \mathcal{P}_{\text{nrel}}$
Question: Is $\mathcal{Q}$ parallel-correct on I under $\boldsymbol{P}_n$?

We also study the parallel correctness problem without reference to a given database instance.

PC($\mathcal{P}_{\text{fin}}$):
Input: CQ $\mathcal{Q}$, $\boldsymbol{P} \in \mathcal{P}_{\text{fin}}$
Question: Is $\mathcal{Q}$ parallel-correct on I under $\boldsymbol{P}$, for all instances $I \subseteq facts(\boldsymbol{P})$?

Here, $facts(\boldsymbol{P})$ denotes the set of facts $\boldsymbol{f}$ with $\boldsymbol{P}(\boldsymbol{f}) \neq \emptyset$.

PC($\mathcal{P}_{\text{nrel}}$):
Input: CQ $\mathcal{Q}$, a natural number n in unary representation
Black box input: $\boldsymbol{P} \in \mathcal{P}_{\text{nrel}}$
Question: Is $\mathcal{Q}$ parallel-correct on I under $\boldsymbol{P}_n$, for all instances $I \subseteq facts(\boldsymbol{P}_n)$?

We quickly discuss how to use distribution policies from $\mathcal{P}_{\text{nrel}}$.

A distribution policy $\boldsymbol{P} \in \mathcal{P}_{\text{nrel}}$ is an NP-testable relation. This means that there exists a (deterministic) algorithm $\mathcal{A}_{\boldsymbol{P}}$ with time bound a polynomial in $\langle \kappa, \boldsymbol{f} \rangle$ that accepts input $(\langle \kappa, \boldsymbol{f} \rangle, x)$ for some string x if and only if $\kappa \in \boldsymbol{P}(\boldsymbol{f})$. We use algorithm $\mathcal{A}_{\boldsymbol{P}}$ as a subroutine in the following algorithms, as described below.

REMARK 3.5 (USE OF SUBROUTINE). *Let V be a valuation for a query $\mathcal{Q}$ with k body atoms and let κ be a node. We assume some additional input string $x = x_1 \circ \cdots \circ x_k$, where each substring x_i has a length polynomial in $V(body_{\mathcal{Q}})$ and the representation size of κ. An algorithm can "test" (w.r.t. x) whether there is a fact in $V(body_{\mathcal{Q}}) = \{\boldsymbol{f}_1, \ldots, \boldsymbol{f}_\ell\}$ that is* not *assigned to node κ under distribution policy $\boldsymbol{P}$, where $\ell \leq k$. To this end, the algorithm invokes $\mathcal{A}_{\boldsymbol{P}}$ as a subroutine with inputs $(\langle \kappa, \boldsymbol{f}_i \rangle, x_i)$ for each $i \in \{1, \ldots, \ell\}$. If any input is rejected, the algorithm accepts, otherwise it rejects. The running time is obviously bounded by the size of $V(body_{\mathcal{Q}})$ and the represention size of κ.*

THEOREM 3.6.

(a) $\text{PC}(\mathcal{P}_{fin})$ and $\text{PCI}(\mathcal{P}_{fin})$ are Π_2^P-complete.

(b) $\text{PC}(\mathcal{P}_{nrel})$ and $\text{PCI}(\mathcal{P}_{nrel})$ are in Π_2^P.

Of course, the upper bounds in Theorem 3.6 also hold if questions of the form "$\kappa \in \boldsymbol{P}(\boldsymbol{f})$?" are answered in polynomial time, or if $\boldsymbol{P}$ is just given as a polynomial time function.

Due to the implicit representation of distributions, we cannot formally claim Π_2^P-hardness for distribution policies from $\mathcal{P}_{\text{nrel}}$. However, in an informal sense, they are, of course, at least as difficult as for $\mathcal{P}_{\text{fin}}$.

PROOF (SKETCH). The upper bounds follow quite directly from Definition 2, or Lemma 3.1 and Proposition 3.4, respectively.

For the lower bound of $\text{PCI}(\mathcal{P}_{\text{fin}})$ we give a polynomial reduction from the Π_2^P-complete problem Π_2-QBF, which can be adapted for $\text{PC}(\mathcal{P}_{\text{fin}})$.

Let φ be an input for Π_2-QBF, i.e., a formula of the form $\forall \mathbf{x} \exists \mathbf{y}\, \psi(\mathbf{x}, \mathbf{y})$. We assume ψ to be a propositional formula in 3-CNF with variables $\mathbf{x} = (x_1, \ldots, x_m)$ and $\mathbf{y} = (y_1, \ldots, y_n)$. Let $C_1, \ldots, C_k$ denote their (disjunctive) clauses, where, for each j, $C_j = (\ell_{j,1} \vee \ell_{j,2} \vee \ell_{j,3})$.

We describe next how the corresponding input instance for $\text{PCI}(\mathcal{P}_{\text{fin}})$, consisting of a query $\mathcal{Q}_\varphi$, a database instance I_φ, and a distribution policy $\boldsymbol{P}_\varphi$, is defined.

The query $\mathcal{Q}_\varphi$ is formulated over variables w_1, w_0, and $x_g, \overline{x}_g, y_h, \overline{y}_h$, for $g \in \{1, \ldots, m\}$ and $h \in \{1, \ldots, n\}$. Intuitively, these variables are intended to represent the Boolean values true and false and the (negated) values of the variables x_g, y_h in ψ, respectively. We overload the notation $\ell_{j,i}$ as follows: if $\ell_{j,i}$ is a negated literal $\neg x$ in C_j, then $\ell_{j,i}$ also denotes the variable $\overline{x}$.

Let $\mathbb{B}^+ \stackrel{\text{def}}{=} \mathbb{B} \setminus \{(0,0,0)\}$ be the set of non-zero Boolean triples and $\mathbb{W}^+ \stackrel{\text{def}}{=} \mathbb{W} \setminus \{(w_0, w_0, w_0)\}$ the set of triples over $\{w_0, w_1\}$ that contain at least one w_1.

We define $\mathcal{Q}_\varphi$ as the query with $head_{\mathcal{Q}_\varphi} = H(x_1, \ldots, x_m)$ and $body_{\mathcal{Q}_\varphi} = Cons \cup Struct(\psi)$, where

$$\begin{aligned} Cons \stackrel{\text{def}}{=}\ & \{\texttt{True}(w_1), \texttt{False}(w_0)\} \\ \cup\ & \{\texttt{Neg}(w_1, w_0), \texttt{Neg}(w_0, w_1)\} \\ \cup\ & \{\texttt{C}_j(\mathbf{w}) \mid j \in \{1, \ldots, k\}, \mathbf{w} \in \mathbb{W}^+\} \end{aligned}$$

is a set of consistency atoms, representing valid combinations of values for Neg-facts and satisfying combinations of values for $\texttt{C}_j$-facts, and

$$\begin{aligned} Struct(\psi) \stackrel{\text{def}}{=}\ & \{\texttt{Neg}(x, \overline{x}) \mid x \in \{x_1, \ldots, x_m, y_1, \ldots, y_n\}\}, \\ \cup\ & \{\texttt{C}_j(\ell_{j,1}, \ell_{j,2}, \ell_{j,3}) \mid \\ & \quad \text{for each clause } C_j = (\ell_{j,1} \vee \ell_{j,2} \vee \ell_{j,3})\} \end{aligned}$$

is a set of atoms representing the logical structure of ψ: it relates variable x_g to $\overline{x}_g$ and also variable y_h to $\overline{y}_h$ for each $g \in \{1, \ldots, m\}$ and $h \in \{1, \ldots, n\}$, respectively. Additionally, it relates all variables that represent literals occurring in the same clause to each other. Furthermore, we define

$$\begin{aligned} I_\varphi \stackrel{\text{def}}{=}\ & \{\texttt{True}(1), \texttt{False}(0), \texttt{Neg}(1,0), \texttt{Neg}(0,1)\} \\ \cup\ & \{\texttt{C}_j(\mathbf{b}) \mid j \in \{1, \ldots, k\}, \mathbf{b} \in \mathbb{B}\}, \end{aligned}$$

which we partition into $I_\varphi^- \stackrel{\text{def}}{=} \{\texttt{C}_j(0,0,0) \mid j \in \{1, \ldots, k\}\}$ and $I_\varphi^+ \stackrel{\text{def}}{=} I_\varphi \setminus I_\varphi^-$.

Moreover, we define $\boldsymbol{P}_\varphi$ to be the finite distribution policy for I_φ over a network $\mathcal{N} = \{\kappa^+, \kappa^-\}$ as

$$\boldsymbol{P}_\varphi(\boldsymbol{f}) = \begin{cases} \{\kappa^+\} & \text{if } \boldsymbol{f} \in I_\varphi^+, \\ \{\kappa^-\} & \text{if } \boldsymbol{f} \in I_\varphi^-. \end{cases}$$

It remains to show that this mapping is a polynomial-time reduction. Obviously, query $\mathcal{Q}_\varphi$, instance I_φ and distribution policy $\boldsymbol{P}_\varphi$ can be computed in polynomial time from φ. □

4. TRANSFERABILITY

Although parallel-correctness provides a direct one-round evaluation algorithm, it still requires a reshuffling of the data for every query. It therefore makes sense, in the context of multiple query evaluation, to consider scenarios in which such reshuffling can be avoided. To this end, we introduce the notion of parallel-correctness transfer which ensures that a subsequent query $\mathcal{Q}'$ can always be evaluated over a distribution for which a query $\mathcal{Q}$ is parallel-correct:

Definition 5. For two queries $\mathcal{Q}$ and $\mathcal{Q}'$ over the same input and output schema, *parallel-correctness transfers from $\mathcal{Q}$ to $\mathcal{Q}'$* when $\mathcal{Q}'$ is parallel-correct under every distribution policy for which $\mathcal{Q}$ is parallel-correct.

As for parallel-correctness we first give a semantical characterization before we study the complexity of parallel-correctness transfer.

LEMMA 4.1. *Parallel-correctness transfers from a CQ $\mathcal{Q}$ to a CQ $\mathcal{Q}'$ if and only if the following holds:*

(C2) for every minimal valuation V' for $\mathcal{Q}'$, there is a minimal valuation V for $\mathcal{Q}$ with $V'(body_{\mathcal{Q}'}) \subseteq V(body_{\mathcal{Q}})$.

The two implications of Lemma 4.1 are shown in Propositions 4.2 and 4.3 below.

PROPOSITION 4.2. *Let $\mathcal{Q}$ and $\mathcal{Q}'$ be CQs. If condition (C2) holds, then, parallel-correctness transfers from $\mathcal{Q}$ to $\mathcal{Q}'$.*

PROOF. Let $\boldsymbol{P}$ be a distribution policy under which $\mathcal{Q}$ is parallel-correct and let I be an instance. Then we show that $\mathcal{Q}'$ is parallel-correct as well on I under $\boldsymbol{P}$. By monotonicity of CQs, $\bigcup_{x \in \mathcal{N}} \mathcal{Q}'(dist_{\boldsymbol{P},I}(x)) \subseteq \mathcal{Q}'(I)$. Thus it suffices to show that for every fact $\boldsymbol{f} \in \mathcal{Q}'(I)$, there is some valuation for $\mathcal{Q}'$ that allows to derive $\boldsymbol{f}$ on one of the chunks of I under $\boldsymbol{P}$. For $\boldsymbol{f} \in \mathcal{Q}'(I)$, there is a minimal valuation V' for $\mathcal{Q}'$ which satisfies on I for $\mathcal{Q}'$ and derives $\boldsymbol{f}$. That is, $V'(body_{\mathcal{Q}'}) \subseteq I$ and $V'(head_{\mathcal{Q}'}) = \boldsymbol{f}$. Next, we show that the facts required by V' for $\mathcal{Q}'$ meet at some node under $\boldsymbol{P}$, which implies that the chunks of I under $\boldsymbol{P}$ indeed allow deriving $\boldsymbol{f}$.

For this, we rely on the assumption that there is a minimal valuation V for $\mathcal{Q}$, where $V'(body_{\mathcal{Q}'}) \subseteq V(body_{\mathcal{Q}})$. Let $J = V(body_{\mathcal{Q}})$. Then, by parallel-correctness of $\mathcal{Q}$ under $\boldsymbol{P}$, there is a valuation W and node $\kappa \in \mathcal{N}$, such that $W(body_{\mathcal{Q}}) \subseteq dist_{\boldsymbol{P},J}(\kappa)$ and $W(head_{\mathcal{Q}}) = V(head_{\mathcal{Q}})$. Because V is minimal and $dist_{\boldsymbol{P},J}(\kappa) \subseteq V(body_{\mathcal{Q}})$, it must be that $V(body_{\mathcal{Q}}) = W(body_{\mathcal{Q}})$. So, $\boldsymbol{P}$ maps all the facts in J onto node κ, implying that all the facts in $V'(body_{\mathcal{Q}'})$ are mapped onto node κ under $\boldsymbol{P}$ (because $V'(body_{\mathcal{Q}'}) \subseteq V(body_{\mathcal{Q}}) = J$).

Hence, $\mathcal{Q}'$ is indeed parallel-correct under the distribution policies for which $\mathcal{Q}$ is parallel-correct. □

PROPOSITION 4.3. *Let $\mathcal{Q}$ and $\mathcal{Q}'$ be CQs. If parallel-correctness transfers from $\mathcal{Q}$ to $\mathcal{Q}'$, then, condition (C2) holds.*

PROOF. The proof is by contraposition. So, we assume that there is a minimal valuation V' for $\mathcal{Q}'$ for which there is no valuation V for $\mathcal{Q}$, where $V'(body_{\mathcal{Q}'}) \subseteq V(body_{\mathcal{Q}})$. Let $m = |V'(body_{\mathcal{Q}'})|$.

We distinguish two cases, depending on whether V' requires only one fact or at least two facts. For both cases we construct a network $\mathcal{N}$ and distribution policy $\boldsymbol{P}$ over $\mathcal{N}$ for which $\mathcal{Q}$ is parallel-correct but $\mathcal{Q}'$ is not, implying that parallel-correctness does *not* transfer from $\mathcal{Q}$ to $\mathcal{Q}'$.

(Case $m = 1$) Let $V'(body_{\mathcal{Q}'}) = \{\boldsymbol{f}\}$. Let $\mathcal{N}$ be a single-node network, i.e., $\mathcal{N} \stackrel{\text{def}}{=} \{\kappa\}$. For $\boldsymbol{P}$ we consider the distribution policy thats skips $\boldsymbol{f}$, that is, maps $\boldsymbol{P}(\boldsymbol{f})$ to the empty set, and maps every other fact in $facts(\mathcal{D})$ onto node κ. By assumption on V', none of the minimal valuations for $\mathcal{Q}$ requires $\boldsymbol{f}$. So it immediately follows by Lemma 3.1 that $\mathcal{Q}$ is parallel-correct under $\boldsymbol{P}$. However, because V' is minimal for $\mathcal{Q}'$, $\mathcal{Q}'$ needs $\boldsymbol{f}$ to derive $V(head_{\mathcal{Q}'})$ when only $\boldsymbol{f}$ is given as input instance. Thus $\mathcal{Q}'$ is not parallel-correct under $\boldsymbol{P}$ which leads to the desired contradiction.

(Case $m \geq 2$) Let $I \stackrel{\text{def}}{=} V'(body_{\mathcal{Q}'}) = \{\boldsymbol{f}_1, \ldots, \boldsymbol{f}_m\}$, $\mathcal{N} \stackrel{\text{def}}{=} \{\kappa_1, \ldots, \kappa_m\}$, and let $\boldsymbol{P}$ be the mapping defined as follows:

- $\boldsymbol{P}(\boldsymbol{g}) = \mathcal{N}$, for every $\boldsymbol{g} \in facts(\mathcal{D}) \setminus I$; and
- $\boldsymbol{P}(\boldsymbol{f}_i) = \mathcal{N} \setminus \{\kappa_i\}$, for every i.

Intuitively, on every instance J, either the facts in J meet on some node under $\boldsymbol{P}$, or $I \subseteq J$. By assumption, none of the minimal valuations for $\mathcal{Q}$ requires all the facts in I, implying that $\mathcal{Q}$ is parallel-correct under $\boldsymbol{P}$. Nevertheless, on instance I under $\boldsymbol{P}$, none of the nodes receives all the facts in I, and there is no valuation that can derive $V'(head_{\mathcal{Q}'})$ for a strict subset of the facts in I (by minimality of V'). So, $\mathcal{Q}'$ is not parallel-correct under $\boldsymbol{P}$ which leads to the desired contradiction. □

The characterisation given by Lemma 4.1 allows us to pinpoint the complexity of parallel-correctness transfers. For a formal statement we define the following algorithmic problem:

PC-TRANS:
Input: CQs $\mathcal{Q}$ and $\mathcal{Q}'$
Question: Does parallel-correctness transfer from $\mathcal{Q}$ to $\mathcal{Q}'$?

In principle, Lemma 4.1, on which the following proofs are based, talks about an infinite number of valuations over the infinite domain **dom**. However, since our queries are generic, the only observable property of the constants used by some valuation is equality/inequality. It therefore suffices to check valuations over an arbitrary finite domain with at least as much constants as valuations for both queries can use. This is stated more explicitly in the following claim.

CLAIM 1. *Let $\mathcal{Q}$ and $\mathcal{Q}'$ be CQs with variables $x_1, \ldots, x_m$ and $y_1, \ldots, y_n$, respectively. Moreover, for $k = m + n$ let $dom_k = \{1, \ldots, k\}$ be a subset of the (countably) infinite set* **dom**.
The following two conditions are equivalent.

1. *For every minimal valuation V' for $\mathcal{Q}'$ over* **dom** *there is a minimal valuation V for $\mathcal{Q}$ over* **dom** *such that $V'(body_{\mathcal{Q}'}) \subseteq V(body_{\mathcal{Q}})$.*
2. *For every minimal valuation V' for $\mathcal{Q}'$ over dom_k there is a minimal valuation V for $\mathcal{Q}$ over dom_k such that $V'(body_{\mathcal{Q}'}) \subseteq V(body_{\mathcal{Q}})$.*

THEOREM 4.4. PC-TRANS *is Π_3^P-complete.*

PROOF (SKETCH). For the upper bound, we note that, by Lemma 4.1, deciding parallel-correctness transfer is equivalent to verifying that for each minimal valuation V' for $\mathcal{Q}'$ there is a minimal valuation V for $\mathcal{Q}$ such that $V'(body_{\mathcal{Q}'}) \subseteq V(body_{\mathcal{Q}})$. This, in turn, is equivalent to checking for each valuation V' for $\mathcal{Q}'$ that it is not minimal, which can be witnessed by another valuation W' that derives the same fact and requires strictly less facts, *or* that there is a minimal valuation V for $\mathcal{Q}$ such that $V'(body_{\mathcal{Q}'_\varphi}) \subseteq V(body_{\mathcal{Q}_\varphi})$. Non-minimality of valuation V can be witnessed by a valuation W. Thanks to Claim 1, all valuations can be restricted to $dom_k = \{1, \ldots, k\}$, where $k = m+n$ and $\mathcal{Q}$, $\mathcal{Q}'$ are queries over variables $x_1, \ldots, x_m$ and $y_1, \ldots, y_n$, respectively.

To prove membership in class Π_3^P, it suffices to show that there is an algorithm with a time bound polynomial in $|\mathcal{Q}| + |\mathcal{Q}'|$ such that for every pair $(\mathcal{Q}, \mathcal{Q}')$ of queries it holds $(\mathcal{Q}, \mathcal{Q}') \in$ PC-TRANS if and only if for every $\mathcal{Q}'$-valuation V' there is a $\mathcal{Q}$-valuation V and a $\mathcal{Q}'$-valuation W' such that for every $\mathcal{Q}$-valuation W, the algorithm accepts $(\langle \mathcal{Q}, \mathcal{Q}' \rangle, V', \langle V, W' \rangle, W)$.

For input $(\langle \mathcal{Q}, \mathcal{Q}' \rangle, V', \langle V, W' \rangle, W)$ the algorithm proceeds as follows. First, it is checked whether W' contradicts the assumed minimality of V', that is, whether $W'(head_{\mathcal{Q}'}) = V'(head_{\mathcal{Q}'})$ as well as $W'(body_{\mathcal{Q}'}) \subsetneq V'(body_{\mathcal{Q}'})$. If this test succeeds, the algorithm accepts because there is no requirement on a non-minimal $\mathcal{Q}'$-valuation. Second, it is checked in an analogous fashion whether W contradicts the assumed minimality of V. If this test succeeds, the algorithm rejects.

Lastly, the algorithm continues with testing $V'(body_{\mathcal{Q}'}) \subseteq V(body_{\mathcal{Q}})$. It accepts in case of satisfaction, and rejects otherwise. All containment tests can be done in polynomial time.

The lower bound is by a reduction from the Π_3^P-complete Π_3-QBF-problem. The reduction is based on the characterization of parallel-correctness transfer by condition (C2) as stated in Lemma 4.1.

Reduction function. Let $\varphi = \forall\mathbf{x}\exists\mathbf{y}\forall\mathbf{z}\,\psi(\mathbf{x},\mathbf{y},\mathbf{z})$ be a formula with a quantifier-free propositional formula ψ in 3-DNF over variables $\mathbf{x} = (x_1,\ldots,x_m)$, $\mathbf{y} = (y_1,\ldots,y_n)$, and $\mathbf{z} = (z_1,\ldots,z_p)$.

Let k be the number of clauses of ψ and, for each $j \in \{1,\ldots,k\}$, let $C_j = (\ell_{j,1} \wedge \ell_{j,2} \wedge \ell_{j,3})$ denote the j-th (conjunctive) clause of ψ.

The reduction function maps φ to a pair $(\mathcal{Q}_\varphi, \mathcal{Q}'_\varphi)$ of CQs that will be described next. It will be obvious that this mapping can be computed in polynomial time. Query $\mathcal{Q}_\varphi$ uses the variables w_1, w_0, which are intended to represent truth and falseness, respectively, the variables of ψ and variables $\overline{u}$, for each variable u of ψ, representing the literal $\neg u$.[5] Besides these variables, query $\mathcal{Q}'_\varphi$ additionally uses the following variables

- s_j, for every $j \in \{1,\ldots,k\}$, intended to represent the truth value of C_j, and
- r_j, for every $j \in \{1,\ldots,k\}$, intended to represent the truth value of $C_1 \vee \cdots \vee C_j$.

We first describe the general construction, give an example explaining its intuition afterwards and finally prove correctness of the reduction.

The queries $\mathcal{Q}_\varphi$ and $\mathcal{Q}'_\varphi$ are defined as follows:

$$\begin{aligned}
head_{\mathcal{Q}_\varphi} &\stackrel{\text{def}}{=} H(x_1,\ldots,x_m,w_1,w_0)\\
body_{\mathcal{Q}_\varphi} &\stackrel{\text{def}}{=} \{\texttt{YVal}_h(w_1), \texttt{YVal}_h(w_0) \mid h \in \{1,\ldots,n\}\}\\
&\cup\ \{\texttt{Res}(w_1)\} \cup \mathit{Fix};
\end{aligned}$$

$$\begin{aligned}
head_{\mathcal{Q}'_\varphi} &\stackrel{\text{def}}{=} H(x_1,\ldots,x_m,y_1,\ldots,y_n,w_1,w_0)\\
body_{\mathcal{Q}'_\varphi} &\stackrel{\text{def}}{=} \{\texttt{YVal}_h(y_h), \texttt{YVal}_h(\overline{y}_h) \mid h \in \{1,\ldots,n\}\}\\
&\cup\ \{\texttt{Res}(w_0), \texttt{Res}(r_k)\} \cup \mathit{Fix} \cup \mathit{Gates} \cup \mathit{Circuit},
\end{aligned}$$

where

$$\mathit{Fix} \stackrel{\text{def}}{=} \{\texttt{XVal}_1(x_1),\ldots,\texttt{XVal}_m(x_m), \texttt{True}(w_1), \texttt{False}(w_0)\}$$

is intended to "fix" truth values for $x_1,\ldots,x_m,w_1,w_0$, while the set

$$\begin{aligned}
\mathit{Gates} &\stackrel{\text{def}}{=} \{\texttt{Neg}(w_0,w_1), \texttt{Neg}(w_1,w_0)\}\\
&\cup\ \{\texttt{And}(w_1,w_1,w_1,w_1), \texttt{And}(w_0,w_1,w_1,w_0),\\
&\quad \texttt{And}(w_1,w_0,w_1,w_0), \texttt{And}(w_0,w_0,w_1,w_0),\\
&\quad \texttt{And}(w_1,w_1,w_0,w_0), \texttt{And}(w_0,w_1,w_0,w_0),\\
&\quad \texttt{And}(w_1,w_0,w_0,w_0), \texttt{And}(w_0,w_0,w_0,w_0)\}\\
&\cup\ \{\texttt{Or}(w_1,w_1,w_1), \texttt{Or}(w_0,w_1,w_1),\\
&\quad \texttt{Or}(w_1,w_0,w_1), \texttt{Or}(w_0,w_0,w_0)\}
\end{aligned}$$

contains all atoms that are consistent with respect to the intended meaning of negation, And- and Or-gates[6] on w_1, w_0, and

$$\begin{aligned}
\mathit{Circuit} &\stackrel{\text{def}}{=} \{\texttt{Neg}(u,\overline{u}) \mid \text{for each variable } u \text{ in } \psi\}\\
&\cup\ \{\texttt{And}(\ell_{j,1},\ell_{j,2},\ell_{j,3},s_j) \mid\\
&\qquad \text{for each clause } C_j = (\ell_{j,1} \wedge \ell_{j,2} \wedge \ell_{j,3})\}\\
&\cup\ \{\texttt{Or}(s_1,s_1,r_1)\}\\
&\cup\ \{\texttt{Or}(r_1,s_2,r_2),\ldots,\texttt{Or}(r_{k-1},s_k,r_k)\}
\end{aligned}$$

is intended to represent a Boolean circuit (with output bit r_k) that evaluates ψ.

[5] If ℓ is a negated literal $\neg u$, we write ℓ also for $\overline{u}$.

[6] The last position in a gate-atom represents the output bit of the gate, the others the input bits.

EXAMPLE 4.5. *We obtain the queries displayed in Figure 1 for* $\varphi = \forall x_1\exists y_1\exists y_2\forall z_1 \Big((x_1\wedge y_1\wedge z_1) \vee (\neg x_1\wedge y_2\wedge z_1)\Big)$.

Note that $\varphi \notin \Pi_3$*-QBF because no truth assignment with* $z_1 \mapsto 0$ *is satisfying for* ψ*. In particular, for the truth assignment* $\beta_{\mathbf{x}} : x_1 \mapsto 1$ *there is no truth assignment* $\beta_{\mathbf{y}}$ *such that for every* $\beta_{\mathbf{z}}$ *it holds* $(\beta_{\mathbf{x}} \cup \beta_{\mathbf{y}} \cup \beta_{\mathbf{z}}) \models \psi$*. We illustrate why* $(\mathcal{Q}_\varphi, \mathcal{Q}'_\varphi) \notin$ PC-TRANS.

Let valuation V *for* $\mathcal{Q}_\varphi$ *be defined by* $V(x_1) \stackrel{\text{def}}{=} \beta_{\mathbf{x}}(x_1) = 1$, $V(w_1) \stackrel{\text{def}}{=} 1$ *and* $V(w_0) \stackrel{\text{def}}{=} 0$*. This valuation is minimal for* $\mathcal{Q}_\varphi$ *(because* $\mathcal{Q}_\varphi$ *is full) and requires the set* $V(body_{\mathcal{Q}_\varphi}) = \{\texttt{YVal}_1(1), \texttt{YVal}_1(0), \texttt{Res}(1), \texttt{XVal}_1(1), \texttt{True}(1), \texttt{False}(0)\}$ *of facts.*

We now argue why there is no minimal valuation V' *for* $\mathcal{Q}'_\varphi$ *such that* $V'(body_{\mathcal{Q}'_\varphi}) \subseteq V(body_{\mathcal{Q}_\varphi})$*. If a valuation* V' *fulfills* $V'(body_{\mathcal{Q}'_\varphi}) \subseteq V(body_{\mathcal{Q}_\varphi})$ *it must map* $w_0 \mapsto 0$, $w_1 \mapsto 1$, $x_1 \mapsto 1$, $r_2 \mapsto 1$*. Furthermore, it must map each of* $(y_1, \overline{y}_1)$ *and* $(y_2, \overline{y}_2)$ *to some pair in* $\{(0,1),(1,0)\}$*. Thus,* V *induces a truth assignment* $\beta_{\mathbf{y}}$ *via* $\beta_{\mathbf{y}}(y_1) \stackrel{\text{def}}{=} V(y_1)$ *and* $\beta_{\mathbf{y}}(y_2) \stackrel{\text{def}}{=} V(y_2)$*. Let* V^* *be the valuation that coincides with* V *on all variables* $w_0, w_i, x_1, \overline{x}_1, y_1, \overline{y}_1, y_2, \overline{y}_2$ *and maps* $z_1 \mapsto 0$ *and maps all other variables to the "correct" values with respect to the semantics of the logical gates in* $\mathcal{Q}_\varphi$*. In particular, since* $(\beta_{\mathbf{x}} \cup \beta_{\mathbf{y}} \cup \beta_{\mathbf{z}}) \not\models \psi$ *(where* $\beta_{\mathbf{z}}(z_1) \stackrel{\text{def}}{=} 0$*), we get* $V^*(r_2) = 0$*. It is now easy to check that* $V^* <_{\mathcal{Q}} V$*, and therefore that* V *is not minimal.*

To complete the proof, we need to show that the mapping $\varphi \mapsto (\mathcal{Q}_\varphi, \mathcal{Q}'_\varphi)$ is indeed a reduction, i.e. that φ is in Π_3-QBF if and only if parallel-correctness transfers from $\mathcal{Q}_\varphi$ to $\mathcal{Q}'_\varphi$.

We start by some observations. We call a valuation for $\mathcal{Q}_\varphi$ or $\mathcal{Q}'_\varphi$ *0-1-valued*, if its range is $\{0,1\}$ and it maps (w_0, w_1) to $(0,1)$ and every pair $(u, \overline{u})$ of variables from ψ to $(0,1)$ or $(1,0)$. A 0-1-valued valuation is called *consistent*, if the values $V(s_j)$ and $V(r_j)$, for $j \in \{1,\ldots,k\}$ are consistent with the values $V(u)$ for variables of ψ, in the obvious sense. That is, $V(s_j) = 1$ if and only if clause C_j evaluates to true for the truth assignment β_V obtained from V and $V(r_j) = 1$ if and only if $C_1 \vee \cdots \vee C_j$ evaluates to true.

It is easy to see that a 0-1-valued valuation V is consistent, if and only if $V(\mathit{Circuit}) \subseteq V(\mathit{Gates})$, because inconsistency requires facts in $V(\mathit{Circuit})$ that are not in $V(\mathit{Gates})$ and likewise the existence of such facts implies inconsistency.

CLAIM 2. *For every 0-1-valued valuation* V *of* $\mathcal{Q}_\varphi$ *the following conditions are equivalent.*

(i) V *is minimal;*

(ii) V *is consistent.*

(only-if). Let $\varphi = \forall\mathbf{x}\exists\mathbf{y}\forall\mathbf{z}\,\psi(\mathbf{x},\mathbf{y},\mathbf{z})$ be a formula with a quantifier-free propositional formula ψ in 3-DNF such that $\varphi \notin \Pi_3$-QBF. We show that there is a minimal valuation V for $\mathcal{Q}_\varphi$ such that each valuation V' for $\mathcal{Q}'_\varphi$ which satisfies $V'(body_{\mathcal{Q}'_\varphi}) \subseteq V(body_{\mathcal{Q}_\varphi})$ is *not* minimal. From that we can conclude by Lemma 4.1 that parallel-correctness does not transfer from $\mathcal{Q}_\varphi$ to $\mathcal{Q}'_\varphi$.

Let $\beta_{\mathbf{x}}$ be a truth assignment for $x_1,\ldots,x_m$ in ψ such that for all truth assignments $\beta_{\mathbf{y}}$ for $y_1,\ldots,y_n$ in ψ there is a truth assignment $\beta_{\mathbf{z}}$ for $z_1,\ldots,z_p$ such that $(\beta_{\mathbf{x}}\cup\beta_{\mathbf{y}}\cup\beta_{\mathbf{z}}) \not\models \psi$.

$$\mathcal{Q}_\varphi : \quad H(x_1, w_1, w_0) \quad \leftarrow \quad \texttt{YVal}_1(w_1), \texttt{YVal}_1(w_0), \texttt{YVal}_2(w_1), \texttt{YVal}_2(w_0), \texttt{Res}(w_1), \texttt{XVal}_1(x_1), \texttt{True}(w_1), \texttt{False}(w_0).$$

$$\mathcal{Q}'_\varphi : \quad H(x_1, x_2, y_1, w_1, w_0) \quad \leftarrow \quad \texttt{YVal}_1(y_1), \texttt{YVal}_1(\overline{y}_1), \texttt{YVal}_2(y_2), \texttt{YVal}_2(\overline{y}_2), \texttt{Res}(w_0), \texttt{Res}(r_2), \texttt{XVal}_1(x_1), \texttt{True}(w_1), \texttt{False}(w_0), \ldots \textit{all atoms from Gates} \ldots, \texttt{Neg}(x_1, \overline{x}_1), \texttt{Neg}(y_1, \overline{y}_1), \texttt{Neg}(y_2, \overline{y}_2), \texttt{Neg}(z_1, \overline{z}_1), \texttt{And}(x_1, y_1, z_1, s_1), \texttt{And}(\overline{x}_1, y_2, z_1, s_2), \texttt{Or}(s_1, s_1, r_1), \texttt{Or}(r_1, s_2, r_2).$$

Figure 1: Output of the reduction function on input $\varphi = \forall x_1 \exists y_1 \exists y_2 \forall z_1 \left((x_1 \wedge y_1 \wedge z_1) \vee (\neg x_1 \wedge y_2 \wedge z_1)\right)$.

Let V be the valuation defined by $V(x_1, \ldots, x_m, w_1, w_0) \stackrel{\text{def}}{=} (\beta_{\mathbf{x}}(x_1), \ldots, \beta_{\mathbf{x}}(x_m), 1, 0)$, which is minimal for $\mathcal{Q}_\varphi$ because $\mathcal{Q}_\varphi$ is full.

Let V' be any valuation for $\mathcal{Q}'_\varphi$ such that $V'(body_{\mathcal{Q}'_\varphi}) \subseteq V(body_{\mathcal{Q}_\varphi})$. In particular, $\texttt{Res}(1) \in V'(body_{\mathcal{Q}'_\varphi})$. Then, valuations V and V' agree on variables $x_1, \ldots, x_m, w_1, w_0$ because each atom in *Fix* is the only atom of $\mathcal{Q}_\varphi$ with its particular relation symbol. Similarly, the $\texttt{YVal}_i$-atoms in $\mathcal{Q}_\varphi$ and $\mathcal{Q}'_\varphi$ ensure that V' maps each pair $(y_i, \overline{y}_i)$ to $(0, 1)$ or $(1, 0)$. Let $\beta_{\mathbf{y}}$ be the truth assignment defined by $\beta_{\mathbf{y}}(y_i) \stackrel{\text{def}}{=} V(y_i)$, for every $i \in \{1, \ldots, n\}$. Since $\varphi \notin \Pi_3$-QBF, there is a truth assignment $\beta_{\mathbf{z}}$ such that $(\beta_{\mathbf{x}} \cup \beta_{\mathbf{y}} \cup \beta_{\mathbf{z}}) \not\models \psi$. Let V^* be the uniquely defined consistent 0-1-valued valuation induced by $(\beta_{\mathbf{x}} \cup \beta_{\mathbf{y}} \cup \beta_{\mathbf{z}})$. Since V^* is consistent, $V^*(\textit{Circuit}) \subseteq V^*(\textit{Gates})$ and therefore $V^*(body_{\mathcal{Q}_\varphi}) \subseteq V(body_{\mathcal{Q}_\varphi})$. Furthermore, since $(\beta_{\mathbf{x}} \cup \beta_{\mathbf{y}} \cup \beta_{\mathbf{z}}) \not\models \psi$, we get $V^*(r_k) = 0$ and therefore $\texttt{Res}(1) \notin V^*(body_{\mathcal{Q}_\varphi})$ and, consequently, $V^*(body_{\mathcal{Q}_\varphi}) \subsetneq V(body_{\mathcal{Q}_\varphi})$, showing that V is not minimal.

(if). Let $\varphi = \forall \mathbf{x} \exists \mathbf{y} \forall \mathbf{z} \psi(\mathbf{x}, \mathbf{y}, \mathbf{z})$ be a formula in Π_3-QBF and let V' be an arbitrary valuation for $\mathcal{Q}'_\varphi$. We will show that there exists a minimal valuation V for $\mathcal{Q}_\varphi$ such that $V'(body_{\mathcal{Q}'_\varphi}) \subseteq V(body_{\mathcal{Q}_\varphi})$, and thus that parallel-correctness transfers from $\mathcal{Q}_\varphi$ to $\mathcal{Q}'_\varphi$, again by Lemma 4.1.

We assume in the following that all quantified variables appear (possibly negated) in ψ. Let $c_0 \stackrel{\text{def}}{=} V'(w_0)$ and $c_1 \stackrel{\text{def}}{=} V'(w_1)$. Since, neither $\mathcal{Q}'_\varphi$ nor $\mathcal{Q}_\varphi$ uses any constant symbols, minimality of V' is not affected, if V' is composed with any bijection of the domain. The same holds for every valuation V and the statement $V'(body_{\mathcal{Q}'_\varphi}) \subseteq V(body_{\mathcal{Q}_\varphi})$, as long as V' and V are composed with the *same* bijection. Therefore, we can assume without loss of generality that $V'(w_0) = 0$ and $V'(w_1) \in \{0, 1\}$.

We distinguish between three cases depending on whether $\mathbf{dom}(V') \subseteq \{0, 1\}$ and $V'(w_1) = 1$.

Case 1 ($\mathbf{dom}(V') \subseteq \{0, 1\}$ and $V'(w_1) = 1$): Let $\beta_{\mathbf{x}}$ be the partial truth assignment for the variables $x_1, \ldots, x_m$ in ψ defined by $\beta_{\mathbf{x}}(x_i) = V'(x_i)$, for every $i \in \{1, \ldots, m\}$. Since, $\varphi \in \Pi_3$-QBF, there exists a partial truth assignment $\beta_{\mathbf{y}}$ for the variables $y_1, \ldots, y_n$ in ψ such that for each partial truth assignment $\beta_{\mathbf{z}}$ for the variables $z_1, \ldots, z_p$ we have $(\beta_{\mathbf{x}} \cup \beta_{\mathbf{y}} \cup \beta_{\mathbf{z}}) \models \psi$. For concreteness let $\beta_{\mathbf{z}}(z_i) \stackrel{\text{def}}{=} 0$, for $i \in \{1, \ldots, p\}$ and $\beta \stackrel{\text{def}}{=} \beta_{\mathbf{x}} \cup \beta_{\mathbf{y}} \cup \beta_{\mathbf{z}}$.

Let V be the uniquely defined 0-1-valued consistent valuation induced by β. Since V is consistent it is also minimal by Claim 2, and as $\beta \models \psi$, $V(r_k) = 1$. Thanks to the latter, $V'(body_{\mathcal{Q}'_\varphi}) \subseteq V(body_{\mathcal{Q}_\varphi})$ follows easily and Case 1 is complete.

Case 2 ($\mathbf{dom}(V') \subseteq \{0, 1\}$ and $V'(w_1) = 0$): Let V be defined by

$$V(u) \stackrel{\text{def}}{=} \begin{cases} V'(u) & \text{if } u \in \{w_0, w_1, x_1, \ldots, x_n\}, \\ 0 & \text{otherwise.} \end{cases}$$

It is easy to see that $V'(body_{\mathcal{Q}'_\varphi}) \subseteq V(body_{\mathcal{Q}_\varphi})$. Furthermore, V' is minimal as every fact from $V(body_{\mathcal{Q}_\varphi})$ either stems from an atom with (only) head variables or is in the unavoidable set $V(\textit{Gates})$.

Case 3 (For some g, $V'(x_g) \notin \{c_0, c_1\}$): We recall that by our assumptions, $c_0 = 0 = V'(w_0)$ and $c_1 = V'(w_1) \in \{0, 1\}$. The following argument works for both subcases, $c_1 = 1$ and $c_1 = 0$. We call a variable x_g *foul* if $V'(x_g) \notin \{c_0, c_1\}$. Likewise, we call a clause *foul* if it contains (positively or negatively) some foul variable. Let G be the set of all indices g for which x_g is foul and J be the set of all indices j of foul clauses. Furthermore, let[7] $a = V'(x_g)$ for the minimal index $g \in G$.

We define valuation V by

$$V(u) \stackrel{\text{def}}{=} \begin{cases} V'(u) & \text{if } u \in \{w_0, w_1, x_1, \ldots, x_m\}, \\ c_1 & \text{if } u \in \{y_1, \ldots, y_n, z_1, \ldots, z_p\}, \\ c_0 & \text{if } u \in \{\overline{y}_1, \ldots, \overline{y}_n, \overline{z}_1, \ldots, \overline{z}_p\}, \\ a & \text{if } u = \overline{x}_g \text{ and } x_g \text{ is foul,} \\ c_0 & \text{if } u = \overline{x}_g \text{ and } V'(x_g) = c_1, \\ c_1 & \text{if } u = \overline{x}_g \text{ and } V'(x_g) = c_0. \end{cases}$$

For variables s_j, $V(s_j) \stackrel{\text{def}}{=} c_1$, if C_j is foul or for all its literals ℓ, it holds $V(\ell) = c_1$, otherwise $V(s_j) \stackrel{\text{def}}{=} c_0$. For variables r_j, $V(r_j) \stackrel{\text{def}}{=} c_1$, if $V(s_i) = c_1$, for some $i \leq j$ and $V(r_j) \stackrel{\text{def}}{=} c_0$, otherwise.

It is clear that $V'(body_{\mathcal{Q}'_\varphi}) \subseteq V(body_{\mathcal{Q}_\varphi})$ holds, but we can not expect that V is minimal. There might be some And-facts in $V(\textit{Circuit})$ resulting from clauses that can be avoided by changing the valuation for some variables z_i. However, we can show that every minimal valuation V^* contained in V fulfills $V'(body_{\mathcal{Q}'_\varphi}) \subseteq V^*(body_{\mathcal{Q}_\varphi})$ and thereby yields (C3).

To this end, let V^* be a minimal valuation such that $V^* \leq_{\mathcal{Q}} V$. We show first that V^* has to produce most facts from $V(body_{\mathcal{Q}_\varphi})$. This is immediate for all facts from $V(\{\texttt{YVal}_h(y_h), \texttt{YVal}_h(\overline{y}_h) \mid h \in \{1, \ldots, n\}\})$, and also for those from $V(\textit{Fix})$, and $V(\textit{Gates})$.

[7]In fact, any value not in $\{c_0, c_1\}$ would do.

Any facts of the form $V(\texttt{Neg}(u,\overline{u}))$ that do not occur in $V(\mathit{Gates})$ are of the form $\texttt{Neg}(V'(x_g),a)$, for some foul variable x_g. As x_g occurs in the head, and there is at most one such fact per foul variable, these facts can not be avoided in $V^*(body_{\mathcal{Q}_\varphi})$. As all facts of the form $V^*(\texttt{Neg}(u,\overline{u}))$ have to be in $V^*(body_{\mathcal{Q}_\varphi})$ and all variables x_i, y_i occur in $head_{\mathcal{Q}_\varphi}$, we can conclude that V^* has to agree with V for all variables of the form $x_i, \overline{x}_i, y_i, \overline{y}_i$ and on w_0 and w_1.

Therefore, it is clear for all facts from $V'(body_{\mathcal{Q}'_\varphi})$ except $\texttt{Res}(c_1)$ that they are captured by $V^*(body_{\mathcal{Q}_\varphi})$. It therefore only remains to show $\texttt{Res}(c_1) \in V^*(body_{\mathcal{Q}_\varphi})$.

Let x_g be the foul variable that was used to define $a \stackrel{\text{def}}{=} V'(x_g)$ and let C_j be some clause in which it occurs. Thus, by definition of V there is an $\texttt{And}$-fact in $V(\mathit{Circuit})$ with value a in one of its first three positions and with c_1 in its fourth position. Furthermore, all $\texttt{And}$-facts in $V(\mathit{Circuit})$ with a-values have c_1 in their fourth position. Therefore, $V^*(\mathit{Circuit})$ needs to contain at least one $\texttt{And}$-fact with a in one of its first three positions and with c_1 in its fourth position. That is, $V^*(s_i) = c_1$, for at least one i. As $V^*(\mathit{Circuit})$ can only contain $\texttt{Or}$-facts from $V(\mathit{Gates})$, it follows that $V^*(r_h) = c_1$, for all $h \geq i$ and, in particular, for $h = k$. Therefore, $\texttt{Res}(c_1) \in V^*(body_{\mathcal{Q}_\varphi})$ and $V'(body_{\mathcal{Q}'_\varphi}) \subseteq V^*(body_{\mathcal{Q}_\varphi})$. □

It is an easy observation that, if we require each valuation of $\mathcal{Q}$ to be minimal, then condition (C2) yields a better, Π_2^P, complexity bound. Surprisingly, in this case, we even get a complexity drop to NP, as will be shown in Theorem 4.8 below. We next introduce the notions needed for this result.

Definition 6. A conjunctive query $\mathcal{Q}$ is *strongly minimal* if all its valuations are minimal.

We give some examples illustrating this definition. In Lemma 4.9, we present a sufficient condition for CQs to be strongly minimal.

EXAMPLE 4.6. *For an example of a strongly minimal CQ, consider query $\mathcal{Q}_1$,*

$$T(x_1,x_2,x_2,x_4) \leftarrow R(x_1,x_2), R(x_2,x_3), R(x_3,x_4).$$

Notice that, by fullness of $\mathcal{Q}_1$, there are no two distinct valuations for $\mathcal{Q}_1$ that derive the same fact. Hence, every valuation of $\mathcal{Q}_1$ must indeed be minimal.

For another example, consider the query $\mathcal{Q}_2$,

$$T() \leftarrow R_1(x_1,x_2), R_2(x_2,x_3), R_3(x_3,x_4).$$

As each atom in the body of $\mathcal{Q}_2$ has a different relation symbol, each valuation of $\mathcal{Q}_2$ yields exactly three different facts and therefore, each valuation is minimal. □

It is easy to see that every strongly minimal CQ is also a minimal CQ, but the converse is not true as witnessed by the query of Example 3.2, which is minimal but not strongly minimal.

The following lemma now provides a characterization of parallel-correctness transfer for strongly minimal queries.

LEMMA 4.7. *Let $\mathcal{Q}'$ be a CQ and let $\mathcal{Q}$ be a strongly minimal CQ. Parallel-correctness transfers from $\mathcal{Q}$ to $\mathcal{Q}'$ if and only if the following holds:*

(C3) there is a simplification θ for $\mathcal{Q}'$ and a substitution ρ for $\mathcal{Q}$ such that $body_{\theta(\mathcal{Q}')} \subseteq body_{\rho(\mathcal{Q})}$.

PROOF. We show that, for strongly minimal $\mathcal{Q}$, (C2) and (C3) are equivalent.

We first show that (C3) implies (C2). It suffices to show that if (C3) holds then for every minimal valuation V' for $\mathcal{Q}'$, there is a valuation V for $\mathcal{Q}$ such that $V'(body_{\mathcal{Q}'}) \subseteq V(body_{\mathcal{Q}})$. By strong minimality of Q, we can then conclude that V is actually minimal.

Let V' be a minimal valuation for $\mathcal{Q}'$ and let θ and ρ be as in (C3). As θ is a simplification, $head_{\theta(\mathcal{Q}')} = head_{\mathcal{Q}'}$ and $body_{\theta(\mathcal{Q}')} \subseteq body_{\mathcal{Q}'}$. Therefore $(V' \circ \theta)$ is also a valuation for $\mathcal{Q}'$ with $(V' \circ \theta)(body_{\mathcal{Q}'}) = V'(body_{\theta(\mathcal{Q}')}) \subseteq V'(body_{\mathcal{Q}'})$ and by minimality of V' the latter inclusion is actually an equality.

By (C3), $body_{\theta(\mathcal{Q}')} \subseteq body_{\rho(\mathcal{Q})}$, therefore V' is a partial valuation for $\rho(\mathcal{Q})$. Let V'' be some arbitrarily chosen extension of V' that is a (total) valuation for $\rho(\mathcal{Q})$. Then,

$$V'(body_{\mathcal{Q}'}) = V'(body_{\theta(\mathcal{Q}')}) = V''(body_{\theta(\mathcal{Q}')})$$
$$\subseteq V''(body_{\rho(\mathcal{Q})}) = (V'' \circ \rho)(body_{\mathcal{Q}}).$$

Thus, $V \stackrel{\text{def}}{=} V'' \circ \rho$ is the desired valuation for $\mathcal{Q}$.

We next show that (C2) implies (C3). Actually, this implication even holds without the assumption that $\mathcal{Q}$ is strongly minimal. Let us therefore assume that (C2) holds. We choose θ as an arbitrary simplification that minimizes $\mathcal{Q}'$. Such a simplification can be found thanks to [7]. In particular, $\theta(\mathcal{Q}')$ is a minimal CQ that is equivalent to $\mathcal{Q}'$.

Let V' be an injective valuation for $\mathcal{Q}'$. We claim that $V' \circ \theta$ is a minimal valuation for $\mathcal{Q}'$. Towards a contradiction, let us assume that there is a valuation V'' such that $V'' <_{\mathcal{Q}'} V' \circ \theta$. Since θ is the identity on the head variables, V' is injective, and V' and V'' agree on $head_{\mathcal{Q}}$, we can conclude that $((V')^{-1} \circ V'')(head_{\mathcal{Q}'}) = head_{\mathcal{Q}'}$, thus $(V')^{-1} \circ V''$ is a homomorphism from $\mathcal{Q}$ to $((V')^{-1} \circ V'')(\mathcal{Q})$. Furthermore, $((V')^{-1} \circ V'')(body_{\mathcal{Q}}) \subseteq body_{\theta(\mathcal{Q})} \subseteq body_{\mathcal{Q}}$, therefore the identity is a homomorphism from $((V')^{-1} \circ V'')(\mathcal{Q})$ to $\mathcal{Q}$. Together, $((V')^{-1} \circ V'')(\mathcal{Q})$ is equivalent to $\mathcal{Q}$. Furthermore, $((V')^{-1} \circ V'')(body_{\mathcal{Q}}) \subsetneq (V')^{-1}(V'(body_{\mathcal{Q}})) = body_{\theta(\mathcal{Q})}$, contradicting the minimality of θ. We thus conclude that $V' \circ \theta$ is indeed a minimal valuation for $\mathcal{Q}'$.

By (C2), there exists a minimal valuation V for $\mathcal{Q}$ such that $V'(body_{\theta(\mathcal{Q}')}) = (V' \circ \theta)(body_{\mathcal{Q}'}) \subseteq V(body_{\mathcal{Q}})$. Now, let f be an extension of $(V')^{-1}$, which maps values that occur in $V(body_{\mathcal{Q}})$ but not in $V'(body_{\mathcal{Q}'})$ in an arbitrary fashion and let $\rho \stackrel{\text{def}}{=} (f \circ V)$. Then,

$$body_{\theta(\mathcal{Q}')} = (V')^{-1}(V'(body_{\theta(\mathcal{Q}')}))$$
$$= f(V'(body_{\theta(\mathcal{Q}')})) = f((V' \circ \theta)(body_{\mathcal{Q}'}))$$
$$\subseteq f(V(body_{\mathcal{Q}})) = \rho(body_{\mathcal{Q}}) = body_{\rho(\mathcal{Q})}.$$

Thus, θ and ρ witness condition (C3). □

THEOREM 4.8. PC-TRANS *restricted to inputs with strongly minimal $\mathcal{Q}$ is* NP*-complete.*

PROOF (SKETCH). The upper bound follows from Lemma 4.7 by the observation that condition (C3) can be checked by a straighforward NP-algorithm. The lower bound follows from Proposition 5.3 below. □

Theorem 4.8 assumes that it is known that $\mathcal{Q}$ is strongly minimal. We complete the picture by investigating the complexity of the problem to decide whether a CQ is strongly minimal.

We first give a lemma that generalizes the above examples into a sufficient (but not necessary) condition for strong minimality. In particular, Lemma 4.9 implies that every full CQ and every CQ without self-joins is strongly minimal. We say that an atom in a CQ is a *self-join atom* when the relation name of that atom occurs more than once in $\mathcal{Q}$. For instance, in the query $T() \leftarrow R(x_1, x_2), R(x_2, x_1)$ both $R(x_1, x_2)$ and $R(x_2, x_1)$ are self-join atoms.

LEMMA 4.9. *Let $\mathcal{Q}$ be a CQ. Then $\mathcal{Q}$ is strongly minimal when the following condition holds: if a variable x occurs at a position i in some self-join atom and not in the head of $\mathcal{Q}$, then all self-join atoms have x at position i.*

PROOF (SKETCH). The proof is by contraposition, i.e., we show that if there is a valuation for $\mathcal{Q}$ which is not minimal then the condition is not satisfied. To this end, let V and V' be valuations for $\mathcal{Q}$ which agree on the head-variables and where $V'(body_{\mathcal{Q}}) \subsetneq V(body_{\mathcal{Q}})$.

Then, there are at least two atoms $A_1 = R(x_1, \ldots, x_k)$ and $A_2 = R(y_1, \ldots, y_k)$ in the body of $\mathcal{Q}$ that collapse under V', but not under V. That is, $V'(A_1) = V'(A_2)$ and $V(A_1) \neq V(A_2)$. So, under V' all the variables in A_1 and A_2 on matching positions must be mapped on the same constant, $V'(x_i) = V'(y_i)$ for each $i \in \{1, \ldots, k\}$, while for V there is a position $j \in \{1, \ldots, k\}$ where this is not the case, $V(x_j) \neq V(y_j)$. Obviously, at least one of these variables must then be a non-head variable. So, either only x_j is a head variable, or only y_j is a head variable, or both are distinct non-head variables. In both cases the condition is not satisfied. □

EXAMPLE 4.10. *For an example of a strongly minimal CQ that does not satisfy the condition in Lemma 4.9, consider query $\mathcal{Q}_3$,*

$$T() \leftarrow R(x_1, x_2), R(x_2, x_1).$$

Notice that $\mathcal{Q}_3$ is indeed strongly minimal, because every valuation for $\mathcal{Q}_3$ either maps x_1 and x_2 on the same value, and thus requires only one fact where both values are equal, or maps x_1 and x_2 onto two distinct values, and thus requires exactly two facts where both values are distinct.

Finally, we establish the complexity of deciding strong minimality.

LEMMA 4.11. *Deciding whether a CQ is strongly minimal is* coNP*-complete.*

PROOF (SKETCH). The complement problem is easily seen to be in NP: for two guessed valuations V^*, V (encoded in length polynomial of the query $\mathcal{Q}$) it can be checked in polynomial time whether $V^* <_{\mathcal{Q}} V$.

A lower bound for the complement problem can be obtained via a reduction from 3SAT. □

5. FAMILIES OF DISTRIBUTION POLICIES

Parallel-correctness transfer can be seen as a generalization of parallel-correctness. In both cases, the goal is to decide whether a query can be correctly evaluated by evaluating it locally at each node. However, for parallel-correctness *transfer*, the question whether $\mathcal{Q}'$ is parallel-correct is not asked for a particular distribution policy but for the *family* of those distribution policies, for which $\mathcal{Q}$ is parallel-correct.[8]

In this section, we study the parallel-correctness problem for other kinds of families of distribution policies that can be associated with a given query $\mathcal{Q}$. In Section 5.1, we will identify classes of families of policies, for which (C3) characterizes parallel-correctness. For these classes we conclude that it is NP-complete to decide, whether for the family $\mathcal{F}$ of policies associated with some given CQ $\mathcal{Q}$, a CQ $\mathcal{Q}'$ is parallel-correct for all distributions from $\mathcal{F}$. In Section 5.2, we will see that this, in particular, holds for the families of distribution policies related to the practical Hypercube algorithm, that was previously investigated in several works [3, 5, 6, 8, 9]. In fact, we even show that this holds for a more general class of distribution policies specified in a declarative formalism.

5.1 Parallel-correctness

We start with the following definition:

Definition 7. A query $\mathcal{Q}$ is *parallel-correct for a family $\mathcal{F}$* of distribution policies if it is parallel-correct under every distribution policy from $\mathcal{F}$.

We call a distribution policy $\boldsymbol{P}$ *$\mathcal{Q}$-generous* for a CQ $\mathcal{Q}$, if, for every valuation V for $\mathcal{Q}$, there is a node κ that contains all facts from $V(body_{\mathcal{Q}})$. A family of distribution policies $\mathcal{F}$ is $\mathcal{Q}$-generous if every policy in $\mathcal{F}$ is. For an instance I, a distribution policy $\boldsymbol{P}$ is called *$(\mathcal{Q}, I)$-scattered* if for each node κ there is a valuation V for $\mathcal{Q}$, such that $dist_{\boldsymbol{P},I}(\kappa) \subseteq V(body_{\mathcal{Q}})$. We then say that a family $\mathcal{F}$ of distribution policies is $\mathcal{Q}$-scattered if $\mathcal{F}$ contains a $(\mathcal{Q}, I)$-scattered policy for every I. A $(\mathcal{Q}, I)$-scattered policy that is also $\mathcal{Q}$-generous yields the finest possible partition of the facts of I and thus, intuitively, scatters them as much as possible.

LEMMA 5.1. *Let $\mathcal{Q}$ be a CQ and let $\mathcal{F}$ be a family of distribution policies that is $\mathcal{Q}$-generous and $\mathcal{Q}$-scattered. Then for every CQ $\mathcal{Q}'$, $\mathcal{Q}'$ is parallel correct for $\mathcal{F}$ if and only if:*

(C3) there is a simplification θ for $\mathcal{Q}'$ and a substitution ρ for $\mathcal{Q}$ such that $body_{\theta(\mathcal{Q}')} \subseteq body_{\rho(\mathcal{Q})}$.

We emphasize that Lemma 5.1 uses the same condition (C3) as Lemma 4.7.

PROOF (SKETCH). (if) Let I be a database for $\mathcal{Q}'$, $\boldsymbol{P}$ a distribution policy from $\mathcal{F}$, and let θ and ρ be as guaranteed by (C3). We show that each fact from $\mathcal{Q}'(I)$ is produced at some node. Let V' be a valuation that yields some fact $\boldsymbol{h} \stackrel{\text{def}}{=} V'(head_{\mathcal{Q}'})$ and let V'' be an arbitrary extension of V' for $\rho(\mathcal{Q})$. As θ is a simplification, $(V' \circ \theta)$ also yields the fact $\boldsymbol{h}$. By (C3) we get $(V' \circ \theta)(body_{\mathcal{Q}'}) = V'(body_{\theta(\mathcal{Q}')}) \subseteq V''(body_{\rho(\mathcal{Q})}) = (V'' \circ \rho)(body_{\mathcal{Q}})$. As $\boldsymbol{P}$ is $\mathcal{Q}$-generous, there is some node κ that has all facts from $(V'' \circ \rho)(body_{\mathcal{Q}})$ and therefore all facts from $(V' \circ \theta)(body_{\mathcal{Q}'})$, and thus $\boldsymbol{h}$ is produced at κ.

(only-if) Suppose $\mathcal{Q}'$ is parallel-correct under all distribution policies in $\mathcal{F}$. Let V' be some injective valuation for $\mathcal{Q}'$. Denote $I \stackrel{\text{def}}{=} V'(body_{\mathcal{Q}'})$ and $\boldsymbol{h} \stackrel{\text{def}}{=} V'(head_{\mathcal{Q}'})$. Let $\boldsymbol{P}$ be

[8] A family of distribution policies is just a set of distribution policies.

some $(\mathcal{Q}, I)$-scattered distribution policy from $\mathcal{F}$. Because $\mathcal{Q}'$ is parallel-correct under $\boldsymbol{P}$, there must be a node κ that outputs $\boldsymbol{h}$ when I is distributed according to $\boldsymbol{P}$. Therefore, there is a valuation W' for $\mathcal{Q}'$ such that κ contains all facts from $W'(\mathit{body}_{\mathcal{Q}'})$ and $W'(\mathit{head}_{\mathcal{Q}'}) = \boldsymbol{h}$. We claim that $\theta \stackrel{\text{def}}{=} (V')^{-1} \circ W'$ is a simplification of $\mathcal{Q}'$. Indeed, this substitution is well-defined thanks to the injectivity of V' and furtermore $((V')^{-1} \circ W')(\mathit{head}_{\mathcal{Q}'}) = \mathit{head}_{\mathcal{Q}'}$ and $((V')^{-1} \circ W')(\mathit{body}_{\mathcal{Q}'}) \subseteq \mathit{body}_{\mathcal{Q}'}$, as $W'(\mathit{body}_{\mathcal{Q}'}) \subseteq I = V'(\mathit{body}_{\mathcal{Q}'})$ and $(V')^{-1}$ maps I back to $\mathit{body}_{\mathcal{Q}'}$.

As $\boldsymbol{P}$ is $(\mathcal{Q}, I)$-scattered, there is a valuation V such that $\mathit{dist}_{\boldsymbol{P},I}(\kappa) \subseteq V(\mathit{body}_{\mathcal{Q}})$. Then, let g be some mapping from $\mathit{img}(V)$ to **var** such that for all $d \in \mathit{img}(W')$, $g(d) = g'(d)$. We define the renaming $\rho \stackrel{\text{def}}{=} g \circ V$ and show that with these choices, $\mathit{body}_{\theta(\mathcal{Q}')} \subseteq \mathit{body}_{\rho(\mathcal{Q})}$, and thus (C3) holds.

Let $R(x_1, \ldots, x_k) \in \mathit{body}_{\theta(\mathcal{Q}')}$. Then, there is an atom $R(y_1, \ldots, y_k) \in \mathit{body}_{\mathcal{Q}'}$ with $W'(R(\bar{y})) \in \mathit{dist}_{\boldsymbol{P},I}(\kappa)$ and, for each i, $x_i = (V')^{-1}(W'(y_i))$. So, as $\mathit{dist}_{\boldsymbol{P},I}(\kappa) \subseteq V(\mathit{body}_{\mathcal{Q}})$, $W'(R(\bar{y})) \in V(\mathit{body}_{\mathcal{Q}})$ and there is an atom $R(z_1, \ldots, z_k) \in \mathit{body}_{\mathcal{Q}}$ such that $W'(R(\bar{y})) = V(R(\bar{z}))$. Clearly, $W'(y_i) = V(z_i)$ for all i. By definition of g, it then follows that $x_i = (V')^{-1}(W'(y_i)) = g(V(z_i))$, for all i. Thus, $R(x_1, \ldots, x_k)$ is in $\mathit{body}_{\rho(\mathcal{Q})}$, as desired. □

THEOREM 5.2. *It is* NP*-complete to decide, for given CQs $\mathcal{Q}$ and $\mathcal{Q}'$, whether $\mathcal{Q}'$ is parallel-correct for $\mathcal{Q}$-generous and $\mathcal{Q}$-scattered families of distribution policies.*

The proof of this theorem shows in particular, that $\mathcal{Q}'$ is either parallel-correct for *all* $\mathcal{Q}$-generous and $\mathcal{Q}$-scattered families of distribution policies or for *none* of them.

PROOF (SKETCH). The upper bound follows immediately from Lemma 5.1 and the fact that (C3) can be checked by an NP-algorithm. Indeed such an algorithm only needs to guess θ and ρ and to verify (in polynomial time) that $\mathit{body}_{\theta(\mathcal{Q}')} \subseteq \mathit{body}_{\rho(\mathcal{Q})}$.

The lower bound follows by Lemma 5.1 and the following Proposition 5.3. □

PROPOSITION 5.3. *It is* NP*-hard to decide, whether for CQs $\mathcal{Q}$ and $\mathcal{Q}'$ condition (C3) holds. This statement remains true if either $\mathcal{Q}$ or $\mathcal{Q}'$ is restricted to acyclic queries. It also remains true if both CQs are Boolean and if $\mathcal{Q}$ is full.*

REMARK 5.4. *The proof of Proposition 5.3 in both cases ($\mathcal{Q}$ acyclic or $\mathcal{Q}'$ acyclic) is by a reduction from graph 3-colorability. The first reduction, in which the input graph is encoded in $\mathcal{Q}'$ and the valid color-assignments in $\mathcal{Q}$ is straightforward. As it only uses a fixed number of colors, $\mathcal{Q}$ can be made acyclic by adding an atom to $\mathcal{Q}$ that contains all allowed colors.*

The second reduction, in which the graph is encoded in $\mathcal{Q}$ and the valid color-assignments in $\mathcal{Q}'$, is a bit more involved.

The reader may now wonder whether NP*-hardness remains when both $\mathcal{Q}$ and $\mathcal{Q}'$ are required to be acyclic. When relations of arbitrary arity are allowed, this is indeed the case: acyclicity is then easily achieved by using one atom containing all variables of the query. Under bounded-arity database schemas, however, the complexity of parallel-correctness transfer for acylic queries remains open.* □

5.2 Hypercube Distribution Policies

In the following, we give a short definition of Hypercube distributions and settle the complexity of the parallel-correctness transfer problem for families $\mathcal{H}(\mathcal{Q})$ of Hypercube distributions for some CQ $\mathcal{Q}$ with the help of the results of Section 5.1. We highlight how Hypercube distributions can be specified in a rule-based fashion, which we consider useful also for more general distributions.

Let $\mathcal{Q}$ be a conjunctive query with variables $x_1, \ldots, x_k$. A collection $H = (h_1, \ldots, h_k)$ of hash functions[9] (called a *hypercube* in the following) determines a *hypercube distribution* $\boldsymbol{P}_H$ for $\mathcal{Q}$ in the following way. For each $i \in \{1, \ldots, k\}$, we let $A_i \stackrel{\text{def}}{=} \mathit{img}(h_i)$ and define the *address space* $\mathcal{A}$ of $\boldsymbol{P}_H$ as the cartesian product $A_1 \times \cdots \times A_k$.

In a nutshell, $\boldsymbol{P}_H$ has one node per address in $\mathcal{A}$ and distributes, for every valuation V of $\mathcal{Q}$, every fact $\boldsymbol{f} = V(A)$, where A is an atom of $\mathcal{Q}$, to all nodes whose address $(a_1, \ldots, a_k)$ satisfies $a_i = h_i(V(x_i))$, for all variables x_i occurring in A.

For the declarative specification of $\boldsymbol{P}_H$ we make use of predicates[10] bucket_i and bucket_i^*, where $\mathit{bucket}_i(a, b)$ holds, if $h_i(a) = b$, and $\mathit{bucket}_i^*(b)$ holds, if $b \in \mathit{img}(h_i)$.

With these predicates, $\boldsymbol{P}_H$ can be specified by stating, for each atom $R(y_1, \ldots, y_m)$ of $\mathcal{Q}$, one rule

$$T_R(z_1, \ldots, z_k; y_1, \ldots, y_m) \leftarrow R(y_1, \ldots, y_m), B_1, \ldots, B_k.$$

Here, for each $i \in \{1, \ldots, k\}$, B_i is $\mathit{bucket}_i(x_i, z_i)$, if x_i occurs in $y_1, \ldots, y_m$, and B_i is $\mathit{bucket}_i^*(z_i)$, otherwise.

The semantics of such a rule is straightforward. For each valuation V of the variables $z_1, \ldots, z_k, x_1, \ldots, x_k$, that makes the body of the rule true, the fact $R(V(y_1), \ldots, V(y_m))$ is distributed to the node with address $(V(z_1), \ldots, V(z_k))$. We emphasize that the variables $y_1, \ldots, y_m$ need not be pairwise distinct and that $\{y_1, \ldots, y_m\} \subseteq \{x_1, \ldots, x_k\}$.

REMARK 5.5. *It is evident that one could use more general rules to specify distribution policies. More than one atom with a database relation could be in the body, and there could be other additional predicates than those derived from hashing functions. Furthermore, the address space could be defined differently.* □

For a CQ $\mathcal{Q}$, we denote by $\mathcal{H}_{\mathcal{Q}}$ the family of distribution policies $\{\boldsymbol{P}_H \mid H \text{ is a hypercube for } \mathcal{Q}\}$.

LEMMA 5.6. *Let $\mathcal{Q}$ be a CQ. Then $\mathcal{H}_{\mathcal{Q}}$ is $\mathcal{Q}$-generous and $\mathcal{Q}$-scattered.*

PROOF. Let $\mathcal{Q}$ be a CQ with $\mathit{vars}(\mathcal{Q}) = \{u_1, \ldots, u_k\}$.

We first show that every policy $\boldsymbol{P}_H \in \mathcal{H}_{\mathcal{Q}}$ is $\mathcal{Q}$-generous. To this end, let H be a hypercube and let V be a valuation for $\mathcal{Q}$. Then, by definition, for the node κ with address $(h_1(V(u_1)), \ldots, h_k(V(u_k)))$, $\kappa \in \boldsymbol{P}_H(\boldsymbol{f})$ for every $\boldsymbol{f} \in V(\mathit{body}_{\mathcal{Q}})$.

We now show that $\mathcal{H}_{\mathcal{Q}}$ is $\mathcal{Q}$-scattered. Thereto, let I be an instance. For every $i \leq k$, we choose $A_i \stackrel{\text{def}}{=} \mathit{adom}(I)$ and let $h_i(a) \stackrel{\text{def}}{=} a$, for every $a \in A_i$. Let κ be an arbitrary node and

[9] A hash function is a partial mapping from **dom** to a finite set whose elements are sometimes referred to as buckets.

[10] For the purpose of specification it is irrelevant whether these predicates are materialized in the database.

let $(a_1, \ldots, a_k)$ be its address. Let V be the valuation mapping u_i to a_i, for each i. Let $R(d_1, \ldots, d_m) \in dist_{\mathbf{P}_H, I}(\kappa)$ thanks to some rule

$$T_R(z_1, \ldots, z_k; y_1, \ldots, y_m) \leftarrow R(y_1, \ldots, y_m), \\ B_1, \ldots, B_k.$$

By definition of the hash functions, every valuation that satisfies the body of this rule, maps x_i to a_i, for every x_i that appears in $R(y_1, \ldots, y_m)$. However, as this valuation coincides with V on $y_1, \ldots, y_m$, it maps $R(y_1, \ldots, y_m)$ to an element of $V(body_{\mathcal{Q}})$. Therefore, $dist_{\mathbf{P}_H, I}(\kappa) \subseteq V(body_{\mathcal{Q}})$. □

COROLLARY 5.7. *It is* NP*-complete to decide, for given conjunctive queries* $\mathcal{Q}, \mathcal{Q}'$, *whether* $\mathcal{Q}'$ *is parallel-correct for* $\mathcal{H}_{\mathcal{Q}}$.

REMARK 5.8. *It is easy to see that Lemma 5.6 and then the upper bound of Corollary 5.7 holds for more general families of distribution policies. As an example, one could add further atoms of* $\mathcal{Q}$ *as "filters" to the bodies of the above rules.* □

6. CONCLUSIONS

We have introduced parallel-correctness as a framework for studying one-round evaluation algorithms for the evaluation of queries under arbitrary distribution policies. We have obtained tight bounds on the complexity of deciding parallel-correctness and the transferability problem for conjunctive queries. For general conjunctive queries, these complexities reside in different levels of the polynomial hierarchy (even when considering Hypercube distributions). Since the considered problems are static analysis problems that relate to queries and not to instances (at least in the case of transferability), such complexities do not necessarily put a burden on practical applicability. Still, it would be interesting to identify fragments of conjunctive queries or particular classes of distribution policies that could render these problems tractable. In addition, it would be interesting to explore more expressive classes of queries like unions of CQs and CQs with negation, and other families of distribution policies.

The notion of parallel-correctness is directly inspired by Hypercube where the result of the query is obtained by aggregating (through union) the evaluation of the original query over the distributed instance. Other possibilities are to consider more complex aggregator functions than union and to allow for a different query than the original one to be executed at computing nodes.

Acknowledgments

We thank Serge Abiteboul, Luc Segoufin, Cristina Sirangelo, and Thomas Zeume for helpful remarks.

7. REFERENCES

[1] S. Abiteboul, R. Hull, and V. Vianu. *Foundations of Databases*. Addison-Wesley, 1995.

[2] F. N. Afrati, P. Koutris, D. Suciu, and J. D. Ullman. Parallel skyline queries. In *ICDT*, pages 274–284, 2012.

[3] F. N. Afrati and J. D. Ullman. Optimizing joins in a map-reduce environment. In *EDBT*, pages 99–110, 2010.

[4] T. J. Ameloot, B. Ketsman, F. Neven, and D. Zinn. Weaker forms of monotonicity for declarative networking: a more fine-grained answer to the CALM-conjecture. In *PODS*, pages 64–75, 2014.

[5] P. Beame, P. Koutris, and D. Suciu. Communication steps for parallel query processing. In *PODS*, pages 273–284, 2013.

[6] P. Beame, P. Koutris, and D. Suciu. Skew in parallel query processing. In *PODS*, pages 64–75, 2014.

[7] A. K. Chandra and P. M. Merlin. Optimal implementation of conjunctive queries in relational data bases. In *STOC*, pages 77–90, 1977.

[8] S. Ganguly, A. Silberschatz, and S. Tsur. A framework for the parallel processing of Datalog queries. In *SIGMOD*, pages 143–152, 1990.

[9] S. Ganguly, A. Silberschatz, and S. Tsur. Parallel bottom-up processing of datalog queries. *J. Log. Program.*, 14(1&2):101–126, 1992.

[10] P. Hell and J. Nesetril. The core of a graph. *Discrete Mathematics*, 109(1-3):117–126, 1992.

[11] P. Koutris and D. Suciu. Parallel evaluation of conjunctive queries. In *PODS*, pages 223–234, 2011.

[12] Spark. http://spark.apache.org.

[13] L. J. Stockmeyer. The polynomial-time hierarchy. *Theor. Comput. Sci.*, 3(1):1–22, 1976.

[14] R. Xin, J. Rosen, M. Zaharia, M. Franklin, S. Shenker, and I. Stoica. Shark: SQL and rich analytics at scale. In *SIGMOD*, 2013.

[15] D. Zinn, T. J. Green, and B. Ludäscher. Win-move is coordination-free (sometimes). In *ICDT*, pages 274–284, 2012.

LogiQL: a Declarative Language for Enterprise Applications

Todd J. Green
LogicBlox, Inc.
1900 Addison St, Suite #200
Berkeley, CA 94704
todd.green@logicblox.com

ABSTRACT

We give an overview of LogiQL, a declarative, Datalog-based language for data management and analytics, along with techniques for efficient evaluation of LogiQL programs, emphasizing theoretical foundations when possible. These techniques include: leapfrog triejoin and its associated incremental maintenance algorithm, which we measure against appropriate optimality criteria; purely-functional data structures, which provide elegant versioning and branching capabilities that are indispensable for LogiQL; and transaction repair, a lock-free concurrency control scheme that uses LogiQL, incremental maintenance, and purely-functional data structures as essential ingredients.

Categories and Subject Descriptors

H.2 [**Database Management**]

General Terms

Algorithms, Design, Languages

Keywords

LogicBlox; LogiQL; Datalog; Leapfrog Triejoin; Incremental Maintenance; Transaction Repair

1. INTRODUCTION

Recent years have witnessed a resurgence of interest in Datalog, not just in academic research but also in industry [9, 1, 13]. As a language residing at an interesting point in the tradeoff between expressive power and algorithmic tractability, it has lately found use in a surprisingly wide range of practical application settings: for example, Datalog-based languages are being used today at Semmle [4] for analysis of large software repositories; in the implementation of VMWare's network virtualization platform (NVP) [17]; for large-scale data processing at Google in the Yedalog project [8]; for distributed, cloud-based applications in Cognitect's Datomic [3]; and as the underpinning of an ambitious attempt to democratize programming in the recently-funded Eve project [2].

PODS'15, May 31–June 4, 2015, Melbourne, Victoria, Australia.

http://dx.doi.org/10.1145/2745754.2745780.

In this tutorial we give a brief overview of LogiQL, a declarative, Datalog-based language for data management and analytics developed at LogicBlox, and explain the appeal of Datalog as the foundation for a practical language for building sophisticated, data-intensive applications. These being used today at some of the largest organizations in the world.

We then discuss techniques for efficient evaluation of LogiQL programs. First, we present the basics of purely functional data structures [24]. These were first developed to cope with the constraints of functional programming languages, but turn out to be enormously useful in a variety of other settings, including database systems, as we shall explain. Next, we overview leapfrog triejoin [27], the workhorse join algorithm in LogicBlox, and its associated incremental view maintenance algorithm [26]. Join evaluation is another topic in which there has been flurry of re-interest, with exciting recent successes [21, 27, 20, 16] in developing algorithms having provable optimality guarantees of various flavors; leapfrog triejoin is one such algorithm. Finally, we give a brief overview of transaction repair [28], a lock-free concurrency control scheme achieving full serializability that uses LogiQL, incremental maintenance, and purely-functional data structures as essential ingredients.

Further details about LogiQL and LogicBlox can be found in a companion paper by Aref et al. [5], from which major portions of this tutorial overview are adapted.

2. LOGIQL

LogiQL is a practical language for building complex enterprise applications involving a mixture of tasks including analytics, transactions, machine learning, and optimization problems. It is a statically typed extension of Datalog that aims to cover the above use cases via a compact, orthogonal set of features while retaining a high-level, declarative character. Conceptually, its relationship to Datalog is like that of functional languages to the lambda calculus.

In this section we describe the core elements of a LogiQL program, namely *predicates*, *derivation rules*, *integrity constraints*, and *reactive rules*.

Predicates. LogicBlox supports predicates (relations) of the form $R(x_1,\ldots,x_n)$ or $R[x_1,\ldots,x_{n-1}] = x_n$ where each attribute x_i has either a primitive type (e.g., int, float, decimal, string, or date) or a user-defined *entity type*.

Each predicate may be declared as being either a *base predicate* (a.k.a. *extensional* or *EDB* predicate or relation), or a *derived predicate* (a.k.a. *intensional* or *IDB* predicate). If left unspecified, the predicate kind (base or derived), as well as the attribute types, are inferred from usage within the program. Base predicates contain input data and derived predicates are *views* over the base data.

Derived predicates default to being materialized. However, if the derivation rule does not use aggregation or recursion, they can be left non-materialized.

Derivation Rules. Derivation rules are used to specify view definitions. LogiQL admits two types of derivation rules.

A *basic derivation rule* is an expression of one of the two forms

$$R(t_1,\ldots,t_n) \leftarrow F$$
$$R[t_1,\ldots,t_{n-1}] = t_n \leftarrow F$$

where R is a derived predicate, $t_1,\ldots,t_n$ are variables and/or constants, and F is a formula containing all variables occurring in $t_1,\ldots,t_n$. The *formula*, here, may be a conjunction of atoms and/or negated atoms. The atoms involve base predicates, derived predicates, and/or built-in predicates such as equality, arithmetic addition, etc. An example of a basic derivation rule is

$$\text{profit}[sku] = z \leftarrow \text{sellingPrice}[sku] = x, \quad \text{buyingPrice}[sku] = y,\ z = x - y.$$

which, using abbreviated syntax, may also be written as the expression

$$\text{profit}[sku] = \text{sellingPrice}[sku] - \text{buyingPrice}[sku].$$

Besides basic derivation rules, LogiQL also supports derivation rules that perform, for instance, aggregation. This is supported in an extensible way via the general construct of a higher order *predicate-to-predicate rule* (*P2P rule*). For example, the P2P rule

$$\text{totalShelf}[\,] = u \leftarrow \text{agg}\ll u = \text{sum}(z)\gg \text{Stock}[p] = x, \quad \text{spacePerProd}[p] = y,\ z = x * y.$$

performs a simple weighted sum-aggregation to compute the total amount of required shelf space, which, using abbreviated syntax, can also be written as:

$$\text{totalShelf}[] += \text{Stock}[p] * \text{spacePerProd}[p].$$

It is worth noting that every view definition definable in the relational algebra can be encoded by means of derivation rules (by introducing auxiliary predicates for intermediate results if necessary).[1] A collection of derivation predicates may be defined by rules with a cyclic dependency graph, in which case the rules in question can be viewed as *recursive* view definitions.

Integrity Constraints. An *integrity constraint* is an expression of the form $F \rightarrow G$ (note the use of a rightward arrow instead of a leftward arrow), where F and G are formulas. Both inclusion dependencies and functional dependencies can be naturally expressed by such expressions. Examples of integrity constraints are:

$$\text{Stock}[p] = v \rightarrow \text{Product}(p), \text{float}(v).$$
$$\text{Product}(p) \rightarrow \text{Stock}[p] = \_.$$
$$\text{totalShelf}[\,] = u, \text{maxShelf}[\,] = v \rightarrow u \leq v.$$

The first constraint can in fact be viewed as a type declaration: it expresses that the key-attribute of the Stock predicate consists of products (Product is a user defined type here), and that the value-attribute is a float. The second constraint is an inclusion dependency that expresses that every product has a stock value. The third constraint expresses that the value of totalShelf[ ] is bounded by the value of maxShelf[ ].

[1] Indeed, it follows from the Immerman-Vardi theorem [15] that every PTIME-computable view definition is expressible.

// Base predicates:

$$\text{spacePerProd}[p] = v \rightarrow \text{Product}(p), \text{float}(v).$$
$$\text{profitPerProd}[p] = v \rightarrow \text{Product}(p), \text{float}(v).$$
$$\text{minStock}[p] = v \rightarrow \text{Product}(p), \text{float}(v).$$
$$\text{maxStock}[p] = v \rightarrow \text{Product}(p), \text{float}(v).$$
$$\text{maxShelf}[\,] = v \rightarrow \text{float}(v).$$

// Derived predicates and rules:

$$\text{Stock}[p] = v \rightarrow \text{Product}(p), \text{float}(v).$$
$$\text{totalShelf}[\,] = v \rightarrow \text{float}(v).$$
$$\text{totalProfit}[\,] = v \rightarrow \text{float}(v).$$
$$\text{totalShelf}[\,] = u \leftarrow \text{agg}\ll u = \text{sum}(z)\gg \text{Stock}[p] = x, \quad \text{spacePerProd}[p] = y,\ z = x * y.$$
$$\text{totalProfit}[\,] \leftarrow \text{agg}\ll u = \text{sum}(z)\gg \text{Stock}[p] = x, \quad \text{profitPerProd}[p] = y,\ z = x * y.$$

// Integrity constraints:

$$\text{Product}(p) \rightarrow \text{Stock}[p] \geq \text{minStock}[p].$$
$$\text{Product}(p) \rightarrow \text{Stock}[p] \leq \text{maxStock}[p].$$
$$\text{totalShelf}[\,] = u, \quad \text{maxShelf}[\,] = v \ \rightarrow u \leq v.$$

Figure 1: Example constraints and rules.

Whereas derivation rules define views, integrity constraints specify the set of legal database states. Traditionally, integrity constraints are used to determine if a transaction succeeds. As we will see below, we also use integrity constraints to encode mathematical optimization problems.

Figure 1 shows an example that involves predicates, derivation rules, and integrity constraints. The program is intended to model a simple retail assortment-planning scenario where the products picked for an assortment cannot take up more space than is available on the shelf.

Reactive Rules. Reactive rules are used to make and detect changes to the database state. They are a special form of derivation rules that refer to versioned predicates and delta predicates [19]. A simple example of a reactive rule is:

$$+\text{sales}[\text{“Popsicle”}, 2015\text{-}01] = 122.$$

which inserts a new fact into the sales predicate. A more interesting example is the following.

$$\hat{\ }\text{price}[\text{“Popsicle”}] = 0.8 * x \leftarrow$$
$$\text{price@}start[\text{“Popsicle”}] = x,$$
$$\text{sales@}start[\text{“Popsicle”}, 2015\text{-}01] < 50,$$
$$+\text{promo}(\text{“Popsicle”}, 2015\text{-}01).$$

This code discounts the price of popsicles if the sales in January 2015 are lower than 50 units, and there is a promotion being created for popsicles.

As we can see from the above examples, reactive rules are derivation rules that may refer to system-provided *versioned predicates* and *delta-predicates* such as $R@start$ (the content of R at the start of the transaction), $+R$ (the set of tuples being inserted into R in the current transaction), $-R$ (the set of tuples being deleted from R in the current transaction). ^R is a shorthand notation for a combination of $+R$ and $-R$. If R is a base predicate, the content of R after

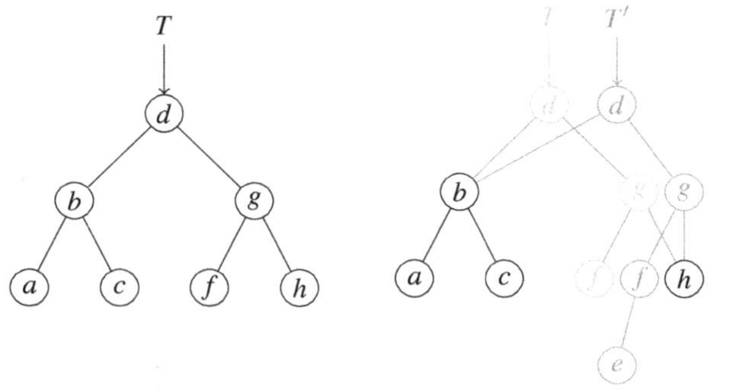

(a) A search tree T. (b) Execution of $T' = \mathsf{insert}(\text{'e'}, T)$.

Figure 2: Consecutive versions of a purely functional search tree.

the transaction is determined by means of the following system-provided *frame rules*:

$$R(x_1,\ldots,x_n) \leftarrow R@start(x_1,\ldots,x_n), !(-R(x_1,\ldots,x_n)).$$
$$R(x_1,\ldots,x_n) \leftarrow +R(x_1,\ldots,x_n).$$

Predictive and prescriptive analytics. LogiQL also contains support for predictive analytics via P2P rules encapsulating a state-of-the-art machine learning library, as well as for prescriptive analytics, where LogiQL constraints are used to define the parameters of optimization problems. For more details see [12].

3. FUNCTIONAL DATA STRUCTURES

Database systems implementations traditionally have employed *mutable* data structures: an insertion of an element to a B-tree, for example, means changing the existing tree in place to accommodate the insertion.

Functional programming languages such as Haskell, on the other hand, forbid the modification of an existing data structure in this way; instead *purely functional data structures* [24] are used. Such data structures are *immutable* (or *persistent*): once constructed, they can never be changed. Updates are implemented by a "copy-on-write" scheme: changes are made by copying the affected nodes of a structure; whiles nodes unaffected by a change are *shared* between the old and new versions. Immutability ensures that such sharing can be done safely.

For example, Figure 2a (from Okasaki [24]) shows a search tree T over some character data. An update "insert e" to the tree yields a new search tree T', shown in Figure 2b. This tree is obtained from T by copying nodes along the path (d,g,f) from the root to the insertion point, with e added below the new copy of f. (Copies are shown in green.) For areas of the tree unaffected by the change, such as the subtree containing b, a, and c or the subtree containing h, the new nodes point to nodes shared with the old tree. The operation remains unchanged in time complexity compared to an imperative implementation, but now involves copying.

Note that after the insertion in the previous example, both versions T and T' of the tree remain available (but take up much less space than $|T|+|T'|$ due to the use of sharing). This versioning capability, while not unique to functional data structures, is extremely useful in the context of database systems implementation.

For instance, the reactive rules described in Section 2 require simultaneous access to multiple versions of a predicate, as in the example seen earlier. By using a purely functional variant of paged B-trees for storing predicates, we satisfy this requirement more or less for free. Moreover, other fundamental operations, such as enumerating differences between successive versions of a predicate, can be implemented efficiently, by exploiting the presence of shared substructure. (The basic idea is that subtrees common to two versions of a predicate can be skipped over in the enumeration.)

As another example, consider the classical `count` technique for view maintenance [11] (closely related to the seminaive evaluation technique for Datalog). In this approach, in order to maintain a view predicate A defined by

$$A(x,y) \leftarrow B(z,x), C(z,y), D(z).$$

we generate *delta rules* for A, which compute the changes A^Δ to A, given changes to its body predicates:

$$A^\Delta(x,y) \leftarrow B^\Delta(z,x), C^{old}(z,y), D^{old}(z).$$
$$A^\Delta(x,y) \leftarrow B^{new}(z,x), C^\Delta(z,y), D^{old}(z).$$
$$A^\Delta(x,y) \leftarrow B^{new}(z,x), C^{new}(z,y), D^\Delta(z).$$
$$A^{new}(x,y) \leftarrow A^{old}(x,y).$$
$$A^{new}(x,y) \leftarrow A^\Delta(x,y).$$

As should be clear from the notation, we require here access different versions of a predicate at the same time. LogicBlox uses a different technique for incremental maintenance (cf. Section 4), but access to predicate versions in that scheme remains crucial.

Finally, there is no reason to stop at using functional data structures only for predicates. Instead, we can use them at all levels of the database system, including for database instances. We can then quickly "branch" a database instance—by making a shallow, copy-on-write version in $O(1)$ time—and perform operations on it in complete isolation from other branches. This immediately provides a form of multi-version concurrency control (MVCC), a single writer and multiple reader concurrency control mechanism that guarantees full serializability [7, 25]. In Section 5 we sketch how we extend this to support concurrent write transactions via the technique of *transaction repair*.

4. LEAPFROG TRIEJOIN

The join algorithm used by LogicBlox, *leapfrog triejoin* (LFTJ), is among the first of a family of new, worst-case optimal join algorithms that have been proposed in the past few years, that depart from the traditional Selinger-style join optimization paradigm, and that come with strong performance guarantees. In the Selinger-style query optimization paradigm, used by all mainstream relational database management systems for the last few decades, queries are evaluated using a tree of binary join operations, and the main task of the optimizer is to decide on the join order as well as on the strategy used to evaluate each individual binary join. Although satisfactory for many workloads, it was recently shown that this approach is inherently sub-optimal. Moreover, analytic workloads increasingly contain graph queries, for which the approach performs particularly poorly. A simple and easily understood example is the query that computes 3-cliques in a graph. Every binary join plan is forced to compute an intermediate result that is potentially much larger than the output of the query. Multiway join algorithms can take advantage of all atoms in the query simultaneously, in order to reduce the search space, leading to better performance, and in fact, provable optimality.

Ngo et al. [21] were the first to present a worst-case optimal join algorithm, building on the work of Atserias, Grohe and Marx [6]. More precisely, their algorithm is worst-case optimal for projection-free conjunctive queries, in the sense that the running time of the

(1,3,4)
(1,3,5)
(1,4,6)
(1,4,8)
(1,4,9)
(1,5,2)
(3,5,2)

(a) Predicate $A(x,y,z)$.

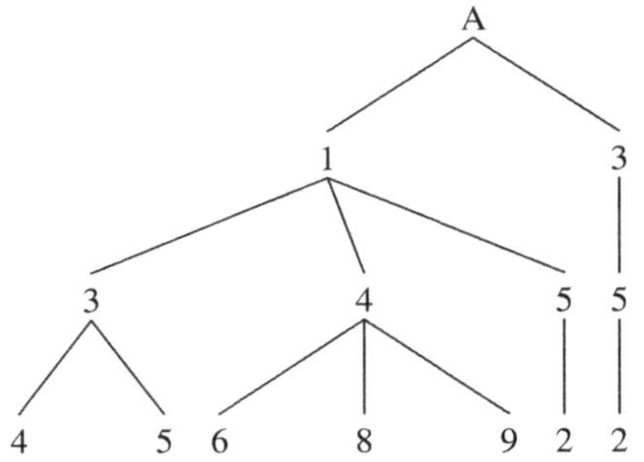

(b) Trie presentation.

Figure 3: Example: Trie presentation of a ternary predicate.

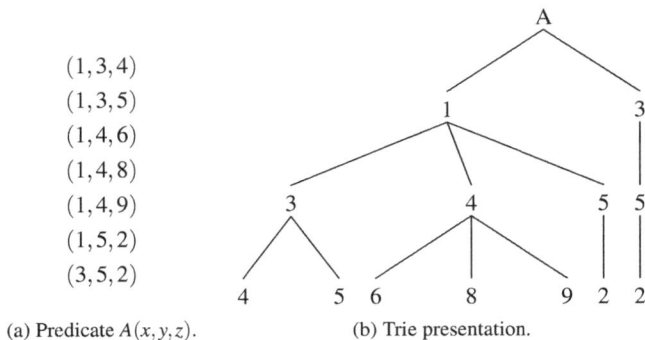

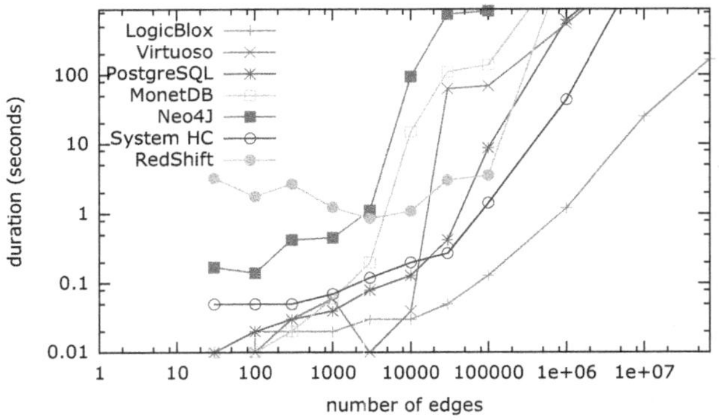

Figure 5: Running time of the 3-clique query on (increasingly larger subsets of) the LiveJournal graph dataset [18] using LogicBlox 4.1.4, Virtuoso 7, PostgreSQL 9.3.4, Neo4j 2.1.5, MonetDB 1.7 (Jan2014-SP3), a commercial in-memory column store (System HC), and RedShift. See [23] for full details and more experiments.

algorithm, on a given input, is bounded in terms of the maximal size of the query result on instance with the cardinality characteristics. Veldhuizen [27] subsequently showed that *Leapfrog Triejoin*, a much simpler multi-way join algorithm, which had already been in use at LogicBlox, is also worst-case optimal in the same sense. Since then, a number of other join algorithms have been proposed in this space [22], including Minesweeper [20] and Tetris [16] for which even stronger optimality theorems hold for various classes of queries.

Scenarios where LFTJ excels particularly compared to other join algorithms are multi-way joins such as the join returning all 3-cliques on the LiveJournal graph dataset, cf. Figure 5. See [23] for full details and more experiments.

We give a high-level description of the LFTJ algorithm and discuss our approach to query optimization, incremental maintenance, and parallel evaluation.

High-Level Description:. LFTJ [27] is essentially an improved, multi-way version of the classical sort-merge join algorithm. It is used to compute the derived predicates (more specifically, it enumerates the satisfying assignments for bodies of derivation rules).

To simplify the presentation, we focus on equi-joins, and we assume that each variable appears at most once in each atom. For example, $R(x,x)$ can be rewritten to $R(x,y), x=y$ to satisfy this requirement.

The algorithm requires a *global variable ordering* that is consistent with the order in which variables occur in the atoms in the query. For instance, in the join $R(a,b), S(b,c), T(a,c)$ we might choose the variable ordering $[a,b,c]$. In cases where no consistent variable order exists, such as for the join $R(a,b,c), S(c,b)$, a secondary index is required on one of the two predicates. For example, if the chosen variable ordering is $[a,b,c]$, a secondary index on S is needed.

The predicates that constitute the input are assumed to be stored sorted in lexicographic order and accessible through a *trie* interface (cf. Figure 3) with efficient support for vertical navigation (up, down) and horizontal navigation (next, seek). The levels in the trie correspond to argument positions of the predicate (from left to right). The output of the LFTJ is itself presented using the same interface, where each level of the trie now corresponds to a variable in the global variable ordering.

Consider the example $R(a,b)$, $S(b,c)$, $T(a,c)$ with the variable ordering $[a,b,c]$. We first apply a "leapfrog join" (described below) to enumerate the values for a that are in both the projections $R(a,\_)$ and $T(a,\_)$. For each successful binding for a, we proceed to the next variable in the chosen order. Again, a leapfrog join is performed to enumerate bindings for b that satisfy both $R(a,b)$ and $S(b,\_)$ (for the current value of a). Finally, for each successful binding of b, we proceed to the variable c, and perform a leapfrog join to enumerate values for c satisfying both $S(b,c)$ and $T(a,c)$ (for the current values of a and b). Each time a leapfrog join finishes, having exhausted its list of possible bindings, we retreat to the previous level and seek another binding for the corresponding variable. Thus, conceptually, we can regard the entire LFTJ run as a backtracking search through a trie of potential variable bindings.

We now describe how a leapfrog join works. For simplicity we consider a join of unary predicates $A_1(x), \ldots, A_k(x)$. The leapfrog join algorithm for unary predicates is of no particular novelty (see, e.g., [14, 10]), but, as we have seen, it serves as the basic building block in the LFTJ algorithm.

The algorithm maintains a priority queue of pointers to input iterators, one for each predicate being joined, where the priority reflects the value at which the iterator is currently positioned. The algorithm repeatedly takes an iterator with the smallest value and performs a seek for the largest value, "leapfrogging" the iterators until they are all positioned at the same value.

Figure 4 illustrates a join of three unary predicates, A, B, and C, with $A = \{0,1,3,4,5,6,7,8,9,11\}$, $B = \{0,2,6,7,8,9\}$, and $C = \{2,4,5,8,10\}$. Initially, the iterators for A, B, and C are positioned at the first elements 0, 0, and respectively 2. Since 2 is the largest from these three values, the iterator for A performs a `seek(2)` which positions the iterator for A at 3. The iterator for B then performs a `seek(3)`, which lands at 6. The iterator for C does `seek(6)`, which lands at 8, and so on. The leapfrog join ends when the iterator for B, while performing `seek(11)`, reaches the end.

Optimization and parallelism. The classic Selinger-style join order optimization does not arise in our multi-way join setting. Instead, when joins are evaluated using LFTJ, query optimization essentially boils down to choosing a good *variable* order. Recall that, depending on the chosen variable order, secondary indices may need to be created and maintained for some predicates.

The LogicBlox query optimizer uses sampling-based techniques: small representative samples of predicates are maintained. These samples are used to compare candidate variable orderings for LFTJ evaluation, and, consequently, also for automatic index creation. Furthermore, the samples are used to determine domain decompositions for automatic parallelization.

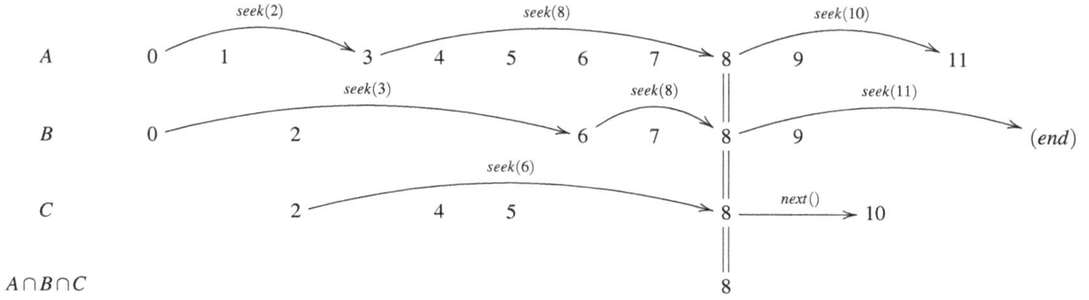

Figure 4: Example of a LFTJ run with unary predicates.

Incremental maintenance. As LFTJ calls the next() and seek() methods of the participating iterators, there is a natural notion of a *sensitivity interval*: an interval where changes may actually affect the result of the LFTJ computation. For instance, in the example in Figure 4, inserting the fact $C(3)$ or deleting the fact $C(4)$ would not affect the computation, given that the seek(6) instruction skips over these values anyway. The sensitivity intervals, i.e., intervals where changes *do* affect the LFTJ computation, for the example in Figure 4 are as follows:

$$A:[-\infty,0],[2,3],[8,8],[10,11]$$
$$B:[-\infty,0],[3,6],[8,8],[11,+\infty]$$
$$C:[-\infty,2],[6,8],[8,10]$$

The sensitivity indices can, in this example, also be viewed as representing an execution trace of the LFTJ algorithm. In the LogicBlox runtime, sensitivity intervals play an important role for both incremental maintenance and concurrent transactions.

As explained in [5], incremental maintenance is of central importance in LogicBlox applications. We support incremental maintenance of derived predicates efficiently by means of an extension of the LFTJ algorithm. The basic setup is as follows. We have a derivation rule such as

$$T(x) \leftarrow A_1(x,y), A_2(y,z), A_3(x,z)$$

and, for each input predicate A_i, we are given an *old* version A_i^{old}, a *new* version A_i^{new}, and a *delta* predicate A_i^{Δ}, where A_i^{Δ} is a set of insertions and deletions that, when applied to A_i^{old}, yields A_i^{new}. We are also given T^{old}, and the task is to compute T^{new} as well as T^{Δ} which is then propagated forward to other rules. Recall that our versioned data structures allow us to compute differences between two versions of a predicate efficiently.

The derivation rule maintenance problem is, conceptually, split into two parts: *maintaining the set of satisfying assignments for the rule body under changes to the input predicates* ("rule body maintenance") and *maintaining the rule head predicate under changes to the set of satisfying assignments for the rule body* ("rule head maintenance"). For recursive LogiQL programs, additional machinery is used to maintain the results of fixpoint computations.

Rule head maintenance is implemented using a variety of data structures for different derivation rules. In the case of the above example, a count predicate is maintained, indicating, for each value a, the number of different ways in which it is derived (i.e,. the number of satisfying assignments of the rule body that support the derivation of that value). For P2P rules performing operations such as aggregation, different data structures are used. Support for efficient *rule body maintenance* is provided by the LFTJ algorithm through the use of *sensitivity indices*. These sensitivity indices maintain sensitivity intervals for a LFTJ run at various levels in the trie and in various contexts (where the context of a sensitivity interval consists of the values for earlier-chosen variables under which the sensitivity occurs). The maintenance algorithm is designed to be optimal in the sense that the cost of maintenance under changes to the input predicates is proportional to the trace-edit distance of the corresponding runs of the LFTJ algorithm [26].

What we have discussed was entirely about maintenance of derived predicates under changes to the input predicates of derivation rules. LogicBlox can also be viewed as performing another, different kind of incremental maintenance, namely under changes to the logic (i.e., the set of derivation rules installed in the database) itself. In practical applications, there may be very large numbers of derived predicates and derivation rules. The corresponding dependency graph tends to be rather intricate as well. When changes are made to the set of derivation rules installed in the workspace, maintaining the content of workspace under these changes is challenging, both in terms as an algorithmic task, and also from a software engineering / architectural standpoint. Our solution to this, interestingly, is to take some of the internal mechanisms in the runtime, such as the construction of the dependency graph of derived predicates, and express these mechanisms themselves by means of declarative rules ("meta-rules") that are incrementally maintained. We will not discuss this further here but refer to reader to [5] for more details.

5. TRANSACTION REPAIR

Recall from Section 3 that our use of purely functional data structures allows us to immediately support single-writer, multiple-reader form of concurrent transactions. In this section we sketch a novel extension of this approach to support concurrent write transactions that was developed at LogicBlox and that is currently being implemented. This novel concurrency control mechanism is called *transaction repair* [28].

For simplicity, consider write transactions that do not install or remove rules, but merely change the content of existing predicates (these are called *exec* transactions in LogiQL). As we have seen earlier, such transactions are specified by means of reactive rules that operate on a branched copy of the workspace, where each database-lifetime predicate R gets, intuitively, renamed to $R@start$ (standing for the content of predicate R at the start of the transaction). The reactive rules take as input these *at-start* predicates as well as other, transaction-lifetime, predicates, and they produce new versions of one or more database-lifetime predicates, which we may denote by $R@final$. At the end of the transaction, assuming that all integrity constraints are satisfied, the changes are committed by performing what is conceptually a simple pointer swap.

Transaction repair takes the perspective that these reactive rules are just another instance of LogiQL derivation rules, and the same incremental maintenance machinery described in Section 4 can be applied to them. In other words, we can treat each predicate $R@final$ as a view that can be maintained incrementally under changes to the input predicates $R@start$. This provides us with a natural conflict resolution strategy: in the case of two concurrent write transactions, T_1, T_2, we apply both transactions to independent branches of the input workspace, and then we incrementally maintain the output of T_2 under the transaction effects of T_1. All the incremental maintenance machinery referred to in the previous section comes into play here. In particular, during the execution of T_2, sensitivity indices are used to record the parts of the workspace T_2 "saw," which allows us to identify and localize conflicts.

The same idea applies in the more general case where we have multiple concurrent write transactions. Note that by construction, transaction repair guarantees fully serializable transaction semantics: the final result is identical to what would have been obtained if the transactions had been executed in sequence.

We have obviously omitted many details here, and we refer to [5, 28] for more details.

6. REFERENCES

[1] http://www.datalog20.org/programme.html.

[2] Beyond Light Table. http://www.chris-granger.com/2014/10/01/beyond-light-table.

[3] Datomic. http://www.datomic.com.

[4] Semmle Ltd. http://www.semmle.com.

[5] Molham Aref, Balder ten Cate, Todd J. Green, Benny Kimelfeld, Dan Olteanu, Emir Pasalic, Todd L. Veldhuizen, and Geoffrey Washburn. Design and implementation of the LogicBlox system. In *SIGMOD*, 2015.

[6] Albert Atserias, Martin Grohe, and Dániel Marx. Size bounds and query plans for relational joins. In *FOCS*, pages 739–748. IEEE Computer Society, 2008.

[7] Philip A. Bernstein and Nathan Goodman. Concurrency control in distributed database systems. *ACM Comput. Surv.*, 13(2):185–221, June 1981.

[8] Brian Chin, Daniel von Dincklage, Vuk Ercegovak, Peter Hawkins, Mark S. Miller, Franz Och, Christopher Olston, and Fernando Pereira. Yedalog: Exploring knowledge at scale. In *SNAPL*, 2015. To appear.

[9] Oege de Moor, Georg Gottlob, Tim Furche, and Andrew Sellers, editors. *Datalog Reloaded: Proceedings of the First International Datalog 2.0 Workshop*. Springer, 2011.

[10] Erik D. Demaine, Alejandro López-Ortiz, and J. Ian Munro. Adaptive set intersections, unions, and differences. In *SODA*, pages 743–752. ACM/SIAM, 2000.

[11] Ashish Gupta, Inderpal Singh Mumick, and V. S. Subrahmanian. Maintaining views incrementally. In *SIGMOD*, pages 157–166, 1993.

[12] Terry Halpin and Spencer Rugaber. *LogiQL: A Query Language for Smart Databases*. CRC Press, 2014.

[13] Shan Shan Huang, Todd J. Green, and Boon Thau Loo. Datalog and emerging applications: An interactive tutorial. In *SIGMOD*, pages 1213–1216, 2011.

[14] Frank K. Hwang and Shen Lin. A simple algorithm for merging two disjoint linearly-ordered sets. *SIAM J. Comput.*, 1(1):31–39, 1972.

[15] Neil Immerman. *Descriptive Complexity*. Springer, 1999.

[16] Mahmoud Abo Khamis, Hung Q. Ngo, Christopher Ré, and Atri Rudra. Joins via geometric resolutions: Worst-case and beyond. In *PODS*, 2015.

[17] Teemu Koponen, Keith Amidon, Peter Balland, Martin Casado, Anupam Chanda, Bryan Fulton, Igor Ganichev, Jesse Gross, Paul Ingram, Ethan Jackson, Andrew Lambeth, Romain Lenglet, Shih-Hao Li, Amar Padmanabhan, Justin Pettit, Ben Pfaff, Rajiv Ramanathan, Scott Shenker, Alan Shieh, Jeremy Stribling, Pankaj Thakkar, Dan Wendlandt, Alexander Yip, and Ronghua Zhang. Network virtualization in multi-tenant datacenters. In *NSDI*, pages 203–216, Seattle, WA, April 2014. USENIX Association.

[18] Jure Leskovec and Andrej Krevl. SNAP Datasets: Stanford large network dataset collection. http://snap.stanford.edu/data, June 2014.

[19] Bertram Ludäscher. *Integration of Active and Deductive Database Rules*, volume 45 of *DISDBIS*. Infix Verlag, St. Augustin, Germany, 1998.

[20] Hung Q. Ngo, Dung T. Nguyen, Christopher Re, and Atri Rudra. Beyond worst-case analysis for joins with minesweeper. In *Proceedings of the 33rd ACM SIGMOD-SIGACT-SIGART Symposium on Principles of Database Systems*, PODS '14, pages 234–245, New York, NY, USA, 2014. ACM.

[21] Hung Q. Ngo, Ely Porat, Christopher Ré, and Atri Rudra. Worst-case optimal join algorithms: [extended abstract]. In *PODS*, pages 37–48. ACM, 2012.

[22] Hung Q. Ngo, Christopher Re, and Atri Rudra. Skew strikes back: New developments in the theory of join algorithms. *Sigmod Record*, 42(4):5–16, 2013.

[23] Dung Nguyen, Molham Aref, Martin Bravenboer, George Kollias, Hung Q. Ngo, Christopher Ré, and Atri Rudra. Join processing for graph patterns: An old dog with new tricks. arXiv:1503.04169, 2015.

[24] Chris Okasaki. *Purely Functional Data Structures*. Cambridge University Press, Cambridge, UK, 1999.

[25] D. P. Reed. Naming and synchronization in a decentralized computer system. Technical report, Cambridge, MA, USA, 1978.

[26] Todd L. Veldhuizen. Incremental maintenance for leapfrog triejoin. *CoRR*, abs/1303.5313, 2013.

[27] Todd L. Veldhuizen. Leapfrog triejoin: A simple, worst-case optimal join algorithm. In *ICDT*, pages 96–106, 2014. Also CoRR abs/1210.0481 (2012).

[28] Todd L. Veldhuizen. Transaction repair: Full serializability without locks. *CoRR*, abs/1403.5645, 2014.

Function Symbols in Tuple-Generating Dependencies: Expressive Power and Computability

Georg Gottlob
University of Oxford
georg.gottlob@cs.ox.ac.uk

Reinhard Pichler
Vienna University of Technology
pichler@dbai.tuwien.ac.at

Emanuel Sallinger
Vienna University of Technology
sallinger@dbai.tuwien.ac.at

ABSTRACT

Tuple-generating dependencies – for short tgds – have been a staple of database research throughout most of its history. Yet one of the central aspects of tgds, namely the role of existential quantifiers, has not seen much investigation so far. When studying dependencies, existential quantifiers and – in their Skolemized form – function symbols are often viewed as two ways to express the same concept. But in fact, tgds are quite restrictive in the way that functional terms can occur.

In this paper, we investigate the role of function symbols in dependency formalisms that go beyond tgds. Among them is the powerful class of SO tgds and the intermediate class of nested tgds. In addition, we employ Henkin quantifiers – a well-known concept in the area of logic – and introduce Henkin tgds to gain a more fine-grained understanding of the role of function symbols in dependencies.

For members of these families of dependency classes, we investigate their expressive power, that is, when one dependency class is equivalently representable in another class of dependencies. In addition, we analyze the computability of query answering under many of the well-known syntactical decidability criteria for tgds as well as the complexity of model checking.

Categories and Subject Descriptors

H.2 [**Database Management**]: General

General Terms

Theory; Algorithms

Keywords

Dependencies; Function Symbols; Expressive Power

PODS'15, May 31–June 4, 2015, Melbourne, Victoria, Australia.

ACM 978-1-4503-2757-2/15/05 ...$15.00.
http://dx.doi.org/10.1145/2745754.2745756 .

1. Introduction

Tuple-generating dependencies – for short tgds – have been a staple of database research throughout most of its history. Tgds appear under many different names in many different areas. They are often called existential rules in the area of artificial intelligence [5, 6]. In the area of data exchange [13] and integration [23], tgds are the most common types of dependencies used for formulating so-called schema mappings, which are high-level specifications of the relationship between two databases.

Yet one of the central aspects of tgds, namely the role of existential quantifiers, has not seen much investigation so far. When studying dependencies, existential quantifiers and – in their Skolemized form – function symbols are often seen as two ways to express the same concept. But in fact, tgds are quite restrictive in the way that functional terms can occur. Consider the following tgd based on employees, their departments and the department managers:

$$\forall e, d\ \mathsf{Emp}(e, d) \to \exists dm\, \mathsf{Mgr}(e, dm)$$

To understand the exact form of existential quantification, let us look at its Skolemized form, where the implicit dependence of the existential quantifier is made explicit using function symbols. That is, the variable dm is replaced by a term based on the function f_{dm}.

$$\exists f_{\mathsf{dm}}\, \forall e, d\ \mathsf{Emp}(e, d) \to \mathsf{Mgr}(e, f_{\mathsf{dm}}(e, d))$$

Observe that any functional term contains the full set of universally quantified variables from the antecedent. More concretely, the function f_{dm} representing the department manager depends on both the department and the employee.

In contrast, what we would probably like to express is that the department manager only depends on the department. That is, the dependency

$$\exists f_{\mathsf{dm}}\, \forall e, d\ \mathsf{Emp}(e, d) \to \mathsf{Mgr}(e, f_{\mathsf{dm}}(d))$$

This dependency cannot be expressed by a logically equivalent set of tgds[1]. However, there are more powerful dependency languages than tgds, most importantly SO tgds [14][2]. The key feature of SO tgds is the use

[1]In Section 4 we will show the stronger result that not even a relaxation of logical equivalence allows the simulation of a similar dependency by a set of tgds.

[2]Note that as originally defined, SO tgds are required to be so-called source-to-target (s-t) dependencies. In the context of this paper, we do not restrict any dependency formalism to s-t unless explicitly mentioned.

of function symbols, and indeed, the above formula is an SO tgd. SO tgds and their subclass plain SO tgds [4] were shown to be particularly suited for expressing composition and inversion of schema mappings, two key operators for schema mapping management [7]. For recent surveys on the many problems studied for schema mappings based on tgds and SO tgds, see e.g. [3, 21].

However, the power of SO tgds comes at a cost: many reasoning tasks become undecidable. For example, even logical equivalence between s-t SO tgds is undecidable [15]. For a survey see e.g. [27].

Yet, there is a middle ground between tgds and SO tgds: nested tgds [16]. Nested tgds were introduced as part of IBM's Clio system [19], which is now part of the InfoSphere BigInsights suite. It has recently been shown that nested tgds have a number of advantages in terms of decidability of reasoning tasks, in particular that equivalence of s-t nested tgds is decidable [22]. Let us now return to our running example. If our schema in addition contains a relation Dep representing departments, then we can express our dependency as the following nested tgd:

$$\forall d\ \mathsf{Dep}(d) \rightarrow \exists dm\,[\forall e\,\mathsf{Emp}(e,d) \rightarrow \mathsf{Mgr}(e,dm)]$$

Looking at our nested tgd in its Skolemized form and normalized to a single implication, again the distinctive feature compared to tgds is the much more flexible use of terms based on function symbols:

$$\exists f_{\mathsf{dm}}\,\forall e,d\ \mathsf{Dep}(d) \wedge \mathsf{Emp}(e,d) \rightarrow \mathsf{Mgr}(e, f_{\mathsf{dm}}(d))$$

We have seen that nested tgds are one way to avoid the complexity of SO tgds, but still be able to model interesting domains. They have however one major restriction: they can only model hierarchical relationships (i.e., the argument lists of Skolem functions must form a tree). However, there are natural relationships that can not be captured by nested tgds. Let us extend our example as follows: for every employee, we want to create an employee ID. We can express this as an SO tgd:

$$\exists f_{\mathsf{eid}}, f_{\mathsf{dm}}\,\forall e,d\ \mathsf{Emp}(e,d) \rightarrow \mathsf{Mgr}(f_{eid}(e), f_{dm}(d))$$

Nested tgds are not able to express this dependency. So how can we gain a more fine-grained understanding of, in general, not hierarchical relationships without resorting to SO tgds? To answer this question, let us look at a well-known formalism from logic which can help us in that regard. In logic, Henkin quantifiers [29, 8] are a tool to gain a fine-grained control over the way function symbols can occur in the Skolemized form of formulas. Let us write our dependency using a (so-called standard) Henkin quantifier:

$$\begin{pmatrix} \forall d\,\exists dm \\ \forall e\,\exists eid \end{pmatrix} \mathsf{Emp}(e,d) \rightarrow \mathsf{Mgr}(eid, dm)$$

where the quantifier prefix means that the existential variable dm only depends on the department d, and the existential variable eid only depends on the employee e. We shall call such Henkin-quantified rules "Henkin tgds".

Altogether, we have described four "families" of tgds so far: tgds as the least expressive, SO tgds as the most expressive and nested tgds and Henkin tgds in between. In Figure 1, we summarize all the classes of tgds relevant in this paper. We will give formal preliminaries for tgds, SO tgds and nested tgds in Section 2. In Section 3 we will formally introduce Henkin tgds as well as discuss normalization of nested tgds. Immediately, this syntactical inclusion diagram raises the question:

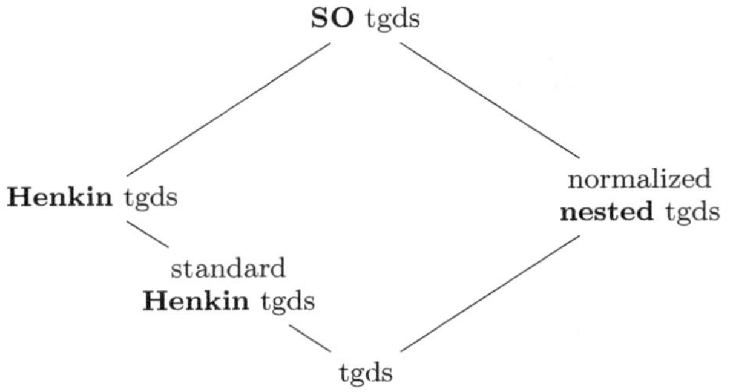

Figure 1: *Hasse diagram of syntactical inclusion between dependency classes in their Skolemized form. An edge denotes that every dependency of the lower class is also a dependency of the upper class.*

- What is the relative expressive power of the given classes? That is, when can we represent tgds from one class as equivalent tgds in another class?

We shall fully answer this question for all classes in Figure 1. It will turn out that the semantical inclusion diagram (given later in Section 4) looks a bit different than the syntactical inclusion diagram in Figure 1.

A central task for database systems is query answering. Given a database, a set of dependencies, and typically a conjunctive query, the task of query answering is to compute the set of certain answers to that conjunctive query. However, query answering for tgds is in general undecidable [20]. Hence, numerous criteria for ensuring decidability have been introduced throughout the last few years. We give an overview by looking at the three major "families" (illustrated in Figure 2).

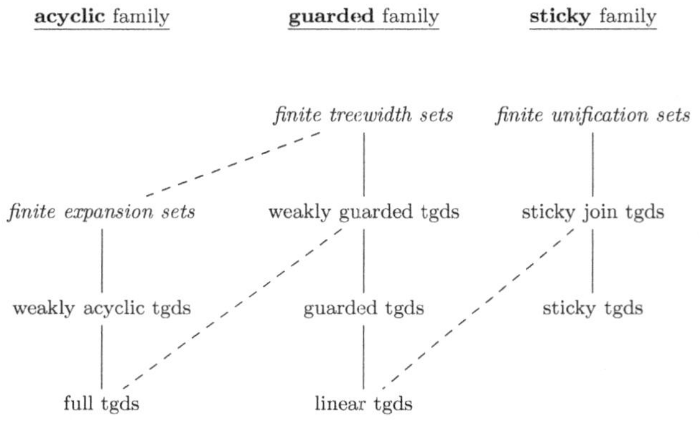

Figure 2: *Hasse diagram based on [24] showing the three major families for decidable query answering of tgds. Solid edges denote inclusions inside the families, dashed edges denote inclusions between the families.*

The best-known family of criteria for ensuring decidable query answering is that of *acyclic*, *weakly acyclic* and *full* tgds [13]. A second family of criteria centers around *guarded* tgds [9], its subset *linear* tgds and its generalization *weakly guarded* tgds [9]. A third family is that of *sticky* tgds [10, 12] The *sticky* and *guarded* (in particular *linear*) based families were combined in the criterion called *sticky join* tgds [11]. A semantic categorization of the different decidable fragments of tgds was done in [5, 6]. The *acyclicity* family is member of tgds with *finite expansion sets* (fes). The *guarded* family is member of tgds with *finite treewidth sets* (fts), a superclass of *fes*. The *sticky* family is member of tgds with *finite unification sets* (fus).

The complex landscape of decidability criteria thus raises the question:

- Where is the decidability/undecidability border for nested, Henkin, and SO tgds, in particular under the three "families" (weakly-)acyclic, guarded and sticky?

Apart from query answering, a second central problem with any logical formalism is model checking. Given a database and a set of dependencies, the task of model checking is to answer whether or not the database satisfies all dependencies.

For tgds, query and combined complexity was shown to be Π_2P-complete [2] (cf. [4]) while – as tgds are first-order formulas – data complexity is in AC_0. For SO tgds, data complexity was shown to be NP-complete [14] and query and combined complexity is known to be NEXPTIME-complete [25]. From these results, we can already derive some bounds for other formalisms, since lower bounds propagate along generalizations and upper bounds propagate along specialization. So the immediate question is:

- What is the precise (data/query/combined) complexity of model checking for nested tgds and Henkin tgds?

Organization and main results. In Section 2, we give preliminaries and in particular recall the classical formalisms of tgds, SO tgds and nested tgds. In Section 3, we introduce Henkin tgds, and discuss normalization of nested tgds. A conclusion and outlook to future work are given in Section 7. Our main results are detailed in Sections 4-6, namely:

- *Expressive Power.* In Section 4, we compare the expressive power of the dependency classes given in Figure 1. Interestingly, we obtain that nested tgds can always be transformed into a logically equivalent set of Henkin tgds. In contrast, we show that a number of inclusions are proper for other classes, in total obtaining a complete picture of the relative expressive power of all classes in Figure 1.
- *Query Answering.* In Section 5, we consider query answering for the dependency classes given in Figure 1. In particular, we show that even when assuming our dependencies to be *both* guarded and sticky, atomic query answering is undecidable for standard Henkin tgds and nested tgds, the two lowest extensions of tgds given in Figure 1. For standard Henkin tgds, undecidability holds even for linear dependencies. In contrast, weak acyclicity guarantees decidability of query answering even for SO tgds. Likewise, imposing a further restriction on linear Henkin tgds leads to decidability. In total, for all discussed dependency classes, we draw a clear border of decidability/undecidability in Figure 2.
- *Model Checking.* In Section 6, we consider the model checking problem. We show that Henkin tgds are NEXPTIME-complete in query and combined complexity and NP-complete in data complexity. Hardness holds even for standard Henkin tgds. We also show that nested tgds are PSPACE-complete in query and combined complexity (while data complexity is known to be in AC_0). Thus we complete the picture of complexity for all the dependency classes in Figure 1.

2. Preliminaries

We assume basic familiarity with logic (predicate logic, Skolemization), complexity and database theory [1].

Schemas, instances, and homomorphisms. A *schema* $\mathcal{R}$ is a finite sequence $\langle R_1, \ldots, R_k \rangle$ of relation symbols, where each R_i has a fixed arity. An *instance* I over $\mathcal{R}$, or an $\mathcal{R}$*-instance*, is a sequence $(R_1^I, \ldots, R_k^I)$, where each R_i^I is a finite relation of the same arity as R_i. We will often use R_i to denote both the relation symbol and the relation R_i^I that instantiates it. A *fact* of an instance I (over $\mathcal{R}$) is an expression $R_i^I(v_1, \ldots, v_m)$ (or simply $R_i(v_1, \ldots, v_m)$), where R_i is a relation symbol of $\mathcal{R}$ and $(v_1, \ldots, v_m) \in R_i^I$.

Sometimes it is beneficial to split a schema into two disjoint parts: Let $\mathcal{S}$ and $\mathcal{T}$ be two schemas with no relation symbols in common. We refer to $\mathcal{S}$ as the *source schema*, and $\mathcal{T}$ as the *target schema*. Similarly, we refer to $\mathcal{S}$-instances as *source instances*, and $\mathcal{T}$-instances as *target instances*. We assume the presence of two kinds of values, namely *constants* and *(labeled) nulls*. We also assume that the active domains of source instances consists of constants; the active domains of target instances may consist of constants and nulls.

Let J_1 and J_2 be two instances. A function h is a *homomorphism* from J_1 to J_2 if the following hold: (i) for every constant c, we have that $h(c) = c$; and (ii) for every relation symbol R in $\mathcal{R}$ and every tuple $(a_1, \ldots, a_n) \in R^{J_1}$, we have that $(h(a_1), \ldots, h(a_n)) \in R^{J_2}$. We use the notation $J_1 \to J_2$ to denote that there is a homomorphism from J_1 to J_2. We say that J_1 is *homomorphically equivalent* to J_2, written $J_1 \leftrightarrow J_2$, if $J_1 \to J_2$ and $J_2 \to J_1$. A minimal subinstance of J that is homomorphically equivalent to J is called a *core* of J. All cores of an instance are isomorphic [18]. Hence, it is justified to speak of *the* core of an instance J, denoted *core*(J).

Tgds. A *tuple-generating dependency* (in short, *tgd*) σ is a first-order sentence of the form

$$\forall \bar{x}(\varphi(\bar{x}) \to \exists \bar{y} \psi(\bar{x}, \bar{y}))$$

where $\varphi(\bar{x})$ is a conjunction of atoms, each variable in $\bar{x}$ occurs in at least one atom in $\varphi(\bar{x})$, and $\psi(\bar{x}, \bar{y})$ is a conjunction of atoms with variables in $\bar{x}$ and $\bar{y}$. If $\bar{y}$ is empty, then σ is called *full*. If φ consists solely of atoms over a schema $\mathcal{S}$ and ψ consists solely of atoms over a schema $\mathcal{T}$, we call σ a *source-to-target* (s-t) tgd. For simplicity, we will often suppress writing the universal quantifiers $\forall\bar{x}$ in formulas of the above form.

SO tgds. *Second-order tgds*, or *SO tgds*, were introduced in [14], where it was shown that SO tgds are needed to specify the composition of an arbitrary number of schema mappings based on s-t tgds. Before we formally define SO tgds, we need to define *terms*. Given collections $\bar{x}$ of variables and $\bar{f}$ of function symbols, a *term (based on $\bar{x}$ and $\bar{f}$)* is defined recursively as follows: (1) Every variable in $\bar{x}$ is a term; (2) If f is a k-ary function symbol in $\bar{f}$ and $t_1, \ldots, t_k$ are terms, then $f(t_1, \ldots, t_k)$ is a term.

A *second-order tuple-generating dependency (SO tgd)* is a formula σ of the form:

$$\exists\bar{f}((\forall\bar{x}_1(\varphi_1 \to \psi_1)) \wedge ... \wedge (\forall\bar{x}_n(\varphi_n \to \psi_n)))$$

where (1) Each member of $\bar{f}$ is a function symbol. (2) Each φ_i is a conjunction of (i) atoms $S(y_1, ..., y_k)$, where S is a k-ary relation symbol and $y_1, \ldots, y_k$ are variables in $\bar{x}_i$, not necessarily distinct, and (ii) equalities of the form $t = t'$ where t and t' are terms based on $\bar{x}_i$ and $\bar{f}$. (3) Each ψ_i is a conjunction of atoms $T(t_1, ..., t_l)$, where T is an l-ary relation symbol and $t_1, \ldots, t_l$ are terms based on $\bar{x}_i$ and $\bar{f}$. (4) Each variable in $\bar{x}_i$ appears in some atomic formula of φ_i.

Let $\mathcal{S}$ be a source schema and $\mathcal{T}$ a target schema. If all φ_i consist solely of atoms over $\mathcal{S}$ and all ψ_i consist solely of atoms over $\mathcal{T}$, we say that σ is *source-to-target*. Note that in the original definition [14], SO tgds are defined to be always source-to-target. In this paper, we do not make that assumption and use the name "SO tgds" to refer to not necessarily s-t dependencies, while we specifically speak of "s-t SO tgds" when it is necessary to refer to the source-to-target case. Let us give an example of an (s-t) SO tgd.

$$\exists f_{\mathsf{mgr}}(\forall e(\mathsf{Emp}(e) \to \mathsf{Mgr}(e, f_{\mathsf{mgr}}(e))) \wedge$$
$$\forall e(\mathsf{Emp}(e) \wedge (e = f_{\mathsf{mgr}}(e)) \to \mathsf{SelfMgr}(e)))$$

The formula expresses the property that every employee has a manager, and if an employee is the manager of himself/herself, then he/she is a self-manager [14].

Note that SO tgds allow for nested terms and for equalities between terms. A nested term is a functional term which contains a functional term as an argument. A *plain SO tgd* is an SO tgd that contains no nested terms and no equalities. For example, the preceding SO tgd is not plain, while the following SO tgd (expressing that if two employees are in some relationship – e.g., working in the same project – also their manager are in some relationship) is plain

$$\exists f_{\mathsf{mgr}}\, \forall e_1, e_2\, (\mathsf{Emps}(e_1, e_2) \to \mathsf{Mgrs}(f_{\mathsf{mgr}}(e_1), f_{\mathsf{mgr}}(e_2)))$$

The properties of plain SO tgds were recently investigated in [4]. In what follows, we will often suppress writing the existential second-order quantifiers and the universal first-order quantifiers in front of SO tgds.

Nested tgds. Fix a partition of the set of first-order variables into two disjoint infinite sets X and Y. A *nested tgd* [14, 28] is a first-order sentence that can be generated by the following recursive definition:

$$\chi ::= \alpha \mid \forall\bar{x}\,(\beta_1 \wedge \ldots \wedge \beta_k \to \exists\bar{y}\,(\chi_1 \wedge \ldots \wedge \chi_\ell))$$

where each $x_i \in X$, each $y_i \in Y$, α is a relational atom, and each β_j is a relational atom containing only variables from X, such that each x_i occurs in some β_j. As an example, the following formula is a nested tgd:

$$\forall d\; \mathsf{Dep}(d) \to \exists dm\, \mathsf{Dep}'(d, dm) \wedge$$
$$[\forall e\, \mathsf{Emp}(e, d) \to \mathsf{Mgr}(e, d, dm)]$$

Note that the choice of brackets (round or square) and the weight of the font (normal or bold) is for emphasizing the nesting structure only and has no syntactical significance.

A nested tgd σ contains a number of *parts* σ_i. Informally, σ_i is an implicational formula that contains conjunctions of atoms on both sides (but no nested implications). As an example, the parts of the preceding nested tgd are

- $\forall d\; \mathsf{Dep}(d) \to \exists dm\, \mathsf{Dep}'(d, dm)$
- $\forall e\, \mathsf{Emp}(e, d) \to \mathsf{Mgr}(e, d, dm)$

In our examples, we refer to parts of nested tgds using labels. The way of inline labeling of parts which we use throughout this paper is illustrated below by a nested tgd τ with three parts τ_1, τ_2, τ_3:

$$\forall d\, \mathsf{Dep}(d) \to \exists d'\, \mathsf{Dep}'(d') \wedge \qquad (\tau_1)$$
$$[\forall g\, \mathsf{Grp}(d, g) \to \exists g' \mathsf{Grp}'(d', g') \wedge \qquad (\tau_2)$$
$$[\forall e\, \mathsf{Emp}(d, g, e) \to \mathsf{Emp}'(d', g', e)]] \qquad (\tau_3)$$

It is often convenient to consider *Skolemized nested tgds*, in which every existential variable y is replaced by the Skolem term $f(\bar{x})$ where f is a fresh function symbol and $\bar{x}$ is the vector of universally quantified variables in the part σ_i in which $\exists y$ occurs, and in the ancestors of σ_i. Note that we assume existential variables in different parts to be renamed apart. The Skolemized version of nested tgd τ above has the following form:

$$\exists \boldsymbol{f_{\mathsf{d}}}, \boldsymbol{f_{\mathsf{g}}}\, \mathsf{Dep}(d) \to \mathsf{Dep}'(f_{\mathsf{d}}(d)) \wedge \qquad (\tau_1)$$
$$[\mathsf{Grp}(d, g) \to \mathsf{Grp}'(f_{\mathsf{d}}(d), f_{\mathsf{g}}(d, g)) \wedge \qquad (\tau_2)$$
$$[\mathsf{Emp}(d, g, e) \to \mathsf{Emp}'(f_{\mathsf{d}}(d), f_{\mathsf{g}}(d, g), e)]] \qquad (\tau_3)$$

Note that syntactically, a Skolemized nested tgd is not necessarily an SO tgd, as it may contain nested implications. However, given a nested tgd it is easy to create a logically equivalent SO tgd where the number of parts of the SO tgd is the same as the number of parts of the nested tgd. Thus one can, informally, consider nested tgds as a subclass of SO tgds. We will discuss this issue in detail in Section 3.

Queries. A conjunctive query (CQ) q over a schema $\mathcal{R}$ with free variables $\bar{y}$ is a logical formula of the form

$$\exists\bar{x}\,(A_1 \wedge \ldots \wedge A_n)$$

where each A_i is a relational atom over $\mathcal{R}$ with variables from $\bar{x} \cup \bar{y}$, where $\bar{x}$ and $\bar{y}$ are disjoint. If $\bar{y}$ is empty, we call q a Boolean conjunctive query. Given a database instance I, the set of answers $q(I)$ to a query q is the set $\{\bar{y} \mid I \models q\}$. Given a set Σ of dependencies and a database instance I, the *certain answers* to a conjunctive query q w.r.t. I are those which are answers over all database instances $\{I' \mid I \subseteq I' \wedge I' \models \Sigma\}$. Given a set of source-to-target dependencies, queries are usually posed against the target schema only.

The *query answering* problem has as input a database instance I, a set of dependencies Σ, a query q and a tuple t. The question is whether t is contained in all certain answers to q w.r.t. I and Σ. The problem is called *atomic query answering* if query q consists of a single atom.

Equivalence. Two sets of dependencies Σ_1 and Σ_2 are called *logically equivalent*, written $\Sigma_1 \equiv \Sigma_2$ or $\Sigma_1 \equiv_{\mathsf{log}} \Sigma_2$, if they have the same models. That is, $I \models \Sigma_1$ holds if and only if $I \models \Sigma_2$ holds. They are called *CQ-equivalent*, written $\Sigma_1 \equiv_{\mathsf{CQ}} \Sigma_2$ if they have the same certain answers over all conjunctive queries q and database instances I. Clearly, logical equivalence implies CQ-equivalence, but the converse does not necessarily hold. Note that logical and CQ-equivalence always consider dependencies over the same schema.

3. Henkin and Normalized Nested tgds

So far we have recalled tgds (the bottom part of Figure 1) and SO tgds (the top part of Figure 1), and we have started giving preliminaries for nested tgds. In this section, our main goal is to introduce Henkin tgds and their various flavors. After that, based on the definition of nested tgds given in the preliminaries, we will discuss how to treat nested tgds as a subclass of SO tgds.

3.1 Henkin tgds

We first introduce Henkin quantifiers and then use them for building dependencies.

A *Henkin quantifier* (cf. [8, 29]) is given by

- a set of first-order quantifiers
- a strict partial order between these quantifiers (i.e., an irreflexive, transitive relation) [3]

The semantics of Henkin quantifiers is given by their Skolemization, that is, the Skolem term of an existential variable contains all universally quantified variables that are preceding the existential variable in the given partial order. For example, recall the following plain SO tgd τ from the introduction:

$$\exists f_{\mathsf{eid}}, f_{\mathsf{dm}}\, \forall e, d\ \mathsf{Emp}(e,d) \rightarrow \mathsf{Mgr}(f_{eid}(e), f_{dm}(d))$$

This dependency could be obtained through Skolemization of the formula

$$Q\ \mathsf{Emp}(e,d) \rightarrow \mathsf{Mgr}(eid, dm)$$

under a Henkin quantifier Q given by the partial order $\prec$ with $\forall e \prec \exists eid$ and $\forall d \prec \exists dm$.

The first important observation is that it is only relevant which universal quantifiers come before an existential quantifier. This is intuitively clear when inspecting the Skolemization of a formula, as the arguments of the Skolem functions for an existential quantifier are purely determined by the scope of the universal quantifiers. This relevant part of the order is called the *essential order* [29].

A Henkin quantifier is called *standard* if

- the strict partial order consists of (disjoint) chains (i.e., it is the disjoint union of a set of linear orders)
- the strict partial order is already an essential order (i.e., every chain consists of universal quantifiers followed by existential quantifiers) [4]

Standard Henkin quantifiers are usually denoted as

$$\begin{pmatrix} \forall \bar{x}_1\ \exists \bar{y}_1 \\ \cdots\ \cdots \\ \forall \bar{x}_n\ \exists \bar{y}_n \end{pmatrix}$$

where $\bar{x}_1$ to $\bar{x}_n$ and $\bar{y}_1$ to $\bar{y}_n$ are vectors of variables, and all variables are distinct. In this notation, each of the rows of the quantifier represents a chain of the strict partial order. For example, our dependency τ:

$$\mathsf{Emp}(e,d) \rightarrow \mathsf{Mgr}(f_{\mathsf{eid}}(e), f_{\mathsf{dm}}(d))$$

can be produced through Skolemization of the formula

$$\begin{pmatrix} \forall d\, \exists dm \\ \forall e\, \exists eid \end{pmatrix} \mathsf{Emp}(e,d) \rightarrow \mathsf{Mgr}(eid, dm)$$

In contrast, note that the following expression σ does *not* contain a standard Henkin quantifier

$$\begin{pmatrix} \forall x_1\ \forall x_2\ \exists y_1 \\ \forall x_2\ \forall x_3\ \exists y_2 \\ \forall x_3\ \forall x_1\ \exists y_3 \end{pmatrix} \varphi(x_1, x_2, x_3, y_1, y_2, y_3)$$

This is the case, since the chains are not disjoint. Note that, in first-order logic (with equality), every positive occurrence of a Henkin quantifier can be expressed by a standard Henkin quantifier [8]. For example, σ can be expressed as:

$$\begin{pmatrix} \forall x_1\ \forall x_2\ \exists y_1 \\ \forall x_2'\ \forall x_3\ \exists y_2 \\ \forall x_3'\ \forall x_1'\ \exists y_3 \end{pmatrix} \begin{array}{r} [x_1 = x_1' \wedge x_2 = x_2' \wedge x_3 = x_3'] \rightarrow \\ \varphi(x_1, x_2, x_3, y_1, y_2, y_3) \end{array}$$

That is, all occurrences of a variable are given unique names and associated using equalities. However, this is not a technique we can use for defining a lightweight subclass of plain SO tgds, since plain SO tgds do not allow equalities in the antecedent. Thus for our purposes, whether we have standard Henkin quantifiers or Henkin quantifiers makes a difference.

We are now ready to give a formal definition of the family of Henkin tgds.

Definition 3.1 *Let $\mathcal{C}$ be a class of Henkin quantifiers, let $\mathcal{Q}$ be a Henkin quantifier from $\mathcal{C}$. Then a $\mathcal{C}$-Henkin tgd is a formula of the form*

$$\mathcal{Q}\ (\varphi(\bar{x}) \rightarrow \psi(\bar{x}, \bar{y}))$$

where $\bar{x}$ consists of universally quantified variables in $\mathcal{Q}$ and $\bar{y}$ consists of existentially quantified variables in $\mathcal{Q}$.

In particular, if $\mathcal{C}$ is the class of all Henkin quantifiers, we simply speak of *Henkin tgds* and if $\mathcal{C}$ is the class of standard Henkin quantifiers, we speak of *standard Henkin tgds*. Furthermore, we will also use the class where the partial order of the Henkin quantifier is tree-structured, hence *tree Henkin tgds* (or more formally,

[3] Sometimes also a non-strict partial order is assumed. Here we follow [29] and assume a strict partial order.

[4] We make the following assumption here which deviates from the definition of [29], to ensure that normal FO quantifiers are standard Henkin quantifiers: A chain may end in multiple existential quantifiers.

every connected component of the graph of the partial order is a tree). From here on, we will always consider the Skolemized form of dependencies.

3.2 Normalized and Simple Nested tgds

So far, we have described all dependency classes in Figure 1, except for nested tgds. This is for a simple reason: In terms of syntax, a nested tgd is not necessarily an SO tgd, as it may contain nested implications. Yet intuitively, one can undo this nesting by applying well-known equivalences from first-order logic. We will formalize this "normalization" now. Let us first consider the following (Skolemized) nested tgd τ as an example:

$$\exists \boldsymbol{f_\mathsf{d}}, \boldsymbol{f_\mathsf{g}}\ \mathsf{Dep}(d) \rightarrow \mathsf{Dep}'(f_\mathsf{d}(d)) \wedge \quad (\tau_1)$$
$$[\mathsf{Grp}(d,g) \rightarrow \mathsf{Grp}'(f_\mathsf{d}(d), f_\mathsf{g}(d,g)) \wedge \quad (\tau_2)$$
$$[\mathsf{Emp}(d,g,e) \rightarrow \mathsf{Emp}'(f_\mathsf{d}(d), f_\mathsf{g}(d,g), e)]] \quad (\tau_3)$$

Intuitively, this nested tgd τ takes a three-level hierarchy of departments, groups and employees, and simply invents identifiers for departments and groups. Let us remove nesting levels one-by-one, starting at the innermost level. By using the fact that $\varphi \rightarrow (\psi \wedge [\varphi_1 \rightarrow \psi_1])$ is equivalent to $[\varphi \rightarrow \psi] \wedge [\varphi \wedge \varphi_1 \rightarrow \psi_1]$ we thus obtain the following two-level nested tgd:

$$\exists \boldsymbol{f_\mathsf{d}}, \boldsymbol{f_\mathsf{g}}\ \mathsf{Dep}(d) \rightarrow \mathsf{Dep}'(f_\mathsf{dep}(d)) \wedge \quad (\tau_1')$$
$$[\mathsf{Grp}(d,g) \rightarrow \mathsf{Grp}'(f_\mathsf{d}(d), f_\mathsf{g}(d,g))] \wedge \quad (\sigma_2)$$
$$[\mathsf{Grp}(d,g) \wedge \mathsf{Emp}(d,g,e) \rightarrow \mathsf{Emp}'(f_\mathsf{d}(d), f_\mathsf{g}(d,g), e)] \quad (\sigma_{23})$$

In particular, we have applied the equivalence to τ_1 and τ_2, obtaining σ_2 and σ_{23}. Let us now remove the outermost nesting level. This time, we have two nested dependencies σ_2 and σ_{23}, but the idea of applying the equivalence remains the same:

$$\exists \boldsymbol{f_\mathsf{d}}, \boldsymbol{f_\mathsf{g}}\ [\mathsf{Dep}(d) \rightarrow \mathsf{Dep}'(f_\mathsf{dep}(d))] \wedge \quad (\sigma_1)$$
$$[\mathsf{Dep}(d) \wedge \mathsf{Grp}(d,g) \rightarrow \mathsf{Grp}'(f_\mathsf{d}(d), f_\mathsf{g}(d,g))] \wedge \quad (\sigma_{12})$$
$$[\mathsf{Dep}(d) \wedge \mathsf{Grp}(d,g) \wedge \mathsf{Emp}(d,g,e) \rightarrow \mathsf{Emp}'(f_\mathsf{d}(d), f_\mathsf{g}(d,g), e)] \quad (\sigma_{123})$$

Thus, we now have a conjunction of three (non-nested) implications, all bound by the same quantifier prefix $\exists f_\mathsf{d}$, f_g or, in other words, a plain SO tgd. In Algorithm 1, we formally describe the transformations we have applied in our example. We thus get the following straightforward definition of normalization.

Definition 3.2 *Let τ be a nested tgd. The* normalized *form of τ is the plain SO tgd $\sigma =$ nested-to-so(τ).*

Using this definition, we speak of *normalized nested tgds*. We now have defined all dependency classes shown in Figure 1. Furthermore, in what follows, it will often be convenient to use the following restriction of SO tgds: We call an SO tgd *simple*, if it contains exactly one SO tgd part. Similarly, we can speak of *simple nested tgds* if a normalized nested tgd consists of only one SO tgd part. For example, our dependency $\sigma =$ nested-to-so(τ) is not a simple nested tgd, as it contains three SO tgd parts.

Algorithm 1: nested-to-so
Input: nested tgd τ in Skolemized form
Output: plain SO tgd σ s.t. $\sigma \equiv_{\log} \tau$

1. Apply the following rewrite step recursively (innermost nesting level to outermost level):

$$\overbrace{\varphi \rightarrow}^{\text{tgd}} (\psi \wedge [\overbrace{\varphi_1 \rightarrow \psi_1}^{\text{plain SO tgd}}] \wedge \ldots \wedge [\overbrace{\varphi_n \rightarrow \psi_n}^{\text{plain SO tgd}}])$$
$$\Downarrow$$
$$\varphi \rightarrow \psi \wedge \bigwedge_{i \in \{1,\ldots,n\}} \underbrace{[\varphi \wedge \varphi_i \rightarrow \psi_i]}_{\text{plain SO tgd}}$$

2. Return σ, which is the result of recursively applying the rewrite rule.

4. Expressive Power

In this section, we investigate the relative expressive power of the dependency classes, that is, when for a given dependency in one class, we can find a logically equivalent set of dependencies in other classes. An overview of this semantical relationship can be found in Figure 3.

In the previous section, we have seen that normalized nested tgds allow the quantification of Skolem function symbols over several dependencies, whereas Henkin tgds only allow quantification over each individual dependency. Nevertheless, quite surprisingly, we shall show in this section that nested tgds can always be expressed as a logically equivalent set of Henkin tgds, indicated by the bold (blue) edge in the Hasse diagram. We shall give this result later in this section. The dotted (red) edges in the Hasse diagram indicate that for a given set of dependencies, not even a CQ-equivalent set of dependencies exists. In particular, all dotted edges together imply that

1. absent (non-implied) edges in the Hasse diagram do not exist. That is, standard Henkin and nested tgds are incomparable with regard to expressive power.
2. all edges denote proper containment. That is, for any two distinct classes, there exists a set of dependencies that separates these two classes.

We now proceed to show the separations (dotted or red edges) in Figure 3. We first separate standard Henkin tgds from nested tgds. We start by giving high-level ideas that will play a major role in the following proofs.

Idea 1: Basic Construction. All of our proofs that a set of dependencies $\Sigma \subseteq \mathcal{C}_1$ is not expressible as a CQ-equivalent set $\Pi \subseteq \mathcal{C}_2$ will proceed by contradiction, in particular along the following general lines:

1. assume that a CQ-equivalent set $\Pi \subseteq \mathcal{C}_2$ exists
2. define an instance I such that our dependencies have to create a particular "large" structure using the specific features of $\mathcal{C}_1$
3. show that $\mathcal{C}_2$ needs to "pass" nulls (values stemming from functional terms) to create the large structure (see Idea 2)
4. show that recursion is of little help for creating the large structure (see Idea 3)
5. derive a contradiction ◁

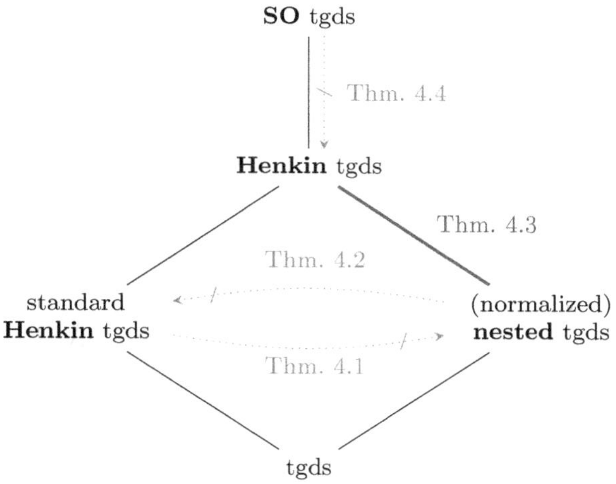

Figure 3: *Hasse diagram of the semantical inclusions between classes. A solid edge denotes that every set of dependencies from the lower class can be expressed as a logically equivalent set of dependencies from the upper class.*

Idea 2: "Passing of Nulls". Every class of dependencies has particular structures of nulls it can generate. As a simple example, nulls generated by a nested tgd have a tree structure, as can be seen in Skolemized form:

$$P(x_1) \wedge Q(x_1, x_2) \rightarrow R(f(x_1), g(x_1, x_2))$$

In this case (i.e., in the case that Skolem terms are at the corresponding positions), we say that the nulls are *directly generated* by our nested tgd. Yet this does not prevent more complex structures to be created by passing of nulls, i.e., dependencies of the form

$$\varphi \wedge R_i(\ldots, x, \ldots) \rightarrow \psi \wedge R_j(\ldots, x, \ldots)$$

where x is bound to a null value that is *passed* from R_i to R_j. Showing that passing of nulls is necessary to create more complex structures is essential in the proofs that follow. $\lhd$

Idea 3: "Recursion Poisoning". Apart from tgds in Σ that exhibit the actual behavior to create our "large" structure, we use dependencies that allow us to add additional atoms into that structure. Assume that our large structure is encoded using facts of the form $R(x_1, x_2, x_3)$. Then we add an additional source of such R facts through the simple copy tgd

$$R'(x_1, x_2, x_3) \rightarrow R(x_1, x_2, x_3)$$

This additional source of R facts allows us to forbid many of the potential recursive dependencies using R, as they would be violated by the "poisoned" facts introduced by the copying tgd. $\lhd$

We are now ready to separate standard Henkin tgds from nested tgds. We start by showing that there are standard Henkin tgds which are not expressible as nested tgds. Note that in Theorem 4.1 (and analogously in the subsequent separation theorems) we actually show a slightly stronger result, namely: even if we restrict standard Henkin tgds to *source-to-target* dependencies and allow *arbitrary* nested tgds, then, in general, standard Henkin tgds cannot be expressed by nested tgds.

Theorem 4.1 *There exists a set Σ of s-t standard Henkin tgds such that there is no set Π of (not necessarily s-t) nested tgds with $\Pi \equiv_{\mathsf{CQ}} \Sigma$.*

Proof (Sketch) Let Σ consist of dependencies

$$\begin{aligned} &P(x_1, x_2) \rightarrow Q(x_1, f(x_1)) \wedge \\ &\quad R(f(x_1), g(x_2)) \wedge S(g(x_2), x_2) && (\sigma_1) \\ &Q'(x_1, x_2) \rightarrow Q(x_1, x_2) && (\sigma_2) \\ &R'(x_1, x_2) \rightarrow R(x_1, x_2) && (\sigma_3) \\ &S'(x_1, x_2) \rightarrow S(x_1, x_2) && (\sigma_4) \end{aligned}$$

In essence, σ_1 is used for encoding the intended behavior, and σ_2 to σ_4 are used for the "recursion poisoning" technique described in Idea 3. Towards a contradiction, assume that there exists a set Π of nested tgds with $\Pi \equiv_{\mathsf{CQ}} \Sigma$. Following Idea 1, we now proceed to constructing our "large" instance I. Let n be greater than the size of Π (the number of atoms contained in Π). We construct the following source instance:

$$I = \{P(\mathsf{a}_i, \mathsf{b}_j) \mid 1 \leq i, j \leq n\}$$

The structure of the intended target instance is sketched below:

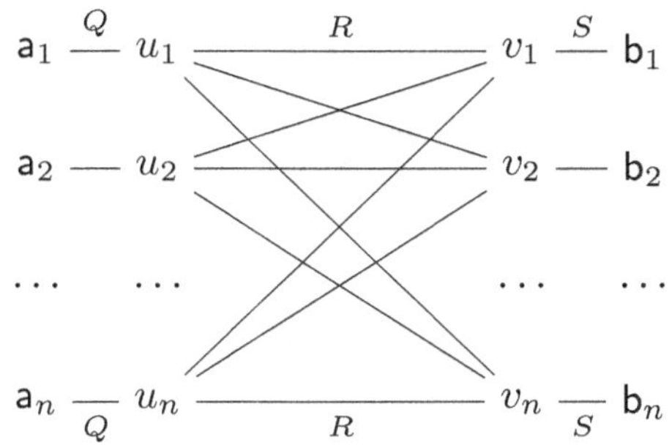

Intuitively, Σ produces a complete bipartite graph encoded through nulls u_i resp. v_j in R. On the left and right sides, this bipartite graph is "protected" by constants through Q and S facts. More formally, the constants contained in Q and S prevent the R facts from being mapped by a homomorphism to a single R fact in the core.

Following Idea 2, our next step is to show that "passing of nulls" is required. The high-level reason for why nested tgds cannot generate the structure shown in the above figure without passing of nulls is as follows: In atoms generated by multiple firings of a nested tgd, there is always a functional dependency between two attributes generated by nulls; e.g., in a normalized nested tgd of the form

$$P(x_1) \wedge Q(x_1, x_2) \rightarrow R(f(x_1), g(x_1, x_2))$$

there is a functional dependency from the attribute generated by g to f (if both functional terms contain the same argument list, then there is a functional dependency in both directions). Thus a nested tgd may directly generate only n of the n^2 edges of our complete bipartite graph, and passing of nulls is required to generate the rest.

We may now use the "recursion poisoning" technique according to Idea 3 to derive a contradiction. While we cannot go into the details (full details can be found in

Algorithm 2: nested-to-henkin
Input: nested tgd τ in Skolemized form
Output: Set Σ of Henkin tgds s.t. $\Sigma \equiv_{\mathsf{log}} \tau$

1. Apply the following rewrite step recursively (innermost nesting level to outermost level):

$$\overbrace{\varphi \rightarrow (\psi}^{\text{tgd}} \wedge \overbrace{[\exists \bar{f}_1\, \varphi_1 \rightarrow \psi_1]}^{\text{tree Henkin tgd}} \wedge \ldots \wedge \overbrace{[\exists \bar{f}_n\, \varphi_n \rightarrow \psi_n]}^{\text{tree Henkin tgd}})$$

$$\Downarrow$$

$$\bigwedge_{I \subseteq \{1,\ldots,n\}} \underbrace{[\exists \bar{f}\, \exists_{i \in I} \bar{f}_i\ \varphi \wedge \bigwedge_{i \in I} \varphi_i \rightarrow \psi \wedge \bigwedge_{i \in I} \psi_i]}_{\text{tree Henkin tgd}}$$

where $\bar{f}$ is the set of Skolem functions representing existential quantifiers of ψ, and all universally quantified variables of φ_i are assumed to be renamed apart.

2. Return $\Sigma = \{\sigma_1, \ldots, \sigma_k\}$ where $\sigma_1 \wedge \ldots \wedge \sigma_k$ is the result of recursively applying the rewriting rule.

the full version) the key idea is to extend source instance I to I' by Q', R' and S' facts that generate (both in Σ and Π) the corresponding Q, R and S facts in the target instance. In Σ, which is source-to-target, these additional target facts are of no concern. Yet in Π, which contains a target tgd τ for the "passing of nulls", the "poisoned" Q, R and S facts cause another triggering of the target tgd τ – thus producing additional facts which are not produced under Σ. This is a contradiction to our assumption that $\Pi \equiv_{\mathsf{CQ}} \Sigma$. □

We now show the reverse direction of the separation, namely that nested tgds are, in general, not expressible as standard Henkin tgds:

Theorem 4.2 *There exists a set Σ of s-t simple nested tgds such that there is no set Π of (not necessarily s-t) standard Henkin tgds with $\Pi \equiv_{\mathsf{CQ}} \Sigma$.*

We now show that the class of nested tgds is semantically contained in the class of tree Henkin tgds. That is, we show the following theorem:

Theorem 4.3 *Let τ be a nested tgd. Then there exists a set $\Sigma =$ nested-to-henkin(τ) of tree Henkin tgds such that $\Sigma \equiv_{\mathsf{log}} \tau$.*

The algorithm nested-to-henkin for converting a nested tgd into a logically equivalent set of Henkin tgds is given as Algorithm 2. Note that Algorithm 2 has the same general structure as Algorithm 1, which we already discussed in detail in Section 3. Let us now look at an example that shows the essence of the algorithm. Assume that we are given the following nested tgd τ (which we already used to illustrate Algorithm 1):

$$\exists \boldsymbol{f}_{\mathsf{d}}, \boldsymbol{f}_{\mathsf{g}}\ \mathsf{Dep}(d) \rightarrow \mathsf{Dep}'(f_{\mathsf{d}}(d)) \wedge \quad (\tau_1)$$
$$[\mathsf{Grp}(d,g) \rightarrow \mathsf{Grp}'(f_{\mathsf{d}}(d), f_{\mathsf{g}}(d,g)) \wedge \quad (\tau_2)$$
$$[\mathsf{Emp}(d,g,e) \rightarrow \mathsf{Emp}'(f_{\mathsf{d}}(d), f_{\mathsf{g}}(d,g), e)]] \quad (\tau_3)$$

Recall that the nested tgd τ takes a three-level hierarchy of departments, groups and employees, and simply invents identifiers for departments and groups. The basic principle of our algorithm nested-to-henkin is to remove nesting levels one-by-one, starting at the innermost level. Following the rewrite step illustrated in Algorithm 2, we thus produce the following two-level nested dependency:

$$\exists \boldsymbol{f}_{\mathsf{d}}\ \mathsf{Dep}(d) \rightarrow \mathsf{Dep}'(f_{\mathsf{dep}}(d)) \wedge \quad (\tau_1')$$
$$[\exists \boldsymbol{f}_{\mathsf{g}}\ \mathsf{Grp}(d,g) \rightarrow \mathsf{Grp}'(f_{\mathsf{d}}(d), f_{\mathsf{g}}(d,g))] \wedge \quad (\sigma_2)$$
$$[\exists \boldsymbol{f}_{\mathsf{g}}\ \mathsf{Grp}(d,g) \wedge \mathsf{Emp}(d,g,e) \rightarrow \mathsf{Grp}'(f_{\mathsf{d}}(d), f_{\mathsf{g}}(d,g)) \wedge \mathsf{Emp}'(f_{\mathsf{d}}(d), f_{\mathsf{g}}(d,g), e)] \quad (\sigma_{23})$$

The critical part of this step is that we have to show that logical equivalence is thus preserved. While the most obvious effect of the rewriting step is the growing number of atoms, the interesting part for logical equivalence is the "splitting" of the quantifiers: originally, we had just one quantifier $\exists f_{\mathsf{d}}$ and now we have two independent ones. Now let us apply the final rewrite step to observe something interesting:

$$\exists \boldsymbol{f}_{\mathsf{d}}, \boldsymbol{f}_{\mathsf{g}}\ \mathsf{Dep}(d) \rightarrow \mathsf{Dep}'(f_{\mathsf{d}}(d)) \quad (\sigma_1)$$
$$\exists \boldsymbol{f}_{\mathsf{d}}, \boldsymbol{f}_{\mathsf{g}}\ \mathsf{Dep}(d) \wedge \mathsf{Grp}(d,g) \rightarrow \mathsf{Dep}'(f_{\mathsf{d}}(d)) \wedge \mathsf{Grp}'(f_{\mathsf{d}}(d), f_{\mathsf{g}}(d,g)) \quad (\sigma_{12})$$
$$\exists \boldsymbol{f}_{\mathsf{d}}, \boldsymbol{f}_{\mathsf{g}}\ \mathsf{Dep}(d) \wedge \mathsf{Grp}(d,g) \wedge \mathsf{Emp}(d,g,e) \rightarrow \mathsf{Dep}'(f_{\mathsf{d}}(d)) \wedge \mathsf{Grp}'(f_{\mathsf{d}}(d), f_{\mathsf{g}}(d,g)) \wedge \mathsf{Emp}'(f_{\mathsf{d}}(d), f_{\mathsf{g}}(d,g), e) \quad (\sigma_{13})$$
$$\exists \boldsymbol{f}_{\mathsf{d}}, \boldsymbol{f}_{\mathsf{g}}\ \mathsf{Dep}(d) \wedge \mathsf{Grp}(d,g) \wedge \mathsf{Emp}(d,g,e) \wedge \mathsf{Grp}(d,g^\star) \rightarrow \mathsf{Dep}'(f_{\mathsf{d}}(d)) \wedge \mathsf{Grp}'(f_{\mathsf{d}}(d), f_{\mathsf{g}}(d,g)) \wedge \mathsf{Emp}'(f_{\mathsf{d}}(d), f_{\mathsf{g}}(d,g), e) \wedge \mathsf{Grp}'(f_{\mathsf{d}}(d), f_{\mathsf{g}}(d,g^\star)) \quad (\sigma_{123})$$

Indeed, the preceding four rules are Henkin tgds. Yet, while we previously had three dependencies, we now have four. The first three of them are verbose but relatively straightforward (simply containing the antecedents and conclusions of τ); the fourth dependency σ_{123} is more complex. To illustrate why σ_{123} is needed, let us look at a specific database instance. The essential parts of this instance are sketched below in hierarchical fashion:

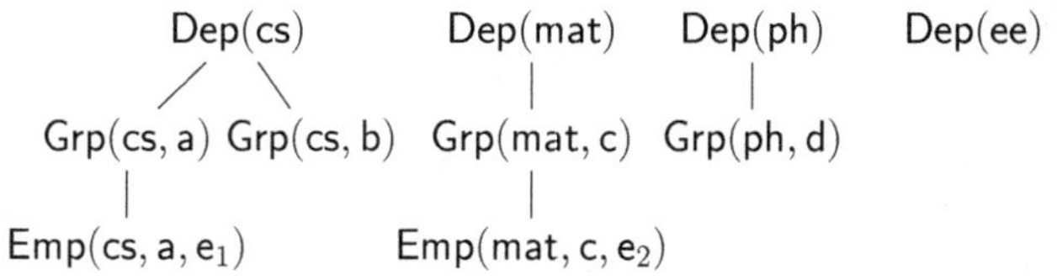

In this example, we see the departments of computer science (cs), mathematics (mat), physics (ph) and electrical engineering (ee). For departments mat, ph and ee, it can be checked that the set Σ' of Henkin tgds is sufficient, but for departments cs there is a problem: Consider an instance I containing all previously given facts with constant cs plus additional facts $\mathsf{Grp}'(n_{\mathsf{cs}}, n_{\mathsf{a}})$ and $\mathsf{Grp}'(n^\star_{\mathsf{cs}}, n_{\mathsf{b}})$, where all arguments are nulls. Notice that in the first atom, we have n_{cs} as the identifier for department cs, and a different identifier $n^\star_{\mathsf{cs}}$ in the second atom. Indeed, we have $I \models \Sigma'$ (since we can assign different values to $f_{\mathsf{d}}(\mathsf{cs})$ in σ_{12} and σ_{13}, as the function symbol is separately quantified in σ_{12} and σ_{13}), but $I \not\models \tau$ (since we can assign only one value to $f_{\mathsf{d}}(\mathsf{cs})$). However, once we add σ_{123}, we have that $\Sigma \equiv_{\mathsf{log}} \tau$.

Let us now make an observation concerning the algorithm nested-to-henkin: In a single step, it may produce exponentially many dependencies (notice that we consider all subsets of the index set I in Algorithm 2). Hence, in total, the algorithm may produce non-elementary (in the nesting depth and the number of parts) many Henkin tgds. While this behavior was not so apparent in our example, let us sketch what happens to a five-level nested tgd:

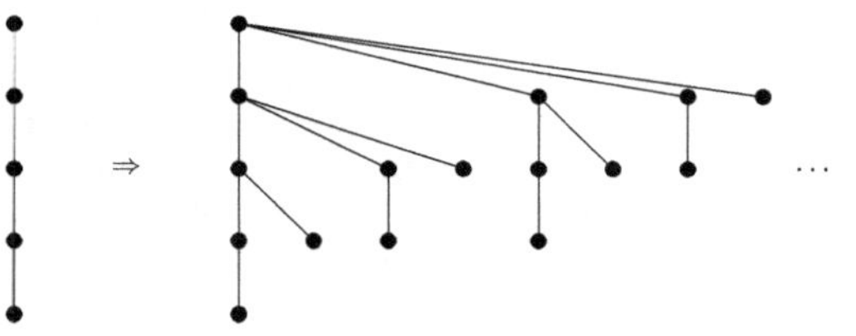

Intuitively, what we see sketched above on the left side is a five-level nested tgd (where each dot denotes a tgd part). On the right side, we see the tree structure covered by the largest Henkin tgd generated by Algorithm 2 (similar to how σ_{123} was the largest Henkin tgd generated by Algorithm 2 for our three-level nested tgd).

Altogether, the algorithm connects nested tgds, Henkin tgds and SO tgds in an interesting way: Obviously, nested tgds have a particular power, namely nesting of implications. SO tgds may emulate this power with only linear blow-up by using one of its powerful features, namely quantifier scope over entire conjunctions of implications (recall the normalization algorithm nested-to-so). Henkin tgds do not have this powerful quantifier scope. Yet, while potentially incurring non-elementary blow-up, they can emulate the power of nested tgds by providing a separate dependency for each possible tree structure of nulls. As future work, it would be interesting to see whether this blowup is indeed unavoidable.

Finally, we show the last missing part for completing Figure 3, namely that there are SO tgds which are not expressible as Henkin tgds:

Theorem 4.4 *There exists an s-t simple plain SO tgd σ such that there is no set Π of (not necessarily s-t) Henkin tgds for which $\Pi \equiv_{\mathsf{CQ}} \sigma$ holds.*

Getting back to the big picture, and in particular Figure 3, notice that the separation results shown in this section also imply separation results for all other edges in Figure 3 that are not covered by explicit results. In particular, since Theorems 4.1 and 4.2 separate standard Henkin tgds and normalized nested tgds from each other, they also separate these two classes from their subclass (tgds) and their superclass (Henkin tgds). So indeed, Figure 3 presents a complete picture of the expressive power of our dependency classes.

5. Query Answering

In this section, we study the problem of query answering. It is structured as follows. First, we show our undecidability results by introducing the problem we are going to reduce from, namely Post's Correspondence Problem. We then give the main ideas of the undecidability proof for linear standard Henkin tgds and show that undecidability also holds for simple nested tgds that are both sticky and guarded. Finally we proceed to decidability. Namely, we discuss that decidability holds in case of weak acyclicity and show that in a limited setting, decidability is also achievable for linear Henkin tgds.

Before we go into the details, let us informally describe what sticky [10] and guarded [9] dependencies are. Note that allowing plain SO tgds rather than ordinary tgds has no effect on the definition of these restrictions.

- a plain SO tgd is called *guarded* if there exists an atom G in the antecedent that contains all variables occurring in the antecedent. That is, assuming φ contains only variables from $\bar{x}$, it is of the form

$$G(\bar{x}) \wedge \varphi(\bar{x}) \rightarrow \psi(\bar{x})$$

- a set of plain SO tgds is called *sticky* if, intuitively speaking, whenever a variable x is joined over, i.e.,

$$R_i(x, \bar{y}_1) \wedge R_j(x, \bar{y}_2) \rightarrow R_k(\bar{z})$$

  it must be contained in all conclusion atoms (i.e., above $x \in \bar{z}$). In addition, x may also "never get lost again", that is, any dependency having R_k in the antecedent must propagate a position where x occurs into all conclusion atoms.

Post's Correspondence Problem (PCP). Post's Correspondence Problem is a classical undecidable problem [26]. It is concerned with strings that can be formed by concatenating certain given words over an alphabet. W.l.o.g., let our alphabet be given by the integers $1, \ldots, k$. An instance of PCP is given by the following two parts:

- the alphabet $A = \{1, \ldots, k\}$
- pairs of words over A: $(w_1^1, w_1^2), \ldots, (w_n^1, w_n^2)$

The question of PCP is whether there exists a non-empty sequence $i_1, \ldots, i_\ell$ of indices s.t.

$$w_{i_1}^1 \cdot w_{i_2}^1 \cdot \ldots \cdot w_{i_\ell}^1 = w_{i_1}^2 \cdot w_{i_2}^2 \cdot \ldots \cdot w_{i_\ell}^2$$

In what follows, let $w_{i,j}^s$ denote the jth character of w_i^s. That is, if the jth character of w_i^s is c, then $w_{i,j}^s = c$.

Idea 1: Basic construction. For representing potential solutions to PCP, we represent two types of information:

- sequence of words selected in the solution
- string obtained by concatenating the selected words

We represent both in a standard way using unary function symbols: for instance, a string $(3, 7, 4, \ldots)$ is represented as a term $f_3(f_7(f_4(\ldots)))$. Selected pairs of words are treated similarly: If e.g. first w_5^1 and w_5^2 were selected, followed by w_8^1 and w_8^2, we represent this as $g_5(g_8(\ldots))$.

The key way to use these data structures to obtain the desired result is as follows. We use two "branches" to represent the first and second string of the PCP, marked by 1 resp. 2 in the first argument of atoms with predicate symbol R. An illustration can be found in Figure 4.

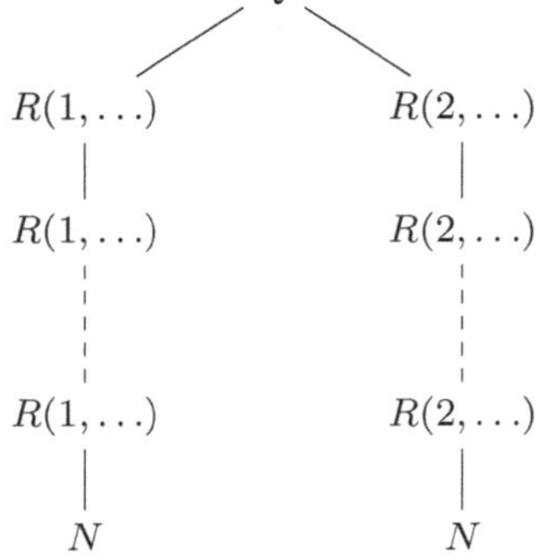

Figure 4: *Intended structure of an instance.*

Both branches start with the empty string and the empty sequence of selected words at the N facts. They then successively select pairs of words and record these selections through R facts. If in the end, both branches produce the same word through the same sequence of selected words, a Q fact is produced. $\lhd$

Idea 2: Representing constants. For our encoding, we need a number of constants for representing e.g. branches, symbols of the alphabet and indexes for words. For representing such constants, the following two properties must be guaranteed:

- symbols that represent the same constant must have the same interpretation
- the sticky property may not be violated

A simple solution to the first issue is to represent the set of constants $\{0, \ldots, d\}$ as a relation N of arity d, where the ith argument represents constant i. This is exactly what the N facts depicted in Figure 4 are used for. The specific solution for also guaranteeing stickiness is as follows. Whenever a fact is introduced, we add a vector of variables representing constants to it:

$$N(\bar{x}) \rightarrow R(\ldots, \bar{x})$$

Whenever a dependency generates a fact, it also includes that vector $\bar{x}$ in that fact. Finally, when the two branches are joined, the join also includes the vector $\bar{x}$ and propagates it to Q. $\lhd$

Idea 3: Applying functions. There is a subtle but critical part when using function symbols in conclusions: For each function symbol, there can only be a single dependency with that function symbol in the conclusion. The reason for this requirement is that it guarantees that the dependencies can actually be obtained from a set of Henkin tgds by Skolemization. However, in our set of dependencies we use function symbols to encode strings. In a naive encoding, we thus have many different dependencies where the same alphabet symbol is added to the string. The solution is a "two-phase" approach.

Say that some R atom should have function f_3 applied to v_1 in its conclusion. In a first phase, we produce a specific fact that contains the information for our desired function application:

$$R(\ldots) \rightarrow F(\ldots, x_3, v_1)$$

In particular, there could be other dependencies that also produce $F(\ldots, x_3, v_1)$ facts. Then, in a second phase, there is one dependency for every function symbol, which applies this function symbol. E.g., for f_3 we have the following dependency:

$$F(\ldots, x_3, y) \rightarrow R(\ldots, f_3(y), \ldots)$$

In this way, we guarantee that for each function symbol, there is only one dependency in which it occurs. $\lhd$

Using these three ideas, it is possible to show that sticky guarded standard Henkin tgds can be used to encode the PCP. Furthermore, through a number of techniques given in detail in the full version, it is possible to further restrict the setting to *linear* Henkin tgds which in total use just two unary function symbols.

Theorem 5.1 *Atomic query answering for sticky linear standard Henkin tgds is undecidable even if only two unary function symbols are allowed in the set of dependencies.*

Another viewpoint of the preceding theorem is that undecidability holds even given just two Henkin tgds, while the rest are full tgds (tgds without existential quantifiers). A slight extension of the above described construction allows us to show undecidability also for nested tgds.

Idea 3$^+$: Nested representation. As we saw in Idea 3, we would like to use Henkin tgds of the form

$$F(\ldots, x_3, y) \rightarrow R(\ldots, f_3(y), \ldots)$$

to apply e.g. function symbol f_3. Unfortunately, this is not the Skolemization of a nested tgd. However, it can be, if we add an additional relation symbol Y as follows:

$$Y(y) \wedge F(\ldots, x_3, y) \rightarrow R(\ldots, f_3(y), \ldots)$$

This is the normalized form of the nested tgd

$$Y(y) \rightarrow \exists z\, [F(\ldots, x_3, y) \rightarrow R(\ldots, z, \ldots)]$$

Hence, we may use nested tgds instead of Henkin tgds (of course, additionally providing tgds that produce corresponding Y facts). Observe that we lose linearity in this way, as we now have two atoms in the antecedent of our normalized nested tgd. However, this is no surprise, as linear nested tgds are just guarded tgds (since linearity prevents nesting) and for guarded tgds we know that query answering is decidable. $\lhd$

Theorem 5.2 *Atomic query answering for sticky guarded simple nested tgds is undecidable even if only two unary function symbols are allowed in dependencies.*

Let us return to the big picture, in particular looking back at the three major "families" of decidable query answering shown in Figure 2. For standard Henkin tgds we have seen that undecidability holds even for sticky and linear, which already rules out decidability for most of the diagram. For nested tgds, we have seen undecidability for sticky and guarded – but not for linear. However, we have discussed in Idea 3$^+$ that query answering is decidable for linear nested tgds.

We have thus drawn the decidability/undecidability in Figure 2 for the two major families of *guarded* and *sticky*, but are still missing the well-known *acyclicity* family. Yet, weak acyclicity and more generally finite expansion sets guarantee, as the name suggests, a finite number of finite instances over which queries can be evaluated. Thus it is implicit in [13, 5] that query answering is decidable even for SO tgds. In total, we have now a clear picture of the border between decidability/undecidability in Figure 2.

We have seen in Theorem 5.1 that query answering is undecidable even for linear Henkin tgds. Below we show that decidability can be achieved by imposing a further restriction.

Proposition 5.3 *Atomic query answering is decidable for linear Henkin tgds if the schema is considered as fixed.*

It would be interesting to see if the result can be extended to conjunctive queries. Note that this result is in a sense optimal for atomic queries: Not fixing the schema yields undecidability by Theorem 5.1. Not requiring the dependencies to be linear yields undecidability by the classical result that query answering is undecidable even for tgds [20].

6. Model Checking

In this section, we discuss the model checking problem of our dependency formalisms. Recall that for tgds and SO tgds, the complexity of model checking is already known [17, 14, 25]. We thus pinpoint the data/query/-combined complexity of nested tgds as well as Henkin tgds. Let us first formally define the model checking problem and its variants.

> MODEL CHECKING($\mathcal{C}$)
> *Query:* A set $\Sigma \subseteq \mathcal{C}$ of dependencies
> *Data:* A model (database instance) I
> *Question:* Does $I \models \tau$ hold?

The data/query/combined complexity of model checking refers to the variant of the problem where the query/data/neither is considered fixed.

We start by considering Henkin tgds and first show NP-completeness in data complexity.

Theorem 6.1 *The model checking problem for Henkin tgds is* NP*-complete in data complexity. Hardness holds even for a single s-t standard Henkin tgd.*

Proof (Sketch) NP-membership is clear, since it holds already for SO tgds [14]. NP-hardness for SO tgds was shown in [14] by a reduction from 3-colorability. However, the resulting SO tgd has the form of the one used in Theorem 4.4, where we showed that it cannot be expressed by a Henkin tgd. We thus show NP-hardness for Henkin tgds by a different reduction from 3-colorability. Let an arbitrary instance of 3-colorability be given by the graph $G = (V_G, E_G)$. We construct an equivalent instance of model checking as (σ, I, J) where σ is a single s-t standard Henkin tgd, I is a source instance and J is a target instance.

Let σ be the following (Skolemized) s-t Henkin tgd

$$V(x) \wedge V(y) \rightarrow T(x, y, f(x), g(y))$$

Let $V^I = V_G$ and let T^J be defined as follows

$$\begin{gathered} E_G \times \{c_1, c_2 \mid c_i \in \{r, g, b\}, c_1 \neq c_2\} \cup \\ \{(v, v) \mid v \in V_G\} \times \{c_1, c_2 \mid c_i \in \{r, g, b\}, c_1 = c_2\} \cup \\ O \times \{c_1, c_2 \mid c_i \in \{r, g, b\}\} \end{gathered}$$

where

$$O = \{(v_1, v_2) \mid v_i \in V_G \wedge v_1 \neq v_2\} \setminus E_G$$

Correctness of the reduction follows from the three lines of the definition of T_J. The first line ensures that both ends of an edge are assigned different colors (where one end's color is given by $f(\cdot)$ and the other's by $g(\cdot)$). The second line ensures that $f(v) = g(v)$ holds for all $v \in V_G$. Finally, the last line ensure that our definition of T_J poses no restriction for any combination not covered by the first two lines (i.e., not an edge and not the same vertex). □

We now show NEXPTIME-completeness of model checking for Henkin tgds in query complexity.

Theorem 6.2 *The model checking problem for Henkin tgds is* NEXPTIME*-complete in query complexity and combined complexity. Hardness holds even for s-t standard Henkin tgds.*

Proof (Sketch) Membership already holds for plain SO tgds [25]. We show hardness by reduction from plain SO tgd model checking, which is known to be NEXPTIME-complete [25]. Let (σ, I, J) be an arbitrary instance of plain SO tgd model checking, where σ is a plain SO tgd, I is a source instance and J is a target instance. In [25], it is implicit that NEXPTIME-hardness holds even if

- $\mathsf{dom}(I) = \mathsf{dom}(J) = \{0, 1\}$
- the arity of predicate symbols is at most 3
- σ consists of a single implication, i.e. is of the form

$$\exists \bar{f}\, \forall \bar{x}\, \varphi(\bar{x}) \rightarrow \psi(\bar{f}, \bar{x})$$

Hence, we assume that our given instance satisfies the three conditions given above. Intuitively, σ might violate one of the following conditions of standard Henkin tgds: ($\star$) every occurrence of a function symbol must have the same argument list ($\star$) the arguments of each Skolem term must be pairwise distinct ($\star$) no variable is allowed to occur as argument of two distinct function symbols. We ensure these properties by a sequence of transformations, which first applies some equivalence-preserving simplifications to the plain SO tgd and then chooses an appropriate extension of the database schema to allow for a transformation of the formula into a standard Henkin tgd. □

We thus have identified the precise data, query, and combined complexity of model checking for Henkin tgds. We now proceed to nested tgds. Since nested tgds are a first-order formalism, data complexity is in AC_0 while combined/query complexity is in PSPACE. We show that the latter bound is tight.

Theorem 6.3 *The model checking problem for nested tgds is* PSPACE*-complete in query and combined complexity. Hardness holds even for s-t simple nested tgds.*

Proof (Sketch) Membership is clear, since it already holds for first-order logic. We show hardness by reduction from the well-known PSPACE-complete problem of QBF satisfiability. Let ψ be an arbitrary QBF. W.l.o.g., we may assume

- ψ is in prenex form, with strict quantifier alternation starting with a universal quantifier and ending with an existential quantifier
- the quantifier-free part of ψ is in 3-CNF

We thus may assume that ψ has the form

$$\forall x_1 \exists y_1 \ldots \forall x_n \exists y_n (c_1 \wedge \ldots \wedge c_n)$$

with $c_i = (l_{i1} \vee l_{i2} \vee l_{i3})$ and l_{ij} is a literal over $\{x_1, \ldots, x_n, y_1, \ldots, y_n\}$. We first define source instance I and target instance J of our model checking problem.

$$\begin{aligned} I &= \{P(1,0), P(0,1)\} \\ J &= \{Q(1,0), Q(0,1)\} \cup \\ &\quad \{C(x_1, x_2, x_3) \mid x \in \{0,1\}\} \setminus \{C(0,0,0)\} \end{aligned}$$

The nested tgd τ of the model checking problem is defined as follows:

$$\begin{aligned} &\forall x_1, \tilde{x}_1\, P(x_1, \tilde{x}) \rightarrow \exists y_1, \tilde{y}_1\, Q(y_1, \tilde{y}_1) \wedge \\ &\quad \forall x_2, \tilde{x}_2\, P(x_2, \tilde{x}) \rightarrow \exists y_2, \tilde{y}_2\, Q(y_2, \tilde{y}_2) \wedge \\ &\quad\quad \ldots \\ &\quad\quad\quad \forall x_n, \tilde{x}_n\, P(x_n, \tilde{x}) \rightarrow \exists y_n, \tilde{y}_n\, Q(y_n, \tilde{y}_n) \wedge \\ &\quad\quad\quad\quad \bigwedge_{i \in \{1,\ldots,m\}} C(l^\star_{i1}, l^\star_{i2}, l^\star_{i3}) \end{aligned}$$

where

$$l^\star_{ij} = \begin{cases} x_\alpha, & \text{if } l_{ij} = x_\alpha \\ \tilde{x}_\alpha, & \text{if } l_{ij} = \neg x_\alpha \\ y_\beta, & \text{if } l_{ij} = y_\beta \\ \tilde{y}_\beta, & \text{if } l_{ij} = \neg y_\beta \end{cases}$$

Intuitively, nested tgds miss two features of QBFs: negation and disjunction. Negation is encoded using symbols of the form x_α for positive literals and $\tilde{x}_\alpha$ for negative literals. Through appropriate definition of relation P and Q in I resp. J, the correct behavior of complementary literals is guaranteed. Similarly, using C atoms we encode clauses (i.e., disjunctions) and guarantee correctness by encoding the correct behavior of disjunction in the C relation of J. □

7. Conclusion

In this work, we have investigated the expressive power and computability of using function symbols in tgds. We have seen that function symbols introduced by different forms of dependencies correspond to different structures underlying the domain that one wants to model. For hierarchically structured domains, nested tgds are often the best choice, while Henkin tgds are well-suited for non-hierarchical domains. Nevertheless, sometimes the full power of SO tgds is required. We observed that

- nested tgds share with SO tgds the power of quantifying over more than one tgd part;
- Henkin tgds share with SO tgds the power of allowing non-tree structured Skolem terms.

Yet, our results revealed a deep semantical connection between these two formalisms, namely: every nested tgd can be expressed as a logically equivalent (tree) Henkin tgd. Still, there is a price to pay for simulating nested tgds by Henkin tgds rather than by (arbitrary) SO tgds:

- Converting nested tgds to logically equivalent SO tgds only leads to a linear blow-up.
- Converting nested tgds to logically equivalent (tree) Henkin tgds may lead to a non-elementary blow-up. While not occurring for typical examples as we saw, this may be a problem for particularly complex settings.

Our results showed that each of our dependency classes has particular features that *cannot* be simulated by a "lower" class in our semantical inclusion diagram (Figure 3), since we proved that the diagram is complete and all inclusions are proper. Altogether, we can conclude from our analysis that great care must be taken when modeling a particular domain by tgds so as to balance expressive power, simplicity of the formalism, and size of the resulting set of dependencies. In summary, our analysis of Henkin and nested tgds has provided a deep insight into the versatile features of SO tgds. The results of our study underline the value of SO tgds, which support the distinguished features of both Henkin and nested tgds.

For the model checking problem, we have pinpointed the data/query/combined complexity of nested tgds and Henkin tgds: for Henkin tgds we proved NEXPTIME-completeness of query/combined complexity and NP-completeness of data complexity. Moreover, we showed that nested tgds are PSPACE-complete in query/combined complexity (and are known to be in AC_0 data complexity).

For query answering under various forms of dependencies, we have provided a complete picture of the decidability/undecidability border in Figure 2 for all dependency classes studied here. We have shown that even the slightest deviation from the way that tgds use function symbols in their Skolemized form yields undecidability: this holds even for the weakest extensions of tgds, simple nested tgds or standard Henkin tgds, and even for two of the best-known families for guaranteeing decidability for tgds (guarded and sticky) together.

Hence our analysis has revealed that the islands of decidability are quite small. One such island is that for a fixed schema, at least linear Henkin tgds allow for decidability. Moreover, we have observed that the third major family, weak acyclicity, guarantees decidability of query answering even for SO tgds.

For future work, the most burning question is how to narrow the gaps between the islands of decidability of query answering under Henkin/nested/SO tgds. We will thus analyze known decidable fragments of various logics (such as, e.g., the two-variable fragment) and investigate their applicability to our setting of query answering under tgds. Moreover, we also have to explore new paradigms that are tailor-made for Henkin/nested/SO tgds and that go beyond known decidability criteria for other logics. Beyond that, it would be interesting to see whether frameworks such as dependence logic yield additional suitable subclasses of SO tgds.

Acknowledgements. This work has been supported by the Austrian Science Fund, projects (FWF):P25207-N23 and (FWF):Y698, the Vienna Science and Technology Fund, project ICT12-015, as well as the Engineering and Physical Sciences Research Council (EPSRC), Programme Grant EP/M025268/ "VADA: Value Added Data Systems – Principles and Architecture".

8. References

[1] S. Abiteboul, R. Hull, and V. Vianu. *Foundations of Databases*. Addison-Wesley, 1995.

[2] S. Amano, L. Libkin, and F. Murlak. Xml schema mappings. In *PODS*, pages 33–42, 2009.

[3] M. Arenas, P. Barceló, L. Libkin, and F. Murlak. *Relational and XML Data Exchange*. Morgan & Claypool Publishers, 2010.

[4] M. Arenas, J. Pérez, J. L. Reutter, and C. Riveros. The language of plain SO-tgds: Composition, inversion and structural properties. *JCSS*, 79(6):763–784, 2013.

[5] J.-F. Baget, M. Leclère, M.-L. Mugnier, and E. Salvat. Extending decidable cases for rules with existential variables. In *IJCAI*, pages 677–682, 2009.

[6] J.-F. Baget, M. Leclère, M.-L. Mugnier, and E. Salvat. On rules with existential variables: Walking the decidability line. *Artif. Intell.*, 175(9-10):1620–1654, 2011.

[7] P. A. Bernstein and S. Melnik. Model management 2.0: manipulating richer mappings. In *SIGMOD*, pages 1–12, 2007.

[8] A. Blass and Y. Gurevich. Henkin quantifiers and complete problems. *Annals of Pure and Applied Logic*, 32(0):1 – 16, 1986.

[9] A. Calì, G. Gottlob, and M. Kifer. Taming the infinite chase: Query answering under expressive relational constraints. *JAIR*, 48:115–174, 2013.

[10] A. Calì, G. Gottlob, and A. Pieris. Advanced processing for ontological queries. *PVLDB*, 3(1):554–565, 2010.

[11] A. Calì, G. Gottlob, and A. Pieris. Query answering under non-guarded rules in datalog+/-. In *RR*, pages 1–17, 2010.

[12] A. Calì, G. Gottlob, and A. Pieris. Towards more expressive ontology languages: The query answering problem. *Artif. Intell.*, 193:87–128, 2012.

[13] R. Fagin, P. G. Kolaitis, R. J. Miller, and L. Popa. Data exchange: semantics and query answering. *Theor. Comput. Sci.*, 336(1):89–124, 2005.

[14] R. Fagin, P. G. Kolaitis, L. Popa, and W. C. Tan. Composing schema mappings: Second-order dependencies to the rescue. *ACM TODS*, 30(4):994–1055, 2005.

[15] I. Feinerer, R. Pichler, E. Sallinger, and V. Savenkov. On the undecidability of the equivalence of second-order tuple generating dependencies. *Inf. Syst.*, 48:113–129, 2015.

[16] A. Fuxman, M. A. Hernández, C. T. H. Ho, R. J. Miller, P. Papotti, and L. Popa. Nested mappings: Schema mapping reloaded. In *VLDB*, pages 67–78, 2006.

[17] G. Gottlob and P. Senellart. Schema mapping discovery from data instances. *J. ACM*, 57(2), 2010.

[18] P. Hell and J. Nešetřil. The Core of a Graph. *Discrete Mathematics*, 109:117–126, 1992.

[19] M. A. Hernández, H. Ho, L. Popa, A. Fuxman, R. J. Miller, T. Fukuda, and P. Papotti. Creating nested mappings with Clio. In *ICDE*, pages 1487–1488, 2007.

[20] D. S. Johnson and A. C. Klug. Testing containment of conjunctive queries under functional and inclusion dependencies. *JCSS*, 28(1):167–189, 1984.

[21] P. G. Kolaitis, M. Lenzerini, and N. Schweikardt, editors. *Data Exchange, Integration, and Streams*, volume 5 of *Dagstuhl Follow-Ups*. Schloss Dagstuhl - Leibniz-Zentrum für Informatik, 2013.

[22] P. G. Kolaitis, R. Pichler, E. Sallinger, and V. Savenkov. Nested dependencies: structure and reasoning. In *PODS*, pages 176–187, 2014.

[23] M. Lenzerini. Data integration: A theoretical perspective. In *PODS*, pages 233–246, 2002.

[24] N. Leone, M. Manna, G. Terracina, and P. Veltri. Efficiently computable datalog programs. In *KR*, 2012.

[25] R. Pichler and S. Skritek. The complexity of evaluating tuple generating dependencies. In *ICDT*, pages 244–255, 2011.

[26] E. L. Post. A variant of a recursively unsolvable problem. *J. Symbolic Logic*, 12(2):255–56, 1946.

[27] E. Sallinger. Reasoning about schema mappings. In *Data Exchange, Integration, and Streams*, pages 97–127, 2013.

[28] B. ten Cate and P. G. Kolaitis. Structural characterizations of schema-mapping languages. In *ICDT*, pages 63–72, 2009.

[29] W. J. Walkoe, Jr. Finite partially-ordered quantification. *J. Symb. Log.*, 35(4):535–555, 1970.

Default Negation for Non-Guarded Existential Rules

Mario Alviano
Dept. of Mathematics and Computer Science
University of Calabria, Italy
alviano@mat.unical.it

Andreas Pieris
Institute of Information Systems
Vienna University of Technology, Austria
pieris@dbai.tuwien.ac.at

ABSTRACT

The problem of query answering under the well-founded and stable model semantics for normal existential rules, that is, existential rules enriched with default negation, has recently attracted a lot of interest from the database and KR communities. In particular, it has been thoroughly studied for classes of normal existential rules that are based on restrictions that guarantee the tree-likeness of the underlying models; a prime example of such a restriction is guardedness. However, little is known about classes of existential rules that significantly deviate from the above paradigm. A prominent example of such a formalism is the class of existential rules that is based on the notion of stickiness, which enforces restrictions on the forms of joins in the rule-bodies. It is the precise aim of the current work to extend sticky existential rules with default negation, and perform an in-depth analysis of the complexity of conjunctive query answering under the well-founded and stable model semantics. We show that an effective way for bridging the gap between stickiness and the well-founded semantics exists, and we provide data and combined complexity results. However, there is no way to reconcile stickiness and the stable model semantics. The reason for this surprising negative result should be found in the fact that sticky existential rules are powerful enough for expressing cartesian products, a construct that forms a prime example of non-guardedness.

Categories and Subject Descriptors

H.2.4 [**Database Management**]: Systems–*query processing, relational databases, rule-based databases*

Keywords

Query Answering; Datalog-based Languages; Default Negation; Well-founded Semantics; Stable Model Semantics; Complexity

1. INTRODUCTION

1.1 Existential Rules and Default Negation

Rule-based languages lie at the core of several areas of central importance to databases, such as data integration and exchange,

PODS'15, May 31–June 4, 2015, Melbourne, Victoria, Australia.

ACM 978-1-4503-2757-2/15/05 ...$15.00.
http://dx.doi.org/10.1145/2745754.2745758.

and data extraction. A prominent rule-based formalism is *Datalog*, that is, function-free first-order Horn logic. The main weakness of this language is its inability to infer the existence of new objects that are not already in the database. *Existential rules* overcome this limitation by extending Datalog with existential quantification in rule-heads. An example of such a rule is

$$\forall X\,(emp(X) \;\rightarrow\; \exists Y\, hasMgr(X,Y) \wedge emp(Y)),$$

which asserts that each employee has a manager who is also an employee. Such rules are also known as *tuple-generating dependencies (TGDs)* or *Datalog*$^{\pm}$ rules.

An algorithmic task that involves TGDs, which is of special interest for databases, is query answering: given a database D, a set Σ of TGDs, and a (Boolean) conjunctive query q, decide whether $D \cup \Sigma \models q$, or, equivalently, whether each model of the logical theory $D \cup \Sigma$ is also a model of q. Unfortunately, query answering under TGDs is undecidable [4], even in the case of fixed sets of TGDs [5], and singleton sets of TGDs [3]. Restrictions are then imposed in order to regain decidability of query answering. There has been a recent and increasing focus on the investigation of such restrictions; see, e.g., [3, 5, 6, 18]. The main decidable classes of TGDs are based on the notions of guardedness [5], acyclicity [11], and stickiness [7]. Apparently, none of these languages can express default negation (a.k.a. negation as failure, denoted $\sim$).

Example 1. Consider the following set Σ of TGDs extended with default negation:

$$\begin{array}{l}\forall X\,(emp(X) \;\rightarrow\; \exists Y\, hasMgr(X,Y) \wedge seniorEmp(Y)),\\ \forall X\,(seniorEmp(X) \;\rightarrow\; emp(X)),\\ \forall X \forall Y\,(emp(X) \wedge emp(Y) \wedge seniorEmp(X) \wedge\\ \qquad {\sim} seniorEmp(Y) \wedge {\sim} sameGrade(X,Y) \;\rightarrow\\ \qquad\qquad moreThan(X,Y)),\\ \forall X \forall Y\,(emp(X) \wedge emp(Y) \wedge {\sim} moreThan(X,Y) \wedge\\ \qquad {\sim} moreThan(Y,X) \;\rightarrow\; sameGrade(X,Y)).\end{array}$$

Σ states the following: (1) each employee has a manager who is a senior employee; (2) usually a senior employee earns more money than a non-senior employee, unless it is known that they are at the same salary grade; and (3) if it is not known that two employees have different salaries, then they are at the same salary grade. TGDs without default negation cannot express (2) and (3). ■

The database and the KR communities have recognized the need for considering TGDs with default negation, called normal. Adding negation to known decidable languages is an intriguing new problem that gave rise to a flourishing research activity the last years. A short discussion on previous approaches to enrich TGDs with default negation follows:

Stratified Negation. Stratified negation for guarded TGDs was investigated in [6], and extended to the more expressive formalism of weakly-guarded TGDs in [1]. Stratified negation is well-behaved in the sense that its addition does not sacrifice decidability, and the complexity remains the same. However, stratified negation is limited, and this has motivated the investigation of more expressive types of negation, namely well-founded and stable model negation. Notice that simple programs like the one given in Example 1 require non-stratified negation.

Well-Founded Negation. Two variants of the well-founded semantics (WFS) for guarded TGDs were considered in [14, 17]. The version of [17] studies the standard WFS for logic programming with function symbols, where it is assumed the unique name assumption (UNA): different Skolem terms are not unifiable. The second variant, called equality-friendly WFS [14], does not use the UNA.

Stable Model Negation. Negation under the stable model semantics for (weakly-)guarded TGDs was recently investigated in [15]. In [2, 19], acyclicity and stratification conditions are proposed for TGDs with negation, which identify languages that have finite and/or unique stable models. The $\mathbb{FDNC}$ programs in [10] combine default negation and function symbols; decidability is obtained by restricting the structure of rules to one of seven predefined forms. A crucial condition that $\mathbb{FDNC}$ programs must satisfy is similar to guardedness.

1.2 Goal and Challenges

Unfortunately, none of the formalisms discussed above is expressive enough to model cases such as Example 1 — the first two TGDs are highly recursive, and thus far from being acyclic, while all the other (normal) TGDs are non-guarded. Interestingly, as we can verify from the formal definition of stickiness given in Section 3, the set of normal TGDs in Example 1 is sticky. However, little is known about the problem of query answering under sticky sets of normal TGDs. Our main goal in this paper is to investigate whether the current gap between stickiness and default negation can be bridged. More precisely, we focus our attention on the well-founded [12] and stable model semantics [13], which are the standard semantics for normal logic programs, and we are interested to understand whether the decidability of conjunctive query answering is preserved, and if it is the case, what is the exact data and combined complexity.

The problems tackled in this paper are technically different than the ones attacked by the other works on query answering under normal TGDs [10, 14, 15, 17, 19]. This is because the model-theoretic properties that guarantee the decidability of conjunctive query answering under guarded and acyclic TGDs are intrinsically different than the ones for sticky sets of TGDs. Guardedness guarantees the tree-likeness of the underlying models, i.e., they are instances of finite treewidth, while acyclicity guarantees their finiteness (and thus, they are trivially tree-like). There exist instead sticky sets of TGDs that admit non-tree-like models.

Example 2. Consider the following set Σ of TGDs:

$$\begin{aligned}\sigma_1 &= \forall X \forall Y\,(p(X,Y) \rightarrow \exists Z\, p(Y,Z) \wedge s(Z))\\ \sigma_2 &= \forall X \forall Y\,(s(X) \wedge s(Y) \rightarrow t(X,Y)).\end{aligned}$$

Σ is sticky but neither acyclic (because of σ_1) nor guarded (because of σ_2). The extension of the binary relation t in an infinite canonical model M of the database $\{p(a,a)\}$ and Σ is an infinite clique, and thus M has infinite treewidth. ∎

Given that sticky sets of TGDs, in general, do not enjoy the tree model property, let alone guardedness and acyclicity, the techniques that are needed for conjunctive query answering under sticky sets of normal TGDs are inherently different than the ones employed for guarded and acyclic normal TGDs. In general, the current algorithms for guarded and acyclic normal TGDs employ forward chaining procedures (similar to the well-known chase). Nevertheless, for sticky sets of normal TGDs it is more convenient to rely on backward chaining (a.k.a. proof-theoretic) procedures, which try to construct, starting from the query, a finite part of a model that entails the query (i.e., a "proof" of the query).

1.3 Our Results

Our contributions can be summarised as follows:

1. We show that sticky sets of TGDs can be extended with well-founded negation preserving decidability of query answering (Theorem 1); this is shown by a reduction to Datalog$^\neg$ query evaluation under the well-founded semantics. Unfortunately, the situation changes dramatically once we concentrate on the stable model semantics, for which we show undecidability of query answering (Theorem 3); this is a rather surprising negative result, which is established by a reduction from the halting problem.
2. For the well-founded semantics, we study the complexity of query answering under sticky sets of normal TGDs, and we show it to be tractable, i.e., in PTIME, in data complexity (Theorem 4), and EXPTIME-complete in combined complexity (Theorem 5). The data complexity upper bound follows from the fact that Datalog$^\neg$ query evaluation under the well-founded semantics is feasible in polynomial time. The combined complexity upper bound is a rather involved result, and is obtained by exhibiting an alternating polynomial space algorithm; the lower bound is inherited from query answering under sticky sets of TGDs.
3. Although the class of sticky sets of normal TGDs forms a natural extension of stickiness with default negation, it is not powerful enough for capturing important database constraints enriched with negation such as normal inclusion dependencies. This led us to investigate a more refined consolidation of stickiness with well-founded negation, and define the so-called 2D-stickiness (the "second dimension" of stickiness). We show that 2D-stickiness reaches the decidability/undecidability frontier of query answering, and we establish precise complexity results: PTIME-complete in data complexity, and 2EXPTIME-complete in combined complexity (Theorem 12). The upper bounds are obtained by a non-trivial extension of the alternating algorithm mentioned above, while the lower bounds by a reduction from query answering under guarded (positive) TGDs.
4. Finally, our algorithmic techniques allowed us to close some interesting open problems, namely the data and combined complexity of linear normal TGDs, that is, normal TGDs with exactly one positive atom, under the well-founded semantics. In particular, we show that the problem is PTIME-complete in data complexity, and 2EXPTIME-complete in combined complexity (Theorem 14).

2. PRELIMINARIES

2.1 General Definitions

We define the following pairwise disjoint (countably infinite) sets: a set $\mathbf{C}$ of *functors* (each of them associated with a nonnegative arity; functors of arity 0 are also called *constants* and constitute the "normal" domain of a database), a set $\mathbf{N}$ of *labeled nulls* (used as placeholders for unknown values, and thus can be also seen as globally existentially quantified variables), and a set $\mathbf{V}$ of (regular) *variables* (used in queries and dependencies). Different functors represent different functions (*unique name assumption*), while different nulls may represent the same value. The set of functors of arity n, for $n \geqslant 0$, is denoted $\mathbf{C}_n$. We denote by $\mathbf{X}$ sequences (or sets, with a slight abuse of notation) of variables $X_1, \ldots, X_k$. Let $[n] = \{1, \ldots, n\}$, for any integer $n \geqslant 1$.

Terms are inductively defined as follows: constants, nulls and variables are terms; $f(t_1, \ldots, t_n)$, where f is an n-ary functor, and $t_1, \ldots, t_n$ are terms, is a term. The set of all terms is denoted $\mathbf{C}^\star$. An *atomic formula* (or simply *atom*) has the form $p(t_1, \ldots, t_n)$, where p is an n-ary predicate, and $t_1, \ldots, t_n$ are terms. For an atom $\underline{a}$, we write $dom(\underline{a})$, $var(\underline{a})$, and $pred(\underline{a})$ for the set of its terms, the set of its variables, and its predicate, respectively; those notations naturally extend to sets of atoms. Atoms and terms not containing variables are called *ground*. For brevity, conjunctions of atoms are often identified with the sets of their atoms. A *database* D is a finite set of atoms such that $dom(D) \subset \mathbf{C}_0$.

A *homomorphism* from a set of atoms A to a set of atoms A' is a mapping $h : \mathbf{C}^\star \to \mathbf{C}^\star$, which is defined on $dom(A)$, such that: $p(t_1, \ldots, t_n) \in A$ implies $p(h(t_1), \ldots, h(t_n)) \in A'$, where $h(f(s_1, \ldots, s_m)) = f(h(s_1), \ldots, h(s_m))$, for each m-ary function f. Given a set of symbols S, A and A' are *S-isomorphic*, written $A \simeq_S A'$, if there exists a bijection $h : \mathbf{C}^\star \to \mathbf{C}^\star$ such that h and h^{-1} are homomorphisms, $h(A) = A'$, $h^{-1}(A') = A$, and both h and h^{-1} are the identity on S. Two atoms $\underline{a}$ and $\underline{a}'$ are S-isomorphic if $\{\underline{a}\}$ and $\{\underline{a}'\}$ are S-isomorphic.

2.2 Normal Rules and TGDs

A *literal* is either an atom (i.e., a positive literal), or an atom preceded by the negation as failure symbol $\sim$ (i.e., a negative literal). An *implication rule* ρ has the form:

$$\forall \mathbf{X} \forall \mathbf{Y} (\varphi(\mathbf{X}, \mathbf{Y}) \to \exists \mathbf{Z}\, \psi(\mathbf{X}, \mathbf{Z})), \qquad (1)$$

where φ and ψ are conjunctions of literals and atoms, respectively, with variables from $(\mathbf{X} \cup \mathbf{Y} \cup \mathbf{Z}) \subset \mathbf{V}$ (and possibly terms from $\mathbf{C}^\star$ not involving nulls). Formula φ is the *body* of ρ, denoted $B(\rho)$, while ψ is the *head* of ρ, denoted $H(\rho)$. Moreover, we denote by $B^+(\rho)$ the set of positive literals in $B(\rho)$, and by $B^-(\rho)$ the set of atoms appearing in negative literals of $B(\rho)$. For brevity, we omit the universal quantifiers in front of implication rules, and use the comma (instead of $\wedge$) for conjoining literals.

We use $\sim.\ell$ to denote the complement of a literal ℓ, i.e., if $\underline{a}$ is an atom, $\sim.\underline{a}$ is the negative literal $\sim\underline{a}$, and $\sim.\sim\underline{a}$ is the positive literal $\underline{a}$. Let $sign(\ell) = +$ if ℓ is positive; otherwise, let $sign(\ell) = -$. For a rule ρ, $\sim.\rho$ is obtained from ρ by replacing each literal ℓ occurring in ρ with $\sim.\ell$; $\rho^\perp$ is obtained from ρ by replacing each negative literal $\sim p(\mathbf{t})$ with $p(\mathbf{t})$, i.e., by eliminating the symbol "$\sim$"; ρ^+ is obtained from ρ by eliminating all the negative literals. Those notations extend to sets of rules in the natural way.

A *normal rule* ρ is an implication rule of the form (1) not containing existential variables. A set Π of normal rules is called *normal program*. A *normal tuple-generating dependency (NTGD)* σ is an implication rule of the form (1) not containing function symbols; if $B^-(\sigma) = \varnothing$, then σ is called TGD. A set of NTGDs can be transformed into a normal logic program by eliminating the existentially quantified variables via *Skolemization*. The Skolemization of a NTGD $\sigma = \varphi(\mathbf{X}, \mathbf{Y}) \to \exists \mathbf{Z}\, \psi(\mathbf{X}, \mathbf{Z})$, denoted $\mathcal{S}(\sigma)$, is a normal rule $\varphi(\mathbf{X}, \mathbf{Y}) \to \psi(\mathbf{X}, \mathbf{f}_\sigma(\mathbf{X}, \mathbf{Y}))$, where $\mathbf{f}_\sigma$ is a vector of function symbols $f_{\sigma,Z}$, one for each $Z \in \mathbf{Z}$. The Skolemization of a set of NTGDs Σ, denoted $\mathcal{S}(\Sigma)$, is the normal program $\{\mathcal{S}(\sigma) \mid \sigma \in \Sigma\}$.

2.3 Semantics for Normal Programs

The main semantics are the well-founded and stable model semantics. Those semantics will be defined for normal programs, and will be applied to Skolemized sets of NTGDs as well. Both semantics under consideration are defined for ground programs; thus, we first need to introduce the notion of grounding. The Herbrand universe of a normal program Π, denoted U_Π, is the set of all terms that can be formed using constants and functors occurring in Π. The Herbrand base of Π, denoted B_Π, is the set of all ground atoms that can be constructed using predicates occurring in Π and terms of U_Π. A ground instance of a rule $\rho \in \Pi$ is obtained from ρ by replacing each variable of ρ by a term from U_Π. The set of all ground instances of rules in Π is denoted $ground(\Pi)$.

A *three-valued interpretation* for Π is a pair (T, N), where $T \subseteq N \subseteq B_\Pi$. Intuitively, T is the set of true atoms, while N is the set of "non-false" atoms; hence, atoms in $(N \setminus T)$ are undefined, while atoms in $(B_\Pi \setminus N)$ are false. If $T = N$ then the interpretation is *total*, or *two-valued*, and will be usually denoted T. An interpretation (T, N) is a model of a ground rule ρ if: (i) $H(\rho) \subseteq N$ whenever $B^+(\rho) \subseteq N$ and $B^-(\rho) \cap T = \varnothing$; and (ii) $H(\rho) \subseteq T$ whenever $B^+(\rho) \subseteq T$ and $B^-(\rho) \cap N = \varnothing$. An interpretation (T, N) is a model of a program Π if it is a model of all rules in $ground(\Pi)$.

2.3.1 Well-Founded Semantics

Two key notions are the *immediate logical consequence operator* and the *greatest unfounded set*. The former is defined as $\mathcal{T}_\Pi^N(T) = \{\underline{a} \in H(\rho) \mid \rho \in ground(\Pi), B^+(\rho) \subseteq T, B^-(\rho) \cap N = \varnothing\}$, where $T \subseteq N \subseteq B_\Pi$. A set A of atoms is an unfounded set for a program Π with respect to an interpretation (T, N) if for each $\rho \in \Pi$ with $H(\rho) \cap A \neq \varnothing$ at least one of the following conditions holds: (i) $B^+(\rho) \not\subseteq N$; or (ii) $B^-(\rho) \cap T \neq \varnothing$; or (iii) $B^+(\rho) \cap A \neq \varnothing$. Intuitively, condition (i) or (ii) holds when ρ is already satisfied because of a false body literal, while condition (iii) guarantees that ρ can be satisfied if all atoms in A are interpreted as false. The greatest unfounded set of Π w.r.t. an interpretation (T, N), denoted $\mathcal{U}_\Pi(T, N)$, is the union of all unfounded sets with respect to (T, N). The well-founded operator is defined as $\mathcal{W}_\Pi(T, N) = (\mathcal{T}_\Pi^N(T),\ B_\Pi \setminus \mathcal{U}_\Pi(T, N))$. The well-founded model of Π, denoted $\mathcal{W}_\Pi^\infty$, is defined as the least fixpoint of the following sequence: $W_0 = \varnothing$; $W_{i+1} = \mathcal{W}_\Pi(W_i)$ for successor ordinal $i + 1$; $W_i = \bigoplus_{j<i} W_j$ for limit ordinal i, where $(T, N) \oplus (T', N') = (T \cup T', N \cap N')$. Each normal program has a unique well-founded model [12].

2.3.2 Stable Model Semantics

The reduct Π^T of a program Π w.r.t. a two-valued interpretation T is the program obtained from $ground(\Pi)$ by first removing all the rules with a false negative body literal, and then eliminating the remaining negative body literals. Formally, $\Pi^T = \{B^+(\rho) \to H(\rho) \mid \rho \in ground(\Pi), B^-(\rho) \cap T = \varnothing\}$. A two-valued interpretation T is a stable model of Π if T is a model of Π, and there is no $T' \subset T$ such that T' is a model of Π^T. Let $SMS(\Pi)$ be the stable models of Π.

2.4 Normal (Boolean) Conjunctive Queries

We add negation to conjunctive queries as follows. An n-ary *normal conjunctive query (NCQ)* q, where $n \geqslant 0$, is a sentence $\exists \mathbf{Y} \bigwedge_{i=1}^m p_i(\mathbf{X}, \mathbf{Y}) \wedge \bigwedge_{j=m+1}^{m+k} \sim p_j(\mathbf{X}, \mathbf{Y})$, where $m \geqslant 1$, $k \geqslant 0$, each atom contains variables from $(\mathbf{X} \cup \mathbf{Y}) \subset \mathbf{V}$ (and possibly constants of $\mathbf{C}_0$), and $|\mathbf{X}| = n$. A 0-ary NCQ is called *normal*

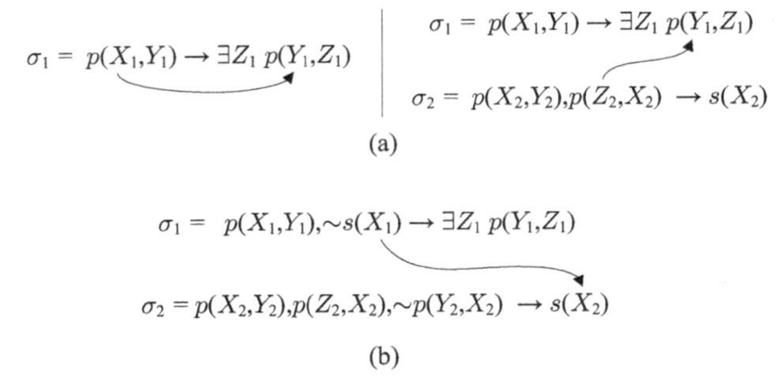

σ1 = p(X1,Y1) → ∃Z1 p(Y1,Z1)
σ1 = p(X1,Y1) → ∃Z1 p(Y1,Z1)
σ2 = p(X2,Y2),p(Z2,X2) → s(X2)
(a)
σ1 = p(X1,Y1),∼s(X1) → ∃Z1 p(Y1,Z1)
σ2 = p(X2,Y2),p(Z2,X2),∼p(Y2,X2) → s(X2)
(b)

Figure 1: Marked variables.

Boolean conjunctive query (NBCQ). We denote by q^+ and q^- the set of atoms occurring in positive and negative literals of q, respectively. The *answer* to an n-ary NCQ q over a three-valued interpretation (T, N), denoted $q(T, N)$, is the set of all tuples of constants $\mathbf{t} \in \mathbf{C}_0^n$ for which there exists a homomorphism h such that $h(q^+) \subseteq T$, $h(\mathbf{X}) = \mathbf{t}$ and $h(q^-) \cap N = \varnothing$. A NBCQ q has only the empty tuple as possible answer, in which case it is said to have a positive answer. Formally, q has a *positive* answer over (T, N), written $(T, N) \models q$, if $q(T, N) \neq \varnothing$.

Consider a database D and a set Σ of NTGDs, and let $\Pi_{D,\Sigma} = ground(D \cup \mathcal{S}(\Sigma))$. The answer to an n-ary NBCQ q over D and Σ under the well-founded semantics is the set of tuples $\{\mathbf{t} \in \mathbf{C}_0^n \mid \mathbf{t} \in q(\mathcal{W}^{\infty}_{\Pi_{D,\Sigma}})\}$. If q is Boolean, then we say that it has a positive answer over D and Σ under the well-founded semantics when $\mathcal{W}^{\infty}_{\Pi_{D,\Sigma}} \models q$, and we write $D \cup \Sigma \models_{WFS} q$. Similarly, the answer to q over D and Σ under the stable model semantics is the set of tuples $\{\mathbf{t} \in \mathbf{C}_0^n \mid \mathbf{t} \in q(T), \text{ for each } T \in SMS(\Pi_{D,\Sigma})\}$. If q is Boolean, then it has a positive answer over D and Σ under the stable model semantics, denoted $D \cup \Sigma \models_{SMS} q$, if $T \models q$, for each $T \in SMS(\Pi_{D,\Sigma})$.

Henceforth, for technical clarity, we focus on NBCQs; however, our results can be easily extended to NCQs. We refer to the problem of deciding whether $D \cup \Sigma \models_x q$, where $x \in \{WFS, SMS\}$, by x-NBCQ answering.

3. STICKY NTGDS: A CASE STUDY

The goal of this section is to investigate how stickiness can be extended with default negation. But let us first recall the class of sticky sets of TGDs, introduced in [7]. Fix a set Σ of TGDs. Henceforth, w.l.o.g., we assume that, for every pair $(\sigma, \sigma') \in \Sigma \times \Sigma$, σ and σ' do not share variables. For notational convenience, given an atom $\underline{a}$ and a variable $X \in var(\underline{a})$, $pos(\underline{a}, X)$ is the set of positions in $\underline{a}$ at which X occurs; recall that a position $p[i]$ identifies the i-th attribute of the predicate p. The definition of stickiness hinges on the notion of marked variables in a set of TGDs.

Definition 1. Consider a TGD $\sigma \in \Sigma$, and a variable X occurring in $B(\sigma)$. We inductively define when X is *marked in* Σ as follows: (i) if there exists $\underline{a} \in H(\sigma)$ such that $X \notin var(\underline{a})$, then X is marked in Σ; and (ii) assuming that there exists $\underline{a} \in H(\sigma)$ such that $X \in var(\underline{a})$, if there exists $\sigma' \in \Sigma$ (not necessarily different than σ) and an atom $\underline{b} \in B(\sigma')$ such that $pred(\underline{a}) = pred(\underline{b})$ and each variable at a position of $pos(\underline{a}, X)$ is marked in Σ, then X is marked in Σ. ■

Example 3. Consider the set Σ consisting of the TGDs:

$$\begin{aligned} \sigma_1 &= p(X_1, Y_1) \rightarrow \exists Z_1\, p(Y_1, Z_1) \\ \sigma_2 &= p(X_2, Y_2), p(Z_2, X_2) \rightarrow s(X_2). \end{aligned}$$

Clearly, the variables X_1, Y_2 and Z_2 are marked in Σ since they do not occur in the head of the TGDs. Now, by induction, we conclude that Y_1 is marked in Σ — Y_1 is marked for the two reasons that are depicted in Figure 1(a). ■

We are now ready to recall when a set of TGDs is sticky:

Definition 2. A set Σ of TGDs is *sticky* if, for each $\sigma \in \Sigma$, and for each variable $V \in var(B(\sigma))$, V is marked in Σ implies V occurs only once in $B(\sigma)$. ■

The TGDs in Example 3 form a sticky set. In fact, σ_1 trivially satisfies the sticky condition since each variable occurs in $B(\sigma_1)$ only once, while σ_2 satisfies the condition since the only variable that occurs in $B(\sigma_2)$ more than once, that is, X_2, is not marked in Σ. Apparently, there are two ways of extending sticky sets of TGDs with default negation that give rise to two classes of NTGDs: either consider or ignore the negative literals during the computation of the marked variables and the check of the stickiness condition.

Definition 3. A set Σ of NTGDs is *sticky* (resp., *sticky*$^+$) if $\Sigma^{\perp}$ (resp., Σ^+) is sticky. ■

Recall that $\Sigma^{\perp}$ is obtained from Σ by replacing each negative literal $\sim p(\mathbf{t})$ with $p(\mathbf{t})$, while Σ^+ is obtained from Σ by eliminating the negative literals. It is straightforward to verify that every sticky set of NTGDs is also sticky$^+$, but not vice-versa.

Example 4. Consider the set Σ consisting of the NTGDs:

$$\begin{aligned} \sigma_1 &= p(X_1, Y_1), \sim s(X_1) \rightarrow \exists Z_1\, p(Y_1, Z_1) \\ \sigma_2 &= p(X_2, Y_2), \underline{p(Z_2, X_2)}, \sim p(X_2, X_2) \rightarrow s(X_2). \end{aligned}$$

Observe that Σ^+ coincides with the set of TGDs given in Example 3, and the set of marked variables in Σ^+ is $\{X_1, Y_1, Y_2, Z_2\}$. The set of marked variables in $\Sigma^{\perp}$ is $\{X_1, X_2, Y_1, Y_2, Z_2\}$, i.e., X_2 is also marked; this is obtained during the inductive step of the computation of the marked variables, as shown in Figure 1(b). Hence, if the underline atom is present, then Σ is sticky$^+$ but not sticky; otherwise, Σ is sticky (and thus sticky$^+$). ■

Our goal, in the rest of this section, is to investigate whether the decidability of query answering under the well-founded and stable model semantics is preserved, after the extension of sticky sets of TGDs with default negation. For technical clarity, in the rest of the paper we consider NTGDs in *normal form*, i.e., NTGDs with just one atom in the head that contains at most one occurrence of an existentially quantified variable. As for TGDs, a set of NTGDs can be transformed in logarithmic space into an equivalent set, w.r.t query answering, of NTGDs in normal form; for the normalization procedure see, e.g., [7]. It is important to say that the employed normalization procedure preserves the sticky and sticky$^+$ conditions. For a NTGD σ in normal form, we denote by $\pi_{\exists}(\sigma)$ the position where its existentially quantified variable occurs; if σ does not contain an existentially quantified variable, then $\pi_{\exists}(\sigma)$ is defined as ε.

3.1 Well-Founded Semantics

We first focus our attention on the well-founded semantics, and show that the decidability of query answering under sticky sets of NTGDs is preserved. This is established by a reduction to Datalog$^\neg$ query evaluation. In particular, given a sticky set Σ of NTGDs, and a NBCQ q, a (finite) Boolean Datalog$^\neg$ query $q_\Sigma = (\Pi, q')$, where q' is a 0-ary auxiliary predicate, can be constructed such that, for every database D, $D \cup \Sigma \models_{WFS} q$ iff $D \cup \Pi \models_{WFS} q'$; the latter is a decidable problem [9], and we get that:

THEOREM 1. *WFS-NBCQ answering under sticky sets of NTGDs is decidable.*

The intuition underlying the rewriting, which essentially extends XRewrite [16] to NTGDs, is given below.

Example 5. Let $q = \exists X \exists Y\, p(X,Y) \wedge r(X)$, and $\mathcal{S}(\Sigma)$ be the set of rules: $\rho_1 = p(X_1,Y_1), \sim u(X_1) \rightarrow r(X_1)$, $\rho_2 = r(X_2) \rightarrow p(f(X_2), X_2)$ and $\rho_3 = t(X_3,Y_3) \rightarrow u(X_3)$. The program Π of the query $q_\Sigma = (\Pi, q')$ is as follows:

$$
\begin{aligned}
\rho_4 &= p(X,Y), r(X) \rightarrow q' \\
\rho_5 &= p(X,Y), p(X,Y_5), \sim q''(X) \rightarrow q' \\
\rho_6 &= u(X) \rightarrow q''(X) \\
\rho_7 &= p(X,Y), \sim q''(X) \rightarrow q' \\
\rho_8 &= r(Y), \sim q'''(Y) \rightarrow q' \\
\rho_9 &= u(f(Y)) \rightarrow q'''(Y) \\
\rho_{10} &= t(X,Y_3) \rightarrow q''(X) \\
\rho_{11} &= t(f(Y),Y_3) \rightarrow q'''(Y).
\end{aligned}
$$

The rule ρ_5 is obtained from ρ_4 by *rewriting* $r(X)$ with ρ_1, which also introduces the subquery ρ_6. The rule ρ_7, instead, is obtained by *reducing* ρ_5, thus allowing for rewriting $p(X,Y)$ with ρ_2. In this case the unifier is $\{X_2 \rightarrow Y, X \rightarrow f(Y)\}$, which would produce $r(Y), \sim q''(f(Y)) \rightarrow q'$. However, in order to avoid functions in negative literals, a new subquery is introduced, as shown by rules ρ_8 and ρ_9. The last rewriting steps produce ρ_{10} and ρ_{11} from ρ_6 and ρ_9, respectively. At this point, since head predicates in Π do not occur in positive bodies, rules whose bodies contain functions are removed. In this case, ρ_9 and ρ_{11} are removed, and the resulting program is Datalog$^\neg$. ■

Unfortunately, the above positive result cannot be extended to sticky$^+$ sets of NTGDs. This is shown by a reduction from the halting problem. Given an arbitrary deterministic Turing machine M, we construct a database D, a sticky$^+$ set Σ of NTGDs (that does not depend on M), and a (positive) BCQ q (also independent of M), such that M halts iff $D \cup \Sigma \models_{WFS} q$. Roughly speaking, the database D encodes the states, the tape alphabet, and the transition function of M. The set Σ of NTGDs simulates the behavior of M. More precisely, the natural numbers and the associated successor and equality relations are modeled, which are used to have access to a certain tape cell at a certain time instant of the computation of M. Moreover, the complement of the aforementioned successor and equality relations is computed — this trick is crucial since it allows us to avoid joins between positive literals, and thus Σ trivially satisfies the sticky$^+$ condition. Having the above ingredients in place, it is then easy to simulate the behavior of M via some simple NTGDs. Using the query q, we check whether a halting configuration can be reached, and the next result follows:

THEOREM 2. *Consider a database D, a sticky$^+$ set Σ of NTGDs, and a BCQ q. The problem of deciding whether $D \cup \Sigma \models_{WFS} q$ is undecidable, even if Σ and q are fixed.*

More precisely, the proof of Theorem 2 shows that WFS-NBCQ answering under sticky$^+$ sets of NTGDs is undecidable even for stratified negation. Let us clarify that the above negative result is not entirely surprising as the sticky$^+$ condition basically violates the key principle of stickiness.

3.2 Stable Model Semantics

Let us now focus on the stable model semantics. Unfortunately, even for sticky sets of NTGDs, SMS-NBCQ answering is undecidable. This is a rather surprising result. Although BCQ answering under sticky sets of TGDs is decidable, and in fact in AC_0 in data complexity [7], a single negative literal in the body of the TGDs is enough to make our problem undecidable under the stable model semantics. Notice that this is not true for guarded TGDs [15], a class of TGDs for which BCQ answering is more difficult than for sticky sets of TGDs. The reason for this unexpected behavior should be found in the fact that sticky sets of NTGDs are powerful enough for expressing cartesian products, i.e., assertions of the form $p(\mathbf{X}), s(\mathbf{Y}) \rightarrow t(\mathbf{X},\mathbf{Y})$, with $\mathbf{X} \cap \mathbf{Y} = \varnothing$, which are a prime example of non-guardedness. By exploiting cartesian products, we can construct infinite grids, while the stable model semantics gives us the power of nondeterministic guessing. This combination leads to the above undesirable behavior.

The above undecidability result is shown by a reduction from the halting problem. More precisely, given an arbitrary deterministic Turing machine M, we construct a database D, a sticky set Σ of NTGDs (that does not depend on M), and a (positive) BCQ q (also independent of M), such that M halts iff $D \cup \Sigma \not\models_{SMS} q$. Intuitively, each stable model of D and Σ encodes an infinite grid, where each row represents a configuration of M with the columns be the cells of the tape. Then, the query q checks whether at least one stable model of D and Σ represents a valid halting computation of M, and the next result follows:

THEOREM 3. *Consider a database D, a sticky set Σ of NTGDs, and a BCQ q. The problem of deciding whether $D \cup \Sigma \models_{SMS} q$ is undecidable, even if Σ and q are fixed.*

3.3 Our Conclusions

From the above analysis, we conclude that:

- An effective way for bridging the gap between stickiness and the well-founded semantics exists. In fact, this requires to take into account the negative literals during the computation of the marked variables and the check whether the sticky condition holds; and
- There is no way to reconcile stickiness and the stable model semantics for query answering purposes. As already said, the reason for this unexpected outcome is the power of stickiness to express cartesian products, and the power of stable model semantics for nondeterministic guessing.

The former gives rise to the problem of pinpointing the exact complexity of WFS-NBCQ answering under sticky sets of NTGDs, which will be the subject of the next section. The latter demonstrates the need of identifying a meaningful fragment of sticky sets of NTGDs that guarantees the decidability of SMS-NBCQ answering — although this is an interesting task, it goes beyond the scope of the current work, and we leave it as an open problem.

4. COMPLEXITY OF STICKY NTGDS

In this section, we investigate the data and the combined complexity of WFS-NBCQ answering under sticky sets of NTGDs. The data complexity is calculated by considering only the database as input, while the set of NTGDs and the query are fixed. The combined complexity considers everything as part of the input. As we shall see, our problem is tractable in the data complexity, namely in PTIME, and EXPTIME-complete in combined complexity.

4.1 Data Complexity

Let us first focus on the data complexity. Recall that the decidability of WFS-NBCQ answering under sticky sets of NTGDs was shown by a reduction to Datalog$^\neg$ query evaluation (see Theorem 1). This reduction depends only on the set of NTGDs and the query, but not on the database; hence, in the data complexity setting, it is feasible in constant time. Since the problem of evaluating a (Boolean) Datalog$^\neg$ query under the well-founded semantics is in PTIME in data complexity [9], we get that:

THEOREM 4. *WFS-NBCQ answering under sticky sets of NTGDs is in* PTIME *in data complexity.*

Unfortunately, the precise complexity of WFS-NBCQ answering under sticky sets of NTGDs is open. However, we conjecture that the constructed Datalog$^\neg$ query can be transformed into a nonrecursive Datalog$^\neg$ query, which implies an AC_0 upper bound.

4.2 Combined Complexity

We now concentrate on the combined complexity of our problem, and show that:

THEOREM 5. *WFS-NBCQ answering under sticky sets of NTGDs is* EXPTIME*-complete in combined complexity.*

The lower bound is inherited from BCQ answering under sticky sets of TGDs [7]. The rest of this section is devoted to establish the desired EXPTIME upper bound. Notice that the machinery employed for the data complexity does not provide an optimal upper bound for the combined complexity, since the obtained Datalog$^\neg$ query is, in general, of double-exponential size; implicit in [16].

4.2.1 Plan of Attack

Our plan of attack is as follows: (1) We first introduce the so-called proof-scheme of a query w.r.t. a database and a set of NTGDs, and show that WFS-NBCQ answering is equivalent to the problem of deciding whether a proof-scheme, called accepting, that fulfills certain syntactic properties exists (Lemma 6). An accepting proof-scheme, which is actually a rooted, infinitely branching, labeled tree, can be conceived as a tree-like representation of the part of the (unique) well-founded model due to which the query is entailed, i.e., the proof of the query (hence the term "proof-scheme"); (2) Having the notion of the proof-scheme in place, we can naturally define the so-called alternating tree, that is, a rooted, finitely branching, labeled tree, that can be understood as a compact representation of a proof-scheme. We establish that an accepting proof-scheme exists iff an accepting alternating tree exists (Lemma 7); (3) Finally, we decide whether an accepting alternating tree exists by employing an alternating polynomial space algorithm (Lemma 10). Since APSPACE $=$ EXPTIME, the desired upper bound follows.

4.2.2 Proof-Scheme

For WFS-NBCQ answering under sticky sets of NTGDs, we can always assume that the query is a positive atomic BCQ, i.e., a query of the form $\exists \mathbf{X}\, p(\mathbf{X})$. Consider a database D, a sticky set Σ of NTGDs, and a NBCQ q of the form $\exists \mathbf{X}\, \varphi(\mathbf{X})$. Clearly, $D \cup \Sigma \models_{WFS} q$ iff $D \cup \Sigma_q \models_{WFS} q^\star$, where $\Sigma_q = \Sigma \cup \{\varphi(\mathbf{X}) \rightarrow p^\star(\mathbf{X})\}$ with $p^\star$ be an auxiliary predicate not occurring in Σ, and $q^\star = \exists \mathbf{X}\, p^\star(\mathbf{X})$; notice that Σ_q is still a sticky set of NTGDs.

Given an atom $\underline{a}$ and a normal program Π, let $\mathit{heads}(\underline{a}, \Pi)$ be the set of rules $\{\rho \in \Pi \mid \underline{a} = H(\rho), B(\rho) \neq \varnothing\}$. In what follows, we consider rooted, infinite, labeled trees, which are directed from the root downwards. The root of a tree T is denoted $\mathit{root}(T)$. Fix a database D, a sticky set Σ of NTGDs, and an atomic BCQ $q = \exists \mathbf{X}\, p(\mathbf{X})$; the formal definition of a proof-scheme follows:

Definition 4. A *proof-scheme* for q w.r.t. D and Σ is an infinitely branching tree $P = (V, E, \lambda_1, \lambda_2)$, where $\lambda_1 : V \rightarrow (B_{D \cup \mathcal{S}(\Sigma)} \cup {\sim}.B_{D \cup \mathcal{S}(\Sigma)})$ and $\lambda_2 : E \rightarrow (\Pi_{D,\Sigma} \cup {\sim}.\Pi_{D,\Sigma})$ are the node and edge labeling functions, respectively, and the following hold:

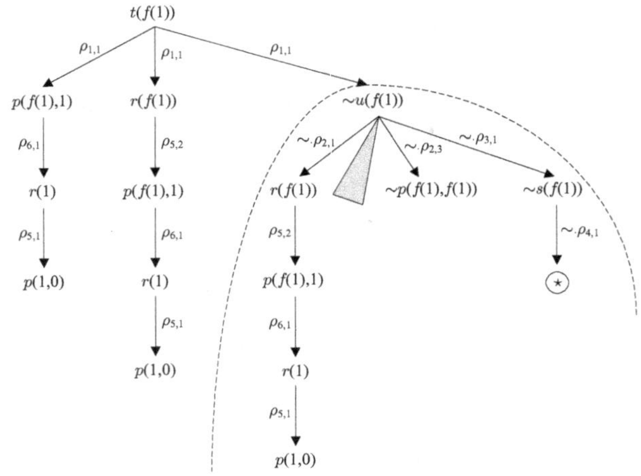

Figure 2: A proof-scheme for Example 6.

1. There exists $\mu : \mathbf{X} \rightarrow U_{D \cup \mathcal{S}(\Sigma)}$ such that $\mu(p(\mathbf{X})) = \lambda_1(\mathit{root}(P))$;
2. For each node $v \in V$:
   (a) if $\lambda_1(v) \in B_{D \cup \mathcal{S}(\Sigma)}$, then: either v is a leaf node, or *there exists* a rule $\rho \in \mathit{heads}(\lambda_1(v), \Pi_{D,\Sigma})$ such that (i) v has $|B(\rho)|$ children, and (ii) *for each* $\underline{b} \in B(\rho)$, there exists a child node u of v such that $\lambda_1(u) = \underline{b}$ and $\lambda_2((v,u)) = \rho$;
   (b) if $\lambda_1(v) \in {\sim}.B_{D \cup \mathcal{S}(\Sigma)}$, then: if v is a leaf node, then $\mathit{heads}({\sim}.\lambda_1(v), \Pi_{D,\Sigma}) = \varnothing$; otherwise, (i) the number of children of v is $|\mathit{heads}({\sim}.\lambda_1(v), \Pi_{D,\Sigma})|$, and (ii) *for each* $\rho \in \mathit{heads}({\sim}.\lambda_1(v), \Pi_{D,\Sigma})$, *there exist* $\underline{b} \in B(\rho)$ and a child node u of v such that $\lambda_1(u) = {\sim}.\underline{b}$ and $\lambda_2((v,u)) = {\sim}.\rho$. ■

An example of a proof-scheme follows:

Example 6. Consider the database $D = \{p(1,0), s(1)\}$, and the set Σ of NTGDs consisting of:

$$
\begin{array}{rcl}
\sigma_1 & = & p(X_1, Y_1), r(X_1), {\sim}u(X_1) \rightarrow t(X_1) \\
\sigma_2 & = & p(X_2, Y_2), {\sim}r(X_2) \rightarrow u(X_2) \\
\sigma_3 & = & s(X_3), {\sim}t(X_3) \rightarrow u(X_3) \\
\sigma_4 & = & u(X_4), {\sim}t(X_4) \rightarrow s(X_4) \\
\sigma_5 & = & p(X_5, Y_5) \rightarrow r(X_5) \\
\sigma_6 & = & r(X_6) \rightarrow \exists Y_6\, p(Y_6, X_6).
\end{array}
$$

Clearly, $\mathcal{S}(\Sigma) = \{\rho_1, \ldots, \rho_6\}$, where $\rho_i = \sigma_i$ for each $i \in \{1, \ldots, 5\}$, and ρ_6 is the rule $r(X_6) \rightarrow p(f(X_6), X_6)$. A small subset of $\Pi_{D,\Sigma}$ follows:

$$
\begin{array}{rcl}
\rho_{D,1} & = & \rightarrow p(1,0) \\
\rho_{D,2} & = & \rightarrow s(1) \\
\rho_{1,1} & = & p(f(1),1), r(f(1)), {\sim}u(f(1)) \rightarrow t(f(1)) \\
\rho_{2,1} & = & p(f(1),0), {\sim}r(f(1)) \rightarrow u(f(1)) \\
\rho_{2,2} & = & p(f(1),1), {\sim}r(f(1)) \rightarrow u(f(1)) \\
\rho_{2,3} & = & p(f(1),f(1)), {\sim}r(f(1)) \rightarrow u(f(1)) \\
\rho_{3,1} & = & s(f(1)), {\sim}t(f(1)) \rightarrow u(f(1)) \\
\rho_{4,1} & = & u(f(1)), {\sim}t(f(1)) \rightarrow s(f(1)) \\
\rho_{5,1} & = & p(1,0) \rightarrow r(1) \\
\rho_{5,2} & = & p(f(1),1) \rightarrow r(f(1)) \\
\rho_{6,1} & = & r(1) \rightarrow p(f(1),1).
\end{array}
$$

A proof-scheme for the query $q = \exists X\ t(X)$ w.r.t. D and Σ is depicted in Figure 2. Nodes labeled by $\star$ are replaced by the subtree under the dashed curve. The shaded subtree of ${\sim}u(f(1))$ represents an infinitely branching tree; $\sim u(f(1))$ has infinitely many children labeled by $r(f(1))$, the edges $(\sim u(f(1)), r(f(1))$ are labeled by ground instances of ρ_2, and each child of $\sim u(f(1))$ is the first node of the path $r(f(1))\rho_{5,2}p(f(1),1)\rho_{6,1}r(1)\rho_{5,1}p(1,0)$. ■

We proceed to define when a proof-scheme is accepting by posing some syntactic restrictions.

Definition 5. Consider a proof-scheme P for q w.r.t. D and Σ, with λ be its node labeling function. P is *accepting* if the following conditions hold: (1) each leaf node v of P with $\lambda(v) \in B_{D \cup \mathcal{S}(\Sigma)}$ is such that $\lambda(v) \in D$, and each node v of P with $\lambda(v) \in \sim.B_{D \cup \mathcal{S}(\Sigma)}$ is such that $\sim.\lambda(v) \notin D$; (2) for every branch π of P without a leaf node, the set $\{v \in \pi \mid \lambda(v) \in B_{D \cup \mathcal{S}(\Sigma)}\}$ is finite. ■

Condition (1) is quite intuitive: all the leaves that are labeled by positive atoms represent database atoms, while all the nodes (including the internal ones) labeled by negative literals refer to non-database atoms. Condition (2) says that all the infinite branches without a leaf must contain finitely many nodes that are labeled by positive atoms; the intuition underlying this condition is as follows.

Assume first that an infinite branch $\pi = v_0 v_1 \dots v_n \dots$ occurs in a proof-scheme P, with λ be its node labeling function, where v_0 is the root node, and $v_n, v_{n+1}, \dots$ are labeled by positive atoms. This implies that the truth of $\lambda(v_i)$ is proved by showing the truth of $\lambda(v_{i+1})$, for each $i \geq n$, which is an unfounded argument because there is no base case. It follows that the query cannot be entailed in this way in the well-founded model; thus, π is considered as non-accepting, and therefore P is non-accepting. Now, if π is such that v_{n-1} is labeled by a positive atom and $v_n, v_{n+1}, \dots$ are labeled by negative literals, then the truth of $\lambda(v_{n-1})$ is proved by showing that $\sim.\lambda(v_n), \sim.\lambda(v_{n+1}), \dots$ are false, which is the case if they belong to some unfounded set not depending on $v_0 \dots v_{n-1}$. Hence, $\lambda(v_{n-1})$ is true, which means that it contributes in the entailment of the query; thus, π is accepting. There is also a third case: branch π may contain infinitely many sign alterations. For simplicity, assume that $sign(\lambda(v_i)) \neq sign(\lambda(v_{i+1}))$ holds for each $i \geq n$, and $sign(\lambda(v_n)) = +$. In this case, for each $i \geq n/2$ (assuming that n is even), the truth of $\lambda(v_{2i})$ is proved by showing the falsity of $\sim.\lambda(v_{2i+1})$, which is in turn proved by showing the truth of $\lambda(v_{2i+2})$. We are again in presence of an unfounded argument because there is no base case, and thus π and P are non-accepting.

Observe that the proof-scheme in Figure 2 is accepting. In particular, all the branches without a leaf node, which are of the form $t(f(1)) \sim u(f(1)) \sim s(f(1)) \sim u(f(1)) \dots$, contain only one positive literal, that is, $t(f(1))$. The next result shows the tight connection between query answering and accepting proof-schemes:

LEMMA 6. *$D \cup \Sigma \models_{WFS} q$ iff there exists an accepting proof-scheme for q w.r.t. D and Σ.*

4.2.3 Alternating Tree

To obtain the desired upper bound, by Lemma 6, it suffices to show that the problem of deciding whether an accepting proof-scheme exists is feasible in exponential time. However, towards this direction, we need to overcome the following two technical difficulties: (i) a proof-scheme is an infinitely branching tree; and (ii) its nodes may be labeled by arbitrarily large Skolem terms. The former can be tackled by encoding the (infinitely many) outgoing edges of a node, labeled with ground instances of the same rule, into a single edge, while the latter can be overwhelmed by using variables, instead of Skolem terms, for labeling the nodes of a proof-scheme (or, in other words, by considering the given NTGDs in their original form with existentially quantified variables). After implementing the above intuitive ideas, we obtain a rooted, finitely branching, labeled tree, called alternating tree, which can be seen as a compact representation of a proof-scheme. Before giving the rather long formal definition, let us briefly explain, via an example, how a proof-scheme can be transformed into an alternating tree.

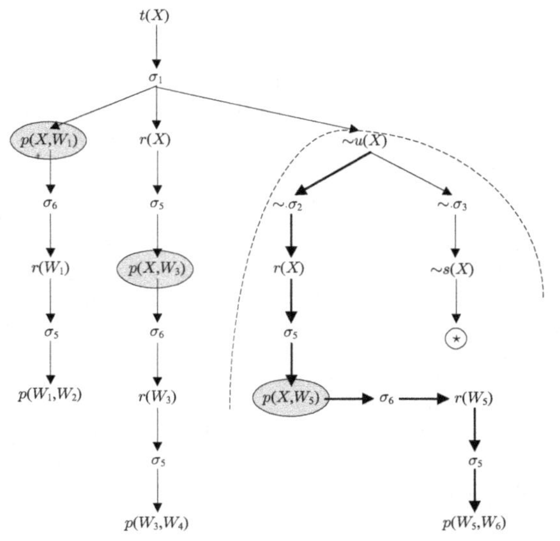

Figure 3: The alternating tree for Example 7.

Example 7. The proof-scheme depicted in Figure 2 can be naturally transformed into the alternating tree shown in Figure 3, where the nodes labeled by $\star$ are replaced by the subtree under the dashed curve. Observe that the query variable X corresponds to the Skolem term $f(1)$, while the shaded nodes represent the atom in the well-founded model where $f(1)$ has been generated; in other words, the shaded nodes refer to the same atom in the well-founded model, and this is captured by the fact that their labels are $\{X\}$-isomorphic atoms. The symbols $W_1, W_2, \dots$ are "fresh" variables that do not occur neither in Σ nor in q. The highlighted path from $\sim u(X)$ down to $p(W_5, W_6)$ encodes the infinitely branching tree rooted at $\sim u(X)$. The alternating tree under consideration is accepting since the leaf nodes, which are labeled by positive atoms, do not contain X (and thus may be database atoms) and can be mapped via a mapping μ to the database atom $p(1,0)$, while μ cannot be extended to a mapping (that is the identity on X) that maps the negative literals occurring in the proof-scheme to the database. Moreover, all the infinite branches without a leaf node contain only one positive atom, that is, $t(X)$. ■

A difference between a proof-scheme and an alternating tree is the fact that in the latter nodes are labeled with literals and TGDs, while edges are not labeled. This is a technicality that will allows us to simplify the alternating algorithm for deciding the existence of an accepting alternating tree.

We now proceed with the formal definition of alternating trees. But let us first introduce some additional notation and terminology. Given two atoms $\underline{a}$ and $\underline{b}$ that unify, we denote by $\mathsf{MGU}(\underline{a}, \underline{b})$ their most general unifier. A term is *bound* in an atom $\underline{a}$ if it is a constant of $\mathbf{C}_0$ or occurs in $\underline{a}$ more than once. Given a NTGD σ and an atom $p(\mathbf{t})$, we say that σ is *T-compatible* with $p(\mathbf{t})$, where $T \subseteq \mathbf{t}$, written as $\sigma \rhd_T p(\mathbf{t})$, if the following conditions hold: (i) $p(\mathbf{t})$ and $H(\sigma)$ unify, and $\mathsf{MGU}(p(\mathbf{t}), H(\sigma))$ is the identity on T; and (ii) for each $i \in [n]$, where n is the arity of p, $\mathbf{t}[i]$ is bound in $p(\mathbf{t})$ implies $p[i] \neq \pi_{\exists}(\sigma)$. Given a set Σ of NTGDs, let $\mathsf{C}_T(p(\mathbf{t}), \Sigma) =$

$\{\sigma \in \Sigma \mid \sigma \rhd_T p(\mathbf{t})\}$; for brevity, whenever Σ is clear from the context, we shall write $\mathsf{C}_T(p(\mathbf{t}))$.

We consider a (countably infinite) set of symbols $\mathbf{\Delta}$ such that $\mathbf{\Delta} \cap (\mathbf{C} \cup \mathbf{N} \cup \mathbf{V}) = \varnothing$. Given a database D, a NTGD σ, and a (finite) set of variables $T \subset \mathbf{V}$, we define $M_{D,\sigma,T}$ as the set of mappings $\{\mu \mid \mu : (var(B(\sigma)) \setminus var(H(\sigma))) \rightarrow (dom(D) \cup T \cup \mathbf{\Delta})\}$. Let $\approx_S$, where S is a (finite) subset of $\mathbf{V}$, be the binary relation on $M_{D,\sigma,T}$ defined as follows: $\mu \approx_S \mu'$ iff $\mu(F) \simeq_S \mu'(F)$, where $F = (var(B(\sigma)) \setminus var(H(\sigma)))$. By definition, $\approx_S$ on $M_{D,\sigma,T}$ is an equivalence relation. The *quotient set* of $M_{D,\sigma,T}$ by $\approx_S$, i.e., the set of all equivalence classes in $M_{D,\sigma,T}$ w.r.t. $\approx_S$, is denoted $M_{D,\sigma,T}/\approx_S$. We denote by $[M_{D,\sigma,T}]_{\approx_S}$ the set of *equivalence class representatives*, that is, a subset of $M_{D,\sigma,T}$ which contains exactly one element, called *representative*, of each equivalence class of $M_{D,\sigma,T}/\approx_S$.

Given a set Σ of NTGDs, let M_Σ be the set of NTGD-mapping pairs $\bigcup_{\sigma \in \Sigma}\{(\sigma, \mu) \mid \mu : var(B(\sigma)) \rightarrow \mathbf{C} \cup \mathbf{V} \cup \mathbf{\Delta}\}$; $\sim\!\cdot M_\Sigma$ is defined in the same way, but its members are pairs of the form $(\sim\!\cdot\sigma, \mu)$. Finally, $B_{D,\Sigma,q}$ is the set of atoms that can be formed using predicates occurring in Σ, constants of $dom(D)$, variables of $var(q)$ and symbols of $\mathbf{\Delta}$. We are now ready to define alternating trees; fix a database D, a sticky set Σ of NTGDs, and an atomic BCQ $q = \exists \mathbf{X}\, p(\mathbf{X})$:

Definition 6. Let $P = (V, E, \lambda)$ be a k-ary tree, where k is the integer $\max\{\max_{\sigma \in \Sigma}\{|B(\sigma)|\}, |\Sigma| \cdot \max_{\sigma \in \Sigma}\{\delta_\sigma\}\}$, with $\delta_\sigma = |[M_{D,\sigma,var(\lambda(root(P)))}]_{\approx var_{>1}(P)}|$ and $var_{>1}(P)$ be the set of variables occurring in more than one branch of P, and λ is the labeling function $V \rightarrow (B_{D,\Sigma,q} \cup \sim\!\cdot B_{D,\Sigma,q} \cup M_\Sigma \cup \sim\!\cdot M_\Sigma)$. We say that P is an *alternating tree* for q w.r.t. D and Σ if the following hold:

1. There exists a mapping $\mu : \mathbf{X} \rightarrow (dom(D) \cup \mathbf{X})$ such that $\mu(p(\mathbf{X})) = \lambda(root(P))$;
2. For each node $v \in V$:

   (a) if $\underline{\lambda(v) \in B_{D,\Sigma,q}}$, then: either v is a leaf node, or v has exactly one child node u, and *there exists* a pair $(\sigma, \mu) \in \mathsf{C}_{var_{>1}(P)}(\lambda(v)) \times M_{D,\sigma,var(\lambda(root(P)))}$ such that (i) $\lambda(u) = (\sigma, \gamma)$, where $\gamma = (\mathsf{MGU}(\lambda(v), H(\sigma)) \cup \mu)$, and u has $|B(\sigma)|$ children, and (ii) *for each* literal $\ell \in B(\sigma)$, there exists a child node w of u such that $\lambda(w) \simeq_{var_{>1}(P)} \gamma(\ell)$;

   (b) if $\underline{\lambda(v) \in \sim\!\cdot B_{D,\Sigma,q}}$, then: if v is a leaf node, then the set $\mathsf{C}_{var_{>1}(P)}(\sim\!\cdot\lambda(v))$ is empty; otherwise, (i) assuming that $\mathsf{C}_{var_{>1}(P)}(\sim\!\cdot\lambda(v)) = \{\sigma_i\}_{i \in [k]}$, v has $\sum_{i \in [k]} \delta_{\sigma_i}$ children, and (ii) *for each* pair (σ, μ) of the set $\mathsf{C}_{var_{>1}(P)}(\sim\!\cdot\lambda(v)) \times [M_{D,\sigma,var(\lambda(root(P)))}]_{\approx var_{>1}(P)}$, there exists a child node u of v such that $\lambda(u) = (\sim\!\cdot\sigma, \gamma)$, where γ is defined as $(\mathsf{MGU}(\sim\!\cdot\lambda(v), H(\sigma)) \cup \mu)$, u has exactly one child node w, and *there exists* $\ell \in B(\sim\!\cdot\sigma)$ such that $\lambda(w) \simeq_{var_{>1}(P)} \gamma(\ell)$;
3. For a variable $X \in var(P)$, we define the set of *critical edges* for X, denoted $critical(X)$, as follows:

$$\left\{ (v,u) \in E \;\middle|\; \begin{array}{l} \lambda(v) \in (B_{D,\Sigma,q} \cup \sim\!\cdot B_{D,\Sigma,q}), \\ \lambda(u) = (\sigma, \cdot) \in (M_\Sigma \cup \sim\!\cdot M_\Sigma), \\ X \in dom(\lambda(v)), \\ \pi_\exists(\sigma) \neq \varepsilon, \\ X \text{ appears in } \lambda(v) \text{ at } \pi_\exists(\sigma) \end{array} \right\}.$$

   For each $X \in var_{>1}(P)$, and for every pair of edges (v_1, u_1), $(v_2, u_2) \in critical(X)$, $\underline{a}_1 \simeq_{var_{>1}(P)} \underline{a}_2$, where $\underline{a}_1$ and $\underline{a}_2$ are the atoms occurring in $\lambda(v_1)$ and $\lambda(v_2)$, respectively. ■

Notice that in the alternating tree P in Figure 3, the shaded nodes are critical for X, and indeed their labels are $\{X\}$-isomorphic. For simplicity, in P, the mappings are omitted in nodes labeled by NTGDs. The accepting condition for alternating trees is similar to the one for proof-schemes (see Definition 5). In what follows, for an alternating tree P, let LV_P^+ be the set of leaf nodes that are labeled by positive literals, and V_P^- the set of nodes (including the internal ones) that are labeled by negative literals.

Definition 7. Consider an alternating tree P for q w.r.t. D and Σ, with λ be its node labeling function. P is *accepting* if: (1) there exists a mapping $\mu : var(\{\lambda(v)\}_{v \in LV^+}) \rightarrow dom(D)$ that is the identity on $var(\lambda(root(P)))$ such that $\mu(\{\lambda(v)\}_{v \in LV^+}) \subseteq D$, and for every $\mu' : (var(\{\lambda(v)\}_{v \in V^-}) \setminus var(\{\lambda(v)\}_{v \in LV^+})) \rightarrow dom(D)$ that is the identity on $var(\lambda(root(P)))$, we have that $(\mu \cup \mu')(\{\lambda(v)\}_{v \in V^-}) \cap D = \varnothing$; and (2) for every branch π of P without a leaf node, the set $\{v \in \pi \mid \lambda(v) \in B_{D,\Sigma,q}\}$ is finite. ■

The next technical result exhibits the strong connection between proof-schemes and alternating trees; let us clarify that stickiness is crucial for the validity of the following lemma:

LEMMA 7. *An accepting proof-scheme exists iff an accepting alternating tree exists, both for q w.r.t. D and Σ.*

4.2.4 An Alternating Algorithm

By Lemmas 6 and 7, our problem is equivalent to the problem of deciding whether an accepting alternating tree exists. Formally speaking, given a database D, a sticky set Σ of NTGDs, and an atomic BCQ q, $D \cup \Sigma \models_{WFS} q$ iff there exists an accepting alternating tree for q w.r.t. D and Σ. The rest of this section is devoted to design an alternating polynomial space algorithm, dubbed WFSQAns, which decides whether an accepting alternating tree exists. In fact, WFSQAns takes as input D, Σ and q, and returns *accept* iff an accepting alternating tree for q w.r.t. D and Σ exists.

Fix a database D, a sticky set Σ of NTGDs, and an atomic BCQ $q = \exists \mathbf{X}\, p(\mathbf{X})$. WFSQAns$(D, \Sigma, q)$ will attempt to construct an accepting alternating tree P for q w.r.t. D and Σ (if it exists). Clearly, P must satisfy the criticality condition (3) given in Definition 6. Therefore, it is crucial to understand which variables may appear in more than one branch of P; in other words, we need to identify what kind of variables may appear in $var_{>1}(P)$. Since Σ is sticky, it is easy to verify that the following holds:

LEMMA 8. *Let P be an alternating tree for q w.r.t. D and Σ. Then, $var_{>1}(P) \subseteq var(q)$.*

Since an alternating tree may contain infinite branches, it is important to understand when it is safe to stop the computation of WFSQAns(D, Σ, q), and check whether the accepting condition given in Definition 7 is satisfied. Towards this direction, we show that the existence of an accepting alternating tree for q w.r.t. D and Σ implies the existence of a *compact* accepting alternating tree for q w.r.t. D and Σ, i.e., the length of a path between two sign alterations is finite. Consider an alternating tree $P = (V, E, \lambda)$ for q w.r.t. D and Σ. A path $v_0u_0v_1u_1 \ldots v_nu_nv_{n+1}u_{n+1}$ occurring in P, where $v_i \in (B_{D,\Sigma,q} \cup \sim\!\cdot B_{D,\Sigma,q})$ and $u_i \in (M_\Sigma \cup \sim\!\cdot M_\Sigma)$ for each $i \in \{0, \ldots, n+1\}$, is called *transitional* if $sign(\lambda(v_0)) \neq sign(\lambda(v_1))$, $sign(\lambda(v_n)) \neq sign(\lambda(v_{n+1}))$, and $sign(\lambda(v_i)) = sign(\lambda(v_{i+1}))$ for each $i \in \{1, \ldots, n-1\}$. It is not difficult to show, via a simple combinatorial argument which exploits stickiness, the following lemma; let m be the number of predicates occurring in Σ, and w the maximum arity over the predicates in Σ:

LEMMA 9. *Assume that there exists an accepting alternating tree for q w.r.t. D and Σ. There exists an accepting alternating tree P for q w.r.t. D and Σ such that, for every transitional path $v_0u_0 \ldots v_{n+1}u_{n+1}$ in P, $n \leqslant m \cdot (2w+1)^w$.*

By exploiting the properties established in the preceding two lemmas, we can design our alternating algorithm.

$\mathsf{WFSQAns}(D, \Sigma, q)$ consists of the following steps:

1. Guess two disjoint sets of variables $S_1 \subseteq \mathbf{X}$ and $S_2 \subset \mathbf{X}$, and a mapping $\mu : S_1 \rightarrow (dom(D) \cup S_2)$.
2. Let $S = \mathbf{X} \setminus S_1$ and $\mu = \mu \cup \{X \rightarrow X \mid X \in S\}$.
3. For each $X \in S$, guess an atom $\underline{a}_X = p(t_1, \ldots, t_n)$, where p is an n-ary predicate in Σ, $(t_1, \ldots, t_n) \in (S \cup dom(D) \cup \mathbf{\Delta})^n$, and X occurs in $\underline{a}_V$ exactly once.
4. Let $Cr = \{(X, \underline{a}_V) \mid X \in S\}$.
5. If $\mathsf{Proof}(\mu(p(\mathbf{X})), D, \Sigma, S, Cr)$ accepts, then *accept*; otherwise, *reject*.

Roughly, the guessed mapping μ represents a homomorphism that maps $p(\mathbf{X})$ to the well-founded model of $\Pi_{D,\Sigma}$. The variables of S symbolize the variables of $p(\mathbf{X})$ that are mapped by μ to terms other than constants of $\mathbf{C}_0$. At step 3, for each variable $X \in S$, we guess an atom that encodes the equality type of the label of the node v, for each critical edge $(v, u) \in critical(X)$, in an accepting alternating tree for q w.r.t. D and Σ. Those atoms will be used by the alternating procedure Proof, which checks for the existence of an accepting alternating tree P (with $root(P) = \mu(p(\mathbf{X}))$) for q w.r.t. D and Σ, to ensure that the criticality condition required by Definition 6 is fulfilled. Intuitively, Proof will construct, in parallel universal computations, the branches of a compact accepting alternating tree for q w.r.t. D and Σ (if it exists).

$\mathsf{Proof}(\ell, D, \Sigma, S, Cr)$ consists of the following steps:

1. $ctr := 0$ and $sign := +$.
2. If $sign = +$, then goto step 3; otherwise, goto step 9.

Positive Literals:

3. If there exists a mapping $\mu : var(\ell) \rightarrow dom(D)$ that is the identity on S such that $\mu(\ell) \in D$, then *accept*.
4. If $ctr > m \cdot (2w + 1)^w$, then *reject*.
5. If $\mathsf{C}_S(\ell) = \varnothing$, then *reject*; otherwise, *guess* a NTGD $\sigma \in \mathsf{C}_S(\ell)$ and a mapping $\mu \in M_{D,\sigma,S}$.
6. If there exists $X \in (var(\ell) \cap S)$ that appears at position $\pi_\exists(\sigma)$ and $\ell \not\approx_S \underline{a}_X$, where $(X, \underline{a}_X) \in Cr$, then *reject*.
7. $\gamma := (\mathsf{MGU}(\ell, H(\sigma)) \cup \mu)$.
8. *Universally select* every literal $\ell \in \gamma(B(\sigma))$ and do the following:
   (a) if $sign = sign(\ell)$, then $ctr := ctr + 1$; otherwise, $sign := sign(\ell)$ and $ctr := 0$.
   (b) Goto step 2.

Negative Literals:

9. If there exists $\mu : var({\sim}\ell) \rightarrow dom(D)$ that is the identity on S such that $\mu({\sim}\ell) \in D$, then *reject*.
10. If $\mathsf{C}_S({\sim}\ell) = \varnothing$, then *accept*.
11. If $ctr > m \cdot (2w + 1)^w$, then *accept*.
12. *Universally select* every pair $(\sigma, \mu) \in \mathsf{C}_S({\sim}\ell) \times [M_{D,\sigma,S}]_{\approx S}$ and do the following:
    (a) If there exists $X \in (var({\sim}\ell) \cap S)$ that appears at position $\pi_\exists(\sigma)$ and ${\sim}\ell \not\approx_S \underline{a}_X$, where $(X, \underline{a}_X) \in Cr$, then *reject*.
    (b) $\gamma := (\mathsf{MGU}({\sim}\ell, H(\sigma)) \cup \mu)$.
    (c) *Guess* a literal $\ell \in \gamma(B({\sim}\sigma))$: if $sign = sign(\ell)$, then $ctr := ctr + 1$; otherwise, $sign := sign(\ell)$ and $ctr := 0$.
    (d) Goto step 2.

It is not difficult to verify that $\mathsf{WFSQAns}(D, \Sigma, q)$ constructs an accepting alternating tree for q w.r.t D and Σ, and thus *accepts*, if it exists, and *rejects* if such a tree does not exist. Regarding the complexity of $\mathsf{WFSQAns}$, observe that it runs in nondeterministic polynomial time with a $\mathcal{C}$-oracle, where $\mathcal{C}$ is a complexity class powerful enough for executing the procedure Proof. At each step of the computation of Proof we need polynomial space, and hence $\mathcal{C}$ = APSPACE. Since APSPACE = EXPTIME and $\text{NP}^{\text{EXPTIME}}$ = EXPTIME, the next technical result follows:

LEMMA 10. *$\mathsf{WFSQAns}$ with input (D, Σ, q) halts after exponentially many steps, and returns accept iff there exists an accepting alternating tree for q w.r.t. D and Σ.*

From Lemmas 6, 7 and 10 we get the desired EXPTIME upper bound, and Theorem 5 follows.

5. TWO-DIMENSIONAL STICKY NTGDS

Although the class of NTGDs investigated in the previous section forms a natural way for extending sticky sets of TGDs with default negation, it is rather limited. Unfortunately, even one of the simplest and most prominent classes of TGDs, namely *inclusion dependencies (IDs)*, enriched with default negation, is not captured by sticky sets of NTGDs. Inclusion dependencies are in fact TGDs with just one atom in the body and one atom in the head, where body-variables (resp., head-variables) occur only once. It is easy to verify that, given an ID, after adding a negative literal in its body, the obtained NTGD is, in general, not sticky. For example, given the ID $p(X, Y) \rightarrow \exists Z\, p(Y, Z)$, by adding the atom ${\sim}s(Y, X)$ in its body, we violate the sticky condition; the variable X, which occurs more than once in the body of the obtained NTGD, is marked.

The above discussion demonstrates the need for devising a more refined combination of stickiness with default negation. More precisely, a class of NTGDs that lies between sticky and sticky$^+$ sets of NTGDs is needed, which fulfills the following criteria: (1) is powerful enough for capturing normal IDs, and ultimately expressing some natural constraints; and (2) guarantees, not only the decidability, but also the tractability of WFS-NBCQ answering in data complexity. Such a formalism are the so-called two-dimensional sticky (or simply 2D-sticky) sets of NTGDs.

5.1 Formal Definition

Before presenting the formal definition of 2D-stickiness, we first need to introduce some auxiliary notions. As already discussed, the reason that makes WFS-NBCQ under sticky$^+$ sets of NTGDs undecidable is basically the fact that the key principle of stickiness is violated. This is due to the marked variables that appear in negative literals; such variables are dubbed dangerous:

Definition 8. Consider a set Σ of NTGDs, and a variable $X \in var(B(\sigma))$, where $\sigma \in \Sigma$. We say that X is *dangerous* in Σ if it is marked in Σ^+, and occurs in $var(B^-(\sigma))$. Let $dvar(\Sigma)$ be the set of variables that are dangerous in Σ. ■

Example 8. Consider the set Σ consisting of the NTGDs:

$$\sigma_1 \;=\; p(X_1, Y_1), {\sim}s(X_1) \rightarrow \exists Z_1\, p(Y_1, Z_1)$$
$$\sigma_2 \;=\; p(X_2, Y_2), p(Z_2, X_2), {\sim}p(Y_2, X_2) \rightarrow s(X_2).$$

The set of marked variables in Σ^+ is $\{X_1, Y_1, Y_2, Z_2\}$ (see Example 4); thus, $dvar(\Sigma) = \{X_1, Y_2\}$. X_2, although it occurs in $B^-(\sigma_2)$, is not dangerous in Σ since it is not marked in Σ^+. ■

Another key notion is the refute set of a positive atom. Let us give the intuition underlying this notion using a simple example.

Consider the set Σ consisting of the NTGDs:

$$\sigma_1 \;=\; \underbrace{p(X_1, Y_1)}_{\underline{a}}, \sim \underbrace{s(X_1)}_{\underline{b}} \rightarrow \exists Z_1\, p(Y_1, Z_1)$$
$$\sigma_2 \;=\; \underbrace{s(X_2)}_{\underline{c}} \rightarrow \exists Y_2\, p(X_2, Y_2).$$

Assuming that $\underline{a}$ is true, in order to conclude that $B(\sigma_1)$ is also true we have to refute $\underline{b}$. Since $\underline{a}$ and $\underline{b}$ share the dangerous variable X_1, we say that $\underline{b}$ belongs to the refute set of $\underline{a}$. Moreover, assuming that $\underline{c}$ is true, which implies that an atom of the form $p(t, t')$ is inferred, it may contribute in making $\underline{a}$ true, and thus (by induction) we say that $\underline{b}$ also belongs to the refute set of $\underline{c}$. Roughly speaking, the refute set of an atom $\underline{a}$ collects all those atoms, containing at least one dangerous variable, that eventually must be refuted, and occur on the same derivation with $\underline{a}$. The refutation of those atoms, which may be arbitrarily many, is the main reason for the undecidability of WFS-NBCQ under sticky$^+$ sets of NTGDs — this is exactly the process that must be tamed in order to regain decidability. In what follows, given an atom $p(\mathbf{t})$ and the position $p[i]$, we denote by $[p(\mathbf{t})]_{p[i]}$ the variable occurring in $p(\mathbf{t})$ at position $p[i]$.

Definition 9. Consider a set Σ of NTGDs, and let X be a variable occurring in the body of some $\sigma \in \Sigma$. The refute set of X w.r.t. Σ, denoted $rset(X, \Sigma)$, is inductively defined as follows: (i) for each $\underline{a} \in B^-(\sigma)$ such that $X \in var(\underline{a})$, $\underline{a} \in rset(X, \Sigma)$; and (ii) assuming that X occurs in $\underline{a} = H(\sigma)$, if there exists $\sigma' \in \Sigma$ and an atom $\underline{b} \in B^+(\sigma')$ with $pred(\underline{a}) = pred(\underline{b})$, then, for each $\pi \in pos(\underline{a}, X)$, the atoms of $rset([\underline{b}]_\pi, \Sigma)$ are added to $rset(X, \Sigma)$. The *refute set* of an atom $\underline{a} \in B^+(\sigma)$ w.r.t. Σ, denoted $rset(\underline{a}, \Sigma)$, is defined as $\bigcup_{X \in (var(\underline{a}) \cap dvar(\Sigma))} rset(X, \Sigma)$. ■

Example 9. Consider the set Σ consisting of the NTGDs:

$$\sigma_1 \;=\; p(X_1, Y_1), \sim s(X_1, Y_1) \rightarrow \exists Z_1\, p(Y_1, Z_1)$$
$$\sigma_2 \;=\; t(X_2, Y_2), s(Y_2, Z_2), \sim p(Y_2, X_2) \rightarrow p(X_2, Y_2).$$

It is easy to verify that

$$rset(X_1, \Sigma) = rset(Y_1, \Sigma) = \{s(X_1, Y_1)\}$$
$$rset(X_2, \Sigma) = rset(Y_2, \Sigma) = \{s(X_1, Y_1), p(Y_2, X_2)\}$$
$$rset(Z_2, \Sigma) = \varnothing.$$

Since $dvar(\Sigma) = \{X_1, X_2\}$, we conclude that

$$rset(p(X_1, Y_1), \Sigma) = \{s(X_1, Y_1)\}$$
$$rset(t(X_2, Y_2), \Sigma) = \{s(X_1, Y_1), p(Y_2, X_2)\}$$
$$rset(s(Y_2, Z_2), \Sigma) = \varnothing.$$

Even if Y_2 occurs in $s(Y_2, Z_2)$, the atoms of $rset(Y_2, \Sigma)$ are not added to $rset(s(Y_2, Z_2), \Sigma)$ since $Y_2 \notin dvar(\Sigma)$. ■

We are now ready to define two-dimensional sticky sets of NTGDs. The key idea underlying this formalism is to relax the sticky condition (without violating the sticky$^+$ condition) in such a way that a dangerous variable may appear more than once in the body a NTGD σ, as long as it does not force an atom of $B^-(\sigma)$ to appear in the refute set of more than one atom of $B^+(\sigma)$, i.e., the atoms of $B^-(\sigma)$ "stick" on one positive atom during the refutation process — this property can be seen as the second dimension of stickiness, and hence the name "two-dimensional" sticky sets of NTGDs.

Definition 10. A set Σ of NTGDs is *two-dimensional sticky* (or *2D-sticky*) if Σ^+ is sticky, and, for every $\underline{a}, \underline{b} \in B^+(\Sigma)$, $\underline{a} \neq \underline{b}$ implies $rset(\underline{a}, \Sigma) \cap rset(\underline{b}, \Sigma) = \varnothing$. ■

Observe that the set of NTGDs given in Example 9 is 2D-sticky. Let us clarify that 2D-sticky sets of NTGDs are strictly more expressive that sticky sets of NTGDs. This can be shown by exploiting the well-known *win-move* program

$$move(X, Y), \sim win(Y) \;\rightarrow\; win(X).$$

It easy to verify that the above NTGD is 2D-sticky. However, it can be shown that it is not expressible as a sticky set of NTGDs. The proof of this inexpressibility result relies on a model-theoretic property of the well-founded model called *sticky property*. Intuitively speaking, the sticky property imposes the following condition: the symbols that are associated (during the application of a NTGD σ) with the body-variables of σ that occur more than once, appear in the generated atom $\underline{a}$, and also in every atom obtained from some derivation that involves $\underline{a}$, thus "sticking" to all such atoms. It is easy to show that sticky sets of NTGDs ensure the sticky property; however, the win-move program is a prime example of a NTGD that violates the sticky property.

The question that comes up is whether we can do better than 2D-stickiness without losing decidability of WFS-NBCQ answering (which is shown in the next section). Unfortunately, even a mild relaxation of 2D-stickiness, which allows an atom to appear in the refute set of two positive body-atoms, makes WFS-NBCQ an undecidable problem. This follows from the fact that Theorem 2 holds even for sticky$^+$ sets Σ of NTGDs such that $B^+(\sigma) \in \{1, 2\}$, for each $\sigma \in \Sigma$. This is a strong indication that 2D-stickiness lies at the decidability/undecidability frontier between sticky and sticky$^+$ sets of NTGDs.

Since normal IDs contain only one positive atom without repetition of variables, we get that:

LEMMA 11. *A set Σ of normal IDs is also 2D-sticky.*

The above lemma immediately implies that 2D-stickiness captures DL-Lite$_{\mathcal{R},\sim}$, that is, the extension of DL-Lite$_{\mathcal{R}}$ with default negation [14]. It is implicit in [14] that every DL-Lite$_{\mathcal{R},\sim}$ TBox can be rewritten, in logarithmic space, into an equivalent (w.r.t. query answering) set of normal IDs. Let us recall that DL-Lite$_{\mathcal{R}}$, proposed in [8], is one of the most widespread description logics, and it forms the OWL 2 QL profile of the Web Ontology Language as standardized by the World Wide Web Consortium (W3C).

5.2 Complexity of 2D-Sticky NTGDs

We proceed to investigate the complexity of 2D-sticky sets of NTGDs, and show that:

THEOREM 12. *WFS-NBCQ answering under 2D-sticky sets of NTGDs is* PTIME*-complete and* 2EXPTIME*-complete in data and combined complexity, respectively.*

5.2.1 Upper Bounds

Our intention is to extend WFSQAns, by adapting the procedure Proof, in order to treat 2D-sticky sets of NTGDs. To this aim, we first need to understand the additional complication caused by 2D-stickiness. Since dangerous variables may appear more than once in a body, new variables, other than query variables, may appear in more than one branch of an alternating tree, and thus Lemma 8 does not hold; this is illustrated by the following example.

Example 10. Consider the 2D-sticky set Σ of NTGDs:

$$\sigma_1 \;=\; t(X_1, Y_1, Z_1), \sim s(X_1, Y_1) \rightarrow \exists W_1\, p(Y_1, W_1)$$
$$\sigma_2 \;=\; u(X_2, Y_2), t(X_2, Y_2, Z_2) \rightarrow s(X_2, Y_2)$$
$$\sigma_3 \;=\; r(X_3, Y_3), \sim v(X_3) \rightarrow \exists Z_3\, t(Z_3, Y_3, X_3).$$

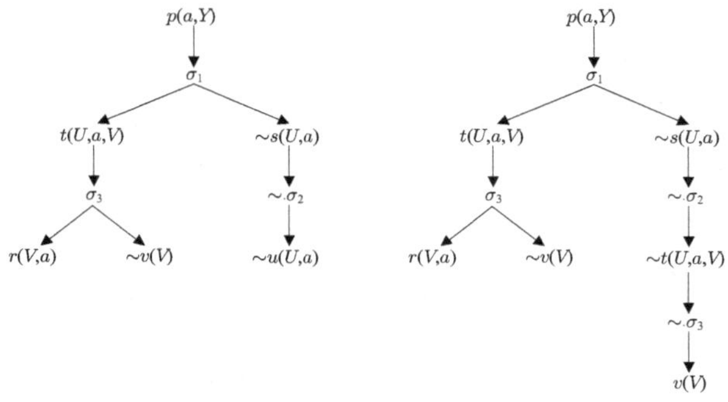

Figure 4: Alternating trees for Example 10.

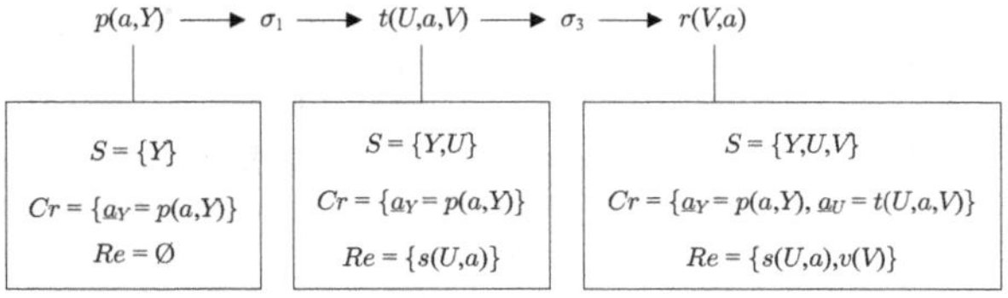

Figure 5: A universal computation of 2DProof**.**

Let $D = \{r(b, a), v(c)\}$ and $q = \exists X \exists Y\, p(X, Y)$. Two alternating trees for q w.r.t. D and Σ are shown in Figure 4. Notice that the left tree is accepting, while the right one is not. Observe that in both trees the variables U and V, which are not query variables, appear in more than one branch. ■

The property established by Lemma 8 implies that for sticky sets of NTGDs the criticality condition (see condition (3) of Definition 6) must be checked only for variables occurring in the given query. Moreover, during the process of deciding whether the special mapping from positive atoms to the database exists, required by the acceptance condition (see condition (1) of Definition 7), it is not necessary to take care of any joins among fresh non-query variables. Those facts allowed us to perform the above crucial checks, during the execution of WFSQAns, locally in each parallel universal computation. This is not true for 2D-sticky sets of NTGDs, and this is the difficulty that we need to overcome.

Luckily, by exploiting the property guaranteed by 2D-stickiness, i.e., a negative atom in the body of a NTGD σ sticks on exactly one positive body-atom of σ during the refutation process, we can overwhelmed the above difficulty, and perform all the required checks locally in each parallel universal computation. Roughly speaking, all the necessary information needed to refute an atom $\underline{a}$ can be obtained by following a single derivation path from the (unique) positive atom to which $\underline{a}$ is attached downwards to the leafs. Once we reach a leaf node (and assuming that the current universal computation is accepting), then we can start, in a new universal computation, the refutation process of $\underline{a}$. Let us illustrate the above ideas by exploiting Example 10.

In Figure 5, we present the execution of a universal computation of the alternating procedure 2DProof (the modified version of Proof). In this new procedure, apart from the set S, which stores the variables that may appear in more than one parallel universal computation (for sticky sets of NTGDs, S contains only query variables), and the set Cr, which stores the atoms that help us to check the criticality condition, we also maintain the set Re, which stores the atoms that eventually must be refuted. Once we reach the negative atom $\sim s(U, a)$, instead of starting immediately the process of its refutation, we store it in Re because we do not have enough information about the variable U — the same is done for the atom $\sim v(V)$ since we know nothing about the variable V. Eventually, once we reach the leaf node labeled by $r(V, a)$, we conclude that this universal computation is accepting since $r(V, a)$ can be mapped, via $\mu = \{V \to b\}$, to the database atom $r(b, a)$. Now, we have all the necessary information for refuting the atoms of Re. More precisely, we know that the variables $\{Y, U\}$ occur in more than one parallel universal computation, V represents the constant b, and the critical atom $\underline{a}_U$ for U is of the form $t(U, a, b)$. Thus, the atoms that we need to refute are $S(U, a)$ and $v(b)$, and this can be done in parallel universal computations.

WFS$_{2D}$QAns is the modified version of WFSQAns that calls the procedure 2DProof instead of Proof. From the above discussion, it is apparent that WFS$_{2D}$QAns(D, Σ, q) constructs an accepting alternating tree for q w.r.t. D and Σ, and thus *accepts*, if it exists, and *rejects* if such a tree does not exist. Regarding the complexity of WFS$_{2D}$QAns, we first need to understand how large are the sets S, Cr and Re. By providing a combinatorial argument, similar to the one for Lemma 9, which exploits the fact that for a 2D-sticky set Σ of NTGDs Σ^+ is sticky, we can show that in a universal computation of 2DProof we do not need to perform more than $\mathcal{O}(m \cdot (2w+1)^w)$ steps, where m is the number of predicates occurring in Σ, and w the maximum arity over the predicates in Σ, before starting the refutation process of the atoms of Re. At each step of a universal computation of 2DProof, we add to S, Cr and Re linearly many objects (in the worst case); in particular, $(b \cdot w)$ objects, where b is the maximum number of literals in the body of a NTGD of Σ. Therefore, the combined size of S, Cr and Re is $\mathcal{O}(b \cdot w \cdot m \cdot (2w + 1)^w)$. Let us now analyze the complexity of WFS$_{2D}$QAns. We first focus on the data complexity.

It can be easily verified that the preliminary steps that must be performed before calling 2DProof are feasible in polynomial time. Although the combined size of S, Cr and Re is constant (since it depends only on Σ), it should not be forgotten that we need to remember some database elements. Since no more that w constants of $dom(D)$ may appear in a universal computation of 2DProof, we conclude that we need logarithmic space for representing them in their binary form. It is well-known that ALOGSPACE coincides with PTIME, and thus WFS$_{2D}$QAns runs in polynomial time when the set of NTGDs and the query are fixed. For the combined complexity, observe that our algorithm runs in nondeterministic polynomial time with a $\mathcal{C}$-oracle, where $\mathcal{C}$ is a complexity class powerful enough for executing the procedure 2DProof. At each step of 2DProof we need exponential space. Since AEXPSPACE $=$ 2EXPTIME and NP$^{\text{2EXPTIME}}$ $=$ 2EXPTIME, the claim follows.

Notice that the PTIME upper bound for the data complexity of 2D-sticky sets of NTGDs immediately implies the same for sticky sets of NTGDs. Thus, the above approach is an alternative way for establishing Theorem 4. However, the proof of Theorem 4 is both conceptually and technically much simpler.

5.2.2 Lower Bounds

The lower bounds are obtained by a reduction from BCQ answering under guarded TGDs. Recall that guarded TGDs are TGDs that have a guard atom in their body, i.e., an atom that contains all the body-variables, and BCQ answering under this formalism is PTIME-hard in data complexity, and 2EXPTIME-hard in combined complexity [5, 6]. We first show that guarded TGDs can be rewritten as normal IDs:

LEMMA 13. *Consider a set Σ of guarded TGDs. We can construct in polynomial time a set Σ' of normal IDs such that, $D \cup \Sigma \models q$ iff $D \cup \Sigma' \models_{WFS} q$, for every D and BCQ q.*

By Lemma 11, a set of normal IDs is trivially 2D-sticky; thus, the preceding lemma immediately implies the desired lower bounds, and Theorem 12 follows.

6. CONSEQUENCES TO LINEAR NTGDS

Although WFS-NBCQ answering has been thoroughly investigated for guarded NTGDs [17], its exact complexity for linear NTGDs, that is, NTGDs with only one positive atom, is still unknown. This formalism is a key subclass of guarded NTGDs that captures normal IDs, and key DLs extended with default negation such as DL-Lite$_{\mathcal{R},\sim}$ [14]. Notably, the algorithmic techniques and results presented above close the complexity of WFS-NBCQ answering under linear NTGDs:

THEOREM 14. *WFS-NBCQ answering under linear NTGDs is* PTIME*-complete in data complexity, and* 2EXPTIME*-complete in combined complexity.*

PROOF. For the upper bounds, by exploiting the construction in the proof of Lemma 13, we can rewrite linear NTGDs into normal IDs. Since, by Lemma 11, a set of normal IDs is 2D-sticky, Theorem 12 implies the desired upper bounds. Regarding the lower bounds, Lemma 13 shows that WFS-NBCQ answering is PTIME-hard in data complexity, and 2EXPTIME-hard in combined complexity, even if we focus on normal IDs. □

Notice that the upper bounds in the above result can be inherited from guarded NTGDs [17]. However, we provide alternative and apparently simpler proofs. Let us recall that BCQ answering under linear TGDs is PSPACE-complete. Since PSPACE $\subset$ 2EXPTIME, the above result shows that linear NTGDs under the well-founded semantics are strictly more expressive than linear TGDs. An interesting question is whether the complexity of query answering changes if we focus on positive linear TGDs and NBCQs. We give an affirmative answer to this question:

THEOREM 15. *WFS-NBCQ answering under (positive) linear TGDs is in* AC_0 *in data complexity, and* EXPTIME*-complete in combined complexity.*

The AC_0 upper bound is implicit in [6], where linear NTGDs with stratified negation are investigated. The EXPTIME upper bound is obtained by exploiting WFSQAns, while the lower bound is shown by a reduction from non-acceptance of an alternating polynomial space Turing machine.

7. CONCLUSIONS

We have extended sticky sets of TGDs with default negation, and we have investigated the problem of query answering for normal Boolean conjunctive queries, focussing on the well-founded and stable model semantics. We have shown that an effective way for bridging the gap between stickiness and the well-founded semantics exists. However, there is no way to reconcile stickiness and the stable model semantics for query answering purposes. An interesting open problem is how to combine the classes of NTGDs considered in this paper with equality-generating dependencies (EGDs).

8. ACKNOWLEDGMENTS

Part of the work of Mario Alviano was performed while visiting the Department of Computer Science, University of Oxford, UK. Part of the work of Andreas Pieris was performed while was postdoctoral researcher at the Department of Computer Science, University of Oxford, UK. Mario Alviano was partly supported by the National Group for Scientific Computation (GNCS-INDAM) and Finanziamento Giovani Ricercatori UNICAL. Andreas Pieris was supported by the EPSRC Grant EP/J008346/1, Austrian Science Fund (FWF), projects P25207-N23 and Y698, and Vienna Science and Technology Fund (WWTF), project ICT12-015.

9. REFERENCES

[1] M. Arenas, G. Gottlob, and A. Pieris. Expressive languages for querying the semantic web. In *PODS*, pages 14–26, 2014.
[2] J. Baget, F. Garreau, M. Mugnier, and S. Rocher. Extending acyclicity notions for existential rules. In *ECAI*, pages 39–44, 2014.
[3] J.-F. Baget, M. Leclère, M.-L. Mugnier, and E. Salvat. On rules with existential variables: Walking the decidability line. *Artif. Intell.*, 175(9-10):1620–1654, 2011.
[4] C. Beeri and M. Y. Vardi. The implication problem for data dependencies. In *ICALP*, pages 73–85, 1981.
[5] A. Calì, G. Gottlob, and M. Kifer. Taming the infinite chase: Query answering under expressive relational constraints. *J. Artif. Intell. Res.*, 48:115–174, 2013.
[6] A. Calì, G. Gottlob, and T. Lukasiewicz. A general Datalog-based framework for tractable query answering over ontologies. *J. Web Sem.*, 14:57–83, 2012.
[7] A. Calì, G. Gottlob, and A. Pieris. Towards more expressive ontology languages: The query answering problem. *Artif. Intell.*, 193:87–128, 2012.
[8] D. Calvanese, G. De Giacomo, D. Lembo, M. Lenzerini, and R. Rosati. Tractable reasoning and efficient query answering in description logics: The DL-Lite family. *J. Autom. Reasoning*, 39(3):385–429, 2007.
[9] E. Dantsin, T. Eiter, G. Georg, and A. Voronkov. Complexity and expressive power of logic programming. *ACM Comput. Surv.*, 33(3):374–425, 2001.
[10] T. Eiter and M. Simkus. FDNC: decidable nonmonotonic disjunctive logic programs with function symbols. *ACM Trans. Comput. Log.*, 11(2), 2010.
[11] R. Fagin, P. G. Kolaitis, R. J. Miller, and L. Popa. Data exchange: Semantics and query answering. *Theor. Comput. Sci.*, 336(1):89–124, 2005.
[12] A. V. Gelder, K. A. Ross, and J. S. Schlipf. The well-founded semantics for general logic programs. *J. ACM*, 38(3):620–650, 1991.
[13] M. Gelfond and V. Lifschitz. The stable model semantics for logic programming. In *ICLP/SLP*, pages 1070–1080, 1988.
[14] G. Gottlob, A. Hernich, C. Kupke, and T. Lukasiewicz. Equality-friendly well-founded semantics and applications to description logics. In *AAAI*, 2012.
[15] G. Gottlob, A. Hernich, C. Kupke, and T. Lukasiewicz. Stable model semantics for guarded existential rules and description logics. In *KR*, 2014.
[16] G. Gottlob, G. Orsi, and A. Pieris. Query rewriting and optimization for ontological databases. *ACM Trans. Database Syst.*, 39(3):25, 2014.
[17] A. Hernich, C. Kupke, T. Lukasiewicz, and G. Gottlob. Well-founded semantics for extended Datalog and ontological reasoning. In *PODS*, pages 225–236, 2013.
[18] N. Leone, M. Manna, G. Terracina, and P. Veltri. Efficiently computable Datalog$^{\exists}$ programs. In *KR*, 2012.
[19] D. Magka, M. Krötzsch, and I. Horrocks. Computing stable models for nonmonotonic existential rules. In *IJCAI*, 2013.

Chase Termination for Guarded Existential Rules

Marco Calautti
DIMES
University of Calabria
calautti@dimes.unical.it

Georg Gottlob
Dept. of Computer Science
University of Oxford
georg.gottlob@cs.ox.ac.uk

Andreas Pieris
Inst. of Information Systems
Vienna Univ. of Technology
pieris@dbai.tuwien.ac.at

ABSTRACT

The chase procedure is considered as one of the most fundamental algorithmic tools in database theory. It has been successfully applied to different database problems such as data exchange, and query answering and containment under constraints, to name a few. One of the central problems regarding the chase procedure is all-instance termination, that is, given a set of tuple-generating dependencies (TGDs) (a.k.a. existential rules), decide whether the chase under that set terminates, for every input database. It is well-known that this problem is undecidable, no matter which version of the chase we consider. The crucial question that comes up is whether existing restricted classes of TGDs, proposed in different contexts such as ontological query answering, make the above problem decidable. In this work, we focus our attention on the oblivious and the semi-oblivious versions of the chase procedure, and we give a positive answer for classes of TGDs that are based on the notion of guardedness. To the best of our knowledge, this is the first work that establishes positive results about the (semi-)oblivious chase termination problem. In particular, we first concentrate on the class of linear TGDs, and we syntactically characterize, via rich- and weak-acyclicity, its fragments that guarantee the termination of the oblivious and the semi-oblivious chase, respectively. Those syntactic characterizations, apart from being interesting in their own right, allow us to pinpoint the complexity of the problem, which is PSPACE-complete in general, and NL-complete if we focus on predicates of bounded arity, for both the oblivious and the semi-oblivious chase. We then proceed with the more general classes of guarded and weakly-guarded TGDs. Although we do not provide syntactic characterizations for its relevant fragments, as for linear TGDs, we show that the problem under consideration remains decidable. In fact, we show that it is 2EXPTIME-complete in general, and EXPTIME-complete if we focus on predicates of bounded arity, for both the oblivious and the semi-oblivious chase. Finally, we investigate the expressive power of the query languages obtained from our analysis, and we show that they are equally expressive with standard database query languages. Nevertheless, we have strong indications that they are more succinct.

PODS'15, May 31–June 4, 2015, Melbourne, Victoria, Australia.

ACM 978-1-4503-2757-2/15/05 ...$15.00.
http://dx.doi.org/10.1145/2745754.2745773.

Categories and Subject Descriptors

F.2.2 [**Analysis of Algorithms and Problem Complexity**]: Nonnumerical Algorithms and Problems—*complexity of proof procedures, computations on discrete structures*; H.2.4 [**Database Management**]: Systems—*relational databases, rule-based databases*

Keywords

Chase Procedure; Termination; Tuple-Generating Dependencies; Existential Rules; Guardedness; Decidability; Complexity

1. INTRODUCTION

1.1 The Chase Procedure

The *chase procedure* (or simply chase) is considered as one of the most fundamental algorithmic tools in databases. It has been successfully applied to a wide range of problems: containment of queries under constraints [2], checking logical implication of constraints [5, 21], computing data exchange solutions [11], and query answering under constraints [6], to name a few. The chase procedure takes as input a database D and a set Σ of constraints and, if it terminates (which is not guaranteed), its result is a finite instance D_Σ that enjoys two crucial properties:

1. D_Σ is a *model* of D and Σ, i.e., it contains D and satisfies the constraints of Σ; and
2. D_Σ is *universal*, i.e., it can be homomorphically embedded into every other model of D and Σ.

In other words, the chase is an algorithmic tool for computing universal models of D and Σ, which can be conceived as representatives of all the other models of D and Σ. This is precisely the reason for the ubiquity of the chase in database theory, as accurately discussed in [9]. Indeed, many key database problems, as the ones above, can be solved by simply exhibiting a universal model.

A central class of constraints, which can be treated by the chase procedure, is the class of *tuple-generating dependencies (TGDs)* (a.k.a. *existential rules*). TGDs are implications of the form

$$\forall \mathbf{X} \forall \mathbf{Y} (\varphi(\mathbf{X}, \mathbf{Y}) \rightarrow \exists \mathbf{Z}\, \psi(\mathbf{Y}, \mathbf{Z})),$$

where φ and ψ are conjunctions of atoms, and they essentially state that the presence of some tuples in an instance implies the existence of some other tuples in the same instance. Given a database D and a set Σ of TGDs, the chase adds new atoms to D (possibly involving nulls that act as witnesses for the existentially quantified variables) until the final result satisfies Σ.

Example 1. Consider the database $D = \{person(Bob)\}$, and the TGD $\forall X (person(X) \rightarrow \exists Y\, hasFather(X, Y) \wedge person(Y))$, which asserts that each person has a father who is also a person. The database atom *triggers* the TGD, and the chase will add in D the atoms $hasFather(Bob, z_1)$ and $person(z_1)$ in order to satisfy it, where z_1 is a (labeled) null representing some unknown value. However, the new atom $person(z_1)$ triggers again the TGD, and the chase is forced to add the atoms $hasFather(z_1, z_2), person(z_2)$, where z_2 is a new null. The result of the chase is the instance

$$\{person(Bob), hasFather(Bob, z_1)\} \cup \bigcup_{i>0} \{person(z_i), hasFather(z_i, z_{i+1})\},$$

where $z_1, z_2, \ldots$ are nulls. ■

1.2 The Challenge of Infinity

As shown by Example 1, the chase procedure may run forever, even for extremely simple databases and constraints. In the light of this fact, there has been a long line of research on identifying syntactic properties on TGDs such that, for every input database, the termination of the chase is guaranteed. A prime example of such a property is *weak-acyclicity* [11], which forms the standard language for data exchange purposes, and guarantees the termination of the semi-oblivious and restricted chase. A similar formalism, called *constraints with stratified-witness*, has been proposed in [10]. Inspired by weak-acyclicity, the notion of *rich-acyclicity* has been proposed in [19], which guarantees the termination of the oblivious chase. Note that the key difference between the various versions of the chase procedure is when a TGD is triggered. Many other sufficient conditions for chase termination can be found in the literature; see, e.g., [9, 16, 18, 22, 24] — this list is by no means exhaustive, and we refer to [17] for a comprehensive survey.

With so much effort spent on identifying sufficient conditions for the termination of the chase procedure, the question that comes up is whether a sufficient condition that is also *necessary* exists. In other words, given a set Σ of TGDs, is it possible to determine whether, for every database D, the chase on D and Σ terminates? This interesting question has been recently addressed in [12], and unfortunately the answer is negative for all the versions of the chase that are usually used in database applications, namely the oblivious, semi-oblivious and restricted chase. The problem remains undecidable even if the database is known; this has been established in [9] for the restricted chase, and it was observed in [22] that the same proof shows undecidability also for the (semi-)oblivious chase.

1.3 Towards Positive Results

Although the chase termination problem is undecidable in general, the proof in [12] does not show the undecidability of the problem for TGDs that enjoy some structural conditions, which in turn guarantee favorable model-theoretic properties. Such a key condition is *guardedness*, a well-accepted paradigm that gives rise to robust rule-based languages [4, 6, 7] that capture important databases constraints such as inclusion dependencies, and lightweight description logics such as DL-Lite [8] and $\mathcal{EL}$ [3]. A TGD is guarded if it has an atom in the left-hand side that contains (or guards) all the universally quantified variables. Guardedness guarantees the tree-likeness of the underlying models, and thus the decidability of central database problems such as query answering under constraints. The question that comes up is whether guardedness has the same positive impact on the chase termination problem:

Question 1: Given a set Σ of guarded TGDs, is it possible to decide whether, for every database D, the chase on D and Σ terminates?

Of course, if the answer to the above question is positive, then the next step is to understand how complex is the problem of determining whether the chase terminates:

Question 2: Given a set Σ of guarded TGDs, what is the exact complexity of deciding whether, for every database D, the chase on D and Σ terminates?

Our main goal in this work is to study in depth the chase termination problem for guarded TGDs, and give answers to the above fundamental questions. In fact, we focus on the (semi-)oblivious versions of the chase, and we show that deciding termination for guarded TGDs is decidable. Surprisingly, this work is to our knowledge the first one that establishes positive results for the chase termination problem. Although the (semi-)oblivious versions of the chase are considered as non-standard ones, they have certain advantages that make them as important as the restricted chase, and thus they deserve our attention. In particular, unlike the restricted chase, the application of a TGD does not require checking if the head of the TGD is already satisfied by the instance, and this guarantees technical clarity and efficiency; see [6, 22] for a discussion on the advantages of the oblivious and semi-oblivious chase.

From our analysis, it turned out that to decide the termination of the chase is inherently different from query answering under guarded TGDs. For our purposes, we had to tame the combinatorial nature of the chase procedure, and understand how different chase derivations affect each other during the construction of the chase. More precisely, we had to understand when a sequence of TGDs gives rise to a valid derivation during the construction of the chase, and whether such a derivation is infinite. These low level issues are irrelevant for query answering, and this is the reason why the chase termination problem is generally considered more challenging than query answering.

It is clear that our positive results immediately give rise to new decidable query languages that can directly exploit the chase procedure. Another goal of the present paper is to clarify the expressiveness of those languages:

Question 3: What is the relative expressive power of the query language obtained from the fragment of guarded TGDs that ensures the termination of the chase?

1.4 Impact

It is interesting to observe that key database problems may benefit from our results. Such problems include: (i) computing data exchange solutions [11], and (ii) answering conjunctive queries in the presence of guarded TGDs [6, 7].

For data exchange, it is vital to use languages that guarantee the termination of the chase, since data exchange solutions must be materialized, and thus explicitly computable. Recall that the main language for data exchange is the class of weakly-acyclic TGDs. However, there are several data exchange scenarios that can be expressed via guarded TGDs, but not via weakly-acyclic TGDs. Our results provide formal algorithmic tools for checking whether a set of guarded TGDs, which is not necessarily weakly-acyclic, is suitable for data exchange purposes.

Regarding query answering, there are decision procedures that allow us to answer conjunctive queries in the presence of guarded TGDs, even if the chase is infinite. The main idea underlying these procedures is to compute an initial finite portion of the chase, whose size depends on the TGDs and the query, and then evaluate the query over this finite instance. It is clear that, by following this approach, for queries of different size we are forced to compute the relevant part of the chase, which is an expensive task. However,

	General	Bounded Arity
Simple Linear	NL-c	NL-c
Linear	PSPACE-c	NL-c
Guarded	2EXPTIME-c	EXPTIME-c
Weakly-Guarded	2EXPTIME-c	EXPTIME-c

Table 1: Complexity of (Semi-)Oblivious Chase Termination.

if we know that the given set of TGDs guarantees the termination of the chase, then we can simply compute once a (finite) universal model, and then evaluate queries directly on that model.

1.5 Summary of Contributions

We first concentrate, in Section 4, on linear and simple linear TGDs, two key subclasses of guarded TGDs. Linear TGDs have only one atom in the left-hand side, while simple linear TGDs do not allow the repetition of variables in the left-hand side. Despite their simplicity, the above classes are powerful enough for capturing prominent database dependencies, and in particular inclusion dependencies, as well as key description logics such as DL-Lite. We syntactically characterize the fragment of linear and simple linear TGDs that ensures the termination of the oblivious and semi-oblivious chase via rich- and weak-acyclicity, respectively. More precisely, we show that a set of simple linear TGDs ensures the termination of the oblivious (resp., semi-oblivious) chase iff it is richly-acyclic (resp., weakly-acyclic). However, for linear TGDs we need to carefully extend rich- and weak-acyclicity. After exposing the reasons why the above acyclicity notions are not powerful enough for our purposes, we introduce *critical-rich-acyclicity* and *critical-weak-acyclicity*, and we show that they characterize the fragment of linear TGDs that guarantees the termination of the oblivious and semi-oblivious chase, respectively.

The above syntactic characterizations, apart from being interesting in their own right, allow us to obtain optimal upper bounds for the chase termination problem under (simple) linear TGDs — we simply need to analyze the complexity of deciding whether a set of (simple) linear TGDs enjoys the above acyclicity-based conditions. In particular, we show that the problem for simple linear TGDs is NL-complete, even for unary and binary predicates, while for linear TGDs is PSPACE-complete, in general, and NL-complete for predicates of bounded arity. For the hardness results, a generic technique, called the looping operator, is proposed, which allows us to obtain lower bounds for the chase termination problem in a uniform way. In fact, the goal of the looping operator is to provide a generic reduction from propositional atom entailment to the complement of chase termination.

We then proceed, in Section 5, with guarded and the more general language of weakly-guarded TGDs. Although there is no way (at least no obvious one) to syntactically characterize the fragments of (weakly-)guarded TGDs that ensure the termination of the chase, it is possible to show that the problem of recognizing the above classes is decidable, and in particular 2EXPTIME-complete, in general, and EXPTIME-complete for predicates of bounded arity. The upper bounds are obtained by exhibiting an alternating algorithm that runs in exponential space, in general, and in polynomial space in case of predicates of bounded arity. The lower bounds are obtained by reductions from the acceptance problem of alternating exponential (resp., polynomial) space clocked Turing machines, i.e., Turing machines equipped with a counter. These reductions are obtained by modifying significantly existing reductions for the problem of propositional atom entailment under (weakly-)guarded TGDs, and then exploiting the looping operator mentioned above. The complexity results in this paper are summarized in Table 1.

Finally, in Section 6, we investigate the expressive power of our languages. In particular, we show that the query language based on the fragment of (simple) linear TGDs that guarantees the termination of the chase has the same expressive power as (simple) linear UCQs (unions of conjunctive queries). Similarly, we show that the query language based on the fragment of (weakly-)guarded TGDs that guarantees the termination of the chase has the same expressive power as (weakly-)guarded Datalog. The above results show that the new languages obtained from our analysis do not provide us with more expressive power compared to the standard database query languages. Nevertheless, we have a strong indication that the fragment of (weakly-)guarded TGDs that guarantees the termination of the chase is more succinct than (weakly-)guarded Datalog.

2. PRELIMINARIES

2.1 General Definitions

We define the following pairwise disjoint sets of symbols: a set $\mathbf{C}$ of *constants* (constitute the "normal" domain of a database), a set $\mathbf{N}$ of *(labeled) nulls* (used as placeholders for unknown values, and thus can be also seen as (globally) existentially quantified variables), and a set $\mathbf{V}$ of (regular) *variables* (used in dependencies). A fixed lexicographic order is assumed on $(\mathbf{C} \cup \mathbf{N})$ such that every null of $\mathbf{N}$ follows all constants of $\mathbf{C}$. We denote by $\mathbf{X}$ sequences (or sets, with a slight abuse of notation) of variables or constants $X_1, \ldots, X_k$, with $k \geqslant 0$. Throughout, let $[n] = \{1, \ldots, n\}$, for any integer $n \geqslant 1$.

A *(relational) schema* $\mathcal{R}$ is a (finite) set of *relational symbols* (or *predicates*), each with its associated arity. We write p/n to denote that p is an n-ary predicate. A *position* $p[i]$ (in a schema $\mathcal{R}$) is identified by a predicate $p \in \mathcal{R}$ and its i-th argument (or attribute). The set of positions of $\mathcal{R}$, denoted by $pos(\mathcal{R})$, is defined as $\{p[i] \mid p/n \in \mathcal{R} \text{ and } i \in [n]\}$. A *term* t is a constant, null or variable. An *atomic formula* (or simply *atom*) has the form $p(\mathbf{t})$, where p is a predicate, and $\mathbf{t}$ a tuple of terms. An atom is called *ground* if all of its terms are constants of $\mathbf{C}$. For an atom $\underline{a}$, we refer to its predicate by $pred(\underline{a})$, and we denote by $dom(\underline{a})$, $var(\underline{a})$ and $pos(\underline{a})$ the set of its terms, the set of its variables, and the set of its positions, respectively. Given a set of positions Π, we denote by $var(\underline{a}, \Pi)$ the set of variables occurring in $\underline{a}$ at positions of Π. Furthermore, given a set of variables $\mathbf{U}$, $pos(\underline{a}, \mathbf{U})$ is the set of positions in $\underline{a}$ at which variables of $\mathbf{U}$ occur. The above notations naturally extend to sets of atoms. Conjunctions of atoms are often identified with the sets of their atoms. An *instance* I is a (possibly infinite) set of atoms of the form $p(\mathbf{t})$, where $\mathbf{t}$ is a tuple of constants and nulls. A *database* D is a finite instance such that $dom(D) \subset \mathbf{C}$.

A *substitution* from a set of symbols S to a set of symbols S' is a function $h : S \to S'$ defined as follows: $\varnothing$ is a substitution (empty substitution), and if h is a substitution, then $(h \cup \{s \to s'\})$ is a substitution, where $(s, s') \in S \times S'$. The *restriction* of h to $T \subseteq S$, denoted as $h_{|T}$, is the substitution $h' = \{t \to h(t) \mid t \in T\}$. A *homomorphism* from a set of atoms A to a set of atoms A' is a substitution $h : (\mathbf{C} \cup \mathbf{N} \cup \mathbf{V}) \to (\mathbf{C} \cup \mathbf{N} \cup \mathbf{V})$ such that: $t \in \mathbf{C}$ implies $h(t) = t$, and $r(t_1, \ldots, t_n) \in A$ implies $h(r(t_1, \ldots, t_n)) = r(h(t_1), \ldots, h(t_n)) \in A'$.

A *tuple-generating dependency (TGD)* σ is a first-order formula $\forall \mathbf{X} \forall \mathbf{Y} (\varphi(\mathbf{X}, \mathbf{Y}) \to \exists \mathbf{Z}\, \psi(\mathbf{X}, \mathbf{Z}))$, where $(\mathbf{X} \cup \mathbf{Y} \cup \mathbf{Z}) \subset \mathbf{V}$, and φ, ψ are conjunctions of atoms; $\varphi(\mathbf{X}, \mathbf{Y})$ is the *body* of σ, denoted $body(\sigma)$, while $\psi(\mathbf{X}, \mathbf{Z})$ is the *head* of σ, denoted $head(\sigma)$. The *frontier* of σ, denoted $fr(\sigma)$, is the set of variables $\mathbf{X}$, and we define $frpos(\sigma)$ as the set of positions $pos(head(\sigma), fr(\sigma))$. Let also $ex(\sigma) = \mathbf{Z}$. Assuming that $head(\sigma) = \underline{a}_1 \wedge \ldots \wedge \underline{a}_k$, let

(σ, i), where $i \in [k]$, be the single-head TGD $body(\sigma) \rightarrow \underline{a}_i$. The schema of set Σ of TGDs, denoted $sch(\Sigma)$, is defined as the set of predicates occurring in Σ. An instance I satisfies σ, written $I \models \sigma$, if the following holds: whenever there exists a homomorphism h such that $h(\varphi(\mathbf{X}, \mathbf{Y})) \subseteq I$, then there exists $h' \supseteq h_{|\mathbf{X}}$ such that $h'(\psi(\mathbf{X}, \mathbf{Z})) \subseteq I$. The instance I satisfies a set Σ of TGDs, written $I \models \Sigma$, if $I \models \sigma$ for each $\sigma \in \Sigma$. For brevity, we omit the universal quantifiers in front of TGDs, and use the comma (instead of $\wedge$) for conjoining atoms. For technical clarity, we focus our attention on constant-free TGDs.

A TGD σ is *guarded* if there exists an atom $\underline{a} \in body(\sigma)$ that contains (or "guards") all the variables of $body(\sigma)$ [6]. The class of guarded TGDs, denoted G, is defined as the family of all possible sets of guarded TGDs. *Weakly-guarded* TGDs extend guarded TGDs by requiring only the body-variables that appear at affected positions, i.e., positions that can host nulls during the chase, to appear in the guard; for the formal inductive definition of affected positions see [6]. The corresponding class is denoted WG. We write $guard(\sigma)$ for the guard of a (weakly-)guarded TGD σ. A key subclass of G are the so-called *linear* TGDs [7], that is, TGDs with just one body-atom (which is automatically a guard), and the corresponding class is denoted L. A set of linear TGDs is called *simple* if there is no repetition of variables in the body of the TGDs, and the corresponding class is denoted SL. It is straightforward to verify that $\mathsf{SL} \subset \mathsf{L} \subset \mathsf{G} \subset \mathsf{WG}$.

2.2 (Semi-)Oblivious TGD Chase Procedure

The *TGD chase procedure* (or simply *chase*) takes as input an instance I and a set Σ of TGDs, and constructs a universal model of I and Σ. The chase works on I by applying the so-called trigger for a set of TGDs on I. In what follows, fix a set Σ of TGDs and an instance I.

Definition 1. A *trigger* for Σ on I is a pair (σ, h), where $\sigma \in \Sigma$ and h is a homomorphism such that $h(body(\sigma)) \subseteq I$. An *application* of (σ, h) to I returns $J = (I \cup h'(head(\sigma)))$, where $h' \supseteq h_{|fr(\sigma)}$ is such that, for each existentially quantified variable $Z \in ex(\sigma)$, $h'(Z) \in \mathbf{N}$ does not occur in I, and follows lexicographically all nulls in I. Such a trigger application is written as $I\langle\sigma, h\rangle J$. ∎

The choice of the type of the next trigger to be applied is crucial since it gives rise to different variations of the chase procedure. In this work, we mainly focus our attention on the *oblivious* [6] and *semi-oblivious* [15, 22] chase.

Oblivious. A finite sequence $I_0, I_1, \ldots, I_n$, where $n \geqslant 0$, is said to be a *terminating oblivious chase sequence* of I_0 w.r.t. a set Σ of TGDs if: (i) for each $0 \leqslant i < n$, there exists a trigger (σ, h) for Σ on I_i such that $I_i\langle\sigma, h\rangle I_{i+1}$; (ii) for each $0 \leqslant i < j < n$, assuming that $I_i\langle\sigma_i, h_i\rangle I_{i+1}$ and $I_j\langle\sigma_j, h_j\rangle I_{j+1}$, $\sigma_i = \sigma_j$ implies $h_i \neq h_j$, i.e., h_i and h_j are different homomorphisms; and (iii) there is no trigger (σ, h) for Σ on I_n such that $(\sigma, h) \notin \{(\sigma_i, h_i)\}_{0 \leqslant i \leqslant n-1}$. In this case, the result of the chase is the (finite) instance I_n. An infinite sequence $I_0, I_1, \ldots$ of instances is said to be a *non-terminating oblivious chase sequence* of I_0 w.r.t. Σ if: (i) for each $i \geqslant 0$, there exists a trigger (σ, h) for Σ on I_i such that $I_i\langle\sigma, h\rangle I_{i+1}$; (ii) for each $i, j > 0$ such that $i \neq j$, assuming that $I_i\langle\sigma_i, h_i\rangle I_{i+1}$ and $I_j\langle\sigma_j, h_j\rangle I_{j+1}$, $\sigma_i = \sigma_j$ implies $h_i \neq h_j$; and (iii) for each $i \geqslant 0$, and for every trigger (σ, h) for Σ on I_i, there exists $j \geqslant i$ such that $I_j\langle\sigma, h\rangle I_{j+1}$; this is known as the fairness condition, and guarantees that all the triggers eventually will be applied. The result of the chase is $\cup_{i \geqslant 0} I_i$.

Semi-oblivious. The semi-oblivious chase is a refined version of the oblivious chase, which avoids the application of some superfluous triggers. Roughly speaking, given a TGD σ, for the semi-oblivious chase, two homomorphisms h and g that agree on the frontier of σ, i.e., $h_{|fr(\sigma)} = g_{|fr(\sigma)}$, are indistinguishable. To formalize this, we first define the binary relation $\sim_\sigma$ on the set of homomorphisms $H_\sigma = \{h \mid h : var(body(\sigma)) \rightarrow (\mathbf{C} \cup \mathbf{N})\}$ as follows: $h \sim_\sigma g$ iff $h_{|fr(\sigma)} = g_{|fr(\sigma)}$. It is easy to verify that $\sim_\sigma$ is an equivalence relation on the elements of H_σ. A (terminating or non-terminating) oblivious chase sequence $I_0, I_1, \ldots$ is called *semi-oblivious* if the following holds: for every $i, j \geqslant 0$ such that $i \neq j$, assuming that $I_i\langle\sigma_i, h_i\rangle I_{i+1}$ and $I_j\langle\sigma_j, h_j\rangle I_{j+1}$, $\sigma_i = \sigma_j = \sigma$ implies $h_i \not\sim_\sigma h_j$, i.e., h_i and h_j belong to different equivalence classes.

Henceforth, we write o-chase and so-chase for oblivious and semi-oblivious chase, respectively.

3. CHASE TERMINATION PROBLEM

We know that, due to the existentially quantified variables, a $\star$-chase sequence, where $\star \in \{\mathsf{o}, \mathsf{so}\}$, may be infinite.

Example 2. Consider the database $D = \{p(a, b)\}$, and

$$\Sigma = \{p(X, Y) \rightarrow \exists Z\, p(Y, Z)\}.$$

There exists only one $\star$-chase sequence of D w.r.t. Σ, where $\star \in \{\mathsf{o}, \mathsf{so}\}$, which is non-terminating, i.e., $I_0, I_1, \ldots$ with

$$\begin{aligned} I_0 &= \{p(a, b)\} \\ I_1 &= \{p(a, b), p(b, z_1)\} \\ I_i &= I_{i-1} \cup \{p(z_{i-1}, z_i)\}, \text{ for } i \geqslant 2, \end{aligned}$$

where $z_1, z_2, \ldots$ are nulls of $\mathbf{N}$. ∎

For a set of TGDs, a key question is whether all or some $\star$-chase sequences are terminating on *all* databases. Before formalizing the above problem, let us recall the following crucial classes of TGDs:

$$\begin{aligned} \mathsf{CT}^\star_\forall &= \{\Sigma \mid \forall D, \text{ all } \star\text{-chase sequences of } D \text{ w.r.t. } \Sigma \text{ are terminating}\} \\ \mathsf{CT}^\star_\exists &= \{\Sigma \mid \forall D, \text{ there exists a terminating } \star\text{-chase sequence of } D \text{ w.r.t. } \Sigma\}. \end{aligned}$$

The decision problems tackled in this work are as follows:

$\forall$-SEQUENCE $\star$-CHASE TERMINATION:
Instance: A set Σ of TGDs.
Question: Does $\Sigma \in \mathsf{CT}^\star_\forall$?

$\exists$-SEQUENCE $\star$-CHASE TERMINATION:
Instance: A set Σ of TGDs.
Question: Does $\Sigma \in \mathsf{CT}^\star_\exists$?

It would be quite beneficial for our later investigation to understand how the above problems are related. To this aim, we recall that $\mathsf{CT}^{\mathsf{o}}_\forall = \mathsf{CT}^{\mathsf{o}}_\exists \subset \mathsf{CT}^{\mathsf{so}}_\forall = \mathsf{CT}^{\mathsf{so}}_\exists$ [15]. This implies that the preceding decision problems coincide for the (semi-)oblivious chase. Henceforth, we refer to the $\star$-chase termination problem, and we write $\mathsf{CT}^\star$ for the classes $\mathsf{CT}^\star_\forall$ and $\mathsf{CT}^\star_\exists$, where $\star \in \{\mathsf{o}, \mathsf{so}\}$.

Another useful notion is the so-called critical database for a set of TGDs [22]. Formally, the *critical database* for a schema $\mathcal{R}$ is the database $D_{\mathsf{c}}(\mathcal{R}) = \{p(\mathsf{c}, \ldots, \mathsf{c}) \mid p \in \mathcal{R} \text{ and } \mathsf{c} \in \mathbf{C}\}$. The critical database for a set Σ of TGDs is defined as the database $D_{\mathsf{c}}(sch(\Sigma))$; for brevity, we will refer to $D_{\mathsf{c}}(sch(\Sigma))$ by $D_{\mathsf{c}}(\Sigma)$. To check for the termination of the (semi-)oblivious chase it suffices to focus on the critical database [22].

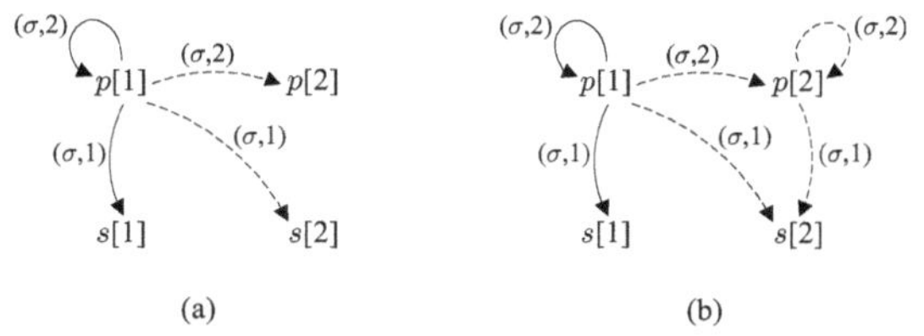

Figure 1: (Extended) dependency graph of Example 3.

4. LINEARITY

We proceed to investigate the (semi-)oblivious chase termination problem for (simple) linear TGDs. The goal of this section is twofold: for every $\star \in \{\mathsf{o}, \mathsf{so}\}$,

1. Syntactically characterize the classes $(\mathsf{CT}^\star \cap \mathsf{SL})$ and $(\mathsf{CT}^\star \cap \mathsf{L})$; and
2. Pinpoint the complexity of the $\star$-chase termination problem for sets of TGDs of (S)L.

For our first goal, we are going to exploit existing syntactic conditions that guarantee the termination of every (semi-)oblivious chase sequence on all databases; in fact, our analysis will build on rich-acyclicity [19] and weak-acyclicity [11]. More precisely, we are going to show that for simple linear TGDs rich-acyclicity (resp., weak-acyclicity) is enough for characterizing $(\mathsf{CT}^\mathsf{o} \cap \mathsf{SL})$ (resp., $(\mathsf{CT}^\mathsf{so} \cap \mathsf{SL})$). However, for (non-simple) linear TGDs this is not the case, and we need to carefully extend rich- and weak-acyclicity. The above syntactic characterizations, apart from being interesting in their own right, allow us to obtain optimal upper bounds for the $\star$-chase termination problem for (S)L, and thus achieving our second goal — we simply need to analyze the complexity of deciding whether a set of (simple) linear TGDs enjoys the above acyclicity-based conditions. But let us first recall those conditions.

Weak- and Rich-Acyclicity

Both weak- and rich-acyclicity are defined via an acyclicity condition on a graph, which encodes how terms are propagated among the positions of the underlying schema during the chase. In fact, weak-acyclicity uses the well-known dependency graph [11], while rich-acyclicity the so-called extended dependency graph [19]. In the sequel, we assume a fixed order on the head-atoms of TGDs.

Definition 2. The *dependency graph* of a set Σ of TGDs is a labeled directed multigraph $DG(\Sigma) = (N, E, \lambda)$, where $N = pos(sch(\Sigma))$, $\lambda : E \rightarrow \Sigma \times \mathbb{N}$, and the edge-set E is as follows: for each $\sigma \in \Sigma$, for each $V \in fr(\sigma)$, and for each $\pi \in pos(body(\sigma), V)$, with $head(\sigma) = \underline{a}_1, \ldots, \underline{a}_k$:

1. for each $i \in [k]$, and for each $\pi' \in pos(\underline{a}_i, V)$, there is a *normal* edge $e = (\pi, \pi') \in E$ with $\lambda(e) = (\sigma, i)$;
2. for each $W \in ex(\sigma)$, for each $i \in [k]$, and for each $\pi' \in pos(\underline{a}_i, W)$, there is a *special* edge $e = (\pi, \pi') \in E$ with $\lambda(e) = (\sigma, i)$;
3. no other edges are in E. ∎

A normal edge (π, π') in the dependency graph keeps track of the fact that a term may propagate from π to π' during the chase. Moreover, a special edge (π, π'') keeps track of the fact that propagation of a value from π to π' also creates a null at position π''.

Example 3. Consider the set Σ consisting of the TGD

$$\sigma = p(X, Y) \rightarrow \exists Z\, s(X, Z), p(X, Z).$$

The graph $DG(\Sigma)$ is depicted in Figure 1(a), where the dashed arrows represent special edges. Observe that the normal edges occur due to the variable X, while the special edges due to the existentially quantified variable Z. ∎

The extended dependency graph of a set Σ of TGDs, introduced in [19], is obtained from the dependency graph of Σ by adding some additional special edges from the positions where non-frontier variables occur to the positions where existentially quantified variables appear. The extended dependency graph of Σ given in Example 2 is shown in Figure 1(b); the additional special edges (dashed arrows) are due to the non-frontier variable Y. Having the above structures in place, we can recall weak- and rich-acyclicity. A set Σ of TGDs is *weakly-acyclic* (resp., *richly-acyclic*) if no cycle in $DG(\Sigma)$ (resp., $EDG(G)$) contains a special edge. The corresponding classes are WA and RA, respectively; clearly, $\mathsf{RA} \subset \mathsf{WA}$.

4.1 Characterizing $(\mathsf{CT}^\mathsf{o} \cap \mathsf{SL})$ and $(\mathsf{CT}^\mathsf{so} \cap \mathsf{SL})$

4.1.1 Oblivious Chase

We start our investigation by showing that rich-acyclicity characterizes the fragment of SL that guarantees the termination of the oblivious chase. In particular, we prove that:

THEOREM 1. $(\mathsf{CT}^\mathsf{o} \cap \mathsf{SL}) = (\mathsf{RA} \cap \mathsf{SL})$.

To establish the above theorem it suffices to show that, for an arbitrary set of TGDs $\Sigma \in \mathsf{SL}$, $\Sigma \in \mathsf{CT}^\mathsf{o}$ iff $\Sigma \in \mathsf{RA}$. The "if" direction has been shown in [19]. Assume now that $\Sigma \notin \mathsf{RA}$. We are going to show that there exists a database D, and a non-terminating o-chase sequence of D w.r.t. Σ, which immediately implies that $\Sigma \notin \mathsf{CT}^\mathsf{o}$. But let us first introduce our generic technical tool, which will be used also for the semi-oblivious chase, and all the other languages that we treat in this work. Given a TGD σ, $\diamond_\sigma^\star$ is defined as $\neq$, if $\star = \mathsf{o}$, and $\not\sim_\sigma$, if $\star = \mathsf{so}$.

Definition 3. A set Σ of TGDs admits an *infinite $\star$-chase derivation*, where $\star \in \{\mathsf{o}, \mathsf{so}\}$, if there exist infinite sequences $I_0, I_1, \ldots$ and $(\sigma_0, h_0), (\sigma_1, h_1), \ldots$, where I_0 is a database, and $\sigma_0, \sigma_1, \ldots \in \Sigma$, such that

1. for each $i \geqslant 0$, $I_i\langle\sigma_i, h_i\rangle I_{i+1}$; and
2. for each $i \neq j \geqslant 0$, $\sigma_i = \sigma_j = \sigma$ implies $h_i \diamond_\sigma^\star h_j$. ∎

It is possible to show that the $\star$-chase termination problem, where $\star \in \{\mathsf{o}, \mathsf{so}\}$, is tantamount to the problem of deciding whether a set of TGDs admits an infinite $\star$-chase derivation.

PROPOSITION 2. *Consider a set Σ of TGDs. $\Sigma \notin \mathsf{CT}^\star$ iff Σ admits an infinite $\star$-chase derivation, where $\star \in \{\mathsf{o}, \mathsf{so}\}$.*

The "only-if" direction is trivial. For the "if" direction, it suffices to show that there exists a database D, and a non-terminating $\star$-chase sequence of D w.r.t. Σ. By hypothesis, we have sequences $I_0, I_1, \ldots$ and $(\sigma_0, h_0), (\sigma_1, h_1), \ldots$ as in Definition 3. A non-terminating $\star$-chase sequence of I_0 w.r.t. Σ is

$$J_0, J_0^1, \ldots, J_0^{k_0}, J_1, J_1^1, \ldots, J_1^{k_1}, J_2, \ldots$$

where,

- $J_0 = I_0$;
- for each $i \geqslant 0$, there exists a trigger (σ, h) for Σ on J_i such that $J_i\langle\sigma, h\rangle J_i^1$;
- for each $i \geqslant 0$ and $1 \leqslant j < k_i$, there exists a trigger (σ, h) for Σ on J_i such that $J_i^j\langle\sigma, h\rangle J_i^{j+1}$;

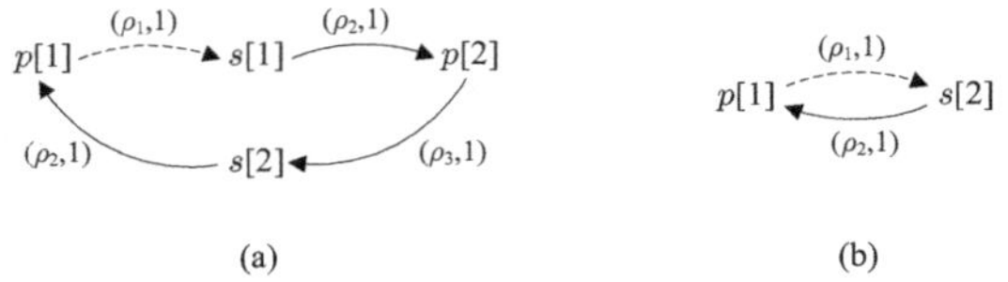

Figure 2: Cycles for Examples 4 and 5.

- for each $i \geqslant 0$, $J_i^{k_i}\langle\sigma_i, h_i\rangle J_{i+1}$; recall that (σ_i, h_i) is a trigger occurring in the sequence obtained by hypothesis;
- for each pair of triggers (σ, h) and (σ', h') considered above, $\sigma = \sigma'$ implies $h \diamond_\sigma^\star h'$; and
- for each $i \geqslant 0$, $k_i \geqslant 0$ is the maximal integer such that the above conditions hold.

Roughly, the above chase sequence constructs the chase in a level-by-level fashion, where level zero is defined as J_0, and the atoms of level i are obtained by applying TGDs on atoms of level $i-1$, by giving priority to the triggers $(\sigma_0, h_0), (\sigma_1, h_1), \ldots$. Thus, the fairness condition is guaranteed, and Proposition 2 follows.

We proceed with the proof of Theorem 1. Recall that we need to show the following: for the set $\Sigma \in \mathsf{SL}$, $\Sigma \notin \mathsf{RA}$ implies $\Sigma \notin \mathsf{CT}^{\mathsf{o}}$. By Proposition 2, it suffices to show that, if $\Sigma \notin \mathsf{RA}$, then Σ admits an infinite o-chase derivation. The rest of this section is devoted to establish that indeed Σ admits an infinite o-chase derivation.

By hypothesis, there exists a cycle in $EDG(\Sigma)$ that contains a special edge; let $(v_0, v_1), (v_1, v_2), \ldots, (v_{n-1}, v_n)$ be such a cycle $(v_0 = v_n)$ with $\lambda((v_i, v_{i+1})) = (\sigma_i, k_i)$, for each $0 \leqslant i < n$. In the sequel, we refer to the above cycle by C. One may claim that, starting from a database D that triggers the TGD σ_0, the cycle C will give rise to an infinite o-chase derivation, which in turn implies that Σ admits an infinite o-chase derivation, as needed. However, such a derivation may be invalid due to the fact that the involved triggers are not distinct. There is no guarantee that the edges of C that are labeled with the same TGD give rise to different triggers.

Example 4. Consider the set $\Sigma' \in \mathsf{SL}$ consisting of

$$\begin{aligned} \rho_1 &= p(X,Y) \rightarrow \exists Z\, s(Z,Z) \\ \rho_2 &= s(X,Y) \rightarrow p(Y,X) \\ \rho_3 &= p(X,Y) \rightarrow s(X,Y). \end{aligned}$$

It is easy to verify that the cycle depicted in Figure 2(a), where the dashed arrow represents a special edge, occurs in $EDG(\Sigma')$. Starting from $I_0 = \{p(c,c)\}$, where $c \in \mathbf{C}$, if we apply the TGDs as dictated by this cycle, we get an infinite sequence of instances $I_0, I_1, \ldots$ with

$$\begin{aligned} I_1 &= I_0 \cup \{s(z_1,z_1)\} \\ I_2 &= I_3 = I_4 = I_1 \cup \{p(z_1,z_1)\} \\ I_5 &= I_4 \cup \{s(z_2,z_2)\} \\ I_6 &= I_7 = I_8 = I_5 \cup \{p(z_2,z_2)\} \\ &\ldots \end{aligned}$$

where $z_1, z_2, \ldots$ are nulls. However, this sequence is not a valid o-chase derivation since, for each $i \in \{1,5,9,13,\ldots\}$, assuming that $I_i\langle\rho_2, h\rangle I_{i+1}$ and $I_{i+2}\langle\rho_2, h'\rangle I_{i+3}$, $h = h' = \{X_2 \rightarrow z_{\lceil \frac{i}{4} \rceil}, Y_2 \rightarrow z_{\lceil \frac{i}{4} \rceil}\}$. Thus, (ρ_2, h), (ρ_2, h') are not distinct, as required by an infinite o-chase derivation. ■

Although C does not necessarily encode a valid infinite o-chase derivation, it is possible to show that in $EDG(\Sigma)$ there exists a cycle C', whose length is less or equal than the length of C, which encodes a valid infinite o-chase derivation. Intuitively speaking, if we avoid to reapply the repeated triggers that are involved in the infinite sequence of instances obtained due to C, then we get a valid o-chase derivation, which corresponds to C'. In fact, C' is one of the shortest cycles in $EDG(\Sigma)$ that contains a special edge. Let us illustrate this via an example that builds on Example 4.

Example 5. Consider the set Σ' given in Example 4. As already discussed above, starting from $I_0 = \{p(c,c)\}$, and applying the TGDs as dictated by the cycle of $EDG(\Sigma)$ shown in Figure 2(a), we obtain an infinite sequence of instances that is not a valid o-chase derivation, since some of the involved triggers are repeated. If we avoid to reapply those triggers, then we get an infinite sequence of instances $J_0 = I_0, J_1, \ldots$ with

$$\begin{aligned} J_1 &= J_0 \cup \{s(z_1,z_1)\} & J_2 &= J_1 \cup \{p(z_1,z_1)\} \\ J_3 &= J_2 \cup \{s(z_2,z_2)\} & J_4 &= J_3 \cup \{p(z_2,z_2)\} \\ &\ldots \end{aligned}$$

where $z_1, z_2, \ldots$ are nulls of $\mathbf{N}$. It is easy to verify that $J_0, J_1, \ldots$ is a valid infinite o-chase derivation, and that this derivation corresponds to the cycle of $EDG(\Sigma')$ depicted in Figure 2(b). This cycle is of length two, and there is no shorter cycle that contains a special edge. ■

From the above discussion, one can exploit the minimal cycles in the extended dependency graph, and show that:

LEMMA 3. *For every set $\Sigma \in \mathsf{SL}$, if $\Sigma \notin \mathsf{RA}$, then Σ admits an infinite o-chase derivation.*

By Proposition 2 and Lemma 3, we immediately get that $\Sigma \notin \mathsf{CT}^{\mathsf{o}}$, and Theorem 1 follows.

4.1.2 Semi-Oblivious Chase

By following a similar approach, we can characterize the fragment of SL that guarantees the termination of the semi-oblivious chase. For a set of TGDs Σ, $\Sigma \in (\mathsf{RA} \cap \mathsf{SL})$ implies $\Sigma \in (\mathsf{CT}^{\mathsf{o}} \cap \mathsf{SL})$, which in turn implies $\Sigma \in (\mathsf{CT}^{\mathsf{so}} \cap \mathsf{SL})$. However, the other direction is, in general, not true. Consider the set Σ given in Example 3. It is easy to verify that $\Sigma \in (\mathsf{CT}^{\mathsf{so}} \cap \mathsf{SL})$, but $\Sigma \notin (\mathsf{RA} \cap \mathsf{SL})$, since in its extended dependency graph, which is depicted in Figure 1, there exists a cycle that contains a special edge.

The main reason why rich-acyclicity is not enough for characterizing $(\mathsf{CT}^{\mathsf{so}} \cap \mathsf{SL})$, is the existence (in the extended dependency graph) of the special edges from the positions where non-frontier variables occur to the positions where existentially quantified variables appear. In fact, those edges encode erroneous propagations of nulls that do not take place during the construction of the semi-oblivious chase. Recall that after eliminating those problematic special edges, we get a graph structure that coincides with the dependency graph. This observation led us to conjecture that weak-acyclicity is enough for characterizing $(\mathsf{CT}^{\mathsf{so}} \cap \mathsf{SL})$. By giving a proof similar to that of Lemma 3, with the difference that we exploit the dependency graph instead of the extended dependency graph, we show that:

LEMMA 4. *For every set $\Sigma \in \mathsf{SL}$, if $\Sigma \notin \mathsf{WA}$, then Σ admits an infinite so-chase derivation.*

By Proposition 2 and Lemma 4, we immediately get that $\Sigma \notin \mathsf{WA}$ implies $\Sigma \notin \mathsf{CT}^{\mathsf{so}}$. Notice that the other direction is implicit in [22], where the same has been shown for a superclass of WA, and the next result follows:

THEOREM 5. $(\mathsf{CT}^{\mathsf{so}} \cap \mathsf{SL}) = (\mathsf{WA} \cap \mathsf{SL})$.

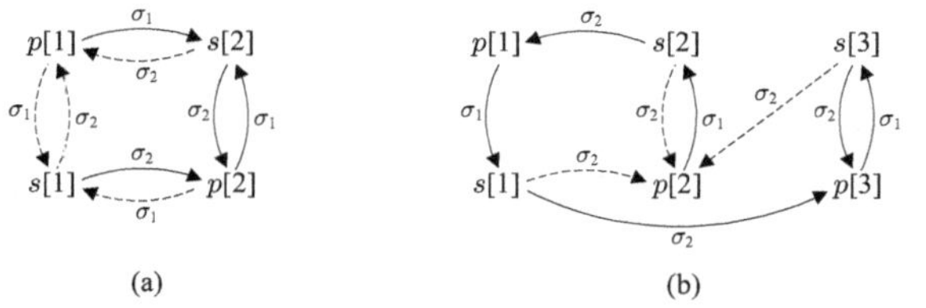

Figure 3: Extended dependency graphs of Examples 6 and 7.

4.1.3 Consequences to Other Formalisms

Despite their simplicity, simple linear TGDs are powerful enough for capturing prominent database dependencies, and in particular *inclusion dependencies*; see, e.g., [1]. It is well-known that inclusion dependencies correspond to simple linear (constant-free) TGDs with just one head-atom without repetition of variables, and we refer to this formalism by ID. Furthermore, simple linear TGDs generalize prominent ontology languages, and in particular DL-Lite$_{\mathcal{R}}$ [8]. In fact, DL-Lite$_{\mathcal{R}}$ (ignoring non-membership and disjointness axioms) corresponds to simple linear TGDs that use only unary and binary predicates; we refer by $\mathsf{DL\text{-}Lite}^{\mathsf{TGD}}$ to this formalism. It is evident that our preceding results on simple linear TGDs immediately imply the following:

COROLLARY 6. *It holds that,*

1. $(\mathsf{CT}^{\star} \cap \mathsf{ID}) = (\mathcal{L}(\star) \cap \mathsf{ID})$,
2. $(\mathsf{CT}^{\star} \cap \mathsf{DL\text{-}Lite}^{\mathsf{TGD}}) = (\mathcal{L}(\star) \cap \mathsf{DL\text{-}Lite}^{\mathsf{TGD}})$,

where $\star \in \{\mathsf{o}, \mathsf{so}\}$, $\mathcal{L}(\mathsf{o}) = \mathsf{RA}$, *and* $\mathcal{L}(\mathsf{so}) = \mathsf{WA}$.

4.2 Characterizing $(\mathsf{CT}^{\mathsf{o}} \cap \mathsf{L})$ and $(\mathsf{CT}^{\mathsf{so}} \cap \mathsf{L})$

4.2.1 Oblivious Chase

We proceed with the characterization of the fragment of L that guarantees the termination of the oblivious chase. Let us first expose, by means of simple examples, the two reasons for which rich-acyclicity is not enough for our purposes.

Example 6. Consider the set $\Sigma \in \mathsf{L}$ consisting of

$$\begin{aligned}\sigma_1 &= p(X,X) \rightarrow \exists Z\, s(Z,X)\\ \sigma_2 &= s(X,X) \rightarrow \exists Z\, p(Z,X).\end{aligned}$$

It is easy to verify that in the extended dependency graph of Σ, depicted in Figure 3(a), there exists a cycle that contains a special edge. However, for every database D, every o-chase sequence of D w.r.t. Σ is terminating. ■

As shown above, the first reason why rich-acyclicity is not enough for characterizing $(\mathsf{CT}^{\mathsf{o}} \cap \mathsf{L})$, is the fact that a cycle in the extended dependency graph does not necessarily encode a chase derivation. Consider, for example, the cycle $(p[1], s[1]), (s[1], p[1])$, where the first edge is labeled by σ_1, and the second edge by σ_2. One expects that, after applying σ_1 during the chase, the obtained atom $\underline{a}$ may trigger σ_2. However, this is not the case, since $\underline{a}$ is necessarily of the form $s(t,t')$, where $t \neq t'$, which means that there is no homomorphism from $body(\sigma_2)$ to $\underline{a}$. The atom $\underline{a}$ is of the above form since, in the head-atom of σ_1, at position $s[1]$ we have an existentially quantified variable, while at position $s[2]$ a frontier variable.

The above informal discussion, demonstrates the need of finding an effective way for guaranteeing that a cycle in the extended dependency graph can indeed be traversed during the construction of the chase, in which case is called active. To this end, we need to understand when, for two single-head linear TGDs σ_1 and σ_2, the atom obtained by applying σ_1 may trigger σ_2. Notice that we focus on single-head TGDs, since, by definition, the edges of the extended dependency graph are labeled by single-head TGDs. The above property is captured by the notion of compatibility. In the sequel, we assume the reader is familiar with the notion of unification. Given two atoms $\underline{a}$ and $\underline{b}$ that unify, we denote by $\mathsf{MGU}(\underline{a}, \underline{b})$ their most general unifier.

Definition 4. Let σ_1 and σ_2 be single-head linear TGDs. Then, σ_1 is *compatible* with σ_2 if: $head(\sigma_1)$ and $body(\sigma_2)$ unify, and for each $X \in var(body(\sigma_2))$, assuming $\Pi = pos(body(\sigma_2), \{X\})$, either $var(head(\sigma_1), \Pi) \subseteq fr(\sigma_1)$, or, $var(head(\sigma_1), \Pi) = \{Z\}$, for some $Z \in ex(\sigma_1)$. ■

Clearly, in Example 6, σ_1 is not compatible with σ_2, and vice-versa. Having the notion of compatibility in place, one may be tempted to claim that a sequence $\sigma_1, \ldots, \sigma_n$ of single-head linear TGDs is active if, for each $i \in [n-1]$, σ_i is compatible with σ_{i+1}. However, this does not capture our intention. Instead, we need to ensure that the resolvent of such a sequence, which is a single-head linear TGD that simulates the behavior of $\sigma_1, \ldots, \sigma_n$, exists.

Definition 5. The *resolvent* of a sequence $\sigma_1, \ldots, \sigma_n$ of single-head linear TGDs, denoted $\mathsf{R}(\sigma_1, \ldots, \sigma_n)$, is inductively defined as follows (for convenience, we write ρ for $\mathsf{R}(\sigma_1, \ldots, \sigma_{n-1})$):

1. $\mathsf{R}(\sigma_1) = \sigma_1$; and
2. $\mathsf{R}(\sigma_1, \ldots, \sigma_n) = \theta(body(\rho)) \rightarrow \theta(head(\sigma_n))$, where $\theta = \mathsf{MGU}(head(\rho), body(\sigma_n))$ if $\rho \neq \bot$ and ρ is compatible with σ_n; otherwise, $\mathsf{R}(\sigma_1, \ldots, \sigma_n) = \bot$.

The sequence $\sigma_1, \ldots, \sigma_n$ is *active* if $\mathsf{R}(\sigma_1, \ldots, \sigma_n) \neq \bot$. ■

Apparently, in order to achieve our goal, we need to extend rich-acyclicity to active-rich-acyclicity, by allowing cycles with special edges to appear in the extended dependency graph, as long as they do not give rise to active sequences of single-head linear TGDs. Unfortunately, active-rich-acyclicity is still not expressive enough for characterizing the fragment of linear TGDs that guarantees the termination of the oblivious chase.

Example 7. Consider the set $\Sigma \in \mathsf{L}$ consisting of

$$\begin{aligned}\sigma_1 &= p(X,Y,Z) \rightarrow s(X,Y,Z)\\ \sigma_2 &= s(X,Y,X) \rightarrow \exists Z\, p(Y,Z,X).\end{aligned}$$

It is easy to verify that in $EDG(\Sigma)$, depicted in Figure 3(b), there exists an active cycle that contains a special edge. For example, $C = (p[2], s[2]), (s[2], p[2])$ gives rise to the sequence σ_1, σ_2. Since σ_1 is compatible with σ_2, we get that $\mathsf{R}(\sigma_1, \sigma_2) \neq \bot$, which in turn implies that C is active. Even if Σ is not actively-richly-acyclic, we can show that, for every D, every o-chase sequence of D w.r.t. Σ is terminating. To this aim, it suffices to verify that every o-chase sequence of the critical database $D_{\mathsf{c}}(\{p, s\})$ w.r.t. Σ is terminating. ■

The above example exposes the second reason why rich-acyclicity is not expressive enough for characterizing $(\mathsf{CT}^{\mathsf{o}} \cap \mathsf{L})$. In particular, even if a cycle in the extended dependency graph is active, which means that it can be traversed at least once during the construction of the chase, it is not guaranteed that it can be traversed infinitely many times, and thus give rise to an infinite chase derivation. Consider, for example, the cycle $C = (p[2], s[2]), (s[2], p[2])$, where the first edge is labeled by σ_1, and the second edge by σ_2. Since C is active, one expects that, starting from $p(\mathsf{c}, \mathsf{c}, \mathsf{c})$, where p is the predicate of $body(\sigma_1)$, we can apply $\sigma_1, \sigma_2, \sigma_1, \ldots$ infinitely many times during the chase. However, after applying $\sigma_1, \sigma_2, \sigma_1, \sigma_2, \sigma_1$, we obtain $\underline{a} = s(t, t', \mathsf{c})$, where $t \neq t'$, and thus there is no homomorphism from $body(\sigma_2)$ to $\underline{a}$. In other words, the cycle C can be traversed twice, but during its third traversal σ_2 is not triggered. The reason for this behavior is the fact that the sequence $\mathsf{R}(\sigma_1, \sigma_2), \mathsf{R}(\sigma_1, \sigma_2), \mathsf{R}(\sigma_1, \sigma_2)$ of length *three* (the chase derivation is blocked during the *third* traversal of C) is not active.

It is clear that we need an effective way for ensuring that an active cycle in the extended dependency graph can be traversed infinitely many times during the construction of the chase. In particular, assuming that an active cycle is labeled by the TGDs $\sigma_1, \ldots, \sigma_n$, we need to ensure that, for every $k > 0$, if $\rho = \mathsf{R}(\sigma_1, \ldots, \sigma_n)$, the sequence $\rho, \ldots, \rho$ of length k is active, in which case $\sigma_1, \ldots, \sigma_n$ is critical. Interestingly, as we shall see below, for ensuring the above criticality condition, we only need to consider sequences of length up to $(\omega_{\sigma_1} + 1)$, where ω_{σ_1} is the arity of the predicate of $body(\sigma_1)$. This leads to the following definition of critical sequences. Henceforth, σ^k denotes the sequence $\sigma, \ldots, \sigma$ of length k:

Definition 6. A sequence $\sigma_1, \ldots, \sigma_n$ of single-head linear TGDs is *critical* if:

1. It is active; and
2. For each $k \in [\omega_{\sigma_1} + 1]$, ρ^k, where $\rho = \mathsf{R}(\sigma_1, \ldots, \sigma_n)$, is active. ■

We proceed to extend rich-acyclicity to critical-rich-acyclicity, which, as we shall see, characterizes $(\mathsf{CT}^{\mathsf{o}} \cap \mathsf{L})$.

Definition 7. Consider $\Sigma \in \mathsf{L}$, and let $EDG(\Sigma) = (N, E, \lambda)$. A cycle $(v_0, v_1), \ldots, (v_{n-1}, v_n)$ in $EDG(\Sigma)$ is called *critical*, if $\lambda((v_0, v_1)), \ldots, \lambda((v_{n-1}, v_n))$ is critical. Σ is *critically-richly-acyclic*, if no critical cycle in $EDG(\Sigma)$ contains a special edge, and the corresponding class is denoted $\mathsf{LCriticalRA}$. ■

The main result of this section follows:

THEOREM 7. $(\mathsf{CT}^{\mathsf{o}} \cap \mathsf{L}) = \mathsf{LCriticalRA}$.

The "if" direction of the above result is shown by giving a proof similar to the one given in [19] for showing that $\Sigma \in \mathsf{RA}$ implies $\Sigma \in \mathsf{CT}^{\mathsf{o}}$. The interesting part is to show that, for a set $\Sigma \in \mathsf{L}$, $\Sigma \notin \mathsf{LCriticalRA}$ implies $\Sigma \notin \mathsf{CT}^{\mathsf{o}}$. By Proposition 2, it suffices to show that, if $\Sigma \notin \mathsf{LCriticalRA}$, then Σ admits an infinite o-chase derivation. This is a rather non-trivial task, which requires some intermediate results.

The equality type of an atom is a set of equalities among positions that perfectly describe its shape. Formally, given a (constant-free) atom $\underline{a} = p(X_1, \ldots, X_n)$, the *equality type* of $\underline{a}$ is defined as $eqtype(\underline{a}) = \{p[i] = p[j] \mid X_i = X_j\}$. For a linear TGD σ, let $eqtype(\sigma) = eqtype(body(\sigma))$. The following lemma establishes a useful property about active sequences and equality types:

LEMMA 8. *Let σ be a single-head linear TGD such that σ^i and σ^{i+1} are active, for some integer $i > 0$, and $eqtype(\mathsf{R}(\sigma^i)) = eqtype(\mathsf{R}(\sigma^{i+1}))$. Then, σ^{i+2} is active, and $eqtype(\mathsf{R}(\sigma^{i+1})) = eqtype(\mathsf{R}(\sigma^{i+2}))$.*

The above result allows us to show that critical cycles can be traversed infinitely many times during the construction of the chase, starting from the critical database. Consider a critical sequence $\sigma_1, \ldots, \sigma_n$ of single-head linear TGDs, and let $\rho = \mathsf{R}(\sigma_1, \ldots, \sigma_n)$. It is not difficult to show that there exists $i \in [\omega_{\sigma_1} + 1]$ such that ρ^i and ρ^{i+1} are active, and $eqtype(\mathsf{R}(\rho^i)) = eqtype(\mathsf{R}(\rho^{i+1}))$. By recursively applying Lemma 8, we conclude that, for every $k > [\omega_{\sigma_1} + 1]$, ρ^k is active. Moreover, since $\sigma_1, \ldots, \sigma_n$ is critical, for every $k \in [\omega_{\sigma_1} + 1]$, ρ^k is active. From the above discussion, we get the following crucial result:

LEMMA 9. *Let $\sigma_1, \ldots, \sigma_n$ be a critical sequence of single-head linear TGDs. Then, for every $k > 0$, ρ^k, where $\rho = \mathsf{R}(\sigma_1, \ldots, \sigma_n)$, is active.*

By using Lemma 9, and the fact that the resolvent of an active sequence of single-head linear TGDs mimics the behavior of the sequence during the chase, starting from the critical database (this can be easily shown by induction on the length of the sequence), we can establish that a minimal critical cycle that contains a special edge gives rise to an infinite chase derivation, which in turn implies the following:

LEMMA 10. *For every set $\Sigma \in \mathsf{L}$, if $\Sigma \notin \mathsf{LCriticalRA}$, then Σ admits an infinite o-chase derivation.*

By Proposition 2 and Lemma 10, we get that $\Sigma \notin \mathsf{LCriticalRA}$ implies $\Sigma \notin \mathsf{CT}^{\mathsf{o}}$, and Theorem 7 follows.

4.2.2 Semi-Oblivious Chase

By applying similar techniques, we can characterize the fragment of L that guarantees the termination of the semi-oblivious chase. To this end, we first need to introduce the notion of critical-weak-acyclicity, which is defined as critical-rich-acyclicity, with the difference that the desired condition is posed on the dependency graph, and not on the extended dependency graph.

Definition 8. A set $\Sigma \in \mathsf{L}$ is *critically-weakly-acyclic*, if no critical cycle in $DG(\Sigma)$ contains a special edge, and the corresponding class is denoted $\mathsf{LCriticalWA}$. ■

As already discussed in Section 4.1.2, the extended dependency graph encodes propagations of nulls that do not take place during the construction of the semi-oblivious chase, and this is exactly the reason why we need to rely on the dependency graph for the characterization of $(\mathsf{CT}^{\mathsf{so}} \cap \mathsf{L})$. By giving a proof similar to that of Lemma 10, with the difference that we exploit the dependency graph instead of the extended dependency graph, we show that:

LEMMA 11. *For every set $\Sigma \in \mathsf{L}$, if $\Sigma \notin \mathsf{LCriticalWA}$, then Σ admits an infinite so-chase derivation.*

By Proposition 2 and Lemma 11, $\Sigma \notin \mathsf{LCriticalWA}$ implies $\Sigma \notin \mathsf{CT}^{\mathsf{so}}$. The proof of the other direction is along the lines of the proof given in [11] for showing that weak-acyclicity guarantees the termination of the restricted chase, and we get that:

THEOREM 12. $(\mathsf{CT}^{\mathsf{so}} \cap \mathsf{L}) = \mathsf{LCriticalWA}$.

4.3 Complexity of Chase Termination

Let us now proceed with our second goal, that is, to pinpoint the complexity of the $\star$-chase termination problem for sets of TGDs of $(\mathsf{S})\mathsf{L}$, where $\star \in \{\mathsf{o}, \mathsf{so}\}$.

4.3.1 Simple Linear TGDs

We first focus on SL, and we show the following:

THEOREM 13. *Consider a set $\Sigma \in \mathsf{SL}$. The problem of deciding whether $\Sigma \in \mathsf{CT}^{\star}$, where $\star \in \{\mathsf{o}, \mathsf{so}\}$, is* NL*-complete, even for unary and binary predicates.*

Upper Bound. To obtain the upper bound, by Theorems 1 and 5, it suffices to show that deciding whether Σ is richly-acyclic (or weakly-acyclic) is in NL.

LEMMA 14. *Consider $\Sigma \in \mathsf{SL}$. The problem of deciding if $\Sigma \in \mathcal{L}$, where $\mathcal{L} \in \{\mathsf{RA}, \mathsf{WA}\}$, is in $NSPACE(\log(\omega \cdot |sch(\Sigma)|))$, where ω is the maximum arity of $sch(\Sigma)$.*

The complement of the problem under consideration can be seen as an instance of graph reachability. In fact, we need to decide whether there exists a node v in the (extended) dependency graph of Σ that is reachable from itself, with the additional condition that the path from v to itself contains at least one special edge. This can be done via a nondeterministic procedure, where at each step needs to remember two consecutive edges of the graph (i.e., three positions of $sch(\Sigma)$), the origin of the traversed cycle (i.e, the position v), and a binary value indicating whether a special edge has been visited or not. All the above elements can be maintained in $\mathcal{O}(\log(\omega \cdot |sch(\Sigma)|))$ space.

Lower Bound. Let us now proceed with the NL-hardness. We first introduce the so-called looping operator, which will allow us to establish a generic complexity tool for proving lower bounds for the chase termination problem. Notice that this tool will be used, not only for simple linear TGDs, but also for all the other languages considered in this work. In fact, the goal of the looping operator is to provide a generic reduction from propositional atom entailment to the complement of chase termination. Recall that an instance of propositional atom entailment consists of a database D, a set Σ of TGDs, and a propositional (i.e., 0-ary) predicate q, and the question is whether $D \cup \Sigma \models q$, or, equivalently, whether q belongs to the result of the chase of D w.r.t. Σ.

Let (D, Σ, q) be an instance of propositional atom entailment. Given an atom $\underline{a} = p(\mathbf{t})$, where $\mathbf{t} = (t_1, \dots, t_n)$, occurring either in D (i.e., $\mathbf{t} \in \mathbf{C}^n$) or in Σ (i.e., $\mathbf{t} \in \mathbf{V}^n$), we define, for some $Y \in \mathbf{V}$ not in Σ, the atomic formula

$$\underline{a}_{\Sigma}^{Y} \;=\; \begin{cases} \exists X_{t_1} \dots \exists X_{t_n}\, p(Y, X_{t_1}, \dots, X_{t_n}), & \mathbf{t} \in \mathbf{C}^n, \\ p(Y, t_1, \dots, t_n), & \mathbf{t} \in \mathbf{V}^n, \end{cases}$$

where $X_{t_1}, \dots, X_{t_n} \in \mathbf{V}$ do not appear in Σ. We define $\Phi_{D,\Sigma}^{Y} = (\bigwedge_{\underline{a} \in D} \underline{a}_{\Sigma}^{Y})$, and Σ^{Y} as the set of TGDs obtained by replacing each atom $\underline{a}$ occurring in Σ with $\underline{a}_{\Sigma}^{Y}$. We are now ready to define the looping operator.

Definition 9. Let (D, Σ, q) be an instance of propositional atom entailment. The application of the *looping operator* on (D, Σ, q) returns the set of TGDs

$$\mathsf{Loop}(D, \Sigma, q) \;=\; \{loop(X, Y) \rightarrow \Phi_{D,\Sigma}^{Y}\} \cup \Sigma^{Y} \cup \{q(Y) \rightarrow \exists Z\, loop(Y, Z)\},$$

where $loop \notin sch(\Sigma)$. A class of TGDs $\mathcal{L}$ is *closed under looping* if, for every instance (D, Σ, q) of propositional atom entailment, where $\Sigma \in \mathcal{L}$, $\mathsf{Loop}(D, \Sigma, q) \in \mathcal{L}$. ■

By using the looping operator, we can transfer, in a uniform way, lower bounds from propositional atom entailment to chase termination. Our generic complexity result follows:

PROPOSITION 15. *Let $\mathcal{L}$ be a class of TGDs that is closed under looping, such that propositional atom entailment for $(\mathsf{CT}^{\star} \cap \mathcal{L})$, where $\star \in \{\mathsf{o}, \mathsf{so}\}$, is $\mathcal{C}$-hard, for a complexity class $\mathcal{C}$ that is closed under log-space reductions. For a set $\Sigma \in \mathcal{L}$, deciding whether $\Sigma \in \mathsf{CT}^{\star}$ is co$\mathcal{C}$-hard.*

To establish the above generic result, it suffices to reduce propositional atom entailment under $(\mathsf{CT}^{\star} \cap \mathcal{L})$ to the complement of chase termination under $\mathcal{L}$. Given a (non-empty) database D, a set $\Sigma \in (\mathsf{CT}^{\star} \cap \mathcal{L})$, and a propositional predicate q, we need to construct in log-space a set $\Sigma' \in \mathcal{L}$ such that, $D \cup \Sigma \models q$ iff there exists a database D' such that a non-terminating $\star$-chase sequence of D' w.r.t. Σ' exists. It can be shown that the above equivalence holds for $\Sigma' = \mathsf{Loop}(D, \Sigma, q)$. The key idea underlying the looping operator can be sketchily described as follows. Consider the simple linear TGD $\sigma = loop(X, Y) \rightarrow \exists Z\, loop(Y, Z)$. It is easy to verify that there exists only one $\star$-chase sequence of $\{loop(a, b)\}$ w.r.t. $\{\sigma\}$, which is non-terminating; for details, see Example 2. Our intention is to mimic the behavior of σ using Σ', with the key difference that an atom of the form $loop(t', t'')$ is obtained by applying σ on an atom $loop(t, t')$ only if $D \cup \Sigma \models q$. This is achieved by "plugging" between $body(\sigma)$ and $head(\sigma)$ the set Σ^{Y}, which, by hypothesis, guarantees the termination of the chase. The given database D is generated by the TGD $loop(X, Y) \rightarrow \Phi_{D,\Sigma}^{Y}$, while the check whether q is entailed is performed by $q(Y) \rightarrow \exists Z\, loop(Y, Z)$. Since, by assumption, $\mathcal{L}$ is closed under looping, $\Sigma' \in \mathcal{L}$, and Proposition 15 follows.

By the Immerman-Szelepcsényi theorem, coNL $=$ NL. Thus, to obtain the NL-hardness for the chase termination problem under simple linear TGDs, since SL is closed under looping, by Proposition 15, it suffices to show that propositional atom entailment under $(\mathsf{CT}^{\star} \cap \mathsf{SL})$ is NL-hard, even for unary and binary predicates. This is shown by giving a reduction from graph reachability. Given a directed graph $G = (N, E)$ and two nodes $s, t \in N$, we construct a database D, a set $\Sigma \in \mathsf{SL}$, and a propositional predicate q such that $D \cup \Sigma \models q$ iff t is reachable from s. The idea is to construct Σ in such a way that its predicate graph coincides with G, while D stores the node s, and q represents the node t. We get that:

LEMMA 16. *Propositional atom entailment under $(\mathsf{CT}^{\star} \cap \mathsf{SL})$, where $\star \in \{\mathsf{o}, \mathsf{so}\}$, is NL-hard, even for unary and binary predicates.*

Theorem 13 follows from Proposition 15, and Lemmas 14 and 16. Notably, $\mathsf{Loop}(D, \Sigma, q)$ belongs to ID and DL-Lite^{TGD}, and thus Theorem 13 holds also for inclusion dependencies and DL-Lite$_{\mathcal{R}}$.

4.3.2 Linear TGDs

We now focus on arbitrary linear TGDs, and we show the following:

THEOREM 17. *Consider a set $\Sigma \in \mathsf{L}$. The problem of deciding whether $\Sigma \in \mathsf{CT}^{\star}$, where $\star \in \{\mathsf{o}, \mathsf{so}\}$, is PSPACE-complete, and NL-complete for predicates of bounded arity.*

Upper Bound. By Theorems 7 and 12, it suffices to show that the problem of deciding whether Σ is critically-richly-acyclic (or critically-weakly-acyclic) can be solved in polynomial space, in general, and in nondeterministic logarithmic space, in case of predicates of bounded arity.

LEMMA 18. *Consider a set $\Sigma \in \mathsf{L}$. The problem of deciding if $\Sigma \in \mathcal{L}$, where $\mathcal{L} \in \{\mathsf{LCriticalRA}, \mathsf{LCriticalWA}\}$, is in NSPACE$(\omega \log(\omega \cdot |sch(\Sigma)|) + \omega \log(\omega \cdot |\Sigma|))$, where ω is the maximum arity over all predicates of $sch(\Sigma)$.*

The above technical lemma is shown by conceiving the complement of our problem as an extended version of graph reachability. In particular, we need to decide whether there exists a node v in the (extended) dependency graph of Σ that is reachable from itself via a critical cycle that contains a special edge. As for Lemma 14, this can be done via a nondeterministic procedure. However, in order to check for the criticality of the traversed cycle, apart from the two consecutive edges, the origin of the cycle, and the binary flag, we also need to remember the resolvent of the TGDs that label the visited edges. Such a resolvent can be computed and maintained in

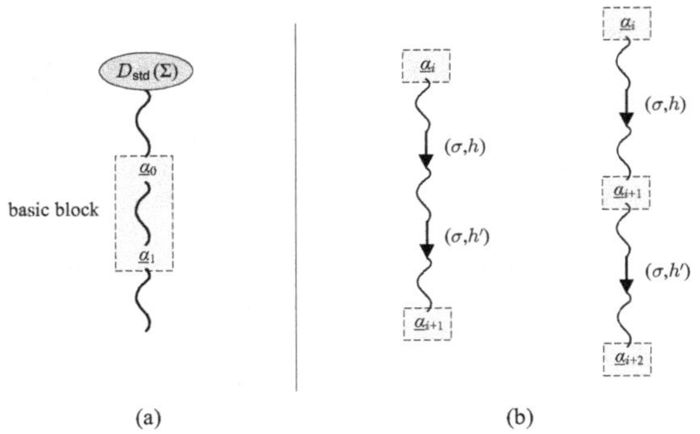

Figure 4: Infinite chase derivation

$\mathcal{O}(\omega \log(\omega \cdot |sch(\Sigma)|) + \omega \log(\omega \cdot |\Sigma|))$ space, and its criticality can be checked using the same space.

Lower Bound. The NL-hardness is immediately inherited from Theorem 13. Concerning the PSPACE-hardness, since L is closed under looping, by Proposition 15, it suffices to show that propositional atom entailment under $(\mathsf{CT}^\star \cap \mathsf{L})$ is PSPACE-hard. This is shown by a reduction from the acceptance problem of a polynomial space Turing machine M.

LEMMA 19. *Propositional atom entailment under* $(\mathsf{CT}^\star \cap \mathsf{L})$, *where* $\star \in \{\mathsf{o}, \mathsf{so}\}$, *is* PSPACE-*hard.*

Theorem 17 follows from Proposition 15, and Lemmas 18 and 19.

5. (WEAK-)GUARDEDNESS

We proceed to investigate the (semi-)oblivious chase termination problem for guarded and weakly-guarded TGDs. Although there is no way (at least no obvious one) to syntactically characterize the classes $(\mathsf{CT}^\star \cap \mathsf{WG})$ and $(\mathsf{CT}^\star \cap \mathsf{G})$, where $\star \in \{\mathsf{o}, \mathsf{so}\}$, as we did for (simple) linear TGDs, it is possible to show that the problem of recognizing the above classes is decidable.

For technical reasons, we focus on *standard databases*, that is, databases that have at least two constants, let's say 0 and 1, that are available via the unary predicates $0(\cdot)$ and $1(\cdot)$, respectively. The results presented below, unless stated otherwise, hold only for standard databases. We show the following:

THEOREM 20. *Consider a set* $\Sigma \in \mathsf{WG}$. *The problem of deciding whether* $\Sigma \in \mathsf{CT}^\star$, *where* $\star \in \{\mathsf{o}, \mathsf{so}\}$, *is* 2EXPTIME-*complete, and* EXPTIME-*complete for predicates of bounded arity. The same holds even if* $\Sigma \in \mathsf{G}$.

The goal of this section is to establish the above result.

5.1 Infinite Chase Derivations

We first focus our attention on weakly-guarded TGDs, and show that the chase termination problem is decidable; this implies that the problem is decidable also for guarded TGDs. By Proposition 2, given a set $\Sigma \in \mathsf{WG}$, to decide whether $\Sigma \notin \mathsf{CT}^\star$ (recall that we focus on standard databases), where $\star \in \{\mathsf{o}, \mathsf{so}\}$, is tantamount to the problem of deciding whether Σ admits an infinite $\star$-chase derivation that starts from a standard database i.e., there exist sequences $I_0, I_1, \ldots$ and $(\sigma_0, h_0), (\sigma_1, h_1), \ldots$ as in Definition 3 with I_0 be a standard database. In what follows, we show that the latter is a decidable problem by presenting an alternating algorithm, called $\star$-$\mathsf{InfiniteDerivation}$.

A General Description. One may be tempted to claim that a set of TGDs Σ admits an infinite $\star$-chase derivation that starts from a standard database iff Σ admits an infinite $\star$-chase derivation that starts from the critical database $D_{\mathsf{c}}(\Sigma)$. However, this is not true since $D_{\mathsf{c}}(\Sigma)$ is *not* a standard database. Nevertheless, the notion of the critical database can be naturally extended to the critical standard database, which is the standard database consisting of all possible atoms that can be formed using predicates of $sch(\Sigma)$ and the constants 0 and 1. Formally, the *critical standard database* for a set Σ of TGDs (not necessarily weakly-guarded), denoted $D_{\mathsf{std}}(\Sigma)$, is defined as the database

$$\{0(0), 1(1)\} \cup \{p(\mathbf{t}) \mid p/n \in sch(\Sigma), \mathbf{t} \in \{0,1\}^n\}.$$

It is clear that the size of $D_{\mathsf{std}}(\Sigma)$ is exponential in general, and polynomial when the maximum arity over all predicates of $sch(\Sigma)$ is fixed. By giving a proof similar to the one in [22] for the critical database, we show the following:

LEMMA 21. *Consider a set* Σ *of TGDs. It holds that,* Σ *admits an infinite* $\star$*-chase derivation that starts from a standard database, where* $\star \in \{\mathsf{o}, \mathsf{so}\}$, *iff* Σ *admits an infinite* $\star$*-chase derivation that starts from* $D_{\mathsf{std}}(\Sigma)$.

Our alternating algorithm, starting from an atom of $D_{\mathsf{std}}(\Sigma)$, and applying nondeterministically chase steps, identifies a finite basic block of a chase derivation (if it exists), which can then be repeated and give rise to an infinite chase derivation; this is graphically illustrated in Figure 4(a). In other words, the algorithm tries to identify an atom $\underline{a}_0$ from which, after applying some valid (depending on the version of the chase) triggers, an atom $\underline{a}_1$ isomorphic to $\underline{a}_0$ is obtained — by isomorphism we mean that, starting from $\underline{a}_0$ and $\underline{a}_1$, we obtain isomorphic atoms. The segment of the derivation between $\underline{a}_0$ and $\underline{a}_1$ is the basic block that we can repeat infinitely many times, and obtain an infinite chase derivation. Before giving the technical details of our algorithm, we need to briefly recall some auxiliary notions and results.

Auxiliary Notions and Results. A set $\Sigma \in \mathsf{WG}$ can be effectively transformed into a set $\Sigma' \in \mathsf{WG}$ such that all the TGDs of Σ' are single-head [6]. It is not difficult to verify that this transformation preserves chase termination, i.e., $\Sigma \in \mathsf{CT}^\star$ iff $\Sigma' \in \mathsf{CT}^\star$, where $\star \in \{\mathsf{o}, \mathsf{so}\}$. Henceforth, for technical clarity, we focus on TGDs with just one atom in the head. Let D be a database, and Σ a set of TGDs. Fix a $\star$-chase sequence $I_0 = D, I_1, \ldots$ of D w.r.t. Σ, for $\star \in \{\mathsf{o}, \mathsf{so}\}$. The instance $\cup_{i \geqslant 0} I_i$, denoted $\star$-$chase(D, \Sigma)$, can be naturally represented as a labeled directed graph $G = (N, E, \lambda)$ as follows: (1) for each atom $\underline{a} \in \star$-$chase(D, \Sigma)$, there exists $v \in N$ such that $\lambda(v) = \underline{a}$; (2) for each $i \geqslant 0$, with $I_i\langle\sigma, h\rangle I_{i+1}$, and for each atom $\underline{a} \in h(body(\sigma))$, there exists $(v, u) \in E$ such that $\lambda(v) = \underline{a}$ and $\{\lambda(u)\} = I_{i+1} \setminus I_i$; and (3) there are no other nodes and edges in G. The *guarded chase forest* of D and Σ, denoted $\mathsf{gcf}(D, \Sigma)$, is the forest obtained from G by keeping only the nodes associated with guard atoms, and their children; for more details, we refer the reader to [6].

Lemma 21 implies that our algorithm has to identify an infinite path in $\mathsf{gcf}(D_{\mathsf{std}}(\Sigma), \Sigma)$. This is achieved by constructing nondeterministically such a path, starting from an atom of $D_{\mathsf{std}}(\Sigma)$, until a basic block that can be repeated is identified. During this process, our algorithm exploits two key results established in [6], where the problem of query answering under (weakly-)guarded TGDs is investigated. Let us recall those results, and explain how they are applied; let D be an arbitrary database:

1. The subtree of $\mathsf{gcf}(D, \Sigma)$ rooted at some atom $\underline{a}$ is determined by the so-called cloud of $\underline{a}$ (modulo renaming of nulls) [6, Theorem 5.16]. The *cloud* of $\underline{a}$ w.r.t. D and Σ, denoted

$cloud(\underline{a}, D, \Sigma)$, is defined as

$$\{\underline{b} \mid \underline{b} \in \star\text{-}chase(D, \Sigma) \text{ and } dom(\underline{b}) \subseteq (dom(D) \cup dom(\underline{a}))\},$$

i.e., the atoms occurring in the result of the chase with constants from D and terms from $\underline{a}$. This result allows us to build the relevant path of $\mathsf{gcf}(D, \Sigma)$. In fact, an atom $\underline{a}$ on this path can be generated by considering only its parent atom $\underline{a}'$ and the cloud of $\underline{a}'$ w.r.t. D and Σ. Whenever a new atom is generated, we nondeterministically guess its cloud, and verify in a parallel universal computation of our algorithm that indeed belongs to the result of the chase.

2. There exists a bound δ, which is double-exponential in the maximum arity ω of $sch(\Sigma)$ (and only ω appears in the second exponent), up to which we have to construct the relevant path of $\mathsf{gcf}(D, \Sigma)$ in order to guarantee that all the obtained atoms are non-isomorphic. This implies that, for our purposes, we simply need to construct the path up to depth $(2 \cdot \delta)$. We use this fact to ensure that our algorithm terminates.

Let us clarify that in [6] only the oblivious chase has been considered, and the above results have been explicitly established for the oblivious chase. Nevertheless, it is not difficult to extend these results to the semi-oblivious chase.

The Alternating Algorithm. We have now all the ingredients in place that are needed to define our algorithm. Given a set $\Sigma = \{\sigma_1, \ldots, \sigma_n\}$ as input, $\star$-$\mathsf{InfiniteDerivation}(\Sigma)$ consists of the following steps:

1. $Cl := D_{\mathsf{std}}(\Sigma)$, $H_{\sigma_i} := \varnothing$, for each $i \in [n]$, $flag := 0$ and $ctr := 0$.
2. Guess an atom $\underline{a} \in D$.
3. Guess a TGD $\sigma \in \Sigma$, and a trigger (σ, h) for Σ on Cl, where $h(guard(\sigma)) = \underline{a}$ and $h \diamond_\sigma^\star h'$, for each $h' \in H_\sigma$; if there is no such a trigger, then *reject*.
4. Let $\underline{a}$ be the atom obtained by applying (σ, h) to Cl, and guess the cloud Cl of $\underline{a}$ w.r.t. D and Σ.
5. Universally goto steps 6 and 7.
6. If Cl is a valid cloud, then *accept*; otherwise, *reject*.
7. $H_\sigma := (H_\sigma \cup \{h\}) \setminus H_{\sigma,\underline{a}}$, where $H_{\sigma,\underline{a}} \subseteq H_\sigma$ is the set of homomorphisms that map a variable of $var(body(\sigma))$ to a term not in $dom(\underline{a})$.
8. If $flag = 0$, then guess to apply or skip the following:
   (a) $loop := (\sigma, \underline{a}, Cl)$ and $flag := 1$.
   (b) $nulls := invent(\underline{a})$, where the latter is the set of nulls invented in $\underline{a}$; if $nulls = \varnothing$, the *reject*.
   (c) Goto step 10.
9. If $flag = 1$, then do the following:
   (a) $nulls := (dom(\underline{a}) \cap nulls) \cup invent(\underline{a})$.
   (b) If $(dom(\underline{a}) \cap nulls) = \varnothing$, then *reject*.
   (c) If $(\sigma, \underline{a}, Cl)$ and $loop$ are the same (modulo bijective null renaming), then *accept*.
10. If $ctr = (2 \cdot \delta)$, then *reject*; otherwise, $ctr := ctr + 1$ and goto step 3.

By construction, $\star$-$\mathsf{InfiniteDerivation}(\Sigma)$, starting from an atom $\underline{a} \in D_{\mathsf{std}}(\Sigma)$, identifies a basic block on a path P in the subtree of $\mathsf{gcf}(D_{\mathsf{std}}(\Sigma), \Sigma)$ rooted at $\underline{a}$, which can be repeated infinitely many times. This allows us to safely conclude that P is an infinite path (or chase derivation), and the algorithm accepts; if such a derivation does not exist, the algorithm terminates and rejects. It remains to explain why this derivation is a valid one, i.e., it does not contain conflicting triggers (depending on the version of the chase).

Consider two triggers (σ, h) and (σ', h') occurring in the obtained infinite $\star$-chase derivation. There are two possible cases: either they occur in the same or in different basic blocks; this is illustrated in Figure 4(b). In the first case, $h \diamond_\sigma^\star h'$ is guaranteed by construction; this is the reason why the set H_σ is maintained during the execution of the algorithm, which stores all the "dangerous" homomorphisms that have been used to trigger σ. In the second case, $h \diamond_\sigma^\star h'$ is guaranteed since the atom $h'(guard(\sigma))$ necessarily contains a null that does not appear in the atom $h(guard(\sigma))$; this is why the set $nulls$ is maintained, which actually stores the nulls that can only appear in the atoms of a certain basic block. From the above discussion, we get the desired result:

PROPOSITION 22. *Consider a set $\Sigma \in \mathsf{WG}$. It holds that, Σ admits an infinite $\star$-chase derivation that starts from a standard database, where $\star \in \{\mathsf{o}, \mathsf{so}\}$, iff $\star$-$\mathsf{InfiniteDerivation}(\Sigma)$ accepts.*

5.2 Complexity of Chase Termination

5.2.1 Upper Bounds

By Propositions 2 and 22, we get that, for a set $\Sigma \in \mathsf{WG}$, $\Sigma \notin \mathsf{CT}^\star$ iff $\star$-$\mathsf{InfiniteDerivation}(\Sigma)$ accepts, where $\star \in \{\mathsf{o}, \mathsf{so}\}$. Therefore, to establish the desired upper bounds, it suffices to show that our alternating algorithm runs in exponential space, in general, and in polynomial space, in the case of predicates of bounded arity; recall that AEXPSPACE = 2EXPTIME and APSPACE = EXPTIME. To this end, we show that the space required for the following tasks is exponential in the maximum arity ω of $sch(\Sigma)$, and polynomial in all the other parameters of the input: (1) maintain $D_{\mathsf{std}}(\Sigma)$ and the cloud of an atom; (2) maintain the set H_σ, where $\sigma \in \Sigma$; (3) maintain the integer value of ctr; and (4) verify that the guessed cloud is valid.

LEMMA 23. *The algorithm $\star$-$\mathsf{InfiniteDerivation}$, where $\star \in \{\mathsf{o}, \mathsf{so}\}$, runs in double-exponential time, in general, and in exponential time, for predicates of bounded arity.*

The upper bounds of Theorem 20 follow from Propositions 2 and 22, and Lemma 23.

5.2.2 Lower Bounds

To establish the desired lower bounds, since G is closed under looping, by Proposition 15, it suffices to show the following:

LEMMA 24. *Propositional atom entailment under $(\mathsf{CT}^\star \cap \mathsf{G})$, where $\star \in \{\mathsf{o}, \mathsf{so}\}$, is 2EXPTIME-hard, and EXPTIME-hard for predicates of bounded arity.*

The 2EXPTIME-hardness is obtained by a significant modification of the proof of Theorem 6.2 in [6], which shows the 2EXPTIME-hardness of propositional atom entailment under arbitrary guarded TGDs (not necessarily in $\mathsf{CT}^\star$). That proof simulates an AEXPSPACE Turing machine that uses no more than 2^n worktape cells; this assumption can be made without affecting the generality of the proof. For proving Lemma 24, we make, w.l.o.g., an additional assumption: we assume the machine contains a counter of 2^{n-1} bits (i.e., the second half of the tape) that is initialized to zero and can count from 0 up to $(2^{2^{n-1}} - 1)$. The counter is incremented by one until either the Turing machine stops, or it reaches the maximal value of $(2^{2^{n-1}} - 1)$, in which case the machine is forced to stop in a rejecting state. This makes sure that the machine cannot cycle and always stops within $\mathcal{O}(2^{2^n})$ steps. Adding counters to Turing machines, giving rise to the concept of *clocked Turing machines*, is a well-known technique; see [20, 25]. The fact that we consider a clocked Turing machine, together with the fact that we focus on standard databases, allows us to construct the double-exponentially many configurations of the machine using a set of TGDs that ensures the termination of the chase, which is not the case in the proof of Theorem 6.2 of [6]. By following a similar approach, we can also show the EXPTIME-hardness in the case of predicates of bounded arity, and Lemma 24 follows.

5.3 Non-Standard Databases

From the above discussion, it is clear that standard databases are crucial for establishing the lower bounds in Proposition 24; in particular, to guarantee that the sets of guarded TGDs employed in the reductions are indeed members of $(\mathsf{CT}^\star \cap \mathsf{G})$, where $\star \in \{\mathsf{o}, \mathsf{so}\}$. Interestingly, the upper bounds stated in Theorem 20 hold also for non-standard databases. This can be shown by slightly modifying $\star$-InfiniteDerivation in such a way that, instead of starting from $D_{\mathsf{std}}(\Sigma)$, where $\Sigma \in \mathsf{WG}$ is the given set of TGDs, starts from the critical database $D_{\mathsf{c}}(\Sigma)$. After applying this modification, it is easy to see that Σ admits an infinite $\star$-chase derivation (that starts from an arbitrary, not necessarily standard database) iff $\star$-InfiniteDerivation(Σ) accepts, and we immediately get the following result for arbitrary databases:

THEOREM 25. *Consider a set $\Sigma \in \mathsf{WG}$. The problem of deciding whether $\Sigma \in \mathsf{CT}^\star$, where $\star \in \{\mathsf{o}, \mathsf{so}\}$, is in 2EXPTIME, and in EXPTIME for predicates of bounded arity.*

The exact complexity of the chase termination problem in case of arbitrary (not necessarily standard databases) is still open.

6. RELATIVE EXPRESSIVE POWER

The results presented above, apart from giving an effective way for deciding the termination of the (semi-)oblivious chase, provide us with new decidable query languages, which are based on guardedness, that can directly exploit the chase procedure. A natural question at this point is whether these new query languages, and in particular the feature of existential quantification, give us more expressive power than existing ones. The goal of the current section is to give an answer to the above crucial question.

Consider a class $\mathcal{L}$ of TGDs. An $\mathcal{L}$ *query* is a pair (Σ, q), where $\Sigma \in \mathcal{L}$, and q is a predicate that does not occur in the body of a TGD in Σ. Given a database D, the *answer* to $Q = (\Sigma, q)$ over D, with q be an n-ary predicate, is defined as the set $ans(Q, D) = \{\mathbf{t} \in \mathbf{C}^n \mid D \cup \Sigma \models q(\mathbf{t})\}$. Given two classes $\mathcal{L}$ and $\mathcal{L}'$ of TGDs, we say that $\mathcal{L}'$ is *more expressive* than $\mathcal{L}$, and we write $\mathcal{L} \rhd \mathcal{L}'$, if, for every $\mathcal{L}$ query Q, we can construct an $\mathcal{L}'$ query Q' such that, for every database D, $ans(Q, D) = ans(Q', D')$. Finally, $\mathcal{L}$ and $\mathcal{L}'$ have the *same expressive power*, written $\mathcal{L} \approx \mathcal{L}'$, if $\mathcal{L} \rhd \mathcal{L}'$ and $\mathcal{L}' \rhd \mathcal{L}$. Recall that our goal is to understand whether the existential quantification gives us more expressive power. Towards this aim, we are going to compare the expressive power of the query languages obtained from our previous analysis on chase termination, with the relevant fragments of Datalog. We write DAT for the family of all Datalog programs, which can be seen as sets of single-head TGDs without existentially quantified variables, and UCQ (unions of conjunctive queries) for the family of all Datalog programs where all the rules have the same head-predicate that does not appear in a rule-body. The main result of this section states that the existential quantification does not add expressive power to the existing Datalog-based languages.

THEOREM 26. *For each $\star \in \{\mathsf{o}, \mathsf{so}\}$,*

1. *$(\mathsf{CT}^\star \cap \mathcal{L}) \approx (\mathsf{UCQ} \cap \mathcal{L})$, where $\mathcal{L} \in \{\mathsf{SL}, \mathsf{L}\}$; and*
2. *$(\mathsf{CT}^\star \cap \mathcal{L}) \approx (\mathsf{DAT} \cap \mathcal{L})$, where $\mathcal{L} \in \{\mathsf{G}, \mathsf{WG}\}$.*

The "$\lhd$" direction is trivial since DAT guarantees the termination of the chase. For the "$\rhd$" direction, we exploit recent rewriting techniques proposed in different contexts [13, 14, 23].

Succinctness. The next question that comes up concerns the succinctness of our new query languages. This challenging problem goes beyond the scope of the current work, and is something that we are currently investigating. Nevertheless, we would like to present a result, which can be seen as a strong indication that the existential quantification allows us to build more succinct queries.

PROPOSITION 27. *Given a $(\mathsf{CT}^\star \cap \mathsf{G})$ query Q, where $\star \in \{\mathsf{o}, \mathsf{so}\}$, there is no $(\mathsf{DAT} \cap \mathsf{G})$ (or even DAT) query Q' that is constructible in polynomial time such that, for every standard database D, $ans(Q, D) = ans(Q', D)$.*

Since EXPTIME $\subsetneq$ 2EXPTIME, the above result follows from Lemma 24, and the fact that Datalog is in EXPTIME in combined complexity. In simple words, Proposition 27 says that, even if $(\mathsf{CT}^\star \cap \mathsf{G})$ is not more succinct than $(\mathsf{DAT} \cap \mathsf{G})$, to construct an equivalent $(\mathsf{DAT} \cap \mathsf{G})$ query of polynomial size will be a hard task.

7. CONCLUSIONS

We show that the (semi-)oblivious chase termination problem for guarded-based TGDs is decidable, and we obtain precise complexity bounds. To the best of our knowledge, this is the first work that establishes positive results about the (semi-)oblivious chase termination problem. The next step is to perform similar analysis focussing on the restricted version of the chase. The nondeterministic nature of the restricted chase makes the chase termination problem even more challenging, and new techniques must be devised. We have some preliminary positive results, and we are currently working towards the full settlement of the problem.

8. ACKNOWLEDGMENTS

Part of the work of M. Calautti was performed while visiting the Department of Computer Science, University of Oxford, UK. Part of the work of A. Pieris was performed while was post-doctoral researcher at the Department of Computer Science, University of Oxford, UK. M. Calautti was supported by the European Commission, European Social Fund and Region Calabria. G. Gottlob was supported by the EPSRC Programme Grant EP/M025268/ "VADA: Value Added Data Systems – Principles and Architecture". A. Pieris was supported by the EPSRC Grant EP/J008346/1, Austrian Science Fund (FWF), projects P25207-N23 and Y698, and Vienna Science and Technology Fund (WWTF), project ICT12-015. We thank the anonymous referees for many helpful comments.

9. REFERENCES

[1] S. Abiteboul, R. Hull, and V. Vianu. *Foundations of Databases*. Addison-Wesley, 1995.

[2] A. V. Aho, Y. Sagiv, and J. D. Ullman. Efficient optimization of a class of relational expressions. *ACM Trans. Database Syst.*, 4(4):435–454, 1979.

[3] F. Baader. Least common subsumers and most specific concepts in a description logic with existential restrictions and terminological cycles. In *IJCAI*, pages 319–324, 2003.

[4] J.-F. Baget, M. Leclère, M.-L. Mugnier, and E. Salvat. On rules with existential variables: Walking the decidability line. *Artif. Intell.*, 175(9-10):1620–1654, 2011.

[5] C. Beeri and M. Y. Vardi. A proof procedure for data dependencies. *J. ACM*, 31(4):718–741, 1984.

[6] A. Calì, G. Gottlob, and M. Kifer. Taming the infinite chase: Query answering under expressive relational constraints. *J. Artif. Intell. Res.*, 48:115–174, 2013.

[7] A. Calì, G. Gottlob, and T. Lukasiewicz. A general Datalog-based framework for tractable query answering over ontologies. *J. Web Sem.*, 14:57–83, 2012.

[8] D. Calvanese, G. De Giacomo, D. Lembo, M. Lenzerini, and R. Rosati. Tractable reasoning and efficient query answering in description logics: The DL-Lite family. *J. Autom. Reasoning*, 39(3):385–429, 2007.

[9] A. Deutsch, A. Nash, and J. B. Remmel. The chase revisisted. In *PODS*, pages 149–158, 2008.

[10] A. Deutsch and V. Tannen. Reformulation of XML queries and constraints. In *ICDT*, pages 225–241, 2003.

[11] R. Fagin, P. G. Kolaitis, R. J. Miller, and L. Popa. Data exchange: Semantics and query answering. *Theor. Comput. Sci.*, 336(1):89–124, 2005.

[12] T. Gogacz and J. Marcinkowski. All-instances termination of chase is undecidable. In *ICALP*, pages 293–304, 2014.

[13] G. Gottlob, G. Orsi, and A. Pieris. Query rewriting and optimization for ontological databases. *ACM Trans. Database Syst.*, 2014.

[14] G. Gottlob, S. Rudolph, and M. Simkus. Expressiveness of guarded existential rule languages. In *PODS*, pages 27–38, 2014.

[15] G. Grahne and A. Onet. Anatomy of the chase. *CoRR*, abs/1303.6682, 2013.

[16] B. C. Grau, I. Horrocks, M. Krötzsch, C. Kupke, D. Magka, B. Motik, and Z. Wang. Acyclicity conditions and their application to query answering in description logics. In *KR*, 2012.

[17] S. Greco, C. Molinaro, and F. Spezzano. *Incomplete Data and Data Dependencies in Relational Databases*. Morgan & Claypool Publishers, 2012.

[18] S. Greco, F. Spezzano, and I. Trubitsyna. Stratification criteria and rewriting techniques for checking chase termination. *PVLDB*, 4(11):1158–1168, 2011.

[19] A. Hernich and N. Schweikardt. CWA-solutions for data exchange settings with target dependencies. In *PODS*, pages 113–122, 2007.

[20] P. M. Lewis, R. E. Stearns, and J. Hartmanis. Memory bounds for recognition of context-free and context-sensitive languages. In *FOCS*, pages 191–202, 1965.

[21] D. Maier, A. O. Mendelzon, and Y. Sagiv. Testing implications of data dependencies. *ACM Trans. Database Syst.*, 4(4):455–469, 1979.

[22] B. Marnette. Generalized schema-mappings: From termination to tractability. In *PODS*, pages 13–22, 2009.

[23] B. Marnette. Resolution and datalog rewriting under value invention and equality constraints. *CoRR*, abs/1212.0254, 2012.

[24] M. Meier, M. Schmidt, and G. Lausen. On chase termination beyond stratification. *PVLDB*, 2(1):970–981, 2009.

[25] R. E. Stearns, J. Hartmanis, and P. M. Lewis. Hierarchies of memory limited computations. In *FOCS*, pages 179–190, 1965.

Recovering Exchanged Data

Gösta Grahne
Concordia University
Montreal, Canada, H3G 1M8
grahne@cs.concordia.ca

Ali Moallemi
Concordia University
Montreal, Canada, H3G 1M8
moa_ali@encs.concordia.ca

Adrian Onet *
Concordia University
Montreal, Canada, H3G 1M8
adrian_onet@yahoo.com

ABSTRACT

The inversion of data exchange mappings is one of the thorniest issues in data exchange. In this paper we study inverse data exchange from a novel perspective. Previous work has dealt with the static problem of finding a target-to-source mapping that captures the "inverse" of a source-to-target data exchange mapping. As we will show this approach has some drawbacks when it comes to actually applying the inverse mapping in order to recover a source instance from a materialized target instance. More specifically *(1):* As is well known, the inverse mappings have to be expressed in a much more powerful language than the mappings they invert. *(2):* There are simple cases where a source instance computed by the inverse mapping misses sound information that one may easily obtain when the particular target instance is available. *(3):* In some cases the inverse mapping can introduce unsound information in the recovered source instance.

To overcome these drawbacks we focus on the dynamic problem of recovering the source instance using the source-to-target mapping as well as a given target instance. Similarly to the problem of finding "good" target instances in forward data exchange, we look for "good" source instances to restore, i.e. to materialize. For this we introduce a new semantics to capture instance based recovery. We then show that given a target instance and a source-to-target mapping expressed as set of tuple generating dependencies, there are chase-based algorithms to compute a representative finite set of source instances that can be used to get certain answers to any union of conjunctive source queries. We also show that the instance based source recovery problem unfortunately is coNP-complete. We therefore present a polynomial time algorithm that computes a "small" set of source instances that can be used to get sound certain answers to any union of conjunctive source queries. This algorithm is then extended to extract more sound information for the case when only conjunctive source queries are allowed.

*Contact author.

PODS'15, May 31–June 4, 2015, Melbourne, Victoria, Australia.

ACM 978-1-4503-2757-2/15/05 ...$15.00.
http://dx.doi.org/10.1145/2745754.2745770.

Categories and Subject Descriptors

H.2.5 [**Heterogeneous Databases**]: Data translation

General Terms

Algorithms; Theory

Keywords

Chase; Date Exchange; Data Repair; Incomplete databases; Complexity

1. INTRODUCTION

Data exchange mappings are now widely used in translating data from one database (the source database) into data in another database (the target database) that has a schema distinct from the source database. A data exchange mapping $\mathcal{M}$ is specified by a triple $(\mathbf{S}, \mathbf{T}, \Sigma)$, where $\mathbf{S}$ and $\mathbf{T}$ are relational schemas such that $\mathbf{S} \cap \mathbf{T} = \emptyset$, and Σ is a set of constraints (typically, formulas in some logic) expressing the relationship between $\mathbf{S}$ (the source schema) and $\mathbf{T}$ (the target schema). A data exchange mapping $\mathcal{M}$ is identified with the set of pairs (I, J), where I is an instance over $\mathbf{S}$, J is an instance over $\mathbf{T}$, and $I \cup J \models \Sigma$. We will henceforth express this by writing $(I, J) \in \mathcal{M}$.

In their seminal paper [13], Fagin et al. proposed the language of tuple generating dependencies (tgds) to represent such schema mappings. The language of tgds was shown to be rich enough to capture most mappings occurring in practice. We recall that a tgd is a first order formula of the form $\forall \bar{x} \forall \bar{y}\ (\alpha(\bar{x}, \bar{y}) \rightarrow \exists \bar{z}\ \beta(\bar{x}, \bar{z}))$, where α and β are conjunctions of relational atoms and $\bar{x}$, $\bar{y}$ and $\bar{z}$ are sequences of variables. For simplicity, when representing tgds we will omit the universal quantifiers. *Source-to-target* tgds (s-t tgds) are those tgds where α contains only relation names from $\mathbf{S}$ and β contains only relation names from $\mathbf{T}$.[1]

In the framework for managing data exchange mappings, Bernstein [10] proposed a set of operators for the mappings. The operators included composition, merging, matching and

[1]Additionally, one may also specify *target constraints.* In this paper we however only consider constraints Σ, where Σ is a (finite) set of s-t tgds.

inverse. Two of these operators has gained a lot of attention in the database community, namely the composition [14, 22, 5, 3, 17, 4, 18] and the inversion of schema mappings [12, 15, 8, 5, 6, 17, 16, 7]. In the case of composition, the semantics of [14] has been widely adopted as standard. As mappings actually are binary relations, the standard composition of $\mathcal{M}$ and $\mathcal{M}'$ is simply $\mathcal{M} \circ \mathcal{M}'$, where $\circ$ is relational composition. In contrast, due to the fact that a straightforward application of the standard algebraic concept of mapping inversion renders most schema mappings non-invertible, several alternative semantics have been proposed. In [12], Fagin et al. defined $\mathcal{M}'$ to be an inverse of a mapping $\mathcal{M}$, if $\mathcal{M} \circ \mathcal{M}' = \{(I, I') : I \subseteq I'\}$, where I and I' are instances over $\mathbf{S}$. This semantics, later named *Fagin-inverse*, turned out to be too restrictive, as even simple source-to-target tgds do not have Fagin-inverses. In a subsequent work Fagin et al. [15] introduced the notion of *quasi-inverse* that does not differentiate between source instances that are equivalent for data exchange. Loosely speaking, $\mathcal{M}'$ is a quasi-inverse of $\mathcal{M}$, if $\mathcal{M} \circ \mathcal{M}' \circ \mathcal{M} = \mathcal{M}$. Even with this relaxation the quasi-inverse remains rather restrictive. To overcome the restrictions, Arenas et al. [8] introduced the notion of a *recovery*. A mapping $\mathcal{M}'$ is a recovery of a mapping $\mathcal{M}$ if $(I, I) \in \mathcal{M} \circ \mathcal{M}'$ for any instance I over $\mathbf{S}$. As there can be several recoveries of a given mapping, Arenas et al. considered the notion of a *maximum recovery*. A mapping $\mathcal{M}'$ is a maximum recovery of $\mathcal{M}$ if $\mathcal{M}'$ is a recovery of $\mathcal{M}$, and for all recoveries $\mathcal{M}''$ of $\mathcal{M}$ it holds that $\mathcal{M} \circ \mathcal{M}' \subseteq \mathcal{M} \circ \mathcal{M}''$. This new operation of maximum recovery relaxed the previous inverse operations, and in [8] it was shown that any mapping specified by a set of source-to-target tgds has a maximum recovery. In the same paper it was also shown that large classes of mappings, including ones containing target dependencies, have maximum recoveries. Unfortunately, the maximum recovery mappings of mappings specified by source-to-target tgds cannot be specified for target-to-source tgds. In [6] Arenas et al. showed that in case one is interested in sound (in the recovery semantics) certain answers for conjunctive queries, the maximum recovery mapping of a mapping expressed by a set of source-to-target tgds can be expressed by a set of target-to-source tgds generalized so that the body of these tgds allows the presence of the inequality predicate ($\neq$) and a special predicate that identifies constants. More recently Fagin et al. [16] introduced the notion of *extended-recovery* mappings that also deals with source instances that contain nulls. In this case it is shown that all mappings specified by source-to-target tgds have an extended-recovery mapping, and that the recovery mapping can be represented by a set of target-to-source tgds with inequalities and the constant predicate allowed to occur in the body, and with disjunctions and Skolem functions in the head (actually second order disjunctive tgds).

Although all these inverses play an important role in the development of the model management framework of Bernstein [10], they are less likely to be used in practice due their complicated structure involving disjunctions, and due to the fact that when actually restoring a source database from a target database, the inverse mapping does not necessarily recover the source completely. For example, let the source-to-target mapping be specified by dependency set $\Sigma = \{R(x, y) \rightarrow S(x), P(y)\}$. In this case the maximum recovery mapping will consist of the following set of target-to-source tgds $\Sigma' = \{\xi'_1, \xi'_2\}$, where:

$$\begin{aligned} \xi'_1 &= S(x) \rightarrow \exists y\, R(x, y); \\ \xi'_2 &= P(y) \rightarrow \exists x\, R(x, y). \end{aligned} \tag{1}$$

Consider target instance $J = \{S(a), P(b_1), \ldots, P(b_n)\}$. In this case chasing J with Σ' will yield source instance

$$I = \{R(a, Y), R(X_1, b_1), \ldots, R(X_n, b_n)\}, \tag{2}$$

where y and the x_i's are nulls. It is however easy to see that the information contained in Σ and J allows us to deduce that the source instance actually must be

$$I' = \{R(a, b_1), R(a, b_2), \ldots, R(a, b_n)\}. \tag{3}$$

We would therefore expect the conjunctive source query $Q(x) = \{(x) : R(x, b_2)\}$ to return tuple (a), which is not the case if the recovered source is I in (2). Similar anomalies plague the other semantics as well. This means that these semantics are not complete even when considering only conjunctive queries.

Another practical issue with the proposed inverse semantics is that these semantics do not seem to be "data-exchange sound." As an example consider the following set of full s-t tgds $\Sigma = \{\xi_1, \xi_2, \xi_3\}$, where:

$$\begin{aligned} \xi_1 &= R(x) \rightarrow T(x); \\ \xi_2 &= R(x) \rightarrow S(x); \\ \xi_3 &= M(x) \rightarrow S(x). \end{aligned} \tag{4}$$

For this example both the maximum recovery [8] and the extended-recovery mapping [16] are logically equivalent with $\Sigma' = \{\xi'_1, \xi'_2\}$, where:

$$\begin{aligned} \xi'_1 &= T(x) \rightarrow R(x); \\ \xi'_2 &= S(x) \rightarrow R(x) \vee M(x). \end{aligned} \tag{5}$$

If we now consider target instance $J = \{S(a)\}$ and use Σ' to restore the source database, we will obtain the following three possible source instances: $I_1 = \{R(a)\}$, $I_2 = \{M(a)\}$ and $I_3 = \{R(a), M(a)\}$. It is easy to observe that neither I_1 nor I_3 can be source instances that would yield target instance J in a data exchange process using Σ and using the extended-chase procedure from [11].

In this paper we will consider the problem of recovering the source instance when the source-to-target mapping and the target instance are given. In the semantics considered a source instance I is a recovery of a target instance J under a set of s-t tgds Σ if the following holds:

1. $I \cup J \models \Sigma$, and
2. all tuples from J are justified through Σ by the existence of some tuples in I.

The second requirement guarantees that all the tuples in J were obtained from instance I. Thus the empty instance will not be considered as recovery even though we have that $\emptyset \cup J \models \Sigma$ for any target instance J and any set of s-t tgds Σ. We note that not all target instances are recoverable given a set of s-t tgds. Consider for example the dependencies in equation (4) and target instance $J = \{T(a)\}$.

It is easy to see that in the general case there might be an infinite number of recovered source instances. We show that there is a chase-based method to construct a finite set of such recoveries, and that this set may be used to get the certain answer for any source UCQ. This chase will be applied with the set of target-to-source tgds obtained from the initial source-to-target tgds by inverting the arrows in the tgds. As we will see our chase is not the standard chase [9, 13]; as it is a more involved computation. There are three main cases that need to be covered by our chase process in order to ensure the soundness (wrt the semantics) and completeness (wrt UCQ certain answers) of the recovered set of instances.

As a first case consider the following source-to-target tgds

$$\Sigma = \{R(x) \to S(x); \\ M(y) \to S(y)\}$$

and target instance $J = \{S(a)\}$. By reversing the arrows we get

$$\Sigma^{-1} = \{S(x) \to R(x); \\ S(y) \to M(y)\}$$

Using the standard chase on J with Σ^{-1} will return instance $I = \{R(a), M(a)\}$. Even though I is a recovery it is not the only one, as $I_1 = \{R(a)\}$ and $I_2 = \{M(a)\}$ also are recoveries of J under Σ. In order to achieve this our chase method will not apply all the existing triggers (homomorphisms from the body of the tgds to the instance) but only enough to be sure that the target instance is covered. The set of triggers chosen will determine the recovery. We note that the target instance and the recovery do not need to be a model of Σ^{-1}. In our example neither I_1 nor I_2 is a model of Σ^{-1} and J.

For the second case consider target instance $J = \{S(a)\}$ and Σ from equation (4). It is easy to see that when chasing instance J with Σ^{-1} we should not trigger the tuple generating dependency $S(x) \to R(x)$. This is because a tuple $R(a)$ in the source instance requires a tuple $T(a)$ in target instance J. Since $T(a) \notin J$ the soundness of the recovery is violated. This led us to the notion of subsumption constraints that we obtain from the set of s-t tgds Σ. The subsumption constraints will ensure that such unsound recoveries do not occur.

Finally, for the third case consider the set of source-to-target tgds $\Sigma = \{\xi_1, \xi_2\}$, where:

$$\begin{aligned} \xi_1 &= R(x, x, y) \to T(x); \\ \xi_2 &= R(v, w, z) \to S(z). \end{aligned} \tag{6}$$

Let $J = \{T(a), S(b)\}$ be the target instance. By simply chasing instance J with Σ^{-1} we will obtain source instance $I = \{R(a, a, X), R(Y, Z, b)\}$, where X, Y and Z are nulls. It is easy to see that I is not a recovery of J under Σ because the existence of tuple $R(a, a, X)$ in the source instance requires the existence of tuple $S(X)$ in the target instance. In this case the chase process needs to be "smart enough" to "see" that the recoveries are instances of the form $I_1 = \{R(a, a, b)\}$, $I_2 = I_1 \cup \{R(Y_2, Z_2, b)\}$, $I_3 = I_2 \cup \{R(Y_3, Z_3, b)\}$, $\ldots$, $I_n = I_{n-1} \cup \{R(Y_n, Z_n, b)\}$, $\ldots$, where the Y_i's and Z_i's are distinct nulls.

The results. First we precisely define the instance recovery semantics, that is, what makes a source instance a valid recovery given a set of source-to-target tgds and a target instance. This semantics contains both the universal solutions [13] and canonical solutions [20]. Next we show that the problem of testing if a target instance J is recoverable under a set of source-to-target tgds Σ is an NP-complete problem (the same complexity also holds when testing if J is a universal or canonical solution for some source instance I and Σ). We then show that in order to obtain complete certain answers for any UCQ query over the source schema it is sufficient to compute a finite number of recoveries. The downside is that the problem of testing if a tuple t is in the certain answer of such a UCQ is coNP-complete, and that the hardness result holds even when the query considered is a conjunctive one. On the other hand, we show that there is a simple tractable algorithm that computes a source instance that is part of *any* recovery. Such a source instance can be used to compute *sound* certain answers to any UCQ. Next the method is extended, retaining tractability, to obtain a source instance that has a homomorphism into every recovery. This source instance can be used to compute sound certain answers to any CQ. We also compare our recoveries with the instances obtained by chasing the target with the inverse/recovery mappings considered in the literature.

Interestingly enough, query answering over the recovered instances is a generalization of query answering over materialized views. Our current work extends the previous work [1] by considering s-t tgds instead of the full GAV dependencies used for views. Also we introduce tractable cases for both the UCQ and CQ query classes.

2. PRELIMINARIES

In this section we introduce the basic technical preliminaries and definitions. More information on relational database theory can be obtained from e.g. [2]. We will consider the complexity classes P, NP and coNP. For the definition of these classes we refer to [23].

A finite mapping f, where $f(a_i) = b_i$, for $i = 1, \ldots, n$, will be represented as $\{a_1/b_1, a_2/b_2, \ldots, a_n/b_n\}$. The composition of mappings f and g is $f \circ g$, defined as $(f \circ g)(x) = f(g(x))$. If f is a mapping with domain A, and $S \subseteq A$, the restriction of f to S is denoted $f|_S$.

A *schema* $\mathbf{R}$ is a finite set $\{R_1, \ldots, R_n\}$ of relational symbols, each R_i having a fixed arity k_i. Let $Cons$ be a countably infinite set of constants, and $Nulls$ a countably infinite set of nulls, such that $Cons \cap Nulls = \emptyset$. An *instance* I of $\mathbf{R}$ is an interpretation that assigns to each relational symbol R_i a finite k_i-ary relation $R_i^I \subset (Cons \cup Nulls)^{k_i}$. An instance I over $\mathbf{R}$ is usually identified with the set of tuples $\{R_i(\bar{a}) : \bar{a} \in R_i^I, R_i \in \mathbf{R}\}$. We denote with $|I|$ the size of I, i.e. the number of tuples in I, and with $dom(I)$ we denote the set of all constants and nulls that occur in I. An instance I, such that $dom(I) \subseteq Cons$ is called a *ground instance.* If I and J are two instances over the same schema $\mathbf{R}$, we denote with $I \subseteq J$ the fact that $R_i^I \subseteq R_i^J$, for all $i \in \{1, \ldots, n\}$.

Let I and J be instances over a schema $\mathbf{R}$. A *homomorphism* from I to J is a mapping h on $Cons \cup Nulls$, identity on $Cons$, and extended to tuples and relations in the natural way, such that $h(R_i^I) \subseteq R_i^J$, for all $i \in \{1, \ldots, n\}$. The existence of a homomorphism between instance I and instance J is denoted $I \to J$.

In data-exchange systems the mapping between the source and the target schema is usually expressed as a set of *source-to-target tuple generating dependencies (s-t tgds).* An s-t tgd

ξ is a first order formula of the form

$$\forall \bar{x} \forall \bar{y}\ \alpha(\bar{x}, \bar{y}) \rightarrow \exists \bar{z}\ \beta(\bar{x}, \bar{z}), \quad (7)$$

where $\alpha(\bar{x}, \bar{y})$ is a conjunction of atoms over the source schema, $\beta(\bar{x}, \bar{z})$ is a conjunction of atoms over the target schema, and $\bar{x}$, $\bar{y}$ and $\bar{z}$ are sequences of variables. In case $\bar{z} = \epsilon$, the tgd is called a *full* tgd. Similarly, in case $\bar{y} = \epsilon$ the tgd is called a *quasi-guarded* tgd. Moreover, by $vars(\xi)$ we mean the set of all variables in $\bar{x}$, $\bar{y}$, and $\bar{z}$. When there is no danger of confusion we will also regard a sequence $\bar{x}$ as a set, and write $x_2 \in \bar{x}$, when for example $\bar{x} = (x_1, x_2, x_3)$. We will also often view a conjunction of atoms as a set of atoms, i.e. as an instance where each variable corresponds to a null value. A source instance I and target instance J is said to *satisfy* dependency ξ, denoted $(I, J) \models \xi$, if $I \cup J$ is a model of ξ in the model-theoretic sense. This is extended to sets of s-t tgds Σ, by stipulating that $(I, J) \models \Sigma$ if $(I, J) \models \xi$ for all $\xi \in \Sigma$. For an s-t tgd ξ of the form (7), by ξ^{-1} we denote the following first order formula, called the *reverse* of ξ:

$$\forall \bar{x} \forall \bar{z}\ \beta(\bar{x}, \bar{z}) \rightarrow \exists \bar{y}\ \alpha(\bar{x}, \bar{y}). \quad (8)$$

Note that if ξ is quasi-guarded, then ξ^{-1} is a full tgd. For a set Σ of s-t tgds we define $\Sigma^{-1} = \{\xi^{-1} : \xi \in \Sigma\}$. In the rest of the paper, we assume without loss of generality, that for each set of s-t tgds every two tgds from that set do not share any variables. For simplicity, we will often omit the universal quantifiers when representing tgds.

Given a source instance I and an s-t tgd ξ of the form $\alpha(\bar{x}, \bar{y}) \rightarrow \exists \bar{z}\ \beta(\bar{x}, \bar{z})$, with $Chase(\xi, I)$ we denote the target instance constructed as follows: Start with $Chase(\xi, I) = I$. For each homomorphism h such that $h(\alpha(\bar{x}, \bar{y})) \subseteq I$, extend h to h' such that $h'(z)$ is a new null that was not used before, for each $z \in \bar{z}$. Then add tuples $h'(\beta(\bar{x}, \bar{z}))$ to $Chase(\xi, I)$. The chase process is extended to a set Σ of s-t tgds by $Chase(\Sigma, I) = \bigcup_{\xi \in \Sigma} Chase(\xi, I)$. It was shown in [13] that $Chase(\Sigma, I) \rightarrow J$ for any target instance J such that $(I, J) \models \Sigma$. If H is a set of homomorphisms from the bodies of tgds in Σ to I, we denote by $Chase_H(\Sigma, I)$ the subset of $Chase(\Sigma, I)$ obtained by using only homomorphisms from H.

A conjunctive query Q over schema $\mathbf{R}$ is an expression of the form $\{(\bar{x}) : \exists \bar{y}\ \alpha(\bar{x}, \bar{y})\}$, where $\alpha(\bar{x}, \bar{y})$ is a conjunction of atoms over $\mathbf{R}$ and $\bar{x}$, $\bar{y}$ are sequences of variables. Given an instance I over schema $\mathbf{R}$, the result of the conjunctive query Q on I is:

$$Q(I) = \{(h(\bar{x})) : h(\alpha(\bar{x}, \bar{y})) \in I \text{ for some homomorphism } h\}. \quad (9)$$

With $Q(I)\downarrow$ we denote the set of those tuples from $Q(I)$ that do not contain any values from $Nulls$. A query with no free variables is called a *Boolean query*. The class of all conjunctive queries is denoted CQ. A *union* Q *of conjunctive queries* over schema $\mathbf{R}$ is an expression of the form

$$\{(\bar{x}) : \exists \bar{y}\ (\alpha_1(\bar{x}, \bar{y}_1) \vee \alpha_2(\bar{x}, \bar{y}_2) \vee \ldots \vee \alpha_n(\bar{x}, \bar{y}_n)), \quad (10)$$

where $\bar{y} = \bar{y}_1 \cup \bar{y}_2 \cup \ldots \cup \bar{y}_n$ and each $\alpha_i(\bar{x}, \bar{y}_i)$ is a conjunction of atoms over $\mathbf{R}$. The result of applying Q on an instance I is defined as

$$Q(I) = \{(h(\bar{x})) : h(\alpha(\bar{x}, \bar{y}_i)) \in I \text{ for some } 1 \leq i \leq n \text{ and homomorphism } h\}. \quad (11)$$

With UCQ is denoted the class of all union of conjunctive queries.

3. INSTANCE BASED RECOVERY

In this section we introduce the notion of *instance based recovery*, not be confused with the notion of a *recovery mapping* introduced by Arenas et al. in [8]. We focus on recovering a source instance I, given a target instance J and an s-t mapping $\mathcal{M}$. This is in contrast with [12, 15, 8, 5, 6, 17, 16, 7] that consider the problem of computing a general target-to-source mapping $\mathcal{M}'$, given a source-to-target mapping $\mathcal{M}$. While such a mapping $\mathcal{M}'$ can be used to compute a source instance from a given target instance, the above cited papers mostly focus on the role of $\mathcal{M}'$ in model management. It turns out that our semantics differs from the semantics previously considered. We argue that our semantics is the natural one for practical data recovery, i.e. for restoring a source instance. In this paper we will focus only on mappings specified by a set of s-t tgds.

DEFINITION 1. **(Minimal solution)** *Given a set of s-t tgds Σ, a source instance I, and a target instance J, we say that J is a minimal solution with respect to Σ and I, if $(I, J) \models \Sigma$ and for any $J' \subset J$, it is the case that $(I, J') \not\models \Sigma$.*

EXAMPLE 1. *Consider $\Sigma = \{S(x) \rightarrow \exists y\ T(x, y)\}$, and target instance $J_1 = \{T(a, b), T(b, c)\}$. In this case J_1 is a minimal solution wrt Σ and $I_1 = \{S(a), S(b)\}$, but J_1 is not a minimal solution wrt Σ and $I_2 = \{S(a)\}$, even though $(I_2, J_1) \models \Sigma$. Note that there are target instances that are not a minimal solution wrt Σ and any source instance I. For example, $J_2 = \{T(a, b), T(a, c)\}$ is not a minimal solution wrt Σ for any source instance I.*

DEFINITION 2. **(Justified solution)** *Given a set of s-t tgds Σ, a target instance J is said to be justified by source instance I under Σ, if*

1. *$(I, J) \models \Sigma$, and*
2. *$J \rightarrow J'$, for some minimal solution J' wrt Σ and I.*

It is easy to see that the *universal solutions* [13] and the *canonical solutions* [20] are justified solutions. On the other hand, there exists justified solutions that are neither universal nor canonical solutions. E.g. instance J_1 in Example 1 is a justified solution by source instance I_1 under Σ, but is not a universal or canonical solution for I_1 and Σ. Note that all the results to be presented hold even if one considers only universal solution (or canonical solution) based semantics, i.e. only universal (canonical) solutions are considered as recoverable. Using the notion of justified solutions, it is clear that it is not possible to find recoveries for all target instances. The following definition describes the target instances for which one may compute recoveries.

DEFINITION 3. **(Valid for recovery)** *Given a set of s-t tgds Σ, a target instance J is said to be valid for recovery under Σ, if there exists a source instance I such that J is justified by I under Σ. Such a source instance I is said to be a recovery for J under Σ. With $\mathsf{REC}(\Sigma, J)$ we denote the set of all recoveries for J under Σ. We thus have*

$$\mathsf{REC}(\Sigma, J) = \{I : J \textit{ is justified for } I \textit{ under } \Sigma\}.$$

Note that the above semantics is more restrictive than the corresponding data-exchange semantics in [13]. Thus, we will not allow mappings that contain empty source instances and non-empty target instances. This restriction is natural as it considers only pairs of instances (I, J) such that each tuple in J is "justified" by the presence of some tuples in I. With this we have the certain answer for Σ and target instance J defined as

$$\mathsf{CERT}(Q, \Sigma, J) = \bigcap_{I \in \mathsf{REC}(\Sigma, J)} Q(I).$$

DEFINITION 4. **($\mathcal{C}$-universal recovery)** *Let $\mathcal{C}$ be a class of queries. A set $\mathcal{I}$ of source instances is said to be a $\mathcal{C}$-*universal recovery*, if*

$$\mathsf{CERT}(Q, \Sigma, J) = \bigcap_{I \in \mathcal{I}} Q(I),$$

for every source query $Q \in \mathcal{C}$,

Because of their importance and frequency of use, the classes of CQ- and UCQ-universal recoveries have been widely studied in most of papers recently published on schema mapping and inversion. Accordingly, in this paper we focus only on the class of CQ- and UCQ-universal recoveries.

4. HOMOMORPHISMS

Let ξ be an s-t tgd of the form $\alpha(\bar{x}, \bar{y}) \to \exists \bar{z}\ \beta(\bar{x}, \bar{z})$, where α and β are conjunctions of predicates over source and target instance, respectively. By $head(\xi)$ we mean the set of atoms in $\beta(\bar{x}, \bar{z})$ and by $body(\xi)$ we mean the set of atoms in $\alpha(\bar{x}, \bar{y})$. Given a target instance J, with $\mathsf{HOM}(\xi, J)$ we denote the set of all homomorphisms $h : dom(head(\xi)) \to dom(J)$, with $h(\beta(\bar{x}, \bar{z})) \subseteq J$. That is,

$$\mathsf{HOM}(\xi, J) = \{h : \ h(\beta(\bar{x}, \bar{z})) \subseteq J\}.$$

We extend this definition to a set Σ of source-to-target tgds, by $\mathsf{HOM}(\Sigma, J) = \bigcup_{\xi \in \Sigma} \mathsf{HOM}(\xi, J)$. Note that because each tgd in Σ contains distinct variables, each homomorphism $h \in \mathsf{HOM}(\Sigma, J)$ uniquely identifies a source-to-target tgd in Σ, which we denoted by ξ_h.

To better visualize the notions introduced in this section we illustrate all the definitions through the following running example:

EXAMPLE 2. *Let $\Sigma = \{\xi, \rho, \sigma\}$, where:*

$$\xi = R(x, x, y) \to \exists z\ S(x, z);$$
$$\rho = R(u, v, w) \to T(w);$$
$$\sigma = D(k, p) \to T(p).$$

For target instance $J = \{S(a, b), T(c), T(d)\}$, the set of all homomorphisms is:

$$\mathsf{HOM}(\Sigma, J) = \{h_1 = \{x/a, z/b\}, h_2 = \{w/c\}, h_3 = \{w/d\}, h_4 = \{p/c\}, h_5 = \{p/d\}\}.$$

Note in the previous example that both homomorphisms h_2 and h_4 cover the same tuple $T(c)$ in J. This brings us to the following definition.

DEFINITION 5. **(Covering of a target instance.)** *Let Σ be a set of s-t tgds and J a target instance. Then*

$$\mathsf{COV}(\Sigma, J) = \{H \subseteq \mathsf{HOM}(\Sigma, J) \ : \ \bigcup_{h \in H} h(head(\xi_h)) = J\}.$$

EXAMPLE 3. *Returning to the set of s-t tgds Σ, target instance J, and set of homomorphisms $\mathsf{HOM}(\Sigma, J)$ from Example 2 we have*

$$\mathsf{COV}(\Sigma, J) = \{\{h_1, h_2, h_3\}, \{h_1, h_2, h_3, h_4\}, \{h_1, h_2, h_5\}, \{h_1, h_4, h_5\}, \{h_1, h_2, h_3, h_4, h_5\}, \{h_1, h_2, h_3, h_5\}, \{h_1, h_3, h_4\}, \{h_1, h_2, h_4, h_5\}, \{h_1, h_3, h_4, h_5\}\}.$$

The intuition behind the covering notion is that the tuples in the target instance can be generated, in a data-exchange process, only using variable mappings from the homomorphisms in one of these coverings. For example, by chasing source instance $I = \{R(a, a, c), D(a, d)\}$ it will generate target instance J by using the covering $\{h_1, h_2, h_5\}$.

In this example we also observe that the source instance may not contain the tuple $R(a, a, a)$, even if homomorphism h_1 will cover tuple $S(a, b)$. This is because, based on the second dependency, the target instance would need to contain tuple $T(a)$ as well. This gives the intuition for the notion of subsumption constraint introduced by the next definitions.

DEFINITION 6. **(Minimal subsummit of a tgd)** *Let Σ be a set of s-t tgds, $\{\xi_1, \ldots, \xi_n\} \subseteq \Sigma$ and ξ_0 a s-t tgd in $\Sigma \setminus \{\xi_1, \ldots, \xi_n\}$. We say that $\{\xi_1, \ldots, \xi_n\}$ is a subsummit for s-t tgd ξ_0, if there are mappings $\theta_i : vars(\xi_i) \to V$, where $V = \mathsf{Vars} \setminus \bigcup_{i=0}^{n} vars(\xi_i)$, such that when each θ_i is extended to be identity on constants and homomorphically to sets of atoms, it holds that*

$$\theta_0(body(\xi_0)) \subseteq \theta_1(body(\xi_1)) \cup \ldots \cup \theta_n(body(\xi_n))$$

We also require that each θ_i, for $i = 1, \ldots, n$, maps each variable y that occurs in $body(\xi_i)$ but not in $head(\xi_i)$ to a unique variable in V. If in addition the inclusion does not hold for any proper subset of $\{\xi_1, \ldots, \xi_n\}$, we say that $\{\xi_1, \ldots, \xi_n\}$ is a minimal subsummit of ξ_0 with $\{\theta_0, \theta_1, \ldots, \theta_n\}$.

Intuitively, the previous definition states that if a source instance I, recovered from a target instance J, triggers the s-t tgds $\{\xi_1, \ldots, \xi_n\}$ in a chase process, then instance I will also trigger dependency ξ_0.

EXAMPLE 4. *Consider the set of source-to-target tgds Σ and instance J from Example 2. It easy to see that for homomorphisms $\theta_0 = \{u/r_1, v/r_1, w/r_2\}$ and $\theta_1 = \{x/r_1, y/r_2\}$ we have $\theta_0(body(\rho)) \subseteq \theta_1(body(\xi))$, meaning that $\{\xi\}$ is a minimal subsummit for ρ with $\{\theta_0, \theta_1\}$. Intuitively the subsummit is stating that the existence of a tuple of the form $R(r_1, r_1, r_2)$ in a source instance recovered by the existence of a tuple in the target instance under relation S and tgd ξ, will also trigger tgd ρ and thus a corresponding tuple $T(r_1)$ will need to exists in the target instance. Note that $\{\rho\}$ can't be a subsummit for ξ for any set of homomorphisms because variables u and v needs to be mapped to distinct values.*

We next define the relationship between subsummits and homomorphisms.

DEFINITION 7. **(Subsumption constraints.)** *Let Σ be a set of s-t tgds. Then*

$$\mathsf{SUB}(\Sigma) = \{\theta_1, \theta_2, \ldots, \theta_n \to \theta_0 : \ \{\xi_1, \ldots, \xi_n\} \subseteq \Sigma \text{ is a minimal subsummit of } \xi_0 \in \Sigma \text{ with } \{\theta_0, \theta_1, \theta_2, \ldots, \theta_n\}\}.$$

From Example 4 we have constraint $\{\theta_1 \to \theta_0\} \subseteq \mathsf{SUB}(\Sigma)$. On the other hand, from the same example we also have $\{\theta_0 \to \theta_1\} \nsubseteq \mathsf{SUB}(\Sigma)$. We next define what it means for a set of homomorphisms to satisfy a subsumption constraint.

DEFINITION 8. **(Model of SUB)** *Let H be a set of homomorphisms and ζ a subsumption constraint of the form $\theta_1, \theta_2, \ldots, \theta_n \to \theta_0$. We say that H is a model of ζ, denoted $H \models \zeta$, if for all $i \in \{1, \ldots, n\}$ and mappings m, such that $(m \circ \theta_i)|_{vars(head(\xi_{h_i}))} = h_i \in H$ there exists an extension m' of m such that $(m' \circ \theta_0)|_{vars(head(\xi_{h_0}))} = h_0 \in H$.*

A subsumption constraint ζ is said to be *tautological* if for any set H of homomorphisms we have $H \models \zeta$. From now on we will consider the set $\mathsf{SUB}(\Sigma)$ containing only non-tautological subsumption constraints. The previous definition is extended to sets Υ of subsumption constraints, by $H \models \Upsilon$ iff $H \models \zeta$, for all $\zeta \in \Upsilon$.

EXAMPLE 5. *Continuing our Example 2 we have, by removing all tautological subsumption constraints, that the set $\mathsf{SUB}(\Sigma)$ equals $\{\theta_1 \to \theta_0\}$. For the set of homomorphisms $H = \{h_1, h_4, h_5\} \in \mathsf{COV}(\Sigma, J)$ we have that $H \not\models \mathsf{SUB}(\Sigma)$. This is because the existence of $h_1 = \{x/a, z/b\}$ in H, based on subsumption constraint $\{\theta_1 \to \theta_0\}$, requires the existence of a homomorphism over variables in ρ in H. Intuitively this restriction states that by using only the homomorphisms in H we will not be able to construct a source instance that will be a recovery for J even if H is a cover for target instance J. On the other hand, the covering $\{h_1, h_2, h_3\}$ is a model of $\mathsf{SUB}(\Sigma)$.*

Let H be a set of homomorphisms, Σ a set of s-t tgds, and I an instance. Recall that $Chase_H(\Sigma, I)$ denotes the result of applying the standard chase with Σ on I, with the restriction that only homomorphisms from H are used to trigger dependencies. For example consider instance $I = \{R(a), R(b)\}$, and the set of source-to-target dependencies

$$\Sigma = \{R(x) \to \exists y\, T(x, y); \quad R(z) \to \exists v\, V(z, v)\}.$$

Let the set of homomorphisms $H = \{\{x/a\}, \{x/b\}\}$. Then we have $Chase_H(\Sigma, I) = \{T(a, X_1), T(b, X_2)\}$, where X_1 and X_2 are new null values. If we consider $H' = \{\{x/a\}, \{z/b\}\}$, we have $Chase_{H'}(\Sigma, I) = \{T(a, X_3), V(b, X_4)\}$, where X_3 and X_4 are new nulls.

The idea is to compute a recovery $Chase_H(\Sigma^{-1}, J)$, for each $H \in \mathsf{COV}(\Sigma, J)$, such that $H \models \mathsf{SUB}(\Sigma)$. However, as seen in the following example, this does not yet guarantee that the result is a recovery of J wrt Σ.

EXAMPLE 6. *Let Σ and J be the set of s-t tgds and target instance from Example 2, and let $H_1 = \{h_1, h_2, h_3\}$. Then $H_1 \in \mathsf{COV}(\Sigma, J)$ and $H_1 \models \mathsf{SUB}(\Sigma)$. Nevertheless, $Chase_{H_1}(\Sigma^{-1}, J) = I'$, where $I' = \{R(a, a, X_1), R(X_2, X_3, c), R(X_4, X_5, d)\}$, is not a recovery of J wrt Σ because we have that $(I', J) \not\models \Sigma$.*

We note that $Chase(\Sigma, I') = J'$, where target instance $J' = \{S(a, a, Z_1), T(X_1), T(c), T(d)\}$. Also there are two homomorphisms g_1 and g_2 from J' to J, where homomorphisms $g_1 = \{Z_1/b, X_1/c\}$ and $g_2 = \{Z_1/b, X_1/d\}$. We can note that $g_1(I') = \{R(a, a, c), R(X_2, X_3, c), R(X_4, X_5, d)\}$ and $g_2(I') = \{R(a, a, d), R(X_2, X_3, c), R(X_4, X_5, d)\}$ are both recoveries of J.

This leads to the following algorithm.

DEFINITION 9. *Let Σ be a set of source-to-target tgds and J a target instance valid for recovery under Σ. Suppose $\mathsf{COV}(\Sigma, J) = \{H_1, \ldots, H_n\}$. Let $Chase_{H_i}(\Sigma^{-1}, J) = I_i$, for each $H_i \models \mathsf{SUB}(\Sigma)$, and let $Chase(\Sigma, I_i) = J_i$. Furthermore, let $\{g_{i1}, \ldots, g_{im_i}\}$ be all homomorphisms from J_i to J that are the identity on $dom(J)$. Then define the set of instances*

$$Chase^{-1}(\Sigma, J) = \bigcup_{1 \le i \le n} \bigcup_{1 \le j \le m_i} \{g_{ij}(I_i)\}.$$

With this we are now ready to state the main theorem of this section.

THEOREM 1. *Let Σ be a set of s-t tgds and J a target instance valid for recovery under Σ. Then*

$$Chase^{-1}(\Sigma, J) \subseteq \mathsf{REC}(\Sigma, J).$$

PROOF. (sketch) It is easy to note that for any set of homomorphisms $H \in \mathsf{COV}(\Sigma, J)$ such that $H \models \mathsf{SUB}(\Sigma, J)$ we have that

$$Chase(\Sigma, Chase_H(\Sigma^{-1}, J)) \to J$$

with homomorphism h identity on the set $dom(J)$. On the other hand, from the construction of h and $Chase_H(\Sigma^{-1}, J)$, it is easy to see that $(h(Chase_H(\Sigma^{-1}, J)), J) \models \Sigma$. Finally, because $H \in \mathsf{COV}(\Sigma, J)$ it follows that each tuple from J is justified by some tuples in $h(Chase_H(\Sigma^{-1}, J))$. Note that h is non-identity only on new nulls created during the creation of $Chase_H(\Sigma^{-1}, J)$. □

Intuitively, Theorem 1 shows that using the special chase $Chase^{-1}$ we get recoveries for Σ and J.

EXAMPLE 7. *Let Σ and J be the set of s-t tgds and instance from Examples 2 and 3. For simplicity we will consider only the set of minimal covers in $\mathsf{COV}(\Sigma, J)$ which are: $H_1 = \{h_1, h_2, h_3\}$, $H_2 = \{h_1, h_2, h_5\}$, $H_3 = \{h_1, h_3, h_4\}$ and $H_4 = \{h_1, h_4, h_5\}$. As mentioned we have $H_4 \not\models \mathsf{SUB}(\Sigma)$, and for any $i \in \{1, 2, 3\}$, we have $H_i \models \mathsf{SUB}(\Sigma)$. Using the notation from Definition 9, $Chase^{-1}$ consists of the following instances:*

$$Chase_{H_1}(\Sigma^{-1}, J) = I_1 = \{R(a, a, X_1), R(X_2, X_3, c), R(X_4, X_5, d)\};$$

$$Chase_{H_2}(\Sigma^{-1}, J) = I_2 = \{R(a, a, Y_1), R(Y_2, Y_3, c), D(Y_4, d)\};$$

$$Chase_{H_3}(\Sigma^{-1}, J) = I_3 = \{R(a, a, Z_1), R(Z_2, Z_3, d), D(Z_4, c)\}.$$

For the target instance $J_1 = Chase(\Sigma, I_1)$, where

$$J_1 = \{S(a, V_1), T(X_1), T(c), T(d)\},$$

we have $J_1 \to J$ with homomorphism $g_{11} = \{V_1/b, X_1/c\}$ and homomorphism $g_{12} = \{V_1/b, X_1/d\}$. Similarly, from source instance I_2 we get homomorphisms $g_{21} = \{V_2/b, Y_1/c\}$ and $g_{22} = \{V_2/b, Y_1/d\}$ and finally from I_3 we get homomorphisms $g_{31} = \{V_3/b, Z_1/c\}$ and $g_{32} = \{V_3/b, Z_1/d\}$.

Based on Definition 9 from these homomorphisms the set $Chase^{-1}(\Sigma, J)$ will contain the following recoveries:

$$g_{11}(I_1) = \{R(a,a,c), R(X_2,X_3,c), R(X_4,X_5,d)\},$$
$$g_{12}(I_1) = \{R(a,a,d), R(X_2,X_3,c), R(X_4,X_5,d)\},$$
$$g_{21}(I_2) = \{R(a,a,c), R(X_2,X_3,c), D(X_4,d)\},$$
$$g_{22}(I_2) = \{R(a,a,d), R(X_2,X_3,c), D(X_4,d)\},$$
$$g_{31}(I_3) = \{R(a,a,c), R(X_2,X_3,d), D(X_4,c)\},$$
$$g_{32}(I_3) = \{R(a,a,d), R(X_2,X_3,d), D(X_4,c)\}$$

Note that the theorem 1 does not guarantee that all possible recoveries are computed. Following Example 2 it is easy to see $I = \{R(a,a,c), R(a,a,d), D(e,c)\} \in \mathsf{REC}(\Sigma, J)$ but obviously $I \notin Chase^{-1}(\Sigma, J)$. Nevertheless, the next theorem shows that the set of instances $Chase^{-1}(\Sigma, J)$ are sufficient for computing the certain answer for any UCQ query.

THEOREM 2. *Let Σ be a set of s-t tgds and target instance J valid for recovery under Σ, then $Chase^{-1}(\Sigma, J)$ is a UCQ-universal recovery of J under Σ.*

PROOF. (sketch) Given two sets of instances $\mathcal{L}$ and $\mathcal{K}$, we write $\mathcal{K} \to \mathcal{L}$ iff $(\forall J \in \mathcal{L} \;\; \exists I \in \mathcal{K} \; : \; I \to J)$. In case $\mathcal{K} \to \mathcal{L}$ and $\mathcal{L} \to \mathcal{K}$, we say that $\mathcal{K}$ and L are homomorphically equivalent and denoted it by $\mathcal{K} \leftrightarrow \mathcal{L}$. In [11] it was shown that $\mathsf{CERT}(Q, \mathcal{K}) = \mathsf{CERT}(Q, \mathcal{L})$ for any UCQ query Q iff $\mathcal{K} \leftrightarrow \mathcal{L}$. It follows that we only need to show that $\mathsf{REC}(\Sigma, J) \leftrightarrow Chase^{-1}(\Sigma, J)$. From Theorem 1 it follows that $\mathsf{REC}(\Sigma, J) \to Chase^{-1}(\Sigma, J)$. Now let $I \in \mathsf{REC}(\Sigma, J)$. Because $Chase^{-1}$ uses sets of homomorphisms that cover the target instance and also from the way $Chase^{-1}$ is constructed, it follows that there exists an instance $I_i \in Chase^{-1}(\Sigma, J)$ such that $I_i \to I$. □

5. COMPLEXITY

We first show that testing if a target instance J is valid for recovery under Σ is NP-complete in the number of tuples in J. We have

PROBLEM:	J-validity.
PARAMETER:	Set Σ of s-t tgds.
INPUT:	Target instance J
QUESTION:	Is J valid for recovery under Σ?

THEOREM 3. *The J-validity problem in NP-complete.*

PROOF. (sketch) Upper bound: It is easy to verify that an instance J is valid for recovery wrt Σ iff there exists a $H \in \mathsf{COV}(\Sigma, J)$, such that $H \vDash \mathsf{SUB}(\Sigma, J)$. Thus one may simply guess a subset H of $\mathsf{HOM}(\Sigma, J)$. The size of H is at most $m \cdot n^k$, where n is the number of tuples in J, m is the number of tgds in Σ, and k is the maximum number of variables in the head of any tgd in Σ. It remains to test if $H \in \mathsf{COV}(\Sigma, J)$ and if $H \vDash \mathsf{SUB}(\Sigma, J)$. It is easy to see that both tests can be done in time polynomial in n.

The lower bound can be inferred directly from the "view consistency" problem that is shown in [1] to be NP-hard even when the view consists of a single GAV dependency. □

The reduction above can also be used to prove the following proposition.

PROPOSITION 1. *Let Σ be a fixed set of s-t tgds and J a target instance. Testing whether J is a universal solution for some source instance I under Σ is NP-complete in the number of tuples in J.*

We saw in the previous section that given a UCQ Q, we can find the certain answer $\mathsf{CERT}(Q, \Sigma, J)$ by computing the set $Chase^{-1}(\Sigma, J)$, and then evaluate Q on this set. It seems that there can be an exponential blow-up when going from J to $Chase^{-1}(\Sigma, J)$. This raises the question whether the blow-up is avoidable. In this section we show that the answer is "no" (assuming P≠NP), by considering the following decision problem.

PROBLEM:	Q-certainty.
PARAMETERS:	Set Σ of s-t tgds, query Q.
INPUT:	Tuple t, target instance J valid for recovery under Σ.
QUESTION:	Is $t \in \mathsf{CERT}(Q, \Sigma, J)$?

We shall see that the problem is coNP-complete when Q is a CQ or a UCQ.

THEOREM 4. *Let Q be a CQ. Then the Q-certainty problem is coNP-complete.*

PROOF. (sketch) For the upper bound we note that the answer is "no" if and only if there exists an instance I in $Chase^{-1}(\Sigma, J)$, such that $t \notin Q(I)$. The instance I can be guessed as follows.

First we generate $\mathsf{SUB}(\Sigma)$. This can be done in polynomial time since the size of Σ is a constant. Then we compute $\mathsf{HOM}(\Sigma, J)$ in time $\mathcal{O}(m \cdot n^k)$, where n is the number of tuples in J, m is the number of tgds in Σ, and k is the maximum number of variables in the head of any tgd in Σ. We also compute, in polynomial time, the instance $Chase_{\mathsf{HOM}(\Sigma,J)}(\Sigma^{-1}, J)$. Let

$$N = Nulls(Chase_{\mathsf{HOM}(\Sigma,J)}(\Sigma^{-1}, J)) \smallsetminus Nulls(J)$$

be the set of "new" nulls. Now the size of N is bounded by $j \cdot m \cdot n^k$, where j is the maximum number of variables in the body of a dependency in Σ. We then guess a mapping h from the new nulls N to $dom(J)$, and guess a subset H of $\mathsf{HOM}(\Sigma, J)$. Before going to the verification phase, we compute $I = Chase_H(\Sigma^{-1}, J) \subseteq Chase_{\mathsf{HOM}(\Sigma,J)}(\Sigma^{-1}, J)$, as well as $Chase(\Sigma, I)$, both in time polynomial in n. It remains to verify that

1. $H \in \mathsf{COV}(\Sigma, J)$,
2. $H \vDash \mathsf{SUB}(\Sigma)$,
3. $\exists$ extension h' of h, identity on $dom(Chase(\Sigma, I)) \smallsetminus N$, such that $h'(Chase(\Sigma, I)) \subseteq J$, and
4. $t \notin h'(I)$.

It is straightforward to show that steps 1, 2 and 4 can be done in time polynomial in n. Step 3 can also be performed in polynomial in n time as Σ is a set of s-t tgds. If all verifications succeed, the answer to the Q-certainty problem in "no," which means that the problem of Q-certainty is in coNP.

The lower bound follows again from [1] where it was shown that already the special case of certain answers to CQs Q using materialized views under CWA when the view is defined as a GAV dependency, is coNP hard. □

We note that the same lower bound and upper bound hold even if Q is a UCQ. We therefore have:

COROLLARY 1. *Let Q be a UCQ. Then the Q-certainty problem is coNP-complete.*

6. TRACTABLE CASES

As saw in the previous section, recovery and certain answer evaluation of CQ and UCQ queries is intractable in the general case. We will now look into some special cases that guarantee tractability. First we give criteria for Σ and J that are sufficient for $\mathsf{REC}(\Sigma, J)$ to contain a unique recovery computable in polynomial time. Such a unique recovery is naturally UCQ-complete. We also give a polynomial time algorithm that materializes a unique instance that gives sound answers to any CQ query.

6.1 Unique recoveries

We shall first look at an example that illustrates the intuition behind unique recoveries.

EXAMPLE 8. *Consider the following dependency that describes a schema evolution in a company.*

Emp(Name, Dept), Bnf(Dept, Benefit) $\rightarrow$
EmpDept(Name, Dept),EmpBnf(Emp, Benefit).

The Emp relation records the department where each employee works, and the Bnf relation lists the benefits (medical insurance, pension contributions, profit sharing, etc.) for all the employees of the given department.

After the data exchange for the new schema is carried out, the company changes its policy to allow an employee to work for more than one department. It therefore decides to restore the database according to the old schema.

It is easy to see that the set $\mathsf{SUB}(\Sigma)$ contains only one constraint, stating that a department gives the same set of benefits to each of its employees.

$$\{Name/v_1, Dept/w, Benefit/u_1\},$$
$$\{Name/v_2, Dept/w, Benefit/u_2\} \rightarrow$$
$$\{Name/v_1, Dept/w, Benefit/u_2\}.$$

Suppose the target instance J is as follows:

J
EmpDept(Joe, HR)
EmpDept(Bill, Sales)
EmpDept(Sue, HR)
EmpBnf(Joe, medical)
EmpBnf(Joe, pension)
EmpBnf(Bill, medical)
EmpBnf(Bill, profit)
EmpBnf(Sue, medical)
EmpBnf(Sue, pension)

It is easy to see that J is valid for recovery under the given dependency and also that it has a unique recovery I:

I
EmpDept(Joe, HR)
EmpDept(Bill, Sales)
EmpDept(Sue, HR)
Bnf(HR, medical)
Bnf(HR, pension)
Bnf(Sales, medical)
Bnf(Sales, profit)

By querying this source instance one may obtain both sound and complete answers. Note that in this example the maximal recovery mapping Σ' [8] for Σ is the same as the maximum CQ recovery mapping [6] for Σ, that is:

EmpDept(Name, Dept) $\rightarrow$
$\exists x$ *Emp(Name, Dept), Bnf(Dept, x);*
EmpBnf(Name, Benefit) $\rightarrow$
$\exists y$ *Emp(Name, y), Bnf(y, Benefit).*

If one now is interested in the benefits of the HR department, that is the conjunctive query Q = Bnf(HR,x), evaluating Q on $Chase(\Sigma', J)$ yields an empty certain answer, whereas using the instance based recovery I the certain answer is {medical, pension}.

We can now introduce the notion of a complete UCQ recovery.

DEFINITION 10. *Let Σ be a set of s-t tgds and J an instance valid for recovery under Σ. A source instance I is said to be a complete UCQ recovery for Σ and J, if $Q(I)\downarrow = \mathsf{CERT}(Q, \Sigma, J)$, for all UCQ queries Q.*

Before presenting a sufficient condition that guarantees the existence of a complete UCQ recovery we need to introduce the following lemma:

LEMMA 1. *Let Σ be a set of s-t tgds such that all the constraints in $\mathsf{SUB}(\Sigma)$ were constructed using only quasi-guarded tgds from Σ. Then*

$$|Chase^{-1}(\Sigma, J)| \leq |\mathsf{COV}(\Sigma, J)|,$$

for any target instance J valid for recovery under Σ.

PROOF. (sketch) The lemma follows from the observation that in case $\mathsf{SUB}(\Sigma)$ is constructed using only quasi-guarded tgds, then $Chase(\Sigma, Chase_H(\Sigma^{-1}, J))$, for $H \in \mathsf{COV}(\Sigma, J)$ and $H \models \mathsf{SUB}(\Sigma)$, will not contain any new nulls generated by the $Chase_H(\Sigma^{-1}, J)$ process. □

Intuitively, the previous lemma states that each covering from $\mathsf{COV}(\Sigma, J)$ that is a model for $\mathsf{SUB}(\Sigma)$ will only generate one recovery using the inverse chase process. Recall that in general, based on Definition 9, for each covering H there maybe an exponential number of recoveries. Consider for example s-t tgds $\Sigma = \{R(x, y) \rightarrow S(x);\ R(u, v) \rightarrow T(v)\}$ and target instance $J = \{S(a), S(b), T(c), T(d)\}$. It is easy to see that with this configuration we have $|\mathsf{COV}(\Sigma, J)| = 1$ and $|Chase^{-1}(\Sigma, J)| = 7$. We say that a set of s-t tgds Σ with the properties from Lemma 1 is *quasi-guarded safe.*

Based on Lemma 1, it seems that a sufficient condition that guarantees the existence of a complete UCQ recovery for a given set of s-t tgd Σ and target instance J, is that there exists only one covering for J under Σ, and that Σ is quasi-guarded safe. The following theorem confirms this intuition.

THEOREM 5. *Let Σ be a set of s-t tgds and J a target instance valid for recovery under Σ. Then there exists an instance I that is a complete UCQ recovery for Σ and J if*

1. $|\mathsf{COV}(\Sigma, J)| = 1$, *and*
2. *Σ is quasi-guarded safe.*

Moreover, the complete UCQ instance I can be computed in time polynomial in the number of tuples in J.

PROOF. (Sketch) Based on Lemma 1 it can be easily noted that the computation of $Chase^{-1}(\Sigma, J)$ becomes deterministic and that it computes a complete UCQ recovery. □

In Example 8 the set of homomorphism constraints $\mathsf{SUB}(\Sigma)$ was constructed from the only tgd in Σ, which was both a full and quasi-guarded. It is easy to see that in case $\mathsf{REC}(\Sigma, J) = \{I\}$, one may use the recovered instance I to obtain both sound and complete answers to any query. Note that the existence of a complete UCQ recovery for Σ and J does not guarantee that $|\mathsf{REC}(\Sigma, J)| = 1$. For this, let $\Sigma = \{R(x, y) \rightarrow S(x)\}$ and $J = \{S(a), S(b), S(c)\}$. In this case there are an infinite number of recoveries but there exists a complete UCQ recovery $I = \{R(a, X_1), R(b, X_2), R(c, X_3)\}$.

The second condition of Theorem 5 is clearly easy to check. The following theorem gives us a necessary and sufficient condition for the first condition to hold.

THEOREM 6. *Let Σ be a set of s-t tgd and J a target instance valid for recovery under Σ. Then $|\mathsf{COV}(\Sigma, J)| = 1$ iff for all $h \in \mathsf{HOM}(\Sigma, J)$ there exists a tuple $t \in J$ such that $t \in h(head(\xi_h))$, and for any homomorphism $h' \in \mathsf{HOM}(\Sigma, J)$, where $h' \neq h$, we have $t \notin h'(head(\xi_{h'}))$.*

PROOF. (sketch) For the if direction, it is easy to see that a covering needs to contain all homomorphisms from $\mathsf{HOM}(\Sigma, J)$, in order to contain all the tuples from J. For the only if direction, if $|\mathsf{COV}(\Sigma, J)| = 1$ the covering contains all the homomorphisms from $\mathsf{HOM}(\Sigma, J)$. This means that by removing any of the homomorphisms, J will not be fully covered. Thus, there exists a tuple covered only by that homomorphism. □

Based on this theorem it is easy to see that testing if $|\mathsf{COV}(\Sigma, J)| = 1$ can be done in quadratic time. There are two important observations to be made:

First, in order to cover more cases, instead of a unique recovery that is UCQ-complete, one can compute a set of $k > 1$ recoveries that is complete for UCQ queries, for a fixed constant k. In Example 8, suppose the target instance has only one employee working for two departments, and each of these two departments offers exactly one benefit (and all the other employees work for exactly one department). In this case there exists a set of two source recoveries $\{I_1, I_2\}$ such that the certain answer $Q(I_1) \cap Q(I_2) = \mathsf{CERT}(Q, \Sigma, J)$, for all UCQ queries Q. By changing the first condition of Theorem 5 to $|\mathsf{COV}(\Sigma, J)| \leq k$, for a fixed k, we can keep the tractability result for a larger class of pairs Σ and J.

Second, even if the first condition Theorem 5 is not satisfied, one may find, in polynomial time, a unique maximal subset J' of J with this property. From J' one can compute a source instance that can be used to get sound answers to any UCQ query. Formally, we have the following theorem.

THEOREM 7. *Let Σ be a set of s-t tgds, and J a target instance valid for recovery under Σ. There is a quadratic (in the number of tuples in J) algorithm that computes a maximal subset J' of J, such that $|\mathsf{COV}(\Sigma, J')| = 1$. Based on J' one may compute in polynomial time a source instance I, such that $Q(I)\!\downarrow\, \subseteq \mathsf{CERT}(Q, \Sigma, J)$, for all UCQ queries Q.*

PROOF. (sketch) For the first part we compute a set K that contains all tuples from J that are covered by only one homomorphism in $\mathsf{HOM}(\Sigma, J)$. After this, instance J' is constructed as $J' = \cup_{t \in K} h_t(head(\xi_{h_t}))$, where h_t is the unique homomorphisms that covers tuple t. For the second part, it can be verified that there exists $I \in \mathsf{REC}(\Sigma, J)$ such that $I' \subseteq I$, where $I' = Chase^{-1}(\Sigma, Chase_H(\Sigma^{-1}, J'))$, and that for all $I'' \in \mathsf{REC}(\Sigma, J)$ we have $I' \rightarrow I''$. □

EXAMPLE 9. *Let $\Sigma = \{\xi_1, \xi_2\}$, where*

$$\xi_1 = R(x, y) \rightarrow S(x), S(y);$$
$$\xi_2 = D(z) \rightarrow T(z).$$

Consider target instance $J = \{S(a), S(b), T(c), T(d)\}$. In this case $J' = \{T(c), T(d)\}$ is the maximal subset of J, such that $|\mathsf{COV}(\Sigma, J')| = 1$. Note that $\mathsf{SUB}(\Sigma) = \varnothing$. The source instance $I = \{D(c), D(d)\}$, that is not a recovery, can be used to get sound answers to any UCQ query. For example for conjunctive query $Q(x) = D(x)$, the result will be $\{c, d\}$.

6.2 Sound CQ answers

In this section we will show that even without any restrictions on the mapping or the target instance one may obtain in polynomial time sound certain answers for any source CQ query. For this we will present a tractable algorithm that computes a "sub-universal" source instance that can be used to obtain the sound answers. Let us first introduce some notation.

Let I_1 and I_2 be instances. A *homomorphic greatest lower bound* of I_1 and I_2, denoted $glb\{I_1, I_2\}$, is an instance K, such that $K \rightarrow I_1$ and $K \rightarrow I_2$, and for all instances L, if $L \rightarrow I_1$ and $L \rightarrow I_2$, then $L \rightarrow K$. This lower bound can be computed as follows [19, 21]: Let ι be an injective mapping from $Nulls \cup Cons$ to $Nulls \cup Cons$, such that

- $\iota(x, x) = x$ for any $x \in Nulls \cup Cons$, and
- $\iota(x, y) = z$ for any $x, y \in Nulls \cup Cons$, with $x \neq y$ and z a new null from $Nulls$.

Initialize $glb\{I_1, I_2\}$ to be the empty instance. For all pairs of tuples

- $(R(x_1, x_2, \ldots, x_k), R(y_1, y_2, \ldots, y_k)) \in I_1 \times I_2$,

the tuple

- $R(\iota(x_1, y_1), \iota(x_2, y_2), \ldots, \iota(x_k, y_k))$

is added to instance $glb\{I_1, I_2\}$. It is easily shown that in case I_1 and I_2 are two ground instances, then we have $Q(glb\{I_1, I_2\})\!\downarrow\, = Q(I_1) \cap Q(I_2)$, for all CQ queries Q. The lower bound is extended to larger sets recursively by the equation $glb\{I_1, I_2, \ldots, I_n\} = glb\{glb\{I_1, I_2, \ldots, I_{n-1}\}, I_n\}$.

Let Σ be a set of s-t tgds, J a target instance valid for recovery under Σ, and $h \in \mathsf{HOM}(\Sigma, J)$. The set of tuples in instance $h(head(\xi_h))$ is denoted J_h. Note that $J_h \subseteq J$. With I_h we then denote the source instance $Chase_{\{h\}}(\Sigma^{-1}, J)$. This notation is extended to sets of homomorphisms $H \subseteq \mathsf{HOM}(\Sigma, J)$, by $J_H = \bigcup_{h \in H} J_h$ and $I_H = \bigcup_{h \in H} I_h$.

DEFINITION 11. *Let Σ be a set of s-t tgds, J a target instance valid for recovery under Σ, and h a homomorphism from $\mathsf{HOM}(\Sigma, J)$. A set of homomorphisms $H \subseteq \mathsf{HOM}(\Sigma, J)$ is said to be a minimal covering for h under Σ and J if*

1. *$J_h \subseteq J_H$, and*
2. *there is no $H' \subset H$ such that $J_h \subseteq J_{H'}$.*

We denote the set of all the minimal coverings for h under Σ and J with $\mathsf{COV}_h(\Sigma, J)$.

Note that based on the previous definition we have that $\{h\} \in \mathsf{COV}_h(\Sigma, J)$, for any $h \in \mathsf{HOM}(\Sigma, J)$. Intuitively any minimal covering $H \in \mathsf{COV}_h(\Sigma, J)$ for a homomorphism h represents an alternative way of obtaining tuples J_h from a source instance in a chase process.

EXAMPLE 10. *Consider the following set of source-to-target tgds $\Sigma = \{\xi_1, \xi_2\}$, where:*

$$\xi_1 = R(x, y) \to S(x);$$
$$\xi_2 = R(z, v) \to S(z), T(v).$$

For target instance $J = \{S(a), T(b_1), \ldots, T(b_n)\}$ we have the set $\mathsf{HOM}(\Sigma, J) =$

$$\{h = \{x/a\},\ h_1 = \{z/a, v/b_1\},\ \ldots,\ h_n = \{z/a, v/b_n\}\}.$$

Based on the previous definition,

$$\mathsf{COV}_h(\Sigma, J) = \{\{h\}, \{h_1\}, \ldots, \{h_n\}\}$$

and $\mathsf{COV}_{h_i}(\Sigma, J) = \{\{h_i\}\}$ for all $i \in \{1, \ldots, n\}$.

From the above example it can be observed that the size of the set $\mathsf{COV}_h(\Sigma, J)$ may be polynomial in the size of target instance J. As we will see next, in order to materialize a CQ-universal source instance we need to compute the *glb* of the source instances generated by homomorphisms from $\mathsf{HOM}(\Sigma, J)$. On the other hand, in [21] it is shown that the size of the *glb* can be exponential in the number of instances. Consequently, in order to keep the tractability of this method, we need to reduce the size of the set for the considered instances.

As an intuition on how the polynomial number of instances can be reduced, note in the previous example that only variable z plays a role in covering homomorphism h, and instead of using source instances $\{R(a, b_1)\}$, $\{R(a, b_2)\}$ to $\{R(a, b_n)\}$ in the *glb* computation, we may use the more generic instance $\{R(a, X)\}$ that was obtain by replacing with new nulls all variables that do not contribute to the covering. In the next paragraphs we introduce some tools needed in this approach.

For a homomorphism h and sequence $\bar{x}$ of variables, with $h_{|\bar{x}}$ we denote the homomorphism h restricted to the variables in $\bar{x}$. Let Σ be a set of s-t tgd's, J a target instance, and h a homomorphism in $\mathsf{HOM}(\Sigma, J)$. Let H and G be sets of homomorphisms in $\mathsf{COV}_h(\Sigma, J)$. The H is said to be *equivalent with G wrt h and Σ*, denoted with $H \equiv_{(h,\Sigma)} G$, if the following conditions hold:

1. $|H| = |G|$, and
2. there exists orderings $h_1, \ldots, h_k$ and $g_1, \ldots, g_k$ of the mappings in H and G, respectively, and k sequences of variables $\bar{x}_1, \ldots, \bar{x}_k$, such that
   - $J_h = \bigcup_{i \in \{1,\ldots,k\}} J_{h_{i|\bar{x}_i}}$, and
   - $J_{h_{i|\bar{x}_i}} = J_{g_{i|\bar{x}_i}}$,

   for all $i \in \{1, \ldots, k\}$.

It is easy to see that $\equiv_{(h,\Sigma)}$ is an equivalence relation. For a set $H \in \mathsf{COV}_h(\Sigma, J)$, with $H_{(h,\Sigma)}$ we denote the set of representatives of the equivalence classes generated by $\equiv_{(h,\Sigma)}$. For a homomorphism $h_i \in H_{(h,\Sigma)}$, with $J_{h_i(h,\Sigma)}$ we denote the instance $f_i(head(\xi_{h_i}))$, where f_i is an extension of $h_{i_{|\bar{x}_i}}$ that assigns a new null value to each variable from $head(\xi_{h_i})$ distinct from the variables in $\bar{x}_i$. We then define the source instance $I_{h_i(h,\Sigma)} = Chase_f(\Sigma^{-1}, J)$ and finally $I_{H(h,\Sigma)} = \bigcup_{h_i \in H_{(h,\Sigma)}} I_{h_i(h,\Sigma)}$.

EXAMPLE 11. *Given the configuration in Example 10 we have $\{h_i\} \equiv_{(h,\Sigma)} \{h_j\}$, for all $i, j \in \{1, \ldots, n\}$. Thus we have $J_{h_i(h,\Sigma)} = \{S(a), T(X_i)\}$, where X_i is a new fresh null. Finally, $I_{\{h_i\}(h,\Sigma)} = \{R(a, X_i)\}$.*

DEFINITION 12. *Let Σ be a set of s-t tgds and target instance J valid for recovery under Σ. Then*

$$I_{\Sigma,J} = \bigcup_{h \in \mathsf{HOM}(\Sigma,J)} glb\{I_{H(h,\Sigma)} : H \in \mathsf{COV}_h(\Sigma, J)\}.$$

The source instance $I_{\Sigma,J}$ can be computed in polynomial time in the size of J as stated below.

THEOREM 8. *Let Σ be a set of s-t tgds and J a target instance valid for recovery under Σ. Then the instance $I_{\Sigma,J}$ can be computed in time $\mathcal{O}(n^m j^{k^2 \ell})$, where n is the size of the domain of J, m is the maximum number of variables occurring in the head of a tgd from Σ, j the maximum number of atoms in the body of a tgd in Σ, k is the largest number of atoms that occur in the head of a tgd in Σ, and ℓ is the total number of tgds in Σ.*

PROOF. (sketch) It is easy to see that the size of the set $\mathsf{HOM}(\Sigma, J)$ is bounded by n^m. Also for each homomorphism $h \in \mathsf{HOM}(\Sigma, J)$ we have $|J_h| < k$ and thus it follows that $|\{I_{H(h,\Sigma)} : H \in \mathsf{COV}_h(\Sigma, J)\}| \leq k^2 \ell$. With this we have $|glb(\{I_{H(h,\Sigma)} : H \in \mathsf{COV}_h(\Sigma, J)\})| \leq j^{k^2 \ell}$ and since the set $\mathsf{HOM}(\Sigma, J)$ is bounded by n^m, the claim of the theorem follows. □

It can be easily observed that in general $I_{\Sigma,J}$ is not a recovery for J under Σ, see Example 12 below. The following theorem shows what makes the source instance $I_{\Sigma,J}$ "CQ sub-universal."

THEOREM 9. *Let Σ be a set of s-t tgds and J a target instance valid for recovery under Σ. Then for all recovered instances $I \in \mathsf{REC}(\Sigma, J)$ we have that $I_{\Sigma,J} \to I$. We also have $Q(I_{\Sigma,J})\downarrow \subseteq \mathsf{CERT}(Q, \Sigma, J)$, for all CQ queries Q.*

PROOF. (sketch) Let $I \in \mathsf{REC}(\Sigma, J)$ and $h \in \mathsf{HOM}(\Sigma, J)$. From the definition of $\mathsf{REC}(\Sigma, J)$ it follows that there exists an instance $I' \subseteq I$ such that $Chase(\xi_h, I') \to J_h$. For the source instance $I'_h = glb(\{I_{H(h,\Sigma)} : H \in \mathsf{COV}_h(\Sigma, J)\})$, we have $I'_h \to I'$. As h was arbitrarily chosen it follows that $I_{\Sigma,J} = \cup_{h \in \mathsf{HOM}(\Sigma,J)} I'_h \to I$. □

The example below illustrates the construction.

EXAMPLE 12. *Let $\Sigma = \{\xi_1, \xi_2, \xi_3\}$ be the set of s-t tgds where:*

$$\xi_1 = R(x, y) \to T(x);$$
$$\xi_2 = U(z) \to S(z);$$
$$\xi_3 = R(v, v) \to T(v), S(v).$$

Consider target instance $J = \{T(a), S(a), S(b)\}$. Clearly J is valid for recovery under Σ. The set of homomorphisms $\mathsf{HOM}(\Sigma, J)$ is $\{h_1 : \{x/a\}, h_2 : \{z/a\}, h_3 : \{z/b\}, h_4 : \{v/a\}\}$. We then have

$$\mathsf{COV}_{h_1}(\Sigma, J) = \{\{h_1\}, \{h_4\}\},$$
$$\mathsf{COV}_{h_2}(\Sigma, J) = \{\{h_2\}, \{h_4\}\},$$
$$\mathsf{COV}_{h_3}(\Sigma, J) = \{\{h_3\}\}, \text{ and}$$
$$\mathsf{COV}_{h_4}(\Sigma, J) = \{\{h_4\}, \{h_1, h_2\}\}.$$

Clearly these are not equivalent homomorphisms sets. For simplicity, we will use the set itself to represent its equivalence class. Corresponding to these homomorphisms we have: $I_{\{h_1\}} = \{R(a, X_1)\}$, $I_{\{h_2\}} = \{U(a)\}$, $I_{\{h_3\}} = \{U(b)\}$, $I_{\{h_4\}} = \{R(a, a)\}$ and finally $I_{\{h_1,h_2\}} = \{R(a, X_2), U(a)\}$, where X_1 and X_2 are distinct null values. Thus, the "CQ sub-universal" instance will be:

$$\begin{aligned} I_{\Sigma,J} =& glb\{I_{\{h_1\}}, I_{\{h_4\}}\} \cup glb\{I_{\{h_2\}}, I_{\{h_4\}}\} \cup \\ & glb\{I_{\{h_3\}}\} \cup glb\{I_{\{h_4\}}, I_{\{h_1,h_2\}}\} \\ =& \{R(a, Y_1), U(b), R(a, Y_2)\} \end{aligned}$$

where Y_1 and Y_2 are distinct null values. Note that even though $(I_{\Sigma,J}, J) \models \Sigma$, the source instance $I_{\Sigma,J}$ is not a recovery for J under Σ, as tuple $S(a)$ from J is not justified by any tuples from $I_{\Sigma,J}$. For the query $Q_1(x) = \{(x) : U(x)\}$, we have $Q_1(I_{\Sigma,J})\downarrow = \{(b)\} \subseteq \mathsf{CERT}(Q_1, \Sigma, J)$. To show that the method is not complete, consider query $Q_2(x) = \{(x) : R(x, x)\}$. For this we have $\mathsf{CERT}(Q_2, \Sigma, J) = \{(a)\}$ and $Q_2(I_{\Sigma,J})\downarrow = \varnothing$.

One may note that for the construction of instance $I_{\Sigma,J}$ the subsumption constraints are not considered. It is still an open problem if one may filter, in polynomial time, the coverings used in Definition 12 based on the subsumption constraint in order to get more sound answers to CQ queries.

As shown in [6], the CQ-maximum recovery mapping can be represented as a set of target-to-source tgds. The following theorem shows that for any set of s-t tgds Σ, target instance J and CQ query Q, the "sub-universal" source instance will return at least the same sound CQ answers over the recoveries as one would obtain by chasing J with the CQ-maximum recovery mapping Σ' obtained from Σ.

THEOREM 10. *Let Σ be a set of s-t tgds, J a target instance valid for recovery under Σ, and let Σ' be the CQ-maximum recovery mapping [6] for Σ. Then it holds that $Q(Chase(\Sigma', J))\downarrow \subseteq Q(I_{\Sigma,J})\downarrow$, for all $Q \in CQ$.*

PROOF. (sketch) Let J be a target instance and Σ' be the CQ-maximum recovery mapping for Σ. It can be easily noted, from the way Σ' is constructed [6], that for any homomorphism f from the body of a tgd $\xi' \in \Sigma'$ into J, one can find homomorphism $h \in \mathsf{HOM}(\Sigma, J)$ such that we have $f(body(\xi')) \subseteq h(head(\xi_h))$, and for any set $H \in \mathsf{COV}_h(\Sigma, J)$, $Chase_f(\xi', J) \to I_{H(h,\Sigma)}$. This means that there is a homomorphism $Chase_{\{f\}}(\xi', J) \to glb\{I_{H(h,\Sigma)} : H \in \mathsf{COV}_h(\Sigma, J)\}$. Extending this to the entire target instance and all dependencies in Σ', it follows that $Chase(\Sigma', J) \to I_{\Sigma,J}$. From this the statement from the theorem follows directly. □

Next example shows that there exists configurations of Σ, J, and Q such that using instance $I_{\Sigma,J}$ we may get strictly more sound information than obtained by chasing J with the CQ-maximum recovery mapping Σ'.

EXAMPLE 13. *Consider the same setting as in Example 12. For Σ, the corresponding CQ-maximum recovery mapping is logically equivalent with $\Sigma' = \{T(x) \to \exists z\ R(x, z)\}$. For target instance J, the source instance obtained by chasing J with Σ' is $I = \{R(a, Z_1)\}$, where Z_1 is a null value. Considering the conjunctive query $Q_3(x) = \{(x) : U(x)\}$, we have $\varnothing = Q_3(I)\downarrow \subset Q_3(I_{\Sigma,J})\downarrow = \{(b)\}$.*

7. CONCLUSIONS

In this paper we proposed a new semantics for the inversion problem in data-exchange. We argue that our instance based recovery is more useful than the previously proposed inversion mappings, as one may recover not only more source data but also only sound data. We introduced a new chase algorithm to compute these recoveries when the initial mapping is given by a set of s-t tgds. The new chase algorithm permits the computation of a finite set of recovered source instances that may be used to get sound and complete answers to any UCQ query over the source schema. On the negative side we showed that getting these answers is coNP-complete even when considering only source CQ queries. Our approach does not have the restriction of only allowing ground instances. We think that our semantics opens the door to new interesting problems, such as finding recoveries after the target instance already has been altered by some operations (in the current work we only consider target instances that were valid for recovery). Another interesting problem is to find syntactical characterizations for the initial source-to-target mapping that will allow tractable computation for CQ (or UCQ) queries over the materialized set of source recoveries.

Acknowledgements

We are grateful to the anonymous referees for detailed and constructive comments.

8. REFERENCES

[1] S. Abiteboul and O. M. Duschka. Complexity of answering queries using materialized views. In *PODS*, pages 254–263, 1998.

[2] S. Abiteboul, R. Hull, and V. Vianu. *Foundations of Databases*. Addison-Wesley, 1995.

[3] M. Arenas, R. Fagin, and A. Nash. Composition with target constraints. In *ICDT*, pages 129–142, 2010.

[4] M. Arenas, R. Fagin, and A. Nash. Composition with target constraints. *Logical Methods in Computer Science*, 7(3), 2011.

[5] M. Arenas, J. Pérez, J. L. Reutter, and C. Riveros. Composition and inversion of schema mappings. *SIGMOD Record*, 38(3):17–28, 2009.

[6] M. Arenas, J. Pérez, J. L. Reutter, and C. Riveros. Inverting schema mappings: Bridging the gap between theory and practice. *PVLDB*, 2(1):1018–1029, 2009.

[7] M. Arenas, J. Pérez, J. L. Reutter, and C. Riveros. Query language-based inverses of schema mappings: semantics, computation, and closure properties. *VLDB J.*, 21(6):823–842, 2012.

[8] M. Arenas, J. Pérez, and C. Riveros. The recovery of a schema mapping: Bringing exchanged data back. *ACM Trans. Database Syst.*, 34(4), 2009.

[9] C. Beeri and M. Y. Vardi. A proof procedure for data dependencies. *J. ACM*, 31(4):718–741, 1984.

[10] P. A. Bernstein. Applying model management to classical meta data problems. In *CIDR*, 2003.

[11] A. Deutsch, A. Nash, and J. B. Remmel. The chase revisited. In *PODS*, pages 149–158, 2008.

[12] R. Fagin. Inverting schema mappings. *ACM Trans. Database Syst.*, 32(4), 2007.

[13] R. Fagin, P. G. Kolaitis, R. J. Miller, and L. Popa. Data exchange: semantics and query answering. *Theor. Comput. Sci.*, 336(1):89–124, 2005.

[14] R. Fagin, P. G. Kolaitis, L. Popa, and W. C. Tan. Composing schema mappings: Second-order dependencies to the rescue. *ACM Trans. Database Syst.*, 30(4):994–1055, 2005.

[15] R. Fagin, P. G. Kolaitis, L. Popa, and W. C. Tan. Quasi-inverses of schema mappings. *ACM Trans. Database Syst.*, 33(2), 2008.

[16] R. Fagin, P. G. Kolaitis, L. Popa, and W. C. Tan. Reverse data exchange: Coping with nulls. *ACM Trans. Database Syst.*, 36(2):11, 2011.

[17] R. Fagin, P. G. Kolaitis, L. Popa, and W. C. Tan. Schema mapping evolution through composition and inversion. In Z. Bellahsene, A. Bonifati, and E. Rahm, editors, *Schema Matching and Mapping*, Data-Centric Systems and Applications, pages 191–222. Springer, 2011.

[18] G. Grahne and A. Onet. Representation systems for data exchange. In *ICDT*, pages 208–221, 2012.

[19] P. Hell and J. Nesetril. *Graphs And Homomorphisms*. Oxford University Press, 2004.

[20] L. Libkin. Data exchange and incomplete information. In *PODS*, pages 60–69, 2006.

[21] L. Libkin. Incomplete information and certain answers in general data models. In *PODS*, pages 59–70, 2011.

[22] A. Nash, P. A. Bernstein, and S. Melnik. Composition of mappings given by embedded dependencies. *ACM Trans. Database Syst.*, 32(1):4, 2007.

[23] C. H. Papadimitriou. *Computational complexity*. Addison-Wesley, 1994.

The (Almost) Complete Guide to Tree Pattern Containment*

Wojciech Czerwiński
University of Warsaw

Wim Martens
Universität Bayreuth

Paweł Parys
University of Warsaw

Marcin Przybyłko
University of Warsaw
University of New Caledonia

ABSTRACT

Tree pattern queries are being investigated in database theory for more than a decade. They are a fundamental and flexible query mechanism and have been considered in the context of querying tree structured as well as graph structured data. We revisit their containment, validity, and satisfiability problem, both with and without schema information. We present a comprehensive overview of what is known about the complexity of containment and develop new techniques which allow us to obtain tractability- and hardness results for cases that have been open since the early work on tree pattern containment. For the tree pattern queries we consider in this paper, it is known that the containment problem does not depend on whether patterns are evaluated on trees or on graphs. This means that our results also shed new light on tree pattern queries on graphs.

Categories and Subject Descriptors

H.2.3 [**Database Management**]: Languages—*query languages*

Keywords

Tree patterns; complexity; XPath; optimization

1. INTRODUCTION

Tree pattern queries are a fundamental building block for many query- and specification languages for tree- and graph-structured data. They have been studied under many names: tree patterns, twig patterns, twig queries, and XPath queries with child and descendant axis. In the context of tree-structured data, they form the core of XPath [7]. XPath is the main mechanism for node selection in XQuery [11] and XSLT [26], the most widely used query languages for XML. In addition, XPath is used for specifying integrity constraints in XML Schema [21], the currently de facto schema language for XML, and it is used in XLink [18] and XPointer [17] for referencing elements in external documents. In the context of graphs, languages based on tree patterns have become popular as well. Nested regular expressions [37] and Graph XPath [30], for example, are heavily inspired on tree patterns and extend them with additional navigational features, negation, or data value comparisons. Tree patterns similar to the ones we consider in this paper are also used to speed up pattern matching algorithms in graphs [14].

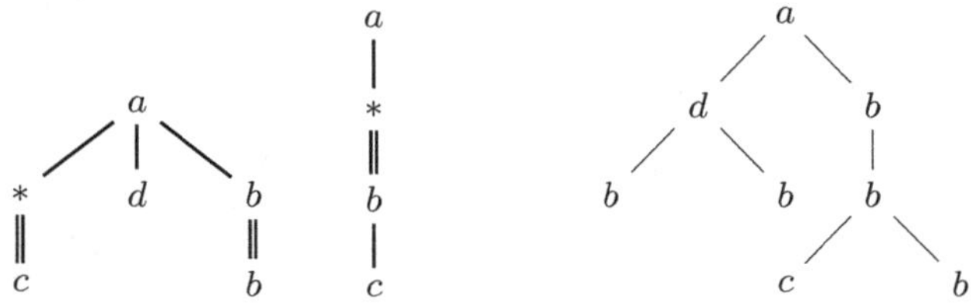

Figure 1: From left to right: two (boolean) tree pattern queries and a tree. Child edges are drawn as single lines and ancestor edges as double lines. Wildcard labels are denoted $*$.

The containment problem for tree patterns and XPath queries is firmly established as an important problem in databases and has been heavily investigated [33, 35, 43, 6, 22, 41, 25]. In this paper we study the tree patterns that were introduced by Miklau and Suciu [33]. These patterns have *wildcards* and allow navigation with *child* and *descendant* axes. Figure 1 contains two tree pattern queries and a tree. The left tree pattern query expresses that the root of the tree should have label a, it has a child of which the label does not matter and which has a c-descendant. The root also has a child with label d and a child with label b which has a b-descendant. The second pattern expresses that the root should be labeled a, it has a child with a b-descendant, which has a c-child. Both tree pattern queries can be matched in the tree on the right. Notice that it is allowed to map different nodes of the tree pattern queries to the same node in the tree.

Even though many variants and extensions of these patterns have been considered in the literature (see, e.g., [19, 5, 16, 24, 9, 29]), a complete picture of the complexity of containment for even this basic kind of tree pattern queries is still lacking. We therefore revisit several variants of containment for tree patterns, with and without schema infor-

*This work was supported by DFG grant MA 4938/2-1 and by Poland's National Science Centre grant no. UMO-2013/11/D/ST6/03075.

PODS'15, May 31–June 4, 2015, Melbourne, Victoria, Australia.

ACM 978-1-4503-2757-2/15/05 ...$15.00.
http://dx.doi.org/10.1145/2745754.2745766.

mation. We also consider validity and satisfiability, which are special cases of containment. However, since validity and satisfiability of tree patterns are trivial in the absence of schemas, we only consider these problems when schemas are present. We only consider schema information in the form of Document Type Definitions (DTDs) [13].

Contribution. We denote the tree patterns as introduced by Miklau and Suciu [33] by TPQ or TPQ(/, //, *). Here, TPQ abbreviates *tree pattern queries*. We consider several fragments, depending on features we allow or disallow. The four features we consider are *child edges* (/), *(proper) descendant edges* (//), *wildcards* (*) and *branching*. We use the term *path queries* or PQ to refer to queries that do not have branching. For example, the second pattern in Figure 1 is a path query. Whenever we talk about a *fragment* of TPQs in this paper, we mean a class that is obtained from TPQs by disallowing zero or more of the four aforementioned features.

We consider containment problems of TPQs with and without DTDs. When DTDs are present, we consider the case where the DTD is part of the input as well as the case where it is fixed. Throughout the paper we consider two forms of containment, namely *strong containment*, in which the root of the pattern is required to match the root of the tree, and *weak containment*, which does not have this requirement.

Unless mentioned otherwise, we treat TPQ*s* as *boolean* queries, i.e., they only return true or false when evaluated. There is a strong connection between containment for boolean TPQ*s* and for (more general) k-ary TPQ*s*, which return k-tuples of nodes. In particular, containment for boolean TPQ*s* is in P if and only if it is in P for k-ary TPQ*s* [33, 27]. However, this connection requires wildcards and branching [27] and therefore does not work out-of-the-box for every fragment of TPQs we consider.

Our main contributions are the following.

(1) We first consider containment without schema information. Here, we complete the picture that was started by Miklau and Suciu [33]. Miklau and Suciu showed, for every fragment $\mathcal{F}$ of TPQs in which child edges are present, whether containment for $\mathcal{F}$-queries is in P or coNP-complete. In addition, they presented a number of results for cases in which the queries can be from different fragments, that is, containment of queries from fragment $\mathcal{F}_1$ in queries from fragment $\mathcal{F}_2$, but the picture was incomplete. One particular, non-trivial case that remained open since this early work is the complexity of path queries (that is, PQ(/, //, *)) in tree pattern queries (that is, TPQ(/, //, *)). We prove that this problem is solvable in P. In fact, we present, for every pair $\mathcal{F}_1$ and $\mathcal{F}_2$ of fragments of TPQs, whether the complexity of containment of queries from $\mathcal{F}_1$ in queries of $\mathcal{F}_2$ is in P or coNP-complete, for weak and for strong containment (Section 3). We obtain new, non-trivial polynomial time results as well as new coNP-completeness results. The aforementioned polynomial time upper bound for containment of path queries in tree pattern queries is the technically most involved result in the section.

(2) We then turn to problems that involve DTD information and present a complete overview of the complexity of satisfiability and validity of fragments of TPQs with schema information (Sections 4 and 5). More precisely we consider the weak and strong satisfiability or validity problem for every fragment of TPQs, with respect to a given DTD or a fixed DTD. For satisfiability, we classify every such variant of the problem either in P or we show that it is NP-complete. For validity, we show that the problem is always either in P or EXPTIME-complete. The EXPTIME-hardness goes back to weak validity of TPQ(/, *) with respect to DTDs [10]; all other cases are in P.

(3) We present an almost complete overview of the most general problem: containment of fragments of TPQ with respect to DTD information (Section 6). We solve a problem that has been open since a decade: containment of PQ(/, //, *) in PQ(/, //, *) with respect to DTDs was mentioned as an open problem in [35]. Until today, not much was known about the precise complexity. It was known to be (trivially) in EXPTIME and the closely related validity problem of PQ(/, //, *) with respect to DTDs was known to be in P [25]. We prove that, perhaps surprisingly, weak containment of PQ(/) in PQ(/, *) with respect to DTDs is already EXPTIME-hard, even when the DTD is fixed. The solution goes through a new variant of tiling problem that we call *triomino tiling* and that may be interesting in its own right. Tiling problems are a commonly used tool for proving complexity lower bounds and ask whether a region can be tiled using a set of tile types, respecting certain *horizontal* and *vertical* constraints. Triomino tiling unifies the horizontal and vertical constraints, which allows us to check both of them at the same time using a single gadget. This property of triomino tiling is crucial for our proof.

(4) We discuss connections between containment of TPQs over graphs and over trees (Section 7). When no schema information is present, it was already observed [33] that the containment problem for TPQs is the same over trees and graphs. That is, we have that TPQ q_1 is contained in TPQ q_2 over trees if and only if it is contained over graphs. We present how this observation can be extended when schema information is present. We discuss several manners how DTDs can be used to specify meta-information on graphs so that the correspondence between trees and graphs also holds for the satisfiability problem. Unfortunately, the correspondence does not seem to carry over already for the validity problem.

Throughout the paper, we summarize our results in tables and present cases for which we prove new insights (to the best of our knowledge) in bold. We stress that the tables are optimized for looking up results and for space in the paper. They often summarize many cases in one cell, which is not optimal for clearly delineating which cases were already known and which are newly solved. Whenever we are aware of a known result that is not implied by a result we prove, we mention it in the text.

We found it striking that, when DTDs are involved, we do not see any complexity difference between the settings where the DTD is fixed or not. All our upper bounds already hold when the DTD is part of the input and all lower bounds hold for fixed DTDs. This shows that, no matter which formalism one uses for describing schema- or meta-information, the hardness results always hold as soon as the formalism is as expressive as a DTD. In fact, the hardness results also hold for DTDs defining *unordered* trees, as in [12].

Many problems are similar in nature to containment, such as, for example, XPath minimization [27], consistent query answering [3], key inference [2], constraint implication [36], computing certain answers in incomplete databases [5, 23]. We believe that the techniques we develop may also be applicable in such closely related scenarios.

We already mentioned that tree patterns can also be used to query graphs instead of trees. Likewise, one can also consider containment of tree patterns on graphs in a similar way as one does on trees. There is a very close connection between these two settings. Miklau and Suciu already observed that, when no schema information is present, containment for tree patterns on graphs *is the same decision problem* than containment for tree patterns on trees [33]. We revisit this correspondence later in the paper.

Related Work. Containment and satisfiability of TPQs was first investigated by Miklau and Suciu [33] who showed, for example, that the containment problem is always in coNP and that its most general version is coNP-complete. However, when one removes wildcards, descendant axes, or branching from TPQs, the problem is in P. Satisfiability and containment of TPQs with respect to DTDs was first studied by Neven and Schwentick [35] and Wood [43]. The results of these papers are surveyed in [38].

Benedikt et al. [6] considered satisfiability of many fragments of XPath, among which also TPQs, with DTD information in many variations, two of which we also consider here ("DTD is fixed" and "DTD is part of the input"). Since some of the query fragments they consider have negation, some of their results imply upper bounds on containment too. Geerts and Fan consider satisfiability of queries with sibling axes [22], which is similar to considering TPQs on words instead of trees.

There is a strong connection between minimization of TPQs [20] and containment in the sense that a large class of TPQs can be solved by a procedure that builds on containment tests. However, it is not clear whether all TPQs can be minimized in this way [27].

Conjunctive queries on trees [24] are closely related to TPQs but can be graph-shaped instead of tree-shaped. Their containment problems are harder than for TPQs. Without schema information, the complexity jumps from coNP to Π_2^P [9] and, with schema information, from EXPTIME to 2EXPTIME [8].

Tree patterns representing XML with incomplete information [5] are also closely related to TPQs and, in fact, are more expressive. For example, they allow navigation in horizontal and vertical direction and have variables to bind data values. Computing *certain answers* over such patterns can be viewed as a form of containment [23]. For these more expressive patterns, Barceló et al. [5] embark on a quest of understanding the tractability frontier of query answering, which is a quest similar to ours. Containment of such patterns was studied in [16].

Finally, we note that the containment problem of tree-pattern-like queries is also relevant on graphs (see, e.g., [29, 44] and the references we already mentioned).

2. PRELIMINARIES

Here, we introduce the necessary definitions concerning graphs, trees, tree pattern queries, and schemas. For a finite set S, we denote by $|S|$ its number of elements.

2.1 Trees and Tree Pattern Queries

We consider trees that are node-labeled, rooted, unranked, and directed from the root downwards. When we do not say that the trees are infinite, resp., unordered, we assume that they have a finite number of nodes, resp., the children of each node are ordered from left to right. Our complexity results do not depend on whether trees are ordered or not. For an arbitrary, possibly infinite set of *labels* Λ, we denote *Λ-trees* as tuples $t = (\mathsf{Nodes}(t), \mathsf{Edges}(t), \mathsf{lab}^t)$, where $\mathsf{Nodes}(t)$ is the set of nodes $\mathsf{Edges}(t) \subseteq (\mathsf{Nodes}(t))^2$ the set of child edges and $\mathsf{lab}^t : \mathsf{Nodes}(t) \to \Lambda$ the labeling function. When t is clear from the context, we sometimes just denote lab^t by lab. The root of t will be denoted $\mathsf{root}(t)$. We define the *size of* t, denoted by $|t|$, to be the number of nodes of t. We denote a tree with root labeled a and subtrees $t_1, \ldots, t_n$ as $a(t_1, \ldots, t_n)$. By $\mathcal{T}_\Lambda$ we denote the set of all ordered, finite Λ-trees. We often simply say *trees* when Λ is clear from the context.

A *path* in tree t is a sequence of nodes $v_0 \cdots v_n$ such that, for each $i = 1, \ldots, n$, we have that $(v_{i-1}, v_i) \in \mathsf{Edges}(t)$. Paths therefore never run upwards, that is, turn towards to the root of t. We say that $v_0 \cdots v_n$ is a path *from* v_0 *to* v_n and that the *length* of the path is n. The *depth* of a node $v \in \mathsf{Nodes}(t)$ is equal to the length of the (unique) path from $\mathsf{root}(t)$ to v. The *depth* of a tree t is then defined as the maximum of the depths of all its nodes.

We will use tree pattern queries with *wildcard*. We will denote the wildcard symbol by $*$. Following the standard conventions, tree pattern queries match trees that only bear labels that are different from $*$ and which we call *letters*.

Definition 2.1 (Tree Pattern Queries). Let Λ be a (possibly infinite) set of labels that contains the wildcard $*$. A *tree pattern query (with wildcards)*, or *TPQ*, over Λ is a tuple $q = (\mathsf{Nodes}(q), \mathsf{Edges}(q), \mathsf{Desc}(q), \mathsf{lab}^q)$ where $\mathsf{Nodes}(q)$ is a finite set of nodes, $\mathsf{Edges}(q) \subseteq (\mathsf{Nodes}(q))^2$ a finite set of edges, and $\mathsf{lab}^q : \mathsf{Nodes}(q) \to \Lambda$ such that $(\mathsf{Nodes}(q), \mathsf{Edges}(q), \mathsf{lab}^q)$ is a tree over Λ. Furthermore, $\mathsf{Desc}(q) \subseteq \mathsf{Edges}(q)$ is the set of *descendant edges*.

Figure 2 contains a tree pattern on the left. Here, the double lines depict edges in Desc and the single lines are edges in Edges $\setminus$ Desc.

Let t be a tree over some arbitrary set of labels Δ that does not contain the wildcard $*$. A *(weak) embedding* of a TPQ q into t is a total mapping m from $\mathsf{Nodes}(q)$ to $\mathsf{Nodes}(t)$ such that

- for every $v \in \mathsf{Nodes}(q)$ such that $\mathsf{lab}(v) \neq *$, we have $\mathsf{lab}(m(v)) = \mathsf{lab}(v)$;
- for every $v_1, v_2 \in \mathsf{Nodes}(q)$
  - if $(v_1, v_2) \notin \mathsf{Desc}$, then $(m(v_1), m(v_2)) \in \mathsf{Edges}(t)$; and
  - if $(v_1, v_2) \in \mathsf{Desc}$, then $m(v_1)$ is a proper ancestor of $m(v_2)$.

An embedding is a *strong embedding* if, additionally, it maps the root of q to the root of t.

The *(weak) language* of q is denoted $L_w(q)$ and consists of all trees t for which there is a weak embedding of q into t. The *strong language* of q is denoted $L_s(q)$ and is defined similarly but requires a strong embedding. Notice that $L_s(q) \subseteq L_w(q)$. In Figure 2, we give an example of an embedding, depicted by dashed lines.

The set of all tree pattern queries is denoted by TPQ or TPQ(/, //, $*$). In this notation, we refer to / as *child edges*, to // as *descendant edges*, and $*$ as *wildcards*. We consider fragments of TPQs that limit the features they can use. If we omit /, then we only consider TPQs q where $\mathsf{Desc}(q) = \mathsf{Edges}(q)$, if we omit //, we assume that $\mathsf{Desc}(q) = \emptyset$, and if we omit $*$, we assume that $\mathsf{lab} : \mathsf{Nodes}(q) \to \Delta$. By PQ we denote the set of *path queries*, which are TPQs q that

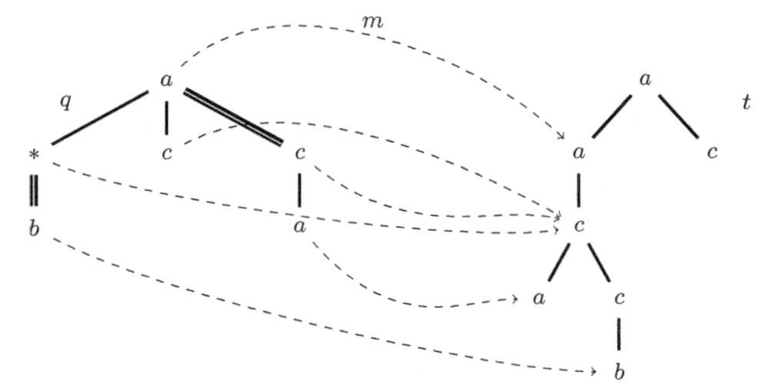

Figure 2: Mapping m is a weak embedding of the TPQ q in the tree t, but it is not a strong embedding, as $m(root(q)) \neq root(t)$. Notice that there exists also a strong embedding of q in t.

do not branch, that is $\mathsf{Edges}(q)$ does not contain any (v, v_1) and (v, v_2) for which $v_1 \neq v_2$. We denote fragments of PQs similar to TPQs. For example, $\mathsf{PQ}(/, *)$ is the set of path queries that use child edges and wildcards.

2.2 Schemas

Throughout the paper, $\Sigma \subseteq \Delta$ always denotes a finite alphabet of letters. We use standard regular expressions using the operators $\cdot$ (concatenation), $+$ (disjunction), and * (Kleene star). For a regular expression r, $L(r)$ is the language of the expression, and $\mathsf{Labels}(r)$ is the set of labels occurring in r. The *size* of a regular expression r, denoted by $|r|$, is defined as the length of its word representation.

In this paper, schemas will be mild variations on Document Type Definitions (DTDs), which we abstract as extended context-free grammars.

DEFINITION 2.2. A *DTD* is a tuple (Σ, d, S_d), where Σ is a finite alphabet, d is a function that maps Σ-symbols to regular expressions over Σ, and $S_d \subseteq \Sigma$ is the set of start symbols. For convenience we sometimes denote (Σ, d, S_d) by d and say that $a \rightarrow r$ *is a rule in* d when $d(a) = r$.

A tree t *satisfies* d if its root is labeled by an element of S_d and, for every node v with label a and children $v_1, \ldots, v_n$ from left to right, the word $\mathsf{lab}(v_1) \cdots \mathsf{lab}(v_n)$ is in the language defined by $d(a)$. By $L(d)$ we denote the language of trees satisfying d. The *size* of a DTD is $|\Sigma| + |S_d| + |d|$ where $|d|$ refers to the size of the representations of the regular string languages. Unless specified otherwise, we represent all such regular string languages by regular expressions. Hence, $|d|$ is the sum of the sizes of all expressions representing languages $d(a)$ for $a \in \Sigma$.

We assume that all DTDs d in this paper are *reduced*, which means that, for every $a \in \Sigma$ there exists a tree in $L(d)$ that contains a. It is well known that, for a DTD that is not reduced, one can find an equivalent reduced one in polynomial time [1, 31].

2.3 Main Decision Problems

We will investigate the complexities of containment, satisfiability and validity of tree pattern queries, possibly with schema information.

In the following, let p and q always denote TPQs and let d denote a DTD. We say that p is weakly contained in q, if $L_w(p) \subseteq L_w(q)$. Similarly, p is strongly contained in q if $L_s(p) \subseteq L_s(q)$. We consider the following problems for TPQs:

W-CONTAINMENT	S-CONTAINMENT
Input: TPQs p, q	Input: TPQs p, q
Q: Is $L_w(p) \subseteq L_w(q)$?	Q: Is $L_s(p) \subseteq L_s(q)$?

We also consider weak and strong containment *with DTD*, in which case we also consider validity and satisfiability as special cases of containment.[1] Weak containment with respect to a DTD is formally defined as follows.

W-CONTAINMENT WITH DTD	
Input:	TPQs p, q, DTD d
Q:	Is $L_w(p) \cap L(d) \subseteq L_w(q)$?

S-CONTAINMENT is defined analogously to W-CONTAINMENT, but it uses L_s instead of L_w everywhere in the definition.

Satisfiability problems can be seen as a special case of containment. For example, we have that $L_w(p) \cap L(d) \not\subseteq \emptyset$ if and only if p is (weakly) satisfiable with respect to d. Formally, W-SATISFIABILITY with respect to a DTD asks, given a TPQ p and DTD d, whether $L_w(p) \cap L(d) \neq \emptyset$. As before, we define S-SATISFIABILITY analogously, with $L_s(p)$ instead of $L_w(p)$. The same holds true for the validity problem with DTDs, which asks whether $L(d) \subseteq L(q)$. So, formally, W-VALIDITY with respect to a DTD asks, given a TPQ q and a DTD d, whether $L(d) \subseteq L_w(q)$. Again, the corresponding S-VALIDITY problem is obtained by taking $L_s(q)$ instead of $L_w(q)$.

In the paper, we also consider variants of the problems in which the DTD is fixed. When we consider a problem with respect to a *fixed DTD* we actually refer to a set of problems. When we prove a hardness bound for such problems, it means that there exists a fixed DTD for which the problem is hard. For example, when we say that W-CONTAINMENT of $\mathsf{TPQ}(//)$ in $\mathsf{PQ}(/)$ w.r.t. fixed DTD is coNP-hard, then we mean that there exists a fixed DTD d_f for which the problem that takes as input a $p \in \mathsf{TPQ}(//)$ and $q \in \mathsf{PQ}(/)$ and asks whether $L_w(p) \cap L(d_f) \subseteq L_w(q)$ is coNP-hard. In fact, in this paper we only show *lower bounds* for problems with fixed DTD.

Weak and Strong Containment. The next observation shows that S-CONTAINMENT and W-CONTAINMENT are equivalent in the case where both queries are allowed to have descendant edges; otherwise it allows us to only present upper bounds for W-CONTAINMENT and lower bounds for S-CONTAINMENT.

OBSERVATION 2.3. *For all fragments $\mathcal{F}_1$ and $\mathcal{F}_2$ of TPQs, there is a polynomial time reduction from* S-CONTAINMENT *of $\mathcal{F}_1$ in $\mathcal{F}_2$ to* W-CONTAINMENT *of $\mathcal{F}_1$ in $\mathcal{F}_2$ (with or without DTD). If $\mathcal{F}_1$ and $\mathcal{F}_2$ both contain $//$, then there is also a polynomial time reduction from* W-CONTAINMENT *of $\mathcal{F}_1$ in $\mathcal{F}_2$ to* S-CONTAINMENT *of $\mathcal{F}_1$ in $\mathcal{F}_2$ (with or without DTD).*

The first reduction boils down to changing the root label of both patters to an unused root symbol r (and appropriately

[1]Without DTD, validity and satisfiability of TPQs are trivial: every query is satisfiable and no query other than $*$ is valid (if one requires trees to have a root node).

updating the DTD). In the second reduction we attach a new r-labeled root with a descendant edge above both patterns. Details are in the appendix.

For the sake of succinctness, when we claim a result about a problem without saying that we mean the weak or strong variant, it means that we claim the result for both. Most often, this will simply be due to Observation 2.3, but sometimes it also just means that the reduction or algorithm only needs a very small adjustment.

General Upper and Lower Complexity Bounds. The containment problem of the most general class, TPQ($/, //, *$) is known to be in coNP, which was shown by Miklau and Suciu [33]. If DTDs are involved, then containment of TPQ($/, //, *$) is in EXPTIME [35].

Regarding lower bounds, satisfiability with respect to a DTD d is always at least as hard as the problem of computing a reduced DTD equivalent to d. Since this problem is P-hard (by a trivial reduction from the emptiness problem of context-free grammars), all decision problems in this paper that involve DTDs in the input are P-hard in general.

3. CONTAINMENT WITHOUT SCHEMA

Containment of TPQs without schema information was studied in the seminal paper of Miklau and Suciu [33] which gives a fairly precise picture of the tractability frontier. In particular, a main message of that paper is that containment of TPQ($/, //, *$) in TPQ($/, //, *$) is coNP-complete (see also Theorem 3.3), whereas the problem becomes tractable if we remove wildcards, descendant edges, or branching from both tree pattern queries. When considering containment of queries p in q and we allow p and q to come from different fragments, then Miklau and Suciu show the following polynomial time bounds.

THEOREM 3.1 (THEOREM 3 IN [33]). *The following problems are in P:*
(1) S-CONTAINMENT *of TPQ($/, *$) in TPQ($/, //, *$);*
(2) S-CONTAINMENT *of TPQ($/, //, *$) in TPQ($/, *$);*
(3) CONTAINMENT *of TPQ($/, //, *$) in TPQ($/, //$);*
(4) CONTAINMENT *of TPQ($/, //, *$) in PQ($/, //, *$).*

Notation-wise, we note that Miklau and Suciu [33] assume that "/" is always present in TPQs, which is why they do not explicitly have it in their notation.

In this paper, we prove the following new polynomial time bounds. One of the new results allows child edges in both patterns and, as such, also fills a remaining gap in [33]. (Indeed, in the notation of Miklau and Suciu, they solved the complexity of all containment problems p in q for all combinations of p and q coming from $\mathrm{XP}^{\{[],//,*\}}$, except the case where p is from $\mathrm{XP}^{\{//,*\}}$.)

THEOREM 3.2. *The following problems are in P:*
(1) CONTAINMENT *of PQ($/, //, *$) in TPQ($/, //, *$);*
(2) CONTAINMENT *of TPQ($//, *$) in TPQ($/, //, *$);*
(3) CONTAINMENT *of TPQ($/, //, *$) in TPQ($//, *$);*
(4) W-CONTAINMENT *of TPQ($/, *$) in TPQ($/, //, *$)*

Cases (1) and (2) are proved by using a dynamic programming approach. The proofs are rather technical and divide patterns into *islands*, which are the maximal subpatterns that are connected by child edges.

Case (3) is proved by a rather standard argument involving canonical trees and case (4) follows almost directly from the corresponding S-CONTAINMENT problem (Theorem 3.1(1)).

Finally, we strengthen the coNP lower bound from Miklau and Suciu to the case where the right pattern only uses child edges.

THEOREM 3.3. *The following problems are coNP-complete:*
(1) CONTAINMENT *of TPQ($/, //$) in TPQ($/, //, *$) [33];*
(2) W-CONTAINMENT *of TPQ($/, //$) in TPQ($/, *$).*

The proof of Theorem 3.3(2) follows the same lines as the proof of Theorem 3.3(2) from [33], which is a reduction from validity of propositional formulas. The main change in our proof is a different construction for the gadgets that encode the truth values, since these gadgets in [33] heavily rely on descendants in patterns. We note that the lower bound only holds for weak containment. For strong containment, the complexity is in P by Theorem 3.2.

We summarize all cases in Table 1. Notice that the table classifies, for every combination of branching, wildcards, child edges, descendant edges and weak/strong containment, whether the containment problem is in P or coNP-hard.

4. SATISFIABILITY WITH SCHEMA

We now turn to containment problems that take schema information into account. The simplest such problems are satisfiability problems. We provide two polynomial-time results.

THEOREM 4.1. *The following problems are in P:*
(1) SATISFIABILITY *of PQ($/, //, *$) w.r.t. a DTD [6];*
(2) SATISFIABILITY *of TPQ($//, *$) w.r.t. a fixed DTD.*

Case (1) immediately follows from a stronger result of Benedikt et al. (Theorem 4.1 in [6]), which shows that the problem remains in P even if unions are added. This case can also be solved by a very simple intersection test of tree automata.

Case (2) of the above theorem was recently proved for an *injective* semantics of TPQs over trees [15]. The proof can be adapted for the non-injective semantics we consider here. Notice that it is crucial for case (2) that the DTD is fixed. Indeed, Wood [43] proved that it is NP-complete to decide whether the language of a given regular expression e over alphabet Σ contains a word that has every letter from Σ.[2] This means that it is already NP-hard to decide whether the language defined by the DTD $r \to e$, containing trees of depth one, has a tree which contains every letter from $\Sigma \setminus \{r\}$. The latter property can be easily expressed by a TPQ($//$). This implies case (1) of the following theorem:

THEOREM 4.2. *The following problems are NP-complete:*
(1) SATISFIABILITY *of TPQ($//$) w.r.t. a DTD [43];*
(2) SATISFIABILITY *of TPQ($/$) w.r.t. a fixed DTD;*
(3) SATISFIABILITY *of TPQ($/, //, *$) w.r.t. a DTD [6].*

We state cases (1) and (2) here for the lower bound and case (3) for the upper bound. We note that Benedikt et al. [6] proved that satisfiability of TPQ($/, *$) with respect to a fixed DTD is NP-complete, which is close to Theorem 4.2(2). In fact, the hardness proof from Benedikt et al. can be adapted so that it does not require wildcard [34],

[2]In fact, Wood's result is stronger. It also holds for expressions that are *deterministic* or *one-unambiguous*, as required in DTDs in practice.

	PQ	TPQ(/,//)	TPQ(/,*)	TPQ(//,*)	TPQ(/,//,*)
PQ			**P** [3.1(1), **3.2(1),(2),(4)**]		
TPQ(/)					
TPQ(//)					
TPQ(/,//)	P [3.1(3),(4)]		**coNP-c [3.3(2)]** / P [3.1(2)]		coNP-c [3.3(1)]
TPQ(/,*)			**P [3.2(4)]** / P [3.1(2)]		**P [3.2(4)]** / P [3.1(1)]
TPQ(//,*)			**P [3.2(2)]** / P [3.1(2)]	**P [3.2(3)]**	**P [3.2(2)]**
TPQ(/,//,*)			**coNP-c [3.3(2)]** / P [3.1(2)]		coNP-c [3.3(1)]

Table 1: Complexities for all combinations of $\mathcal{F}_1$ in $\mathcal{F}_2$, where $\mathcal{F}_1$ and $\mathcal{F}_2$ are fragments of TPQ. When two complexities are listed, then the left one is for weak containment and the right one for strong containment. Results in bold are new, to the best of our knowledge.

which would also imply Theorem 4.2(2). However, the construction we present here can also be used to show Theorem 6.3, which we do not know how to do by tweaking the proof in [6]. We present a complete overview of the complexity of satisfiability in Table 2.

We provide a proof sketch of case (2) of Theorem 4.2.

Proof sketch (case 2). The proof is by reduction from 4-partition, which is defined as follows. We are given a number 2^K for some $K \in \mathbb{N}$, and a multiset S' of cardinality $4 \cdot 2^L$ for some $L \in \mathbb{N}$, containing positive integers. The question to answer is whether one can partition S' into $\frac{|S'|}{4}$ sub-multisets so that the sum of the numbers in each of them is 2^K. It can be shown that 4-partition is NP-complete by reduction from the well-known 3-partition problem.

We now reduce 4-partition to our problem. To this end, consider an instance 2^K, S' (with $|S'| = 4 \cdot 2^L$) of 4-partition. We construct a fixed DTD d and pattern $p \in$ TPQ(/) such that p is strongly satisfiable w.r.t. d if and only if there is a solution to the given instance of 4-partition.

The DTD is very simple: it just says that the alphabet is $\{a, b, c, d, e\}$ where each node labeled by a has exactly two children, and each other node is a leaf.

We define sets T_i of (unordered) trees, inductively on i, as follows. The set T_0 consists of the four trees with one node, with a label from $\{b, c, d, e\}$. When T_i is known, we define T_{i+1} to be all trees consisting of a root labeled by a, which is attached to two different unordered subtrees from T_i. Notice that each tree in T_i is perfectly balanced: each leaf is at depth exactly i. The trees in T_i can be also considered as tree patterns. Such pattern strongly embeds into exactly one unordered tree (itself) when taking the DTD restriction into account. Indeed, we cannot add any other node, since each a may have only two children and the leaf labels occur only at the leaves. Furthermore, we cannot merge any two subtrees since they always have to be different. We fix the smallest number M for which $|T_M| \geq 2^{K+L}$. We have that

$$|T_0| = 4, \qquad |T_{i+1}| = \frac{1}{2}|T_i|(|T_i| - 1).$$

Notice that, as i increases, the number $|T_i|$ is almost squared, so $|T_i|$ grows double-exponentially faster than i. This means that, for sufficiently large instances, M will be smaller than $K + L$, so we can use 2^{K+L} trees from T_M to construct our pattern, and it will be polynomial (recall that 2^K is given in unary).

We are now ready to describe the pattern p. From the root we create $|S'|$ paths, each of length L (each of them

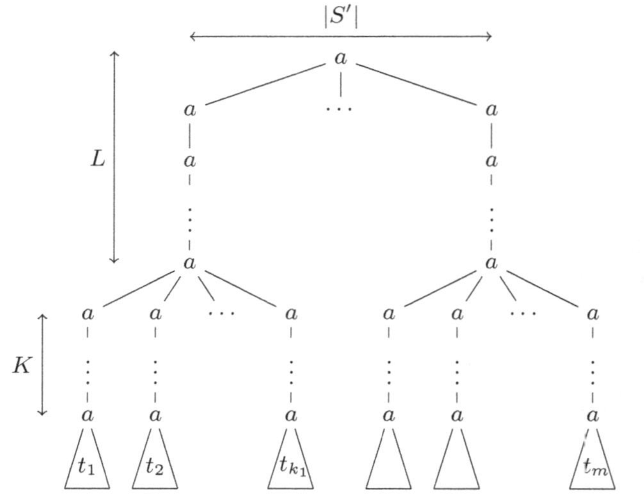

Figure 3: Structure of the pattern p in the proof of Theorem 4.2(2). All the t_j are different trees.

corresponds to one number from S'). At the end of the path corresponding to a number k we create k paths of length K. At the end of each such path, we attach a tree from T_M that occurs nowhere else in the whole pattern p. Figure 3 has a graphical presentation of p.

This concludes the reduction. It can be shown that $L(d) \cap L_s(p) \neq \emptyset$ if and only if $L(d) \cap L_w(p) \neq \emptyset$ if and only if the instance of 4-partition has a solution. □

5. VALIDITY WITH SCHEMA

For the validity problem, we do not present any new deep results, only an observation that closes a small gap between the results that were presented by Hashimoto et al. [25] and Björklund et al. [10]. We summarize the strongest results here, for the sake of completeness and present a complete overview in Table 3.

Theorem 5.1. *The following problems are in P:*
(1) Validity of PQ(/,//,) w.r.t. a DTD [25];*
(2) Validity of TPQ(/,//) w.r.t. a DTD [25];
(3) S-Validity of TPQ(/,) w.r.t. a DTD [25];*
(4) Validity of TPQ(//,) w.r.t. a DTD [25];*
(5) Validity of TPQ(/,//,) w.r.t. a fixed DTD.*

DTD:	fixed	not fixed
PQ	P [4.1(1)]	
TPQ(/)	**NP-c [4.2(2)]**	
TPQ(//)	**P [4.1(2)]**	NP-c [4.2(1)]
TPQ(/, //)	**NP-c [4.2(2)**,(3)]	
TPQ(/, *)	NP-c [4.2(2),(3)]	
TPQ(//, *)	**P [4.1(2)]**	NP-c [4.2(1),(3)]
TPQ(/, //, *)	NP-c [4.2(3)])	

Table 2: Complexity of satisfiability for fragments of TPQs. Results in bold are new, to the best of our knowledge.

	strong	weak	DTD fixed
PQ	P [5.1]		**P [5.1]**
TPQ(/, //)	P [5.1]		
TPQ(/, *)	P [5.1]	EXPTIME-c [5.2]	
TPQ(//, *)	P [5.1]		
TPQ(/, //, *)	EXPTIME-c [5.2]		

Table 3: Complexity of validity for fragments of TPQs w.r.t. a DTD.

Cases (1–4) are proved in Theorem 3 of [25]. Case (5) can be efficiently solved due to the constant language defined by the DTD; we prove it in the appendix. The fixed DTD in case (5) is rather crucial. Without it, weak validity for TPQ(/, *) immediately jumps to EXPTIME, as the following theorem shows.

THEOREM 5.2 (THEOREM 12 IN [10]). *W-VALIDITY of TPQ(/, *) w.r.t. a DTD is EXPTIME-complete.*

From this theorem, we also immediately know that S-VALIDITY of TPQ(/, //, *) with respect to a DTD is EXPTIME-complete.

6. CONTAINMENT WITH SCHEMA

The containment problem with schema information is the most general problem we consider. The solutions for Theorem 6.1(4) and Theorem 6.6 are technically most involved results of this paper.

6.1 Polynomial Time Fragments

THEOREM 6.1. *The following are in P:*
*(1) CONTAINMENT of PQ(/, //, *) in PQ(/, //);*
*(2) CONTAINMENT of PQ(/, //, *) in TPQ(//, *);*
*(3) S-CONTAINMENT of PQ(/, //, *) in TPQ(/, *);*
*(4) W-CONTAINMENT of PQ(/, //, *) in TPQ(/);*
all w.r.t. a DTD.

The proofs for cases (1), (2), and (3) rely on the following observation.

OBSERVATION 6.2. *Let Σ be a finite alphabet and let q be a query in (1) PQ(/, //); (2) TPQ(//, *); or in (3) TPQ(/, *). Then we can construct in polynomial time a non-deterministic tree automaton for the language $\mathcal{T}_\Sigma \setminus L_s(q)$.*

Cases (1)–(3) of Theorem 6.1 now follow by reduction to the emptiness problem of non-deterministic tree automata. Indeed, for $p \in$ PQ(/, //, *) and DTD d one can construct in polynomial time a non-deterministic tree automaton for $L_s(p) \cap L(d)$. This means that, in all three cases, we can obtain in polynomial time a non-deterministic tree automaton that accepts the empty language if and only if $L_s(p) \cap L(d) \subseteq L_s(q)$. Since emptiness testing of non-deterministic tree automata is in P, this gives a P solution to the problem. The P upper bounds for weak containment in cases (1) and (2) are immediate from Observation 2.3. We note that Neven and Schwentick [35] already showed that containment of PQ(/, //) in PQ(/, //) w.r.t. DTD is in P, which is very close to Theorem 6.1(1).

Case (4), however involves a non-trivial argument. Let $p \in$ PQ(/, //, *), $q \in$ TPQ(/), and let d be a DTD. Notice that the automaton recognizing $\mathcal{T}_\Sigma \setminus L_w(q)$ may be of exponential size, thus we have to proceed differently from cases (1)–(3). In a first stage, whenever in q we have two siblings with the same label, we merge them. Although this changes $L_w(q)$, it is easy to see that it does not influence the containment question. In a second stage, we remove redundant subqueries of q. Namely, it may happen that we can remove some subquery of q obtaining some q', so that whenever q' can be embedded into a tree from $L(d)$, then the whole q can be embedded as well. After this cleaning stage, we have one of two mutually exclusive situations. One possibility is that the pattern q is a path (or is very similar to a path); then we have case (1). The opposite case is that in q we have some branching. Then we can prove that the containment never holds. Indeed, to obtain a tree t from $(L_w(p) \cap L(d)) \setminus L_w(q)$ we are quite restricted only while arranging the path into which p will be embedded. However, into this path at most one path of q embeds. Outside of this path in t we can place arbitrary subtrees satisfying d, so we place there subtrees into which the rest of q cannot be embedded. Such subtrees exist, since otherwise the rest of q would be redundant, but all redundant subqueries were already removed during the second stage.

In fact the most difficult part is to check whether q is (weakly) equivalent to its part q' w.r.t. our DTD d. At first glance this looks hopeless, as this is just the W-CONTAINMENT problem of TPQ(/) in TPQ(/) w.r.t. a DTD, which by Theorem 6.3 is in general coNP-hard. Luckily, our pattern q is not arbitrary: there are no two siblings labeled the same (thanks to the first stage). The crux of the proof is to reduce the equivalence problem in this special case to multiple smaller instances of the (slightly generalized) containment question of PQ(/) in TPQ(/) w.r.t. a DTD. Thanks to that, we can proceed by dynamic programming.

6.2 Hard Fragments

We will prove there are two ingredients that make the containment problem w.r.t. DTDs hard, even when the DTD is constant. These two ingredients are
(1) branching in the left pattern and
(2) right patterns of the form $//a/*/*/\cdots/*/b$.
Branching in the left pattern immediately renders containment with schema coNP-hard. The underlying reason is that already satisfiability of TPQ(/) with a fixed DTD is NP-complete (Theorem 4.2); and that our proof can be adapted for the case where the left pattern only has //-edges. The second source of hardness is when the right pattern can express "there is an a-node which is (exactly) k levels above a b-node". In this case the complexity even jumps to EX-

	PQ (/), PQ (//), PQ (/,//)	PQ (/,*)	PQ (//,*)	PQ (/,//,*)
PQ (/), PQ (//), PQ(/,//,*)	**P [6.1(1)]** and [35]	**EXPT.-c [6.6(1),(2)] / P [6.1(3)]**	**P [6.1(2)]**	**EXPT.-c [6.6(1),(2)] / EXPT.-c [6.6(3),(4)]**
TPQ (/), TPQ (//), TPQ(/,//,*)	**coNP-c [6.3,6.4(1)]**	**EXPT.-c [6.6(1),(2)] / coNP-c [6.3(1),(2), 6.4(3)]**	**coNP-c [6.3(3),(4),6.4(2)]**	**EXPT.-c [6.6(1),(2)] / EXPT.-c [6.6(3),(4)]**

Table 4: Complexity of containment TPQs w.r.t. a DTD; right pattern is a PQ. When two complexities are listed, the first is for weak containment and the second for strong containment. The results hold for the case where the DTD is part of the input and for the case where the DTD is fixed. Fields in bold have at least one new result, to the best of our knowledge.

	TPQ (/)	TPQ (//)	TPQ (/,//)	TPQ (/,*)	TPQ (//,*)	TPQ (/,//,*)
PQ (/), PQ (//), PQ(/,//,*)	**P [6.1(4)] / P [6.1(3)]**	**P [6.1(2)]**	in EXPT.	**EXPT.-c [6.6(1),(2)] / P [6.1(3)]**	**P [6.1(2)]**	**EXPT.-c [6.6(1),(2)] / EXPT.-c [6.6(3),(4)]**
TPQ (/), TPQ (//), TPQ (/,//,*)	**coNP-h [6.3] / coNP-c [6.3,6.4(3)]**	**coNP-c [6.3,6.4(2)]**	**coNP-h [6.3]**	**EXPT.-c [6.6(1),(2)] / coNP-c [6.3,6.4(3)]**	**coNP-c [6.3,6.4(2)]**	**EXPT.-c [6.6(1),(2)] / EXPT.-c [6.6(3),(4)]**

Table 5: Complexity of containment TPQs w.r.t. a DTD; right pattern is a TPQ. Notation and remarks are the same as in Table 4.

PTIME, which is already the highest possible complexity class for TPQ containment. We found it rather surprising that such a seemingly inexpressive query makes containment so hard even when the DTD is fixed.

THEOREM 6.3. *The following are coNP-hard:*
(1) CONTAINMENT *of TPQ(/) in PQ(/);*
(2) CONTAINMENT *of TPQ(//) in PQ(/);*
(3) CONTAINMENT *of TPQ(/) in PQ(//);*
(4) CONTAINMENT *of TPQ(//) in PQ(//);*
all w.r.t. a fixed DTD.

For cases (1)–(3), it does not follow from Observation 2.3 that weak and strong containment have the same complexity, but we merged them for succinctness. The proofs are very similar. Cases (1) and (3) are immediate from Theorem 4.2(2). The other cases can be obtained from adapting the proof of Theorem 4.2(2), as follows. Recall that in this proof we were using a DTD ensuring that each internal node (but no leaf) of a tree is labeled by a, and we were reducing an instance of the 4-PARTITION problem into satisfiability of a pattern p that has each leaf on the same depth, say n. We notice that such pattern p is satisfiable if and only if $L_w(p') \cap L(d) \not\subseteq L_w(q)$, where p' is the pattern obtained from p by changing all child edges into descendant edges, and q is a path consisting of $n+1$ nodes labeled by a (connected either by child edges or by descendant edges, depending on the considered fragment). Indeed, any tree in $L_s(p) \cap L(d)$ is in $L_w(p')$ and not in $L_w(q)$ (because of the depth). On the other hand, any tree $t \in L_w(p') \cap L(d) \setminus L_w(q)$ has depth at most n, so an embedding of p' into t maps every descendant edge into a child edge, and hence p embeds into t as well. This gives a reduction to (the negation of) the problem considered in case (2) or (4).

For many cases, we can also prove coNP-completeness:

THEOREM 6.4. *The following are coNP-complete:*
(1) CONTAINMENT *of TPQ(/,//,*) in PQ(/,//);*
(2) CONTAINMENT *of TPQ(/,//,*) in TPQ(//,*);*
(3) S-CONTAINMENT *of TPQ(/,//,*) in TPQ(/,*);*
all w.r.t. a DTD.

These coNP upper bounds follow from two observations. The first one is Observation 6.2. The second one concerns S-SATISFIABILITY of TPQ(/,//,*) in the language of a tree automaton:

OBSERVATION 6.5. SATISFIABILITY *of a TPQ(/,//,*) w.r.t. a non-deterministic tree automaton is in NP.*

The proof of the observation is a rather standard "small model" argument. The result follows immediately from, e.g., Theorem 8 in [8]. We finish the proof of Theorem 6.4 as follows. Observation 6.2 says that, in all three cases, we can build a non-deterministic tree automaton for the language of all trees that satisfy the DTD and do not satisfy the right pattern. In all three cases, containment holds if and only if the left pattern is not satisfiable w.r.t. this tree automaton, which is in coNP by Observation 6.5.

The following theorem involves the technically most difficult hardness proof of the paper. The proof goes through a variant of tiling problems that we call *triomino tiling.* Whereas standard tiling problems [42] use *horizontal* and *vertical* constraints, triomino tiling unifies these to a single kind of constraint in the shape of an *L-triomino.*[3] A triomino constraint restricts how a cell, its horizontal neighbor and its vertical neighbor can be tiled. Our main reason to go through triomino tiling is because it allows us to check the horizontal and vertical constraints *at the same time, and using only the right pattern.* We believe that the triomino tiling problem may be useful in its own respect. We present details in the Appendix.

[3]Readers familiar with Tetris may know the term *tetromino*, which are the "blocks", consisting of four squares, that appear in the game. A triomino has three squares.

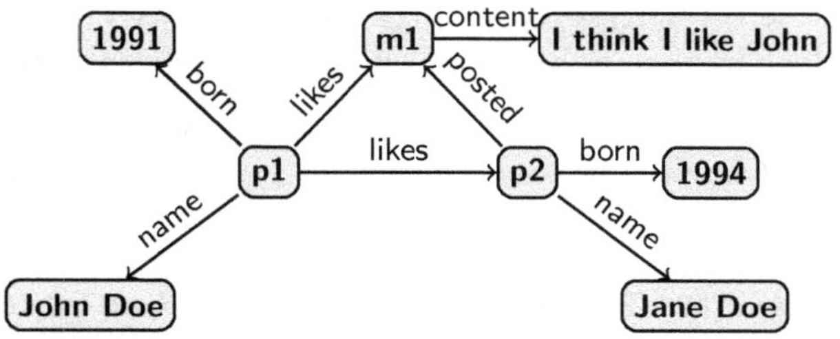

(a) A toy graph database about a social network.

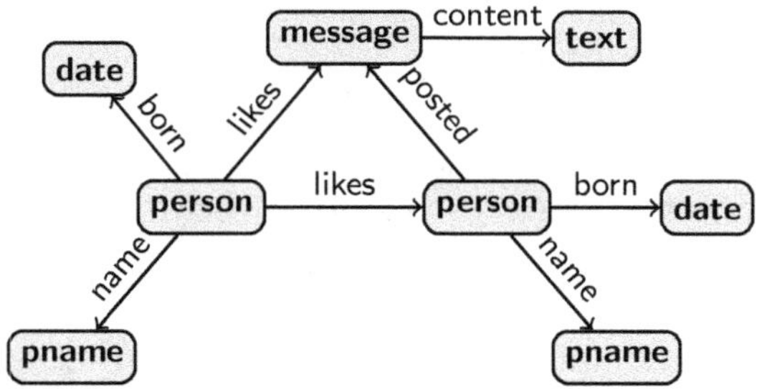

(b) Abstraction of the graph database in (a), only bearing node types and edge labels.

Figure 4: A graph database (4(a)) and its abstraction as a typed graph (4(b)).

THEOREM 6.6. *The following are EXPTIME-complete:*
(1) W-CONTAINMENT *of* PQ(/) *in a* PQ(/, *)*;*
(2) W-CONTAINMENT *of* PQ(//) *in a* PQ(/, *)*;*
(3) S-CONTAINMENT *of* PQ(/) *in a* PQ(/, //, *)*;*
(4) S-CONTAINMENT *of* PQ(//) *in a* PQ(/, //, *)*;*
all w.r.t. a fixed DTD.

7. TREES VERSUS GRAPHS

We explain how the complexity results in the paper can be interpreted in the context of graph databases. We consider two possible abstractions of graph databases in this section. The first is a node-labelled graph and the second is a node- and edge-labelled graph. We note that the standard models of graph databases in the literature are edge-labelled rather than node-labelled (e.g., [4, 30, 32]), but this does not make a difference when transferring our kind of results. In the node- and edge-labelled model, edges will be triples consisting of two nodes and a label (as usual) and nodes will be labelled by a function called type. The intuition is that if a graph represents a social network, for example, we assume that nodes already have information on whether they represent a person, message, or photo. The relations between nodes are modelled as directed edges, e.g., *person x likes message y* is modelled as a directed edge from node x to node y labelled likes, and nodes x and y carry the type person and message respectively. An example graph and its abstraction with types is presented in Figure 4.

7.1 No Schema Information

First we explain the connection to the setting where we do not consider DTDs. Let Γ be a finite alphabet of *types*. A *graph* G over Γ is a triple $(\mathsf{Nodes}(G), \mathsf{Edges}(G), \mathsf{type}^G)$ where $\mathsf{Nodes}(G)$ is a finite set of nodes, $\mathsf{Edges}(G) \subseteq (\mathsf{Nodes}(G))^2$, and $\mathsf{type}^G : \mathsf{Nodes}(G) \to \Gamma$. When G is clear from the context, we often also denote type^G as type. It is a *rooted graph* if it has a special node $\mathsf{root}(G) \in \mathsf{Nodes}(G)$.

A *(weak) embedding* m of a TPQ q (over the letters Γ) on a graph G is defined analogously as on trees, except that we consider $\mathsf{type}(m(v))$ instead of $\mathsf{lab}(m(v))$ and, if $(v_1, v_2) \in \mathsf{Desc}(q)$, then we require that there is a directed path in G from $m(v_1)$ to $m(v_2)$. If G is a rooted graph, then m is a *strong embedding* of q if it is a weak embedding on G and $m(\mathsf{root}(q)) = \mathsf{root}(G)$. We can now define the weak and strong graph languages of q analogously as we did over trees. The small difference is that the strong graph language is a set of *rooted graphs*. Once these notions are established, the definitions of S-CONTAINMENT and W-CONTAINMENT of TPQs over graphs are again analogous as for trees. The next proposition, which was already observed by Miklau and Suciu [33], says that with these definitions, the W-CONTAINMENT and S-CONTAINMENT problems are independent of whether TPQs are interpreted over graphs or over trees.

PROPOSITION 7.1 (SECTION 5.3 IN [33]). *For all fragments $\mathcal{F}_1$ and $\mathcal{F}_2$ of TPQs we consider in this paper, the* W-CONTAINMENT *(resp.,* S-CONTAINMENT*) problem of $\mathcal{F}_1$ in $\mathcal{F}_2$ over graphs is the same as the* W-CONTAINMENT *(resp.,* S-CONTAINMENT*) problem of $\mathcal{F}_1$ in $\mathcal{F}_2$ over trees.*

The proposition implies that all complexity results in Section 3 also hold for TPQs over node-labelled graphs. If one considers *graph databases* [4], that is, graphs in which the edges are triples coming from $\mathsf{Nodes}(G) \times \Sigma \times \mathsf{Nodes}(G)$, and one defines the semantics of TPQs as in Libkin et al. [30], the proposition holds as well.

7.2 Typed Graphs and Schema Information

We extend Proposition 7.1 so that it also connects to satisfiability w.r.t. DTDs. We have to adjust DTDs a little bit since they are not the most natural model for meta-information on graphs. We take some inspiration from Shape Expressions [40, 39]. However, a crucial difference with [40] is that we assume that nodes already have types. That is, in a social network, nodes already have types such as person or message associated to them.

We feel that there are two natural ways of interpreting DTDs over typed graphs. In the first, the DTD only reasons about the types of nodes. In the second we consider graphs that have labelled edges and nodes with associated types and the DTD reasons about pairs consisting of node- and edge labels. We explain both variants next.

Nodes Only. In the first variant, we say that a graph G satisfies a DTD (Γ, d, S_d) *under nodes-only semantics* if, for every node u of G with $\mathsf{type}(u) = a$ and neighbors $\{v_1, \ldots, v_n\} = \{v \mid (u, v) \in \mathsf{Edges}(G)\}$, there exists a permutation σ of $\{1, \ldots, n\}$ such that $\mathsf{type}(v_{\sigma(1)}) \cdots \mathsf{type}(v_{\sigma(n)}) \in L(d(a))$. Finally, if $\mathsf{root}(G)$ exists, we additionally require that $\mathsf{type}(\mathsf{root}(G)) \in S_d$.

Formally, this means that we consider the neighbors of a node in a graph to be unordered and, therefore, we also consider the regular expressions in DTDs to define an unordered language. Here, we need to make a brief discussion about complexity. Testing if a given word (or multiset of labels) is in the language of an unordered regular expression, that is, testing if the above permutation σ exists, is NP-complete [28]. In fact, this is a reason why unordered regular expressions do not seem suitable out of the box for schemas for unordered XML and why the research on the design of schema languages for unordered XML considers restricted regular expressions, see [12]. However, NP-completeness of this problem does not influence the complexity of TPQ containment. The reason is that, since tree pattern queries are already unordered, it does not matter for the complexity of TPQ containment whether they are interpreted on ordered or unordered structures.

We define the nodes-only semantics of TPQs to be the same one as we used for Proposition 7.1. Then we have the following correspondence between graphs and trees:

PROPOSITION 7.2. *For all fragments $\mathcal{F}$ of TPQs we consider in this paper, under the nodes-only semantics of DTDs and TPQs on graphs, the* W-SATISFIABILITY *(resp.,* S-SATISFIABILITY*) problem of $\mathcal{F}$ with respect to DTDs over graphs is the same as the* W-SATISFIABILITY *(resp.,* S-SATISFIABILITY*) problem of $\mathcal{F}$ over trees.*

We note that this proposition requires that the DTDs are *reduced*, which is a condition we assume throughout the paper. Unfortunately there is no longer a strong correspondence for the VALIDITY and CONTAINMENT problems. Actually, we think that already for VALIDITY the complexities may even be different. We comment on this in the conclusions.

Nodes and Edges. The second way of tweaking DTDs for graphs deals with node- and edge labels and is a little bit more technical. First we say how we see such graphs. We let Γ be a finite alphabet of *types* as before and we additionally consider a finite alphabet Σ of *edge labels*, disjoint from Γ. A *typed graph* over (Σ, Γ) is a tuple $G = (\mathsf{Nodes}(G), \mathsf{Edges}(G), \mathsf{type})$ where $\mathsf{Nodes}(G)$ and the mapping $\mathsf{type} : \mathsf{Nodes}(G) \to \Gamma$ are as before, but $\mathsf{Edges}(G) \subseteq (\mathsf{Nodes}(G) \times \Sigma \times \mathsf{Nodes}(G))$.

For typed graphs, we consider DTDs that also reason about pairs of node- and edge labels. More precisely, it uses the alphabet $\Gamma \cup (\Sigma \times \Gamma)$ and its rules are of a restricted form. We first provide an example.

EXAMPLE 7.3. Consider the rules

$$\begin{array}{ll} \mathsf{person} \to (\mathsf{born}, \mathsf{date})(\mathsf{name}, \mathsf{pname})(\mathsf{posted}, \mathsf{message})^* & \\ \qquad\qquad (\mathsf{likes}, \mathsf{message})^*(\mathsf{likes}, \mathsf{person})^* & \\ (\mathsf{born}, \mathsf{date}) & \to \mathsf{date} \\ (\mathsf{name}, \mathsf{pname}) & \to \mathsf{pname} \\ (\mathsf{posted}, \mathsf{message}) & \to \mathsf{message} \\ (\mathsf{likes}, \mathsf{message}) & \to \mathsf{message} \\ (\mathsf{likes}, \mathsf{person}) & \to \mathsf{person} \\ \mathsf{message} & \to (\mathsf{content}, \mathsf{text}) \\ (\mathsf{content}, \mathsf{text}) & \to \mathsf{text} \end{array}$$

When we don't explicitly write a rule for a symbol s, we implicitly assume to have the rule $\mathsf{s} \to \varepsilon$. Notice the difference between rules that only have a type on the left and rules that have a pair on the left. Intuitively, the former rules define the kind of outgoing edges that are allowed from nodes in the graph and the latter rules say, for each edge, the type of node they should point to. (We have these two kinds of rules due to the limited expressive power of DTDs; a DTD can define only one right-hand-side per left-hand symbol.) So, the reason is that a DTD can only control the 1-neighborhood of a node, not the 2-neighborhood.

On a typed graph, the first six rules express that each person has an outgoing edges labelled born that points to a node of type date and an outgoing edge labelled name that points to a node of type pname. Furthermore, a person can have outgoing edges labelled likes that can point to nodes of type message or person and it can have outgoing edges labelled posted that point to nodes of type message. The last two rules express that each message has an outgoing content edge to a text-node. The typed graph in Figure 4(b) satisfies the DTD.

Formally, we say that a DTD is a *graph DTD* if it is of the form $(\Gamma \cup (\Sigma \times \Gamma), d, S_d)$ and the rules in d are only of the form $a \to r$ with $a \in \Gamma$ in $r \in \mathcal{R}(\Sigma \times \Gamma)$ or of the form $(e, a) \to a$ for $e \in \Sigma$ and $a \in \Gamma$.

A typed graph G satisfies d *under nodes/edges semantics* if all the following hold:

- for every node u of G with $\mathsf{type}(u) = a$ and incident edges $\{e_1, \ldots, e_n\} = \{(u, a_i, v_i) \mid (u, a_i, v_i) \in \mathsf{Edges}(G)\}$, there exists a permutation σ of $\{1, \ldots, n\}$ such that $(a_{\sigma(1)}, \mathsf{type}(v_{\sigma(1)})) \cdots (a_{\sigma(n)}, \mathsf{type}(v_{\sigma(n)})) \in L(d(a))$;
- for every edge $e = (u, a, v)$ of G, we have that $\mathsf{type}(v) \in L(d((a, \mathsf{type}(v))))$; and
- if $\mathsf{root}(G)$ exists, then $\mathsf{type}(\mathsf{root}(G)) \in S_d$.

We now explain when a TPQ matches a graph under nodes/edges semantics. Intuitively, this is done by translating the graph to a node-labelled graph and then take the same semantics as we already defined. Formally, let $G = (\mathsf{Nodes}(G), \mathsf{Edges}(G), \mathsf{type}^G)$. We associate to G a node-labelled graph $G_N = (\mathsf{Nodes}(G_N), \mathsf{Edges}(G_N), \mathsf{type}^{G_N})$ over $\Gamma \cup (\Sigma \times \Gamma)$, which is obtained from G as follows:

- $\mathsf{Nodes}(G_N) := \mathsf{Nodes}(G) \uplus \{n_e \mid e \in \mathsf{Edges}(G)\}$;
- $\mathsf{Edges}(G_N) := \{(u, n_e), (n_e, v) \mid e = (u, a, v) \in \mathsf{Edges}(G)\}$;
- for every $u \in Nodes(G)$, $\mathsf{type}^{G_N}(u) := \mathsf{type}^G(u)$;
- for every $n_e \in \mathsf{Nodes}(G_N)$ with $e = (u, a, v)$, we define $\mathsf{type}^{G_N}(n_e) := (a, \mathsf{type}^G(v))$; and
- if $\mathsf{root}(G)$ exists, then $\mathsf{root}(G_N) := \mathsf{root}(G)$.

We now say that G satisfies a TPQ q *under nodes/edges semantics* if G_N satisfies q. Notice that, as in graph DTDs, the TPQ q uses letters from $\Gamma \cup (\Sigma \times \Gamma)$.

PROPOSITION 7.4. *For all fragments $\mathcal{F}$ of TPQs we consider in this paper, under the nodes/edges semantics of DTDs and TPQs on graphs, the* W-SATISFIABILITY *(resp.,* S-SATISFIABILITY*) problem of $\mathcal{F}$ with respect to DTDs over graphs is the same as the* W-SATISFIABILITY *(resp.,* S-SATISFIABILITY*) problem of $\mathcal{F}$ over trees.*

Similarly to Proposition 7.2, this proposition does not generalize to VALIDITY or CONTAINMENT. We are still working on the question which *complexity* results carry over.

8. DISCUSSION AND FUTURE WORK

We made significant progress in the investigation of the complexity of containment of TPQs over trees. The only table that still contains cases that are not yet classified as either "tractable" or complete for a complexity class containing NP or coNP is Table 5.

In Section 7 we discussed a close correspondence between the containment problem for trees and the problem for graphs. In this respect, our biggest open question is to which extent the results for trees can be carried over to graphs for the containment and validity problems with schema information. We know that the validity problem is not the same for trees than for graphs. For example, over trees, the query $a//b$ is valid for the DTD with rules $a \to a + b$ and $b \to \varepsilon$, but this is not true over graphs. The challenge consists of dealing with schemas that are recursive, i.e., allow cycles in graphs.

In this work we presented a manageable amount of existing and newly discovered results that seem to be quite powerful for classifying the complexity of tree pattern containment problems. Research is not about considering large amounts of cases and solving all of them but, only as an illustration, when one would consider all variations of TPQ fragments, weak/strong containment, with fixed DTD or not as "different", then the results mentioned in this paper classify 856 different cases out of 916 total as either in P or complete for a higher complexity class. When one does not care about completeness for the higher class, then 892 cases are classified. Given the rich literature on tree pattern containment, we feel that, in addition to the newly obtained technical results, our work also contributes in making a clearer picture of the problem.

Acknowledgments. We thank Filip Murlak for pointing us to [15] and the anonymous reviewers of PODS 2015 for many helpful remarks.

9. REFERENCES

[1] J. Albert, D. Giammerresi, and D. Wood. Normal form algorithms for extended context free grammars. *Theoretical Computer Science*, 267(1–2):35–47, 2001.

[2] M. Arenas, J. Daenen, F. Neven, M. Ugarte, J. Van den Bussche, and S. Vansummeren. Discovering XSD keys from XML data. In *International Conference on Management of Data (SIGMOD)*, pages 61–72, 2013.

[3] M. Arenas and L. Libkin. XML data exchange: Consistency and query answering. *J. ACM*, 55(2), 2008.

[4] P. Barceló. Querying graph databases. In *Principles of Database Systems (PODS)*, pages 175–188, 2013.

[5] P. Barceló, L. Libkin, A. Poggi, and C. Sirangelo. XML with incomplete information. *Journal of the ACM*, 58(1):4, 2010.

[6] M. Benedikt, W. Fan, and F. Geerts. XPath satisfiability in the presence of DTDs. *Journal of the ACM*, 55(2), 2008.

[7] A. Berglund, S. Boag, D. Chamberlin, M. F. Fernández, M. Kay, J. Robie, and J. Siméon. XML Path Language (XPath) 2.0. Technical report, World Wide Web Consortium, January 2007. W3C Recommendation, http://www.w3.org/TR/2007/REC-xpath20-20070123/.

[8] H. Björklund, W. Martens, and T. Schwentick. Optimizing conjunctive queries over trees using schema information. In *International Symposium on Mathematical Foundations of Computer Science (MFCS)*, pages 132–143, 2008.

[9] H. Björklund, W. Martens, and T. Schwentick. Conjunctive query containment over trees. *Journal of Computer and System Sciences*, pages 450–472, 2010.

[10] H. Björklund, W. Martens, and T. Schwentick. Validity of tree pattern queries with respect to schema information. In *Mathematical Foundations of Computer Science (MFCS)*, pages 171–182, 2013.

[11] S. Boag, D. Chamberlin, M. F. Fernández, D. Florescu, J. Robie, and J. Siméon. XQuery 1.0: An XML query language. Technical report, World Wide Web Consortium, January 2007. W3C Recommendation, http://www.w3.org/TR/2007/REC-xquery-20070123/.

[12] I. Boneva, R. Ciucanu, and S. Staworko. Schemas for unordered XML on a DIME. *CoRR*, abs/1311.7307, 2013.

[13] T. Bray, J. Paoli, C. M. Sperberg-McQueen, E. Maler, and F. Yergeau. Extensible Markup Language XML 1.0 (fifth edition). Technical report, World Wide Web Consortium (W3C), November 2008. W3C Recommendation, http://www.w3.org/TR/2008/REC-xml-20081126/.

[14] J. Cheng, J. X. Yu, B. Ding, P. S. Yu, and H. Wang. Fast graph pattern matching. In *International Conference on Data Engineering, (ICDE)*, pages 913–922, 2008.

[15] C. David, N. Francis, and F. Murlak. Consistency of injective tree patterns. In *Foundations of Software Technology and Theoretical Computer Science (FSTTCS)*, pages 279–290, 2014.

[16] C. David, A. Gheerbrant, L. Libkin, and W. Martens. Containment of pattern-based queries over data trees. In *International Conference on Database Theory (ICDT)*, pages 201–212, 2013.

[17] S. DeRose, E. Maler, and R. Daniel. XML pointer language (XPointer) version 1.0. Technical report, World Wide Web Consortium (W3C), 2001.

[18] S. DeRose, E. Maler, D. Orchard, and N. Walsh. XML linking language (XLink) version 1.1. Technical report, World Wide Web Consortium (W3C), 2010.

[19] D. Figueira. *Reasoning on Words and Trees with Data.* PhD thesis, École Normale Supérieure de Cachan, 2010.

[20] S. Flesca, F. Furfaro, and E. Masciari. On the minimization of XPath queries. *Journal of the ACM*, 55(1), 2008.

[21] S. Gao, C. M. Sperberg-McQueen, H. Thompson, N. Mendelsohn, D. Beech, and M. Maloney. W3C XML Schema Definition Language (XSD) 1.1 part 1: Structures. Technical report, World Wide Web Consortium, April 2009. W3C Recommendation, http://www.w3.org/TR/2009/CR-xmlschema11-1-20090430/.

[22] F. Geerts and W. Fan. Satisfiability of XPath queries with sibling axes. In *International Symposium on Database Programming Languages (DBPL)*, pages 122–137, 2005.

[23] A. Gheerbrant, L. Libkin, and C. Sirangelo. Reasoning about pattern-based XML queries. In *International Conference on Web Reasoning and Rule Systems (RR)*, pages 4–18, 2013.

[24] G. Gottlob, C. Koch, and K. U. Schulz. Conjunctive queries over trees. *Journal of the ACM*, 53(2):238–272, 2006.

[25] K. Hashimoto, Y. Kusunoki, Y. Ishihara, and T. Fujiwara. Validity of positive XPath queries with wildcard in the presence of DTDs. In *Database Programming Languages (DBPL)*, 2011.

[26] M. Kay. XSL Transformations (XSLT) version 2.0. Technical report, World Wide Web Consortium,

January 2007. W3C Recommendation, http://www.w3.org/TR/2007/REC-xslt20-20070123/.

[27] B. Kimelfeld and Y. Sagiv. Revisiting redundancy and minimization in an XPath fragment. In *Extending Database Technology (EDBT)*, pages 61–72, 2008.

[28] E. Kopczynski and A. W. To. Parikh images of grammars: Complexity and applications. In *IEEE Symposium on Logic in Computer Science (LICS)*, pages 80–89, 2010.

[29] E. V. Kostylev, J. L. Reutter, and D. Vrgoč. Containment of data graph queries. In *International Conference on Database Theory (ICDT)*, pages 131–142, 2014.

[30] L. Libkin, W. Martens, and D. Vrgoč. Querying graph databases with XPath. In *International Conference on Database Theory (ICDT)*, pages 129–140, 2013.

[31] W. Martens, F. Neven, and T. Schwentick. Complexity of decision problems for XML schemas and chain regular expressions. *Siam Journal on Computing*, 39(4):1486–1530, 2009.

[32] A. O. Mendelzon and P. T. Wood. Finding regular simple paths in graph databases. *SIAM Journal on Computing*, 24(6):1235–1258, 1995.

[33] G. Miklau and D. Suciu. Containment and equivalence for a fragment of XPath. *Journal of the ACM*, 51(1):2–45, 2004.

[34] F. Murlak. Personal communication.

[35] F. Neven and T. Schwentick. On the complexity of XPath containment in the presence of disjunction, DTDs, and variables. *Logical Methods in Computer Science*, 2(3), 2006.

[36] M. Niewerth and T. Schwentick. Reasoning about XML constraints based on xml-to-relational mappings. In *International Conference on Database Theory (ICDT)*, pages 72–83, 2014.

[37] J. Pérez, M. Arenas, and C. Gutierrez. nsparql: A navigational language for RDF. *Journal of Web Semantics*, 8(4):255–270, 2010.

[38] T. Schwentick. XPath query containment. *Sigmod RECORD*, 33(1):101–109, 2004.

[39] Shape expressions. http://www.w3.org/2001/sw/wiki/ShEx.

[40] S. Staworko, I. Boneva, J. E. Labra Gayo, S. Hym, E. G. Prud'hommeaux, and H. Solbrig. Complexity and expressiveness of ShEx for RDF. In *International Conference on Database Theory (ICDT)*, 2015.

[41] B. ten Cate and C. Lutz. The complexity of query containment in expressive fragments of XPath 2.0. *Journal of the ACM*, 56(6), 2009.

[42] P. van Emde Boas. The convenience of tilings. In *Complexity, Logic and Recursion Theory*, volume 187 of *Lecture Notes in Pure and Applied Mathematics*, pages 331–363. Marcel Dekker Inc., 1997.

[43] P. T. Wood. Containment for XPath fragments under DTD constraints. In *International Conference Database Theory (ICDT)*, 2003. Full version, obtained through personal communication.

[44] Q. Zeng, X. Jiang, and H. Zhuge. Adding logical operators to tree pattern queries on graph-structured data. *PVLDB*, 5(8):728–739, 2012.

APPENDIX

A. TRIOMINO TILING

A *triomino tiling system* is a tuple $S = (T, C, t_f)$ where T is a finite set of *tile types*, $C \subseteq T^3$ a set of *triomino constraints*, and $t_f \in T$ is a *final tile*. An instance of the triomino tiling problem consists of a word $s \in T^*$. Let $s = a_1 \cdots a_n$ such that each $a_i \in T$. A *correct tiling* for S with start s is a function $\lambda : \{1, \ldots, m\} \to T$ for some $m \geq n$ such that

- the start is s, that is $\lambda(i) = a_i$ for every $i \leq n$;
- the triomino constraints are fulfilled, that is, for all $i \in \{1, \ldots, m-n\}$ it holds that $(\lambda(i), \lambda(i+1), \lambda(i+n)) \in C$ and
- the final tile is correct, that is, $\lambda(m) = t_f$.

The analogy with triomino blocks is best seen when thinking of the positions $1, \ldots, m$ as coordinates in an $n \times k$ grid, for some $k \in \mathbb{N}$. Here, each position i corresponds to the coordinate in row $\lceil i/n \rceil$ and column (i modulo n).

The problem CorridorTriominoTiling(S) asks, given a word s, whether there exists a correct tiling for S with start s.

Remark A.1. *There exists a triomino tiling system S such that* CorridorTriominoTiling*(S) is PSPACE-complete.*

Remark A.1 can be shown by reduction from the well-known corridor tiling problem. The remark implies, in particular, that the triomino tiling problem is already hard if the set of tiles is constant.

B. PROOF SKETCH FOR THEOREM 6.6

We present the main lines of a reduction from corridor triomino tiling to containment. This sketch already shows that containment is PSPACE-hard and already contains many important ingredients of the full proof, which is a reduction from a two-player variant of corridor triomino tiling. (The two-player version is EXPTIME-complete.)

Fix a triomino tiling system $S = (T, C, t_f)$ such that CorridorTriominoTiling(S) is PSPACE-hard. From now on, we simply refer to CorridorTriominoTiling(S) as CTT.

For a given instance $s \in T^*$ for CTT we show how to construct patterns p, q and a DTD d such that there exists a solution for s if and only if $L_w(p) \cap L(d) \not\subseteq L_w(q)$. This will show PSPACE-hardness of the considered inclusion problem.

High level description. We will encode correct tilings by trees that conform to a DTD d, into which a pattern p can be weakly embedded, but into which a pattern q cannot be weakly embedded. Pattern p will ensure that the start s is correct. The DTD together with the pattern q will ensure that a tree is indeed a correct encoding of a tiling that also fulfils the constraints and ends with the final tile.

Every node in such a tree will be either on the *trunk* or on a *branch*. The alphabet Σ of the DTD is a disjoint union of Σ_{tr}, called the *trunk alphabet* (containing *trunk letters*) and Σ_{br}, called the *branch alphabet* (containing *branch letters*). We note that Σ will be a fixed, constant-size set. The schema ensures that the root is on the trunk and, for every node on the trunk, its parent, if it exists, is also on the trunk and at most one of its children is on the trunk. So, in every tree that conforms to the DTD, the trunk is a path from the root, that does not necessarily end in a leaf. We use the term *ℓ-nodes* to refer to nodes labeled with $\ell \in \Sigma$. Denote the depth of a node u by depth(u). For $j \in \mathbb{N}$, the j-ancestor of a node u is the ancestor v of u such that depth(v) $=$ depth(u) $- j$. In this case we also call u a *j-descendant* of v.

Tiles are encoded as words of length $k = |T| + 4$ written on the trunk, where T is the set of tiles from the triomino tiling system S. The whole trunk is an encoding of a tiling in the following sense: from the root downwards, first the first tile is encoded, then the second tile is encoded, etc.; at the bottom part of the trunk the last tile of the tiling is encoded.

Recall that triomino constraints should be checked between a tile, its successor, and the tile n positions further. The pattern q in our reduction depends only on the length of the input s and is otherwise the same for every instance: it is a PQ($/, *$) starting with letter a, then having $kn + 2$ wildcards and at the bottom ending with letter b. Note that q does not embed into a tree t if and only if no $(kn + 3)$-ancestor of a b-node is labeled by a.

Branch nodes are used to ensure that the encoding is correct. They enforce the occurrence of many b-nodes, which strongly restrict the possible forms of the trees in the language of the DTD.

Encoding of a tile. Let $T = \{t_1, \ldots, t_{|T|}\}$, where $t_f = t_{|T|}$. We define $\Sigma_{\text{tr}} = \{\#, a, c_1, \ldots, c_{|T|}, d_1, \ldots, d_{|T|-1}, e_1, \ldots, e_{|T|}, f\}$. For every tile there is a unique length k word over Σ_{tr} which encodes that tile. Recall that $k = |T| + 4$. More precisely, the tile t_i, for $i \leq |T| - 2$, is encoded by the word

$$w_i = c_i\, d_{i-1} \cdots d_1\, a\, e_{k-i-3} e_{k+i-4} \cdots e_1\, aa.$$

Note that w_i always has exactly three letters a, at positions $i+1$, $k-1$, and k. Letters $c_1, \ldots, c_{k-4}, d_1, \ldots, d_{k-5}$ are the *first block letters* and $e_1, \ldots, e_{k-4}$ are the *second block letters*. Observe also that none of the blocks is empty and that, in a correct encoding, the only place where aa occurs is at the end of a tile.

There is one special situation, for the final tile. The tile $t_{|T|}$ is encoded as $c_{k-4} d_{k-5} \cdots d_1\, a\, f$. Intuitively, the letter f indicates that there we reached the end of the tiling encoding and therefore the end of the trunk. Note also that the encoding of the final tile is of length $k-2$, so it is shorter than the others. This does not introduce any problems, since the final tile occurs once, at the end of the trunk.

Ensuring the constraints. The triomino constraint $(\lambda(i), \lambda(i+1), \lambda(i+n)) \in C$ imposes that the choice of a tile $\lambda(i+n)$ is restricted w.r.t. tiles $\lambda(i)$ and $\lambda(i+1)$. In the trunk, the encodings of $\lambda(i)$ and $\lambda(i+1)$ are, respectively, nk and $(n-1)k$ levels above the encoding of $\lambda(i+n)$.

Triomino constraints are enforced as follows. For every triple $j = (j_1, j_2, j_3)$ such that $(t_{j_1}, t_{j_2}, t_{j_3})$ is not in C, that is, $(t_{j_1}, t_{j_2}, t_{j_3})$ is forbidden by the constraints, we have a special letter $g_j \in \Sigma_{\text{br}}$, which is responsible for forbidding that triple. (The number of such letters g_j is constant, since T as well as C are constant.) The DTD enforces that the letter g_j always occurs as a child of the letter c_{j_3}. In the DTD we have the following rule

$$g_j \to g_{j,1} + g_{j,2},$$

where $g_{j,1}, g_{j,2} \in \Sigma_{\text{br}}$ are responsible for forbidding the tile t_{j_1} occurring exactly n tiles above and forbidding the tile t_{j_2} occurring exactly $n-1$ tiles above, respectively. That means that the letter $g_{j,1}$ should prevent a $(kn + 2 - j_1)$-ancestor labeled by a, while $g_{j,2}$ should prevent a $(k(n-1) + 2 - j_2)$-ancestor labeled by a. Preventing an ℓ-ancestor labeled by a is realized by having a $(kn + 3 - \ell)$-descendant labeled by b, since the pattern q forbids a $kn + 3$-ancestor of a b-node to be labeled by a. Therefore each $g_{j,1}$ labeled node has a $kn{+}3{-}(kn{+}2{-}j_1) = j_1{+}1$-descendant labeled by b and each $g_{j,2}$ labeled node has a $kn{+}3{-}(k(n{-}1){+}2{-}j_2) = k{+}j_2{+}1$-descendant labeled by b. This is realized by the rules

$$g_{j,1} \to b_{j_1}, \qquad g_{j,2} \to b_{k+j_2},$$
$$b_i \to b_{i-1} \text{ for every } i > 1, \qquad b_1 \to b.$$

Notice that, since j_1, k, and j_2 are constant numbers, these rules are also constant.

Start s. For a tree to be a correct encoding of the tiling instance it has to be ensured that the beginning of the tree starts with s. We enforce it by the pattern p together with the DTD. Pattern p is of the form $\#a w_{j_1} w_{j_2} \cdots w_{j_n}$, where $\#$ is a special symbol occurring nowhere else and the start s is of the form $t_{j_1} t_{j_2} \cdots t_{j_n}$. Furthermore, the DTD requires $\#$ to be the root of the tree, that is $S_d = \{\#\}$. Notice that, due to this unique root symbol, if p weakly embeds into a tree in $L(d)$, then it also strongly embeds into this tree.

Ensuring the correct form. The last and technically most involved condition that has to be checked is that only trees that are of the form mentioned above belong to $(L_w(p) \cap L(d)) \setminus L_w(q)$. This condition is needed to assure that $(L_w(p) \cap L(d)) \setminus L_w(q)$ is nonempty if and only if there is some correct tiling for the instance s.

More precisely, we will enforce that the letters from Σ_{tr} form a path of the form $\#a w_{i_1} w_{i_2} \ldots w_{i_\ell}$ for some $\ell \in \mathbb{N}$ and the last letter of w_{i_ℓ} equals f. The fact that the letters from Σ_{tr} form a path is already enforced by the DTD. Now we show how it is ensured that, on the trunk,

(a) the *aa-block*, that is, the two consecutive a letters, is repeated every k nodes,

(b) in between of every two such aa-blocks the word

$$c_i d_{i-1} \cdots d_1 a e_{k-3-i} \cdots e_1$$

is written, and

(c) below the last aa-block the word $c_{k-4} d_{k-5} \cdots d_1 a f$ is written.

We will ensure (a), (b), and (c) by restricting positions on which letters can occur in the trunk. This will be realized by forcing the property that i-ancestors, for appropriately chosen i, of nodes labeled by some concrete letter cannot be a-nodes.

For $x_1 \leq x_2 \leq x_3 \in \mathbb{N}$ we say that a node u is $(x_1, \hat{x}_2, x_3)$-free if none of its i-ancestors for $i \in (\{x_1, \ldots, x_3\} \setminus \{x_2\})$ is labeled by letter a. Node u in the tree is (x_1, x_3)-*1-free* if it is $(x_1, \hat{x}_2, x_3)$-free for some $x_2 \in \{x_1, \ldots, x_3\}$.

We show now how to ensure that a node is $(nk{-}x, nk{-}y)$-1-free, for constants x, y, that is, x and y do not depend on the instance of CTT. Due to the structure of q, note that it is sufficient to ensure that, for all but one i such that $x{+}3 \leq i \leq y{+}3$, there is some i-descendant labeled by letter b. Consider the following rules of the DTD, which aim at making every $d_{(x,z,y)}$-node $(nk{-}x{+}1, \widehat{nk - z + 1}, nk{-}y{+}1)$-free and every $d_{(x,y)}$-node $(nk - x, nk - y)$-1-free:

$$d_{(x,z,y)} \to b_{x+1} b_{x+2} \cdots b_z b_{z+2} \cdots b_y b_{y+1}$$

(where the sequence on the right is the one consisting of precisely all b_i for $i \in \{x+1, \ldots, z\} \cup \{z+2, \ldots, y+1\}$, so only $z+1$ is missing) and

$$d_{(x,y)} \to d_{(x,x,y)} + d_{(x,x+1,y)} + \cdots + d_{(x,y-1,y)} + d_{(x,y,y)}.$$

Recall that each b_i-node has an i-descendant b-node. As such, the freeness of the $d_{(x,z,y)}$-nodes and the 1-freeness of $d_{(x,y)}$-nodes is immediate.

Notice that, for a node labeled by a trunk letters $\#$, c_i, d_i, e_i, or f, it is determined which trunk letter will label its child. Therefore in order to stabilize the trunk we have only to demand that the child of an a-node is the correct one. There are only four possibilities for a label of a node that has an a-labeled parent: letters a, c_i, e_i, and f. Thus we demand that

(1) every c_i-node is $(nk, nk-(k-3))$-1-free,

(2) every e_i-node is $(nk-(i+2), nk-(k+i-1))$-1-free,

(3) the f-node is $(nk-3, nk-k)$-1-free, similarly to an e_1-node, and

(4) every a-node that has an a-labeled parent is $(nk-1, nk-(k-2))$-1-free.

We can ensure this by enforcing that c_i-nodes always have a sibling labeled by $d_{(0,k-3)}$, e_i-nodes always have a sibling labeled by $d_{(i+2,k+i-1)}$, f-nodes always have a sibling labeled by $d_{(3,k)}$, and a-nodes that have an a-labeled parent always have a sibling labeled by $d_{(1,k-2)}$.

Notice that conditions (1)–(4) indeed assure conditions (a) and (b). Condition (c) is also assured, as f-node has to occur at some moment, because this is the only way how the trunk can be finished. In that case conditions (1)–(4) indeed imply (c). The left pattern enforces that indeed a prefix of the trunk is of the form $\#aw_{i_1}w_{i_2}\ldots w_{i_n}$. Then we can show that every next letter on the trunk is placed correctly. As said before, for a trunk node labeled by a letter other than a, its child being on the trunk is always correctly labeled. In the case of an a-node conditions (1)–(4) assure that the child is appropriately chosen, depending on the shift of the considered node with respect to the period of length k.

Formal definition. We now write the whole definition of the patterns p and q and the DTD.

Pattern p was, in fact, already formally defined before and is of the form $\#aw_{j_1}w_{j_2}\cdots w_{j_n}$, where $\#$ is the special symbol occurring nowhere else and the initial row s is of the form $t_{j_1}t_{j_2}\ldots t_{j_n}$. Since p does not contain descendant edges or a wildcard, we have that $p \in \mathsf{PQ}(/)$.

Pattern q is of the form $a *^{(kn+2)} b$, where again all edges are short. So, $q \in \mathsf{PQ}(/, *)$.

We now turn to the definition of the DTD (Σ, d, S_d). As mentioned before, we have that $S_d = \{\#\}$. The alphabet Σ of the DTD consists of the two parts Σ_{tr} and Σ_{br}:

$$\Sigma_{\text{tr}} = \{\#, a, c_1, \ldots, c_{k-4}, d_1, \ldots, d_{k-5}, e_1, \ldots, e_{k-4}, f\}$$

and

$$\begin{aligned}\Sigma_{\text{br}} = \{&b, b_1, \ldots, b_{2k-4}\}\\ &\cup \{d_{(x,y)}, d_{(x,y,z)} \mid 0 \le x \le z \le y \le 2k-5\}\\ &\cup \{g_j, g_{j,1}, g_{j,2} \mid j = (j_1, j_2, j_3) \in \mathbb{N}^3\\ &\qquad \text{and } (t_{j_1}, t_{j_2}, t_{j_3}) \notin C\}.\end{aligned}$$

The rules in the DTD are the following:

$$\begin{aligned}&\# \to a, &&\\ &d_i \to d_{i-1} \text{ for } i>1, && d_1 \to a,\\ &e_i \to e_{i-1} \text{ for } i>1, && e_1 \to a,\\ &f \to \varepsilon. &&\end{aligned}$$

Let $s_i = g_{j^1}g_{j^2}\ldots g_{j^r}$, where $j^1, \ldots, j^r$ are all the triples of the form (k_1, k_2, i) for which $(t_{k_1}, t_{k_2}, t_i) \notin C$. We have also the rules:

$$c_i \to d_{i-1}s_i \text{ for } i>1, \qquad c_1 \to as_1,$$

and

$$\begin{aligned}a \to ad_{(1,k-2)} &+ \Big(\bigcup_{1\le i\le k-4} c_i d_{(0,k-3)}\Big)\\ &+ \Big(\bigcup_{3\le i\le k-4} e_i d_{(i+2,k+i-1)}\Big) + fd_{(3,k)}\Big).\end{aligned}$$

The letters from Σ_{br} have the following rules:

$$\begin{aligned}&b_i \to b_{i-1} \text{ for every } i>1, && b_1 \to b,\\ &b \to \varepsilon, && g_j \to g_{j,1} + g_{j,2},\\ &g_{j,1} \to b_{j_1}, && g_{j,2} \to b_{k+j_2},\end{aligned}$$

where we assume that $j = (j_1, j_2, j_3) \in \mathbb{N}^3$. The more complicated ones are:

$$d_{(x,y,z)} \to b_{x+1}b_{x+2}\cdots b_z b_{z+2}\cdots b_y b_{y+1},$$

$$d_{(x,y)} \to d_{(x,x,y)} + d_{(x,x+1,y)} + \ldots + d_{(x,y-1,y)} + d_{(x,y,y)}$$

for all $0 \le x \le z \le y \le 2k-5$. We note that actually, not all of these last rules are needed.

Efficient Evaluation and Approximation of Well-designed Pattern Trees

Pablo Barceló
Center for Semantic Web Research & Dept. of Comp. Science, University of Chile
pbarcelo@dcc.uchile.cl

Reinhard Pichler
Faculty of Informatics
Vienna University of Technology
pichler@dbai.tuwien.ac.at

Sebastian Skritek
Faculty of Informatics
Vienna University of Technology
skritek@dbai.tuwien.ac.at

ABSTRACT

Conjunctive queries (CQs) fail to provide an answer when the pattern described by the query does not exactly match the data. CQs might thus be too restrictive as a querying mechanism when data is semistructured or incomplete. The semantic web therefore provides a formalism – known as *well-designed pattern trees* (WDPTs) – that tackles this problem: WDPTs allow us to match patterns over the data, if available, but do not fail to give an answer otherwise. Here we abstract away the specifics of semantic web applications and study WDPTs over arbitrary relational schemas.

Our language properly subsumes the class of CQs. Hence, WDPT evaluation is intractable. We identify structural properties of WDPTs that lead to tractability of various variants of the evaluation problem. For checking if a WDPT is equivalent to one in our tractable class, we prove 2EXPTIME-membership. As a corollary, we obtain fixed-parameter tractability of (variants of) the evaluation problem. Our techniques also allow us to develop a theory of approximations for WDPTs.

Categories and Subject Descriptors

H.2.3 [**Database Management**]: Languages—*Query Languages*

General Terms

Algorithms, Theory

Keywords

RDF; well-designed pattern trees; efficient query answering; containment; subsumption; approximations

1. INTRODUCTION

Conjunctive queries (CQs) constitute the core of the query languages for relational databases and also the most intensively studied querying mechanism in the database theory community. But CQs suffer from a serious drawback when dealing with information that is semistructured or incomplete, or when users do not have a good understanding of the schema that underlies the data: CQs fail to provide an answer when the pattern described by the query does not exactly match the data.

The semantic web therefore provides formalisms to overcome this problem [20]. We concentrate on the simplest such formalism, which corresponds to the {AND,OPT}-fragment of SPARQL – the standard query language for the semantic web data model (RDF). This fragment allows the user not only to specify patterns by taking conjunctions of atoms (using the AND-operator) – in the same way as CQs do – but also to match patterns over the data, if available, without failing to give an answer otherwise. This is precisely the role of the OPT-operator, which allows for optional matching and essentially corresponds to the left-outer join operator in the relational algebra.

Example 1. Consider the following {AND,OPT}-SPARQL query that is posed over a database that stores information about bands and records:[1]

$$\Big(((x, \texttt{recorded\_by}, y)\ \mathsf{AND}\ (x, \texttt{published}, \text{“after\_2010”})) \ \mathsf{OPT}\ (x, \texttt{NME\_rating}, z) \Big)\ \mathsf{OPT}\ (y, \texttt{formed\_in}, z'). \quad (1)$$

This query retrieves all pairs (b, r) such that r is a record of band b that was published during this decade. This is specified by the pattern $(x, \texttt{recorded\_by}, y)$ AND $(x, \texttt{published\_in}, \text{“after\_2010”})$. Furthermore, whenever possible this query also retrieves (one or both of) the following pieces of data: the rating t of record r as declared by the NME magazine and the year t' in which band b was formed. In other words, in addition to (b, r) we also retrieve t and/or t' if they can be found in the database. This is specified by the atoms $(x, \texttt{NME\_rating}, z)$ and $(y, \texttt{formed\_in}, z')$ following the respective OPT-operators.

Pérez et al. noticed that a non-constrained interaction of the operators AND and OPT in SPARQL may lead to undesired behavior [18]. This motivated the definition of a better behaved syntactic restriction of the language, known as *well-designed* {AND,OPT}-SPARQL. In particular, the query in Example 1 is well-designed. Among other things,

[1]Note that we are using here the more algebraic-style notation of [18] rather than the official SPARQL syntax of [20].

PODS'15, May 31–June 4, 2015, Melbourne, Victoria, Australia.
Copyright © 2015 ACM 978-1-4503-2757-2/15/05 ...$15.00.
http://dx.doi.org/10.1145/2745754.2745767 .

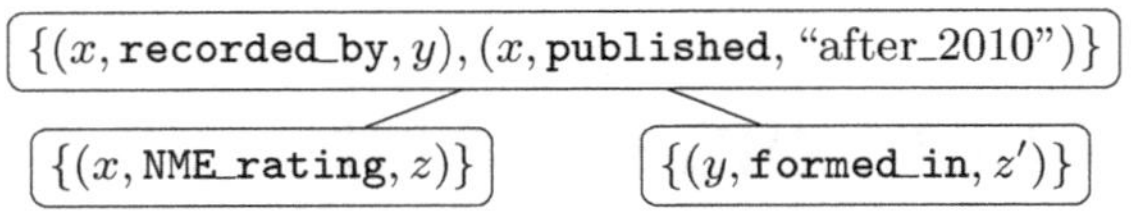

{(x, recorded_by, y), (x, published, "after_2010")}
{(x, NME_rating, z)}
{(y, formed_in, z')}

Figure 1: WDPT representing query (1) from Example 1.

queries in this fragment are more natural than the full language [18], allow for lower complexity of evaluation [18], and lend themselves to optimization techniques [17, 19]. Moreover, they allow for a natural tree representation, known as *well-designed pattern trees*, or WDPTs [17].

Intuitively, a WDPT p consists of a tree T rooted in a distinguished node r and a function that labels each node of T with a set of RDF atoms. The condition of being well-designed imposes that appearances of the same variable in different nodes of T must be connected. Each node of a WDPT p represents a conjunction of atoms, while the nesting of optional matching is represented by the tree structure of p. For instance, the query in Example 1 can be represented as the WDPT in Figure 1.

The semantics of WDPT p is as follows. With each subtree T' of T rooted in r we associate a CQ $r_{T'}$ defined by the conjunction of all atoms in the nodes of T'. The evaluation of WDPT p over database $\mathcal{D}$ consists then of all "maximal" answers to the CQs of the form $r_{T'}$. That is, we take the union of all answers to the CQs of the form $r_{T'}$, for T' a subtree of T rooted in r, and then remove all those answers that are "extended" by some other answer in the set. We revisit Example 1 to illustrate these ideas.

Example 2. Consider an RDF database $\mathcal{D}$ consisting of triples ("Our_love", `recorded_by`, "Caribou"), ("Our_love", `published`, "after_2010"), ("Swim", `recorded_by`, "Caribou"), ("Swim", `published`, "after_2010"), ("Swim", `NME_ranking`, "2"). The evaluation over $\mathcal{D}$ of the WDPT in Figure 1, and, therefore, of the query in (1), consists of partial mappings μ_1 and μ_2 defined on variables x, y, z, z' such that: (1) μ_1 is only defined on x and y in such a way that $\mu_1(x) =$ "Our_love" and $\mu_2(y) =$ "Caribou", and (2) μ_2 is defined on x, y and z in such a way that $\mu_1(x) =$ "Swim", $\mu_2(y) =$ "Caribou", and $\mu_2(z) =$ "2".

The expressive power of WDPTs is limited due to the absence of projection, a feature that CQs enjoy. Consequently, WDPTs are often enhanced with projection as a way to increase their expressiveness and to obtain a proper extension of the class of CQs over RDF vocabularies [17, 19]. In this paper we concentrate on this extended class of WDPTs.

Example 3. For the WDPT from Example 1, one might decide to project out the variable x. This would result in restricting the mappings μ_1 and μ_2 from Example 2 to μ_1' and μ_2' in such a way that: (1) μ_1' is only defined on y with $\mu_1'(y) =$ "Caribou", and (2) μ_2' is defined on y and z and it holds that $\mu_2'(y) =$ "Caribou" and $\mu_2'(z) =$ "2".

Our view is that WDPTs are of interest not only for semantic web applications, but also for every application that needs to handle semistructured or incomplete data. This motivates our study of WDPTs over arbitrary relational schemas, abstracting away from the specifics of the semantic web data model – RDF – which only allows for triples in the nodes of WDPTs (or, in other words, relational atoms over a single ternary relation).

Despite the importance of WDPTs, very little is known about some fundamental problems related to them. In particular, no in-depth study has been carried out regarding efficient evaluation of these queries, a problem that permeates the literature on CQs and its extensions [21, 12, 13, 16, 5]. Likewise, restrictions on WDPTs to decrease the complexity of basic static query analysis tasks [19] such as testing containment are largely unexplored. Topics strongly related to the identification of tractable fragments of query evaluation are semantic query optimization and query approximation. There we ask if some query is equivalent to or can at least be "approximated" by a query from a tractable class. These questions have recently received quite some interest in case of CQs and conjunctive regular path queries over graph databases [10, 5, 4]. So far, nothing is known in case of WDPTs.

The main goal of this work is to initiate a systematic study of tractable fragments of WDPTs for query evaluation and to apply these fragments to fundamental questions in the areas of query analysis, semantic optimization, and approximation.

Efficient evaluation of WDPTs. Evaluation of WDPTs is defined in terms of CQ evaluation, which is an intractable problem in general. Therefore, our goal of identifying tractable classes of WDPTs naturally calls for a restriction of the classes of CQ patterns allowed in them. In particular, there has been a flurry of activity around the topic of determining which classes of CQs admit efficient evaluation that could be reused in our scenario [21, 12, 13]. We concentrate here on two of the most fundamental classes: those of bounded *treewidth* [8, 10] and *hypertreewidth* [13]. We denote by $\mathsf{TW}(k)$ and $\mathsf{HW}(k)$ the CQs of treewidth and hypertreewidth at most k, for $k \geq 1$. Queries in these classes even lie in the parallelizable class LOGCFL [12, 13].

The restriction to tractable classes of CQ-evaluation has already been successfully applied in the context of WDPTs without projection. It is known, in particular, that a very mild condition known as *local tractability* leads to efficient evaluation [17]. This condition enforces each node in the WDPT to contain a set of relational atoms from one of our tractable classes of CQs, namely $\mathsf{TW}(k)$ or $\mathsf{HW}(k)$. Nevertheless, it is also known that this condition does not lead to tractability for the more expressive WDPTs with projection that we study here [17]. Then the question remains: When is the evaluation of WDPTs tractable or, more precisely, which natural conditions can be added to local tractability to achieve tractable WDPT evaluation? We shall identify such a condition – called *bounded interface* – that limits by a constant the number of variables that each node in a WDPT can share with its children. Notably, similar conditions have been recently applied to obtain reasonable bounds for the containment problem of Datalog into unions of CQs [6]).

Due to the nature of WDPTs, two other evaluation problems – called the *partial* and *maximal* evaluation problems – are of importance [18, 2]. The first one refers to checking whether a mapping μ is a *partial answer* to the evaluation $p(\mathcal{D})$ of a WDPT p over a database $\mathcal{D}$; i.e., whether there is a mapping $\mu' \in p(\mathcal{D})$ that "extends" μ. The second problem asks if μ is maximal among all answers in $p(\mathcal{D})$. (In the presence of projection, it may happen that some partial mapping and also a proper extension of this mapping are solutions of a WDPT. E.g., in Example 3, μ_1' and also its extension μ_2' are solutions.) We shall identify tractable fragments also for these problems by introducing the notion of *global tractability*. Here, we restrict every CQ $r_{T'}$ represented by a subtree T' of the WDPT T to belong to $\mathsf{TW}(k)$ or $\mathsf{HW}(k)$. We show that global tractability suffices to ensure tractability of the latter problems even though it is a weaker condition than local tractability plus bounded interface.

Containment and subsumption. Containment is a crucial static analysis task that amounts to checking whether the evaluation of a query q is necessarily contained in the evaluation of another query q' (often written as $q \subseteq q'$). The containment problem for CQs is known to be NP-complete [7]. In contrast, it becomes undecidable for WDPTs [19] and remains so even for our restriction to local tractability and bounded interface. The same holds for the equivalence problem (i.e., checking whether the evaluation of q necessarily coincides with the evaluation of q').

It is known that WDPT containment may display some unintuitive behavior, which motivated the introduction of a meaningful variant of it known as *subsumption* [3]. This is the problem of checking whether every answer of a WDPT p over any database $\mathcal{D}$ can be "extended" to an answer of WDPT p' over $\mathcal{D}$ (we denote this by $p \sqsubseteq p'$). The corresponding notion of equivalence is then *subsumption-equivalence*, where we ask if both directions $p \sqsubseteq p'$ and $p' \sqsubseteq p$ hold. In sharp contrast to containment, subsumption for WDPTs is known to be decidable and complete for the class Π_2^P [17]. Subsumption-equivalence can be shown to have the same behavior. We will investigate in this context whether restrictions to tractable classes of WDPT evaluation alleviate the complexity of checking subsumption or subsumption-equivalence. Our main result will be that the restriction to tractable classes of query evaluation allows us to reduce the complexity to coNP but not any further.

Semantic optimization of WDPTs. We introduce several syntactic restrictions on WDPTs that lead to tractability of (variants of) evaluation. As a general method for finding larger classes of queries with good evaluation properties, one typically explores the *semantic space* defined by the syntactical restrictions that yield tractability; this space is defined by all queries that are equivalent to one in the well-behaved class (see, e.g., [10, 4, 5]). In this context the following are the two most important questions:

1. Is it decidable to check whether a query is equivalent to one in the well-behaved syntactically defined class?
2. Can the evaluation problem be solved more efficiently for queries equivalent to one in a well-behaved class?

Positive answers to these questions have been provided in the context of CQs [10] and conjunctive regular path queries over graph databases [5]. For example, regarding question (1) it is known that verifying if a CQ is equivalent to one in $\mathsf{TW}(k)$ is in NP. For question (2) it can be proved that the evaluation problem for those CQs that are equivalent to one in $\mathsf{TW}(k)$ is in PTIME [10]. Here we investigate these questions for WDPTs.

Some care is required in fixing the appropriate setting for this investigation. For instance, since classical equivalence is undecidable for WDPTs we have to content ourselves with the relaxed notion of equivalence based on subsumption introduced earlier. But subsumption-equivalence only preserves partial and maximal answers. We shall therefore focus on the partial and maximal evaluation problems and choose global tractability as the corresponding tractability criterion of WDPTs. Our main finding will be a positive answer to both questions (1) and (2) above in this setting.

Approximations of WDPTs. When a query q is not equivalent to one in a well-behaved class $\mathcal{Q}$ it might be convenient to compute a $\mathcal{Q}$-*approximation* of q. This is a query $q' \in \mathcal{Q}$ that is maximal (with respect to $\subseteq$) among all queries in $\mathcal{Q}$ that are contained in q. Intuitively, q' is sound with respect to q (since $q' \subseteq q$) and provides the best approximation to q among all queries in $\mathcal{Q}$ that are sound for $\mathcal{Q}$.

The notion of approximations is by now well-understood in the context of CQs [4]. For instance, $\mathsf{TW}(k)$-approximations of CQs always exist and can be computed in single-exponential time. These results allow us to explain the role of approximations. In general, the evaluation of a CQ q on a database $\mathcal{D}$ is of the order $|\mathcal{D}|^{O(|q|)}$, which might be prohibitively expensive for a large dataset $\mathcal{D}$ even if q is small. On the other hand, the previous properties imply that computing and running an approximation of a CQ q on a database $\mathcal{D}$ takes time $O(|\mathcal{D}| \cdot 2^{t(|q|)})$, for some polynomial $t : \mathbb{N} \to \mathbb{N}$. This is much faster than $|\mathcal{D}|^{O(|q|)}$ on large databases. Thus, if the quality of the approximation is good, we may prefer to run this faster query instead of q.

Our techniques allow us to develop a thorough theory of approximations for WDPTs. Again, we define approximations via subsumption instead of containment. Furthermore, we look for approximations by WDPTs of the globally tractable classes. Our main finding is that approximations in these classes always exist, can be computed in double-exponential time, and have at most single-exponential size.

Unions of WDPTs. We finally study unions of WDPTs (UWDPTs) as a natural extension of WDPTs. For the variants of query evaluation considered here, all results on WDPTs easily carry over to UWDPTs. In contrast, for semantic optimization and approximation by tractable classes of UWDPTs, we shall reveal a huge difference between WDPTs and UWDPTs. By establishing a close connection between UWDPTs and unions of CQs, we can apply the theory of approximations of CQs to WDPTs. This will allow us to prove significantly better complexity bounds for the problems studied in the context of semantic optimization and approximation.

Organization and main results. In Section 2, we recall some basic notions and results on CQs and WDPTs. A conclusion and outlook to future work are given in Section 7. Our main results are detailed in Sections 3 – 6, namely:

- The problem of finding tractable classes of WDPTs is studied in Section 3. Our main result states that WDPTs which enjoy local tractability and bounded interface can be evaluated in LOGCFL. Since our classes properly contain CQs of bounded treewidth and hypertreewidth, we obtain relevant extensions of these well-known tractable classes of CQs. We also study two further variants of query evaluation, namely partial evaluation and maximal evaluation. We show that global tractability suffices to ensure tractability of these two problems. Interestingly, it does not suffice to obtain tractability for the exact evaluation problem. In fact, we show that global tractability is a strictly weaker condition than local tractability plus bounded interface.

- We dedicate Section 4 to the study of containment and subsumption. Subsumption has already been known to be Π_2^P-complete [17]. We establish the same complexity classification for subsumption-equivalence and show that Π_2^P-completeness of both subsumption and subsumption-equivalence continues to hold even under the restriction to local tractability. This complexity is then shown to drop to coNP-completeness under the further restriction of the WDPTs to global tractability. In case of testing subsumption $p \sqsubseteq p'$, we also identify a significant asymmetry in that coNP-membership only depends on the restriction of p', while p may be an arbitrary WDPT.

- Section 5 contains our investigation of semantic optimization and approximations. Our main finding in terms of semantic optimization is that the problem of checking whether a WDPT is subsumption-equivalent to one in our tractable classes is decidable in $\text{NEXPTIME}^{\text{NP}}$. From this we get as immediate corollary that the partial and maximal evaluation problems for those WDPTs which are subsumption-equivalent to one in a tractable classes are *fixed-parameter tractable* (taking the size of the WDPT as parameter).[2] As far as the approximation in the globally tractable classes of WDPTs is concerned, we show that such approximations always exist, can be computed in double-exponential time, and have at most single-exponential size. We also prove that the exponential blowup in the size of a WDPT approximation cannot be avoided. The total time for computing and running an approximation of a WDPT p on a database $\mathcal{D}$ thus takes time $O(|\mathcal{D}| \cdot 2^{2^{t(|p|)}})$, for some polynomial $t : \mathbb{N} \to \mathbb{N}$. For big $\mathcal{D}$, this is in general faster than directly evaluating p over $\mathcal{D}$.

- In Section 6 we study the extension of WDPTs to unions of WDPTs. For the variants of query evaluation considered here, all results on WDPTs easily carry over to UWDPTs. We can thus establish for UWDPTs the analogous tractability results as for WDPTs. For instance, unions of WDPTs that are locally tractable and have bounded interface can be evaluated in LOGCFL. The same holds for unions of globally tractable WDPTs in the context of partial and maximal evaluation. In contrast, for semantic optimization and approximation by tractable classes of UWDPTs, we shall reveal a huge difference between WDPTs and UWDPTs. More precisely, we obtain better bounds for the complexity of (1) checking whether a UWDPT ϕ is equivalent to a union ϕ' of tractable WDPTs, and (2) checking if a union ϕ' of tractable WDPTs is an approximation of a UWDPT ϕ. In fact, both problems are Π_2^P-hard. Depending on whether we define global tractability via treewidth or hypertreewidth, we get an upper bound of Π_2^P or Π_3^P, respectively. This is in stark contrast to single WDPTs, where we essentially obtained double exponential upper bounds for the analogous problems.

Proof sketches for most results are provided in Appendix A. Full proofs will be provided in a full version.

[2]Recall that the evaluation problem for a class $\mathcal{Q}$ of queries is fixed-parameter tractable w.r.t. the size of the query, if there exists a computable function $f : \mathbb{N} \to \mathbb{N}$ and a constant $k \geq 1$ such that evaluating a query $q \in \mathcal{Q}$ over a database $\mathcal{D}$ can be done in time $O(|\mathcal{D}|^k \cdot f(|q|))$.

2. PRELIMINARIES

Conjunctive queries. Let $\mathbf{U}$ and $\mathbf{X}$ be disjoint countably infinite sets of constants and variables, respectively. Assume that σ is a relational schema. A *relational atom* over σ is an expression of the form $R(\bar{v})$, where R is a relation symbol in σ of arity $n > 0$ and $\bar{v}$ is an n-tuple over $\mathbf{X} \cup \mathbf{U}$. A *database* $\mathcal{D}$ over σ is a set of relational atoms without variables over σ.

A *conjunctive query* (CQ) q over σ is a rule of the form:

$$\text{Ans}(\bar{x}) \leftarrow R_1(\bar{v}_1), \ldots, R_m(\bar{v}_m), \quad (2)$$

where each $R_i(\bar{v}_i)$ $(1 \leq i \leq m)$ is a relational atom in σ and $\bar{x}$ is a tuple of distinct variables among the ones that appear in the $\bar{v}_i$'s. We often write this CQ as $q(\bar{x})$ in order to denote that $\bar{x}$ is the tuple of *free* variables of q.

The semantics of CQs is defined in terms of *homomorphisms*. Let $\mathcal{D}$ be a database over σ. A homomorphism from a CQ $q(\bar{x})$ of the form (2) to $\mathcal{D}$ is a partial mapping $h : \mathbf{X} \to \mathbf{U}$ such that $R_i(h(\bar{v}_i)) \in \mathcal{D}$,[3] for $1 \leq i \leq m$. We denote by $h_{\bar{x}}$ the restriction of h to the variables in $\bar{x}$. The *evaluation* $q(\mathcal{D})$ of $q(\bar{x})$ over $\mathcal{D}$ is the set of all mappings of the form $h_{\bar{x}}$, such that h is a homomorphism from q to $\mathcal{D}$.[4]

For comparing partial mappings, the notion of subsumption is useful: let $h, h' : \mathbf{X} \to \mathbf{U}$ be partial mappings, and assume that X and X' are the subsets of $\mathbf{X}$ where h and h' are defined, respectively. Then we say that h is *subsumed* by h', denoted $h \sqsubseteq h'$, if $X \subseteq X'$ and $h(x) = h'(x)$, for each $x \in X \cap X'$. If $h \sqsubseteq h'$ but it is not the case that $h' \sqsubseteq h$, then we write $h \sqsubset h'$.

Pattern trees. When data is inherently incomplete, it is convenient to work with a proper extension of the class of CQs known as *pattern trees.* Intuitively, a pattern tree allows the user to specify patterns over the data that should be recovered, if available, but do not force the query to fail to give an answer otherwise.

We concentrate here on the class of *well-designed* pattern trees (WDPTs), which has received considerable attention in the semantic web literature. As shown in [17], WDPTs provide an intuitive representation of well-designed {AND,OPT}-SPARQL [18]. WDPTs have been used extensively in analyzing query evaluation and in static query analysis of SPARQL [17, 18, 19].

Intuitively, the nodes of a WDPT represent CQs (called "basic graph patterns" in the semantic web context) while the tree structure of a WDPT represents the nesting of optional matching. We formalize the class of WDPTs below.

Definition 1. (WDPTs) A *well-designed pattern tree* (WDPT) over a relational schema σ is a tuple $(T, \lambda, \bar{x})$, such that the following holds:

1. T is a tree rooted in a distinguished node r and λ maps each node t in T to a set of relational atoms over σ.

2. For every variable y that appears in T, the set of nodes of T where y is mentioned is connected.

3. We have that $\bar{x}$ is a tuple of distinct variables mentioned in T, which correspond to the *free variables* of the WDPT.

[3]As usual, we write $h(v_1, \ldots, v_n)$ for $(h(v_1), \ldots, h(v_n))$, and define $h(u) = u$ for each constant $u \in \mathbf{U}$.

[4]Our definition of $q(\mathcal{D})$ slightly departs from the traditional one in which $q(\mathcal{D})$ is the set of all tuples of the form $h(\bar{x})$, for h a homomorphism from q to $\mathcal{D}$.

We say that $(T, \lambda, \bar{x})$ is *projection-free*, if $\bar{x}$ contains all variables mentioned in T.

Pairs (T, λ) that satisfy condition (1) correspond to the natural extension of pattern trees studied in the semantic web context to arbitrary schemas. Condition (2) is the one that defines well-designedness [18]. Projection-free WDPTs are of importance in the semantic web context [17, 18].

Assume $p = (T, \lambda, \bar{x})$ is a WDPT over σ. We write r to denote the root of T. Given a subtree T' of T rooted in r, we define $q_{T'}$ to be the CQ $\text{Ans}(\bar{y}) \leftarrow R_1(\bar{v}_1), \ldots, R_m(\bar{v}_m)$, where the $R_i(\bar{v}_i)$'s are the relational atoms that label the nodes of T', i.e.,

$$\{R_1(\bar{v}_1), \ldots, R_m(\bar{v}_m)\} = \bigcup_{t \in T'} \lambda(t),$$

and $\bar{y}$ are all the variables that are mentioned in T'.

We write $|p|$ to denote the *size* of p in standard relational notation – which corresponds to the size of CQ q_T. By slight abuse of notation, we often identify nodes and subtrees in p with their labels. For example, we shall speak of a homomorphism from subtree T' to subtree T'' to refer to a mapping between the atoms occurring in the labels of the nodes in these subtrees.

Semantics of WDPTs. We define the semantics of WDPTs by naturally extending their interpretation under semantic web vocabularies [17, 19]. The intuition behind the semantics of a WDPT $(T, \lambda, \bar{x})$ is as follows. Each subtree T' of T rooted in r describes a pattern, namely CQ $q_{T'}$. A mapping h satisfies (T, λ) over a database $\mathcal{D}$, if it is "maximal" among the mappings that satisfy the patterns defined by the subtrees of T. This means, h satisfies the pattern defined by some subtree T' of T, and there is no way to "extend" h to satisfy the pattern of a bigger subtree T'' of T. The evaluation of WDPT $(T, \lambda, \bar{x})$ over $\mathcal{D}$ corresponds then to the projection over the variables in $\bar{x}$ of the mappings h that satisfy (T, λ) over $\mathcal{D}$. We formalize this next.

Definition 2. (Semantics of WDPTs) Let us consider a WDPT $p = (T, \lambda, \bar{x})$ and a database $\mathcal{D}$ over σ.

- A *homomorphism* from p to $\mathcal{D}$ is a partial mapping $h : \mathbf{X} \to \mathbf{U}$, for which it is the case that there is a subtree T' of T rooted in r (the distinguished root node of T) such that $h \in q_{T'}(\mathcal{D})$.
- The homomorphism h is *maximal* if there is no homomorphism h' from p to $\mathcal{D}$ such that $h \sqsubset h'$.

The *evaluation* of WDPT $p = (T, \lambda, \bar{x})$ over $\mathcal{D}$, denoted $p(\mathcal{D})$, corresponds to all mappings of the form $h_{\bar{x}}$, such that h is a maximal homomorphism from p to $\mathcal{D}$.

Notice that WDPTs properly extend CQs. In fact, assume $q(\bar{x})$ is a CQ of the form $\text{Ans}(\bar{x}) \leftarrow R_1(\bar{v}_1), \ldots, R_m(\bar{v}_m)$. Then $q(\bar{x})$ is equivalent to WDPT $p = (T, \lambda, \bar{x})$, where T consists of a single node r and $\lambda(r) = \{R_1(\bar{v}_1), \ldots, R_m(\bar{v}_m)\}$. In other words, $q(\mathcal{D}) = p(\mathcal{D})$, for each database $\mathcal{D}$. We typically do not distinguish between a CQ and the single node WDPT that represents it. On the other hand, as illustrated in Example 1, WDPTs express interesting properties that cannot be expressed as CQs.

RDF well-designed pattern trees. By the nature of semantic web vocabularies, WDPTs are defined in such context over a schema that consists of a single ternary relation. We call these *RDF WDPTs*. As recalled above, RDF WDPTs are equal in expressive power to well-designed SPARQL restricted to the AND and OPT operators [17, 18]. All lower bounds obtained in our paper can be proven to hold even for RDF WDPTs. Hence, all our results continue to hold in the RDF scenario.

3. EFFICIENT EVALUATION OF WDPTS

In this section we study the complexity of the evaluation problem for different classes $\mathcal{C}$ of WDPTs. This problem is formally defined as follows:

PROBLEM :	$\text{EVAL}(\mathcal{C})$.
INPUT :	A database $\mathcal{D}$ and a WDPT $p \in \mathcal{C}$ over σ, and a partial mapping $h : \mathbf{X} \to \mathbf{U}$.
QUESTION :	Is $h \in p(\mathcal{D})$?

The complexity of $\text{EVAL}(\mathcal{C})$ has been studied for the case when $\mathcal{C}$ is the class $\mathcal{C}_{\text{all}}$ of all WDPTs or the class $\mathcal{C}_{\text{pf}}$ of projection-free WDPTs. This is summarized next:

THEOREM 1. *The following hold:*

1. $\text{EVAL}(\mathcal{C}_{\text{all}})$ *is* Σ_2^P*-complete [17].*
2. $\text{EVAL}(\mathcal{C}_{\text{pf}})$ *is* coNP*-complete [18].*

That is, the evaluation problem is intractable (coNP-hard) even for the simple class of projection-free WDPTs. For the class of all WDPTs the complexity jumps to the second-level of the polynomial hierarchy. This raises the need for understanding which classes of WDPTs can be evaluated in polynomial time.

Evaluation of WDPTs is defined in terms of CQ evaluation, which is an intractable problem in general. Therefore, our goal of identifying tractable classes of WDPTs naturally calls for a restriction of the classes of CQ patterns allowed in them. This idea has already been successfully applied for obtaining tractable classes of projection-free WDPTs [17]. Extending this to the class of WDPTs with projection requires new conditions, which we develop in this section. It is important first, however, to review some of the classes of CQs that can be evaluated efficiently.

3.1 Tractable evaluation for CQs

The evaluation problem for a class $\mathcal{C}$ of CQs, denoted CQ-$\text{EVAL}(\mathcal{C})$, is defined analogously to the case of WDPTs. That is, CQ-$\text{EVAL}(\mathcal{C})$ is the problem of checking if $h \in q(\mathcal{D})$, given a database $\mathcal{D}$, a CQ $q \in \mathcal{C}$ and a partial mapping $h : \mathbf{X} \to \mathbf{U}$.

It is known that, without further restrictions, the evaluation problem for CQs is intractable; in particular, CQ-$\text{EVAL}(\mathcal{C})$ is NP-complete when $\mathcal{C}$ is the class of all CQs [7]. Due to a myriad of papers in the last two decades, we have by now a very good understanding of which classes of CQs admit tractable evaluation. In this work, we concentrate on two of the most fundamental tractable classes of CQs: the class of CQs of bounded *treewidth* [8] and of bounded *hypertreewidth* [13], respectively, which are defined next.

CQs of bounded treewidth. A tractable class of CQs can be obtained by restricting the *treewidth* of the *hypergraph* of queries [8]. A hypergraph H is a pair (V, E), where V is a finite set of nodes and E is a finite set of *hyperedges*, i.e., subsets of V.

A *tree decomposition* of a hypergraph $H = (V, E)$ is a pair (S, ν), where S is a tree and $\nu : S \to 2^V$, that satisfies the following: (1) For each $u \in V$ the set $\{s \in S \mid u \in \nu(s)\}$ is a connected subset of S, and (2) each hyperedge of E is contained in one of the sets $\nu(s)$, for $s \in S$. The *width* of (S,ν) is $(\max\{|\nu(s)| \mid s \in S\}) - 1$. The *treewidth* of H is the minimum width of its tree decompositions. Intuitively, the treewidth of H measures its *tree-likeness*. If H is an undirected graph, then H is acyclic iff it is of treewidth one.

Let q be the CQ $\text{Ans}(\bar{x}) \leftarrow R_1(\bar{v}_1), \ldots, R_m(\bar{v}_m)$. Its underlying hypergraph H_q is the pair (V, E), where V is the set of variables mentioned in q and E consists precisely of the sets of variables in the atoms $R_i(\bar{v}_i)$, for $1 \leq i \leq m$. For example, for the CQ $\text{Ans}() \leftarrow R(x,y,z), R(x,v,v), E(v,z)$, the hyperedges are $\{x,y,z\}$, $\{x,v\}$, and $\{v,z\}$. The treewidth of CQ q is the treewidth of H_q. We denote by $\mathsf{TW}(k)$ the class of CQs of treewidth at most k, for $k \geq 1$.

Example 4. Consider the CQ $\text{Ans}() \leftarrow E(x_1,x_2), \ldots, E(x_{n-1},x_n)$ for $n \geq 3$. This CQ is in $\mathsf{TW}(1)$, since its hypergraph is a path, and, thus, acyclic. Adding the atom $E(x_1,x_n)$ increases the treewidth to two. Adding all atoms of the form $E(x_i,x_j)$, for $1 \leq i,j \leq n$, yields a CQ whose hypergraph is a clique of size n. Its treewidth is $n-1$.

It follows from [8] (see also [10]) that evaluating CQs in $\mathsf{TW}(k)$, for $k \geq 1$, is a tractable problem:

THEOREM 2. *Let $k \geq 1$. Then* CQ-EVAL($\mathsf{TW}(k)$) *can be solved in* PTIME.

CQs of bounded hypertreewidth. The notion of treewidth is too restrictive when the arity of the schemas is not fixed in advance. In order to overcome this limitation, Gottlob et al. [13] proposed studying syntactic restrictions of the class of CQs based on *hypertree decompositions* of their hypergraphs. The analogue of treewidth in this context is the notion of hypertreewidth, which, like the former, leads to tractability of query evaluation.

A *hypertree decomposition* of a hypergraph $H = (V,E)$ is a triple (S,ν,κ), where S is a tree, ν is a map from S to 2^V, and κ is a map from S to 2^E, such that:

1. (S,ν) is a tree decomposition of H.
2. $\nu(s) \subseteq \bigcup \kappa(s)$ holds for every $s \in S$.

The *width* of (S,ν,κ) is defined as $\max_{s \in S} |\kappa(s)|$. The *hypertreewidth* of a hypergraph is the minimum width over all its hypertree decompositions.

The hypertreewidth of q is the hypertreewidth of H_q. We denote by $\mathsf{HW}(k)$ the class of all CQs with hypertreewidth at most k. Notably, $\mathsf{HW}(1)$ corresponds to the well-studied class AC of *acyclic* CQs [21]. Moreover, bounded treewidth is subsumed by bounded hypertreewidth; in particular, $\mathsf{TW}(k) \subseteq \mathsf{HW}(k+1)$, for every $k \geq 1$ [1]. On the other hand, as the next example shows, even $\mathsf{HW}(1) = \mathsf{AC}$ is not subsumed by any of the $\mathsf{TW}(k)$'s.

Example 5. Consider a class $\mathcal{C} = \{\theta_n \mid n \geq 2\}$ of CQs, where $\theta_n := \text{Ans}() \leftarrow \bigwedge_{1 \leq i < j \leq n} E(x_i,x_j), T_n(x_1,\ldots,x_n)$. It is easy to show that every CQ $\theta_n \in \mathcal{C}$ is in AC. On the other hand, the treewidth of the CQs in $\mathcal{C}$ is not bounded by any constant.

Evaluation of CQs of bounded hypertreewidth is not only polynomial but can be solved in the parallelizable complexity class LOGCFL, that lies in between NL and AC_1. Formally, this corresponds to the class of languages that can be reduced in logarithmic space to a context free language.

THEOREM 3. *[13] The problem* CQ-EVAL($\mathsf{HW}(k)$) *is complete for* LOGCFL *under logspace reductions, for every* $k \geq 1$.

Notice that this improves over the bound in Theorem 2 for the classes of CQs of bounded treewidth.

Remark. For historical reasons, hypertree decompositions are called *generalized* hypertree decompositions in the literature, and, correspondingly, hypertreewidth is known as generalized hypertreewidth [14]. Hypertreewidth is then obtained by imposing an extra condition on generalized hypertree decompositions. This condition ensures the tractability of the *recognizability* problem, i.e., determining if a hypergraph is of hypertreewidth k, for a fixed $k \geq 1$. For us, it is convenient to work with the more general and intuitive notion of hypertreewidth defined above.

3.2 Tractable evaluation of WDPTs

We now return to the main question of this section: When is the evaluation of WDPTs tractable? A condition that has been shown to help identifying relevant tractable fragments of WDPTs is *local tractability* [17]. This refers to restricting the CQ defined by each node in a WDPT to belong to a tractable class.

- **Local tractability:** Let $\mathcal{C}$ be a class of CQs for which CQ-EVAL($\mathcal{C}$) is tractable. A WDPT $(T,\lambda,\bar{x})$ is *locally in* $\mathcal{C}$, if for each node $t \in T$ such that $\lambda(t) = \{R_1(\bar{v}_1),\ldots,R_m(\bar{v}_m)\}$ the CQ $\text{Ans}() \leftarrow R_1(\bar{v}_1),\ldots,R_m(\bar{v}_m)$ is in $\mathcal{C}$.

  We write ℓ-$\mathcal{C}$ for the set of all WDPTs that are locally in $\mathcal{C}$.

It is known that local tractability leads to tractability of evaluation for projection-free WDPTs:

THEOREM 4. *[17] Let $\mathcal{C}$ be a class of CQs such that* CQ-EVAL($\mathcal{C}$) *is in* PTIME, *and assume $\mathcal{C}'$ is the class of projection-free WDPTs in ℓ-$\mathcal{C}$. Then* EVAL($\mathcal{C}'$) *is in* PTIME.

On the other hand, this result does not hold in the presence of projection, even when $\mathcal{C}$ is of bounded treewidth:

THEOREM 5. *[17]* EVAL(ℓ-$\mathsf{TW}(k)$) *and* EVAL(ℓ-$\mathsf{HW}(k)$) *are* NP*-complete for every* $k \geq 1$.

This raises the question of which further restrictions on WDPTs are needed to achieve tractability. Here we identify a natural such restriction, called *bounded interface*. Intuitively, this restricts the number of variables shared between a node in a WDPT and its children.

- **Bounded interface:** Let $c \geq 1$. A WDPT $(T,\lambda,\bar{x})$ has *c-bounded interface*, if for each node $t \in T$ with children $t_1,\ldots,t_k$ it is the case that the number of variables that appear both in a relational atom in $\lambda(t)$ and in a relational atom in $\lambda(t_i)$, for some $1 \leq i \leq k$, is at most c.

  We denote $\mathsf{BI}(c)$ the set of WDPTs of c-bounded interface.

Example 6. Let p be the WDPT from Figure 1. Then $p \in \ell$-$\mathsf{TW}(1)$ and $p \in \mathsf{BI}(2)$: Since each node contains exactly two variables, the treewidth of each node is trivially

1. Concerning the number of shared variables, observe that x occurs in both the root node and its first child, while y occurs in the root node and its second child. WDPT p thus has a 2-bounded interface.

Notice that the effect of bounding the interface of each node in a WDPT $(T, \lambda, \bar{x})$ is a restriction on the shape of the CQs of the form $q_{T'}$ (for every subtree T' of T rooted in r) that define the semantics of $(T, \lambda, \bar{x})$. In particular, c-bounded interface implies that the number of variables shared between two atoms $R(\bar{v})$ and $R'(\bar{v}')$ in $q_{T'}$ that come from different nodes of T' is at most c. Interestingly, similar restrictions on the number of variables shared by different atoms of CQs have been recently applied for obtaining reasonable bounds for the problem of containment of Datalog into unions of CQs [6].

Our main result of the section states that local tractability and bounded interface yield tractability of WDPT evaluation:

Theorem 6. *Let $\mathcal{C}$ be a class of CQs for which* CQ-Eval($\mathcal{C}$) *is in* PTime *and $c \geq 1$ a positive integer. Then* Eval(ℓ-$\mathcal{C} \cap \mathsf{BI}(c)$) *is also in* PTime.

Recall that the evaluation problem for the CQ classes $\mathsf{TW}(k)$ and $\mathsf{HW}(k)$, for $k \geq 1$, is not only tractable but can be solved in the parallelizable class LogCFL. In fact, the PTime-algorithm for WDPT-evaluation in the proof of Theorem 6 can be refined to a LogCFL-algorithm, provided that the corresponding CQ-evaluation problem is in LogCFL. We thus obtain the following:

Theorem 7. *Let $\mathcal{C}$ be a class of CQs for which* CQ-Eval($\mathcal{C}$) *is in* LogCFL *and $c \geq 1$ a positive integer. Then* Eval(ℓ-$\mathcal{C} \cap \mathsf{BI}(c)$) *is also in* LogCFL. *In particular,* Eval(ℓ-$\mathsf{TW}(k) \cap \mathsf{BI}(c)$) *and* Eval($\ell$-$\mathsf{HW}(k) \cap \mathsf{BI}(c)$) *are in* LogCFL *for each $k, c \geq 1$.*

Notice that CQs can be considered as special case of WDPTs consisting of the root node only. Hence, $\mathsf{TW}(k) \subseteq \ell$-$\mathsf{TW}(k) \cap \mathsf{BI}(c)$ and $\mathsf{HW}(k) \subseteq \ell$-$\mathsf{HW}(k) \cap \mathsf{BI}(c)$ hold for each $c \geq 1$. Therefore, Theorem 7 tells us that ℓ-$\mathsf{TW}(k) \cap \mathsf{BI}(c)$ and ℓ-$\mathsf{HW}(k) \cap \mathsf{BI}(c)$ define relevant extensions of $\mathsf{TW}(k)$ and $\mathsf{HW}(k)$, respectively, that do not increase the complexity of evaluation. It follows from [12] that both Eval(ℓ-$\mathsf{TW}(k) \cap \mathsf{BI}(c)$) and Eval($\ell$-$\mathsf{HW}(k) \cap \mathsf{BI}(c)$) are LogCFL-hard under logspace reductions.

3.3 Partial evaluation of WDPTs

Given the nature of WDPTs, it is also interesting to check whether a mapping h is a *partial* answer to the WDPT p over $\mathcal{D}$ [18], i.e., whether h can be "extended" to some answer h' to p over $\mathcal{D}$. This gives rise to the partial evaluation problem for $\mathcal{C}$ defined as follows.

PROBLEM :	Partial-Eval($\mathcal{C}$).
INPUT :	A database $\mathcal{D}$ and a WDPT $p \in \mathcal{C}$ over σ, and a partial mapping $h : \mathbf{X} \to \mathbf{U}$.
QUESTION :	Is there $h' \in p(\mathcal{D})$ such that $h \sqsubseteq h'$?

Partial evaluation is tractable for the class of projection-free WDPTs [18]. In contrast, if projection is allowed, then partial evaluation is intractable even under local tractability:

Proposition 1. *[17]* Partial-Eval(ℓ-$\mathsf{TW}(k)$) *is* NP-*complete for every $k \geq 1$.*

Recall from Theorem 7 that the conjunction of local tractability and bounded interface leads to efficient (exact) evaluation of WDPTs. It is easy to modify the proof of Theorem 7 to show that also Partial-Eval(ℓ-$\mathsf{TW}(k) \cap \mathsf{BI}(c)$) and Partial-Eval($\ell$-$\mathsf{HW}(k) \cap \mathsf{BI}(c)$) are in LogCFL. However, partial evaluation is seemingly easier than exact evaluation. Hence, the question naturally arises if tractability of partial evaluation of WDPTs can be ensured by a weaker condition. Indeed, we give a positive answer to this question below. This condition will be referred to as *global tractability*. Intuitively, it states that there is a bound on the treewidth (resp., hypertreewidth) of the CQs defined by the different subtrees of a WDPT $(T, \lambda, \bar{x})$ rooted in r.

- **Global tractability:** Let $\mathcal{C}$ be $\mathsf{TW}(k)$ or $\mathsf{HW}(k)$, for $k \geq 1$. A WDPT $(T, \lambda, \bar{x})$ is *globally in $\mathcal{C}$*, if for each subtree T' of T rooted in r it is the case that the CQ $q_{T'}$ is in $\mathcal{C}$.

  We denote with g-$\mathcal{C}$ the set of all WDPTs that are globally in $\mathcal{C}$.

The following proposition formally states that global tractability is a strictly weaker condition than the conjunction of local tractability and bounded interface. The first part of the proposition shows that local tractability plus bounded interface imply global tractability, while the second part shows that the opposite is not the case:

Proposition 2. *The following hold:*

1. *Let $k, c \geq 1$. Then:*
   - ℓ-$\mathsf{TW}(k) \cap \mathsf{BI}(c) \subseteq g$-$\mathsf{TW}(k + 2c)$.
   - ℓ-$\mathsf{HW}(k) \cap \mathsf{BI}(c) \subseteq g$-$\mathsf{HW}(k + 2c)$.
2. *For every $k \geq 1$ there is a family C_k of WDPTs in g-$\mathsf{TW}(k)$ (resp., in g-$\mathsf{HW}(k)$) such that $C_k \not\subseteq \mathsf{BI}(c)$, for each $c \geq 1$.*

We now formally prove that global tractability leads to tractability of the partial evaluation problem for WDPTs:

Theorem 8. Partial-Eval(g-$\mathsf{TW}(k)$) *and* Partial-Eval(g-$\mathsf{HW}(k)$) *are in* LogCFL *for every $k \geq 1$.*

It remains to answer the question if global tractability also suffices to ensure tractability of (exact) evaluation for WDPTs. Below we show that this is not the case.

Proposition 3. Eval(g-$\mathsf{TW}(k)$) *and* Eval(g-$\mathsf{HW}(k)$) *are* NP-*complete for every $k \geq 1$.*

3.4 Semantics based on maximal mappings

The semantics of projection-free WDPTs is only based on *maximal* mappings, i.e., mappings that are not subsumed by any other mapping in the answer. This is no longer the case in the presence of projection as it has already been shown in Example 2 in the introduction.

Recent work on query answering for SPARQL under entailment regimes has established the need for a semantics for WDPTs that is uniquely based on maximal mappings [2]. This semantics is formalized as follows. Assume $\mathcal{D}$ is a database and p is a WDPT over σ. The *evaluation of p over $\mathcal{D}$ under maximal mappings*, denoted $p_m(\mathcal{D})$, corresponds to the restriction of $p(\mathcal{D})$ to those mappings $h \in p(\mathcal{D})$ that are maximal with respect to $\sqsubseteq$.

Example 7. Let p be the WDPT from Figure 1, but assume the answers to be projected to $\bar{x} = \{y, z\}$, and $\mathcal{D}$ the database from Example 2. Then $p(\mathcal{D}) = \{\mu_1, \mu_2\}$ with $\mu_1(y) = \mu_2(y) =$ "*Caribou*" and $\mu_2(z) =$ "2", while $p_m(\mathcal{D}) = \{\mu_2\}$.

This naturally leads to the following decision problem:

PROBLEM :	MAX-EVAL($\mathcal{C}$).
INPUT :	A database $\mathcal{D}$ and a WDPT $p \in \mathcal{C}$ over σ, and a partial mapping $h : \mathbf{X} \to \mathbf{U}$.
QUESTION :	Is $h \in p_m(\mathcal{D})$?

It follows from [2] that MAX-EVAL($\mathcal{C}$) is intractable when $\mathcal{C}$ is the class of all WDPTs (more precisely, this problem is complete for the class DP, i.e., the class of languages that correspond to the intersection of a language in NP and one in CONP). To obtain tractability in this case it is sufficient to impose global tractability, which is exactly the same condition that yields tractability of partial evaluation for WDPTs (as stated in Theorem 8):

THEOREM 9. *MAX-EVAL(g-TW(k)) and MAX-EVAL(g-HW(k)) are in* LOGCFL *for every $k \geq 1$.*

Analogously to PARTIAL-EVAL, local tractability is not sufficient to ensure tractability of MAX-EVAL:

PROPOSITION 4. *For every $k \geq 1$ the problems MAX-EVAL(ℓ-TW(k)) and MAX-EVAL(ℓ-HW(k)) are DP-complete.*

4. CONTAINMENT AND SUBSUMPTION

Query containment and query equivalence are among the most fundamental problems in static query analysis, i.e., given two queries q_1 and q_2, one wants to test if – for any database $\mathcal{D}$ – the condition $q_1(\mathcal{D}) \subseteq q_2(\mathcal{D})$ or $q_1(\mathcal{D}) = q_2(\mathcal{D})$, respectively, holds. If this is the case, we write $q_1 \subseteq q_2$ or $q_1 \equiv q_2$, respectively. For CQs, these problems are NP-complete in the general case [7] and LOGCFL-complete if we restrict the CQs to one of the classes TW(k) or HW(k) [8, 13].

A detailed study of containment and equivalence of RDF WDPTs was carried out in [19]. In sharp contrast to the case of CQs, it was shown that both problems are undecidable. Now the question remains if the restriction to tractable fragments of WDPT evaluation can help. An inspection of the undecidability proofs in [19] shows that this is not the case. We thus get:

THEOREM 10 (IMPLICIT IN [19]). *The containment and equivalence problems of WDPTs are undecidable. The undecidability holds even if both WDPTs are from ℓ-TW(k) $\cap$ BI(c) for arbitrary $k \geq 1$ and appropriately chosen constant c.*

In [3], it was observed that query containment of WDPTs may display an unintuitive behavior. Consequently, *subsumption* is proposed as a variant of containment: a WDPT p_1 is subsumed by p_2 (written as $p_1 \sqsubseteq p_2$) if, for every database $\mathcal{D}$, every answer $h \in p_1(\mathcal{D})$ is subsumed by an answer $h' \in p_2(\mathcal{D})$ [3]. Additionally, we define *subsumption-equivalence* (denoted as $p_1 \equiv_s p_2$) if both $p_1 \sqsubseteq p_2$ and $p_2 \sqsubseteq p_1$ hold. We thus study the following problems.

PROBLEM :	SUBSUMPTION($\mathcal{C}_1, \mathcal{C}_2$).
INPUT :	Two WDPTs $p_1 \in \mathcal{C}_1$ and $p_2 \in \mathcal{C}_2$ over σ.
QUESTION :	Does $p_1 \sqsubseteq p_2$ hold?

PROBLEM :	$\sqsubseteq$-EQUIVALENCE($\mathcal{C}_1, \mathcal{C}_2$).
INPUT :	Two WDPTs $p_1 \in \mathcal{C}_1$ and $p_2 \in \mathcal{C}_2$ over σ.
QUESTION :	Does $p_1 \equiv_s p_2$ hold?

In [17], the Π_2^P-completeness of SUBSUMPTION($\mathcal{C}_1, \mathcal{C}_2$) was proved where $\mathcal{C}_1$ and $\mathcal{C}_2$ denote the class of arbitrary WDPTs. It was also shown that Π_2^P-hardness holds even if we restrict both $\mathcal{C}_1$ and $\mathcal{C}_2$ to projection-free WDPTs.

The problem $\sqsubseteq$-EQUIVALENCE($\mathcal{C}_1, \mathcal{C}_2$) has not been studied so far. However, in [2] a closely related problem based on the "'maximal mappings" semantics from Section 3.4 was studied – the so-called MAXEQUIVALENCE($\mathcal{C}_1, \mathcal{C}_2$)-problem: Given two WDPTs $p \in \mathcal{C}_1$, $p' \in \mathcal{C}_2$, does $p_m(\mathcal{D}) = p'_m(\mathcal{D})$ hold for every database $\mathcal{D}$? In other words, we check if two WDPTs p and p' have the same *maximal* solutions over any database $\mathcal{D}$. If this is the case, we write $p \equiv_{\max} p'$. This problem was shown to be Π_2^P-complete in [2]. An inspection of the proof in [2] shows that Π_2^P-hardness holds even if one of the classes $\mathcal{C}_i$ is restricted to ℓ-TW(k) $\cap$ BI(c) with $k = c = 2$. Below, we show that $\sqsubseteq$-EQUIVALENCE($\mathcal{C}_1, \mathcal{C}_2$) and MAXEQUIVALENCE($\mathcal{C}_1, \mathcal{C}_2$) are equivalent problems. In this way, we establish Π_2^P-completeness also for $\sqsubseteq$-EQUIVALENCE($\mathcal{C}_1, \mathcal{C}_2$).

PROPOSITION 5. *For any classes $\mathcal{C}_1, \mathcal{C}_2$ of WDPTs, the problems MAXEQUIVALENCE($\mathcal{C}_1, \mathcal{C}_2$) and $\sqsubseteq$-EQUIVALENCE($\mathcal{C}_1$, $\mathcal{C}_2$) are equivalent, i.e., for all $p \in \mathcal{C}_1$ and $p' \in \mathcal{C}_2$, we have*

$$p \equiv_s p' \quad \Leftrightarrow \quad p \equiv_{\max} p'.$$

We then immediately obtain the following:

COROLLARY 1. *Let $\mathcal{C}_1, \mathcal{C}_2$ be the class of arbitrary WDPTs. Then the problem $\sqsubseteq$-EQUIVALENCE($\mathcal{C}_1, \mathcal{C}_2$) is Π_2^P-complete. It remains Π_2^P-hard even if one of the classes $\mathcal{C}_i$ is restricted to ℓ-HW(k) $\cap$ BI(c) (or to ℓ-TW(k) $\cap$ BI(c)) with $k = c = 2$.*

Now the natural question is if the restriction of $\mathcal{C}_1, \mathcal{C}_2$ to tractable classes of WDPT evaluation also leads to a lower complexity of SUBSUMPTION($\mathcal{C}_1, \mathcal{C}_2$) and $\sqsubseteq$-EQUIVALENCE($\mathcal{C}_1$, $\mathcal{C}_2$). This question is answered below.

THEOREM 11. *SUBSUMPTION($\mathcal{C}_1, \mathcal{C}_2$) is* CONP*-complete for the following classes $\mathcal{C}_1, \mathcal{C}_2$ of WDPTs:*

1. CONP*-membership holds even if $\mathcal{C}_1$ is the class of arbitrary WDPTs and $\mathcal{C}_2 \subseteq g$-HW($k$) for any $k \geq 1$.*

2. CONP*-hardness holds even if $\mathcal{C}_1, \mathcal{C}_2 \subseteq \ell$-HW($k$) $\cap$ BI(c) (or, likewise, if $\mathcal{C}_1, \mathcal{C}_2 \subseteq \ell$-TW($k$) $\cap$ BI(c)) holds for any $k \geq 1$ and $c = 1$.*

Membership is proved using techniques from [17]. Hardness uses a straightforward reduction from VALIDITY. We next give a similar complexity classification for $\sqsubseteq$-EQUIVALENCE.

THEOREM 12. *$\sqsubseteq$-EQUIVALENCE($\mathcal{C}_1, \mathcal{C}_2$) is* CONP*-complete for the following classes $\mathcal{C}_1, \mathcal{C}_2$ of WDPTs:*

1. CONP*-membership holds even if $\mathcal{C}_1, \mathcal{C}_2 \subseteq g\text{-HW}(k)$ for any $k \geq 1$.*
2. CONP*-hardness holds even if $\mathcal{C}_1, \mathcal{C}_2 \subseteq \ell\text{-HW}(k) \cap \text{BI}(c)$ (or, likewise, if $\mathcal{C}_1, \mathcal{C}_2 \subseteq \ell\text{-TW}(k) \cap \text{BI}(c)$) holds for any $k \geq 1$ and $c = 2$.*

PROOF SKETCH. Membership follows from the CONP-membership of SUBSUMPTION($\mathcal{C}$) in Theorem 11. Hardness is proved by a reduction from VALIDITY. To ensure $p_1 \equiv_s p_2$ in case of a valid formula ϕ, we need an involved construction. In particular, the selection of a particular truth assignment for the variables in X is encoded by the selection of $2m$ (with $m = |X|$) descendants of the root of p_2 from a collection of $3m$ possible descendants, which are arranged in a subtree of depth m. □

Theorems 11 and 12 together with the Π_2^P-completeness results of [17] and Corollary 1 have left a small gap: What if both $\mathcal{C}_1$ and $\mathcal{C}_2$ are locally tractable classes? We close this gap below.

PROPOSITION 6. *The problems* SUBSUMPTION*($\mathcal{C}_1, \mathcal{C}_2$) and $\sqsubseteq$-*EQUIVALENCE*($\mathcal{C}_1, \mathcal{C}_2$) remain Π_2^P-complete even if both $\mathcal{C}_1$ and $\mathcal{C}_2$ are restricted to $\ell\text{-HW}(k)$ or to $\ell\text{-TW}(k)$ with $k \geq 2$.*

5. SEMANTIC OPTIMIZATION OF WDPTS

In Section 3, we developed conditions that lead to tractability for several variants of the WDPT evaluation problem. In this section, we study the *semantic space* defined by these conditions; that is, the space of WDPTs that are equivalent to a WDPT in a class syntactically defined via treewidth or hypertreewidth.

First we have to fix the right notion of *equivalence*. By Theorem 10 we know that strict equivalence ("$\equiv$") is undecidable even for the most restricted fragments of WDPTs considered here. Hence, we have to be contented with a relaxed notion of equivalence – *subsumption equivalence* ("$\equiv_s$") introduced above.

But then we also have to choose the appropriate variant of WDPT evaluation: subsumption equivalence preserves *partial* and *maximal* solutions. Hence, we shall focus on the PARTIAL-EVAL($\mathcal{C}$) and MAX-EVAL($\mathcal{C}$) problems here. It should be noted that the MAX-EVAL, PARTIAL-EVAL and EVAL problems coincide for CQs, i.e., WDPTs consisting of the root node only.

Finally, we determine the right syntactical restriction on WDPTs to ensure tractability of these problems. By Theorems 8 and 9, the restriction to $g\text{-TW}(k)$ or $g\text{-HW}(k)$ for constant k is sufficient. At this point, the discussion of a significant difference between treewidth and hypertreewidth is in order: It will turn out convenient to choose our fragment of CQs in such a way that it is closed under taking *arbitrary* subqueries. While $\text{TW}(k)$ enjoys this property, $\text{HW}(k)$ does not. We therefore restrict $\text{HW}(k)$ to the class $\text{HW}'(k)$ consisting of all CQs q such that each subquery q' of q has hypertreewidth at most k. In [15], this restricted notion of hypertreewidth was called β-hypertreewidth in analogy with β-acyclicity introduced in [11]. We thus define the class

$$\text{WB}(k) \;=\; g\text{-}\mathcal{C}(k), \quad \text{for } k \geq 1,$$

with either $\mathcal{C}(k) = \text{TW}(k)$ or $\mathcal{C}(k) = \text{HW}'(k)$. The acronym WB stands for *well-behaved.* Most results presented below hold for both choices of $\mathcal{C}(k)$. These results will thus simply be stated for $\text{WB}(k)$ without distinguishing between $g\text{-TW}(k)$ and $g\text{-HW}'(k)$. However, there are also some results (in particular upper bounds) where the concrete choice of $\mathcal{C}(k)$ does make a difference in that an additional NP-oracle is needed in case of $\mathcal{C}(k) = g\text{-HW}'(k)$. The oracle is used to verify that some WDPT indeed is in $g\text{-HW}'(k)$. The problem here is that it is not known if, for given k, it can be can be tested efficiently if β-hypertreewidth $\leq k$ holds.

The semantic space defined by classes of the form $\text{WB}(k)$ is formally defined below.

Definition 3. ($\mathcal{M}(\text{WB}(k))$) Let $k \geq 1$. We denote by $\mathcal{M}(\text{WB}(k))$ the class of WDPTs p for which there is a WDPT $p' \in \text{WB}(k)$ such that $p \equiv_s p'$.

We show that these classes are decidable. We then apply this result to show that the partial and maximal evaluation problems for WDPTs in $\mathcal{M}(\text{WB}(k))$ are fixed-parameter tractable (when taking the size of the WDPT as the parameter). This is an improvement with respect to the corresponding evaluation problems for arbitrary WDPTs and even for CQs. For the latter, no fixed-parameter tractable algorithm is believed to exist. Finally, we study the notion of $\text{WB}(k)$-approximation for WDPTs.

5.1 Decidability of WB(k) modulo equivalence

We start by stating the decidability of our notion:

THEOREM 13. *Let $k \geq 1$. There is a* NEXPTIME^{NP} *algorithm that, given a WDPT p, decides if p is in $\mathcal{M}(\text{WB}(k))$, and, if this is the case, constructs a WDPT p' in $\text{WB}(k)$ of at most exponential size in p such that $p \equiv_s p'$. The* NP*-oracle is omitted if $\text{WB}(k) = g\text{-TW}(k)$.*

The proof of this result follows from the next lemma:

LEMMA 1. *Let p and p' be WDPTs such that $p' \sqsubseteq p$ and $p' \in \text{WB}(k)$. Then there exists $p'' \in \text{WB}(k)$ such that (1) $p' \sqsubseteq p'' \sqsubseteq p$, and (2) the size of p'' is at most exponential in the size of p.*

We now explain how Theorem 13 follows from Lemma 1. Assume p is in $\mathcal{M}(\text{WB}(k))$, i.e., there is a WDPT p' in $\text{WB}(k)$ such that $p \equiv_s p'$. Since $p' \sqsubseteq p$ and $p' \in \text{WB}(k)$, we have from Lemma 1 that there is a WDPT $p'' \in \text{WB}(k)$ such that (1) $p' \sqsubseteq p'' \sqsubseteq p$, and (2) the size of p'' is at most exponential in the size of p. We conclude that $p \equiv_s p''$ since $p \sqsubseteq p' \sqsubseteq p'' \sqsubseteq p$. Hence, if p is in $\mathcal{M}(\text{WB}(k))$, then there is a WDPT p' in $\text{WB}(k)$ with $p \equiv_s p'$ and the size of p' is at most exponential in the size of p. Then the NEXPTIME^{NP} algorithm in Theorem 13 simply guesses such p' and checks (1) if $p' \in \text{WB}(k)$ and (2) if it is subsumption-equivalent to p. Condition (1) requires an NP-oracle if $\text{WB}(k) = g\text{-HW}'(k)$. Condition (2) is satisfied if certain (exponentially many) homomorphisms exist [17]: they can be guessed alongside p' itself and do not increase the complexity.

While the upper bound in Theorem 13 might not be optimal, we can prove that the problem is at least on the second-level of the polynomial hierarchy:

PROPOSITION 7. *Let $k > 1$. The problem of checking whether a WDPT p belongs to $\mathcal{M}(\mathsf{WB}(k))$ is Π_2^P-hard.*

Notice that this establishes a difference with the analogous problem of checking whether a CQ is equivalent to one in a tractable class: For each $k \geq 1$, checking whether a CQ q is equivalent to some CQ q' in $\mathsf{TW}(k)$ or $\mathsf{HW}'(k)$ is in NP [10].

Evaluation for WDPTs in $\mathcal{M}(\mathsf{WB}(k))$. An important corollary of Theorem 13 is the following fixed-parameter tractability result:

COROLLARY 2. *Let $k \geq 1$. Then the problems* PARTIAL-EVAL($\mathcal{M}(\mathsf{WB}(k))$) *and* MAX-EVAL($\mathcal{M}(\mathsf{WB}(k))$) *are fixed-parameter tractable (when taking the size of the WDPT as the parameter).*

5.2 WB(k)-Approximations of WDPTs

When a query q is not equivalent to one in a well-behaved class $\mathcal{Q}$, it might be useful to compute an *approximation* of q in $\mathcal{Q}$ [4]. Recall that this is a query $q' \in \mathcal{Q}$ that is *maximally contained* in q with respect to all queries in $\mathcal{Q}$. In other words, $q' \subseteq q$, and there is no $q'' \in \mathcal{Q}$ such that $q' \subset q'' \subseteq q$. For the reasons given before, we define approximations in the WDPT context not in terms of containment, but subsumption. Throughout this section we assume that WDPTs *do not contain constants*. The reason is that the notion of approximations with constants is problematic and not even well understood in the CQ context [4].

We now define approximations in the WDPT context. We write $p \sqsubset p'$ to denote that $p \sqsubseteq p'$ but $p \not\equiv_s p'$.

Definition 4. ($\mathsf{WB}(k)$-approximations) Let $k \geq 1$. Assume p and p' are WDPTs such that $p' \in \mathsf{WB}(k)$. Then p' is a $\mathsf{WB}(k)$*-approximation* of p if (1) $p' \sqsubseteq p$, and (2) there is no $p'' \in \mathsf{WB}(k)$ such that $p' \sqsubset p'' \sqsubseteq p$.

Existence of approximations. The most important question in the context of approximations is whether approximations always exist [4, 5]. The techniques developed in Lemma 1 allow us to prove that this is indeed the case in the WDPT scenario. Furthermore, for each WDPT, an exponential size approximation can be constructed in double-exponential time:

THEOREM 14. *Let $k \geq 1$. There is a double-exponential time algorithm that, given a WDPT p, constructs an exponential size $\mathsf{WB}(k)$-approximation p' of p.*

Complexity. In order to better understand the complexity of computing approximations, we study the following decision problem: Given WDPTs p and p' such that $p' \in \mathsf{WB}(k)$, for $k \geq 1$, is p' a $\mathsf{WB}(k)$-approximation of p? We call this problem $\mathsf{WB}(k)$-APPROXIMATION. The next proposition establishes some upper and lower bounds for the problem.

PROPOSITION 8. *The following hold:*

1. $\mathsf{WB}(k)$-APPROXIMATION *is in* CONEXPTIME^{NP} *for each $k \geq 1$. The* NP*-oracle is omitted if* $\mathsf{WB}(k) = g\text{-}\mathsf{TW}(k)$.

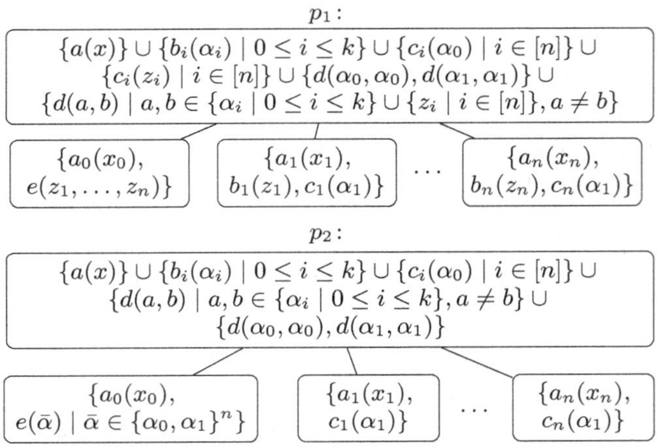

Figure 2: Exponential blow-up from p_1 to p_2.

2. $\mathsf{WB}(k)$-APPROXIMATION *is Π_2^P-hard for each $k > 1$.*

3. *If the input of the problem includes the promise that $p' \sqsubseteq p$, then* $\mathsf{WB}(k)$-APPROXIMATION *is Σ_2^P-hard for each $k > 1$.*

Again, this shows that our problem is harder than an analogous problem for CQs: For each $k \geq 1$, the problem of checking whether a CQ q is a $\mathsf{TW}(k)$-approximation of CQ q' is DP-complete. If, in addition, the input includes the promise that $q \subseteq q'$, then the problem becomes CONP-complete [4].

Size of approximations. We have seen above that approximations always exist even though Lemma 1 only allowed us to give an exponential upper bound on their size. The proof of that lemma centered around the properties of subsumption – without making use of the specific properties of approximations. One may thus ask if exponential size is indeed attainable by approximations. We give an affirmative answer to this question. This establishes another sharp contrast with CQs, where every $\mathsf{TW}(k)$-approximation is equivalent to one of polynomial size [4].

THEOREM 15. *For every $k \geq 2$, there exists a sequence of pairs of WDPTs $(p_1^{(n)}, p_2^{(n)})$, such that (1) $p_2^{(n)}$ is a* $\mathsf{WB}(k)$-approximation *of $p_1^{(n)}$, and (2) $p_2^{(n)}$ is necessarily* exponentially bigger *than $p_1^{(n)}$. More precisely, we have*

$$|p_1^{(n)}| = O(n^2) \quad \textit{and} \quad |p_2^{(n)}| = \Omega(2^n),$$

and, for every WDPT $p_3^{(n)} \in \mathsf{WB}(k)$ with $p_2^{(n)} \sqsubseteq p_3^{(n)} \sqsubseteq p_1^{(n)}$, we have $|p_3^{(n)}| \geq |p_2^{(n)}|$.

PROOF SKETCH. Let $k \geq 1$ and $n \geq 1$. Consider the WDPTs $p_1^{(n)}$ and $p_2^{(n)}$ in Figure 2 with free variables $X = \{x, x_0, \ldots, x_n\}$. For the sake of readability, we omit superscript (n) from now on. Clearly, p_2 is exponentially bigger than p_1 and $p_2 \sqsubseteq p_1$ hold. Actually, we do not insist that p_2 is indeed a $\mathsf{WB}(k)$-approximation of p_1. It suffices to show that for every WDPT $p_3 \in \mathsf{WB}(k)$ with $p_2 \sqsubseteq p_3 \sqsubseteq p_1$, we have $|p_3| \geq |p_2|$.

We briefly discuss the main ideas of this construction. The WDPT p_1 is outside $\mathsf{WB}(k)$ due to a big clique of size $k+1+n$

(i.e., the d-atoms) in the root. The WDPT p_2 is obtained by instantiating all variables z_i to one of the two values α_0 or α_1. This is enforced by the fact that (by the condition $p_2 \in \mathsf{WB}(k)$) the big clique has to be shrunk to at most $k+1$ vertices and (by the condition $p_2 \sqsubseteq p_1$) there must exist a homomorphism from the root of p_1 to the root of p_2.

The variables z_i in the atom $e(z_1, \ldots, z_n)$ in the first leaf node of p_1 have to be instantiated in the same way. Again consider the condition $p_2 \sqsubseteq p_1$. As in the proof sketch of Lemma 1, this requires the existence of certain homomorphisms from subtrees of p_1 to subtrees of p_2. We thus consider every subtree p_2' of p_2 consisting of the root, the first leaf and an arbitrary subset of the remaining leaf nodes. We have to find a homomorphism from the corresponding subtree p_1' of p_1 (i.e., p_1' has the same free variables as p_2') into p_2'. It turns out that those variables z_i such that the leaf with atom $b_1(z_i)$ is contained in p_2' have to be mapped to α_1 while the other z_i's have to be mapped to α_0. Therefore, the first leaf of p_2 indeed has to contain all 2^n possible instantiations of atom $e(z_1, \ldots, z_n)$, resulting in an exponential blow-up. □

6. UNIONS OF WDPTS

Closing WDPTs under union constitutes one of the basic extensions of the language [18, 19]. Formally, a *union of WDPTs* (UWDPT) is an expression ϕ of the form $\bigcup_{1 \le i \le n} p_i$, where each p_i is a WDPT over σ. (Notice that we do not require different p_i's to have the same set of free variables). The evaluation of ϕ over database $\mathcal{D}$, denoted $\phi(\mathcal{D})$, corresponds to the set $\bigcup_{1 \le i \le n} p_i(\mathcal{D})$.

As before, we write $\phi \sqsubseteq \phi'$, for UWDPTs ϕ and ϕ', if for every database $\mathcal{D}$ and partial mapping $h \in \phi(\mathcal{D})$ it is the case that there is $h' \in \phi'(\mathcal{D})$ such that $h \sqsubseteq h'$. Similarly, we write $\phi \equiv_s \phi'$ whenever $\phi \sqsubseteq \phi'$ and $\phi' \sqsubseteq \phi$, and $\phi \sqsubset \phi'$ if $\phi \sqsubseteq \phi'$ but $\phi \not\equiv_s \phi'$.

If $\mathcal{C}$ is a class of WDPTs, we denote by $\bigcup$-EVAL($\mathcal{C}$) the problem of determining if $h \in \phi(\mathcal{D})$, for ϕ a union of WDPTs in $\mathcal{C}$, $\mathcal{D}$ a database, and $h : \mathbf{X} \to \mathbf{U}$ a partial mapping. Similarly, we define $\bigcup$-PARTIAL-EVAL($\mathcal{C}$) and $\bigcup$-MAX-EVAL($\mathcal{C}$). It is immediate that unions of WDPTs from a well-behaved class $\mathcal{C}$ in terms of (variants of) evaluation preserve the good properties of $\mathcal{C}$:

THEOREM 16. *The following hold for each $k \ge 1$ assuming $\mathcal{C}(k) = \mathsf{TW}(k)$ or $\mathsf{HW}(k)$:*

1. *The problem $\bigcup$-EVAL(ℓ-$\mathcal{C}(k) \cap \mathsf{BI}(c)$) is in LOGCFL for each $c \ge 1$.*
2. *$\bigcup$-PARTIAL-EVAL(g-$\mathcal{C}(k)$) and $\bigcup$-MAX-EVAL(g-$\mathcal{C}(k)$) are in LOGCFL.*

In other words, the additional expressive power of UWDPTs compared with WDPTs has no effect on our variants of the evaluation problem. We look next at semantic optimization into well-behaved classes of UWDPTs. It will turn out that there the extension from WDPTs to UWDPTs makes a huge difference.

Semantic optimization of UWDPTs. Following Section 5, we concentrate on unions of WDPTs from $\mathsf{WB}(k) = g$-$\mathcal{C}(k)$, where $\mathcal{C}(k)$ is either $\mathsf{TW}(k)$ or $\mathsf{HW}'(k)$. We thus define:

$$\mathsf{UWB}(k) = \{ \bigcup_{1 \le i \le n} p_i \mid p_i \in \mathsf{WB}(k), \text{for each } 1 \le i \le n\}.$$

Analogously, we define the classes $\mathcal{M}(\mathsf{UWB}(k))$ of UWDPTs that are $\equiv_s$-equivalent to queries in $\mathsf{UWB}(k)$:

$$\mathcal{M}(\mathsf{UWB}(k)) = \{\phi \mid \phi \equiv_s \phi', \text{ for some } \phi' \text{ in } \mathsf{UWB}(k)\}.$$

We prove below that the class $\mathcal{M}(\mathsf{UWB}(k))$ is not only decidable but allows for a nice characterization. To present this characterization, we introduce some useful notation first.

Given a WDPT $p = (T, \lambda, \bar{x})$ and a subtree T' of T rooted in r, we denote by $r_{T'}$ the CQ $\text{Ans}(\bar{x}') \leftarrow R_1(\bar{v}_1), \ldots, R_m(\bar{v}_m)$, where $\{R_1(\bar{v}_1), \ldots, R_m(\bar{v}_m)\}$ is the set of all relational atoms in T' and $\bar{x}'$ is the set of variables that appear in $\bar{x}$ and in some $\bar{v}_i$, for $1 \le i \le m$. In other words, $r_{T'}$ is exactly as $q_{T'}$, only that we now take the projection over those variables from the $R_i(\bar{v}_i)$'s that appear free in p. Let us then define:

$$\phi_{\text{cq}} = \bigcup_{p=(T,\lambda,\bar{x})\in\phi} \; \bigcup_{T' \text{ a subtree of } T \text{ rooted in } r} r_{T'}.$$

It is not hard to see that $\phi \equiv_s \phi_{\text{cq}}$ holds.

Example 8. Consider the RDF WDPT p introduced in Example 1, and the projection onto the variables $\{y, z, z'\}$ introduced in Example 3. When replacing the triple patterns by binary atoms, we get p_{cq} as the union of the following CQs:

- $\text{Ans}(y) \leftarrow \texttt{rec\_by}(x, y), \texttt{publ}(x, \text{“after\_2010”})$.
- $\text{Ans}(y, z) \leftarrow \texttt{rec\_by}(x, y), \texttt{publ}(x, \text{“after\_2010”}), \texttt{NME\_ranking}(x, z)$.
- $\text{Ans}(y, z') \leftarrow \texttt{rec\_by}(x, y), \texttt{publ}(x, \text{“after\_2010”}), \texttt{formed\_in}(y, z')$.
- $\text{Ans}(y, z, z') \leftarrow \texttt{rec\_by}(x, y), \texttt{publ}(x, \text{“after\_2010”}), \texttt{NME\_rating}(x, z), \texttt{formed\_in}(y, z')$.

Here we use `rec_by` and `publ` as abbreviation for `recorded_by` and `published`, respectively.

With ϕ_{cq} we have a useful tool for our further analysis of the class $\mathcal{M}(\mathsf{UWB}(k))$. In particular, this allows us to give the following characterization of $\mathcal{M}(\mathsf{UWB}(k))$.

PROPOSITION 9. *Let $k \ge 1$. A UWDPT ϕ is in $\mathcal{M}(\mathsf{UWB}(k))$ iff ϕ_{cq} is $\sqsubseteq$-equivalent to a union of CQs in $\mathcal{C}(k)$.*

Applying Proposition 9 we obtain the following:

THEOREM 17. *The following hold for each $k \ge 1$:*

1. *The problem of checking if a UWDPT ϕ is in $\mathcal{M}(\mathsf{UWB}(k))$ is in Π_2^P if $\mathcal{C}(k) = \mathsf{TW}(k)$, and in Π_3^P if $\mathcal{C}(k) = \mathsf{HW}'(k)$ For $k > 1$ either problem is Π_2^P-hard.*
2. *There is an EXPTIME algorithm that, given ϕ in $\mathcal{M}(\mathsf{UWB}(k))$, constructs a union ϕ' of (possibly exponentially many) WDPTs in $\mathsf{WB}(k)$ such that (1) each WDPT in ϕ' is of polynomial size, and (2) $\phi \equiv_s \phi'$.*

Notice the stark contrast of this result with the problem of checking whether a WDPT p is in $\mathcal{M}(\mathsf{WB}(k))$, for which we could only obtain a NEXPTIME^{NP} upper bound in Theorem 13.

Evaluation for UWDPTs in $\mathcal{M}(\mathsf{UWB}(k))$. Analogously to the case of Corollary 2, it follows from Theorem 17 that the maximal and partial evaluation problems for queries in $\mathcal{M}(\mathsf{UWB}(k))$ are fixed-parameter tractable:

COROLLARY 3. *Let* $k \geq 1$. *Then* $\bigcup$-PARTIAL-EVAL($\mathcal{M}$(UWB(k))) *and* $\bigcup$-MAX-EVAL($\mathcal{M}$(UWB(k))) *are fixed-parameter tractable (when considering the size of the UWDPT as parameter).*

UWB(k)-approximations. As in the case of Section 5.2, we study approximations for UWDPTs without constants. Fix $k \geq 1$. Let ϕ, ϕ' be UWDPTs such that $\phi' \in$ UWB(k). Analogously to Definition 4, we have that ϕ' is a UWB(k)-approximation of ϕ if (1) $\phi' \sqsubseteq \phi$, and (2) there is no UWDPT $\phi'' \in$ UWB(k) such that $\phi' \sqsubset \phi'' \sqsubseteq \phi$.

The previous machinery allows us to develop a theory of approximations for UWDPTs. First of all, we can prove that approximations always exist and can be computed in exponential time. Second, approximations are unique up to $\equiv_s$-equivalence and consist of (possibly exponentially many) WDPTs of polynomial size (actually, these WDPTs are even CQs).

THEOREM 18. *There is an* EXPTIME *algorithm that, given a UWDPT* ϕ, *constructs a union* ϕ' *of (possibly exponentially many) WDPTs in* WB(k) *such that (1) each WDPT in* ϕ' *is of polynomial size, and (2)* ϕ' *is the unique (up to* $\equiv_s$*-equivalence)* UWB(k)*-approximation of* ϕ.

These techniques also allow us to find reasonable bounds for the problem of checking if ϕ' is a UWB(k)-approximation of ϕ. This problem is called UWB(k)-APPROXIMATION.

PROPOSITION 10. *The problem* UWB(k)-APPROXIMATION *is in* Π_2^P *if* $\mathcal{C}(k)$ = TW(k), *and in* Π_3^P *if* $\mathcal{C}(k)$ = HW′(k). *For* $k \geq 1$ *either problem is* Π_2^P*-hard.*

This is again in stark contrast with the problem of checking if a WDPT ϕ' is a WB(k)-approximation of ϕ, for which we could only obtain a CONEXPTIME upper bound in Proposition 8.

7. CONCLUSION

In this work we have studied well-designed pattern trees (WDPTs) as a natural extension of conjunctive queries (CQs) by optional matching. We have considered WDPTs over arbitrary relational schemas here. However, all our results also apply to the corresponding fragment of the semantic web query language SPARQL by restricting the schema to a single ternary relation.

We have extended the search for tractable query evaluation and tractable query analysis from CQs to WDPTs. It has turned out that additional restrictions are required to ensure tractability of query evaluation of WDPTs. In Table 1, we give an overview of the complexities. The five rows refer to the five problems EVAL, PARTIAL-EVAL, MAX-EVAL, subsumption ($\sqsubseteq$), and subsumption-equivalence ($\equiv_s$). Completeness results are abbreviated with "c". The results marked with references are (at least implicitly) proved in previous work. Arrows indicate that the non-trivial part of these results carries over from the more special case ($\leftarrow$) or from the more general case ($\rightarrow$), respectively.

We have then applied our tractable classes of query evaluation to study semantic optimization and to initiate a theory of approximation of WDPTs. To this end, we have defined the classes WB(k) and UWB(k) of (unions) of "well-behaved" queries. Above all, we have managed to prove

	general	l-$\mathcal{C}(k)$	g-$\mathcal{C}(k)$	l-$\mathcal{C}(k) \cap$ BI(k)
EVAL	Σ_2^P [17]	NP [17]	NP	LOGCFL
P-EVAL	$\leftarrow$	NP [17]	LOGCFL	$\rightarrow$
M-EVAL	$\leftarrow$	DP	LOGCFL	$\rightarrow$
$\sqsubseteq$	$\leftarrow$	Π_2^P	CONP	CONP
$\equiv_s$	$\leftarrow$	Π_2^P	CONP	CONP

Table 1: Complexity of WDPT evaluation and query analysis (all entries denote completeness).

	lower b.	upper bound
WB(k)-MEMBERSHIP	Π_2^P	NEXPTIME^{NP}
WB(k)-APPROXIMATION	Π_2^P	CONEXPTIME^{NP}
UWB(k)-MEMBERSHIP	Π_2^P	Π_3^P
UWB(k)-APPROXIMATION	Π_2^P	Π_3^P

Table 2: Semantic Optimization of WDPTs: lower- and upper bounds of the complexity.

fixed-parameter tractability of query evaluation for (unions of) WDPTs that are $\equiv_s$-equivalent to a query in WB(k) or UWB(k), respectively. Further problems studied in this context are WB(k) / UWB(k)-MEMBERSHIP (is a WDPT resp. a union of WDPTs $\equiv_s$-equivalent to a well-behaved one?) and WB(k) / UWB(k)-APPROXIMATION (is a WDPT resp. a union of WDPTs an approximation of the other?). Preliminary complexity results for these tasks are displayed in Table 2. The upper bounds refer to the case WB(k) = *g*-HW′(k). For WB(k) = *g*-TW(k), the NP-oracle can be omitted and Π_3^P drops to Π_2^P, respectively.

Several lines of future work should be pursued. As far as query evaluation and query analysis are concerned, we yet have to identify a natural fragment of WDPTs that guarantees tractable subsumption and subsumption-equivalence. Towards a theory of semantic optimization of WDPTs, we have only made the first steps here. A better understanding of the nature of WB(k)- and UWB(k)-approximations is needed to close the gaps in Table 2. For instance, we conjecture that there always exists some approximation of polynomial size and that the complexity of WB(k)-APPROXIMATION drops to the polynomial hierarchy. The situation of WDPTs is much more involved than for CQs, where the analogous problems come down to simple containment tests.

Acknowledgments

The work of Pablo Barceló is funded by the Millenium Nucleus Center for Semantic Web Research under grant NC120004. Part of this work was done while Reinhard Pichler and Sebastian Skritek were visiting Pablo Barceló on invitation by the Millenium Nucleus Center for Semantic Web Research. Reinhard Pichler and Sebastian Skritek were supported by the Vienna Science and Technology Fund (WWTF) through project ICT12-015 and by the Austrian Science Fund (FWF):P25207-N23.

8. REFERENCES

[1] I. Adler, G. Gottlob, and M. Grohe. Hypertree width and related hypergraph invariants. *Eur. J. Comb.*, 28(8):2167–2181, 2007.

[2] S. Ahmetaj, W. Fischl, R. Pichler, M. Simkus, and S. Skritek. Towards reconciling SPARQL and certain answers. To appear in WWW 2015.

[3] M. Arenas and J. Pérez. Querying semantic web data with SPARQL. In *PODS*, pages 305–316, 2011.

[4] P. Barceló, L. Libkin, and M. Romero. Efficient approximations of conjunctive queries. *SIAM J. Comput.*, 43(3):1085–1130, 2014.

[5] P. Barceló, M. Romero, and M. Y. Vardi. Semantic acyclicity on graph databases. In *PODS*, pages 237–248, 2013.

[6] P. Barceló, M. Romero, and M. Y. Vardi. Does query evaluation tractability help query containment? In *PODS*, pages 188–199, 2014.

[7] A. K. Chandra and P. M. Merlin. Optimal implementation of conjunctive queries in relational data bases. In *STOC*, pages 77–90, 1977.

[8] C. Chekuri and A. Rajaraman. Conjunctive query containment revisited. *Theor. Comput. Sci.*, 239(2):211–229, 2000.

[9] S. A. Cook and P. McKenzie. Problems complete for deterministic logarithmic space. *J. Algorithms*, 8(3):385–394, 1987.

[10] V. Dalmau, P. G. Kolaitis, and M. Y. Vardi. Constraint satisfaction, bounded treewidth, and finite-variable logics. In *CP*, pages 310–326, 2002.

[11] R. Fagin. Degrees of acyclicity for hypergraphs and relational database schemes. *J. ACM*, 30(3):514–550, 1983.

[12] G. Gottlob, N. Leone, and F. Scarcello. The complexity of acyclic conjunctive queries. *J. ACM*, 48(3):431–498, 2001.

[13] G. Gottlob, N. Leone, and F. Scarcello. Hypertree decompositions and tractable queries. *J. Comput. Syst. Sci.*, 64(3):579–627, 2002.

[14] G. Gottlob, Z. Miklós, and T. Schwentick. Generalized hypertree decompositions: NP-hardness and tractable variants. *J. ACM*, 56(6), 2009.

[15] G. Gottlob and R. Pichler. Hypergraphs in model checking: Acyclicity and hypertree-width versus clique-width. *SIAM J. Comput.*, 33(2):351–378, 2004.

[16] M. Grohe and D. Marx. Constraint solving via fractional edge covers. *ACM Transactions on Algorithms*, 11(1):4, 2014.

[17] A. Letelier, J. Pérez, R. Pichler, and S. Skritek. Static analysis and optimization of semantic web queries. *ACM Trans. Database Syst.*, 38(4):25, 2013.

[18] J. Pérez, M. Arenas, and C. Gutierrez. Semantics and complexity of SPARQL. *ACM Trans. Database Syst.*, 34(3), 2009.

[19] R. Pichler and S. Skritek. Containment and equivalence of well-designed SPARQL. In *PODS'14*, pages 39–50, 2014.

[20] E. Prud'hommeaux and A. Seaborne. SPARQL Query Language for RDF. W3C Recommendation, Jan. 2008.

[21] M. Yannakakis. Algorithms for acyclic database schemes. In *VLDB*, pages 82–94, 1981.

APPENDIX

A. ADDITIONAL PROOF DETAILS

A.1 Proof (sketches) for Section 3

PROOF SKETCH OF THEOREM 6. Given a WDPT $p \in \ell$-$\mathcal{C} \cap \mathsf{BI}(c))$, a database $\mathcal{D}$ and a partial mapping h, the main idea of the polynomial time algorithm is to construct a Boolean acyclic CQ q on a new database $\mathcal{D}'$ such that $q(\mathcal{D}') = \mathit{true}$ iff $h \in p(\mathcal{D})$.

The CQ q is constructed from $p = (T, \lambda, \bar{x})$ as follows: Let $\bar{x}'$ be the subset of variables from $\bar{x}$ on which h is defined, and let T' be the minimal subtree of T that contains $\bar{x}'$ (and no more variables from $\bar{x}$). Moreover, let T'' be the *maximal* subtree of T that contains $\bar{x}'$ but no additional variable from $\bar{x}$. By the well-designedness of p, these subtrees are uniquely defined. For every node $t \in T'$, let $\bar{y}_t$ be the set of existentially quantified variables that appear both in $\lambda(t)$ and in $\lambda(t_i)$, for some child node t_i of t. We invent a new relation symbol R_t or arity $|\bar{y}_t|$ and define $q = \text{Ans}() \leftarrow \bigwedge_{t \in T'} R_t(\bar{y}_t)$.

Database $\mathcal{D}'$ is defined in two steps: First, for every node $t \in T'$, we compute all mappings g on the variables $\bar{y}_t$, such that $g \cup h$ can be extended to a homomorphism from $\lambda(t)$ into $\mathcal{D}$, i.e., g contains all instantiations of the (existentially quantified) "interface" variables consistent with solution candidate h. We define an intermediate database $\mathcal{D}''$ as the set of all atoms $R_t(g(\bar{y}))$. One can check that $\mathcal{D}''$ fulfills the following property: $q(\mathcal{D}'') = \mathit{true}$ iff h can be extended to a solution in $p(\mathcal{D})$.

In the second step, we make sure that h can be combined with some mapping on the existentially quantified variables in T', such that no extension to further free variables is possible. To this end, we compute analogous relations R_t also for each node $t \in T'' \setminus T'$. These relations are filled in a bottom-up manner from the leaves of T'' until the leaves of T' are reached. But now we store the additional information for every tuple in R_t indicating if the instantiation of the variables $\bar{y}$ necessarily leads to an extension to some free variable occurring below T''. By deleting from $\mathcal{D}''$ all atoms $R_t(g(\bar{y}))$ with this property, we guarantee that condition $q(\mathcal{D}') = \mathit{true}$ implies that $h \in p(\mathcal{D})$. □

PROOF OF THEOREM 8. Observe that for deciding if h can be extended to some answer $h' \in p(\mathcal{D})$, it suffices to identify some homomorphism $\hat{h}$ from p to $\mathcal{D}$ s.t. $\hat{h}_{\bar{z}} = h$ (where $\bar{z}$ are the variables on which h is defined), i.e., $\hat{h}$ does not need not to be maximal. The problem can thus be solved by (1) identifying the minimal subtree T' of T that contains (at least) all variables from $\bar{z}$; and (2) deciding if $\hat{q}_{T'}(\mathcal{D}) \neq \emptyset$ where $\hat{q}_{T'}$ is derived from $q_{T'}$ by replacing each variable $z \in \bar{z}$ with $h(z)$. Clearly, $\hat{q}_{T'} \in \mathsf{TW}(k)$ (or $\mathsf{HW}(k)$, respectively). Step (1) can be done in LOGSPACE [9], while step (2) fits into LOGCFL [13]. □

PROOF SKETCH OF PROPOSITION 3. We only sketch the lower bound and concentrate on the case $k = 1$. We use a reduction from 3-colorability. Assume $G = (V, E)$ is an undirected graph such that $V = \{v_1, \ldots, v_n\}$ and $E = \{e_1, \ldots, e_m\}$. Let $\mathcal{D} = \{c(1,1), c(2,2), c(3,3)\}$ be a database. We define a WDPT $p = (T, \lambda, \bar{x})$ such that:

- T consists of a root r with children n_j^1, n_j^2 and n_j^3, for each $1 \leq j \leq m$.
- $\lambda(r) = \{c(u_i, u_i) \mid 1 \leq i \leq n\} \cup \{c(x,x)\}$, where x and the u_i's are variables.

- $\lambda(n_j^k) = \{c(u_{j_1}, k), c(u_{j_2}, k), c(x_j^k, x_j^k)\}$, for each $1 \leq j \leq m$ such that $e_j = \{v_{j_1}, v_{j_2}\}$ and $1 \leq k \leq 3$, where the x_j^k's are variables.
- The free variables in $\bar{x}$ are x and all variables of the form x_j^k, for $1 \leq j \leq m$ and $1 \leq k \leq 3$.

We also define a partial mapping $h : \mathbf{X} \rightarrow \mathbf{U}$ that satisfies $h(x) = 1$ and is undefined elsewhere.

Clearly, $\mathcal{D}$, p and h can be constructed in polynomial time from G. Furthermore, p belongs to g-TW(1) and g-HW(1). We claim that G is 3-colorable iff $h \in p(\mathcal{D})$. This follows directly from the following observation. For every mapping λ from the u_i's to $\{1, 2, 3\}$, it is the case that $h \cup \lambda$ is a maximal homomorphism from p to $\mathcal{D}$ iff λ is a valid 3-coloring of G. The reason why the latter holds is simple. Assume first that λ does not encode a valid 3-coloring of G. Then for some $e_j = \{v_{j_1}, v_{j_2}\}$ it is the case that $\lambda(u_{j_1}) = \lambda(u_{j_2})$. Assume without loss of generality that $\lambda(u_{j_1}) = \lambda(u_{j_2}) = 1$ (the other two cases are analogous). Then $h \cup \lambda \cup h'$ is a homomorphism from p to $\mathcal{D}$, where h' maps x_j^1 to 1. On the other hand, if λ is a valid 3-coloring then clearly no such extension exists. □

A.2 Proof (sketches) for Section 5

Proof of Lemma 1. Let $p = (T, \lambda, \bar{x})$ and $p' = (T_1, \lambda_1, \bar{x}_1)$ be WDPTs such that $p' \sqsubseteq p$ and $p' \in \mathsf{WB}(k)$. We can transform p' into a WDPT $p'' = (T_2, \lambda_2, \bar{x}_1)$ with the desired properties:

First, we restrict the number of nodes in T_1. To this end, we determine the set N of those nodes in T_1 which introduce at least one free variable, i.e., a variable from $\bar{x}_1$ that occurs in this node but not in its parent. Then we delete all nodes that are not on a path from the root to some node in N. Moreover, we may merge every node n with its child node n' if n contains no free variable and n' is the only child of n. We thus end up with a tree T_2 whose number of nodes is linearly bounded in the size of p. Note that it is precisely this merging of nodes where the closure under taking subgraphs of the class $\mathsf{WB}(k)$ is needed.

We then restrict the number of atoms in the labeling λ_1. Recall from [17] that the subsumption test $p' \sqsubseteq p$ requires the existence of certain homomorphisms from certain subtrees of p to subtrees of p'. The number of homomorphisms needed corresponds to the number of subtrees of T_2. Labelling λ_2 is then essentially obtained from λ_1 by deleting all atoms that do not occur in the image of any of these homomorphisms. Here we get an exponential blow-up due to the number of subtrees (and, hence, of homomorphisms) that have to be considered. □

Proof of Corollary 2. From Theorem 13, there is a $\text{NEXPTIME}^{\text{NP}}$ algorithm that, given a WDPT p in $\mathcal{M}(\mathsf{WB}(k))$, constructs an exponential size p' in $\mathsf{WB}(k)$ such that $p \equiv_s p'$. Therefore, in order to check whether a partial mapping $h : \mathbf{X} \rightarrow \mathbf{U}$ is a partial answer to p over $\mathcal{D}$, for p a WDPT in $\mathcal{M}(\mathsf{WB}(k))$ and $\mathcal{D}$ a database, we can construct p' using the previous algorithm and then check whether h is a partial answer to p' over $\mathcal{D}$ (since this is equivalent with the fact that h is a partial answer to p over $\mathcal{D}$). The latter can be solved in polynomial time in the size of $\mathcal{D}$ and p' from Theorem 9. We conclude that Partial-Eval($\mathcal{M}(\mathsf{WB}(k))$) can be solved in time $O(f(|p|) + |\mathcal{D}|^c \cdot 2^{t(|p|)})$, where $f : \mathbb{N} \rightarrow \mathbb{N}$ is a double-exponential function, $t : \mathbb{N} \rightarrow \mathbb{N}$ is a polynomial, and $c \geq 1$ is a constant. A similar argument shows that Max-Eval($\mathcal{M}(\mathsf{WB}(k))$) is fixed-parameter tractable. □

Proof sketch of Theorem 14. It follows from the proof of Lemma 1 that there is a polynomial $t : \mathbb{N} \rightarrow \mathbb{N}$, such that the $\mathsf{WB}(k)$-approximations of a WDPT p are precisely the maximal elements (with respect to $\sqsubseteq$) of the set of WDPTs in $\mathsf{WB}(k)$ that are subsumed by p and whose size is at most $2^{t(|p|)}$. It follows from [4] that this set is nonempty, and therefore it contains at least one maximal element. Furthermore, each such maximal element can be computed in double-exponential time from p. □

A.3 Proof (sketches) for Section 6

Proof sketch of Proposition 9. For the right-to-left direction observe that ϕ_{cq} is $\equiv_s$-equivalent to a union of CQs in $\mathcal{C}(k)$, i.e., a union of single-node WDPTs in $\mathsf{WB}(k)$.

For the left-to-right direction assume that ϕ is $\equiv_s$-equivalent to a UWDPT ϕ^* in $\mathsf{UWB}(k)$. Then $\phi \equiv_s \phi^* \equiv_s \phi_{\mathrm{cq}} \equiv_s \phi^*_{\mathrm{cq}}$. But for unions of CQs we have that $\equiv_s$ is the same as $\equiv$, and hence $\phi_{\mathrm{cq}} \equiv \phi^*_{\mathrm{cq}}$. Moreover, since each WDPT in ϕ^* is in $\mathsf{WB}(k)$, it follows that ϕ^*_{cq} is indeed a union of CQs in $\mathcal{C}(k)$. □

Proof of Theorem 17. Let ϕ^r_{cq} be the union of CQs that is obtained by removing from ϕ_{cq} every CQ q that is contained in another CQ q' in ϕ_{cq}. By Proposition 9, query ϕ is in $\mathcal{M}(\mathsf{UWB}(k))$ iff ϕ_{cq} is equivalent to a union of CQs in $\mathcal{C}(k)$. It is easy to prove that this is the case iff each CQ in ϕ^r_{cq} is equivalent to a CQ in $\mathcal{C}(k)$ [5].

This gives us the following non-deterministic algorithm to check if $\phi \notin \mathcal{M}(\mathsf{UWB}(k))$:

Guess a CQ $q \in \phi_{\mathrm{cq}}$ (all of them are of polynomial size);
check that (1) $q \not\subseteq q'$ for every other CQ q' in ϕ_{cq}, and
(2) q is not equivalent to a CQ in $\mathcal{C}(k)$.

Clearly, (1) can be checked in coNP, and the same holds for (2) in case of $\mathcal{C}(k) = \mathsf{TW}(k)$ (see, e.g., [4]). For $\mathcal{C}(k) = \mathsf{HW}'(k)$, step (2) can be checked in Π_2^P, thus giving us the desired Π_2^P- and Π_3^P-algorithms, respectively.

The proof of the second part of the theorem is similar. □

Proof sketch of Theorem 18. By $\phi \equiv_s \phi_{\mathrm{cq}}$, we can apply results on approximations of unions of CQs from [4]. Let $\phi_{\mathrm{cq-app}}$ denote the union of all $\mathcal{C}(k)$-approximations of the CQs in ϕ_{cq}. A crucial result in [4] is that the $\mathcal{C}(k)$-approximation of a union of CQs can be obtained as the union of the approximations. Moreover, it follows from further results in [4] that $\phi_{\mathrm{cq-app}}$ is nonempty and contains at most a single-exponential number of CQs. Furthermore, each CQ in $\phi_{\mathrm{cq-app}}$ can be assumed to be of polynomial size. Hence, $\phi_{\mathrm{cq-app}}$ is the desired UWDPT ϕ'. □

Proof of Proposition 10. Hardness follows from the Π_2^P-hardness of Subsumption, which holds as long as the restriction to $\mathsf{WB}(k)$ only applies to the WDPT on the left-hand side. Now look at the membership: Given two UWDPTs ϕ', ϕ, to test if ϕ' is a $\mathsf{UWB}(k)$-approximation of ϕ, we first check that $\phi' \sqsubseteq \phi$ holds, which can be done in Π_2^P [19]. If this is the case, the proof of Theorem 18 tells us that ϕ' is a $\mathsf{UWB}(k)$-approximation of ϕ iff $\phi_{\mathrm{cq-app}} \sqsubseteq \phi'$, where $\phi_{\mathrm{cq-app}}$ again denotes the union of all $\mathcal{C}(k)$-approximations of the CQs in ϕ_{cq}. Checking if the latter is the case can be done in Π_2^P for $\mathcal{C}(k) = \mathsf{TW}(k)$ and in Π_3^P for $\mathcal{C}(k) = \mathsf{HW}(k)$. □

BonXai: Combining the simplicity of DTD with the expressiveness of XML Schema

Wim Martens
Universität Bayreuth

Frank Neven
Hasselt University and transnational University of Limburg

Matthias Niewerth
Universität Bayreuth

Thomas Schwentick
TU Dortmund University

ABSTRACT

While the migration from DTD to XML Schema was driven by a need for increased expressivity and flexibility, the latter was also significantly more complex to use and understand. Whereas DTDs are characterized by their simplicity, XML Schema Definitions (XSDs) are notoriously difficult. In this paper, we introduce the XML specification language BonXai which possesses most features of XSDs, including its expressivity, while retaining the simplicity of DTDs. In brief, the latter is achieved by sacrificing the explicit use of types in favor of simple patterns expressing contexts for elements. The goal of BonXai is by no means to replace XML Schema, but rather to provide a simpler DTD-like alternative to schema designers that do not need the explicit use of types. Therefore, BonXai can be seen as a practical front-end for XML Schema. A particular strong point of BonXai is its solid foundation rooted in a decade of theoretical work around pattern-based schemas. We present in detail the formal model for BonXai and discuss translation algorithms to and from XML Schema.

Categories and Subject Descriptors

H.2.3 [**Database Management**]: Languages—*Data Description Languages (DDL)*

General Terms

Design, Languages, Algorithms

Keywords

XML; BonXai; Schema Language

1. INTRODUCTION

Through its endorsement by the W3C, XML Schema [24] is nowadays adopted as the industry wide standard for the specification of XML schema languages. XML Schema can be considered as the replacement of DTDs with added expressivity and flexibility regarding namespaces, modularization, and datatypes. As an unfortunate side effect, the migration to XML Schema has also a negative impact on usability. Indeed, while DTDs are praised for their simplicity, XML Schema is notoriously difficult. It is designed to be machine-readable rather than human-readable and the central document of its specification (Part 1 of the specification) already consists of 100 pages of intricate text [9]. In their book, Møller and Schwartzbach discuss the comprehensibility of XML Schema as follows [19] (p. 156):

> *XML Schema is generally too complicated and hard to use by non-experts. This is a problem since many non-experts need to be able to read schemas to write valid instance documents.*

The goal of BonXai is to address this point by reconciling the expressivity and many features of XML Schema with the simplicity of DTDs. Whereas BonXai builds upon many ideas from existing schema languages, its most important feature, distinguishing itself from other schema languages, is its ability to serve as a front-end for XML Schema. Not only can BonXai schemas be readily transformed to and from XML Schema, but a BonXai schema itself can also be used to inspect, analyze and provide a deeper understanding of the corresponding XML Schema Definitions (henceforth, XSDs).

The purpose of this paper is to present a schema language for XML, called BonXai, specifically tailored as a practical schema design language, not to replace XML Schema but in support of the development of XML Schemas.

One of the most significant changes in the migration from DTDs to XML Schema is the introduction of types. The latter addition not only allows for a development style closely resembling object-oriented design and thereby facilitating modularization (for instance, through derivation and substitution), but types also significantly increase the structural expressiveness of schemas by allowing element definitions to depend on the context in which they appear. Surprisingly, studies reveal that XSDs occurring in practice hardly take advantage of the additional structural expressivity over DTDs [1]. In fact, most real world XSDs are structurally equivalent to a DTD. While the precise cause of the latter restricted use is unclear (we are not aware of any studies that tried to explain this), plausible explanations are that users do not know how to wield the extra expressiveness of XML Schema or that it is too cumbersome to write sophisticated and precise schemas when weighed against their

PODS'15, May 31–June 4, 2015, Melbourne, Victoria, Australia.

ACM 978-1-4503-2757-2/15/05 ...$15.00.
http://dx.doi.org/10.1145/2745754.2745774.

obvious benefits. Actually, Møller and Schwartzbach assert that the introduction of types is a major aspect complicating the design of XSDs (pg. 156) [19]:

> *One important factor of the complexity of the language is the type mechanism. Even without type derivations and substitution groups, this notion of types adds an extra layer of complexity: an element in the instance document has a* name, *some element declaration in the schema then assigns a* type *to this element name, and finally, some type definition then gives us the* constraints *that must be satisfied for the given element. In DTD, an element name instead directly identifies the associated constraints.*

In other words, the use of types to express structural constraints could be beyond the average user. The main idea underlying BonXai is to remove the need to use types to express structural constraints by adding those constraints as primitives to the language. That is, BonXai allows users to express contexts for elements by simple patterns without the need to explicitly specify and define complex types. Regardless of why one believes that many XSDs in practice are structurally equivalent to DTDs, BonXai should make schema development and XSD development easier.

We stress once more that the objective of BonXai is by no means to replace XML Schema, but rather to provide a simple way to specify and manipulate a large class of XML Schemas that only adds as much additional complication beyond DTDs as needed. Therefore, BonXai can also be seen as a practical front-end for XML Schema, i.e., "XML Schema for human beings". Indeed, as already mentioned above, the automatic translation into (and from) XML Schema is an important feature which distinguishes BonXai from other schema languages for XML. While several good alternatives for XML Schema exist, most notably DSD, Schematron and Relax NG [6, 23, 22], each with their own user base, they cannot be directly compiled into XML Schema for the simple reason that they can define schemas that are not representable as XSDs. We give a comparison with contemporary schema languages in Section 3.3.

An additional strength of BonXai is its solid foundation which is rooted in pattern-based schemas [16, 17] and which facilitates reasoning and transformation algorithms [10, 12]. Martens et al. [17] have shown that the increase in structural expressiveness from DTDs to XSDs lies in the ability to specify element definitions relative to a certain context. Whereas DTDs are restricted to element definitions relative to the name of the element, XSDs can specify element definitions relative to the path of element names from the root leading to that element.

We present a formal model for the core of BonXai and give formal descriptions of algorithms that translate back and forth between XML Schema and BonXai. These algorithms illustrate why the two languages are expressively equivalent. We analyze the worst-case blow-ups in these translations and show why our algorithms are worst-case optimal. Furthermore, we discuss practically relevant fragments of XML- and BonXai Schemas in which the conversions are particularly efficient.

As a reality check, we implemented the BonXai system in a tool [15] that allows, among other things, to parse BonXai schemas, validate XML against them and highlights matching rules, and can translate back and forth between BonXai and XML Schema.

Outline. This paper combines a practical language's exposition with an explanation of the underlying theory. We hope that in this way a reader who is familiar with either the practical or theoretical side can easily get an understanding of the other side as well. Section 2 provides a light-weight introduction to BonXai through a comparison with XML Schema that avoids notions from theoretical computer science and only requires a basic understanding of DTDs and XML Schema. In Section 3, we discuss more features of BonXai and its implementation, and consider its relationship with other XML schema languages. Section 4 introduces the formal model for BonXai and discusses the translations into and from XML Schema. We conclude in Section 5.

2. BONXAI BY EXAMPLE

In this section, we compare the ability of DTDs and XSDs to specify element definitions relative to a context and discuss how the latter influenced the design of BonXai.

Document Type Definitions (DTDs) constitute the first schema language for XML and are most well-known for their simplicity. Basically, DTDs are a grammar-based formalism where element declarations are entirely context insensitive. That is, the *content model* for an element is solely dependent on the name of that element.

We will now discuss a toy markup language that we will use to discuss the main features of XML Schema and BonXai. We first describe the markup language and an example document informally and then we will define a DTD, XML Schema, and BonXai schema for it.

EXAMPLE 2.1 (AN EXAMPLE DOCUMENT). *Consider the XML tree in Figure 1 with content formatted in a fictional markup language. The* `document` *is divided into three parts:* `template`, `userstyles` *(which contains user-defined style definitions), and* `content`. *The* `content` *part contains the actual text of the document, with markup (bold, font changes, etc.). Inside* `content`, *the text is structured by* `section` *elements, which can be nested to form subsections, etc.*

The `template` *element should describe the default formatting of the text within* `content`. *One could think that* `template` *defines ACM SIG style, for example. Within* `template`, *the default formatting of sections is specified within the* `section` *child of* `template` *and the default formatting of subsections within the* `section` *grandchild. So, a difference between* `template` *and* `content` *is that, in* `template`, *there is at most one* `section` *element per nesting depth. For the sake of the example, the rationale is that the default formatting of all sections at the same level should be the same. Furthermore,* `template` *does not contain text since all the actual text is within* `content`.

The `userstyles` *element contains a list of* `style` *elements. Each such* `style` *element should be thought of as being either some user-defined style (e.g., a fancy font for bold mathematics). Each* `style` *element has a unique name, which can be referred to from within* `content`. *Our example uses only one user-defined style:* `userdefined1`.

We chose our example such that it has elements within `content` and within `template` that have the same element names but different semantics, notably, the `section` element.

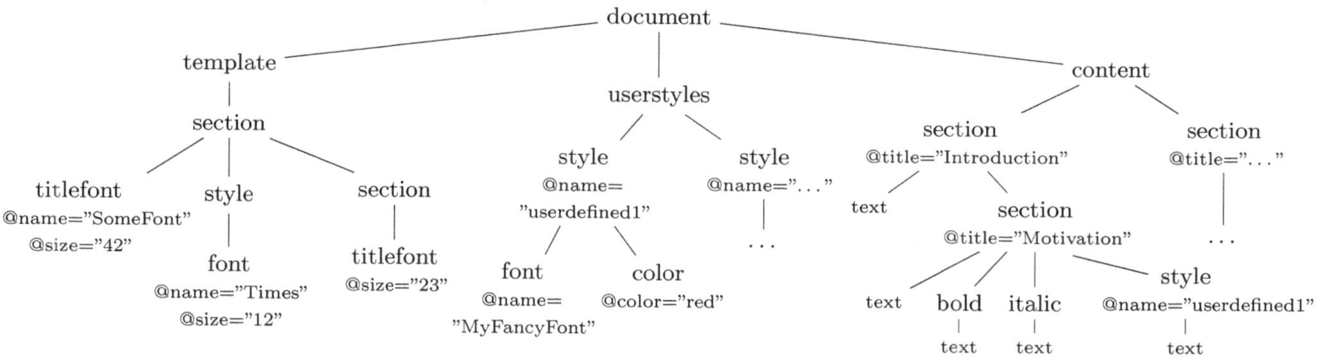

Figure 1: Example XML document.

```
<!ELEMENT document   (template, userstyles, content)>
<!ELEMENT template   section>
<!ELEMENT userstyles style*>
<!ELEMENT content    section*>
<!ENTITY % markup    "bold|italic|font|style|color">
<!ELEMENT section    (#PCDATA|titlefont|section|
                                        %markup;)*>
<!ATTLIST section    title CDATA #IMPLIED>
<!ELEMENT bold       (#PCDATA|%markup;)*>
<!ELEMENT italic     (#PCDATA|%markup;)*>
<!ELEMENT font       (#PCDATA|%markup;)*>
<!ATTLIST font       name CDATA #IMPLIED
                     size CDATA #IMPLIED>
<!ELEMENT style      (#PCDATA|%markup;)*>
<!ATTLIST style      name CDATA #IMPLIED>
<!ELEMENT titlefont  EMPTY>
<!ATTLIST titlefont  name CDATA #IMPLIED
                     size CDATA #IMPLIED>
<!ELEMENT color      (#PCDATA|%markup;)*>
<!ATTLIST color      color CDATA #REQUIRED>
```

Figure 2: A DTD describing the XML document in Figure 1.

Similarly, `style` has a different semantics if it is used within `userstyles`, within `template`, or within `content`. DTDs do not have the expressive power to take these differences into account and must define a common content model for all elements with the same name. That is, a DTD can only define one rule for `section`, independent of where a `section` element occurs in the document.

EXAMPLE 2.2 (DTD FOR EXAMPLE 2.1). *A complete DTD for which the XML document is valid is given in Figure 2. Note the use of the entity* `markup` *that allows us to write the schema more succinctly. We present this entire DTD because it is instructive to compare it with the XSD which we expose next and with the BonXai schema which we define later and is equivalent to the XSD.*

We next develop an XSD for our example markup language which is able to differentiate the elements with the same name but different semantics. Specifically, XSDs can take context into account through the explicit use of types.

EXAMPLE 2.3 (XSD FOR EXAMPLE 2.1). *A fragment of an XSD for the markup language of Example 2.1 is presented in Figure 3. Figure 3 contains the definition of the root* `document` *node. Similar to the DTD, it has a group* `markup` *(at the end) to avoid any unnecessary verbosity. All our type names start with a capital* T *so that the reader can easily distinguish them from element names.*

The XSD distinguishes between two types *of sections:* Tsection *and* TtemplateSection. *The former should be used within* `content` *and the latter one within* `template`. *The type of a* `section` *element is determined by the type of its parent. That is, when the parent of such an element is labeled* `content` *or is a* `section` *element with type* Tsection, *the section can contain text and markup. On the other hand, if the parent is labeled* `template` *or is a* `section` *with type* TtemplateSection, *the* `section` *element cannot contain text, it can only contain formatting instructions. Similarly, the XSD should contain three types that can be used for* `style`*:* TtemplateStyle *(for* `style` *elements below* `template`*),* TnamedStyle *(for* `style` *elements below* `userstyles`*, and* TstyleRef *(for* `style` *elements below* `content`*).*

The tree representation of XML documents is crucial for understanding the expressiveness of XML Schema and, therefore, also the expressiveness of BonXai. Intuitively, XML Schema can distinguish between elements of the same name when they have different labels on the path to the root of the XML tree, the so-called *ancestor path.*[1] So, XML Schema can distinguish the `section` elements within `content` from those within `template`, for example. Indeed, the former have labels `section content document` on the path to the root, whereas the latter have `section template document`. (Similarly, XML Schema can also distinguish between `style` within `userstyles`, within `template`, or within `content`.) In [17], it was shown that the kind of constraint which can be put on such an ancestor path by an XSD can always be captured by a regular expression and, in over 98% of the XSDs in the study, even by so-called linear XPath expressions [12], which are Core XPath expressions that do not branch.[2] The latter insight influences the design of BonXai to make such contexts explicit through the addition of patterns over ancestor paths.

[1]This property of XML Schema originates from the Element Declarations Consistent constraint, which is enforced by the XML Schema Specification [9] (Section 3.8.6.3) prohibits the use of the same element occurring in the same content model with different types. A detailed discussion on the implications of this constraint can be found in [17, 16].
[2]Consequently, linear XPath expressions can only reason about *paths* in trees.

```
<?xml version="1.0" encoding="UTF-8" standalone="no"?>
<xs:schema xmlns="http://mydomain.org/namespace"
     xmlns:xs="http://www.w3.org/2001/XMLSchema"
     elementFormDefault="qualified"
     targetNamespace="http://mydomain.org/namespace">
 <xs:element name="document">
  <xs:complexType>
   <xs:sequence>
    <xs:element name="template">
     <xs:complexType>
      <xs:sequence>
       <xs:element name="section" minOccurs="0"
                          type="TtemplateSection"/>
      </xs:sequence>
     </xs:complexType>
    </xs:element>
    <xs:element name="userstyles">
     <xs:complexType>
      <xs:sequence>
       <xs:element name="style" minOccurs="0"
           maxOccurs="unbounded" type="TnamedStyle"/>
      </xs:sequence>
     </xs:complexType>
    </xs:element>
    <xs:element name="content">
     <xs:complexType>
      <xs:sequence>
       <xs:element name="section" minOccurs="0"
             maxOccurs="unbounded" type="Tsection"/>
      </xs:sequence>
     </xs:complexType>
    </xs:element>
   </xs:sequence>
  </xs:complexType>
 </xs:element>
 <xs:complexType name="TtemplateSection">
  <xs:sequence>
   <xs:element name="titlefont" type="TtemplateFont"
                               minOccurs="0"/>
   <xs:element name="style"    type="TtemplateStyle"
                               minOccurs="0"/>
   <xs:element name="section"  type="TtemplateSection"
                               minOccurs="0"/>
  </xs:sequence>
 </xs:complexType>
 <xs:complexType name="Tsection" mixed="true">
  <xs:choice minOccurs="0" maxOccurs="unbounded">
   <xs:group ref="markup"/>
   <xs:element name="section" type="Tsection"/>
  </xs:choice>
  <xs:attribute name="title" type="xs:string"
                               use="required"/>
 </xs:complexType>
 <xs:group name="markup">
  [...]
 </xs:group>
 [...]
</xs:schema>
```

Figure 3: An XSD for the XML tree in Fig. 1.

We now discuss two BonXai schemas for the running example's markup language. The BonXai schema in Figure 4 is equivalent to the DTD given in Figure 2, while the BonXai schema in Figure 5 exploits the additional expressiveness of BonXai to be equivalent to the (full version of the) XSD of Figure 3.

Both examples use a compact syntax inspired by Relax NG [22]. Like a DTD, a BonXai schema is a collection of rules. The right-hand side of a rule denotes a content model as usual. The left-hand side can be either a label or a regular expression if more expressiveness is needed. We use a regular expression syntax which resembles XPath expressions since this allows users to also write linear XPath expression on left-hand sides. The semantics is that for an XML document to match the schema, the children of nodes in the document selected by a left-hand side expression when evaluated from the root, should match the content model denoted in the right-hand side of the rule. For instance, the rule

```
template//section = { element titlefont?,
                      element style?, element section? }
```

stipulates that `section` elements occurring somewhere below a `template` element can contain a `titlefont` child, a `style` child, and a `section` child, whereas the rule

```
content//section = mixed {  attribute title,
                       (element section|group markup)*}
```

stipulates that elements occurring somewhere below a `content` element should contain a title and may contain text (indicated by the keyword `mixed`) with markup. The keyword `mixed` allows mixed content, i.e., it is allowed to interleave text with XML tags. In the BonXai schema in Figure 5, `/` and `//` stand for the XPath axes "child" and "descendant", respectively. We denote concatenation, disjunction, Kleene star, and "optional" by ",", "|", "*", and "?", as in DTDs. The operator "&" stands for unordered concatenation, which is known as `xs:all` in XSD. If an expression does not start with `/` or `//`, we implicitly assume that it starts with `//`. This way, simple lables are just a special case of regular expressions.

```
target namespace http://mydomain.org/namespace
namespace xs = http://www.w3.org/2001/XMLSchema
global { document }
groups {
 group markup = { element bold | element italic |
       element font | element style | element color }
}
grammar {
 document    = { element template, element userstyles,
                 element content }
 template    = { element section }
 userstyles = { (element style)* }
 content     = { (element section)* }
 section = mixed { attribute title,(element section |
                  element titlefont | group markup)* }
 bold      = mixed { (group markup)* }
 italic    = mixed { (group markup)* }
 font      = mixed { attribute name, attribute size,
                      (group markup)* }
 style     = mixed { attribute name, (group markup)* }
 titlefont =       { attribute name, attribute size }
 color     = mixed { attribute color, (group markup)* }
 @name     = { type xs:string }
 @color    = { type xs:string }
 @title    = { type xs:string }
 @size     = { type xs:integer }
}
```

Figure 4: A BonXai schema equivalent to the DTD in Figure 2.

```
target namespace http://mydomain.org/namespace
namespace xs = http://www.w3.org/2001/XMLSchema
global { document }
groups {
 attribute-group fontattr = { attribute name?, attribute size? }
 group markup = { ( element bold | element italic | element font | element style | element color )* }
}
grammar {
 document                                   = { element template, element userstyles, element content }
 content                                    = { (element section)* }
 template                                   = { (element section)? }
 userstyles                                 = { (element style)* }
 content//section                           = mixed { attribute title, (element section | group markup)* }
 content//style                             = mixed { attribute name, group markup }
 content//font                              = mixed { attribute-group fontattr, group markup }
 content//color                             = mixed { attribute color, group markup }
 (bold|italic)                              = mixed { group markup }
 template//section                          = { element titlefont?, element style?, element section? }
 template//style                            = { element font? & element color? }
 userstyles/style                           = { attribute name, element font? & element color? }
 (userstyles|template)//color               = { attribute color }
 (userstyles|template)//(font|titlefont)    = { attribute-group fontattr }
 (@name| @color|@title)                     = { type xs:string }
 @size                                      = { type xs:integer }
}
```

Figure 5: A BonXai schema equivalent to the (partial) XSD from Figure 3.

The main difference with the corresponding XSD is that contexts are now defined explicitly. Another way of viewing the difference between XSD and BonXai is top-down versus bottom-up. XSDs carry all relevant information about the root-path in a top-down fashion, encoded in types, while BonXai, instead, looks upward from a node, thus separating types from their inference. Furthermore, as XSDs employ types, context has to be specified in terms of automata, while BonXai can use the more user-friendly regular expressions or linear XPath expressions.

3. BONXAI, THE PRACTICAL LANGUAGE

In Subsection 3.1, we present BonXai in more detail but do not intend to discuss every feature of the language and its relationship with XML Schema here. Instead, we provide a high-level overview and refer the reader to [14] for further details. We just discuss a few BonXai-specific matters (ancestor patterns, child patterns, and priorities) and then argue how BonXai seamlessly incorporates most of XML Schema language features (like differentiation between elements/attributes, simple types, element- and attribute groups, namespaces, constraints, schema imports, mixed types, default values, anytype/anyattribute).

Subsection 3.2 explains BonXai's priority system. As mentioned in the introduction, the design of BonXai is influenced by existing XML schema languages. We discuss these in Subsection 3.3.

3.1 The BonXai Schema Specification Language

BonXai schemas consist of up to five blocks. First comes the *namespace block*, declaring all namespaces used in the schema. The second block is called the *global block* and specifies which element names can occur at the root of documents that match the schema. Third, there is an optional *group block*, which can declare the equivalent of XSD groups. The fourth block is called the *grammar block* and is the actual core of the schema. The grammar block contains the definitions of the rules that define the structure of documents. Finally, there is an optional *constraints block* which defines integrity constraints.

Global Element Names: Elements that are declared `global` in a BonXai schema can occur as root elements in XML documents that match the schema. In our running example, there is a single such element, called `document`.

Ancestor Patterns: A rule within the grammar-block of a BonXai schema is of the form

`<ancestor pattern> = <child pattern>`

The ancestor pattern (left of the equality sign) describes the context of the rule and should be matched against paths in the tree that start from the root. Ancestor patterns are variants of regular expressions, built from element names and attribute names (i.e. names starting with @). The regular expressions have the operators union (|), concatenation (/), descendant (//), Kleene star (∗), one-or-more (+), and zero-or-one (?). Sub-patterns can be grouped using round brackets. For compatibility with XML Schema, we need that, if attribute names appear, they occur at the end of ancestor patterns. For example, `(/a/a)*(@c|@d)` is allowed (and specifies `c`- and `d`-attributes for even-depth nodes that are labeled `a` and only have `a`-labeled ancestors), but `/a/@b/c` is not allowed. (Indeed, in XML, attributes cannot have children.)

For convenience, a pattern that does not start with either / or // is implicitly assumed to start with //. This allows to just use an element name as ancestor pattern to match all elements of this name, as in DTDs.

Child Patterns: In its simplest form, a child pattern is a regular expression describing the content model of a set of elements. To allow some other features (e.g. groups) and not introducing ambiguity, all element names have to be prefixed with the keyword `element`. Regular expressions in child patterns are built using concatenation (`,`), union (`|`), interleaving(`&`), Kleene closure (`*`), one-or-more (`+`), zero-or-one (`?`) and counting (`{n,m}`). The upper bound of counters may be `*` instead of a number to express that there is no upper bound. Sub-expressions can be grouped using round brackets. The use of the interleaving operator is restricted, to reflect the restrictions imposed by the all-pattern of XML Schema. (The restrictions for XML Schema are described in Section 3.8.2 in [9].) In plain words, these restrictions say that no content model should use an interleaving operator and at the same time a union or a concatenation operator. Furthermore, in content models containing an interleaving operator, counters are only allowed directly above element declarations in the syntax tree of the regular expression.

Priorities: It is possible to define BonXai rules such that two or more rules match the same path. When such a multiple match occurs, BonXai gives priority to the rule that occurs last in the schema. To illustrate, assume that we would change the ancestor pattern `content//section` to `section`. Then we would have the rules

```
section = mixed {attribute title,
                (element section|group markup)*}
template//section = { element titlefont?,
                element style?, element section? }
```

in the schema. Both rules are matched by a `section` element that is below a `template` element. In cases like this, the rule that occurs last in the schema takes priority. Here, `template//section` takes priority and therefore the semantics of the modified schema are the same as the semantics of the original schema. The rationale behind priorities is that a developer can first write down rules that generally apply in the schema and write down the special cases and exceptions later. We introduced priorities in BonXai because they were required for ensuring full compatibility with XML Schema's expressive power. We explain priorities in more detail in Section 3.2.

Integrity Constraints, etc.: BonXai allows to express the same integrity constraints as XML Schema (i.e., unique, key, and keyref). The term "keyref" is taken from XML Schema, where it denotes a foreign key constraint.

BonXai's current implementation also models *attributes*, *groups*, *namespaces*, *mixed and nillable content models*, *references to foreign namespaces*, *wildcards*, and *annotations*.

3.2 Priorities in BonXai

In this subsection, we explain some fine points of the priority-based semantics of rules in BonXai schemas. Priorities were mainly introduced to avoid compatibility problems with XML Schema. However, we think they can also be convenient, as we will explain below.

In the theory of pattern-based schemas for XML (of which BonXai is an example), two alternative semantics for multiple matches of rules have been investigated [10, 12]: existential semantics and universal semantics. We say that the *ancestor-pattern of rule* `r = {s}` *matches a node* n in an XML tree, if the string of element names from the root of the document to n matches the regular expression `r`. The two semantics can now informally be defined as follows:

- Universal semantics: for each node n in the XML tree and each rule `r = {s}` for which the ancestor pattern matches n, the children of n must match `s`.
- Existential semantics: for each node n in the XML tree, there must be at least one rule `r = {s}` for which the ancestor pattern matches n and the children of n match `s`.

Thus, under universal semantics, we would require a matching element to match *all* content model definitions of relevant rules and under existential semantics, we would require a matching element to match *at least one* content model definition of a relevant rule. Unfortunately, neither semantics can be applied while retaining at the same time compatibility with the Unique Particle Attribution (UPA) rule of the W3C XML Schema specification [9, Section 3.8.6.4]. In a nutshell, UPA requires content model definitions to be *deterministic regular expressions* [2]. Furthermore, translating BonXai schemas under the universal or existential semantics to XSDs, requires deterministic regular expressions to be closed under finite unions and finite intersections, respectively, which is not the case [2, 3, 13]. As an aside we mention that deterministic regular expressions are not closed under complement.

A "quick and dirty" solution could be to require ancestor patterns in rules to have an empty intersection. However, we feel that this would be very user-unfriendly. Consider again our running example in Figure 5. The two ancestor patterns `template//section` and `content//section` have a non-empty intersection since both could, in theory, match a word that has an occurrence of `template`, followed by `content`, followed by `section` (even though such a word cannot occur as a path in trees defined by the schema). Changing the two ancestor patterns to mend this problem would make the schema less readable and require users to have deeper expertise in formal language theory.

We show in Section 4 that the priority-based semantics of BonXai does not have the expressivity problems of universal or existential semantics, by giving conversion algorithms from the core of BonXai to XML Schema and back; and by observing that the Unique Particle Attribution constraint is preserved. Furthermore, we feel that priorities make sense when designing schemas (specify general rules first, special cases later) and lead to more readable schemas. Therefore, a sensible way of using priorities is for cases where, for a set of elements with the same name, most of the elements have the same content model, but there are a few exceptions. (Notice that, if two ancestor patterns define regular expressions that end with different element names, the intersection of the rules is always empty and priorities are irrelevant.)

We conclude this section with a use case for priorities: schema evolution. In our running example, sections can be nested arbitrarily deeply. Assume that we want to change the schema such that the nesting depth of sections is at most three. In the BonXai schema in Figure 5, this can be achieved by inserting the rule

```
content/section/section/section =
                { attribute title, group markup }
```

at the end of the rules that start with `content`. The semantics of this rule would be that subsubsections only have a title attribute and markup, but no `section` children.

If one would want to perform the equivalent change directly in XML Schema, one would be required to make three complex types for sections below `content`: one for each allowed nesting depth. The change would introduce much more clutter.

3.3 A Comparison With Other Schema Languages for XML

As already stated before, BonXai borrows concepts from several existing schema languages for XML. The purpose of this section is to give an overview of the most well-known of those languages and discuss their relationship with BonXai.

Following [19], DSD2 [6] (Document Structure Description 2.0) is a language developed by the University of Aarhus and AT&T Research Labs whose primary goal is to be simple yet expressive. Like BonXai, DSD2 is based on rules which must be satisfied for every element in the input document. BonXai and DSD2 are incomparable in how context is defined. While DSD2 is far more expressive than DTDs, its exact expressiveness in formal language theoretic terms is unclear. It allows context to be defined in terms of Boolean expressions which can refer to structural predicates like *parent* and *ancestor*, but, unlike BonXai, also allows to look downward using predicates like *child* and *descendant*. BonXai on the other hand harnesses the full power of regular languages on the ancestor path, while DSD2 seems to remain within the star-free regular languages (on the ancestor path). For this reason, DSD2, on a structural level, is incomparable to XML Schema.

Relax NG [22] has been developed within the Organization for the Advancement of Structured Information Standards (OASIS). Like DSD2, its main goal is to combine simplicity with expressivity. In formal language theoretic terms, the expressiveness of Relax NG corresponds to the unranked regular tree languages which strictly includes XML Schema [20, 17]. Like XML Schema, Relax NG is grammar based and utilizes types to define context. However, Relax NG schemas are not restrained by the Unique Particle Attribution constraint or the Element Declarations Consistent constraint. So, unlike XSDs and therefore BonXai, the context of an element in Relax NG can depend on the complete tree. As BonXai strives for simplicity it utilizes a readable compact syntax which is inspired by that of Relax NG.

Schematron [23] is a rule-based language based on patterns, rules and assertions. Basically, an assertion is a pair (ϕ, m) where ϕ is an XPath expression and m an error message. The error message is displayed when ϕ fails. A rule groups various assertions together and defines by means of an XPath expression a context in which the grouped assertions are evaluated. Patterns then group various rules together. Schematron is not so much intended as a stand-alone schema language but can be used in cooperation with existing schema languages. BonXai shares the use of XPath-expressions with Schematron, although BonXai restricts them to a very small subset (linear expressions) to ensure compatibility with XML Schema.

Co-constraints is an overloaded term which generally refers to a mechanism for verifying data interdependencies. While DSD, Schematron, and Relax NG quite naturally allow to express co-constraints, XSDs are rather limited in this respect. The latter motivated the formulation of extensions of DTDs and XSDs, named DTD++ [8] and SchemaPath [4], with XPath expressions to express co-existence and co-absence of element names and attributes. These extensions share with BonXai the use of XPath to express conditions but differ from BonXai in that they increase the expressiveness beyond that of XML Schema.

4. THEORY: BONXAI VERSUS XSD

In this section, we explain the underlying theory behind BonXai. In particular, we provide

- a compact and clear formal model of core BonXai schemas, stripped of features that are unimportant for analysing conversion algorithms;
- a formal back and forth translation procedure between core XML Schema and core BonXai;
- an analysis of the blow-up of these conversions; and
- proof of worst-case optimality for the conversions.

Our aim is to provide a precise mathematical description of BonXai's core which abstracts away from unavoidable cosmetics like namespaces and data types, and which offers a quick understanding of the essentials of the language. The presentation of the translations between BonXai and XML Schema fulfills a similar purpose and, in addition, makes the relation between BonXai and XML Schema apparent. In particular, the translation provides insight to where one language can be more succinct than the other.

4.1 A Formal Model for BonXai Schemas

Before we introduce the formal model for the core of BonXai, we first establish some basic terminology and notation.

Basic Terminology.

We view an XML document as a finite, rooted, ordered, labeled, unranked tree D. We assume a finite alphabet (that is, a finite set) EName of *element names* from which the nodes of XML trees take their labels, that is, each node v of D carries exactly one label $\text{lab}(v) \in \mathsf{EName}$. By $a, b, c, \ldots$ we denote elements from EName. For a node v, we denote by $\text{anc-str}^D(v)$ the *ancestor-string* of v in D which is given by the concatenation of the labels of the nodes on the path from the root of D to v. More formally, the ancestor-string of v in D is the string $\text{lab}(v_1) \cdots \text{lab}(v_n)$, where v_1 is the root of D, $v_n = v$, and v_{i+1} is a child of v_i for each $i = 1, \ldots, n-1$. We denote by $\text{ch-str}^D(v)$ the concatenation of the labels of the children of v in D. More formally, if the children of v are $u_1, \ldots, u_m$ from left to right, then $\text{ch-str}^D(v) = \text{lab}(u_1) \cdots \text{lab}(u_m)$. We note that $\text{ch-str}^D(v)$ is sometimes also called the *content* of node v. We omit D in the notation of ancestor- or child-strings when D is clear from the context.

EXAMPLE 4.1. *Consider the* `section` *child* v *of the element* `template` *in the tree of Figure 1. Then*

$$\text{anc-str}(v) = \texttt{document template section}$$
$$\text{ch-str}(v) = \texttt{titlefont style section}.$$

We assume familiarity with finite automata and only discuss notation here. We denote a (nondeterministic) finite automaton or NFA as a tuple $A = (Q, \mathsf{EName}, \delta, q_0, F)$ where Q is its finite set of states, EName is the alphabet, $\delta : (Q \times \mathsf{EName}) \to 2^Q$ is the transition function, $q_0 \in Q$ is the initial state and $F \subseteq Q$ is the set of accepting states. An NFA is *deterministic* if $\delta(q, a)$ contains at most one state for each $q \in Q$ and $a \in \mathsf{EName}$. The *language* of A (i.e., the set of words accepted by A) is defined in the standard manner. The *size* of A, denoted $|A|$, is the number of states of A. Sometimes we use finite automata without accepting states. We then simply write them as $A = (Q, \mathsf{EName}, \delta, q_0)$. We sometimes use $A(w)$ as an abbreviation the set of states that A can reach after reading w.

We use regular expressions r with the following syntax

$$r ::= \varepsilon \mid \emptyset \mid a \mid rr \mid r + r \mid (r)? \mid (r)^+ \mid (r)^*,$$

where ε denotes the empty string and a ranges over symbols in the alphabet EName. Sometimes we also use the symbol $\cdot$ for regular expression concatenation to improve readability. For a set $S = \{a_1, \ldots, a_n\} \subseteq \mathsf{EName}$ we sometimes abbreviate the disjunction $(a_1 + \cdots + a_n)$ by S. As usual, we write $L(r)$ for the language defined by regular expression r. We define the *size* of regular expression r to be its total number of alphabet symbol occurrences. For example, both expressions aaa and $a(b + c)?$ have size three.

A Formal Model for BonXai's Core.

Now we define *BonXai Schema Definitions (BXSDs)*, which are a formal model for the core of BonXai schemas. The difference between the BonXai schema specification language and BXSDs is that the former can be used in our implementation [15] and has most of the XML Schema Language features to make it usable in practice, whereas the latter is a stripped down version that we use here to study translations between BonXai and XML Schema. For instance, the BonXai language supports integrity constraints, but we do not define these in BXSDs since they are trivial to translate from and to XSD.

Our definition of BonXai Schema Definitions requires expressions s_i to be *deterministic* [2]. This restriction is necessary to make BXSDs expressively equivalent to XSDs, due to the UPA condition mentioned in Subsection 3.2. We note that such expressions are sometimes referred to as *one-unambiguous* [2]. We do not formally introduce deterministic regular expressions here, as BXSDs and XSDs have exactly the same restrictions and our conversion algorithms therefore do not alter the regular expressions of the content models. Given the lacking closure of DRE under Boolean operations noted in Subsection 3.2, it is however crucial, that none of the conversion algorithms presented in Subsection 4.2 construct unions, intersections, or complements of content models.

DEFINITION 1. A *BonXai Schema Definition (BXSD)* is a pair $B = (\mathsf{EName}, S, R)$ where $S \subseteq \mathsf{EName}$ is a set of start elements and R is an ordered list $r_1 \to s_1, \ldots, r_n \to s_n$ of rules, where

- all r_i are regular expressions over EName and
- all s_i are deterministic regular expressions over the alphabet EName.

For each $i = 1, \ldots, n$, we say that the rule $r_i \to s_i$ has *index* i. Let D be an XML document and u a node of D. A rule $r_i \to s_i$ is *relevant* for u if i is the largest index such that $\text{anc-str}^D(u) \in L(r_i)$. Notice that a node u has at most one relevant rule in B. An XML document D conforms to the BXSD B if the label of $\text{root}(D)$ is in S and, for each node $u \in \text{Nodes}(D)$, if $r_i \to s_i$ is relevant for u, then $\text{ch-str}^D(u) \in L(s_i)$. The definition of relevant rules reflects the priority system in BonXai: rules with a higher index have higher priority.

EXAMPLE 4.2. *The formal abstraction of the BonXai schema in Figure 5 is the BXSD $B = (\mathsf{EName}, S, R)$ where*

- EName = *{document, template, userstyles, content, section, style, title}*
- S = *{document}*
- *R is the ordered list containing rules (parts omitted):*

$$\begin{aligned}
//document &\to template\ userstyles\ content\\
//content &\to section^*\\
//template &\to section\\
//userstyles &\to style^*\\
//content//section &\to (bold + \cdots + section)^*\\
&\vdots\\
//template//section &\to titlefont?\ style?\ section?\\
&\vdots
\end{aligned}$$

Here, we wrote the left-hand-sides of BonXai rules as in Section 2. Formally, in this section, // abbreviates the regular expression EName^*.

4.2 Translations Between Schemas

Before we discuss how to translate back and forth between XML Schema and BonXai, we give our abstraction of an XML Schema, closely following the definition from [20, 17, 16].

A Formal Model for Core XSDs.

An XML Schema uses a finite set of element names and complex type names. We therefore fix finite sets EName and Types of *element names* and *complex type names*, respectively. The set TEname of *typed element names* is then defined as $\{a[t] \mid a \in \mathsf{EName}, t \in \mathsf{Types}\}$. In an XML Schema, a typed element name $a[t]$ could, for example, be written as `<xs:element name="a" type="t"/>`.

DEFINITION 2. An *XSchema Definition (XSD)* is a tuple $X = (\mathsf{EName}, \mathsf{Types}, \rho, T_0)$ where EName and Types are finite sets of elements and types, respectively, ρ is mapping from Types to regular expressions over alphabet TEname, and $T_0 \subseteq \mathsf{TEname}$ is a set of typed start elements. Furthermore, the following two conditions hold:

Element Declarations Consistent (EDC) There are no typed elements $a[t_1]$ and $a[t_2]$ in a regular expression $\rho(t)$ with $t_1 \neq t_2$. Furthermore, there are no typed elements $a[t_1]$ and $a[t_2]$ in T_0 with $t_1 \neq t_2$.

Unique Particle Attribution (UPA) Each regular expression $\rho(t)$ is deterministic.

We sometimes also refer to $\rho(t)$ as the *content model associated to t*. The EDC constraint can be found in [9, Section 3.8.6.3] and the UPA constraint in [9, Section 3.8.6.4].

A *typing* of an XML document D w.r.t. X associates, to each node u of D, a type of the schema. Formally, a typing of D w.r.t. X is a mapping μ from $\text{Nodes}(D)$ to TEname. A typing μ is *correct* if it satisfies the following three conditions:

- $\mu(\text{root}(D)) \in T_0$.
- For each node $u \in \text{Nodes}(D)$, we have $\mu(u) \in \{\text{lab}(u)[t] \mid t \in \mathsf{Types}\}$.
- For each node $u \in \text{Nodes}(D)$ with children $u_1, \ldots, u_n$ from left to right, we have $\mu(u_1) \cdots \mu(u_n) \in L(\mu(u))$.

An XML document D conforms to an XSD X if there exists a *correct typing μ of D w.r.t. X*. Notice that typings are unique due to the EDC condition, that is, there can be at most one correct typing for a given document D w.r.t. a given XSD X.

4.2.1 Translation from XML Schema to BonXai

We present a translation algorithm from XSDs to BXSDs. This algorithm is the core of a procedure that we implemented to translate XML Schema into BonXai [15]. The algorithm consists of two phases. The first phase converts an XSD into an intermediate data structure, which is called a *DFA-based XSD*. We will define such a DFA-based XSD formally, because it is a representation of schemas that is very convenient in proofs. In the second phase, the DFA-based XSD is translated to the BXSD.

DFA-based XSDs were introduced in [16] (Definition 6) as an alternative characterization of XML Schema Definitions. We now define DFA-based XSDs as in [16], with a minor difference: due to the UPA condition, we require their content models to be deterministic regular expressions.

DEFINITION 3. A *DFA-based XSD (with deterministic content models)* is a tuple (A, S, λ), where $A = (Q, \mathsf{EName}, \delta, q_0)$ is a DFA with initial state q_0 and without final states such that q_0 has no incoming transitions, $S \subseteq \mathsf{EName}$ is the set of allowed root element names and λ is a function mapping each state in $Q \setminus \{q_0\}$ to a deterministic regular expression over EName. Furthermore, for every state $q \in Q$ and every element name a occurring in $\lambda(q)$, we have that $\delta(q, a)$ is non-empty.

In the remainder of the paper, S usually equals $\{a \mid \delta(q_0, a) \neq \emptyset\}$. (The intuition is that, for each element $a \in S$, the automaton A can read a string that starts with a. Since S is simply the set of root elements, λ does not map q_0 to a regular expression.) However, we sometimes use fully defined DFAs (which are DFAs in which $|\delta(q, a)| = 1$ for every state q and label a) and therefore we need to explicitly mention S in general. Since we *only* consider DFA-based XSDs with deterministic content models in this paper, we henceforth simply refer to them as *DFA-based XSDs*.

An XML document D *satisfies* (A, S, λ) if the root node is labelled with an element name from S and, for every node u, $A(\text{anc-str}^t(u)) = \{q\}$ implies that $\text{ch-str}^D(u)$ is in the language defined by $\lambda(q)$.

We now explain how to translate a given XSD $X = (\mathsf{EName}, \mathsf{Types}, \rho, T_0)$ into an equivalent DFA-based XSD A in linear time. The procedure is outlined in Algorithm 1 and resembles procedures in [17, 10], which were developed for different models of XSDs.[3] It has the following property.

LEMMA 4 (ADAPTED FROM LEMMA 7 IN [10]). *Each XSD can be translated into an equivalent DFA-based XSD in linear time.*

We now show how to translate DFA-based XSDs into equivalent BXSDs. The translation is in Algorithm 2 and is similar to the proof of Theorem 7.1 ((a) $\Rightarrow$ (d)) in [17].

LEMMA 5. *Each DFA-based XSD (A, S, λ) can be translated into an equivalent BXSD B with linearly many rules in $|A|$.*

Notice that the ordering of the rules in R in Algorithm 2 is arbitrary. The reason why the ordering is not important is that the priorities in BonXai are irrelevant in the schema. Indeed, for each pair of states $q_1 \neq q_2$ from A, we have that $L(r_{q_1}) \cap L(r_{q_2}) = \emptyset$, because A is a DFA. Furthermore, the BXSD B can have regular expressions that are exponentially

[3]One consequence of the slightly different models of XSDs is that the translation in [10] is quadratic, whereas it is linear in our case.

Algorithm 1 Translating an XSD to an equivalent DFA-based XSD.

Input: XSD $X = (\mathsf{EName}, \mathsf{Types}, \rho, T_0)$
Output: DFA-based XSD $(A = (Q, \mathsf{EName}, \delta, q_0), S, \lambda)$ equivalent to X

$S := \{a \mid \exists t \in \mathsf{Types} \text{ such that } a[t] \in T_0\}$
$Q := \{q_0\} \uplus \mathsf{Types}$
For each $a[t] \in T_0$, $\delta(q_0, a) := t$
For each $t_1 \in \mathsf{Types}$ and $a \in \mathsf{EName}$ such that $a[t_2]$ occurs in $\rho(t_1)$, $\delta(t_1, a) := t_2$
For each $t \in \mathsf{Types}$, $\lambda(t) := \mu(\rho(t))$
▷ $\mu(\rho(t))$ is obtained from $\rho(t)$ by replacing every $a[t']$ with a

Algorithm 2 Translating a DFA-based XSD into an equivalent BXSD.

Input: DFA-based XSD $(A = (Q, \mathsf{EName}, \delta, q_0), S, \lambda)$
Output: BXSD $B = (\mathsf{EName}, S, R)$ equivalent to X

for every state $q \in Q$ **do**
  $r_q :=$ a reg. expression for $(Q, \mathsf{EName}, \delta, q_0, \{q\})$
  $s_q := \lambda(q)$
$R := r_{q_1} \to s_{q_1}, \ldots, r_{q_n} \to s_{q_n}$, where $\{q_1, \ldots, q_n\} = Q$

larger than $|A|$ in general. This cannot be avoided[4] because A is a DFA and the worst-case conversion from a DFA to a regular expression is well-known to be exponential [7]. In Section 4.4 we discuss classes of schemas that capture most cases in practice and that do not lead to such a blow-up.

4.2.2 Translation from BonXai to XML Schema

The translation from BonXai to XML Schema follows a similar overall outline as the reverse translation of Section 4.2.1. Again, we use DFA-based XSDs as an intermediate representation in the translation. That is, we first translate BXSDs into DFA-based XSDs and translate the latter to XSDs. However, the present translation is more technical than the one before.

Algorithm 3 describes the translation of BXSDs into DFA-based XSDs.

LEMMA 6. *Each BXSD B can be translated into an equivalent DFA-based XSD (A, S, λ) for which $|A|$ is at most exponential in $|B|$.*

It should be noted that Algorithm 3 is optimized for readability and not for efficiency. It is straightforward to change it such that it only computes reachable states of A. Note that whether a state is reachable also depends on the right-hand sides of the rules, because a transition $\delta(p, a)$, for which the label a does not occur in $\lambda(p)$, can never be taken in a conforming document.

The final translation we need is the one from DFA-based XSDs into XSDs. It is summarized in Algorithm 4 and has linear running time.

LEMMA 7 (ADAPTED FROM LEMMA 7 IN [10]). *Each DFA-based XSD can be translated into an equivalent XSD in linear time.*

We note that the XSD that results from Algorithm 4 can be "minimized" efficiently using a minor adaptation of the

[4]Proving that an exponential blow-up cannot be avoided is more technical than just this observation, see Section 4.3.

Algorithm 3 Translating a BXSD to an equivalent DFA-based XSD.

```
Input: BXSD B = (EName, S, R = r_1 → s_1, ..., r_n → s_n)
Output: DFA-based XSD (A, S, λ) equivalent to B
for each i = 1, ..., n do
    A_i := minimal complete DFA
                    (Q_i, EName, δ_i, q_0^i, F_i) for L(r_i)
A := A_1 × ··· × A_n        ▷ A has state set Q_1 × ··· × Q_n
for each (q_1, ..., q_n) ∈ Q_1 × ··· × Q_n do
    if ∃i ∈ {1, ..., n} such that q_i ∈ F_i then
        i := largest number such that q_i ∈ F_i
        λ((q_1, ..., q_n)) := s_i
    else
        λ((q_1, ..., q_n)) := (EName)*
```

Algorithm 4 Translating a DFA-based XSD to an equivalent XSD.

```
Input: DFA-based XSD (A = (Q, EName, δ, q_0), S, λ)
Output: XSD X = (EName, Types, ρ, T_0)
                              equivalent to (A, S, λ)
Types := Q
T_0 := {a[δ(q_0, a)] | a ∈ S, δ(q_0, a) ≠ ∅}
for each state q ∈ Q do
    r_q := expression obtained from λ(q) by replacing
                         each symbol a with a[δ(q, a)]
    ρ(q) = r_q
```

minimization algorithm for XSDs from [18]. (More formally, it is possible to efficiently produce an XSD such that the set Types is minimal among all equivalent XSDs. Also, the expressions r_q do not become larger.) The difference with the minimization algorithm from [18] would be that the deterministic regular expressions r_q should not be minimized. (In fact, it is not clear how to efficiently minimize a deterministic regular expression — if it would be possible to do this efficiently, the whole resulting XSD could be minimized in polynomial time by the algorithm from [18].)

4.3 Worst-Case Optimality of the Translation Algorithms

We now prove that both translation algorithms are worst-case optimal. In particular, we show that both conversions from the previous section can lead to exponential size blow-ups in general. In Section 4.4 we exhibit fragments that are prevalent in practice for which the conversions are efficient.

4.3.1 From XML Schema to BonXai

When converting an XML Schema (XSD) to a BonXai Schema Definition (BXSD) using the procedures in Lemmas 4 and 5 it is possible that the BXSD is exponentially larger than the XSD. The source of this exponential blow-up lies in Algorithm 2 which is used in Lemma 5. More precisely, line 1 constructs a regular expression equivalent to a DFA, which is well known to be exponential in the worst case [7].

We will now show that this blow-up cannot be avoided in general, which means that, in this sense, our conversion algorithm is worst-case optimal. Recall, however, that our conversion which we showed in Lemma 5 does not produce a large number of rules in the BXSD. Indeed, if the DFAs that Algorithm 2 encounters on line 2 only produce polynomially large regular expressions, then the whole conversion is polynomial as well. We discuss a particularly relevant such case in Section 4.4.

The following theorem is the most technical result in the paper. Its proof leverages a technique from [7]. The hard part of our proof is to show that the exponential blowup cannot be avoided by a clever use of the priorities in BonXai.

THEOREM 8. *There exists a family* $(X_n)_{n\in\mathbb{N}}$ *of XSDs such that, for each* n, X_n *has size* $O(n^2)$ *but the smallest BXSD equivalent to* X_n *has size at least* $2^{\Omega(n)}$.

PROOF SKETCH. Essentially, one needs to show that there exists a family of DFA-based XSDs $(X_n)_{n\in\mathbb{N}}$ such that every BXSD in which the left-hand-sides of rules reflect the DFA-types of the X_n requires exponential-size regular expressions. This means that we need to exhibit the existence of a family of DFAs such that the smallest equivalent regular expressions are necessarily exponential, even when they can exploit the limited negation of BonXai's priority system. To achieve this, we significantly extend and strengthen a technique of Ehrenfeucht and Zeiger [7] who showed that there is a class of languages $(Z_n)_{n\in\mathbb{N}}$, such that Z_n can be accepted by a DFA of size $O(n^2)$ but cannot be defined by a regular expression of size smaller than 2^{n-1}.

For every $n \in \mathbb{N}$ we let $\Sigma_n = \{a_{ij} \mid i, j \in \{1, \ldots, n\}\}$. We call i the *source* and j the *target* of a symbol a_{ij}. We define Z_n as

$$Z_n = \{w_1 \cdots w_m \in \Sigma_n^* \mid \forall i \in \{1, \ldots, m-1\}, \exists j, k, l \text{ such that } w_i w_{i+1} = a_{jk} a_{kl}\}.$$

That is, in every word in Z_n, the target of a symbol and the source of the following symbol must be equal. Every word $w \in \Sigma_n^* \setminus Z_n$ has a first symbol $a_{i\ell}$ whose target ℓ does not coincide with the source of the following symbol. We call ℓ the error index of w.

We now construct a family $(X_n)_{n\in\mathbb{N}}$ of XSDs, such that X_n is of size $O(n^2)$ and the smallest BXSD equivalent to X_n has size $2^{\Omega(n)}$. We define X_n by its DFA-based XSD (A_n, S_n, λ_n). To this end, we let $S_n = \Sigma_n$ and choose the components of $A_n = (Q \cup Q', \Sigma_n, \delta, q_1)$ as follows.

- $Q = \{q_i | 1 \le i \le n\}$ and $Q' = \{q'_i | 1 \le i \le n\}$;
- for every $q_i \in Q$ and $a_{j\ell} \in \Sigma$, $\delta(q_i, a_{j\ell}) = \begin{cases} q_\ell & \text{if } i = j \\ q'_i & \text{if } i \neq j \end{cases}$
- and, for every $q'_i \in Q'$ and $a_{j\ell} \in \Sigma$, $\delta(q'_i, a_{j\ell}) = q'_i$,
- for every $q_i \in Q$, $\lambda(q_i) = \varepsilon \cup \Sigma$,
- for every $q'_\ell \in Q$, $\lambda(q'_\ell) = \varepsilon \cup \Sigma \cup \{a_{\ell\ell} a_{\ell\ell}\}$.

In other words, A_n is a DFA that tests whether a word is in Z_n and remembers, for words not in Z_n, their error index.

The documents valid with respect to X_n are thus characterized by the following two properties.

- All label sequences over Σ_n are allowed in paths.
- The only allowed kind of branching is binary branching of the form $a_{ij} \to a_{\ell\ell} a_{\ell\ell}$ below nodes whose ancestor path contains a Z_n-error with error index ℓ.

We note that, as branching can only take place below an error, and the first error of a path is unique, in every document there can be binary branching $a_{\ell\ell} a_{\ell\ell}$ with at most one kind of symbols.

It is straightforward that X_n is of size $O(n^2)$. It can be shown that every equivalent BXSD B is of size $2^{\Omega(n)}$. □

4.3.2 From BonXai to XML Schema

We prove that the translation from BXSDs to XSDs is worst-case optimal.

THEOREM 9. *There exists a family of BXSDs $(B_n)_{n \in \mathbb{N}}$ such that, for each n, the BXSD B_n has size $O(n)$ but the smallest XSD equivalent to B_n has size at least 2^n.*

PROOF SKETCH. Let $n \in \mathbb{N}$ be arbitrary. Let $B_n = (\mathsf{EName}_n, S_n, R_n)$ be the BXSD with

$$\mathsf{EName}_n = \{a, a_1, \ldots, a_n, b_1, \ldots, b_n\},$$

$S_n = \{a_1, \ldots, a_n\}$, and R_n consisting of the following rules:

$$\begin{array}{rcl} //a & \to & \varepsilon \\ //(b_1 + \cdots + b_n) & \to & \varepsilon \\ //(a_1 + \cdots + a_n) & \to & (a + a_1 + \cdots + a_n) \\ //a_1//a_1//a & \to & b_1 \\ //a_2//a_2//a & \to & b_2 \\ \vdots & \vdots & \vdots \\ //a_n//a_n//a & \to & b_n \end{array}$$

Here we wrote the regular expressions on the left-hand-side of rules as in Section 2 with // as an abbreviation for EName^*. This schema defines a set of unary (i.e., non-branching) trees and its semantics is the following. If the ancestor path of an a-element contains, for each $1 \leq i \leq n$, at most one a_i element, its content model is ε. Otherwise, if j is the largest number such that a_j occurs at least two times on the path to the a element, then this a element has b_j as a child.

It can be proved with techniques from [18] that the smallest XSD equivalent to the above BXSD is exponentially large in n. Intuitively, in order to decide which b_i is the child under an a, the types of the XSD needs to keep track of the largest j, for which a_j has already occurred twice, and, worse, the set of $i > j$, for which a_i has already occurred once. □

4.4 Efficient Translations for Fragments

Even though the translations between XSD and BonXai in Sections 4.2.1 and 4.2.2 are provably optimal, they can be exponential in the worst case. In this section, we argue why we do not expect this to be a problem in practice. In particular, we prove that the translation is polynomial for a restriction of XSDs that accounts for the overwhelming majority of schemas in practice. An examination of 225 XSDs from the Web revealed that in more than 98% the content model of an element only depends on the label of the element itself, the label of its parent, and the label of its grandparent [17]. This motivates the study of the following class of DFA-based XSDs.

DEFINITION 10. A DFA-based XSD is *k-suffix*, if the type of an element only depends of the last k symbols of its ancestor string. More precisely, a DFA-based XSD (A, S, λ) with $A = (Q, \mathsf{EName}, \delta, q_0)$ is k-suffix based if $A(w_1 a_1 \cdots a_k) = A(w_2 a_1 \cdots a_k)$ for all strings w_1, w_2 over EName and symbols $a_1, \ldots, a_k \in \mathsf{EName}$.

Hence, 98% of the XSDs in the aforementioned study have a corresponding 3-suffix DFA-based XSD. Actually, this DFA-based XSD can be obtained simply by applying the construction of Lemma 4 to the given XSD. Furthermore, according to Lemmas 4 and 7, the translations between XSDs and DFA-based XSDs are straightforward and very efficient. We therefore do not revisit these constructions and focus on translations between (k-suffix) DFA-based XSDs and BXSDs. The BXSDs corresponding to this class of schemas can be defined as follows.

DEFINITION 11. A regular language L is a *suffix language* if $L = \{w\}$ or $L = L(\mathsf{EName}^* w)$ for some word w. It is a *k-suffix language* if, additionally, $|w| \leq k$. A BXSD (EName, S, R) is *k-suffix based* if, for every rule $r \to s$ in R, the left-hand side r is a k-suffix language.

The following theorem considers the translation from k-suffix based BXSDs and k-suffix DFA-based XSDs. It is similar in flavor to Proposition 5.2 in [12], but considers rules with a priority system as in BonXai. Kasneci and Schwentick avoided this issue by assuming that rules have pairwise disjoint left-hand-side languages.

THEOREM 12. *Each k-suffix based BXSD can be translated in polynomial time into an equivalent k-suffix DFA-based XSD of linear size.*

We now consider the reverse direction. An important difference with Theorem 12 is that this direction is exponential in k, that is, it needs k to be constant in order to be polynomial. However, as we noted before, in 98% of the schemas occurring in the practical study of [17], we see that $k \leq 3$.

THEOREM 13. *Let k be a constant. Each k-suffix DFA-based XSD can be translated in polynomial time into an equivalent k-suffix based BXSD.*

Finally, we note that it is easy to decide if a given XSD can be translated efficiently into a BXSD, i.e., whether it corresponds to a k-suffix DFA-based XSD (where k can either be fixed in advance or not). Questions of this kind were investigated in [5, 11, 21].

5. CONCLUSIONS

We introduced BonXai with the explicit goal of reconciling the expressivity of XML Schema with the simplicity of DTDs, thereby creating a de facto human-readable front-end for XSDs and providing a means to simplify XSD development. BonXai is a full-fledged schema language with many features and a formal specification [14]. The language can be employed in various scenarios (c.f., [15]) ranging from the creation of novel XSDs to debugging of existing XSDs. Furthermore, BonXai is built on a solid theoretical foundation which is rooted in pattern-based schemas [16, 17] and which facilitates transformation algorithms and their analysis. While transforming between BonXai and XML Schema can have high complexity in the worst case, our investigations show that for a very large and practically relevant class this is never the case. At the moment, BonXai cannot yet specify simple types natively. This means that in order to use simple types in BonXai one has to define them in an XSD which is then to be imported in the BonXai schema. Adding native support for simple type would probably be one of the most desirable extensions of the current language.

Acknowledgments

We acknowledge the financial support of grant number MA 4938/2-1 from the Deutsche Forschungsgemeinschaft (Emmy Noether Nachwuchsgruppe).

6. REFERENCES

[1] G. J. Bex, F. Neven, and J. Van den Bussche. DTDs versus XML Schema: A practical study. In *International Workshop on the Web and Databases (WebDB)*, pages 79–84, 2004.

[2] A. Brüggemann-Klein and D. Wood. One-unambiguous regular languages. *Information and Computation*, 142(2):182–206, 1998.

[3] P. Caron, Y. Han, and L. Mignot. Generalized one-unambiguity. In *International Conference on Developments in Language Theory (DLT)*, pages 129–140, 2011.

[4] C. S. Coen, P. Marinelli, and F. Vitali. Schemapath, a minimal extension to XML Schema for conditional constraints. In *International World Wide Web Conference (WWW)*, pages 164–174, 2004.

[5] W. Czerwiński, W. Martens, and T. Masopust. Efficient separability of regular languages by subsequences and suffixes. In *International Colloquium on Automata, Languages and Programming (ICALP)*, pages 150–161, 2013.

[6] DSD. Document structure description (DSD). `http://www.brics.dk/DSD/`, 2002.

[7] A. Ehrenfeucht and H. P. Zeiger. Complexity measures for regular expressions. *Journal of Computer and System Sciences*, 12(2):134–146, 1976.

[8] D. Fiorello, N. Gessa, P. Marinelli, and F. Vitali. DTD++ 2.0: Adding support for co-constraints. In *Extreme Markup Languages*, 2004.

[9] S. Gao, C. Sperberg-McQueen, H. Thompson, N. Mendelsohn, D. Beech, and M. Maloney. W3C XML Schema definition language (XSD) 1.1 part 1: Structures. `www.w3.org/TR/2012/REC-xmlschema11-1-20120405/`, April 2012.

[10] W. Gelade and F. Neven. Succinctness of pattern-based schema languages for XML. *Journal of Computer and System Sciences*, 77(3):505–519, 2011.

[11] P. Hofman and W. Martens. Separability by short subsequences and subwords. In *International Conference on Database Theory (ICDT)*, 2015.

[12] G. Kasneci and T. Schwentick. The complexity of reasoning about pattern-based XML schemas. In *International Symposium on Principles of Database Systems (PODS)*, pages 155–164, 2007.

[13] K. Losemann, W. Martens, and M. Niewerth. Descriptional complexity of deterministic regular expressions. In *International Symposium on Mathematical Foundations of Computer Science (MFCS)*, pages 643–654, 2012.

[14] W. Martens, V. Mattick, M. Niewerth, S. Agarwal, N. Douib, O. Garbe, D. Günther, D. Oliana, J. Kroniger, F. Lücke, T. Melikoglu, K. Nordmann, G. Özen, T. Schlitt, L. Schmidt, J. Westhoff, and D. Wolff. Design of the BonXai schema language. Available at www.theoinf.uni-bayreuth.de/download/bonxai-spec.pdf, Manuscript 2014.

[15] W. Martens, F. Neven, M. Niewerth, and T. Schwentick. Developing and analyzing XSDs through bonXai. *International Conference on Very Large Data Bases (VLDB)*, 5(12):1994–1997, 2012.

[16] W. Martens, F. Neven, and T. Schwentick. Simple off the shelf abstractions of XML Schema. *Sigmod RECORD*, 36(3):15–22, 2007.

[17] W. Martens, F. Neven, T. Schwentick, and G. J. Bex. Expressiveness and complexity of XML Schema. *ACM Transactions on Database Systems*, 31(3):770–813, 2006.

[18] W. Martens and J. Niehren. On the minimization of XML Schemas and tree automata for unranked trees. *Journal of Computer and System Sciences*, 73(4):550–583, 2007.

[19] A. Møller and M. Schwartzbach. *An introduction to XML and web technologies.* Addison-Wesley, 2006.

[20] M. Murata, D. Lee, M. Mani, and K. Kawaguchi. Taxonomy of XML schema languages using formal language theory. *ACM Transactions on Internet Technology*, 5(4):660–704, 2005.

[21] T. Place, L. van Rooijen, and M. Zeitoun. Separating regular languages by piecewise testable and unambiguous languages. In *International Symposium on Mathematical Foundations of Computer Science (MFCS)*, pages 729–740, 2013.

[22] RelaxNG. Relax NG specification. `http://www.relaxng.org/spec-20011203.html`, 2001.

[23] Schematron. Schematron. `http://www.schematron.com/`, 1999.

[24] C. Sperberg-McQueen and H. Thompson. XML Schema. `http://www.w3.org/XML/Schema`, 2005.

Compact Summaries over Large Datasets

Graham Cormode
University of Warwick
G.Cormode@Warwick.ac.uk

ABSTRACT

A fundamental challenge in processing the massive quantities of information generated by modern applications is in extracting suitable representations of the data that can be stored, manipulated and interrogated on a single machine. A promising approach is in the design and analysis of compact summaries: data structures which capture key features of the data, and which can be created effectively over distributed data sets. Popular summary structures include the count distinct algorithms, which compactly approximate item set cardinalities, and sketches which allow vector norms and products to be estimated. These are very attractive, since they can be computed in parallel and combined to yield a single, compact summary of the data. This tutorial introduces the concepts and examples of compact summaries.

Categories and Subject Descriptors

E.1 [**Data**]: Data Structures

General Terms

Algorithms, Theory

Keywords

summaries, sketches, approximate counting

PODS'15, May 31–June 4, 2015, Melbourne, Victoria, Australia.

http://dx.doi.org/10.1145/2745754.2745781.

1. INTRODUCTION

Business and scientific communities all agree that "big data" holds both tremendous promise, and substantial challenges [8]. There is much potential for extracting useful intelligence and actionable information from the large quantities of data generated and captured by modern information processing systems. Big data challenges involve not only the sheer volume of the data, but the fact that it can represent a complex variety of entities and interactions between them, and new observations that arrive, often across multiple locations, at high velocity. Examples of applications that generate big data include:

Physical Data from sensor deployments and scientific experiments—astronomy data from modern telescopes generates terabytes of data each night, while the data collected from a single particle physics experiment is too big to store;

Medical Data, as we can now sequence whole genomes economically, generating data sets of the order of 200TB in one example [7];

Activity Data, as human activity data is captured and stored in ever greater quantities and detail: interactions from online social networks, locations from GPS, Internet activity etc.

Across all of these disparate settings, certain common themes emerge. The data in question is large, and growing. The applications seek to extract patterns, trends or descriptions of the data. Ensuring the scalability of systems, and the timeliness and veracity of the analysis is vital in many of these applications. In order to realize the promise of these sources of data, we need new methods that can handle them effectively.

While such sources of big data are becoming increasingly common, the resources to process them (chiefly, processor speed, fast memory and slower disk) are growing at a slower pace. The consequence of this trend is that there is an urgent need for more effort directed towards capturing and processing data in many critical applications. Careful planning and scalable architectures are needed to fulfill the requirements of analysis and information extraction on big data. In response to these needs, new computational paradigms are being adopted to deal with the challenge of big data. Large scale distributed computation is a central piece: the scope of the computation can exceed what is feasible on a single machine, and so clusters of machines work together in parallel. On top of these architectures, parallel algorithms are designed which can take the complex task and break it into independent pieces suitable for distribution over multiple machines.

A central challenge within any such system is how to compute and represent complex features of big data in a way that can be processed by many single machines in parallel. A vital component is to be able to build and manipulate a *compact summary* of a large amount of data. This powerful notion of a small summary, in all its many and varied forms, is the subject of this tutorial. The idea of a summary is a natural and familiar one. It should represent something large and complex in a compact fashion. Inevitably, a summary must dispense with some of the detail and nuance of the object which it is summarizing. However, it should also preserve some key features of the object in a very accurate fashion. Effective compact summaries are often *approximate* in their answers to queries and *randomized*.

The theory of compact summaries can be traced back over four decades. A first example is the Morris Approximate Counter, which approximately counts quantities up to magnitude n using $O(\log \log n)$ bits, rather than the $\lceil \log n \rceil$ bits to count exactly [15]. Subsequently, there has been much interest in summaries in the context of *streaming algorithms*: these are algorithms that process data in the form of a stream of updates, and whose associated data structures can be seen as a compact summary [16]. More recently, the more general notion of *mergeable summaries* has arisen: summaries that can be computed on different portions of a dataset in isolation, then subsequently combined to form a summary of the union of the inputs [1]. It turns out that a large number streaming algorithms entail a mergeable summary, hence making this class of objects a large and interesting one.

There has been much effort expended on summary techniques over recent years, leading to the invention of powerful and effective summaries which have found applications in Internet Service Providers [5], Search Engines [17, 12], and beyond.

2. TUTORIAL OUTLINE

This short tutorial will introduce the notion of summaries, and outline ideas behind some of the most prominent examples, which may include:

- Counts, approximate counts [15], and approximate frequencies [14]
- Count distinct, set cardinality, and set operations [9, 10]
- Random projections with low-independence vectors to give *sketch* data structures [3, 4, 6]
- Summaries for medians and order statistics [11, 13]
- Linear summaries for graphs: connectivity, bipartiteness and sparsification [2]
- Summaries for matrix and linear algebra operations [18]
- Problems for which no compact summary can exist, via communication complexity lower bounds.

Acknowledgments

This work supported in part by a Royal Society Wolfson Research Merit Award, funding from the Yahoo Research Faculty Research and Engagement Program, and European Research Council (ERC) Consolidator Grant ERC-CoG-2014-647557.

3. REFERENCES

[1] Pankaj Agarwal, Graham Cormode, Zengfeng Huang, Jeff Phillips, Zheiwei Wei, and Ke Yi. Mergeable summaries. In *ACM Principles of Database Systems*, 2012.

[2] Kook Jin Ahn, Sudipto Guha, and Andrew McGregor. Analyzing graph structure via linear measurements. In *ACM-SIAM Symposium on Discrete Algorithms*, 2012.

[3] N. Alon, Y. Matias, and M. Szegedy. The space complexity of approximating the frequency moments. In *ACM Symposium on Theory of Computing*, pages 20–29, 1996.

[4] M. Charikar, K. Chen, and M. Farach-Colton. Finding frequent items in data streams. In *Procedings of the International Colloquium on Automata, Languages and Programming (ICALP)*, 2002.

[5] G. Cormode, F. Korn, S. Muthukrishnan, T. Johnson, O. Spatscheck, and D. Srivastava. Holistic UDAFs at streaming speeds. In *ACM SIGMOD International Conference on Management of Data*, pages 35–46, 2004.

[6] G. Cormode and S. Muthukrishnan. An improved data stream summary: The Count-Min sketch and its applications. *Journal of Algorithms*, 55(1):58–75, 2005.

[7] Kathleen Cravedi, Tera Randall, and Larry Thompson. 1000 genomes project data available on Amazon Cloud. *NIH News*, March 2012.

[8] Kenneth Cukier. Data, data everywhere. *The Economist*, February 2010.

[9] P. Flajolet and G. N. Martin. Probabilistic counting algorithms for database applications. *Journal of Computer and System Sciences*, 31:182–209, 1985.

[10] Philippe Flajolet, É. Fusy, Olivier Gandouet, and Frederic Meunier. Hyperloglog: The analysis of a near-optimal cardinality estimation algorithm. In *International Conference on Analysis of Algorithms*, 2007.

[11] M. Greenwald and S. Khanna. Space-efficient online computation of quantile summaries. In *ACM SIGMOD International Conference on Management of Data*, 2001.

[12] Sergey Melnik, Andrey Gubarev, Jing Jing Long, Geoffrey Romer, Shiva Shivakumar, Matt Tolton, and Theo Vassilakis. Dremel: Interactive analysis of web-scale datasets. In *International Conference on Very Large Data Bases*, pages 330–339, 2010.

[13] A. Metwally, D. Agrawal, and A. El Abbadi. Efficient computation of frequent and top-k elements in data streams. In *International Conference on Database Theory*, 2005.

[14] J. Misra and D. Gries. Finding repeated elements. *Science of Computer Programming*, 2:143–152, 1982.

[15] Robert Morris. Counting large numbers of events in small registers. *Communications of the ACM*, 21(10):840–842, 1977.

[16] S. Muthukrishnan. *Data Streams: Algorithms and Applications*. Now Publishers, 2005.

[17] Rob Pike, Sean Dorward, Robert Griesemer, and Sean Quinlan. Interpreting the data: Parallel analysis with sawzall. *Dynamic Grids and Worldwide Computing*, 13(4):277–298, 2005.

[18] David Woodruff. Sketching as a tool for numerical linear algebra. *Foundations and Trends in Theoretical Computer Science*, 10(1-2):1–157, 2014.

Defining Relations on Graphs: How Hard is it in the Presence of Node Partitions?

M. Praveen[*]
Chennai Mathematical Institute
Chennai, India
praveenm@cmi.ac.in

B. Srivathsan[*]
Chennai Mathematical Institute
Chennai, India
sri@cmi.ac.in

ABSTRACT

Designing query languages for graph structured data is an active field of research. Evaluating a query on a graph results in a relation on the set of its nodes. In other words, a query is a mechanism for defining relations on a graph. Some relations may not be definable by any query in a given language. This leads to the following question: given a graph, a query language and a relation on the graph, does there exist a query in the language that defines the relation? This is called the definability problem. When the given query language is standard regular expressions, the definability problem is known to be PSPACE-complete.

The model of graphs can be extended by labeling nodes with values from an infinite domain. These labels induce a partition on the set of nodes: two nodes are equivalent if they are labeled by the same value. Query languages can also be extended to make use of this equivalence. Two such extensions are Regular Expressions with Memory (REM) and Regular Expressions with Equality (REE).

In this paper, we study the complexity of the definability problem in this extended model when the query language is either REM or REE. We show that the definability problem is EXPSPACE-complete when the query language is REM, and it is PSPACE-complete when the query language is REE. In addition, when the query language is a union of conjunctive queries based on REM or REE, we show coNP-completeness.

Categories and Subject Descriptors

F.4.3 [**Formal Languages**]: Classes defined by grammars or automata; H.2.3 [**Languages**]: Query languages

General Terms

Theory

*Partially funded by a grant from Infosys Foundation

PODS'15, May 31–June 4, 2015, Melbourne, Victoria, Australia.

ACM 978-1-4503-2757-2/15/05 ...$15.00.
http://dx.doi.org/10.1145/2745754.2745764.

Keywords

graphs with data; regular data path queries; definability; regular expressions with memory; regular expressions with equality

1. INTRODUCTION

Graph structures representing data have found many applications like semantic web [22, 15], social networks [23] and biological networks [18]. One model of graph structured data consists of a set of nodes labeled by values from some infinite domain and directed edges between the nodes labeled by letters from a finite alphabet. For example, a graph representing a social network may have a node for each member. There may be directed edges labeled *friend* between two nodes if the corresponding members are friends in the network. Nodes could be labeled by the name of the corresponding member's favourite movie. These labels from the infinite domain partition the set of nodes of the graph. Two nodes are equivalent if they have the same label. An active field of research is designing languages for querying such graphs, using both the structure of the graph and the partition induced by labels from the infinite domain [20, 4].

We will use the term *data graphs* for the model where nodes carry labels from an infinite domain (a nomenclature from [20]). The labels themselves are called *data values*. One way of querying data graphs is to simply specify a language L of strings. Each string in L has data values in odd positions and a letter from the finite alphabet in even positions. Evaluating a query specified by such a language on a data graph returns the set of all pairs of nodes $\langle q_1, q_2 \rangle$ such that there is a path from q_1 to q_2 labeled by a string in the specified language. Register automata [16, 24, 21] are extensions of standard finite state automata for handling data values from infinite domains. Using register automata as the formalism to specify languages, Libkin and Vrgoč studied the complexity of evaluating queries on data graphs [20]. There, the main reason behind the choice of register automata over other formalisms is to obtain tractable complexity for the query evaluation problem. Aiming towards a practically usable query language, extensions of standard regular expressions were introduced in [20]. They are named regular expressions with memory (REM) and (less expressive) regular expressions with equality (REE). REM are expressively equivalent to register automata [19]. The complexity of query containment for these have also been studied [17].

Here we study the complexity of the definability problem: given a data graph and a set of pairs of nodes, check if the set can be obtained as the evaluation of some query on the data graph. One of the motivations for this study is the extraction of schema mappings, which we illustrate by an example. Given a data graph representing a social network, suppose we want to create another graph where two nodes are in the *movieLink* relation if they represent people having the same favourite movie and who are linked by a series of friends. There is a correspondence between the two graphs; in general such correspondences are called schema mappings. This particular schema mapping is specified by saying that the relation *movieLink* is exactly the relation returned by evaluating the query *friend** on the original graph, with the additional condition that the two nodes have the same data value (i.e., the same favourite movie). Given the original data graph and the relation *movieLink*, suppose we want to algorithmically build the specification of the schema mapping using some query language. Then we need to check if the query language is capable of defining the *movieLink* relation — this is the definability problem. Using example instances of source and target schemas for deriving appropriate source-to-target mappings have been explored in relational databases [11, 14, 10, 2]. Research on schema mappings for graph databases has started [7, 5], though data values and extraction from example graphs have not been considered till now to the best of our knowledge. Example instances have also been used to derive "wrapper" queries for extraction of relevant information from data sources [13].

Contributions We study the complexity of the definability problem in data graphs, using either REM or REE as query languages. We prove the following results.

1. The definability problem with REM as the query language is EXPSPACE-complete.
2. The definability problem for REM with k memory locations is in SPACE($\mathcal{O}(n\delta^k)$), where n is the number of nodes and δ is the number of data values used in the data graph.
3. The definability problem for REE is PSPACE-complete.
4. The definability problem for union of conjunctive queries based on REM or REE is coNP-complete.

For the upper bounds, we have to overcome some challenges. In the presence of data values, standard language theoretic tools like complementation, determinization and decidability of language inclusion do not work. We have to understand how data values affect definability, so that we can appeal directly to the more fundamental idea of pumping lemma, which still works in the presence of data values. For the lower bounds, we identify how small data graphs can count exponentially large numbers using data values, which otherwise require exponentially large graphs. The proofs omitted in the main body of this paper can be found in the appendix.

Related work Apart from derivation of mappings [11, 14, 10, 2], studies have also been made of using data examples to illustrate the semantics of schema mappings [1]. In [8], the problem of deriving schema mappings from data examples is studied from the perspective of algorithmic learning theory.

In [3], the complexity of the definability problem for graph query languages is studied, but they do not consider data values. Their main result is that definability using regular expressions in PSPACE-complete. They also give upper and lower bounds for various fragments of conjunctive queries based on regular expressions. We do not study conjunctive queries or their fragments but instead give tight bounds for union of conjunctive queries, which also apply to the setting of [3] where there are no data values.

The problem of query containment for fragments and extensions of REM and REE have been studied in [17]. A query e_1 is contained in another query e_2 if the set defined by e_1 is a subset of the set defined by e_2 on all data graphs. It is shown in [17] that for some fragments of REM and REE, query containment is respectively EXPSPACE-complete and PSPACE-complete. These are similar to the bounds we get for the definability problem. However, the upper bounds in [17] apply only to the positive fragments of REM and REE, where tests for inequality of data values are not allowed (query containment in the general case is undecidable). There is no obvious way to use those techniques here, since we allow the full syntax for REM and REE. For the EXPSPACE lower bound, the authors of [17] use techniques similar to those used in [6] to prove EXPSPACE lower bound for checking the emptiness of parameterized regular expressions, closely related to REM. The EXPSPACE lower bound in [6] is based on succinctly reducing the emptiness of intersection of several expressions to the emptiness of a single expression. Here, we need to use a different approach, since we deal with the definability problem and can not rely on intersections.

2. PRELIMINARIES

We will recall the basic definitions. The model of graphs with node labels from an infinite domain are called data graphs in [20]. We will follow the same nomenclature here. We will also make use of many other notations from [20].

Let Σ be a finite alphabet and let $\mathcal{D}$ be a countably infinite set of data values. We write $[n]$ for the set $\{0, 1, \dots, n\}$.

Definition 1 (Data graph) A *data graph* over Σ and $\mathcal{D}$ is a triple $G = (V, E, \rho)$ where:

- V is a finite set of nodes,
- $E \subseteq V \times \Sigma \times V$ is a set of edges with labels in Σ,
- $\rho : V \to \mathcal{D}$ maps every vertex to a data value.

Example 2 Figure 1 gives an example of a data graph over $\Sigma = \{a\}$ and $\mathcal{D} = \mathbb{N}$, the set of natural numbers. However, a given graph would use only a finite set of data values. The role of data values will become clearer when we define query languages for such data graphs. We will use this graph as a running example throughout this section.

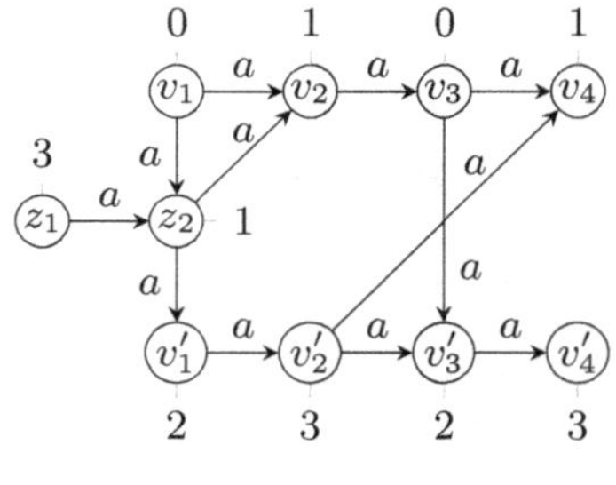

Figure 1: Example of a data graph over a unary alphabet $\Sigma = \{a\}$ and using data values $\{0, 1, 2, 3\}$.

A *path* in G is a sequence $\xi = v_1 a_1 v_2 a_2 \dots v_{m-1} a_{m-1} v_m$ of nodes in V alternating with letters in Σ such that (v_i, a_i, v_{i+1}) is in E for all $i < m$. The *data path* w_ξ corresponding to a path ξ is the sequence $\rho(v_1)a_1\rho(v_2)a_2 \dots \rho(v_{m-1})a_{m-1}\rho(v_m)$ obtained by replacing every node in ξ by its associated data value. We say that a data path w *connects* node u to v if there is a path $\xi = u a_1 u_1 \dots a_{m-1} v$ in G such that $w_\xi = w$. We write $u \xrightarrow{w} v$ in this case.

In general, a data path is a sequence $d_0 a_0 d_1 a_1 \dots a_{m-1} d_m$ of data values in $\mathcal{D}$ alternating with letters in Σ, starting and ending with data values. The set of all data paths over Σ and $\mathcal{D}$ is denoted by $\Sigma[\mathcal{D}]^*$. A *data language* $L \subseteq \Sigma[\mathcal{D}]^*$ is a set of data paths. Given two data paths $w_1 = d_0 a_0 d_1 \dots a_{m-1} d_m$ and $w_2 = d'_0 b_0 d'_1 \dots b_{l-1} d'_l$ where the last data value of w_1 coincides with the first data value of w_2 ($d_m = d'_0$), the *concatenation* $w_1 \cdot w_2$ is the data path $d_0 a_1 d_1 \dots a_{m-1} d_m b_0 d'_1 \dots b_{l-1} d'_l$. This naturally extends to concatenations of many data paths. We will often write $w_1 w_2$ instead of $w_1 \cdot w_2$.

We will now define two formalisms to characterize data languages. These formalisms would then be used to define query languages for data graphs. Since $\mathcal{D}$ could be infinite, these formalisms cannot check for the exact data value. They can however check for equality of two data values. The first formalism is *regular expressions with memory.* They are extensions of standard regular expressions over the finite alphabet Σ, introduced in [20]. They are equipped with *registers,* that can store data values along a data path. The stored data values can be used to impose conditions on the data values allowed in future positions of the data path.

Definition 3 Given a set of registers $r_1, r_2, \dots, r_k$, the set $\mathcal{C}_k$ of conditions is given by the following grammar:

$$c := \top \mid r_i^= \mid r_i^{\neq} \mid c \vee c \mid c \wedge c \mid \neg c, \quad 1 \le i \le k$$

The satisfaction is defined with respect to a data value $d \in \mathcal{D}$ and a tuple $\tau = (d_1, \dots, d_k) \in (\mathcal{D} \cup \bot)^k$ called an *assignment*: $d, \tau \models \top$ always, $d, \tau \models r_i^=$ iff $d_i = d$ and $d, \tau \models r_i^{\neq}$ iff $d_i \neq d$. The $\bot$ symbol is used to denote an empty register. It satisfies $\bot \neq d$ for every data value $d \in \mathcal{D}$. Satisfaction for the logical operators is as usual.

Definition 4 (Regular expressions with memory) Let Σ be a finite alphabet and $r_1, \dots, r_k$ a set of registers. Then, *regular expressions with memory (REM)* are defined by the following grammar:

$$e := \varepsilon \mid a \mid e + e \mid e \cdot e \mid e^+ \mid e[c] \mid \downarrow \overline{r}.e$$

where $a \in \Sigma$, $c \in \mathcal{C}_k$ and $\overline{r}$ is a tuple of registers.

We will use k-REM to denote the set of regular expressions with memory that use at most k registers. Let σ be an assignment. We will denote by $\sigma[\overline{r} \to d]$ the assignment obtained from σ by assigning d to the registers in $\overline{r}$. The semantics of k-REMs are as follows, reproduced from [20].

Definition 5 (Semantics of k-REMs) Suppose e is a k-REM, w is a data path in $\Sigma[\mathcal{D}]^*$ and $\sigma, \sigma' \in (\mathcal{D} \cup \bot)^k$ are assignments of the k registers used in e. The relation $(e, w, \sigma) \vdash \sigma'$ is defined by induction on the structure of e:

$$\begin{array}{rl}
(\varepsilon, w, \sigma) \vdash \sigma' & \text{if } w = d \text{ for some } d \in \mathcal{D} \text{ and } \sigma = \sigma' \\
(a, w, \sigma) \vdash \sigma' & \text{if } w = d_1 a d_2 \text{ and } \sigma' = \sigma \\
(e_1 + e_2, w, \sigma) \vdash \sigma' & \text{if } (e_1, w, \sigma) \vdash \sigma' \text{ or } (e_2, w, \sigma) \vdash \sigma' \\
(e_1 \cdot e_2, w, \sigma) \vdash \sigma' & \text{if } w = w_1 \cdot w_2 \text{ and } \exists\, \sigma_1 \in (\mathcal{D} \cup \bot)^k \\
 & \text{s. t. } (e_1, w_1, \sigma) \vdash \sigma_1 \\
 & \text{and } (e_2, w_2, \sigma_1) \vdash \sigma' \\
(e^+, w, \sigma) \vdash \sigma' & \text{if } w = w_1 w_2 \dots w_l \\
 & \text{and } \exists\, \sigma_0, \dots, \sigma_l \in (\mathcal{D} \cup \bot)^k \text{ s.t.} \\
 & (e, w_i, \sigma_i) \vdash \sigma_{i+1} \text{ for } i \in [l-1] \\
 & \text{and } \sigma_0 = \sigma,\ \sigma_l = \sigma' \\
(e[c], w, \sigma) \vdash \sigma' & \text{if } (e, w, \sigma) \vdash \sigma' \text{ and } \sigma', d \models c \\
 & \text{where } d \text{ is the last data value in } w \\
(\downarrow \overline{r}.e, w, \sigma) \vdash \sigma' & \text{if } (e, w, \sigma[\overline{r} \to d]) \vdash \sigma' \\
 & \text{where } d \text{ is the first value in } w
\end{array}$$

The *language* of a k-REM e is defined as follows:

$$\mathcal{L}(e) = \{\, w \in \Sigma[\mathcal{D}]^* \mid (e, w, \bot^k) \vdash \sigma \text{ for some } \sigma \}$$

where $\bot^k$ denotes the assignment that has $\bot$ in every register.

Example 6 The REM $\downarrow r_1 \cdot a \cdot [r_1^=]$ uses one register. The language of this 1-REM consists of all data paths of the form dad where the first and last data values are the same. The 2-REM $\downarrow r_1 \cdot a \cdot \downarrow r_2 \cdot b \cdot a[r_1^=] \cdot b[r_2^{\neq}]$ contains data paths of the form $d_1 a d_2 b d_3 a d_4 b d_5$ where $d_1 = d_4$ and $d_2 \neq d_5$.

The next formalism for characterizing data languages is another extension of standard regular expressions, called *regular expressions with equality,* again introduced in [20]. These are less powerful than REMs, since checking the equivalences between data values is restricted to a certain form.

Definition 7 (Regular expressions with equality) Let Σ be a finite alphabet and $\mathcal{D}$ a countably infinite set of data values. A *regular expression with equality (REE)* is constructed from the following grammar:

$$e := \varepsilon \mid a \mid e + e \mid e \cdot e \mid e^+ \mid e_= \mid e_{\neq}$$

where a belongs to Σ. The language $\mathcal{L}(e)$ of an REE is defined as follows:

$$\begin{array}{rcl}
\mathcal{L}(\varepsilon) & = & \{\, d \mid d \in \mathcal{D}\} \\
\mathcal{L}(a) & = & \{\, d_1 a d_2 \mid d_1, d_2 \in \mathcal{D}\} \\
\mathcal{L}(e_1 + e_2) & = & \mathcal{L}(e_1) \cup \mathcal{L}(e_2) \\
\mathcal{L}(e_1 \cdot e_2) & = & \mathcal{L}(e_1) \cdot \mathcal{L}(e_2) \\
\mathcal{L}(e^+) & = & \{\, w_1 \cdots w_l \mid l \ge 1 \text{ and each } w_i \in \mathcal{L}(e) \,\} \\
\mathcal{L}(e_=) & = & \{\, d_1 a_1 d_2 \dots a_{m-1} d_m \in \mathcal{L}(e) \mid d_1 = d_m\} \\
\mathcal{L}(e_{\neq}) & = & \{\, d_1 a_1 d_2 \dots a_{m-1} d_m \in \mathcal{L}(e) \mid d_1 \neq d_m\}
\end{array}$$

Example 8 The language of the REE $((a)_{\neq} \cdot (b)_{\neq})_{\neq}$ contains data paths $d_1 a d_2 b d_3$ such that $d_1 \neq d_2$, $d_2 \neq d_3$ and $d_1 \neq d_3$.

We call a bijection $\pi : \mathcal{D} \to \mathcal{D}$ an automorphism on $\mathcal{D}$, since it preserves (in)equality.

Definition 9 Let $\pi : \mathcal{D} \mapsto \mathcal{D}$ be an automorphism on $\mathcal{D}$. For a data path $w = d_0 a_0 d_1 a_1 \dots d_m$ over $\Sigma[\mathcal{D}]^*$, we denote by $\pi(w)$ the data path $\pi(d_0)a_0\pi(d_1)a_1 \dots \pi(d_m)$ obtained by applying the automorphism π on the data values of w.

An important property of REM and REE is that they cannot distinguish between automorphic data paths, just like register automata [16].

Fact 10 ([16, 19]) For every REM or REE e, and for every data path $w \in \mathcal{L}(e)$ and automorphism $\pi : \mathcal{D} \to \mathcal{D}$, $\pi(w)$ is also in $\mathcal{L}(e)$.

2.1 Query languages for data graphs

The above two formalisms can be used to define query languages for data graphs.

Definition 11 (Regular data path queries) An expression $Q = x \xrightarrow{e} y$ is a *regular data path query*, when e is either a standard regular expression, or an REM or an REE. Given a data graph G, the result of the query $Q(G)$ is the set of pairs of nodes $\langle u, v\rangle$ such that there exists a data path from u to v that belongs to $\mathcal{L}(e)$. The query is called *regular data path query with memory ($RDPQ_{mem}$)* or *regular data path query with equality ($RDPQ_{=}$)* depending on whether e is an REM or an REE. If e is a standard regular expression, the query is called a *regular path query (RPQ)*.

A *relation* on the set of nodes in the graph is a set of tuples of same arity. We will say that a relation S on a data graph G is *defined* by a query Q if S equals $Q(G)$.

Example 12 Evaluating the RPQ $Q_1 : x \xrightarrow{aaa} y$ on the data graph in Figure 1 results in the relation $S_1 = \{ \langle v_1, v_4\rangle, \langle v_1, v_3'\rangle, \langle v_1, v_3\rangle, \langle v_1, v_2'\rangle, \langle v_2, v_4'\rangle, \langle z_1, v_3\rangle, \langle z_1, v_2'\rangle, \langle z_2, v_4\rangle, \langle z_2, v_3'\rangle, \langle v_1', v_4'\rangle \}$. This is the set of all pairs of nodes connected by aaa. Neither $S_2 = \{\langle v_1, v_4\rangle, \langle v_1', v_4'\rangle\}$ nor $S_3 = \{\langle v_1, v_3\rangle\}$ can be defined using RPQs. To see why, consider S_2. The only path connecting v_1' to v_4' is aaa. But this path connects many other pairs apart from the ones in S_2. Hence to restrict to the pairs in S_2, we need to make use of data values. A similar argument will tell us that to define S_3, we need to consider data values.

The relation S_2 can be defined by the RDPQ_{mem} $Q_2 : x \xrightarrow{e_2} y$, where $e_2 = \downarrow r_1 \cdot a \cdot \downarrow r_2 \cdot a[r_1^=] \cdot a[r_2^=]$. The REM e_2 contains all data paths $d_1 a d_2 a d_3 a d_4$ such that $d_1 = d_3$ and $d_2 = d_4$. From Figure 1, it can be checked that the only data paths in the graph satisfying this expression are: $w_1 : 0a1a0a1$ and $w_2 : 2a3a2a3$, and they connect $\langle v_1, v_4\rangle$ and $\langle v_1', v_4'\rangle$ respectively. Hence $Q_2(G) = S_2$, thus defining the relation S_2. Note that the two words w_1 and w_2 are automorphic images and hence cannot be distinguished by REMs (c.f. Fact 10).

The expression e_2 is a 2-REM (uses 2 registers r_1 and r_2). Let us see why S_2 cannot be defined using a 1-REM. Suppose e is a 1-REM used in a query defining S_2. As the only data path connecting v_1' to v_4' is $2a3a2a3$, $\mathcal{L}(e)$ should contain the data path $2a3a2a3$. Moreover, the data paths $0a1a0a2$ and $1a2a3a2$ should not be in $\mathcal{L}(e)$, since $v_1 \xrightarrow{0a1a0a2} v_3'$ and $z_2 \xrightarrow{1a2a3a2} v_3'$. Since the prefix of $2a3a2a3$ (to be included) and $0a1a0a2$ (to be excluded) up to the first three data values are automorphic, the only way to add $2a3a2a3$ to $\mathcal{L}(e)$ and eliminate $0a1a0a2$ from $\mathcal{L}(e)$ is to check in e that the second and fourth data values are equal. This will still not eliminate $1a2a3a2$. To eliminate $1a2a3a2$, one has to add the condition that the first and third data values are equal. So we need to compare the first data value to the third, and second data value to the fourth. This kind of an "interleaved" check needs 2 registers as in the REM e_2 above. For the same reason, S_2 cannot be defined using $\text{RDPQ}_=$.

The relation S_3 can be defined using the $\text{RDPQ}_=$ $Q_3 : x \xrightarrow{e_3} y$ with $e_3 = (a \cdot (a)_= \cdot a)_=$ In the data graph of Figure 1, the only data path satisfying e_3 is $w_5 : 0a1a1a0$. that connects $\langle v_1, v_3\rangle$. Both the checks in e_3: first data value equals fourth data value, and second equals third, are required to eliminate the following words: $w_6 : 3a1a1a0$ and $w_7 : 1a2a3a1$, that connect $\langle z_1, v_3\rangle$ and $\langle z_2, v_4\rangle$ which are not in S_3. Hence for similar reasons as mentioned in the above paragraph, S_3 cannot be defined by an RDPQ_{mem} that uses a 1-REM. A 2-REM would work though.

We will also study a standard extension of query languages: union of conjunctive queries.

Definition 13 (Conjunctive data path queries) A *conjunctive regular data path query (CRDPQ)* is an expression of the form

$$Ans(\overline{z}) := \bigwedge_{1 \le i \le m} x_i \xrightarrow{e_i} y_i, \tag{1}$$

where $m \ge 0$, x_i, y_i are variables and $\overline{z}$ is a tuple of variables among $\overline{x}$ and $\overline{y}$ and either every e_i is an REM, or every e_i is an REE. The semantics of a CRDPQ Q of the form (1) over a data graph $G = (V, E, \rho)$ is defined as follows. Given a valuation $\mu : \bigcup_{1 \le i \le m} \{x_i, y_i\} \to V$, we write $(G, \mu) \models Q$ if $\langle \mu(x_i), \mu(y_i)\rangle$ is in the answer of $x_i \xrightarrow{e_i} y_i$ on G, for each $i = 1, \dots, m$. Then $Q(G)$ is the set of all tuples $\mu(\overline{z})$ such that $(G, \mu) \models Q$. The number of variables in $\overline{z}$ is the *arity* of Q. A *union of conjunctive regular data path queries* (UCRDPQ) is a finite set $Q = \{Q_1, \dots, Q_k\}$ of CRDPQs $Q_1, \dots, Q_k$, which are all of the same arity. For a data graph G, $Q(G)$ is the set $Q_1(G) \cup \dots \cup Q_k(G)$.

Example 14 We will work on the same graph from Figure 1. Consider the following CRDPQ Q_4: $Ans(x_1, y_1) := x_1 \xrightarrow{a} y_1 \wedge x_1 \xrightarrow{a} y_2 \wedge y_2 \xrightarrow{a} y_1$ The only valuation μ satisfying the above conditions is: $\mu(x_1) = v_1$, $\mu(y_1) = v_2$ and $\mu(y_2) = z_2$. The result $Q_4(G)$ would hence be the relation $\{ \langle v_1, v_2\rangle \}$. Note that this relation cannot be defined using RDPQ_{mem} or $\text{RDPQ}_=$. The only data paths connecting $\langle v_1, v_2\rangle$ are $0a1$ and $0a1a1$. The former data path cannot be used to distinguish $\langle v_1, v_2\rangle$ as it connects $\langle v_3, v_4\rangle$ as well and the latter one cannot be used since an automorphic data path $3a1a1$ connects $\langle z_1, v_2\rangle$. From Fact 10, we know that REMs and REEs cannot differentiate between automorphic data paths.

Consider another query Q_5: $Ans(x_1, y_1, x_2) := x_1 \xrightarrow{(a)_{\neq}} y_1 \wedge x_2 \xrightarrow{(a)_{\neq}} y_1$. The above query uses REEs in its individual regular data path queries. The result $Q_5(G)$ would be: $\{ \langle v_1, z_2, z_1\rangle, \langle v_3, v_4, v_2'\rangle, \langle v_3, v_3', v_2'\rangle \}$ The query singles out the "pattern" of x_1 and x_2 converging into y_1, where the label of y_1 is different from those of x_1 and x_2.

2.2 Definability problems

From the examples, we can infer that RDPQ_{mem} and $\text{RDPQ}_{=}$ can define more relations than RPQ. In addition, RDPQ_{mem} can define more relations than $\text{RDPQ}_{=}$. CRDPQs can define even more than RDPQ_{mem}. Restricting to RDPQ_{mem}, using k registers we can define relations that are not possible with $k-1$ registers. It is also not difficult to construct examples of graphs and relations that are not definable using any of the query languages that we have seen. This motivates us to look at the following definability problems. The input is a data graph G and a relation S on the set of nodes in G.

RDPQ_{mem}-*definability:* Does there exist an RDPQ_{mem} Q s.t. $Q(G) = S$?

k-RDPQ_{mem}-*definability:* Does there exist an RDPQ_{mem} Q which uses at most k registers s.t. $Q(G) = S$?

$\text{RDPQ}_{=}$-*definability:* Does there exist an $\text{RDPQ}_{=}$ Q s.t. $Q(G) = S$?

UCRDPQ-definability: Does there exist a UCRDPQ Q s.t. $Q(G) = S$?

In the subsequent sections, we study the complexity of the above problems. For the last problem, we do not make a distinction between UCRDPQs using REM or REE, as we will see that the complexity stays the same in both cases.

Speciality of the equivalence relation As stated before, the data values induce an equivalence relation on the set of nodes, where two nodes are equivalent when they have the same label. Each letter a from the finite alphabet Σ also induces a binary relation on the set of nodes: the pair $\langle u, v\rangle$ is in this relation when there is an edge labeled a from u to v. Given that data values also induce a binary relation, why is it that we can not solve the definability problem by simply treating the equivalence relation as an extra letter in the finite alphabet and using the techniques developed for RPQs? The reason is that query languages give a special privilege to the equivalence relation: it can be used to relate positions that are far apart in a data path, while the binary relation induced by a letter in the finite alphabet can only relate successive positions. Hence, as seen in Example 12, some relations that can be defined by RDPQ_{mem} can not be defined by RPQ, even if we add the equivalence relation as an extra letter in the finite alphabet. However, a more sophisticated extension of the graph will allow us to use this idea, as explained in the beginning of the next section.

3. QUERIES USING REGULAR EXPRESSIONS WITH MEMORY

In this section we study the RDPQ_{mem}-definability and the k-RDPQ_{mem}-definability problems. Fix a data graph G and a binary relation S on the vertices in G. We denote the set of data values in G by $\mathcal{D}_G$. The goal is to decide if S is RDPQ_{mem}-definable. We start with some basic observations about the strengths and weaknesses of REMs.

If w is a data path and $\pi : \mathcal{D}_G \to \mathcal{D}_G$ is an automorphism on $\mathcal{D}_G$, we have seen in Fact 10 that no REM can distinguish between w and $\pi(w)$. On the other hand, if two data paths are not automorphic, then they can be distinguished by an REM. We denote by $[w]$ the set of all data paths automorphic to w.

Lemma 15 For every data path w, there is an REM $e_{[w]}$ such that $\mathcal{L}(e_{[w]}) = [w]$.

PROOF. Suppose $d_1, \ldots, d_k$ are the distinct data values occurring in w. The required REM $e_{[w]}$ uses k registers $r_1, \ldots, r_k$. Essentially, at the first position where the data value d_i appears, $e_{[w]}$ stores d_i in the register r_i. In every subsequent position where d_i appears, it is compared against the value stored in r_i. Formally, $e_{[w]}$ is defined as follows by induction on length of w: $e_{[d_i]} \;=\; \downarrow r_i$.

$$e_{[wad_i]} \quad = \quad \begin{cases} e_{[w]} \cdot a[r_i^{=}] & \text{if } d_i \text{ occurs in } w \\ e_{[w]} \cdot a \cdot \downarrow r_i.\varepsilon & \text{otherwise} \end{cases}$$

For every data value d_i occurring in w, $e_{[w]}$ notes all the positions having the data value d_i. Using this, it is routine to prove that any data path w' is in $\mathcal{L}(e_{[w]})$ iff w' is automorphic to w. □

Combining Fact 10 and Lemma 15, we infer that two data paths can be distinguished by an REM iff they are not automorphic. This suggests the following procedure for checking RDPQ_{mem}-definability. For simplicity, suppose that we want to define the singleton set $\{\langle u, v\rangle\}$. Suppose there is a data path w connecting u to v. The expression $e_{[w]}$ will not define the set $\{\langle u, v\rangle\}$ iff there is an automorphism π such that $\pi(w)$ connects u' to v' for some $\langle u', v'\rangle \neq \langle u, v\rangle$. The automorphism π is obstructing $e_{[w]}$ from defining $\{\langle u, v\rangle\}$, but this obstruction is not explicit in the data graph G. It *is* explicit in $G_{\pi^{-1}}$ (obtained from G after replacing every data value d by $\pi^{-1}(d)$), since w connects u' to v' in $G_{\pi^{-1}}$. All such obstructions will be explicit in G_{aut}, the disjoint union of G_π for all automorphisms π. A little more work will allow us to drop the special treatment given to data values and treat them as usual letters from a finite alphabet in G_{aut}. The RDPQ_{mem}-definability problem on G can be reduced to the RPQ-definability problem on G_{aut}. The PSPACE-completeness of RPQ-definability [3] will then give an EXPSPACE upper bound for RDPQ_{mem}-definability. This approach however does not throw light on the role of registers in definability, nor does it give precise bounds in the case where the number of registers is fixed.

In the next sub-section, we make some observations on $k - \text{RDPQ}_{\text{mem}}$-definability, which are counterparts of the above observations on RDPQ_{mem}-definability.

3.1 RDPQ_{mem}-definability with bounded number of registers

If w is a data path with k distinct data values, we saw in Lemma 15 that there is a REM $e_{[w]}$ whose language is exactly $[w]$. The number of registers used in $e_{[w]}$ is k. If we restrict the number of registers to less than k, then there may not be an expression whose language is exactly $[w]$. Still, the expression $e_{[w]}$ (which uses k registers) has a simple syntactic form, which we would like to capture and use in scenarios where there are fewer registers.

Definition 16 (Basic REM) A *basic k-REM* is a k-REM of the form $\downarrow \overline{r}_1.a_1[c_1]\cdot \downarrow \overline{r}_2.a_2[c_2] \cdots \downarrow \overline{r}_m.a_m[c_m]$, where $a_i \in \Sigma$, $c_i \in \mathcal{C}_k$ and $\overline{r}_i$ are tuples from $r_1, \ldots, r_k$.

Basic k-REMs can also be thought of as those built without using the rules $e := e^+$ and $e := e + e$. We considered defining a singleton set $\{\langle u, v\rangle\}$ for simplicity. We would like to retain the simplicity but handle arbitrary sets, which is the purpose of the following definition.

Definition 17 Suppose G is a data graph, S is a binary relation on the set of nodes of G and $\langle u, v\rangle \in S$. A *$k$-REM witness for $\langle u, v\rangle$ in S* is a basic k-REM e satisfying the following conditions.

1. (Connecting path) $u \xrightarrow{w} v$ for some $w \in \mathcal{L}(e)$.
2. (No extraneous pairs) If any data path in $\mathcal{L}(e)$ connects some u' to some v', then $\langle u', v'\rangle \in S$.

If an arbitrary k-REM e defines S and $\langle u, v\rangle \in S$, then there is a data path $w \in \mathcal{L}(e)$ connecting u to v. If e is of the form $e_1 e_2^+ e_3$, there is an m such that $\mathcal{L}(e_1 e_2^m e_3)$ contains w. Continuing this process of removing iterations in e, while still retaining w in the language will result in a k-REM witness for $\langle u, v\rangle$ in S.

Lemma 18 If S is definable, then it is definable by a union of $|S|$ k-REM witnesses.

Now suppose we are trying to define S using $k-\mathrm{RDPQ_{mem}}$ and let $\langle u, v\rangle \in S$. Assume there is a data path w connecting u to v and there is a basic k-REM e such that $w \in \mathcal{L}(e)$. If e is not a k-REM witness for $\langle u, v\rangle$ in S, then there is a data path $w' \in \mathcal{L}(e)$ connecting u' to v' for some $\langle u', v'\rangle \neq \langle u, v\rangle$. The data path w' is obstructing e from being a witness and we need a structure where such obstructions are explicit. Since we are dealing with k-REMs, the structure would have to keep track of possible values stored in the k registers. The following definition and lemma are similar to the way the semantics of REM over a data graph is defined in [17].

Definition 19 (Assignment graph) Let k be a natural number. To a data graph $G = (V, E, \rho)$ over finite alphabet Σ and data values $\mathcal{D}_G$ we associate a transition system $\mathcal{T}_G = (Q_G, \rightarrow_G)$ called the *k-assignment graph*. Its set of states is $Q_G = V \times (\mathcal{D}_G \cup \bot)^k$. The transitions are of the form $\downarrow \overline{r}.a[c]$, where $\overline{r}$ is a (possibly empty) tuple of variables from $r_1, \ldots, r_k$, $a \in \Sigma$ and c is a condition in $\mathcal{C}_k$. There is a transition $(v, \sigma) \xrightarrow{\downarrow \overline{r}.a[c]}_G (v', \sigma')$ if $(v, a, v') \in E$, $\sigma' = \sigma[\overline{r} \rightarrow \rho(v)]$ and $\rho(v'), \sigma' \models c$.

A sequence of the form $(v_0, \sigma_0) \xrightarrow{\downarrow \overline{r}_1.a_1[c_1]}_G (v_1, \sigma_1) \rightarrow_G \cdots \xrightarrow{\downarrow \overline{r}_m.a_m[c_m]}_G (v_m, \sigma_m)$ in $\mathcal{T}_G$ is called a run from (v_0, σ_0) to (v_m, σ_m). The sequence $\downarrow \overline{r}_1.a_1[c_1] \cdots \downarrow \overline{r}_m.a_m[c_m]$ is a basic k-REM. Hence, we can think of runs in $\mathcal{T}_G$ as being of the form $(u, \sigma) \xrightarrow{e}_G (v, \sigma')$, where e is the basic k-REM formed by the labels of the sequence of transitions connecting (u, σ) to (v, σ'). This observation leads to the following connection between runs in the assignment graph and data paths in G belonging to the languages of basic REMs.

Lemma 20 Let e be a basic k-REM. Let $\sigma : \{r_1, \ldots, r_k\} \rightarrow \mathcal{D}_G \cup \{\bot\}$ and $\sigma' : \{r_1, \ldots, r_k\} \rightarrow \mathcal{D}_G \cup \{\bot\}$ be some assignments. The following are equivalent.

1. A data path w connects u to v in G and $(e, w, \sigma) \vdash \sigma'$.
2. There exists a run $(u, \sigma) \xrightarrow{e}_G (v, \sigma')$ in $\mathcal{T}_G$.

Suppose we are trying to define a set S on the data graph G using $k-\mathrm{RDPQ_{mem}}$. The above lemma allows us to think of k-REM witnesses in terms of runs in $\mathcal{T}_G$. A basic k-REM e is a k-REM witness for $\langle u, v\rangle$ in S iff it satisfies the following conditions.

1. $(u, \bot^k) \xrightarrow{e}_G (v, \sigma)$ for some assignment σ, to satisfy condition 1 of Definition 17 (connecting path).
2. If $(u', \bot^k) \xrightarrow{e}_G (v', \sigma)$ for some nodes u', v' and some assignment σ, then $\langle u', v'\rangle \in S$, to satisfy condition 2 of Definition 17 (no extraneous pairs).

Checking that a basic k-REM e is a witness thus reduces to checking that e connects a pair in $\mathcal{T}_G$ and does not connect certain other pairs. This observation allows us to use the pigeon hole principle to prove the existence of short witnesses.

Lemma 21 Suppose G is a data graph with δ distinct data values, n nodes $v_1, \ldots, v_n$ and S is a binary relation on the set of nodes. If there is a k-REM witness for $\langle v_p, v_q\rangle$ in S, there is one of length $\mathcal{O}\left(2^{n^2 \delta^k}\right)$.

PROOF. For sets of states $Q_1, \ldots, Q_n, Q'_1, \ldots, Q'_n \subseteq Q_G$, we write $\langle Q_1, \ldots, Q_n\rangle \xrightarrow{e}_G \langle Q'_1, \ldots, Q'_n\rangle$ if $Q'_i = \{(v', \sigma') \mid (v, \sigma) \xrightarrow{e}_G (v', \sigma') \text{ for some } (v, \sigma) \in Q_i\}$ for every $i = 1, \ldots, n$. Suppose e is a k-REM witness for $\langle v_p, v_q\rangle$ in S. Let $e = e_1 \cdot e_2 \cdots e_m$, where every e_i is of the form $\downarrow \overline{r}_i a_i.[c_i]$. Consider the sequence:

$$\langle \{(v_1, \bot^k)\}, \ldots, \{(v_n, \bot^k)\}\rangle \xrightarrow{e_1}_G \langle Q_1^1, \ldots, Q_n^1\rangle \quad (2)$$
$$\xrightarrow{e_2}_G \cdots \xrightarrow{e_m}_G \langle Q_1^m, \ldots, Q_n^m\rangle \ .$$

The set Q_i^j is the set of all states reachable from $(v_i, \bot^k)$ along the path $e_1 \cdots e_j$ in $\mathcal{T}_G$. If there are $j < j'$ such that $\langle Q_1^j, \ldots, Q_n^j\rangle = \langle Q_1^{j'}, \ldots, Q_n^{j'}\rangle$, then removing the part of this sequence between j and j' will lead to the same final tuple $\langle Q_1^m, \ldots, Q_n^m\rangle$. We claim that after this removal, the resulting k-REM $e_1 \cdots e_j \cdot e_{j'+1} \cdots e_m$ is a k-REM witness for $\langle v_p, v_q\rangle$ in S. The reason is as follows: from Lemma 20, the following two conditions are equivalent to the original hypothesis that e is a k-REM witness for $\langle v_p, v_q\rangle$ in S.

1. For some assignment σ, $(v_q, \sigma) \in Q_p^m$.
2. For any $i = 1, \ldots, n$ and any $(v, \sigma) \in Q_i^m$, $(v_i, v) \in S$.

Hence, any basic k-REM that ends in the same n-tuple $\langle Q_1^m, \ \ldots \ , Q_n^m\rangle$ is also a k-REM witness for $\langle v_p, v_q\rangle$ in S. As long as there are duplicate tuples along the sequence (2), we can remove part of it to get a shorter witness. By pigeon hole principle, we conclude that there is a witness no longer than the total number of distinct tuples $\langle Q_1, \ldots, Q_n\rangle$.

There are at most $n(\delta + 1)^k$ states in $\mathcal{T}_G$. Hence, there are at most $2^{n^2(\delta+1)^k}$ tuples $\langle Q_1, \ldots, Q_n\rangle$. From the argument in the previous paragraph, we infer that if there is a k-REM witness for $\langle v_p, v_q\rangle$ in S, there is one of length at most $2^{n^2(\delta+1)^k}$. □

For graphs without data considered in [3], the solution to RPQ-definability looks at the graph as a finite automaton. This paves the way for using language theoretic tools, which are ultimately based on a pumping argument. In our case, we cannot view a data graph directly as a register automaton. Hence we need to construct the assignment graph on which we can apply the pumping argument.

Theorem 22 *The* $k-\text{RDPQ}_{\text{mem}}$*-definability problem is in* $\text{NSPACE}(\mathcal{O}(n^2\delta^k))$*, where* n *is the number of nodes and* δ *is the number of distinct data values.*

3.2 RDPQ_{mem}-definability

We can now tackle RDPQ_{mem}-definability, where there is no bound on the number of registers.

Lemma 23 Suppose G is a data graph with δ distinct data values. A relation S is RDPQ_{mem}-definable if and only if it is δ-RDPQ_{mem}-definable.

The next theorem follows from the previous two results.

Theorem 24 RDPQ_{mem}*-definability is in* EXPSPACE.

Next we give a matching lower bound.

Theorem 25 *The* RDPQ_{mem}*-definability problem in data graphs is* EXPSPACE*-hard.*

PROOF. We reduce the exponential width corridor tiling problem to the RDPQ_{mem}-definability problem. An instance of the tiling problem consists of a set T of tile types, a relation $C_h \subseteq T \times T$ of horizontally compatible tile types and a relation $C_v \subseteq T \times T$ of vertically compatible tile types, an initial tile type t_i, a final tile type t_f and a number n (in unary). The problem is to check if there exists a number R and a tiling $\tau : [R] \times [2^n - 1] \to T$ that is *legal* — $\tau(0,0) = t_i$, $\tau(R, 2^n - 1) = t_f$, $(\tau(i,j), \tau(i,j+1)) \in C_h$ and $(\tau(i,j), \tau(i+1,j)) \in C_v$ for all i, j. The intention here is that $\tau(i,j)$ is the tile type at the ith row j^{th} column of a corridor with $R+1$ rows and 2^n columns. This problem is known to be EXPSPACE-complete (e.g., see [25]). To be precise, we need to allow any exponential function in place of 2^n. Our proof works in that case also; we use 2^n to reduce notational clutter.

Let $\overline{T} = \{\overline{t} \mid t \in T\}$ be a disjoint copy of T. Given an instance of the tiling problem, we reduce it to the RDPQ_{mem}-definability problem in data graphs, where the finite alphabet is $T \cup \overline{T} \cup \{\$, \alpha\}$. A tiling τ is encoded by data paths in the language of the following REM:

$$\begin{array}{lllllll}
\$\cdot & \downarrow r_n\cdot & \alpha\cdot & \downarrow r_{n-1}\cdot & \alpha\cdots\alpha\cdot & \downarrow r_1\cdot & \tau(0,0) \\
 & [r_n^=]\cdot & \alpha & [r_{n-1}^=]\cdot & \alpha\cdots\alpha & [r_1^{\neq}]\cdot & \tau(0,1) \\
 & [r_n^=]\cdot & \alpha & \cdots\alpha & [r_2^{\neq}]\cdot\alpha & [r_1^=]\cdot & \tau(0,2) \\
 & & & & \vdots & & \\
 & [r_n^{\neq}]\cdot & \alpha & [r_{n-1}^{\neq}]\cdot & \alpha\cdots\alpha & [r_1^{\neq}]\cdot & \overline{\tau(0,2^n-1)} \\
 & [r_n^=]\cdot & \alpha & [r_{n-1}^=]\cdot & \alpha\cdots\alpha & [r_1^=]\cdot & \tau(1,0) \\
 & & & & \vdots & & \\
 & [r_n^{\neq}]\cdot & \alpha & [r_{n-1}^{\neq}]\cdot & \alpha\cdots\alpha & [r_1^{\neq}]\cdot & \overline{\tau(R,2^n-1)}\cdot \quad \$
\end{array} \tag{3}$$

The expression lists the tile types used in the tiling sequentially from left column to right column, bottom row to top row. The first n data values are stored in the registers $r_n, \ldots, r_1$. In later positions, $[r_k^=]$ (resp. $[r_k^{\neq}]$) indicates that the kth bit is 0 (resp. 1). The n conditions preceding $\tau(i,j)$ in the expression denote the binary representation of j. Tile types in the last column are represented by letters in $\overline{T}$, so that we need not check them for horizontal compatibility with the next tile. The data graph is the disjoint union of two graphs $p_1 \xrightarrow{\$} \boxed{\text{illegal tilings}} \xrightarrow{\$} q_1$ and $p_2 \xrightarrow{\$} \boxed{\text{all tilings}} \xrightarrow{\$} q_2$ satisfying the following conditions.

1. Any data path starting and ending with the letter \$ may only connect p_1 to q_1 or p_2 to q_2.

2. Every tiling can be encoded by some data path connecting p_2 to q_2.

3. None of the data paths connecting p_1 to q_1 are encodings of legal tilings.

4. For every data path w connecting p_2 to q_2 that is not the encoding of a legal tiling, there exists a data path automorphic to w connecting p_1 to q_1.

We claim that there exists a legal tiling iff $\{\langle p_2, q_2\rangle\}$ is RDPQ_{mem}-definable. Indeed, suppose there exists a legal tiling τ. Conditions 1, 2 and 3 ensure that the REM in (3) defines $\{\langle p_2, q_2\rangle\}$. Conversely, suppose $\{\langle p_2, q_2\rangle\}$ is definable. There exists a defining REM e and a data path w in $\mathcal{L}(e)$ connecting p_2 to q_2. If w does not encode a legal tiling, then condition 4 above implies that there is a data path w' automorphic to w (and hence in $\mathcal{L}(e)$) connecting p_1 to q_1, contradicting the hypothesis that e defines $\{\langle p_2, q_2\rangle\}$. Hence, w encodes a legal tiling. The data graph can be constructed in polynomial time (details follow) and hence the RDPQ_{mem}-definability problem in data graphs is EXPSPACE-hard. At a high level, the strategy of this proof is similar to that of [17, Theorem 3.7] in the sense that a small gadget differentiates between the set of all tilings and the set of illegal tilings. However, [17, Theorem 3.7] can not be used here directly, since that is about containment of one query in another while we are concerned about the definability of a relation in a given data graph. There is also a subtle difference between the proof strategies which will be highlighted in the details that follow.

We now give the details of the data graph. Nodes are denoted by circles, with data values written outside. The data values of some nodes are skipped when they are not important. The data values $d_n, e_n, \ldots, d_1, e_1$ are all distinct. The portion of the data graph containing p_2 and q_2 is as follows.

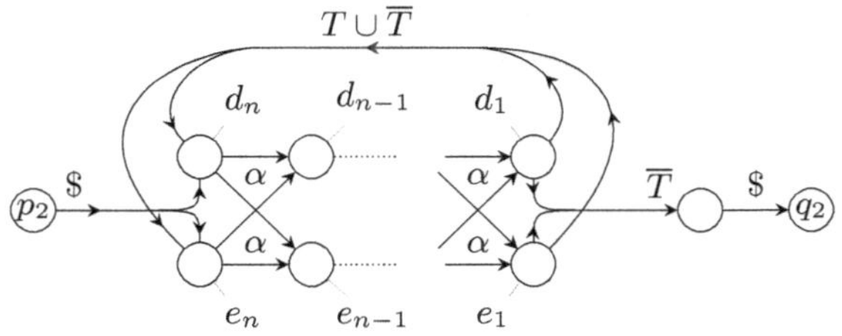

For every data path connecting p_2 to q_2 that is not the encoding of a legal tiling, we now add automorphic data paths connecting p_1 to q_1 through gadgets. This will ensure that the data graph satisfies condition 4 above. We also ensure that every path we add satisfies conditions 1 and 3.

• *In a data path* w *connecting* p_2 *to* q_2*, the sequence of* n *data values preceding* $\tau(0,1)$ *does not represent* 1. This could be due to any one (or more) of the n bits being wrong; following is the gadget for checking that the kth bit is 1 (at node q) instead of 0. There are n such gadgets, one for each bit.

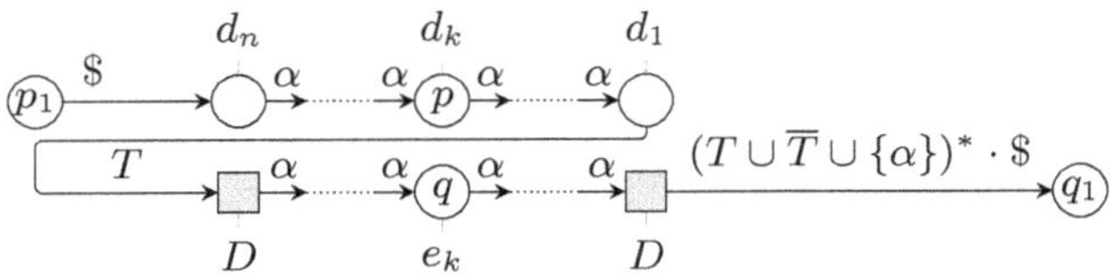

The gadget simply checks that the kth data value preceding $\tau(0,1)$ in the data path w (e_k at node q) is unequal to the kth data value preceding $\tau(0,0)$ (d_k at node p). This will ensure that the kth bit preceding $\tau(0,1)$ is 1 instead of 0. If the kth data value preceding $\tau(0,0)$ is e_k, the gadget can still imitate w modulo an automorphism that interchanges d_k and e_k. In the above diagram, every gray box marked D is actually a gadget with $2n$ nodes, with each node having a distinct data value from the set $\{d_n, e_n, \ldots, d_1, e_1\}$. For every edge coming in to a gray box, there is an edge coming in to each of the $2n$ nodes. For every edge coming out of a gray box, there is an edge coming out of each of the $2n$ nodes. The edge coming in to the node q_1 is labeled by the REM $(T \cup \overline{T} \cup \{\alpha\})^* \cdot \$$, whose language consists of all the data paths having exactly one occurrence of the letter \$, which occurs at the end. A gadget admitting exactly this set of data paths can be easily designed using polynomially many nodes; the gadget is not shown in the diagram since it is easier to understand the expression.

- *Some sequence of n conditions does not encode the successor of the preceding n conditions.* The following gadget checks that the kth bit flips from 1 (in node 2) to 0 (in node 4) but the $(k+1)^{\text{th}}$ bit stays at 0 (in nodes 1 and 3). There are $\mathcal{O}(n)$ such gadgets for checking all such errors.

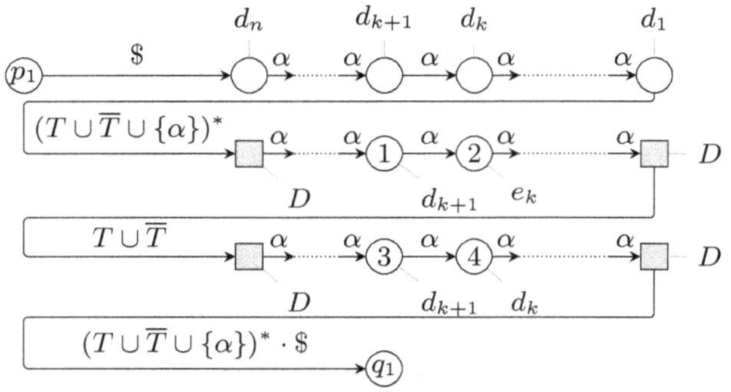

- *The sequence of n conditions before a letter in $\overline{T}$ does not represent $2^n - 1$.* This can be due to any one (or more) of the bits being 0 instead of 1. The following gadget checks that the kth bit is 0 (at node q). There are n such gadgets, one for each bit.

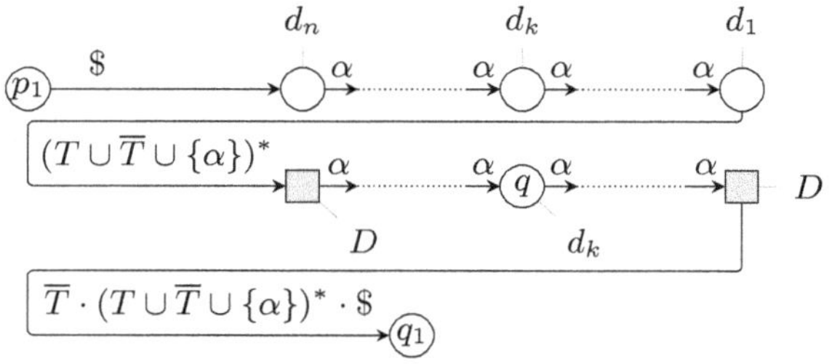

- *The n conditions before a letter in T represent $2^n - 1$.*

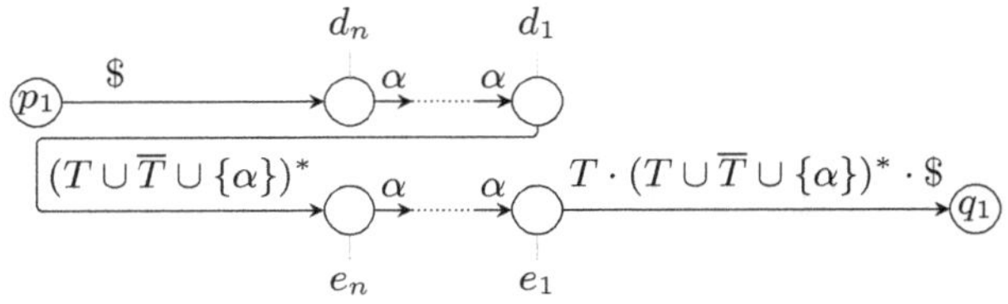

- *The tiling does not begin with the tile type t_i.*

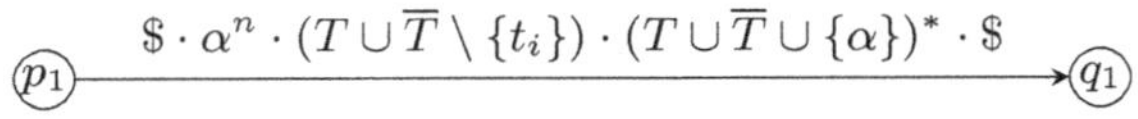

- *The tiling does not end with the tile type t_f.*

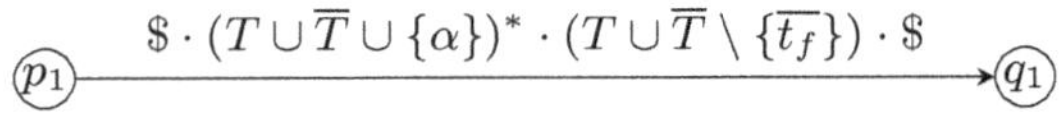

- *Two adjacent tiles in the same row are not horizontally compatible.* The following gadget checks that the tile type t_2 is adjacent to the horizontally incompatible tile type t_1 in the same row. There is one such gadget for every pair (t_1, t_2) of horizontally incompatible tile types.

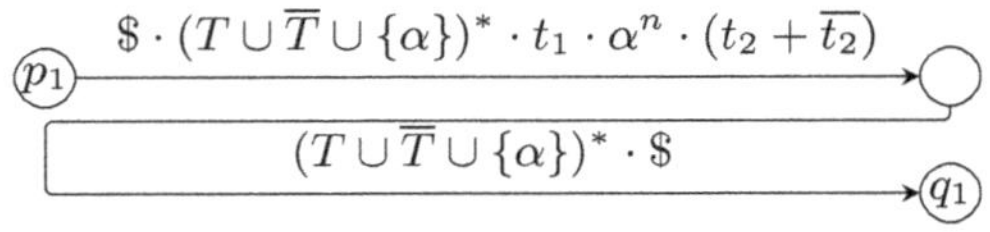

- *Two adjacent tiles in the same column are not vertically compatible.* The gadget below checks that the tile type t_2 (seen just after node 2) is adjacent to the vertically incompatible tile type t_1(seen just after node 1) in the last column. The tiles are matched from the same column, since the data values seen just before $\overline{t_1}$ are same as the data values seen just before $\overline{t_2}$. The tiles are matched from adjacent rows, since $\overline{t_1}$ is the only letter from $\overline{T}$ allowed between the nodes 1 and 2. There is one such gadget for every pair (t_1, t_2) of vertically incompatible tile types.

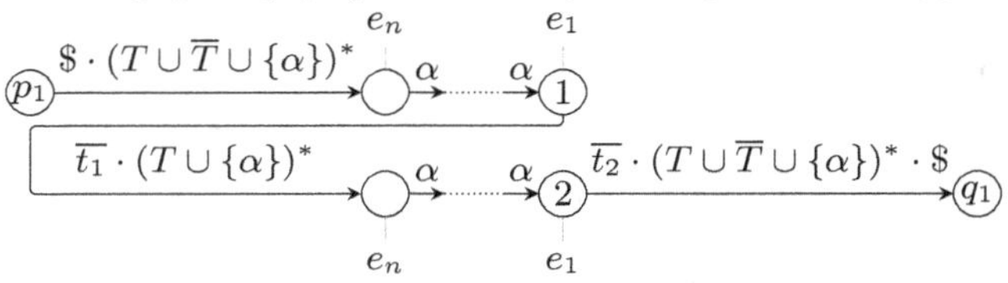

We now highlight a subtle difference between this proof and that of [17, Theorem 3.7]. There, to check that the distance between two positions is exactly 2^n, a gadget checks n bits of the first position against n bits of the second position. There the gadget is built using REM and hence it can check the bits individually for equality. Here, we need to build a similar gadget using data graphs. If we did this check by matching each bit explicitly, the gadget would be exponentially larger. We avoid it by observing that we need not admit the exact data path encoding an illegal tiling, but only an *automorphic copy.* Thus, if a data path has the data value d_1 just before $\overline{t_1}$ and $\overline{t_2}$, the above gadget will still catch it through an automorphism that interchanges d_1 and e_1.

The gadget below checks that the tile type t_2 is adjacent to the vertically incompatible tile type t_1 in a column other than the last one. There is one such gadget for every pair (t_1, t_2) of vertically incompatible tile types.

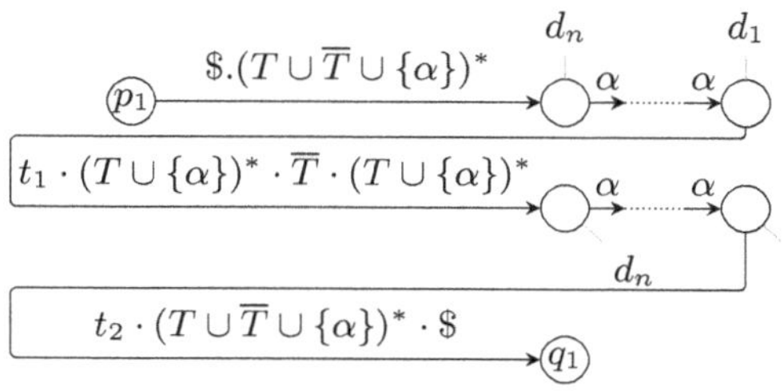

□

4. QUERIES USING REGULAR EXPRESSIONS WITH EQUALITY

We study the RDPQ$_=$-definability problem in this section. These are queries using REE. As seen before, REE have the additional $e_=$ and $e_{\neq}$ constructs on top of standard regular expressions. In Example 12, we have seen that they are less powerful than REM in defining relations. However, due to $e_=$ and $e_{\neq}$, they can define more relations than RPQs.

In Section 3, we have shown that RDPQ$_{\mathrm{mem}}$-definability is EXPSPACE-complete. RPQ-definability is known to be PSPACE-complete [3]. We will now prove that RDPQ$_=$-definability is PSPACE-complete as well.

The main idea is the following observation. Suppose we have an expression $e_1 \cdot e_2$. If e_1 and e_2 are REMs, it is possible that there is a register getting bound in e_1 by $\downarrow r$, and used in a condition in e_2. So one cannot reason about $e_1 \cdot e_2$ by independently reasoning about e_1 and e_2. Such a situation does not arise with REE. The relation defined by $e_1 \cdot e_2$ can in fact be obtained as a composition of the relations defined by e_1 and e_2. This makes it possible to solve the problem in PSPACE.

For this section, fix a data graph $G = (V, E, \rho)$ over edge alphabet Σ. Let $\mathsf{Bin} = V \times V$ be the set of binary relations over V. Our first goal would be to define operators over the set Bin and to generate relations in a hierarchical manner by making use of these operators in a certain way.

Definition 26 Given two relations $S_1, S_2 \in \mathsf{Bin}$, we define the following operators:

$$\begin{aligned} S_1 + S_2 &= \{\langle u,v\rangle \mid \langle u,v\rangle \in S_1 \text{ or } \langle u,v\rangle \in S_2\} \\ S_1 \circ S_2 &= \{\langle u,v\rangle \mid \exists z : \langle u,z\rangle \in S_1 \text{ and } \langle z,v\rangle \in S_2\} \\ S^= &= \{\langle u,v\rangle \in S \mid \rho(u) = \rho(v)\} \\ S^{\neq} &= \{\langle u,v\rangle \in S \mid \rho(u) \neq \rho(v)\} \end{aligned}$$

The $+$ and $\circ$ are the *union* and *composition* operators. We call $S^=$ and $S^{\neq}$ as the *=-restriction* and the *≠-restriction* respectively. From the definitions, it is easy to see that $+$ is commutative and associative. Furthermore, the operator $\circ$ is associative and distributes over $+$.

For an REE e, let us write S_e for the binary relation defined by it: $S_e = \{\langle u,v\rangle \in V \times V \mid \exists w \in \mathcal{L}(e) \text{ s.t. } u \xrightarrow{w} v\}$.

Definition 27 Consider the set Bin of binary relations. We will define a sequence $L_0, L_1, \ldots$ of subsets of Bin, called *levels*, as follows:

$$\begin{aligned} B_0 &= \{S_\varepsilon\} \cup \{S_a \mid a \in \Sigma\} \\ L_0 &= \text{closure of } B_0 \text{ under } + \text{ and } \circ \\ \text{for } i \geq 1,\ B_i &= \{S^= \mid S \in L_{i-1}\} \cup \{S^{\neq} \mid S \in L_{i-1}\} \cup L_{i-1} \\ L_i &= \text{closure of } B_i \text{ under } + \text{ and } \circ \end{aligned}$$

Intuitively, the set B_0 consists of those relations that are defined using the atomic expressions ε and a. The set L_0 closes these relations under union and composition. The base sets B_1 of the next level are formed by adding to L_0 the $=$ and $\neq$-restrictions of relations in L_0. These are now closed under union and composition to get the set L_1. This process continues. Of course, this cannot continue beyond 2^{n^2} steps, which is the total number of relations in Bin. The next lemma further restricts it to n^2 steps.

Lemma 28 For all $j \geq n^2$, $L_j = L_{n^2}$.

PROOF. To every newly added relation in L_i, we will associate a relation in L_{i-1} having at least one extra pair of nodes. As the new relations that are added become strictly smaller each time we go up a level, no new relations can be added beyond L_{n^2}.

A newly added relation S in L_i is either in B_i, or formed by union of compositions of relations from B_i:

$$\begin{aligned} S &= T_1 + T_2 + \cdots + T_m \quad \text{where } m \leq n^2 \qquad (4) \\ \text{and each } T_j &= (R_1 \circ R_2 \circ \ldots \circ R_p) \quad \text{s.t. } p \leq 2^{n^2}, \text{ and} \\ & \qquad R_k \in B_i \text{ for } k \leq p. \end{aligned}$$

The bounds on m and p above follow from the fact that each relation can have at most n^2 pairs. For the relations $S^=$ or $S^{\neq}$ added in B_i let us associate the set $S \in L_{i-1}$. They are added only if they are strict subsets of S. This means there exists a pair $\langle u,v\rangle \in S$ that does not belong to $S^=$ and another pair $\langle u',v'\rangle \in S$ that does not belong to $S^{\neq}$. Hence the cardinalities of $S^=$ and $S^{\neq}$ are strictly lesser than S.

Let T be a relation obtained by union of compositions of relations in B_i. The relation T is new only if some of the relations in the underlying composition according to (4) are the new basic sets $S^=$ and $S^{\neq}$. Consider the relation T' where each of these $S^=$ and $S^{\neq}$ is replaced by the corresponding relation S. Clearly $T \subseteq T'$. Moreover T is added only if it is different from T'. This shows that T' has at least one pair more than T. □

The motive behind defining these operations and the hierarchy of relations is that this procedure resembles the way REEs are constructed from its grammar.

Lemma 29 For every two REE e and f, we have: $S_e + S_f = S_{e+f}$, $S_e \circ S_f = S_{ef}$, $S_e^= = S_{e_=}$ and $S_e^{\neq} = S_{e_{\neq}}$.

The proof of the above lemma is quite straightforward from the definitions. However, the lemma is significant because it allows to reason about S_{ef} by independently reasoning about S_e and S_f. As mentioned before, this property is not true for REMs. The above lemma can be used to show the important property that all REE-definable relations can be generated by this hierarchical construction that repeatedly applies the $=$ and $\neq$ restrictions and closes under $+$ and $\circ$.

Lemma 30 A relation is RDPQ$_=$-definable iff it belongs to level L_{n^2}.

Let us define the *height* of a relation S to be the least i such that $S \in L_i$. The fact that the height of an RDPQ$_=$ definable relation is polynomially bounded can be used to give a PSPACE upper bound.

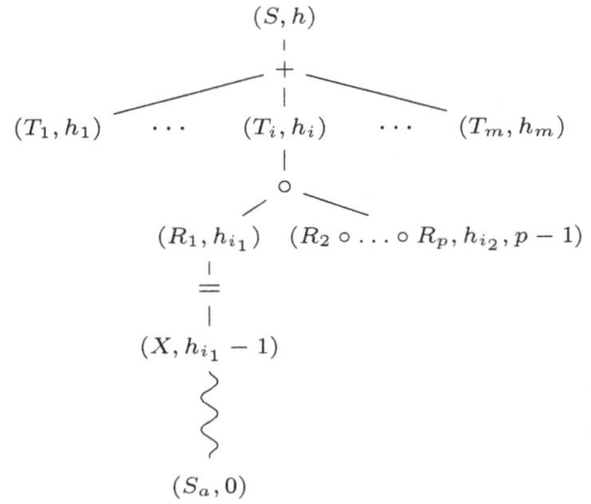

Figure 2: A part of execution of the algorithm for $\mathrm{RDPQ}_=$ **definability**

Lemma 31 $\mathrm{RDPQ}_=$ definability problem is in PSPACE.

PROOF. The inputs are a data graph G and a binary relation S. We will describe a non-deterministic algorithm that decides in polynomial space if S is $\mathrm{RDPQ}_=$-definable. Due to Lemma 30, checking if S is $\mathrm{RDPQ}_=$ definable is equivalent to checking if S belongs to L_{n^2}. We will now explain how the algorithm can check the membership of S in L_{n^2}.

Every relation in L_{n^2} has appeared due to a sequence of computations starting from the basic relations S_ε and S_a for each $a \in \Sigma$. Thanks to (4), there is a specific structure to this computation that allows to look at it as a "computation tree". Nodes in this tree are relations in L_{n^2} and the children of a node are different relations in the same or smaller level that are used to construct the parent relation through the operations $+$, $\circ$, or the $=$ and $\neq$ restrictions. The leaves are the basic sets S_ε and S_a.

A naive approach would be to guess this entire computation tree and check two things: are leaves of the form S_a or S_ε, and is each node either the union, composition or one of the (in)equality restrictions of its children. These checks can be done in polynomial time. However, we cannot hope to maintain the entire tree in PSPACE as compositions can have exponentially many children (4).

Instead of guessing the entire tree, the algorithm guesses, in a certain way, a path in the tree along with the children of each node in this path: if the node is a union of $T_1, \ldots, T_m$, all these relations are guessed as children (there are only polynomially many); if a node is a composition of $R_1, \ldots, R_p$, two children are guessed - the relation R_1 and the composed relation $R_2 \circ \cdots \circ R_p$. The former is a proper child in the computation tree, and the latter is a different relation which needs to be further decomposed to get the actual children in the computation tree. The algorithm also maintains the number the decompositions left: so the child would be $(R_2 \circ \cdots \circ R_p, p-1)$. Storing $p-1$ needs only polynomially many bits. This is the main idea. Additionally, the algorithm maintains the height of each node (see Figure 2). Each time an $=$ or $\neq$ restriction happens, the height reduces by one. At the leaf level, it is checked if the relation is one of S_ε or S_a. Nodes whose heights have been certified can be removed: that is, leaf nodes can be removed after the basic check, and non-leaf nodes are removed once all its children are checked. Hence at any point of time, the algorithm maintains some structure like Figure 2. Since the height is polynomial, this can be done in PSPACE. □

The PSPACE-hardness of RPQ-definability [3] can be easily extended to give the same lower bound for $\mathrm{RDPQ}_=$-definability.

Theorem 32 *$\mathrm{RDPQ}_=$-definability is PSPACE-complete.*

5. UNION OF CONJUNCTIVE QUERIES

In this section, we study the complexity of the definability problem for data graphs using UCRDPQs. The notion of homomorphisms has been used in relational databases to characterize relations definable by union of conjunctive queries. We will now adapt it to data graphs.

Definition 33 Let $G = (V, E, \rho)$ be a data graph and $h : V \to V$ be a mapping. We call h a *data graph homomorphism* if it satisfies the following two conditions.

1. (Single step compatibility) For every $p, q \in V$ and $a \in \Sigma$, $p \xrightarrow{a} q$ implies $h(p) \xrightarrow{a} h(q)$.
2. (Data compatibility of reachable nodes) For every $p, q \in V$, if q is reachable from p, then $\rho(p) = \rho(q) \Leftrightarrow \rho(h(p)) = \rho(h(q))$.

Intuitively, a data graph homomorphism h ensures that if there is an edge labeled a from p to q, there is also an edge labeled a from $h(p)$ to $h(q)$, thus preserving the relations induced by the letters in the finite alphabet. In addition, suppose there is a path from p to q. Then the data values at p and q are same if, and only if, the data values at $h(p)$ and $h(q)$ are same. This preserves the relations induced by (in)equality of data values. The following result characterizes UCRDPQ-definable sets in terms of data graph homomorphisms.

Lemma 34 Let $G = (V, E, \rho)$ be a data graph and S be a relation of any arity. Then the following are equivalent.

1. The set S is UCRDPQ-definable.
2. For every data graph homomorphism h and every tuple $\overline{p} \in S$, $h(\overline{p})$ also belongs to S.

PROOF. ($1 \Rightarrow 2$). Suppose $S = Q_1(G) \cup \cdots \cup Q_k(G)$, where $Q_1, \ldots, Q_k$ are CRDPQs. Suppose Q_j is of the form (1)(in Definition 13) and $\overline{p} \in Q_j(G)$. Let h be a data graph homomorphism. We will prove that $h(\overline{p}) \in Q_j(G)$. From the semantics of CRDPQs, we infer that there is a valuation $\mu : \cup_{1\le i\le m}\{x_i, y_i\} \to V$ such that $(G, \mu) \models Q_j$ and $\overline{p} = \mu(\overline{z})$. Let $h \circ \mu$ be the valuation such that $h \circ \mu(x) = h(\mu(x))$ for all x. It is enough to prove that $(G, h \circ \mu) \models Q_j$ — in that case, $h(\overline{p}) = h \circ \mu(\overline{z}) \in Q_j(G)$. Now let us prove that $(G, h\circ\mu) \models Q_j$. Since Q_j is of the form (1) and $(G, \mu) \models Q_j$, we infer that for every $i = 1, \ldots, m$, there is a data path $w_i \in \mathcal{L}(e_i)$ from $\mu(x_i)$ to $\mu(y_i)$. It is enough to prove that there is a data path w_i' automorphic to w_i from $h \circ \mu(x_i)$ to $h\circ\mu(y_i)$ for every $i = 1, \ldots, m$ — in that case $(G, h\circ\mu) \models Q_j$. So suppose w_i is the data path associated with the path $\mu(x_i) \xrightarrow{a_1} p_2 \xrightarrow{a_2} \cdots \xrightarrow{a_{l-1}} p_l \xrightarrow{a_l} \mu(y_i)$, where $p_2, \ldots, p_l$ are the intermediate nodes in the path from $\mu(x_i) = p_1$ to $\mu(y_i) = p_{l+1}$. Since h is a data graph homomorphism, we infer from the single step compatibility property that G has a path $h \circ \mu(x_i) \xrightarrow{a_1} h(p_2) \xrightarrow{a_2} \cdots \xrightarrow{a_{l-1}} h(p_l) \xrightarrow{a_l} h \circ \mu(y_i)$, where $h(p_2), \ldots, h(p_l)$ are intermediate nodes in a path from $h \circ \mu(x_i)$ to $h \circ \mu(y_i)$. We claim that the data path w_i' associated with this path is automorphic to w_i. If not, there would be positions j_1 and j_2 such that $\rho(p_{j_1}) = \rho(p_{j_2})$ but $\rho(h(p_{j_1})) \neq \rho(h(p_{j_2}))$ (or vice-versa), violating the data compatibility property of the data graph homomorphism h. Thus, w_i' is a data path automorphic to w_i from $h \circ \mu(x_i)$ to $h \circ \mu(y_i)$. This concludes the proof that $h(\overline{p}) \in S$.

($2 \Rightarrow 1$) Suppose $V = \{p_1, \ldots, p_n\}$. Let $\overline{x} = \langle x_1, \ldots, x_n \rangle$. Let $\phi_G(\overline{x})$ be defined as follows.

$$\phi_G(\overline{x}) = \bigwedge_{(p_i,a,p_j)\in E} x_i \xrightarrow{a} x_j \;\wedge \bigwedge_{(p_i,p_j)\in(\Sigma^+)_=(G)} x_i \xrightarrow{(\Sigma^+)_=} x_j$$
$$\wedge \bigwedge_{(p_i,p_j)\in(\Sigma^+)_{\neq}(G)} x_i \xrightarrow{(\Sigma^+)_{\neq}} x_j$$

In the above definition, $(\Sigma^+)_=$ is an REE; $(\Sigma^+)_=(G)$ is the set of pairs of nodes (p_i, p_j) such that p_j is reachable from p_i and both nodes have the same data value. Similarly, $(\Sigma^+)_{\neq}(G)$ is the set of pairs of nodes (p_i, p_j) such that p_j is reachable from p_i and the two nodes have different data values. The valuation that assigns p_i to x_i for every $i = 1, \ldots, n$ satisfies all the conditions in $\phi_G(\overline{x})$. If a valuation μ for $\overline{x}$ satisfies all the conditions in $\phi_G(\overline{x})$, then the mapping $h_\mu : V \to V$ such that $h_\mu(p_i) = \mu(x_i)$ is a data graph homomorphism. Let S' be the set of tuples defined by the UCRDPQ $\{Ans(\langle x_{i_1}, \ldots, x_{i_r}\rangle) := \phi_G(\overline{x}) \mid \langle p_{i_1}, \ldots, p_{i_r}\rangle \in S\}$. We claim that $S' = S$, which will prove that S is UCRDPQ-definable.

($S \subseteq S'$): For every $\langle p_{i_1}, \ldots, p_{i_r}\rangle \in S$, we have that $\langle p_{i_1}, \ldots, p_{i_r}\rangle \in Ans(\langle x_{i_1}, \ldots, x_{i_r}\rangle) := \phi_G(\overline{x})(G) \subseteq S'$.

($S' \subseteq S$): Suppose $\langle p_{j_1}, \ldots, p_{j_r}\rangle \in S'$. Then there is some $\langle p_{i_1}, \ldots, p_{i_r}\rangle \in S$ and a valuation μ for $\overline{x}$ such that μ satisfies all the conditions in $\phi_G(\overline{x})$ and $\langle p_{j_1}, \ldots, p_{j_r}\rangle = \langle \mu(x_{i_1}), \ldots, \mu(x_{i_r})\rangle$. The mapping $h_\mu : V \to V$ such that $h_\mu(p_i) = \mu(x_i)$ is a data graph homomorphism. Now we have $\langle p_{j_1}, \ldots, p_{j_r}\rangle = \langle \mu(x_{i_1}), \ldots, \mu(x_{i_r})\rangle$ and in addition $\langle \mu(x_{i_1}), \ldots, \mu(x_{i_r})\rangle = \langle h_\mu(p_{i_1}), \ldots, h_\mu(p_{i_r})\rangle$. Hence, we have $\langle p_{j_1}, \ldots, p_{j_r}\rangle = h_\mu(\langle p_{i_1}, \ldots, p_{i_r}\rangle) \in S$; the last inclusion follows from condition 2 of the lemma, as $\langle p_{i_1}, \ldots, p_{i_r}\rangle \in S$. □

Readers familiar with Global as View (GAV) schema mappings for relational databases may note some similarities with the above result. For a data graph G, consider the relational database D_G over the domain V consisting of all the binary relations that are definable by RDPQs. For a set of tuples S over V, let D_S be the relational database consisting of the single relation S. Then S is UCRDPQ-definable on G iff some GAV schema mapping fits the source database D_G and the target database D_S. A characterization using homomorphisms similar to the one in Lemma 34 is given for GAV schema mappings in [9, 2]. Here, we extend the notion of homomorphisms to include data value compatibility. A coNP-completeness result for a subclass of GAV schema mappings is given in [9]. We give a similar result for UCRDPQ-definability below. However, there is no obvious way of directly using the upper bound in [9] here, since the relational database D_G may be exponentially larger than G. Preservation under homomorphism is a fundamental concept, which appears in other contexts as well, for example querying databases with incomplete information [12].

Theorem 35 *UCRDPQ-definability is* coNP*-complete.*

PROOF. We first prove the coNP upper bound. Given a data graph $G = (V, E, \rho)$ and a set of tuples S, we can guess a mapping $h : V \to V$, verify that it is a data graph homomorphism and that there is some tuple $\overline{p} \in S$ such that $h(\overline{p}) \notin S$. If S is not UCRDPQ-definable, then Lemma 34 ensures that at least one of the guesses will succeed. On the other hand, if S is UCRDPQ-definable, then none of the guesses will succeed.

For the coNP lower bound, we reduce the unsatisfiability problem for Boolean 3-CNF formulas to the UCRDPQ-definability problem. This part of the proof is an adaptation of a similar proof from [9] about relational databases (which can have ternary relations) to data graphs (which can only have binary relations). Given a 3-CNF formula F consisting of clauses $C_1, \ldots, C_m$ over the variables $p_1, \ldots, p_n$, we map it to the data graph shown in Fig. 3. All nodes have the same data value, which is not shown explicitly.

There is only one node ①, but the same node is drawn (dotted) at many places in the diagram to avoid the clutter of too many edges. Same comment applies to all the nodes drawn dotted. There is an edge labeled γ from all nodes R_i^j to R_{i+1}^k, but most of the edges are grayed out and the label γ is not shown to reduce clutter. Same applies to edges from L_i^j to L_{i+1}^k. In the diagram, the clause C_1 is assumed to be $(p_1 \vee \neg p_2 \vee p_3)$. From every clause node C_i, there are edges labeled l_1, l_2 and l_3 to the nodes corresponding to the literals occurring in C_i. Only the edges from C_1 are shown and others are not shown. From every node R_i^j and L_i^j, there is an edge labeled l_k to either 0 or 1, depending on the kth most significant bit of the binary representation of j. Only the edges from L_1^0, R_1^1, R_1^2 and R_1^7 are shown. Others are not shown. We claim that the given Boolean 3-CNF formula F is not satisfiable iff the set of tuples of nodes $S = \{\langle C_1\rangle, \ldots, \langle C_m\rangle\} \cup \{\langle L_i^j\rangle \mid 1 \leq i \leq m, 0 \leq j \leq 7\}$ is UCRDPQ-definable.

Suppose there is an assignment $sa : \{p_1, \ldots, p_n\} \to \{0, 1\}$ satisfying F. Consider the graph mapping h that maps the node p_i to the node $sa(p_i)$ and $\overline{p}_i$ to $1 - sa(p_i)$. For every $i = 1, \ldots, m$, h maps the node C_i to the node R_i^j; here j is the number whose binary representation is the one formed by the three literals of the clause C_i according to the satisfying assignment sa. All other nodes are mapped to themselves by h. This mapping h is a data graph homomorphism and $h(\langle C_1\rangle) = \langle R_1^j\rangle$ for some j. Since $\langle C_1\rangle \in S$ and $\langle R_1^j\rangle \notin S$, we infer from Lemma 34 that S is not UCRDPQ-definable.

Conversely, suppose F is not satisfiable. Let h be any data graph homomorphism. We will prove that $h(\langle p\rangle) \in S$ for every tuple $\langle p\rangle \in S$. Since the only node with a self edge labeled $\top$ (resp. $\perp$) is 1 (resp. 0), 1 (resp. 0) is mapped to itself by h. Due to the self edges labeled l and the edges labeled l_1, l_2 and l_3, h maps L_1^j to itself for every $j = 0, \ldots, 7$. The edges labeled γ, l_1, l_2, l_3 then force h to map L_i^j to itself for every i, j. It remains to prove that $h(\langle C_i\rangle) \in S$ for every $i = 1, \ldots, m$. Due to the edges labeled β and the self edges labeled γ, h maps p_1 to either itself or to 1 or to 0. If h maps p_1 to itself, then the edges labeled α and β force h to map p_i to itself (and $\overline{p}_i$ to itself) for every $i = 1, \ldots, n$. The edges labeled l_1, l_2 and l_3 then force h to map C_i to itself for every $i = 1, \ldots, m$. On the other hand, if h maps p_1 to 1 or 0, the edges labeled α force h to map $\overline{p}_1$ to $1 - h(p_1)$. The edges labeled α and β then force h to map p_i to 1 or 0 and

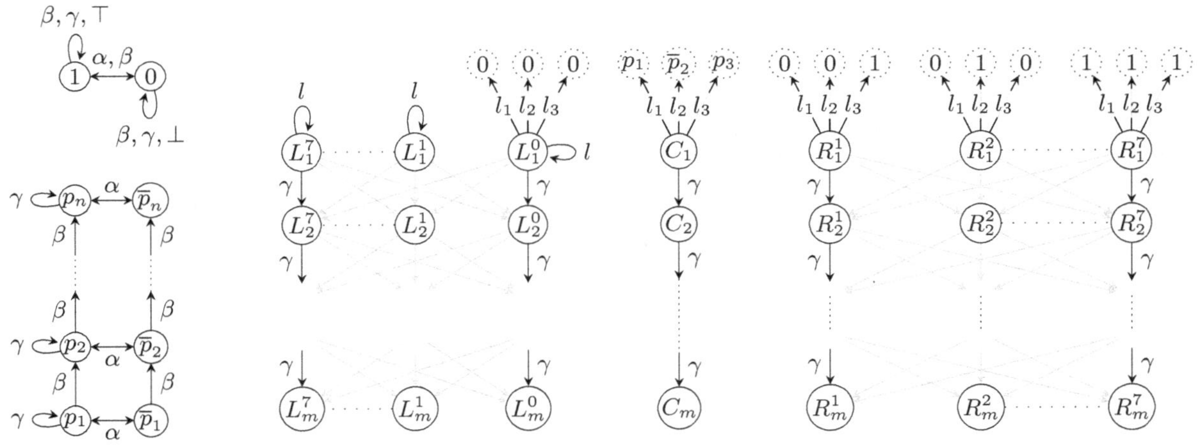

Figure 3: Data graph for the lower bound of UCRDPQ-definability

$\overline{p}_i$ to $1 - h(p_i)$ for every $i = 1, \ldots, n$. The homomorphism h thus determines a truth assignment for $p_1, \ldots, p_n$. For every $i = 1, \ldots, m$, the edges labeled l_1, l_2 and l_3 force h to map C_i to either L_i^j or R_i^j; here j is the number whose binary representation is the one formed by the three literals of the clause C_i according to the truth assignment determined by h. If h maps C_i to R_i^* (R_i^* could be any one of R_i^1, $\ldots$, R_i^7) for some $i = 1, \ldots, m$, then the edges labeled γ force h to map C_i to R_i^* for every $i = 1, \ldots, m$. This implies that the truth assignment determined by h assigns at least one literal to *true* in every clause, contradicting the hypothesis that F is not satisfiable. Hence h maps C_i to L_i^* for every $i = 1, \ldots, m$. Since this holds for every data graph homomorphism, we conclude that $h(\langle p \rangle) \in S$ for every data graph homomorphism h and every tuple $\langle p \rangle \in S$. Hence, we can conclude from Lemma 34 that S is UCRDPQ-definable. □

6. DISCUSSION

A natural question to ask is how to synthesize a query that defines a given relation. In principle, the decision procedures in the paper can be converted into a procedure to synthesize a defining query. However such queries would not have an interesting structure. For instance, in the REM and REE cases, the synthesized queries do not make use of the star operator. Moreover, the lower bound for the decision problem implies that the worst case size of the defining queries will be doubly exponential for REMs, and exponential for REEs. In the UCRDPQ case, the defining query described in Lemma 34 essentially constructs the whole data graph using conditions and then picks out the required tuples. This does not capture the essence of conjunctive queries, which is to identify patterns that are much smaller than the graphs themselves.

A possible future direction would be to find a notion of "good" queries and reformulate the definability problem to ask for the existence of "good" defining queries.

In some application domains, data graphs may have a special structure (such as not too many cycles). An orthogonal direction would be to study the definability problem for such data graphs.

7. REFERENCES

[1] B. Alexe, B. T. Cate, P. G. Kolaitis, and W-C Tan. Characterizing schema mappings via data examples. *ACM Trans. Database Syst.*, 36(4):23:1–23:48, 2011.

[2] B. Alexe, B. T. Cate, P. G. Kolaitis, and W-C Tan. Designing and refining schema mappings via data examples. In *SIGMOD*, pages 133–144, 2011.

[3] T. Antonopoulos, F. Neven, and F. Servais. Definability problems for graph query languages. In *ICDT*, pages 141–152, 2013.

[4] P. Barceló. Querying graph databases. In *PODS*, pages 175–188, 2013.

[5] P. Barceló, J. Pérez, and J. Reutter. Schema mappings and data exchange for graph databases. In *ICDT*, pages 189–200, 2013.

[6] P. Barceló, J. Reutter, and L. Libkin. Parameterized regular expressions and their languages. *Theor. Comput. Sci.*, 474:21–45, 2013.

[7] D. Calvanese, G. De Giacomo, M. Lenzerini, and M. Y. Vardi. Simplifying schema mappings. In *ICDT*, pages 114–125, 2011.

[8] B. T. Cate, V. Dalmau, and P. G. Kolaitis. Learning schema mappings. *ACM Trans. Database Syst.*, 38(4):28:1–28:31, 2013.

[9] B. T. Cate, P. G. Kolaitis, and W-C Tan. Database constraints and homomorphism dualities. In *CP*, pages 475–490, 2010.

[10] A. Das Sarma, A. Parameswaran, H. Garcia-Molina, and J. Widom. Synthesizing view definitions from data. In *ICDT*, pages 89–103, 2010.

[11] G.H.L. Fletcher, M. Gyssens, J. Paredaens, and D. V. Gucht. On the expressive power of the relational algebra on finite sets of relation pairs. *IEEE Trans. Knowledge and Data Engg.*, 21(6):939–942, 2009.

[12] A. Gheerbrant, L. Libkin, and C. Sirangelo. When is naive evaluation possible? In *PODS*, pages 75–86, 2013.

[13] G. Gottlob, C. Koch, R. Baumgartner, M. Herzog, and S. Flesca. The Lixto data extraction project: Back and forth between theory and practice. In *PODS*, pages 1–12, 2004.

[14] G. Gottlob and P. Senellart. Schema mapping discovery from data instances. *J. ACM*, 57(2):6:1–6:37, 2010.
[15] C. Gutierrez, C. Hurtado, and A. Mendelzon. Foundations of semantic web databases. *JCSS*, 77(3):520–541, 2011.
[16] M. Kaminski and N. Francez. Finite-memory automata. *Theor. Comp. Sc.*, 134(2):329 – 363, 1994.
[17] E.V. Kostylev, J.L. Reutter, and D. Vrgoč. Containment of data graph queries. In *ICDT*, pages 131–142, 2014.
[18] U. Leser. A query language for biological networks. *Bioinformatics*, 21(suppl 2):ii33–ii39, 2005.
[19] L. Libkin and D. Vrgoč. Regular expressions for data words. In *Logic for Programming, Artificial Intelligence, and Reasoning*, volume 7180 of *LNCS*, pages 274–288. 2012.
[20] L. Libkin and D. Vrgoč. Regular path queries on graphs with data. In *ICDT*, pages 74–85, 2012.
[21] F. Neven, T. Schwentick, and V. Vianu. Finite state machines for strings over infinite alphabets. *ACM TOCL*, 5(3):403–435, 2004.
[22] J. Pérez, M. Arenas, and C. Gutierrez. Semantics and complexity of SPARQL. *ACM Trans. Database Syst.*, 34(3), 2009.
[23] R. Ronen and O. Shmueli. Soql: A language for querying and creating data in social networks. In *ICDE*, pages 1595–1602, 2009.
[24] H. Sakamoto and D. Ikeda. Intractability of decision problems for finite-memory automata. *Theor. Comp. Sc.*, 231(2):297 – 308, 2000.
[25] P. van Emde Boas. The convenience of tilings. In *Complexity, Logic and Recursion Theory*, pages 331–363. Marcel Dekker Inc., 1997.

APPENDIX

A. PROOFS FROM SECTION 3

PROOF (LEMMA 18). Suppose a k-REM e defines S and $\langle u, v\rangle \in S$. We will show that there exists a k-REM witness for $\langle u, v\rangle$ in S, which will prove the lemma.

Since e defines S, there is a data path $w \in \mathcal{L}(e)$ connecting u to v. Without loss of generality, we can assume that e is of the form $e_1 + e_2 + \cdots + e_m$ for some $m \geq 1$ such that each e_i is union-free, that is each e_i is constructed using the grammar for REMs without the $e := e + e$ rule. The data path w belongs to $\mathcal{L}(e_i)$ for some $i \in \{1, \ldots, m\}$. If e_i is a basic k-REM, then we are done. Otherwise, e_i is of the form $f_1 \cdot (f_2)^+ \cdot f_3$ where f_1, f_2 and f_3 are union free k-REMs. As $w \in \mathcal{L}(e_i)$, from the semantics of k-REMs, there exists a number α such that w satisfies the k-REM obtained by α iterations of f_2. More precisely, there exist data paths $x \in \mathcal{L}(f_1)$, $y_1, \ldots, y_\alpha \in \mathcal{L}(f_2)$ and $z \in \mathcal{L}(f_3)$ such that $w = x \cdot y_1 \cdots y_\alpha \cdot z$.

Let us write $(f_2)^\alpha$ for the k-REM obtained by concatenating f_2 α times. If $f_1(f_2)^\alpha f_3$ is basic, then we are done. Otherwise continue this process of "unfolding" to get a basic k-REM e'. Since w is in $\mathcal{L}(e')$, e' satisfies the first condition of Definition 17 (connecting path). Since $\mathcal{L}(e') \subseteq \mathcal{L}(e)$ and e defines S, e' satisfies the second condition of Definition 17 (no extraneous pairs). Hence, e' is a k-REM witness for $\langle u, v\rangle$ in S, which finishes the proof. □

PROOF (LEMMA 20). By an induction on the number of blocks of the form $\downarrow \overline{r}.a[c]$ in e. Suppose $e = \downarrow \overline{r}.a[c]$. If there is a data path w as in the lemma, then $(u, a, v) \in E$ and by the semantics of REMs, $\sigma' = \sigma[\overline{r} \to \rho(u)]$ and $\rho(v), \sigma' \models c$. Hence $(u, \sigma) \xrightarrow{\downarrow \overline{r}.a[c]}_G (v, \sigma')$. Conversely, let us suppose $(u, \sigma) \xrightarrow{\downarrow \overline{r}.a[c]}_G (v, \sigma')$ in $\mathcal{T}_G$. By definition of $\mathcal{T}_G$, we have $(u, a, v) \in E$, $\sigma' = \sigma[\overline{r} \to \rho(u)]$ and $\rho(v), \sigma' \models c$. Hence, $\rho(u)a\rho(v)$ is a data path connecting u to v in G and $(\downarrow \overline{r}.a[c], \rho(u)a\rho(v), \sigma) \vdash \sigma'$.

For the induction step, suppose $e = \downarrow \overline{r}.a[c] \cdot e'$. If there is a data path w as in the lemma, then $w = \rho(u)a\rho(u_0) \cdot w'$ for some node u_0 and a data path w' connecting u_0 to v in G. In addition, by the semantics of REMs, there is some assignment σ_0 such that $(\downarrow \overline{r}.a[c], \rho(u)a\rho(u_0), \sigma) \vdash \sigma_0$ and $(e', w', \sigma_0) \vdash \sigma'$. Now we can use an argument similar to the one in the base case to infer that $(u, \sigma) \xrightarrow{\downarrow \overline{r}.a[c]}_G (u_0, \sigma_0)$ and use the induction hypothesis to infer that $(u_0, \sigma_0) \xrightarrow{e'}_G (v, \sigma')$. Hence, $(u, \sigma) \xrightarrow{e}_G (v, \sigma')$. Conversely, suppose $(u, \sigma) \xrightarrow{e}_G (v, \sigma')$ in $\mathcal{T}_G$. This run can be split as follows: $(u, \sigma) \xrightarrow{\downarrow \overline{r}.a[c]} (u_0, \sigma_0) \xrightarrow{e'}_G (v, \sigma')$ for some node u_0 and assignment σ_0. Then we can argue as in the base case to infer that the data path $\rho(u)a\rho(u_0)$ connects u to u_0 in G and $(\downarrow \overline{r}.a[c], \rho(u)a\rho(u_0), \sigma) \vdash \sigma_0$. We can use the induction hypothesis to infer that there is a data path w' connecting u_0 to v in G and $(e', w', \sigma_0) \models \sigma'$. Hence, the data path $\rho(u)a\rho(u_0) \cdot w'$ connects u to v in G and $(e, \rho(u)a\rho(u_0) \cdot w', \sigma) \vdash \sigma'$. □

PROOF (THEOREM 22). Suppose we are trying to define the set S. From Lemma 18, it is enough to check that there are $|S|$ k-REM witness, one for each pair $\langle u, v\rangle$ in S. From Lemma 21, we infer that it is enough to check for witnesses of length at most $2^{n^2(\delta+1)^k}$. We will now give a non-deterministic algorithm to do this in space $\mathcal{O}(n^2\delta^k)$.

First we note that given a tuple $\langle Q_1, \ldots, Q_n\rangle$ of subsets of Q_G and a k-REM $e = \downarrow \overline{r}a.[c]$, we can compute in space polynomial in $(n\delta^k)$ the tuple $\langle Q'_1, \ldots, Q'_n\rangle$ such that $\langle Q_1, \ldots, Q_n\rangle \xrightarrow{e}_G \langle Q'_1, \ldots, Q'_n\rangle$. Suppose $v_1, \ldots, v_n$ are the nodes of G. Now we give a non-deterministic algorithm to check if there exists a k-REM witness for $\langle v_1, v_p\rangle$ in S of length at most $2^{n^2(\delta+1)^k}$. The algorithm maintains a counter initialized to 0 and a tuple of subsets of Q_G, initialized to $\langle\{(v_1, \perp^k)\}, \ldots, \{(v_n, \perp^k)\}\rangle$. The algorithm performs the following steps as long as the counter does not exceed $2^{n^2(\delta+1)^k}$.

1. Increment the counter.
2. Guess a k-REM $e = \downarrow \overline{r}a.[c]$.
3. Replace current tuple $\langle Q_1, \ldots, Q_n\rangle$ with $\langle Q'_1, \ldots, Q'_n\rangle$, where $\langle Q_1, \ldots, Q_n\rangle \xrightarrow{e} \langle Q'_1, \ldots, Q'_n\rangle$.
4. Check if $(v_p, \sigma) \in Q'_1$ for some assignment σ and that for every $i = 1, \ldots, n$ and for every $(v', \sigma) \in Q'_i$, the pair $\langle v_i, v'\rangle$ belongs to S. If yes, accept and terminate. If not, go back to step 1.

From the proof of Lemma 21, we conclude that some run of the above non-deterministic algorithm will accept if there is a k-REM witness for $\langle v_1, v_p\rangle$ in S. If there is no such witness, then clearly no run will accept. The algorithm needs space to store the counter, the tuple of subsets of Q_G and the space to compute the successor tuple. The counter can be implemented in space $\mathcal{O}(n^2\delta^k)$ using binary counting. One state of Q_G needs $(\log n \cdot k \cdot \log \delta)$ bits. There are at most $n(\delta+1)^k$ states in Q_G. Hence, the tuple of subsets and the space needed for intermediate computations can all be accommodated in space $\mathcal{O}(n^2\delta^k)$. □

PROOF (LEMMA 23). The right to left implication is obvious. For the other direction, suppose S is $k-\text{RDPQ}_{\text{mem}}$-definable for some k. From Lemma 18, for every pair $\langle u,v\rangle \in S$, there is a k-REM witness e for $\langle u,v\rangle$ in S. Hence, there exists a data path $w \in \mathcal{L}(e)$ connecting u to v. From Lemma 15, $e_{[w]}$ is a δ-REM and from Fact 10, $\mathcal{L}(e_{[w]}) \subseteq \mathcal{L}(e)$. Hence, $e_{[w]}$ is a δ-REM witness for $\langle u,v\rangle$ in S. Such witnesses exist for every pair in S and hence, S is $\delta-\text{RDPQ}_{\text{mem}}$-definable. □

PROOF (THEOREM 24). From Lemma 23, it is equivalent to checking $\delta-\text{RDPQ}_{\text{mem}}$-definability, where δ is the number of distinct data values in the given data graph. From Theorem 22, $\delta-\text{RDPQ}_{\text{mem}}$-definability is in $\text{NSPACE}(\mathcal{O}(n^2\delta^\delta))$. From Savitch's theorem, we then get a deterministic exponential space algorithm. □

B. PROOFS FROM SECTION 4

PROOF (LEMMA 30). We prove the left-to-right direction by an induction on the structure of REE. Relations S_ε and S_a definable by the basic REE ε and a already belong to L_0, and hence belong to L_{n^2}. For REE e and f, let S_e and S_f belong to L_{n^2}.

By Lemma 29, we have $S_{e+f} = S_e + S_f$ and $S_{ef} = S_e \circ S_f$. As L_{n^2} is closed under $+$ and $\circ$, the relations S_{e+f} and S_{ef} belong to L_{n^2} as well. The relation $S_{e_=}$ equals $S_e^=$. Since S_e belongs to L_{n^2}, the relation $S_e^=$ would be present in B_{n^2+1} by definition and hence in the level L_{n^2+1}. But by Lemma 28, this means that $S_e^=$ belongs to L_{n^2} as well. Similar argument holds for $S_e^{\neq}$.

The right-to-left direction can be proved by an easy induction on the level number, once again using Lemma 29. □

PROOF (THEOREM 32). The PSPACE upper bound comes from Lemma 31. For the lower bound, consider the RPQ-definability problem: given a graph H and a relation T on H, is T definable by a regular expression? This problem is known to be PSPACE-complete [3]. We will show that RPQ-definability can be reduced to $\text{RDPQ}_=$ definability.

Consider the data graph H' obtained from H by attaching the same data value to all the nodes. Consider the $\text{RDPQ}_=$ definability of the same set T. If T is RPQ-definable on H, then clearly T would be $\text{RDPQ}_=$ definable on H' as well using the same expression. Suppose T is $\text{RDPQ}_=$ definable on H' using the expression e. Without loss of generality, assume that T is non-empty. We claim that the REE defining T on H' will not have sub-expressions of the form $f_{\neq}$. This is because $f_{\neq}$ defines the empty relation and hence can be eliminated from the defining REE. Secondly observe that for the graph H', no matter which REE f we choose, $S_f = S_{f_=}$. Hence all sub-expressions of the form $f_=$ in e can be modified to f and still the defined set remains the same. This way, we have obtained a regular expression that defines H'. The same regular expression would define T on H as well.

□

Querying Big Data by Accessing Small Data

Wenfei Fan[1,3] Floris Geerts[2] Yang Cao[1,3] Ting Deng[3] Ping Lu[3]
[1]University of Edinburgh [2]University of Antwerp [3]Beihang University
{wenfei@inf, yang.cao@}.ed.ac.uk, floris.geerts@ua.ac.be, {dengting, luping}@buaa.edu.cn

ABSTRACT

This paper investigates the feasibility of querying big data by accessing a bounded amount of the data. We study boundedly evaluable queries under a form of access constraints, when their evaluation cost is determined by the queries and constraints only. While it is undecidable to determine whether FO queries are boundedly evaluable, we show that for several classes of FO queries, the bounded evaluability problem is decidable. We also provide characterization and effective syntax for their boundedly evaluable queries.

When a query Q is not boundedly evaluable, we study two approaches to approximately answering Q under access constraints. (1) We search for upper and lower envelopes of Q that are boundedly evaluable and warrant a constant accuracy bound. (2) We instantiate a minimum set of variables (parameters) in Q such that the specialized query is boundedly evaluable. We study problems for deciding the existence of envelopes and bounded specialized queries, and establish their complexity for various classes of FO queries.

Categories and Subject Descriptors: H.2.1 [**Database Management**]: Logical Design – *Data Models*; H.2.4 [**Database Management**]: Systems – *Query Processing*

General Terms: Theory, Languages, Algorithms

Keywords: Big data; query answering; complexity

1. INTRODUCTION

Querying big data is cost prohibitive. Indeed, a linear scan of a dataset D of PB size (10^{15} bytes) takes days using a solid state drive with a read speed of 6GB/s, and it takes years if D is of EB size (10^{18} bytes) [18].

Given a query Q and a dataset D, can we efficiently compute query answers $Q(D)$ when D is big? There has been work tackling this question [11, 12, 17]. One idea is to capitalize on a set $\mathcal{A}$ of access constraints, which are a combination of indices and cardinality constraints commonly found in practice. Under $\mathcal{A}$, we study *boundedly evaluable* queries Q, such that for all datasets D that satisfy constraints in $\mathcal{A}$, there exists $D_Q \subseteq D$ such that

- $Q(D_Q) = Q(D)$, and
- the time for identifying D_Q and hence the size $|D_Q|$ of D_Q are determined by Q and $\mathcal{A}$ only.

The need for studying bounded evaluability is evident: if Q is boundedly evaluable, then $Q(D)$ can be computed by accessing (identifying and fetching) a small D_Q by using the indices in $\mathcal{A}$, in time determined by Q and $\mathcal{A}$, *not by* the size of D, no matter how big D grows. Experimenting with real-life data, we find that a large number of queries are boundedly evaluable under a small number of simple access constraints, and that such queries can be efficiently answered in big datasets that satisfy the constraints [11, 12].

Example 1.1: On the dataset D_0 of all traffic accidents in the UK from 1979 to 2005 [1], we find that 77% of conjunctive queries (CQ, *a.k.a.* SPC) are actually boundedly evaluable under a set of 84 simple access constraints, and for such queries, our query plans take 9 seconds on average as opposed to more than 14 hours by MySQL [12].

As an example, consider a query Q_0 to find the ages of drivers who were involved in an accident in Queen's Park district on May 1, 2005. The query is defined on three (simplified) relations Accident(aid, district, date), Casualty(cid, aid, class, vid) and Vehicle(vid, driver, age), recording accidents (where and when), casualties (class and vehicle), and vehicles (including driver information such as age), respectively. Query Q_0 is a conjunctive query written as

$$\begin{aligned} Q_0(x_a) = \exists\ & \mathsf{aid}, \mathsf{cid}, \mathsf{class}, \mathsf{vid}, \mathsf{dri} \\ & (\mathsf{Accident}(\mathsf{aid}, \text{"Queen's Park"}, \text{"1/5/2005"}) \wedge \\ & \mathsf{Casualty}(\mathsf{cid}, \mathsf{aid}, \mathsf{class}, \mathsf{vid}) \wedge \mathsf{Vehicle}(\mathsf{vid}, \mathsf{dri}, x_a)). \end{aligned}$$

It is costly to compute $Q_0(D_0)$ directly: the Accident, Casualty and Vehicle relations have more than 7.5, 10 and 13.5 million tuples, respectively. Nonetheless, a closer examination of D_0 reveals the following cardinality constraints:

ψ_1: Accident (date $\rightarrow$ aid, 610)
ψ_2: Casualty (aid $\rightarrow$ vid, 192)
ψ_3: Accident (aid $\rightarrow$ (district, date), 1)
ψ_4: Vehicle (vid $\rightarrow$ (driver, age), 1)

The first two constraints state that from 1979 to 2005, at most 610 accidents happened within a single day, and each accident involved at most 192 vehicles, respectively. Constraint ψ_3 says that aid is a key for Accident; similarly for ψ_4. These constraints are discovered by simple aggregate queries on D_0. Indices can be built on D_0 based on ψ_1 such

PODS'15, May 31–June 4, 2015, Melbourne, Victoria, Australia.

http://dx.doi.org/10.1145/2745754.2745771.

that given a date, it returns all the ids of those accidents (at most 610) that happened on the particular day; similarly for ψ_2–ψ_4. We refer to the cardinality constraints and their indices put together as *access constraints.*

Given these access constraints, we can compute $Q_0(D_0)$ by accessing at most 234850 tuples from D_0, instead of millions. (1) We identify and fetch at most 610 aid's of Accident tuples with date = "1/5/2005", using the index built on ψ_1. (2) For each aid, we fetch its Accident tuple using the index for ψ_3. We select a set T_1 of tuples with district = "Queen's Park". (3) For each tuple $t \in T_1$, we fetch a set T_2 of at most 192 vid's from Casualty tuples with aid = t[aid], with the index for ψ_2. (4) For each $s \in T_2$, we find a Vehicle tuple with vid = s[vid], using the index for ψ_4. These tuples suffice for computing $Q_0(D_0)$, $610 + 610 \times 192 \times 2$ in total, all fetched using indices. In fact, the chances are that we need to access $610 \times 2 \times 2 = 3050$ tuples only, since accidents involved two vehicles on average. Better still, no matter how big D_0 grows, as long as D_0 satisfies ψ_1–ψ_4 (possibly with cardinality bounds mildly adjusted), $Q_0(D_0)$ can be computed by accessing a small number of tuples determined by Q_0 and the bounds in ψ_1–ψ_4 only. Thus Q_0 is *boundedly evaluable under access constraints* ψ_1–ψ_4.

This approach is also effective when querying graphs. Experimenting with real-life Web graphs of billions of nodes and edges, we find that 60% of graph pattern queries via subgraph isomorphism are boundedly evaluable under simple access constraints, and that our bounded-evaluation approach outperforms conventional subgraph isomorphism methods by *4 orders of magnitude* on average [11]. □

These experimental findings verify that the bounded evaluability analysis yields a practical approach to optimizing queries on big data. The effectiveness of the approach is particularly evident for personalized searches. For example, a typical query of Graph Search, Facebook [16] is to "find me all my friends in NYC who like cycling", which only needs data relevant to a designated person (*i.e.,* "me").

However, to make effective use of the approach, several questions have to be settled. (1) Can we decide whether a query is boundedly evaluable under given access constraints? We know that this problem is undecidable for first-order logic queries (FO) [17]. Is it decidable for practical fragments of FO? (2) When queries are not boundedly evaluable, can we "approximate" them with boundedly evaluable queries that warrant reasonable approximation bounds?

Contributions. This paper tackles these questions.

Bounded evaluability. We start with a study of *the bounded evaluability problem,* denoted by BEP. Given a query Q and a set $\mathcal{A}$ of access constraints, BEP is to decide whether Q is boundedly evaluable under $\mathcal{A}$. Intuitively, it is to determine whether it is feasible to compute exact answers to Q in big datasets D by accessing a bounded amount of data from D.

It is known that BEP is undecidable for FO [17]. Hence we study BEP for several classes of FO queries, including CQ, unions of conjunctive queries (UCQ), and positive existential FO queries ($\exists$FO$^+$; *a.k.a.* SPJU). The good news is that BEP is decidable for these practical query classes. The bad news is that BEP is EXPSPACE-complete for CQ and $\exists$FO$^+$.

The complexity of BEP suggests that we develop an *effective syntax* of boundedly evaluable queries in CQ. We show that for a given set $\mathcal{A}$ of access constraints over a relational schema $\mathcal{R}$, there exists a class of CQ queries over $\mathcal{R}$ that are *covered by* $\mathcal{A}$, such that (a) it is in PTIME to decide whether a CQ is covered by $\mathcal{A}$; (b) all CQ queries covered by $\mathcal{A}$ are boundedly evaluable under $\mathcal{A}$; and (c) every boundedly evaluable CQ Q under $\mathcal{A}$ is $\mathcal{A}$-equivalent to a CQ Q' covered by $\mathcal{A}$. Here Q is $\mathcal{A}$-equivalent to Q' if for all database instances D of $\mathcal{R}$ that satisfy $\mathcal{A}$, $Q(D) = Q'(D)$. The effective syntax tells us what makes a query in CQ boundedly evaluable, and helps us design boundedly evaluable queries. Moreover, boundedly evaluable CQ queries in practice are often covered and can be syntactically checked [12]. This provides us with a PTIME method to check the bounded evaluability of conjunctive queries, which are perceived as "the most fundamental and the most widely used queries" [22].

We also extend the notion of covered queries to UCQ and $\exists$FO$^+$, and show that covered queries also provide an effective syntax for their boundedly evaluable queries. We study *the covered query problem* (CQP), to decide whether a query is covered by $\mathcal{A}$, and hence, to help us syntactically check whether a query is boundedly evaluable. We show that CQP is in PTIME for CQ, and is Π_2^p-complete for UCQ and $\exists$FO$^+$.

Boundedly evaluable envelopes. When a query Q is not boundedly evaluable under $\mathcal{A}$, we study two approaches to approximately answering Q in big data.

One approach is by means of envelopes, following [14]. We search for two queries Q_l and Q_u in the same query language of Q, such that (a) Q_l and Q_u are boundedly evaluable under $\mathcal{A}$, (b) for all datasets D, if D satisfies $\mathcal{A}$, then $Q_l(D) \subseteq Q(D) \subseteq Q_u(D)$, and (c) $|Q(D) - Q_l(D)| \leq N_l$ and $|Q_u(D) - Q(D)| \leq N_u$ for constants N_l and N_u derived from Q and constants in $\mathcal{A}$. Here $|S|$ denotes the cardinality of a set S. We refer to Q_l and Q_u as *lower and upper envelopes* of Q under $\mathcal{A}$, respectively. Intuitively, envelopes approximate Q: they guarantee a constant approximation bound, and are boundedly evaluable under $\mathcal{A}$.

Envelopes do not always exist. This motivates us to study *the upper and lower envelopes problems*, denoted by UEP and LEP, respectively. Given a query Q that is not boundedly evaluable under $\mathcal{A}$, UEP (resp. LEP) is to determine whether there exists an upper (resp. lower) envelope of Q under $\mathcal{A}$. To avoid the high complexity of checking BEP, we study envelopes that are covered by $\mathcal{A}$ when Q is in CQ, UCQ or $\exists$FO$^+$. We establish the complexity of UEP and LEP for CQ, UCQ, $\exists$FO$^+$and FO, from NP-complete to undecidable.

Bounded query specialization. The other approach is by specializing queries to achieve bounded evaluability. A query Q in an e-commerce system often comes with a set X of parameters (variables) indicating, *e.g.,* price range and make of a product, which are expected to be instantiated with values of users' choice before Q is executed. Personalized searches of Graph Search [16] are also parameterized queries in which a variable for "person" (*i.e.,* "me") is instantiated by users of the query. We refer to $Q(\bar{x} = \bar{c})$ as a *specialized query* of Q, when a tuple $\bar{x}$ of parameters of X is instantiated with constants $\bar{c}$, referred to as a *valuation* of $\bar{x}$.

We study *the query specialization problem,* denoted by QSP. Given a positive integer k and a query Q that is not boundedly evaluable under $\mathcal{A}$ and comes with a set X of parameters, it is to decide whether there exists a tuple $\bar{x}$ of at most k parameters in X such that $Q(\bar{x} = \bar{c})$ is covered by $\mathcal{A}$ for all valuations $\bar{c}$ of $\bar{x}$, and hence, boundedly evaluable. We provide the complexity of QSP for CQ, UCQ, $\exists$FO$^+$and

FO, ranging over NP-complete, Π_2^p-complete and undecidable. Better still, when $\mathcal{A}$ and a query Q in FO satisfy certain conditions, Q can always be boundedly specialized.

Summary. We study bounded evaluability for computing exact query answers and approximate query answers. We identify several problems for bounded evaluability, and develop their complexity bounds. The complexity results help practitioners assess the difficulty of the bounded evaluability analysis for practical query classes. We also provide characterizations for these problems, to help practitioners develop efficient query plans. Observe that for parameterized queries, it is an *one-time* cost to compute envelopes and bounded specialized queries, although intractable, since these queries remain unchanged and only their parameters are instantiated with different values. The computation can be conducted *offline* when developing the queries.

A variety of (syntactic) characterizations, algorithms and reductions are used to prove these results. Some of the proofs are highly nontrivial. In particular, under access constraints, the satisfiability and containment analyses of queries are a departure from the classical Homomorphism Theorem [13] for CQ and the characterization of [32] for UCQ. These have to be revisited to deal with challenges analogous to what indefinite databases introduce [27,28,34].

Related work. We classify previous work as follows.

Scale independence. The study of bounded evaluability is motivated by the idea of scale independence [6]. The latter aims to guarantee that a bounded amount of work is required to execute all queries in an application, regardless of the size of the underlying data. To enforce scale independence, users may specify bounds on the amount of data accessed and the size of intermediate results; when more data is needed, only top-k tuples are retrieved to meet the bounds [5].

The idea was formalized in [17]. A query Q is called *scale independent* in a dataset D *w.r.t.* a bound M if there is $D_Q \subseteq D$ such that $Q(D) = Q(D_Q)$ and $|D_Q| \leq M$. Access constraints were introduced in [17]. A notion of $\bar{x}$-scale independence was also proposed in [17], to characterize queries $Q(\bar{x}, \bar{y})$ that, for all databases D that satisfy access constraints and for each tuple $\bar{a}$ of values for $\bar{x}$, $Q(\bar{x} = \bar{a}, D)$ can be computed in time dependent on $\mathcal{A}$ and Q only. It showed that x-scale independence is undecidable for FO, and developed syntactic rules as a sufficient condition for deciding the x-scale independence of FO queries under access constraints.

When $\bar{x}$ is empty, *i.e.,* when no instantiation of $\bar{x}$ is required, $\bar{x}$-scale independence was studied in [12], referred to as *effective boundedness*. The notion of effective boundedness is based on *a restricted form* of query plans in which data is fetched before any relational operations. It showed that it is in PTIME to decide whether a CQ Q is effectively bounded under $\mathcal{A}$, *i.e.,* it has a restricted query plan. With real-life data, the approach was experimentally evaluated for CQ in [12] and for graph pattern queries in [11].

This work extends the prior work in the following. (1) We extend access constraints of [12,17], by allowing cardinality bounds to be specified by a (sublinear) function in the size of the underlying data. (2) While [17] has mostly focused on scale independence in *a given database*, we focus on bounded evaluability on *all databases* that satisfy access constraints, like x-scale independence. We also give characterizations for bounded evaluability of queries for various fragments of FO. (3) We study generic query plans that are not allowed by [12]. To see the difference, BEP is EXPSPACE-hard for CQ, as opposed to PTIME for its effective boundedness [12]. To cope with the high complexity of BEP, we give an effective syntax for boundedly evaluable CQ, which is not studied in [12,17]. (4) When exact query answers are beyond reach, we study approximate query answering based on bounded evaluability, which were not considered in [12,17], except a special case of QSP [12]. (5) In the general setting, BEP and QSP have not been studied for CQ, UCQ and $\exists$FO$^+$, and none of CQP, UEP and LEP has been considered in [12,17].

Related to access schema is the notion of access patterns, which require that a relation can only be accessed by providing certain combinations of attribute values. Query processing under limited access patterns has been well studied, *e.g.,* [8,15,29,30]. In contrast, access schemas combine indices and cardinality constraints. Our goal is to characterize what queries are boundedly evaluable with access schema, rather than to study the complexity or executable plans for answering queries under access patterns [8,15,29,30].

Approximate query answering. There has been work on approximate query answering, by means of (1) data synopses that given a query Q on a dataset D, compute $Q(D_s)$ in a synopsis D_s of D, such as histograms [24,25], wavelets [21,35] and sampling [3,7]; (2) budgeted search [4,23,36] that terminates the run of an algorithm when reaching a predefined budget (cost or accuracy) and returns intermediate answers. As opposed to the prior work, the study of bounded evaluability aims to (a) fetch $D_Q \subseteq D$ for each query Q based on access constraints, rather than to use a "one-size fits-all" synopsis to answer all queries posed on D, and (b) guarantee accuracy bound for *non-aggregate* queries.

Closer to our work is query-driven approximation [9,14,19,20] that uses a "cheaper" query Q_a instead of Q and computes $Q_a(D)$ as approximate answers to Q in D, *e.g.,* UCQ for recursive datalog [14], tractable queries for CQ [9,20], and (revised) graph simulation for subgraph isomorphism [19]. Following the absolute approximation scheme of [14], we study boundedly evaluable envelopes (UEP and LEP). The problem studied in [14] is to approximate datalog programs with UCQ; it is very different from UEP and LEP considered in this work, which aim to find bounded evaluable envelopes for various FO fragments under access constraints.

Related to specialized queries are query suggestion [26] and parameterized queries, which instantiate parameters with values possibly from a list of suggested keywords. Related to QSP is the $\bar{x}$-controllability problem studied in [17], to find a minimum set $\bar{x}$ of variables in a query Q such that Q can be verified $\bar{x}$-scale independent by the syntactic rules of [17]. It differs from QSP in that $\bar{x}$-scale independence is defined by syntactic rules, as opposed to covered queries. Hence for FO, the $\bar{x}$-controllability problem is in NP, while QSP is undecidable. A special case of QSP was also studied in [12] for CQ, when all variables of Q are treated as parameters. It is based on effective boundedness, as opposed to bounded evaluability. In addition, we also study QSP for UCQ and $\exists$FO$^+$, which are not considered in [12].

Organization. Access constraints and bounded evaluability are defined in Section 2. We study the bounded evaluability of queries in Section 3. For approximate query answering, we investigate boundedly evaluable envelopes in Section 4, and bounded query specialization in Section 5. Open problems for future work are identified in Section 6.

2. BOUNDEDLY EVALUABLE QUERIES

We next define access constraints, query plans and boundedly evaluable queries over a relational schema.

A relational schema $\mathcal{R}$ consists of a collection of relation schemas $(R_1, \ldots, R_n)$, where each relation schema R_i has a fixed set of attributes. We assume a countably infinite domain $\mathbf{D}$ of data values, on which instances of $\mathcal{R}$ are defined. For an instance D of $\mathcal{R}$, we use $|D|$ to denote its size, measured as the total *number of tuples* in D.

Query classes. We study the following queries [2].

- Conjunctive queries (CQ), built up from relation atoms $R_i(\bar{x})$ (for $R_i \in \mathcal{R}$), and equality atoms $x = y$ or $x = c$ (for constant c), by closing them under conjunction $\wedge$ and existential quantification $\exists$.
- Unions of conjunctive queries (UCQ) of the form $Q = Q_1 \cup \cdots \cup Q_k$, where for all $i \in [1, k]$, Q_i is in CQ, referred to as a CQ *sub-query* of Q.
- Positive existential FO queries ($\exists$FO$^+$, SPJU of select-project-join-union queries), built from relation atoms and equality atoms by closing under $\wedge$, $\vee$ and $\exists$. For a query Q in $\exists$FO$^+$, a CQ *sub-query* of Q is a CQ sub-query in the UCQ equivalence of Q.
- First-order logic queries (FO), built from atomic formulas by using $\wedge$, $\vee$, negation $\neg$, $\exists$ and $\forall$.

If $\bar{x}$ is the tuple of free variables of Q, we will write $Q(\bar{x})$. Given a query $Q(\bar{x})$ with $|\bar{x}| = m$ and a database D, the answer to Q in D, denoted by $Q(D)$, is the set $\{\bar{a} \in adom(D)^m \mid D \models Q(\bar{a})\}$, where the active domain, $adom(D)$, consists of all constants appearing in D or Q.

Access schema. An *access schema* $\mathcal{A}$ over a relational schema $\mathcal{R}$ is a set of *access constraints* of the form:

$$R(X \to Y, N),$$

where R is a relation schema in $\mathcal{R}$, X and Y are sets of attributes of R, and N is a natural number.

A relation instance D of R *satisfies* the constraint if

- for any X-value $\bar{a}$ in D, $|D_Y(X = \bar{a})| \leq N$, where $D_Y(X = \bar{a}) = \{t[Y] \mid t \in D, t[X] = \bar{a}\}$; and
- there exists an *index on* X *for* Y that given an X-value $\bar{a}$, retrieves $D_Y(X = \bar{a})$.

For instance, ψ_1–ψ_4 given in Example 1.1 together with their indices are access constraints. An access constraint is a combination of a cardinality constraint and an index on X for Y. It tells us that given any X-value, there exist at most N distinct corresponding Y-values, and these Y values can be efficiently retrieved by using the index.

We say that D *satisfies* access schema $\mathcal{A}$, denoted by $D \models \mathcal{A}$, if D satisfies all the constraints in $\mathcal{A}$.

Query plans. To define boundedly evaluable queries, we first present corresponding query plans. Consider a query Q in the relational algebra over schema $\mathcal{R}$, defined in terms of projection operator π, selection σ, Cartesian product $\times$, union $\cup$, set difference $-$ and renaming ρ (see, *e.g.*, [2] for details). A *query plan* for Q is a sequence

$$\xi(Q, \mathcal{R}): \ T_1 = \delta_1, \ \ldots, \ T_n = \delta_n,$$

such that (1) for all instances D of $\mathcal{R}$, $T_n = Q(D)$, and (2) for all $i \in [1, n]$, δ_i is one of the following:

- $\{a\}$, where a is a constant in Q; or
- $\mathsf{fetch}(X \in T_j, R, Y)$, where $j < i$, and T_j has attributes X; for each $\bar{a} \in T_j$, it retrieves $D_{XY}(X = \bar{a})$ from D, and returns $\bigcup_{\bar{a} \in T_j} D_{XY}(X = \bar{a})$; or
- $\pi_Y(T_j)$, $\sigma_C(T_j)$ or $\rho(T_j)$, for $j < i$, a set Y of attributes in T_j, and condition C defined on T_j; or
- $T_j \times T_k$, $T_j \cup T_k$ or $T_j - T_k$, for $j < i$ and $k < i$.

The result $\xi(D)$ of applying $\xi(Q, \mathcal{R})$ to D is T_n.

A query plan $\xi(Q, \mathcal{R})$ is said to be *boundedly evaluable under an access schema* $\mathcal{A}$ if (1) for each $\mathsf{fetch}(X \in T_j, R, Y)$ in it, there exists a constraint $R(X \to Y', N)$ in $\mathcal{A}$ such that $Y \subseteq X \cup Y'$, and (2) the length n of $\xi(Q, \mathcal{R})$ (*i.e.*, the number of operations) is bounded by an exponential in $|\mathcal{R}|$, $|\mathcal{A}|$ and $|Q|$, which are the sizes of $\mathcal{R}$, $\mathcal{A}$ and Q, respectively, *independent of* dataset D. Indeed, a query plan longer than exponential in $|\mathcal{R}|$, $|\mathcal{A}|$ and $|Q|$ is hardly practical.

Intuitively, if $\xi(Q, \mathcal{R})$ is boundedly evaluable under $\mathcal{A}$, then for all instances D of $\mathcal{R}$ that satisfy $\mathcal{A}$, $\xi(Q, \mathcal{R})$ tells us how to fetch $D_Q \subseteq D$ with the indices in $\mathcal{A}$ such that $Q(D) = Q(D_Q)$, where D_Q is the set of all tuples fetched from D by following $\xi(Q, \mathcal{R})$. Better still, D_Q is *bounded*: $|D_Q|$ is determined by Q and constants in $\mathcal{A}$ only. Moreover, the time for identifying and fetching D_Q also depends on Q and $\mathcal{A}$ only (assuming that given an X-value $\bar{a}$, it takes $O(N)$ time to fetch $D_{XY}(X = \bar{a})$ in D with the index in $R(X \to Y, N)$). For instance, a boundedly evaluable query plan for Q_0 is given in Example 1.1 under access constraints ψ_1–ψ_4.

Boundedly evaluable queries. Consider a query Q in a language $\mathcal{L}$ and an access schema $\mathcal{A}$, both over the same relational schema $\mathcal{R}$. We say that Q is *boundedly evaluable under* $\mathcal{A}$ if it has a boundedly evaluable query plan $\xi(Q, \mathcal{R})$ under $\mathcal{A}$ such that in each $T_i = \delta_i$ of $\xi(Q, \mathcal{R})$,

- if $\mathcal{L}$ is CQ, then δ_i is a fetch, π, σ, $\times$ or ρ operation;
- if $\mathcal{L}$ is UCQ, δ_i can be fetch, π, σ, $\times$ or ρ, and there is $k \leq |Q|$ such that the last $k - 1$ operations of $\xi(Q, \mathcal{R})$ are $\cup$, and $\cup$ does not appear anywhere else in $\xi(Q, \mathcal{R})$;
- if $\mathcal{L}$ is $\exists$FO$^+$, then δ_i is fetch, π, σ, $\times$, $\cup$ or ρ; and
- if $\mathcal{L}$ is FO, δ_i can be fetch, π, σ, $\times$, $\cup$, $-$ or ρ

One can verify the following: if Q is boundedly evaluable under $\mathcal{A}$, then for *all* instances D of $\mathcal{R}$ that satisfy $\mathcal{A}$, there exists $D_Q \subseteq D$ such that (a) $Q(D_Q) = Q(D)$; (b) the time for identifying and fetching D_Q is determined by Q and $\mathcal{A}$ only; and (c) the size $|D_Q|$ is also *independent of* $|D|$.

General access constraints. We also study access constraints in its general form, defined as follows:

$$R(X \to Y, s(\cdot)),$$

where $s(\cdot)$ is a (sublinear) function in $|D|$.

An instance D of R *satisfies* the constraint if for any given X-value $\bar{a}$, we can retrieve $D_Y(X = \bar{a})$ from D by using an index on X for Y, such that $|D_Y(X = \bar{a})| \leq s(|D|)$.

That is, $|D_Y(X = \bar{a})|$ is bounded by a function in $|D|$, *e.g.*, $\log(|D|)$, rather than by a constant. We refer to these as access constraints *with non-constant cardinality*. Constraints $R(X \to Y, N)$ are a special form when $s(\cdot)$ is a constant N, and are referred to access constraints with *constant cardinality* or simply access constraints. Access constraints with non-constant cardinality are easier to be satisfied, and still allow us to query big data by accessing a small fraction D_Q of the data, although $|D_Q|$ is no longer independent of $|D|$.

To simplify the discussion, we focus on access constraints $R(X \to Y, N)$ with constant cardinality in the sequel. Nonetheless, the characterizations and complexity results of Section 3 remain intact on access constraints with non-constant cardinality, as long as function $s(\cdot)$ is PTIME computable. Similarly, the results on QSP (Section 5) also hold in the presence of the general access constraints.

3. DECIDING BOUNDED EVALUABILITY

We study *the bounded evaluability problem*, denoted by BEP($\mathcal{L}$) for a query class $\mathcal{L}$ and stated as follows:

- INPUT: A relational schema $\mathcal{R}$, an access schema $\mathcal{A}$ over $\mathcal{R}$ and a query $Q \in \mathcal{L}$ over $\mathcal{R}$.
- QUESTION: Is Q boundedly evaluable under $\mathcal{A}$?

While BEP(FO) is undecidable [17], we show that for several practical fragments of FO, BEP is decidable. However, the complexity bounds of BEP for these query classes are rather high (Section 3.1). To cope with these, we develop an effective syntax for boundedly evaluable queries in CQ. The syntax is given in terms of a notion of covered queries, which can be checked in PTIME. We extend the notion of covered queries to UCQ and $\exists\text{FO}^+$, to characterize their boundedly evaluable queries. We also provide complexity for deciding whether their queries are covered (Section 3.2).

3.1 Characterizing Bounded Evaluability

No matter how desirable, it is nontrivial to decide whether a query is boundedly evaluable, even for CQ.

Example 3.1: (1) Consider an access schema $\mathcal{A}_1$ and a query Q_1 defined over a relation schema $R_1(A, B, E, F)$:

$$\mathcal{A}_1 = \{\varphi_1 = R_1(A \to B, N_1),\ \varphi_2 = R_1(E \to F, N_2)\},$$
$$Q_1(x, y) = \exists x_1, x_2 \big(R(x_1, x, x_2, y) \wedge x_1 = 1 \wedge x_2 = 1\big).$$

Under $\mathcal{A}_1$, Q_1 is seemingly boundedly evaluable: given an instance D_1 of schema R_1, values $x_1 = 1$ and $x_2 = 2$, we can extract x values from D_1 by using φ_1, and y values by φ_2. However, there exists no bounded query plan for Q_1: $\mathcal{A}_1$ does not provide us with indices to check whether these x and y values come from the same tuples in D_1.

(2) Consider $\mathcal{A}_2$ and Q_2 defined on $R_2(A, B)$:

$$\mathcal{A}_2 = \{\varphi_3 = R_2(A \to B, 1)\},$$
$$Q_2(x) = \exists x_1, x_2 \big(R_2(x, x_1) \wedge R_2(x, x_2) \wedge x_1 = 1 \wedge x_2 = 2\big).$$

Query Q_2 is boundedly evaluable under $\mathcal{A}_2$, although $\mathcal{A}_2$ does not help us retrieve x values from an instance D_2 of R_2. To see why Q_2 is bounded, note that given any x value, it is impossible to find both $(x, 1)$ and $(x, 2)$ in D_2 that satisfies $\mathcal{A}_2$, because of φ_3. Therefore, $Q_2(D_2) = \emptyset$, *i.e.*, Q_2 is not satisfiable by instances D_2 of R_2 that satisfy $\mathcal{A}_2$. Hence a query plan for empty query suffices to answer Q_2 in D_2.

(3) Consider $\mathcal{A}_3$ and Q_3 defined on $R_3(A, B, C)$:

$$\mathcal{A}_3 = \{\varphi_4 = R_3(\emptyset \to C, 1),\ \varphi_5 = R_3(AB \to C, N)\},$$
$$Q_3(x, y) = \exists x_1, x_2, z_1, z_2, z_3 \big(R_3(x_1, x_2, x) \wedge R_3(z_1, z_2, y) \wedge R_3(x, y, z_3) \wedge x_1 = 1 \wedge x_2 = 1\big).$$

At first glance, Q_3 is not boundedly evaluable under $\mathcal{A}_3$, since $\mathcal{A}_3$ does not help us check $R(z_1, z_2, y)$. However, Q_3 is "$\mathcal{A}_3$-equivalent" to Q'_3, *i.e.*, for any instance D_3 of R_3, if $D_3 \models \mathcal{A}_3$, then $Q_3(D_3) = Q'_3(D_3)$, where

$$Q'_3(x, x) = R_3(1, 1, x) \wedge R_3(x, x, x).$$

Query Q'_3 is boundedly evaluable under $\mathcal{A}_3$. Hence, Q_3 is boundedly evaluable under $\mathcal{A}_3$ since a boundedly evaluable query plan for Q'_3 is also a query plan for Q_3.

To see that Q_3 is "$\mathcal{A}_3$-equivalent" to Q'_3, observe the following: for any instance D_3 that satisfies $\mathcal{A}_3$, (a) by φ_4, x, y and z_3 must take the same (unique) value c_0 from D_3, which can be fetched by using the index built for φ_4; hence $R_3(x, y, z_3)$ becomes $R_3(x, x, x)$; and (b) $\exists z_1, z_2(R_3(1, 1, x) \wedge R_3(z_1, z_2, y))$ is equivalent to $R_3(1, 1, x)$; thus $R_3(z_1, z_2, y)$ can be removed. Moreover, Q'_3 is boundedly evaluable under $\mathcal{A}_3$ since by φ_5, we can check whether $(1, 1, x)$ and (x, x, x) are in D_3 when $x = c_0$, using the index for φ_5. □

Impact of access constraints. The complications are introduced partly by access constraints. Consider an access schema $\mathcal{A}$ and a query Q, both defined over the same relational schema $\mathcal{R}$. We say that Q is *$\mathcal{A}$-satisfiable* if there exists an instance D of $\mathcal{R}$ such that $D \models \mathcal{A}$ and $Q(D) \neq \emptyset$.

When Q is a query in CQ, it is in PTIME to decide whether there exists D such that $Q(D) \neq \emptyset$ (satisfiability; cf. [2]). In contrast, $\mathcal{A}$-satisfiability is intractable for CQ.

Lemma 3.2: It is NP-complete to decide whether a query in CQ is $\mathcal{A}$-satisfiable for an access schema $\mathcal{A}$. □

To prove this, we need the following notation. Consider a tableau (T_Q, u) representing a CQ Q (see, *e.g.*, [2]). A valuation θ of (T_Q, u) is a mapping from variables in T_Q to (not necessarily distinct) constants in $\mathbf{D}$. We use $\theta(T_Q)$ to denote the instance obtained by applying θ to variables in T_Q. We call $\theta(T_Q)$ an *$\mathcal{A}$-instance* of Q if $\theta(T_Q) \models \mathcal{A}$. There are possibly exponentially many $\mathcal{A}$-instances of Q up to isomorphism, analogous to representative instances in indefinite data [27, 28, 34]. This is why the $\mathcal{A}$-satisfiability of CQ is more intriguing to check than the satisfiability.

Proof sketch. For the upper bound, we give an NP algorithm that, given (T_Q, u) and $\mathcal{A}$, (a) guesses a valuation θ of tableau (T_Q, u), and (2) checks whether $\theta(T_Q) \models \mathcal{A}$ and $\theta(u)$ is well defined; it returns true if so.

The lower bound is verified by reduction from 3SAT. Given a propositional formula ψ, 3SAT decides whether ψ is satisfiable. It is known to be NP-complete (cf. [31]). □

Recall that query containment and equivalence are NP-complete for CQ, by the Homomorphism Theorem [13]. These classical results on containment and equivalence of CQ no longer hold in the presence of an access schema $\mathcal{A}$. More specifically, we say that a query Q_1 is *$\mathcal{A}$-contained* in query Q_2, denoted by $Q_1 \sqsubseteq_{\mathcal{A}} Q_2$, if for all instances D of $\mathcal{R}$ such that $D \models \mathcal{A}$, $Q_1(D) \subseteq Q_2(D)$. We say that Q_1 and Q_2 are *$\mathcal{A}$-equivalent*, denoted by $Q_1 \equiv_{\mathcal{A}} Q_2$, if $Q_1 \sqsubseteq_{\mathcal{A}} Q_2$ and $Q_2 \sqsubseteq_{\mathcal{A}} Q_1$. Then for CQ, the $\mathcal{A}$-containment and $\mathcal{A}$-equivalence problems are Π_2^p-complete, rather than NP-complete. That is, the presence of access constraints makes the containment and equivalence analyses harder for CQ.

Lemma 3.3: For access schema $\mathcal{A}$ and queries Q_1 and Q_2 in CQ, (1) $Q_1 \sqsubseteq_{\mathcal{A}} Q_2$ if and only if either Q_1 is not $\mathcal{A}$-satisfiable, or for all $\mathcal{A}$-instances $\theta(T_Q)$ of Q_1, $\theta(u) \in Q_2(\theta(T_Q))$; and (2) it is Π_2^p-complete to decide (a) whether $Q_1 \sqsubseteq_{\mathcal{A}} Q_2$ and (b) whether $Q_1 \equiv_{\mathcal{A}} Q_2$. □

Proof sketch. (1) To determine whether $Q_1 \sqsubseteq_{\mathcal{A}} Q_2$, we need to consider (possibly exponentially many) $\mathcal{A}$-instances of Q_1, rather than a "canonical instance" of Q_1 as in [13]. Statement 1 can be verified based on the definition of $Q_1 \sqsubseteq_{\mathcal{A}} Q_2$ and the monotonicity of CQ, since $\mathcal{A}$-instances of Q_1 are instances that satisfy $\mathcal{A}$, on which Q_2 can be applied.

(2) It suffices to show that it is Π_2^p-complete to decide whether $Q_1 \sqsubseteq_{\mathcal{A}} Q_2$, from which the complexity of $Q_1 \equiv_{\mathcal{A}} Q_2$ follows. For the upper bound, we give an Σ_2^p algorithm to determine whether $Q_1 \not\sqsubseteq_{\mathcal{A}} Q_2$, by checking whether Q_1 is $\mathcal{A}$-satisfiable (in NP) and there exists an $\mathcal{A}$-instance $\theta(T_Q)$ of Q_1 such that $\theta(u) \notin Q_2(\theta(T_Q))$ (in Σ_2^p).

The lower bound is verified by reduction from $\forall^*\exists^*$3CNF, which is Π_2^p-complete [33]. The $\forall^*\exists^*$3CNF problem is to decide, given a sentence $\varphi = \forall X \exists Y \psi$, whether φ is true, where ψ is an instance of 3SAT defined over $X \cup Y$. The reduction uses $Q_1(X)$ and $Q_2(X)$ to "compute" truth assignments for X such that $\exists Y \psi$ is false and true, respectively. □

Complexity. As opposed to BEP(FO), the BEP analysis is decidable for CQ, although it is highly nontrivial.

Theorem 3.4: BEP(CQ) is EXPSPACE-complete. □

Proof sketch. The lower bound is verified by reduction from the non-emptiness problem for parameterized regular expressions with certainty semantics, which is shown to be EXPSPACE-complete in [10]. A parameterized regular expression is an extension of conventional regular expressions over alphabet Σ by including variables, which are mapped to symbols in Σ. Given such a parameterized regular expression e, we construct a CQ Q and an access schema $\mathcal{A}$, such that Q has a boundedly evaluable query plan under $\mathcal{A}$ if and only if there exists a string that is in the languages of e under all possible valuations of its variables.

For the upper bound, we develop an NEXPSPACE algorithm: it guesses a query plan ξ of exponential size, and checks whether ξ is (a) boundedly evaluable under $\mathcal{A}$ and (b) "$\mathcal{A}$-equivalent" to Q, *i.e.*, for all instances D that satisfy $\mathcal{A}$, $\xi(D) = Q(D)$. To check (b), we show that from a boundedly evaluable ξ, an "$\mathcal{A}$-equivalent" CQ Q' can be computed in PTIME in the size of ξ, and checks whether $Q \equiv_{\mathcal{A}} Q'$ by using the algorithm given in the proof of Lemma 3.3. Since EXPSPACE = NEXPSPACE, BEP(CQ) is in EXPSPACE. □

Adding unions. We next study BEP for UCQ and $\exists$FO$^+$. While BEP(CQ) is nontrivial, the presence of union makes the bounded evaluability analysis more intriguing. Recall that for two UCQ $Q = \bigcup_{i \in [1,m]} Q_i$ and $Q' = \bigcup_{j \in [1,n]} Q'_j$, $Q \subseteq Q'$ if and only if for each Q_i, there exists Q'_j such that $Q_i \subseteq Q'_j$ [32]. This result of [32] no longer holds when we consider $\mathcal{A}$-containment $\sqsubseteq_{\mathcal{A}}$ under an access schema $\mathcal{A}$.

Example 3.5: Consider a relation schema $R(X)$, an access schema $\mathcal{A}$ with $R(\emptyset \to X, 2)$, and queries below:

$$Q(x) = \exists y(Q_c(\,) \wedge Q_\psi(x, y)),$$
$$Q_c(\,) = \exists y_1, y_2(R(y_1) \wedge y_1 = 1 \wedge R(y_2) \wedge y_2 = 0),$$
$$Q'(x) = Q_1(x) \cup Q_2(x),$$
$$Q_1(x) = \exists y(Q_\psi(x, y) \wedge y = 1),$$
$$Q_2(x) = \exists y(Q_\psi(x, y) \wedge y = 0),$$

where Q_ψ is a CQ, and Q_c and $\mathcal{A}$ ensure that an R relation encodes Boolean domain $\{0, 1\}$. Then one can verify that $Q \sqsubseteq_{\mathcal{A}} Q'$. However, $Q \not\sqsubseteq_{\mathcal{A}} Q_1$ and $Q \not\sqsubseteq_{\mathcal{A}} Q_2$.

As another example, consider $R'(A, B, C)$, $\mathcal{A}'$ consisting of $R'(A \to B, N)$ only, and a query $Q = Q_1 \cup Q_2$, where

$$Q_1(y) = \exists x, z(R'(x, y, z) \wedge x = 1),$$
$$Q_2(y) = \exists x, z(R'(x, y, z) \wedge x = 1 \wedge z = y).$$

Then under $\mathcal{A}'$, Q_1 and Q are boundedly evaluable, but Q_2 is not. Hence a CQ sub-query of a boundedly evaluable UCQ Q may not be boundedly evaluable itself, as long as it is contained in other sub-queries of Q. □

The lemma below characterizes the bounded evaluability of UCQ under an access schema. It also tells us how to determine whether a query Q in $\exists$FO$^+$is boundedly evaluable, since a query in $\exists$FO$^+$is equivalent to a query in UCQ.

Lemma 3.6: Under an access schema $\mathcal{A}$, a UCQ Q is boundedly evaluable if and only if Q is $\mathcal{A}$-equivalent to a UCQ $Q' = Q_1 \cup \cdots \cup Q_k$ such that for each $i \in [1, k]$, CQ subquery Q_i is boundedly evaluable under $\mathcal{A}$. □

We next show that BEP is decidable for UCQ and $\exists$FO$^+$.

Corollary 3.7: BEP is EXPSPACE-complete for $\exists$FO$^+$. □

Proof sketch. The lower bound follows from Theorem 3.4. For the upper bound, we give an NEXPSPACE (EXPSPACE) algorithm for checking BEP($\exists$FO$^+$), by "decomposing" an $\exists$FO$^+$query into a union of "elementary queries" such that their tableaux satisfy $\mathcal{A}$, and by using Lemma 3.6. □

3.2 Effective Syntax

While BEP is decidable for CQ and $\exists$FO$^+$, its complexity is too high for us to make practical use of bounded evaluability analysis. This motivates us to develop an effective syntax for their boundedly evaluable queries, with lower complexity.

Effective syntax for CQ. Example 3.1 suggests that to decide whether a CQ Q is boundedly evaluable under an access schema $\mathcal{A}$, we need to check (a) whether Q is "$\mathcal{A}$-equivalent" to a CQ Q' that is boundedly evaluable under $\mathcal{A}$, or (b) whether the indices for constraints in $\mathcal{A}$ "cover" attributes corresponding to variables in Q. We now formalize what queries Q in CQ are "covered by" $\mathcal{A}$, *i.e.*, when the cardinality constraints and indices in $\mathcal{A}$ provide us with sufficient information to fetch tuples for answering Q.

Covered variables. We first look at variables in Q that have to be "covered by" $\mathcal{A}$. Denote by var(Q) the set of all variables that occur in Q, either free or bound. Assume *w.l.o.g.* that Q is safe, *i.e.*, each variable in var(Q) is equal to either a variable occurring in a relation atom or a constant in Q. We also assume that queries are satisfiable, *i.e.*, each variable can be equal to at most one constant; and moreover, we assume *w.l.o.g.* that only variables appear in relation atoms of Q, while constants are in equality atoms.

For a variable $x \in$ var(Q), we denote by eq(x, Q) the set of all variables in Q that are equal to x as determined by equality atoms of the form $y = z$ in Q, and the transitivity of equality. We define eq$^+$(x, Q) as the extension of eq(x, Q) by including variables y such that $x = y$ can be inferred also from conditions $z = c$ for some constant c (*e.g.*, $x = c$ and $y = c$). We refer to x as a *constant variable* if eq(x, Q) contains a variable y such that $y = c$ occurs in Q.

A variable x is called *data-dependent* if eq(x, Q) contains variables that occur in relation atoms of Q, and it is called *data-independent* otherwise. A CQ $Q(\bar{x})$ can be equivalently written as $Q_{dd}(\bar{x}_1) \wedge Q_{di}(\bar{x}_2)$ such that $\bar{x} = (\bar{x}_1, \bar{x}_2)$, $\bar{x}_1$ and $\bar{x}_2$ are disjoint, and Q_{dd} and Q_{di} consist solely of data-dependent and independent variables, respectively.

Example 3.8: Consider a query:

$$Q(x, y, u, v) = R(x, y) \wedge x = 1 \wedge x = y \wedge u = 1 \wedge u = v.$$

Then $\mathsf{eq}(x, Q) = \{x, y\}$ and $\mathsf{eq}^+(x, Q) = \{x, y, u, v\}$. Note that x and y are data-dependent, but u is not, although $u \in \mathsf{eq}^+(x, Q)$. It is to define data-independent variables that we separate $\mathsf{eq}(x, Q)$ from $\mathsf{eq}^+(x, Q)$. □

We next define the set $\mathsf{cov}(Q, \mathcal{A})$ of *variables covered by* $\mathcal{A}$. Intuitively, $\mathsf{cov}(Q, \mathcal{A})$ contains all variables in Q whose values are determined by Q or by $\mathcal{A}$. We define

$$\mathsf{cov}(Q, \mathcal{A}) = \mathsf{cov}(Q_{dd}, \mathcal{A}) \cup \mathsf{cov}(Q_{di}, \mathcal{A}),$$

where $\mathsf{cov}(Q_{di}, \mathcal{A}) = \mathsf{var}(Q_{di})$, since the values of such variables do not need to be retrieved from a database D, or to be verified with data in D. We define $\mathsf{cov}(Q_{dd}, \mathcal{A})$ inductively, starting from $\mathsf{cov}_0(Q_{dd}, \mathcal{A}) = \emptyset$. When $i > 0$, we say that an access constraint $\varphi = R(X \to Y, N)$ is *applicable* to an atom $R(\bar{x}, \bar{y}, \bar{z})$ in Q_{dd} if the following conditions are satisfied:

- variables $\bar{x}$ correspond to X, and either are already in $\mathsf{cov}_{i-1}(Q, \mathcal{A})$ or are constant variables; and
- $\bar{y}$ corresponds to Y, and there exists a variable y in $\bar{y}$ such that y is not yet in $\mathsf{cov}_{i-1}(Q, \mathcal{A})$.

We define $\mathsf{cov}_i(Q_{dd}, \mathcal{A})$ by extending $\mathsf{cov}_{i-1}(Q_{dd}, \mathcal{A})$ with the following after each application of a constraint:

- variables in $\mathsf{eq}^+(x, Q_{dd})$ for all constant variables x in $\bar{x}$ that are not already in $\mathsf{cov}_{i-1}(Q, \mathcal{A})$; and
- variables in $\mathsf{eq}^+(y, Q_{dd})$ for each $y \in \bar{y}$.

Note that by using eq^+ instead of eq, we ensure that whenever variable x is covered and $x = c$ holds, then all other variables that are equal to constant c are covered as well. We define $\mathsf{cov}(Q_{dd}, \mathcal{A}) = \mathsf{cov}_k(Q_{dd}, \mathcal{A})$ when $\mathsf{cov}_k(Q_{dd}, \mathcal{A}) = \mathsf{cov}_{k+1}(Q, \mathcal{A})$, *i.e.*, as "the fixpoint".

The lemma below ensures that $\mathsf{cov}(Q, \mathcal{A})$ is well defined, regardless of the order in which constraints in $\mathcal{A}$ are applied.

Lemma 3.9: For any CQ Q and access schema $\mathcal{A}$ over a relational schema $\mathcal{R}$, $\mathsf{cov}(Q, \mathcal{A})$ is uniquely determined and can be computed in PTIME in $|Q|$, $|\mathcal{R}|$ and $|\mathcal{A}|$. □

Covered queries. We are now ready to define covered queries. A CQ $Q(\bar{x})$ is *covered by* $\mathcal{A}$ if

(a) its free variables are covered, *i.e.*, $\bar{x} \subseteq \mathsf{cov}(Q, \mathcal{A})$;

(b) for all non-covered variables $y \notin \mathsf{cov}(Q, \mathcal{A})$, y is non-constant and only occurs once in Q; and

(c) each relation atom $R(\bar{w})$ in Q is *indexed* by $\mathcal{A}$, *i.e.*, there is a constraint $R(Y_1 \to Y_2, N)$ in $\mathcal{A}$ such that (a) all variables in $\bar{w}$ corresponding to attributes Y_1 must be covered, and (b) let $\bar{y}$ be $\bar{w}$ excluding bound variables that only occur once in Q; then each y in $\bar{y}$ corresponds to an attribute in $Y_1 \cup Y_2$.

Intuitively, condition (a) ensures that the values of all free variables of Q are either constants in Q or can be retrieved from a database instance with indices in $\mathcal{A}$. Conditions (b) and (a) together assert that non-covered variables are existentially quantified and do not participate in "joins"; hence, for any instance D of $\mathcal{R}$, $Q(D)$ does not depend on what values these variables take. Condition (c) requires that when we need $t[Y]$ values of an R tuple t to answer Q, the values of all attributes in Y come from the same tuple t and can be retrieved (checked) by using an index in $\mathcal{A}$.

Example 3.10: Query Q_3 of Example 3.1 is covered by $\mathcal{A}_3$: (a) $\mathsf{cov}(Q_3, \mathcal{A}_3) = \{x, y, z_3, x_1, x_2\}$, including all free variables x and y; (b) while z_1 and z_2 are uncovered, they satisfy condition (b), and thus their values has no impact on answers to Q_3; and (c) relations $R(x_1, x_2, x)$ and $R(x, y, z_3)$ are indexed by φ_5, and $R(z_1, z_2, y)$ is indexed by φ_4.

In contrast, query Q_1 of Example 3.1 is not covered by $\mathcal{A}_1$: Q_1 does not satisfy condition (c), since relation atom $R(x_1, x, x_2, y)$ is not indexed by any constraint in $\mathcal{A}_1$.

As another example, query Q_0 of Example 1.1 is covered by $\mathcal{A}_0$ consisting of ψ_1–ψ_4. Indeed, its free variable x_a is covered, non-covered variables cid and class occur only once in Q_0, and all its relation atoms are indexed: Accident by ψ_3, Casualty by ψ_2 and Vehicle by ψ_4. □

Effective syntax. Covered CQ queries provide us with an effective syntax for boundedly evaluable CQ queries. In our experiments with real-life data [12], we find that most boundedly evaluable CQ queries are covered.

Theorem 3.11: For an access schema $\mathcal{A}$ and a CQ Q.

(1) Q is boundedly evaluable under $\mathcal{A}$ if and only if Q is $\mathcal{A}$-equivalent to a CQ Q' that is covered by $\mathcal{A}$;

(2) if Q is covered by $\mathcal{A}$, then Q is boundedly evaluable under $\mathcal{A}$; and

(3) checking whether Q is covered by $\mathcal{A}$ is in PTIME in $|Q|$, $|\mathcal{A}|$ and $|\mathcal{R}|$, where $\mathcal{R}$ is the relational schema over which Q and $\mathcal{A}$ are defined. □

Proof sketch. The proof is a little involved, and needs the following lemmas, which are verified with constructive proofs, *i.e.*, by developing algorithms needed. Consider query plans, an access schema $\mathcal{A}$ and queries over a relational schema $\mathcal{R}$.

(a) Every boundedly evaluable query plan ξ under $\mathcal{A}$ for a CQ determines a CQ Q_ξ such that Q_ξ is covered by $\mathcal{A}$ and for all instances D of $\mathcal{R}$, if $D \models \mathcal{A}$, then when ξ is applied to D, $\xi(D) = Q_\xi(D)$. This is verified by induction on the length of ξ, constructing Q_ξ step by step.

(b) If a CQ Q is covered by $\mathcal{A}$, then Q is boundedly evaluable under $\mathcal{A}$. This is verified by generating a boundedly evaluable query plan ξ for Q, mimicking each step of the evaluation of Q with an operation in ξ.

From Lemmas (a) and (b), statement (1) follows. Statement (2) follows from Lemma (b). Statement (3) follows from Lemma 3.9 and the fact that checking conditions (b) and (c) of covered queries can be done in PTIME. □

Example 3.12: The notion of coverage characterizes what makes a CQ boundedly evaluable. For instance, Q_0 of Example 1.1 is covered by $\mathcal{A}_0$, and Q_3 of Example 3.1 is covered by $\mathcal{A}_3$. As shown earlier, both queries are boundedly evaluable. The characterization is, however, not purely syntactic. Some boundedly evaluable CQ queries may not be covered, but are $\mathcal{A}$-equivalent to a covered query in CQ. For example, Q_2 of Example 3.1 is not covered by $\mathcal{A}_2$: its free variable x is not in $\mathsf{cov}(Q_2, \mathcal{A}_2)$. Nonetheless, Q_2 is $\mathcal{A}_2$-equivalent to a query $Q_2'(x) = (x = 1 \wedge x = 2)$, which is covered by $\mathcal{A}_2$ since its variable is data-independent. □

Effective syntax for $\exists\mathsf{FO}^+$. We now extend the notion of covered queries to $\exists\mathsf{FO}^+$(and hence UCQ). A query Q in $\exists\mathsf{FO}^+$is *covered* by an access schema $\mathcal{A}$ if for each Q_i of its CQ sub-queries, either (a) Q_i is covered, or (b) for all $\mathcal{A}$-instances $\theta(T_Q)$ of Q_i, there is $j \in [1, k]$ such that $\theta(u) \in Q_j(\theta(T_Q))$ and Q_j is covered by $\mathcal{A}$.

Covered queries are also an effective syntax for boundedly evaluable queries in $\exists\text{FO}^+$. Indeed, the corollary below follows from Theorem 3.11 and Lemma 3.6.

Corollary 3.13: (1) An $\exists\text{FO}^+$query is boundedly evaluable under an access schema $\mathcal{A}$ if and only if it is $\mathcal{A}$-equivalent to an $\exists\text{FO}^+$query that is covered by $\mathcal{A}$. (2) Each $\exists\text{FO}^+$query covered by $\mathcal{A}$ is boundedly evaluable under $\mathcal{A}$. □

Deciding coverage. We study the *query coverage problem*, denoted by $\text{CQP}(\mathcal{L})$ and stated as follows.

- INPUT: $\mathcal{R}$, $\mathcal{A}$ and Q as in BEP.
- QUESTION: Is Q covered by $\mathcal{A}$?

In practice, the analysis of CQP helps us syntactically check whether Q is boundedly evaluable under an access schema.

By Theorem 3.11, CQP is in PTIME for CQ, as opposed to EXPSPACE-complete for BEP. It provides us with a tractable syntactic method to check the bounded evaluability of CQ. However, CQP is nontrivial when it comes to UCQ and $\exists\text{FO}^+$, although it is easier than its BEP counterparts.

Theorem 3.14: CQP is
- in PTIME for CQ; and
- Π_2^p-complete for UCQ and $\exists\text{FO}^+$. □

Alternatively, one can define a query Q in $\exists\text{FO}^+$to be covered if each of its CQ sub-query is covered. If so, CQP(UCQ) is in PTIME and CQP($\exists\text{FO}^+$) is coNP-complete, down from Π_2^p-complete. We opt to adopt a more general notion of covered queries for $\exists\text{FO}^+$, to include most boundedly evaluable UCQ and $\exists\text{FO}^+$queries found in practice.

Proof sketch. We show that CQP is in Π_2^p for $\exists\text{FO}^+$and Π_2^p-hard for UCQ. For the upper bound, we develop an Σ_2^p algorithm that checks whether a query Q in $\exists\text{FO}^+$ is not covered by an access schema. The lower bound is verified by reduction from the $\forall^*\exists^*$3CNF problem; it is a revision of its counterpart given in the proof of Lemma 3.3. □

Generalization. Access constraints with non-constant cardinality (Section 2) do not make our lives harder.

Corollary 3.15: All the results of this section (Theorems 3.11, 3.4 and 3.14, Lemmas 3.2, 3.3, 3.9, 3.6, as well as Corollaries 3.7 and 3.13) also hold under access constraints of the general form $R(X \to Y, s(\cdot))$. □

4. QUERY DRIVEN APPROXIMATION

When a query Q is boundedly evaluable under an access schema $\mathcal{A}$, in all datasets D that satisfy $\mathcal{A}$, we can compute $Q(D)$ by accessing a bounded amount of data. If Q is not boundedly evaluable, however, it may be cost-prohibitive to compute exact answers to Q in D. In light of this, we study how to compute approximate query answers to Q following the absolute approximation scheme of [14]. Below we first present envelopes based on bounded evaluability in Section 4.1. We then study the existence of upper and lower envelopes in Sections 4.2 and 4.3, respectively.

4.1 Boundedly Evaluable Envelopes

Consider an access schema $\mathcal{A}$ and a query Q, both defined over a relational schema $\mathcal{R}$, where Q is in query language $\mathcal{L}$, and Q is not boundedly evaluable under $\mathcal{A}$.

We want to find queries Q_l and Q_u in $\mathcal{L}$ such that

(a) Q_l and Q_u are boundedly evaluable under $\mathcal{A}$; and

(b) for all instances D of $\mathcal{R}$ that satisfy $\mathcal{A}$,
- $Q_l(D) \subseteq Q(D) \subseteq Q_u(D)$, and
- $|Q(D) - Q_l(D)| \leq N_l$, $|Q_u(D) - Q(D)| \leq N_u$,

where N_l and N_u are constants derived from Q and constants in $\mathcal{A}$. We refer to Q_u and Q_l as *upper* and *lower envelopes* of Q under $\mathcal{A}$, respectively, and call N_u (resp. N_l) an *approximation bound* of Q_u (resp. Q_l) *w.r.t.* Q.

Intuitively, upper and lower envelopes approximate query Q. Given any instance D of $\mathcal{R}$, as long as $D \models \mathcal{A}$, $Q_u(D)$ and $Q_l(D)$ can be efficiently computed by accessing a bounded amount of data. Better still, $Q_u(D)$ and $Q_l(D)$ are not too far from the exact answers $Q(D)$: $Q_u(D)$ includes all tuples in $Q(D)$, and it has at most N_u tuples that are not in $Q(D)$; moreover, all tuples in $Q_l(D)$ are also in $Q(D)$, and at most N_l tuples in $Q(D)$ are not in $Q_l(D)$.

Example 4.1: Consider a relation schema $R(A, B)$, an access schema $\mathcal{A}$ consisting of a single constraint $R(A \to B, N)$ for a constant N, and two queries in CQ:

$$Q_1(x) = \exists y, z, w\big(R(w, x) \wedge R(y, w) \wedge R(x, z) \wedge w = 1\big);$$
$$Q_2(x, y) = \exists w\big(R(w, x) \wedge R(y, w) \wedge w = 1\big).$$

Then Q_1 is not boundedly evaluable under $\mathcal{A}$. However, it has upper envelope Q_u and lower envelope Q_l:

$$Q_u(x) = \exists y, z\big(R(1, x) \wedge R(x, z)\big),$$
$$Q_l(x) = \exists y, z\big(R(1, x) \wedge R(y, 1) \wedge R(x, y) \wedge R(x, z)\big).$$

Indeed, Q_u and Q_l are covered by $\mathcal{A}$ and are boundedly evaluable. Moreover, for any instance D of R, if $D \models \mathcal{A}$, then $|Q_u(D) - Q_1(D)| \leq N$ and $|Q_1(D) - Q_l(D)| \leq N$.

In contrast, Q_2 is not boundedly evaluable under $\mathcal{A}$, and it has neither upper nor lower envelope. □

As we have seen in Example 4.1, a query may not have upper or lower envelopes, *e.g.,* Q_2. This suggests that we study problems for deciding whether a query Q has envelopes under an access schema, to help us determine whether it is possible to approximate Q with boundedly evaluable queries that warrant constant approximation bounds.

However, the problems for deciding the existence of envelopes for a given query Q are even harder than BEP, the problem for deciding the bounded evaluability of Q. In light of this we consider envelopes of certain syntactic forms, to get lower complexity for the decision problems.

4.2 Deciding Upper Envelopes

We first define upper envelopes of a certain syntactic form, and then study the associated decision problem.

Query relaxation. Assume a relational schema $\mathcal{R}$ over which our queries and access schemas are defined.

A *relaxation* of a CQ $Q(\bar{x}) = \exists\bar{y}\psi(\bar{x}, \bar{y})$ is a CQ $Q'(\bar{x}) = \exists\bar{y}'\psi'(\bar{x}, \bar{y}')$ such that $\bar{y}' \subseteq \bar{y}$, and moreover, every atomic formula in ψ' is an atomic formula in ψ.

For instance, query Q_u given in Example 4.1 is a relaxation of Q_1. Intuitively, Q' is obtained by removing tuples from the tableau representing Q. Note that Q and Q' have the same set of free variables and $Q \subseteq Q'$. Hence $Q \sqsubseteq_{\mathcal{A}} Q'$ for any access schema $\mathcal{A}$ defined over $\mathcal{R}$.

We extend the notion of relaxation to $\exists\text{FO}^+$. A *relaxation* of an $\exists\text{FO}^+$query Q is a query Q' in $\exists\text{FO}^+$such that each CQ sub-query Q'_i of Q' is a relaxation of a CQ sub-query of Q.

Decision problem. The *upper envelope problem* for a query class $\mathcal{L}$, denoted by UEP($\mathcal{L}$), is stated as follows.

- INPUT: A relational schema $\mathcal{R}$, an access schema $\mathcal{A}$ over $\mathcal{R}$, and a query $Q \in \mathcal{L}$ over $\mathcal{R}$ that is not boundedly evaluable under $\mathcal{A}$.
- QUESTION: Does there exist an upper envelope Q_u of Q under $\mathcal{A}$? In particular, when $\mathcal{L}$ is CQ, UCQ or $\exists FO^+$, it is to decide whether there exists Q_u that is a relaxation of Q and is covered by $\mathcal{A}$.

That is, whenever possible, we search for upper envelopes that can be syntactically checked, to reduce the cost of checking their bounded evaluability. By Corollary 3.13, a covered query is boundedly evaluable.

Characterization. What queries can have an upper envelope? We start with a condition that is necessary for the existence of both upper and lower envelopes.

A query Q is *bounded under* $\mathcal{A}$ if there exists a constant c determined by Q and $\mathcal{A}$ such that for *all* instances D of $\mathcal{R}$, if $D \models \mathcal{A}$, then there exists $D_Q \subseteq D$, where

(a) $Q(D_Q) = Q(D)$; and

(b) $|D_Q| \leq c$, *i.e.*, $|D_Q|$ is independent of $|D|$.

Hence, there exists a constant c_r such that $|Q(D)| \leq c_r$.

The notion of boundedness is weaker than the notion of boundedly evaluability. A boundedly evaluable query is also bounded, but a bounded query may *not* be boundedly evaluable, *i.e.*, it does not necessarily have an boundedly evaluable query plan. For instance, query Q_1 of Example 4.1 is bounded, but it is not boundedly evaluable.

Recall that query Q_2 of Example 4.1 is not bounded, and it does not have an envelope. This is not a coincidence. Indeed, boundedness is a necessary condition for a query to have an envelope, as shown by the lemma below.

Lemma 4.2: Under an access schema $\mathcal{A}$,

(a) if a query Q has an (upper or lower) envelope, then Q must be bounded;

(b) a CQ $Q(\bar{x})$ is bounded if and only if all free variables $\bar{x}$ of Q are covered by $\mathcal{A}$; and

(c) a query Q in $\exists FO^+$ is bounded if and only if every CQ sub-query of Q is bounded. □

Proof sketch. If Q has an envelope Q', then Q' is boundedly evaluable and hence for all instances D that satisfy $\mathcal{A}$, $|Q(D)| \leq c$ for a constant c. Thus if Q is not bounded, Q' does not have a constant approximation bound for Q' *w.r.t.* Q. From this statement (a) follows.

Statements (b) and (c) are verified based on the monotonicity of CQ and $\exists FO^+$. Note that statement (c) only holds for bounded queries. In contrast, for a boundedly evaluable query in $\exists FO^+$, some of its CQ sub-queries may *not* be boundedly evaluable, as Example 3.5 demonstrates. □

For a CQ Q that is not boundedly evaluable under $\mathcal{A}$, UEP asks whether we can make Q covered by removing relation atoms, and hence removing variables that are not covered by $\mathcal{A}$. For instance, query Q_1 of Example 4.1 has a relation atom $R(y, w)$ with variable y that is not covered. We remove $R(y, w)$ and get an upper envelope Q_u that is covered.

When Q is in $\exists FO^+$, the lemma below characterizes UEP for $\exists FO^+$, which can be verified based on the definitions of query relaxations and covered queries for $\exists FO^+$.

Lemma 4.3: Under an access schema $\mathcal{A}$, a query Q in $\exists FO^+$ has an upper envelope that is a relaxation and covered if and only if for each CQ sub-query Q_i of Q, either Q_i has a covered relaxation, or for any $\mathcal{A}$-instance $\theta(T_Q)$ of Q_i, there exists a covered relaxation Q'_j of a CQ sub-query Q_j such that $\theta(u) \in Q'_j(\theta(T_Q))$. □

Complexity. We next give the complexity of UEP($\mathcal{L}$). To make the picture complete, we also study UEP(FO) in which an upper envelope Q_u is simply defined to be a boundedly evaluable FO query such that $Q \sqsubseteq_{\mathcal{A}} Q_u$ and Q_u has a constant approximation bound *w.r.t.* Q.

While UEP is intractable for CQ and $\exists FO^+$, its analyses are much simpler than their BEP counterparts.

Theorem 4.4: Under an access schema, UEP is

- NP-complete for CQ;
- Π_2^p-complete for UCQ and $\exists FO^+$; and
- undecidable for FO. □

Proof sketch. (1) *Lower bounds.* We show that UEP is NP-hard, Π_2^p-hard and undecidable for CQ, UCQ and FO by reductions from X3C, $\forall^*\exists^*$3CNF and the complement of the satisfiability problem for FO, respectively. The X3C problem (exact cover by 3-sets) is to determine, given a set X with $3q$ elements and a collection C of 3-element subsets of X, whether C contains an exact cover C' of X, *i.e.*, $C' \subseteq C$ such that every element of X occurs in exactly one subset of C'. It is NP-complete (cf. [31]). The satisfiability problem for FO is to decide, given an FO query Q over a relational schema $\mathcal{R}$, whether there is an instance D of $\mathcal{R}$ such that $Q(D) \neq \emptyset$. It is undecidable (cf. [2]).

It should be remarked that while UEP(UCQ) has the same complexity as CQP(UCQ), the reduction for UEP is more involved than its counterpart for CQP.

(2) *Upper bounds.* We develop an NP algorithm for checking whether a CQ has a relaxation that is covered by $\mathcal{A}$, based on Theorem 3.11. Capitalizing on Lemma 4.3, we develop an Σ_2^p algorithm to check whether a query in $\exists FO^+$ does *not* have a relaxation that is covered by $\mathcal{A}$. □

4.3 Deciding Lower Envelopes

Analogous to the analysis of upper envelopes, we study lower envelopes of a certain syntactic form.

Query expansion. Assume a positive integer k. A *k-expansion* of a CQ $Q(\bar{x}) = \exists\bar{y}\psi(\bar{x},\bar{y})$ is a CQ $Q'(\bar{x}) = \exists\bar{y}'\psi'(\bar{x},\bar{y}')$ such that $\bar{y} \subseteq \bar{y}'$, every atomic formula in ψ is an atomic formula in ψ', and moreover, ψ' contains at most k relation atoms that do not occur in ψ.

Intuitively, let (T_Q, u) be the tableau representation of Q, and T'_Q be a tableau obtained by adding at most k additional tuples to T_Q. Then Q' is a CQ represented by (T'_Q, u). For instance, query Q_l given in Example 4.1 is an 1-expansion of query Q_1. Observe that $Q' \subseteq Q$ and $Q' \sqsubseteq_{\mathcal{A}} Q$ for any access schema $\mathcal{A}$ that is defined over the same relational schema $\mathcal{R}$ on which queries Q and Q' are defined.

We define a *k-expansion* of a query Q in $\exists FO^+$ to be a query Q' in $\exists FO^+$ such that each CQ sub-query of Q' is a k-expansion of a CQ sub-query of Q.

Decision problem. We now state the *lower envelope problem* for a query class $\mathcal{L}$, denoted by LEP($\mathcal{L}$).

- INPUT: $\mathcal{R}$, $\mathcal{A}$, Q as in UEP, and a natural number k.
- QUESTION: Does there exist a lower envelope Q_l of Q under $\mathcal{A}$ that is $\mathcal{A}$-satisfiable? In particular, when $\mathcal{L}$ is CQ, UCQ or $\exists$FO$^+$, it is to decide whether there exists a lower envelope Q_l that is a k-expansion of Q and is covered by $\mathcal{A}$.

We refer to Q_l as a *k-expansion lower envelope*.

We require Q_l to be $\mathcal{A}$-satisfiable to rule out "trivial" lower envelopes. Note that when a CQ Q is bounded under $\mathcal{A}$, empty query $Q_\emptyset$ would have been a lower envelope of Q. Such a trivial envelope is not very useful. We do not impose the condition on upper envelopes, since an upper envelope Q_u is guaranteed $\mathcal{A}$-satisfiable. Indeed, UEP is studied for Q that is not boundedly evaluable under $\mathcal{A}$; hence Q must be $\mathcal{A}$-satisfiable. By $Q \sqsubseteq_{\mathcal{A}} Q_u$, Q_u is also $\mathcal{A}$-satisfiable.

Characterization. For a CQ Q that is not boundedly evaluable, LEP is to decide whether we can make Q covered by adding additional relation atoms. Intuitively, when Q contains variables that are not covered, we add relation atoms to make them covered, as illustrated by Q_l of Example 3.10. When Q contains relation atoms $R(\bar{y})$ that are not indexed by $\mathcal{A}$ (see the definition of covered queries in Section 3.1), sometimes we can "split" $R(\bar{y})$ into $R(\bar{y}_1) \wedge \ldots \wedge R(\bar{y}_n)$ such that $\bar{y} = (\bar{y}_1, \ldots, \bar{y}_n)$ and each $R(\bar{y}_i)$ is indexed.

Example 4.5: Consider a relation schema $R(A, B, C)$, an access schema $\mathcal{A}$ and a CQ Q defined as follows:

$$\mathcal{A} = \{R(A \to B, N), R(B \to C, 1)\},$$
$$Q(x, y) = R(1, x, y).$$

Then Q is not covered by $\mathcal{A}$, since $R(1, x, y)$ is not indexed by $\mathcal{A}$. Nonetheless, its 1-expansion below is covered:

$$Q'(x, y) = \exists z_1, z_2 \big(R(1, x, z_1) \wedge R(z_2, x, y)\big).$$

One can verify that Q' is indexed and $Q' \equiv_{\mathcal{A}} Q$. □

For query Q in $\exists$FO$^+$, a characterization for the existence of lower envelopes is given as follows, which can be verified by using the definitions of covered queries and k-expansions.

Lemma 4.6: Under an access schema $\mathcal{A}$, a query Q in $\exists$FO$^+$has a k-expansion lower envelope if and only if (a) Q is bounded under $\mathcal{A}$, and (b) there exists a CQ sub-query Q_i of Q such that it has a k-expansion that is covered by $\mathcal{A}$ and is $\mathcal{A}$-satisfiable. □

Complexity. Compared to UEP($\mathcal{L}$), LEP($\mathcal{L}$) has a lower complexity when $\mathcal{L}$ is UCQ or $\exists$FO$^+$.

Theorem 4.7: Under an access schema $\mathcal{A}$, LEP is

- NP-complete for CQ and UCQ;
- DP-complete for $\exists$FO$^+$; and
- undecidable for FO. □

Proof sketch. (1) *Lower bounds.* We show that LEP is NP-hard, DP-hard and undecidable for CQ, $\exists$FO$^+$and FO, by reduction from X3C, SAT-UNSAT and the complement of the satisfiability problem for FO, respectively. SAT-UNSAT is to decide, given a pair (φ_1, φ_2) of 3SAT instances, whether φ_1 is satisfiable and φ_2 is not satisfiable. It is DP-complete (cf. [31]). The reduction from SAT-UNSAT makes use of nested union in $\exists$FO$^+$query, which is not supported by UCQ.

(2) *Upper bounds.* Based on Lemmas 4.2 and 4.6, we develop an algorithm to check whether a query has a lower envelope that is a k-expansion, $\mathcal{A}$-satisfiable and covered. It is in NP for UCQ. In contrast, it is in DP for $\exists$FO$^+$since it uses a coNP oracle to check whether Q is bounded, and an NP oracle to check whether Q has a covered k-expansion. □

General constraints. When access constraints with non-constant cardinality are considered, the notion of bounded queries needs to be revised to accommodate cardinality functions, and the results of this section do not carry over directly to access constraints of the general form.

5. BOUNDED QUERY SPECIALIZATION

For a query Q that is not boundedly evaluable, the chances are that Q will become boundedly evaluable when its users instantiate some parameters of Q. This suggests another strategy to process costly queries based on bounded evaluability. As remarked in Section 1, parameterized queries are common in e-commerce systems and personalized searches, and such queries are typically specialized by instantiating some of its parameters when being issued by its users. Below we study QSP, the query specialization problem.

5.1 Query Specialization

We first present (bounded) query specialization.

Specialized queries. First consider $Q(\bar{y}) = \exists \bar{z}\ \psi(\bar{y}, \bar{z})$ in CQ, where ψ is quantifier free, and $\bar{z}$ consists of bound variables. The *parameters* of Q, denoted by X, may include both free variables of $\bar{y}$ and bound variables of $\bar{z}$. Such parameters are typically *designated* by the provider of Q.

A *specialized query* $Q(\bar{x} = \bar{c})$ of Q is defined as $\exists \bar{z}(\psi(\bar{y}, \bar{z}) \wedge \bar{x} = \bar{c})$, where $\bar{x}$ is a tuple of parameters in X, and $\bar{c}$ is a tuple of constants with $|\bar{x}| = |\bar{c}|$. Here we use $|\bar{x}|$ to denote the arity of $\bar{x}$, and refer to $\bar{c}$ as a *valuation* of $\bar{x}$. That is, we specialize Q by instantiating parameters $\bar{x}$.

Example 5.1: Consider query Q defined on relations Accident, Casualty and Vehicle given in Example 1.1:

$$\begin{aligned} Q(x_a) = \exists\ & \text{aid, date, district, cid, class, vid, dri} \\ & (\text{Accident(aid, district, date)} \wedge \\ & \text{Casualty(cid, aid, class, vid)} \wedge \text{Vehicle(vid, dri, } x_a)). \end{aligned}$$

It has two parameters date and district in X, identified by the designer of Q. Given a valuation (c_1, c_2) of (date, district), the specialized query $Q(\text{date} = c_1, \text{district} = c_2)$ of Q is to find the ages of drivers who were involved in an accident in district c_2 on day c_1. For instance, Q(date = "1/5/2005", district = "Queen's Park") is query Q_0 given in Example 1.1.

Under access constraints ψ_1–ψ_4 of Example 1.1, (1) Q is *not* boundedly evaluable itself, since free variable x_a is not covered; but (2) $Q(\text{date} = c_1)$ is boundedly evaluable for *all* valuations c_1 of date; *i.e.*, instantiating a single parameter makes the specialized queries boundedly evaluable. □

For an FO query Q, consider its DNF form: $Q(\bar{y}) = P_1 z_1 \ldots P_n z_n \psi(\bar{y}, \bar{z})$, where P_i is either $\exists$ or $\forall$, and $\bar{z}$ denotes $(z_1, \ldots, z_n)$. Its *parameters* in X may be variables from $\bar{y}$ and $\bar{z}$. A *specialized query* $Q(\bar{x} = \bar{c})$ of Q is defined as $P_1 z_1 \ldots P_n z_n (\psi(\bar{y}, \bar{z}) \wedge \bar{x} = \bar{c})$, where $\bar{x}$ is a tuple of parameters in X, and $\bar{c}$ is a valuation of $\bar{x}$.

Bounded query specialization. Consider query Q that is not boundedly evaluable under an access schema $\mathcal{A}$, with a parameter set X. We say that Q can be *boundedly specialized* *under $\mathcal{A}$ with $\bar{x}$* if $\bar{x}$ is a tuple of parameters from X such that (a) $Q(\bar{x} = \bar{c})$ is boundedly evaluable under $\mathcal{A}$ for *all valuations* $\bar{c}$ of $\bar{x}$, and (b) there exists at least one valuation $\bar{c}$ of $\bar{x}$ such that $Q(\bar{x} = \bar{c})$ is $\mathcal{A}$-satisfiable.

Intuitively, condition (a) asks for $Q(\bar{x} = \bar{c})$ to be generic regardless of what valuations are used, and condition (b) requires the specialized query to be sensible.

Some queries Q may not be boundedly specialized. For instance, recall query Q from Example 5.1. If its set X of parameters consists of district only, one can verify that Q may not be boundedly specialized under constraints ψ_1–ψ_4. Moreover, if Q can be boundedly instantiated, we naturally want to instantiate a minimum set of parameters in X.

Decision problem. Hence we study the *query specialization problem*, denoted by $\mathsf{QSP}(\mathcal{L})$ for a query language $\mathcal{L}$.

- INPUT: A relational schema $\mathcal{R}$, an access schema $\mathcal{A}$ over $\mathcal{R}$, a query $Q \in \mathcal{L}$ defined over $\mathcal{R}$ that is not boundedly evaluable under $\mathcal{A}$, a set X of parameters in Q, and a natural number k.
- QUESTION: Can Q be boundedly specialized under $\mathcal{A}$ with a tuple $\bar{x}$ from X such that $|\bar{x}| \leq k$? In particular, when $\mathcal{L}$ is CQ, UCQ or $\exists$FO$^+$, it is to decide whether there exists $\bar{x}$ such that $|\bar{x}| \leq k$ and $Q(\bar{x} = \bar{c})$ is covered by $\mathcal{A}$ for all valuations $\bar{c}$ of $\bar{x}$.

The study of QSP aims to help us decide what access schema to maintain and what parameters to instantiate, to make specialized queries boundedly evaluable.

When $\mathcal{L}$ is CQ, UCQ or $\exists$FO$^+$, we ask for specialized queries $Q(\bar{x} = \bar{c})$ that are covered by $\mathcal{A}$, to reduce the cost of the QSP analysis. By Corollary 3.13, $Q(\bar{x} = \bar{c})$ is boundedly evaluable under $\mathcal{A}$. Without the syntactic restriction, $\mathsf{QSP}(\mathcal{L})$ has complexity higher than $\mathsf{BEP}(\mathcal{L})$ when $\mathcal{L}$ is, *e.g.,* CQ, and is too costly to be practical.

Remark. Both QSP and LEP aim to restrict a query Q and make it boundedly evaluable. However, QSP approaches bounded evaluability by instantiating parameters, while LEP is by imposing additional relation atoms on Q. Moreover, LEP requires that $|Q(D) - Q_l(D)| \leq N_l$ with a constant N_l for all instances D that satisfy $\mathcal{A}$. In light of this, Q has to be bounded to get a lower envelope, whereas this is not required by QSP. As will be seen shortly, $\mathsf{QSP}(\mathcal{L})$ and $\mathsf{LEP}(\mathcal{L})$ have different complexity for UCQ and $\exists$FO$^+$.

5.2 Deciding Bounded Specialization

We next study the complexity of $\mathsf{QSP}(\mathcal{L})$. It is nontrivial to identify parameters $\bar{x}$ of Q for instantiation and make specialized $Q(\bar{x} = \bar{c})$ boundedly evaluable.

Example 5.2: Consider a relational schema $\mathcal{R}$, an access schema $\mathcal{A}$ and a CQ Q over $\mathcal{R}$: (1) $\mathcal{R}$ consists of $R_i(A, B_1, B_2, B_3)$ for $i \in [1, n]$, (2) $\mathcal{A}$ defines 4 constraints on each R_i: $R_i(A \to (B_1, B_2, B_3), 1)$, $R_i(B_1 \to A, 1)$, $R_i(B_2 \to A, 1)$ and $R_i(B_3 \to A, 1)$; and (3) Q is

$$\exists \bar{y}, \bar{z}\big(\textstyle\bigwedge_{i\in[1,n]} R_i(1, 1, 1, 1) \wedge \bigwedge_{i\in[1,n]} R_i(y_i, z_{i1}, z_{i2}, z_{i3})\big).$$

One can verify that the Boolean query $Q()$ is not boundedly evaluable under $\mathcal{A}$. Now let X be $\bar{y}$ and k be a positive integer. We want to know whether Q can be boundedly specialized with $\bar{x}$ from X and $|\bar{x}| \leq k$.

In the proof of Theorem 5.3, we use $\mathcal{R}$, $\mathcal{A}$ and Q to encode an instance of the minimum set cover problem (MSC). Given a collection C of subsets of a finite set S and a natural number k, MSC is to decide whether there exists a cover C' of C with $|C'| \leq k$. Assume $C = \{C_i \mid i \in [1, n]\}$ and $|S| = |\bar{z}|$. Then each R_i encodes a subset $C_i \in C$, $y_i \in \bar{y}$ indicates C_i, and z_{i1}, z_{i2} and z_{i3} denote elements in C_i. Moreover, C contains a cover C' with $|C'| \leq k$ if and only if Q can be boundedly specialized with $\bar{x}$ from X and $|\bar{x}| \leq k$. This illustrates why QSP analysis is nontrivial. □

Theorem 5.3 gives the complexity of QSP. While $\mathsf{QSP}(\mathcal{L})$ has the same complexity as $\mathsf{UEP}(\mathcal{L})$, the proofs are quite different from their counterparts for UEP. Compared to LEP, the QSP analysis is more complicated for UCQ and $\exists$FO$^+$.

Theorem 5.3: QSP is

- NP-complete for CQ; and
- Π_2^p-complete for UCQ and $\exists$FO$^+$; and
- undecidable for FO. □

Proof sketch. (1) *Lower bounds.* We show that QSP is NP-hard, Π_2^p-hard and undecidable for CQ, UCQ and FO by reduction from MSC, $\forall^*\exists^*$3CNF and the complement of the satisfiability problem for FO, respectively. It is known that MSC is NP-complete (cf. [31]). In contrast to the reductions of Theorem 4.7, the reductions here encode what variables can be instantiated and ensure that all instantiations of these variables yield a covered specialized query. For instance, Example 5.2 outlines a reduction from MSC for CQ.

(2) *Upper bounds.* We develop NP and Π_2^p algorithms for checking QSP for CQ and $\exists$FO$^+$, respectively. The algorithms make use of Theorem 3.11 and a lemma: if Q is $\mathcal{A}$-satisfiable, then for all tuples $\bar{x}$ of parameters of Q, there exists a valuation $\bar{c}$ of $\bar{x}$ such that $Q(\bar{x} = \bar{c})$ is $\mathcal{A}$-satisfiable. □

A syntactic condition. Is it possible to maintain an access schema $\mathcal{A}$ over a relational schema $\mathcal{R}$ such that bounded specialization is always within reach under $\mathcal{A}$ for all FO queries defined over $\mathcal{R}$? The answer is affirmative.

We say that $\mathcal{A}$ *covers* $\mathcal{R}$ if for each relation schema R in $\mathcal{R}$, there exists an access constraints $R(X \to (Y, N))$ in $\mathcal{A}$ such that for each attribute B of R, either $B \in X$ or $B \in Y$, *i.e.,* indices are built on B or for B. We say that an FO query Q is *fully parameterized* if its set X of parameters includes all variables in Q. These suffice for bounded specialization.

Proposition 5.4: Under an access schema $\mathcal{A}$ that covers a relational schema $\mathcal{R}$, all fully parameterized FO queries defined over $\mathcal{R}$ can be boundedly specialized. □

Generalization. The results of this section carry over to access constraints with non-constant cardinality.

Corollary 5.5: Theorem 5.3 and Proposition 5.4 also hold on access constraints of the form $R(X \to Y, s(\cdot))$. □

6. CONCLUSION

We have investigated how to query big data by leveraging bounded evaluability, to compute exact answers if possible, and approximate answers otherwise by means of envelopes and bounded query specialization. We have identified several problems associated with bounded evaluability, and provided their complexity and characterizations. The main complexity results are summarized in Table 1, annotated with their corresponding theorems.

Queries	BEP($\mathcal{L}$)	CQP($\mathcal{L}$)	UEP($\mathcal{L}$)	LEP($\mathcal{L}$)	QSP($\mathcal{L}$)
CQ	EXPSPACE-c (Th. 3.4)	PTIME (Th. 3.11)	NP-c (Th. 4.4)	NP-c (Th. 4.7)	NP-c (Th. 5.3)
UCQ	EXPSPACE-c (Cor. 3.7)	Π_2^p-c (Th. 3.14)	Π_2^p-c (Th. 4.4)	NP-c (Th. 4.7)	Π_2^p-c (Th. 5.3)
$\exists$FO$^+$	EXPSPACE-c (Cor. 3.7)	Π_2^p-c (Th. 3.14)	Π_2^p-c (Th. 4.4)	DP-c (Th. 4.7)	Π_2^p-c (Th. 5.3)
FO	undecidable [17]	not defined for FO	undecidable (Th. 4.4)	undecidable (Th. 4.7)	undecidable (Th. 5.3)

Table 1: Complexity for reasoning about bounded evaluability ($\mathcal{C}$-c indicates $\mathcal{C}$-complete)

This work suggests a strategy to answer queries on big data as follows. (1) We develop and maintain an access schema $\mathcal{A}$ for an application. (2) Given a dataset D that satisfies $\mathcal{A}$, for all queries Q posed over D, we first check whether Q is boundedly evaluable under $\mathcal{A}$ or covered by $\mathcal{A}$; if so, we compute exact answers $Q(D)$ by accessing a bounded amount of data; otherwise we compute approximate query answers, by using envelopes or by interacting with users to get a boundedly specialized query.

One topic for future work is identify an effective syntax for boundedly evaluable FO queries. Another topic is to study UEP and LEP under general access constraints. A third topic is to study, given a query Q in a language $\mathcal{L}$, whether Q has envelopes in another language $\mathcal{L}'$, *e.g.,* to find envelopes in CQ for an FO query. Finally, it is interesting to explore envelopes with approximation ratios measured in terms of precision and recall, instead of absolute approximation [14].

Acknowledgments. Fan is supported in part by NSFC 61133002, 973 Program 2012CB316200, Shenzhen Peacock Program 1105100030834361, Guangdong Innovative Research Team Program 2011D005, EPSRC EP/J015377/1 and EP/M025268/1, and a Google Faculty Research Award. Cao and Deng are supported in part by NSFC 61421003 and 973 Program 2014CB340302.

7. REFERENCES

[1] *http://data.gov.uk/dataset/road-accidents-safety-data.*

[2] S. Abiteboul, R. Hull, and V. Vianu. *Foundations of Databases.* Addison-Wesley, 1995.

[3] S. Agarwal, H. Milner, A. Kleiner, A. Talwalkar, M. I. Jordan, S. Madden, B. Mozafari, and I. Stoica. Knowing when you're wrong: building fast and reliable approximate query processing systems. In *SIGMOD*, 2014.

[4] S. Agarwal, B. Mozafari, A. Panda, H. Milner, S. Madden, and I. Stoica. BlinkDB: Queries with bounded errors and bounded response times on very large data. In *EuroSys*, 2013.

[5] M. Armbrust, K. Curtis, T. Kraska, A. Fox, M. J. Franklin, and D. A. Patterson. PIQL: Success-tolerant query processing in the cloud. *PVLDB*, 5(3), 2011.

[6] M. Armbrust, A. Fox, D. A. Patterson, N. Lanham, B. Trushkowsky, J. Trutna, and H. Oh. SCADS: Scale-independent storage for social computing applications. In *CIDR*, 2009.

[7] B. Babcock, S. Chaudhuri, and G. Das. Dynamic sample selection for approximate query processing. In *SIGMOD*, 2003.

[8] V. Bárány, M. Benedikt, and P. Bourhis. Access patterns and integrity constraints revisited. In *ICDT*, 2013.

[9] P. Barceló, L. Libkin, and M. Romero. Efficient approximations of conjunctive queries. *SICOMP*, 43(3):1085–1130, 2014.

[10] P. Barceló, J. L. Reutter, and L. Libkin. Parameterized regular expressions and their languages. *TCS*, 474:21–45, 2013.

[11] Y. Cao, W. Fan, and R. Huang. Making pattern queries bounded in big graphs. In *ICDE*, 2015.

[12] Y. Cao, W. Fan, and W. Yu. Bounded conjunctive queries. *PVLDB*, 2014.

[13] A. K. Chandra and P. M. Merlin. Optimal implementation of conjunctive queries in relational data bases. In *STOC*, 1977.

[14] S. Chaudhuri and P. G. Kolaitis. Can datalog be approximated? *JCSS*, 55(2):355–369, 1997.

[15] A. Deutsch, B. Ludäscher, and A. Nash. Rewriting queries using views with access patterns under integrity constraints. *TCS*, 371(3), 2007.

[16] Facebook. Introducing Graph Search. *https://en-gb.facebook.com/about/graphsearch*, 2013.

[17] W. Fan, F. Geerts, and L. Libkin. On scale independence for querying big data. In *PODS*, 2014.

[18] W. Fan, F. Geerts, and F. Neven. Making queries tractable on big data with preprocessing. *PVLDB*, 2013.

[19] W. Fan, J. Li, S. Ma, N. Tang, Y. Wu, and Y. Wu. Graph pattern matching: From intractability to polynomial time. *PVLDB*, 3(1):1161–1172, 2010.

[20] R. Fink and D. Olteanu. On the optimal approximation of queries using tractable propositional languages. In *ICDT*, 2011.

[21] M. N. Garofalakis and P. B. Gibbons. Wavelet synopses with error guarantees. In *SIGMOD*, 2004.

[22] G. Gottlob, S. T. Lee, G. Valiant, and P. Valiant. Size and treewidth bounds for conjunctive queries. *JACM*, 59(3), 2012.

[23] R. Haenni and N. Lehmann. Resource bounded and anytime approximation of belief function computations. *IJAR*, 31, 2002.

[24] Y. E. Ioannidis and V. Poosala. Histogram-based approximation of set-valued query-answers. In *VLDB*, 1999.

[25] H. V. Jagadish, N. Koudas, S. Muthukrishnan, V. Poosala, K. C. Sevcik, and T. Suel. Optimal histograms with quality guarantees. In *VLDB*, 2009.

[26] M. P. Kato, T. Sakai, and K. Tanaka. Structured query suggestion for specialization and parallel movement: effect on search behaviors. In *WWW*, 2012.

[27] A. Klug. On conjunctive queries containing inequalities. *J. ACM*, 35(1):146–160, 1988.

[28] P. G. Kolaitis, D. L. Martin, and M. N. Thakur. On the complexity of the containment problem for conjunctive queries with built-in predicates. In *PODS*, 1998.

[29] C. Li. Computing complete answers to queries in the presence of limited access patterns. *VLDB J.*, 12(3), 2003.

[30] A. Nash and B. Ludäscher. Processing first-order queries under limited access patterns. In *PODS*, 2004.

[31] C. H. Papadimitriou. *Computational Complexity.* Addison-Wesley, 1994.

[32] Y. Sagiv and M. Yannakakis. Equivalences among relational expressions with the union and difference operators. *J. ACM*, 27(4):633–655, 1980.

[33] L. J. Stockmeyer. The polynomial-time hierarchy. *TCS*, 3(1):1–22, 1976.

[34] R. van der Meyden. The complexity of querying indefinite data about linearly ordered domains. *JCSS*, 54(1), 1997.

[35] J. S. Vitter and M. Wang. Approximate computation of multidimensional aggregates of sparse data using wavelets. In *SIGMOD*, 1999.

[36] S. Zilberstein. Using anytime algorithms in intelligent systems. *AI magazine*, 17(3), 1996.

Skyline Queries with Noisy Comparisons

Benoit Groz[*†]
benoit.groz@lri.fr

Tova Milo[*]
milo@cs.tau.ac.il

[*]Tel Aviv University, School of Computer Science
Tel Aviv
Israel

[†]Univ Paris-Sud, LRI, UMR 8623, and INRIA
Orsay, F-91405
France

ABSTRACT

We study in this paper the computation of skyline queries - a popular tool for multicriteria data analysis - in the presence of noisy input. Motivated by crowdsourcing applications, we present the first algorithms for skyline evaluation in a computation model where the input data items can only be compared through noisy comparisons. In this model comparisons may return wrong answers with some probability, and confidence can be increased through independent repetitions of a comparison. Our goal is to minimize the number of comparisons required for computing or verifying a candidate skyline, while returning the correct answer with high probability. We design output-sensitive algorithms, namely algorithms that take advantage of the potentially small size of the skyline, and analyze the number of comparison rounds of our solutions. We also consider the problem of predicting the most likely skyline given some partial information in the form of noisy comparisons, and show that optimal prediction is computationally intractable.

1. INTRODUCTION

The rapid expansion of data generated by web users, sensor networks, and other noisy/uncertain data sources, raises new challenges for decision support systems. We focus in this paper on the computation of skyline queries - a popular tool for multicriteria data analysis - in the presence of noisy input. Given a set of data items, the skyline is the subset of items (a.k.a. Pareto optima) that are not "dominated", where an item is dominated if there is another item that is superior for every criterion. For instance, consider a scenario in which we wish to identify which cities offer the highest salaries together with high quality education. The skyline and dominated items are as illustrated in Figure 1.

Skyline queries are traditionally viewed as a problem of computing maximal vectors in a multidimensional space $\mathbb{R}^d$; data items correspond to points and each criterion corresponds to one dimension. Much research has been devoted to efficient skyline computation in the presence of exact data.

PODS'15, May 31–June 4, 2015, Melbourne, Victoria, Australia.

ACM 978-1-4503-2757-2/15/05 ...$15.00.
http://dx.doi.org/10.1145/2745754.2745775 .

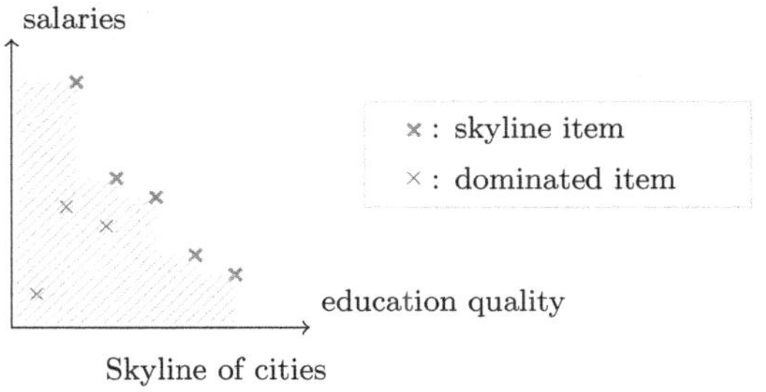

Figure 1: Skyline example

For the noisy case, the main approaches so far deal with the computational complexity of skyline queries when the input is a set of points with uncertain location. In contrast, we consider here a different setting where no information is given a priori about point location and points can only be compared, through noisy comparisons, along each dimension. We study the complexity of skyline computation here in terms of the required number of such comparisons.

This setting is motivated by the processing of skyline queries in crowdsourcing scenarios. In such settings, uncertainty is inherent, numerical estimates are not always relevant, and the focus lies in general on the cost of interaction with the crowd rather than computational complexity. To illustrate, let us consider a crowdsourcing scenario based on the example from Figure 1. Information about the average salary or schooling in different cities may be missing and people may not be able to return numerical estimates. Instead, comparing different cities may be more natural (Marcus et al. [34], for instance, show that comparisons provide more accurate rankings than ratings in certain Crowdsourcing experiments). Therefore to compute the skyline with the help of the crowd we can ask people questions of the form "is the education system superior in city x or city y?" or "can I expect a better salary in city x or city y". Of course, people are likely to make mistakes, and so each question is typically posed to multiple people. Our objective is to minimize the number of questions that need to be issued to the crowd, while returning the correct skyline with high probability.

We refer to our computation model as the *noisy comparison model*. We assume that items are fully ordered along each dimension. The order is unknown but items can be compared through oracles $(<_i)_{i\leq d}$, where $<_i$ compares a pair of items on dimension i. Each call to the comparison oracle would intuitively be implemented in our crowd scenario by asking a new person to compare two items on a particular dimension. In order to take into account noisy answers, we model queries to the comparison oracle as i.i.d. random boolean variables that may return an erroneous answer with probability bounded away from 1/2, e.g., $p < 1/3$. The assumption here is that there is an underlying ground truth, but the oracle may make mistakes. We thus design algorithms to mitigate those mistakes. Our cost model reports the number of oracle calls required for skyline computation, rather than computational complexity. Our assumption that error is bounded away from 1/2 makes sense for real-life scenarios as it is hard to distinguish error probabilities close to 1/2 from statistical noise.

Of course the model is a simplification of actual crowd behavior and evaluating skyline queries on a real crowd raises many further issues which we leave for future work, such as estimating the error rate of workers and dealing with varying error rates. Nevertheless the formal results in this paper may serve as a yardstick on what could be expected from the performance of algorithms in refined crowdsourcing models.

Contributions. In this paper, we provide the first algorithms for skyline queries in the noisy comparison model, and evaluate their performance with respect to the following parameters:

- the number of input items n
- the dimension (number of criteria) d
- the error probability tolerated for the result δ
- the (unknown) skyline cardinality k

Specifically, we show that if we want our algorithms to return the correct answer with probability at least $1 - \delta$

- we can check if a candidate set of k items is the skyline with $O(dnk \log \frac{1}{\delta})$ or $O(dn \log \frac{dk}{\delta})$ comparisons,
- the skyline can be computed with $O(dkn \log(dk/\delta))$, $O(dk^2 n \log(k/\delta))$ or $O(dn \log \frac{dn}{\delta})$ comparisons.
- $\Omega(n \log \frac{k}{\delta})$ comparisons are necessary to check a candidate skyline in the worst case (hence also to compute the skyline).

These algorithms rely on sorting, binary search, and maxima procedures from the literature. The complexity of the corresponding problems in presence of noisy comparisons has indeed been established in [16] as $\Theta(n \log(n/\delta))$, $\Theta(\log(n/\delta))$, and $\Theta(n \log(1/\delta))$. Our results thus show that naïvely sorting the data along all dimensions and computing the skyline based on the corresponding orders is optimal for constant d when $k = \Omega(n)$, and we provide more efficient solutions when this is not the case.

We also analyze the number of rounds #rounds required by our algorithms when all comparisons whose execution has been decided at some point of the algorithm are processed in a single round in parallel. This measure is in particular relevant for crowdsourcing scenarios where questions are issued in batches, hence the number of successive batches provides some measure on the time required to complete the scenario. Obtaining low #rounds for sorting-based algorithms proved challenging. The first (and so far unique) efficient parallel sorting algorithm in presence of noise derives from the notoriously complex AKS comparator circuit network, which achieves an optimal #rounds of $O(\log n)$ rounds. We also design a simpler algorithm that does not rely on the AKS network, runs in (optimal) $O(n \log \frac{n}{\delta})$ noisy comparison, and uses $O(n^{\alpha})$ rounds for any (arbitrarily small) constant $\alpha > 0$.

To achieve our results, this paper slightly extends several results from the skyline [28] and fault-tolerant sorting [32] literature to fit our arbitrary dimension and arbitrary precision setting. Finally, to complete the picture, we also consider an incremental scenario where some noisy comparisons were already performed, and the task is to process or complement the collected information in order to compute the most likely skyline. We thus prove that results from [19] about maxima computation can be extended to show that in presence of arbitrary sorting information (a multiset of noisy comparison results), it is Θ_2^p-hard for every dimension d to:

- compute the most likely skyline
- decide which additional comparison will most increase our confidence on the skyline.

This setting may in particular be relevant for our Crowdsourcing scenario if one endeavours to make the best of the comparison data available instead of computing this information from scratch.

Organization. Section 2 introduces formally our model and the problems we investigate. The results from the literature that we exploit in this paper (e.g., sorting and searching with noisy comparisons) are introduced in Section 2, whereas Section 7 provides a broader overview of related work. Section 3 investigates the complexity of verifying a candidate skyline, and those techniques are exploited in Section 4 to devise algorithms for computing skylines. The latency of our algorithms is analyzed in Section 5. Finally, Section 6 is devoted to our hardness results for the optimal exploitation of available information in skyline computation.

2. TECHNICAL PRELIMINARIES

Comparison-based results for computing skylines in the noiseless case typically rely on sorting and max algorithms and bounds [31]. In this section we first present our computation model. Then we survey skyline problems in the noiseless case. Finally we discuss sorting and max algorithms and bounds with noisy comparisons.

2.1 Model and Notations

Let S denote a set of n items. We assume these items admit a full (but not necessarily strict) order $\leq_i$ along d dimensions $i \in \{1, \ldots, d\}$. These implicit orders are not known and can only be discovered through queries of the form "is item v' superior to item v along dimensions i; i.e., $v \leq_i v'$?". We also write $v \preceq v'$ to denote that $v \leq_i v'$ for each $i \leq d$. When $v \preceq v'$ and there is some $i \leq d$ such that $v <_i v'$, we say that v' *dominates* v, which we denote by $v \preccurlyeq v'$. The notation extends to any set of items C: $v \preccurlyeq C$ iff there exists some $v' \in C$ such that $v \preccurlyeq v'$. Finally, we denote the lexicographic order among items with $<_{\text{lex}}$: $v <_{\text{lex}} v'$ iff there is $j \leq d$ satisfying both (1) for all $i < j$, $v \leq_i v'$, and (2) $v <_j v'$.

DEFINITION 1. *Given a set of d-dimensional items S, the* skyline *of S is the set of items that are not dominated (we assume that two items can not coincide):*

$$Sky(S) = \{v \in S \mid \forall v' \in S \setminus \{v\}, \exists i \leq d.\, v >_i v'\}.$$

REMARK 1. *Skylines are a generalization to multiple dimensions of the maximum problem: for $d = 1$, the skyline $Sky(S)$ is the maximal item of S. We therefore only consider the case $d \geq 2$ in the proofs.*

Noisy comparison model. The *noisy* comparison model assumes we are given access to an oracle that takes as input a pair of items v, v' together with a dimension $i \leq d$, and answers with probability at least[1] $1 - p$ whether $v \leq_i v'$, where p is a fixed constant $p < 1/2$ (say, $p \leq 1/3$). We assume that oracle queries are independent, so that repeating a query decreases the probability of error. The *noiseless* comparison model corresponds to the particular case where $p = 0$.

We shall also consider the more limited *noisy boolean variable* model from [16] where the algorithm takes as input a set of boolean variables and an oracle providing with error probability $p \leq 1/3$ the correct value of the variables. The latter can be considered as a noisy comparison model where each item can only be compared to a specific item representing variable "0".

The problems we consider in these models take as input a parameter δ called the *tolerance*, and the algorithms must return the correct answer with error probability at most δ. Henceforth we shall abbreviate error probability as err. pr. and omit to mention that error probability is obviously allowed to be smaller than δ.

Complexity measure. Our focus is on the worst case *oracle complexity*; the number of calls to the comparison oracle. But at each step of their execution, our algorithms may require extensive computation, based on previous comparison answers, to decide which comparisons should be asked next or which answer should be returned. Unless specified otherwise, our upper bounds will therefore deal with *computational complexity*. The latter of course bounds from above oracle complexity.

Problems of interest. The problem that we wish to investigate is the following:

Skyline computation problem:
Input: S: set of n items, δ: tolerance
Objective: compute Sky(S) with error probability δ.

Before we tackle this Skyline computation problem, we shall address the simpler problem of checking a candidate skyline:

Skyline verification problem:
Input: S: set of n items, C: candidate set, δ: tolerance
Objective: Check $C = $ Sky(S) with error probability δ.

We shall in particular investigate *output sensitive* algorithms, namely algorithms whose complexity depends on the number k of items in the skyline. Of course, we do not assume prior knowledge of this number, so the algorithm has to guess the value of k.

2.2 Complexity of noiseless skylines

Before going into the noisy model we first recall results for the noiseless case. Most results in the literature analyze the computational complexity of skyline queries rather than oracle complexity. But the lower bounds generally count the comparisons required to compute the skyline, and conversely a few algorithms guarantee a low oracle complexity under some restrictions.

Of course the oracle complexity is at most $O(dn \log n)$ since sorting the input along all dimensions solves any problem w.r.t. oracle complexity. For $d = 2$ a tight lower bound of $f_{\text{sort}}(n) + n - 1$ on the oracle complexity was proved by Yao [45], where $f_{\text{sort}}(n)$ denotes the number of comparisons required to sort n items. For $d = 3$, an upper bound of $2n \log_2 n + O(n)$ comparisons follows from Kung et al's algorithm [31]; a lower constant factor than the naïve sorting approach, but one checks easily that Kung et al's algorithm does not guarantee better constant factors for oracle complexity than naïve sorting beyond $d = 3$. A bound of $n \log_2 k + O(n\sqrt{\log k})$ was recently established [11], matching the information-theoretic lower bound of $n \log_2 k$ comparisons [28].

We are not aware of results on the oracle complexity of skyline for higher dimension. The question of computing an asymptotic equivalent for the oracle complexity of skylines beyond $d = 2$ is actually left open in [11]. For arbitrary large d, a few algorithms nevertheless outperform the naïve sorting approach in terms of computational and (thereby also) oracle complexity when k is small enough.

A standard skyline algorithm allows to compute the skyline in $O(dnk)$. For this we can for instance maintain a partial skyline S_i for $i = 0, \ldots, k$ containing the i greatest skyline points for lexicographic order, together with the set R_i of points that are not dominated by S_i ($S_0 = \emptyset$, R_0 is the whole input). At step i we compute S_{i+1} in $O(dn)$ from S_i by adding the largest item of R_i for lexicographic order, then compute R_{i+1} from R_i, also in $O(dn)$ by removing all items that are dominated by this largest item. This algorithm is essentially the one we shall adopt in presence of noisy comparison, except that we will not maintain R_i due to the higher cost of this screening operation in presence of noise. When R_i is not available, the computation of S_{i+1} from S_i and the set of all input items has a higher cost, though.

A shrewder algorithm with low computational complexity for small values of k and d has been proposed by Kirkpatrick and Seidel [28], based on a Divide and Conquer paradigm. The authors only investigate the complexity for constant d, but we outline in the Appendix an analysis for arbitrary dimensions:

THEOREM 1 (ADAPTED FROM [28]). *The skyline can be computed in $O(d^2 n \log^{d-2} k)$ (computational complexity)*[2].

[1]The algorithms are robust to an adversary oracle that could return a correct answer instead of an incorrect one.

[2]Throughout the paper, we abuse notations and write $d-2$ for $\max(1, d-2)$, $d-3$ for $\max(1, d-3)$, etc.

2.3 Computing in the noisy comparison model

While skyline computation has not been previously studied (to the best of our knowledge) in the noisy comparison model, several other operators were investigated: the OR problem decides if one of n boolean input variables is `true`, whereas MAX returns the maximum of the n items, SORTING returns the input items in sorted order, and TOP-k returns the k largest items (in arbitrary order). Finally, BINARY SEARCH takes as input (1) an ordered list S of n items and (2) another item v, and returns the successor of v in S.

LEMMA 1 ([16]). *The problems above can be computed within the following bounds for computational complexity, which are tight even for oracle complexity:*

OR	$\Theta(n \log \frac{1}{\delta})$
MAX	$\Theta(n \log \frac{1}{\delta})$
SORTING	$\Theta(n \log \frac{n}{\delta})$
Binary search	$\Theta(\log \frac{n}{\delta})$
TOP-k	$\Theta(n \log \frac{\min(k,n-k)}{\delta})$

Actually, it is obvious that any algorithm for the noiseless case with complexity $f(n)$ can be turned into an algorithm with tolerance δ in presence of noise by repeating each comparison requested by the algorithm $\log(f(n)/\delta)$ times and taking majority vote: each noiseless comparison will thus be simulated by a comparison with tolerance $\delta/f(n)$, hence an overall error of δ by union bound [16]. The bounds of Lemma 1 show that for the problems considered we can do better.

The algorithms above assume the input oracle has constant error probability. While our access to data is limited to noisy comparisons, we shall consider any procedure computing some boolean condition (with the help of such comparisons) as an additional oracle that can be exploited by other queries. Our algorithms thus compute compositions of boolean queries, etc. In order to optimize the cost of such compositions, we investigate the cost of *trust-preserving* algorithms, whose tolerance is determined by that of the input oracle(s): for all $\delta < 1/3$ the output must be correct with err. pr. at most δ if the input oracle(s) has err. pr. δ. Trust-preserving algorithms can be pipelined; as observed in [36] for the similar ϵ-fault-tolerant model: a trust-preserving algorithm for the composition of functions (e.g. boolean functions) can be obtained through the composition of trust-preserving algorithms for these functions. In the case of OR, Newman provided a simple trust-preserving algorithm in linear time.

LEMMA 2 ([36]). *OR can be computed in $O(n)$ with a trust-preserving algorithm that returns the variable of minimal index among the true ones (if any).*

We can derive from this simple algorithm a *trust-preserving* algorithm for MAX. Assume w.l.o.g. the input oracle has err. pr. $\delta < 1/6$. We observe that we can simulate a comparison with err. pr. $\delta/2$ by majority of 3 comparisons having err. pr. δ. Furthermore the maximum of 4 items can be computed with err. pr. $\delta/2$ in $c = O(1)$.

LEMMA 3. *MAX can be computed in $O(n)$ with a trust-preserving algorithm, as illustrated in Algorithm 1.*

Algorithm 1: Algorithm $T(n, \delta)$

1 Partition input items into groups of 4 (last group may be smaller), AND compute with err. pr. $\delta/2$ the max within each group.
2 Apply recursively $T(n/4, \delta/2)$ to these $n/4$ candidate maxima (if $n > 4$).

PROOF. The cost of $T(n, \delta)$ satisfies the equation below: $C(n, \delta) = c \cdot \lceil n/4 \rceil + C(n/4, \delta/2) \leq c \cdot n + 3 \cdot C(n/4, \delta) = O(n)$. We show by induction that $T(n, \delta)$ errs with probability at most δ: the probability that the maximum has been unduly eliminated in step 1 is $\delta/2$, and the probability that it is eliminated in step 2 is also $\delta/2$ by induction hypothesis, hence an overall tolerance δ. □

Alternatively a slightly stronger result can be obtained as follows: [18] shows that MAX can be computed with a deterministic noisy tournament tree in $O(\log \log n)$ rounds, with $O(n)$ comparisons. A simple analysis of their proof shows the algorithm to be trust-preserving (we only need to maintain the dependency on ϵ throughout their proof).

In our skyline algorithm we repeatedly compute the maximal item (for $<_1$) that is not dominated by larger items. For this, we will use the following lemma:

LEMMA 4. *Let S denote a set of n items, P a boolean property on S, and $<$ a total order on S. Given an oracle that decides P with tolerance δ in time $\alpha(\delta)$, and a similar oracle with tolerance δ for $<$ in $\beta(\delta)$, one can compute $\max\{v \in S \mid v$ satisfies $P\}$ with tolerance δ in $O((\alpha(\delta) + \beta(\delta))n)$.*

PROOF. One can simply view the problem as the search of the maximum for a modified total order; $<^P$, defined from P by:

- $v <^P v'$ if $v < v' \wedge P(v')$
- $v <^P v'$ if $\neg P(v) \wedge P(v')$
- when $\neg P(v) \wedge \neg P(v')$, say v and v' are ties (any arbitrary choice would do)

We can clearly simulate in $O(\alpha(\delta) + \beta(\delta))$ an oracle with tolerance δ for $<^P$, using the oracles for $<$ and P. Furthermore, the maximum for P is the item we are looking for, therefore we can solve our problem by executing the max-algorithm of Lemma 3 on order $<^P$. □

We show in the next two sections how our skyline problems can be solved using the results about sorting and computing maxima with noisy comparisons.

3. SKYLINE VERIFICATION PROBLEM.

Dominance tests are a cornerstone of our skyline algorithms. We therefore begin our exposition of skyline algorithms with two procedures for dominance testing.

LEMMA 5. *Let $C \subseteq S, v \in S$.*

1. *We can check $v \preceq C$ with err. pr. δ in $O(d|C| \log \frac{1}{\delta})$*
2. *When the order of C is known along each dimension, we can check whether $v \preceq C$ in $O(d \log \frac{d|C|}{\delta})$ oracle complexity, with err. pr. δ .*

PROOF. (1) The first procedure views dominance testing as the composition of OR queries: $v \preceq C$ is equivalent to $\bigvee_{w \in C} \bigwedge_{i \le d} v \le_i w$. Each dominance test $v \preceq w = \bigwedge_{i=1}^{d} v \le_i w$ can be checked in $O(d)$ with err. pr. 1/3 using the OR algorithm from Lemma 1. Using these tests as the basic oracle of the OR algorithm, we can check $\bigvee_{w \in C} v \preceq w$ in $O(d|C| \log \frac{1}{\delta})$.

(2) Alternatively, assume we know the ordering $<_i$ for C in every dimension $i \le d$. We can then compute with err. pr. δ/d for each $i \in \{1, \dots, d\}$ the successor for $<_i$ of v in C. Using the binary search algorithm of Lemma 1, each successor can be computed with err. pr. δ/d in $O(\log \frac{d|C|}{\delta})$. We then deduce whether $v \preceq C$ without further oracle comparisons (though with possibly large computational cost). □

We are now ready to address the problem of checking a candidate skyline. We develop two algorithms that mostly differ on which procedure from Lemma 5 they adopt for dominance queries. The algorithms simply check the two properties (1) $C = \mathrm{Sky}(C)$ and (2) $\mathrm{Sky}(S) \subseteq C$ with err. pr. $\delta/2$. Both properties can be viewed as boolean combinations of dominance tests:

- $C = \mathrm{Sky}(C)$ iff $\bigwedge_{v \neq v' \in C} \neg(v \preceq v')$
- $C \supseteq \mathrm{Sky}(S)$ iff $\bigwedge_{v \in S} v \preceq C$.

Our first algorithm uses the first procedure of Lemma 5 for the dominance tests, whereas our second algorithm, presented below as Algorithm 2, first sorts C along all dimensions and then relies on binary search to process dominance queries

THEOREM 2. *Let $C \subseteq S$, we can check if $C = Sky(S)$*

1. *in $O(dn|C| \log \frac{1}{\delta})$ (computational complexity)*
2. *or with $O(dn \log \frac{d|C|}{\delta})$ oracle complexity.*

PROOF. We first observe that the two conditions above are necessary and sufficient to guarantee $\mathrm{Sky}(S) = C$.
(1) Each dominance test $v \preceq C$ can be checked in $O(d|C|)$ with err. pr. 1/3 using the first procedure of Lemma 5. Using these tests as the basic oracle for the OR algorithm, we check $C \supseteq \mathrm{Sky}(S)$ in $O(n|C| \log \frac{1}{\delta})$ calls to this dominance test, which yields $O(dn|C| \log \frac{1}{\delta})$. We use similarly the OR algorithm to check $C = \mathrm{Sky}(Cs)$ with the same complexity. Computational and Oracle complexity are the same for this algorithm.

(2) Line 1 of Algorithm 2 runs in $O(d|C| \log(d|C|/\delta))$ according to Lemma 1 (which in turn summarizes results from [16]). In line 2 we then check $C = \mathrm{Sky}(C)$ without any further call to the comparison oracle. When the orders computed in line 1 are correct, we can simulate in $O(d \log(d|C|/\delta))$ (oracle complexity) an oracle that for each item $v \in S$ checks with err. pr. $\delta/2$ if v is dominated by C, according to Lemma 5. Using this oracle, we can then check $\bigvee_{v \in S} v \preceq C$ with err. pr. $\delta/2$ in $O(n \cdot d \log(d|C|/\delta))$, by Newman's trust-preserving OR algorithm (see Lemma 2). This yields an overall oracle complexity of $O(dn \log(d|C|/\delta))$ for the algorithm. The computational complexity, however, may be higher due to the dominance tests and skyline computation on C (see discussion in Section 7). □

We do not have tight bounds for checking skylines in the general case, but we next prove that the second bound in

Algorithm 2: Skyline verification(S, C, δ)

1 Sort C along each dimension with err. pr. $\delta/(2d)$
2 **if** $C \neq \mathrm{Sky}(C)$ according to these orderings
3   **return false**
4 **else** Check $\bigwedge_{v \in S} v \preceq C$ with err. pr. $\delta/2$

Theorem 2 is optimal for constant d, whereas the first one is optimal for constant $|C|$.

PROPOSITION 1. *Let $C \subseteq S$. Checking if $C = Sky(S)$ has oracle complexity $\Omega(n \log |C| + dn \log(1/\delta))$.*

PROOF. The $\Omega(n \log_2 |C|)$ lower bound is actually a particular case of stronger bounds from the literature [4, 28]. We can also prove it directly from the information-theoretic bound in the noiseless case with $d = 2$, adapting the argument of Yao: even when items can be dominated by at most one item from C, there are at least $|C|^{n-|C|} \cdot |C|!$ possible ways to order items of C and assign each remaining items to its dominating point in C. Any algorithm checking the skyline must gather information sufficient to distinguish two such configurations, and therefore performs $\Omega(n \log_2 |C|)$ oracle comparisons (details are left for the Appendix).

The $\Omega(dn \log \frac{1}{\delta})$ lower bound derives from an immediate reduction of OR: assume that we wish to compute the disjunction of $d \times n$ noisy variables $x_{i,j}$ ($i \le n, j \le d$). Let $C = \{v_0\}$ denote the unique tuple with value 1 on dimension $d+1$ and 0 on the others. For each $i \in \{1, \dots, n\}$, let v_i denote the tuple $(x_{i,1}, \dots, x_{i,d}, 0)$. The disjunction is true if and only if $C \neq \mathrm{Sky}(S)$, which concludes our reduction. □

4. COMPUTING SKYLINE.

After the last section discussing skyline candidate verification, we now investigate the complexity of skyline computation. The oracle complexity of skyline computation (or actually any problem) is bounded from above by the complexity of sorting.

Algorithm 3: Full sort skyline algorithm(S, δ)

Sort C along each dimension with err. pr. δ/d
Deduce the skyline, assuming all orders are correct.

THEOREM 3. *Algorithm 3 computes Sky(S) with oracle complexity $O(dn \log(dn/\delta))$.*

PROOF. Each dimension can be sorted with err. pr. δ/d in $O(n \log(dn/\delta))$ according to Lemma 1. By union bound, all orders are then correct with err. pr. δ, so that any standard algorithm for noiseless skylines can compute the skyline based on these orders without further oracle calls. □

By reduction from skyline verification (Proposition 1), this is again optimal for constant d when the skyline contains $k = \Omega(n^c)$ $(c > 0)$ items. We next turn our attention to output-sensitive algorithms, namely algorithms that perform better when k is small. Recall that k denotes the number of items belonging to the skyline. Our output-sensitive algorithms for computing the skyline rely on the following auxiliary procedure:

Algorithm 4: Skysample$(S, \hat{k}, \delta)$

```
1  S_0 ← ∅
2  for i in 0, ..., k̂ − 1
3      Compute z ← max_{<lex} {v | v ⊀ S_i} with err. pr. δ/k̂
4      if z = ∅ return S_i
5      else S_{i+1} ← S_i ∪ z
6  return S_k̂

Oracle for <lex(v, v', δ):
7  Find l ← min{i | v <_i v'} with err. pr. δ/2
8  Find L ← min{i | v >_i v'} with err. pr. δ/2
9  if (L = Null or l ≼ L)
10     return true
11 else
12     return false
```

PROPOSITION 2. *Depending on the procedure adopted for dominance testing in line 3, Algorithm 4 computes the first* $\min(|Sky(S)|, \hat{k})$ *points of the skyline in decreasing lexicographic order*

1. *in* $O(dk^2 n \log(\hat{k}/\delta))$ *(computational complexity)*
2. *or with* $O(dkn \log(d\hat{k}/\delta))$ *oracle complexity.*

PROOF. Let S_i denote the set comprising the i items of Sky(S) having the highest rank for $<_{\text{lex}}$. Lines 7 to 12 show how an oracle for lexicographic comparison can be simulated in $O(d)$ with err. pr. 1/3, using Newman's OR algorithm (see Lemma 2). Using this oracle for lexicographic order and the oracle for dominance testing of Lemma 5 as basic oracles for the max-algorithm of Lemma 4, lines 3 to 5 compute iteratively S_{i+1} from S_i with the requested complexity:

(1) Using the first procedure for dominance testing of Lemma 5 we get the new skyline item with err. pr. $\delta/\hat{k}$ in $O(d \cdot i \cdot n \log(\hat{k}/\delta))$. Overall, we thus get k skyline items with err. pr. δ in $O(\sum_{i<k} d \cdot i \cdot n \log(\hat{k}/\delta)) = O(dk^2 n \log(\hat{k}/\delta))$.

(2) Using the second procedure of Lemma 5 yields the new skyline item with err. pr. $\delta/\hat{k}$ in $O(dn \log(d\hat{k}/\delta))$. Overall, we can thus get with err. pr. δ a set of k skyline items in $O(\sum_{i<k} dn \log(d\hat{k}/\delta)) = O(dkn \log(d\hat{k}/\delta))$. □

Remark: For $d = 2$, dominance tests are essentially trivial, so the problem can be solved in a simpler way in the sense that the algorithm needs only use MAX/OR algorithms and not binary insertion. The complexity of the first algorithm is lowered to $O(kn \log(\hat{k}/\delta))$.

We next present our main algorithm for computing skylines with noisy comparisons. The idea is to exploit the SkySample algorithm from Proposition 2, but since the value of k is not known in advance, we must be careful to set a small enough value of $\hat{k} \geq k$ in order to guarantee low complexity. We thus use Chan's trick [9] to "guess" k by binary search with increasing candidate values: the ith call to SkySample uses $k_i = 2^{2^i}$ instead of k, and $\delta/2^i$ instead of δ.

THEOREM 4. *Algorithm 5 computes Sky(S)*

1. *in* $O(dk^2 n \log(k/\delta))$ *(computational complexity)*
2. *or with* $O(dkn \log(dk/\delta))$ *oracle complexity.*

Algorithm 5: Skyline computation(S, δ)

```
i ← 1;  k_i ← 4;  compl←false
while compl= false
    R ← SkySample(S, k_i, δ/2^i)
    if |R| < k_i
        compl←true
    else
        i ← i + 1
        k_i ← 2^{2^i}
return R
```

PROOF. The probability of returning a wrong answer at round i is $\delta/2^i$. By union bound, the error probability sums up to at most $\sum_{i \leq \lfloor \log\log k \rfloor} \delta/2^i \leq \delta$ overall.

(1) Using the first procedure for dominance testing in Proposition 2, the computational (hence oracle) complexity of the algorithm is at most $O(dn \sum_{i=1}^{\lfloor \log\log k \rfloor} k_i^2 \log(k_i \cdot 2^i/\delta)) + O(dk^2 n \log(k/\delta)) = O(dk^2 n \log(k/\delta))$.

(2) Alternatively, if we use the second procedure for dominance testing instead, the oracle complexity of Algorithm 5 is in $O(dn \sum_{i=1}^{\lfloor \log\log k \rfloor} k_i \log(dk_i \cdot 2^i/\delta)) + O(dkn \log(dk/\delta))$, which amounts to $O(dkn \log(dk/\delta))$. □

5. DELAY IN TERMS OF ROUNDS

In the algorithms above, some oracle calls depend on the result of previous calls. This may become an issue in, e.g., crowdsourcing scenarios where tasks involve substantial delays. We therefore analyze the number of rounds required by each algorithm when all comparisons are processed simultaneously in a same round, unless their execution is determined by the outcome of some comparison that has not been processed yet, in which case it is left for future rounds. A formal definition of this number of rounds #rounds can be found in [18].

Before presenting our results we survey some previous work on #rounds for binary search and sorting, and improve some of these results, then use the improved bounds to analyze our skyline algorithms.

5.1 Parallel algorithms with noise: sorting

Feige et al. [16] already investigate the question of parallelism for MAX and Sorting with noisy comparisons when using a maximum of n processors. In our setting we instead focus on the model of Newman [36] and Goyal and Saks [18]. This model, which they apply to the MAX and OR problems, does not restrict the number of simultaneous comparisons. This model seems more relevant for our crowd scenario as we can recruit additional workers when needed. In particular, Newman [36] shows a trust-preserving OR algorithm in $O(n \log(1/\delta))$ with $O(\log^* n)$ rounds. Goyal and Saks [18] prove a corresponding $\Omega(\log^* n)$ lower bound and also propose a trust-preserving MAX algorithm in $O(n)$ with $O(\log\log n)$ rounds (the algorithm is presented for constant tolerance, but a careful analysis of their proof shows it is error preserving). The $O(n \log n)$ sorting algorithm of Feige et al. [16] mentioned in Lemma 1 relies on binary search to sort items incrementally by insertion, and therefore requires $\Omega(n \log(n/\delta))$ rounds as their binary search algorithm requires $O(\log(n/\delta))$. We first show that #rounds of binary search can be lowered to $O(\log n)$.

THEOREM 5. *Binary Search can be solved with err. pr. δ in time $O(\log(n/\delta))$ and **with** $O(\log n)$ **rounds**.*

LEMMA 6 (CHERNOFF BOUND). *Let $X_1, \ldots, X_k$ denote i.i.d. 0-1 variables with $\Pr(X_i = 1) = \rho$, where $\rho < 1/2$. Then we have*

$$\Pr(\sum_{i=1}^{k} X_i \geq k/2) \leq (2\rho e)^{k/2} e^{-\rho k}$$

PROOF. This is the standard Chernoff bound with $\mu = \rho k$, $1 + \delta = 1/(2\rho)$.

$$\Pr(\sum_{i=1}^{k} X_i \geq (1+\delta)\mu) \leq \left(e^{\delta}/(1+\delta)^{1+\delta}\right)^{\mu}$$
$$\leq e^{\delta\mu}(2\rho)^{k/2}$$
$$\leq e^{k/2-\rho k}(2\rho)^{k/2}$$

□

We next prove the theorem.

PROOF (ADAPTED FROM [16]). When $\delta \geq 1/n$ the result is obvious since the $O(\log(n/\delta))$ rounds of [16] satisfies our bound. We therefore restrict our attention to the case $\delta < 1/n$. Given a comparison oracle with error probability $p < 1/3$, we can use majority vote to simulate a comparison oracle with error probability at most $2^{-\log(1/\delta)/\log n}/(2e)$, in $O(\log(1/\delta)/\log n)$ and with constant number of rounds. We then process all comparisons of the binary search algorithm described in [16] with this oracle.

This algorithm interprets a binary search as a random walk down the binary search tree. In short, let $x_1 \leq x_2 \leq \cdots \leq x_n$ denote the n input items in sorted order. We fix $x_0 = -\infty$ and $x_{n+1} = \infty$. For each $i \leq n$, the ith leaf of the tree is associated to the interval $[x_i, x_i + 1)$ and the interval of an internal node is the union of both children intervals. The random walk starts at the root of the tree. Each step of the algorithm compares the value of the item searched with the bounds of the children intervals and proceeds to the corresponding child. In case of a contradiction (the node appears to be outside both children intervals) the walk backtracks to the parent of the current node. Finally, when a leaf is reached, since there are no children to move to, a counter is incremented instead when the comparisons confirm the interval, and decremented if the comparisons contradict the interval.

Using our comparison oracle, we make sure the probability that each step of the random walk moves toward the correct destination with err. pr. at most $\rho = 2^{-\log(1/\delta)/\log n}/(2e)$. By the Chernoff bound therefore, after $k = 2\log n$ steps the probability that the walk does not terminate at the correct leaf is at most $(2\rho e)^{k/2} = (2^{-\log(1/\delta)/\log n})^{\log n} = \delta$. The cost of the whole algorithm is clearly $O(\log(1/\delta))$ and #rounds is $O(\log n)$. □

The next results show that very efficient parallel algorithms can be obtained while maintaining the number of comparisons within the optimal $O(n \log(n/\delta))$ bound.

THEOREM 6. *SORTING can be solved **with err. pr.** δ in time $O(n\log(n/\delta))$ and with $O(\log n)$ rounds.*

PROOF (ADAPTED FROM [32]). The proof almost literally follows the proof of [32], replacing error $1/n^2$ by δ (we assume $\delta < 1/n^2$). Their sorting algorithm relies on a recursive application of some AKS partial-sorting network whose properties are described in the following lemma.

LEMMA 7 (COROLLARY 2.1 IN [32]). *Let X be a set of size m and let $\beta = 1 - 1/(8\log 6)$. Given a comparison oracle with err. pr. ρ for any (not necessarily constant) $\rho < 1/3$, we can compute with err. pr. at most $\rho^{\Theta(\log m)}$, in time[3] $O(m \log m)$ and with $O(\log m)$ rounds, a partition of X into disjoint sets $\{S, X_1, \ldots, X_{\overline{m}}\}$ where $\overline{m} = \Theta(m^{1-\beta})$, $|S| = O(m^{3/4})$, and $|X_1| = \cdots = |X_{\overline{m}}| = \Theta(m^{\beta})$ such that the items in X_i are smaller than items in X_j for all $i < j$.*

Step 1- Using Lemma 7, we compute with err. pr $\delta/10$ a partition $X = S \cup X_1 \cup X_2 \cup \cdots \cup X_{\overline{n}}$ such that all the items in X_i are smaller than all the items in X_j for $i < j$, where $\overline{n} = \Theta(n^{1-\beta})$. To obtain such accuracy we need for some constant c to make sure that $\rho^{c \log n} \leq \delta/10$. This can be guaranteed via majority vote by repeating each comparison $O(\log\delta/\log n)$ times, thus lowering ρ to $2^{\log(\delta/10)/(c\log n)}$. The cost of applying this step is at most $O(n\log(1/\delta))$, and #rounds remains $O(\log n)$.

Step 2 and 3- Using Lemma 3 we compute in parallel for all $i \leq \overline{n}$ the maximum item M_i of X_i with tolerance $\delta/(10\overline{n})$. We then sort $P = S \cup \{M_1, \ldots, M_{\overline{n}}\}$ using parallel MergeSort [13], repeating each comparison via majority vote so that P is sorted with err. pr $\delta/10$. Based on the sorted order of P, we can derive the approximately correct position for each item in S. In particular, we partition X as

$$X = \bigcup_{1 \leq i \leq \overline{n}} Y_i$$

where $Y_i = X_i \cup \{s \in S \mid M_{i-1} < s \leq M_i\}$ for $i < \overline{n}$ and $Y_{\overline{n}} = X_{\overline{n}} \cup \{s \in S \mid s > M_{\overline{n}-1}\}$ (and M_0 is assumed to be $-\infty$). One checks easily $|Y_i| = \Theta(n^{\beta})$. Since $|P| = O(n^{3/4})$ the cost of computing maxima and sorting P, thus building the partition, is $O(n\log(n/\delta))$ and #rounds is $O(\log n)$.

Step 4- To sort the items within Y_i recursively, we use an adaptive approach. In parallel, we recursively sort Y_i with tolerance δ^{β}. Let p_0 denote the probability that there are 2 or more unsorted groups.

$$p_0 \leq \binom{\overline{n}}{2}\delta^{2\beta}$$
$$\leq 0.5n^{2(1-\beta)} \cdot \delta^{2\beta}$$
$$\leq \delta/2$$

The last derivation is justified by $2\beta - 1 > 2(1-\beta)$ together with $\delta < 1/n$. Observe that δ decreases at the same rate as n so $\delta < 1/n$ is maintained through the recursive calls.

Step 5 and 6- We now detect which groups of the form Y_i remain unsorted. We check the correctness of the order reported by the recursive sorting algorithm for each i in parallel. This is achieved with err. pr. $\delta/10$ by comparing each pair of adjacent items $O(\log(n/\delta))$ times. With probability at least $1 - \delta/10$, we will detect the (probably) unique unsorted group, with constant number of rounds. We then sort this group using MergeSort, repeating each comparison via majority vote so that the group is sorted with err. pr $\delta/10$. The number of items contained in the unsorted group is at most $O(n^{\beta})$, so the cost of this sorting step is $O(n\log(n/\delta))$ and #rounds is $O(\log n)$.

[3]It's not clear to me how the AKS (i.e., the expanders) are computed efficiently. But it must be feasible otherwise their Theorem 5.1 would not hold

Summing over all steps, we check immediately that the algorithm has error probability at most δ. The cost $C(n,\delta)$ and number of rounds $T(n,\delta)$ of the algorithm satisfy:

$$C(n,\delta) = n^{1-\beta}C(n^\beta,\delta^\beta) + O(n\log(n/\delta))$$

$$T(n,\delta) = T(n^\beta,\delta^\beta) + O(\log n)$$

This gives $C(n,\delta) \in O(n\log(n/\delta))$ and $T(n) \in O(\log n)$. $\square$

As the AKS network [5] on which this algorithm is based is notoriously complex [42], we propose another sorting algorithm in $O(n\log(n/\delta))$ that requires more rounds asymptotically but is based on a much simpler binary insertion merging procedure and therefore may be more practical. We decompose our algorithm into β stages, as illustrated in Figure 2. At stage $k \in \{0,\dots,\beta-1\}$, the algorithm receives a partition of the input into sorted groups of size $n^{\frac{k}{\beta}}$ (input sets at stage 0 are singletons, and the last group may be smaller). During this stage, the algorithm computes a partition into sorted groups of size $n^{\frac{k+1}{\beta}}$ by merging $j = n^{\frac{1}{\beta}}$ groups one by one. Let $S_1,\dots,S_j$ denote the groups to be merged. In order to merge S_i into $\bigcup_{h<i} S_h$, we execute in parallel $n^{\frac{k}{\beta}}$ binary searches with err. pr. $\delta/(\beta n)$; one for each item in S_i.

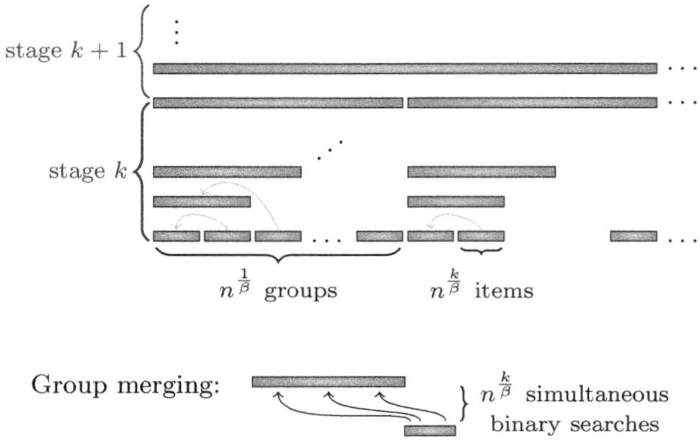

Figure 2: Parallel sort with noisy comparisons

THEOREM 7. *For every $\alpha > 0$, SORTING can be solved in $O(n\log\frac{n}{\delta})$ with $O(n^\alpha)$ rounds with a simple merging approach based on parallel insertion.*

PROOF. The binary searches within each stage can be processed in parallel because the order of items in S_h is already known, and will not be contradicted as long as the binary searches return correct answers. Over the whole execution of the algorithm, at most βn binary searches are executed (β per item), hence (1) by union bound all insertions are correct with err. pr. at most δ, and (2) the complexity of the algorithm is in $O(\beta n\log(n/\delta))$. The number of rounds during each stage is $O(n^{\frac{1}{\beta}}\log n)$ according to Theorem 5. Taking $\beta = 1 + \lfloor 1/\alpha \rfloor$ thus concludes the proof. $\square$

5.2 Parallel algorithms with noise: skylines

We next analyze the number of rounds required by each of our skyline algorithms, when multiple comparisons can be processed simultaneously. The maximal number of comparisons in a round is roughly equal to the average number of comparisons per round (number of comparisons divided by number of rounds), as detailed in the proof (deferred to the Appendix).

THEOREM 8. *Analyzing #rounds for our algorithms yields the following results:*

- *One can check a candidate skyline C in:*

Oracle complexity	*Rounds*
$dn\lvert C\rvert\log(1/\delta)$	$\log^*(d)\cdot\log^*(n)\cdot\log^*(\lvert C\rvert)$
$dn\log(d\lvert C\rvert/\delta)$	$\log^* n\cdot\log\lvert C\rvert$

- *One can compute the skyline in:*

Oracle complexity	*Rounds*
$dn\log(dn/\delta)$	$\log n$
$dk^2n\log(k/\delta)$	$k\cdot\log\log n\cdot\log^*(d)\cdot\log^*(k)$
$dkn\log(dk/\delta)$	$k\cdot\log\log n\cdot\log k$

where every entry is implicitly an asymptotic $O()$, and complexity refers to oracle *complexity.*

We can similarly analyze the number of simultaneous comparisons per round. We omit exact expressions.

6. EXPLOITING AVAILABLE DATA

Up until now we studied algorithms that query a comparison oracle to find the correct skyline (with a low probability of error *a priori*). We next turn our attention to the setting where some comparison information is already available and the objective is to exploit this information in an optimal way with respect to computational complexity. In this new approach, we now assume that on each dimension all orders have equal probability a priori, but the (noisy) comparison information adds to our knowledge on the hidden order, which raises the question of computing the most likely skylines given the information available. This fits for instance a scenario where the computation may be interrupted after it runs out of time or resources. It is also justified in [19] as a model of CrowdSourcing that is simpler to implement when human workers do not behave as predicted and fail to answer some of the questions due to unacceptable response time or lack of knowledge.

We henceforth call the result of a comparison a *vote*; for instance: "$v <_i v'$". Two questions of interest in our model are (1) how can we compute the most likely skyline given a multiset of votes (without executing any further comparison), and (2) given a multiset of votes, which pairs of objects should we compare next with the oracle (and on which dimension) to maximize our information on Sky(S). Formally, we first define problem MLsky and show it is computationally intractable in general. We then do the same for NVsky. Those two problems, standing respectively for Maximum Likelihood and Next Vote, generalize to multiple dimensions problems from [19] about maxima computation. Those problems were proved hard when $d = 1$ [19] but the case $d = 1$ is somewhat particular and it does not seem easy to cast it as a particular case of higher dimension skylines: the nature of the problem changes a bit from $d \geq 2$, with the number of possible skylines raising from n to 2^n... So we next explain how those hardness results extend to arbitrary dimension.

Maximum Likelihood Skyline (MLsky):
Input: p: err. pr., $M \in (\mathbb{N}^{S\times S})^d$: input votes
Objective: compute the most likely skyline; $P \subseteq S$ that maximizes $\Pr(\text{Sky}(S) = P \mid M)$.

We first detail our setting and conventions. To simplify the proofs we assume that objects admit a full and *strict* ordering along each dimension, and we also assume that all $(n!)^d$ d-tuples of orders are equally likely a priori (before any votes are known). The proofs generalize however to the case where ties would be allowed.

The comparison oracle again errs with probability at most p on each execution independently, for some $p \leq 1/3$. Given any d-tuple v and $k \leq d$, $v.k$ shall denote the kth entry of v. The entries of $M.k$ count the answers of the oracle for the corresponding comparisons on dimension k: $(M.k)_{i,j}$ is the number of times the oracle answered "$i <_k j$". Using Bayes rule we can determine the probability a posteriori of a possible world, given the list M of vote matrices. The *possible worlds* are all d-tuples specifying an order for each dimension. To each possible world π corresponds a skyline, denoted $\text{Sky}(\pi)$, which can be computed in polynomial time using skyline algorithms on noiseless comparisons. The probability $\Pr(\text{Sky}(S) = P \mid M)$ can thus be derived by summing possible worlds in which P is the skyline:

$$\begin{aligned}\Pr(\text{Sky}(S) = P \mid M) &= \sum_{\pi:\text{Sky}(\pi)=P} \Pr(\pi \mid M) \\ &= \sum_{\pi:\text{Sky}(\pi)=P} \Pr(M \mid \pi) \cdot \Pr(\pi) / \Pr(M)\end{aligned}$$

$\Pr(\pi)/\Pr(M)$ does not depend on π, so the most likely skyline P is obtained by maximizing

$$\sum_{\pi:\text{Sky}(\pi)=P} \Pr(M \mid \pi) = \sum_{\pi:\text{Sky}(\pi)=P} \prod_{i=1}^{d} \Pr(M.i \mid \pi.i).$$

The probabilities $\Pr(M.i \mid \pi.i)$ can easily be computed [19]. The number of possible worlds, however, is exponential, even for $d = 1$, so this only provides an exponential algorithm (though in polynomial space) for computing $\Pr(\text{Sky}(S) = P)$. We next show that a polynomial algorithm is unlikely.

When $d = 1$, the problem MLsky is actually the problem of computing the most likely maximum in elections. When p is small enough, the most likely maximum coincides with the winner elected by the Kemeny voting rule [19]. The determination of the Kemeny winner is Θ_2^p-complete [23], where Θ_2^p is the class of problems solvable by a polynomial Turing machine with a logarithmic number of calls to an NP oracle. The hardness result even holds when the input votes are guaranteed to elect a single Kemeny winner. We exploit this to show that MLsky is Θ_2^p hard for every dimension d.

PROPOSITION 3. *MLsky is Θ_2^p-hard* **for every** *d.*

PROOF. The proof works by reduction from the unique Kemeny winner problem. We assume that votes are the same along all dimensions and guarantee a unique Kemeny winner x (obviously the same in all dimensions). We then show in the Appendix that when p is small enough, the most likely skyline consists of a single item, corresponding to the Kemeny winner x. □

We next turn our attention to the Next vote problem which decides "which comparison should be asked next" as specified in [19]. The Next vote problem computes which comparison should be executed next to maximize the expected probability that the maximum-likelihood skyline is correct. More formally, the probability that we can compute correctly the skyline after asking the additional comparison between x and y on dimension i is given by:

$$\begin{aligned}&\max_{P_0} \sum_{\pi:\text{Sky}(\pi)=P_0} \Pr(\pi \mid M \wedge x >_i y) \Pr(x >_i y \mid M) \\ &+ \max_{P_0} \sum_{\pi:\text{Sky}(\pi)=P_0} \Pr(\pi \mid M \wedge x <_i y) \Pr(x <_i y \mid M)\end{aligned}$$

Applying Baye's Rule and removing irrelevant factors, one checks easily that to maximize this probability we need to maximize

$$\begin{aligned}F_{x,y,i} = &\max_{P_0} \sum_{\pi:\text{Sky}(\pi)=P_0} \Pr(M \wedge x >_i y \mid \pi) \\ &+ \max_{P_0} \sum_{\pi:\text{Sky}(\pi)=P_0} \Pr(M \wedge x <_i y \mid \pi)\end{aligned}$$

We can now formally define the Next Vote problem and claim it is computationally intractable (the proof is deferred to the Appendix).

Next Vote for Skyline (NVsky):
Input: p: err. pr., $M \in (\mathbb{N}^{S\times S})^d$: input votes
Objective: compute the next comparison to ask; $(x, y, i) \in S^2 \times \{1, \ldots, d\}$ that maximizes $F_{x,y,i}$.

PROPOSITION 4. *NVsky is Θ_2^p-hard* **for every** *d.*

The proofs generalize to the case when ties are allowed because both hardness results rely on a reduction from the (unique) Kemeny winner problem, the complexity of which is not affected by ties [23, 22]. The fact that the two problems studied above are computationally hard motivates future study of possible approximation schemes that would be computable in polynomial time and yet provide reasonable quality guarantees.

Similarly, the other hardness results from [19] about computing the maximum imply hardness of the corresponding problems for skylines. For instance, they show that computing the associated probabilities for those two problems (computing the probability that the most likely skyline is indeed the skyline - resp., will be the skyline after the next vote is processed) is $\#P$-hard.

7. RELATED WORK

Skyline algorithms. As mentioned in the introduction, skyline queries (a.k.a. maximal vectors or Pareto maxima) have been the subject of extensive study in databases, computational geometry and multicriteria optimization. Almost all results focus on the computational complexity in the absence of noise, although lower bounds are proved through oracle complexity.

The history of worst-case-oriented comparison-based algorithms is interwoven with the history of convex hull algorithms [31, 28, 4, 11]. Kung et al. [31] proposed a Divide and Conquer algorithm with worst case complexity

$O(d^2 n \log^{d-2} n)$. Kirkpatrick and Seidel then adapted the algorithm into an output-sensitive algorithm with complexity $O(d^2 n \log^{d-2} k)$, and with even better complexity when $k \ll \sqrt{n}$. These results are optimal when $d \in \{2, 3\}$ in the comparison model [31, 45], and even in the algebraic decision tree model [28]. For $d = 2$ and $d = 3$ the results were recently strengthened with instance-optimal algorithms [4]. Chan and Lee [11] raised the question of determining the oracle complexity of skyline queries, and investigate the constant factors in the $O(n \log k)$ complexity for $d = 2$ and $d = 3$. For arbitrary values of d, Sheng and Tao recently showed that skylines can be computed in $O(n \log^{d-2} n)$ computational complexity with a minor adaptation of Kung et al's algorithm [31], thus removing a d^2 factor.

Skylines can be computed faster in the RAM model [10, 2] or when the dimension is very large [47]. In particular, the skyline can be computed in $O(n \log^{d-3} n)$ expected time [10] on RAM. For $d = n$, an $O(n^{2.684})$ algorithm can be obtained through matrix multiplication techniques [35, 47]. These approaches do not seem to lower oracle-complexity because the first step of the matrix-multiplication approach is actually to sort all items along each dimension, and the RAM algorithms similarly assume rank-space reduction of the input.

After the skyline was suggested as a new operator to express preferences [7], the database community investigated the integration of this operator in database systems [12], and the performance of skyline algorithms in theory and practice in various settings [7, 30, 17]. Further from our purpose, other related problems (sampling, datastructures for subspace skyline or dominance reporting, layers of skyline), computational models and evaluation criteria have been considered, such as I/O efficient algorithms in external memory [43, 24], average-case analysis [6, 17] or progressive computation [37].

Parallel sort and parallel skyline. The number of rounds necessary to compute OR and MAX queries with optimal (linear) complexity was recently proven to be respectively $\Theta(\log^* n)$ and $\Theta(\log \log n)$ [18, 36]. Minimizing latency to compute with noisy comparisons more complex queries such as selection [18], top-k [15] or sorting [16] was formulated as an open question. The only parallel sorting algorithms in $O(n \log(n/\delta))$ with noisy comparisons we are aware of are a randomized algorithm [16] and an EREW-PRAM algorithm [32] with tolerance $\delta = 1/n^c$ for constant c. The deterministic PRAM algorithm is based on a fault-tolerant adaptation of the AKS circuits [5]. This is in sharp contrast with the noiseless case where several sorting algorithms with optimal $O(\log n)$ latency have been proposed [39, 13, 14]. Several algorithms have been suggested to leverage parallelism in (noiseless) skyline computation, see [1] and references therein, though again they generally partition the data according to the rank of items, hence seem to be of little help in our setting.

Maximum Likelihood for maxima. The problem of computing winners in elections has been investigated under a maximum likelihood perspective since -at least- the works of Condorcet [46]. When the probability of error is low, the maximum corresponds to the Kemeny winner and is therefore hard to compute [19].

Skyline algorithms with noisy information. The problem of computing skylines under noisy information was only investigated recently, though related results appeared earlier in the literature about multicriteria optimization, where the number of points needs not be finite. For instance, Papadimitriou and Yannakakis [38] show that any –possibly infinite– set of Pareto-optimal points in $\mathbb{Q}^d$ can be approximated up to any multiplicative factor $\epsilon > 0$ with a "small" set of solution points, and subsequent work [44] investigates algorithms and bounds when the objective is to minimize the size of the approximated solution. Similar bounds and results were established for the approximation of skylines, where the instance is a finite set of n points [29]: a smallest ϵ-approximation (cover) of the skyline can be computed greedily in two dimensions, but this problem becomes NP-hard from $d = 3$. However one can always find an ϵ-approximation of the skyline that is larger than the minimal one by a factor at most $\log n$, or even by a constant factor when $d = 3$.

Pei et al. [40] introduce the ρ-skyline as the set of points that have probability at least ρ to belong to the skyline, and propose heuristics for their computation. The ρ-skyline has mostly been investigated in the "locational" model where the location of each of the n uncertain points is independently defined by a discrete probability distribution over k possible points: each uncertain point P is thus defined as (1) a k-tuple of probabilities summing up to one, together with (2) a k-tuple of vectors in $\mathbb{R}^d$ representing the corresponding locations. The ρ-skyline can then be computed in $(nk)^{2-1/d}$, or alternatively in $O(\min(n, k) nk \log(nk))$ [3]. Afshani et al. [3] also devise some approximation algorithms for ρ-skylines. More heuristic approaches have also been suggested for skyline computation on incomplete or imprecise data [27, 33].

Alternative noisy comparison model. Multiple models have been developed that aim to guarantee some form of fault-tolerance in computation. Variations of the noisy comparison model have been investigated in particular on decision trees [16, 18, 26] and broadcast networks [36] for sorting problems [16], maxima computation [16, 18] and boolean function evaluation [16, 26, 36, 18].

Sorting and selection problems were also considered in other noise models; some assume for instance an upper bound k on the number of errors instead of random errors [41]. Another extends the noisy comparison model in the context of clustering and top-k query processing through Crowdsourcing [15], so that the probability of error depends on some distance function between the items compared: the motivation for this extension being that crowd workers are more likely to make mistakes when two items are similar. Many results also deal with the particular case where the algorithm must be implemented as a network of comparators. The questions and techniques considered in Section 6 are connected to optimization problems such as minimum feedback-arc set on graphs, and related voting theory questions [8]. Hardness results and heuristics have recently been suggested for those problems in the framework of crowdsourcing [19].

8. CONCLUSION AND FUTURE WORK

We introduced several algorithms and bounds for skyline queries with noisy comparisons. We showed that sorting the full dataset is asymptotically optimal when the dimension is fixed and the skyline contains at least a constant fraction of the input. But efficient algorithms can be obtained when the skyline cardinality is small.

The quadratic or cubic number of comparisons required by our algorithms may surprise in view of the traditionally lower complexity claimed for noiseless skylines. To explain this gap, we point out that (1) traditional skyline bounds generally hide constants depending on d as d is generally fixed (and often limited to $d \leq 3$), and (2) most skyline algorithms rely on Divide and Conquer schemes that do not work well in presence of noisy comparisons. Specifically, two bottlenecks here are the accurate computation of the *screening* (identifying all dominated points) and sorting procedures: identifying all dominated items or sorting accurately a large number of non-trivial subsets both have the same complexity as sorting the whole input set.

Our algorithms and bounds on the number of comparisons mostly build upon the literature of sorting and searching with noisy comparisons. The gap between those algorithms and lower bounds highlight numerous open questions, in both the output-sensitive and general cases. First of all, can skylines be computed with cost $o(nk)$ in the planar case, or even for any constant d? How does the number of comparison vary with d? Can we establish some tradeoff between rounds and questions similar to the one observed for maxima queries?

Getting the right value of error parameters is a typical issue, e.g., in probabilistic databases. In crowdsourcing scenarios for example, the simplest approach adopted by practitioners is to sample users on a set of questions for which the answers are known. Of course there are more sophisticated schemes and this is an interesting question but outside the scope of this paper. Other possible directions for future works include the analysis of average-case and other models of computations, for instance restricting the comparisons authorized to a subset of all item pairs and dimensions [20, 21, 25], hybrid models allowing both comparisons and numerical values, etc. The model should also be extended in several directions to address issues of real-world crowdsourcing scenarios: taking into account varying error rates among users, dependencies between dimensions and correlation between errors, etc.

Acknowledgements

This work has been partially funded by the European Research Council under the FP7, ERC grant MoDaS, agreement 291071, and by the Israel Ministry of Science.

9. REFERENCES

[1] F. N. Afrati, P. Koutris, D. Suciu, and J. D. Ullman. Parallel skyline queries. In *ICDT*, pages 274–284, 2012.

[2] P. Afshani. Fast computation of output-sensitive maxima in a word ram. In *SODA*, pages 1414–1423, 2014.

[3] P. Afshani, P. K. Agarwal, L. Arge, K. G. Larsen, and J. M. Phillips. (approximate) uncertain skylines. *Theory Comput. Syst.*, 52(3):342–366, 2013.

[4] P. Afshani, J. Barbay, and T. M. Chan. Instance-optimal geometric algorithms. In *FOCS*, pages 129–138, 2009.

[5] M. Ajtai, J. Komlós, and E. Szemerédi. Sorting in c log n parallel sets. *Combinatorica*, 3(1):1–19, 1983.

[6] J. L. Bentley, K. L. Clarkson, and D. B. Levine. Fast linear expected-time algorithms for computing maxima and convex hulls. *Algorithmica*, 9(2):168–183, 1993.

[7] S. Börzsönyi, D. Kossmann, and K. Stocker. The skyline operator. In *ICDE*, pages 421–430, 2001.

[8] M. Braverman and E. Mossel. Noisy sorting without resampling. In *SODA*, pages 268–276, 2008.

[9] T. M. Chan. Optimal output-sensitive convex hull algorithms in two and three dimensions. *Discrete & Computational Geometry*, 16(4):361–368, 1996.

[10] T. M. Chan, K. G. Larsen, and M. Patrascu. Orthogonal range searching on the ram, revisited. In *SOCG*, pages 1–10, 2011.

[11] T. M. Chan and P. Lee. On constant factors in comparison-based geometric algorithms and data structures. In *30th Annual Symposium on Computational Geometry, SOCG'14, Kyoto, Japan, June 08 - 11, 2014*, page 40, 2014.

[12] J. Chomicki, P. Ciaccia, and N. Meneghetti. Skyline queries, front and back. *SIGMOD Record*, 42(3):6–18, 2013.

[13] R. Cole. Parallel merge sort. *SIAM J. Comput.*, 17(4):770–785, 1988.

[14] R. Cole. Correction: Parallel merge sort. *SIAM J. Comput.*, 22(6):1349, 1993.

[15] S. B. Davidson, S. Khanna, T. Milo, and S. Roy. Using the crowd for top-k and group-by queries. In *ICDT*, pages 225–236, 2013.

[16] U. Feige, P. Raghavan, D. Peleg, and E. Upfal. Computing with noisy information. *SIAM J. Comput.*, 23(5):1001–1018, 1994.

[17] P. Godfrey, R. Shipley, and J. Gryz. Algorithms and analyses for maximal vector computation. *VLDB J.*, 16(1):5–28, 2007.

[18] N. Goyal and M. Saks. Rounds vs. queries tradeoff in noisy computation. *Theory of Computing*, 6(1):113–134, 2010.

[19] S. Guo, A. G. Parameswaran, and H. Garcia-Molina. So who won?: dynamic max discovery with the crowd. In *SIGMOD Conference*, pages 385–396, 2012.

[20] A. Gupta and A. Kumar. Sorting and selection with structured costs. In *FOCS*, pages 416–425, 2001.

[21] A. Gupta and A. Kumar. Where's the winner? max-finding and sorting with metric costs. In *APPROX-RANDOM*, pages 74–85, 2005.

[22] E. Hemaspaandra, L. A. Hemaspaandra, and J. Rothe. Hybrid elections broaden complexity-theoretic resistance to control. *CoRR*, abs/cs/0608057, 2006.

[23] E. Hemaspaandra, H. Spakowski, and J. Vogel. The complexity of kemeny elections. *Theor. Comput. Sci.*, 349(3):382–391, 2005.

[24] X. Hu, C. Sheng, Y. Tao, Y. Yang, and S. Zhou. Output-sensitive skyline algorithms in external memory. In *SODA*, pages 887–900, 2013.

[25] Z. Huang, S. Kannan, and S. Khanna. Algorithms for the generalized sorting problem. In *FOCS*, pages 738–747, 2011.

[26] C. Kenyon and V. King. On boolean decision trees with faulty nodes. *Random Struct. Algorithms*, 5(3):453–464, 1994.

[27] M. E. Khalefa, M. F. Mokbel, and J. J. Levandoski. Skyline query processing for incomplete data. In *ICDE*, pages 556–565, 2008.

[28] D. G. Kirkpatrick and R. Seidel. Output-size sensitive algorithms for finding maximal vectors. In *SOCG*, pages 89–96, 1985.

[29] V. Koltun and C. H. Papadimitriou. Approximately dominating representatives. *Theor. Comput. Sci.*, 371(3):148–154, 2007.

[30] D. Kossmann, F. Ramsak, and S. Rost. Shooting stars in the sky: An online algorithm for skyline queries. In *VLDB*, pages 275–286, 2002.

[31] H. T. Kung, F. Luccio, and F. P. Preparata. On finding the maxima of a set of vectors. *J. ACM*, 22(4):469–476, 1975.

[32] F. T. Leighton, Y. Ma, and C. G. Plaxton. Breaking the theta (n $\log^2$ n) barrier for sorting with faults. *J. Comput. Syst. Sci.*, 54(2):265–304, 1997.

[33] C. Lofi, K. E. Maarry, and W.-T. Balke. Skyline queries in crowd-enabled databases. In *EDBT*, pages 465–476, 2013.

[34] A. Marcus, E. Wu, D. R. Karger, S. Madden, and R. C. Miller. Human-powered sorts and joins. *PVLDB*, 5(1):13–24, 2011.

[35] J. Matousek. Computing dominances in e^n. *Inf. Process. Lett.*, 38(5):277–278, 1991.

[36] I. Newman. Computing in fault tolerant broadcast networks and noisy decision trees. *Random Struct. Algorithms*, 34(4):478–501, 2009.

[37] D. Papadias, Y. Tao, G. Fu, and B. Seeger. Progressive skyline computation in database systems. *ACM Trans. Database Syst.*, 30(1):41–82, 2005.

[38] C. H. Papadimitriou and M. Yannakakis. On the approximability of trade-offs and optimal access of web sources. In *FOCS*, pages 86–92, 2000.

[39] M. Paterson. Improved sorting networks with o(log n) depth. *Algorithmica*, 5(1):65–92, 1990.

[40] J. Pei, B. Jiang, X. Lin, and Y. Yuan. Probabilistic skylines on uncertain data. In *VLDB*, pages 15–26, 2007.

[41] A. Pelc. Searching games with errors - fifty years of coping with liars. *Theor. Comput. Sci.*, 270(1-2):71–109, 2002.

[42] J. I. Seiferas. Sorting networks of logarithmic depth, further simplified. *Algorithmica*, 53(3):374–384, 2009.

[43] C. Sheng and Y. Tao. Worst-case i/o-efficient skyline algorithms. *ACM Trans. Database Syst.*, 37(4):26, 2012.

[44] S. Vassilvitskii and M. Yannakakis. Efficiently computing succinct trade-off curves. *Theor. Comput. Sci.*, 348(2-3):334–356, 2005.

[45] F. F. Yao. On finding the maximal elements in a set of plane vectors. Technical Report UIUCDCS-R-74-667, University of Illinois, 1974.

[46] H. P. Young. Condorcet's Theory of Voting. *American Political Science Review*, 82:1231–1244, 1988.

[47] R. Yuster. Efficient algorithms on sets of permutations, dominance, and real-weighted apsp. In *SODA*, pages 950–957, 2009.

Appendix

Proof of Theorem 1

We next evaluate the dependence on d of the output-sensitive algorithm of Kirpatrick and Seidel. We recall that most results in [28] only hold for constant d. In particular, the proofs of their Lemma 3.1 and Theorem 3.1 are not valid for non-constant d in spite of the deceptive d factors maintained along these proofs.

We follow closely the proof of [28] and only highlight the results on which we depart from the original proof. Adopting the notations of [28], let $C_d(k,n)$ denote the complexity of computing the skyline of n items when the (unknown) number of skyline items[4] is k, and let $F_d(r,s)$ denote the complexity of determining which items of S are dominated by some item(s) of R when $S, R \subseteq \mathbb{R}^d$, $|S| = s$, $|R| = r$. Let also $G_d(r,s,t)$ denote the complexity of Algorithm SCREEN as defined in [28].

The algorithm Max1 in [28] proceeds as follows to compute the skyline of a d-dimensional n-items set T:

- partition T around the median for lexicographic order into S and R such that $x <_{\text{lex}} y$ for all $(x,y) \in S \times R$
- compute recursively $M(R) = \text{Max1}(R)$
- remove from S the items dominated by $\text{Max1}(R)$
- compute $M(S) = \text{Max1}(S)$
- return $M(R) \cup M(S)$.

The partition can be computed in $O(nd)$ using a linear selection algorithm, with lexicographic comparisons of cost $O(d)$ each. We thus deduce, by setting $r = |M(R)|$:

LEMMA 8 (FROM LEMMA 2.2 IN [28]). *When parameter r ranges over $\{1,\ldots,\min(k-1,n/2)\}$,*

$$C_d(k,n) \le \max_r (C_d(r,n/2) + F_{d-1}(r,n/2) + C_d(k-r,n/2) + O(dn))$$

Following the proof in [28] and taking care of the cost $O(d)$ for lexicographic comparisons, we also show easily that:

LEMMA 9 (FROM LEMMA 3.1 IN [28]). *For all values of d we have:*

(i) $G_d(1,s,t) \in O(ds)$

(ii) For $d \ge 3$ and $2 \le t \le r$:

$$G_d(r,s,t) \in O(d^2(s + r(t-1)^{d-3})(\log r)(\log_t r)^{d-3}).$$

We imediately deduce:

LEMMA 10 (FROM COROLLARY 3.1 IN [28]). *For all values of d we have:*

$$F_d(r,s) \in O(d^2(r+s)(\log r)^{d-2}).$$

We next turn to the proof of the theorem, which is where we differ most from the original proof. For $d = 2, 3$ the complexity of skyline computation is $C_d(k,n) = O(n \log k)$ [28], and we next prove the theorem for $d \ge 4$ by induction. By Lemmas 8 and 9, when r ranges over $\{1,\ldots,\min(k-1,n/2)\}$,

$$C_d(k,n) \le \max_r (C_d(r,n/2) + C_d(k-r,n/2) + O(d^2 n \log^{d-3} r))$$

We distinguish two cases:

[4]for consistency with our paper we denote this variable by k instead of v.

Case 1: $d-3 \geq \log r$. Then by induction there are constants $c, c' > c$ such that

$$\begin{aligned} C_d(k,n) \leq & \max_r (c'd^2 n(\log^{d-2} r + \log^{d-2}(k-r))/2 \\ & + c(d^2 n \log^{d-3} r)) \\ \leq & c'd^2 n(1+\log^{d-2}(k-1))/2 \\ & + c(d^2 n \log^{d-3} k) \\ \leq & c'd^2 n(\log^{d-2} k) \end{aligned}$$

The middle step is justified because $r \mapsto \log^{d-2} r$ is convex and increasing, hence $r \mapsto \log^{d-2} r + \log^{d-2}(k-r)$ reaches its maximum in our range for $r=1$.

Case 2: $d-3 \leq \log r$. Then by induction there are constants $c, c' > c$ such that

$$\begin{aligned} C_d(k,n) \leq & \max_r (c'd^2 n(\log^{d-2} r + \log^{d-2}(k-r))/2 \\ & + c(d^2 n \log^{d-3} r)) \\ \leq & c'd^2 n(\log^{d-2}(k/2)) \\ & + c(d^2 n \log^{d-3} k) \\ \leq & c'd^2 n(\log^{d-2} k) \end{aligned}$$

The middle step is justified because $r \mapsto \log^{d-2} r$ is concave.

We have thus shown that for some constant c', $C_d(k,n) \leq c'd^2 n(\log^{d-2} k)$ which concludes our proof. □

Proof of Proposition 1

The $\Omega(n \log_2 |C|)$ lower bound is actually a particular case of stronger bounds from the literature: Kirkpatrick and Seidel [28] show a $\Omega(n \log_2 |C|)$ lower bound for the stronger *algebraic decision tree model* by reduction from the multiset size verification problem. Afshani et al [4] prove a refined $n\mathcal{H}(S)$ bound in the comparison tree model for $d=2$, where $\mathcal{H}(S)$ is the entropy-like expression defined as follows. $\mathcal{H}(S)$ is the minimal value of $\sum_k (|S_k|/n)\log(n/|S_k|)$ for a partition $(S_k)_k$ of S such that each subset S_k is either a singleton or an axis-aligned box. But the weaker bound that we need can be proved directly through an information-theoretic argument adapting the proof of Yao [45]: There are at least $|C|^{n-|C|} \cdot |C|!$ possible ways to order items of C and assign each remaining items to its dominating point in C such that each item is dominated by at most one item from C. Any deterministic algorithm that given an arbitrary input S, C checks if C is the skyline of S must gather information sufficient to distinguish two such configurations, and therefore performs $\Omega(n \log_2 |C|)$ oracle comparisons. To see why two configurations as above must be distinguished: let $<_1, <_2$ be some orderings of S such that $C = \mathrm{Sky}(S)$ and each item is dominated by at most one item from C. We next show that

1. for every $v' \notin \mathrm{Sky}(S)$ the comparisons of any skyline verification algorithm must allow to determine some $v \in C$ such that $v' \prec v$
2. the comparisons must order all items of $\mathrm{Sky}(S)$ on both $<_1$ and $<_2$.

For each $v \in C$ let D_v be the set of items $v' \prec v$ such that the comparisons performed by the algorithm do not allow to determine $v' <_1 v$. If $D_v \neq \emptyset$ then we can shift all items v' of D_v so that $v' >_1$ without falsifying the results of any comparison performed, to the effect that D_v now contributes to $\mathrm{Sky}(S)$. This provides an instance which the algorithm cannot distinguish from S, whose skyline differs from C. A contradiction. The same is true on $<_2$ which concludes the proof of the first property. The second property is established similarly. □

Proof of Theorem 8

The only part of our algorithms that we actually parallelize are essentially the dominance checking and sorting procedures. We therefore revisit the procedures for dominance checking and then deduce #rounds for our algorithms. The first procedure for dominance checking in Lemma 5 can clearly be executed in $O(\log^*(d) \cdot \log^*(|C|))$ rounds each involving at most $O(d|C| \log \frac{1}{\delta})$ simultaneous comparisons. The second procedure requires $\log \frac{d|C|}{\delta}$ rounds, each involving at most $O(d \log \frac{d}{\delta} / \log |C|)$ simultaneous comparisons.

Skyline candidate verification:

1. The composition of the 3 applications of the OR algorithm presented in Theorem 2 can clearly be executed in $O(\log^*(d) \cdot \log^*(n) \cdot \log^*(|C|))$ rounds.
2. We can sort C along all dimensions with $O(\log |C|)$ rounds, according to Theorem 6. Each oracle call can then be processed in $O(\log^* n \cdot \log |C|)$ rounds.

Skyline computation: The first item below discusses the trivial approach that sorts the whole dataset whereas the second and third items analyze #rounds for the procedures in Proposition 2 and thereby Theorem 4. The oracle for lexicographic order can be implemented in $O(\log^* d)$ rounds, and therefore has no impact on cost since both procedures for domination oracles require more.

1. We can sort the whole dataset along all dimensions with $O(\log n)$ rounds, according to Theorem 6.
2. The procedure for dominance testing through composition of OR queries requires $O(\log^*(d) \cdot \log^*(k))$ rounds. Thus, each new point can be computed in $O(\log\log n \cdot \log^*(d) \cdot \log^*(k))$ rounds. This yields a total of $O(k \cdot \log\log n \cdot \log^*(d) \cdot \log^*(k))$ rounds for SkySample, hence for the computation of skylines too.
3. To minimize the number of rounds we compute the ordering of S_{i+1} from that of S_i, inserting the new point through binary search, hence #rounds $= k \log(dk/\delta)$ for sorting partial skylines. Then each oracle call for dominance test can be processed in $O(\log(\hat{k}))$ rounds. This yields a total of $O(k \cdot \log\log n \cdot \log \hat{k})$ rounds for SkySample, hence the result. □

Proof of Proposition 3

Before we discuss the proof, we first present the *Kemeny Winner problem*. The input consists of an $n \times n$ vote matrix M with $M_{i,j}$ counting the number of votes for $i < j$. As in our noisy comparison problems, votes can contradict each others, but in contrast to our problems, there are no probabilities involved. The rankings that contradict the fewest votes are called *Kemeny permutations*, and the *Kemeny Winner problem* is the problem of deciding whether there is some Kemeny permutation in which the given object is ranked first. The *unique Kemeny Winner problem* is the same problem restricted to instances for which the Kemeny Winner is unique. Both the Kemeny Winner [23] and the unique Kemeny Winner [22, Appendix] problems are Θ_2^p-

hard (and actually Θ_2^p-complete when votes are given as a *list* of preference rankings [23, 22]).

PROOF (ADAPTED FROM [19]). We adapt to arbitrary d the proof from [19]. As already mentioned, for $d = 1$ the result is immediate from [19] which proves that by setting $p < 1 - 1/(1 + \frac{1}{n!})$, any most likely maximum is a Kemeny winner. To the best of our knowledge, our extension of this hardness result to skylines in arbitrary dimension is new.

To extend the proof to arbitrary values of d, we use instead a reduction from the unique Kemeny Winner problem and set $p < 1 - 1/(1 + \frac{1}{n!(2d+1)})$. From the vote matrix M_{Kem} that guarantees a unique Kemeny winner, we build a tuple of d identical matrices $M.1 = \cdots = M.d = M_{\text{Kem}}$. From the argument in [19, Theorem 2], one deduces easily that the most likely skyline consists of a single item; the Kemeny winner. We say that a possible world π is *Kemeny* if for all $i \leq d$ $\pi.i$ is a Kemeny permutation. We wish to prove that the probability of Kemeny possible worlds exceeds that of non-Kemeny worlds when p is small enough.

On each dimension i, for any Kemeny permutation π' and non-Kemeny π'',

$$\Pr(\pi.i = \pi' \mid M) \cdot \frac{p}{1-p} \geq \Pr(\pi.i = \pi'' \mid M)$$

Summing over non-Kemeny permutations, we deduce:

$$\Pr(\pi.i = \pi' \mid M) \cdot n! \cdot \frac{p}{1-p} \geq \sum_{\pi'' \text{not Kemeny}} \Pr(\pi.i = \pi'' \mid M)$$

Consequently, when $p < 1 - 1/(1 + \frac{1}{n!(2d)})$, the probability that $\pi.i$ is not Kemeny is strictly less than $1/(2d)$. Hence a probability greater than $1/2$ that π is Kemeny. By construction of M, when π is Kemeny, the skyline $\text{Sky}(\pi)$ consists of a single item; the Kemeny winner of M_{Kem}. Therefore, the most likely skyline is the Kemeny winner of M_{Kem}. □

Proof of Proposition 4 (adapted from [19])

The proof for arbitrary d exploits exactly the same ideas as the one for $d = 1$ in [19], but considering several dimensions opens more possibilities for the choice of the next comparison, and our proof also fixes some imprecisions[5]. In order to generalize the result to higher dimensions, we again replace the reduction from the Kemeny winner problem with a reduction from the *unique* Kemeny winner problem, and replicate the vote matrix along all dimensions.

We are given an $n \times n$ vote matrix W for which we are guaranteed there exists a unique Kemeny winner. We first replicate along all dimensions this matrix to create a new matrix W', then add an additional item v to W', such that for all dimensions $i \leq d - 1$, $W'[i]$ contains a vote $v >_i w$ for every item w. Finally, we replicate 3 times each vote in W' so that adding a new vote will never turn a non-Kemeny permutation into a Kemeny one. Note that this replication step preserves Kemeny permutations, and thereby the Kemeny winner. By definition, v is the Kemeny winner in $W'[j]$ for all $j < d$, and one of the two Kemeny winners in $W'[d]$. Recall, however, that our goal is to return a Kemeny winner in W, not in $W'[d]$.

Let us show that the Next Vote problem on W' returns the comparison on dimension d of v and v' where v' is the Kemeny winner in W. We first observe that $\Pr(W' \wedge x >_i y \mid \pi) = \Pr(W' \mid \pi) \Pr(x >_i y \mid \pi)$ for all x, y and i. Let (x, y, i) be the comparison returned by the next vote problem on W', comparing x and y on dimension i. We want to show that $\{x, y\} = \{v, v'\}$ and $i = d$. We assume that the probability of error p is small enough that the probabilities associated to non-Kemeny possible worlds are negligible. More formally, let $P_1 = \{\pi \mid \exists j \leq d.\ \pi.i \text{ is not Kemeny for } W'[i]\}$ and let $\pi_{Kem} \notin P_1$. Then we assume p is small enough that $\Pr(W' \mid \pi_{Kem}) > \sum_{\pi \in P_1} \Pr(W' \mid \pi)$. We also assume that $\Pr(W' \mid \pi_{Kem})(1-p) > \sum_{\pi}(W' \mid \pi_{Kem})np$. Let $i = d, x = v, y = v'$, let c be the number of Kemeny permutations in W, and let π_0 be an arbitrary Kemeny permutation of W. Let π_1 denote the possible world such that $\pi_1.j$ is obtained by placing v on top of π_0 for all $j \leq d$. Let also π_j $(2 \leq j \leq n+1)$ be the possible world that only differs from π_1 on dimension d, such that $\pi_j.d$ is obtained from π_0 by inserting v on the jth position.

For the values of i, x, y specified above we thus obtain

$$\begin{aligned} F_{v,v',d} \geq & \sum_{\pi:\text{Sky}(\pi)=\{v\}} \Pr(W' \wedge v >_d v' \mid \pi) \\ & + \sum_{\pi:\text{Sky}(\pi)=\{v,v'\}} \Pr(W' \wedge v <_d v' \mid \pi) \\ \geq & \sum_{\pi:\text{Sky}(\pi)=\{v\}} \Pr(W' \mid \pi)(1-p) \\ & + \sum_{\pi:\text{Sky}(\pi)=\{v,v'\}} \Pr(W' \mid \pi)(1-p) \\ \geq & (c + cn)c^{d-1} \Pr(W' \mid \pi_1)(1-p) \end{aligned}$$

Let us justify the derivation. By construction, the most likely skyline in W can either be $\{v, v'\}$ or $\{v\}$, depending on whether $v <_d v'$. In every Kemeny possible world π for $W' \wedge v >_d v'$, v is the maximal item in every dimension so $\text{Sky}(\pi) = \{v\}$; the most likely skyline is $P_0 = \text{Sky}(\pi)$. In every Kemeny possible world π for $W' \wedge v <_d v'$, v is the maximal and v' the second item in every dimension except in dimension d where v' is first and the position of v is arbitrary. In this case the most likely skyline is $P_0 = \{v, v'\}$. Consider the left term first: there are c^d Kemeny possible worlds π such that $\text{Sky}(\pi) = \{v\}$. The probability of getting votes W' and vote $x >_i y$ given any such possible world equals $\Pr(W' \mid \pi_1)(1-p)$. Now, we observe that $\Pr(W' \mid \pi_j) = \Pr(W' \mid \pi_1)$ for all $j \geq 2$ so the second term, $\sum_{\pi:\text{Sky}(\pi)=\{v,v'\}} \Pr(W' \mid \pi)(1-p)$, is at least $nc^d \Pr(W' \mid \pi_1)(1-p)$. This justifies the derivation above.

On the other hand, we next show that $F_{x,y,i}$ is smaller for every other value of $\{x, y\}$ and i. We first recall that by construction any additional vote can only reduce or preserve the set of Kemeny permutations and observe that $P_0 = \{v, v'\}$ becomes a most likely skyline for both $W' \wedge x <_i y$ and $W' \wedge x >_i y$. This is because for both comparison outcomes there are as many Kemeny possible worlds consistent with the outcome that satisfy $v' >_d v$ as there are that satisfy $v' <_d v$. Then it is clear that every Kemeny permutation for $W[i]$ (hence every Kemeny possible world) is contradicted by one of $x <_i y$ or $x >_i y$. As a consequence $F_{x,y,i}$ is equal to $nc^d \Pr(W' \mid \pi_1)((1-p) + p)$ plus negligible contributions from non-Kemeny possible worlds. This is smaller than $F_{v,v',d}$ since $np \ll 1 - p$. □

[5]in particular, we insist that $W \wedge a$ is the conjunction of events W and a, not a vote matrix obtained by combining the vote multisets W and a.

The Communication Complexity of Distributed Set-Joins with Applications to Matrix Multiplication

Dirk Van Gucht[1] Ryan Williams[2*] David P. Woodruff[3] Qin Zhang[1]

[1]Indiana University Bloomington
[2]Stanford University
[3]IBM Almaden

ABSTRACT

Given a set-comparison predicate $\mathcal{P}$ and given two lists of sets $\mathcal{A} = (A_1, \ldots, A_m)$ and $\mathcal{B} = (B_1, \ldots, B_m)$, with all $A_i, B_j \subseteq [n]$, the *$\mathcal{P}$-set join* $\mathcal{A} \bowtie^{\mathcal{P}} \mathcal{B}$ is defined to be the set $\{(i,j) \in [m] \times [m] \mid \mathcal{P}(A_i, B_j)\}$ ($[n]$ denotes $\{1, 2, \ldots, n\}$). When $\mathcal{P}(A_i, B_j)$ is the condition "$A_i \cap B_j \neq \emptyset$" we call this the *set-intersection-not-empty join* (a.k.a. the composition of $\mathcal{A}$ and $\mathcal{B}$); when $\mathcal{P}(A_i, B_j)$ is "$A_i \cap B_j = \emptyset$" we call it the *set-disjointness join*; when $\mathcal{P}(A_i, B_j)$ is "$A_i = B_j$" we call it the *set-equality join*; when $\mathcal{P}(A_i, B_j)$ is "$|A_i \cap B_j| \geq T$" for a given threshold T, we call it the *set-intersection threshold join*. Assuming $\mathcal{A}$ and $\mathcal{B}$ are stored at two different sites in a distributed environment, we study the (randomized) communication complexity of computing these, and related, set-joins $\mathcal{A} \bowtie^{\mathcal{P}} \mathcal{B}$, as well as the (randomized) communication complexity of computing the exact and approximate value of their size $k = |\mathcal{A} \bowtie^{\mathcal{P}} \mathcal{B}|$. Combined, our analyses shed new insights into the quantitative differences between these different set-joins. Furthermore, given the close affinity of the *natural join* and the set-intersection-not-empty join, our results also yield communication complexity results for computing the natural join in a distributed environment.

Additionally, we obtain new algorithms for computing the distributed set-intersection-not-empty join when the input and/or output is sparse. For instance, when the output is k-sparse, we improve an $\tilde{O}(kn)$ communication algorithm of (Williams and Yu, SODA 2014). Observing that the set-intersection-not-empty join is isomorphic to *Boolean matrix multiplication* (BMM), our results imply new algorithms for fundamental graph theoretic problems related to BMM. For example, we show how to compute the transitive closure of a directed graph in $\tilde{O}(k^{3/2})$ time, when the transitive closure contains at most k edges. When $k = O(n)$, we obtain a (practical) $\tilde{O}(n^{3/2})$ time algorithm, improving a recent $\tilde{O}(n \cdot n^{\frac{\omega+1}{4}})$ time algorithm (Borassi, Crescenzi, and Habib, arXiv 2014) based on (impractical) fast matrix multiplication, where $\omega \geq 2$ is the exponent for matrix multiplication.

*Supported by NSF CCF-1212372.

PODS'15, May 31–June 4, 2015, Melbourne, Victoria, Australia.

ACM 978-1-4503-2757-2/15/05 ...$15.00.
http://dx.doi.org/10.1145/2745754.2745779.

1. INTRODUCTION

In this paper we study the complexity of a variety of distributed set-join operations in the natural setting of two-party communication complexity.

In this introduction, we first specify the different set-joins we consider. We next turn to their distributed computation, and then provide a summary of the main results regarding their communication complexities. We obtain both positive and negative results. For the set-intersection, set-equality, and at-least-T set-joins, we obtain positive results by showing that efficiency gains in communication can be achieved through the use of sophisticated protocols. We also show that several of these protocols are optimal. On the other hand, for the set-disjointness join, and its affiliated superset and subset joins, we obtain negative results: we prove lower bounds on their communication complexity which establish that, in general, the best one can do for these set-joins is to send all the data from one site to the other site and then, at that site, perform the set-join without further communication.

In addition to our communication complexity results, we also describe new and positive results about the computation of Boolean matrix multiplication and transitive closure that follow from the algorithmic techniques developed for computing distributed set-intersection joins (i.e., composition and natural join).

1.1 Set-Joins

Among the most common tasks in querying data are finding associations/links between two data sources. Two classic cases of such tasks are computing the *composition* and the *natural join* of two relations[10].[1] More specifically, let $\mathcal{A}$ be a relation defined over attributes (I, L) and let $\mathcal{B}$ be a relation defined over attributes (L, J). Let $[z]$ denote $\{1, 2, \ldots, z\}$ for a natural number z. Assume for simplicity that $dom(I) = dom(J) = [m]$, and $dom(L) = [n]$. Then $\mathcal{A} \subseteq [m] \times [n]$ and $\mathcal{B} \subseteq [n] \times [m]$. The *composition* of $\mathcal{A}$ and $\mathcal{B}$ and the *natural join* of $\mathcal{A}$ and $\mathcal{B}$ are respectively defined

[1]The composition and the natural join were first introduced to the database community by Codd in his 1970 celebrated paper on the Relational Model [10]. Actually, compared to the natural join, the composition operator has a much longer history: its definition and properties were first studied by De Morgan, Schröder, Peirce, and Tarski in the late 19th and early 20th centuries [35]. More recently, since composition can be considered as the canonical graph traversal/navigation operation, it has been studied intensively in the context of semi-structured tree and graph databases [2, 14, 42]. Furthermore, since repeated application of the composition operation corresponds to determining graph connectivity, it is at the core of computing the *transitive closure* of a graph.

as

$$\mathcal{A} \circ \mathcal{B} := \{(i,j) \mid \exists \ell : (i,\ell) \in \mathcal{A} \;\&\; (\ell,j) \in \mathcal{B}\}, \text{ and}$$
$$\mathcal{A} \bowtie \mathcal{B} := \{(i,\ell,j) \mid (i,\ell) \in \mathcal{A} \;\&\; (\ell,j) \in \mathcal{B}\}.$$

Clearly, one can view the natural join as an *adornment* of the composition, i.e., for each composition pair $(i,j) \in \mathcal{A} \circ \mathcal{B}$, the natural join adorns (i,j) with its corresponding *witnesses* ℓ. The composition operator can also be viewed as *Boolean matrix multiplication* when $\mathcal{A}$ and $\mathcal{B}$ are construed as Boolean matrices in a natural way; see the discussion in Section 1.3.

The composition and natural join operations can be defined in an alternative way: if we let A_i be the "projection/witness" set $\{\ell \mid (i,\ell) \in \mathcal{A}\}$ and let B_j be $\{\ell \mid (\ell,j) \in \mathcal{B}\}$, then we have

$$\mathcal{A} \circ \mathcal{B} = \{(i,j) \mid A_i \cap B_j \neq \emptyset\}, \text{ and}$$
$$\mathcal{A} \bowtie \mathcal{B} = \{(i,\ell,j) \mid \ell \in A_i \cap B_j\}.$$

Because of the not-empty set-intersection conditions present in the definition of the composition and the natural join, we will call them generically *set-intersection-not-empty joins*, or more succinctly, *set-intersection joins*. We will reserve the acronym SIJ for the composition and when necessary, explicitly refer to the natural join.

Set-intersection joins are by no means the only set-joins one may consider. Imagine, for example, that $\mathcal{A}$ stores job-applicants and their skills and that $\mathcal{B}$ stores the required skills of job-openings. In this case, a useful relationship between a job-applicant and a job-opening may exist if *all* of the skills of an applicant include (contain) all the skills required for a job. We may also wish that these skills are precisely the same. Formally, we want to compute the sets $\{(i,j) \mid A_i \supseteq B_j\}$ and $\{(i,j) \mid A_i = B_j\}$, which we call the *superset join* and the *set-equality join*, respectively.

There are other set-joins of this flavor one may consider. Table 1 summarizes the set-joins of interest for this paper. Besides the set-intersection, superset, and set-equality joins, we consider the *Subset Join* $\mathcal{A} \bowtie^{\subseteq} \mathcal{B}$ which can be viewed as an inverse of the superset join, the *Set-Disjointness Join* $\mathcal{A} \bowtie^{\cap=\emptyset} \mathcal{B}$ which can be viewed as the negation of the set-intersection joins, the *Not-Superset Join* $\mathcal{A} \bowtie^{\not\supseteq} \mathcal{B}$ and the *Not-Subset Join* $\mathcal{A} \bowtie^{\not\subseteq} \mathcal{B}$ which can be viewed as negations of the superset and subset joins, respectively, and the At-Least-T join $\mathcal{A} \bowtie^{\geq T} \mathcal{B}$ which joins the A_i and B_j pairs whose intersection contain at least T elements.

Clearly, not all these set-joins paper are independent. Indeed, straightforward equivalences between the above permit us to focus only on four classes of set-joins: the set-intersection, set-disjointness, set-equality, and at-least-T join operations.[2] Observe that, since, $\mathcal{A} \bowtie^{=} \mathcal{B} = (\mathcal{A} \bowtie^{\subseteq} \mathcal{B}) \cap (\mathcal{A} \bowtie^{\supseteq} \mathcal{B})$, we could also omit the set-equality join from our study. We will see however that it is more insightful if we consider the set-equality join as a primitive set-join in its own right.

Applications, logical and algebraic properties, algorithms and data structures (and their implementations), and empirical studies of some or all of these set-joins have been described in [3,5,9,13,16–18,23,26,28,36–38,46].

One of the main threads that runs through these papers is that, compared to the set-intersection joins, the class of the super, subset, and set-disjointness joins are considered and suspected to be computationally more expensive in time and space utilization, even though we are not aware of formal proof of this. We therefore think that our communication-complexity results are particularly meaningful since they **do** indeed formally prove, and therefore inform and substantiate, these suspected computational differences.

1.2 Distributed Set-Joins and their Communication Complexity

Distributed computations of several set-joins have been studied extensively. Mishra and Eich [29] (Section 5) and Kossman [21]) surveyed distributed set-intersection joins (principally, natural joins). More recently, and primarily because of the introduction of MapReduce, there has been renewed interest in the distributed and parallel computations of such joins (see for example [1,6,33].) On the other hand, there is far less work on distributed and parallel computation for the other set-joins operations we consider in this paper: we mention here the work in [4,24,43] wherein algorithms, data structures, and implementation are described for set-joins other than set-intersection joins.

In this paper, we study the complexity of distributed set-join operations in the natural setting of two-party communication complexity. One party, Alice, holds the collection $\mathcal{A} = \{A_1,\ldots,A_m\}$, and another party, Bob, holds $\mathcal{B} = \{B_1,\ldots,B_{m'}\}$ in another remote location. To ease the presentation we assume $m = m'$, but all our results can be easily adapted to the case where $m \neq m'$. Alice and Bob wish to exchange a *minimum* number of bits in order to determine information about a set-join operation on $\mathcal{A}$ and $\mathcal{B}$ (or compute the set-join itself, if that is a small set). We allow Alice and Bob to occasionally make random choices in their algorithms. Informally, we call the minimum number of bits needed to be exchanged to compute an operation with high probability (as a function of n and m) the *randomized communication complexity* of that operation. Further background and definitions are in Section 2.

We prove new upper and lower bounds on the communication required to compute these set-joins, building on sophisticated algorithms and tools from prior work. Our results establish formal quantitative differences between the complexities of these various set-join operations; in particular, their respective communication complexities are not the same.

We are aware of only one other theoretical result with a similar type of message: namely, Leinders and Van den Bussche [23] exhibit a way in which the set-intersection join and the superset-join can be seen as quantitatively different. Consider the problem of determining if $|\mathcal{A} \bowtie \mathcal{B}| > 0$ and the problem of determining if $|\mathcal{A} \bowtie^{\supseteq} \mathcal{B}| > 0$. Establishing that $|\mathcal{A} \bowtie \mathcal{B}| > 0$ is equivalent to establishing $|\mathcal{A} \ltimes \mathcal{B}| > 0$.[3] Since the size of $\mathcal{A} \ltimes \mathcal{B}$ is linear in the size of $\mathcal{A}$ and $\mathcal{B}$, the decision problem $|\mathcal{A} \bowtie \mathcal{B}| > 0$ can be solved in linear space, even though the size of $\mathcal{A} \bowtie \mathcal{B}$ itself may be quadratic. In sharp contrast, Leinders and Van den Bussche showed that for **any** expression E in the relational algebra with the prop-

[2]Recalling that $A_i, B_j \subseteq [n]$, let $\overline{A_i} = [n] - A_i$ and $\overline{B_j} = [n] - B_j$. Then (1) the conditions $A_i \supseteq B_j$ and $\overline{A_i} \cap B_j = \emptyset$ are equivalent; (2) the conditions $A_i \subseteq B_j$ and $A_i \cap \overline{B_j} = \emptyset$ are equivalent; (3) the conditions $A_i \not\supseteq B_j$ and $\overline{A_i} \cap B_j \neq \emptyset$ are equivalent; and (4) the conditions $A_i \not\subseteq B_j$ and $A_i \cap \overline{B_j} \neq \emptyset$ are equivalent.

[3]Recall that $\mathcal{A} \ltimes \mathcal{B}$, i.e. the semi-join of $\mathcal{A}$ and $\mathcal{B}$, is $\{(i,\ell) \mid \ell \in A_i \;\&\; A_i \cap B \neq \emptyset\}$, where $B = \pi_{[L]}(\mathcal{B})$, i.e, the set of ℓ-values in all L columns of $\mathcal{B}$.

Name	Notation	Definition
Natural Join	$\mathcal{A} \bowtie \mathcal{B}$	$\{(i,\ell,j) \mid \ell \in A_i \cap B_j\}$
Composition	$\mathcal{A} \bowtie^{\cap\neq\emptyset} \mathcal{B}$	$\{(i,j) \mid A_i \cap B_j \neq \emptyset\}$
Superset Join	$\mathcal{A} \bowtie^{\supseteq} \mathcal{B}$	$\{(i,j) \mid A_i \supseteq B_j\}$
Set-Equality Join	$\mathcal{A} \bowtie^{=} \mathcal{B}$	$\{(i,j) \mid A_i = B_j\}$
Subset Join	$\mathcal{A} \bowtie^{\subseteq} \mathcal{B}$	$\{(i,j) \mid A_i \subseteq B_j\}$
Set-Disjointness Join	$\mathcal{A} \bowtie^{\cap=\emptyset} \mathcal{B}$	$\{(i,j) \mid A_i \cap B_j = \emptyset\}$
Not-Superset Join	$\mathcal{A} \bowtie^{\not\supseteq} \mathcal{B}$	$\{(i,j) \mid A_i \not\supseteq B_j\}$
Not-Subset Join	$\mathcal{A} \bowtie^{\not\subseteq} \mathcal{B}$	$\{(i,j) \mid A_i \not\subseteq B_j\}$
At-Least-T-Join	$\mathcal{A} \bowtie^{\geq T} \mathcal{B}$	$T \in \mathbb{N}, \{(i,j) \mid \lvert A_i \cap B_j\rvert \geq T\}$

Table 1: Joins considered in this paper.

erty that $|\mathcal{A} \bowtie^{\supseteq} \mathcal{B}| > 0$ is equivalent to $|E| > 0$, such an E must have a sub-expression which, when evaluated, generates an intermediate result whose size is *quadratic* in the size of $\mathcal{A}$ and $\mathcal{B}$. In other words, in contrast with the set-intersection join, there is no linear space expression E in the relational algebra for the $|\mathcal{A} \bowtie^{\supseteq} \mathcal{B}| > 0$ decision problem for the superset join.

1.3 Main Results

To describe the main results about the communication-complexity of a set-join, we need to define its *enumerative version* and its *counting version.* Given a set-join $\mathcal{A} \bowtie^{\mathcal{P}} \mathcal{B}$, its enumerative version refers to the communication-complexity of determining (enumerating) the set of pairs $\{(i,j)|\mathcal{P}(A_i, B_j)\}$, and its counting version refers to the communication-complexity of determining the count $k = |\{(i,j)|\mathcal{P}(A_i, B_j)\}|$ of this set. For the counting version, we furthermore discern between the *exact* and the *approximate* determination of k.

Notice that a lower bound on the counting version implies a lower bound on the corresponding enumerative version, and analogously, an upper bound on the enumerative version implies and upper bound on its corresponding counting version. Actually, in many cases, the enumerative and counting versions are the same. Therefore, in the statements of our results we will not always explicitly differentiate between them.

The main contributions of our paper are

1. to the best of our knowledge, the first formal evidence of the suspected quantitative differences between the "hardness" of computing different set-join operations in terms of a computational complexity model;
2. the determination of matching lower and upper communication bound for the enumerative set-intersection join;
3. the determination of an output-sensitive upper communication bound for the enumerative natural join;
4. the determination of upper and lower communication bounds for approximating the size of set-intersection join;
5. the determination of matching lower and upper communication bound for the enumerative and counting versions of superset, subset, set-disjointness, and set-equality set-join operations; and
6. new algorithmic techniques and insights for Boolean matrix multiplication (isomorphic to set-intersection join), which lead to an improved algorithm for the fundamental problem of computing transitive closure of a directed graph in terms of running time.

Our main results for various joins are described in Table 2. In the rest of this section we illustrate our main results in more details. Below are some global notations we use in our paper.

- n to denote the size of the item universe,
- m to denote the number of tuples in a table to be joined,
- k to denote the size of the output,
- s to denote the sparsity of each tuple in the set-joins; that is,
  $s = \max\{|A_i|, |B_j| \mid i, j \in [m]\}$.

For a matrix M, let $M_{i,j}$ denote the entry at i-th row and j-th column; let $M_{i,*}$ denote the i-th row and let $M_{*,j}$ denote the j-th column. Let $\mathbf{nnz}(M)$ denote the number of non-zero entries in M. For simplicity, we use $\tilde{O}(f)$ to denote $f \cdot \text{poly}\log(fmn)$. That is, $\tilde{O}$ suppresses polylogarithmic factors. We use $\tilde{\Theta}(f)$ to denote at most $\tilde{O}(f)$ and at least $\Omega(f)$.

An isomorphic way to view the composition operator $\mathcal{A} \circ \mathcal{B}$ is as a *Boolean matrix multiplication* (BMM). Construe $\mathcal{A}$ as an $m \times n$ Boolean matrix P such that $P_{i,\ell} = 1$ if and only if $(i, \ell) \in \mathcal{A}$. Similarly, construe $\mathcal{B}$ as an $n \times m$ matrix Q such that $Q_{\ell,j} = 1$ if and only if $(\ell, j) \in \mathcal{B}$. Then $(P \cdot Q)_{i,j} \geq 1$ if and only if $(i,j) \in \mathcal{A} \circ \mathcal{B}$.

We start with our results on the set-intersection join (i.e., Boolean matrix multiplication). We first consider computing the set-intersection join exactly, presenting what we consider to be the main result of this paper; certainly it is the most surprising. Recent work on the communication complexity of matrix multiplication demonstrated that, when Alice (holding $\mathcal{A} = \{A_1, \ldots, A_m\}, A_i \subseteq [n]$) and Bob (holding $\mathcal{B} = \{B_1, \ldots, B_m\}, B_j \subseteq [n]$) construe $\mathcal{A}$ and $\mathcal{B}$ as $m \times n$ and $n \times m$ matrices, respectively, they can compute their product $\mathcal{A} \cdot \mathcal{B}$ over an arbitrary finite field with randomized communication $\tilde{O}(kn)$, where k is the number of nonzeroes in the matrix product [44]. Intuitively, this upper bound looks essentially optimal. It seems impossible to attain $o(kn)$ communication: shouldn't Alice and Bob need to communicate $\Omega(n)$ bits in the worst case, for every nonzero entry in the output (exchanging the relevant n-bit vectors)? Here, we show that $o(kn)$ communication is in fact possible, and the communication algorithms can be efficiently implemented as well.

	enumeration / exact counting		c-approximate counting	
	upper bound	lower bound	upper bound	lower bound
set-intersection join (composition), not-superset/not-subset join	$\tilde{\Theta}(\min(ms, \sqrt{skn}) + n)$ *		$\tilde{O}(n/\epsilon^2)$ ($c = 1+\epsilon$)	$\Omega(n/\epsilon^2)$ (1-way, $c = 1+\epsilon$) $\Omega(n/\epsilon^{\frac{2}{3}})$ (2-way, $c = 1+\epsilon$)
set-equality join	$\Theta(m \operatorname{ilog}^{\Theta(r)} m + \log\log n)$		$\Theta(m \operatorname{ilog}^{\Theta(r)} m + \log\log n)$ (any $c > 0$)	
set-disjointness join subset/superset join	$\Theta(mn)$		$\Theta(mn)$ (any $c > 0$)	
at-least-T join	$\Theta(mn)$		$O(mn)$	$\Omega(mn)$ (1-way, any $c > 0$) $\Omega(m\sqrt{nT})$ (2-way, any $c > 0$)

Table 2: Our results for joins. *This result also applies to natrual join after converting it to the form of set-intersection join by projections (see discussions in Section 1.1). $\tilde{O}(f)$ denotes $f \cdot \operatorname{poly}\log(fmn)$; $\tilde{\Theta}(f)$ denotes at most $\tilde{O}(f)$ and at least $\Omega(f)$; and $\operatorname{ilog}^r m$ means $\log \ldots \log m$ with r logs.

Result 1 (Theorem 3 in Section 3) *The randomized communication complexity of computing set-intersection join (equivalently, computing the product of two Boolean matrices $P \in \{0,1\}^{m\times n}$ and $Q \in \{0,1\}^{n\times m}$) is $\tilde{O}(\sqrt{k} \cdot n)$, when n is the universe size and k is the output join size. Furthermore, if the sparsity of $\mathcal{A}, \mathcal{B}$ is at most s, we can obtain an algorithm with $\tilde{O}(\min(ms, \sqrt{skn}) + n)$ bits of communication. Finally, this algorithm is optimal, up to polylogarithmic factors.*

The algorithm (Algorithm 1) in Theorem 3 applies both the Count-Sketch algorithm [12] and the ℓ_0-sketch algorithm [20] in novel ways. The high-level idea is to consider two kinds of column vectors that may appear in the output matrix: columns which are "sparse" and columns which are "dense". Roughly speaking, "dense" columns have at least $\sqrt{k}$ non-zeroes, and "sparse" columns are those which are not dense. First, we can determine which resulting columns will be sparse and dense using an ℓ_0-sketch, requiring little communication between the two parties. Dense columns can be handled efficiently by having Bob send $O(\sqrt{k})$ of the relevant columns to Alice (there are $O(\sqrt{k})$ columns with greater than $\sqrt{k}$ nonzeroes in the output matrix, by simple counting). Sparse columns can be computed using a Count-Sketch matrix with only $\tilde{O}(\sqrt{k})$ rows: Alice can multiply such a matrix with her own, and send the resulting $\tilde{O}(\sqrt{k}n)$ data to Bob, who can then recover the sparse columns of the matrix product.

As a "by-product", which is in fact fundamental for databases, this algorithm plus a post-processing (Algorithm 2 in Section 3) can output all witnesses of all set-intersections, that is, all ℓ's s.t. $\ell \in A_i \cap B_j$ for any $A_i \in \mathcal{A}, B_j \in \mathcal{B}$, which in fact solves the corresponding natural join problem (see the discussion on the equivalence between natural join and set-intersection join in Section 1.1).

Result 2 (Corollary 1 in Section 3) *Under the notations in Result 1, the algorithm can also be used to solve the corresponding natural join problem with $\tilde{O}(\min(ms, \sqrt{skn}) + n)$ communication.*

With more algorithmic cleverness, this algorithm can be efficiently implemented as well:

Result 3 (Theorem 13 in Section 4) *There is a randomized algorithm for multiplying $P \in \{0,1\}^{m\times n}$ and $Q \in \{0,1\}^{n\times m}$ that runs in $\tilde{O}(k + k^{1/2}(\mathbf{nnz}(P) + \mathbf{nnz}(Q)))$ time and succeeds with probability $1 - 1/n$, where k is the number of nonzero entries in the output.*[4]

Result 3 has natural applications in situations where one anticipates that the output may be sparse. For example, in Section 4 we can readily apply Result 3 to obtain:

Result 4 (Corollary 4 in Section 4) *There is a randomized algorithm for computing the transitive closure of an $n \times n$ Boolean matrix A which runs in $\tilde{O}(k^{1.5})$ time and succeeds with probability $1 - 1/n$, where k is the number of edges in the transitive closure.*

Hence any transitive closure which contains $O(\mathbf{nnz}(A))$ edges can be computed in $\tilde{O}(\mathbf{nnz}(A)^{1.5})$ time. This, in the case that $\mathbf{nnz}(A) \le n$, improves over a recent result of Borassi, Crescenzi, and Habib [7], who achieved $\tilde{O}(\mathbf{nnz}(A) \cdot n^{\frac{\omega+1}{4}})$ time, where $\omega \approx 2.373$ is the exponent of fast matrix multiplication. Moreover, their algorithm relies on fast matrix multiplication algorithms while ours does not, and so ours presumably have practical advantages. One can recognize whether a given graph is a comparability graph in the same time as computing the transitive closure, as observed in [7]. (See Section 4 for more details.) Corollary 4 therefore improves the algorithm of [7] for this task as well.

Next, we turn to approximating the *size* of the set-intersection join. Let c-SIJ be the communication problem of approximating the number of pairs (i, j) such that $A_i \cap B_j \ne \varnothing$ to within a multiplicative factor of c. We give nearly tight upper and lower bounds on the *one-way* communication complexity of this problem, where all messages are sent from Alice to Bob, and Bob computes the answer. The true answer is surprisingly low:

Result 5 (Theorem 5, 6 in Section 3) *The one-way randomized communication of $(1+\epsilon)$-SIJ is $\tilde{\Theta}(n/\epsilon^2)$.*

The upper bound applies the ℓ_0-sketch algorithm ([20]) in a simple way; the lower bound follows by a reduction from the Indexing function (see the Section 2 for definitions). We note that since our upper bound is a sketching algorithm and our lower bound is for 1-way communication, they apply to the *data stream model* of computation in which one sees the sets A_i and B_j one at a time in an arbitrary order and one

[4]The algorithm can be implemented in any reasonable computational model with random access to the input, such as the RAM model.

would like to compute $(1+\epsilon)$-SIJ using a small amount of memory. Our results imply that $\tilde{\Theta}(n/\epsilon^2)$ bits of memory is necessary and sufficient.

In the general (two-way) communication setting, we can still prove a lower bound depending on n and ϵ, although we do not have a better upper bound than that for 1-way communication.

Result 6 (Theorem 7 in Section 3) *The randomized communication complexity of $(1+\epsilon)$-SIJ is at least $\Omega(n/\epsilon^{2/3})$.*

A main question left open by this work is to close this gap for two-way approximate set-intersect join.

Finally, we consider a few other joins. In the Set-Equality Join (EQJ) problem, Alice and Bob wish to compute all pairs (i,j) such that $A_i = B_j$. We notice that the complexity of this enumerative problem is the same as the counting version. In fact, we show that a lower bound for the counting version matches an upper bound for the enumerative version. We thus use EQJ for the two versions interchangeably. In its approximation version, which we call c-EQJ, Alice and Bob wish to compute the *number* of such pairs (i,j) within a multiplicative factor of c. Recent work on the communication complexity of set intersection implies fairly tight results on the communication complexity of these two problems:

Result 7 (Theorem 8, 9 and Corollary 2 in Section 3) *The randomized communication complexity of EQJ is at least $\Omega(m \operatorname{ilog}^{\Theta(r)} m + \log\log n)$ and is at most $O(m \operatorname{ilog}^r m + \log\log n)$, where $\operatorname{ilog}^r = \log\log\cdots\log m$ (with r logs) denotes the* log *function iterated r times. Analogous results hold for c-EQJ for any constant $c > 0$.*

Then we turn to the Set-Disjointness Join (SDJ) problem, where Alice and Bob wish to compute all pairs (i,j) such that $A_i \cap B_j = \emptyset$. Again, we notice that the enumerative version has the same complexity as the counting version of this problem. More precisely, the lower bound for the counting version is high enough to match the trivial enumerative upper bound that Alice simply ships all her data to Bob. We thus use SDJ for the two versions interchangeably. In this case, we can show there is no substantially better communication algorithm than the one in which one party sends all their data to the other.

Result 8 (Theorem 10 in Section 3) *The randomized communication complexity of SDJ is $\Omega(mn)$. Analogous results hold for the c-approximation version c-SDJ for any constant $c > 0$.*

We also look at the At-Least-T Join (ATJ) problem, where T is a non-negative integer known in advance and Alice and Bob wish to output (or count, again they have the same complexity) those (i,j) such that $|A_i \cap B_j| \geq T$. Via a simple reduction to SDJ, this requires $\Omega(mn)$ communication. More interestingly, we consider the c-ATJ problem in which the players would like to approximate the number of such pairs up to a multiplicative factor of c. Here we can prove lower bounds:

Result 9 (Theorem 11, 12 in Section A) *For every $c > 1$, the randomized one-way communication complexity of c-ATJ is $\Omega(mn)$, and assuming $\kappa \log m \leq T \leq 99n/100$, for a constant $\kappa > 0$, the randomized two-way communication complexity of c-ATJ is $\Omega(m\sqrt{nT})$.*

2. BACKGROUND ON SKETCHES AND COMMUNICATION COMPLEXITY

In this section we introduce a few sketching algorithms from the data stream literature and some concepts in communication complexity that are needed in this paper. Please refer to the survey of Muthukrishnan [31] for more background on data steams and the book [22] for more knowledge on communication complexity. For background on approximation and randomized algorithms, please refer to the classic book [30].

Sketches. The idea being that a sketch provides a faithful but (much) smaller summary representation of a data object and that a reconstruction function has the ability to yield back a good approximation of the initial data object or some function (like the ℓ_0 norm) of this data object. Since sketches are smaller than the original data objects, they can be communicated with fewer bits. Furthermore, this communication preserves in a good way the original data object.

We will make use of a few linear sketches from the literature. Let κ be an integer. We say that a vector v is κ-sparse if v has at most κ non-zeros in its components.

Lemma 1 ([12], Count-Sketch) *For any positive integer n, $\delta \in (0,1)$, and integer $\kappa \in [n]$, there is a distribution on random matrices $S \in \mathbb{R}^{O(\kappa \cdot \log 1/\delta) \times n}$ and a reconstruction function* $\texttt{Rec}(\cdot)$*, such that*

1. *Given any κ-sparse vector $x \in \mathbb{R}^n$,* $\texttt{Rec}(\cdot)$ *can take Sx, and give x exactly with probability $1-\delta$. In addition,* $\texttt{Rec}(\cdot)$ *can take Sx and a parameter i, and output the i-th bit of x in $\tilde{O}(1)$ time.*
2. *The column sparsity of S is bounded by $O(\log n)$.*

Lemma 2 ([20], ℓ_0-sketch) *For any positive integer n, $\epsilon \in (0,1)$, and $\delta \in (0,1)$, there is a distribution on random matrices $M \in \mathbb{R}^{O(1/\epsilon^2 \cdot \log(1/\delta)) \times n}$ and a reconstruction function* $\texttt{Rec}(\cdot)$*, such that given any $x \in [N]^n$ (N is the maximum value of coordinates in x),* $\texttt{Rec}(Mx)$ *gives a $(1+\epsilon)$-approximation of $\mathbf{nnz}(x)$ with probability $1-\delta$. Furthermore, we can truncate the real number in each entry of M to $\log(Nn)$ bits without affecting the approximation ratio.*

Communication Complexity. In this paper we consider the classical model of two-party communication complexity. Here we briefly recall some standard notions. Let $\mathcal{X}$ and $\mathcal{Y}$ be sets of strings. One party, Alice, is given $x \in \mathcal{X}$ and another party Bob is given $y \in \mathcal{Y}$, and they want to jointly compute some function $f : \mathcal{X} \times \mathcal{Y} \to \mathcal{Z}$, by exchanging messages according to a randomized algorithm Π. We allow Alice and Bob to use both private randomness (coins). Let r_A and r_B be the private coins used by Alice and Bob respectively. We use $\Pi_{xyr_Ar_B}$ to denote the transcript (i.e., the concatenation of messages) when Alice and Bob run Π on the input (x,y) using private coins r_A, r_B respectively, and $\Pi(x,y,r_A,r_B)$ denotes the output of the algorithm. We will omit x, y, r_A, r_B when clear from context. We say Π is a δ-error algorithm if for all $(x,y) \in \mathcal{X} \times \mathcal{Y}$,

$$\mathbf{Pr}_{r_A,r_B}[\Pi(x,y,r_A,r_B) \neq f(x,y)] \leq \delta.$$

Let $|\Pi|$ be the bit-length of the transcript. The *communication cost* of Π is $\max_{x,y,r_A,r_B} |\Pi_{xyr_Ar_B}|$. The δ-error randomized communication complexity of f, denoted by $R_\delta(f)$, is the minimal cost of any δ-error algorithm for f.

Let μ be a distribution over the inputs, and let $(X, Y) \sim \mu$. A deterministic algorithm Π computes f with error probability δ on μ if $\mathbf{Pr}_{(X,Y)\sim\mu}[\Pi(X,Y) \neq f(X,Y)] \leq \delta$. The *$\delta$-error μ-distributional communication complexity of* f, denoted by $D^\mu_\delta(f)$, is the minimum communication complexity of a deterministic algorithm that computes f with error probability δ on μ. Yao's Lemma [47] says that for any function f and any $\delta > 0$, $R_\delta(f) \geq \max_\mu D^\mu_\delta(f)$. Therefore to prove randomized communication lower bounds, one can choose an input distribution μ, then prove distributional communication lower bounds under μ.

For a problem $f : \mathcal{X} \times \mathcal{Y} \to \{0, 1\}$, by a standard Chernoff bound argument, it holds that for any constant $\delta > 0$, $R_{1/3}(f) = \Omega(R_\delta(f)/\log(1/\delta)) = \Omega(R_\delta(f))$.

We use $R^\to_\delta(f)$ to denote *one-way* communication complexity where communication is either only from Alice to Bob or from Bob to Alice, and use $R^{(r)}_\delta(f)$ to denote *two-way* communication complexity using r rounds of communication. In a round of communication, only one player speaks to the other player, so Alice sends a single message to Bob or Bob sends a single message to Alice.

In our lower bound reductions, we allow parties to use potentially infinite amounts of public coins in algorithms (that is, Alice and Bob have free access to a shared, potentially infinite, public random string). Denote the corresponding randomised communication complexity by R^{pub}_δ where δ is the error parameter as before. Such coins can be "removed" (replaced with private randomness) by Newman's theorem. The increases on the communication cost and error probability are negligible in our applications.

Theorem 1 (Newman's Theorem [32]) *Let $f : \{0,1\}^t \times \{0,1\}^t \to \mathbb{N}$ be a function. For every $\delta > 0$ and every $\epsilon > 0$, $R_{\epsilon+\delta}(f) \leq R^{pub}_\epsilon(f) + O(\log t + \log \delta^{-1})$, where R^{pub} denotes the randomized communication complexity with public coins.*

We will need two well-known problems in communication complexity for proving our lower bounds by reductions.

Indexing. In the Indexing communication problem for $t \in \mathbb{N}$, Alice holds $x = \{0,1\}^t$, and Bob holds an index $i \in [t]$. The goal is for Bob to compute x_i. It is known that this problem effectively requires Alice to send her entire input to Bob, in the one-way communication setting:

Lemma 3 (see, e.g., [22]) $R^\to_{1/2-\delta}$*(Indexing) $\geq \Omega(t)$ for any constant $\delta > 0$.*

Set-intersection (SI). In the SI communication problem for $t \in \mathbb{N}$, Alice has $x = (x_1, \ldots, x_t) \in \{0,1\}^t$, and Bob has $y = (y_1, \ldots, y_t) \in \{0,1\}^t$. They want to compute

$$\mathrm{SI}(x, y) = \begin{cases} 1, & \text{if } \exists \ell \in [t] \text{ s.t. } x_\ell = y_\ell = 1, \\ 0, & \text{otherwise.} \end{cases}$$

We will use the following hard input distribution for SI:

Distribution ν (Razborov [39]). With probability $1/2$, x and y are random among all pairs of non-intersecting strings each of Hamming weight exactly $t/4$, while with probability $1/2$, x and y intersect in a unique uniformly randomly chosen i, and each x and y have Hamming weight exactly $t/4$.

Lemma 4 ([39]) *D^ν_δ(SI) $\geq \Omega(t)$ for a sufficiently small constant δ.*

3. COMMUNICATION COMPLEXITY OF SET JOINS

3.1 Exact Computation of Set-Intersection Join

As mentioned earlier, we can think of Alice having a matrix $P \in \{0,1\}^{m\times n}$ where $P_{i,\ell} = 1$ if A_i has item ℓ, and Bob having a matrix $Q \in \{0,1\}^{n\times m}$ where $Q_{\ell,j} = 1$ if B_j has item ℓ. Then, the set-intersection join (SIJ) is simply the Boolean matrix multiplication $R = P \cdot Q$. Let $k = \mathbf{nnz}(R) = |\{(i,j) \mid A_i \cap B_j \neq \emptyset\}|$ be the size of the output of an SIJ instance.

One-way Communication. First we show an $\Omega(mn)$ bound for SIJ when $m = O(n)$, matching the trivial algorithm where Alice sends all her data to Bob.

Theorem 2 $R^\to_{1/3}$*(SIJ) $= \Omega(mn)$ for $m = O(n)$.*

PROOF. The proof is by a reduction from the Indexing problem of size mn. We can view Alice's mn-bit input vector as an $m \times n$ Boolean matrix by partitioning the vector to chunks of size n as rows, and Bob's index $\ell \in [mn]$ as an (i,j)-pair where $i = \lfloor \ell/n \rfloor$ and $j = \ell - \lfloor \ell/n \rfloor \cdot n$.

Suppose first that $m < n/2$. We make the first m columns of Alice's matrix P be the $m \times m$ identity matrix. On the next $n/2$ columns, we place $\min\{ms, nk\}$ random $0/1$ entries in a block diagonal matrix with blocks of size $k \times s$ (recall that s is the tuple sparsity and k is the join output size). The rest $n/2 - m$ columns are just left to be all 0. Then Bob can make use of an algorithm for SIJ to do the following:

- Query $\mathbf{nnz}(P_{*,j})$ by creating an $n \times m$ matrix Q in which all but the first column is 0. In the first column, put a 1 in the j-th position.
- Query $\mathbf{nnz}(P_{*,i} + P_{*,j})$ by creating an $n \times m$ matrix Q in which all but the first column is 0. In the first column, put a 1 in the i-th position and the j-th position.

Thus Bob can compute the (i,j)-th entry of matrix P for any $i \in [m]$ and $j \in \{m+1, \ldots, n\}$ by comparing $\mathbf{nnz}(P_{*,j})$ and $\mathbf{nnz}(P_{*,i} + P_{*,j})$. By reducing from the Indexing problem we obtain an $\Omega(mn)$ lower bound. □

Remark 1 The above lower bound does not hold in the case when $m \gg n$: for instance, if $n, s = O(1)$ but $k = \Omega(m)$. (This could happen if P has $O(1)$ random non-zero columns.) In this case there is an upper bound of $2^n = O(1)$: one can just prepare an answer for each possible query set B_j. The above lower bound would be $\min\{ms, nt\} = \Omega(m)$, which cannot hold.

Two-way Communication. In the following, suppose $\mathcal{A}$ and $\mathcal{B}$ have *sparsity* s, i.e., there are at most s non-zeroes in each A_i, B_j. (Note that $s \leq n$.) In contrast to the one-way setting, the case of two-way communication becomes extremely interesting. We show that there is a two-round algorithm with communication cost $\tilde{O}(\min(ms, \sqrt{skn}) + n)$.

Theorem 3 $R^{(2)}_{2/m}$*(SIJ) $= \tilde{O}(\min(ms, \sqrt{skn}) + n)$. This bound also holds if we require to output for each $(i,j) \in [m]^2$, all the witnesses ℓ such that $\ell \in A_i \cap B_j$.*

Algorithm 1: Exact Algorithm for Set-Intersection Join

Input : Alice has a matrix $P \in \mathbb{N}^{m \times n}$ with rows representing $A_1, \ldots, A_m$, and Bob has a matrix $Q \in \mathbb{N}^{n \times m}$ with columns representing $B_1, \ldots, B_m$. Let $R \leftarrow PQ \in \mathbb{N}^{m \times m}$.

Output: $k \leftarrow \mathbf{nnz}(R)$

1 Set $s \leftarrow \max\{\mathbf{nnz}(A_i), \mathbf{nnz}(B_i) \mid i \in [m]\}$. Set $k_A \leftarrow 0, k_B \leftarrow 0$;
2 Alice and Bob approximate the number of non-zero entries in columns $R_{*,1}, \ldots, R_{*,m}$ up to a factor of 2 using Algorithm 3 (setting $\epsilon = 1$). Let $\tilde{k}_j$ be the 2-approximation of $\mathbf{nnz}(R_{*,j})$, and let $\tilde{k} \leftarrow \sum_{j \in [m]} \tilde{k}_j$;
3 **if** $s\tilde{k} < n$ **then**
4   Set $L = \emptyset$;
5   Let $H \leftarrow \{j \mid \tilde{k}_j > 0\}$;
6   **foreach** $j \in H$ **do**
7   Bob sends $Q_{*,j}$ to Alice;
8   Alice computes $\mathbf{nnz}(R) = \sum_{j \in H} \mathbf{nnz}(PQ_{*,j})$.
9 **else if** $s\tilde{k} \geq n$ **then**
10   Let $H \leftarrow \{j \mid \tilde{k}_j > \sqrt{s\tilde{k}/n}\}$, and $L \leftarrow [m] \backslash H$;
11   **foreach** $j \in H$ **do**
12   Bob sends $Q_{*,j}$ to Alice;
13   Alice computes $R_{*,j} = P \cdot Q_{*,j}$, and sets $k_A \leftarrow k_A + \mathbf{nnz}(R_{*,j})$;
14   Alice samples a random matrix $S \in \mathbb{R}^{O(\sqrt{s\tilde{k}/n} \cdot \log m) \times m}$ according to Lemma 1 (setting $\delta \leftarrow 1/(nm^3)$), and sends $Z \leftarrow SP$ to Bob;
15   Bob computes $k_B \leftarrow \sum_{j \in L} \mathbf{nnz}(\texttt{Rec}(ZQ_{*,j}))$ according to Lemma 1, and sends it back to Alice;
16   Alice outputs $k \leftarrow k_A + k_B$.

Algorithm 2: Post-processing to Compute All Pairs (i, j), All Witnesses ℓ s.t. $\ell \in A_i \cap B_j$

`/* All notations follow Algorithm 1 */`
1 **foreach** $j \in H$ **do**
2   Alice computes for all $i \in [m]$, the $A_i \cap B_j$;
3 **foreach** $j \in L$ **do**
4   **foreach** $i \in [m]$ **do**
5   **foreach** $\ell \in B_j$ **do**
6   Bob removes ℓ from B_j, getting $Q'_{*,j}$, computes $R'_{*,j} = \texttt{Rec}(ZQ'_{*,j})$; `/* Z is sent to Bob at Line 14 of Algorithm 1 */`
7   **if** $R_{i,j} \neq R'_{*,j}$ **then**
8   declares $\ell \in A_i \cap B_j$;
9   Bob adds ℓ back to B_j.

We have the following immediate corollary for natural join. Let us first recall the relationship between natural join and set-intersection join. In the natural join, Alice has a relation $\mathcal{A} \subseteq [m] \times [n]$, and Bob has a relation $\mathcal{B} \subseteq [n] \times [m]$. They want to compute $\mathcal{A} \bowtie \mathcal{B}$. Now we make the following "rewrite" of the input: For each $i, j \in [m]$, let $A_i = \{\ell \mid (i, \ell) \in \mathcal{A}\}$ and $B_j = \{\ell \mid (\ell, j) \in \mathcal{B}\}$ be the projection sets of $\mathcal{A}, \mathcal{B}$ on $[m]$. It is straightforward to observe that $(\mathcal{A}' = \{A_1, \ldots, A_m\}, \mathcal{B}' = \{B_1, \ldots, B_m\})$ becomes an input to the set-intersection join. Still let $s = \max\{|A_i|, |B_j| \mid i, j \in [m]\}$ be the sparsity of sets.

Corollary 1 *Under the notations above, Alice and Bob can compute the natural join $\mathcal{A} \bowtie \mathcal{B}$ exactly in 2 rounds with probability $(1 - 2/m)$ using $\tilde{O}(\min(ms, \sqrt{skn}) + n)$ bits of communication.*

PROOF. (of Theorem 3) The algorithm is described in Algorithm 1, where $\tilde{k}_j, \tilde{k}$ are defined, and P, Q are the matrix representations of $\mathcal{A}, \mathcal{B}$. Now we give the analysis.

First note that Line 2 only costs $\tilde{O}(n)$ bits of communication by Theorem 5 (see Section 3.2; note that here $\epsilon = 1$).

Suppose now that $s\tilde{k} < n$, or $sk < n$ (note that $k \leq \tilde{k} \leq 2k$). The number of columns of R containing a non-zero entry is at most k. These columns can be determined with $\tilde{O}(n)$ communication using Lemma 2, since a column contains a non-zero entry if and only if $\tilde{k}_j > 0$. Given the identities of these columns j in R, Bob can send the corresponding $Q_{*,j}$, which requires only s communication since columns of Q are s-sparse. Hence, Bob can send all such columns of Q using at most $k \cdot s \cdot \log n = \tilde{O}(n)$ communication. Hence, if $sk < n$, the upper bound is $\tilde{O}(n)$, as desired.

Suppose then that $s\tilde{k} \geq n$. We can show an $O(\min(ms, \sqrt{skn}))$ upper bound. Since each $\tilde{k}_j$ $(j \in [m])$ is a 2-approximation of k_j, the number of columns in $H = \{j \mid \tilde{k}_j > \sqrt{sk/n}\}$ can be at most $2k/(\sqrt{sk/n}) = 2\sqrt{kn/s}$. For each $j \in H$, if Bob sends $Q_{*,j}$ to Alice, then Alice can compute $R_{*,j} = PQ_{*,j}$. The total communication for all such columns, given that the columns of Q are s-sparse, is at most $2\sqrt{kn/s} \cdot s = 2\sqrt{skn}$. All remaining columns of R have at most $\sqrt{sk/n}$ non-zero entries. Alice chooses a random Count-Sketch matrix S with $\kappa = \sqrt{s\tilde{k}/n}$ according to Lemma 1, computes SP, and sends this to Bob. This requires $\tilde{O}(\sqrt{sk/n} \cdot n) = \tilde{O}(\sqrt{skn})$ bits of communication.

Finally, note that if $ms < \sqrt{skn}$, Alice can alternatively just send P to Bob using $O(ms \log n)$ communication, since the rows of P are s-sparse.

The error of Algorithm 1 comes from two places. The first is the error introduced by the call of Algorithm 3 at Line 2, which is bounded by $1/m$ by Theorem 5. The second error comes from Line 14 and 15. By setting $\delta = 1/(nm^3)$ in Lemma 1 and apply a union bound on columns with indices in L, we can also bound this error by $1/m$.

For the communication rounds, Lines 2 and 14 can be done simultaneously in the first round (from Alice to Bob), and Lines 7 (or 12) and 15 can be done simultaneously in the second round (from Bob to Alice).

Algorithm 2 shows that we can in fact compute for all pairs $(i, j) \in [m]^2$, all the witnesses ℓ such that $\ell \in A_i \cap B_j$ using a post-processing (without any further communication) after running Algorithm 1. For any $j \in H$, Alice can compute the witnesses ℓ for all (i, j) $(i \in [m])$ trivially since Bob has sent the whole column $Q_{*,j}$ (i.e., the set B_j) to her. For any $j \in L$, for any $i \in [m]$ Bob can recover all the witnesses ℓ in $A_i \cap B_j$ as follows: for each $\ell \in B_j$, Bob first removes ℓ from B_j by setting the corresponding cell $Q_{\ell,j} = 0$ (getting $Q'_{*,j}$), and compute $R'_{*,j} = \texttt{Rec}(ZQ'_{*,j})$.

Now for each $i \in [m]$, if $R_{i,j} \neq R'_{i,j}$, then we conclude that $\ell \in A_i \cap B_j$. Note that we perform at most nm^2 such tests, thus by a union bound all tests succeed with probability $1 - 1/(nm^3) \cdot (nm^2) = 1 - 1/m$.

Note that at the end of Algorithm 2, the sets $A_i \cap B_j$ $(i, j \in [m])$ are disjointly distributed at Alice and Bob. They need to spend another $\tilde{O}(k)$ bits of communication in the worst case if Alice (or Bob) would like to obtain all the witnesses. □

Remark 2 (Not-Superset Join and Not-Subset Join) As mentioned in the introduction, the not-superset join (outputting all (i, j) such that $A_i \not\supseteq B_j$) can be thought as the complement of the set-intersection join: one can convert $\mathcal{A} = \{A_1, \ldots, A_m\}$ to $\mathcal{A}' = \{A'_1, \ldots, A'_m\}$ such that $A'_i = [n] - A_i$ for each $i \in [m]$, and then solve the set-intersection join on $\mathcal{A}'$ and $\mathcal{B}$. There is one issue: sets in $\mathcal{A}'$ may not have sparsity s (typically $\ll n$). However, we have noticed that our upper bound in Theorem 3 still holds since Algorithm 1 only requires sets in $\mathcal{B}$ to have sparsity s (or only sets in $\mathcal{A}$ by exchanging the positions of Alice and Bob). The above argument also implies to not-subset join by symmetry.

Surprising as the above algorithm is, there is a matching lower bound up to polylogarithmic factors:

Theorem 4 $R_{1/3}(SIJ) = \Omega(\min(ms, \sqrt{skn}) + n)$.

PROOF. For the $\Omega(n)$ lower bound, let $s, k \leq n$ and put an instance of n-bit SI on the diagonal of P and Q. Here we use $m \leq n$. If $m > n$ we only use the upper $n \times n$ submatrix.

It remains to show a lower bound of $\min(ms, \sqrt{skn})$. We can assume $sk > n$, as otherwise this minimum is less than the n lower bound just established. Notice that if $ms = \sqrt{skn}$, then $m = \sqrt{kn/s}$. It therefore suffices to assume that $\sqrt{kn/s} < m$ and show a $\sqrt{skn}$ lower bound. Indeed, if $m < \sqrt{kn/s}$, then we can both reduce k and n by the same multiplicative factor g, obtaining k' and n', so that $sk' > n'$ still holds and g is chosen large enough so that $m = \sqrt{k'n'/s}$. Reducing n to n' corresponds to restricting to the first n' columns of P and first n' rows of Q. As s is unchanged, and when $m = \sqrt{k'n'/s}$ we have $ms = \sqrt{sk'n'}$, by showing a $\sqrt{sk'n'}$ lower bound we obtain the desired ms lower bound.

Hence, it suffices to show a $\sqrt{skn}$ lower bound under the assumption that $\sqrt{kn/s} < m$. Set $t = \sqrt{nk/s}$. We construct P and Q as follows: In P only the first t rows are non-zero and in Q only the first t columns are non-zero. We partition coordinates $[n]$ into n/s disjoint groups each of size s. We place the first SI instance on the first row of P and first column of Q into the first group of s coordinates. We place the second independent SI instance on the second row of P and second column of Q into the second group of s coordinates. After processing n/s independent SI instances, we wrap back around to the first group of s coordinates, and second group of s coordinates, and continue. Note in total we plant t independent SI instances. Doing things in this way ensures that the inner product of the i-th row of P with the j-th column of Q is only non-zero if they both have SI instances placed on the same group of s coordinates. For each i, only an s/n fraction of the j have this property. As there are t different choices of i and j, this makes the number of non-zero entries of R equal to $t^2 \cdot s/n$, which is at most k by our choice of t.

If we can exactly determine $\mathbf{nnz}(R)$, then we can figure out the number of the t planted SI instances which evaluated to 0, since all cross-pairs (i, j) $(i \neq j)$ of SI instances will intersect with probability $1 - o(1)$ (similar to Claim 1 in Section 3.3). We will know from the proof of Theorem 10 that just determining the OR of t SI instances has complexity the same as solving a single SI instance of size $t \cdot s$. Therefore we obtain a lower bound of $\Omega(ts) = \Omega(\sqrt{skn})$. □

Algorithm 3: $(1 + \epsilon)$-Approximation Algorithm for Set-Intersection Join

Input : Alice has $P \in \mathbb{N}^{m \times n}$ with rows representing $A_1, \ldots, A_m$, and Bob has $Q \in \mathbb{N}^{n \times m}$ with columns representing $B_1, \ldots, B_m$.

Output: A $(1 + \epsilon)$-approximation of $|\{(i, j) \mid A_i \cap B_j \neq \emptyset\}|$.

$\delta \leftarrow 1/m^2$;

Alice samples a random sketching matrix $M \in \mathbb{R}^{O(1/\epsilon^2 \cdot \log(1/\delta)) \times m}$ according to Lemma 2, and sends $Z \leftarrow MP$ to Bob;

Bob outputs $\sum_{j \in [m]} \mathtt{Rec}(ZQ_{*,j})$.

3.2 Approximate Counting for Set-Intersection Join

One-way Communication. We can use the ℓ_0-sketch (Lemma 2) to design a simple one-way algorithm for approximating SIJ to within $1 + \epsilon$, for every $\epsilon > 0$:

Theorem 5 *For all* $\epsilon > 0$, $R^{\rightarrow}_{1/m}((1 + \epsilon)\text{-}SIJ) = \tilde{O}(n/\epsilon^2)$.

PROOF. The algorithm is described in Algorithm 3. Now we give the analysis.

First, note that $\mathtt{Rec}(ZQ_{*,j}) = \mathtt{Rec}(MPQ_{*,j}) = \mathtt{Rec}(MR_{*,j})$. By Lemma 2, $\mathtt{Rec}(MR_{*,j})$ computes $\mathbf{nnz}(R_{*,j})$ up to a multiplicative error $(1 + \epsilon)$ with probability $(1 - 1/m^2)$ for each $j \in [m]$. Therefore Algorithm 3 computes $\mathbf{nnz}(R)$ up to $(1 + \epsilon)$-approximation with probability $(1 - 1/m)$ by a union bound. Finally, note that Alice only needs to send the matrix Z, which is $O(n/\epsilon^2 \cdot \log m \log(mn))$ bits by Lemma 2 (here we set $N = O(m)$). □

We can prove a matching lower bound for this approximation problem (up to polylog factors):

Theorem 6 $R^{\rightarrow}_{1/3}((1 + \epsilon)\text{-}SIJ) = \Omega(n/\epsilon^2)$.

We need the following lemma of Jayram et al. [19]. Let $\Delta(a, b)$ be the hamming distance between two bitstrings $a, b \in \{0, 1\}^{1/\epsilon^2}$.

Lemma 5 ([19]) *Let x be a random bitstring of length $\gamma = 1/\epsilon^2$, and let i be a random index in $[\gamma]$. Choose γ public random bitstrings $r^1, \ldots, r^\gamma$, each of length γ. Create γ-length bitstrings a, b as follows:*

- *For each $j \in [\gamma]$, $a_j = \text{majority}\{r^j_k \mid \text{indices } k \text{ for which } x_k = 1\}$.*
- *For each $j \in [\gamma]$, $b_j = r^j_i$.*

Then with success probability $1/2 + \delta$ for a constant $\delta > 0$, we can determine the value of x_i from any $c\sqrt{\Delta(a,b)}$-additive approximation to $\Delta(a,b)$, provided $c > 0$ is a sufficiently small constant.

PROOF. We give a reduction from Indexing. Alice has a random bitstring y of length $(n-\gamma)\cdot\gamma$, which is partitioned to $n-\gamma$ contiguous groups $y^1, \ldots, y^{n-\gamma}$. She creates her matrix $P \in \{0,1\}^{\gamma\times n}$ as follows: she uses public coins to choose random bitstrings $r^1, \ldots, r^\gamma$, each of length γ. For the leftmost $\gamma \times \gamma$ submatrix of P, in the i-th column for each $i \in [\gamma]$, Alice uses $r^1, \ldots, r^\gamma$ and the value i to create the γ-length bitstring b according to Lemma 5 and assigns it to this column. Next, in the remaining $n-\gamma$ columns of P, in the j-th column for each $j \in \{\gamma+1, \ldots, n\}$, Alice uses $y^{j-\gamma}$ and $r^1, \ldots, r^\gamma$ to create the γ-length bitstring a according to Lemma 5 and assigns it to this column.

Bob has an index $\ell = i + (j-\gamma-1)\cdot\gamma$ ($i \in [\gamma], j \in \{\gamma+1, \ldots, n\}$), and he wants to learn the ℓ-th coordinate of y. This is a standard Indexing problem, and by Lemma 3 Alice has to send $\Omega(|y|) = \Omega(n/\epsilon^2)$ bits to get a success probability $(1/2+\delta)$ for any constant $\delta > 0$. For the reduction, Bob creates his matrix $Q \in \{0,1\}^{n\times\gamma}$ in which all but the first column is 0. In the first column, he puts a 1 in the i-th position and the j-th position. Then in $P \cdot Q$ all but the first column is 0, and the first column is equal to $P_{*,i} + P_{*,j}$. Note that $(P_{*,i}, P_{*,j})$ corresponds to a pair of (a,b) created from $r^1, \ldots, r^\gamma$ and $x = y^{j-\gamma}$ (and $x_i = (y^{j-\gamma})_i = y_\ell$) in Lemma 5. Also note that $(P_{*,i} + P_{*,j})_t = 1$ if and only if $P_{t,i} \neq P_{t,j}$. Therefore from a $(1+c_\epsilon\epsilon)$-approximation of $\mathbf{nnz}(PQ) = \mathbf{nnz}(P_{*,i} + P_{*,j})$ for a sufficiently small constant c_ϵ, and exact values $\mathbf{nnz}(P_{*,i}), \mathbf{nnz}(P_{*,j})$ (Alice can send Bob all $\mathbf{nnz}(P_{*,k}$ $(k \in [n]))$ using $O(n\log(1/\epsilon)) = o(n/\epsilon^2)$ bits which is negligible in the reduction), one can compute $\Delta(P_{*,i}, P_{*,j})$ up to an additive error $c_\epsilon\epsilon\cdot\mathbf{nnz}(PQ) \leq c\sqrt{\Delta(P_{*,i}, P_{*,j})}$ (note that both $\mathbf{nnz}(PQ)$ and $\Delta(P_{*,i}, P_{*,j})$ are in the order $\Theta(1/\epsilon^2)$) for a sufficiently small constant c_ϵ, and consequently y_ℓ with probability $1/2+\delta$ for a constant δ by Lemma 5. This completes the reduction. The one-way communication complexity of $(1+\epsilon)$-SIJ follows from Lemma 3. □

Two-way Communication. While we do not have a better upper bound than given by Theorem 5, we can still prove a non-trivial lower bound using the recent work [45].

Theorem 7 *$R_\delta((1+\epsilon)$-SIJ$) = \Omega(n/\epsilon^{2/3})$ for a sufficiently small constant δ.*

PROOF. We start by choosing a hard input distribution ψ for SIJ: for each $i \in [m]$, we first choose $(A_i, B_i) \sim \mu$ (see its definition in Section 2), and then pick a special coordinate $\ell \in [n]$ uniformly at random and replace (A_i^ℓ, B_i^ℓ) with $\{0,1\}^2$ uniformly at random.

Let SUM$(\mathcal{A}, \mathcal{B}) = \sum_{i\in[m]}$ SI(A_i, B_i). In [45] the following is shown.

Lemma 6 ([45]) *Any randomized algorithm that computes SUM up to an additive error $\sqrt{m}/2$ with probability δ for a sufficiently small constant δ needs $\Omega(mn)$ bits of communication.*

We now establish a relationship between SIJ and SUM: For a fixed pair $(i,j), i \neq j$, the probability that $A_i \cap B_j = \emptyset$ is at most $(1-1/16)^{n-1} \leq 2^{-\Omega(n)}$ (ignoring the special coordinate ℓ). By a union bound, with error probability at most $m^2 \cdot 2^{-\Omega(n)} = o(1)$ (assuming $n = \Omega(\log m)$), we have SIJ$(\mathcal{A}, \mathcal{B}) =$ SUM$(\mathcal{A}, \mathcal{B}) + m(m-1)$. By this equality and Lemma 6, we conclude that any randomized algorithm that computes SIJ up to an additive error $\sqrt{m}/2$ with probability δ' for a sufficiently small constant δ' needs $\Omega(mn)$ bits of communication. Since SIJ$(A,B) \leq m^2$, the theorem follows by setting $m = \epsilon^{-2/3}$. □

3.3 Other Types of Joins

Set-Equality Join. Consider the EQJ problem where Alice has sets $A_1, \ldots, A_m$, and Bob has sets $B_1, \ldots, B_m$. They want to compute all pairs (i,j) such that $A_i = B_j$ (or count the number of such pairs, which has the same complexity). This is just the problem of computing the intersection of sets $\mathcal{A} = \{A_1, \ldots, A_m\}$ and $\mathcal{B} = \{B_1, \ldots, B_m\}$, where the elements of sets $\mathcal{A}$ and $\mathcal{B}$ are themselves sets. The communication complexity of set intersection is known, with near-tight upper and lower bounds in terms of the number of rounds. We can assume that $\mathcal{A}$ and $\mathcal{B}$ are sets, rather than multisets, and the players can each locally solve the EQJ problem by also exchanging the multiplicities of each of their sets A_i and B_j, which can be done by each communicating $O(m)$ bits (since the sum of the multiplicities is m).

Theorem 8 *([8]) $R_{1/3}^{(r)}$(EQJ) $= O(m \operatorname{ilog}^r m + \log\log n)$, where $\operatorname{ilog}^r = \log\log\cdots\log m$ (with r logs). denotes the $\log$ function iterated r times.*

The upper bound is almost matched by the following lower bound.

Theorem 9 *([40]) $R_{1/3}^{(r)}$(EQJ) $= \Omega(m \operatorname{ilog}^{cr} m + \log\log n)$, where $c > 0$ is a fixed constant.*

Let c-EQJ denote the problem of approximating the number of pairs (i,j) such that $A_i = B_j$ up to a multiplicative factor of c. We notice that the above lower bound for EQJ in fact holds just to check if $\mathcal{A} \cap \mathcal{B} = \emptyset$, and therefore implies:

Corollary 2 *$R_{1/3}^{(r)}$(c-EQJ) $= \Omega(m \operatorname{ilog}^{cr} m + \log\log n)$ for a fixed constant $c > 0$.*

Set-Disjoint Join, Subset Join and Superset Join. In the Set-Disjoint-Join (SDJ) problem, where Alice and Bob wish to compute all pairs (i,j) such that $A_i \cap B_j = \varnothing$. We show that for SDJ there is no better algorithm than the trivial one in which Alice just sends all her data to Bob. The lower bound in fact holds for the case where Alice and Bob just want to count the number of such pairs (i,j), or even whether there exists a pair (i,j) such that $A_i \cap B_j = \varnothing$, and thus any constant multiplicative approximation of counting the number of such pairs has the same complexity.

Theorem 10 *$R_{1/3}$(SDJ) $= \Omega(mn)$. The lower bound also holds for any multiplicative approximation of SDJ.*

Due to the equivalence of SDJ and subset join (SubJ) and superset join (SupJ), (e.g., $A_i \supseteq B_j \Leftrightarrow \overline{A_i} \cap B_j = \emptyset$), we have the following corollary.

Corollary 3 $R_{1/3}(SubJ) = R_{1/3}(SupJ) = \Omega(mn)$. *The lower bound also holds for any multiplicative approximations of SubJ and SupJ.*

PROOF. Due to the space constraints, we delay the proof to Appendix B.1. □

At-Least-T Join. We will show the following two results for At-Least-T Join (ATJ) and its c-approximation counting version c-ATJ. We comment that Algorithm 1 and 2 for SIJ can also be used to solve ATJ since they can output (thus count the number of) all the witnesses of each intersecting pair (A_i, B_j) $(i, j \in [m])$.

Theorem 11 *For* $T \geq \log m$, $R^{\rightarrow}_{1/3}(c\text{-}ATJ) = \Omega(mn)$.

Theorem 12 *There is a constant* $\kappa > 0$ *so that for any* $\kappa \log m \leq T \leq 99n/100$ *it holds that* $R_{1/3}(c\text{-}ATJ) = \Omega(m\sqrt{nT})$.

Due to the space constraints, we delay this section to Appendix A.

4. IMPROVED ALGORITHM FOR OUTPUT-SENSITIVE MATRIX MULTIPLICATION, AND TRANSITIVE-CLOSURE

In this section we show that the algorithm for computing the non-zero entries of $P \cdot Q$ in Section 3 can be further improved to algorithmically compute the transitive closure for sparse graphs very efficiently, when the output of the transitive closure (i.e., the number of edges in the transitive closure) is sparse.

Output-sensitive matrix multiplication algorithms have been studied in several prior works. The standard column-row approach to matrix multiplication takes time $O(kn + n^2)$ [41] where n is the dimension of the matrices, and k is the number of nonzeroes in the output. Pagh [34] improved this to $\tilde{O}(\mathbf{nnz}(P) + \mathbf{nnz}(Q) + kn)$ time over the real numbers with a randomized algorithm. Williams and Yu [44] show that Alice and Bob (with separate matrices) can compute their product with an $\tilde{O}(kn)$ communication algorithm; their construction works over any field. Lingas [25] shows how to compute output-sensitive Boolean matrix multiplication in $\tilde{O}(n^2 \cdot k^{\omega/2-1}) \leq O(n^2 \cdot k^{0.19})$ time, which is useful when the input matrices and output matrix are dense.

Theorem 13 *There is a randomized algorithm for the Boolean matrix multiplication of* $P \in \{0,1\}^{m\times n}$ *and* $Q \in \{0,1\}^{n\times m}$ *that runs in* $\tilde{O}(k + k^{1/2}(\mathbf{nnz}(P) + \mathbf{nnz}(Q)))$ *time and succeeds with probability* $1 - 1/n$, *where* $k = \mathbf{nnz}(PQ)$, *that is, the number of nonzero entries in the output.*[5]

PROOF. The algorithm is similar to the two-way algorithm for SIJ in Section 3. We first estimate the number of non-zero entries k_j in each column of $R_{*,j}$ up to a factor of 2; using the approximation algorithm for SIJ (Theorem 5), this can be done in $\tilde{O}(\mathbf{nnz}(P) + \mathbf{nnz}(Q) + k)$ time. Following the notations in Algorithm 1, let $\tilde{k}_j$ be the 2-approximation of k_j. Let $H = \{j \mid \tilde{k}_j > \sqrt{k}\}$ and $L = [n]\backslash H$. That is, we divide the columns of the product $R_{*,j}$ into two types: those which are "dense" (in the set H) and those which are "sparse" (in the set L). Note that $|H| = O(\sqrt{k})$, by a counting argument.

For those $j \in H$ (those column indices with a "dense" number of non-zeroes), we compute the non-zero entries in $R_{*,j}$ by directly multiplying $Q_{*,j}$ with each $P_{i,*}$ $(i \in [n])$, which can be done in $O(\mathbf{nnz}(P) + \mathbf{nnz}(Q))$ time. Since $|H| \leq O(\sqrt{k})$, the total running time of computing $\{R_{*,j} \mid j \in H\}$ is at most $O(\sqrt{k} \cdot (\mathbf{nnz}(P) + \mathbf{nnz}(Q))$.

For those $j \in L$ (with a "sparse" number of non-zeroes), we build a Count-Sketch matrix S with $\sqrt{k}\log^2 n$ rows; in particular, we set $\kappa = \sqrt{k}\log n$ and $\delta = 1/n^{10}$ in Lemma 1. Then we compute $Z = (S \cdot P) \cdot Q$. Next, for each $j \in L$ we try to reconstruct the non-zero entries in $R_{*,j}$ from $Z_{*,j}$ using Lemma 1 (note that $Z = S \cdot R$). It is easy to see that the running time of computing the non-zero entries in Z is bounded by $\tilde{O}(\sqrt{k}(\mathbf{nnz}(P) + \mathbf{nnz}(Q))$, by first multiplying $S \cdot P$ and then multiplying Q with the result. However, the recovery procedure $\texttt{Rec}(\cdot)$ for Count-Sketch in Lemma 1 is slow, a priori: the naive way to recover each x_i in the n-bit vector x has running time at least $\Omega(n)$. In the following, we show how to augment the sketching step to speed up the recovery using a dyadic interval trick which has been used before in several places (for example, [11]).

We first recall the definition of *dyadic intervals* of $[n]$. Assume that n is a factor of 2, otherwise we can always pad dummy items. The dyadic intervals are $(\log n + 1)$ partitions of $[n]$: $\mathcal{I}_0 = (1, 2, \ldots), \mathcal{I}_1 = (\{1,2\}, \{3,4\}, \ldots), \mathcal{I}_2 = (\{1,2,3,4\}, \{5,6,7,8\}, \ldots), \ldots, \mathcal{I}_{\log n} = (\{1, 2, \ldots, n\})$. We have the following lemma regarding Count-Sketch and dyadic intervals.

Lemma 7 *Let* $x \in \mathbb{N}^n$ *be a vector with at most* κ *non-zero entries. Let* $\mathcal{I} = \{\mathcal{I}_0, \ldots, \mathcal{I}_{\log n}\}$ *be dyadic intervals of* $[n]$. *Denote* $x^{\mathcal{I}_0} = (x)$, $x^{\mathcal{I}_1} = (x_1 + x_2, x_3 + x_4, \ldots)$, $x^{\mathcal{I}_2} = (x_1 + x_2 + x_3 + x_4, \ldots)$ *and so on. For* $0 \leq \ell \leq \log n$, *let* $S_\ell \in \mathbb{R}^{\kappa \log(n^{10}) \times 2^\ell}$ *be a Count-Sketch matrix. There exists an algorithm that can recover* x *from* $S_0 \cdot x^{\mathcal{I}_0}, \ldots, S_{\log n} \cdot x^{\mathcal{I}_{\log n}}$ *with probability* $1 - 1/n^7$, *using* $\tilde{O}(\kappa)$ *time.*

PROOF. The algorithm is as follows:

1. Consider a binary tree whose leaves are $\{1, 2, \ldots, n\}$, with each interval node corresponding to the interval formed by the leaves of its subtree. That is, the root corresponds to $x_1^{\mathcal{I}_{\log n}}$, the left child of the root corresponds to $x_1^{\mathcal{I}_{\log n-1}}$, the right child of the root corresponds to $x_2^{\mathcal{I}_{\log n-1}}$, and so on.
2. Recover $x_1^{\mathcal{I}_{\log n}}$ from $S_{\log n} x^{\mathcal{I}_{\log n}}$; if $x_1^{\mathcal{I}_{\log n}} > 0$ then mark the root *red*.
3. Start from the root and proceed level by level top-down. For each red node in this level, for each of its two child nodes (say the child node is the i-th node at level ℓ), mark it red if $x_i^{\mathcal{I}_\ell} > 0$, which can be recovered from $S_\ell x^{\mathcal{I}_\ell}$.
4. All leaves marked red correspond to non-zero entries in x.

[5] The algorithm can be implemented in any reasonable computational model with random access to the input, such as the RAM model.

Note that the above algorithm essentially probes κ root-leaf paths in the tree each of length at most $O(\log n)$; and for each path, the time spent on each node in the path is $\tilde{O}(1)$ by Lemma 1. Also by Lemma 1, we can recover $x_i^{\mathcal{I}_\ell}$'s at each probed node with probability $1 - 1/n^{10}$ (recall that we have set $\delta = 1/n^{10}$). The overall success probability follows from a union bound on all probed nodes. □

In our setting, we view each $R_{*,j}$ $(j = 0, 1, \ldots, \log n)$ as a vector of sparsity at most $\ell = \sqrt{k}$. However we cannot create $(R_{*,j})^{\mathcal{I}_0}, \ldots, (R_{*,j})^{\mathcal{I}_{\log n}}$ directly and then apply Count-Sketch matrices $S_0, \ldots, S_{\log n}$, since $R_{*,j} = P \cdot Q_{*,j}$ is the vector we want to compute. We can instead sum up the corresponding rows of P according to dyadic intervals, obtaining $P_0, P_1, \ldots, P_{\log n}$ where P_i is a $2^i \times n$ matrix, and then apply $S_0, S_1 \ldots, S_{\log n}$ on P_i's. We can apply Lemma 7 to recover non-zero entries of each $R_{*,j}$ from the sketches $S_0 \cdot P_0 \cdot Q_{*,j}$, $S_1 \cdot P_1 \cdot Q_{*,j}$, ..., $S_{\log n} \cdot P_{\log n} \cdot Q_{*,j}$. In this way we can recover all non-zero entries in R with success probability $1 - 1/n^{10} \cdot \tilde{O}(n^2) \geq 1 - 1/n^7$, by a union bound.

Now let us analyze the running time for this modified recovery procedure in our setting. First, it takes $O(\mathbf{nnz}(P))$ time to implicitly (that is, only specify non-zero entries) compute each P_i $(0 \leq i \leq \log n)$, since P is sparse. Second, applying S_i on each P_i takes $\tilde{O}(\ell \cdot \mathbf{nnz}(P)) = \tilde{O}(\sqrt{k} \cdot \mathbf{nnz}(P))$ time each. Third, for each $i = 0, 1, \ldots, \log n$, it takes $\tilde{O}(\sqrt{k} \cdot \mathbf{nnz}(Q))$ time to compute $S_i \cdot P_i \cdot Q$. To sum up, it takes $\tilde{O}(\sqrt{k}(\mathbf{nnz}(P) + \mathbf{nnz}(Q))$ time to compute $\{S_0 \cdot P_0 \cdot Q, S_1 \cdot P_1 \cdot Q, \ldots, S_{\log n} \cdot P_{\log n} \cdot Q\}$, from which we can recover each column of R.

Corollary 4 *There is a randomized algorithm for computing the transitive closure of an $n \times n$ Boolean matrix M which runs in $\tilde{O}(k^{1.5})$ time and succeeds with probability $1 - 1/n$, where k is the number of edges in the transitive closure.*

PROOF. Every power M^i must contain at most k nonzeros, including $M^1 = M$ itself. Therefore, if we compute M^n by repeated squaring for $\log n$ times using the algorithm of Theorem 13, we can ensure a running time of

$$\tilde{O}\left(k + k^{1/2} \cdot \left(\max_{i=1,\ldots,n} \mathbf{nnz}(M^i)\right)\right) \leq \tilde{O}(k^{1.5}).$$

□

As noted by Borassi, Crescenzi, and Habib [7], efficient algorithms for transitive closures have further applications themselves, such as checking whether a given graph is a *comparability graph*. Given any partial order P on n elements, the *comparability graph of P* is the undirected graph with n nodes (one for each element in P) and an edge between two nodes if and only if they are comparable in P. The class of comparability graphs is simply the class of all graphs obtainable from a partial order P in this manner. Recognizing whether a given input graph can be modelled by some partial order P in this way is called the *comparability graph recognition* problem, and is very old (see discussion in [7]). To our knowledge, the previous best known algorithms ran in $O(mn)$ time (m is the number of edges of the graph) by Golumbic in 1977 [15], and $O(n^\omega)$ time where $\omega \geq 2$ is the matrix multiplication exponent (cf. [27]).

Our algorithm implies a rather quick solution to this problem for sparse graphs, avoiding fast matrix multiply:

Corollary 5 *There is a randomized algorithm for comparability graph recognition running in $\tilde{O}(m^{1.5})$ time, where m is the number of edges in the given graph.*

5. CONCLUDING REMARKS

In this section we discuss how to extend our results on set-intersection join to multiparty, as well as a few problems left open by our work and some future research directions.

We can generalize set-intersection join to the *multiparty* setting. Let $O^1, \ldots, O^t$ be t parties. We still have two collections of sets $A = (A_1, ..., A_m)$ and $B = (B_1, ..., B_m)$, but they are distributed across t players. That is, each O^i has $A^i \subseteq A$ and $B^i \subseteq B$, where $\{A^1, \ldots, A^t\}$ is a partition of A and $\{B^1, \ldots, B^t\}$ is a partition of B. The t parties want to compute SIJ$(\mathcal{A}, \mathcal{B})$.

This generalization can be solved easily using the "linearity" of Algorithm 1. Let $P \in \{0,1\}^{m \times n}$ be the matrix representation of A, and let $P^i \in \{0,1\}^{m \times n}$ $(i \in [t])$ be the matrix representing the subset $A^i \subseteq A$ (pad all '0' in rows do not correspond A^i). Similarly, let $Q \in \{0,1\}^{n \times m}$ be the matrix representation of B, and let $Q^i \in \{0,1\}^{n \times m}$ $(i \in [t])$ be the matrix representing the subset $B^i \subseteq B$. In the first step, Player O^1 sends SP^1 to player O^2 (S is a Count-Sketch same as that in Algorithm 1), and then O^2 computes $S(P^1 + P^2)$ and sends it to O^3, and so on. At the end O^t can compute SP where $P = P^1 + \cdots + P^t$. In the second step, O^t sends SP to each party $O^1, \ldots, O^{t-1}$, and the t parties use the same way to compute $SP \cdot Q$. Next, the parties can use the same way to compute MPQ where M is ℓ_0-sketch. Given SPQ and MPQ, we run Algorithm 1 to recover the columns with small number of non-zeros, and for remaining columns have the parties who possess them directly transmit these. The total communication cost is at most t times that for the 2-party case (Theorem 3).

There are many problems left open by this work. The biggest technical question left open is to close the gap between the upper bound $\tilde{O}(n/\epsilon^2)$ and the lower bound $\Omega(n/\epsilon^{2/3})$ for $(1+\epsilon)$-SIJ in the 2-way communication model. Another natural question is whether we can extend this line of research to more expressive queries. Finally, it will be interesting to investigate whether this line of work could lead to asymptotically faster algorithms for Boolean matrix multiplication that do not rely on heavy un-implementable algebra (like the last 30 years of work on the subject). That would be a major advance for both theory and practice. There are other potential applications which rely on Boolean matrix multiplication as well (triangle detection/counting, context-free grammar parsing, etc.) which are worth pursuing further.

6. REFERENCES

[1] F. N. Afrati and J. D. Ullman. Optimizing joins in a map-reduce environment. In *EDBT*, pages 99–110, 2010.

[2] R. Angles and C. Gutiérrez. Survey of graph database models. *ACM Comput. Surv.*, 40(1), 2008.

[3] A. Arasu, V. Ganti, and R. Kaushik. Efficient exact set-similarity joins. In *VLDB*, pages 918–929, 2006.

[4] A. Badia and M. Dobbs. Supporting quantified queries in distributed databases. *IJPEDS*, 29(5):421–459, 2014.

[5] A. Badia, D. VanGucht, and M. Gyssens. Querying with generalized quantifiers. In *Applications of Logic Databases*, pages 235–258, 1993.

[6] S. Blanas, J. M. Patel, V. Ercegovac, J. Rao, E. J. Shekita, and Y. Tian. A comparison of join algorithms for log processing in mapreduce. In *SIGMOD*, pages 975–986, 2010.

[7] M. Borassi, P. Crescenzi, and M. Habib. Into the square - on the complexity of quadratic-time solvable problems. *CoRR*, 2014.

[8] J. Brody, A. Chakrabarti, R. Kondapally, D. P. Woodruff, and G. Yaroslavtsev. Beyond set disjointness: the communication complexity of finding the intersection. In *PODC*, pages 106–113, 2014.

[9] J. Claußen, A. Kemper, G. Moerkotte, and K. Peithner. Optimizing queries with universal quantification in object-oriented and object-relational databases. In *VLDB*, pages 286–295, 1997.

[10] E. F. Codd. A relational model of data for large shared data banks. *Commun. ACM*, 13(6):377–387, 1970.

[11] G. Cormode and S. Muthukrishnan. An improved data stream summary: the count-min sketch and its applications. *J. Algorithms*, 55(1):58–75, 2005.

[12] G. Cormode and S. Muthukrishnan. Combinatorial algorithms for compressed sensing. In *SIROCCO*, pages 280–294, 2006.

[13] M. Dadashzadeh. An improved division operator for relational algebra. *Inf. Syst.*, 14(5):431–437, 1989.

[14] G. H. L. Fletcher, M. Gyssens, D. Leinders, J. VandenBussche, D. VanGucht, S. Vansummeren, and Y. Wu. Relative expressive power of navigational querying on graphs. In *ICDT*, pages 197–207, 2011.

[15] M. C. Golumbic. The complexity of comparability graph recognition and coloring. *Computing*, 18(3):199–208, 1977.

[16] G. Graefe and R. L. Cole. Fast algorithms for universal quantification in large databases. *ACM Trans. Database Syst.*, 20(2):187–236, 1995.

[17] S. Helmer and G. Moerkotte. Evaluation of main memory join algorithms for joins with set comparison join predicates. In *VLDB*, pages 386–395, 1997.

[18] P. Hsu and D. S. P. Jr. Improving SQL with generalized quantifiers. In *ICDE*, pages 298–305, 1995.

[19] T. S. Jayram, R. Kumar, and D. Sivakumar. The one-way communication complexity of hamming distance. *Theory of Computing*, 4(1):129–135, 2008.

[20] D. M. Kane, J. Nelson, and D. P. Woodruff. An optimal algorithm for the distinct elements problem. In *PODS*, pages 41–52, 2010.

[21] D. Kossmann. The state of the art in distributed query processing. *ACM Comput. Surv.*, 32(4):422–469, 2000.

[22] E. Kushilevitz and N. Nisan. *Communication complexity*. Cambridge: Cambridge Univ, 1997.

[23] D. Leinders and J. VandenBussche. On the complexity of division and set joins in the relational algebra. *J. Comput. Syst. Sci.*, 73(4):538–549, 2007.

[24] G. Li, D. Deng, J. Wang, and J. Feng. PASS-JOIN: A partition-based method for similarity joins. *PVLDB*, 5(3):253–264, 2011.

[25] A. Lingas. A fast output-sensitive algorithm for boolean matrix multiplication. In *ESA*, pages 408–419, 2009.

[26] N. Mamoulis. Efficient processing of joins on set-valued attributes. In *SIGMOD*, pages 157–168, 2003.

[27] R. M. McConnell and J. Spinrad. Linear-time modular decomposition and efficient transitive orientation of comparability graphs. In *SODA*, pages 536–545, 1994.

[28] S. Melnik and H. Garcia-Molina. Adaptive algorithms for set containment joins. *ACM Trans. Database Syst.*, 28:56–99, 2003.

[29] P. Mishra and M. H. Eich. Join processing in relational databases. *ACM Comput. Surv.*, 24(1):63–113, 1992.

[30] R. Motwani and P. Raghavan. *Randomized Algorithms*. Cambridge University Press, New York, NY, USA, 1995.

[31] S. Muthukrishnan. Data streams: Algorithms and applications. *Foundations and Trends in Theoretical Computer Science*, 1(2), 2005.

[32] I. Newman. Private vs. common random bits in communication complexity. *Inf. Process. Lett.*, 39(2), 1991.

[33] A. Okcan and M. Riedewald. Processing theta-joins using mapreduce. In *SIGMOD*, pages 949–960, 2011.

[34] R. Pagh. Compressed matrix multiplication. In *ITCS*, pages 442–451, 2012.

[35] V. R. Pratt. Origins of the calculus of binary relations. In *LICS*, pages 248–254, 1992.

[36] K. Ramasamy, J. M. Patel, J. F. Naughton, and R. Kaushik. Set containment joins: The good, the bad and the ugly. In *VLDB*, pages 351–362, 2000.

[37] R. Rantzau. *Query processing concepts and techniques for set containment tests*. PhD thesis, University of Stuttgart, 2004.

[38] S. Rao, A. Badia, and D. VanGucht. Providing better support for a class of decision support queries. In *SIGMOD*, pages 217–227, 1996.

[39] A. A. Razborov. On the distributional complexity of disjointness. *Theor. Comput. Sci.*, 106(2):385–390, 1992.

[40] M. Saglam and G. Tardos. On the communication complexity of sparse set disjointness and exists-equal problems. In *FOCS*, pages 678–687, 2013.

[41] C. Schnorr and C. R. Subramanian. Almost optimal (on the average) combinatorial algorithms for boolean matrix product witnesses, computing the diameter (extended abstract). In *RANDOM*, pages 218–231, 1998.

[42] B. ten Cate and M. Marx. Navigational xpath: calculus and algebra. *SIGMOD Record*, 36(2):19–26, 2007.

[43] R. Vernica, M. J. Carey, and C. Li. Efficient parallel set-similarity joins using mapreduce. In *SIGMOD*, pages 495–506, 2010.

[44] R. Williams and H. Yu. Finding orthogonal vectors in discrete structures. In *SODA*, pages 1867–1877, 2014.

[45] D. P. Woodruff and Q. Zhang. An optimal lower bound for distinct elements in the message passing model. In *SODA*, pages 718–733, 2014.

[46] C. Xiao, W. Wang, X. Lin, and J. X. Yu. Efficient similarity joins for near duplicate detection. In *WWW*, pages 131–140, 2008.

[47] A. C.-C. Yao. Probabilistic computations: Toward a unified measure of complexity (extended abstract). In *FOCS*, pages 222–227, 1977.

APPENDIX

A. AT-LEAST-T JOIN

Consider the ATJ problem where Alice has sets $A_1, \ldots, A_m$, and Bob has sets $B_1, \ldots, B_m$ all from a universe $[n]$. They want to compute the number of (i, j) pairs for which $|A_i \cap B_j| \geq T$, for a parameter $T > 0$. By padding each set with $T - 1$ common elements, Theorem 10 implies an $\Omega(mn)$ lower bound on the two-way randomized communication complexity of this problem, that is, no non-trivial algorithm exists.

The situation becomes more interesting if we want to approximate the number of (i, j) pairs for which $|A_i \cap B_j| \geq T$ up to a multiplicative factor of $c > 1$, which we call c-ATJ. To obtain a lower bound for the randomized communication of this problem for any approximation factor c, it suffices to obtain a lower bound for the problem of determining if there exists a pair (i, j) for which $|A_i \cap B_j| \geq T$. We call the latter problem $\exists$-ATJ. We give tight bounds for the one-way communication of this problem below, as well as a lower bound for the two-way communication of this problem which is tight if $T = \Omega(n)$ and m and n are polynomially related. By the aforementioned connection, we obtain the same lower bounds for c-ATJ.

Theorem 14 (restatement of Theorem 11) *For $T \geq \log m$, $R^{\rightarrow}_{1/3}(c\text{-ATJ}) = \Omega(mn)$.*

PROOF. We reduce from the Indexing problem to $\exists$-ATJ. In our reduction, Bob has a single non-empty set B_1. In each of Alice's sets A_i, in its characteristic vector on the first $r = 2T$ coordinates, she places a new *distinct* vector with $T - 1$ ones. Assuming $T \geq \log m$, it is possible to do this, since in that case there are $\binom{2T}{T-1} > m$ such vectors. This ensures that the characteristic vectors of any two sets $A_j, A_{j'}$ with $j \neq j'$ agree on at most $T - 2$ ones among the first r coordinates. On the remaining $n - r$ coordinates of the characteristic vectors of each of her m sets she places her input bits to the Indexing problem. Hence, we can embed an instance of Indexing on $(m - r)n = \Omega(mn)$ bits in Alice's vectors.

If Bob is interested in the i-th bit of the characteristic vector of A_j in the Indexing problem, in his set B_1 he puts the prefix corresponding to A_j in the first r coordinates, then he adds the single coordinate i to A_j. Then the only set this can intersect in T positions is A_j. But this happens if and only if i occurs in A_j. □

Theorem 15 (restatement of Theorem 12) *There is a constant $\kappa > 0$, so that for any $\kappa \log m \leq T \leq 99n/100$, it holds that $R_{1/3}(c\text{-ATJ}) = \Omega(m\sqrt{nT})$.*

PROOF. We reduce from SI on size $m\sqrt{nT/8}$ sets. That is, Alice is given $x \in \{0,1\}^{m\sqrt{nT/8}}$, while Bob is given $y \in \{0,1\}^{m\sqrt{nT/8}}$, and the players would like to determine if there exists an ℓ for which $x_\ell = y_\ell = 1$ (see Section 2 for a definition and discussion of SI).

We can partition x into m contiguous substrings

$$x^1, \ldots, x^m \in \{0,1\}^{\sqrt{nT/8}},$$

and similarly partition y into m contiguous substrings

$$y^1, \ldots, y^m \in \{0,1\}^{\sqrt{nT/8}}.$$

For each $i \in [m]$, we use the public randomness to define a random injection $f^i : [\sqrt{nT/8}] \rightarrow [n - 48T]$, where we assume $\sqrt{nT/8} \leq n - 48T$ (we remove this assumption below). The f^i are independent for the different i.

We define the following event $\mathcal{E}_{i,j}$ for $i \neq j \in [m]$: $|f^i(x^i) \cap f^j(y^j)| > T/2$, where $|f^i(x^i) \cap f^j(y^j)|$ denotes the number of coordinates ℓ for which $f^i(x^i)_\ell = f^j(y^j)_\ell = 1$. Since f^i is an injection, the number of coordinates $\ell \in [n - 48T]$ for which $f^i(x^i)_\ell = 1$ is at most $\sqrt{nT/8}$, and similarly the number of coordinates ℓ in $[n - 48T]$ for which $f^j(x^j)_\ell = 1$ is at most $\sqrt{nT/8}$.

We compute $\mathbf{Pr}[|f^i(x^i) \cap f^j(y^j)| > T/2]$. This probability cannot decrease if $f^i(x^i)$ and $f^j(y^j)$ are 1 on the maximum possible number of coordinates, namely, $\sqrt{nT/8}$. Then the probability $|f^i(x^i) \cap f^j(y^j)|$ exceeds $T/2$ can be upper bounded by the following process: we choose the $\sqrt{nT/8}$ ones of $f^j(y^j)$ one at a time. Each time we choose a one, there are at most $\sqrt{nT/8}$ positions it could collide with in $f^i(x^i)$, out of at least $n - 48T - \sqrt{nT/8} \geq n/2$ remaining positions, where we assume $48T + \sqrt{nT/8} \leq n/2$ (we remove this assumption below). Hence, $\mathbf{Pr}[|f^i(x^i) \cap f^j(y^j)| > T/2]$ is upper bounded by $\mathbf{Pr}[Z > T/2]$, where Z is the sum of $\sqrt{nT/8}$ independent indicator random variables each with success probability $\sqrt{nT/8}/(n/2)$. Hence, $\mathbf{E}[Z] = T/4$. By a Chernoff bound,

$$\mathbf{Pr}[Z > T/2] \leq \exp(-\Theta(T)) \leq \frac{1}{10m^2},$$

where the second inequality uses that $T \geq \kappa \log m$ for a sufficiently large constant $\kappa > 0$. By a union bound $\mathbf{Pr}[\mathcal{E}] > \frac{9}{10}$, which we condition on.

For each $i \in [m]$, we also choose a random subset S^i of $[48T]$ with $|S^i| = T - 1$. Note that for $i \neq j$,

$$\begin{aligned}
\mathbf{Pr}[|S^i \cap S^j| \geq T/2] &\leq \binom{T-1}{T/2}\left(\frac{1}{48}\right)^{T/2} \\
&\leq \left(\frac{2Te}{T}\right)^{T/2}\left(\frac{1}{48}\right)^{T/2} \\
&\leq \left(\frac{2e}{48}\right)^{T/2} \\
&< \left(\frac{1}{4}\right)^{T} \\
&\leq \frac{1}{m^2},
\end{aligned}$$

where the fist inequality follows by a union bound over all possibilities of intersecting in at least $T/2$ positions, the second inequality follows from the inequality $\binom{n}{k} \leq (ne/k)^k$, and the final inequality uses that $T \geq \log m$. It follows by a union bound that there exist sets $S^1, \ldots, S^m$ with $|S^i| = T - 1$ and $|S^i \cap S^j| < T/2$ for all $i \neq j \in [m]$. We fix a choice of $S^1, \ldots, S^m$ which has this property. Note that our choice of $S^1, \ldots, S^m$ is done independently of our choice of $f^1, \ldots, f^m$.

For each $i \in [m]$, we define $A_i \subseteq [n]$ to be the set whose characteristic vector is $f(x^i)$ on the first $n - 48T$ coordinates, and which equals S^i on the remaining $48T$ coordinates. Similarly, define $B_i \subseteq [n]$ to be the set whose characteristic vector is $f(y^i)$ on the first $n - 48T$ coordinates, and which equals S^i on the remaining $48T$ coordinates.

For $i \neq j$, we have

$$|A_i \cap B_j| = |f^i(x^i) \cap f^j(y^j)| + |S^i \cap S^j| \leq \frac{T}{2} + \frac{T}{2} - 1 < T.$$

On the other hand, we have

$$|A_i \cap B_i| = |x^i \cap y^i| + T - 1,$$

where $|x^i \cap y^i|$ denotes the number of coordinates ℓ for which $x^i_\ell = y^j_\ell = 1$. It follows that the $\exists$-ATJ problem on inputs $A_1, \ldots, A_m$ and $B_1, \ldots, B_m$ is equal to 1 if and only if there is an ℓ for which $x_\ell = y_\ell = 1$. Hence, a protocol for $\exists$-SITJ which errs with probability $1/5$ can be used to solve SI with error probability at most $1/5 + 1/10 < 1/3$, and so $R_{1/5}(c\text{-ATJ}) \geq R_{1/5}(\exists\text{-ATJ}) \geq R_{1/3}(\text{SI}) = \Omega(m\sqrt{nT})$. Note that $R_{1/3}(c\text{-ATJ}) = \Omega(R_{1/5}(c\text{-ATJ}))$ since a protocol which errs with probability $1/3$ can be made to err with probability $1/5$ by repeating the protocol independently $O(1)$ times and outputting the majority outcome.

It remains to discuss the two assumptions in the above proof, (1) $\sqrt{nT/8} \leq n - 48T$ and (2) $48T + \sqrt{nT/8} \leq n/2$. Both assumptions are satisfied provided that $T \leq cn$ for a sufficiently small constant $c > 0$. This is always possible to assume, since given $T \leq 99n/100$ and n, we can replace (n, T) with $(n - (1-\gamma)T, \gamma T)$ for arbitrarily small constant $\gamma > 0$ and pad each of the sets A_i, B_j in the above with $(1-\gamma)T$ common elements. Since $T \leq 99n/100$, for sufficiently small γ the ratio $(\gamma T)/(n - (1-\gamma)T)$ is at most c, while n and T change by constant factors, so the same conclusion of the $\Omega(m\sqrt{nT})$ lower bound holds. □

B. OMITTED PROOFS

B.1 Proof for Theorem 10

We reduce from the SI problem with a universe of size mn. That is, Alice and Bob have vectors $x, y \in \{0,1\}^{mn}$ and would like to determine if there is an $\ell \in [mn]$ for which $x_\ell = y_\ell = 1$, in which case we say x and y intersect. We use the distribution ν on (x, y) (see Section 2).

Break x into m contiguous strings $x^1, \ldots, x^m \in \{0,1\}^n$, and set A_i such that x^i is the characteristic vector of A_i. Similarly, break y into m contiguous strings $y^1, \ldots, y^m \in \{0,1\}^n$ and set B_j such that y^j is the characteristic vector of B_j.

Claim 1 *With probability $1 - m^2 \cdot e^{-\Omega(n)}$ over $(x, y) \sim \nu$, for all $i \neq j$, x^i intersects y^j.*

PROOF. For fixed i and j, by a Chernoff bound, the Hamming weights of x^i and of y^j are at least $n/5$ with probability at least $1 - e^{-\Omega(n)}$. Conditioned on the Hamming weights of x^i and y^j, the positions of the 1s in x^i and y^j are independent, since $i \neq j$. Hence, for any fixing of Hamming weights of value at least $n/5$, the probability x^i does not intersect y^j is at most the probability that a random set $B \subset [n]$ of size $n/5$ does not contain an element in $[n/5]$, which is at most $(4/5)^{n/5} = e^{-\Omega(n)}$. The claim follows by a union bound over the $\binom{m}{2}$ pairs (i, j). □

If $\text{SI}(x, y) = 1$, then one additional pair (x^i, y^i) will intersect, otherwise if $\text{SI}(x, y) = 0$, then all additional pairs (x^i, y^i) will not intersect. These cases can be distinguished by an algorithm for SDJ since by Claim 1, $\text{SDJ}(\mathcal{A}, \mathcal{B}) = m - \text{SI}(x, y)$ with probability $1 - o(1)$. Lemma 4 states that $D^\nu_\delta(\text{SI}) = \Omega(mn)$, for a constant error probability $\delta > 0$, yielding the theorem.

Joins via Geometric Resolutions: Worst-case and Beyond

Mahmoud Abo Khamis
University at Buffalo, SUNY
mabokham@buffalo.edu

Hung Q. Ngo
University at Buffalo, SUNY
hungngo@buffalo.edu

Christopher Ré
Stanford University
chrismre@cs.stanford.edu

Atri Rudra
University at Buffalo, SUNY
atri@buffalo.edu

ABSTRACT

We present a simple geometric framework for the relational join. Using this framework, we design an algorithm that achieves the fractional hypertree-width bound, which generalizes classical and recent worst-case algorithmic results on computing joins. In addition, we use our framework and the same algorithm to show a series of what are colloquially known as beyond worst-case results. The framework allows us to prove results for data stored in Btrees, multidimensional data structures, and even multiple indices per table. A key idea in our framework is formalizing the inference one does with an index as a type of geometric resolution; transforming the algorithmic problem of computing joins to a geometric problem. Our notion of geometric resolution can be viewed as a geometric analog of logical resolution. In addition to the geometry and logic connections, our algorithm can also be thought of as backtracking search with memoization.

Categories and Subject Descriptors

H.2.4 [**Database Management**]: Systems—*Relational databases*

General Terms

Algorithms, Theory

Keywords

Relational join; Resolution; Bounded-width join queries; Indices; Beyond worst-case analysis

1. INTRODUCTION

Efficient processing of the natural join operation is a key problem in database management systems [1, 26, 42]. A large number of algorithms and heuristics for computing joins have been proposed and implemented in database systems, including Block-Nested loop join, Hash-Join, Grace, Sort-merge, index-nested, double pipelined, PRISM, etc. [9, 10, 20, 24]. In addition to their role in database management, joins (or variants) are powerful enough to capture many fundamental problems in logic and constraint satisfaction [25,36], or subgraph listing problems [32,33] which are central in social [40,41] and biological network analysis [30,37].

Not surprisingly, there has been a great deal of work on joins in various settings. A celebrated result is Yannakakis' algorithm, which shows that acyclic join queries can be computed in linear time [44] in data complexity (modulo a log factor). Over the years, this result was generalized to successively larger classes of queries based on various notions of widths: from *treewidth* (tw) [12, 38], *degree of acyclicity* [22, 23], *query width* (qw) [11], to *generalized hypertree width* (ghw) [19, 39]. From the bound of Atserias, Grohe and Marx [6, 21] (AGM bound), and its algorithmic proof [32], we recently know that there is a class of join algorithms that are optimal in the worst case, in the sense that for each join query the algorithm runs in time linear in the size of the worst-case output [32, 33, 43]. Combining a worst-case optimal join algorithm with Yannakakis' algorithm yields an algorithm running in time $\tilde{O}(N^{\text{fhtw}} + Z)$, where fhtw stands for *fractional hypertree width* [21], a more general notion than the widths mentioned above, and Z is the output size.

However, worst-case can be pathological. For example, input relations are typically already pre-processed and stored in sophisticated indices to facilitate fast query answering (in even *sub-linear* time). Motivated by this, recent work has gone beyond worst-case analysis to notions that are closer to *instance or pointwise* optimality. These beyond worst-case results have as their starting point the work of Demaine et al. [14] and Barbay and Kenyon [7, 8], who designed beyond worst-case algorithms for set intersection and union problems, which were recently extended to join processing [31].[1]

As one might expect, the algorithms that achieve the above varied results are themselves varied; they make a wide range of seemingly incompatible assumptions: data are indexed or not; the measures are worst-case or instance-based; they may rely on (or ignore) detailed structural information about the query or cardinality information about the underlying tables. With all this variety, our first result may be surprising:

[1]This algorithm has been implemented in a commercial database system, LogicBlox, with promising but initial results. In our preliminary experimental results, the new algorithm on some queries on real social network data showed up to two, even three orders of magnitude speedup over several existing commercial database engines [34].

PODS'15, May 31–June 4, 2015, Melbourne, Victoria, Australia.

ACM 978-1-4503-2757-2/15/05 ...$15.00.
http://dx.doi.org/10.1145/2745754.2745776.

we recover all of the above mentioned results with a single, simple algorithm.[2]

Our central algorithmic idea is to cast the problem of evaluating a join over data in indices as a geometric problem; specifically, we reduce the join problem to a problem (defined below) in which one covers a rectangular region of a multi-dimensional space (with dimension equal to the number of attributes of the join) with a set of rectangular boxes. These boxes represent regions in the space in which we know output tuples are *not* present. Such rectangles are a succinct way to represent the information conveyed by these data structures. We illustrate these ideas by an example.

Example 1.1. Consider the relation $R(A, B) = \{4\} \times \{1, \ldots, 7\} \cup \{1, \ldots, 7\} \times \{4\}$, which is illustrated in Figure 1a. For now assume that R is stored in a B-tree with attribute order (A, B). Any two consecutive tuples (a, b_1) and (a, b_2) in R give rise to the box with its A side being the singleton interval $[a, a]$ and its other side being the interval (b_1, b_2). For example the gap box between the tuples $(4, 4)$ and $(4, 5)$ in Figure 1a is denoted by the blue box in Figure 1b. Consecutive tuples (a_1, b_1) and (a_2, b_2) for $a_1 \neq a_2$ give rise to bigger rectangles. Figure 1b illustrates all the gap boxes generated from this R. Suppose we want to compute the join $R(A, B) \bowtie S(B, C)$ for some other relation S. Then, the gap boxes from R will span all values in the C-dimension. Similarly, the gap boxes for S span all values in the A-dimension. And the output tuples are precisely the tuples (a, b, c) which do not fall into any gap boxes, from both indices of R and S.

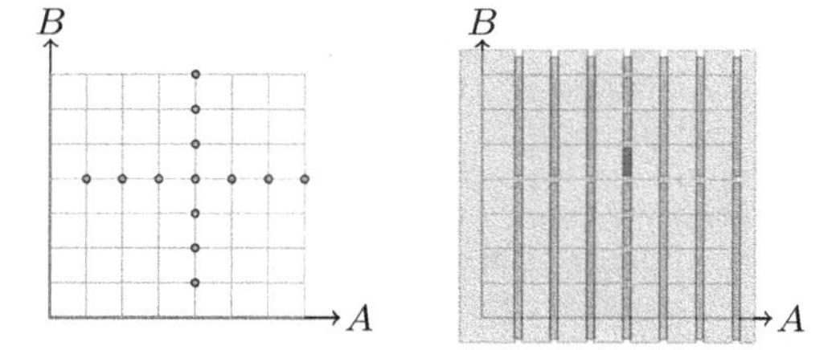

(a) Tuples of $R(A, B)$ (b) Gap boxes from (A, B)-ordered Btree

Figure 1: A relation and the corresponding gap boxes from sorted order (A, B).

Throughout this paper we will think of the data as integers for convenience, but our results assume only that the domains of attributes are discrete and ordered. For technical reasons, we will assume that the boxes are *dyadic boxes*, i.e., rectangles whose endpoints and side lengths can be encoded as powers of 2. Importantly, a dyadic interval can be thought of as a bitstring, which allows many geometric operations such as containment and intersection to be reduced to string operations that take time linear in the length of strings and so logarithmic in the size of the data. This encoding does increase the number of gap boxes, but by only a polylogarithmic factor in the input data size. With this idea, the central problem in this work is the *box cover problem*, which informally is defined as follows. (Formal definition is in Section 3.)

> Given a set of dyadic boxes $\mathcal{A}$, i.e. the gaps from the data,[3] our goal is to list all the points that are not covered by any box in $\mathcal{A}$.

The core of our algorithm solves essentially the Boolean version of the box cover problem, where in addition to the set of boxes $\mathcal{A}$, one is also given a target box $\mathbf{b}$ and the goal is to check if $\mathbf{b}$ is covered by the union of boxes in $\mathcal{A}$. Our algorithm for the Boolean box cover problem is recursive, with the following steps: We first check if any box $\mathbf{a} \in \mathcal{A}$ contains $\mathbf{b}$. If such $\mathbf{a}$ exists, we return it as a witness that $\mathbf{b}$ is covered. If not, then we split the box $\mathbf{b}$ into two halves $\mathbf{b}_1$ and $\mathbf{b}_2$ and recurse. In the recursive steps, we either find a point in the target box that is not covered (in which case we return it as a witness that the target box is not covered), or we discover two boxes $\mathbf{w}_1, \mathbf{w}_2 \in \mathcal{A}$ that contain $\mathbf{b}_1$ and $\mathbf{b}_2$ respectively. We then construct a single box $\mathbf{w}$ by combining $\mathbf{w}_1$ and $\mathbf{w}_2$ such that $\mathbf{w}$ contains $\mathbf{b}$, we add $\mathbf{w}$ to $\mathcal{A}$, [4] and we return it as a witness that $\mathbf{b}$ is covered. This algorithm needs to answer three questions:

- *How to find a box* $\mathbf{a} \in \mathcal{A}$ *containing the target box* $\mathbf{b}$ *if such a box exists?* This search procedure should be efficient, ideally in polylogarithmic time in the data size. Dyadic encoding of gap boxes makes this goal possible. Our algorithm stores boxes in $\mathcal{A}$ in a (multilevel) dyadic tree data structure.
- *How to split the input box* $\mathbf{b}$ *into* $\mathbf{b}_1$ *and* $\mathbf{b}_2$*?* A first natural scheme is to go in a fixed attribute order. We show that this scheme is sufficient to recover all the results mentioned earlier in this section. However, we also show that this approach is fundamentally limited. In particular, we show a novel alternate scheme that is able to achieve much stronger per-instance guarantees.
- *How to combine* $\mathbf{w}_1$ *and* $\mathbf{w}_2$ *to form* $\mathbf{w}$*?* The combine operation has two competing goals: it should be *complete* in that it can infer $\mathbf{b}$ (or a box that contains $\mathbf{b}$) and it should be *efficient* in that it should take at most polylogarithmic time in the data. For that purpose, we introduce a notion called *geometric resolution* (Figure 6). We show that this framework is complete and the resolution operation can be implemented efficiently as a simple operation on bitstrings. In conjunction with the efficient search procedure, this implies that the running time of the algorithm is the number of such resolutions (up to polylogarithmic factors in the data size). Thus, we can reason about the geometry of these covers instead of the algorithmic steps.[5]

In our first contribution, we show that our algorithm – named Tetris– is able to recover the worst-case algorithmic results shown in the top-half of Table 1, and the recent beyond-worst-case results of [31].

[2]We are unable to recover the more recent notions of widths, in particular, the notion of *submodular width* [29]. See Section 2 for a more detailed discussion.

[3]We note that our algorithms assume an oracle access to $\mathcal{A}$ and some of our algorithms essentially minimize the number of accesses to the oracle.

[4]$\mathcal{A}$ is assumed to be a global variable: all levels of the recursion access the same $\mathcal{A}$. See Section 4.2.1.

[5]This should be contrasted with traditional logical resolution that can potentially require $\Omega(N)$ time for a single step due to large clauses. At a high level, logical resolution is resolving *combinatorial* rectangles while our notion resolves geometric rectangles. See [2] for more.

Join Query	Run time	Recovers(R)/Subsumes(S)
	WORST-CASE RESULTS	
α-acyclic	$N + Z$	Yannakakis [44] (R)
Arbitrary	$N + \mathsf{AGM}$	[32,43] (R)
'width' w^*	$N^{w^*} + Z$	[11,12,19,32,43,44] (S)
	CERTIFICATE BASED RESULTS	
treewidth w	$\|\mathcal{C}_\Box\|^{w+1} + Z$	New and [31] (S)
treewidth 1	$\|\mathcal{C}_\Box\| + Z$	New

Table 1: Overview of our upper bounds achieved by the *same* algorithm called Tetris. The run times are up to polylogarithmic factors and either in terms of the total input size N or in the size of the optimal certificate $\mathcal{C}_\Box$ as well as the output size Z. In the above, the bounded width $w^* = \text{fhtw} \leqslant \text{ghw} \leqslant \text{qw} \leqslant \text{tw} + 1$. Our worst-case result on fractional hypertree width (fhtw) implies the other worst-case results on various notions of widths. Our result for treewidth w queries subsumes that of [31] since the latter only works for indices with mutually consistent sort orders. AGM denotes the AGM-bound for the query [6].

Our second contribution is to use these insights to go beyond known results. In previous work on beyond-worst-case analysis, one made an assumption that indexes were consistent with a single global ordering of attributes; a constraint that is not often met in practice. Our first results remove this restriction, which we believe argues for the power of the above framework. In particular, we reason about multiple Btrees on the same relation, multidimensional index structures like KD-trees and RTrees, and even sophisticated dyadic trees. In turn, this allows us to extend beyond-worst case analysis to a larger set of indexing schemes and, conceptually, this brings us closer to a theory of how indexing and join processing impact one another.

The idea of beyond worst-case complexity is captured by a natural notion of geometric certificate. In particular, a minimum-sized subset $\mathcal{C}_\Box \subseteq \mathcal{A}$ whose union is the same as the union of all input gap boxes in $\mathcal{A}$ is called a *gap box certificate* for the join problem. For beyond worst-case results, $|\mathcal{C}_\Box|$ is the analogous quantity to input size N that is used in the worst-case results.

There are several reasons for our current certificate framework to use only 'gap' boxes and not input tuples (or more generally boxes that contain the input tuples). First, gap boxes directly generalize the results from [31], where it was shown that $|\mathcal{C}_\Box|$ is in the same order as the minimum number of comparisons that a comparison-based join algorithm has to perform in order to be certain that the output is correct. Second, we expect the input data to be very sparse in the ambient space. In particular, we show in this paper that $|\mathcal{C}_\Box| = O(N)$ and there are classes of input instances for which $|\mathcal{C}_\Box| = o(N)$ (or even $O(1)$). Third, gap boxes in some sense capture differences between different input indices. The same relation indexed in different ways give different sets of gap boxes which can all be used in evaluating the join. Last but not least, our move to use gaps rather than the input tuples themselves has a strong parallel with using proof by contradiction to prove logical statements. In hindsight, this parallel is precisely what results in the strong connection between our framework and resolution (indeed resolution is a specific form of proof by contradiction).

We show that for queries with treewidth 1 (i.e. query graphs are forests), we can compute them in $\tilde{O}(|\mathcal{C}_\Box| + Z)$ time[6], where Z is the output size. For general treewidth w join queries, we obtain a weaker runtime of $\tilde{O}(|\mathcal{C}_\Box|^{w+1} + Z)$.

We also develop a new and intriguing result, where we obtain a runtime of $\tilde{O}(|\mathcal{C}_\Box|^{n/2} + Z)$ for a query with n attributes. This subsumes and greatly extends the results on 3-cliques from previous work to all queries on n attributes (including n-cliques). Moreover, it shows that in some sense the clique queries remain the hardest for beyond worst-case analysis as well. Our geometric framework plays a crucial role in this result, both in the analysis and the design of our algorithm.

Finally, we also use our framework to provide lower bounds on the number of geometric resolutions that any algorithm needs. In particular, we consider three variants of geometric resolution in this paper. The most general kind (which is not as powerful as general logical resolution) resolves geometric boxes, which we call GEOMETRIC RESOLUTION. We are able to recover all of the results in Table 1 with a weaker form of geometric resolution called ORDERED GEOMETRIC RESOLUTION, which corresponds to geometric resolution but when we only combine boxes in a fixed attribute order. We also consider an even more special case TREE ORDERED GEOMETRIC RESOLUTION, which corresponds to ordered geometric resolution when we do *not* cache the outcome of any resolution. Figure 2 summarizes where our upper and lower bounds fit in these classes of resolution.

There is an intriguing connection between our framework and DPLL with clause learning used for #SAT. We address this further in Section 4.2.4.

All the omitted material can be found in the full version of the paper [2].

2. RELATED WORK

In a seminal work [44], Yannakakis showed that if the query is acyclic (or more precisely α-acyclic in Fagin's terminology [15]) then it can be evaluated in time $\tilde{O}(N + Z)$, where N is the input size (in terms of data complexity), and Z is the output size. Researchers have expanded the classes of tractable queries using an increasingly finer structural measure called the 'width' of the query, measuring how 'far' from being acyclic a query is. If the query 'width' is bounded by a constant, then the problem is tractable in the data complexity sense. The width notion progressed from *treewidth* (tw) [12,38], *degree of acyclicity* [22,23], *query width* (qw) [11], *hypertree width* and *generalized hypertree width* [19,39].

Worst-case optimal join algorithms. Atserias, Grohe, and Marx (AGM henceforth) [6,21] derived a bound on the output size (the number of tuples in the output) using *both* the structural information about the query *and* the input relation sizes. Their bound is a function of the input relation sizes and a fractional edge cover of the hypergraph representing the query. By solving a linear program, we can obtain the best possible bound for the output size. We refer to this best bound as the *AGM bound.* AGM also showed that their bound is tight (in data complexity) by constructing a family of instances for which the output size is in the order of the

[6]In this paper $\tilde{O}$ will hide poly-log N factors as well as factors that just depend on the query size, which is assumed to be a constant.

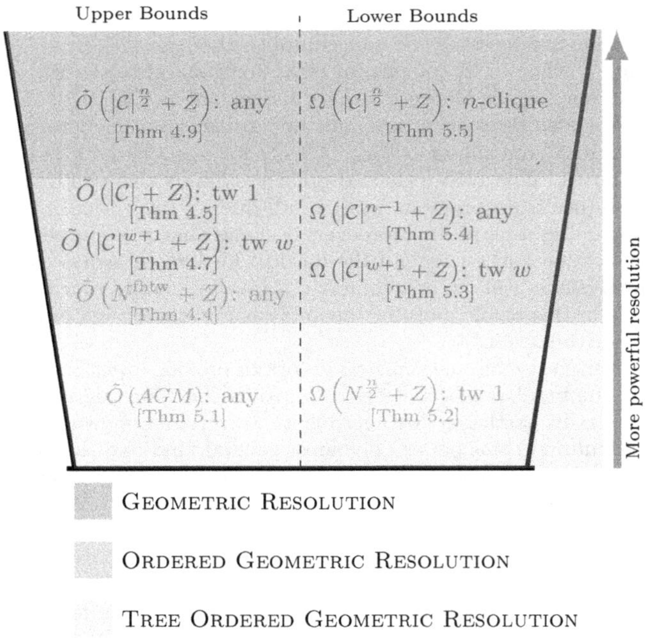

Figure 2: An overview of our results and the resolution framework. Bounds for worst-case complexity are denoted by orange (where N is the size of the largest relation) and certificate-based results are presented in green (where $\mathcal{C}$ is the optimal certificate). AGM denotes the bound on the output due to AGM and Z denotes the size of the output (per-instance basis). The bounds are presented in format time:query, where *any* denotes an arbitrary query on n attributes, *tw* w denotes a query on n attributes with treewidth w $(1 < w < n-1)$ and *n-clique* denotes the n-variable clique query.

bound. Similar but slightly weaker bounds were proven by Alon [4] and Friedgut and Kahn [17]. All of these results were proved via entropy-based arguments.

An algorithm whose worst-case runtime matches the AGM bound would be *worst-case optimal*. Such an algorithm was derived by Ngo, Porat, Ré, and Rudra (NPRR henceforth). Soon after, the Leapfrog Triejoin algorithm [43] was shown to run within the AGM bound. An even simpler but generic skeleton of a class of join algorithms which generalized both NPRR and Leapfrog Triejoin was shown to run within AGM bound [33].

Marx introduced yet another more general notion of width called *adaptive width* [28], which is equivalent to *submodular width* [27], and we are unable to recover this tighter notion of width using the results of this paper.

Beyond worst-case for joins with Minesweeper. Beyond worst-case analysis in databases was formalized by Fagin et al.'s algorithm [16] for searching scored items in a database. These per instance guarantees are desirable, though they are very hard to achieve: there have been relatively few such results [3]. More relevantly, for the sorted set intersection problem, Demaine, López-Ortiz, and Munro [14], with followups by Barbay and Kenyon [7,8] devised the notion of a *certificate* or a *proof*, which is a set of comparisons necessary to certify that the output is correct. An algorithm running in time proportional to the minimum certificate size (up to a log-factor and in data complexity) can be considered instance-optimal among comparison-based algorithms.[7]

The work of Demaine et al. and Barbay et al. was extended to general join queries [31] by defining the notion of a *comparison certificate* for a join problem, which roughly speaking is a set of propositional comparison statements about the input, such that two inputs satisfy the same set of propositional statements if and only if they have the same output. Intuitively, the minimum size of a comparison certificate is the minimum amount of work a comparison-based join algorithm has to do to correctly compute the output. A major technical assumption needed in prior work [31] was that all relations are indexed by BTrees according to a single *global attribute order* (GAO) index. For example, if the GAO is A, B, C, D (attributes participating in the query), and $R(A, C)$ is an input relation, then the BTree/trie for R has to branch on A before C. In this work, we are able to handle more general indexes (KD-trees, dyadic trees and multiple indices per relation) and do not require this assumption. To the best of our knowledge, the current work and that in [31] are the only two instances that present (near) instance optimal results for a large class of problems.

The analysis from [31] implies that we can use a 'box certificate' in place of a 'comparison certificate' because a box certificate has size at most the size of a comparison certificate (see [2]). This result inspired our investigation into the world of geometric certificates in this paper. Indeed we were able to generalize the results from [31] because the box certificates we considered in this paper are more general than the GAO-consistent boxes in [31].

Connections to DPLL. As we will see in Section 4.2.4 Tetris is essentially a version of the DPLL algorithm. We would like to stress that the novelty of our work is to (i) adapt this well-known framework to a geometric view of joins and (ii) prove sharp bounds on the run time of Tetris.

Computational geometry. The box cover problem seems to be a natural problem in computational geometry. However, the closest problem we can find is the STRIPS-COVER-BOX problem [18], where we want to know whether a collection of strips cover a given axis-parallel rectangle. The strips are infinitely long, but they can have any orientation.

3. PRELIMINARIES

We give an overview of the strong connection between indices and gap boxes in Section 3.1 and then move on to our geometric notion of certificates in Section 3.2. We formally define our main geometric problem BCP in Section 3.3.

3.1 Gap boxes and indices

We informally describe the idea of gap boxes that capture database indices. The set of gap boxes depends intimately on the indices that store the relations. For example, for the relation in Figure 1a, Figure 1b shows the gap boxes generated by a BTree that uses the sort order (A, B). Figure 3a shows the gap boxes for the same relation when stored in a BTree with sort order (B, A). Note that the different sort order

[7]As was observed in [31], the log factor loss is necessary when dealing with comparison based algorithms.

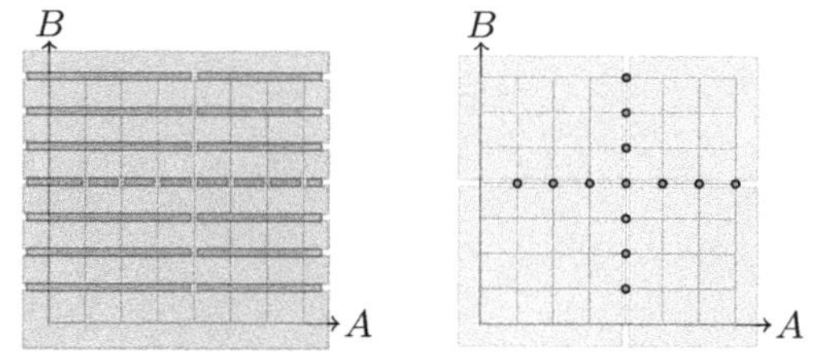

(a) (B, A)-consistent gap boxes (b) Gap-boxes in R from quad-trees

Figure 3: The gap boxes for the relation in Figure 1a from sorted order (B, A) and from a quad-tree type index.

manifests itself in a completely different set of boxes. Finally, Figure 3b represents the boxes for the same relation when stored in a quad-tree. In addition to a completely different set of boxes from those in Figures 1b and 3a, the number of boxes is also much smaller. We will see another example for three attributes soon.

3.2 Geometric Certificates

For any attribute A, $\mathbf{D}(A)$ denotes its domain. For any join query Q, let atoms(Q) denote the set of constituting relations; in other words, we can write Q as $Q = \Join_{R \in \text{atoms}(Q)} R$. For any relation R (Q included), vars(R) denotes the set of its attributes.

We assume each input relation R is already indexed using some data structure that satisfies the following property. The data structure stores a collection $\mathcal{B}(R)$ of gap boxes whose union contains all points in $\prod_{A \in \text{vars}(R)} \mathbf{D}(A)$ which are *not* tuples in R. Note that there can be multiple indices per relation. Gap boxes from all those indices contribute to $\mathcal{B}(R)$. By filling out the coordinates not in vars(R) with "wild cards" (i.e. each one of those coordinates spans the entire dimension), we can without loss of generality view $\mathcal{B}(R)$ as a collection of gap boxes in the output space $\prod_{A \in \text{vars}(Q)} \mathbf{D}(A)$.

We begin with the notion of certificate. The size of the smallest such certificate will replace the input size as the measure of complexity of an instance in our beyond worst-case results.

Definition 3.1 (Box certificate). A *box certificate* for Q is a subset of gap boxes from $\bigcup_{R \in \text{atoms}(Q)} \mathcal{B}(R)$ that cover every tuple not in the output. We use $\mathcal{C}_\square$ to denote a box certificate of minimum size for the instance.

We would like to stress the point above that the size of the smallest box certificate is intimately tied to the kind of index being used. In particular, for certain instances the certificate sizes might be much smaller for more powerful kinds of indices. This should be contrasted with the worst-case results of [32, 43] where BTrees with a single sort order are enough to obtain the optimal worst-case results (and using more powerful indices like quad-trees does not improve the results). Further, our algorithms do not assume the knowledge of $\mathcal{C}_\square$ though they implicitly compute a box certificate $\mathcal{C}$ such that $|\mathcal{C}| = \tilde{O}(\mathcal{C}_\square)$.

For a more thorough discussion of indices, gap boxes, various notions of certificates and how they relate to box certificates, please see [2]. In particular, we can show that the notion of a box certificate is finer than the notion of comparison-based certificate used in [31].

Dyadic boxes. For simplicity, but without any loss of generality, let us assume the domain of each attribute is the set of all binary strings of length d, i.e. $\mathbf{D}(A) = \{0,1\}^d$, for every $A \in \text{vars}(Q)$. This is equivalent to saying that the domain of each attribute is the set of all integers from 0 to $2^d - 1$. Since d is the number of bits needed to encode a data value of the input, d is logarithmic in the input size.

Definition 3.2 (Dyadic interval). A *dyadic interval* is a binary string x of length $|x| \leqslant d$. This interval represents all the binary strings y such that $|y| = d$ and x is a prefix of y. Translating to the integral domain, the dyadic interval represents all integers in the range $[x2^{d-|x|}, (x+1)2^{d-|x|} - 1]$. Here, we view x as the integer corresponding to the bit string. The empty string $x = \lambda$ is a dyadic interval consisting of all possible values in the domain. (This serves as a wild-card.) If $|x| = d$, then it is called a *unit dyadic interval*, which represents a point in the domain.

Definition 3.3 (Dyadic box). Let vars(Q) $= \{A_1, \dots, A_n\}$. A *dyadic box* is an n-tuple of dyadic intervals: $\mathbf{b} = \langle x_1, \dots, x_n \rangle$. If all components of $\mathbf{b}$ are unit dyadic intervals, then $\mathbf{b}$ represents a *point* in the output space. The dyadic box is the set of all tuples $\mathbf{t} = (t_1, \dots, t_n) \in \prod_{i=1}^n \mathbf{D}(A_i)$ such that t_i belongs to the dyadic interval x_i, for all $i \in [n]$.

Note again that some dyadic intervals can be λ, matching arbitrary domain values; also, a dyadic box $\mathbf{b}$ contains a dyadic box $\mathbf{b}'$ if each of $\mathbf{b}$'s components is a prefix of the corresponding component in $\mathbf{b}'$. The set of all dyadic boxes forms a partially ordered set (poset) under this containment.

It is straightforward to show that every (not necessarily dyadic) box in n dimensions can be decomposed into a disjoint union of at most $(2d)^n = \tilde{O}(1)$ dyadic boxes. In particular, for every box certificate, there is a dyadic box certificate of size at most a factor of $\tilde{O}(1)$ larger. Henceforth, we will assume that all boxes are dyadic boxes. This assumption is also crucial for the discovery of an optimal box certificate. In particular, the number of dyadic boxes containing a given tuple is always at most $\tilde{O}(1)$. (See [2] for the details.)

3.3 The Box Cover Problem

We assume the input index data structure(s) for an input relation R can return in $\tilde{O}(1)$-time the set of all dyadic gap boxes in $\mathcal{B}(R)$ containing a given tuple in $\prod_{A \in \text{vars}(R)} \mathbf{D}(A)$. This assumption holds for most of the common indices in relational database management systems such as BTree or trie. The objective of a general join algorithm is to list the set of all output tuples. Our join algorithm will attempt to take full advantage of the gaps stored in the input indices: it tries to compute/infer a collection of dyadic boxes whose union contains all tuples in $\prod_{A \in \text{vars}(Q)} \mathbf{D}(A)$ except the output tuples. (The smallest such collection is called a (dyadic) box certificate as defined in Definition 3.1.) Recall that an output tuple *is also* a (unit) dyadic box. Hence, the output dyadic boxes and the gap boxes together fill the entire output space. Consequently, we can think of a join algorithm as an algorithm that tries as fast as possible to fill up the entire output space with dyadic boxes of various shapes and sizes.

Abstracting away from the above idea, we first define a problem called the *box-cover problem* (or BCP).

Definition 3.4 (Box Cover Problem). Given a set $\mathcal{A}$ of (dyadic) boxes, list all tuples *not* covered by any box in $\mathcal{A}$, i.e.

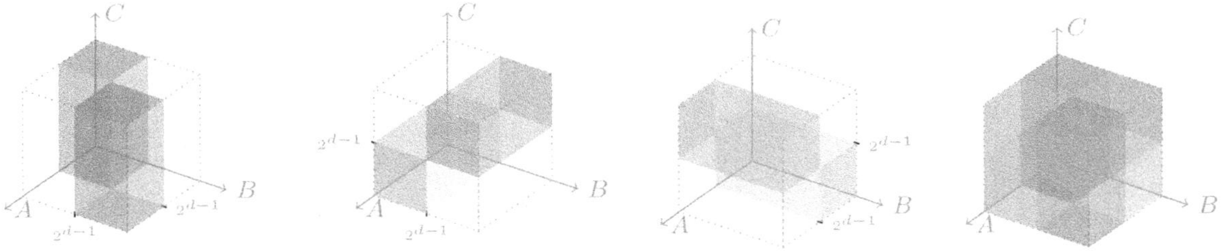

(a) Gap boxes for R (b) Gap boxes for S (c) Gap boxes for T (d) Union of all gap boxes

Figure 4: The first three figures show the gap boxes for $R(A, B), S(B, C)$ and $T(A, C)$ where each relation has the tuples in the dyadic boxes $0 \times 1 \cup 1 \times 0$, where recall $b \in \{0, 1\}$ denotes the dyadic interval corresponding to all length d bitstrings that start with b. The last figure shows the union of all the gap boxes. Since the boxes cover all of the bounding box (which is denoted by the dashed gray box), the output is empty.

list all tuples $\mathbf{t}$ such that $\mathbf{t} \notin \mathbf{b}$ for every $\mathbf{b} \in \mathcal{A}$. Define the (box) *certificate* for the instance $\mathcal{A}$ of BCP to be the smallest subset $\mathcal{C}_\Box \subseteq \mathcal{A}$ such that $\bigcup_{\mathbf{b} \in \mathcal{C}_\Box} \mathbf{b} = \bigcup_{\mathbf{b} \in \mathcal{A}} \mathbf{b}$.

Given a join query Q, $\mathcal{B}(Q)$ denotes the set of all gap boxes from the input indices, i.e. $\mathcal{B}(Q) = \bigcup_{R \in \text{atoms}(Q)} \mathcal{B}(R)$. The following is straightforwardly true.

Proposition 3.5. *On input $\mathcal{A} = \mathcal{B}(Q)$, the output of* BCP *is exactly the same as the output of the join query Q. And, $|\mathcal{C}_\Box(\mathcal{B}(Q))| = |\mathcal{C}_\Box(Q)|$.*

We illustrate the connection between the triangle query $Q_\Delta = R(A, B) \bowtie S(B, C) \bowtie T(A, C)$ and the corresponding instance for the BCP. Consider the instance for Q_Δ in which R has pairs $(a, b) \in \{0, 1\}^d \times \{0, 1\}^d$ such that the first bits (or MSBs) of a and b are complements of each other. In this case, the gaps in R can be represented in a dyadic tree as depicted in Figure 4a: there are two gap boxes corresponding to all triples (a, b, c) such that the first bits of a and b are 0 and 1 respectively.[8] Further, let $(b, c) \in S$ ($(a, c) \in T$ resp.) if and only if the first bits of b and c (a and c resp.) are different. The corresponding gap boxes are depicted in Figures 4b and 4c. Then the BCP instance corresponds to the six gap boxes the union of which covers the entire output space (as depicted in Figure 4d), since the output of Q_Δ is empty for the given instance. See Figure 5 for another instance for the same join query when the output is non-empty.

Definition 3.6 (Support of a dyadic box)**.** Let $\mathbf{b} = \langle x_1, \ldots, x_n \rangle$ be a dyadic box. Its *support*, denoted by $\text{support}(\mathbf{b})$, is the set of all attributes A_i for which $x_i \neq \lambda$. It follows that, if $\mathbf{b} \in \mathcal{B}(R)$ for some relation R, then the $\text{support}(\mathbf{b}) \subseteq \text{vars}(R)$.

Definition 3.7 (Supporting hypergraph of a set of boxes)**.** Let $\mathcal{A}$ be a collection of dyadic boxes. The *supporting hypergraph of $\mathcal{A}$*, denoted by $\mathcal{H}(\mathcal{A})$, is the hypergraph whose vertex set is the set $\mathcal{V}$ of all attributes participating in boxes of $\mathcal{A}$, and whose edge set is the set of all $\text{support}(\mathbf{b})$, $\mathbf{b} \in \mathcal{A}$.

Proposition 3.8. *Let Q be any join query, and* tw *denote* tree-width, *then* $\text{tw}(\mathcal{H}(\mathcal{B}(Q))) \leqslant \text{tw}(Q)$.

Proof. For every box $\mathbf{b} \in \mathcal{B}(Q)$, we have $\text{support}(\mathbf{b}) \subseteq \text{vars}(R)$ for some $R \in \text{atoms}(Q)$. Thus, every edge of the hypergraph $\mathcal{H}(\mathcal{B}(Q))$ is a subset of some edge of the hypergraph of Q. This means every tree decomposition of the hypergraph of Q is a tree decomposition of the hypergraph $\mathcal{H}(\mathcal{B}(Q))$. The proposition follows trivially. $\Box$

[8]By contrast one gap box in Figure 4a would correspond to roughly 2^{d-1} gap boxes if R was stored in a BTree.

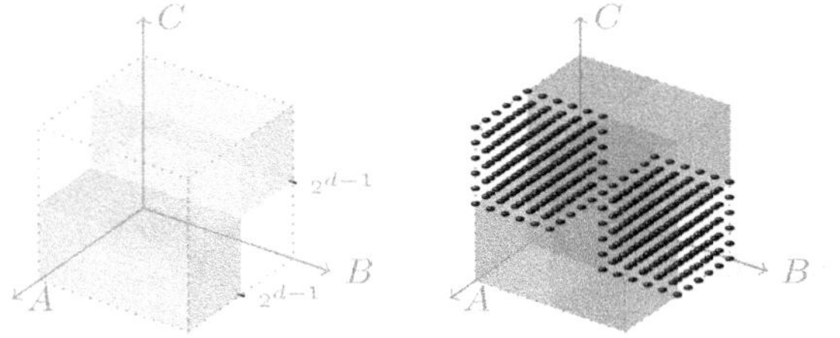

(a) Gap boxes for T' (b) Output points marked

Figure 5: Boxes for BCP instance corresponding to $R \bowtie S \bowtie T'$ with R and S as in Figure 4 and $T' = 0 \times 0 \cup 1 \times 1$ (boxes for T' shown on the left). The union of the boxes along with the output tuples are marked out in the right figure.

A dyadic segment x is *non-trivial* if $x \neq \lambda$ and x is not a unit segment. Let $\mathcal{A}$ be a set of dyadic boxes on attribute set $\mathcal{V} = \{A_1, \ldots, A_n\}$. A *global attribute order* (GAO) is an ordering σ of attributes in $\mathcal{V}$.

Definition 3.9 (GAO-consistent boxes)**.** Let $\mathcal{A}$ be a set of dyadic boxes on $\mathcal{V}$ and σ be a GAO on $\mathcal{V}$. Then, $\mathcal{A}$ is said to be *σ-consistent* if the following conditions are met: (a) For every box $\mathbf{b} = \langle x_1, \ldots, x_n \rangle \in \mathcal{A}$, there is at most one x_i for which x_i is non-trivial. (b) For every box $\mathbf{b} = \langle x_1, \ldots, x_n \rangle \in \mathcal{A}$, if x_i is non-trivial, then $x_j = \lambda$ for all j such that A_j comes after A_i in σ.

Note that if Q is a join query whose input relations are indexed consistently with a GAO σ, then $\mathcal{B}(Q)$ is σ-consistent. (See [31] for the definition of GAO-consistent indices. In short, the search tree for each relation is indexed using an attribute order consistent with the GAO.)

4. UPPER BOUNDS

We formally define the notion of geometric resolution in Section 4.1. Our main algorithm Tetris is presented in Section 4.2. We present rederivations of existing results using

Tetris in Section 4.3 (worst-case results) and in Section 4.4 (beyond-worst case results, which recover and generalize results from [31]). Finally, we present our new beyond worst-case result that works for arbitrary queries in Section 4.5.

4.1 Geometric Resolution

Our algorithm uses the framework of *geometric resolution*, which is a special case of logical resolution. The two input *clauses* to geometric resolution are two dyadic boxes, say,

$$\mathbf{w}_1 = \langle y_1, \ldots, y_n \rangle \text{ and } \mathbf{w}_2 = \langle z_1, \ldots, z_n \rangle$$

that have to satisfy the following two properties: (1) There exists a position $\ell \in [n]$ and a string x such that $y_\ell = x0$ and $z_\ell = x1$ (where x can be λ and xb denotes the concatenation of string x and bit b); and (2) For every other $j \in [n] \backslash \{\ell\}$, either y_j is a prefix of z_j or z_j is a prefix of y_j.

The result of the geometric resolution or the *resolvent* is the dyadic box

$$\mathbf{w} = \langle y_1 \cap z_1, \ldots, y_{\ell-1} \cap z_{\ell-1}, x, y_{\ell+1} \cap z_{\ell+1}, \ldots, y_n \cap z_n \rangle,$$

where we use $y_i \cap z_i$ to denote the *longer* of the two strings y_i, z_i. Geometrically, $\mathbf{w}_1$ and $\mathbf{w}_2$ are adjacent in the ℓth dimension, and in the other dimensions we are taking the intersection of those two dyadic segments which are contained in one another. For the rest of the paper, unless we explicitly mention otherwise, whenever we say resolution we mean geometric resolution. Pictorially this can be visualized for $n = 2$ as in Figure 6.

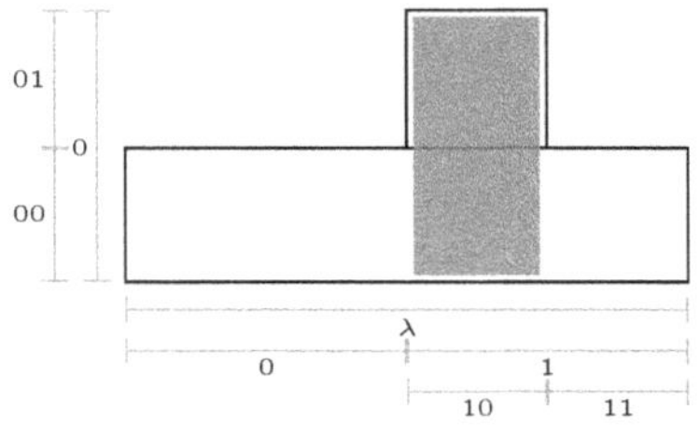

Figure 6: Geometric resolution on the vertical axis between two dyadic rectangles $\langle \lambda, 00 \rangle$ (bottom box) and $\langle 10, 01 \rangle$ (top box). The result ($\langle 10, 0 \rangle$) is highlighted and is drawn slightly smaller than its correct size for illustration purposes.

We briefly explain the name 'resolution.' In propositional logic, the resolution of two clauses C_1 and C_2 is a clause C_3 such that every truth assignment satisfying both C_1 and C_2 must satisfy C_3. The geometric resolution of two boxes $\mathbf{w}_1$ and $\mathbf{w}_2$ is a box $\mathbf{w}_3$ such that every point *not* covered by either $\mathbf{w}_1$ nor $\mathbf{w}_2$ must not be covered by $\mathbf{w}_3$.

Proposition 4.1 (Completeness of geometric resolution). *Given a set of boxes $\mathcal{A}$ such that the union of all the boxes in $\mathcal{A}$ covers some box $\mathbf{b}$, there exists a sequence of geometric resolutions on $\mathcal{A}$ that results in a box $\mathbf{b}'$ that contains $\mathbf{b}$.*

The crux of this paper is to show that one can efficiently find a small sequence of geometric resolutions that solves BCP. The inputs to most of the resolutions made by our algorithms will have an even more restricted structure:

$$\mathbf{w}_1 = \langle y_1, \ldots, y_{\ell-1}, x_\ell 0, \lambda, \ldots, \lambda \rangle \quad (1)$$
$$\mathbf{w}_2 = \langle z_1, \ldots, z_{\ell-1}, x_\ell 1, \lambda, \ldots, \lambda \rangle, \quad (2)$$

where for every $i < \ell$, either y_i or z_i is a prefix of the other.

Definition 4.2 (Ordered geometric resolution). Given two dyadic boxes $\mathbf{w}_1$ and $\mathbf{w}_2$ of the format shown in (1) and (2), the *ordered geometric resolution* of $\mathbf{w}_1$ and $\mathbf{w}_2$ is the dyadic box

$$\mathbf{w} = \langle y_1 \cap z_1, \ldots, y_{\ell-1} \cap z_{\ell-1}, x_\ell, \lambda, \ldots, \lambda \rangle \quad (3)$$

We say that $\mathbf{w}$ is the result of resolving $\mathbf{w}_1$ and $\mathbf{w}_2$ *on attribute A_ℓ*. (Note that x_ℓ might be λ.)

4.2 The Algorithm

Our algorithm for BCP at its core solves essentially the Boolean version of the BCP using a sub-routine called TetrisSkeleton. The sub-routine is then repeatedly invoked by the *outer* algorithm – Tetris – to compute the output of the BCP instance.

4.2.1 The Core Algorithm

The Boolean version of BCP is the following problem: given a set of dyadic boxes $\mathcal{A}$ and a target box $\mathbf{b}$, determine if $\mathbf{b}$ is covered by the (union of) boxes in $\mathcal{A}$. TetrisSkeleton solves this problem by not only answering YES or NO, but also generating an *evidence* for its answer:

- If $\mathbf{b}$ is covered by $\mathcal{A}$, then output a box $\mathbf{w}$ that covers $\mathbf{b}$ such that $\mathbf{w}$ is covered by the union of boxes in $\mathcal{A}$.
- If $\mathbf{b}$ is not covered by $\mathcal{A}$, then output a point/tuple in $\mathbf{b}$ that is not covered by any box in $\mathcal{A}$.

TetrisSkeleton has a very natural recursive structure. We fix a splitting attribute order (SAO) of the query, say $(A_1, \ldots, A_n)$. Following this order, we find the first dimension on which $\mathbf{b}$ is *thick* and thus can be split into two halves $\mathbf{b}_1$ and $\mathbf{b}_2$. If we can find an uncovered point in either half, then we can immediately return. Otherwise, we have recursively found two boxes $\mathbf{w}_1$ and $\mathbf{w}_2$, each of which covers one half of $\mathbf{b}$. Each box may not cover $\mathbf{b}$ as a whole. Hence, we resolve the two boxes $\mathbf{w}_1$ and $\mathbf{w}_2$ by creating a maximal box $\mathbf{w} \subseteq \mathbf{w}_1 \cup \mathbf{w}_2$, making sure that $\mathbf{w}$ covers both $\mathbf{b}_1$ and $\mathbf{b}_2$; hence, $\mathbf{w}$ covers $\mathbf{b}$. Figure 7 illustrates the main idea.

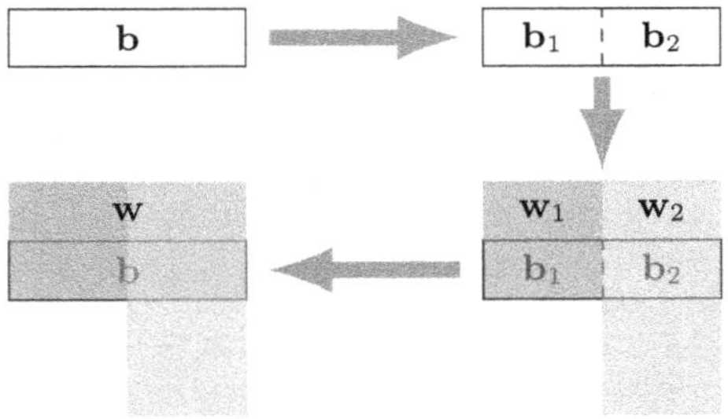

Figure 7: Illustration of main resolution step.

TetrisSkeleton is presented in Algorithm 1. There are three extra things that Algorithm 1 does over the basic outline above. First, we handle the base cases when $\mathbf{b}$ is already covered by a box in $\mathcal{A}$ itself in lines 1 and 2 (see [2] on how we can implement this step in $\tilde{O}(1)$ time using a *multi-level dyadic tree* data structure) and when $\mathbf{b}$ is a unit box that is not covered by any box in $\mathcal{A}$ (and hence cannot be covered by any boxes derived from $\mathcal{A}$ either) in lines 3 and 4. Second, we check boundary conditions in lines 11 and 16.

Algorithm 1 TetrisSkeleton ($\mathbf{b}$)

Precondition: A global set of boxes $\mathcal{A}$ ▷ Our knowledge base
Precondition: Pick a splitting attribute order (SAO) $(A_1, \ldots, A_n)$
Input: Target box $\mathbf{b}$
Output: A pair $(v, \mathbf{w})$, where $\mathbf{w}$ is a cover box for $\mathbf{b}$ if v is TRUE, and an uncovered point if v is FALSE

1: **If** there is a box $\mathbf{a} \in \mathcal{A}$ such that $\mathbf{a} \supseteq \mathbf{b}$ **then**
2: **Return** $(\text{TRUE}, \mathbf{a})$
3: **else If** $\mathbf{b}$ is a unit box **then**
4: **Return** $(\text{FALSE}, \mathbf{b})$
5: **else**
6: $(\mathbf{b}_1, \mathbf{b}_2) \leftarrow$ Split-First-Thick-Dimension($\mathbf{b}$)
7: ▷ Cut $\mathbf{b}$ into two equal halves
8: $(v_1, \mathbf{w}_1) \leftarrow$ TetrisSkeleton($\mathbf{b}_1$)
9: **If** v_1 is FALSE **then**
10: **Return** $(\text{FALSE}, \mathbf{w}_1)$
11: **else If** $\mathbf{w}_1 \supseteq \mathbf{b}$ **then**
12: **Return** $(\text{TRUE}, \mathbf{w}_1)$
13: $(v_2, \mathbf{w}_2) \leftarrow$ TetrisSkeleton($\mathbf{b}_2$) ▷ Backtracking
14: **If** v_2 is FALSE **then**
15: **Return** $(\text{FALSE}, \mathbf{w}_2)$
16: **else If** $\mathbf{w}_2 \supseteq \mathbf{b}$ **then**
17: **Return** $(\text{TRUE}, \mathbf{w}_2)$
18: $\mathbf{w} \leftarrow$ Resolve($\mathbf{w}_1, \mathbf{w}_2$) ▷ Geometric resolution of $\mathbf{w}_1, \mathbf{w}_2$
19: $\mathcal{A} \leftarrow \mathcal{A} \cup \{\mathbf{w}\}$ ▷ Cache the resolution
20: **Return** $(\text{TRUE}, \mathbf{w})$

Finally, in line 19, we add back the result of resolution from line 18 to $\mathcal{A}$. (The last step is crucial in proving most of our results.) We defer a more detailed discussion on Resolve and Split-First-Thick-Dimension to the end of this section.

4.2.2 The Outer Algorithm: Tetris

The TetrisSkeleton algorithm was designed for the Boolean BCP. We now present the simple idea that allows us to use TetrisSkeleton as a sub-routine and solve the general BCP problem. The input to the general BCP problem is a set of boxes $\mathcal{B}$ to which we have oracle access. The *oracle* represents the pre-built database indices of input relations from a join query. In particular, given a unit box $\mathbf{w}$, the oracle can return the set of boxes in $\mathcal{B}$ containing $\mathbf{w}$ in $\tilde{O}(1)$-time. (See [2] for more.)

Algorithm 2, named Tetris, solves BCP by continuously calling TetrisSkeleton on input $\mathcal{A}$, called the knowledge base, with the target box being the universal box $\mathbf{b} = \langle \lambda, \ldots, \lambda \rangle$. We will explain how different initializations of $\mathcal{A}$ lead to different guarantees in later sections.

After each invocation of TetrisSkeleton, $\mathcal{A}$ is amended with a few more boxes and the next invocation of TetrisSkeleton is on the enlarged knowledge base $\mathcal{A}$. Apart from resolvents that are cached by TetrisSkeleton in $\mathcal{A}$, Tetris amends $\mathcal{A}$ with two types of boxes: output (unit) boxes and boxes from $\mathcal{B}$. To be more specific, if TetrisSkeleton returns $(\text{TRUE}, \mathbf{w})$, then we know there are no tuples to output and we can stop. However, if TetrisSkeleton returns $(\text{FALSE}, \mathbf{w})$, then we check if $\mathbf{w}$ is *not* covered by any box in $\mathcal{B}$. If so, we know $\mathbf{b}$ is an output point and we can output that point and amend $\mathcal{A}$ with $\mathbf{b}$. Otherwise we know that $\mathcal{A}$ was not properly initialized in which case we amend $\mathcal{A}$ with boxes in $\mathcal{B}$ that cover $\mathbf{b}$ and repeat.

Algorithm 2 Tetris ($\mathcal{B}$)

Input: Oracle access to a set of boxes $\mathcal{B}$.
Output: All tuples not covered by any box in $\mathcal{B}$.

1: Initialize($\mathcal{A}$)
2: $(v, \mathbf{w}) \leftarrow$ TetrisSkeleton($\langle \lambda, \ldots, \lambda \rangle$)
3: **While** $v = \text{FALSE}$ **do**
4: $\mathcal{B}' \leftarrow \{\mathbf{b} \in \mathcal{B} \mid \mathbf{b} \supseteq \mathbf{w}\}$ ▷ from the oracle
5: **If** $\mathcal{B}' = \varnothing$ **then**
6: **Report** $\mathbf{w}$ as an output tuple
7: $\mathcal{B}' \leftarrow \{\mathbf{w}\}$
8: $\mathcal{A} \leftarrow \mathcal{A} \cup \mathcal{B}'$ ▷ Amend the knowledge base
9: $(v, \mathbf{w}) \leftarrow$ TetrisSkeleton($\langle \lambda, \ldots, \lambda \rangle$)

4.2.3 Recursion and Resolution

We next flesh out the two key operations that were not specified in the description of Algorithm 1: how to split a box $\mathbf{b}$ into two halves in line 6, and how to resolve two *witnesses* $\mathbf{w}_1$ and $\mathbf{w}_2$ in line 18.

We first explain what the Split-First-Thick-Dimension routine does. Consider a dyadic box $\mathbf{b} = \langle x_1, x_2, \ldots, x_n \rangle$. If $|x_i| = d$, then x_i represents a unit dyadic segment, which corresponds to a flat slice through the A_i-dimension. The box $\mathbf{b}$ is flat and is not splittable along such dimension. The first thick dimension is the smallest value $\ell \in [n]$ for which $|x_\ell| < d$. Because $\mathbf{b}$ is not a unit box, there must exist such an ℓ. In that case, the call

$$(\mathbf{b}_1, \mathbf{b}_2) \leftarrow \text{Split-First-Thick-Dimension}(\mathbf{b})$$

in line 6 of Algorithm 1 returns the following pair:

$$\begin{aligned} \mathbf{b}_1 &= \langle x_1 \;,\; \ldots \;,\; x_{\ell-1} \;,\; x_\ell 0 \;,\; x_{\ell+1} \;,\; \ldots \;,\; x_n \rangle \\ \mathbf{b}_2 &= \langle x_1 \;,\; \ldots \;,\; x_{\ell-1} \;,\; x_\ell 1 \;,\; x_{\ell+1} \;,\; \ldots \;,\; x_n \rangle. \end{aligned}$$

Note again that by definition $|x_i| = d$ for all $i < \ell$. It is easy to implement the above bitstring operation in $O(dn)$ time, which by our convention is $\tilde{O}(1)$ time.

Next, we explain the resolution step. Resolve is geometric resolution as defined in Section 4.1. Note that by the time Resolve is called in line 18 we know none of $\mathbf{w}_1$ and $\mathbf{w}_2$ covers $\mathbf{b}$. There are a lot of boxes we can infer from $\mathbf{w}_1$ and $\mathbf{w}_2$ if those two boxes are general dyadic boxes that can overlap in peculiar ways. However, TetrisSkeleton forces $\mathbf{w}_1$ and $\mathbf{w}_2$ to be somewhat special, making resolution much more intuitive and clean. In Lemma B.1, we show that all the resolutions in line 18 are ordered geometric resolutions (see Definition 4.2).

We now state the key analytical tool that will be used throughout this paper to bound the runtime of our algorithm in different settings. The tool is a very simple but important combinatorial lemma that says the following: hiding behind the potential poly-log factor in $\tilde{O}$, we can bound the runtime of Tetris by the number of resolutions it performs. The main observation is that in *most* cases when the algorithm backtracks, it does one resolution. The amount of work it does modulo the recursive calls is $\tilde{O}(1)$: inserting a new box, querying for boxes containing a box, and resolving. Finally, line 19 and line 1 make sure that we are not repeating any resolution more than once. (The full proof is in Appendix B.1.)

Lemma 4.3 (Runtime is bounded by #resolutions). *Let M denote the total number of resolutions performed by Algorithm 2. Then, the total runtime of Algorithm 2 is $\tilde{O}(M)$.*

4.2.4 Tetris *as DPLL with clause learning*

We briefly explain how Tetris can be viewed as a form of DPLL with clause learning. A tuple in the output space is an n-dimensional dyadic box each of whose components is a string of length d. When viewed as a bit-string, this tuple is a truth assignment. A dyadic gap box $\mathbf{w}$ under this view can be encoded with a clause, containing all tuples *not* belonging to $\mathbf{w}$. Under this encoding, geometric resolution becomes a particular form of propositional logic resolution. The resolvent of a geometric resolution is a new clause that was inferred and cached in the computation. Hence, Tetris can be cast as a DPLL algorithm for #SAT with a fixed variable ordering and with a particular way of learning new clauses. (It is for #SAT because the algorithm keeps running even after a satisfying assignment is found. See [2] for more.)

4.3 Worst-case Results

The initialization of the knowledge base $\mathcal{A}$ has a crucial implication in terms of the kind of runtime result Tetris is able to attain. In this section, we discuss one extreme where we can load the knowledge base $\mathcal{A}$ with *all* boxes from the input set of boxes $\mathcal{B}$. For notational convenience, we call Tetris with this specific instantiation of Initialize to be Tetris-Preloaded.

It turns out that Tetris-Preloaded achieves the following type of runtime guarantee: given a join query Q, under some assumption about the type of boxes in $\mathcal{B}(Q)$, Tetris-Preloaded runs in time at most the maximum AGM-bound on a bag of any tree decomposition of Q. And we can construct $\mathcal{B}(Q)$ satisfying the assumption in time linear in the input relations' sizes.

Since the AGM-bound result requires some lengthy definitions, we state below a slightly weaker result, in terms of the fractional hypertree width of the query Q. We prove our full (stronger) result in [2].

Theorem 4.4 (Tetris-Preloaded achieves fractional hypertree width bound). *Let Q be a join query, N the total number of input tuples, fhtw the fractional hypertree width of the query, and Z the total number of output tuples. Then, there exists a global attribute order (GAO) σ such that the following holds. Suppose for all $R \in atoms(Q)$, $\mathcal{B}(R)$ is σ-consistent. Then, by setting SAO to be σ,* Tetris-Preloaded *on input $\mathcal{B}(Q)$ runs in time $\tilde{O}(N + N^{fhtw} + Z)$.*

Recall that Tetris uses ordered geometric resolution. It turns out that Tree Ordered Geometric Resolution is enough to recover the AGM bound (see Theorem 5.1). However, Tree Ordered Geometric Resolution is not powerful enough to recover Theorem 4.4 (see Theorem 5.2).

4.4 Beyond Worst-case Results

Our algorithm Tetris not only can recover some existing results as we have seen, but also leads to new results, as presented in this section. In particular, we show that Tetris can extend the bounded treewidth results of [31], which only hold for GAO-consistent input indices, to handle cases of arbitrary input indices, including sophisticated indices such as dyadic trees (and multiple indices per relation).

The crux of *beyond worst-case* guarantee is for the runtime of the algorithm to be measured in the finer notion of (box) certificate size $|\mathcal{C}_\Box|$ of the BCP instance, instead of input size. It is easy to construct arbitrarily large input instances for which the certificate size is $\tilde{O}(1)$. (See [2].) Consequently, preloading the knowledge base $\mathcal{A}$ with all boxes from $\mathcal{B}$ as we did with Tetris-Preloaded is no longer an option.

To obtain certificate-based results, we can only load the boxes from $\mathcal{B}$ into $\mathcal{A}$ that are absolutely needed. In particular, we go the other extreme and set $\mathcal{A} \leftarrow \emptyset$ in Initialize($\mathcal{A}$) (and let lines 4 and 8 in Algorithm 2 load the required boxes from $\mathcal{B}$ into $\mathcal{A}$). For notational convenience, we use Tetris-Reloaded to refer to Tetris with this specific instantiation of Initialize.

In the following results, we use the well-known fact that if a hypergraph (or a query) has treewidth w, then there is a vertex ordering (or an attribute ordering) that has an *elimination width* w; and, this ordering can be computed in $\tilde{O}(1)$-time in data complexity. We get a near-optimal result for treewidth-1 queries. (Proofs are in Appendix A.)

Theorem 4.5 ($\tilde{O}(|\mathcal{C}_\Box| + Z)$-runtime for treewidth 1). *For any set of boxes $\mathcal{B}$ with $\mathrm{tw}(\mathcal{H}(\mathcal{B})) = 1$, by setting SAO to be the attribute ordering with elimination width 1,* Tetris-Reloaded *solves* BCP *on input $\mathcal{B}$ in time $\tilde{O}(|\mathcal{C}_\Box| + Z)$.*

Along with Propositions 3.8 and 3.5, the above result implies the following:

Corollary 4.6. Tetris-Reloaded *evaluates any join query Q with treewidth 1 in time $\tilde{O}(|\mathcal{C}_\Box| + Z)$.*

Note that a treewidth of 1 implies that all relations are binary. In [2], we show that as soon as there is a relation of arity $\geqslant 3$, a runtime of $\tilde{O}(|\mathcal{C}_\Box| + Z)$ is not possible modulo the hardness of 3SUM.

For general treewidths, we prove a slightly weaker result.

Theorem 4.7 ($\tilde{O}(|\mathcal{C}_\Box|^{w+1} + Z)$-runtime for treewidth w). *For any set of boxes $\mathcal{B}$ with $\mathrm{tw}(\mathcal{H}(\mathcal{B})) = w$, by setting SAO to be the attribute ordering with elimination width w,* Tetris-Reloaded *solves* BCP *on input $\mathcal{B}$ in time $\tilde{O}(|\mathcal{C}_\Box|^{w+1} + Z)$.*

Along with Propositions 3.8 and 3.5, the above result implies the following:

Corollary 4.8. Tetris-Reloaded *evaluates any join query Q with treewidth w in time $\tilde{O}(|\mathcal{C}_\Box|^{w+1} + Z)$.*

4.5 Arbitrary queries

We now show that an enhancement of Tetris gives an improved beyond worst-case result for arbitrary join queries. In particular, we show the following result (see [2] for a more general result):

Theorem 4.9. *For any integer $n \geqslant 2$, the problem* BCP *on n dimensions can be solved in time $\tilde{O}(|\mathcal{C}_\Box|^{n/2} + Z)$.*

Theorem 5.4 shows that this result cannot be achieved by an algorithm that only performs ordered geometric resolution (like Tetris), no matter which SAO is choosen. The main reason is that it might get stuck in resolving boxes along a fixed dimension due to the fixed SAO, while it could have covered the entire space faster by dynamically switching to resolutions in other dimensions.

We get around this bottleneck by transforming the input boxes into boxes in a higher-dimensional space, then applying Tetris. The idea is to carefully construct this map so that the amount of work per dimension is balanced out. It is worth noting that we are still using the same algorithm Tetris, under a transformed input. Since the analysis of the algorithm is quite involved, we sketch in this section some of the key ideas by making some assumptions about the input. In particular, in this section we assume that the algorithm is given as its input the box certificate of the instance of the BCP, which we will denote by $\mathcal{C}$. We will also refer to this version of the BCP as the *offline* case of the problem. At the end of the section, we outline how we can remove this restriction, leaving the full description to [2].

4.5.1 Divide and conquer

To build intuition, we start off with a very special case. Call the input box set $\mathcal{C}$ *balanced* if there exists an attribute X and a partition P_X of the domain $\mathbf{D}(X)$ into $\tilde{O}(\sqrt{|\mathcal{C}|})$ many (disjoint) dyadic intervals such that (i) for each box $\mathbf{b} \in \mathcal{C}$, the interval $\pi_X(\mathbf{b})$ is contained in one of the intervals in P_X and (ii) for each interval $x \in P_X$, the number of boxes $\mathbf{b} \in \mathcal{C}$ such that $\pi_X(\mathbf{b}) \subseteq x$ is also bounded by $\tilde{O}(\sqrt{|\mathcal{C}|})$. The idea is that, when $\mathcal{C}$ is balanced we can solve $\tilde{O}(\sqrt{|\mathcal{C}|})$ independent sub-instances of BCP, one for each *layer* $x \in P_X$; each sub-instance has an input box set of size $\tilde{O}(\sqrt{|\mathcal{C}|})$. This divide and conquer strategy is useful because Tetris can solve BCP on $\mathcal{B}$ in time $\tilde{O}(|\mathcal{B}|^{n-1} + Z)$ (Theorem A.8). This means if we apply Tetris to each of the $\tilde{O}(\sqrt{|\mathcal{C}|})$ independent subproblems, and then output the union of the results, then we have an overall run time of $\tilde{O}(\sqrt{|\mathcal{C}|} \cdot (\sqrt{|\mathcal{C}|})^{n-1} + Z) = \tilde{O}(|\mathcal{C}|^{n/2} + Z)$, as desired. In general, the above is too strong a condition.

To rectify this situation, we perform a conceptually simple pre-processing step. We design a procedure called Balance that takes as input the certificate $\mathcal{C}$ (recall that we are in the offline case). It outputs a box set $\mathcal{C}'$ of the same size. $\mathcal{C}'$ has a specific SAO such that if one runs Tetris on $\mathcal{C}'$ with this SAO, then one ends up with the desired $\tilde{O}(|\mathcal{C}|^{n/2} + Z)$ runtime. Thus, armed with the balancing procedure, our final algorithm has a very simple structure as illustrated in Algorithm 3.

Algorithm 3 Tetris-Preloaded-LB

Input: A set of boxes $\mathcal{C}$
Output: Output tuples for the BCP on $\mathcal{C}$
1: $\mathcal{B} \leftarrow$ Balance($\mathcal{C}$)
2: **Return** Tetris-Preloaded($\mathcal{B}$)

4.5.2 Load-balancing with Balance

To sketch out how load-balancing works, we make one further simplifying assumption that we are trying to solve only the Boolean version of BCP: given the set of boxes $\mathcal{C}$, does the union of the boxes in $\mathcal{C}$ cover the entire output space? We begin by formalizing certain notions that we used in defining a balanced $\mathcal{C}$ above.

Definition 4.10 (Dimension partition). A *partition* P of $\mathbf{D} = \{0, 1\}^d$ is a collection of disjoint dyadic intervals whose union is exactly $\mathbf{D}$. Given a dimension X of the BCP, an *X-partition* is a partition of the domain $\mathbf{D}(X)$. We will typically use P_X to denote a partition along dimension X.

Geometrically, a partition along dimension X divides the output space into $|P_X|$ layers, one for each interval x in P_X. An input gap box whose X-component is disjoint from x will not affect whether the x-layer is covered. Hence, to verify whether the x-layer is covered, we can ignore all gap boxes that do not intersect x. If the remaining set of gap boxes is small, then this verification is fast. At the same time, we do not want too many layers because that certainly increases the total amount of verification work. This balancing act leads to our first idea: we find a dimension partition that is somehow balanced.

More concretely, given a set of boxes $\mathcal{C}$ and a dyadic interval x on the domain $\mathbf{D}(X)$, define two sets:

$$\mathcal{C}_{\subset x}(X) = \{\mathbf{b} \in \mathcal{C} \mid \pi_X(\mathbf{b}) \subsetneq x\} \quad (4)$$
$$\mathcal{C}_{\supseteq x}(X) = \{\mathbf{b} \in \mathcal{C} \mid \pi_X(\mathbf{b}) \supseteq x\}. \quad (5)$$

Note that, for every box $\mathbf{b} \in \mathcal{C} \backslash (\mathcal{C}_{\subset x}(X) \cup \mathcal{C}_{\supseteq x}(X))$, the dyadic interval $\pi_X(\mathbf{b})$ is completely disjoint from the interval x.

Definition 4.11 (Balanced dimension partition). Let $\mathcal{C}$ be the set of input gap boxes, and X be any attribute. A *balanced X-partition* is an X-partition P_X such that

$$|P_X| = \tilde{O}(\sqrt{|\mathcal{C}|})$$
$$|\mathcal{C}_{\subset x}(X)| \leqslant \sqrt{|\mathcal{C}|}, \text{ for every } x \in P_X.$$

Given a set $\mathcal{C}$ of input gap boxes and an arbitrary attribute X, we can show that a balanced X-partition can be computed in time $\tilde{O}(|\mathcal{C}|)$. (See [2].) Furthermore, if there exists a balanced X-partition (for some dimension X) such that for every $x \in P_X$, we also have $|\mathcal{C}_{\supseteq x}(X)| \leqslant \tilde{O}(\sqrt{|\mathcal{C}|})$ and $\mathcal{C}_{\supseteq x}(X) \cap \mathcal{C}_{\supseteq x'}(X) = \varnothing$ for every $x \neq x' \in P_X$, then $\mathcal{C}$ is balanced. So, to have a balanced partition, two fairly strong conditions are required. We next introduce two ideas to relax these requirements.

First, the requirement that $\mathcal{C}_{\supseteq x}(X)$ be disjoint for distinct $x \in P_X$ is not strictly required for the divide and conquer strategy to go through. In particular, for each $x \in P_X$ we can create the sub-instance of BCP by copying every box $\mathbf{b} \in \mathcal{C}_{\supseteq x}(X)$ and replacing $\pi_X(\mathbf{b})$ by x (for each copy). These new boxes along with $\mathcal{C}_{\subset x}(X)$ form a sub-instance. Now we can solve each sub-instance separately as before. Now, if $|\mathcal{C}_{\supseteq x}(X)| \leqslant \tilde{O}(\sqrt{|\mathcal{C}|})$ for every $x \in P_X$, then we would be done.

Second, unfortunately in general $|\mathcal{C}_{\supseteq x}(X)|$ could be as large as $\Omega(|\mathcal{C}|)$. The copying trick to divide the BCP instance into disjoint sub-instances for each $x \in P_X$ is too expensive when $n > 3$. However, when $n = 3$, note that we have $|P_X|$ disjoint BCP instances on dimension 2. In two dimensions, thanks to Theorem A.8, we know Tetris can solve the sub-instance of BCP in time $\tilde{O}(|\mathcal{C}|)$, which would lead to the desired $\tilde{O}(|\mathcal{C}|^{3/2})$ time (since $|P_X| \leqslant \tilde{O}(\sqrt{|\mathcal{C}|})$). Applying naively, this trick will lead to an overall runtime of $\tilde{O}(|\mathcal{C}|^{n-3/2})$, which matches our desired bound of $\tilde{O}(|\mathcal{C}|^{n/2})$ only for $n = 3$.

For general n we use the following natural recursive strategy. We divide up the original BCP on n dimensions to $|P_X|$ many disjoint BCP problems (with the copying trick as above) on $n-1$ dimensions (i.e. on all dimensions except X). If a sub-problem has size $\tilde{O}(\sqrt{|\mathcal{C}|})$ then we can run Tetris directly. Otherwise we recurse on each of the sub-problems. However, there are two technical issues we need to solve to properly implement this recursive strategy.

First, in the discussion above, we did not talk about boxes in $\mathcal{C}_{\subset x}(X)$ for $x \in P_X$. In particular, to define the disjoint $(n-1)$-dimensional sub-problems, we have to perform all possible resolutions of boxes in $\mathcal{C}_{\subset x}(X)$ and only retain those boxes $\mathbf{b}$ such that $\pi_X(\mathbf{b}) = x$ for the sub-problem corresponding to $x \in P_X$. Theorem A.8 implies that the number of such boxes could potentially be as large as $\tilde{O}(|\mathcal{C}|^{(n-1)/2})$. When $n = 3$, this is still not a problem. However when $n > 3$, we will need to reason about such boxes carefully. (In particular, we cannot consider a sub-problem on $\tilde{O}(|\mathcal{C}|^{(n-1)/2})$ many boxes.)

Second, we also need to be careful about the number of times we apply the copying trick above. Some of the boxes that need to be copied might themselves be previous copies, in which case the copying effect would be accumulated. In particular, it is possible for the outcome of a resolution (call it $\mathbf{b}$) among boxes in $\mathcal{C}_{\subset x}(X)$ for $x \in P_X$ to become a box in $\mathcal{C}_{\supseteq y}(Y)$ for $y \in P_Y$, where Y is some dimension that is encountered later in the recursion. Now in this case, we have to be careful when we copy $\mathbf{b}$ while applying the copying trick for dimension Y.

To tackle the issues above, our final implementation of Balance ends up mapping the BCP on n dimension to a BCP on $2n-2$ dimensions. Note that in this case we cannot use the simple analysis we used for balanced certificates earlier: since even if we can get $\sqrt{|\mathcal{C}|}$ disjoint problems with certificate size $\sqrt{|\mathcal{C}|}$, each sub-problem will be in $2n-3$ dimensions. Tetris on each sub-problem will take time $\tilde{O}(|\mathcal{C}|^{n-2})$, which is generally too costly. Thus, for our Balance function, we have to do a more careful analysis. We would like to stress that Algorithm 3 is still valid: just that the earlier intuitive analysis needs to be tweaked a fair bit.

We present the full analysis of Algorithm 3 along with the complete definition of Balance in [2]. The analysis is a bit involved since we have to carefully analyze the number of input boxes each witness depends on. As alluded to earlier, resolvents from earlier levels of recursive calls can interact with resolutions at lower levels of recursions, which foils a straightforward recursive analysis. However, we prove a recursive structural lemma on how resolvents are supported by appropriate number of boxes from previous resolutions, which is enough to appropriately bound the total number of resolutions.

For the *online* version of the problem where the certificate is not given as input, we use the same strategy as Tetris-Reloaded: load boxes from the input $\mathcal{B}$ only when necessary. The number of boxes loaded is $\tilde{O}(|\mathcal{C}|)$. Since we are now loading boxes on the go, the notion of a balanced set of boxes changes over time as new boxes are added. For example, a dyadic interval $x \in P_X$ might define a *good* layer whose sub-problem can be solved efficiently for a while, but as new boxes come the layer might eventually become overloaded. Furthermore, the notion of balancedness depends on the total number of boxes. Thus, a *bad* layer might also become good after some time if new boxes do not intersect this layer. We take care of the above key issues by periodically re-adjusting the partitions and show that the total amount of readjustments is not too high.

5. LOWER BOUNDS AND EXTENSIONS

In this section, we clarify the classes of geometric resolution that are needed to compute various classes of BCP (and hence joins) and prove their limitations. Then, we prove some conditional lower bounds showing that the restrictions in our beyond worst-case results are necessary. Finally, we present some extensions where we prove sharper upper bounds that depend more on the query structure (but only hold for weaker forms of certificates). Omitted proofs can be found in [2].

5.1 Limitations of Resolution Strategies

So far in this paper, we have seen the class of geometric resolution in Section 4.5. This is the most general class of resolution we will use in this paper. Recall from Section 1 that we denote this class of resolution by GEOMETRIC RESOLUTION. In Sections 4.3 and 4.4, we saw a subclass of GEOMETRIC RESOLUTION: ordered geometric resolutions. Recall from Section 1 that we denote this class of resolutions by ORDERED GEOMETRIC RESOLUTION. It turns out that another subclass of ORDERED GEOMETRIC RESOLUTION, which we call TREE ORDERED GEOMETRIC RESOLUTION is also an interesting class. TREE ORDERED GEOMETRIC RESOLUTION (as mentioned in Section 1) is the subclass of ORDERED GEOMETRIC RESOLUTION that only re-uses the input gap boxes: in other words, if an intermediate box has to be used more than once, then all the set of resolutions leading up to the intermediate box has to be repeated.[9]

Figure 2 summarizes the power and limitations of the three classes of resolution above. All of our lower bounds (which we present next) follow by constructing explicit hard examples with an empty output for various classes of resolution that we consider in this paper. (Note that for these hard examples any resolution strategy will have to generate the box $\langle\lambda,\ldots,\lambda\rangle$.)

We begin with the power of TREE ORDERED GEOMETRIC RESOLUTION. We show that one can modify Tetris so that no resolution results are ever cached (this essentially corresponds to running Algorithm 2 but without line 19 in Algorithm 1) so that one can achieve the AGM bound. Note that this change implies that the modified algorithm falls under TREE ORDERED GEOMETRIC RESOLUTION. This implies that:

Theorem 5.1 (TREE ORDERED GEOMETRIC RESOLUTION achieves AGM bound). *Let Q be a join query, N the total number of input tuples, and AGM(Q) the best AGM bound for this instance. Then there exists a scheme in* TREE ORDERED GEOMETRIC RESOLUTION *that computes Q with $\tilde{O}(\mathsf{AGM}(Q))$ many resolutions.*

Now recall that Tetris uses ORDERED GEOMETRIC RESOLUTION and in particular, by Theorem 4.4 Tetris is powerful enough to recover the fractional hypertreewidth bound. In turn, this implies that ORDERED GEOMETRIC RESOLUTION is enough to compute the BCP on boxes with treewidth 1. Next, we argue that TREE ORDERED GEOMETRIC RESOLUTION is not powerful enough to recover such a result.

Theorem 5.2. *There exists a query Q with treewidth 1 such that every* TREE ORDERED GEOMETRIC RESOLUTION *algorithm on input $\mathcal{B}(Q)$ needs to make $\Omega(N^{n/2})$ many resolutions, where N is the number of input tuples.*

[9]The qualifier TREE comes from the following fact. We can consider any set of resolutions in GEOMETRIC RESOLUTION (and hence ORDERED GEOMETRIC RESOLUTION) as a DAG–each box is a node and the inputs to a resolution point towards the output of the resolution. TREE ORDERED GEOMETRIC RESOLUTION is the subset of ORDERED GEOMETRIC RESOLUTION, where the resolution DAG is a tree.

We now move to ORDERED GEOMETRIC RESOLUTION. Since Tetris only uses ORDERED GEOMETRIC RESOLUTION, Theorem 4.7 immediately implies that there exists an ORDERED GEOMETRIC RESOLUTION algorithm that can solve the BCP on boxes with treewidth w with $\tilde{O}(|\mathcal{C}_\square|^{w+1} + Z)$ many resolutions. Next, we show that this in general is the best possible.

Theorem 5.3. *There exists a set $\mathcal{B}$ of boxes with $1 < \mathsf{tw}(\mathcal{H}(\mathcal{B})) < n - 1$ such that any* ORDERED GEOMETRIC RESOLUTION *algorithm that solves the* BCP *on $\mathcal{B}$ needs to make $\Omega(|\mathcal{C}_\square(\mathcal{B})|^{w+1})$ many resolutions.*

We have already seen that we can prove bounds of the form $\tilde{O}(|\mathcal{C}_\square|^{w} + Z)$ for the special case of $w = 1$ (Theorem 4.5) and $w = n - 1$ (Theorem A.8). Next, we show the upper bound for $w = n - 1$ is the best possible.

Theorem 5.4. *There exists a set $\mathcal{B}$ of boxes on n dimensions such that any* ORDERED GEOMETRIC RESOLUTION *algorithm that solves the* BCP *on $\mathcal{B}$ needs to make $\Omega(|\mathcal{C}_\square(\mathcal{B})|^{n-1})$ many resolutions.*

Note that the above implies that our move to GEOMETRIC RESOLUTION to obtain the bound of $\tilde{O}(|\mathcal{C}_\square|^{n/2} + Z)$ for the BCP problem on dimension n was necessary. It is natural to wonder if this bound can be further improved. We show that this is not possible with GEOMETRIC RESOLUTION.

Theorem 5.5. *For every $n \geqslant 3$, there exists an instance for the* BCP *on n dimensions on which every* GEOMETRIC RESOLUTION *algorithm needs to make $\Omega(|\mathcal{C}_\square|^{n/2})$ many resolutions.*

The proof of Theorem 5.5 follows by a volume argument. We construct the boxes so that resolving any two of them results in a box with a small volume in the output tuples space. Thus, to cover the box $\langle \lambda, \ldots, \lambda \rangle$ one needs to perform a lot of geometric resolutions.

Another natural question is whether GEOMETRIC RESOLUTION is strictly less powerful than general resolution. In [2], we show that this indeed is the case by showing that general resolution can solve the hard instance for the proof of Theorem 5.5 with $\tilde{O}(|\mathcal{C}_\square|)$ many general resolutions. However, we do not know if general resolution can solve all BCP instances on n dimensions with $o(|\mathcal{C}_\square|^{n/2})$ resolutions.

5.2 Other Results

A natural question we have not addressed so far is whether we can extend Theorem 4.5 to all β-acyclic queries. These queries do admit linear time algorithms but for the weaker comparison based certificate [31]. In [2], we show that under the 3SUM conjecture, one cannot hope for such a result for box certificates for β-acyclic queries if relations are allowed arities of 3.

Finally, we are able to prove upper bounds with better dependence on the query than the result in Section 4.5 *if* we work with weaker notions of certificates. See [2].

6. CONCLUSION

We presented a simple geometric resolution system that allowed us to derive algorithms that match the efficiency of several of the best known algorithms for worst-case analysis and to derive new results for beyond worst-case analysis. Of purely conceptual interest, these rederivations in our simple framework unify and -we argue- simplify their presentation. More technically, our notion of certificate supports a wide range of indexing schemes, compared to previous work that essentially focused on Btrees with a total attribute order. We are excited about further opportunities to more carefully study the impact of indexing on query performance. In addition, we made a connection to proof complexity via geometric resolution that we believe may further strengthen the connection between constraint satisfaction and database join processing. We conclude with two technical questions. First, as observed by [31] it is not possible to obtain a certificate based result with the fhtw in the exponent. It is a very interesting question to figure out the 'correct' notion of fractional cover for certificate-based results. Second, it would be interesting to extend the results of [35] to the certificate setting.

Acknowledgments

We thank Paul Beame for clarifying the relation of our notion of geometric resolution with general resolution.

MAK's research is supported in part by NSF grant CCF-1161196. HQN's research is supported in part by NSF grants CNF-1409551 and CCF-1319402. CR gratefully acknowledges the support of DARPA's XDATA Program under No. FA8750-12-2-0335, DEFT Program under No. FA8750-13-2-0039, DARPA's MEMEX program under No. FA8750-14-2-0240, NSF CAREER Award No. IIS-1353606, CCF-1356918 and EarthCube Award under No. ACI-1343760, the ONR N000141210041 and N000141310129, the Sloan Research Fellowship, the Moore Foundation Data Driven Investigator award, and gifts from American Family Insurance, Google, Lightspeed Ventures, and Toshiba. AR's research is supported in by part by NSF grants CCF-0844796 and CCF-1319402.

7. REFERENCES

[1] S. Abiteboul, R. Hull, and V. Vianu. *Foundations of Databases*. Addison-Wesley, 1995.

[2] M. Abo Khamis, H. Q. Ngo, C. Ré, and A. Rudra. Joins via Geometric Resolutions: Worst-case and Beyond. *ArXiv e-prints*, Feb. 2015.

[3] P. Afshani, J. Barbay, and T. M. Chan. Instance-optimal geometric algorithms. In *FOCS*, pages 129–138, 2009.

[4] N. Alon. On the number of subgraphs of prescribed type of graphs with a given number of edges. *Israel J. Math.*, 38(1-2):116–130, 1981.

[5] S. Arnborg and A. Proskurowski. Linear time algorithms for NP-hard problems restricted to partial k-trees. *Discrete Appl. Math.*, 23(1):11–24, 1989.

[6] A. Atserias, M. Grohe, and D. Marx. Size bounds and query plans for relational joins. In *FOCS*, pages 739–748. IEEE Computer Society, 2008.

[7] J. Barbay and C. Kenyon. Adaptive intersection and t-threshold problems. In *SODA*, pages 390–399, 2002.

[8] J. Barbay and C. Kenyon. Alternation and redundancy analysis of the intersection problem. *ACM Transactions on Algorithms*, 4(1), 2008.

[9] S. Blanas, Y. Li, and J. M. Patel. Design and evaluation of main memory hash join algorithms for multi-core CPUs. In *SIGMOD*, pages 37–48. ACM, 2011.

[10] S. Chaudhuri. An overview of query optimization in relational systems. In *PODS*, pages 34–43. ACM, 1998.
[11] C. Chekuri and A. Rajaraman. Conjunctive query containment revisited. *Theor. Comput. Sci.*, 239(2):211–229, 2000.
[12] R. Dechter and J. Pearl. Tree-clustering schemes for constraint-processing. In H. E. Shrobe, T. M. Mitchell, and R. G. Smith, editors, *AAAI*, pages 150–154. AAAI Press / The MIT Press, 1988.
[13] R. Dechter and J. Pearl. Tree clustering for constraint networks. *Artificial Intelligence*, 38(3):353–366, 1989.
[14] E. D. Demaine, A. López-Ortiz, and J. I. Munro. Adaptive set intersections, unions, and differences. In *SODA*, pages 743–752, 2000.
[15] R. Fagin. Degrees of acyclicity for hypergraphs and relational database schemes. *J. ACM*, 30(3):514–550, 1983.
[16] R. Fagin, A. Lotem, and M. Naor. Optimal aggregation algorithms for middleware. In *Proceedings of the Twentieth ACM SIGMOD-SIGACT-SIGART Symposium on Principles of Database Systems*, PODS '01, pages 102–113, New York, NY, USA, 2001. ACM.
[17] E. Friedgut and J. Kahn. On the number of copies of one hypergraph in another. *Israel J. Math.*, 105:251–256, 1998.
[18] A. Gajentaan and M. H. Overmars. On a class of $o(n^2)$ problems in computational geometry. *Comput. Geom. Theory Appl.*, 45(4):140–152, May 2012.
[19] G. Gottlob, N. Leone, and F. Scarcello. Robbers, marshals, and guards: game theoretic and logical characterizations of hypertree width. *J. Comput. Syst. Sci.*, 66(4):775–808, 2003.
[20] G. Graefe. Query evaluation techniques for large databases. *ACM Computing Surveys*, 25(2):73–170, June 1993.
[21] M. Grohe and D. Marx. Constraint solving via fractional edge covers. In *SODA*, pages 289–298. ACM Press, 2006.
[22] M. Gyssens, P. Jeavons, and D. A. Cohen. Decomposing constraint satisfaction problems using database techniques. *Artif. Intell.*, 66(1):57–89, 1994.
[23] M. Gyssens and J. Paredaens. A decomposition methodology for cyclic databases. In *Advances in Data Base Theory*, pages 85–122, 1982.
[24] C. Kim, T. Kaldewey, V. W. Lee, E. Sedlar, A. D. Nguyen, N. Satish, J. Chhugani, A. Di Blas, and P. Dubey. Sort vs. hash revisited: fast join implementation on modern multi-core CPUs. *Proc. VLDB Endow.*, 2(2):1378–1389, Aug. 2009.
[25] P. G. Kolaitis and M. Y. Vardi. Conjunctive-query containment and constraint satisfaction. *J. Comput. Syst. Sci.*, 61(2):302–332, 2000.
[26] D. Maier. *The Theory of Relational Databases.* Computer Science Press, 1983.
[27] D. Marx. Tractable hypergraph properties for constraint satisfaction and conjunctive queries. In *STOC*, pages 735–744, 2010.
[28] D. Marx. Tractable structures for constraint satisfaction with truth tables. *Theory Comput. Syst.*, 48(3):444–464, 2011.
[29] D. Marx. Tractable hypergraph properties for constraint satisfaction and conjunctive queries. *J. ACM*, 60(6):42, 2013.
[30] R. Milo, S. Shen-Orr, S. Itzkovitz, N. Kashtan, D. Chklovskii, and U. Alon. Network motifs: simple building blocks of complex networks. *Science*, 298(5594):824–827, October 2002.
[31] H. Q. Ngo, D. T. Nguyen, C. Ré, and A. Rudra. Beyond worst-case analysis for joins with Minesweeper. In *PODS*, pages 234–245, 2014.
[32] H. Q. Ngo, E. Porat, C. Ré, and A. Rudra. Worst-case optimal join algorithms: [extended abstract]. In *PODS*, pages 37–48, 2012.
[33] H. Q. Ngo, C. Ré, and A. Rudra. Skew strikes back: New developments in the theory of join algorithms. In *SIGMOD RECORD*, pages 5–16, 2013.
[34] D. Nguyen, M. Aref, M. Bravenboer, G. Kollias, H. Q. Ngo, C. Ré, and A. Rudra. Join Processing for Graph Patterns: An Old Dog with New Tricks. *ArXiv e-prints*, 2015.
[35] D. Olteanu and J. Zavodny. Size bounds for factorised representations of query results. *ACM Transactions on Database Systems*, 2014. To appear.
[36] C. H. Papadimitriou and M. Yannakakis. On the complexity of database queries. In *PODS*, pages 12–19, 1997.
[37] N. Przulj, D. G. Corneil, and I. Jurisica. Modeling interactome: scale-free or geometric? *Bioinformatics*, 20(18):3508–3515, 2004.
[38] N. Robertson and P. D. Seymour. Graph minors. II. Algorithmic aspects of tree-width. *J. Algorithms*, 7(3):309–322, 1986.
[39] F. Scarcello. Query answering exploiting structural properties. *SIGMOD Record*, 34(3):91–99, 2005.
[40] S. Suri and S. Vassilvitskii. Counting triangles and the curse of the last reducer. In *WWW*, pages 607–614, 2011.
[41] C. E. Tsourakakis. Fast counting of triangles in large real networks without counting: Algorithms and laws. In *ICDM*, pages 608–617. IEEE Computer Society, 2008.
[42] J. D. Ullman. *Principles of Database and Knowledge-Base Systems, Volume II.* Computer Science Press, 1989.
[43] T. L. Veldhuizen. Triejoin: A simple, worst-case optimal join algorithm. In *ICDT*, pages 96–106, 2014.
[44] M. Yannakakis. Algorithms for acyclic database schemes. In *VLDB*, pages 82–94, 1981.

APPENDIX

A. OMITTED PROOFS FROM SECTION 4.4

We will bound the runtime of Tetris-Reloaded on instances with bounded treewidth, proving both Theorems 4.7 and 4.5. To analyze the runtime of Tetris-Reloaded, we first argue that the number of accesses it makes to $\mathcal{B}$ is of the correct order:

Lemma A.1. *The total number of boxes that* Tetris-Reloaded *loads from* $\mathcal{B}$ *into* $\mathcal{A}$ *(in line 4) is* $\tilde{O}(|\mathcal{C}_{\Box}|)$.

Proof. In each iteration of Tetris-Reloaded, if $\mathbf{w}$ is an output point, then no box from $\mathcal{B}$ is loaded into $\mathcal{A}$. If $\mathbf{w}$ is not an output point, there must be at least one box from $\mathcal{C}_\square$ that covers $\mathbf{w}$. Moreover, no box from $\mathcal{C}_\square$ is loaded twice. Hence, the total number of iterations that load boxes from $\mathcal{B}$ is at most $|\mathcal{C}_\square|$. The number of boxes that are loaded from $\mathcal{B}$ in each iteration (i.e. the size of $\mathcal{B}'$) is $\tilde{O}(1)$, completing the proof. □

From Lemma 4.3, the runtime of Tetris is in the order of the number of resolutions $\mathbf{w} = \mathsf{Resolve}(\mathbf{w}_1, \mathbf{w}_2)$ it performs. We call the box $\mathbf{w}$ a *resolvent* (box). It is not hard to see that a box cannot be a resolvent twice. Hence, it is sufficient to bound the total number of resolvents. We develop a simple technique for bounding the total number of resolvents Tetris encounters.

A.1 The integral cover support lemma

In the context of Tetris-Reloaded, a box $\mathbf{a}$ is called an *input gap box* if it was loaded from $\mathcal{B}$ into $\mathcal{A}$ (i.e. if $\mathbf{a} \in \mathcal{B}'$) at some point in time during the execution of the algorithm. Note that we load into the knowledge base $\mathcal{A}$ either gap boxes from $\mathcal{B}$, or an output (unit) box. We distinguish between two types of resolvents. We call a resolvent $\mathbf{w} = \mathsf{Resolve}(\mathbf{w}_1, \mathbf{w}_2)$ an *output resolvent* if either $\mathbf{w}_1$ or $\mathbf{w}_2$ is an output box, or (recursively) if either $\mathbf{w}_1$ or $\mathbf{w}_2$ is an output resolvent. Other resolvents are called *gap box resolvents.*

Definition A.2 (Projection of a box onto some support)**.** Let $\mathbf{b} = \langle x_1, \dots, x_n\rangle$ be any dyadic box, and V be some subset of attributes. Then, the projection of $\mathbf{b}$ onto V, denoted by $\pi_V(\mathbf{b})$, is the box $\overline{\mathbf{b}} = \langle y_1, \dots, y_n\rangle$ where

$$y_i = \begin{cases} x_i & \text{if } i \in V \\ \lambda & \text{if } i \notin V. \end{cases}$$

Definition A.3 (Resolvent supported on an integral cover)**.** Let $\mathbf{w}$ be a gap box resolvent. Let S be a subset of $\mathsf{support}(\mathbf{w})$, and $\mathbf{a}$ be an input gap box. Then, $\mathbf{w}$ is said to be *supported by* $\mathbf{a}$ *on* S if $\pi_S(\mathbf{a}) \supseteq \pi_S(\mathbf{w})$. (Geometrically, the shadow of $\mathbf{w}$ on the coordinate subspace of the variables in S contains the shadow of $\mathbf{a}$ on the same subspace.) An *integral cover* of $\mathsf{support}(\mathbf{w})$ is a collection of subsets of $\mathsf{support}(\mathbf{w})$, say $S_1, \dots, S_c$, such that

$$S_1 \cup \dots \cup S_c = \mathsf{support}(\mathbf{w}).$$

The resolvent $\mathbf{w}$ is said to be *supported on an integral cover* $S_1, \dots, S_c$ if for each $i \in [c]$, $\mathbf{w}$ is supported by some input gap box on S_i.

Note that the collection $\{S_1, \dots, S_c\}$ viewed as a hypergraph forms an integral (edge) cover of the ground set $\mathsf{support}(\mathbf{w})$.

Lemma A.4 (The integral cover support lemma)**.** *Suppose there is a positive integer* $c \in [n]$ *such that every gap box resolvent* $\mathbf{w}$ *is supported by an integral cover of size at most* c*. Then,* Tetris-Reloaded *runs in time* $\tilde{O}(|\mathcal{C}_\square|^c + Z)$.

Proof. Noting Theorem B.4, we only need to show that the number of gap box resolvents is at most $\tilde{O}(|\mathcal{C}_\square|^c)$. The total number of boxes that Tetris-Reloaded loads from $\mathcal{B}$ into $\mathcal{A}$ is $\sum_{\mathcal{B}'} |\mathcal{B}'|$. For a given subset K of the n attributes of $\mathcal{B}$, there are only $\tilde{O}(1)$ possible integral covers of size c. For each such integral cover $\{S_1, \dots, S_c\}$, there are at most $\tilde{O}((\sum_{\mathcal{B}'} |\mathcal{B}'|)^c)$ witnesses $\mathbf{w}$ supported on this integral cover. (This is because given an integral cover of size c along with c input gap boxes , there are maximally $\tilde{O}(1)$ witnesses supported on this integral cover by those c input gap boxes.) By Lemma A.1, $(\sum_{\mathcal{B}'} |\mathcal{B}'|)^c = \tilde{O}(|\mathcal{C}_\square|^c)$. The number of possible choices of K is also $\tilde{O}(1)$, which completes the proof. □

A.2 Proof of Theorem 4.7

Definition A.5 ($\mathsf{support}(A_k)$ and the induced width of a GAO)**.** Let $\mathcal{H}_n = (\mathcal{V}, \mathcal{E})$ be a hypergraph whose vertex set is $\mathcal{V} = \{A_1, \dots, A_n\}$. Let $\sigma = (A_1, \dots, A_n)$ be a GAO for the vertices (attributes) in $\mathcal{V}$. The support of A_n (denoted by $\mathsf{support}(A_n)$) is the union of all hyperedges in $\mathcal{H}_n$ that contain A_n. Construct $\mathcal{H}_{n-1}$ from $\mathcal{H}_n$ by inserting $\mathsf{support}(A_n)$ as a new hyperedge, and then removing A_n from the vertex set and from all the hyperedges of $\mathcal{H}_n$. Then, define $\mathsf{support}(A_{n-1})$ as the union of all hyperedges containing A_{n-1} in $\mathcal{H}_{n-1}$. We keep constructing hypergraphs $\mathcal{H}_k$ and defining the supports of A_k, for $k = n-2, \dots, 1$ in the same way:

- $\mathsf{support}(A_k)$ is the union of all hyperedges of $\mathcal{H}_k = (\mathcal{V}_k, \mathcal{E}_k)$ that contain A_k.
- $\mathcal{H}_{k-1}$ is constructed from $\mathcal{H}_k$ by adding a new hyperedge $\mathsf{support}(A_k)$ to $\mathcal{H}_k$ and removing the vertex A_k from $\mathcal{H}_k$.

The quantity

$$w = \max_{k\in[n]} |\mathsf{support}(A_k)| - 1 \tag{6}$$

is called the *induced width* of $\sigma = (A_1, \dots, A_n)$ (with respect to the hypergraph $\mathcal{H}$). Furthermore, if $\mathcal{H}$ has treewidth w, then there exists a GAO with induced width w. This follows from the well-known fact that the smallest induced treewidth (over all elimination orders) of a hypergraph is the same as the treewidth of the hypergraph (see, e.g., [5, 13]). Such a GAO with optimal induced width can be computed in time exponential in the size of $\mathcal{H}$.

Lemma A.6. *Let* $\mathcal{B}$ *be a set of boxes over the attributes* $\{A_1, \dots, A_n\}$ *and suppose that we run* Tetris-Reloaded *on* $\mathcal{B}$ *with SAO* $\sigma = (A_1, \dots, A_n)$*. Let* $\mathbf{w}$ *be an input gap box or a gap box resolvent, and suppose that the last non-*λ *component of* $\mathbf{w}$ *is on attribute* A_k *(i.e.* $k = \max\{i \mid A_i \in \mathsf{support}(\mathbf{w})\}$*). Then*

$$\mathsf{support}(\mathbf{w}) \subseteq \mathsf{support}(A_k).$$

Proof. We prove this lemma by induction. If $\mathbf{w}$ is an input gap box, then clearly $\mathsf{support}(\mathbf{w}) \in \mathcal{E}_k$. For the inductive step, suppose $\mathbf{w}$ is the resolution of $\mathbf{w}_1$ and $\mathbf{w}_2$ on attribute A_k, where the induction hypothesis is $\mathsf{support}(\mathbf{w}_1) \subseteq \mathsf{support}(A_k)$ and $\mathsf{support}(\mathbf{w}_2) \subseteq \mathsf{support}(A_k)$.

If the last non-λ component of $\mathbf{w}$ is on A_k, then by Lemma B.1

$$\mathsf{support}(\mathbf{w}) \subseteq \mathsf{support}(\mathbf{w}_1) \cup \mathsf{support}(\mathbf{w}_2) \subseteq \mathsf{support}(A_k).$$

If the resolution turns the kth component of $\mathbf{w}$ into a λ, then $\mathsf{support}(\mathbf{w}) \subseteq \mathsf{support}(A_k) - \{A_k\}$. Suppose the last non-$\lambda$ component of $\mathbf{w}$ is on $A_{k'}$, then $A_{k'} \in \mathsf{support}(A_k) - \{A_k\}$, and hence $\mathsf{support}(\mathbf{w})$ is a hyperedge of the graph $\mathcal{H}_{k'}$. This means $\mathsf{support}(\mathbf{w}) \subseteq \mathsf{support}(A_{k'})$ as desired. □

Proof of Theorem 4.7. We apply Lemma A.4. We will show that for every witness $\mathbf{w}$ which is a either an input gap box or a gap box resolvent, its support $\text{support}(\mathbf{w})$ is the union of $w+1$ singleton sets $V_1, \ldots, V_{w+1}$ such that for each set V_i, $\pi_{V_i}(\mathbf{a}) \subseteq \pi_{V_i}(\mathbf{w})$ for some input gap box $\mathbf{a}$.

From Lemma A.6 and Equation (6), it follows that $\text{support}(\mathbf{w}) \leqslant w+1$. Therefore, it is sufficient to prove the following claim: every non-λ component of $\mathbf{w}$ is a prefix of some component of an input gap box $\mathbf{a}$.

The claim is proved easily by induction. For the base case, if $\mathbf{w}$ is an input gap box, then clearly the claim holds. For the inductive step, suppose $\mathbf{w} = \text{Resolve}(\mathbf{w}_1, \mathbf{w}_2)$ where the claim holds for $\mathbf{w}_1$ and $\mathbf{w}_2$, and the resolution is on attribute A_k. The claim holds for $\mathbf{w}$ because every non-λ component of $\mathbf{w}$ is either the same as that of $\mathbf{w}_1$ or of $\mathbf{w}_2$, except for the component corresponding to A_k which is a prefix of the component from $\mathbf{w}_1$ (and $\mathbf{w}_2$). □

A.3 Proof of Theorem 4.5

Given a hypergraph $\mathcal{H}$ (or a query Q), there exists a GAO with induced width 1 if and only if $\mathcal{H}$ is a forest (all relations in Q have arity at most 2, and Q is α-acyclic [10]). When the induced width is 1, by definition $\text{support}(A_k) \leqslant 2$ for all $k \in [n]$.

The essence of the proof of Theorem 4.5 is to make use of the fact that when resolving $\mathbf{w}_1$ and $\mathbf{w}_2$ with support of size at most 2, we end up with a resolvent $\mathbf{w}$ which contains either $\mathbf{w}_1$ or $\mathbf{w}_2$ or both. (See Figure 6 for an illustration.)

Lemma A.7 (2D-resolution expands). *Suppose* Tetris *performs* $\mathbf{w} = \text{Resolve}(\mathbf{w}_1, \mathbf{w}_2)$ *such that*

$$|\textit{support}(\mathbf{w}_1) \cup \textit{support}(\mathbf{w}_2)| \leqslant 2.$$

Then, the resulting box $\mathbf{w}$ *contains either* $\mathbf{w}_1$ *or* $\mathbf{w}_2$ *or both.*

Proof. Given two strings x_1, x_2 and two boxes $\mathbf{w_1}, \mathbf{w_2}$ WLOG of the form:

$$\begin{aligned} \mathbf{w}_1 &= \langle \lambda \ , \quad x_1 \quad , \lambda \ , \lambda \ , x_2 0 \ , \lambda \rangle \\ \mathbf{w}_2 &= \langle \lambda \ , \ \text{prefix}(x_1) \ , \lambda \ , \lambda \ , x_2 1 \ , \lambda \rangle \end{aligned}$$

The resolvent of $\mathbf{w}_1$ and $\mathbf{w}_2$ is

$$\mathbf{w} = \langle \lambda \ , x_1 \ , \lambda \ , \lambda \ , x_2 \ , \lambda \rangle.$$

Hence, $\mathbf{w}$ contains $\mathbf{w}_1$. □

Proof of Theorem 4.5. In light of Lemma A.4, we will show that every gap box resolvent $\mathbf{w}$ is supported by *one* input gap box on $\text{support}(\mathbf{w})$. In particular, we will use induction to show that $\mathbf{a} \subseteq \mathbf{w}$ for some input gap box $\mathbf{a}$. If $\mathbf{w}$ was an input gap box, then the above obviously holds. We can use that as a base case.

Tetris selects a SAO with elimination width 1. From Lemma A.6 and Equation (6), any two boxes $\mathbf{w}_1$ and $\mathbf{w}_2$ that are resolved (on any dimension) satisfy $|\text{support}(\mathbf{w}_1) \cup \text{support}(\mathbf{w}_2)| \leqslant 2$. From Lemma A.7, every resolution $\mathbf{w} = \text{Resolve}(\mathbf{w}_1, \mathbf{w}_2)$ results in a box $\mathbf{w}$ containing either $\mathbf{w}_1$ or $\mathbf{w}_2$. Hence, by induction every gap box resolvent contains an input gap box. □

The following theorem can be proved in the same way as above (a combination of Lemmas A.4 and A.7). We state it here for completeness. Its proof is in [2].

[10]When all relations have arity $\leqslant 2$, α-acyclicity and β-acyclicity coincide.

Theorem A.8 (Tetris-Reloaded runs in time $\tilde{O}(|\mathcal{C}_\Box|^{n-1}+Z)$). *For any set of boxes $\mathcal{B}$ in n dimensions,* Tetris-Reloaded *solves* BCP *on input $\mathcal{B}$ in time $\tilde{O}(|\mathcal{C}_\Box|^{n-1}+Z)$. Here, $\mathcal{C}_\Box$ is any optimal box certificate for the instance, and Z is the output size.*

B. KEY TOOLS FOR RUNTIME ANALYSIS

Lemma B.1 (All resolutions are ordered). *If the initial call to* TetrisSkeleton *is with the universal box* $\mathbf{b} = \langle \lambda, \ldots, \lambda \rangle$, *then the following hold:*

(i) At any point in time, the box $\mathbf{b}$ *to be split must have the form*

$$\mathbf{b} = \langle x_1 \ , \ \ldots \ , \ x_{\ell-1} \ , \ x_\ell \ , \ \lambda \ , \ \ldots \ , \ \lambda \rangle \tag{7}$$

where $\ell \in [n]$ and $x_1, \ldots, x_{\ell-1}$ are strings of length d (maximal-length strings), and $|x_\ell| < d$.

(ii) every time we are calling Resolve $(\mathbf{w}_1, \mathbf{w}_2)$, *the two witnesses have the format shown in (1) and (2).*

In particular, it is sufficient for Resolve *to apply ordered resolution.*

Proof. We prove (i) by induction. The universal box certainly has the claimed format. When we split a box $\mathbf{b}$ (in line 6 of Algorithm 1) that has the format (7), $\mathbf{b}_1$ and $\mathbf{b}_2$ will be:

$$\begin{aligned} \mathbf{b}_1 &= \langle x_1 \ , \ \ldots \ , \ x_{\ell-1} \ , \ x_\ell 0 \ , \ \lambda \ , \ \ldots \ , \ \lambda \rangle \\ \mathbf{b}_2 &= \langle x_1 \ , \ \ldots \ , \ x_{\ell-1} \ , \ x_\ell 1 \ , \ \lambda \ , \ \ldots \ , \ \lambda \rangle \end{aligned}$$

This completes the proof of the invariant. To see (ii), note that when we call $\text{Resolve}(\mathbf{w}_1, \mathbf{w}_2)$, we know $\mathbf{w}_1$ covers $\mathbf{b}_1$ but not $\mathbf{b}$ (due to line 11 in Algorithm 1), and $\mathbf{w}_2$ covers $\mathbf{b}_2$ but not $\mathbf{b}$ (due to line 16 in Algorithm 1). It follows that $\mathbf{w}_1$ and $\mathbf{w}_2$ must be of the forms (1) and (2), respectively. □

B.1 Proof of Lemma 4.3

Proof. We begin with the simplifying assumption that Tetris calls TetrisSkeleton only once. In this case if M is the number of resolutions made, we will prove that TetrisSkeleton (and hence Tetris) runs in time $\tilde{O}(M+1)$. Later on in the proof, we will see how to get rid of this assumption.

TetrisSkeleton can be thought of as a depth-first traversal of a binary tree whose nodes are dyadic boxes. Calling TetrisSkeleton $(\mathbf{b})$ corresponds to visiting node $\mathbf{b}$ in this binary tree. As soon as TetrisSkeleton visits a node $\mathbf{b}$, it checks whether $\mathbf{b}$ is covered by some dyadic box $\mathbf{a}$ in $\mathcal{A}$ and whether $\mathbf{b}$ is a point (lines 1 and 3 of Algorithm 1): If $\mathbf{b}$ is either covered or a point, then TetrisSkeleton backtracks directly without visiting any children of $\mathbf{b}$, in which case $\mathbf{b}$ is a *leaf node* of the visited binary tree. If $\mathbf{b}$ is neither covered nor a point, then TetrisSkeleton recursively visits its children $\mathbf{b}_1$ and $\mathbf{b}_2$, in which case $\mathbf{b}$ is an *internal node*. TetrisSkeleton spends $\tilde{O}(1)$ at each node it visits. In any full binary tree, the number of leaf nodes is equal to one plus the number of internal nodes. Therefore, to bound the runtime of TetrisSkeleton, we only need to bound the number of internal nodes it visits (i.e. the number of recursive calls of TetrisSkeleton in which the execution reaches line 6).

Moreover, whenever TetrisSkeleton returns from visiting a leaf with a FALSE (in line 4), then (thanks to lines 9 and 14) it will keep backtracking while passing this FALSE upwards the tree until it reaches the root. Because the depth of any node in the tree is $\tilde{O}(1)$, the total number of internal nodes that return FALSE is $\tilde{O}(1)$. (This term contributes to the $+1$ term in our final bound of $\tilde{O}(M+1)$.) Therefore, to bound the runtime of TetrisSkeleton, we only need to bound the number of internal nodes that return TRUE (i.e. the number of recursive calls that return in lines 12, 17 or 20). We will be referring to those nodes as TRUE *internal nodes.*

While TetrisSkeleton is traversing the tree, new boxes are being created by resolution and added to $\mathcal{A}$ (in lines 18 and 19). We will be referring to those boxes as *resolution boxes.* We will show that the total number of TRUE internal nodes is within a $\tilde{O}(1)$ factor from the total number of resolution boxes. And to do that, we will establish a mapping between TRUE internal nodes and resolution boxes such that this mapping satisfies the following two conditions:

- No resolution box is mapped to more than $\tilde{O}(1)$ TRUE internal nodes.
- Every TRUE internal node is mapped to at least one resolution box.

During the traversal, TetrisSkeleton makes sure not to visit any internal node $\mathbf{b}$ that is already covered by some box $\mathbf{a}$ in $\mathcal{A}$ (TetrisSkeleton might still visit $\mathbf{b}$ as a leaf node, but thanks to line 1, the execution will never make it to line 6 in order for $\mathbf{b}$ to become an internal node). However, when a new resolution box $\mathbf{w}$ is added to $\mathcal{A}$, the current internal node $\mathbf{b}$ that is being visited might already be covered by $\mathbf{w}$. If this happens, then (thanks to line 1) TetrisSkeleton will keep backtracking upwards the tree until it reaches a node that is not covered by $\mathbf{w}$, and it will never visit any internal node that is covered by $\mathbf{w}$ ever after. The depth of the tree is $\tilde{O}(1)$. Therefore, from the moment a new resolution box $\mathbf{w}$ is added to $\mathcal{A}$, TetrisSkeleton will traverse no more than $\tilde{O}(1)$ TRUE internal nodes that are covered by $\mathbf{w}$. We define the mapping between resolution boxes and TRUE internal nodes as follows: Every resolution box $\mathbf{w}$ is mapped to all TRUE internal nodes that are covered by $\mathbf{w}$ and that are traversed by TetrisSkeleton after $\mathbf{w}$ is added to $\mathcal{A}$. From this definition, we can see that no resolution box is mapped to more than $\tilde{O}(1)$ TRUE internal nodes.

Before TetrisSkeleton returns from visiting any internal node $\mathbf{b}$ with TRUE, $\mathbf{b}$ must be covered by some box in $\mathcal{A}$ (in lines 12, 17 and 20, $\mathbf{b}$ is covered by $\mathbf{w}_1, \mathbf{w}_2$ and $\mathbf{w}$, which all have been added to $\mathcal{A}$). Moreover, this box could not have existed in $\mathcal{A}$ from the very beginning because earlier in line 1 TetrisSkeleton could not find any box in $\mathcal{A}$ that covers $\mathbf{b}$. In other words, this box must be a resolution box that $\mathbf{b}$ can be mapped into. Therefore, every TRUE internal node is mapped to at least one resolution box.

Finally, we consider the case when Tetris calls TetrisSkeleton more than once. The proof of Lemma A.1 suggests that the total number of iterations of Tetris[11] (and hence the total number of calls to TetrisSkeleton) is bounded by $(|\mathcal{C}_\square| + Z)$. Note that the last call to TetrisSkeleton returns (TRUE, $\langle\lambda,\dots,\lambda\rangle$), indicating that $\langle\lambda,\dots,\lambda\rangle$ is covered. At that time, Tetris would have implicitly built a resolution proof of $\langle\lambda,\dots,\lambda\rangle$ using the Z output unit boxes along with at least $|\mathcal{C}_\square|$ input boxes. Hence, $|\mathcal{C}_\square| + Z = \tilde{O}(M)$. □

[11]Even though Lemma A.1 is referring to Tetris-Reloaded, it can be easily verified that the bound of $(|\mathcal{C}_\square| + Z)$ on the number of iterations applies to Tetris in general.

B.2 The gap box resolution bound

In the context of joins (and BCP), when we resolve two boxes $\mathbf{w}_1$ and $\mathbf{w}_2$, each one of them could be either an input gap box or an output box (the latter is the box $\mathbf{b}$ added due to lines 7 and 8 in Algorithm 2) or a result of a previous resolution.

Definition B.2 (gap box resolution). A *gap box resolution* is any resolution where each one of the two boxes to be resolved is either an input gap box or a result of a previous gap box resolution (i.e., a gap box resolution does not involve any output box, neither directly nor indirectly). The result of a gap box resolution is called a *gap box resolvent.*

An *output box resolution* is any resolution that is not a gap box resolution. The result of an output box resolution is called an *output resolvent.*

Definition B.3 (Prefix of a box). Given any box $\mathbf{b}$:

$$\mathbf{b} \quad = \quad \langle x_1 \ , \ \dots \ , \ x_n \rangle$$

(where $x_1, \dots, x_n$ are strings of arbitrary length), we define a *prefix* of $\mathbf{b}$ to be any box $\mathbf{b}'$ that has the form:

$$\mathbf{b}' \quad = \quad \langle x_1 \ , \ \dots \ , \ x_{\ell-1} \ , \ \text{prefix}(x_\ell) \ , \ \lambda \ , \ \dots \ , \ \lambda \rangle$$

where $\ell \in [n]$.

Theorem B.4 (The gap box resolution bound). *An invocation of* Tetris *runs in time $\tilde{O}(X + Z)$, where X is the total number of gap box resolutions that have been performed, and Z is the total number of output tuples of* BCP.

Proof. We will use Lemma 4.3, and bound the runtime by bounding the number of resolutions. The number of gap box resolutions is X. Next, we bound the number of output box resolutions.

We will prove the following claim: For every witness $\mathbf{w}$ that is either an output box or an output resolvent, there is some output box $\mathbf{z}$ such that $\mathbf{w}$ is a prefix box of $\mathbf{z}$. Because every box has $\tilde{O}(1)$ possible prefix boxes, proving the claim will bound the number of output box resolutions by $\tilde{O}(Z)$, as desired.

This claim can be proved by induction. The base case clearly holds. For the inductive step, suppose that $\mathbf{w} =$ Resolve$(\mathbf{w}_1, \mathbf{w}_2)$ where the claim holds for at least one of $\mathbf{w}_1$ or $\mathbf{w}_2$. Without loss of generality, let the claim hold for $\mathbf{w}_1$. $\mathbf{w}_1$ must be a prefix box of some output box $\mathbf{z}$. $\mathbf{z}$ is a unit box (i.e. a point) and hence has the form

$$\mathbf{z} \quad = \quad \langle t_1 \ , \ \dots \ , \ t_n \rangle$$

where $t_1, \dots, t_n$ are strings of maximal-length d. In Algorithm 2, the calls to TetrisSkeleton are with the universal box $\mathbf{b} = \langle\lambda, \dots, \lambda\rangle$. According to Lemma B.1, all performed resolutions are going to be ordered. In particular, $\mathbf{w}_1$ and $\mathbf{w}_2$ must have the form shown in (1) and (2). Since $\mathbf{w}_1$ is a prefix box of $\mathbf{z}$, $\mathbf{w}_1$ and $\mathbf{w}_2$ will have the form

$$\begin{aligned} \mathbf{w}_1 &= \langle t_1 \ , \ \dots \ , \ t_{\ell-1} \ , \ x_\ell 0 \ , \ \lambda \ , \ \dots \ , \ \lambda \rangle \\ \mathbf{w}_2 &= \langle p_1 \ , \ \dots \ , \ p_{\ell-1} \ , \ x_\ell 1 \ , \ \lambda \ , \ \dots \ , \ \lambda \rangle \end{aligned}$$

where $\ell \in [n]$, and p_i is a prefix of t_i for all $i \in [\ell - 1]$. The output resolvent $\mathbf{w}$ will be

$$\mathbf{w} \quad = \quad \langle t_1 \ , \ \dots \ , \ t_{\ell-1} \ , \ x_\ell \ , \ \lambda \ , \ \dots \ , \ \lambda \rangle,$$

which is a prefix of $\mathbf{w}_1$ and hence $\mathbf{z}$. Therefore, the claim holds for $\mathbf{w}$. □

External Memory Stream Sampling

Xiaocheng Hu Miao Qiao Yufei Tao

CUHK
Hong Kong

ABSTRACT

This paper aims to understand the I/O-complexity of maintaining a *big sample set*—whose size exceeds the internal memory's capacity—on a data stream. We study this topic in a new computation model, named the *external memory stream* (EMS) *model*, that naturally extends the standard external memory model to stream environments. A suite of EMS-indigenous techniques are presented to prove matching lower and upper bounds for with-replacement (WR) and without-replacement (WoR) sampling on append-only and time-based sliding window streams, respectively. Our results imply that, compared to RAM, the EMS model is perhaps a more suitable computation model for studying stream sampling, because the new model separates different problems by their hardness in ways that could not be observed in RAM.

Categories and Subject Descriptors

F.2.2 [**Analysis of algorithms and problem complexity**]: Nonnumerical Algorithms and Problems

Keywords

Stream; Sampling; I/O-Efficient Algorithms; Lower Bound

1. INTRODUCTION

Uniform sampling on data streams is a fundamental topic that has been extensively studied, but under the assumption that the sample set fits in (internal) memory [3, 4, 8, 19]. In this work, we do away with the assumption, and aim to understand the I/O complexity of maintaining *big* sample sets.

1.1 Motivation of Big Sampling

Big sampling—acquiring a sample set whose size exceeds the memory's capacity—is hardly a new concept. Jermaine et al. [12] were the first to design algorithms to do so by taking disk accesses into account; and their work has triggered a line of research [7, 12, 15, 16, 18] on this topic. The importance of big sampling is reflected in the fact that, the sample size must grow rapidly with the cardinality of the "ground" input set to allow high accuracy in many analytic tasks. Next, we explain this in two areas where sampling has been widely applied: subset-size estimation, and designing approximation algorithms.

PODS'15, May 31–June 4, 2015, Melbourne, Victoria, Australia.

Http://dx.doi.org/10.1145/2745754.2745757.

Estimation with Bounded Relative Errors. Consider the following basic estimation problem. Let S be a set of n elements. Given a *predicate* which can be any function $f : S \to \{0, 1\}$, we want to estimate the number k of elements $e \in S$ with $f(e) = 1$. Clearly, the entire S must be stored if a precise k is demanded for an arbitrary predicate.

Suppose that it suffices to derive an estimate $\hat{k}$ such that, with probability at least $1-\delta$, the relative error $|k-\hat{k}|/k$ is at most ϵ. This problem can be solved by taking s samples *with replacement* (namely, each sample is uniformly distributed in S independently), and obtaining $\hat{k}$ by first counting and then scaling up the number of samples e with $f(e) = 1$. How large should s be? A standard application of Chernoff bounds shows $s = O(\frac{n}{\epsilon^2 k} \log \frac{1}{\delta})$.

To strike a balance between the space usage and the smallest k supported, a threshold Δ is set such that the guarantee holds for all $k \geq \Delta$. The number of samples required is thus $O(\frac{n}{\epsilon^2 \Delta} \log \frac{1}{\delta})$. Δ is typically in relation to n, e.g., $\Delta = n^{0.99}$ (as n grows, a predicate needs to retrieve more elements to be protected by the guarantee), making $O(\frac{n^{0.01}}{\epsilon^2} \log \frac{1}{\delta})$ samples necessary, namely, *polynomial* to n. Note that here ϵ is not necessarily a constant: in some applications the number of samples may be fixed, in which case the value of ϵ (i.e., guarantee-able error bound) needs to increase with n.

Note that the exemplified Δ was deliberately chosen to be very large; in reality, Δ is often much smaller, but this can only *increase* the sample size.

Approximation Algorithms. Uniform sampling is a common tool in designing algorithms for finding approximate answers to problems whose exact results are expensive to compute. For example, in *triangle counting*, we are given a graph $G = (V, E)$, and want to count the number of 3-vertex cliques in G. In the streaming version of the problem, the edges of G arrive continuously; the goal is to maintain an estimate of the number of triangles that has a relative error at most ϵ with a probability at least $1 - \delta$. Currently the best algorithm [17] requires space

$O(\frac{1}{\epsilon^2} \log \frac{1}{\delta} \cdot \frac{|E| d_{max}}{t})$, where d_{max} is the maximum degree of a vertex in G, and t is the number of triangles in G. The algorithm at its core samples $O(\frac{1}{\epsilon^2} \log \frac{1}{\delta} \cdot \frac{|E| \cdot d_{max}}{t})$ edges of E (in a strategic manner that uses uniform sampling as a black box). The number of samples can be very large, when either d_{max} is large or t is small.

1.2 The External Memory Stream Model

Big sampling perhaps makes the best sense on big data, which are characterized by "3V": (high) volume, velocity, and variety. The first two V's imply that big-data sampling is an external memory problem, and simultaneously, also a data stream problem.

We propose an extension of the standard *external memory* (EM) model [1] to the stream scenario. A machine is equipped with internal memory of M words, and a disk of an unbounded size which has been formatted into *blocks* of size B words. It holds that $M \geq 2B$. The data *stream* is defined to be an unbounded sequence of elements, with each element fitting in a word. An algorithm is allowed the following operations. First, it may perform an I/O to exchange a block of data between the memory and the disk. Second, it may perform any CPU calculation on the data inside the memory. Third, it may perform a PULL operation to fetch the next element from the stream, which will be placed inside the memory, overwriting a word there. This element is said to have *arrived*, and disappears forever from the stream.

We measure the *time* of an algorithm as the number of I/Os it performs, and its *space* as the number of disk blocks it occupies. CPU calculation and the PULL operation are for free. We will refer to the above as the *external memory stream* (EMS) *model*.

Allowing PULL to be I/O-free is consistent with the fact that, when fetched from a network socket, a stream element is always saved into memory in the existing operating systems. In fact, the "directly-into-memory" feature is not really new, and finds its counterpart in the conventional EM model as well. Specifically, one may compare PULL to an "insertion" to an EM structure. Such insertions are (implicitly) assumed to be given in memory; this assumption is crucial in, for example, the analysis of online *buffer trees* [2, 20].

What differentiates the EMS model from the EM model is, in our opinion, the amount of space consumption. Suppose that currently N stream elements constitute the input to a computation problem. We would typically be interested in algorithms that consume *far less* than N/B blocks, but more than M words (to avoid degenerating into traditional stream algorithms in RAM).

1.3 Problem Definitions and Previous Results

Let P be a ground set of N elements. There are two standard definitions of sample set:

- A *without-replacement* (WoR) *sample set* with size R can be any of the $\binom{N}{R}$ size-R subsets of P with the same probability.[1]
- A *with-replacement* (WR) *sample set* with size R is a sequence of R elements, each of which is taken uniformly at random from P independently.

Note that the element ordering is irrelevant for a WoR sample set, but matters for a WR sample set.

We revisit, in the EMS model, two problems that have received considerable attention in RAM. The first one is:

> **Problem 1: Full Stream Sampling.** Maintain a WoR or WR sample set of size R on all the elements that have arrived.

In RAM, the WoR version of Problem 1 can be optimally solved with *reservoir sampling* [19], which uses $O(R)$ space, processes each incoming element in $O(1)$ time, and reports a sample set in $O(R)$ time. As a folklore, a size-R WoR sample set can be converted to a WR sample set of the same size in $O(R)$ time. Therefore, all the performance guarantees of reservoir sampling carry over to the WR version of Problem 1 as well.

In the scenario where the sample set does not fit in memory, previous work on Problem 1 did not explicitly consider the EMS model. Nevertheless, some of the solutions developed can be adapted to work in this model with good guarantees. The *geometric file* of Jermaine et al. [12, 18] processes a stream of N elements with total cost of $O(\frac{R^2}{MB} \log \frac{N}{R})$ expected I/Os, and consumes $O(R/B)$ space at all times, such that a sample set of size R can be output at any moment in $O(R/B)$ I/Os. Gemulla and Lehner [7] presented an improved algorithm that (when adapted to EMS) has the same space and sample reporting cost as the geometric file, but can process N stream elements with $O(\frac{R}{B} \log \frac{N}{R})$ expected I/Os in total.

There have been no explicit studies on maintaining massive WR sample sets. However, the folklore RAM algorithm for size-R WoR-to-WR conversion can be implemented in $perm(R) = \Theta(\min\{R, \frac{R}{B} \log_{M/B} \frac{R}{B}\})$ I/Os in EM.[2] Hence, the algorithm of [7] can also output a size-R WR sample set in $perm(R)$ I/Os.

An interesting question then arises: *is it possible to carry out a size-R WoR-to-WR conversion in o(perm(R)) I/Os?* Recently, a negative answer has been provided in [10] for the special case where R is as large as the size of the ground set. The argument of [10], unfortunately, does not extend to general values of R.

> **Problem 2: Time-Based Sliding Window Sampling.** Each element e from the stream now carries a real-valued *timestamp* t_e, which is non-descending, namely, $t_e \geq t_{e'}$ where e' is the element arriving right before e. Define a *sliding window* as the set of elements whose timestamps fall in $[t_{now} - \tau, t_{now}]$, where $\tau > 0$ is a fixed real-valued parameter and t_{now} is the timestamp of the last arrived element. The objective is to maintain a WoR or WR sample set with size R of the current sliding window.

Let n be the length of the current sliding window. Note that n may vary with time from 1 to any arbitrarily

[1]Specially, we regard a WoR sample set of size $R > N$ to be P itself.

[2]$perm(R)$ is the number of I/Os needed to permute R elements in EM [1].

problem	model	cost of handling N elements	space	WoR sample reporting	WR sample reporting	source	remark
Prob. 1	RAM	$O(N)$	$O(R)$	$O(R)$	$O(R)$	[19]	
Prob. 1	EMS	$O(\frac{R}{B}\log\frac{N}{R})^\dagger$	$O(R/B)$	$O(R/B)$	$O(perm(R))$	[7]	
Prob. 1	EMS	$\Omega(\frac{R}{B}\log\frac{N}{R})^\dagger$	trivially $\Omega(R/B)$	trivially $\Omega(R/B)$	$\Omega(perm(R))^\ddagger$	**new**	**optimal**
Prob. 2	RAM	$O(N)$	$O(R\log n)$	$O(R)$	$O(R)$	[4]	n = window length
Prob. 2	RAM/EMS		$\Omega(R\log\frac{n}{R})$ elements			[8]	
Prob. 2	RAM	$O(N)$	$O(R\log\frac{n}{R})$	$O(R)$	$O(R)$	**new**	**optimal**
Prob. 2	EMS	$\Theta(N/B)$	$O(\frac{R}{B}\log\frac{n}{R})$	$\Theta(R/B)$	$\Theta(perm(R))^\ddagger$	**new**	**optimal**

†Expected. ‡The lower bound applies to the element-processing cost in the 3rd column.

Table 1: Summary of our and previous results

large integer. In RAM, Braverman et al. [4] described an algorithm that uses $O(R\log n)$ space, processes each element in $O(1)$ amortized time, and reports a WoR (hence, also WR) sample set in $O(R)$ time. In [8], Gemulla and Lehner proved that any algorithm solving Problem 2 must store $\Omega(R\log\frac{n}{R})$ elements.[3] In other words, there is a tiny gap between the lower bound and the space of [4].

Problem 2 has not been investigated in the scenario where the sample set is disk resident. Currently the only approach to solve the problem in the EMS model is to run the RAM algorithm of [4] by treating the disk as virtual memory, but the approach obviously suffers from severe I/O penalty.

1.4 Our Results

We resolve the I/O complexities of both problems in the EMS model. For Problem 1, our contributions are on lower bounds:

THEOREM 1. *In the EMS model, when $N \geq R \geq cM$ with c being a sufficiently large constant,*

1. *any algorithm solving the WoR or WR version of Problem 1 must perform $\Omega(\frac{R}{B}\log\frac{N}{R})$ expected I/Os to process N stream elements.*
2. *any algorithm that uses $o(perm(R)\cdot\log\frac{N}{R})$ expected I/Os to process N stream elements must incur $\Omega(perm(R))$ I/Os to return a WR sample set.*

Therefore, the algorithm of [7], as well as its WR extension described in Section 1.3, is already optimal. Note that the theorem officially separates WoR sampling from WR sampling—conditioned on spending $O(\frac{R}{B}\log\frac{N}{R})$ I/Os processing N stream elements, a WoR sample set can be reported in $O(R/B)$ I/Os, whereas a WR one requires $\Omega(perm(R))$ I/Os to report. This, interestingly, implies that the folklore WoR-to-WR conversion algorithm is already the best in EM:

COROLLARY 1. *In the EM model, when $R \geq cM$ with c being a sufficiently large constant, any algorithm converting a size-R WoR sample set of a ground set P into a size-R WR sample set of P must incur $\Omega(perm(R))$ I/Os.*

On Problem 2, we attack upper and lower bounds simultaneously, and conquer both by designing an optimal EMS algorithm, as shown in next two theorems:

[3]Gemulla and Lehner claimed $\Omega(R\log N)$ in [8], but a close look at their proof reveals that their lower bound is actually $\Omega(R\log\frac{n}{R})$.

THEOREM 2. *For Problem 2, there is an EMS algorithm that performs $O(N/B)$ I/Os to process N stream elements, uses $O(\frac{R}{B}\log\frac{n}{R})$ space (where n is the length of the current sliding window), and outputs at any moment a WoR sample set in $O(R/B)$ I/Os, and a WR sample set in $O(perm(R))$ I/Os.*

THEOREM 3. *When $N \geq cR$ and $R \geq cM$ with c being a sufficiently large constant,*

1. *any algorithm solving the WoR or WR version of Problem 2 must perform $\Omega(N/B)$ expected I/Os to process N stream elements.*
2. *any algorithm that uses $o(perm(R)\cdot(N/R))$ expected I/Os to process N stream elements must incur $\Omega(perm(R))$ expected I/Os to return a WR sample set.*

The above statements are true regardless of τ.

Note that the space optimality of Theorem 2 follows from the space lower bound $\Omega(R\log\frac{n}{R})$ of [8].

Our algorithm for Problem 2 adopts novel ideas beyond the solution of Braverman et al. [4]. Perhaps the fastest (and yet convincing) way to illustrate this is to point out that, setting $B = 1$ and M to an appropriate constant, our algorithm also works in RAM, where we improve the result of Braverman et al. [4]:

COROLLARY 2. *For Problem 2, in the RAM model, there is an algorithm that uses $O(R\log\frac{n}{R})$ space (where n is the length of the current sliding window), processes each stream element in $O(1)$ amortized time, and outputs at any moment a WoR sample set in $O(R)$ time.*

This is the first RAM algorithm for Problem 2 that is optimal for *all* values of n and R. Table 1 gives a quick summary of our and previous results.

EMS vs. RAM. By comparing the results of Problems 1 and 2, one can see the differences in their I/O complexities. In particular, while Problem 2 requires $\Theta(1/B)$ amortized I/Os per element, it is possible to lower the corresponding cost to $O(\frac{1}{B}\frac{R\log N}{N})$ for Problem 1. Such a separation is absent in RAM, where an algorithm obviously needs to pay at least constant time just to look at an element. This has two implications. First, the $O(1)$-time "optimality" in RAM (for element processing) hardly touches the essence of the problems. Second, efficiency is a far more important issue in the EMS model than in RAM (where attention focuses primarily on space usage and seldom on efficiency).

Note also that the above separation owes to the I/O-free PULL operation in the EMS model—if an algorithm was forced to read the stream from the disk, the element-processing cost would be vacuously dominated by $\Omega(N/B)$ for both problems.

Remarks. The selection of Problems 1 and 2 is a careful one. Problem 1 (due to its relative simplicity) is the best for demonstrating our lower bound techniques. Problem 2, on the other hand, demands new ideas to design an efficient EMS algorithm, even given its state-of-the-art solution in RAM. In fact, the methods developed in this paper can be applied to settle other sampling problems optimally in the EMS model as well, e.g., *sequence-based sliding window sampling* [4].

2. PRELIMINARIES

Let us start with three basic algorithms that will be needed frequently throughout the paper:

2.1 Offline WoR Sampling in EM

In this problem, we are given a *static* ground set P in an array (hence, $|P|$ is known). The goal is to obtain a size-R WoR sample set of P.

Here is a simple algorithm [6, 13] performing $O(|P|/B)$ I/Os. For the j-th ($1 \le j \le |P|$) element of P, add it to the sample set with probability $(R-x)/(|P|-j+1)$, where x is the number of samples already taken from the first $j-1$ elements of P.

2.2 WoR-to-WR Conversion in EM

In this problem, we are given a size-R WoR sample set S of a ground set P. The goal is to convert S into a size-R WR sample set of P.

Next, we show how to do so in $O(perm(R))$ I/Os, assuming $n = |P|$ and $R \le n$.[4] Our algorithm executes in three steps:

- Generate an array A of size R. First, set $A[1] = 1$ and $J = 1$. Then, in ascending order of $i \in [2, R]$, decide $A[i]$ by choosing uniformly at random an integer $z \in [1, n]$. If $z \le J$, set $A[i] = z$; otherwise, set $A[i] = J+1$ and increase J by 1.

- Take a size-J WoR sample set T of S (using the algorithm in Section 2.1). Randomly permute the elements of T in $O(perm(R))$ I/Os [9].

- Create an array Q of size R where $Q[j]$ ($1 \le j \le R$) is the $A[j]$-th element of T. It can be done in $O(perm(R))$ I/Os.

Q is returned as the final WR sample set. See appendix for a correctness proof.

2.3 Full Stream Sampling in EMS

In this subsection, we review the algorithm of [7] for solving Problem 1, which can be regarded as an implementation of reservoir sampling in the EMS model.

[4]If $R > n$, then $S = P$, in which case the problem is straightforward.

Handling Incoming Elements. The first R stream elements constitute the initial WoR sample set S. Create an empty linked list L at this point.

Given the i-th ($i \ge R+1$) stream element e, we add e to L with probability R/i, and discard e otherwise. When $|L| = R$, update the WoR sample set S by performing a *merge* of L and S (to be explained shortly). The algorithm then empties L and continues as described above.

A merge of L and S is carried out as follows:

- Perform a "clean-up" to possibly shrink L by inspecting its elements in reverse arrival order. At the beginning, $x = 0$. For the j-th ($1 \le j \le |L|$) most-recently arrived element e of L, toss a coin with head probability x/R. If it heads, remove e from L; otherwise, retain e in L, and increase x by 1.

- Take a WoR sample set S' of size $R - |L|$ from S in $O(R/B)$ I/Os with offline sampling.

- Reset $S = S' \cup L$.

The cost of a merge is $O(R/B)$ I/Os.

The algorithm uses $O(R/B)$ space at all times. It processes N elements with $O(N/B)$ I/Os in the *worst* case. The expected cost, on the other hand, is much lower. To see this, note that after N elements there have been in expectation $\sum_{i=R+1}^{N}(R/i) = O(R\log(N/R))$ insertions into L. Therefore, the algorithm has launched in expectation $O(\log(N/R))$ merges, which perform in total $O(\frac{R}{B}\log\frac{N}{R})$ expected I/Os.

WoR Sample Set Any Time. To report a WoR sample set before $|L|$ reaches R, simply perform a merge of S and L right away, and return the resulting S. The cost is $O(R/B)$.

3. HARDNESS OF PERMUTATION IN EMS

In this section, we will formulate and study a problem called *(N, R)-permutation*. Not only does this problem explain the hardness of WR sampling in the EMS model (as shown in the next section), but also it sheds light on some subtle but crucial differences between the EM and EMS models from a technical point of view.

The problem is defined as follows. The input is a stream of N elements. Denote by P the set of those elements. Given the value of N and an integer $R \le N$, an algorithm should

- either *succeed* by writing to the disk a random R-permutation[5] of P, namely, any of the $\frac{N!}{(N-R)!}$ R-permutations is output with the same chance,

- or declare *failure*.

The algorithm must succeed with at least a constant probability.

The problem admits a solution that never fails, and terminates in $O(perm(R))$ I/Os. We can first take a size-R WoR sample set S of P. Since N is known, this is in fact offline sampling, and can be completed in $O(R/B)$ I/Os (see

[5]An R-permutation is an ordered list of R distinct elements in P.

Section 2.1). After that, we output a random permutation of S in $O(perm(R))$ I/Os.

The rest of the subsection will prove that it is impossible to do any better, even by failing:

LEMMA 1. *When $R \geq 2M$, any algorithm solving the (N, R)-permutation problem must incur $\Omega(perm(R))$ I/Os in expectation.*

EMS Subtlety. Permutation is one of the most fundamental problems in EM, and also one of the best understood, with lower bounds already established in various contexts [1, 11, 14]. Unfortunately, all the techniques behind those lower bounds can be used to prove only bounds far worse than the one in Lemma 1 in the EMS model. This, interestingly, is not due to the looseness of those techniques, but rather, due to an inherent difference between the EM and EMS models.

In general, a permutation lower bound in EM is proved by observing that an I/O cannot generate too many new permutations, which, in turn, relies on the fact that in EM *no new elements can enter memory between two I/Os.* This is no longer true in the EMS model: new elements may be added to the memory by the PULL operation, even though no I/O is performed. As a consequence, an I/O may potentially create a huge number of new permutations, thus significantly weakening the power of the existing arguments.

In what follows, we will present an EMS-indigenous technique to derive Lemma 1.

Producing One R-Permutation. Let us first look at a different problem in the EMS model which we call *one-R-permutation.* The input stream is a sequence of R pairs of the form (e_i, p_i), where e_i is an element drawn from a certain domain, and p_i is an integer in $[1, R]$. It is required that $p_1, p_2, ..., p_R$ are distinct. The output is a permutation π of $e_1, e_2 ..., e_R$ in the disk where e_i is placed at the p_i-th position of π, for each $i \in [1, R]$.

This problem is in fact a disguise of the classic problem of permuting R elements in EM. Notice that $\Omega(R/B)$ is a clearly a lower bound for one-R-permutation. Hence, one can reduce the EM permutation problem to one-R-permutation, by simulating a stream with a scan of the R elements in the input. The opposite reduction is also straightforward: in the EMS model, one can first spend $O(R/B)$ I/Os storing all the incoming R elements, and then, solve one-R-permutation as a permutation problem in EM. It thus follows that the *worst-case* I/O complexity is $\Theta(perm(R))$ for one-R-permutation.

However, it is not the worst case that will interest us in the subsequent discussion; instead, we will be concerned with *every instance* of the problem. Specifically, for every possible sequence $(p_1, ..., p_R)$, we will need the *smallest* I/O cost of all the possible strategies for producing the target permutation π. For example, when $p_1, ..., p_R$ happen to be in ascending order, then an *optimal strategy* would spend only $\lceil R/B \rceil$ I/Os. Interestingly, we do not need to design the optimal strategy for each $(p_1, ..., p_R)$; it suffices to know that it definitely *exists.*

Proof of Lemma 1. The crux of our proof is to show that, given an algorithm $\mathcal{A}$ solving the (N, R)-permutation problem in H expected I/Os, we can design an algorithm $\mathcal{A}'$ in the EM model to produce a random permutation of R elements in $O(H)$ expected I/Os. The latter problem has a lower bound of $\Omega(perm(R))$ expected I/Os[6]. It will thus follow that $H = \Omega(perm(R))$.

From now on, we will fix the arrival order of the elements in P. Denote by c the success probability of $\mathcal{A}$. Let S be an arbitrary size-R subset of P. We denote by $cost(\mathcal{A} \mid S)$ the expected I/O cost of $\mathcal{A}$, under the event that the algorithm succeeds by outputting an R-permutation with elements only from S. The probability of the event is $\mathbf{Pr}[S] = c/\binom{N}{R}$ for any S. We have:

$$H \geq \sum_{\forall S} cost(\mathcal{A} \mid S) \cdot \mathbf{Pr}[S].$$

Let $S^\star$ be the S with the smallest $cost(\mathcal{A} \mid S)$. Thus:

$$\begin{aligned} H &\geq \sum_{\forall S} cost(\mathcal{A} \mid S^\star) \cdot \mathbf{Pr}[S] \\ &= cost(\mathcal{A} \mid S^\star) \sum_{\forall S} \mathbf{Pr}[S] \\ &= c \cdot cost(\mathcal{A} \mid S^\star). \end{aligned} \quad (1)$$

Henceforth, we will view $S^\star$ as a sequence where its elements are arranged by arrival order in the stream.

Next we design an algorithm $\mathcal{A}^\star$ which may fail with probability $1 - c$, but when it does not, it *always* produces a random permutation of $S^\star$. Furthermore, the expected cost of $\mathcal{A}^\star$ is at most H. For this purpose, we take the view that a randomized algorithm has free access to a sequence of random bits, such that the algorithm's execution is deterministic once all those bits are fixed. For every such sequence Σ of fixed bits, we design the (deterministic) behavior of $\mathcal{A}^\star$ conditioned on Σ:

- If $\mathcal{A}$ fails on Σ, we instruct $\mathcal{A}^\star$ to fail immediately without performing any I/O.
- If the output of $\mathcal{A}$ (given Σ) is a permutation $\pi^\star$ of $S^\star$, we instruct $\mathcal{A}^\star$ to take an optimal strategy to solve the one-R-permutation instance that aims to produce $\pi^\star$ from the stream sequence $S^\star$ (recall how we view $S^\star$ as a sequence). Such a strategy always exists, as explained before.
- The remaining case is that the output of $\mathcal{A}$ (given Σ) is a permutation π of an element set $S \neq S^\star$. Let us regard S as a sequence of its elements sorted by arrival order. We resort to the following one-one mapping from the elements of S to those of $S^\star$: for each $i \in [1, R]$, the i-th element of S maps to the i-th element of $S^\star$. The mapping converts π into a permutation $\pi^\star$ of $S^\star$. We instruct $\mathcal{A}^\star$ to follow an optimal strategy to solve the one-R-permutation instance that aims to produce $\pi^\star$ from the stream sequence $S^\star$.

We claim that the algorithm $\mathcal{A}^\star$ thus designed serves our purposes. First, it is clear that $\mathcal{A}^\star$ succeeds with probability c, and when it does, it always outputs a permutation of $S^\star$. Second, $\mathcal{A}^\star$ (if succeeds) returns a random permutation of $S^\star$ because (i) $\mathcal{A}$ outputs a random R-permutation of P and

[6]Proof: Combine Yao's Minimax theorem and the permutation lower bound of Aggarwal and Vitter [1].

(ii) the same number of R-permutations of P are mapped to each permutation of $S^\star$ output by $\mathcal{A}^\star$.

It remains to analyze the expected cost $H^\star$ of $\mathcal{A}^\star$. By definition:

$$H^\star = \sum_{\forall \text{ permutation } \pi^\star \text{ of } S^\star} optcost(\pi^\star) \cdot \frac{c}{R!} \quad (2)$$

where $optcost(\pi^\star)$ is the cost of an optimal strategy solving the one-R-permutation problem that produces $\pi^\star$ from the stream sequence $S^\star$. Denote by $cost(\mathcal{A} \mid \pi^\star)$ the expected cost of $\mathcal{A}$ under the condition that $\mathcal{A}$ outputs $\pi^\star$. It holds by definition of $optcost(\pi^\star)$ that $optcost(\pi^\star) \le cost(\mathcal{A} \mid \pi^\star)$. Therefore:

$$\begin{aligned}(2) &\le c \sum_{\forall \text{ permutation } \pi^\star \text{ of } S^\star} cost(\mathcal{A} \mid \pi^\star)\frac{1}{R!} \\ &= c \cdot cost(\mathcal{A} \mid S^\star) \\ \text{(by (1))} &\le H.\end{aligned}$$

We are now ready to design the promised algorithm $\mathcal{A}'$ in the EM model which, given a set X of R elements, outputs a random permutation of X. We simply create a (virtual) data stream of length N where the elements of X are placed at the same positions as the elements of $S^\star$ in the input stream of $\mathcal{A}^\star$. Since the contents of the elements outside X are irrelevant, we can generate such a stream by reading X in $O(R/B)$ I/Os. Then, $\mathcal{A}'$ repetitively runs $\mathcal{A}^\star$ on that stream until it succeeds (when it does, the output is guaranteed to be a random permutation of X). The total expected cost of $\mathcal{A}'$ is $O(R/B + H^\star) = O(H)$, where the equality used the fact that $H = \Omega(R/B)$ when $R \ge 2M$. We thus complete the proof of Lemma 1.

4. HARDNESS OF FULL STREAM SAMPLING

In this section, we will explain why it is impossible to do any better than the algorithm of [7] (see Section 2.3), by presenting a proof of Theorem 1. As required by the theorem, we assume that $N \ge R \ge cM$ with c being a sufficiently large constant.

We say that the i-th element of the stream has *sequence number* i. Divide the stream into *epochs* such that epoch 1 includes the first R elements of the stream, and epoch $j \ge 2$ covers elements with sequence numbers in

$$[1 + 2^{j-2}R, 2^{j-1}R].$$

Note that, at the end of each epoch $j \ge 2$, epoch j accounts for exactly half of the elements that have arrived.

Element Processing. We will first prove Statement 1 of the theorem. We will argue that any algorithm $\mathcal{A}$ must perform $\Omega(R/B)$ expected I/Os in each of the $\Theta(\log \frac{N}{R})$ epochs, which brings the total cost to $\Omega(\frac{R}{B} \log \frac{N}{R})$.

Consider first WoR sampling, for which we choose $c = 3$. For the first epoch, since $\mathcal{A}$ must remember all the first R elements, it needs $\Omega((R - M)/B) = \Omega(R/B)$ I/Os to write at least $R - M$ elements to the disk. For each epoch $j \ge 2$, if a sample request arises at the end of the epoch, with half probability, $\mathcal{A}$ must return at least $R/2$ samples from epoch j (recall that epoch j covers half of the already-arrived elements). Therefore, with half probability, $\mathcal{A}$ must have written at least $R/2 - M = \Omega(R)$ of samples from epoch j to the disk, necessitating $\Omega(R/B)$ I/Os.

The above argument can be extended to WR sampling, for which we choose $c = 9$. For each epoch $j \ge 3$, imagine that we, at the end of the epoch, request $\mathcal{A}$ to return a size-R sample set stored in an array Q. We observe:

LEMMA 2. *For each $z \in [1, R]$, $Q[z]$ has at least $1/4$ probability to satisfy two conditions simultaneously: (i) it comes from epoch j, and (ii) $Q[z]$ is unique in Q (i.e., there does not exist $z' \ne z$ with $Q[z'] = Q[z]$).*

PROOF. First, $Q[z]$ clearly has half probability to come from epoch j. Conditioned on $Q[z]$ originating from epoch j, next we show that it is unique in Q with at least half probability. This will prove the correctness of the lemma.

Epoch $j \ge 3$ has at least $2R$ elements by definition. As the elements of Q are independent, $Q[z]$ equals one of the other $R - 1$ elements with probability at most $(R-1)/2R < 1/2$. □

COROLLARY 3. *With at least $1/7$ probability, Q contains at least $R/8$ unique elements coming from epoch j.*

PROOF. Otherwise, the expected number of unique elements from the epoch is strictly smaller than $\frac{1}{7} \cdot R + \frac{6}{7} \cdot \frac{R}{8} = R/4$, contradicting Lemma 2. □

Therefore, with probability at least $1/7$, $\mathcal{A}$ must spend at least $(R/8 - M)/B = \Omega(R/B)$ I/Os writing $R/8$ elements from epoch j to the disk.

WR Reporting. Next we will prove Statement 2 of Theorem 1, namely, if $\mathcal{A}$ spends $o(perm(R) \cdot \log \frac{N}{R})$ expected I/Os processing N stream elements, it must incur $\Omega(perm(R))$ I/Os returning a WR sample set.

Our hard *workload* includes the stream constructed at the beginning of the section, and a WR sample request at the end of each epoch $j \ge 3$. We claim that the total I/O cost of processing the entire workload is $\Omega(perm(R) \cdot \log \frac{N}{R})$ in expectation, which suffices for establishing Statement 2 (because there are $O(\log \frac{N}{R})$ sample requests).

Our proof of the claim is a corollary of Lemma 1. Fix an arbitrary epoch $j \ge 3$. Let H be the total expected I/O cost of $\mathcal{A}$ in processing the elements of the epoch and the sample request at the end of the epoch. By Corollary 3, with probability at least $1/7$, the WR sample set Q fetched at the end of epoch j contains at least $R/8$ distinct elements from epoch j. The sequence of those $R/8$ elements in Q is a random $(R/8)$-permutation of the elements in the epoch. Choosing $c = 16$, we ensure $R/8 \ge 2M$; and hence, $H = \Omega(perm(R/8)) = \Omega(perm(R))$ by Lemma 1. It thus follows that $\Omega(perm(R) \cdot \log \frac{N}{R})$ expected I/Os are needed to process the entire workload.

5. TIME-BASED SLIDING WINDOW SAMPLING

We now set off to tackle Problem 2 defined in Section 1.3. An element is said to be *alive* if it falls in the current sliding window, and *expired* otherwise.

As a major obstacle in overcoming Problem 2, an algorithm often does *not* know the number n of alive elements, but nonetheless would need to make decisions based on n. This is especially true in the so-called *two-bucket sampling problem* which, as identified by Braverman et al. [4], is a subproblem vital to settling Problem 2. We present a new algorithm to solve the subproblem I/O-efficiently in Section 5.1. In Section 5.2, we combine this algorithm with ideas from the *exponential histogram* [5] to solve Problem 2. Finally, we analyze the hardness of Problem 2 in Section 5.3.

5.1 Two-Bucket Sampling

Problem. Let U_1 and U_2 be two subsequences of the data stream satisfying the following 5 conditions:

1. They are disjoint and consecutive (i.e., the first element in U_2 arrived directly after the last element in U_1)
2. They together cover all the alive elements; and U_1 covers at least one alive element (but perhaps also some expired elements). In other words, if we denote by α and β the lengths of U_1 and U_2, respectively, then n can be anywhere from $\beta+1$ to $\alpha+\beta$.
3. $\alpha \geq R$ and $\beta \geq 2\alpha$.
4. We have taken two size-R WoR sample sets T_1 and S_1 of U_1, and a size-R WoR sample set S_2 of U_2, such that T_1, S_1, S_2 are independent from each other.
5. Each sample $e \in T_1$ also carries an *index*: if e is the i-th element of U_1, then its index equals i.

Our goal is to compute a size-R WoR sample set S of the current sliding window in $O(R/B)$ I/Os.

Algorithm. We denote by γ the number of alive elements in U_1; in other words, $n = \beta + \gamma$. Remember that the value of γ is unknown (which renders n unknown). The following is a crucial lemma, whose proof is non-trivial, and hence, deferred to the end of the subsection:

LEMMA 3. *Given values c_1, c_2 satisfying $0 \leq c_1 \leq c_2 \leq R$, a Bernoulli trial returns a binary random variable that equals 1 with probability $\frac{\alpha-c_1}{\beta+\gamma-c_2}$, and 0 with the remaining probability. Given T_1, we can support R independent Bernoulli trials, each with its own c_1, c_2. The total number of I/Os required is $O(R/B)$.*

Next we describe our algorithm for two-bucket sampling. First, generate a random number Y defined as follows. Imagine taking a size-R WoR sample set from the set of integers in $[1, \beta+\gamma]$; Y equals the number of sampled integers falling in $[1, \alpha]$. Y can be easily obtained by repeating the following step R times ($Y = 0$ initially): cast a coin with head probability $\frac{\alpha-Y}{\beta+\gamma-j}$, where j is the number of times the step is already performed ($j = 0$ for the first time); increase Y by 1 if the coin heads. By Lemma 3, the generation of Y requires $O(R/B)$ I/Os.

Second, take a size-Y WoR sample set $\hat{S}_1$ of S_1. Then, our final S is the union of (i) the alive elements of $\hat{S}_1$ (we can tell if an element is alive from its timestamp)—denote by h the number of them—and (ii) a size-$(R-h)$ WoR sample set of S_2. Since only offline WoR sampling is performed, both $\hat{S}_1$ and S can be produced in $O(R/B)$ I/Os.

Correctness. Let X be a random variable equal to the output of our algorithm. Fix an arbitrary size-R subset S of the current sliding window. We will prove that

$$\mathbf{Pr}[X = S] = 1/\binom{\beta+\gamma}{R}.$$

Define $X' = X \cap U_1, X'' = X \cap U_2, S' = S \cap U_1$, and $S'' = S \cap U_2$. Thus:

$$\begin{aligned}\mathbf{Pr}[X = S] &= \mathbf{Pr}[X'' = S'' \mid X' = S'] \cdot \mathbf{Pr}[X' = S'] \\ &= \frac{1}{\binom{\beta}{R-|S'|}} \cdot \mathbf{Pr}[X' = S']\end{aligned}$$

We analyze $\mathbf{Pr}[X' = S']$ by expanding it:

$$\begin{aligned}&\mathbf{Pr}[X' = S'] \\ = &\sum_{y=|S'|}^{R} \mathbf{Pr}[X' = S' \mid Y = y] \cdot \mathbf{Pr}[Y = y] \\ = &\sum_{y=|S'|}^{R} \frac{\binom{\alpha-\gamma}{y-|S'|}}{\binom{\alpha}{y}} \cdot \frac{\binom{\alpha}{y}\binom{\beta+\gamma-\alpha}{R-y}}{\binom{\beta+\gamma}{R}} \\ = &\frac{1}{\binom{\beta+\gamma}{R}} \sum_{y=|S'|}^{R} \binom{\alpha-\gamma}{y-|S'|}\binom{\beta-(\alpha-\gamma)}{R-y} \\ = &\frac{\binom{\beta}{R-|S'|}}{\binom{\beta+\gamma}{R}}.\end{aligned}$$

It thus follows that $\mathbf{Pr}[X = S] = 1/\binom{\beta+\gamma}{R}$, as desired.

Proof of Lemma 3. We will first tackle another subproblem—which we call *random seeding*—whose goal is to compute from T_1 an array *rand* of size R defined as follows:

- Each cell $rand[j]$ ($1 \leq j \leq R$) stores a pair (b, i), where i is a random variable drawn uniformly from $[1, \alpha]$, and b is a bit that equals 1 if the i-th element of U_1 is alive, or 0 otherwise (hence, $\mathbf{Pr}[b = 1] = \gamma/\alpha$).
- The R cells of *rand* are independent from each other.

This subproblem can be trivially solved in $O(R)$ time in RAM. Specifically, we can obtain from T_1 a size-R WR sample set of U_1 in $O(R)$ time. Given a $j \in [1, R]$, let e be the j-th element in the WR sample set. We then set $rand[j] = (b, i)$ with i being the index of e, and b indicating whether e is alive (which we can tell from its timestamp). In EM, however, this strategy takes $\Theta(perm(R))$ I/Os which is the cost to produce the WR sample set. Next, we present an alternative solution with I/O cost $O(R/B)$.

Our algorithm is designed based on the WoR-to-WR conversion algorithm in Section 2.2. First, generate the array A as described in Section 2.2, and accordingly, the value of J (i.e., the number of distinct values in A). Then, take a size-J WoR sample set of T from T_1. Recall that the algorithm of Section 2.2 would now produce a random permutation of T—denote that permutation as Π. We can no longer afford to do the same (because it requires $O(perm(R))$ I/Os). The key change here is to determine only the positions of two special elements of T in Π, as explained next.

Define e_l as the element with the largest index of all the expired elements in T. Denote by i_l the index of e_l; if e_l does not exist, then $i_l = 0$. Similarly, define e_r as the element with the smallest index of all the alive elements in T. Denote by i_r the index of e_r; if e_r does not exist, then $i_r = \alpha + 1$. It is clear that e_l, e_r, i_l, and i_r can be obtained by scanning T once in $O(J/B) = O(R/B)$ I/Os.

Recall that we cannot afford to generate Π; instead, we only generate the position p_l of e_l in Π, and the position of p_r of e_r in Π. Specifically, the integer p_l is chosen from $[1, J]$ uniformly at random, after which p_r is chosen from $[1, J] \setminus \{p_l\}$ uniformly at random.

Next, generate the *rand* array as follows. First, for each j where $A[j] = p_l$ (or p_r), place i_l (or i_r, resp.) in the second field of $rand[j]$. Second, for every remaining $j \in [1, R]$, place an integer drawn uniformly at random from $[1, \alpha] \setminus [i_l, i_r]$ in the second field of $rand[j]$. At this moment, every cell of *rand* contains in its second field an integer i that is in $[1, i_l] \cup [i_r, \alpha]$. We finalize the cell as $(1, i)$ if $i \geq i_r$, or $(0, i)$ otherwise. The above steps can be accomplished in $O(R/B)$ I/Os.

LEMMA 4. *The rand array produced by our algorithm fulfills the requirements of random seeding.*

PROOF. We denote by I the sequence of indexes in the *rand* array produced by our algorithm (namely, for each $j \in [1, R]$, if $rand[j] = (b, i)$, then $I[j] = i$). Fix an arbitrary sequence $V \in [1, \alpha]^R$. We will prove that $\mathbf{Pr}[I = V] = 1/\alpha^R$, which is sufficient to establish the lemma.

Recall that U_1 contains γ alive elements. Precisely, the elements of U_1 with indexes in $[1, \alpha - \gamma]$ have expired, while those with indexes $[\alpha - \gamma + 1, \alpha]$ are alive. Given a sequence $\Sigma \in [1, \alpha]^R$, let us define four values: (i) $i_l(\Sigma)$ is the largest integer in Σ that is at most $\alpha - \gamma$ (if no such integer exists, $i_l(\Sigma) = 0$), (ii) $i_r(\Sigma)$ is the smallest integer in Σ that is at least $\alpha - \gamma + 1$ (if no such integer exists, $i_r(\Sigma) = \alpha + 1$), (iii) $c_l(\Sigma)$ is the number of times that $i_l(\Sigma)$ appears in Σ, and (iv) $c_r(\Sigma)$ is the number of times that $i_r(\Sigma)$ appears in Σ. Given integers i_1, i_2, z_1, z_2, we denote by $X(i_1, i_2, z_1, z_2)$ the set of all sequences $\Sigma \in [1, \alpha]^R$ such that $i_l(\Sigma) = i_1, i_r(\Sigma) = i_2, c_l(\Sigma) = z_1$, and $c_r(\Sigma) = z_2$.

Our algorithm conceptually decides a random permutation Π of T as follows: (i) the positions of e_l and e_r are determined as described earlier, and then (ii) randomly permute the other elements of T over the remaining positions. Π, in turn, determines a WR sample set Q together with the array A, as described by our WoR-to-WR algorithm in Section 2.2. From Q, we can define a sequence $Q' \in [1, \alpha]^R$ where $Q'[j]$ $(1 \leq j \leq R)$ is the index of element $Q[j]$. Notice that Q' distributes uniformly at random from $[1, \alpha]^R$. We can now write $\mathbf{Pr}[I = V]$ into the following:

$$
\begin{aligned}
&\mathbf{Pr}[I = V] \\
= &\sum_{i_1, i_2, z_1, z_2} \Big(\mathbf{Pr}[I = V \mid Q' \in X(i_1, i_2, z_1, z_2)] \cdot \\
&\mathbf{Pr}[Q' \in X(i_1, i_2, z_1, z_2)]\Big)
\end{aligned}
$$

There are two crucial observations. First, if Q' belongs to $X(i_1, i_2, z_1, z_2)$, then so does I. In other words, $\mathbf{Pr}[I = V \mid Q' \in X(i_1, i_2, z_1, z_2)]$ is positive *only if* $i_1 = i_l(V)$, $i_2 = i_r(V)$, $z_1 = c_l(V)$, and $z_2 = c_r(V)$. Second, conditioned on that Q' belongs to $X(i_l(V), i_r(V), c_l(V), c_r(V))$, the I returned by our algorithm is drawn uniformly at random from $X(i_l(V), i_r(V), c_l(V), c_r(V))$. It thus follows that

$$
\begin{aligned}
&\mathbf{Pr}[I = V] \\
= \;&\mathbf{Pr}[I = V \mid Q' \in X(i_l(V), i_r(V), c_l(V), c_r(V))] \cdot \\
&\mathbf{Pr}[Q' \in X(i_l(V), i_r(V), c_l(V), c_r(V))] \\
= \;&\frac{1}{|X(i_l(V), i_r(V), c_l(V), c_r(V))|} \cdot \\
&\frac{|X(i_l(V), i_r(V), c_l(V), c_r(V))|}{\alpha^R} \\
= \;&1/\alpha^R.
\end{aligned}
$$

□

Next, we show how to perform a Bernoulli trial using only a single pair (b, i) in the *rand* array, which will then complete the proof of Lemma 3 because the array allows us to perform R such independent trials. In fact, we will explain how to generate from (b, i) a binary random variable Y that equals 1 with probability $\frac{\beta - c_2}{\beta + \gamma - c_2}$. With Y, a Bernoulli trial can be supported by casting another coin with head probability $\frac{\alpha - c_1}{\beta - c_2}$ (note that $\frac{\alpha - c_1}{\beta - c_2} \leq 1$ under the condition $0 \leq c_1 \leq c_2 \leq R \leq \alpha \leq \beta/2$).

Motivated by [4], we generate Y from (b, i) by the following procedure. If $b = 0$, then immediately we set $Y = 1$. Otherwise, we toss a coin with head probability $\frac{\alpha\beta'}{(\beta' + \alpha - i)(\beta' + \alpha - i + 1)}$, where $\beta' = \beta - c_2$. We set $Y = 0$ if the coin heads, or $Y = 1$ otherwise.

LEMMA 5. $\mathbf{Pr}[Y = 1] = \frac{\beta - c_2}{\beta + \gamma - c_2}$.

PROOF. We will instead prove $\mathbf{Pr}[Y = 0] = \gamma/(\beta' + \gamma)$. This is true because

$$
\begin{aligned}
\mathbf{Pr}[Y = 0] &= \sum_{j = \alpha - \gamma + 1}^{\alpha} \mathbf{Pr}[Y = 0 \mid i = j] \cdot \mathbf{Pr}[i = j] \\
&= \sum_{j = \alpha - \gamma + 1}^{\alpha} \frac{\alpha\beta'}{(\beta' + \alpha - j)(\beta' + \alpha - j + 1)} \cdot \frac{1}{\alpha} \\
&= \sum_{j=0}^{\gamma - 1} \frac{\beta'}{(\beta' + j)(\beta' + j + 1)} \\
&= \beta' \cdot \sum_{j=0}^{\gamma - 1} \left(\frac{1}{\beta' + j} - \frac{1}{\beta' + j + 1}\right) \\
&= \beta' \cdot \left(\frac{1}{\beta'} - \frac{1}{\beta' + \gamma}\right) = \frac{\gamma}{\beta' + \gamma}.
\end{aligned}
$$

□

5.2 Algorithm for Problem 2

This subsection explains our solution to Problem 2.

Merging WoR Sample sets. We will often need to solve a subproblem defined as follows. Let P_1 and P_2 be two disjoint sets of elements, whose cardinalities are known. Let S_1 and S_2 be size-R WoR sample sets of P_1 and P_2, respectively. The goal is to obtain a size-R sample set S of $P_1 \cup P_2$. Assuming that S_1 and S_2 are stored in arrays, next we describe an algorithm that achieves this goal with $O(R/B)$ I/Os.

First, we obtain the number s_1 (or s_2) of samples to take from S_1 (or S_2, resp.). For this purpose, we first set $s_1 = s_2 = 0$, $n_1 = |P_1|$ and $n_2 = |P_2|$. Then, repeat the following two step R times: Cast a coin with head probability $\frac{n_1}{n_1+n_2}$—if the coin heads, increase s_1 and decrease n_1 each by 1; otherwise, increase s_2 and decrease n_2 each by 1. After s_1 and s_2 are ready, we simply take a size-s_1 sample set S'_1 from S_1, and a size-s_2 sample set S'_2 from S_2 using offline sampling (Section 2.1). Then, we return S in an array that concatenates S'_1 and S'_2.

Structure. We tackle Problem 2 by dividing a suffix of the stream into a list of subsequences $U_1, U_2, ..., U_m, buf$ that satisfy all the following conditions:

$P1$: These subsequences are disjoint and consecutive: The first element of U_{i+1} succeeds the last element of U_i ($1 \le i \le m-1$), and the first element of *buf* succeeds the last element of U_m. We refer to each of $U_1, ..., U_m$ as a *bucket*.

$P2$: The length $|buf|$ of *buf* can be anywhere between 0 and $2R$. The length of a bucket, however, must be $2^j R$ for some integer $j \ge 0$. Moreover, $|U_i| \ge |U_{i'}|$ if $i < i'$.

$P3$: If $|buf| < R$, then $m = 0$ (i.e., no bucket exists).

$P4$: If $|U_1| = 2^j R$ for some $j \ge 1$, then for each $j' \in [0, j]$, there is at least one but at most two buckets with length $2^{j'} R$.

$P5$: U_1 must contain at least one alive element.

The above conditions imply $m = O(\log(n/R))$ where n is the number of alive elements currently.

A bucket U of length $2^j R$ with $j \ge 1$ defines a *left* and a *right sub-bucket* whose lengths are both $2^{j-1} R$. These buckets form a partition of U with the left sub-bucket covering the older elements in U. A bucket of length R does not define any sub-buckets.

We maintain a structure that stores the following information.

- For each bucket U, store its length, and the oldest and newest elements covered. They are the *boundary elements* of U. Store the same for each sub-bucket of U.

- For each bucket U, store 3 independent size-R WoR sample sets of the elements covered by U. If U has sub-buckets, for each sub-bucket U', store 3 independent size-R WoR sample sets of the elements covered by U'. In other words, there are up to 9 WoR sample sets associated with U and its sub-buckets. All these sample sets are independent from *buf*, and from the WoR sample sets of all other buckets and their sub-buckets.

- Define a *super-bucket* $U^\star$ as the subsequence that concatenates $U_2, U_3, ..., U_m$ and *buf* (i.e., excluding U_1). Store 3 independent size-R WoR sample sets of the elements covered by $U^\star$. These sample sets are independent from those of U_1 and its sub-buckets.

It is clear from the above description that the space of our structure is $O(\frac{R}{B} \log \frac{n}{R})$.

Producing a Sample Set. We first explain how to obtain a size-R WoR sample set S from our structure. If $m = 0$ or $|U_1| = R$, then the current sliding window has $O(R)$ elements, in which case we can simply run offline WoR sampling to compute S in $O(R/B)$ I/Os.

Now consider that U_1 has length $2^j R$ for some $j \ge 1$. By Properties $P3$ and $P4$, the super-bucket $U^\star$ must have length at least $R + \sum_{k=0}^{j-1} 2^k R = 2^j R$. Denote by U_1^{left} and U_1^{right} the left and right sub-buckets of U_1, respectively. Next, we identify two subsequences V_1 and V_2 by distinguishing two cases:

- *Case 1: the oldest alive element is in* U_1^{left}. Set $V_1 = U_1^{left}$, and V_2 to the subsequence formed by concatenating U_1^{right} and $U^\star$. Obtain a WoR sample set of V_2 by merging a WoR sample set of U_1^{right} with that of $U^\star$ in $O(R/B)$ I/Os.

- *Case 2: the oldest alive element is in* U_1^{right}. Set $V_1 = U_1^{right}$ and $V_2 = U^\star$.

In both cases, it is ensured that $2|V_1| \le |V_2|$. We then produce the target S by performing two-bucket sampling on V_1 and V_2 in $O(R/B)$ I/Os.

We compute a size-R WR sample set from S by running our algorithm in Section 2.2 for converting a WoR sample set to a WR one. There is one subtle issue that deserves clarification. Recall that our conversion algorithm requires generating R binary random variables X of the form: X takes 1 with probability c/n, and 0 otherwise, where c is an integer in $[0, R-1]$, and n is the number of alive elements currently. The subtlety is that we do not know the value of n. This issue can be resolved by resorting to Lemma 3, where the values of α, β, and γ satisfy $\alpha = |V_1|$ and $\beta = |V_2|$. To generate an X, we first perform a Bernoulli trial with $c_1 = c_2 = 0$ to obtain a binary random variable Y. If $Y = 0$, we immediately set $X = 0$. Consider now $Y = 1$; we toss a coin with head probability c/α, and set X to 1 if the coin heads, or to 0 otherwise. It is easy to verify that $Y = 1$ with probability $c/(\beta + \gamma) = c/n$.

The above discussion also explains why we chose to maintain 3 independent WoR sample sets for each bucket: the two-bucket sampling requires 2 sample sets of V_1 (see Section 5.1), one from V_2, while the WoR-to-WR conversion demands another one from V_1.

Maintenance. It remains to explain how to update our structure upon the arrival of a new element e at time t_{now}. If U_1 does not exist, we discard the elements in *buf* that have expired. Otherwise we first discard all the buckets in which all the elements have expired, and then, recompute the WoR sample sets of $U^\star$ by merging those of the current $U_2, U_3, ..., U_m$ and *buf*. If the new U_1 has size $2^j R$, the cost of merging is $O(2^j R/B)$. We amortize this cost on the elements in the old (just discarded) U_1, each of which bears only $O(1/B)$ I/Os.

Now we update the WoR sample sets of $U^\star$ with e using the algorithm of [7] in Section 2.3, which requires $O(1/B)$ I/Os per element. Next, add e into *buf*. If $|buf| < 2R$, our update algorithm finishes. Otherwise, we remove the first R elements of *buf*, and make them into a new bucket of length R. If at this moment the number of buckets with length R is at most 2, our update algorithm finishes.

In general, when there are 3 buckets with the same length $2^j R$ for some $j \geq 0$, we fix it by combining the oldest two—denoted as U_1' and U_2'—of those buckets into a new bucket U with length $2^{j+1}R$. Specifically, the WoR sample set of U is obtained by merging those of U_1' and U_2', while U_1' and U_2' now serve as the sub-buckets of U. The sub-buckets of U_1' and U_2' can now be discarded. The merging may result in 3 buckets with length $2^{j+1}R$, which is fixed in the same manner. Standard analysis of the exponential histogram [5] shows that all the merging increases the amortized cost of each element by $O(1/B)$.

Finally, if the above merging results in a new U_1, we discard the WoR sample sets of $U^\star$, and recompute them from the WoR sample sets of $U_2, U_3, ..., U_m$, and *buf* in $O(2^j R/B)$ I/Os, assuming $|U_1| = 2^j R$. We charge the cost on the $\Omega(2^j R/B)$ elements that were newly added to U_1, so that each of them bears $O(1/B)$ I/Os.

In summary, our maintenance algorithm performs $O(1/B)$ amortized I/Os per element. We thus have completed the whole proof of Theorem 2.

5.3 Lower Bounds

Next, we will show that our algorithm in Section 5.2 is optimal by establishing Theorem 3. As required by the theorem, we assume that $N \geq cR$ and $R \geq cM$ with c being a sufficiently large constant. Our proof is similar to the one in Section 4.

Our discussion will focus on a data stream where the timestamp of the i-th ($i \geq 1$) element is $\lfloor i/R \rfloor(\tau + 1)$. That is, the first R elements are associated with timestamp 0, the next R with timestamp $\tau+1$, still the next R with timestamp $2(\tau + 1)$, and so on.

Define an *epoch* $j \geq 1$ to be the sequence of elements with timestamp $(j - 1)(\tau + 1)$ ($j = 0, 1, 2, ...$). In other words, each epoch has size R; and the total number of epochs is $O(N/R)$. Note that a WoR or WR sample set issued at the end of epoch j must contain elements only in this epoch.

Element Processing Cost. We now prove Statement 1 of Theorem 3. We will argue that any algorithm $\mathcal{A}$ must perform $\Omega(R/B)$ expected I/Os in each epoch, and hence, $\Omega(N/B)$ expected I/Os for all epochs.

Consider first WoR sampling. At the end of epoch j ($= 1, 2, ...$), $\mathcal{A}$ must be keeping all the R elements in this epoch (because it must return all these elements for a sample request issued at this moment). Therefore, for $R \geq 3M$, $\mathcal{A}$ must have written $\Omega(R/B)$ I/Os during the epoch.

For WR sampling, imagine issuing a sample request at the end of epoch j. By Lemma 3 of [10], when R is large enough, with at least half probability this request fetches $\Omega(R)$ distinct elements in epoch j. This means that, with at least half probability, $\mathcal{A}$ must have written $\Omega(R/B)$ I/Os during the epoch when c is sufficiently large.

WR Reporting. Next we prove Statement 2 of Theorem 3, namely, if $\mathcal{A}$ spends $o(perm(R)\cdot\frac{N}{R})$ expected I/Os processing N stream elements, it must incur $\Omega(perm(R))$ I/Os returning a WR sample set.

Our hard *workload* includes the aforementioned stream and a WR sample request at the end of each epoch. We claim that $\mathcal{A}$ must incur $\Omega(perm(R) \cdot \frac{N}{R})$ expected I/Os to process the entire workload, which is sufficient to establish Statement 2 (because there are $O(N/R)$ sample requests).

Let H be the expected number of I/Os needed to process epoch j ($= 1, 2, ...$) and the sample request at the end of epoch j. As mentioned earlier, with at least half probability, the WR sample set Q returned by $\mathcal{A}$ has at least $\Omega(R)$ distinct elements, all of which must be in epoch j. The sequence of those elements in Q is a random $\Omega(R)$-permutation of the elements in epoch j. When c is sufficiently large, by Lemma 1 we know $H = \Omega(perm(R))$. It thus follows that $\Omega(perm(R)\cdot\frac{N}{R})$ expected I/Os are needed to process the entire workload.

ACKNOWLEDGEMENTS

This work was supported in part by Grants GRF 4168/13 and GRF 142072/14 from HKRGC.

6. REFERENCES

[1] A. Aggarwal and J. S. Vitter. The input/output complexity of sorting and related problems. *CACM*, 31(9):1116–1127, 1988.

[2] L. Arge. The buffer tree: A technique for designing batched external data structures. *Algorithmica*, 37(1):1–24, 2003.

[3] B. Babcock, M. Datar, and R. Motwani. Sampling from a moving window over streaming data. In *SODA*, pages 633–634, 2002.

[4] V. Braverman, R. Ostrovsky, and C. Zaniolo. Optimal sampling from sliding windows. *JCSS*, 78(1):260–272, 2012.

[5] M. Datar, A. Gionis, P. Indyk, and R. Motwani. Maintaining stream statistics over sliding windows. *SIAM J. of Comp.*, 31(6):1794–1813, 2002.

[6] C. Fan, M. Muller, and I. Rezucha. Development of sampling plans by using sequential (item-by-item) selection techniques and digital computers. *Am. Stat. Assn. J.*, 57:387–402, 1962.

[7] R. Gemulla and W. Lehner. Deferred maintenance of disk-based random samples. In *EDBT*, pages 423–441, 2006.

[8] R. Gemulla and W. Lehner. Sampling time-based sliding windows in bounded space. In *SIGMOD*, pages 379–392, 2008.

[9] J. Gustedt. Efficient sampling of random permutations. *Journal of Discrete Algorithms*, 6(1):125–139, 2008.

[10] X. Hu, M. Qiao, and Y. Tao. Independent range sampling. In *PODS*, pages 246–255, 2014.

[11] D. A. Hutchinson, P. Sanders, and J. S. Vitter. Duality between prefetching and queued writing with parallel disks. *SIAM J. of Comp.*, 34(6):1443–1463, 2005.

[12] C. Jermaine, A. Pol, and S. Arumugam. Online maintenance of very large random samples. In *SIGMOD*, pages 299–310, 2004.

[13] T. Jones. A note on sampling a tape-file. *CACM*, 5(6):343, 1962.

[14] Y. Matias, E. Segal, and J. S. Vitter. Efficient bundle sorting. *SIAM J. of Comp.*, 36(2):394–410, 2006.

[15] S. Nath and P. B. Gibbons. Online maintenance of very large random samples on flash storage. *PVLDB*, 1(1):970–983, 2008.

[16] S. Nath and P. B. Gibbons. Online maintenance of very large random samples on flash storage. *VLDB J.*, 19(1):67–90, 2010.
[17] A. Pavan, K. Tangwongsan, S. Tirthapura, and K. Wu. Counting and sampling triangles from a graph stream. *PVLDB*, 6(14):1870–1881, 2013.
[18] A. Pol, C. M. Jermaine, and S. Arumugam. Maintaining very large random samples using the geometric file. *VLDB J.*, 17(5):997–1018, 2008.
[19] J. S. Vitter. Random sampling with a reservoir. *ACM Trans. Math. Softw.*, 11(1):37–57, 1985.
[20] K. Yi. Dynamic indexability and the optimality of B-trees. *JACM*, 59(4), 2012.

Correctness of the Algorithm in Section 2.1

We will prove the algorithm's correctness by induction on R. The case of $R = 1$ is obvious. Next, assuming that the algorithm is correct for $R = k$, we will prove the same for $R = k + 1$. Specifically, given an arbitrary sequence $V \in P^{k+1}$, we want to prove that $\mathbf{Pr}[Q = V] = 1/n^{k+1}$ (Q is the output of our algorithm).

Denote by $Q_{\leq k}$ (or $A_{\leq k}$) the prefix of Q (or A) including its first k elements. From our inductive assumption, we know that $\mathbf{Pr}[Q_{\leq k} = V_{\leq k}] = 1/n^k$ (observe that $Q_{\leq k}$ is produced in the same way as running our algorithm for $R = k$). Next, we will show that $\mathbf{Pr}[Q[k+1] = V[k+1] \mid Q_{\leq k} = V_{\leq k}] = 1/n$, which will then complete the proof.

Let $J^\star$ be the value of J right before the generation of $A[k+1]$. Define $T_{\leq J^\star}$ as the length-$J^\star$ prefix of T (recall that T is an array storing a random permutation of its elements). We now distinguishes two cases:

Case 1: $V[k+1]$ appears in $V_{\leq k}$. In this case, $Q[k+1] = V[k+1]$ if and only if $A[k+1]$ equals the position of $V[k+1]$ in $T_{\leq J^\star}$, which happens with probability $1/n$.

Case 2: $V[k+1]$ does not appear in $V_{\leq k}$. In this case, $Q[k+1] = V[k+1]$ if and only if (i) $A[k+1] = J^\star + 1$, which happens with probability $\frac{n-J^\star}{n}$, and (ii) $V[k+1] = T[J^\star+1]$, which happens with probability $\frac{1}{n-J^\star}$. The two independent conditions happen simultaneously with probability $1/n$.

Vertex and Hyperedge Connectivity in Dynamic Graph Streams

Sudipto Guha*
University of Pennsylvania
sudipto@seas.upenn.edu

Andrew McGregor†
University of Massachusetts
mcgregor@cs.umass.edu

David Tench
University of Massachusetts
dtench@cs.umass.edu

ABSTRACT

A growing body of work addresses the challenge of processing dynamic graph streams: a graph is defined by a sequence of edge insertions and deletions and the goal is to construct synopses and compute properties of the graph while using only limited memory. Linear sketches have proved to be a powerful technique in this model and can also be used to minimize communication in distributed graph processing.

We present the first linear sketches for estimating vertex connectivity and constructing hypergraph sparsifiers. Vertex connectivity exhibits markedly different combinatorial structure than edge connectivity and appears to be harder to estimate in the dynamic graph stream model. Our hypergraph result generalizes the work of Ahn et al. (PODS 2012) on graph sparsification and has the added benefit of significantly simplifying the previous results. One of the main ideas is related to the problem of reconstructing subgraphs that satisfy a specific sparsity property. We introduce a more general notion of graph degeneracy and extend the graph reconstruction result of Becker et al. (IPDPS 2011).

Categories and Subject Descriptors

F.2 [**Analysis of Algorithms & Problem Complexity**]

General Terms

Algorithms, Theory

Keywords

data streams; graph sketching; vertex connectivity; hypergraphs; sparsification

1. INTRODUCTION

Massive graphs arise in many applications. Popular examples include the web-graph, social networks, and biological networks but, more generally, graphs are a natural abstraction whenever we have information about both a set of basic entities and relationships between these entities. Unfortunately, it is not possible to use existing algorithms to process many of these graphs; many of these graphs are too large to be stored in main memory and are constantly changing. Rather, there is a growing need to design new algorithms for even basic graph problems in the relevant computational models.

In this paper, we consider algorithms in the dynamic data stream and linear sketching models. In the dynamic data stream model, a sequence of edge insertions and deletions defines an input graph and the goal is to solve a specific problem on this graph given only one-way access to the input sequence and limited working memory. While insert-only graph streaming has been an active area of research for over a decade, it is only relatively recently algorithms have been found that handle insertions and deletions [2–4, 16, 19, 20, 24]. The main technique used in these algorithms is *linear sketching* where a random linear projection of the input graph is maintained as the graph is updated. To be useful, we need to be able to a) store the projection of the graph in small space and b) solve the problem of interest given only the projection of the graph. While linear sketching is a classic technique for solving statistical problems in the data stream model, it was long thought unlikely to be useful in the context of combinatorial problems on graphs. Not only do linear sketches allow us to process edge deletions (a deletion can just be viewed as a "negative" insertion) but the linearity of the resulting data structures enables a rich set of algorithmic operations to be performed after the sketch has been generated. Linear sketches are also a useful technique for reducing communication when processing distributed graphs. For a recent survey of graph streaming and sketching see [25].

1.1 Our Contributions and Related Work

We present sketch-based dynamic graph algorithms for three basic graph problems: computing vertex connectivity, graph reconstruction, and hypergraph sparsification. All our algorithms run in (low) polynomial time, typically linear in the number of edges. However, our primary focus is on space complexity, as is the convention in much of the data streams literature. In what follows, let n denote the number of vertices in the graph.

Vertex Connectivity. To date, the main success story for graph sketching has been about edge connectivity, i.e., estimating how many edges need to be removed to disconnect the graph, and estimating the size of cuts. In this paper we present the first dynamic graph stream algorithms for vertex connectivity, i.e., estimating how many *vertices* need to be removed to disconnect the graph. While it can be shown that edge connectivity is an upper bound for vertex connectivity, the vertex connectivity of a graph can be much smaller. Furthermore, the combinatorial structure relevant to both

*Supported by NSF Awards CCF-1117216.

†Supported by NSF Awards CCF-0953754, IIS-1251110, CCF-1320719, and a Google Research Award.

PODS'15, May 31–June 4, 2015, Melbourne, Victoria, Australia.

http://dx.doi.org/10.1145/2745754.2745763.

quantities is very different. For example, edge-connectivity is transitive[1] whereas vertex-connectivity is not. A celebrated result by Karger [21] bounds the number of near minimum cuts whereas no analogous bound is known for vertex removal. Feige et al. [14] discuss issues that arise specific to vertex connectivity in the context of approximation algorithms and embeddings.

In Section 3, we present two sketch-based algorithms for vertex connectivity. The first algorithm uses $O(kn \operatorname{polylog} n)$ space and constructs a data structure such that, at the end of the stream, it is possible to test whether the removal of a queried set of at most k vertices would disconnect the graph. We prove that this algorithm is optimal in terms of its space use. The second algorithm estimates the vertex connectivity up to a $(1+\epsilon)$ factor using $O(\epsilon^{-1} kn \operatorname{polylog} n)$ space where k is an upper bound on the vertex connectivity.

No stream algorithms were previously known that supported both edge insertions and deletions. Existing approaches either use $\Omega(n^2)$ space [28] or only handle insertions [13]. With only insertions, Eppstein et al. [13] proved that $O(kn \operatorname{polylog} n)$ space was sufficient. Their algorithm drops an inserted edge $\{u, v\}$ iff there already exists k vertex-disjoint paths between u and v amongst the edges stored thus far. Such an algorithm fails in the presence of edge deletions since some of the vertex disjoint paths that existed when an edge was ignored need not exist if edges are subsequently deleted.

Graph Reconstruction. Our next result relates to reconstructing graphs rather than estimating properties of the graph. Becker et al. [5] show that is possible to reconstruct a d-degenerate graph given an $O(d \operatorname{polylog} n)$ size sketch of each row of the adjacency matrix of the graph. In Section 4, we define the d-cut-degeneracy and show that the strictly larger class of graphs that satisfy this property can also be reconstructed given an $O(d \operatorname{polylog} n)$-size sketch of each row. Moreover, even if the graph is not d-cut-degenerate we show that we can find all edges with a certain connectivity property. This will be an integral part of our algorithm for hypergraph sparsification. For this purpose, we also prove the first dynamic graph stream algorithms for hypergraph connectivity in this section. We also extend the vertex connectivity results to hypergraphs.

Hypergraph Sparsification. Hypergraph sparsification is a natural extension of graph sparsification. Given a hypergraph, the goal is to find a sparse weighted subgraph such that the weight of every cut in the subgraph is within a $(1+\epsilon)$ factor of the weight of the corresponding cut in the original hypergraph. Estimating hypergraph cuts has applications in video object segmentation [17], network security analysis [30], load balancing in parallel computing [8], and modelling communication in parallel sparse-martix vector multiplication [7].

Kogan and Krauthgamer [23] recently presented the first stream algorithm for hypergraph sparsification in the insert-only model. In Section 5, we present the first algorithm that supports both edge insertions and deletions. The algorithm uses $O(n \operatorname{polylog} n)$ space assuming that size of the hyperedges is bounded by a constant. This result is part of a growing body of work on processing hypergraphs in the data stream model [12, 23, 26, 27, 29]. There are numerous challenges in extending previous work on graph sparsification [3, 4, 16, 19, 20] to hypergraph sparsification and we discuss these in Section 5. In the process of overcoming these challenges, we also identify a simpler approach for graph sparsification in the data stream model.

[1]If it takes at least k edge deletions to disconnect u and v and it takes at least k edge deletions to disconnect v and w, then it takes at least k edge deletions to disconnect u and w.

2. MODELS AND PRELIMINARIES

Graphs Preliminaries. A hypergraph is specified by a set of vertices $V = \{v_1, \ldots, v_n\}$ and a set of subsets of V called hyperedges. In this paper we assume all hyperedges have cardinality at most r for some constant r. The special case when all hyperedges have cardinality exactly two corresponds to the standard definition of a graph. All graphs and hypergraphs discussed in this paper will be undirected. It will be convenient to define the following notation: Let $\delta_G(S)$ be the set of hyperedges that cross the cut $(S, V \setminus S)$ in the hypergraph G where we say a hyperedge e crosses $(S, V \setminus S)$ if $e \cap S \neq \emptyset$ and $e \cap (V \setminus S) \neq \emptyset$. For any hyperedge e, define $\lambda_e(G)$ to be the minimum cardinality of a cut that includes e. A *spanning graph* $H = (V, E)$ of a hypergraph $G = (V, E)$ is a subgraph such that $|\delta_H(S)| \geq \min(1, |\delta_G(S)|)$ for every $S \subset V$.

Linear Sketches and Applications. All the algorithms presented in this paper use linear sketches.

DEFINITION 1 (LINEAR SKETCHES). *A linear measurement of a hypergraph on n vertices is defined by a set of coefficients $\{c_e : e \in \mathcal{P}_r(V)\}$ where $\mathcal{P}_r(V)$ is the set of all subsets of V of size at most r. Given a hypergraph $G = (V, E)$, the evaluation of this measurement is defined as $\sum_{e \in E} c_e$. A* sketch *is a collection of (non-adaptive) linear measurements. The cardinality of this collection is referred to as the* size *of the sketch. We will assume that the magnitude of the coefficients c_e is $\operatorname{poly}(n)$. We say a linear measurement is* local *for node v if the measurement only depends on hyper-edges incident to v, i.e., $c_e = 0$ for all hyper-edges that do not include v. We say a sketch is* vertex-based *if every linear measurement is local to some node.*

Linear sketches have long been used in the context of data stream models because it is possible to maintain a sketch of the stream incrementally. Specifically, if the next stream update is an insertion or deletion of an edge, we can update the sketch by simply adding or subtracting the appropriate set of coefficients. Sketches are also useful in distributed settings. In particular, the model considered by Becker et al. [5] was as follows: suppose there are $n+1$ players $P_1, \ldots, P_n$ and Q. The input for player P_i is the set of (hyper-)edges that include the ith vertex of a graph G. Player Q wants to compute something about this graph such as determining whether G connected. To enable this, each of the players $P_1, \ldots, P_n$ simultaneously sends a message about their input to Q such that the set of these n messages contains sufficient information to complete Q's computation. In the case of randomized protocols, we assume that all players have access to public random bits. The goal is to minimize the maximum length of the n messages that are sent to Q. If a vertex-based sketch exists for the problem under consideration, then for each linear measurement, there is a single player that can evaluate this message and send it to Q.

3. VERTEX CONNECTIVITY

A natural approach to determining vertex connectivity could be to try to mimic the algorithm of Cheriyan et al. [11]. They showed that the union of k disjoint "scan first search trees" (a generalization of breadth-first search trees) can be used to determine if a graph is k vertex connected. A similar approach worked in data stream model for the case of edge-connectivity (which we discuss in further detail in the next section) but in that case the trees to be constructed could be arbitrary. Unfortunately, we can show (see appendix) that any algorithm for constructing a scan-first search tree in the data stream model requires $\Omega(n^2)$ space even when there are no edge deletions.

To avoid this issue, we take a different approach based on finding arbitrary spanning trees for the induced graph on a random subset of vertices.[2] We will use the following result for finding these spanning trees.

THEOREM 2 (AHN ET AL. [2]). *For a graph on n vertices, there exists a vertex-based sketch of size $O(n \operatorname{polylog} n)$ from which we can construct a spanning forest with high probability.*

Note that in this section we restrict our attention to graphs rather than hypergraphs. However, in the next section we will explain how the vertex connectivity results extend to hypergraphs.

3.1 Warm-Up: Vertex Connectivity Queries

For $i = 1, 2, \ldots, R := 16 \cdot k^2 \ln n$, let G_i be a graph formed by deleting each vertex in G with probability $1 - 1/k$. Let T_i be an arbitrary spanning forest of G_i and define $H = T_1 \cup T_2 \cup \ldots \cup T_R$.

LEMMA 3. *Let S be an arbitrary collection of at most k vertices. With high probability, $H \setminus S$ is connected iff $G \setminus S$ is connected.*

PROOF. First we note that H has the same set of vertices as G with high probability. This follows because the probability a given vertex is not in H is $(1 - 1/k)^R \leq \exp(-16 \cdot k \cdot \ln n) = n^{-16k}$ and hence by an application of the union bound, all vertices in G are also in H with probability at least $1 - n^{-(16k-1)}$. Then since H is a subgraph of G, then $G \setminus S$ disconnected implies $H \setminus S$ disconnected. It remains to prove that $G \setminus S$ connected implies $H \setminus S$ connected.

Assume $G \setminus S$ is connected. Consider an arbitrary pair of vertices $s, t \notin S$ and let $s = v_0 \to v_1 \to v_2 \to \ldots \to v_\ell = t$ be a path between s and t in $G \setminus S$. Then note that there is a path between v_i and v_{i+1} in $H \setminus S$ if there exists G_i such that $G_i \cap S = \emptyset$ and $v_i, v_{i+1} \in H \setminus S$. This follows because if $\{v_i, v_{i+1}\} \in G_i$ and $G_i \cap S = \emptyset$ then $T_i \setminus S$ either contains $\{v_i, v_j\}$ or a path between between v_i and v_j. Hence,

$$\mathbb{P}\left[v_i \text{ and } v_{i+1} \text{ are connected in } T_i \setminus S\right] \geq 1/k^2(1-1/k)^k$$

and therefore

$$\begin{aligned} & \mathbb{P}\left[v_i \text{ and } v_{i+1} \text{ are disconnected in } T_i \setminus S \text{ for all } i \in [R]\right] \\ \leq \quad & (1 - 1/k^2(1-1/k)^k)^R \leq 1/n^4 \ . \end{aligned}$$

Taking the union bound over all $\ell < n$ pairs $\{v_i, v_{i+1}\}$, we conclude that s and t are connected in $H \setminus S$ with probability at least $1 - 1/n^3$. By applying the union bound again, with probability at least $1 - 1/n^2$, s is connected in $H \setminus S$ to all other vertices. □

Our algorithm constructs a spanning forest for each of $G_1, \ldots, G_R$ using the algorithm referenced in Theorem 2. Note that since each G_i has $O(n/k)$ vertices with high probability, we can construct these R trees in $R \times O(n/k \operatorname{polylog} n) = O(nk \operatorname{polylog} n)$ space. This gives us the following theorem.

THEOREM 4. *There is a sketch-based dynamic graph algorithm that uses $O(kn \operatorname{polylog} n)$ space to test whether a set of vertices S of size at most k disconnects the graph. The query set S is specified at the end of the stream.*

We next prove that the above query algorithm is space-optimal.

THEOREM 5. *Any dynamic graph algorithm that allows us to test, with probability at least $3/4$, whether a queried set of at most k vertices disconnects the graph requires $\Omega(kn)$ space.*

PROOF. The proof is by a reduction from the communication problem of indexing [1]. Suppose Alice has a binary string $x \in \{0,1\}^{(k+1) \times n}$ indexed by $[k+1] \times [n]$ and Bob wants to compute $x_{i,j}$ for some index $(i,j) \in [k+1] \times [n]$ that is unknown to Alice. This requires $\Omega(nk)$ bits to be communicated from Alice to Bob if Bob is to be successful with probability at least $3/4$. Consider the protocol where the players create a bipartite graph on vertices $L \cup R$ where $L = \{l_1, \ldots, l_{k+1}\}$ and $R = \{r_1, \ldots, r_n\}$. Alice adds edges $\{l_i, r_j\}$ for all pairs (i,j) such that $x_{i,j} = 1$. Alice runs the algorithm and sends the state to Bob. Bob adds edges $\{r_\ell, r_{\ell'}\}$ for all $\ell, \ell' \neq j$ and deletes all vertices in L except l_i. Now r_j is connected to the rest of the graph iff the $x_{i,j} = 1$. □

3.2 Vertex Connectivity

For $i = 1, 2, \ldots, R := 160 \cdot k^2 \epsilon^{-1} \ln n$, let G_i be a graph formed by deleting each vertex in G with probability $1 - 1/k$. As before, let T_i be an arbitrary spanning forest of G_i and define $H = T_1 \cup T_2 \cup \ldots \cup T_R$.

THEOREM 6. *Let S be a subset of V of size k. Consider any pair of vertices $u, v \in V \setminus S$ such that there are at least $(1+\epsilon)k$ vertex-disjoint paths between u and v in G. Then,*

$$\mathbb{P}\left[u \text{ and } v \text{ are connected in } G_S\right] \geq 1 - 4/n^{10k}$$

where $G_S = \cup_{i \in U(S)} G_i$ and $U(S) = \{i : G_i \cap S = \emptyset\}$ is the set of sampled graphs with no vertices in S.

PROOF. We first argue that $|U(S)|$ is large with high probability. Then $\mathbb{E}\left[|U(S)|\right] = (1 - 1/k)^k R \geq R/4$. By an application of the Chernoff bound:

$$\mathbb{P}\left[|U(S)| \leq 1/2 \times R/4\right] \leq e^{-1/4 \times R/4 \times 1/3} < 1/n^{10k} \ .$$

In the rest of the proof we condition on event $|U(S)| \geq r := R/8$.

Note that there are $t \geq \epsilon k$ vertex-disjoint paths between u and v in $G \setminus S$. Call these paths $P_1, \ldots, P_t$. For each P_i, let a_i be the edge incident to u, let c_i be the edge incident to v, and let B_i be the remaining edges in P_i. Note that a_i and c_i need not be distinct and B_i could be empty.

CLAIM 1. *The followings three probabilities are each larger than $1 - 1/n^{10k}$:*

$$\mathbb{P}\left[a_i \in G_S \text{ for at least } 3t/4 \text{ values of } i\right]$$

$$\mathbb{P}\left[B_i \subseteq G_S \text{ for at least } 3t/4 \text{ values of } i\right]$$

$$\mathbb{P}\left[c_i \in G_S \text{ for at least } 3t/4 \text{ values of } i\right] \ .$$

PROOF. Each edge in B_i is not present in G_S with probability $(1 - 1/k^2)^r$. Hence, by the union bound, $\mathbb{P}\left[B_i \not\subseteq G_S\right] \leq |B_i|(1 - 1/k^2)^r$. Also by the union bound,

$$\begin{aligned} & \mathbb{P}\left[B_i \not\subseteq G_S \text{ for more than } t/4 \text{ values of } i\right] \\ < \quad & \binom{t}{t/4} (n(1-1/k^2)^r)^{t/4} \\ < \quad & e^{t \ln 2 + (\ln n - r/k^2)t/4} < 1/n^{10k} \ . \end{aligned}$$

---

[2]We note that the idea of subsampling vertices was recently explored by Censor-Hillel et al. [9,10]. They showed that if each vertex of a k-vertex-connected graph is subsampled with probability $p = \Omega(\sqrt{\log n/k})$ then the resulting graph has vertex connectivity $\Omega(kp^2)$. We do not make use of this result in our work as it does not lead to an approximation factor better than $\sqrt{k}$.

The proofs for a_i and c_i are entirely symmetric so we just consider a_i. Consider the set $U'(S) = U(S) \cap \{j : u \in G_j\}$. Note that for $j \in U'(S)$ we have $\mathbb{P}[a_i \in G_j] = 1/k$ and by the union bound,

$$\begin{aligned} & \mathbb{P}\left[a_i \notin \cup_{j \in U'(S)} G_j \text{ for at least } t/4 \text{ values of } i\right] \\ \leq & \binom{t}{t/4}(1-1/k)^{|U'(S)|t/4} \\ \leq & 2^t \exp\left(\frac{-|U'(S)|t}{(4k)}\right) . \end{aligned}$$

Let E be the event that $|U'(S)| \leq |U(S)|/(2k)$. Then, by an application of the Chernoff bound:

$$\begin{aligned} & \mathbb{P}[a_i \notin G_S \text{ for at least } t/4 \text{ values of } i] \\ \leq & \mathbb{P}[E] \\ & + \mathbb{P}\left[a_i \notin \cup_{j \in U'(S)} G_j \text{ for at least } t/4 \text{ values of } i \mid \neg E\right] \\ \leq & \exp(-1/4 \times |U(S)|/k \times 1/3) \\ & + \mathbb{P}\left[a_i \notin \cup_{j \in U'(S)} G_j \text{ for at least } t/4 \text{ values of } i \mid \neg E\right] \\ \leq & \exp(-1/4 \times r/k \times 1/3) + 2^t \exp(-r/(2k) \times t/(4k)) \\ < & 1/n^{10k} . \end{aligned}$$

□

It follows from the claim that there exists i such that $P_i \in G_S$ (and therefore u and v are connected in G_S) with probability at least $1 - 3/n^{10k}$. The conditioning on $|U(S)| \geq r$ decreases this by another $1/n^{10k}$.

COROLLARY 7. *If G is $(1+\epsilon)k$-vertex-connected then H is k-vertex-connected with high probability. If H is k-vertex connected then G is k-vertex connected.*

PROOF. The first part of the corollary follows from Theorem 6 by applying the union bound over all $O(n^k)$ subsets of size at most k and $O(n^2)$ choices of u and v. Note that u and v connected in G_S implies u and v are connected in H since H includes a spanning forest of G_S. The second part is implied by the fact H is a subgraph of G. □

As in the previous section, our algorithm is simply to construct H be using the algorithm referenced in Theorem 2 to construct $T_1, \ldots, T_R$. We can then run any vertex connectivity algorithm on H in post-processing. Since each G_i has $O(n/k)$ vertices with high probability, we can construct these R trees in $R \times O(n/k \cdot \text{polylog}\, n) = O(nk\epsilon^{-1} \text{polylog}\, n)$ space. This gives us the following theorem.

THEOREM 8. *There is a sketch-based dynamic graph algorithm that uses $O(kn\epsilon^{-1} \text{polylog}\, n)$ space to distinguish $(1+\epsilon)k$-vertex connected graphs from k-connected graphs.*

4. RECONSTRUCTING HYPERGRAPHS

We next present sketches for reconstructing cut-degenerate hypergraphs. Recall that a hypergraph is d-degenerate if all induced subgraphs have a vertex of degree at most d. Cut-degeneracy is defined as follows.

DEFINITION 9. *A hypergraph is* d-cut-degenerate *if every induced subgraph has a cut of size at most d.*

The following lemma establishes that this is a strictly weaker property than d-degeneracy.

LEMMA 10. *Any hypergraph that is d-degenerate is also d-cut-degenerate. There exists graphs that are d-cut-degenerate but not d-degenerate.*

PROOF. Since the degree of a vertex v is exactly the size of the cut $(\{v\}, V \setminus \{v\})$ it is immediate that d-degeneracy implies d-cut-degeneracy. For an example that d-cut-degenerate does not imply it is d-degenerate consider the graph G on eight vertices $\{v_1, v_2, v_3, v_4, u_1, u_2, u_3, u_4\}$ with edges $\{v_i, v_j\}, \{u_i, u_j\}$ for all i, j except $i = 1, j = 4$ and edges $\{v_1, u_1\}$ and $\{v_4, u_4\}$. Then G has minimum degree 3 and is therefore not 2-degenerate while it is 2-cut-degenerate. □

Becker et al. [5] showed how to reconstruct a d-degenerate graph in the simultaneous communication model if each player sends an $O(d\, \text{polylog}\, n)$ bit message. We will show that it is also possible to reconstruct any d-cut-degenerate with the same message complexity. Even if the graph is not cut-degenerate, we show that is possible to reconstruct all edges with a certain connectivity property. We will subsequently use this fact in Section 5.

4.1 Skeletons for Hypergraphs

We first review the existing results on constructing k-skeletons [2] that we will need for our new results. In doing so, we generalize the previous work to the case of hypergraphs. In particular, this leads to the first dynamic graph algorithm for determining hypergraph connectivity.

DEFINITION 11 (k-SKELETON). *Given a hypergraph $H = (V, E)$, a subgraph $H' = (V, E')$ is a* k-skeleton *of H if for any $S \subset V$, $|\delta_{H'}(S)| \geq \min(|\delta_H(S)|, k)$.*

In particular, any spanning graph is a 1-skeleton and it can be shown that $F_1 \cup F_2 \cup \ldots \cup F_k$ is a k-skeleton [2] of G if F_i is a spanning graph of $G \setminus (\cup_{j=1}^{i-1} F_j)$. The next lemma establishes that given an arbitrary k-skeleton of a graph we can exactly determine the set of edges with $\lambda_e(G) \leq k-1$.

LEMMA 12. *Let H be a k-skeleton of G then $\lambda_e(H) \leq k-1$ iff $\lambda_e(G) \leq k-1$.*

PROOF. Since H is a subgraph $\lambda_e(H) \leq \lambda_e(G)$ and hence $\lambda_e(G) \leq k-1$ implies $\lambda_e(H) \leq k-1$. Using the fact that H is a k-skeleton $\lambda_e(H) \geq \min(k, \lambda_e(G))$ and hence, if $\lambda_e(H) \leq k-1$ it must be that $\lambda_e(G) \leq k-1$. □

Constructing Spanning Graphs. For each vertex $v_i \in V$, define the vector $\mathbf{a}^i \in \{-1, 0, 1, 2, \ldots, r-1\}^d$ where $d = \sum_{i=2}^{r} \binom{n}{i}$ is the number of possible hyperedges of size at most r:

$$\mathbf{a}^i_e = \begin{cases} |e| - 1 & \text{if } i = \min e \text{ and } e \in E \\ -1 & \text{if } i \in e \setminus \min e \text{ and } e \in E \\ 0 & \text{otherwise} \end{cases}$$

where e ranges over all subsets of V of size between 2 and r and $\min e$ denotes the smallest ID of a node in e. Observe that these vectors have the property that for any subset of vertices $\{v_i\}_{i \in S}$, the non-zero entries of $\sum_{i \in S} \mathbf{a}^i$ correspond exactly to $\delta(S)$. This follows because the only subsets of

$$\{|e| - 1, \underbrace{-1, -1, \ldots, -1}_{|e|-1}\}$$

that sum to zero are the empty set and the entire set. Hence, the e-th coordinate of $\sum_{i \in S} \mathbf{a}^i$ is zero iff either $e \notin E$ or $e \subset S$ or $e \subset V \setminus S$.

The rest of algorithm proceeds exactly as in the case of (non-hyper) graphs [2] and a reader that is very familiar with the previous work should feel free to skip the remainder of Section 4.1. We construct the sketches $M\mathbf{a}^1, \ldots, M\mathbf{a}^n$ where M is chosen according to a distribution over matrices $\mathbb{R}^{k \times d}$ where $k = \text{polylog}(d)$. The distribution has the property that for any $\mathbf{a} \in \mathbb{R}^d$, it is possible to determine the index of a non-zero entry of $\mathbf{a}$ given $M\mathbf{a}$ with probability $1 - 1/\text{poly}(n)$. Such as distribution is known to exist by a result of Jowhari et al. [18]. Given $M\mathbf{a}^1, \ldots, M\mathbf{a}^n$ we can find an edge across an arbitrary cut $(S, V \setminus S)$. To do this, we compute $\sum_{i \in S} M\mathbf{a}^i = M(\sum_{i \in S} \mathbf{a}^i)$. We can then determine the index of a non-zero entry of $\sum_{i \in S} \mathbf{a}^i$ which corresponds to an element of $\delta(S)$ as required. It may appear that to test connectivity we need to test all $2^{n-1} - 1$ possible cuts. Since the failure probability for each cut is only inverse polynomial in n this would be problematic. However, it is possible to be more efficient and only test $O(n)$ cuts. See Ahn et al. [2] for details.

THEOREM 13 (SPANNING GRAPH SKETCHES). *There exists a vertex-based sketch $\mathcal{A}$ of size $O(n \,\text{polylog}\, n)$ such that we can find a spanning graph of a hypergraph G from $\mathcal{A}(G)$ with high probability.*

Note the above theorem can be substituted for Theorem 2 and the resulting algorithms for vertex connectivity go through for hypergraphs unchanged.

Constructing k-skeletons. As mentioned above, it suffices to find $F_1, \ldots, F_k$ such that F_i is a spanning graph of $G \setminus (\cup_{j=1}^{i-1} F_j)$. Do to this we use k independent spanning graph sketches $\mathcal{A}^1(G)$, $\mathcal{A}^2(G), \ldots, \mathcal{A}^k(G)$ as described in the previous section. We may construct F_1 from $\mathcal{A}^1(G)$ because this is the functionality of a spanning graph sketch. Assuming we have already constructed $F_1, \ldots, F_{i-1}$ we can construct F_i from:

$$\mathcal{A}^i(G - F_1 - F_2 \ldots - F_{i-1}) = \mathcal{A}^i(G) - \sum_{j=1}^{i-1} \mathcal{A}^i(F_j) .$$

THEOREM 14 (k-SKELETON SKETCHES). *There exists a vertex-based sketch $\mathcal{B}$ of size $O(kn \,\text{polylog}\, n)$ such that we can find of a k-skeleton a hypergraph G from $\mathcal{B}(G)$ with high probability.*

4.2 Beyond k-Skeletons

One might be tempted as ask whether it was necessary to use k independent spanning graph sketches $\mathcal{A}^1, \ldots, \mathcal{A}^k$ rather that reuse a single sketch $\mathcal{A}$. If each application of the sketch $\mathcal{A}$ fails to return a spanning graph with probability δ, one might hope to use the union bound to argue that the probability that $\mathcal{A}$ fails on any of the inputs $G, G - F_1, G - F_1 - F_2, \ldots, G - F_1 - \ldots - F_{k-1}$ is at most $k\delta$. *But this would not be a valid application of the union bound!* The union bound states that for any *fixed* set of t events $B_1, \ldots, B_t$, we have $\mathbb{P}[B_1 \cup \ldots \cup B_t] \leq \sum_i \mathbb{P}[B_i]$. The issue is that the events in the above example are not fixed, i.e., they can not be specified a priori, since spanning graph F_i is determined by the randomness in the sketch.[3] We belabor this point because, while the union bound was not applicable in the above case, we will need it to prove our next result in a situation that is only subtly different and yet the union bound *is* valid.

[3]Another way to see that using the same sketch cannot work is that if it were possible to repeatedly remove each spanning graph from the sketch of the original graph, we would be able to reconstruct the entire graph using only a sketch of size $O(n \,\text{polylog}\, n)$. Clearly this is not possible because it requires at $\Omega(n^2)$ bits to specify an arbitrary graph on n vertices.

4.2.1 *Finding the light edges*

Given a graph $G = (V, E)$ and a postive integer k, recursively define

$$E_i = \{e \in E : \lambda_e(G \setminus \bigcup_{j=1}^{i-1} E_i) \leq k\}$$

and denote the union of these sets as:

$$\text{light}_k(G) = \bigcup_{i \geq 1} E_i .$$

Note that if G is d cut-degenerate then $\text{light}_d(G) = E$. Furthermore, there is at most n values of i such that E_i is non-empty since removing each non-empty set E_i from the graph increases the number of connected components.

Suppose $\mathcal{B}(G)$ is a sketch that returns an arbitrary $(k+1)$-skeleton of G with failure probability $\delta = 1/\text{poly}(n)$. Then, since $E_1, E_2, \ldots, E_n$ are sets defined solely by the input graph (and not any randomness in a sketch) we can specify the fixed events

$$B_i = \text{"We fail to return a } (k+1)\text{-skeleton sketch of } G - E_1 - \ldots - E_i \text{ given } \mathcal{B}(G - E_1 - \ldots - E_i)\text{"}$$

and therefore use the union bound to establish that the probability that we find a $(k+1)$-skeleton of each of the relevant graphs with failure probability at most $n\delta = 1/\text{poly}(n)$.

We can therefore find the sets $E_1, E_2, \ldots, E_n$ as follows. Let S_i be an arbitrary $(k+1)$ skeleton of $G - E_1 - \ldots E_{i-1}$. Assuming we have already determined $E_1, \ldots, E_{i-1}$, we can find S_i using:

$$\mathcal{B}(G - E_1 - E_2 \ldots - E_{i-1}) = \mathcal{B}(G) - \sum_{j=1}^{i-1} \mathcal{B}(E_j) .$$

Then, by appealing to Lemma 12, we know that we can then uniquely determine E_i given S_i.

THEOREM 15. *There exists a vertex-based sketch of size $\tilde{O}(kn)$ from which $\text{light}_k(G)$ can be reconstructed for any hypergraph G. In the case of a k-cut-degenerate graph, this is the entire graph.*

4.2.2 *What are the light edges?*

In this section, we restrict our attention to graphs rather than hypergraphs and show that the set of edges in $\text{light}_k(G)$ can be defined in terms of the notion of *strong connectivity* introduced by Benczúr and Karger [6].

LEMMA 16. $\text{light}_k(G) = \{e : k_e \leq k\}$ *where $k_{\{u,v\}}$ is the maximum k such that there is a set $S \subset V$ including u and v such that the induced graph on S is k-edge-connected.*

PROOF. Define t_e to be the minimum value of k such that $e \in \text{light}_k(G)$. We prove that $t_e = k_e$ and the result follows. To show $k_e \geq t_e$ suppose $t_e = t$ and then note that e survives when we recursively remove edges with edge connectivity $t-1$. But the remaining components in this graph are at least $(t-1)+1 = t$ connected so $k_e \geq t$. To show that $k_e \leq t_e$, suppose $k_e = k$. Then there exists a vertex induced subgraph H containing e that is k-connected. But when we recursively remove edges with edge connectivity at most $k-1$ then no edge in H can be removed. Hence, $t_e > (k-1)$ and so $t_e \geq k$. □

5. HYPERGRAPH SPARSIFICATION

In this final section, we present a vertex-based sketch for constructing a sparsifier of a hypergraph. This yields the first dynamic graph stream algorithm for constructing a sparsifier of a hypergraph. As an added bonus, our approach gives an algorithm and analysis that is significantly simpler than previous work on the specific case of graph sparsification [3, 16].

DEFINITION 17 (HYPERGRAPH SPARSIFIER). *A weighted subgraph $H = (V, E', w)$ of a hypergraph $G = (V, E)$ is a* sparsfier *if for all $S \subset V$, $\sum_{e \in \delta_H(S)} w(e) = (1 \pm \epsilon)|\delta_G(S)|$.*

Previous approaches to sparsification in the dynamic stream model relied on work by Fung et al. [15]. To construct a *graph* sparsifier, they showed that it was sufficient to independently sample every edge in the graph with probability $O(\epsilon^{-2}\lambda_e^{-1} \log n)$. Using their work required coopting their machinery and modifying it appropriately (e.g., replacing Chernoff arguments with careful Martingale arguments). Another downside to the previous approach is that the Fung et al. result does not seem to extend to the case of hypergraphs.[4]

Using our new-found ability (see the previous section) to find the entire set of edges that are not k-strong, we present an algorithm that a) has a simpler, and almost self-contained, analysis and b) extends to hypergraphs. Our approach is closer in spirit to Benczúr and Karger's original work on sparsification [6] which in turn is based on the following result by Karger [22]: if we sample each edge with probability $p \geq p^* = c\epsilon^{-2}\lambda^{-1} \log n$ where λ is the cardinality of the minimum cut and $c \geq 0$ is some constant, and weight the sampled edges by $1/p$ then the resulting graph is a sparsifier with high probability.

The idea behind our algorithm is as follows. For a hypergraph G, if we remove the hyperedges $\text{light}_k(G)$ where $k = 2c\epsilon^{-2} \log n$, then every connected component in the remaining hypergraph has minimum cut of size greater than $2c\epsilon^{-2} \log n$. Hence, for each of these components $p^* \leq 1/2$. Therefore, the graph formed by sampling the hyperedges in $G \setminus \text{light}_k(G)$ with probability 1/2 (and doubling the weight of sampled hyperedges) and adding the set of hyperedges in $\text{light}_k(G)$ with unit weights is a sparsifier of G. We then repeat this process until there are no hyperedges left to sample.

Algorithm.

1. Generate a series of graphs $G_0, G_1, G_2 \ldots$ where G_i is formed by deleting each hyperedge in G_{i-1} independently with probability 1/2 and $G_0 = G$.

2. For $i = 0, 1, 2, \ldots, \ell = 3 \log n$:

   (a) Let $F_i = \text{light}_k(H_i)$ where $k = O(\epsilon^{-2}(\log n + r))$ where $H_i = G_i \setminus (F_0 \cup F_1 \cup F_2 \cup \ldots \cup F_{i-1})$

3. Return $\bigcup_{i=0}^{\ell} 2^i \cdot F_i$ where $2^i \cdot F_i$ is the set of hyperedges in F_i where each is given weight 2^i.

Analysis. The following lemma uses an argument due to Karger [21] combined with a hypergraph cut counting result by Kogan and Krauthgamer [23].

LEMMA 18. *$2H_{i+1} \cup F_i$ is a $(1 + \epsilon)$-sparsifier for H_i.*

PROOF. It suffices to prove that $2H_{i+1}$ is a $(1 + \epsilon)$-sparsifier for $H_i \setminus F_i$. Furthermore, it suffices to consider each connected component of $H_i \setminus F_i$ separately.

Let C be an arbitrary connected component of $H_i \setminus F_i$ and note that C has a minimum cut of size at least k. Let C' be the graph formed by deleting each hyperedge in C with probability $1/2$. Consider a cut of size t in C and let X be the number of hyperedges in this cut that are in C'. Then $\mathbb{E}[X] = t/2$ and by an application of the Chernoff bound, $\mathbb{P}[|X - t/2| \geq \epsilon t/2] \leq 2\exp(-\epsilon^2 t/6)$.

The number of cuts of size at most t is $\exp(O(rt/k + t/k \cdot \log n))$ by appealing to a result by Kogan and Krauthgamer [23]. By an application of the union bound, the probability that there exists a cut of size t such that the number of hyperedges in corresponding cut in C' is not $(1 \pm \epsilon)t/2$ is at most

$$2\exp(-\epsilon^2 t/6) \cdot \exp(O(rt/k + t/k \cdot \log n)) .$$

This probability is less than $1/n^{10}$ if $k \geq c\epsilon^{-2}(\log n + r)$ for some sufficiently large constant c. Hence, taking the union bound over all $t \geq k$ ensures that with probability at least $1/n^8$, for every cut in C, the fraction of edges in the corresponding cut in C' is $(1 \pm \epsilon)/2$. □

THEOREM 19. *$\bigcup_{i=0}^{\ell} 2^i \cdot F_i$ is a $(1+\epsilon)^\ell$-sparsifier of G where $\ell = 3 \log n$.*

PROOF. The theorem follows by repeatedly applying Lemma 18. Specifically,

1. $F_{\ell-1}$ is a $(1 + \epsilon)$ sparsifier for $H_{\ell-1}$ since H_ℓ is the empty graph with high probability.

2. $2H_{\ell-1} \cup F_{\ell-2}$ is a $(1+\epsilon)$-sparsifier for $H_{\ell-2}$ and so $2F_{\ell-1} \cup F_{\ell-2}$ is a $(1 + \epsilon)^2$-sparsifier for $H_{\ell-2}$

3. $2H_{\ell-2} \cup F_{\ell-3}$ is a $(1+\epsilon)$-sparsifier for $H_{\ell-3}$ and so $4F_{\ell-1} \cup 2F_{\ell-2} \cup F_{\ell-3}$ is a $(1 + \epsilon)^3$-sparsifier for $H_{\ell-3}$

We continue in this way until we deduce $\bigcup_{i=0}^{\ell} 2^i \cdot F_i$ is a $(1 + \epsilon)^\ell$-sparsifier for $H_0 = G_0$. □

By re-parameterizing $\epsilon \leftarrow \epsilon/(2\ell)$ and using the sketches from Section 4, we establish the next theorem.

THEOREM 20. *There exists a vertex-based sketch of size $\tilde{O}(\epsilon^{-2} n)$ from which we can construct a $(1 + \epsilon)$ hypergraph sparsifier.*

Acknowledgements. We thank Jennifer Chayes for prompting us to investigate hypergraph connectivity.

6. REFERENCES

[1] F. M. Ablayev. Lower bounds for one-way probabilistic communication complexity and their application to space complexity. *Theor. Comput. Sci.*, 157(2):139–159, 1996.

[2] K. J. Ahn, S. Guha, and A. McGregor. Analyzing graph structure via linear measurements. In *Twenty-Third Annual ACM-SIAM Symposium on Discrete Algorithms, SODA 2012*, pages 459–467, 2012.

[3] K. J. Ahn, S. Guha, and A. McGregor. Graph sketches: sparsification, spanners, and subgraphs. In *31st ACM SIGMOD-SIGACT-SIGART Symposium on Principles of Database Systems*, pages 5–14, 2012.

[4] K. J. Ahn, S. Guha, and A. McGregor. Spectral sparsification in dynamic graph streams. In *APPROX*, pages 1–10, 2013.

[5] F. Becker, M. Matamala, N. Nisse, I. Rapaport, K. Suchan, and I. Todinca. Adding a referee to an interconnection network: What can(not) be computed in one round. In *25th IEEE International Symposium on Parallel and Distributed Processing, IPDPS 2011*, pages 508–514, 2011.

[4]For the reader familiar with Fung et al. [15], the issue is finding a suitable definition of cut-projection for hypergraphs and then proving a bound on the number of distinct cut-projections.

[6] A. A. Benczúr and D. R. Karger. Approximating s-t minimum cuts in $\tilde{O}(n^2)$ time. In *STOC*, pages 47–55, 1996.

[7] Ü. V. Çatalyürek and C. Aykanat. Hypergraph-partitioning-based decomposition for parallel sparse-matrix vector multiplication. *IEEE Trans. Parallel Distrib. Syst.*, 10(7):673–693, 1999.

[8] Ü. V. Çatalyürek, E. G. Boman, K. D. Devine, D. Bozdag, R. T. Heaphy, and L. A. Riesen. A repartitioning hypergraph model for dynamic load balancing. *J. Parallel Distrib. Comput.*, 69(8):711–724, 2009.

[9] K. Censor-Hillel, M. Ghaffari, G. Giakkoupis, B. Haeupler, and F. Kuhn. Tight bounds on vertex connectivity under vertex sampling. In *ACM-SIAM Symposium on Discrete Algorithms, SODA 2015*, 2015.

[10] K. Censor-Hillel, M. Ghaffari, and F. Kuhn. A new perspective on vertex connectivity. In *Twenty-Fifth Annual ACM-SIAM Symposium on Discrete Algorithms, SODA 2014, Portland, Oregon, USA, January 5-7, 2014*, pages 546–561, 2014.

[11] J. Cheriyan, M. Y. Kao, and R. Thurimella. Scan-first search and sparse certificates: an improved parallel algorithm for k-vertex connectivity. *SIAM Journal on Computing*, 22(1):157–174, 1993.

[12] Y. Emek and A. Rosén. Semi-streaming set cover - (extended abstract). In *ICALP*, pages 453–464, 2014.

[13] D. Eppstein, Z. Galil, G. F. Italiano, and A. Nissenzweig. Sparsification - a technique for speeding up dynamic graph algorithms. *J. ACM*, 44(5):669–696, 1997.

[14] U. Feige, M. Hajiyaghayi, and J. R. Lee. Improved approximation algorithms for minimum-weight vertex separators. *Proc. of STOC*, 2005.

[15] W. S. Fung, R. Hariharan, N. J. A. Harvey, and D. Panigrahi. A general framework for graph sparsification. In *STOC*, pages 71–80, 2011.

[16] A. Goel, M. Kapralov, and I. Post. Single pass sparsification in the streaming model with edge deletions. *CoRR*, abs/1203.4900, 2012.

[17] Y. Huang, Q. Liu, and D. N. Metaxas. Video object segmentation by hypergraph cut. In *2009 IEEE Computer Society Conference on Computer Vision and Pattern Recognition (CVPR 2009), 20-25 June 2009, Miami, Florida, USA*, pages 1738–1745, 2009.

[18] H. Jowhari, M. Saglam, and G. Tardos. Tight bounds for lp samplers, finding duplicates in streams, and related problems. In *PODS*, pages 49–58, 2011.

[19] M. Kapralov, Y. T. Lee, C. Musco, C. Musco, and A. Sidford. Single pass spectral sparsification in dynamic streams. In *FOCS*, 2014.

[20] M. Kapralov and D. P. Woodruff. Spanners and sparsifiers in dynamic streams. In *ACM Symposium on Principles of Distributed Computing, PODC '14, Paris, France, July 15-18, 2014*, pages 272–281, 2014.

[21] D. R. Karger. Random sampling in cut, flow, and network design problems. In *STOC '94: Proceedings of the twenty-sixth annual ACM symposium on Theory of computing*, pages 648–657, New York, NY, USA, 1994. ACM.

[22] D. R. Karger. Random sampling in cut, flow, and network design problems. In *STOC*, pages 648–657, 1994.

[23] D. Kogan and R. Krauthgamer. Sketching cuts in graphs and hypergraphs. In *6th Innovations in Theoretical Computer Science*, 2015.

[24] K. Kutzkov and R. Pagh. Triangle counting in dynamic graph streams. In *Algorithm Theory - SWAT 2014 - 14th Scandinavian Symposium and Workshops, Copenhagen, Denmark, July 2-4, 2014. Proceedings*, pages 306–318, 2014.

[25] A. McGregor. Graph stream algorithms: a survey. *SIGMOD Record*, 43(1):9–20, 2014.

[26] J. Radhakrishnan and S. Shannigrahi. Streaming algorithms for 2-coloring uniform hypergraphs. In *Algorithms and Data Structures - 12th International Symposium, WADS 2011, New York, NY, USA, August 15-17, 2011. Proceedings*, pages 667–678, 2011.

[27] B. Saha and L. Getoor. On maximum coverage in the streaming model & application to multi-topic blog-watch. In *SIAM International Conference on Data Mining, SDM 2009, April 30 - May 2, 2009, Sparks, Nevada, USA*, pages 697–708, 2009.

[28] P. Sankowski. Faster dynamic matchings and vertex connectivity. In *Eighteenth Annual ACM-SIAM Symposium on Discrete Algorithms, SODA 2007, New Orleans, Louisiana, USA, January 7-9, 2007*, pages 118–126, 2007.

[29] H. Sun. Counting hypergraphs in data streams. *CoRR*, abs/1304.7456, 2013.

[30] Y. Yamaguchi, A. Ogawa, A. Takeda, and S. Iwata. Cyber security analysis of power networks by hypergraph cut algorithms. In *2014 IEEE International Conference on Smart Grid Communications*, 2014.

APPENDIX

A. SCAN-FIRST TREES

A scan first search tree (SFST) of a graph [11] is defined as follows: The tree is initially empty, all vertices except the root (chosen arbitrarily) are *unmarked*, and all vertices are *unscanned*. At each step we *scan* an marked but unscanned vertex. For each vertex x that is being scanned, all edges from x to unmarked neighbors of x are added to the tree and the unmarked neighbors are marked. This continues until no marked but unscanned vertices remain.

THEOREM 21. *Any data stream algorithm that constructs a SFST with probability at least $3/4$ requires $\Omega(n^2)$ space.*

PROOF. The proof is by a reduction from the communication problem of indexing [1]. Suppose Alice has a binary string $x \in \{0,1\}^{n^2}$ indexed by $[n] \times [n]$ and Bob wants to compute $x_{i,j}$ for some index $(i,j) \in [n] \times [n]$ that is unknown to Alice. This requires $\Omega(n^2)$ bits to be communicated from Alice to Bob if Bob is to learn $x_{i,j}$ with probability at least $3/4$. Suppose we have a data stream algorithm for constructing an SFST. Alice creates a graph on nodes $T \cup U \cup V \cup W$ where $T = \{t_1, \ldots, t_n\}, U = \{u_1, \ldots, u_n\}, V = \{v_1, \ldots, v_n\}$, and $W = \{w_1, \ldots, w_n\}$. She adds edges $\{t_k, u_\ell\}$ and $\{v_\ell, t_k\}$ for each ℓ, k such that $x_{\ell,k} = 1$. Alice runs the scan-first search algorithm and sends the contents of her memory to Bob. Bob adds the edge $\{u_i, v_i\}$. Note that any SFST includes all neighbors of u_i or v_i. In particular, $x_{i,j} = 1$ iff at least one of $\{t_j, u_i\}$ or $\{v_i, w_j\}$ is present in the SFST constructed. Hence, the algorithm must have used $\Omega(n^2)$ space. □

Fast and Near–Optimal Algorithms for Approximating Distributions by Histograms

Jayadev Acharya
MIT
jayadev@csail.mit.edu

Ilias Diakonikolas
University of Edinburgh
ilias.d@ed.ac.uk

Chinmay Hegde
MIT
chinmay@csail.mit.edu

Jerry Li
MIT
jerryzli@csail.mit.edu

Ludwig Schmidt
MIT
ludwigs@mit.edu

ABSTRACT

Histograms are among the most popular structures for the succinct summarization of data in a variety of database applications. In this work, we provide fast and near-optimal algorithms for approximating arbitrary one dimensional data distributions by histograms.

A k-histogram is a piecewise constant function with k pieces. We consider the following natural problem, previously studied by Indyk, Levi, and Rubinfeld [ILR12] in PODS 2012: Given samples from a distribution p over $\{1, \ldots, n\}$, compute a k-histogram that minimizes the ℓ_2-distance from p, up to an additive ε. We design an algorithm for this problem that uses the information–theoretically minimal sample size of $m = O(1/\varepsilon^2)$, runs in sample–linear time $O(m)$, and outputs an $O(k)$– histogram whose ℓ_2-distance from p is at most $O(\mathrm{opt}_k) + \epsilon$, where opt_k is the minimum ℓ_2-distance between p and any k-histogram. Perhaps surprisingly, the sample size and running time of our algorithm are independent of the universe size n.

We generalize our approach to obtain fast algorithms for multi-scale histogram construction, as well as approximation by piecewise polynomial distributions. We experimentally demonstrate one to two orders of magnitude improvement in terms of empirical running times over previous state-of-the-art algorithms.

1. Introduction

In recent years, we have witnessed the proliferation of massive datasets in a variety of scientific and technological domains. Moreover, our inferential goals on the gathered data have become increasingly ambitious. A classical approach to deal with this phenomenon involves constructing *succinct synopses* of the data. In most settings, the use of synopses is essential when exploring massive datasets; see the recent survey [CGHJ12] for an extensive treatment. As expected, a compact representation of a very large dataset may be *lossy* in general. For a given synopsis structure, we are interested in the *space* it requires, the *error* it introduces (quantifying how well it preserves the desired properties of the data), and the *time* needed for its construction and operation. Understanding the precise tradeoff between these criteria has been an important goal in database research and beyond for the last two decades.

In this work, we design efficient algorithms for the compact representation of data distributions by *histograms*. Formally, a k-histogram over the universe $[n]$ is a piecewise constant function with k interval pieces. The parameter k is a natural measure of the space requirement, since a k-histogram can be represented with $O(k)$ numbers. Informally speaking, for a data distribution p over $[n]$, a k-histogram h is a "good" representation of p if $p(i)$ – i.e., the relative frequency of item i in the data – is "close" to $h(i)$. Histograms constitute the oldest and most widely used method for the succinct approximation of data. In the context of databases, they were first proposed in [Koo80], and have since been extensively studied in a variety of applications [GMP97, JKM+98, CMN98, TGIK02, GGI+02, GSW04, GKS06, ILR12].

Our approach can be extended, more generally, to approximating distributions by *piecewise polynomials*. Piecewise polynomial functions are a natural generalization of histograms, where the data distribution in each interval is represented by a degree-d polynomial (i.e., histograms correspond to the special case $d = 0$). A piecewise polynomial with k intervals and degree d is represented by $O(k(d + 1))$ numbers, and hence the product $k(d + 1)$ is a natural measure of its space requirements. Due to their flexibility, piecewise polynomials can provide an even more succinct approximation to data than histograms and have been previously considered as a synopsis structure in this context (see, e.g., [GKS06]). We note that piecewise polyno-

PODS'15, May 31–June 4, 2015, Melbourne, Victoria, Australia.

http://dx.doi.org/10.1145/2745754.2745772 .

mials have received significant attention in other scientific disciplines, including approximation theory [Che66] and statistics (see, e.g., [Sil86, WW83, SHKT97, WN07, CDSS14a, CDSS14b] and references therein).

A common error metric used for fitting a histogram to the data is the "sum squared error", also known as the *V–optimal* measure [IP95]. Here, the goal is to construct a synopsis structure that minimizes the ℓ_2–norm from the underlying data distribution. Most existing works in this area assume that the data distribution p is provided explicitly in the input, and hence the corresponding algorithms inherently incur at least a *linear* dependence on the universe size n. In an early work on this topic, Jagadish *et al.* [JKM+98] provided a dynamic programming algorithm that runs in time $O(kn^2)$ and outputs the best V–optimal histogram of a one-dimensional data distribution over $[n]$. Subsequent results [TGIK02, GGI+02, GKS06] achieved a series of improvements to the running time by focusing on near-optimal solutions. The culmination of this research is the work of Guha *et al.* [GKS06], who gave a $(1+\delta)$ multiplicative approximation to the best V–optimal histogram running in time $O(n + k^3 \log^2 n/\delta^2)$.

When handling massive datasets that range from petabytes to exabytes in size, the requirement that our algorithms read the entire input is unrealistic. A standard way to obtain a small representative subset of the input involves *random sampling* from the data (see [CD14] for a recent tutorial). Ideally, we would like to draw a small number of samples from our data set and efficiently post–process the samples to obtain an accurate representation of the underlying data distribution. Observe that choosing a uniformly random element from a multi-set D over $[n]$ is equivalent to drawing i.i.d. samples from the underlying distribution p of relative frequencies. Hence, the problem of constructing an optimal histogram (or piecewise polynomial) representation under a given metric is essentially equivalent to the problem of *learning* (i.e., performing density estimation) an arbitrary discrete distribution over $[n]$ with respect to this metric.

In recent work, Indyk *et al.* [ILR12] studied the histogram construction problem in the aforementioned random sampling framework. Their main result is an additive ε-approximation algorithm for this problem with running time $O((k^5/\varepsilon^8)\cdot\log^2 n)$. The sample complexity of their algorithm is logarithmic in the domain size n, and quadratic in the number k of histogram pieces. The authors of [ILR12] posed as an open question whether the running time of their algorithm can be improved and whether the logarithmic dependence on n in the sample complexity is necessary.

In this work, we design simple, highly efficient algorithms for approximating data distributions by histograms (and piecewise polynomials) in the ℓ_2-norm using random samples. Our algorithms have information–theoretically optimal sample complexity (independent of the domain size n), run in sample–linear time, and output a histogram (or piecewise polynomial) whose number of intervals and accuracy are within a small constant factor of the best possible. In particular, for the case of histograms, our algorithm runs in time $O(1/\varepsilon^2)$, *independent of both n and k*. In the following section we formally state our results and provide a detailed comparison with prior work.

2. Our Results and Techniques

2.1 Basic Definitions.

We consider distributions over $[n] := \{1,\ldots,n\}$, which are functions $p : [n] \to [0,1]$ such that $\sum_{i=1}^{n} p(i) = 1$, where $p(i)$ is the probability of element i under p. For convenience, we will use p to denote the distribution with mass function $p(i)$. The ℓ_2-norm of a function $f : [n] \to \mathbb{R}$ is $\|f\|_2 := \sqrt{\sum_{i=1}^{n} f(i)^2}$. The ℓ_2-distance between functions $f, g : [n] \to \mathbb{R}$ is defined as $\|f-g\|_2$. Let $\mathcal{D}_n$ denote the class of all probability distributions over $[n]$. A function (or distribution) $f : [n] \to \mathbb{R}$ is s-sparse if f is nonzero for at most s points, i.e., $|\{i \in [n] \mid f(i) \neq 0\}| \leq s$. For a function f and a set $I \subseteq [n]$, we define f_I as the restriction of f to I; namely, for $i \in I$, we have $f_I(i) := f(i)$, and for $i \notin I$, $f_I(i) := 0$.

Interval Partitions and k-Histograms. Fix a partition of $[n]$ into a set of disjoint intervals $\mathcal{I} = \{I_1,\ldots,I_\ell\}$. For such a partition $\mathcal{I}$ we denote the number of intervals by $|\mathcal{I}|$, i.e., $|\mathcal{I}| = \ell$. For an interval $J \subseteq [n]$, we denote its cardinality or length by $|J|$, i.e., if $J = [a,b]$, with $a \leq b \in [n]$, then $|J| = b-a+1$. A *k-histogram* is a piecewise constant function $h : [n] \to \mathbb{R}$ with at most k interval pieces, i.e., there exists a partition $\mathcal{I} = \{I_1,\ldots,I_k\}$ of $[n]$ into k intervals I_j, $j \in [k]$, with corresponding values v_j such that $h(i) = v_j$ for all $i \in I_j$. In addition, if h is a probability distribution, then it is referred to as a k-histogram distribution. We use $\mathcal{H}_k^n$ to denote the class of all k-histogram distributions over $[n]$.

Given m independent samples $\{s_j\}_{j=1}^{m}$ drawn from a distribution $p \in \mathcal{D}_n$, the *empirical distribution* $\widehat{p}_m$ over $[n]$ is the discrete distribution defined as follows: for all $i \in [n]$, $\widehat{p}_m(i) := |\{j \in [m] \mid s_j = i\}|/m$.

Agnostic Histogram ℓ_2–Learning. We cast our histogram construction problem within the framework of distribution estimation. More specifically, we study the following learning problem: Fix parameters $\alpha, \beta \geq 1$. Given m i.i.d. draws from a distribution $p \in \mathcal{D}_n$, and parameters $k \in \mathbb{Z}_+$, $\delta, \varepsilon > 0$, our goal is to output a hypothesis $h \in \mathcal{H}_t^n$ with $t \leq \alpha \cdot k$ such that with probability at least $1-\delta$ our hypothesis satisfies $\|h-p\|_2 \leq \beta \cdot \mathrm{opt}_k + \varepsilon$, where $\mathrm{opt}_k := \min_{h' \in \mathcal{H}_k^n} \|h'-p\|_2$. That is, the algorithm outputs a t-histogram distribution h whose ℓ_2–error from p is almost as small as the minimum error attainable by any k-histogram.

The approximation factors α and β quantify the performance of the learning algorithm; the former quantifies the number of interval pieces of the constructed histogram (space), while the latter quantifies the achieved accuracy. To measure the complexity, we are interested in the number of samples drawn from p (sample complexity), and the total running time of the algorithm (computational complexity). The "gold standard" in this context is an algorithm achieving an optimal performance guarantee (i.e., $\alpha = 1$, $\beta = 1$) that uses an information–theoretically minimum sample size and runs in sample–linear time.

2.2 Main Results.

As our main contribution, we design a fast constant–factor approximation algorithm for the aforementioned histogram construction problem. Formally, we obtain:

THEOREM 2.1 (MAIN). *There is an algorithm that, given k, $0 < \varepsilon, \delta < 1$ draws $m = O((1/\varepsilon^2) \cdot \log(1/\delta))$ samples from an arbitrary $p \in \mathcal{D}_n$, runs in time $O(m)$, and with probability at least $1-\delta$ outputs a $5k$-histogram h such that $\|h - p\|_2 \leq 2 \cdot \mathrm{opt}_k + \varepsilon$. Moreover, any algorithm for this problem requires $\Omega((1/\varepsilon^2) \cdot \log(1/\delta))$ samples from p, independent of its running time.*

That is, the algorithm uses an information theoretically minimal sample size (up to a constant), runs in sample–linear time (independent of n), and outputs a histogram representation whose number of intervals and accuracy are within a small constant factor of the best possible.

Our algorithm is simple, easy to implement, and works well in practice. Our experimental evaluation (Section 5) shows that it outperforms previous approaches by at least one order of magnitude. Moreover, our algorithmic approach is quite robust, generalizing effortlessly to *multi-scale* histogram construction, as well as approximation by piecewise polynomial functions. Before we elaborate on these extensions, let us provide a brief explanation of our techniques.

At a high-level, our algorithm can be "decoupled" into two independent stages. In the first stage, we draw $m = O((1/\varepsilon^2) \cdot \log(1/\delta))$ samples from p and construct the empirical distribution $\widehat{p}_m$. In the second stage, we post-process $\widehat{p}_m$ to obtain an $O(k)$-histogram distribution h that approximately minimizes the ℓ_2–distance from $\widehat{p}_m$. While this decoupling approach seems intuitive, its correctness relies crucially on the structure of the ℓ_2–norm.[1] The second stage exploits the $O(m)$–sparsity of the empirical distribution to remove the dependence on n in the running time. We remark that a black-box application of previous algorithms to post-process $\widehat{p}_m$ would lead to super-linear running times (see Section 2.3). We stress that it is by no means obvious how to perform the second stage in time $O(m)$ – i.e., linear in the sparsity of $\widehat{p}_m$ – and this is the main algorithmic contribution of our work.

Our algorithm for implementing the second stage (Algorithm 1 in Section 3.2) is based on an iterative greedy approach. Starting from $\widehat{p}_m$ (itself an $O(m)$-histogram), in each iteration the algorithm merges pairs of consecutive intervals according to a natural notion of error that the merging operation would incur. In particular, it merges all pairs *except* the ones with largest error. The algorithm terminates when the number of remaining intervals is $O(k)$, and the constructed histogram is obtained by "flattening" the empirical distribution with respect to the final set of intervals.

In most applications, the desired value of k (number of intervals in the output histogram) is *a priori* unknown. Instead, the underlying goal is merely to efficiently compute a succinct representation of the data with a few pieces (i.e., small enough value of k) and small error (i.e., small enough value of opt_k). There is a *trade-off* between these two criteria and it is important to design algorithms that capture this tradeoff. A straightforward adaptation of Algorithm 1 can be used to approximately capture the *entire* Pareto curve between k and opt_k, while still running in linear time. In particular, we show (see Section 3.4):

THEOREM 2.2 (MULTI-SCALE HISTOGRAM). *There is an algorithm that, given $0 < \varepsilon, \delta < 1$ draws $m = O((1/\varepsilon^2) \cdot \log(1/\delta))$ samples from an arbitrary $p \in \mathcal{D}_n$, runs in time $O(m)$, and has the following performance guarantee: With probability at least $1 - \delta$,* for every k, $1 \leq k \leq m$, *it outputs a t-histogram h_t with $t \leq 8k$ and an error estimate e_t such that (i) $\|h_t - p\|_2 \leq 2 \cdot \mathrm{opt}_k + \varepsilon$, and (ii) $\|h_t - p\|_2 - \varepsilon \leq e_t \leq \|h_t - p\|_2 + \varepsilon$.*

Note that for all $1 \leq k \leq m$ the above algorithm gives us an accurate estimate e_t of the true error $\|h_t - p\|_2$. This is useful for selecting the value of k such that the desired tradeoff between number of intervals and accuracy is achieved.

Finally, we remark that our iterative greedy approach can be generalized to efficiently fit more general classes of functions to the data, such as piecewise polynomials. A (k, d)-piecewise polynomial is a piecewise polynomial function f with k interval pieces $\{I_1, \ldots, I_k\}$ such that f agrees with a degree-d polynomial within each I_j. The piecewise polynomial approximation algorithm is very similar to Algorithm 1. The new technical ingredient is an efficient routine to "project" the data (in a given interval) on the class of degree-d polynomials. We design a fast iterative routine for this subproblem by exploiting properties of discrete Chebyshev polynomials. Specifically, we prove the following:

THEOREM 2.3 (PIECEWISE POLYNOMIALS). *There is an algorithm that, given k, d, and $0 < \varepsilon, \delta < 1$, draws $m = O((1/\varepsilon^2) \cdot \log(1/\delta))$ samples from an arbitrary $p \in \mathcal{D}_n$, runs in time $O(m \cdot (d+1)^2)$, and with probability at least $1 - \delta$ outputs a $(5k, d)$-piecewise polynomial f such that $\|f - p\|_2 \leq 2 \cdot \mathrm{opt}_{k,d} + \varepsilon$, where $\mathrm{opt}_{k,d}$ is the minimum ℓ_2-distance between p and any (k, d)–piecewise polynomial.*

2.3 Comparison with Previous Work.

As mentioned in the introduction, the majority of prior work on histogram construction assumes that the data distribution p is explicitly provided as the input. Jagadish *et al.* [JKM+98] used dynamic programming to compute the best V–Optimal k-histogram of a distribution over $[n]$ in time $O(n^2 k)$. Regarding approximation algorithms, the most relevant reference is the work of Guha *et al.* [GKS06], who gave a $(1 + \delta)$-multiplicative approximation that runs in time $O(n + k^3 \log^2 n/\delta^2)$. (See [GKS06] for references on several other approxima-

[1]Notably, such a decoupling into sampling and optimization fails for other metrics, e.g., the ℓ_1–norm [CDSS14a, CDSS14b].

tion algorithms based on alternative approaches, such as wavelet–based techniques.)

[JKM+98] also give a greedy algorithm for the *dual* version of the histogram construction problem. That is, given a bound b on the ℓ_2-error, output a histogram whose error is at most b with the minimum number of pieces k^*. Their algorithm runs in $O(n)$ time and outputs a $3k^*$-histogram with error at most $3b$. We remark that a black-box application of this algorithm to solve the primal problem will necessarily lead to super-linear running times, as it requires an appropriate binary search procedure on the error parameter.

Our sampling stage can be combined with the above approaches to obtain qualitatively better results. In particular, by applying the dynamic programming approach [JKM+98] to the empirical distribution $\widehat{p}_m$, we obtain a k-histogram with error at most $\mathrm{opt}_k + \varepsilon$. This guarantee corresponds to $\alpha = \beta = 1$, which is optimal. The major disadvantage is the resulting running time of $\Theta(m^2 k)$, which is prohibitively large for most applications. Moreover, our experiments indicate that this approach may sometimes result in over-fitting. Similarly, post-processing the empirical distribution using the approximation algorithm of [GKS06] gives a k-histogram with error at most $(1+\delta)\cdot\mathrm{opt}_k+\varepsilon$, i.e., $\alpha = 1$ and $\beta = 1 + \delta$. The running time of this approach is $\Omega(m + k^3 \log^2 m/\delta^2)$.[2] The second term in this expression makes this approach sub-optimal; this is reflected in the experimental comparison in Section 5. Finally, we point out that an adaptation of the dual greedy algorithm in [JKM+98] for m-sparse signals would also lead to a running time super-linear in m. In addition, this approach does not generalize to piecewise polynomial approximation and our experiments show that it empirically performs worse both in terms of approximation ratio and in terms of running time.

[ILR12] studied the agnostic histogram ℓ_2–learning problem in the same framework as ours. Their main result is an algorithm that, given sample access to an arbitrary data distribution p over $[n]$, computes an $O(k\log(1/\varepsilon))$-histogram whose ℓ_2–distance from p is opt_k. That is, they achieve an (α, β) approximation guarantee, where $\alpha = O(\log(1/\varepsilon))$ and $\beta = 1$. Their algorithm has sample complexity $\widetilde{O}((k^2/\varepsilon^4)\log n)$ and running time $\widetilde{O}((k^5/\varepsilon^8)\cdot\log^2 n)$. In comparison, our algorithm in Theorem 2.1 achieves $\alpha = 5$, $\beta = 2$, and has both sample complexity and running time of $O(1/\varepsilon^2)$.

Finally, we mention a different set of histogram approximation algorithms developed in [GSW04] that run in linear time. However, these algorithms provide guarantees for so-called *relative error* measures. As far as we know, none of these approaches imply results for the ℓ_2-learning problem that we consider.

Paper Structure. In Section 3.1 we provide tight upper and lower bounds on the sample complexity of our histogram learning problem. In Section 3.2 we present our main histogram construction algorithm establishing Theorems 2.1 and 2.2. In Section 3.4 we present the generalization of our algorithm to multi-scale histogram construction. In Section 4 we present the generalization of our algorithm to more general functions, including piecewise polynomials. Finally, in Section 5 we describe our experimental evaluation and compare with previous approaches. For the sake of readability, some proofs are deferred to an appendix.

[2] It is unclear whether an adaptation of [GKS06] to m-sparse signals over $[n]$ can lead to running time independent of n.

3. Near-optimal Histogram Approximation

In this section we describe our algorithms for histogram approximation establishing Theorems 2.1 and 2.2.

3.1 Tight Bounds on Sample Complexity.

The following simple theorem establishes the sample upper bound of $O((1/\varepsilon^2)\cdot\log(1/\delta))$ and justifies our two stage learning approach:

THEOREM 3.1. *Let $p \in \mathcal{D}_n$. For any constants $\alpha, \beta \geq 1$ there is an algorithm that, given k and $0 < \varepsilon, \delta < 1$, draws $m = O((1/\varepsilon^2)\cdot\log(1/\delta))$ samples from p and with probability at least $1-\delta$ outputs a hypothesis $h \in \mathcal{H}_t^n$ with $t \leq \alpha\cdot k$ such that $\|h - p\|_2 \leq \beta\cdot\mathrm{opt}_k(p) + \beta\varepsilon$.*

We require the following simple lemma:

LEMMA 3.1. *Fix $0 < \varepsilon, \delta < 1$. Let $p \in \mathcal{D}_n$ and let $\widehat{p}_m$ be the empirical distribution formed by considering $m = \Omega\left((1/\varepsilon^2)\cdot\log(1/\delta)\right)$ samples. Then, with probability at least $1-\delta$, we have that $\|\widehat{p}_m - p\|_2 \leq \varepsilon$.*

PROOF. For $i \in [n]$, let n_i be the number of occurrences of element i among the m samples. Note that $n_i \sim \mathrm{Binom}(m, p(i))$, hence $\mathrm{Var}[n_i] = mp(i)\,(1-p(i))$. Since $\widehat{p}_m(i) = n_i/m$ we can write

$$\begin{aligned}\mathbb{E}[\|\widehat{p}_m - p\|_2^2] &= \sum_{i=1}^{n}\mathbb{E}\left[(\widehat{p}_m(i) - p(i))^2\right]\\ &= (1/m^2)\cdot\sum_{i=1}^{n}\mathbb{E}\left[(n_i - mp(i))^2\right]\\ &= (1/m^2)\cdot\sum_{i=1}^{n}\mathrm{Var}[n_i]\\ &= (1/m)\cdot\sum_{i=1}^{n}p(i)\cdot(1-p(i))\\ &< 1/m.\end{aligned}$$

Consider the random variable $Y = \|\widehat{p}_m - p\|_2$. Jensen's inequality implies that

$$\mathbb{E}[Y] \leq \sqrt{\mathbb{E}[Y^2]} < 1/\sqrt{m} \leq \varepsilon/4.$$

We can write $Y = g(s_1, \ldots, s_m)$, where $s_j \sim p$ and the samples s_j, $j \in [m]$, are mutually independent. Note that the function g satisfies the following Lipschitz property:

$$|\,g(s_1,\ldots,s_j,\ldots,s_m) - g(s_1,\ldots,s_j',\ldots,s_m)\,| \leq \frac{2}{m}$$

for any $j \in [m]$ and $s_1, \ldots, s_m, s_j' \in [n]$ because changing a single sample moves only $1/m$ of the empirical probability mass. Hence, McDiarmid's inequality [McD89] implies that

$$\Pr[Y > \mathbb{E}[Y] + \eta] \leq \exp(-\eta^2 m/2).$$

The lemma follows from our choice of parameters by setting $\eta = \varepsilon/4$. □

PROOF OF THEOREM 3.1. The algorithm proceeds in two stages:

(i) Construct the empirical distribution $\widehat{p}_m$, and

(ii) Compute and output $h \in \mathcal{H}_t^n$ such that

$$\|h - \widehat{p}_m\|_2 \leq \beta \cdot \mathrm{opt}_k(\widehat{p}_m) .$$

We now sketch correctness. By Lemma 3.1, with probability at least $1 - \delta$ over the samples, we will have that $\|p - \widehat{p}_m\|_2 \leq \varepsilon$. We henceforth condition on this event. Since $\|p - \widehat{p}_m\|_2 \leq \varepsilon$, it follows that $|\mathrm{opt}_k(p) - \mathrm{opt}_k(\widehat{p}_m)| \leq \varepsilon$. The proposition follows by an application of the triangle inequality. □

Theorem 3.1 reduces the histogram construction problem for the distribution p to essentially the same problem for the empirical $\widehat{p}_m$ with an additive loss in the error guarantee. The main algorithmic ingredient lies in efficiently implementing Step (ii). In the following subsection, we design an algorithm (Algorithm 1) that implements the second step in time $O(m)$, while achieving approximation guarantees of $\alpha = 5$ and $\beta = 2$. We remark that an entirely analogous proposition (with an identical proof) holds for constructing piecewise polynomial approximations.

We also prove a matching information-theoretic lower bound of $\Omega((1/\varepsilon^2) \cdot \log(1/\delta))$ for the sample complexity of our learning problem. Our lower bound applies even for the very special case of $k = 2$ and $\mathrm{opt}_k = 0$.

THEOREM 3.2. *Fix $0 < \varepsilon, \delta < 1/2$. Any algorithm with sample access to an arbitrary $p \in \mathcal{D}_n$ that agnostically learns p to ℓ_2-distance ε with probability $1-\delta$ must use $m = \Omega\left((1/\varepsilon^2) \cdot \log(1/\delta)\right)$ samples.*

PROOF. Let p_1 and p_2 be 2-histogram distributions on $[n]$, such that $p_1(1) = 1/2+\varepsilon = p_2(2)$, $p_1(2) = 1/2 - \varepsilon = p_2(1)$, and for all $i \in \{3, \ldots, n\}$, $p_1(i) = p_2(i) = 0$. Then, $\|p_1 - p_2\|_2 = 2\sqrt{2}\varepsilon$. We consider the following special case of our agnostic learning problem: We are given sample access to a distribution p over $[n]$ and we are promised that the underlying distribution is either p_1 or p_2. Our goal is to learn the distribution p with probability at least $1 - \delta$. We will prove a sample lower bound of $\Omega\left((1/\varepsilon^2) \cdot \log(1/\delta)\right)$ for this problem. Note that, since both p_1 and p_2 are 2-histograms (i.e., $\mathrm{opt}_2 = 0$) with effective support the set $\{1, 2\}$, we can assume without loss of generality that our hypothesis is a 2-histogram supported on $\{1, 2\}$. Hence, the parameters α and β in the definition of agnostic learning are irrelevant for this special case.

To prove our result, we consider the following (essentially equivalent) hypothesis testing problem. Given m independent samples from $p \in \{p_1, p_2\}$ decide whether the underlying distribution is p_1 or p_2 with error probability at most δ. We call this the problem of *distinguishing* between p_1 and p_2.

Formally, we use this hypothesis testing problem to prove our lower bound. We show:

(*a*) If p_1 and p_2 cannot be distinguished with m samples with probability at least $1 - \delta$, then the ℓ_2 error of any learning algorithm that succeeds with probability $1 - \delta$ is at least ε.

(*b*) p_1 and p_2 cannot be distinguished with probability $1-\delta$ with fewer than $\Omega((1/\varepsilon^2) \cdot \log(1/\delta))$ samples.

Proof of (*a*)**:** We show the contrapositive. Suppose there is an algorithm $\mathcal{A}$ that with probability at least $1 - \delta$ outputs a hypothesis q with ℓ_2 error at most ε. We claim that the following tester distinguishes p_1 and p_2 with probability at least $1 - \delta$:

$$\begin{array}{ll} p_1, & \text{if } \|p_1 - q\|_2 < \|p_2 - q\|_2 \\ p_2, & \text{otherwise.} \end{array}$$

Indeed, by the triangle inequality we have that

$$\max\{\|p_1 - q\|_2, \|p_2 - q\|_2\} > \sqrt{2}\varepsilon.$$

Therefore, if the underlying distribution is p_i and q satisfies $\|p_i - q\|_2 < \varepsilon$, the tester correctly distinguishes p_1 and p_2.

Proof of (*b*)**:** It is a well-known lemma in hypothesis testing (see, e.g., Theorem 4.7, Chapter 4 of [BY02]) that any hypothesis tester that distinguishes between p_1 and p_2 with probability of error δ must use at least

$$\Omega\left(\frac{1}{h^2(p_1, p_2)} \cdot \log(1/\delta)\right)$$

samples, where $h(p_1, p_2)$ denotes the Hellinger distance between p_1 and p_2. Recall that the Hellinger distance between distributions p and q over a finite set $\mathcal{X}$ is defined as [LCY00]

$$h(p, q) \stackrel{\text{def}}{=} \sqrt{\frac{1}{2} \sum_{x \in \mathcal{X}} \left(\sqrt{p(x)} - \sqrt{q(x)}\right)^2}.$$

Therefore, for p_1 and p_2, we have

$$\begin{aligned} h^2(p_1, p_2) &= \frac{1}{2} \sum_{1 \leq x \leq n} \left(\sqrt{p_1(x)} - \sqrt{p_2(x)}\right)^2 \\ &= 1 - \sqrt{1 - 4\varepsilon^2} \\ &= \frac{4\varepsilon^2}{1 + \sqrt{1 - 4\varepsilon^2}} \\ &\leq 2\varepsilon^2, \end{aligned}$$

which completes the proof. □

3.2 Near-optimal Histograms in Input Sparsity Time.

In this subsection, we describe our main algorithm for approximating an arbitrary discrete function with a histogram under the ℓ_2-norm. Our algorithm runs in input sparsity time and achieves approximation error and number of pieces (of the output histogram) that are both optimal up to constant factors. Formally, we study the following problem: Given an s-sparse function $q : [n] \to \mathbb{R}$ and a parameter k, compute a k-histogram h' such that $\|q - h'\|_2 = \mathrm{opt}_k$. To achieve $O(s)$ running time, we allow the output to consist of up to $O(k)$ pieces and are willing to accept an approximation guarantee of $O(\mathrm{opt}_k)$. Our algorithm will offer a trade-off between the constants hidden in the $O(\cdot)$-notation.

Before introducing the algorithm, let us concern ourselves with the following simple problem: for a single fixed interval I and a function q supported on I, find the value c which minimizes $\sum_{i\in I}(c - q(i))^2$. This corresponds to finding the best 1-histogram approximation to q over I. An easy calculation shows that $c = \frac{1}{|I|}\sum_{i\in I} q(i)$ is the minimizing value. This motivates the following definition.

DEFINITION 3.1 (FLATTENING). *For any interval* I, *let* $\mu_q(I) = \frac{1}{|I|}\sum_{i\in I} q(i)$ *be the value of the best 1-histogram approximation to* q *on* I. *Furthermore, let* $err_q(I) = \sum_{i\in I}(q(i) - \mu_q(I))^2$ *denote the* ℓ_2*-squared error incurred by this approximation. If* $\mathcal{I} = \{I_1, \ldots, I_s\}$ *is a partition of* $[n]$, *we let* $\bar{q}_{\mathcal{I}} : [n] \to \mathbb{R}$ *be the function given by* $\bar{q}_{\mathcal{I}}(x) = \mu_q(I_i)$ *if* $x \in I_i$. *We call this function the* flattening *of* q *over* $\mathcal{I}$. *By the discussion above,* $\bar{q}_{\mathcal{I}}(x)$ *is the best fit to* q *among all functions that are constant on each of the intervals* $I_1, \ldots, I_s$.

Our algorithm works as follows: We start by representing the s-sparse input function q as an $O(s)$ histogram (by assigning a separate interval to each nonzero and each contiguous block of zeros). We call the corresponding set of $O(s)$ intervals $\mathcal{I}^0$. Note that this representation is exact, i.e., $\bar{q}_{\mathcal{I}^0} = q$. Then, we repeatedly perform the following steps: given the current set of intervals $\mathcal{I}^j = \{I_1, \ldots, I_{s_j}\}$, we pair up consecutive intervals and form $I'_u = I_{2u-1} \cup I_{2u}$ for all $1 \le u \le \frac{s_j}{2}$. For each such pair of intervals, we compute the error incurred by I'_u with respect to the input function, i.e., $\mathrm{err}_q(I'_u)$. Using these error values, we find the new intervals I'_u with the $O(k)$ largest $\mathrm{err}_q(I'_u)$. For each interval with large error, we include its two components I_{2u-1} and I_{2u} in $\mathcal{I}^{j+1}$, i.e., we do *not* merge these two intervals in the current iteration. For the remaining intervals (i.e., the ones with smaller error), we include I'_u in $\mathcal{I}^{j+1}$, i.e., we merge the two subintervals. We repeat this process as long as $\mathcal{I}^j$ has more than $O(k)$ intervals. Our final $O(k)$-histogram is the flattening of q over the final set of intervals produced.

At a high level, our algorithm succeeds for the following reason: Let q^* be the optimal k-histogram approximation to q. Intuitively, we accumulate error beyond opt_k when we flatten an interval where q^* has a jump, since on these intervals we diverge from the optimal solution. However, while we may accidentally flatten an interval containing a jump of q^*, this mistake cannot contribute a large error because we only flatten intervals when the resulting error is small compared to the other merging candidates.

For a formal description of our algorithm, see the pseudocode given in Algorithm 1. In addition to the parameter k, our algorithm has two additional parameters that quantify trade-offs between the different objectives: (i) The parameter δ controls the trade-off between the approximation ratio achieved by our algorithm and the number of pieces in the output histogram. (ii) The parameter γ controls the trade-off between the running time and the number of pieces in the output histogram. For details regarding the parameters, see the analysis in the following subsection.

3.3 Analysis of Algorithm 1.

We begin our analysis by establishing the desired approximation guarantee.

THEOREM 3.3. *Let* $q : [n] \to \mathbb{R}$ *be an* s*-sparse function. Moreover, let* $\mathcal{I}$ *be the partition of* $[n]$ *returned by* CONSTRUCTHISTOGRAM(q, k, δ, γ). *Then*

$$|\mathcal{I}| \le \left(2 + \frac{2}{\delta}\right)k + \gamma \quad \text{and} \quad \|\bar{q}_{\mathcal{I}} - q\|_2 \le \sqrt{1+\delta}\cdot \mathrm{opt}_k ,$$

where $\mathrm{opt}_k = \min\|q' - q\|_2$ *and* q' *ranges over all* k*-histograms.*

PROOF. Let $\mathcal{I} = \{I_1, \ldots, I_{k'}\}$ be the partition of $[n]$ returned by CONSTRUCTHISTOGRAM. By construction, we have that $k' \le (2 + \frac{2}{\delta})k + \gamma$. Furthermore, let q^* be a k-histogram with optimal error, i.e., $\|q^* - q\|_2 = \mathrm{opt}_k$. We denote the corresponding partition of $[n]$ with $\mathcal{I}^* = \{I_1^*, \ldots, I_k^*\}$.

Note that we can decompose the error incurred by $\bar{q}_{\mathcal{I}}$ into the error on the individual intervals:

$$\|\bar{q}_{\mathcal{I}} - q\|_2^2 = \sum_{i=1}^{k'} \|(\bar{q}_{\mathcal{I}})_{I_i} - q_{I_i}\|_2^2 = \sum_{i=1}^{k'} \mathrm{err}_q(I_i) .$$

This enables us to analyze the error $\|\bar{q}_{\mathcal{I}} - q\|_2$ in two parts: (i) the intervals I_i which are fully contained in an interval of the optimal k-histogram I_j^*, and (ii) the intervals I_i that intersect at least two intervals I_j^* and I_{j+1}^*. The intervals in case (i) do not contain a "jump" of the optimal histogram q^* and hence our approximation on those intervals is at least as good as q^*. On the other hand, the intervals in case (ii) contain a jump of q^*, but we can bound the error from these intervals because our algorithm does not merge the intervals with large errors. We separately analyze the two cases.

Case (i). Let F be the set of intervals output by our algorithm that do not contain a "jump" of the best k-histogram q^*, i.e., $F = \{i \in [k'] \mid I_i \subseteq I_j^* \text{ for some } j \in [k]\}$. For each $i \in F$, we have defined the value of $\bar{q}_{\mathcal{I}}$ on I_i so that $\|(\bar{q}_{\mathcal{I}})_{I_i} - q_{I_i}\|_2$ is minimized among 1-histograms on I_i. Since q^* is also a 1-histogram on I_i, we have $\|(\bar{q}_{\mathcal{I}})_{I_i} - q_{I_i}\|_2 \le \|q^*_{I_i} - q_{I_i}\|_2$. Summing over all $i \in F$ gives

$$\begin{aligned} \sum_{i\in F} \|(\bar{q}_{\mathcal{I}})_{I_i} - q_{I_i}\|_2^2 &\le \sum_{i\in F} \|q^*_{I_i} - q_{I_i}\|_2^2 \\ &\le \|q^* - q\|_2^2 \\ &\le \mathrm{opt}_k^2 . \end{aligned} \tag{1}$$

Case (ii). We now consider the set of intervals containing a jump of the k-histogram q^*, i.e., $J = \{i \in [k'] \mid I_i \not\subseteq I_j^* \text{ for all } j \in [k]\}$. Since q^* is a k-histogram,

Algorithm 1 Approximating with histograms by merging.

1: **function** ConstructHistogram(q, k, δ, γ)
2: ▷ *We assume that q is given as the sorted set of nonzeros $\{(i_1, y_1), \ldots, (i_s, y_s)\}$ such that $y_j = q_{i_j}$.*
3: $J \leftarrow \bigcup_{j=1}^{j \leq s} \{i_j - 1, i_j, i_j + 1\}$
4: ▷ Set of relevant indices.
5: ▷ *Precompute partial sums for fast mean and error computation.*
6: $r_j \leftarrow \sum_{i_u \leq j} y_u$ for $j \in J$
7: $t_j \leftarrow \sum_{i_u \leq j} y_u^2$ for $j \in J$
8: ▷ *Initial histogram.*
9: Let $\mathcal{I}^0 \leftarrow \{I_1, \ldots, I_{s_0}\}$ be the initial partition of $[n]$ defined by the set J.
10: ▷ *Iterative greedy merging (we start with $j = 0$).*
11: **while** $|\mathcal{I}^j| > (2 + \frac{2}{\delta})k + \gamma$ **do**
12: Let s_j be the current number of intervals.
13: ▷ *Compute the errors for merging neighboring pairs of intervals.*
14: **for** $u \in \{1, 2, \ldots, \frac{s_j}{2}\}$ **do**
15: $e_u \leftarrow \mathrm{err}_q(I_{2u-1} \cup I_{2u})$
16: Let L be the set of u with the $(1 + \frac{1}{\delta})k$ largest e_u and M be the set of the remaining u.
17: $\mathcal{I}^{j+1} \leftarrow \bigcup_{u \in L} \{I_{2u-1}, I_{2u}\}$
18: ▷ Keep the intervals with large merging errors.
19: $\mathcal{I}^{j+1} \leftarrow \mathcal{I}^{j+1} \cup \{I_{2u-1} \cup I_{2u} \mid u \in M\}$
20: ▷ Merge the remaining intervals.
21: $j \leftarrow j + 1$
22: **return** $\mathcal{I}^j$

we have $|J| \leq k$. For each I_i with $i \in J$, there are two sub-cases: (a) I_i is one of the initial intervals in $\mathcal{I}^0$, (b) I_i was created in some iteration of the algorithm. In case (a), we clearly have $\|(\bar{q}_\mathcal{I})_{I_i} - q_{I_i}\|_2 = 0$, so we focus our attention on case (b).

Consider the iteration in which I_i was created. Since I_i is the result of merging two smaller intervals, the error $\mathrm{err}_q(I_i)$ was not among the $(1 + \frac{1}{\delta})k$ largest errors. Let L be the set of indices with the largest errors, so $\mathrm{err}_q(I_i) \leq \mathrm{err}_q(I_j)$ for all $j \in L$ (see line 16 of Alg. 1). At most k of the intervals in L can contain a jump of q^*, so at least $\frac{k}{\delta}$ intervals in L are contained in an interval in $\mathcal{I}^*$. Let L' be this set of intervals, i.e., $L' = \{j \in L \mid I_j \subseteq I_u^* \text{ for some } u \in [k]\}$. Using a similar optimality argument as in Case (i), we have that

$$\sum_{j \in L'} \mathrm{err}_q(I_j) \;=\; \sum_{j \in L'} \|(\bar{q}_\mathcal{I})_{I_j} - q_{I_j}\|_2^2 \;\leq\; \mathrm{opt}_k^2 .$$

Since $|L'| \geq \frac{k}{\delta}$, this implies that

$$\min_{j \in L'} \mathrm{err}_q(I_j) \leq \frac{\delta}{k} \mathrm{opt}_k^2 .$$

Therefore, we have that $\mathrm{err}_q(I_i) \leq \frac{\delta}{k}\mathrm{opt}_k^2$ because $\mathrm{err}_q(I_i)$ was not among the largest errors. Hence we have:

$$\sum_{i \in J} \|(\bar{q}_\mathcal{I})_{I_i} - q_{I_i}\|_2^2 \;\leq\; |J| \cdot \frac{\delta}{k}\mathrm{opt}_k^2 \;\leq\; \delta \cdot \mathrm{opt}_k^2 . \qquad (2)$$

Since $F \cup J = [k']$, we can now combine Eq. (1) and Eq. (2) to get our final approximation guarantee:

$$\|\bar{q}_\mathcal{I} - q\|_2^2 \;=\; \sum_{i \in F} \|(\bar{q}_\mathcal{I})_{I_i} - q_{I_i}\|_2^2 + \sum_{i \in J} \|(\bar{q}_\mathcal{I})_{I_i} - q_{I_i}\|_2^2$$
$$\leq\; \mathrm{opt}_k^2 + \delta \cdot \mathrm{opt}_k^2 \;=\; (1 + \delta) \cdot \mathrm{opt}_k^2 . \quad \square$$

Next, we consider the running time of our algorithm. Intuitively, each iteration of the merging algorithm takes time linear in the current number of intervals by using the precomputed partial sums (see line 7 of Alg. 1) and a linear-time selection algorithm [CSRL01, p. 189]. Moreover, every iteration of the merging algorithm reduces the number of intervals by a constant factor as long as the number of intervals is larger than $(1 + \frac{1}{\delta})k$. Therefore, the total running time of our algorithm is bounded by the time complexity of the first iteration, which is $O(s)$. We show this more formally below.

Theorem 3.4. *Let $q : [n] \to \mathbb{R}$ be an s-sparse function. Then* ConstructHistogram(q, k, δ, γ) *runs in time*

$$O\left(s \,+\, k\left(1 + \frac{1}{\delta}\right) \log\left(\frac{(1 + 1/\delta)k}{\gamma}\right)\right) .$$

Proof. Consider J, r_j, and t_j as defined in ConstructHistogram. Clearly, all three quantities can be computed in $O(s)$ time. Moreover, precomputing the partial sums allows us to compute $\mathrm{err}_q(I)$ in constant time if the endpoints of I are contained in J. In particular, let $I = \{a, a+1, \ldots, b\}$ with $a, b \in J$. Then

$$\mathrm{err}_q(I) = \sum_{i \in I} q(i)^2 - \frac{1}{|I|}\left(\sum_{i \in I} q(i)\right)^2$$
$$= t_b - t_a + y_a^2 - \frac{1}{b - a + 1}(r_b - r_a + y_a)^2 ,$$

which we can evaluate in constant time. Since our algorithm only constructs intervals with endpoints in the set J, this allows us to quickly evaluate all instances of err_q over the course of the algorithm.

Next, we show that for all j, the $(j+1)$-th iteration of the loop in ConstructHistogram can be performed in time $O(s_j)$ (recall $s_j = |\mathcal{I}^j|$ is the number of intervals active in the j-th iteration). As outlined above, the e_u can be computed in $O(s_j)$ total time. Moreover, we can find the set L containing the $(1+1/\delta)k$-th largest e_u in linear time: first, we find the $(1+1/\delta)k$-th largest single e_u using a linear time selection algorithm [CSRL01, p. 189]. Then, we can find all elements in L in one further pass over the e_u, checking whether the current e_u is larger than the threshold value of the $(1+1/\delta)k$-th largest single e_u. After this, we can easily create the set $\mathcal{I}^{j+1}$ in linear time and hence the entire iteration can be performed in time $O(s_j)$.

Moreover, for all $j \geq 1$ until we terminate, we have that

$$s_{j+1} = \frac{s_j - (2+2/\delta)k}{2} + \left(2 + \frac{2}{\delta}\right) k = \frac{s_j + (2+2/\delta)k}{2} . \quad (3)$$

The first equality follows by construction, since in each iteration of the loop, we keep $(2+\frac{2}{\delta})k$ intervals from the previous iteration and merge the remaining pairs into one new interval per pair. Starting with $s_0 = s$, and applying Equation 3 j times, we obtain that for all j until the algorithm terminates,

$$s_j = 2^{-j}s + (1 - 2^{-j}) \left(2 + \frac{2}{\delta}\right) k . \quad (4)$$

In particular, this implies that the algorithm terminates after at most $\lambda = \log(s/\gamma)$ iterations. Let $\lambda' = \log((2+2/\delta)k+s) - \log((2+2/\delta)k)$. By a straightforward manipulation, we see that for all $j \leq \lambda'$, we have $2^{-j}s \geq (1-2^{-j})(2+2/\delta)k$, and for all $j > \lambda'$, the opposite direction holds. By the arguments above, it follows that the total runtime of ConstructHistogram(q, k, δ, γ) is $O(\sum_{j=1}^{\lambda} s_j)$. The proof follows from the following sequence of inequalities:

$$\begin{aligned}
\sum_{j=0}^{\lambda} s_j &= \sum_{j=0}^{\lambda'} s_j + \sum_{j=\lambda'+1}^{\lambda} s_j \\
&\leq 2\sum_{j=0}^{\lambda'} 2^{-j}s + 2 \sum_{j=\lambda'+1}^{\lambda} (1-2^{-j}) \left(2+\frac{2}{\delta}\right) k \\
&\leq 4s + (\lambda - \lambda') \left(2 + \frac{2}{\delta}\right) k \\
&\leq 4s + \log\left(\frac{(2+2/\delta)k}{\gamma}\right) \left(2+\frac{2}{\delta}\right) k , \quad (5)
\end{aligned}$$

where the last line is obtained by expanding the expression for $\lambda - \lambda'$ and using the fact $(2+2/\delta)k \geq 0$. □

Thus, we have:

Corollary 3.1. *For any constant $c > 0$, ConstructHistogram$(q, k, \delta, c(2+2/\delta)k)$ runs in time $O(s)$ and returns a $(1+c)(2+2/\delta)k$-histogram.*

Proof. Following the analysis of Theorem 3.4, when we plug in $\gamma = c(2+2/\delta)k$ into Equation 5, we get that

$$\sum_{j=0}^{\lambda} s_j \leq 4s + \log\left(\frac{1}{c}\right)\left(2+\frac{2}{\delta}\right) k.$$

We can assume that $(2+2/\delta)k \leq s$ since otherwise the input $\mathcal{I}^0$ is already $(2+2/\delta)k$-flat. Hence, we have $\sum_{j=0}^{\lambda} s_j = O(s)$ which completes the proof. □

With the parameterization in Corollary 3.1, the algorithm runs in linear time for *all* values of k. The reason for this parameterization is that the merging algorithm makes increasingly slower progress as the number of intervals decreases (and hence the fraction of intervals which are not merged increases). In fact, for the regime $k = O(\frac{s}{\log s})$, the algorithm runs in time $O(s)$ for any $\gamma \geq 1$.

3.4 Multi-scale Histogram Construction.

Our previously described algorithm (Algorithm 1) requires a priori knowledge of the parameter k, i.e., the desired number of intervals in the output histogram approximation. We show that a variant of Algorithm 1, which we call ConstructHierarchicalHistogram, works *without* knowledge of k and produces good histogram approximations for all values of $k \geq 1$. The guarantees for the running time, number of histogram intervals, and approximation error are similar to those of Algorithm 1.

As before, our algorithm works for arbitrary s-sparse functions. We start with a histogram consisting of $O(s)$ intervals and reduce the number of intervals by a fourth in each iteration of the algorithm. At any stage, suppose the intervals are $I_1, \ldots, I_{s'}$. As before, we pair the intervals as I_{2i+1}, I_{2i} and compute the approximation errors of the merged intervals. We keep *half* of the pairs corresponding to the *largest* errors and merge the remaining $\frac{s'}{2}$ pairs of intervals. This reduces the number of intervals from s' to $\frac{3s'}{4}$. A detailed pseudocode for this variant of the merging algorithm is given in Alg. 2. We have:

Theorem 3.5. *Let $q : [n] \to \mathbb{R}$ be an s-sparse function. Moreover, let $\mathcal{I}^0, \mathcal{I}^1, \ldots, \mathcal{I}^L$ be the partitions of $[n]$ returned by* ConstructHierarchicalHistogram(q). *Then given any $1 \leq k \leq s$, there is an $\mathcal{I}^j$ with $|\mathcal{I}^j| \leq 8k$ and*

$$\|\bar{q}_{\mathcal{I}^j} - q\|_2 \leq 2 \cdot \mathrm{opt}_k ,$$

where $\mathrm{opt}_k = \min \|q' - q\|_2$ and q' ranges over all k-histograms. Moreover, the algorithm runs in $O(s)$ time.

We remark that a *single* run of Algorithm 2 produces a hierarchical histogram that achieves a constant-factor approximation guarantee for *any* target number of histogram pieces.

Proof of Theorem 3.5. We first prove the claimed running time of our algorithm. In each iteration, the number of intervals reduces by a fourth, and the number of initial intervals is $O(m)$. Moreover, we can output $\mathcal{I}^j$

Algorithm 2 Learning histograms by hierarchical merging.

function ConstructHierarchicalHistogram(q)
    ▷ *We assume that q is given as the sorted set of nonzeros $\{(i_1, y_1), \ldots, (i_s, y_s)\}$ such that $y_j = q_{i_j}$.*
    ▷ *Set of relevant indices.*
    $J \leftarrow \bigcup_{j=1}^{j \leq s} \{i_j - 1, i_j, i_j + 1\}$
    ▷ *Initial histogram.*
    Let $\mathcal{I}^0 \leftarrow \{I_1, \ldots, I_{s_0}\}$ be the initial partition of $[n]$ defined by the set J.
    ▷ *Iterative greedy merging.*
    $j \leftarrow 0$
    while $|\mathcal{I}^j| \geq 8$ **do**
        Let s_j be the current number of intervals.
        ▷ *Compute the errors for merging neighboring pairs of intervals.*
        for $u \in \{1, 2, \ldots, \frac{s_j}{2}\}$ **do**
            $e_u \leftarrow \mathrm{err}_q(I_{2u-1} \cup I_{2u})$
        Let L be the set of u with the $\frac{s_j}{4}$ largest e_u and M be the set of the remaining u.
        ▷ *Keep the intervals with the large merging errors.*
        $\mathcal{I}^{j+1} \leftarrow \bigcup_{u \in L} \{I_{2u-1}, I_{2u}\}$
        ▷ *Merge the remaining intervals.*
        $\mathcal{I}^{j+1} \leftarrow \mathcal{I}^{j+1} \cup \{I_{2u-1} \cup I_{2u} \mid u \in M\}$
        $j \leftarrow j + 1$
    return $\mathcal{I}^0, \mathcal{I}^1, \ldots, \mathcal{I}^j$

in each iteration in time linear in the current number of intervals. Therefore, the total running time satisfies,

$$T(s) = T\left(\frac{3s}{4}\right) + O(s).$$

We start with m steps, and therefore the algorithm runs in time $O(m)$.

We now turn our attention to the approximation guarantee. Suppose we want to match the approximation error of a k-histogram. Consider the iteration of our algorithm in which the number of intervals drops below $8k$ for the first time. We output the corresponding partition $\mathcal{I}^j$, which by definition satisifies $|I_j| \leq 8k$. For the approximation error, we follow the proof of Theorem 3.3: we consider the set of intervals that contain a "jump" of an optimal k-histogram approximation q^*. Since there were at least $8k$ intervals before this iteration, we form $4k$ pairs of intervals and do not merge at least $2k$ pairs of intervals with the largest errors. At least k of those intervals do not contain a jump and thus contribute an error of at most opt_k. This also holds for any previous iteration of the algorithm. Therefore, each interval containing a jump contributes at most $\frac{\mathrm{opt}_k}{k}$ error, and the total contribution of all intervals containing a jump is at most opt_k. Combined with the contribution from intervals containing no jump (also at most opt_k in total), the final approximation error is $2 \cdot \mathrm{opt}_k$. □

4. A Generalized Merging Algorithm and Fitting Piecewise Polynomials

In this section we adapt Algorithm 1 to work for more general classes of functions, in particular, piecewise polynomials. These results establish Theorem 2.3.

4.1 An Oracle Version of Algorithm 1.

Note that Algorithm 1 relies only on the following property of piecewise constant functions: given an interval I and a function f, we can efficiently find the constant function with minimal ℓ_2 error to f on I. We can extend this idea to fit more general types of functions (for example, the class of piecewise polynomials.) We formalize this intuition in the following definitions.

Definition 4.1 (Projection Oracle). *Let $\mathcal{F}$ be any set of functions from $[n]$ to $\mathbb{R}$. $\mathcal{O}$ is a* projection oracle *for $\mathcal{F}$ if it takes as input an interval I and a function $f : I \to \mathbb{R}$, and outputs a function $g^* \in \mathcal{F}$ and a value v such that*

$$v = \|g_I^* - f\|_2 \leq \inf_{g \in \mathcal{F}_J} \|g_I - f\|_2 .$$

Definition 4.2. *A function $f : [n] \to \mathbb{R}$ is a k-piecewise $\mathcal{F}$-function if there exists a partition of $[n]$ into k disjoint intervals $\{I_1, \ldots, I_k\}$ so that for each i, $f_{I_i} = (g_i)_{I_i}$, for some $g_i \in \mathcal{F}$.*

For example, suppose $\mathcal{F}$ is the set of all constant functions on $[n]$. Then there is a trivial projection oracle $\mathcal{O}$ for $\mathcal{F}$: for any function $f : I \to \mathbb{R}$, the optimal flat approximator to f is the function which is constantly

$\mu_f(I)$ (as we argued in Section 3.2). The error of this approximation is $\text{err}_f(I)$ and is also easy to calculate. Thus, one way of describing Algorithm 1 is as follows: given input function q, in each iteration, we compute the best estimator for q from $\mathcal{F}$ using $\mathcal{O}$ on each merged interval and its associated error. Subsequently, we merge all intervals except those with top $O(k)$ errors, and repeat the process.

The idea of the generalized merging algorithm is the following. For general classes of functions $\mathcal{F}$, at each iteration, we first call the corresponding projection oracle $\mathcal{O}$ over consecutive pairs of intervals to find the best fit in $\mathcal{F}$ over this larger interval. We also calculate the ℓ_2-error of the approximation using $\mathcal{O}$. As in Algorithm 1, we merge all intervals except those with large errors. This general algorithm, which we call
ConstructGeneralHistogram($q, k, \delta, \gamma, \mathcal{O}$), is conceptually similar to Algorithm 1 except that we use a projection oracle instead of a flattening step. Assuming the existence of such an oracle, we can formally state our main result for approximation with k-piecewise $\mathcal{F}$-functions.

Theorem 4.1. *Let $q : [n] \to \mathbb{R}$ be s-sparse. Let $\mathcal{F}$ be any set of functions on $[n]$ to $\mathbb{R}$ as above, and let $\mathcal{O}$ be a projection oracle for $\mathcal{F}$ which, given any s'-sparse function q' on a subinterval of I, runs in time $O(\alpha s')$. Then* ConstructGeneralHistogram($q, k, \delta, \gamma, \mathcal{O}$) *runs in time*

$$O\left(\alpha\left(s + k\left(1+\frac{1}{\delta}\right)\log\left(\frac{(1+1/\delta)k}{\gamma}\right)\right)\right)$$

and outputs a k'-piecewise $\mathcal{F}$-function $f : [n] \to \mathbb{R}$ where

$$k' \leq \left(2+\frac{2}{\delta}\right)k+\gamma$$

and which satisfies $\|f - q\|_2 \leq (1+\delta)\cdot\|f' - q\|_2$ where f' ranges over all k-piecewise $\mathcal{F}$-functions.

The proof of Theorem 4.1 is a simple adaptation of the proof of Theorem 3.3.

4.2 Finding the best fit polynomial on a subinterval.

We now specialize Theorem 4.1 to piecewise polynomial approximation. Let us first restate this problem in the terminology introduced above. Fix an interval $I = [a, b] \subseteq [n]$. It will be convenient to represent functions $w : I \to \mathbb{R}$ as vectors $v = (v_1, \ldots, v_{b-a+1})$, where $v_i = w(a+i-1)$. For a fixed interval I, the vector representation of a function is uniquely defined. Hence, throughout this section we will blur the distinction between a function and its vector representation.

We define $\mathcal{P}_d(I)$ to be the set of $v \in \mathbb{R}^{|I|}$ such that there exists a degree-d polynomial $p : \mathbb{R} \to \mathbb{R}$ such that for all $i \in I$, $v_i = p(a+i-1)$, and $\mathcal{P}_d = \mathcal{P}_d([n])$. We construct an efficient procedure $\text{FitPoly}_d(I, q)$ (see Algorithm 3 in the appendix) that takes as input an interval $I \subseteq [n]$ and a function $q : I \to \mathbb{R}$, and finds the best approximation of the function within the interval with a degree-d polynomial. In particular, we will prove:

Theorem 4.2. *There exists a projection oracle* FitPoly_d *for $\mathcal{P}_d$, which, given an interval I and an s-sparse function $q : I \to \mathbb{R}$, runs in time $O(d^2 s)$.*

Theorems 4.1 and 4.2 give our desired result, which we now state for completeness:

Corollary 4.1. *Let $q : [n] \to \mathbb{R}$ be s-sparse. Then,* ConstructGeneralHistogram($q, k, \delta, \gamma, \text{FitPoly}_d$) *runs in time*

$$O\left(d^2\left(s + k\left(1+\frac{1}{\delta}\right)\log\left(\frac{(1+1/\delta)k}{\gamma}\right)\right)\right),$$

and outputs a t-piecewise degree-d polynomial function $f : I \to R$, such that $t \leq \left(2+\frac{2}{\delta}\right)k+\gamma$ and $\|f - q\|_2 \leq (1+\delta)\cdot\|f' - q\|_2$ where f' ranges over all k-piecewise degree-d polynomials.

Note that, as in Corollary 3.1, for a natural choice of parameters δ and γ, the running time becomes $O(d^2 s)$. It remains to prove Theorem 4.2, which we defer to the appendix. The core of algorithm is a fast projection onto the space of degree-d polynomials via the orthonormal basis of discrete Chebyshev polynomials [Sze89]. The key technical ingredient is a subroutine which evaluates these basis polynomials at s points in time $O(d^2 s)$. This compares favorably to the $O(d^\omega s)$ time algorithm given in [GKS06] (where ω is the matrix multiplication constant).

5. Experimental Evaluation

In order to evaluate the empirical performance of our algorithm, we conduct several experiments on real and synthetic data. As with our analysis, we split the empirical evaluation into two parts: "offline" histogram approximation (where we assume that the full data distribution is explicitly present), and histogram approximation from sampled data. All experiments in this section were conducted on a laptop computer from 2010, using an Intel Core i7 CPU with 2.66 GHz clock frequency, 4 MB of cache, and 8 GB of RAM. We used the Debian GNU/Linux distribution and **g++** 4.8 as compiler with the `-O3` flag (all algorithms were implemented in C++). All reported running times are averaged over at least 10 trials (and up to 10^4 trials for algorithms with a fast running time).

5.1 Histogram approximation.

Due to the large amount of prior work on histogram approximation, we focus on the most relevant algorithms in our comparison. Moreover, we study the performance in the case of *dense* input, i.e., we make no assumptions about the number of nonzeros, since most prior algorithms work in this setting. We denote the size of the dense input with n. Note that our merging algorithm (Alg. 1) is directly applicable to dense inputs, which can be represented as an n-sparse function. We run the following histogram approximation schemes:

`exactdp` An exact dynamic program with running time $O(n^2k)$ [JKM+98].

`dual` A variant of the linear time algorithm for the dual problem given in [JKM+98]. Since the target error is not known in the primal version of the problem, this variant incurs an extra logarithmic factor due to a binary search over opt.

`merging` Our algorithm as outlined in Alg. 1. We use parameters $\delta = 1{,}000$ and $\gamma = 1.0$ so that our algorithm produces a histogram with $2k+1$ pieces.

`merging2` The same algorithm as `merging`, but using $k' = \frac{k}{2}$ as input. Hence the resulting histogram has $k + 1$ pieces.

`fastmerging` A variant of Alg. 1 with a more aggressive merging scheme that merges larger groups of intervals in the early iterations.[3] We also use $\delta = 1{,}000$ and $\gamma = 1.0$ for fastmerging.

`fastmerging2` The same algorithm as `fastmerging`, but using $k' = \frac{k}{2}$ as input. Similar to `merging2`, the resulting histogram has $k + 1$ pieces.

We run the algorithms on two synthetic and one real-world data set with input sizes ranging from $n = 1{,}000$ to 16,384 (see Fig. 1). We have chosen the same real-world data set as in [GKS06] so that our results are comparable to the results given there. For the `hist` and `poly` data sets, we run the algorithms with $k = 10$. For the `dow'` dataset, we use $k = 50$.

Table 1 contains detailed results for our experiments. Our algorithms are several orders of magnitude faster than the exact dynamic program. Interestingly, our algorithms also achieve a very good approximation ratio. Note that for `merging` and `fastmerging`, the approximation ratio is *better* than 1.0 on the `poly` and `dow` data sets. The reason is that the algorithms produce histograms with $2k+1$ pieces, which makes a better approximation than that achieved by `exactdp` possible. In particular, the empirical results are significantly better than those predicted by our theoretical analysis, which only guarantees a very large constant factor for $\delta = 1{,}000$. Further, both the `merging2` and `fastmerging2` variants still achieve a good approximation ratio while using only $k + 1$ pieces in the output histogram.

Compared to `dual`, all variants of our algorithm achieve a better approximation ratio (by a factor close to 1.75 on the `dow` data set). Moreover, the `fastmerging` variants are roughly ten times faster than the `dual` algorithm on the two larger data sets.

The fastest algorithm in [GKS06] is AHIST-L-Δ, which achieves an approximation ratio of about 1.003 for the `dow` data set with $n = 16{,}384$ and $k = 50$. This approximation ratio is better than `merging2` and `fastmerging2`, but worse than `merging` and `fastmerging` (note however that AHIST-L-Δ uses exactly k pieces in the output histogram). All of our algorithms are significantly faster: the reported running time of AHIST-L-Δ on `dow` is larger than one second, which is more than 1,000 times larger than the running time of our algorithms. While the running times are not directly comparable due to different CPUs and compilers, a comparison of running times of `exactdp` in our experiments with those in [GKS06] shows that our speedup due to CPU and compiler is around 3×. Even assuming a generous 10×, our algorithms are still more than two orders of magnitude faster than AHIST-L-Δ.

[3]One can show that with a more aggressive merging, the `fastmerging` algorithm performs only $O(\log\log n)$ rounds of merging, as opposed to $O(\log n)$ as in the "binary" merging algorithm given in Alg. 1. However, the total running time is determined by the first round of merging and remains $O(n)$.

5.2 Histogram approximation from samples.

In addition to offline histogram approximation, we also study the performance of our algorithms for the histogram learning problem. We use the same data sets as in Figure 1, but normalize them to form a probability distribution. Due to the slow running time of `exactdp`, we also subsample the `poly` and `dow` data sets by a factor of 4 and 16 respectively (using uniformly spaced samples) so that all data sets have a support of size roughly 1,000. We call the resulting data sets `hist'`, `poly'`, and `dow'`, and use the same values of k as in the offline histogram approximation experiments.

Figure 2 shows the results of the histogram learning experiments. In order to reduce clutter in the presentation of our results, we only perform sampling experiments with the `exactdp`, `merging`, and `merging2` algorithms. Our histogram approximation algorithms demonstrate very good empirical performance and often achieve a better approximation error than `exactdp`. The results indicate that the additional time spent on constructing an exact histogram fit to the empirical distribution does not lead to a better approximation to the true underlying distribution.

Acknowledgements.

The authors would like to thank Piotr Indyk for helpful discussions. I.D. was supported by a Marie Curie CIG, EPSRC grant EP/L021749/1, and a SICSA grant. J.A., C.H., and L.S. were supported by a grant from the MIT-Shell Energy Initiative. J.L. was supported by NSF grant CCF-1217921 and DOE grant DE-SC0008923.

6. References

[BY02] Z. Bar-Yossef. *The Complexity of Massive Data Set Computations*. PhD thesis, University of California, Berkeley, 2002.

[CD14] G. Cormode and N. Duffield. Sampling for big data: A tutorial. In *ACM KDD*, 2014.

[CDSS14a] S. Chan, I. Diakonikolas, R. Servedio, and X. Sun. Efficient density estimation via piecewise polynomial approximation. In *STOC*, pages 604–613, 2014.

[CDSS14b] S. Chan, I. Diakonikolas, R. Servedio, and X. Sun. Near-optimal density estimation in near-linear time using variable-width histograms. In *NIPS*, pages 1844–1852, 2014.

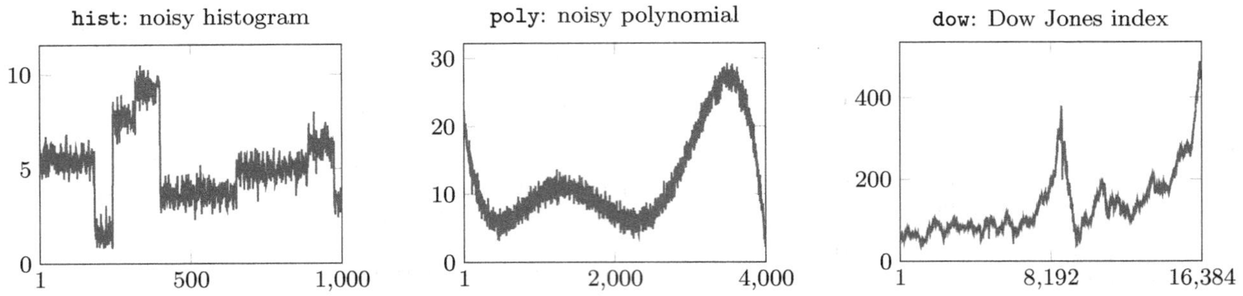

Figure 1: Data sets for the offline histogram approximation experiments. (left) `hist` is a histogram consisting of 10 pieces contaminated with Gaussian noise ($n = 1000$). (middle) `poly` is a degree 5 polynomial, also contaminated with Gaussian noise ($n = 4000$). (right) `dow` is a time series of Dow-Jones Industrial Average (DJIA) daily closing values ($n = 16384$).

		exactdp	merging	merging2	fastmerging	fastmerging2	dual
hist	Error (ℓ_2)	16.1	16.4	16.6	17.0	21.5	25.8
	Error (relative)	**1.00**	**1.02**	**1.03**	**1.06**	**1.34**	**1.60**
	Time (milliseconds)	55.391	0.038	0.037	0.020	0.014	0.108
	Time (relative)	**3,910**	**2.7**	**2.6**	**1.4**	**1.0**	**7.6**
poly	Error (ℓ_2)	105.1	85.9	111.6	85.6	111.7	124.0
	Error (relative)	**1.00**	**0.82**	**1.06**	**0.81**	**1.06**	**1.18**
	Time (milliseconds)	858.064	0.112	0.112	0.048	0.041	0.446
	Time (relative)	**20,924**	**2.7**	**2.7**	**1.2**	**1.0**	**10.9**
dow	Error (ℓ_2)	904.0	733.1	1,046.1	727.5	1,079.1	1,838.1
	Error (relative)	**1.00**	**0.81**	**1.16**	**0.80**	**1.19**	**2.03**
	Time (milliseconds)	73576.921	0.510	0.478	0.205	0.173	1.849
	Time (relative)	**425,540**	**3.0**	**2.8**	**1.2**	**1.0**	**10.7**

Table 1: Results of the algorithms on the three data sets in Fig. 1. The relative errors are reported as ratios compared to the error achieved by `exactdp`. For the relative running times, the baseline is `fastmerging2`.

[CGHJ12] G. Cormode, M. Garofalakis, P. Haas, and C. Jermaine. Synopses for massive data: Samples, histograms, wavelets, sketches. *Foundations and Trends in Databases*, 2012.

[Che66] E. Cheney. *Introduction to Approximation Theory.* McGraw-Hill, New York, New York, 1966.

[CMN98] S. Chaudhuri, R. Motwani, and V. Narasayya. Random sampling for histogram construction: How much is enough? In *ACM SIGMOD*, 1998.

[CSRL01] T. Cormen, C. Stein, R. Rivest, and C. Leiserson. *Introduction to Algorithms.* 2nd edition, 2001.

[GGI+02] A. Gilbert, S. Guha, P. Indyk, Y. Kotidis, S. Muthukrishnan, and M. Strauss. Fast, small-space algorithms for approximate histogram maintenance. In *STOC*, 2002.

[GKS06] S. Guha, N. Koudas, and K. Shim. Approximation and streaming algorithms for histogram construction problems. *ACM Trans. Database Syst.*, 2006.

[GMP97] P. Gibbons, Y. Matias, and V. Poosala. Fast incremental maintenance of approximate histograms. In *VLDB*, 1997.

[GSW04] S. Guha, K. Shim, and J. Woo. REHIST: Relative error histogram construction algorithms. In *VLDB*, 2004.

[ILR12] P. Indyk, R. Levi, and R. Rubinfeld. Approximating and Testing k-Histogram Distributions in Sub-linear Time. In *PODS*, 2012. Corrected version available as ECCC TR11-171.

[IP95] Y. Ioannidis and V. Poosala. Balancing histogram optimality and practicality for query result size estimation. In *ACM SIGMOD*, 1995.

[JKM+98] H. Jagadish, N. Koudas, S. Muthukrishnan, V. Poosala, K. Sevcik, and T. Suel. Optimal histograms with quality guarantees. In *VLDB*, 1998.

[Koo80] R. Kooi. *The Optimization of Queries in Relational Databases.* PhD thesis, 1980.

[LCY00] L. Le Cam and G. L. Yang. *Asymptotics in statistics: some basic concepts.* Springer, 2000.

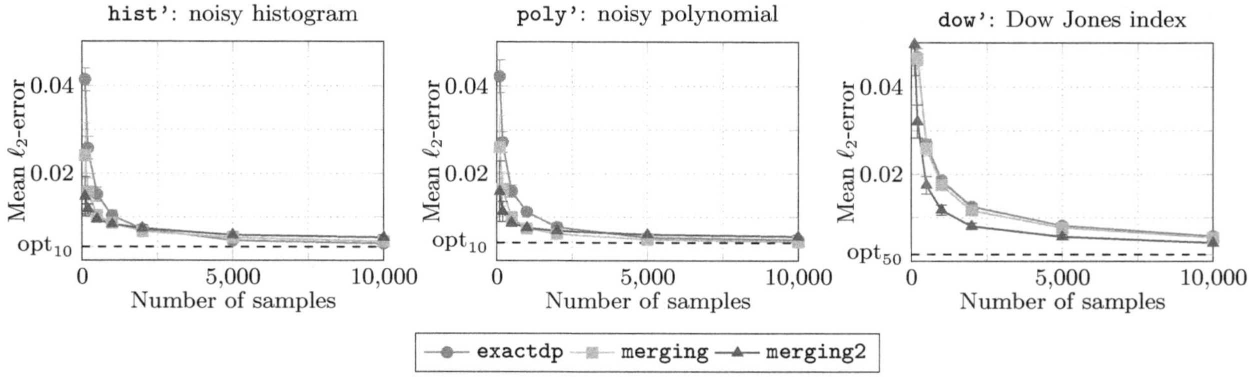

Figure 2: Resuls of the histogram learning experiments for three different data sets (see Figure 1). Every data point is the mean error over 20 trials and the error bars indicate one standard deviation. The opt_k values are the approximation error of the best k-histogram fit to the underlying distribution.

[McD89] C. McDiarmid. On the method of bounded differences. In *Surveys in Combinatorics 1989*, pages 148–188. London Mathematical Society Lecture Notes, 1989.

[SHKT97] C. J. Stone, M. H. Hansen, C. Kooperberg, and Y. K. Truong. Polynomial splines and their tensor products in extended linear modeling: 1994 wald memorial lecture. *Ann. Statist.*, 25(4):1371–1470, 1997.

[Sil86] B. Silverman. *Density Estimation.* Chapman and Hall, London, 1986.

[Sze89] G. Szegö. *Orthogonal Polynomials*, volume XXIII of *American Mathematical Society Colloquium Publications.* A.M.S, 1989.

[TGIK02] N. Thaper, S. Guha, P. Indyk, and N. Koudas. Dynamic multidimensional histograms. In *ACM SIGMOD*, 2002.

[WN07] R. Willett and R. Nowak. Multiscale poisson intensity and density estimation. *IEEE Trans. Info. Theory*, 2007.

[WW83] E. J. Wegman and I. W. Wright. Splines in statistics. *Journal of the American Statistical Association*, 78(382):pp. 351–365, 1983.

APPENDIX

A. Proofs and Description of FitPoly$_d$

We now describe FITPOLY$_d$, and prove Theorem 4.2. In particular, we show how to perform the projection of q onto $\mathcal{P}_d(I)$ in time $O(d^2 s)$, where s is the sparsity of q.

Fix an interval $[a, b] = I \subseteq [n]$. Then, $\mathcal{P}_d(I)$, the class of all polynomials of degree at most d, is a $(d+1)$-dimensional linear subspace spanned by the vectors $x_0, \ldots, x_d$ where x_j is the vector associated with the function $f_j(x) = x^j$, that is, $x_j = (a^j, (a+1)^j, \ldots, b^j)$. By the linear transform $x \to x - a$, each x_j can be written as a linear combination of the vectors $y_j = (0^j, 1^j, 2^j, \ldots, (|I| - 1)^j)$. We henceforth assume that the interval of interest is $I = [0, b-1]$.

Now the problem of finding the best-fit polynomial to q becomes equivalent to finding $v \in \mathcal{P}_d(I)$ that minimizes $\|v - q\|_2^2$. This is exactly the problem of finding the projection of q onto the vector space $\mathcal{P}_d(I)$. We do so by appealing to the theory of discrete orthogonal polynomials.

DEFINITION A.1. *The* discrete Chebyshev, *or* Gram *polynomial of degree r for the interval $[0, \ldots, b-1]$ is the polynomial given by*

$$t_r(y) = \frac{1}{W_r} r! \cdot \Delta^r \left(\binom{y}{r} \binom{y-b}{r} \right) \tag{6}$$

where Δ is the forward difference operator on functions given by $\Delta f(x) \stackrel{def}{=} f(x+1) - f(x)$, $\binom{x}{r}$ is the generalized binomial coefficient, and

$$W_r = \frac{b \cdot (b^2 - 1)^{\underline{r^2}}}{(2r+1)}$$

where $y^{\underline{r}} \stackrel{def}{=} y(y-1)\ldots(y-r+1)$ denotes the rth falling power.

It is well known [Sze89] that $\{t_r\}_{r=0}^d$ forms an orthonormal basis for $\mathcal{P}$. Thus, for any function q, the projection of q onto $\mathcal{P}_d(I)$ is given by $q(x) = \sum_{r=0}^d a_r t_r(x)$ where

$$a_r = \sum_{i=0}^{b-1} q(i) \cdot t_r(i), \tag{7}$$

and by Parseval's theorem, the error of the projection is given by $\|q\|_2^2 - \sum_{r=0}^d a_r^2$. FITPOLY$_d$ computes a_r and the error using these formulas. The formal pseudocode is given in Algorithm 3.

The crucial subroutine is EVALUATEGRAM(x, d, b), which compute the values $t_r(x)$ for $r = 0, \ldots, d$, for any fixed $x \in [0, b-1]$, in time $O(d^2)$. The formal pseudocode for EVALUATEGRAM(x, d, b) is given in Algorithm 4.

LEMMA A.1. EVALUATEGRAM(x, d, b) *computes $t_0(x), \ldots, t_d(x)$ in time $O(d^2)$.*

Algorithm 3 Projecting an s-sparse vector on to $\mathcal{P}_d([0, b-1])$.

function FITPOLY$_d(q, b)$
  ▷ *We assume that q is given as the sorted set of nonzeros $\{(i_1, y_1), \ldots, (i_s, y_s)\}$ such that $y_j = q_{i_j}$.*
  ▷ *Set of relevant indices.*
  ▷ *Compute values of $t_r(i)$ for $i = i_1, \ldots, i_s$*
  $v_i \leftarrow$ EVALUATEGRAM(i, d, b) for $i = i_1, \ldots, i_s$
  ▷ *Compute inner product of q with t_r for all $r = 0, \ldots, d$*
  for $r = 0, \ldots, d$ **do**
    $a_r \leftarrow \sum_{j=1}^{s} y_j v_{i_j}(r)$
  ▷ *Compute the error of the projection*
  $\text{err} = \sum_{j=1}^{s} y_j^2 - \sum_{r=0}^{d} a_r^2$
  return $([a_0, \ldots, a_r], \text{err})$

PROOF. EVALUATEGRAM(x, d, b) computes the quantities $t_0(x), \ldots, t_d(x)$ as follows. For fixed r, we can evaluate $\binom{y}{r}$ for $y = x, x+1, \ldots, x+r$ in time $O(d)$ since $\binom{y}{r} = y^{\underline{r}}/r!$. We can evaluate $r!$ and $x^{\underline{r}}$, for all $r \leq d$, in time $O(d)$. Moreover, given $y^{\underline{r}}$, in constant time we can compute $(y+1)^{\underline{r}} = (y+1) \cdot y^{\underline{r}}/(y-r+1)$. Thus we can evaluate $r!$ and $y^{\underline{r}}$ in time $O(d)$ for $y = x, x+1, \ldots, x+r$, and $\binom{y}{r}$ for $y = x, x+1, \ldots, x+r$ and for all r in time $O(d^2)$. Similarly, we can find $\binom{y-b}{r}$ for $y = x, x+1, \ldots, x+r$ and for all r in time $O(d^2)$. It is straightforward to compute all the $(b^2-1)^{\underline{r^2}}$ in time $O(d^2)$ from the formula, and thus we can compute all the W_r in time $O(d^2)$ as well.

Therefore, we can compute the values of $\nu_r(y) := \binom{y}{r}\binom{y-b}{r}$ at $y = x, \ldots, x+r$, $r!$, and W_r for all r simultaneously in total time $O(d^2)$. Through similar methods as those described above, we can also compute $\binom{r}{j}$ for all $0 \leq r \leq d$ and for all $0 \leq j \leq r$ in time $O(d^2)$. Given that we know these values, we conclude that we can evaluate $t_r(x)$ in time $O(d^2)$, since for any x, we have

$$\begin{aligned} t_r(x) &= \frac{1}{W_r} r! \cdot \Delta^r\left(\nu_r(x)\right) \\ &= \frac{1}{W_r} r! \sum_{j=0}^{r} (-1)^j \binom{r}{j} \nu_r(x+r-i). \end{aligned}$$

This concludes the proof. □

We are now in a position to prove Theorem 4.2.

THEOREM 4.2. *There exists a projection oracle* FITPOLY$_d$ *for $\mathcal{P}_d$, which, given an interval I and an s-sparse function $q : I \to \mathbb{R}$, runs in time $O(d^2 s)$.*

PROOF. We first run EVALUATE-GRAM(i_j, d, b) for $j = 1, \ldots, s$. We now have access to the values $t_r(i_j)$ for all $r = 0, \ldots, d$ and all $j = 1, \ldots, d$. Given these values, computing the a_r for the original function q is simple: if q is supported on points $i_1, \ldots, i_s$, we evaluate $t_r(i_j)$, for all $0 \leq r \leq d$ and for all $j = 1, \ldots, s$. We then apply Equation 7, $a_r = \sum_{j=1}^{s} q(i_j) t_r(i_j)$, and compute the error using Parseval's theorem as described above. This procedure takes time $O(d^2 s)$. □

Algorithm 4 $\textsc{EvaluateGram}(x, d, b)$ returns v_x, a function on $0, \ldots, d$ so that $v_x(r) = t_r(x)$, where t_r is the Gram polynomial of degree r on the interval $[0, b-1]$ as defined in Equation 6. Throughout the description of the algorithm, since we have to evaluate certain mathematical expressions that depend on b and r, we will denote by \bar{a} any value a which we have computed.

1: **function** $\textsc{EvaluateGram}(x, d, b)$
2: \triangleright *Evaluate* W_r *for* $r = 0, \ldots, d$
3: $\overline{(b^2 - 1)^{\underline{0}}} \leftarrow 1$
4: **for** $r = 1, \ldots, d$ **do**
5: $\overline{(b^2 - 1)^{\underline{r^2}}} \leftarrow \overline{(b^2 - 1)^{\underline{(r-1)^2}}} \cdot \prod_{j=(r-1)^2+1}^{r} (b2 - 1 - j)$
6: **for** $r = 0, \ldots, d$ **do**
7: $W_r \leftarrow \frac{b \cdot \overline{(b^2-1)^{\underline{r^2}}}}{(2r+1)}$
8: \triangleright *Evaluate* $r!$ *for* $r = 0, \ldots, d$
9: $\overline{0!} \leftarrow 1$
10: **for** $r = 1, \ldots, d$ **do**
11: $\overline{r!} \leftarrow r \cdot \overline{(r-1)!}$
12: \triangleright *Evaluate* $\binom{r}{j}$ *for* $r = 0, \ldots, d$ *and* $j \leq r$
13: **for** $r = 0, \ldots, d$ **do**
14: $\overline{\binom{r}{0}} \leftarrow 1$
15: $\overline{\binom{r}{r}} \leftarrow 1$
16: **for** $j = 1, \ldots, r - 1$ **do**
17: $\overline{\binom{r}{j}} \leftarrow \overline{\binom{r-1}{j}} + \overline{\binom{r-1}{j-1}}$
18: \triangleright *Evaluate* $\nu_r(i)$ *for* $r = 0, \ldots, d$ *and for all* $i = 0, \ldots, r$
19: **for** $r = 0, \ldots, d$ **do**
20: \triangleright *Evaluate* $\binom{y}{r}$ *for all* $y = x, \ldots, x + r$
21: $\overline{\binom{x}{r}} \leftarrow x^{\underline{r}}/r!$
22: **for** $i = 1, \ldots, r$ **do**
23: $\overline{\binom{x+i}{r}} \leftarrow (x + i + 1) \cdot \overline{\binom{x+i}{r}}/(x + i - r + 1)$
24: \triangleright *Evaluate* $\binom{y-b}{r}$ *for all* $y = x, \ldots, x + r$
25: $\overline{\binom{x-b}{r}} \leftarrow (x - b)^{\underline{r}}/r!$
26: **for** $i = 1, \ldots, r$ **do**
27: $\overline{\binom{x-b+i+1}{r}} \leftarrow (x - b + i + 1) \cdot \overline{\binom{x-b+i}{r}}/(x - b + i - r + 1)$
28: **for** $i = 1, \ldots, r$ **do**
29: $\overline{t_r(i)} \leftarrow \overline{\binom{x+i}{r}} \cdot \overline{\binom{x-b}{r}}$
30: \triangleright *Evaluate* $\nu_x(r) = t_r(x)$ *for* $r = 0, \ldots, d$
31: **for** $r = 0, \ldots, d$ **do**
32: $\nu_x(r) \leftarrow \frac{1}{W_r} r! \sum_{j=0}^{r} (-1)^j \overline{\binom{r}{j}} \cdot \overline{t_r(x + r - i)}$
33: **return** ν_x

On Top-k Range Reporting in 2D Space

Saladi Rahul
University of Minnesota
USA
sala0198@umn.edu

Yufei Tao
Chinese University of Hong Kong
Hong Kong
taoyf@cse.cuhk.edu.hk

ABSTRACT

Orthogonal range reporting (ORR) is a classic problem in computational geometry and databases, where the objective is to preprocess a set P of points in $\mathbb{R}^2$ such that, given an axis-parallel rectangle q, all the points in $P \cap Q$ can be reported efficiently. This paper studies a natural variant of the problem called *top-k ORR*, where each point $p \in P$ carries a *weight* $w(p) \in \mathbb{R}$. Besides q, a query also specifies an integer $k \in [1, |P|]$, and needs to report the k points in $q \cap P$ with the largest weights. We present optimal or near-optimal structures for solving the top-k ORR problem in the pointer machine and external memory models. As a side product, our structures give new space-query tradeoff for the *orthogonal range max* problem, which is a special case of top-k ORR with $k = 1$.

Categories and Subject Descriptors

F.2.2 [**Analysis of algorithms and problem complexity**]: Nonnumerical Algorithms and Problems—*computations on discrete structures*; H.3.1 [**Information storage and retrieval**]: Content analysis and indexing—*indexing methods*

Keywords

Top-k; Range Reporting; Approximate Weight Threshold

1. INTRODUCTION

In the *orthogonal range reporting* (ORR) problem, we want to preprocess a set P of points in $\mathbb{R}^2$ into a structure such that, given an axis-parallel rectangle q, all the points in $P \cap q$ can be reported efficiently. This is a classic problem in computational geometry that has been very well understood.

In this work, we study a natural variant of the problem called *top-k orthogonal range reporting* (or top-k ORR) which is defined as follows. Each point $p \in P$ is associated with a distinct *weight* $w(p) \in \mathbb{R}$. Besides q, a query also specifies an integer $k \in [1, n]$ where $n = |P|$. The query returns the k points in $q \cap P$ with the largest weights (see Figure 1).[1] The objective, as before, is to store P in a structure of small size to answer all queries efficiently.

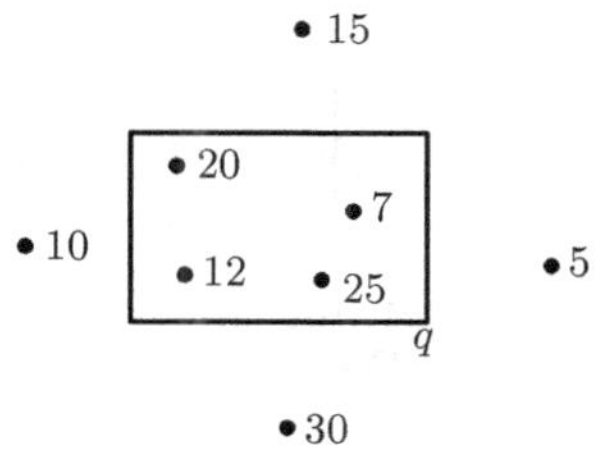

Figure 1: The number beside each point indicates its weight. A top-k ORR query with $k = 2$ and a search region q as shown returns the points with weights 20 and 25.

As an interesting special case, top-1 ORR (i.e., fixing $k = 1$) is also known as the *orthogonal range max* problem.

Pratical Motivation. Top-k ORR is important in applications where a user is interested in only the *best few* objects in terms of weights, as opposed to all the objects in a query region. As a representative example in spatial databases, consider each point as the location of a hotel, with the point's weight corresponding to the restaurant's rating. A top-10 ORR query that would be frequently issued at a website like *hotel.com* is "find the 10 best rated hotel in the Manhattan area". It is not hard to see plenty of other applications of this sort in various domains. In particular, top-k ORR serves as a top-k extension of queries of the following form in relational databases: `select max(`A_1`) from table where` $A_2 \in [x_1, x_2]$ `and` $A_3 \in [y_1, y_2]$.

Computation Models. We are interested in structures of both internal and external memory. For internal memory, our structure works under the pointer machine model. Depending on the types of CPU calculation allowed, Chazelle [9] refined the model into several variants. Unless otherwise stated, by "pointer machine", we refer to the most primitive of his variants—called *elementary pointer machine* (EPM)—which allows only comparisons and $+$.

For external memory, we resort to the standard model defined by Aggarwal and Vitter [6]. In this model, a machine

[1]That objects have distinct weights is a standard assumption in the previous top-k studies [4, 21]. Otherwise, what would be a top-k result becomes ambiguous (just imagine the extreme case where all objects have the same weight).

PODS'15, May 31–June 4, 2015, Melbourne, Victoria, Australia.

Http://dx.doi.org/10.1145/2745754.2745777.

problem	space	query	source	model	remark
2-sided top-k ORR	$O(n)$	$O(\log n + k)$	**new**	EPM	optimal
	$O(n/B)$	$O(\log_B n + k/B)$	**new**	EM	optimal
3-sided top-k ORR	$O(n\frac{\log n}{\log\log n})$	$O(\log n + k)$	**new**	EPM	optimal
	$O(\frac{n}{B}\frac{\log n}{\log\log_B n})$	$O(\log_B n + k/B)$	**new**	EM	optimal
4-sided top-k ORR	$O(n\log^2 n)$	$O(\log^2 n + k)$	[18]	EPM	
	$O(n\log^2 n)$	$O(\log n + k\log\log n)$	[18]	EPM	ordered reporting
	$O(n\frac{\log n}{\log\log n})$	$O(\log n + k)$	**new**	EPM	optimal
	$O(\frac{n}{B}\frac{\log n\cdot(\log\log B)^2}{\log\log_B n})$	$O(\log_B n + k/B)$	**new**	EM	
	$O(n/B)$	$O(\sqrt{n/B} + k/B)$	**new**	EM	non-replicate, optimal
orthogonal range max	$O(n)$	$O(\log^3 n)$	[9]	EPM	
	$O(n)$	$O(\log^2 n)$	[9]	APM	
	$O(n\log^2 n)$	$O(\log n)$	folklore	EPM	
	$O(n\frac{\log n}{\log\log n})$	$O(\log n)$	**new**	EPM	
	$O(n/B)$	$O(\log_B^2 n)$	[5]	EM	
	$O(\frac{n}{B}\log n)$	$O(\log_B n)$	[20]	EM	
	$O(\frac{n}{B}\frac{\log n}{\log\log_B n})$	$O(\log_B n)$	**new**	EM	

Table 1: Comparison of our and previous results (EPM = elementary pointer machine, APM = arithmetic pointer machine, and EM = external memory)

has memory of M words, and a disk that has been formatted into *blocks* of size B words (it always holds that $M \geq 2B$). An I/O exchanges a block of data between the disk and the memory. The space of a structure is the number of blocks occupied, whereas the cost of an algorithm is the number of I/Os performed. CPU calculation is free.

1.1 Previous Results

In this subsection, we will review the existing structures on the top-k ORR problem and the orthogonal range max problem. Focus will be placed on the pointer-machine and external memory models, but we will also briefly mention the state-of-the-art relevant results in the RAM (random access machine) model for the two problems.

Top-k ORR. This problem, in spite of its practical importance, has not been extensively studied. On pointer machines, the only results we are aware of are due to Rahul et al. [18]. They propose two structures, both consuming $O(n\log^2 n)$ space[2], but answering a query in $O(\log^2 n + k)$ and $O(\log n + k\log\log n)$ time, respectively. On a RAM, Navarro and Nekrich [15] gave a structure of $O(n)$ space and $O(\log^{1+\epsilon} n + k\log^{\epsilon} n)$ query time.

On the other hand, one-dimensional top-k ORR—where the points of P are on a line and a query region q is an interval—has received more attention. On pointer machines, combining Frederickson's heap selection algorithm [11] with a priority search tree [14] gives a structure of $O(n)$ size and $O(\log n + k)$ query time. In external memory, Afshani et al. [4] presented a structure of $O(n/B)$ space that answers a query in $O(\log_B n + k/B)$ I/Os. In the scenario where the n points of P are in the range $[1, O(n)]$, Brodal et al. [8] developed an optimal RAM structure of $O(n)$ space and $O(k)$ query time. See also the work of Karpinski and Nekrich [13] for a colored version of 1d top-k ORR.

In this work, the k points in the result of a top-k query can be reported in an arbitrary order. In the *ordered* version of the problem, the result points must be output in ascending order of weight. In 2D space, the $O(\log n + k\log\log n)$ query time structure of [18] and the structure of [15] (both mentioned earlier) were actually designed for the ordered version. See [4, 8, 13] for the corresponding results in 1D space. Furthermore, while the current paper assumes that the input set is static, update-efficient top-k structures have also appeared in the literature recently, e.g., [19, 23].

[2]All logarithms have base 2 by default.

Orthogonal Range Max. For this problem, Chazelle [9] developed a pointer-machine structure of $O(n)$ size and $O(\log^3 n)$ query time. In a more powerful model—*arithmetic pointer machine* (APM) which allows comparisons, $+$, $-$, $\times$, $\div$, and bit-shifting—he [9] also gave an $O(n)$-size structure with $O(\log^2 n)$ query time. In the same paper, Chazellel [9] also gave several RAM structures with different space-query tradeoffs.

When the search region q is *2-sided*—namely, in the form $(-\infty, x] \times (-\infty, y]$—orthogonal range max can be reduced to the *point location* problem, which can be solved by a pointer machine structure of $O(n)$ size and $O(\log n)$ query time. Using range-tree ideas, this leads to a pointer machine structure of $O(n\log^2 n)$ size and $O(\log n)$ query time for general (i.e., *4-sided*) queries.

In external memory, Agarwal et al. [5] presented a structure of $O(n/B)$ space and $O(\log_B^2 n)$ query cost. When the query region is *3-sided*—in the form $[x_1, x_2] \times (-\infty, y]$—Sheng and Tao [20] obtained a structure of $O(n/B)$ space and $O(\log_B n)$ query cost. This gives rise to a structure of $O(\frac{n}{B}\log n)$ space that answers a 4-sided query in $O(\log_B n)$ I/Os.

1.2 Our Contributions

Results. Table 1 compares our main results to the relevant existing results. It is worth mentioning that our pointer machine structure for the orthogonal range max problem is the first achieving a space-query-time product of $o(n\log^2 n)$.

New Technique: Δ-AWT. A common approach [4, 21] to answer a top-k ORR query is to find a threshold σ, such that at least k but at most $O(k)$ points $p \in P$ (i) fall in the query region q, and (ii) have weights $w(p) \geq \sigma$. After this, one can retrieve all the points satisfying conditions (i) and (ii) using a 5-sided[3] orthogonal range query in the 3D space of x, y, and weight. The 5-sided range query can report only $O(k)$ points, and incurs $O(\log n)$ additional time by resorting to a structure of [3]. Finally, the top-k points can be found from those $O(k)$ points with k-selection.

In this work, we extend the above methodology, and propose to look at a new type of queries:

> Given an axis-parallel rectangle q and an integer k, a Δ-*approximate weight threshold* (Δ-AWT) query returns a value σ such that at least k but at most $O(k+\Delta)$ points $p \in P$ satisfy: $p \in q$, and $w(p) \geq \sigma$ (if $|P \cap q| < k$, then the query should return $-\infty$). Here, Δ is an integer in $[1, n]$ that is fixed for all queries.

Note that σ does *not* need to be the weight of any point in P.

To see the relevance of Δ-AWT to top-k ORR, fix $\Delta = \log n$. Given a top-k ORR query, we first answer a Δ-AWT query with the same q and k. Let σ be the Δ-AWT output. Proceed with a 5-sided query as described in the conventional approach. This 5-sided query returns at most $O(k + \Delta) = O(\log n + k)$ points, which has no impact on the overall running time $O(\log n + k)$.

Δ-AWT turns out to be an interesting problem in itself. When $\Delta = \omega(1)$, it may be possible to use structures of *sublinear* sizes to process Δ-AWT queries efficiently. In particular, when q is 2-sided, a Δ-AWT query can be answered in $O(\log(n/\Delta))$ time using a pointer machine structure of $O(n/\Delta)$ space—both the space and query costs are optimal, as we will prove in the next section. It is such space savings that allow us to obtain neat 3- and 4-sided Δ-AWT structures that pave the way to solving top-k ORR.

2. 2-SIDED Δ-AWT

This section serves as a proof for our first main result:

THEOREM 1. *The following statements are true:*

1. *Any structure correctly solving 2-sided Δ-AWT queries must store $\Omega(n/\Delta)$ words in the worst case. Restricting to the pointer machine model, any structure must incur $\Omega(\log(n/\Delta))$ query time in the worst case.*
2. *There is a pointer machine structure of $O(n/\Delta)$ size that answers a 2-sided Δ-AWT query in $O(\log(n/\Delta))$ time.*

Lower Bounds. To prove Statement 1 of the above theorem, we consider that a machine word has t bits, and that the weight domain is the integer range $[0, 2^t - 1]$. Let c be a constant such that, given a Δ-AWT query with parameters q and k, the structure returns a value σ ensuring at least k but at most $c(k + \Delta)$ points $p \in P$ satisfy $p \in q$ and $w(p) \geq \sigma$, provided that $|P \cap q| \geq k$. Define $\lambda = c(1 + \Delta) + 1$. We will assume that n is multiple of λ, that 2^t is a multiple of both n and n/λ, and that $2^t \geq n^2$.

It suffices to look at a set P of one-dimensional points, where the i-th ($i \in [1, n]$) point p_i has coordinate i. To decide the weights of these points, we divide P into n/λ *groups* of equal size: $P_1, ..., P_{n/\lambda}$, where P_j ($j \in [1, n/\lambda]$) consists of the points from coordinate $(j-1)\lambda + 1$ to $j\lambda$. Likewise, divide the weight domain into n/λ *chunks* of equal size $s = 2^t\lambda/n$, such that the j-th chunk ($j \in [1, n/\lambda]$) is the range $[(j-1)s, js - 1]$.

The weights of the points in each group are generated independently. To describe the generation for group P_j (for any $j \in [1, n/\lambda]$), let $\pi_1, ..., \pi_\lambda$ be the points of P_j in ascending order, and $v_1, ..., v_s$ the values of chunk j in descending order. Then:

- The weight $w(\pi_1)$ of π_1 is picked from $\{v_{z\lambda} \mid z = 1, 2, ..., s/\lambda\}$ uniformly at random. Define $X_j = w(\pi_1)$ for the purpose of our analysis later.
- Then, for each $z' = 2, ..., \lambda$, the weight $w(\pi_{z'})$ of $\pi_{z'}$ is set to $w(\pi_1) - (z' - 1)$.

The above construction endows P with two properties:

- For any $j_1 < j_2$, the points of group P_{j_1} have weights strictly smaller than those of group P_{j_2}.
- In group P_j (of any j), the points have weights $X_j, X_j - 1, ..., X_j - (\lambda - 1)$, respectively, with X_j being a multiple of λ.

Now consider a one-dimensional Δ-AWT query with $q = (-\infty, j\lambda]$ (note that this is a degenerated 2-sided rectangle) and $k = 1$, where j is an integer from 1 to n/λ. The structure must return a value $\sigma_j \in (X_j - (\lambda - 1), X_j]$ due to the reasons below:

- P has a point (in group j) that is covered by q, and has weight X_j. Hence, no value higher than X_j can be returned.
- If $\sigma_j \leq X_j - (\lambda - 1)$, then all the points of P_j are covered by q, and have weights at least σ_j. This violates the requirement Δ-AWT because $|P_j| = \lambda > c(1 + \Delta)$.

It thus follows that, the query algorithm can decide precisely the value of X_j as the nearest multiple of λ that is at least σ_j.

Therefore, the structure serves as an encoding of random variables $(X_1, X_2, ..., X_{n/\lambda})$. Note that each X_j ($j \in [1, n/\lambda]$) has an entropy of $\log_2(s/\lambda)$ bits. Due the independence of the n/λ variables, we know that the structure must contain $(n/\lambda)\log_2(s/\lambda) = (n/\lambda)\log_2(2^t/n)$ bits in the worst case. When $2^t \geq n^2$, this is at least $\Omega((n/\lambda)\log(2^t))$ bits, namely, $\Omega(n/\Delta)$ words.

The query lower bound in Statement 1 can be established by the following argument. First recall that any pointer machine structure can be modeled as a directed graph where each node stores $O(1)$ words. Consider running the n/λ queries as mentioned earlier, one for each $j \in [1, n/\lambda]$. Remove from the structure all nodes that are never touched by any of the queries. From the space lower bound, we know that at least $\Omega(n/\Delta)$ nodes remain. Any query algorithm must start from a unique node (called the *root*) of the structure, and at each node, can choose from any of its out-neighbors as the next hop. Since each node has $O(1)$ out-neighbors, we know that at least one node requires $\Omega(\log(n/\Delta))$ hops from the root.

Remark. Note that the $\Omega(n/\Delta)$ space lower bound is not restricted to pointer machine structures. It holds for any

[3]A 5-sided rectangle in 3D space has the form $[x_1, x_2] \times [y_1, y_2] \times [z, \infty)$.

RAM/EM structure. Furthermore, our information theoretic argument essentially has shown that randomization does not help: any structure must use $\Omega(n/\lambda)$ space in expectation.

Upper Bounds. Inspired by [4], we now describe a pointer machine structure matching the aforementioned lower bounds, assuming without loss of generality that n/Δ is a power of 2. First, convert each point $p = (x, y)$ in P to a 3D point (x, y, z) where $z = w(p)$. Let P' be the set of 3D points thus obtained. In general, given two 3D points $p_1 = (x_1, y_1, z_1)$ and $p_2 = (x_2, y_2, z_2)$, we say that p_1 *dominates* p_2 if $x_1 \le x_2$, $y_1 \le y_2$, $z_1 \le z_2$, and at least one equality does not hold. Also, we say that p_1 is *lower* than p_2 if $z_1 < z_2$.

Let S be a set of points in $\mathbb{R}^3$. We say that S is a *shallow τ-cutting* of P' if it has the following properties:

P1: S has $O(n/\tau)$ points.

P2: Each point in S dominates $O(\tau)$ points in P'.

P3: Any point p (which is not necessarily in P') dominating at most τ points in P' is dominated by at least a point in S.

As shown in [1], such an S exists for any $\tau \in [1, n]$.

Let $h = \log_2(n/\Delta)$. We obtain sets $S_1, ..., S_{h+1}$ where S_i ($i \in [1, h+1]$) is a shallow $(2^{i-1}\Delta)$-cutting of P'. On each S_i, we create a structure to answer *probing queries* of the form: given a 2D point $\pi = (x, y)$, find the lowest point $p \in S_i$ such that $x(p) \le x$ and $y(p) \le y$, where $x(p)$ and $y(p)$ are the x- and y-coordinates of p, respectively. Note that this is essentially a 2-sided orthogonal range max query, and thus, can be answered in logarithmic time by a linear size structure (see the literature review in Section 1). Since the sizes of $S_1, ..., S_{h+1}$ decrease geometrically, the total space of all these structures is dominated by the one on S_1, namely, $O(n/\Delta)$ by Property ***P1***.

To answer a Δ-AWT query with parameters $q = [x, \infty) \times [y, \infty)$ and k, we check whether $k < \Delta$. If so, we manually increase k to Δ before proceeding. When $k \ge \Delta$, we first determine the smallest i such that $2^i\Delta \ge k$. Then, perform a probing query on S_{i+1} with $\pi = (x, y)$. Let p be the point returned by this probing query. We return $z(p)$ (i.e., the z coordinate of p) as the answer for the Δ-AWT query.

LEMMA 1. *The probing query definitely returns a point p. Furthermore, $z(p)$ is a correct answer for the Δ-AWT query.*

PROOF. Let z be a value such that $p' = (x, y, z)$ dominates exactly k points in P'; if z does not exist, we set $z = -\infty$. In any case, p' dominates at most $k \le 2^i\Delta$ points in P'. Hence, by Property ***P3***, we know that S_{i+1} definitely contains a point dominating p', implying that the probing query cannot return an empty result. Furthermore, it also implies that p (that output of the probing query) definitely dominates p'.

Next, we prove the second part of the lemma focusing on the scenario where $k \ge \Delta$. First, if $z = -\infty$, it follows that $|P \cap q| < k$ and that $z(p)$ must be $-\infty$. Hence, our algorithm correctly returns $-\infty$.

The subsequent discussion considers $z \ne -\infty$ (and hence, p' dominates k points in P'). As $z(p) \le z$, point $(x, y, z(p))$ must dominate at least k points of P'. On the other hand,

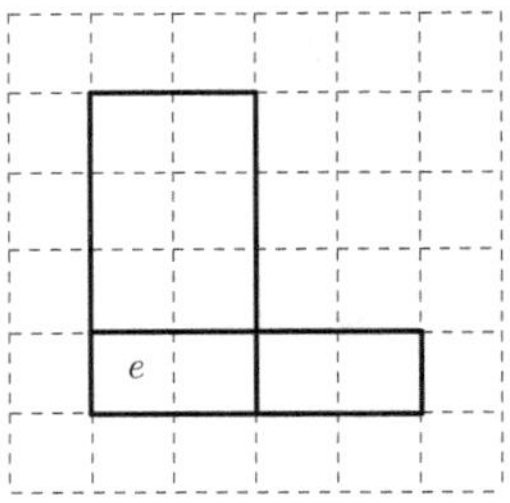

Figure 2: Two dyadic rectangles of e in solid edges

$(x, y, z(p))$ cannot dominate more points of P' than p does (because $x(p) \le x$ and $y(p) \le y$). Property ***P2*** guarantees that p dominates $O(2^i\Delta) = O(2k) = O(k + \Delta)$ points of P'. This completes the proof. □

At first glance, the above query algorithm seems to require division to determine the smallest i such that $2^i\Delta \ge k$, contradicting our goal of designing a structure on an elementary pointer machine. This can be fixed by creating a binary search tree on the $h+1$ values Δ, 2Δ, $2^2\Delta$, ... $2^h\Delta$ so that at query time we can find i by finding the successor of k in this tree using $O(\log h)$ time. In this way, the query algorithm relies on only comparisons. The overall query cost is dominated by the time of a probing query, which is $O(\log(n/\Delta))$. We now conclude the proof of Theorem 1.

3. 4-SIDED Δ-AWT AND TOP-K ORR

In this section, we will present a structure for solving 4-sided Δ-AWT queries, and then, explain how the structure can be utilized to settle top-k ORR. Let us start with an easy lemma:

LEMMA 2. *There is a pointer machine structure of $O(\frac{n}{\Delta}\log\frac{n}{\Delta})$ size that answers a 3-sided Δ-AWT query in $O(\log(n/\Delta))$ time. There is also a pointer machine structure of $O(\frac{n}{\Delta}\log^2\frac{n}{\Delta})$ size that answers a 4-sided Δ-AWT query in $O(\log(n/\Delta))$ time.*

PROOF. By standard range-tree ideas. □

The 4-sided structure in the above lemma is not powerful enough for obtaining our final result on top-k ORR. Next, we improve it by reducing its space to $O(\frac{n}{\Delta}\log^2\frac{n}{\Delta}/\log\log\frac{n}{\Delta})$. We achieve this by combining the standard approach of using a logarithmic-fanout range tree with new ideas based on dyadic rectangles.

Structure. Without loss of generality, we assume that n is a multiple of Δ. Divide the data space into n/Δ vertical slabs such that each slab covers exactly Δ points of P. Set $f = \log(n/\Delta)$. Create an f-ary tree T on these slabs, each of which corresponds to a leaf node in T. Given a node u in T, we will use $slab(u)$ to denote the slab of u (if u is an internal node, $slab(u)$ is the union of the slabs of its children). Define $P_u = P \cap slab(u)$, and $n_u = |P_u|$.

We associate each internal node u with several secondary structures. Let $m = \Delta\log^3(n/\Delta)$. Impose an $f \times \frac{n_u}{m}$ grid G_u on P_u, such that each column of G_u is the slab of a child of u, whereas each row covers $\Theta(m)$ points in P_u. For each column, create a *column structure* which is a 3-sided structure of Lemma 2 on the points of P_u in the column. For each row, create a *row structure* which which is a 4-sided structure of Lemma 2 on the points of P_u in the row.

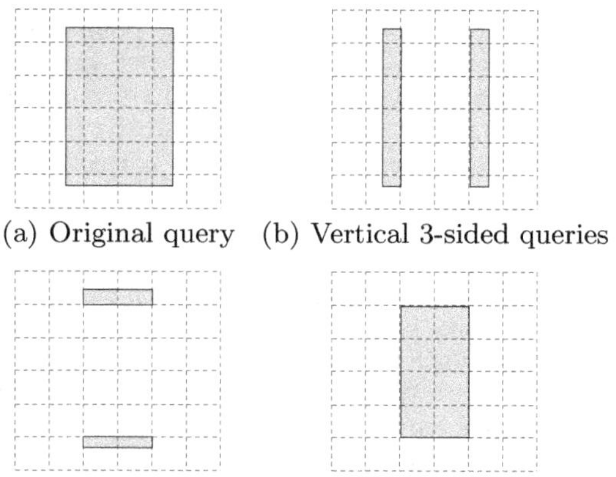

(a) Original query (b) Vertical 3-sided queries

(c) Horizontal 3-sided queries (d) Grid query

Figure 3: Partitioning a query rectangle

Now consider a cell e in G_u. Let r be a rectangle whose edges are aligned with the column and row boundaries of G_u. In other words, r is tiled by a set of cells in G_u. Let a (b) be the number of columns (rows) of G_u that r covers. We say that r is a *dyadic* $a \times b$ *rectangle of* e if it satisfies two conditions:

- Both a and b are powers of 2.
- e is covered by r, and is located at one of the 4 corners of r.

See Figure 2 for an example. Note that e has $O(\log f \cdot \log(n_u/m)) = O(\log\log(n/\Delta) \cdot \log(n/\Delta))$ dyadic rectangles. For each such rectangle r, we store a *sketch*, which consists of the Δ-th largest, (2Δ)-th largest, $(2^2\Delta)$-th largest ... of the weights of the points in $r \cap P$. In other words, e is associated with $O(\log\log(n/\Delta) \cdot \log(n/\Delta))$ sketches, each of size $O(\log(n/\Delta))$.

Overall, the column structures of u occupy $O((n_u/\Delta)\log(n_u/\Delta))$ space, and its row structures occupy $O(\frac{n_u}{m}\frac{m}{\Delta}\log^2\frac{m}{\Delta}) = O(\frac{n_u}{\Delta}(\log\log\frac{n_u}{\Delta})^2)$ space. G_u has fn_u/m cells, each of which needs $O(\log^2\frac{n}{\Delta}\log\log\frac{n}{\Delta})$ space for its sketches. Hence, all the sketches of all cells in G_u occupy in total

$$O\left(\log\frac{n}{\Delta} \cdot \frac{n_u}{\Delta\log^3(n/\Delta)} \cdot \log^2\frac{n}{\Delta}\log\log\frac{n}{\Delta}\right)$$

$$= O\left(\frac{n_u}{\Delta}\log\log\frac{n}{\Delta}\right)$$

space. In summary, all the secondary structures at each level of T use $O((n/\Delta)\log(n/\Delta))$ space. T has $O(\log\frac{n}{\Delta}/\log\log\frac{n}{\Delta})$ levels, and thus, needs $O(\frac{n}{\Delta}\log^2\frac{n}{\Delta}/\log\log\frac{n}{\Delta})$ space.

Query. We now explain how to answer a 4-sided AWT query with parameters q and $k \geq \Delta$ (if $k < \Delta$, simply increase k to Δ before proceeding). If q completely falls within the slab of a leaf node in T, we finish by returning $-\infty$. Otherwise, we use the following algorithm to answer q at the highest node u at which q intersects at least two columns in G_u. Note that u can be found in $O(\log(n/\Delta))$ time.

If q is completely contained in a row of G_u, we answer it using the corresponding row structure in $O(\log m) = O(\log\log(n/\Delta))$ time. Otherwise, q can be divided into two *vertical 3-sided* queries, two *horizontal 3-sided* queries, and a *grid query*, as illustrated in Figure 3. For each resulting query—let q' be its search rectangle—we compute the outcome of the Δ-AWT query with parameters q' and k on P. Specifically, let σ_{v1}, σ_{v2} be the outcomes of the two vertical 3-sided queries, σ_{h1}, σ_{h2} be the outcomes of the two horizontal 3-sided queries, and σ_g be the outcome of the grid query. We return $\sigma = \max\{\sigma_{v1}, \sigma_{v2}, \sigma_{h1}, \sigma_{h2}, \sigma_g\}$ as the final answer.

It is easy to see that σ_{v1}, σ_{v2} can be obtained using two column structures at u in $O(\log\frac{n_u/f}{\Delta}) = O(\log(n/\Delta))$ time, and σ_{h1}, σ_{h2} can be obtained using two row structures at u in $O(\log(m/\Delta)) = O(\log\log(n/\Delta)$ time. Next, we explain how to compute σ_g.

Denote by g the search rectangle of the grid query. Suppose that g spans a columns and b rows of G_u. Denote by a' and b' the largest powers of 2 at most a and b, respectively. Let e_1, e_2, e_3, and e_4 be the top-left, top-right, bottom-left, and bottom-right corners of g, respectively. Let r_1 be the dyadic $a' \times b'$ rectangle of e_1, having e_1 at its top-left corner. Similarly, let r_2, r_3, r_4 be the dyadic $a' \times b'$ rectangles having e_2, e_3, e_4 at their top-right, bottom-left, and bottom-right corners, respectively. Note that r_1, r_2, r_3 and r_4 may overlap, as is exemplified in Figure 4 using r_1 and r_4.

Let i be the lowest integer such that $2^i\Delta \geq k$. We set σ_{g1} to the i-th largest weight in the sketch of r_1, if the sketch has size at least i; otherwise, $\sigma_{g1} = -\infty$. Likewise, let σ_{g2}, σ_{g3}, and σ_{g4} be decided in the same manner from r_2, r_3, and r_4, respectively. Then, σ_g is determined as $\max\{\sigma_{g1}, \sigma_{g2}, \sigma_{g3}, \sigma_{g4}\}$.

To implement the above algorithm in $O(\log(n/\Delta))$ time on an (elementary) pointer machine, the only technicality worth mentioning is to derive a' and b' from a and b, respectively, on an elementary pointer machine. The crucial observation is that both a and b can distribute only inside the range $[1, n/\Delta]$. Hence, we can index with a binary search tree all the powers of 2 within that range. Then, a' (b') is simply the predecessor of a (b) in this tree.

LEMMA 3. *The answer σ thus computed is correct.*

PROOF. It suffices to show that σ_g is a correct answer for the Δ-AWT query with parameters g and k. First, if $\sigma_g = -\infty$, it means that $\sigma_{g1} = \sigma_{g2} = \sigma_{g3} = \sigma_{g4} = -\infty$. Thus, g can cover at most $4k$ points of P, in which case $\sigma_g = -\infty$ is correct.

Consider that $\sigma_g \neq -\infty$. Suppose without loss of generality that $\sigma_g = \sigma_{g1}$. By the definition of σ_{g1}, at least k points in $P \cap r_1$ have weights no less than σ_{g1}. Thus, at least k points in g have weights no less than σ_g.

Let c_i ($i = 1, 2, ..., 4$) be the number of points in $P \cap r_i$ having weights at least σ_{gi}. We know that $c_i = O(k)$. Let c be the number of points in $P \cap g$ having weights at least σ_g. If a point is not counted by any of $c_1, ..., c_4$, it cannot be counted by c either. Hence, $c \leq \sum_{i=1}^{4} c_i = O(k)$. □

The above discussion has established:

LEMMA 4. *There is a pointer machine structure of $O(\frac{n}{\Delta}\log^2\frac{n}{\Delta}/\log\log\frac{n}{\Delta})$ size that answers a 4-sided Δ-AWT query in $O(\log(n/\Delta))$ time.*

Remark. We can improve the space of our 3-sided structure in Lemma 2 to $O(\frac{n}{\Delta}\log\frac{n}{\Delta}/\log\log\frac{n}{\Delta})$, and accordingly,

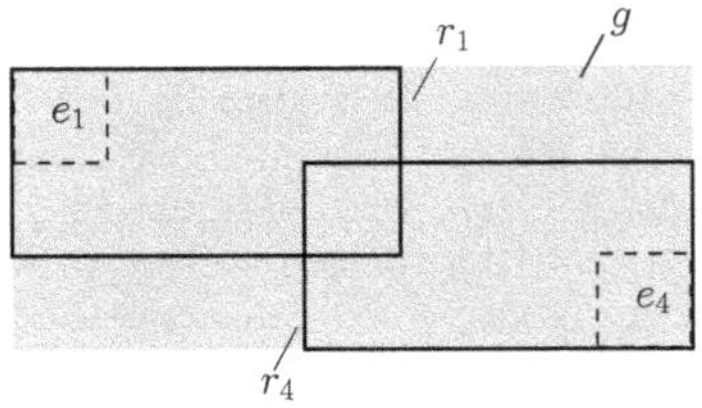

Figure 4: Covering a grid query with dyadic rectangles

improve the space of our 4-sided structure in Lemma 4 to $O(\frac{n}{\Delta}(\log \frac{n}{\Delta}/\log\log \frac{n}{\Delta})^2)$. We leave the details to the full version because, as discussed below, Lemma 4 already suffices for obtaining optimal top-k ORR structures.

Top-k ORR. We now proceed to discuss top-k ORR queries. If queries are 2-sided, we can answer them in $O(\log n + k)$ time using a structure of $O(n)$ size. For this purpose, we build a structure $\mathcal{T}$ of Theorem 1 with $\Delta = \log n$ on P. Given a top-k ORR query with a 2-sided rectangle q, we first perform Δ-AWT search on $\mathcal{T}$ to obtain a threshold σ. Then, all the points in $P \cap q$ with weights at least σ can be obtained in $O(\log n + \Delta + k) = O(\log n + k)$ time using a 3D dominance structure [1] which uses $O(n)$ space.

For 4-sided queries, a similar approach gives a structure of $O(n \log n/\log\log n)$ space and $O(\log n + k)$ query time. Specifically, we create a structure $\mathcal{T}$ of Lemma 4 with $\Delta = \log n$. Note that $\mathcal{T}$ consumes $O(n \log n/\log\log n)$ space. Given a top-k ORR query with parameters q and k, we perform Δ-AWT search on $\mathcal{T}$ to obtain a threshold σ. Then, all the points in $P \cap q$ with weights at least σ can be obtained in $O(\log n + k)$ time using a 3D 5-sided range reporting structure [3] which uses $O(n \log n/\log\log n)$ space.

One may wonder what happens to 3-sided top-k ORR. Interestingly, there is no hope to improve upon the bounds obtained above for 4-sided queries. In general, for 3-sided top-k ORR, it is impossible to use $o(n \log n/\log\log n)$ space if one wishes for a query time of $O(\log^c n + k)$ for any constant c. This can be proved with the following argument. Consider the so-called $Q(3,1)$ *range reporting* problem as defined in [2]: let P' be a set of n points in $\mathbb{R}^3$; we want to store P' in a structure such that, given a rectangle $q = [x_1, x_2] \times [y, \infty) \times [z, \infty)$, we can report all the points in $P' \cap q$ efficiently. It is known (from a lower bound in [10]) that every structure with $O(\log^c n + k')$ query time (where $k' = |P' \cap q|$) must use $\Omega(n \log n/\log\log n)$ space. However, as we show below, any 3-sided top-k ORR structure with query time $O(\log^c n + k)$ can be deployed to answer a $Q(3,1)$ query in $O(\log^c n + k')$ time. This means that the 3-sided top-k ORR structure must use $\Omega(n \log n/\log\log n)$ space.

Now we explain a reduction from $Q(3,1)$ to 3-sided top-k ORR. Let us regard each point $p' = (x, y, z)$ in P' as a 2D point $p = (x, y)$ with weight $w(p) = z$. Let P be the set of 2D points thus obtained. Store P in a 3-sided top-k ORR structure $\mathcal{T}$. Given a $Q(3,1)$ query $q = [x_1, x_2] \times [y, \infty) \times [z, \infty)$, we answer it with a series of 3-sided top-k ORR queries on $\mathcal{T}$ as follows. The search regions of all these queries are fixed to $[x_1, x_2] \times [y, \infty)$. The i-th ($i \geq 1$) query is issued with k set to $2^{i-1} \log^c n$. Let S_i be the set of points fetched by this query. Define z_i as the $(2^{i-1} \log^c n)$-th largest weight of the points in S_i if $|S_i| \geq 2^{i-1} \log^c n$, or set $z_i = -\infty$ otherwise. Report all the points in S_i whose weights are between $[\max\{z, z_i\}, z_{i-1}]$ (let $z_0 = \infty$ for the boundary case $i = 1$). The algorithm stops as soon as z_i falls below z.

It is clear that the above algorithm correctly reports all the points in $q \cap P'$. Next, we argue that the query cost is $O(\log n + k')$ where $k' = |q \cap P'|$. Define $k_i = 2^{i-1} \log^c n$ for $i \geq 1$, and $k_0 = 0$. Let ρ be the total number of 3-sided top-k ORR queries issued. For each $i \in [1, \rho - 1]$, the i-th query reports $k_i - k_{i-1} \geq k_i/2$ points, and incurs cost $O(\log^c n + k_i)$ which is $O(k_i)$ because all of k_1, ..., $k_{\rho-1}$ must be at least $\log^c n$. We can therefore amortize the time onto the $k_i/2$ points reported, so that each point gets charged only $O(1)$ cost. Regarding the ρ-th query, observe that k_ρ is at most $2k'$ if $\rho \geq 2$ (because $k_{\rho-1}$ is at most k'). If $\rho = 1$, then $k_\rho = \log^c n$. In any case, the time of the ρ-th query is bounded by $O(\log^c n + k_\rho) = O(\log^c n + k')$.

THEOREM 2. *The following statements are true:*

1. *There is a pointer machine structure of $O(n)$ size that answers a 2-sided top-k ORR query in $O(\log n + k)$ time.*
2. *For any constant c, a pointer machine structure that answers a 3-sided top-k ORR query in $O(\log^c n + k)$ time must use $\Omega(n \log n/\log\log n)$ space.*
3. *There is a pointer machine structure of $O(n \log n/\log\log n)$ size that answers a 4-sided top-k ORR query in $O(\log n + k)$ time.*

4. TOP-K ORR IN EXTERNAL MEMORY

In this section, we adapt the pointer machine results of the previous section to external memory. Our main technical novelty can be summarized as:

- Proof of an $\Omega(\log_B(n/\Delta))$ lower bound for Δ-AWT queries. Recall that the query lower bound in Theorem 1 applies only to pointer machines. However, an EM structure does not need to be pointer-based; instead, an algorithm can choose at its free will to access any block of the structure—a piece of luxury that a pointer machine structure does not have. This discrepancy prevents the pointer-machine's query cost argument from being applicable in EM.
- Working with Δ-AWT structures that store just as many words as the ones on pointer machines.
- Obtain a space-economical structure that can answer a 5-sided range reporting query in 3D space using $O(\log_B n + k/B)$ I/Os.

4.1 Query Lower Bound on 2-Sided Δ-AWT

The first statement of Theorem 1 implies that any EM structure solving the 2-sided Δ-AWT problem must occupy $\Omega(n/(B\Delta))$ blocks. In this subsection, we prove:

THEOREM 3. *For any $\Delta \in [1, n]$, an external memory structure of $O(n/(B\Delta))$ space must incur $\Omega(\log_B(n/\Delta))$ I/Os answering a 2-sided Δ-AWT query in the worst case.*

We will give a reduction from the *predecessor search* problem to 2-sided Δ-AWT with an interesting use of an upper bound result of [7] on *one-dimensional range reporting.*

Let t be the number of bits in a word. We consider that the input of predecessor search is a set S of n integers in $[0, \frac{2^t-1}{\Delta}]$; given an integer $x \in [0, \frac{2^t-1}{\Delta}]$, a query returns the predecessor of x in S, namely, $\max\{v \in S \mid v \leq x\}$. Without loss of generality, let us assume that 0 always belongs to S, so that the predecessor of x definitely exists. According to a result of Patrascu and Thorup [17], when $B \geq t$ and 2^t is sufficiently large compared to n, any structure using $O(n/B)$ space must incur $\Omega(\log_B n)$ I/Os answering a predecessor query in the worst case.

In 1D range reporting, the goal is to preprocess the set S aforementioned so that, given a range I inside $[0, 2^t - 1]$, a query can report all the elements in $S \cap I$ efficiently. In [7], Alstrup et al. described a structure of $O(n/B)$ space that answers such a query in $O(1+k'/B)$ I/Os, where $k' = |S \cap I|$.

At a high level, our reduction from predecessor search to 2-sided Δ-AWT works as follows. Given a predecessor query with parameter x, we will somehow perform a Δ-AWT query to obtain an interval $I = [x', x]$ with the guarantee that $|S \cap I| \in [1, O(1)]$. Then, we can retrieve all the elements of $S \cap I$ in $O(1)$ I/Os, after which the predecessor of x can be obtained from only these elements. Next, we describe the details.

Let $v_1, ..., v_n$ be the integers of S in ascending order. Define $S' = \{v_i\Delta \mid i \in [1,n]\}$. Note that each element of S' is in $[0, 2^t - 1]$. Then, we create a set P of $n\Delta$ points from S'. Specifically, for each $i \in [1,n]$, add to P the following Δ points: $(v_i\Delta, v_i\Delta + j)$ with weight $v_i\Delta + j$ for $j = 0, ..., \Delta - 1$—we say that these Δ points form the *group* of v_i.

We create a 2-sided Δ-AWT structure T of optimal space on P; in other words, T occupies $O(\frac{n\Delta}{\Delta B}) = O(n/B)$ blocks. Given a predecessor query with parameter x on S, we perform a 2-sided Δ-AWT query with parameters $q = (-\infty, x\Delta] \times (-\infty, \infty)$ and $k = \Delta$. Suppose that the Δ-AWT query returns a value σ. We set $x' = \lceil \sigma/\Delta \rceil$. We argue that $I = [x', x]$ is an interval we are looking for:

LEMMA 5. *$|S \cap I|$ has at least 1 and at most $O(1)$ elements.*

PROOF. Let v_i be the predecessor of x in S. Then, the points in the group of v_i have the Δ largest weights among all the points in $P \cap q$. Therefore, $\sigma \leq v_i\Delta$ (otherwise, less than $k = \Delta$ points in $P \cap q$ have weights at least σ). Hence, $x' \leq v_i$, meaning that $S \cap I$ has at least one element.

Let j be the largest integer such that $v_j \geq x'$. We know that all the $(i-j+1)\Delta$ points in the groups of $x_j, x_{j+1}, ..., x_i$ fall in $P \cap q$ and have weights at least σ. By definition of Δ-AWT, at most $O(k + \Delta) = O(\Delta)$ such points can exist. Hence, $i - j + 1 = O(1)$. □

It thus follows from the above definition that T must incur $\Omega(\log_B n)$ I/Os answering a 2-sided Δ-AWT query. Since T is created on a set P of size $n\Delta$, we thus conclude the proof of Theorem 3.

4.2 Δ-AWT Structures

This subsection is devoted to I/O-efficient Δ-AWT structures. First of all, the discussion in Section 2 directly leads to:

LEMMA 6. *There is an external memory structure of $O(n/(B\Delta))$ space that answers a 2-sided Δ-AWT query in $O(\log_B(n/B))$ I/Os.*

PROOF. It suffices to point out that there is a 3D dominance structure of $O(n/B)$ space that answers a query in $O(\log_B n + k'/B)$ I/Os, where k' is the output size [1]. □

The situation with 3- and 4-sided AWT, on the other hand, is more interesting. Take 3-sided as an example. Our pointer machine structure uses $O(\frac{n}{\Delta} \log \frac{n}{\Delta})$ words. By the standard wisdom behind the existing I/O-efficient techniques, one would probably expect an EM structure of $O(\frac{n}{B\Delta} \log_B \frac{n}{\Delta})$ blocks. However, the existence of such a structure implies an internal memory structure that uses only $O(\frac{n}{\Delta} \log_B \frac{n}{\Delta})$ words! Note that we have the luxury to increase B arbitrarily such that by using $B = (n/\Delta)^c$ for any $c \in (0, 1]$, we actually get an internal memory structure of $O(n/\Delta)$ size for 3-sided Δ-AWT—an ambitious goal whose achievement still remains elusive to us.

The hidden message behind the above discussion is that we should instead try to work with an EM structure that uses as many words as its internal-memory counterpart (e.g., for 3-sided, this means an EM structure of $O(\frac{n}{B\Delta} \log \frac{n}{\Delta})$ blocks—note that the logarithm has base 2). If one accepts this as the new goal, then it is not hard to derive:

LEMMA 7. *There is an external memory structure of $O(\frac{n}{B\Delta} \log^2 \frac{n}{\Delta} / \log\log \frac{n}{\Delta})$ space that answers a 4-sided Δ-AWT query in $O(\log_B(n/\Delta))$ I/Os.*

PROOF. Trivially applying the pointer machine structures already meets the space requirement, but the query cost is $O(\log(n/\Delta))$. The log base can be increased to B by the standard technique of grouping nodes of multiple levels of an f-ary tree into a block when $f \leq B$. □

The above lemma allows us to obtain optimal top-k ORR structures in external memory. The key is to set Δ to $B \log_B n$. Recall that by the reasoning described in Section 3, we will eventually rely on a 5-sided range reporting structure with query cost $O(\log_B n + k'/B)$, where k' is the number of points returned. Hence, by setting $\Delta = B \log_B n$, a top-k Δ-AWT query returns a threshold σ that will ensure $k' = O(k+\Delta) = O(k+B \log_B n)$, such that $O(\log_B n+k'/B)$ is just $O(\log_B n + k/B)$.

LEMMA 8. *When $\Delta = B \log_B n$, the space complexity in Lemma 7 is $O(\frac{n}{B} \frac{\log n}{\log\log_B n})$.*

PROOF. See the appendix. □

To close the deal, we need:

LEMMA 9. *We can store n 3D points in a structure of $O(\frac{n}{B} \frac{\log n \cdot (\log\log B)^2}{\log\log_B n})$ space such that a 5-sided range reporting query can be answered in $O(\log_B n + k'/B)$ I/Os, where k' is the number of points reported.*

PROOF. See Section 4.3. □

Now we claim:

THEOREM 4. *The following statements are true in external memory:*

1. *There is a structure of $O(n/B)$ space that answers a 2-sided top-k ORR query in $O(\log_B n + k/B)$ I/Os.*

2. *For any constant c, a structure that answers a 3-sided top-k ORR query in $O(\log_B^c n + k/B)$ I/Os must use $\Omega(\frac{n}{B}\frac{\log n}{\log\log_B n})$ space.*

3. *There is a structure of $O(\frac{n}{B}\frac{\log n}{\log\log_B n})$ size that answers a 3-sided top-k ORR query in $O(\log_B n + k/B)$ I/Os.*

4. *There is a structure of $O(\frac{n}{B}\frac{\log n\cdot(\log\log B)^2}{\log\log_B n})$ size that answers a 4-sided top-k ORR query in $O(\log_B n+k/B)$ I/Os.*

PROOF. The proof follows the same argument for Theorem 2 but with a few changes. To prove Statement 1, the 3D dominance structure is the I/O-efficient one proposed in [1]. In the argument for statement 2, we should set k_i to $2^{i-1}B\log_B^c n$ instead. For Statement 3, we use the $Q(3,1)$-structure of [2] in external memory. For Statement 4, the 5-sided range reporting structure is the one in Lemma 9. □

4.3 5-Sided Range Reporting

This subsection proves Lemma 9 by giving such a structure. Recall that the input is a set P' of n points in $\mathbb{R}^3$. Given a 5-sided rectangle $q = [x_1, x_2] \times [y_1, y_2] \times (-\infty, z]$, a query returns all the points in $P' \cap q$. In external memory, the best result we are aware of is a structure of $O(\frac{n}{B}(\frac{\log n}{\log\log_B n})^2)$ space and $O(\log_B n+k'/B)$ query cost due to Afshani et al. [2] (see [16] for an alternative result when the points fall on a 3D grid). Note that Lemma 9 strictly improves this result.

The next lemma is easy:

LEMMA 10. *For any parameter $\lambda \in [B, |P'|]$, there is an external memory structure of $O(\frac{|P'|}{B}\log^2(|P'|/\lambda))$ space that answers a 5-sided range reporting query in $O(\lambda/B + \log_B|P'| + k'/B)$ I/Os, where k' is the number of points reported.*

PROOF. Applying range-tree ideas to the 3D dominance structure of [1] yields a structure of $O(\frac{|P'|}{B}\log|P'|)$ space that supports 4-sided range reporting (i.e., the query region has the form $(-\infty, x] \times [y_1, y_2] \times (-\infty, z]$) in $O(\log_B |P'|)$ I/Os plus the minimum output cost. Note that the query cost has base B instead of base 2. The space can be brought down to $O(\frac{|P'|}{B}\log(|P'|/\lambda))$ by using fat leaves of size λ in the base tree. The query cost has an additive term of $O(\lambda/B)$ because we may need to scan the points in a leaf. Applying the same idea again on this structure gives the lemma. □

Our structure of Lemma 9 leverages the above fact to bootstrap an adapted version of a pointer machine structure of [3]. Define $\mathcal{F}^{(1)}(n) = \sqrt{nB}\log n$, and $\mathcal{F}^{(i+1)}(n) = \mathcal{F}^{(1)}(\mathcal{F}^{(i)}(n))$ for $i \geq 1$. Let $\mathcal{F}^*(n)$ be the smallest integer i such that $\mathcal{F}^{(i)}(n) \leq B\log^{0.99} n \cdot (\log B + 3\log\log n)^2$. We have:

LEMMA 11. $\mathcal{F}^*(n) = \log\frac{\log n}{\log\log_B n} + O(1)$.

PROOF. Note that $\mathcal{F}^{(i)}(n) \leq B\log^2 n{\cdot}n^{1/2^i}$. Hence, when $i = \lceil \log\frac{\log n}{\log\log_B n}\rceil$, $\mathcal{F}^{(i)}(n) < B\log^3 n$. One can then verify that $\mathcal{F}^{(2)}(B\log^3 n) \leq B\log^{0.99} n \cdot (\log B + 3\log\log n)^2$ (see the appendix for details). □

Structure. Set $\theta = \sqrt{n/(B\log^2 n)}$. We impose an orthogonal grid G in the xy-plane with θ rows and θ columns, such that each row (column) covers the xy-projections of no more than $\sqrt{nB}\log n$ points in P'. For each row (column) of G, we build a structure of [1] to answer 3D dominance queries on the points of P' whose xy-projections fall in that row (column).

Given two points in $\mathbb{R}^3$, (same as in Section 2) we say that the former is *lower* if it has a smaller z-coordinate. Let e be a cell in G, and $P'(e)$ be the set of points in P' whose xy-projections fall in e. We store the points of $P'(e)$ in a linked list sorted by z-coordinate. The B-th lowest point in $P'(e)$ is called the *sentinel* of e; note that if $|P'(e)| < B$, no sentinel is defined for e. Let the *pilot set* of e be the lowest B points in $P'(e)$. Let Π be the union of the pilot sets of all the cells e in G. We create a structure of Lemma 10 on Π with $\lambda = B$, and refer to it as a *pilot structure*. Since $|\Pi| \leq B\theta^2 = O(B\frac{n/B}{\log^2 n}) = O(n/\log^2 n)$, the pilot structure uses $O(n/B)$ space.

We then recursively apply the above construction on the subproblem defined by each row and column, respectively (namely, on the set of points of P' whose xy-projections fall in that row or column). Note that, on each sub-problem, θ should be calculated by setting n to the size of that subproblem (i.e., θ decreases with the subproblem's size). Recursion completes when a sub-problem has at most $B\log^{0.99} n\cdot(\log B + 3\log\log n)^2$ points, on which we build a structure of Lemma 10 with $\lambda = B\log_B n$. If we amortize the space of this structure onto those $B\log^{0.99} n\cdot(\log B + 3\log\log n)^2$ points, the amount of space that each point accounts for is

$$O\left(\frac{1}{B}\log^2\frac{B\log^{0.99} n\cdot(\log B + 3\log\log n)^2}{B\log_B n}\right)$$
$$= \quad O((\log\log B)^2/B).$$

Let h be the number of levels in the recursion. Standard analysis shows that the overall space consumption is $O(2^h\frac{|P'|}{B}(\log\log B)^2)$, which is $O(\frac{n}{B}\frac{\log n\cdot(\log\log B)^2}{\log\log_B n})$ by Lemma 11.

Query. We will first explain how to perform range reporting using 4-sided rectangles of the form $q = [-\infty, x] \times [y_1, y_2] \times (-\infty, z]$. If q falls completely within a row of G, we recursively answer the query on the subproblem defined by that row. At the end of recursion, we are looking at no more than $B\log^{0.99} n\cdot(\log B + 3\log\log n)^2$ points; by Lemma 10, we answer the query in $O(\lambda/B + 1 + \log_B\log_B n) = O(\log_B n)$ I/Os plus the minimum output cost.

Now consider that q intersects at least two rows of G. The query can be partitioned into (i) two *row queries*, each being a 3D dominance query whose search region falls in a row on the xy-plane (see Figure 5a), (ii) a *grid-query*, a 4-sided query whose search region is aligned on the grid in the xy-plane (Figure 5b), and (iii) a *vertical query*, another 4-sided query whose search region falls in a column of G on the xy-plane (Figure 5c). We answer the row queries directly using the 3D dominance structures of the corresponding rows, and send the vertical query to the subproblem defined by that column. Next, we explain how to answer the grid query.

Let g be the (3D) search region of the grid query. We first search the pilot structure to report all the points stored there that fall in g. Furthermore, for each cell e whose sentinel has been reported, we jump to the linked list of $P'(e)$, and

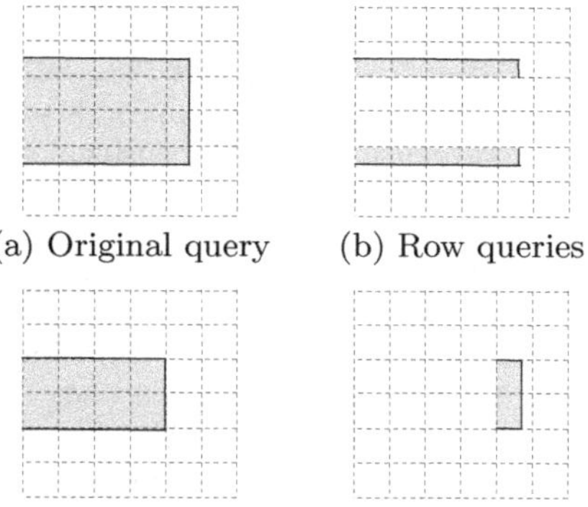

(a) Original query (b) Row queries

(c) Grid query (d) Vertical query

Figure 5: Answering a 4-sided query

report the non-pilot points in $P'(e) \cap g$ in ascending order of z-coordinate.

If we denote $Q(m)$ as the query cost (only the output independent part) on a problem of size m. Then, it follows from the above discussion that $Q(m) = O(\log_B n)$ if $m \leq B \log^{0.99} n \cdot (\log B + 3 \log\log n)^2$; otherwise:

$$Q(m) \quad = \quad Q(\mathcal{F}^{(1)}(m)) + O(\log_B m)$$

Setting $i = \mathcal{F}^*(m)$, we have:

$$\begin{aligned} Q(m) &= O(\log_B n) + \sum_{j=1}^{i} O(\log_B(\mathcal{F}^{(j)}(m))) \\ &= O(\log_B n) + \sum_{j=1}^{i} O\left(\log_B(B \log^2 m \cdot m^{1/2^j})\right) \end{aligned}$$

$$\begin{aligned} &= O(\log_B n) + \sum_{j=1}^{i} O\left(1 + \log_B \log m + \frac{1}{2^j} \log_B m\right) \\ &= O(\log_B n) + \mathcal{F}^*(m) \cdot O(1 + \log_B \log m) \end{aligned}$$

where the second equality used the fact that $\mathcal{F}^{(j)}(m) \leq B \log^2 m \cdot m^{1/2^j}$. Therefore:

$$\begin{aligned} Q(n) &= O(\log_B n) + \mathcal{F}^*(n) \cdot O(\log_B \log n) \\ &= O(\log_B n) + O(\log\log n) \cdot O(\log_B \log n) \\ &= O(\log_B n). \end{aligned}$$

Following the discussion of [3], a 5-sided query can be reduced to four 4-sided queries (which are can be processed as above) and a grid query whose search region is aligned on the grid G in the xy-plane. The grid query can be answered in $O(\log_B n)$ I/Os plus the linear output cost in the same way as we answered a query of Figure 5c. This completes the proof of Lemma 9.

4.4 Orthogonal Range Max

When k is fixed to 1, we can remove the $(\log\log B)^2$ factor in Statement 4 of Theorem 4. Furthermore, the structure can be made much simpler by utilizing the linear size structure of [20] for 3-sided range max—even without resorting to Δ-AWT.

THEOREM 5. *There is a structure of* $O(\frac{n}{B} \frac{\log n}{\log\log_B n})$ *space that answers an orthogonal range max query in* $O(\log_B n)$ *I/Os.*

PROOF. Let P be the input set of points in $\mathbb{R}^2$. Build a B-tree T on their x-coordinates with internal fanout $f = \log_B n$. Let u be an internal node. Naturally, u corresponds to a vertical slab in $\mathbb{R}^2$, which is divided into f smaller slabs by its children. Let P_u be the points of P in the slab of u, and let $n_u = |P_u|$. Create a structure on the points of P_u in each child slab to answer 3-sided orthogonal range max queries in $O(\log_B n)$ I/Os. Impose an $f \times \frac{n_u}{m}$ grid G_u with $m = \log^3 n$ in the same way as explained in Section 3. For each dyadic rectangle, store the maximum weight of the points of P_u in the rectangle. As there are $f \frac{n_u}{m} \log f \cdot \log n \leq n_u$ dyadic rectangles, doing so requires $O(n_u/B)$ space. Finally, within each row of G_u, build the orthogonal range max structure of [5] (see Table 1) on the points of P_u in that row.

The overall space is $O(\frac{n}{B} \frac{\log n}{\log\log_B n})$. The query algorithm proceeds in essentially the same manner as described in Section 3. It is easy to see that the query cost is $O(\log_B n)$ (notice that within each row, the structure of [5] requires only $O((\log_B \log n)^2) = O(\log_B n)$ I/Os). $\square$

It is worth mentioning that the simplicity of our structure does *not* carry over to the pointer machine model, where it remains unknown whether there is an $O(n)$-size structure that can answer a 3-sided query in $O(\log n)$ time. In other words, we still need to go through Δ-AWT to obtain the claimed orthogonal range max structure in Table 1.

5. LINEAR SPACE TOP-K ORR

In this section, we give a top-k ORR structure in external memory that uses $O(n/B)$ space, and answers a query in $O(\sqrt{n/B} + k/B)$ I/Os. This tradeoff can be proven to be optimal among the class of so-called "non-replicate" structures as will be discussed later.

LEMMA 12. *We can store n 3D points in a structure of* $O(n/B)$ *space such that a 5-sided range reporting query can be answered in in* $O(\sqrt{n/B} + k'/B)$ *I/Os, where* k' *is the number of points reported.*

PROOF. This can be achieved by combining ideas of the kd-tree and the priority search tree. Build a kd-tree on the projections of the points of P onto the xy-plane. The tree has $O(n/B)$ leaves, each containing between $B/2$ and B points. In each node u, we store B *pilot points*, which are the B points with the highest z-coordinates that are not pilot points in any proper ancestor of u. Clearly, the space occupied is $O(n/B)$ blocks. Recall that each node u can be thought of as being associated with a 2D minimum bounding rectangle (MBR) of all the points in its subtree.

Consider a query with search region $q' = [x_1, x_2] \times [y_1, y_2] \times [z, \infty)$. Let q be the xy-projection of q'. We search the kd-tree with q in the standard way to obtain a canonical set S of $O(\sqrt{n/B})$ nodes whose MBRs together cover q. At each node which is an ancestor of at least one node in S, we scan all its pilot points to report those lying in q'. Let v be a child of a canonical node in S. Report the pilot points of v whose z-coordinates are at least z. If all the pilot points of v are reported, we recursively repeat this procedure at the two children of v. Standard analysis shows that the algorithm performs $O(\sqrt{n/B} + k'/B)$ I/Os. $\square$

THEOREM 6. *There is a structure of* $O(n/B)$ *space that answers a 4-sided top-k ORR query in* $O(\sqrt{n/B} + k/B)$ *I/Os.*

PROOF. We only need a Δ-AWT structure of Lemma 7 with $\Delta = \sqrt{n/B}$, and a 5-sided reporting structure of Lemma 12. □

Remark on Non-Replication. Let P be the input set of n 2D points to the traditional orthogonal range reporting problem. Suppose that a query is required to report the ids of the points in the result. This means that a structure must also store point ids. A structure is said to be *non-replicate* [12, 22] if the id of each point is stored only once. In general, each point in P is associated an *information field* of L words, such that a query is required to report the information fields of all the result points. A structure is non-replicate [22] if it uses at most $O(n/B) + nL/B$ blocks (which implies that the information field of each point can be stored only once).

Our structure of Theorem 6 is a non-replicate one—in the structure of Lemma 12, we associate each node u in the kd-tree with $1 + xL/B$ blocks storing the information fields of the $x \in [1, B]$ pilot points of u. The space cost of the top-k ORR structure becomes $O(n/B) + nL/B$, whereas its query cost is $O(\sqrt{n/B} + kL/B)$. This is optimal following a lower bound of [22] and our reduction from (traditional) ORR to top-k ORR in Section 3.

ACKNOWLEDGEMENTS

This work was supported in part by Grants GRF 4168/13 and GRF 142072/14 from HKRGC.

6. REFERENCES

[1] Peyman Afshani. On dominance reporting in 3D. In *Proceedings of European Symposium on Algorithms (ESA)*, pages 41–51, 2008.

[2] Peyman Afshani, Lars Arge, and Kasper Dalgaard Larsen. Orthogonal range reporting in three and higher dimensions. In *Proceedings of Annual IEEE Symposium on Foundations of Computer Science (FOCS)*, pages 149–158, 2009.

[3] Peyman Afshani, Lars Arge, and Kasper Dalgaard Larsen. Orthogonal range reporting: query lower bounds, optimal structures in 3-d, and higher-dimensional improvements. In *Proceedings of Symposium on Computational Geometry (SoCG)*, pages 240–246, 2010.

[4] Peyman Afshani, Gerth Stolting Brodal, and Norbert Zeh. Ordered and unordered top-k range reporting in large data sets. In *Proceedings of the Annual ACM-SIAM Symposium on Discrete Algorithms (SODA)*, pages 390–400, 2011.

[5] Pankaj K. Agarwal, Lars Arge, Jun Yang, and Ke Yi. I/O-efficient structures for orthogonal range-max and stabbing-max queries. In *Proceedings of European Symposium on Algorithms (ESA)*, pages 7–18, 2003.

[6] Alok Aggarwal and Jeffrey Scott Vitter. The input/output complexity of sorting and related problems. *Communications of the ACM (CACM)*, 31(9):1116–1127, 1988.

[7] Stephen Alstrup, Gerth Stølting Brodal, and Theis Rauhe. Optimal static range reporting in one dimension. In *Proceedings of ACM Symposium on Theory of Computing (STOC)*, pages 476–482, 2001.

[8] Gerth Stolting Brodal, Rolf Fagerberg, Mark Greve, and Alejandro Lopez-Ortiz. Online sorted range reporting. In *International Symposium on Algorithms and Computation (ISAAC)*, pages 173–182, 2009.

[9] Bernard Chazelle. A functional approach to data structures and its use in multidimensional searching. *SIAM Journal of Computing*, 17(3):427–462, 1988.

[10] Bernard Chazelle. Lower bounds for orthogonal range searching: I. the reporting case. *Journal of the ACM (JACM)*, 37(2):200–212, 1990.

[11] Greg N. Frederickson. An optimal algorithm for selection in a min-heap. *Information and Computation*, 104(2):197–214, 1993.

[12] Kothuri Venkata Ravi Kanth and Ambuj K. Singh. Optimal dynamic range searching in non-replicating index structures. In *Proceedings of International Conference on Database Theory (ICDT)*, pages 257–276, 1999.

[13] Marek Karpinski and Yakov Nekrich. Top-k color queries for document retrieval. In *Proceedings of the Annual ACM-SIAM Symposium on Discrete Algorithms (SODA)*, pages 401–411, 2011.

[14] Edward M. McCreight. Priority search trees. *SIAM Journal of Computing*, 14(2):257–276, 1985.

[15] Gonzalo Navarro and Yakov Nekrich. Top-k document retrieval in optimal time and linear space. In *Proceedings of the Annual ACM-SIAM Symposium on Discrete Algorithms (SODA)*, pages 1066–1077, 2012.

[16] Yakov Nekrich. I/O-efficient point location in a set of rectangles. In *Latin American Symposium on Theoretical Informatics (LATIN)*, pages 687–698, 2008.

[17] Mihai Patrascu and Mikkel Thorup. Time-space trade-offs for predecessor search. In *Proceedings of ACM Symposium on Theory of Computing (STOC)*, pages 232–240, 2006.

[18] Saladi Rahul, Prosenjit Gupta, Ravi Janardan, and K. S. Rajan. Efficient top-k queries for orthogonal ranges. In *Proceedings of International Workshop on Algorithms and Computation (WALCOM)*, pages 110–121, 2011.

[19] Saladi Rahul and Ravi Janardan. A general technique for top-k geometric intersection query problems. *IEEE Transactions on Knowledge and Data Engineering (TKDE)*, 26(12):2859–2871, 2014.

[20] Cheng Sheng and Yufei Tao. New results on two-dimensional orthogonal range aggregation in external memory. In *Proceedings of ACM Symposium on Principles of Database Systems (PODS)*, pages 129–139, 2011.

[21] Cheng Sheng and Yufei Tao. Dynamic top-k range reporting in external memory. In *Proceedings of ACM Symposium on Principles of Database Systems (PODS)*, 2012.

[22] Yufei Tao. Indexability of 2d range search revisited: constant redundancy and weak indivisibility. In *Proceedings of ACM Symposium on Principles of Database Systems (PODS)*, pages 131–142, 2012.

[23] Yufei Tao. A dynamic I/O-efficient structure for one-dimensional top-k range reporting. In *Proceedings of ACM Symposium on Principles of Database Systems (PODS)*, pages 256–265, 2014.

APPENDIX

Proof of Lemma 8

When $\Delta = B \log_B n$, we have

$$\begin{aligned}
\frac{n}{B\Delta} \frac{\log^2 \frac{n}{\Delta}}{\log\log \frac{n}{\Delta}} &\leq \frac{n}{B^2 \log_B n} \cdot \frac{\log^2 n}{\log\log n} \\
&= \frac{n \log B \cdot \log n}{B^2 \log\log n} \\
&\leq \frac{n}{B} \frac{\log n}{B^{0.99} \log\log n} \\
&= O\left(\frac{n}{B} \frac{\log n}{\log\log_B n}\right).
\end{aligned}$$

Additional Details in the Proof of Lemma 11

Here are the details of showing $\mathcal{F}^{(2)}(B\log^3 n) \leq B\log^{0.99} n \cdot (\log B + 3\log\log n)^2$. By definition:

$$\begin{aligned}
\mathcal{F}^{(1)}(B\log^3 n) &= \sqrt{B\log^3 nB} \cdot \log(B\log^3 n) \\
&= B\log^{1.5} n \cdot (\log B + 3\log\log n).
\end{aligned}$$

Hence,

$$\begin{aligned}
&\mathcal{F}^{(2)}(B\log^3 n) \\
= \;&\mathcal{F}^{(1)}(B\log^{1.5} n \cdot (\log B + 3\log\log n)) \\
= \;&\sqrt{B\log^{1.5} n \cdot (\log B + 3\log\log n) \cdot B} \\
&\log(B\log^{1.5} n \cdot (\log B + 3\log\log n)) \\
= \;&B\log^{0.75} n \cdot (\log B + 3\log\log n)^{0.5} \\
&(\log B + 1.5\log\log n + \log(\log B + 3\log\log n)) \\
< \;&B\log^{0.75} n \cdot (\log B + 3\log\log n)^{1.6}.
\end{aligned}$$

Dynamic Data Structures for Document Collections and Graphs

J. Ian Munro
Cheriton School of Computer Science
University of Waterloo
imunro@uwaterloo.ca.

Yakov Nekrich
Cheriton School of Computer Science
University of Waterloo
ynekrich@uwaterloo.ca

Jeffrey Scott Vitter
Department of Electrical Engineering & Computer Science
University of Kansas
jsv@ku.edu.

ABSTRACT

In the dynamic indexing problem, we must maintain a changing collection of text documents so that we can efficiently support insertions, deletions, and pattern matching queries. We are especially interested in developing efficient data structures that store and query the documents in compressed form. All previous compressed solutions to this problem rely on answering rank and select queries on a dynamic sequence of symbols. Because of the lower bound in [Fredman and Saks, 1989], answering rank queries presents a bottleneck in compressed dynamic indexing. In this paper we show how this lower bound can be circumvented using our new framework. We demonstrate that the gap between static and dynamic variants of the indexing problem can be almost closed. Our method is based on a novel framework for adding dynamism to static compressed data structures. Our framework also applies more generally to dynamizing other problems. We show, for example, how our framework can be applied to develop compressed representations of dynamic graphs and binary relations.

Categories and Subject Descriptors

F2.2 [**Analysis of Algorithms and Problem Complexity**]: Nonnumerical Algorithms and Problems—*Sorting and searching*; H.3.1 [**Information Storage and Retrieval**]: Content Analysis and Indexing—*Indexing methods*

Keywords

Compressed Data Structures; Text Indexes; Graph Data Structures

1. INTRODUCTION

Motivated by the preponderance of massive data sets (so-called "big data"), it is becoming increasingly useful to store data in compressed form and moreover to manipulate and query the data while in compressed form. For that reason, such compressed data structures have been developed in the context of text indexing, graph representations, XML indexes, labeled trees, and many other applications. In this paper we describe a general framework to convert known static compressed data structures into dynamic compressed data structures. We show how this framework can be used to obtain significant improvements for two important dynamic problems: maintaining a dynamic graph and storing a dynamic collection of documents. We expect that our general framework will find further applications.

In the indexing problem, we keep a text or a collection of texts in a data structure, so that, given a query pattern, we can list all occurrences of the query pattern in the texts. This problem is one of the most fundamental in the area of string algorithms. Data structures that use $O(n \log n)$ bits of space can answer pattern matching queries in optimal time $O(|P| + \text{occ})$, where $|P|$ denotes the length of the query pattern P and occ is the number of occurrences of P. Because of the large volumes of data stored in text data bases and document collections, we are especially interested in data structures that store the text or texts in compressed form and at the same time can answer pattern matching queries efficiently. Compressed indexing problem was extensively studied in the static scenario and during the last two decades significant progress has been achieved; we refer to a survey [30] for an overview of previous results in this area.

In the dynamic indexing problem, also known as the library management problem, we maintain a collection of documents (texts) in a data structure under insertions and deletions of texts. It is not difficult to keep a dynamic collection of texts in $O(n)$ words (i.e., $O(n \log n)$ bits) and support pattern matching queries at the same time. For instance, we can maintain suffixes of all texts in a suffix tree; when a new text is added or deleted, we add all suffixes of the new text to the suffix tree (respectively, remove all suffixes of the deleted text from the suffix tree). We refer the reader to the full version of this paper [29] for a more detailed description of the $O(n \log n)$-bit solution. The problem of keeping a dynamic document collection in compressed form is however more challenging. Compressed data structures for the library management problem were considered in a number of papers [9, 25, 8, 25, 23, 26, 15, 24, 16, 20, 32, 31]. In spite of previous work, the query times of previously described dynamic data structures significantly exceed the query times of the best static indexes. In this paper we show that the gap between the static and the dynamic variants

PODS'15, May 31–June 4, 2015, Melbourne, Victoria, Australia.

http://dx.doi.org/10.1145/2745754.2745778 .

of the compressed indexing problem can be closed or almost closed. Furthermore we show that our approach can be applied to the succinct representation of dynamic graphs and binary relations that supports basic adjacency and neighbor queries. Again our technique significantly reduces the gap between static and dynamic variants of this problem.

These problems arise often in database applications. For example, reporting or counting occurrences of a string in a dynamic collection of documents is an important operation in text databases and web browsers. Similar tasks also arise in data analytics. Suppose that we keep a search log and want to find out how many times URLs containing a certain substring were accessed. Finally the indexing problem is closely related to the problem of substring occurrence estimation [33]. The latter problem is used in solutions of the substring selectivity estimation problem [10, 21, 22]; we refer to [33] for a more extensive description. Compressed storage schemes for such problems help us save space and boost general performance because a larger portion of data can reside in the fast memory. Graph representation of data is gaining importance in the database community. For instance, the set of subject-predicate-object RDF triples can be represented as a graph or as two binary relations [12]. Our compressed representation applied to an RDF graph enables us to support basic reporting and counting queries on triples. An example of such a query is given x, to enumerate all the triples in which x occurs as a subject. Another example is, given x and p, to enumerate all triples in which x occurs as a subject and p occurs as a predicate.

Previous Results. Static Case.

We will denote by $|T|$ the number of symbols in a sequence T or in a collection of sequences; $T[i]$ denotes the i-th element in a sequence T and $T[i..j] = T[i]T[i+1]\dots T[j]$. Suffix trees and suffix arrays are two handbook data structures for the indexing problem. Suffix array keeps (references to) all suffixes $T[i..n]$ of a text T in lexicographic order. Using a suffix array, we can find the range of suffixes starting with a query string P in $t_{\mathrm{range}} = O(|P| + \log n)$ time; once this range is found, we can locate each occurrence of P in T in $t_{\mathrm{locate}} = O(1)$ time. A suffix tree is a compact trie that contains references to all suffixes $T[i..n]$ of a text T. Using a suffix trie, we can find the range of suffixes starting with a query string P in $t_{\mathrm{range}} = O(|P|)$ time; once this range is found, we can locate every occurrence of P in T in $t_{\mathrm{locate}} = O(1)$ time. A large number of compressed indexing data structures are described in the literature; we refer to [30] for a survey. These data structures follow the same two-step procedure for answering a query: first, the range of suffixes that start with P is found in $O(t_{\mathrm{range}})$ time, then we locate each occurrence of P in T in $O(t_{\mathrm{locate}})$ time. Thus we report all occ occurrences of P in $O(t_{\mathrm{range}} + \mathrm{occ} \cdot t_{\mathrm{locate}})$ time. We can also extract any substring $T[i..i+\ell]$ of T in $O(t_{\mathrm{extract}})$ time. Data structures supporting queries on a text T can be extended to answer queries on a collection $\mathcal{C}$ of texts: it suffices to append a unique symbol $\$_i$ at the end of every text T_i from $\mathcal{C}$ and keep the concatenation of all T_i in the data structure.

We list the currently best and selected previous results for static text indexes with asymptotically optimal space usage in Table 1. All listed data structures can achieve different space-time trade-offs that depend on parameter s: an index typically needs about $nH_k + o(n\log\sigma) + O(n\log n/s)$ bits and t_{locate} is proportional to s. Henceforth H_k denotes the k-th order empirical entropy and σ denotes the alphabet size[1]. We assume that $k \le \alpha\log_\sigma n - 1$ for a constant $0 < \alpha < 1$. H_k is the lower bound on the average space usage of any statistical compression method that encodes each symbol using the context of k previous symbols [27]. The currently fastest such index of Belazzougui and Navarro [6] reports all occurrences of P in $O(|P| + s \cdot \mathrm{occ})$ time and extracts a substring of length ℓ in $O(s+\ell)$ time. Thus their query time depends only on the parameter s and the length of P. Some recently described indices [3, 6] achieve space usage $nH_k + o(nH_k) + o(n)$ or $nH_k + o(nH_k) + O(n)$ instead of $nH_k + o(n\log\sigma)$.

If we are interested in obtaining faster data structures and can use $\Theta(n\log\sigma)$ bits of space, then better trade-offs between space usage and time are possible [18, 19]. For the sake of space, we describe only one such result. The data structure of Grossi and Vitter [19] uses $O(n\log\sigma)$ bits and reports occurrences of a pattern in $O(|P|/\log_\sigma n + \log^\varepsilon n + \mathrm{occ}\log^\varepsilon n)$ time; see Table 3. We remark that the fastest data structure in Table 1 needs $\Omega(n\log^{1-\varepsilon} n)$ space to obtain the same time for t_{locate} as in [19]. If a data structure from Table 1 uses $O(n\log\sigma)$ space, then $t_{\mathrm{locate}} = \Omega(\log_\sigma n)$.

Dynamic Document Collections.

In the dynamic indexing problem, we maintain a collection of documents (strings) under insertions and deletions. An insertion adds a new document to the collection, a deletion removes a document from the collection. For any query substring P, we must return all occurrences of P in all documents. When a query is answered, relative positions of occurrences are reported. To be precise, we must report all pairs (doc, off), such that P occurs in a document *doc* at position *off*. We remark that relative positions of P (with respect to document boundaries) are reported. Hence an insertion or a deletion of a document does not change positions of P in other documents. Indexes for dynamic collections of strings were also studied extensively [9, 25, 8, 23, 26, 15, 24, 16, 20, 32, 31]. The fastest previously known result for the case of large alphabets is described in [31]. Their data structure, that builds on a long line of previous work, uses $nH_k + o(n\log\sigma) + O(n\log n/s) + O(\rho\log n)$ bits of space, where ρ is the number of documents; queries are answered in $O(|P|\log n/\log\log n + \mathrm{occ}\cdot s\cdot\log n/\log\log n)$ time and updates are supported in $O(\log n + |T_u|\log n/\log\log n)$ amortized time, where T is the document inserted into or deleted from the collection. See Table 2 for some other previous results.

An important component of previous dynamic solutions is a data structure supporting rank and select queries: a sequence S over an alphabet $\Sigma = \{1,\dots,\sigma\}$ is kept in a data structure so that the i-th occurrence of a symbol $a \in \Sigma$ and the number of times a symbol a occurs in $S[1..i]$ for any $1 \le i \le n$ can be computed. Thus progress in dynamic indexing was closely related to progress in dynamic data structures for rank and select queries. In [31] the authors obtain a

[1]Let S be an arbitrary string over an alphabet $\Sigma = \{1,\dots,\sigma\}$. A *context* $s_i \in \Sigma^k$ is an arbitrary string of length k. Let $n_{s_i,a}$ be the number of times the symbol a is preceded by a context s_i in S and $n_{s_i} = \sum_{a\in\Sigma} n_{s_i,a}$. Then $H_k = -\sum_{s_i\in\Sigma^k}\sum_{a\in\Sigma} n_{s_i,a}\log\frac{n_{s_i,a}}{n_{s_i}}$ is the k-th order empirical entropy of S.

Ref.	Space ($+O(n\frac{\log n}{s})$)	t_{range}	t_{locate}	t_{extract}	σ
[18]	$nH_k + o(n\log\sigma)$	$O(\lvert P\rvert\log\sigma + \log^4 n)$	$O(s\log\sigma)$	$O((s+\ell)\log\sigma)$	
[34]	$nH_k + o(n\log\sigma)$	$O(\lvert P\rvert\log n)$	$O(s)$	$O(s+\ell)$	
[13]	$nH_k + o(n\log\sigma)$	$O(\lvert P\rvert\frac{\log\sigma}{\log\log n})$	$O(s\frac{\log\sigma}{\log\log n})$	$O((s+\ell)\frac{\log\sigma}{\log\log n})$	
[5]	$nH_k + o(n\log\sigma)$	$O(\lvert P\rvert\log\log\sigma)$	$O(s\log\log\sigma)$	$O((s+\ell)\log\log\sigma)$	
[3]	$nH_k + o(nH_k) + o(n)$	$O(\lvert P\rvert\frac{\log\sigma}{\log\log n})$	$O(s\frac{\log\sigma}{\log\log n})$	$O((s+\ell)\frac{\log\sigma}{\log\log n})$	
[3]	$nH_k + o(nH_k) + o(n)$	$O(\lvert P\rvert\log\log\sigma)$	$O(s\log\log\sigma)$	$O((s+\ell)\log\log\sigma)$	
[3]	$nH_k + o(nH_k) + o(n)$	$O(\lvert P\rvert)$	$O(s)$	$O(s+\ell)$	$\log^{\text{const}} n$
[6]	$nH_k + o(nH_k) + O(n)$	$O(\lvert P\rvert)$	$O(s)$	$O(s+\ell)$	

Table 1: Asymptotically optimal space data structures for static indexing. Occurrences of a string P can be found in $O(t_{\text{range}} + t_{\text{locate}}\cdot\text{occ})$ time. A substring $T[i..i+\ell]$ of T can be extracted in $O(t_{\text{extract}})$ time. Results are valid for any $k \le \alpha\log_\sigma n - 1$ and $0 < \alpha < 1$.

Ref.	Space ($+O(n\frac{\log n}{s}) + \rho\log n$)	t_{range}	t_{locate}	t_{extract}	Insert/ Delete	σ
[8]	$O(n)$	$O(\lvert P\rvert\log n)$	$O(\log^2 n)$	$O((\log n+\ell)\log n)$	$O(\lvert T_u\rvert\log n)$	const
[25]	$nH_k + o(n\log\sigma)$	$O(\lvert P\rvert\log n\log\sigma)$	$O(s\log n\log\sigma)$	$((s+\ell)\log n\log\sigma)$	$O(\lvert T_u\rvert\log n\log\sigma)$	
[31]	$nH_k + o(n\log\sigma)$	$O(\lvert P\rvert\log n)$	$O(s\log n)$	$O((s+\ell)\log n)$	$O(\lvert T_u\rvert\log n)$	
[31]	$nH_k + o(n\log\sigma)$	$O(\lvert P\rvert\frac{\log n}{\log\log n})$	$O(s\log n/\log\log n)$	$O((s+\ell)\frac{\log n}{\log\log n})$	$O(\log n + \lvert T_u\rvert\frac{\log n}{\log\log n})^{\mathbf{A}}$	
Our	$nH_k + o(n\log\sigma)$	$O(\lvert P\rvert\log\log n)$	$O(s)$	$O(s+\ell)$	$O(\lvert T_u\rvert\log^{1+\varepsilon} n)$	$\log^{\text{const}} n$
Our	$nH_k + o(n\log\sigma)$	$O(\lvert P\rvert\log\log n\log\log\sigma)$	$O(s\log\log\sigma)$	$O((s+\ell)\log\log\sigma)$	$O(\lvert T_u\rvert\log^\varepsilon n)$/ $O(\lvert T_u\rvert(\log^\varepsilon n + s))$	
Our	$nH_k + o(n\log\sigma)$	$O(\lvert P\rvert\log\log n)$	$O(s)$	$O(s+\ell)$	$O(\lvert T_u\rvert\log^\varepsilon n)^{\mathbf{R}}$/ $O(\lvert T_u\rvert(\log^\varepsilon n + s)^{\mathbf{R}}$	

Table 2: Asymptotically optimal space data structures for dynamic indexing. The same notation as in Table 1 is used. Randomized update procedures that achieve specified cost in expectation are marked with R. Amortized update costs are marked with A. T_u denotes the document that is inserted into (resp. deleted from) the data structure during an update operation. In previous papers on dynamic indexing only the cases of $s = \log n$ or $s = \log_\sigma n\log\log n$ was considered, but extension to an arbitrary value of s is straightforward.

dynamic data structure that supports rank and select in $O(\log n/\log\log n)$ time. By the lower bound of Fredman and Saks [14], this query time is optimal in the dynamic scenario. It was assumed that the solution of the library management problem described in [31] achieves query time that is close to optimal.

Our Results.

In this paper we show that the lower bound on dynamic rank-select problem can be circumvented and describe data structures that need significantly less time to answer queries. Our results close or almost close the gap between static and dynamic indexing. If the alphabet size $\sigma = \log^{O(1)} n$, we can obtain an $(nH_k + o(n\log\sigma) + O(n\frac{\log n}{s}))$-bit data structure that answers queries in $O(|P|\log\log n + \text{occ}\cdot s)$ time; updates are supported in $O(|T_u|\log^{1+\varepsilon} n)$ time, where T_u denotes the document that is inserted into or deleted from the index. Our second data structure supports updates in $O(|T_u|\log^\varepsilon n)$ expected time and answers queries in $O(|P|\log\log n + \text{occ}\cdot s)$ time for an arbitrarily large alphabet[2]. If the update procedure is deterministic, then queries are answered in $O((|P|\log\log n + \text{occ}\cdot s)\log\log\sigma)$ time and updates are supported in $O(|T_u|\log^\varepsilon n)$ worst-case time. See Table 2. If $O(n\log\sigma)$ bits of space are available, then our dynamic data structure matches the currently fastest static result of Grossi and Vitter [19]. We can report all occurrences of a pattern P in $O(|P|/\log_\sigma n + \log^\varepsilon n + \text{occ}\cdot\log^\varepsilon n)$ time. This is the first compressed dynamic data structure that achieves $t_{\text{range}} = o(|P|)$ if $\sigma = n^{o(1)}$. Compared to the fastest previous data structure that needs the same space, we achieve $O(\log n\log_\sigma n)$ factor improvement in query time. A variant of this data structure with deterministic update procedure answers queries in $O(|P|(\log\log n)^2/\log_\sigma n + \log n + \text{occ}\cdot\log^\varepsilon n)$ time. See Table 3.

Our data structures can also count occurrences of a pattern P in $O(t_{\text{count}})$ time. For previously described indexes $t_{\text{count}} = t_{\text{range}}$. In our case, $t_{\text{count}} = t_{\text{range}} + \log n/\log\log n$ or $t_{\text{count}} = (t_{\text{range}} + \log n/\log\log n)\log\log n$. Times needed to answer a counting query are listed in Table 4. However, if our data structures support counting queries, then update times grow slightly, as shown in Table 4.

All of the above mentioned results are obtained as corollaries of two general transformations. Using these transformations, that work for a very broad class of indexes, we can immediately turn almost any static data structure with good pre-processing time into an index for a dynamic collection of texts. The query time either remains the same or increases by a very small multiplicative factor. Our method can be applied to other problems where both compressed representation and dynamism are desirable.

[2]Dynamic indexes also need $O(\rho\log n)$ bits to navigate between documents, where ρ is the number of documents. Since $\rho\log n$ is usually negligible in comparison to n, we ignore this additive term, except for Tables 2 and 3, to simplify the description.

Binary Relations and Graphs.

One important area where our techniques can also be used is compact representation of directed graphs and binary relations. Let $R \subseteq L \times O$ be a binary relation between labels from a set L and objects from a set O. Barbay et al. [5] describe a compact representation of a static binary relation R (i.e., the set of object-label pairs) that consists of a sequence S_R and a bit sequence B_R. S_R contain the list of labels related to different objects and is ordered by object. That is, S_R lists all labels related to an object o_1, then all labels related to an object o_2, etc. The binary sequence B_R contains unary-encoded numbers of labels related to objects o_1, o_2, ... Barbay et al [5] showed how S_R and B_R can be used to support basic queries on binary relations, such as listing or counting all labels related to an object, listing or counting all objects related to a label, and telling whether a label and an object are related. Their method reduces queries on a binary relation R to rank, select, and access queries on S_R and B_R. Another data structure that stores a static binary relation and uses the same technique is described in [2]. Static compact data structures described in [5, 2] support queries in $O(\log\log\sigma_l)$ time per reported datum, where σ_l is the number of labels. For instance, we can report labels related to an object (resp. objects related to a label) in $O((k+1)\log\log\sigma_l)$ time, where k is the number of reported items; we can tell whether an object and a label are related in $O(\log\log\sigma_l)$ time. In [31], the authors describe a dynamization of this approach that relies on dynamic data structures answering rank and select queries on dynamic strings S_R and B_R. Again the lower bound on dynamic rank queries sets the limit on the efficiency of this approach. Since we need $\Omega(\log n/\log\log n)$ time to answer rank queries, the data structure of Navarro and Nekrich [31] needs $O(\log n/\log\log n)$ time per reported item, where n is the number of object-label pairs in R. Updates are supported in $O(\log n/\log\log n)$ amortized time and the space usage is $nH + \sigma_l\log\sigma_l + t\log t + O(n + \sigma_l\log\sigma_l)$ where n is the number of pairs, H is the zero-order entropy of the string S_R, σ_l is the number of labels and t is the number of objects.In [31] the authors also show that we can answer basic adjacency and neighbor queries on a directed graph by regarding a graph as a binary relation between nodes. Again reporting and counting out-going and in-going neighbors of a node can be performed in $O(\log n)$ time per delivered datum.

In this paper we show how our method for dynamizing compressed data structures can be applied to binary relations and graphs. Our data structure supports reporting labels related to an object or reporting objects related to a label in $O(\log\log n\cdot\log\log\sigma_l)$ time per reported datum. We support counting queries in $O(\log n)$ time and updates in $O(\log^{\varepsilon} n)$ worst-case time. The same query times are also achieved for the dynamic graph representation. The space usage of our data structures is dominated by nH where n is the number of pairs in a binary relation or the number of edges in a graph and H is the zero-order entropy of the string S_R defined above. Thus the space usage of our data structure matches that of [31] up to lower-order factors. At the same time we show that reporting queries in a dynamic graph can be supported without dynamic rank and select queries.

Overview.

The main idea of our approach can be described as follows. The input data is distributed among several data structures. We maintain a fraction of the data in an uncompressed data structure that supports both insertions and deletions. We bound the number of elements stored in uncompressed form so that the total space usage of the uncompressed data structure is affordable. Remaining data is kept in several compressed data structures that do not support updates. New elements (respectively new documents) are always inserted into the uncompressed data structure. Deletions from the static data structures are implemented by the lazy deletions mechanism: when a deletion takes place, then the deleted element (respectively the document) is marked as deleted. We keep positions of marked elements in a data structure, so that all elements in a query range that are not marked as deleted can be reported in $O(1)$ time per element. When a static structure contains too much obsolete data (because a certain fraction of its size is marked as deleted), then this data structure is purged: we create a new instance of this data structure that does not contain deleted elements. If the uncompressed data structure becomes too big, we move its content into a (new) compressed data structure. Organization of compressed data structures is inspired by the logarithmic method, introduced by Bentley and Saxe [7]: the size of compressed data structures increases geometrically. We show that re-building procedures can be scheduled in such way that only a small fraction of data is kept in uncompressed form at any given time. Since the bulk of data is kept in static data structures, our approach can be viewed as a general framework that transforms static compressed data structures into dynamic ones.

In Section 2 we describe Transformation 1; Transformation 1, based on the approach outlined above, can be used to turn a static indexing data structure into a data structure for dynamic collection of documents with amortized update cost. The query costs of the obtained dynamic data structure are the same as in the underlying static data structure. In Section 3 we describe Transformation 2 that turns a static indexing data structure into a dynamic data structure with worst-case update costs. We use more sophisticated division into sub-collections and slightly different re-building procedures in Transformation 2. In Section 4 we describe how to obtain new solutions of the dynamic indexing problem using our static-to-dynamic transformations. Finally Section 5 contains our data structures for dynamic graphs and binary relations.

2. DYNAMIC DOCUMENT COLLECTIONS

In this section we show how a static compressed index $\mathcal{I}_s$ can be transformed into a dynamic index $\mathcal{I}_d$. $\mathcal{C}$ will denote a collection of texts $T_1, \ldots, T_\rho$. We say that an index $\mathcal{I}_s$ is $(u(n), w(n))$-constructible if there is an algorithm that uses $O(n\cdot w(n))$ additional workspace and constructs $\mathcal{I}_s$ in $O(n\cdot u(n))$ time. Henceforth we make the following important assumptions about the static index $\mathcal{I}_s$. $\mathcal{I}_s$ needs at most $|S|\phi(S)$ bits of space for any symbol sequence S and the function $\phi(\cdot)$ is monotonous: if any sequence S is a concatenation of S_1 and S_2, then $|S|\phi(S) \geq |S_1|\phi(S_1) + |S_2|\phi(S_2)$. We also assume that $\mathcal{I}_s$ reports occurrences of a substring in $\mathcal{C}$ using the two-step method described in the introduction: first we identify the range $[a, b]$ in the suffix array, such that all suffixes that start with P are in $[a, b]$; then we find the

Ref.	t_{range}	t_{locate}	t_{extract}	Update	σ
[19]	$O(\|P\|/\log_\sigma n + \log^\varepsilon n)$	$O(\log^\varepsilon n)$	$O(\ell/\log_\sigma n)$	static	
[8]	$O(\|P\| \log n)$	$O(\log^2 n)$	$O((\log n + \ell)\log n)$	$O(\|T_u\| \log n)$	const
[31]	$O(\|P\| \log n)$	$O(\log n \log_\sigma n)$	$O((\log_\sigma n + \ell)\log n)$	$O(\|T_u\| \log n)$	
Our	$O(\|P\|/\log_\sigma n + \log^\varepsilon n)$	$O(\log^\varepsilon n)$	$O(\ell/\log_\sigma n)$	$O(\|T_u\| \log^\varepsilon n)^{\mathbf{R}}$	
Our	$O(\|P\|(\log\log n)^2/\log_\sigma n + \log n)$	$O(\log^\varepsilon n)$	$O(\ell/\log_\sigma n)$	$O(\|T_u\| \log^\varepsilon n)$	

Table 3: $O(n\log\sigma)$-bit indexes. Dynamic data structures need additional $\rho\log n$ bits. Randomized update costs are marked with R.

Space	Counting	Updates	σ
$nH_k + o(n\log\sigma)$	$O(\|P\| \log\log n + \log n)$	$O(\|T_u\| \log n)$	$\log^{\text{const}} n$
$nH_k + o(n\log\sigma)$	$O((\|P\| \log\log\sigma \log\log n + \log n)$	$O(\|T_u\| \log n)$	
$nH_k + o(n\log\sigma)$	$O((\|P\| \log\log n + \log n)$	$O(\|T_u\| \log n)^{\mathbf{R}}$	
$O(n\log\sigma)$	$O(\|P\|/\log_\sigma n + \log n/\log\log n)$	$O(\|T_u\| \log n)^{\mathbf{R}}$	
$O(n\log\sigma)$	$O(\|P\|(\log\log n)^2/\log_\sigma n + \log n)$	$O(\|T_u\| \log n)$	

Table 4: Costs of counting queries for our data structures. Randomized update costs are marked with R. The first three rows correspond to the last three rows in Table 2, the last two rows correspond to the last two rows in Table 3.

positions of suffixes from $[a, b]$ in the document(s). These operations will be called range-finding and locating. Moreover the rank of any suffix $T_i[l..]$ in the suffix array can be found in time $O(t_{\text{SA}})$. The class of indexes that satisfy these conditions includes all indexes that are based on compressed suffix arrays or the Burrows-Wheeler transform. Thus the best currently known static indexes can be used in Transformation 1 and the following transformations described in this paper.

Our result can be stated as follows.

TRANSFORMATION 1. *Suppose that there exists a static $(u(n), w(n))$-constructible index $\mathcal{I}_s$ that uses $|S|\phi(S)$ space for any document collection S. Then there exists a dynamic index $\mathcal{I}_d$ that uses $|S|\phi(S)+O(|S|(\frac{\log\sigma}{\tau}+w(n)+\frac{\log\tau}{\tau}))$ space for a parameter $\tau = O(\log n/\log\log n)$; $\mathcal{I}_d$ supports insertions and deletions of documents in $O(u(n)\log^\varepsilon n)$ time per symbol and $O(u(n)\cdot\tau + t_{\text{SA}} + \log^\varepsilon n)$ time per symbol respectively. Update times are amortized. The asymptotic costs of range-finding, extracting, and locating are the same in $\mathcal{I}_s$ and $\mathcal{I}_d$.*

We start by showing how to turn a static index into a semi-dynamic deletion-only index using $O((n/\tau)\log\tau)$ additional bits. Then we will show how to turn a semi-dynamic index into a fully-dynamic one.

Supporting Document Deletions.

We keep a bit array B whose entries correspond to positions in the suffix array SA of $\mathcal{C}$. $B[j] = 0$ if $SA[j]$ is a suffix of some text T_f, such that T_f was already deleted from $\mathcal{C}$ and $B[j] = 1$ otherwise. We keep a data structure V that supports the following operations on B: *zero*(j) sets the j-th bit in B to 0; *report*(j_1, j_2) reports all 1-bits in $B[j_1..j_2]$. V is implemented using Lemma 3, so that *zero*(i) is supported in $O(\log^\varepsilon n)$ time and *report*(j_1, j_2) is answered in $O(k)$ time, where k is the number of output bit positions. If B contains at most n/τ zeros, then B and V need only $O((n\log\tau)/\tau)$ bits. Lemma 3 is proved in Section A.1.

When a document T_f is deleted, we identify the positions of T_f's suffixes in SA and set the corresponding bits in B to 0. When the number of symbols in deleted documents equals (n/τ), we re-build the index for $\mathcal{C}$ without deleted documents in $O(n \cdot u(n))$ time. The total amortized cost of deleting a document is $O(u(n)\tau + t_{\text{SA}} + \log^\varepsilon n)$ per symbol. To report occurrences of some string P in $\mathcal{C}$, we identify the range $[s..e]$ such that all suffixes in $SA[s..e]$ start with P in $O(t_{\text{range}})$ time. Using V, we enumerate all j, such that $s \le j \le e$ and $B[j] = 1$. For every such j, we compute $SA[j]$ in $O(t_{\text{locate}})$ time.

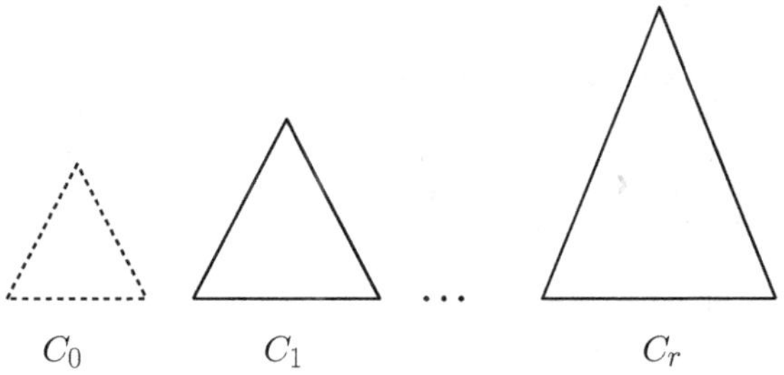

Figure 1: Sub-collections $\mathcal{C}_i$ for dynamizing a deletion-only index. A data structure for $\mathcal{C}_0$ is fully-dynamic and stores documents in uncompressed form.

Fully-Dynamic Index.

We split $\mathcal{C}$ into a constant number of sub-collections $\mathcal{C}_0, \mathcal{C}_1, \ldots, \mathcal{C}_r$ such that $|\mathcal{C}_i| \le \max_i$ for all i. The maximum size of the i-th sub-collection, $\max_i$, increases geometrically: $\max_0 = 2n/\log^2 n$ and $\max_i = 2(n/\log^2 n)\log^{\varepsilon\cdot i} n$ for a constant $\varepsilon > 0$; see Fig. 1. There is no lower bound on the number of symbols in a sub-collection $\mathcal{C}_i$; for instance, any $\mathcal{C}_i$ can be empty. Our main idea is to store $\mathcal{C}_0$ in uncompressed form and $\mathcal{C}_i$ for $i \ge 1$ in semi-static deletion-only data structures. Insertions into $\mathcal{C}_i$ for $i \ge 1$ are supported by re-building the semi-static index of $\mathcal{C}_i$. We also re-build all sub-collections when the total number of elements is increased by a constant factor (global re-build).

We store the document collection $\mathcal{C}_0$ in uncompressed form. Suffixes of all documents in $\mathcal{C}_0$ are kept in an (uncompressed) suffix tree $\mathcal{D}_0$. We can insert a new text T into $\mathcal{D}_0$ or delete T from $\mathcal{D}_0$ in $O(|T|)$ time. Using $\mathcal{D}_0$, all occurrences of a pattern P in $\mathcal{C}_0$ can be reported in $O(|P| + \text{occ})$ time. Since $|\mathcal{C}_0| \le 2n/\log^2 n$, we need $O(n/\log n)$ bits to store $\mathcal{C}_0$. For completeness we describe the data structure for $\mathcal{C}_0$ in the full version of this paper [29]

Every $\mathcal{C}_i$ for $i \ge 1$ is kept in a semi-dynamic data structure described in the first part of this section. Let $size(i)$ denote the total length of all undeleted texts in $\mathcal{C}_i$. When a new document T must be inserted, we find the first (smallest) collection $\mathcal{C}_j$ such that $\sum_{i=0}^{j} size(i) + |T| \le \max_j$ where $\max_j = 2(n/\log^2 n)\log^{\varepsilon \cdot j} n$. That is, we find the first subcollection $\mathcal{C}_j$ that can accommodate the new text T and all preceding subcollections without exceeding the size limit. If $j = 0$, we insert the new text into $\mathcal{C}_0$. Otherwise, if $j \ge 1$, we discard the old indexes for all $\mathcal{C}_i$ where $0 \le i \le j$, set $\mathcal{C}_j = (\cup_{i=0}^{j}\mathcal{C}_i) \cup T$ and construct a new semi-static index for $\mathcal{C}_j$. If $\sum_{i=0}^{j} size(i) + |T| > \max_j$ for all j, we start a global re-build procedure: all undeleted texts from old sub-collections are moved to the new sub-collection $\mathcal{C}_r$ and parameters $\max_i$ are re-calculated; new sub-collections $\mathcal{C}_i$ for $0 \le i < r$ are initially empty after the global re-build.

We start a global re-build procedure when the total number of elements is at least doubled. Hence, the amortized cost of a global re-build is $O(u(n))$. The amortized cost of re-building sub-collections can be analyzed as follows. When a sub-collection $\mathcal{C}_j$ is re-built, we insert all symbols from subcollections $\mathcal{C}_i$, $0 \le i < j$ and the new text T into $\mathcal{C}_j$. Our insertion procedure guarantees that $\sum_{i=1}^{j-1} size(j) + |T| > \max_{j-1}$. We need $O(\max_j \cdot u(n))$ time to construct a new index for $\mathcal{C}_j$. The cost of re-building $\mathcal{C}_j$ can be distributed among the new text symbols inserted into $\mathcal{C}_j$. Since $\max_{j-1} = \max_j / \log^{\varepsilon} n$, the amortized cost of inserting a new symbol into $\mathcal{C}_j$ is $O(u(n) \cdot \log^{\varepsilon} n)$. Every text is moved at most once to any subcollection $\mathcal{C}_j$ for any j such that $1 \le j \le \lceil 2/\varepsilon \rceil$. Hence the total amortized cost of an insertion is $O((1/\varepsilon)u(n) \cdot \log^{\varepsilon} n)$ per symbol.

A query is answered by querying all non-empty subcollections $\mathcal{C}_i$ for $i = 0, 1, \ldots, r$. Since $r = O(1)$, query times are the same as in the underlying static index. Splitting a collection into sub-collection does not increase the space usage because the function $\phi(\cdot)$ is monotonous. We need $O((n/\tau)\log \tau)$ bits to keep data structures V for all $\mathcal{C}_i$. Another $O(nw(n))$ bits are needed for global and local rebuilds. Finally we need $O((n/\tau)\log \sigma)$ bits to store the symbols from deleted documents. Since there are no more than $O(n/\tau)$ deleted symbols, we use $O((n/\tau)\log \sigma) + o(n \log \sigma)$ additional bits to store them; a more detailed analysis is given in the full version [29]. Hence, the total space overhead of our dynamic index is $O(n(w(n) + (\log \sigma + \log \tau)/\tau))$.

3. WORST-CASE UPDATES

In this section we will prove the following result.

TRANSFORMATION 2. *Suppose that there exists a static $(u(n), w(n))$-constructible index $\mathcal{I}_s$ that uses $|S|\phi(S)$ space for any document collection S. Then there exists a dynamic index $\mathcal{I}_d$ that uses $|S|\phi(S) + O(|S|\frac{\log \sigma + \log \tau + w(n)}{\tau})$ space for any parameter $\tau = O(\log n/\log\log n)$; $\mathcal{I}_d$ supports insertions and deletions of documents in $O(u(n)\log^{\varepsilon} n)$ time per symbol and $O(u(n) \cdot (\log^{\varepsilon} n + \tau \log \tau) + t_{SA})$ time per symbol respectively. The asymptotic costs of range-finding increases by $O(\tau)$; the costs of extracting and locating are the same in $\mathcal{I}_s$ and $\mathcal{I}_d$.*

We use the index of Transformation 1 as the starting point. First we give an overview of our data structure and show how queries can be answered. Then we describe the procedures for text insertions and deletions.

Overview.

The main idea of supporting updates in worst-case is to maintain several copies of the same sub-collection. An old copy of $\mathcal{C}_j$ is locked while a new updated version of $\mathcal{C}_{j+1}$ that includes $\mathcal{C}_j$ is created in the background. When a new version of $\mathcal{C}_{j+1}$ is finished, we discard an old locked sub-collection. When a new document $\mathcal{T}$ must be inserted, we insert it into $\mathcal{C}_0$ if $|\mathcal{C}_0| + |T| \le \max_0$. Otherwise we look for the smallest $j \ge 0$, such that $\mathcal{C}_{j+1}$ can accommodate both $\mathcal{C}_j$ and T; then we move both T and all documents from $\mathcal{C}_j$ into $\mathcal{C}_{j+1}$[3]. If the new document T is large, $|T| \ge \max_j/2$, we can afford to re-build $\mathcal{C}_{j+1}$ immediately after the insertion of T. If the size of T is smaller than $\max_j/2$, re-building of $\mathcal{C}_{j+1}$ is postponed. For every following update, we spend $O(\log^{\varepsilon} n \cdot u(n))$ time per symbol on creating the new version of $\mathcal{C}_{j+1}$. The old versions of $\mathcal{C}_j$, $\mathcal{C}_{j+1}$ are retained until the new version is completed. If the number of symbols that are marked as deleted in $\mathcal{C}_j$ exceeds $\max_j/2$, we employ the same procedure for moving $\mathcal{C}_j$ to $\mathcal{C}_{j+1}$: $\mathcal{C}_j$ is locked and we start the process of constructing a new version $\mathcal{C}_{j+1}$ that contains all undeleted documents from $\mathcal{C}_j$.

The disadvantage of delayed re-building is that we must keep two copies of every document in $\mathcal{C}_j \cup \mathcal{C}_{j+1}$ until new $\mathcal{C}_{j+1}$ is completed. In order to reduce the space usage, we keep only a fraction of all documents in sub-collections $\mathcal{C}_i$. All $\mathcal{C}_i$ for $0 \le i \le r$ will contain $O(n/\tau)$ symbols, where τ is the parameter determining the trade-off between space overhead and query time. The remaining documents are kept in top sub-collections $\mathcal{T}_1, \ldots, \mathcal{T}_g$ where $g \le 2\tau$. Top sub-collections are constructed using the same delayed approach. But once $\mathcal{T}_i$ is finished, no new documents are inserted into $\mathcal{T}_i$. We may have to re-build a top collection or merge it with another $\mathcal{T}_j$ when the fraction of deleted symbols exceeds a threshold value $1/\tau$. We employ the same rebuilding-in-the-background approach. However, we will show that the background procedures for maintaining $\mathcal{T}_i$ can be scheduled in such a way that only one $\mathcal{T}_j$ is re-built at any given moment. Hence, the total space overhead due to re-building and storage of deleted elements is bounded by an additive term $O(n(\log \sigma + w(n))/\tau)$.

Data Structures.

We split a document collection $\mathcal{C}$ into subcollections $\mathcal{C}_0$, $\mathcal{C}_1, \ldots, \mathcal{C}_r, \mathcal{L}_1, \ldots, \mathcal{L}_r$ and top subcollections $\mathcal{T}_1, \ldots, \mathcal{T}_g$ where $g = O(\tau)$. We will also use auxiliary collections $\mathcal{N}_1, \ldots, \mathcal{N}_{r+1}$ and temporary collections $Temp_1, \ldots, Temp_r$. $Temp_i$ are also used to answer queries but each non-empty

[3]Please note the difference between Transformations 1 and 2. In Transformation 1 we look for the sub-collection $\mathcal{C}_j$ that can accommodate the new document and *all* smaller sub-collections $\mathcal{C}_0, \ldots, \mathcal{C}_{j-1}$. In Transformation 2 we look for the sub-collection $\mathcal{C}_{j+1}$ that can accommodate that can accommodate the new document and the preceding sub-collection $\mathcal{C}_j$. We made this change in order to avoid some technical complications caused by delayed re-building.

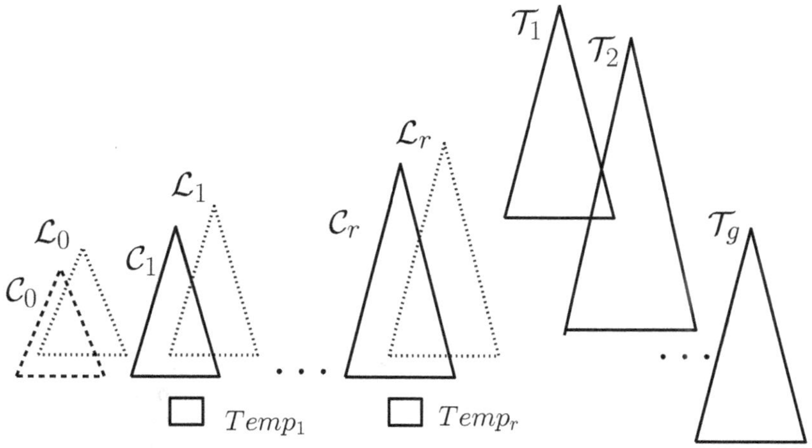

Figure 2: Dynamization with worst-case update guarantees. Only main sub-collections used for answering queries are shown. $\mathcal{L}'_r$ and auxiliary collections $\mathcal{N}_i$ are not shown.

$Temp_i$ contains exactly one document; $Temp_i$ are used as temporary storage for new document that are not yet inserted into "big" collections. The sizes of sub-collections can be defined as a function of parameter n_f such that $n_f = \Theta(n)$; the value of n_f changes when n becomes too large or too small. Let $\max_i = 2(n_f/\log^2 n)\log^{i\varepsilon} n$. We maintain the invariant $|\mathcal{C}_i| \leq \max_i$ for all i, $0 \leq i \leq r$, but r is chosen in such way that $n_f/\log^{2-r\varepsilon} n_f = n_f/\tau$. Every $\mathcal{T}_i$ contains $\Omega(n_f/\tau)$ symbols. If $\mathcal{T}_i$ contains more than one text, then its size is at most $4n_f/\tau$; otherwise $\mathcal{T}_i$ can be arbitrarily large. When a collection $\mathcal{C}_j$ is merged with $\mathcal{C}_{j+1}$, the process of re-building $\mathcal{C}_j$ can be distributed among a number of future updates (insertions and deletions of documents). During this time $\mathcal{C}_j$ is locked: we set $\mathcal{L}_j = \mathcal{C}_j$ and initialize a new empty sub-collection $\mathcal{C}_j$. When a new subcollection $\mathcal{N}_{j+1} = \mathcal{C}_{j+1} \cup \mathcal{C}_j$ is completed, we set $\mathcal{C}_{j+1} = \mathcal{N}_{j+1}$ and discard old $\mathcal{C}_{j+1}$ and $\mathcal{L}_j$. A query is answered by querying all non-empty $\mathcal{C}_i$, $\mathcal{L}_i$, $Temp_i$, and $\mathcal{T}_i$. Therefore the cost of answering a range-finding query grows by $O(\tau)$. The costs of locating and extracting are the same as in the static index. We show main sub-collections used by our method on Figure 2.

Insertions.

When a document T is inserted, we consider all j, such that $0 \leq j \leq r$ and the data structure $\mathcal{L}_j$ is not empty. For every such j, we spend $O(|T|\log^{\varepsilon} n \cdot u(n))$ units of time on constructing $\mathcal{N}_{j+1}$. If $\mathcal{N}_{j+1}$ for some $0 \leq j \leq r-1$ is completed, we set $\mathcal{C}_{j+1} = \mathcal{N}_{j+1}$ and $\mathcal{N}_{j+1} = Temp_{j+1} = \emptyset$; if $\mathcal{N}_{r+1}$ is completed, we set $\mathcal{T}_{g+1} = \mathcal{N}_{r+1}$, increment the number of top collections g, and set $\mathcal{N}_{r+1} = Temp_{r+1} = \emptyset$. Then we look for a sub-collection that can accommodate the new document T. If $|T| \geq n/\tau$, we create the index for a new sub-collection $\mathcal{T}_i$ that contains a single document T. If $|T| < n/\tau$, we look for the smallest index j, such that $|\mathcal{C}_{j+1}| + |\mathcal{C}_j| + |T| \leq \max_{j+1}$. That is, $\mathcal{C}_{j+1}$ can accommodate both the preceding sub-collection $\mathcal{C}_j$ and T. If $|T| \geq \max_j/2$, we set $\mathcal{C}_{j+1} = \mathcal{C}_j \cup \mathcal{C}_{j+1} \cup T$ and create an index for the new $\mathcal{C}_{j+1}$ in $O(|\mathcal{C}_{j+1}| \cdot u(n)) = O(|T|\log^{\varepsilon} n \cdot u(n))$ time. If $|T| < \max_j/2$, the collection $\mathcal{C}_j$ is locked. We set $\mathcal{L}_j = \mathcal{C}_j$, $\mathcal{C}_j = \emptyset$ and initiate the process of creating $\mathcal{N}_{j+1} = \mathcal{C}_j \cup \mathcal{C}_{j+1} \cup T$. The cost of creating the new index for $\mathcal{N}_{j+1}$ will be distributed among the next $\max_j$ update operations. We also create a temporary static index $Temp_{j+1}$ for the text T in $O(|T|u(n))$ time. This procedure is illustrated on Fig. 3. If the index j is not found and $|\mathcal{C}_i| + |\mathcal{C}_{i+1}| + |T| > \max_{i+1}$ for all i, $0 \leq i < r$, we lock $\mathcal{C}_r$ (that is, set $\mathcal{L}_r = \mathcal{C}_r$ and $\mathcal{C}_r = \emptyset$) and initiate the process of constructing $\mathcal{N}_{r+1} = \mathcal{L}_r \cup T$. We also create a temporary index $Temp_{r+1}$ for the document T in $O(|T|u(n))$ time.

Deletions.

Indexes for sub-collections $\mathcal{C}_i$, $1 \leq i \leq r$, and $\mathcal{T}_j$, $1 \leq j \leq g$, support lazy deletions in the same way as in Section 2: when a document is deleted from a sub-collection, we simply mark the positions of suffixes in the suffix array as deleted and set the corresponding bits in the bit vector B to 0. Augmenting an index so that lazy deletions are supported is done in exactly the same way as in Section 2.

We will need one additional sub-collection $\mathcal{L}'_r$ to support deletions. If a sub-collection $\mathcal{C}_j$ for $1 \leq j \leq r-1$ contains $\max_j/2$ deleted elements, we start the process of re-building $\mathcal{C}_j$ and merging it with C_{j+1}. This procedure is the same as in the case of insertions. We lock $\mathcal{C}_j$ by setting $\mathcal{L}_j = \mathcal{C}_j$ and $\mathcal{C}_j = \emptyset$. The data structure $\mathcal{N}_{j+1} = \mathcal{C}_{j+1} \cup \mathcal{L}_j$ will be re-built during the following $\max_j/2$ updates. If a sub-collection $\mathcal{C}_r$ contains $\max_r/2$ deleted symbols, we set $\mathcal{L}'_r = \mathcal{C}_r$ and $\mathcal{C}_r = \emptyset$. The sub-collection $\mathcal{L}'_r$ will be merged with the next sub-collection $\mathcal{T}_i$ to be re-built.

If a collection $\mathcal{T}_i$ contains a single document and this document is deleted, then $\mathcal{T}_i$ is discarded. We also bound the number of deleted symbols in any $\mathcal{T}_i$ by n_f/τ. This is achieved by running the following background process. After each series of $n_f/(2\tau\log\tau)$ symbol deletions, we identify $\mathcal{T}_j$ that contains the largest number of deleted symbols. During the next $n_f/(2\tau\log\tau)$ symbol deletions we build the new index for $\mathcal{T}_j$ without the deleted symbols. At the same time we remove the deleted symbols from $\mathcal{L}'_r$ if $\mathcal{L}'_r$ exists. If $\mathcal{L}'_r$ exists and contains at least $n_f/2\tau$ undeleted symbols, we create an index for a new sub-collection $\mathcal{T}'_{g+1}$ and increment the number g of top collections. If $\mathcal{L}'_r$ exists, but contains less than $n_f/2$ undeleted symbols, we merge $\mathcal{L}'_r$ with the largest $\mathcal{T}_j$ that contains more than one document and split the result if necessary: if the number of undeleted symbols in $\mathcal{L}'_r \cup \mathcal{T}_j$ does

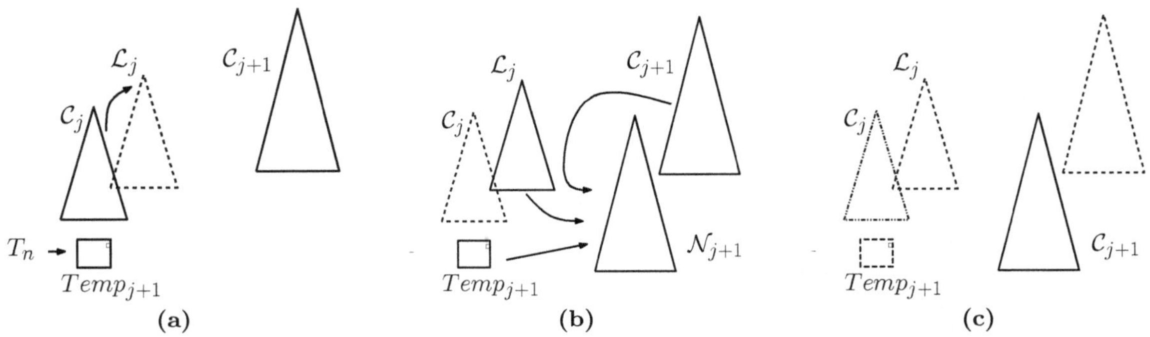

Figure 3: Suppose that $\mathcal{C}_{j+1}$ is the first sub-collection that can accommodate both $\mathcal{C}_j$ and a new document T_n. If $\mathcal{C}_j$ must be rebuilt in the background, we "rename" $\mathcal{C}_j$ to $\mathcal{L}_j$ and initialize another (initially empty) $\mathcal{C}_j$. New document T_n is put into a separate collection $Temp_{j+1}$ (a). A background process creates a new collection $\mathcal{N}_{j+1}$ that contains all documents from $\mathcal{L}_j$, $\mathcal{C}_{j+1}$ and $Temp_{j+1}$ (b). When $\mathcal{N}_{j+1}$ is finished, we discard $\mathcal{C}_{j+1}$, $\mathcal{L}_j$ and $Temp_{j+1}$, and set $\mathcal{C}_{j+1} = \mathcal{N}_{j+1}$ (c). Our procedure guarantees that $\mathcal{N}_{j+1}$ is completed before the new sub-collection $\mathcal{C}_j$ must be re-built again.

not exceed $2n_f/\tau$, we construct an index for $T_j \cup \mathcal{L}'_r$ without deleted symbols; otherwise, we split $T_j \cup \mathcal{L}'_r$ into two parts T_j^1, T_j^2 and create indexes for the new sub-collections. Our method guarantees us that the number of deleted elements in any collection $\mathcal{T}_i$ does not exceed $O(n_f/\tau)$ as follows from a Theorem of Dietz and Sleator [11].

LEMMA 1 ([11], THEOREM 5). *Suppose that $x_1, \ldots, x_g$ are variables that are initially zero. Suppose that the following two steps are iterated: (i) we add a non-negative real value a_i to each x_i such that $\sum a_i = 1$ (ii) set the largest x_i to 0. Then at any time $x_i \le 1 + h_{g-1}$ for all i, $1 \le i \le g$, where h_i denotes the i-th harmonic number.*

Let m_i be the number of deleted elements in the i-th top collection $\mathcal{T}_i$ and $\delta = n_f/(2\tau \log \tau)$. We define $x_i = m_i/\delta$. We consider the working of our algorithm during the period when the value of n_f is fixed. Hence, δ is also fixed and the number of variables x_i is $O(\tau)$ (some x_i can correspond to empty collections). Every iteration of the background process sets the largest x_i to 0. During each iteration $\sum x_i$ increases by 1. Hence, the values of x_i can be bounded from above by the result of Lemma 1: $x_i \le 1 + h_{2\tau}$ for all i at all times. Hence $m_i = O((n_f/2\tau \log \tau) \log \tau) = O(n_f/\tau)$ for all i because $h_i = O(\log i)$. Thus the fraction of deleted symbols in each $\mathcal{T}_i$ is $O(1/\tau)$.

It is easy to show that the sub-collections that we use are sufficient for our algorithm. When a sub-collection $\mathcal{L}_j$ is initialized, $\mathcal{C}_j$ is empty. The situation when $\mathcal{C}_j$ cannot accommodate a new document T_n and a preceding sub-collection $\mathcal{C}_{j-1}$ can happen only after $\max_j - \sum_{t=1}^{j-1} \max_t$ new symbol insertions. Since we spend $O(\log^\varepsilon n \cdot u(n))$ time for constructing $\mathcal{N}_{j+1}$ with each new symbol insertion, we can choose constants in such a way that construction of $\mathcal{N}_{j+1}$ is finished (and $\mathcal{L}_j$ is discarded) after $\max_j/2 < \max_j - \sum_{t=1}^{j-1} \max_t$ symbol insertions. The situation when $\mathcal{C}_j$ contains $\max_j/2$ deleted symbols can happen after at least $\max_j$ new symbol updates ($\max_j/2$ insertions and $\max_j/2$ deletions). Hence, the collection $\mathcal{L}_j$ is discarded before $\mathcal{C}_j$ has to be locked again. In our description of update procedures we assumed that the parameter n_f is fixed. We can maintain the invariant $n_f = \Theta(n)$ using standard methods; for completeness we will provide a description in the full version [29].

The space overhead caused by storing copies of deleted elements is bounded by $O(n/\tau)$: all $\mathcal{C}_i$ contain $O(n/\tau)$ symbols and at most every second symbol in each $\mathcal{C}_i$ is from a deleted document; the fraction of deleted symbols in each $\mathcal{T}_i$ does not exceed $O(1/\tau)$. By the same argument, at any moment of time at most $O(n/\tau)$ symbols are in sub-collections that are re-built. Hence re-building procedures running in the background need $O(nw(n)/\tau)$ bits of space. Since each $\mathcal{T}_i$ contains at most $O(|\mathcal{T}_i|/\tau)$ deleted symbols, we can store the data structure V, which enables us to identify undeleted elements in any range of the suffix array and is implemented as described in Lemma 3, using $O(|\mathcal{T}_i| \log \tau/\tau)$ bits. Data structures V for all $\mathcal{T}_i$ need $O(n \log \tau/\tau)$ bits. Hence, the total space overhead of $\mathcal{I}_d$ compared to $\mathcal{I}_s$ is $O(n\frac{w(n)+\log \tau+\log \sigma}{\tau})$ bits.

Counting Occurrences.

Our dynamic indexes can be easily extended so that pattern counting queries are supported.

THEOREM 1. *We can augment the indexes $\mathcal{I}_d$ of Transfomations 1- 2 with $O((n \log \tau)/\tau)$ additional bits so that all occurrences of a pattern can be counted in $O(t_{\text{count}})$ time, where $t_{\text{count}} = (t_{\text{range}} + \log n/\log\log n)(r + \tau)$ and τ is defined as in the proofs of respective Transformations. If counting is supported, update times are increased by $O(\log n/\log\log n)$ additive term per symbol.*

PROOF. Every semi-dynamic index for a sub-collection $\mathcal{C}_i$ (respectively $\mathcal{T}_i$) already keeps a vector B that enables us to identify the suffixes of already deleted documents in the suffix array. We also store each B in a data structure of Navarro and Sadakane [32] that supports rank queries in $O(\log n/\log\log n)$ time and updates in $O(\log n/\log\log n)$ time. If B contains $O(|B|/\tau)$ zero values, then the structure of [32] needs $O((|B|/\tau) \log \tau)$ bits. Using this data structure, we can count the number of 1's in any portion $B[a..b]$ of B in the same time. To answer a counting query, we first answer a range-finding query in every sub-collection. For every non-empty range that we found, we count the number of 1's in that range. Finally, we sum the answers for all sub-collections. Since a range-finding query returns the range of all suffixes that start with a query pattern and each

1 in V corresponds to a suffix of an undeleted document, our procedure is correct. □

4. DYNAMIC INDEXES

To obtain our results on dynamic document collections, we only need to plug some currently known static indexes into Transformations 1 and 2. We prove the statements about constructibility of static indexes in the full version of this paper [29].

The static index of Belazzougui and Navarro, described in [6], is $(\log^{\varepsilon} n, \log \sigma)$-constructible. Their index achieves $t_{\text{range}} = O(|P|)$, $t_{\text{extract}} = O(s+\ell)$, and $t_{\text{SA}} = t_{\text{locate}} = O(s)$ for arbitrarily large alphabets; it needs $nH_k + O(n\frac{\log n}{s}) + O(n\frac{H_k}{\log\log n}) + O(n)$ bits. We apply Transformation 2 with $\tau = \log\log n$. The construction algorithm for this index relies on randomized algorithm for constructing an mmphf functions [6]; therefore the update procedures of our dynamic data structure also rely on randomization in this case. The resulting dynamic index uses $nH_k + O(n\frac{\log n}{s}) + O(n\frac{\log \sigma}{\log\log n}) + O(n)$ bits. This index achieves $t_{\text{range}} = O(|P|\log\log n)$, $t_{\text{extract}} = O(s+\ell)$, $t_{\text{locate}} = O(s)$. Insertions and deletions are supported in $O(|T|\log^{\varepsilon} n)$ time and $O(|T|(\log^{\varepsilon} n + s))$ expected time respectively. If counting queries are also supported, then $t_{\text{count}} = O(|P|\log\log n + \log n)$ and updates take $O(|T|\log n)$ expected time.

The index of Barbay et al. [3, 2] is also $(\log^{\varepsilon} n, \log \sigma)$-constructible and uses $nH_k + O(n\frac{\log n}{s}) + o(n\log\sigma)$ bits. If the alphabet size $\sigma = \log^{O(1)} n$, this index achieves $t_{\text{range}} = O(|P|)$, $t_{\text{extract}} = O(s+\ell)$, and $t_{\text{locate}} = O(s)$; it uses $nH_k + O(n\frac{\log n}{s}) + o(n\log\sigma)$ bits. If we set $\tau = \log\log n$ and apply Transformation 2, we obtain a dynamic data structure with $t_{\text{range}} = O(|P|\log\log n)$, $t_{\text{extract}} = O(s+\ell)$, and $t_{\text{SA}} = t_{\text{locate}} = O(s)$. For an arbitrary alphabet size σ, the index of Barbay et al. [3, 2] achieves $t_{\text{range}} = O(|P|\log\log\sigma)$, $t_{\text{extract}} = O((s+\ell)\log\log\sigma)$, and $t_{\text{SA}} = t_{\text{locate}} = O(s\log\log\sigma)$. Again we set $\tau = \log\log n$ and apply Transformation 2. We obtain a dynamic index that has query costs $t_{\text{range}} = O(|P|\log\log\sigma\log\log n)$, $t_{\text{extract}} = O((s+\ell)\log\log\sigma)$, and $t_{\text{SA}} = t_{\text{locate}} = O(s\log\log\sigma)$. Insertions and deletions are supported in $O(|T|\log^{\varepsilon} n)$ time and $O(|T|(\log^{\varepsilon} n + s))$ time respectively. If counting queries are also supported, then $t_{\text{count}} = O(|P|\log\log n\log\log\sigma + \log n)$ (resp. $t_{\text{count}} = O(|P|\log\log n + \log n)$ if $\sigma = \log^{O(1)} n$) and updates take $O(|T|\log n)$ time.

The index of Grossi and Vitter [19] is $(\log^{\varepsilon} n, \log\sigma)$-constructible. It achieves $t_{\text{locate}} = O(\log^{\varepsilon} n)$, $t_{\text{range}} = O(|P|/\log_{\sigma} n + \log^{\varepsilon} n)$ and $t_{\text{extract}} = O(\ell/\log_{\sigma} n)$. We apply Transformation 2 with $\tau = 1/\delta$ for a constant δ. The resulting dynamic index uses $O(n\log\sigma(1+1/\delta)) = O(n\log\sigma)$ bits and has the following query costs: $t_{\text{locate}} = O(\log^{\varepsilon} n)$, $t_{\text{range}} = O(|P|/\log_{\sigma} n + \log^{\varepsilon} n)$, $t_{\text{extract}} = O(\ell/\log_{\sigma} n)$. As shown in the full version [29], in this case the data structure for uncompressed sequence $\mathcal{C}_0$ relies on hashing. Therefore the update procedure is randomized. Updates are supported in $O(|T|\log^{2\varepsilon} n)$ expected time, but we can replace ε with $\varepsilon/2$ in our construction and reduce the update time to $O(|T|\log^{\varepsilon} n)$. If counting queries are also supported, then $t_{\text{count}} = O(|P|/\log_{\sigma} n + \log n/\log\log n)$ and updates take $O(|T|\log n)$ expected time. If we want to support updates using a deterministic procedure, then the cost of searching in $\mathcal{C}_0$ grows to $O(|P|(\log\log n)^2/\log_{\sigma} n + \log n)$. In this case $t_{\text{range}} = t_{\text{count}} = O(|P|(\log\log n)^2/\log_{\sigma} n + \log n)$, $t_{\text{locate}} = O(\log^{\varepsilon} n)$, and $t_{\text{extract}} = O(\ell/\log_{\sigma} n)$.

5. DYNAMIC GRAPHS AND BINARY RELATIONS

Let R denote a binary relation between t objects and σ_l labels. In this section we denote by n the cardinality of R, i.e., the number of object-label pairs. We will assume that objects and labels are integers from intervals $[1, \sigma_l]$ and $[1, t]$ respectively. Barbay et al. [4] showed how a static relation R can be represented by a string S. A dynamization of their approach based on dynamic data structures for rank and select queries is described in [31].

Let M be a matrix that represents a binary relation R; columns of R correspond to objects and rows correspond to matrices. The string S is obtained by traversing M columnwise (i.e., objectwise) and writing the labels. An additional bit string N encodes the numbers of labels related to objects: $N = 1^{n_1}01^{n_2}0\ldots1^{n_t}$, where n_i is the number of labels related to the i-th object. Using rank, select, and access queries on N and S, we can enumerate objects related to a label, enumerate labels related to an object, and decide whether an object and a label are related.

Deletion-Only Data Structure.

We keep R in S and N described above; S and N are stored in static data structures. If a pair (e, l) is deleted from R, we find the element of S that encodes this pair and mark it as deleted. We record marked elements (i.e. pairs that are deleted but are still stored in the data structure) in a bit vector D: $D[i] = 0$ if and only if the pair $S[i]$ is marked as deleted. We maintain the data structure of Lemma 3 on D. Moreover we keep D in a data structure described in [17]; this data structure enables us to count the number of 1-bits in any range of D. For each label a we also keep a data structure D_a. D_a is obtained by traversing the a-th row of M: if $M[a,j] \neq 0$, then we append 0 to D_a if (a,j) is marked as deleted; if $M[a,j] \neq 0$ and (a,j) is not marked as deleted, we append 1 to D_a. For each D_a we also maintain data structures for reporting and counting 1-bits described above. Finally we record indices of deleted labels and objects in two further bit sequences. The static data structures on S and N are implemented as in[2], so that rank and select queries are answered in $O(\log\log\sigma_l)$ time and any $S[i]$ or $N[i]$ can be retrieved in constant time.

If we need to list labels related to an object i, we first find the part of S that contains these labels. Let $l = \text{rank}_1(\text{select}_0(i-1, N), N)$ and $r = \text{rank}_1(\text{select}_0(i, N), N)$. We list all elements of $S[l..r]$ that are not marked as deleted by enumerating all 1-bits in $D[l..r]$. Then we access and report $S[i_1]$, $S[i_2]$, ..., $S[i_f]$, where i_1, i_2, ..., i_f are positions of 1-bits in $D[l..r]$. In order to list objects related to a label a, we find positions of 1-bits in D_a. Then we access and report $\text{select}_a(j_1, S)$, $\text{select}_a(j_2, S)$, ..., where j_1, j_2, ... denote positions of 1-bits in D_a. In order to determine whether an object i and a label a are related, we compute $d = \text{rank}_a(r, S) - \text{rank}_a(l, S)$, where l and r are as defined above. If $d = 0$, then the object i and the label a are not related. If $d = 1$, we compute $j = \text{select}_a(\text{rank}_a(r, S), S)$; i and a are related if and only if $D[j] = 1$.

When (e, l) is deleted, we find the position j of (e, l) in S and set $D[j] = 0$; j can be found with a constant number of rank and select queries. We also set $D_a[j'] = 0$ for $j' = \mathrm{rank}_a(S, j)$. When an empty label or an empty object is removed, we simply record this fact by adding it to a compact list of empty labels (resp. empty objects). When the number of pairs that are marked as deleted exceeds n/τ, we start the process of re-building the data structure. The cost of re-building is distributed among the following updates; we will give a more detailed description in the exposition of the fully-dynamic data structure.

Fully-Dynamic Data Structure.

We split a binary relation R, regarded as a set of object-label pairs, into subsets and keep these subsets in data structures $\mathbb{C}_0$, $\mathbb{C}_1$, ..., $\mathbb{C}_r$, $\mathbb{L}_1$, ..., $\mathbb{L}_r$, and $\mathbb{T}_1$, ..., $\mathbb{T}_g$ for $g = \Theta(\tau)$. We set the parameter $\tau = \log\log n$. Only $\mathbb{C}_0$ is stored in a fully-dynamic data structure, but we can afford to keep $\mathbb{C}_0$ in $O(\log n)$ bits per item because it contains only a small fraction of pairs. All other pairs are stored in deletion-only data structures described above. Distribution of pairs among subsets and procedures for re-building deletion-only data structures are the same as in Section 3. To simplify a description, we will not distinguish between a subset and a data structure that stores it.

$\mathbb{C}_0$ contains at most $\max_0 = 2n/\log^2 n$ pairs. Each structure $\mathbb{C}_i$ for $r \geq i \geq 1$ contains at most $\max_i = 2n/\log^{2-i\varepsilon} n$ pairs. Every $\mathbb{T}_i$ contains at most $2n/\tau$ pairs. Data structure $\mathbb{C}_0$ contains object-label pairs in uncompressed form and uses $O(\log n)$ bits per pair. For every object i that occurs in $\mathbb{C}_0$ we keep a list L_i that contains all labels that occur in pairs $(i, \cdot) \in \mathbb{C}_0$; for each label a that occurs in $\mathbb{C}_0$ we keep a list of objects that occur in pairs $(\cdot, a) \in \mathbb{C}_0$. Using these lists we can enumerate all objects related to a label or labels related to an object in $\mathbb{C}_0$ in $O(1)$ time per datum. If we augment lists L_i with predecessor data structures described in [1], we can also find out whether an object i and a label a are related in $O((\log\log\sigma_l)^2)$ time.

All pairs in $\mathbb{C}_1$,$\mathbb{L}_1$,..., $\mathbb{C}_r$, $\mathbb{L}_r$, and $\mathbb{T}_1$, $\mathbb{T}_\tau$ are kept in deletion-only data structures described above. A new object-label pair (i, a) is inserted into $\mathbb{C}_0$ if $\mathbb{C}_0$ contains less than $\max_0$ pairs. Otherwise we look for the smallest j, $0 \leq j < r$, such that $|\mathbb{C}_{j+1}|+|\mathbb{C}_j|+1 \leq \max_{j+1}$. We lock $\mathbb{C}_j$ by setting $\mathbb{L}_j = \mathbb{C}_j$, $\mathbb{C}_j = \emptyset$ and initiate the process of creating $\mathbb{N}_{j+1} = \mathbb{C}_j \cup \mathbb{C}_{j+1} \cup \{(i, a)\}$. If $|\mathbb{C}_{i+1}|+|\mathbb{C}_i|+1 \leq \max_{i+1}$ for all $i < r$, we lock $\mathbb{C}_r$ and start the process of constructing $\mathbb{N}_{j+1} = \mathbb{C}_r \cup \{(i, a)\}$. The cost of creating $\mathbb{N}_j$ is distributed among the next $\max_j$ updates in the same way as in Section 3. We observe that data structures $Temp_i$ are not needed now because each update inserts only one element (pair) into the relation R. We guarantee that each structure $\mathbb{C}_i$ for some $1 \leq i \leq r$ contains at most $\max_i /2$ pairs marked as deleted and $\mathbb{T}_i$ for $1 \leq i \leq r$ contains an $O(1/\tau)$ fraction of deleted pairs. Procedures for re-building data structures that contain too many pairs marked as deleted are the same as in Section 3.

Our fully-dynamic data structure must support insertions and deletions of new objects and labels. An object that is not related to any label or a label that is not related to any object can be removed from a data structure. This means that both the number of labels σ_l and the number of objects t can change dynamically. Removing and inserting labels implies changing the alphabets of strings S that are used in deletion-only data structures. Following [31] we store two global tables, NS and SN; SN maps labels to integers bounded by $O(\sigma_l)$ (global label alphabet) and NS maps integers back to labels. We also keep bitmaps GC_i and GT_i, GL_i, and GN_i for all subsets C_i, L_i, N_i, and T_i. $GC_i[j] = 1$ if the label that is assigned to integer j occurs in $\mathbb{C}_i$ and $GC_i[j] = 0$ otherwise; GT_i, GL_i, and GN_i keep the same information for subsets $\mathbb{T}_i$, $\mathbb{L}_i$, and $\mathbb{N}_i$. Using these bit sequences we can map the symbol of a label in the global alphabet to the symbol of the same label in the effective alphabet[4] used in one of subsets. When a label a is deleted, we mark $SN[a]$ as free. When a new label a' is inserted, we set $SN[a']$ to a free slot in SN (a list of free slots is maintained). When some subset, say $\mathbb{C}_i$ is re-built, we also re-build the bit sequence GC_i.

In order to list objects related to a label a, we first report all objects that are related to $SN[a]$ and stored in $\mathbb{C}_0$. Then we visit all subsets $\mathbb{C}_i$, $\mathbb{L}_i$, and $\mathbb{T}_i$ and report all objects related to $\mathrm{rank}_1(SN[a], GC_i)$, $\mathrm{rank}_1(SN[a], GL_i)$, and $\mathrm{rank}_1(SN[a], GT_i)$ respectively. We remark that a global symbol of a label can be mapped to a wrong symbol in the local effective alphabet. This can happen if some label a' is removed and its slot in $SN[]$ is assigned to another label a but the bitmap of say GC_i is not yet re-built. In this case $\mathrm{rank}_1(SN[a], GC_i)$ will map a to the symbol for the wrong label a'. But a' can be removed only if all object-label pairs containing a' are deleted; hence, all pairs (i, a') in $\mathbb{C}_i$ are marked as deleted and the query to $\mathbb{C}_i$ will correctly report nothing. We can report labels related to an object and tell whether a certain object is related to a certain label using a similar procedure. We visit $O(\log\log n)$ data structures in order to answer a query. In all data structures except for $\mathbb{C}_0$, we spend $O(\log\log\sigma_l)$ time per reported datum. An existential query on $\mathbb{C}_0$ takes $O((\log\log\sigma_l)^2)$ time; all other queries on $\mathbb{C}_0$ take $O(1)$ time per reported datum. Hence all queries are answered in $O(\log\log n \log\log\sigma_l)$ time per reported datum. A counting query takes $O(\log n/\log\log n)$ time in each subset. Hence, we can count objects related to a label or labels related to an object in $O(\log n)$ time.

All bit sequences D and D_a in all subsets use $O((n/\tau)\log\tau)$ bits. Every string S stored in a deletion-only data structure needs $|S|H_0(S)+o(|S|\log\sigma_l)$ bits. Hence all strings S use at most $nH + o(n\log\sigma_l)$ bits, where $H = \sum_{1\leq a\leq\sigma_l} \frac{n_i}{n}\log\frac{n}{n_i}$. Bit sequences GC_i, GL_i, and GT_i use $O(\sigma_l\tau) = o(n\log\sigma_l)$ bits. Now we consider the space usage of bit sequences N stored in deletion-only data structures. Let m_i denote the number of pairs in a data structure $\mathbb{T}_i$. N consists of m_i 1's and t 0's. If $m_i > t$, then the bit sequence N stored as a part of $\mathbb{T}_i$ uses $m_i\log\frac{m_i+t}{m_i} = O(m_i)$ bits. If $t \geq m_i$, N uses $O(m_i\log\tau)$ bits because $m_i = \Theta(n/\tau)$. Hence all N stored in all $\mathbb{T}_i$ use $O(n\log\tau)$ bits. In our data structure we set $\tau = \log\log n$. If $\sigma_l = \Omega(\log^{1/4} n)$, $O(n\log\tau) = o(n\log\sigma_l)$. Otherwise $t = \Omega(n/\log n)$ because $n \leq t\cdot\sigma_l$; if $t = \Omega(n/\log n)$, $O(n\log\tau) = o(t\log t)$. Data structures that are re-built at any moment of time contain $O(n/\tau)$ elements and use $O(\frac{n}{\tau}\log\sigma_l) = o(n\log\sigma_l)$ bits. Extra space that we need to store elements marked as deleted is bounded by $o(n\log\sigma_l)$; this can be shown in the same way as in Section 3.

THEOREM 2. *A dynamic binary relation that consists of n pairs relating t objects to σ_l labels can be stored in $nH + o(n\log\sigma_l) + o(t\log t) + O(t + n + \sigma_l\log n)$ bits where $H =$*

[4] An effective alphabet of a sequence S contains only symbols that occur in S at least once.

$\sum_{1\le a\le\sigma_l}\frac{n_a}{n}\log\frac{n}{n_a}$ *and* n_a *is the number of objects related to a label* a*. We can determine whether an object and a label are related in* $O(\log\log\sigma_l\log\log n)$ *time and report all objects related to a label (resp. all labels related to an object) in* $O((k+1)\log\log\sigma_l\log\log n)$ *time, where* k *is the number of reported items. We can count objects related to a label or labels related to an object in* $O(\log n)$ *time. Updates are supported in* $O(\log^{\varepsilon} n)$ *time.*

Directed graph is a frequently studied instance of a binary relation. In this case both the set of labels and the set of objects are identical with the set of graph nodes. There is an edge from a node u to a node v if the object u is related to the label v.

THEOREM 3. *A dynamic directed graph that consists of* σ_l *nodes and* $n\ge\sigma_l$ *edges can be stored in* $nH+o(n\log\sigma_l)+O(n+\sigma_l\log n)$ *bits where* $H=\sum_{1\le a\le\sigma_l}\frac{n_a}{n}\log\frac{n}{n_a}$ *and* n_a *is the number of outgoing edges from node* a*. We can determine if there is an edge from one node to another one in* $O(\log\log\sigma_l\log\log n)$ *time and report all neighbors (resp. reverse neighbors) of a node in* $O((k+1)\log\log\sigma_l\log\log n)$ *time, where* k *is the number of reported nodes. We can count neighbors or reverse neighbors of a node in* $O(\log n)$ *time. Updates are supported in* $O(\log^{\varepsilon} n)$ *time.*

6. CONCLUSIONS

In this paper we described a general framework for transforming static compressed indexes into dynamic ones. We showed that, using our framework, we can achieve the same or almost the same space and time complexity for dynamic indexes as was previously obtained by static indexes. Our framework is applicable to a broad range of static indexes that includes a vast majority of currently known results in this area. Thus, using our techniques, we can easily modify almost any compressed static index, so that insertions and deletions of documents are supported. It will likely be possible to apply our framework to static indexes that will be obtained in the future. Our approach also significantly reduces the cost of basic queries in compact representations of dynamic graphs and binary relations. We expect that our ideas can be applied to the design of other compressed data structures.

Acknowledgments.

The authors wish to thank Djamal Belazzougui for clarifying the construction time of the static index in [6] and Gonzalo Navarro for explaining some technical details of dynamic indexes used in [26].

7. REFERENCES

[1] A. Andersson and M. Thorup. Dynamic ordered sets with exponential search trees. *J. ACM*, 54(3):13, 2007.

[2] J. Barbay, F. Claude, T. Gagie, G. Navarro, and Y. Nekrich. Efficient fully-compressed sequence representations. *Algorithmica*, 69(1):232–268, 2014.

[3] J. Barbay, T. Gagie, G. Navarro, and Y. Nekrich. Alphabet partitioning for compressed rank/select and applications. In *Proc. 21st ISAAC*, pages 315–326 (part II), 2010.

[4] J. Barbay, A. Golynski, J. I. Munro, and S. S. Rao. Adaptive searching in succinctly encoded binary relations and tree-structured documents. *Theoretical Computer Science*, 387(3):284–297, 2007.

[5] J. Barbay, M. He, J. I. Munro, and S. S. Rao. Succinct indexes for strings, binary relations and multi-labeled trees. *ACM Transactions on Algorithms*, 7(4):article 52, 2011.

[6] D. Belazzougui and G. Navarro. Alphabet-independent compressed text indexing. In *Proc. 19th Annual European Symposium on Algorithms (ESA 2011)*, pages 748–759, 2011.

[7] J. L. Bentley and J. B. Saxe. Decomposable searching problems i: Static-to-dynamic transformation. *J. Algorithms*, 1(4):301–358, 1980.

[8] H. Chan, W.-K. Hon, T.-H. Lam, and K. Sadakane. Compressed indexes for dynamic text collections. *ACM Transactions on Algorithms*, 3(2):article 21, 2007.

[9] H.-L. Chan, W.-K. Hon, and T.-W. Lam. Compressed index for a dynamic collection of texts. In *Proc. 15th CPM*, LNCS 3109, pages 445–456, 2004.

[10] S. Chaudhuri, V. Ganti, and L. Gravano. Selectivity estimation for string predicates: Overcoming the underestimation problem. In *Proc. 20th International Conference on Data Engineering, (ICDE 2004)*, pages 227–238, 2004.

[11] P. F. Dietz and D. D. Sleator. Two algorithms for maintaining order in a list. In *Proc. 19th Annual ACM Symposium on Theory of Computing (STOC 1987)*, pages 365–372, 1987.

[12] J. D. Fernández, M. A. Martínez-Prieto, and C. Gutierrez. Compact representation of large RDF data sets for publishing and exchange. In *Proc. 9th International Semantic Web Conference, (ISWC 2010)*, pages 193–208, 2010.

[13] P. Ferragina, G. Manzini, V. Mäkinen, and G. Navarro. Compressed representations of sequences and full-text indexes. *ACM Transactions on Algorithms*, 3(2):article 20, 2007.

[14] M. Fredman and M. Saks. The cell probe complexity of dynamic data structures. In *Proc. 21st STOC*, pages 345–354, 1989.

[15] R. González and G. Navarro. Improved dynamic rank-select entropy-bound structures. In *Proc. 8th LATIN*, LNCS 4957, pages 374–386, 2008.

[16] R. González and G. Navarro. Rank/select on dynamic compressed sequences and applications. *Theoretical Computer Science*, 410:4414–4422, 2009.

[17] R. González and G. Navarro. Rank/select on dynamic compressed sequences and applications. *Theor. Comput. Sci.*, 410(43):4414–4422, 2009.

[18] R. Grossi, A. Gupta, and J. S. Vitter. High-order entropy-compressed text indexes. In *Proc. 14th SODA*, pages 841–850, 2003.

[19] R. Grossi and J. S. Vitter. Compressed suffix arrays and suffix trees with applications to text indexing and string matching. *SIAM J. Comput.*, 35(2):378–407, 2005.

[20] M. He and J. I. Munro. Succinct representations of dynamic strings. In *Proc. 17th SPIRE*, pages 334–346, 2010.

[21] H. V. Jagadish, R. T. Ng, and D. Srivastava. Substring selectivity estimation. In *Proc. 18th ACM SIGACT-SIGMOD-SIGART Symposium on Principles of Database Systems (PODS 1999)*, pages 249–260, 1999.

[22] P. Krishnan, J. S. Vitter, and B. R. Iyer. Estimating alphanumeric selectivity in the presence of wildcards. In *Proceedings of the 1996 ACM SIGMOD International Conference on Management of Data (SIGMOD1996)*, pages 282–293, 1996.

[23] S. Lee and K. Park. Dynamic rank-select structures with applications to run-length encoded texts. In *Proc. 18th CPM*, LNCS 4580, pages 95–106, 2007.

[24] S. Lee and K. Park. Dynamic rank/select structures with applications to run-length encoded texts. *Theoretical Computer Science*, 410(43):4402–4413, 2009.

[25] V. Mäkinen and G. Navarro. Dynamic entropy-compressed sequences and full-text indexes. In *Proc. 17th CPM*, LNCS 4009, pages 307–318, 2006.

[26] V. Mäkinen and G. Navarro. Dynamic entropy-compressed sequences and full-text indexes. *ACM Transactions on Algorithms*, 4(3):article 32, 2008.

[27] G. Manzini. An analysis of the burrows-wheeler transform. *J. ACM*, 48(3):407–430, 2001.

[28] C. W. Mortensen, R. Pagh, and M. Patrascu. On dynamic range reporting in one dimension. In *Proc. 37th Annual ACM Symposium on Theory of Computing (STOC)*, pages 104–111, 2005.

[29] J. I. Munro, Y. Nekrich, and J. S. Vitter. Dynamic data structures for document collections and graphs. *CoRR*, abs/1503.05977, 2015.

[30] G. Navarro and V. Mäkinen. Compressed full-text indexes. *ACM Comput. Surv.*, 39(1), 2007.

[31] G. Navarro and Y. Nekrich. Optimal dynamic sequence representations. In *Proc. 24th Annual ACM-SIAM Symposium on Discrete Algorithms (SODA 2013)*, pages 865–876, 2013.

[32] G. Navarro and K. Sadakane. Fully-functional static and dynamic succinct trees. *ACM Transactions on Algorithms*, 10(3):article 16, 2014.

[33] A. Orlandi and R. Venturini. Space-efficient substring occurrence estimation. In *Proc. 30th ACM SIGMOD-SIGACT-SIGART Symposium on Principles of Database Systems (PODS 2011)*, pages 95–106, 2011.

[34] K. Sadakane. New text indexing functionalities of the compressed suffix arrays. *J. Algorithms*, 48(2):294–313, 2003.

APPENDIX

A.1. REPORTING 1-BITS IN A BIT VECTOR

We show how to store a bit vector with a small number of zeros in small space, so that all 1-values in an arbitrary range can be reported in optimal time. This result is used by our method that transforms a static index into an index that supports deletions. We start by describing an $O(n)$-bit data structure. Then we show how space usage can be reduced to $O((n\log\tau)/\tau)$

LEMMA 2. *There exists an $O(n)$-bit data structure that supports the following operations on a bit vector B of size n: (i) $zero(i)$ sets $B[i]=0$ (ii) $report(s,e)$ enumerates all j such that $s\le j\le e$ and $B[j]=1$. Operation $zero(i)$ is supported in $O(\log^{\varepsilon} n)$ time and a query $report(s,e)$ is answered in $O(k)$ time, where k is the number of output bit positions.*

PROOF. We divide the vector B into words $W_1,\ldots, W_{\lceil |B_i|/\log n\rceil}$ of $\log n$ bits. We say that a word W_t is non-empty if at least one bit in W_t is set to 1. We store the indices of all non-empty words in a data structure that supports range reporting queries in $O(k)$ time, where k is the number of reported elements, and updates in $O(\log^{\varepsilon} n)$ time [28]. For every word W_i we can find the rightmost bit set to 1 before the given position p or determine that there is no bit set to 1 to the right of p in $O(1)$ time. This can be done by consulting a universal look-up table of size $o(n)$ bits. To report positions of all 1-bits in $B[s..e]$, we find all non-empty words whose indices are in the range $[\lceil s/\log n\rceil, \lfloor e/\log n\rfloor]$. For every such word, we output the positions of all 1-bits. Finally, we also examine the words $W_{\lfloor s/\log n\rfloor}$ and $W_{\lceil e/\log n\rceil}$ and report positions of 1-bits in these two words that are in $B[s..e]$. The total query time is $O(k)$. Operation $zero(i)$ is implemented by setting the bit $i-\lfloor i/\log n\rfloor\log n$ in the word $W_{\lceil i/\log n\rceil}$ to 0. If $W_{\lceil i/\log n\rceil}$ becomes empty, we remove $\lceil i/\log n\rceil$ from the range reporting data structure. □

LEMMA 3. *Let B be a bit vector of size n with at most $O(\frac{n}{\tau})$ zero values for $\tau=O(\log n/\log\log n)$. B can be stored in $O(n\frac{\log\tau}{\tau})$-bit data structure that supports the following operations on B: (i) $zero(i)$ sets $B[i]=0$ (ii) $report(s,e)$ enumerates all j such that $s\le j\le e$ and $B[j]=1$. Operation $zero(i)$ is supported in $O(\log^{\varepsilon} n)$ time and a query $report(s,e)$ is answered in $O(k)$ time, where k is the number of output bit positions.*

PROOF. We divide B into words W_i of τ bits. Indices of non-empty words are stored in the the data structure B', implemented as in Lemma 2. Every word W_i is represented as follows: we store the number of zeros in W_i using $O(\log\tau)$ bits. A subword with f zeros, where $0\le f\le\tau$, is encoded using $f(\log\tau)$ bits by specifying positions of 0-bits. For every word W_i we can find the rightmost bit set to 1 before the given position p or determine that there is no bit set to 1 to the right of p in $O(1)$ time. This can be done by consulting a universal look-up table of size $o(n)$ bits. Query processing is very similar to Lemma 2. To report 1-bits in $B[s..e]$, we find all non-empty words whose indices are in the range $[\lceil l/\tau\rceil, \lfloor r/\tau\rfloor]$. For every such word, we output the positions of all 1-bits. Finally, we also examine the words $W_{\lfloor s/\tau\rfloor}$ and $W_{\lceil e/\tau\rceil}$ and report positions of 1-bits in these two words that are in $B[s..e]$.

Operation $zero(i)$ is implemented by setting the corresponding bit in some word W_i to 0 and changing the word encoding. If W_i becomes empty, the i-th bit in B' is set to 0. Issues related to memory management can be resolved as in [31].

We need $O(n/\tau)$ bits to store the data structure B' for non-empty words. Let n_f denote the number of words with f zero values. All words W_i need $\sum_{f=1}^{\tau} n_f \cdot f \cdot \log \tau = \log \tau \sum n_f \cdot f = O((n/\tau) \log \tau)$ because $\sum n_f \cdot f = O(n/\tau)$. $\square$

Join Dependency Testing, Loomis-Whitney Join, and Triangle Enumeration

Xiaocheng Hu Miao Qiao Yufei Tao

CUHK
Hong Kong

ABSTRACT

In this paper, we revisit two fundamental problems in database theory. The first one is called *join dependency (JD) testing*, where we are given a relation r and a JD, and need to determine whether the JD holds on r. The second problem is called *JD existence testing*, where we need to determine if there exists *any* non-trivial JD that holds on r.

We prove that JD testing is NP-hard even if the JD is defined *only* on binary relations (i.e., each with only two attributes). Unless P = NP, this result puts a negative answer to the question whether it is possible to efficiently test JDs defined exclusively on *small* (in terms of attribute number) relations. The question has been open since the classic NP-hard proof of Maier, Sagiv, and Yannakakis in JACM'81 which requires the JD to involve a relation of $\Omega(d)$ attributes, where d is the number of attributes in r.

For JD existence testing, the challenge is to minimize the computation cost because the problem is known to be solvable in polynomial time. We present a new algorithm for solving the problem I/O-efficiently in the external memory model. Our algorithm in fact settles the closely related *Loomis-Whitney (LW) enumeration problem*, and as a side product, achieves the optimal I/O complexity for the *triangle enumeration problem*, improving a recent result of Pagh and Silvestri in PODS'14.

Categories and Subject Descriptors

F.2.2 [**Analysis of algorithms and problem complexity**]: Nonnumerical Algorithms and Problems; H.2.4 [**Database Management**]: Systems—*Relational databases*

Keywords

Join Dependency; Loomis-Whitney Join; Triangle Enumeration

1. INTRODUCTION

Given a relation r of d attributes, a key question in database theory is to ask if r is *decomposable*, namely, whether r can be projected onto a set S of relations with less than d attributes such that the natural join of those relations equals precisely r. Intuitively, a *yes* answer to the question implies that r contains a certain form of redundancy. Some of the redundancy may be removed by decomposing r into the smaller (in terms of attribute number) relations in S, which can be joined together to restore r whenever needed. A *no* answer, on the other hand, implies that the decomposition of r based on S will lose information, as far as natural join is concerned.

Join Dependency Testing. The above question (as well as its variants) has been extensively studied by resorting to the notion of *join dependency* (JD). To formalize the notion, let us refer to d as the *arity* of r. Denote by $R = \{A_1, A_2, ..., A_d\}$ the set of names of the d attributes in r. R is called the *schema* of r. Sometimes we may denote r as $r(R)$ or $r(A_1, A_2, ..., A_d)$ to emphasize on its schema. Let $|r|$ represent the number of tuples in r.

A JD *defined on* R is an expression of the form

$$J = \bowtie[R_1, R_2, ..., R_m]$$

where (i) $m \geq 1$, (ii) each R_i ($1 \leq i \leq m$) is a subset of R that contains at least 2 attributes, and (iii) $\cup_{i=1}^{m} R_i = R$. J is *non-trivial* if none of $R_1, ..., R_m$ equals R. The *arity* of J is defined to be $\max_{i=1}^{m} |R_i|$, i.e., the largest size of $R_1, ..., R_m$. Clearly, the arity of a non-trivial J is between 2 and $d - 1$.

Relation r is said to *satisfy* J if

$$r = \pi_{R_1}(r) \bowtie \pi_{R_2}(r) \bowtie ... \bowtie \pi_{R_m}(r)$$

where $\pi_X(r)$ denotes the projection of r onto an attribute set X, and $\bowtie$ represents natural join. We are ready to formally state the first two problems studied in this paper:

PROBLEM 1. [λ-JD Testing] *Given a relation r and a join dependency J of arity at most λ that is defined on the schema of r, we want to determine whether r satisfies J.*

PROBLEM 2. [JD Existence Testing] *Given a relation r, we want to determine whether there is any non-trivial join dependency J such that r satisfies J.*

Note the difference in the objectives of the above problems. Problem 1 aims to decide if r can be decomposed according to a *specific* set J of projections. On the other hand, Problem 2 aims to find out if there is any way to decompose r at all.

Computation Model. Our discussion on Problem 1 will concentrate on proving its NP-hardness. For this purpose, we will describe all our reductions in the standard RAM model.

For Problem 2, which is known to be polynomial time solvable (as we will explain shortly), the main issue is to design fast

PODS'15, May 31–June 4, 2015, Melbourne, Victoria, Australia.

Http://dx.doi.org/10.1145/2745754.2745768.

algorithms. We will do so in the *external memory* (EM) model [2], which has become the de facto model for analyzing I/O-efficient algorithms. Under this model, a machine is equipped with M words of memory, and an unbounded disk that has been formatted into *blocks* of B words. It holds that $M \geq 2B$. An *I/O operation* exchanges a block of data between the disk and the memory. The *cost* of an algorithm is defined to be the number of I/Os performed. CPU calculation is for free.

To avoid rounding, we define $\lg_x y = \max\{1, \log_x y\}$, and will describe all logarithms using $\lg_x y$. In all cases, the value of an attribute is assumed to fit in a single word.

Loomis-Whitney Enumeration. As will be clear later, the JD existence-testing problem is closely related to the so-called *Loomis-Whitney (LW) join*. Let $R = \{A_1, A_2, ..., A_d\}$ be a set of d attributes. For each $i \in [1, d]$, define $R_i = R \setminus \{A_i\}$, that is, removing A_i from R. Let $r_1, r_2, ..., r_d$ be d relations such that r_i ($1 \leq i \leq d$) has schema R_i. Then, the natural join $r_1 \bowtie r_2 \bowtie ... \bowtie r_d$ is called an LW join. Note that the schema of the join result is R.

We will consider LW joins in the EM model, where traditionally a join must write out all the tuples in the result to the disk. However, the result size can be so huge that the number of I/Os for writing the result may (by far) overwhelm the cost of the join's rest execution. Furthermore, in some applications of LW joins (e.g., for solving Problem 2), it is not necessary to actually write the result tuples to the disk; instead, it suffices to *witness* each result tuple once in the memory.

Because of the above, we follow the approach of [14] by studying an *enumerate* version of the problem. Specifically, we are given a memory-resident routine $emit(.)$ which requires $O(1)$ words to store. The parameter of the routine is a tuple t of d values $(a_1, ..., a_d)$ such that a_i is in the domain of A_i for each $i \in [1, d]$. The routine simply sends out t to an outbound socket with no I/O cost. Then, our problem can be formally stated as:

PROBLEM 3. [LW Enumeration] *Given relations $r_1, ..., r_d$ as defined earlier where $d \leq M/2$, we want to invoke $emit(t)$ once and exactly once for each tuple $t \in r_1 \bowtie r_2 \bowtie ... \bowtie r_d$.*

As a noteworthy remark, if an algorithm can solve the above problem in x I/Os using $M - B$ words of memory, then it can also report the entire LW join result of K tuples (i.e., totally Kd values) in $x + O(Kd/B)$ I/Os.

Triangle Enumeration. Besides being a stepping stone for Problem 2, LW enumeration has relevance to several other problems, among which the most prominent one is perhaps the *triangle enumeration problem* [14] due to its large variety of applications (see [8, 14] and the references therein for an extensive summary).

Let $G = (V, E)$ be an undirected simple graph, where V (or E) is the set of vertices (or edges, resp.). A *triangle* is defined as a clique of 3 vertices in G. We are again given a memory-resident routine $emit(.)$ that occupies $O(1)$ words. This time, given a triangle Δ as its parameter, the routine sends out Δ to an outbound socket with no I/O cost (this implies that all the 3 edges of Δ must be in the memory at this moment). Then, the triangle enumeration problem can be formally stated as:

PROBLEM 4. [Triangle Enumeration] *Given graph G as defined earlier, we want to invoke $emit(\Delta)$ once and exactly once for each triangle Δ in G.*

Observe that this is merely a special instance of LW enumeration with $d = 3$ where $r_1 = r_2 = r_3 = E$ (with some straightforward care to avoid emitting a triangle twice in no extra I/O cost).

1.1 Previous Results

Join Dependency Testing. Beeri and Vardi [5] proved that λ-JD testing (Problem 1) is NP-hard if $\lambda = d - o(d)$; recall that d is the number of attributes in the input relation r. Maier, Sagiv, and Yannakakis [11] gave a stronger proof showing that λ-JD testing is still NP-hard for $\lambda = \Omega(d)$ (more specifically, roughly $2d/3$). In other words, (unless P = NP) no polynomial-time algorithm can exist to verify every JD $\bowtie [R_1, R_2, ..., R_m]$ on r, when one of $R_1, ..., R_m$ has $\Omega(d)$ attributes.

However, the above result does not rule out the possibility of efficient testing when the JD has a small arity, namely, *all* of $R_1, ..., R_m$ have just a few attributes (e.g., as few as just 2). Small-arity JDs are important because many relations in reality can eventually be losslessly decomposed into relations with small arities. By definition, for any $\lambda_1 < \lambda_2$, the λ_1-JD testing problem may only be easier than λ_2-JD testing problem because an algorithm for the latter can be used to solve the former problem, but not the vice versa. The ultimate question, therefore, is whether 2-JD testing can be solved within polynomial time. Unfortunately, that the arity of J being $\Omega(d)$ appears to be an inherent requirement in the reductions of [5, 11].

We note that a large body of beautiful theory has been developed on *dependency inference*, where the objective is to determine whether a target dependency can be inferred from a set Σ of dependencies (see [1, 10] for excellent guides into the literature). When the target dependency is a join dependency, the inference problem has been proven to be NP-hard in a variety of scenarios, most notably: (i) when Σ contains one join dependency and a set of functional dependencies [5, 11], (ii) when Σ is a set of multi-valued dependencies [6], and (iii) when Σ has one domain dependency and a set of functional dependencies [9]. The proofs of [5, 11] are essentially the same ones used to establish the NP-hardness of $\Omega(d)$-JD testing, while those of [6, 9] do not imply any conclusions on λ-JD testing.

JD Existence Testing and LW Join. There is an interesting connection between JD existence testing (Problem 2) and LW join. Let $r(R)$ be the input relation to Problem 2, where $R = \{A_1, A_2, ..., A_d\}$. For each $i \in [1, d]$, define $R_i = R \setminus \{A_i\}$, and $r_i = \pi_{R_i}(r)$. Nicolas showed [13] that r satisfies at least one non-trivial JD *if and only if* $r = r_1 \bowtie r_2 \bowtie ... \bowtie r_d$. In fact, since it is always true that $r \subseteq r_1 \bowtie r_2 \bowtie ... \bowtie r_d$, Problem 2 has an answer *yes* if and only if $r_1 \bowtie r_2 \bowtie ... \bowtie r_d$ returns exactly $|r|$ result tuples.

Therefore, Problem 2 boils down to evaluating the result size of the LW join $r_1 \bowtie r_2 \bowtie ... \bowtie r_d$. Atserias, Grohe, and Marx [4] showed that the result size can be as large as $(n_1 n_2 ... n_d)^{\frac{1}{d-1}}$, where $n_i = |r_i|$ for each $i \in [1, d]$. They also gave a RAM algorithm to compute the join result in $O(d^2 \cdot (n_1 n_2 ... n_d)^{\frac{1}{d-1}} \cdot \sum_{i=1}^{n} n_i)$ time. Since apparently $n_i \leq n = |r|$ $(1 \leq i \leq d)$, it follows that their algorithm has running time $O(d^2 \cdot n^{d/(d-1)} \cdot dn) = O(d^3 \cdot n^{2+o(1)})$, which in turn means that Problem 2 is solvable in polynomial time. Ngo et al. [12] designed a faster RAM algorithm to perform the LW join (hence, solving Problem 2) in $O(d^2 \cdot (n_1 n_2 ... n_d)^{\frac{1}{d-1}} + d^2 \sum_{i=1}^{d} n_i)$ time.

Problems 2 and 3 become much more challenging in external memory (EM). The algorithm of [12] (similarly, also the algorithm of [4]) is unaware of data blocking, relies heavily on hashing, and can entail up to $O(d^2 \cdot (n_1 n_2 ... n_d)^{\frac{1}{d-1}} + d^2 \sum_{i=1}^{d} n_i)$ I/Os. When d is small, this may be even worse than a naive generalized blocked-nested loop, whose I/O complexity for $d = O(1)$ is $O(n_1 n_2 ... n_d / (M^{d-1} B))$ I/Os. Recall that B and M are the sizes of a disk block and memory, respectively.

Triangle Enumeration. Problem 4 has received a large amount of attention from the database and theory communities (see [8] for a survey). Recently, Pagh and Silvestri [14] solved the problem in EM with a randomized algorithm whose I/O cost is $O(|E|^{1.5}/(\sqrt{M}B))$ *expected*, where $|E|$ is the number of edges in the input graph. They also presented a sophisticated de-randomization technique to convert their algorithm into a deterministic one that performs $O(\frac{|E|^{1.5}}{\sqrt{M}B} \cdot \log_{M/B} \frac{|E|}{B})$ I/Os. An I/O lower bound of $\Omega(|E|^{1.5}/(\sqrt{M}B))$ has been independently developed in [8, 14] on the *witnessing* class of algorithms.

1.2 Our Results

Section 2 will establish our first main result:

THEOREM 1. *2-JD testing is NP-hard.*

The theorem officially puts a negative answer to the question whether a small-arity JD can be tested efficiently (remember that 2 is already the smallest possible arity). As a consequence, we know that Problem 2 is NP-hard for *every* value $\lambda \in [2, d-1]$. Our proof is completely different from those of [5, 11], and is based on a novel reduction from the *Hamiltonian path problem*.

Our second main result is an I/O-efficient algorithm for LW enumeration (Problem 3). Let $r_1, r_2, ..., r_d$ be the input relations; and set $n_i = |r_i|$. In Section 3, we will prove:

THEOREM 2. *There is an EM algorithm that solves the LW enumeration problem with I/O complexity:*

$$O\Big(sort\Big[d^{3+o(1)}\Big(\frac{\Pi_{i=1}^{d} n_i}{M}\Big)^{\frac{1}{d-1}} + d^2 \sum_{i=1}^{d} n_i\Big]\Big).$$

where function $sort(x)$ *equals* $(x/B)\lg_{M/B}(x/B)$.

The main difficulty in obtaining the above theorem is that we *cannot* materialize the join result, because (as mentioned before) the result may have up to $(\Pi_{i=1}^{d} n_i)^{1/(d-1)}$ tuples such that writing them all to the disk may necessitate $\Omega(\frac{d}{B}(\Pi_{i=1}^{d} n_i)^{1/(d-1)})$ I/Os. This is why the problem is more challenging in EM (than in RAM where it is affordable, in fact even compulsory, to list out the entire join result [4, 12]). We overcome the challenge with a delicate piece of recursive machinery, and prove its efficiency through a non-trivial analysis.

As our third main result, we prove in Section 4 an improved version of Theorem 2 for $d = 3$:

THEOREM 3. *There is an EM algorithm that solves the LW enumeration problem of* $d = 3$ *with I/O complexity* $O(\frac{1}{B}\sqrt{\frac{n_1 n_2 n_3}{M}} + sort(n_1 + n_2 + n_3))$.

By combining the above two theorems with the reduction from JD existence testing to LW enumeration described in Section 1.1, we obtain the first non-trivial algorithm for I/O-efficient JD existence testing (Problem 2):

COROLLARY 1. *Let* $r(R)$ *be the input relation to the JD existence testing problem, where* $R = \{A_1, ..., A_d\}$. *For each* $i \in [1, d]$, *define* $R_i = R \setminus \{A_i\}$, *and* n_i *as the number of tuples in* $\pi_{R_i}(r)$. *Then:*

- *For* $d > 3$, *the problem can be solved with the I/O complexity in Theorem 2.*
- *For* $d = 3$, *the I/O complexity can be improved to the one in Theorem 3.*

Finally, when $n_1 = n_2 = n_3 = |E|$, Theorem 3 directly gives a new algorithm for triangle enumeration (Problem 4), noticing that $sort(|E|) = O(|E|^{1.5}/(\sqrt{M}B))$:

COROLLARY 2. *There is an algorithm that solves the triangle enumeration problem optimally in* $O(|E|^{1.5}/(\sqrt{M}B))$ *I/Os.*

Our triangle enumeration algorithm is deterministic, and strictly improves that of [14] by a factor of $O(\lg_{M/B}(|E|/B))$. Furthermore, the algorithm belongs to the witnessing class [8], and is the first (deterministic algorithm) in this class achieving the optimal I/O complexity for all values of M and B.

2. NP-HARDNESS OF 2-JD TESTING

This section will establish Theorem 1 with a reduction from the *Hamiltonian path problem*. Let $G = (V, E)$ be an undirected simple graph[1] with a vertex set V and an edge set E. Set $n = |V|$ and $m = |E|$. Without loss of generality, assume that each vertex $v \in V$ is uniquely identified by an integer id in $[1, n]$, denoted as $id(v)$. A *path* of length ℓ in G is a sequence of ℓ vertices $v_1, v_2, ..., v_\ell$ such that E has an edge between v_i and v_{i+1} for each $i \in [1, \ell - 1]$. The path is *simple* if no two vertices in the path are the same. A *Hamiltonian path* is a simple path in G of length n (such a path must pass each vertex in V exactly once). Deciding whether G has a Hamiltonian path is known to be NP-hard [7].

Let R be a set of n attributes: $\{A_1, A_2, ..., A_n\}$. We will create $\binom{n}{2}$ relations. Specifically, for each pair of i, j such that $1 \le i < j \le n$, we generate a relation $r_{i,j}$ with attributes A_i, A_j. The tuples in $r_{i,j}$ are determined as follows:

- *Case* $j = i + 1$: Initially, $r_{i,j}$ is empty. For each edge E between vertices u and v, we add two tuples to $r_{i,j}$: $(id(u), id(v))$ and $(id(v), id(u))$. In total, $r_{i,j}$ has $2m$ tuples.
- *Case* $j \ge i + 2$: $r_{i,j}$ contains $n(n-1)$ tuples (x, y), for all possible integers x, y such that $x \ne y$, and $1 \le x, y \le n$.

In general, the total number of tuples in the $r_{i,j}$ of all possible i, j is $O(nm + n^4) = O(n^4)$.

Define:

$$\text{CLIQUE} = \text{the output of the natural join of all } r_{i,j} \; (1 \le i < j \le n).$$

For example, for $n = 3$, CLIQUE $= r_{1,2} \bowtie r_{1,3} \bowtie r_{2,3}$. In general, CLIQUE is a relation with schema R.

LEMMA 1. *G has a Hamiltonian path if and only if* CLIQUE *is not empty.*

PROOF. Direction If. Assuming that CLIQUE is not empty, next we show that G has a Hamiltonian path. Let $(id(v_1), id(v_2), ..., id(v_n))$ be an arbitrary tuple in CLIQUE. It follows that:

[1]Recall that a graph is *simple* if it has at most one edge between any two vertices.

- For every $i \in [1, n-1]$, $(id(v_i), id(v_{i+1}))$ is a tuple in $r_{i,i+1}$, indicating that E has an edge between v_i and v_{i+1}.
- For every i, j such that $j \geq i+2$, $(id(v_i), id(v_j))$ is a tuple in $r_{i,j}$, indicating that $id(v_i) \neq id(v_j)$, i.e., $v_i \neq v_j$.

We thus have found a Hamiltonian path $v_1, v_2, ..., v_n$ in G.

Direction Only-If. Assuming that G has a Hamiltonian path, next we show that CLIQUE is not empty. Let $v_1, v_2, ..., v_n$ be any Hamiltonian path in G. It is easy to verify that $(id(v_1), id(v_2), ..., id(v_n))$ must appear in CLIQUE. □

For each pair of i, j satisfying $1 \leq i < j \leq n$, define an attribute set $R_{i,j} = \{A_i, A_j\}$. Denote by J the JD that "corresponds to" CLIQUE, namely:

$$J = \bowtie[R_{i,j}, \forall i, j \text{ s.t. } 1 \leq i < j \leq n].$$

For instance, for $n = 3$, $J = \bowtie[R_{1,2}, R_{1,3}, R_{2,3}]$. Note that J has arity 2, and $R = \cup_{i,j} R_{i,j}$ in general.

Next, we will construct from G a relation r^* of schema R such that CLIQUE is empty *if and only if* r^* satisfies J. The construction of r^* takes time polynomial to n (and hence, also to m because $m \leq n^2$).

Initially, r^* is empty. For *every* tuple t in *every* relation $r_{i,j}$ ($1 \leq i < j \leq n$), we will insert a tuple t' into r^*. Recall that $r_{i,j}$ has schema $\{A_i, A_j\}$. Suppose, without loss of generality, that $t = (a_i, a_j)$. Then, t' is determined as follows:

- $t'[A_i] = a_i$ ($t'[A_i]$ is the value of t' on attribute A_i)
- $t'[A_j] = a_j$
- For any $k \in [1, n]$ but $k \neq i$ and $k \neq j$, $t'[A_k]$ is set to a *dummy value* that appears only once in the whole r^*.

Since (as mentioned before) there are $O(n^4)$ tuples in the $r_{i,j}$ of all i, j, we know that r^* has $O(n^4)$ tuples, and hence, can be built in $O(n^5)$ time.

LEMMA 2. CLIQUE *is empty if and only if* r^* *satisfies* J.

PROOF. We first point out three facts:

1. Every tuple in r^* has $n-2$ dummy values.
2. Define $r^*_{i,j} = \pi_{A_i, A_j}(r^*)$ for i, j satisfying $1 \leq i < j \leq n$. Clearly, $r^*_{i,j}$ and $r_{i,j}$ share the same schema $R_{i,j}$. It is easy to verify that $r_{i,j}$ is exactly the set of tuples in $r^*_{i,j}$ that do *not* contain dummy values.
3. Define:

$$\text{CLIQUE}^* = \text{the output of the natural join of all } r^*_{i,j} \ (1 \leq i < j \leq n).$$

Then, r^* satisfies J if and only if $r^* = \text{CLIQUE}^*$.

Equipped with these facts, we now proceed to prove the lemma.

Direction If. Assuming that r^* satisfies J, next we show that CLIQUE is empty. Suppose, on the contrary, that $(a_1, a_2, ..., a_n)$ is a tuple in CLIQUE. Hence, (a_i, a_j) is a tuple in $r_{i,j}$ for any i, j satisfying $1 \leq i < j \leq n$. As neither a_i nor a_j is dummy, by Fact 2, we know that (a_i, a_j) belongs to $r^*_{i,j}$. It thus follows that $(a_1, a_2, ..., a_n)$ is a tuple in CLIQUE*. However, by Fact 1, $(a_1, a_2, ..., a_n)$ cannot belong to r^*, thus giving a contradiction against Fact 3.

Direction Only-If. Assuming that CLIQUE is empty, next we show that r^* satisfies J. Suppose, on the contrary, that r^* does not satisfy J, namely, $r^* \neq \text{CLIQUE}^*$ (Fact 3). Let $(a^*_1, a^*_2, ..., a^*_n)$ be a tuple in CLIQUE* but not in r^*. We distinguish two cases:

- *Case 1: none of* $a^*_1, ..., a^*_n$ *is dummy.* This means that, for any i, j satisfying $1 \leq i < j \leq n$, (a^*_i, a^*_j) is a tuple in $r_{i,j}$ (Fact 2). Therefore, $(a^*_1, a^*_2, ..., a^*_n)$ must be a tuple in CLIQUE, contradicting the assumption that CLIQUE is empty.
- *Case 2:* a^*_k *is dummy for at least one* $k \in [1, n]$. Since every dummy value appears exactly once in r^*, we can identify a unique tuple t^* in r^* such that $t^*[A_k] = a^*_k$. Next, we will show that t^* is precisely $(a^*_1, a^*_2, ..., a^*_n)$, thus contradicting the assumption that $(a^*_1, a^*_2, ..., a^*_n)$ is not in r^*, which will then complete the proof.

  Consider any i such that $1 \leq i < k$. That $(a^*_1, a^*_2, ..., a^*_n)$ is in CLIQUE* implies that (a^*_i, a^*_k) is in $r^*_{i,k}$. However, because in r^* the value a^*_k appears only in t^*, it must hold that $t^*[A_i] = a^*_i$. By a similar argument, for any j such that $k < j \leq n$, we must have $t^*[A_j] = a^*_j$. It thus follows that $(a^*_1, a^*_2, ..., a^*_n)$ is precisely t^*.

□

From the above discussion, we know that any 2-JD testing algorithm can be used to check whether CLIQUE is empty (Lemma 2), and hence, can be used to check whether G has a Hamiltonian path (Lemma 1). We thus conclude that 2-JD testing is NP-hard.

3. LW ENUMERATION

The discussion from the previous section has eliminated the hope of efficient JD testing no matter how small the JD arity is (unless P = NP). We therefore switch to the less stringent goal of JD *existence* testing (Problem 2). Based on the reduction described in Section 1.1, next we concentrate on LW enumeration as formulated in Problem 3, and will establish Theorem 2.

Let us recall a few basic definitions. We have a "global" set of attributes $R = \{A_1, A_2, ..., A_d\}$. For each $i \in [1, d]$, let $R_i = R \setminus \{A_i\}$. We are given relations $r_1, r_2, ..., r_d$ where r_i ($1 \leq i \leq d$) has schema R_i. The objective of LW enumeration is that, for every tuple t in the result of $r_1 \bowtie r_2 \bowtie ... \bowtie r_d$, we should invoke $emit(t)$ once and exactly once. We want to do so I/O-efficiently in the EM model, where B and M represent the sizes (in words) of a disk block and memory, respectively.

For each $i \in [1, d]$, set $n_i = |r_i|$, and define $dom(A_i)$ as the domain of attribute A_i. Given a tuple t and an attribute A_i (in the schema of the relation containing t), we denote by $t[A_i]$ the value of t on A_i. Furthermore, we assume that each of $r_1, ..., r_d$ is given in an array, but the d arrays do not need to be consecutive.

3.1 Basic Algorithms

Let us first deal with two scenarios under which LW enumeration is easier. The first situation arises when there is an n_i (for some $i \in [1, d]$) satisfying $n_i = O(M/d)$. In such a case, we call $r_1 \bowtie r_2 \bowtie ... \bowtie r_d$ a *small join*.

LEMMA 3. *Given a small join, we can emit all its result tuples in* $O(d + sort(d \sum_{i=1}^{d} n_i))$ *I/Os.*

PROOF. See appendix. □

The second scenario takes a bit more efforts to explain. In addition to $r_1, ..., r_d$, we accept two more input parameters:

- an integer $H \in [1, d]$
- a value $a \in dom(A_H)$.

It is required that a should be the *only* value that appears in the A_H attributes of $r_1, ..., r_{H-1}, r_{H+1}, ..., r_d$ (recall that r_H does not have A_H). In such a case, we call $r_1 \bowtie r_2 \bowtie ... \bowtie r_d$ a *point join*.

LEMMA 4. *Given a point join, we can emit all its result tuples in $O(d + sort(d^2 n_H + d\sum_{i\in[1,d]\setminus\{H\}} n_i))$ I/Os.*

PROOF. See appendix. □

We will denote the algorithm in the above lemma as PTJOIN$(H, a, r_1, r_2, ..., r_d)$.

3.2 The Full Algorithm

This subsection presents an algorithm for solving the general LW enumeration problem. We will focus on $n_1 > 2M/d$; if $n_1 \le 2M/d$, simply apply Lemma 3 because this is a small-join scenario.

Define:

$$U = \left(\frac{\prod_{i=1}^{d} n_i}{M}\right)^{\frac{1}{d-1}} \quad (1)$$

$$\tau_i = \frac{n_1 n_2 ... n_i}{(U \cdot d^{\frac{1}{d-1}})^{i-1}} \quad \text{for each } i \in [1, d]. \quad (2)$$

Notice that $\tau_1 = n_1$ and $\tau_d = M/d$.

Our general algorithm is a recursive procedure JOIN$(h, \rho_1, ..., \rho_d)$, which has three requirements:

- h is an integer in $[1, d]$;
- Each ρ_i $(1 \le i \le d)$ is a subset of the tuples in r_i.
- The size of ρ_1 satisfies:

$$|\rho_1| \le \tau_h. \quad (3)$$

JOIN$(h, \rho_1, ..., \rho_d)$ emits all result tuples in $\rho_1 \bowtie ... \bowtie \rho_d$. The original LW enumeration problem can be settled by calling JOIN$(1, r_1, ..., r_d)$.

3.2.1 Case $\tau_h \le 2M/d$

In this case, by the requirements of JOIN$(h, \rho_1, ..., \rho_d)$, it holds that $|\rho_1| \le \tau_h = O(M/d)$. Hence, we can directly apply the small-join algorithm in Lemma 3 to carry out the LW enumeration.

3.2.2 Case $\tau_h > 2M/d$

Denote by H the smallest integer in $[h+1, d]$ such that $\tau_H < \tau_h/2$. H always exists because $\tau_d = M/d < \tau_h/2$. Given a value $a \in dom(A_H)$, we define

$$freq(a) = \text{number of tuples } t \text{ in } \rho_1 \text{ with } t[A_H] = a.$$

Now we introduce:

$$\Phi = \{a \in dom(A_H) \mid freq(a) > \tau_H/2\}. \quad (4)$$

Let t^* be a result tuple of $\rho_1 \bowtie ... \bowtie \rho_d$. Conceptually, t^* is given a color: (i) *red*, if $t^*[A_H] \in \Phi$, or (ii) *blue*, otherwise.

Our strategy is to emit red and blue tuples separately. Towards this purpose, for each $i \in [1, d] \setminus \{H\}$, we partition ρ_i into:

$$\rho_i^{red} = \{\text{tuple } t \text{ in } \rho_i \mid t[A_H] \in \Phi\}$$
$$\rho_i^{blue} = \{\text{tuple } t \text{ in } \rho_i \mid t[A_H] \notin \Phi\}$$

To emit red tuples, it suffices to consider $\rho_1^{red}, ..., \rho_{H-1}^{red}, \rho_H, \rho_{H+1}^{red}, ..., \rho_d^{red}$. Likewise, to emit blue tuples, it suffices to consider $\rho_1^{blue}, ..., \rho_{H-1}^{blue}, \rho_H, \rho_{H+1}^{blue}, ..., \rho_d^{blue}$. Next, we will elaborate on how to do so.

Remark. The set Φ, as well as ρ_i^{red} and ρ_i^{blue} for each $i \in [1, d] \setminus \{H\}$, can be produced by sorting each ρ_i on A_H. More specifically, each element to be sorted is a tuple of $d-1$ values where d can be as large as $M/2$. Using an EM string sorting algorithm of [3], all the sorting can be completed with $O(d + sort(d\sum_{i\in[1,d]\setminus\{H\}} |\rho_i|))$ I/Os in total.

Emitting Red Tuples. For every $a \in \Phi$, we aim to emit the red tuples t^* with $t^*[A_H] = a$ separately. Define for each $i \in [1, d] \setminus \{H\}$:

$$\rho_i^{red}[a] = \text{set of tuples } t \text{ in } \rho_i^{red} \text{ with } t[A_H] = a.$$

The tuples of $\rho_i^{red}[a]$ are stored consecutively in the disk because we have sorted ρ_i^{red} by A_H earlier. All the red tuples t^* with $t^*[A_H] = a$ can be emitted by:

$$\text{PTJOIN}(H, a, \rho_1^{red}[a], ..., \rho_{H-1}^{red}[a], \rho_H, \rho_{H+1}^{red}[a], ..., \rho_d^{red}[a]).$$

Emitting Blue Tuples. First, divide $dom(A_H)$ into $q = O(1 + |\rho_1|/\tau_H)$ *disjoint* intervals $I_1, I_2, ..., I_q$ with the following properties:

- $I_1, I_2, ..., I_q$ are in ascending order[2].
- For each $j \in [1, q]$, define:

  $$\rho_1^{blue}[I_j] = \text{set of tuples in } \rho_1^{blue} \text{ whose } A_H\text{-values fall in } I_j$$

  If $j < q$, we require $\tau_H/2 \le |\rho_1^{blue}[I_j]| \le \tau_H$. Regarding $\rho_1^{blue}[I_q]$, we require $1 \le |\rho_1^{blue}[I_q]| \le \tau_H$.

Because ρ_1 has been sorted by A_H, all the $I_1, ..., I_q$ and $\rho_1^{blue}[I_1], ..., \rho_1^{blue}[I_q]$ can all be obtained with one scan of ρ_1.

Next, for each $i \in [2, d] \setminus \{H\}$, we produce for each $j \in [1, q]$:

$$\rho_i^{blue}[I_j] = \text{set of tuples in } \rho_i^{blue} \text{ whose } A_H\text{-values fall in } I_j.$$

Because ρ_i^{blue} has been sorted by A_H, all the $\rho_i^{blue}[I_1], \rho_i^{blue}[I_2], ..., \rho_i^{blue}[I_q]$ can be obtained by scanning synchronously ρ_i^{blue} and $\{I_1, ..., I_q\}$ once.

Finally, to emit all the blue tuples, we simply recursively call our algorithm for each $j \in [1, q]$:

$$\text{JOIN}(H, \rho_1^{blue}[I_j], ..., \rho_{H-1}^{blue}[I_j], \rho_H, \rho_{H+1}^{blue}[I_j], ..., \rho_d^{blue}[I_j]).$$

Note that the requirements for calling JOIN are fulfilled—in particular, $|\rho_1^{blue}[I_j]| \le \tau_H$, due to the way $I_1, ..., I_q$ were determined.

3.3 Analysis

Define a sequence of integers as follows:

- $h_1 = 1$;
- After h_i has been defined $(i \ge 1)$:
  - if $\tau_{h_i} > 2M/d$, then define h_{i+1} as the smallest integer in $[1 + h_i, d]$ satisfying $\tau_{h_{i+1}} < \tau_{h_i}/2$;
  - otherwise, h_{i+1} is undefined.

Denote by w the largest integer with h_w defined.

Recall that our LW enumeration algorithm starts by calling the JOIN procedure with JOIN$(1, r_1, ..., r_d)$, which recursively makes

[2]An interval $[x, y]$ *precedes* another $[x', y']$ if $y < x'$.

$$f(\ell,\rho_1,...,\rho_d) = \begin{cases} O(d) & \text{if } \ell = w \\ O(d\cdot\mu_\ell) + \sum_{j=1}^{q} f(\ell+1, \rho_1^{blue}[I_j], ..., \rho_{h_{\ell+1}-1}^{blue}[I_j], \rho_{h_{\ell+1}}, \rho_{h_{\ell+1}+1}^{blue}[I_j], ..., \rho_d^{blue}[I_j]) & \text{if } \ell < w \end{cases}$$

$$g(\ell,\rho_1,...,\rho_d) = \begin{cases} d\sum_{i=1}^{d}|\rho_i| & \text{if } \ell = w \\ d^2\mu_\ell|\rho_{h_{\ell+1}}| + d\sum_{i=1}^{d}|\rho_i| + \sum_{j=1}^{q} g(\ell+1, \rho_1^{blue}[I_j], ..., \rho_{h_{\ell+1}-1}^{blue}[I_j], \rho_{h_{\ell+1}}, \rho_{h_{\ell+1}+1}^{blue}[I_j], ..., \rho_d^{blue}[I_j]) & \text{if } \ell < w \end{cases}$$

Figure 1: Definitions of $f(h,\rho_1,...,\rho_d)$ and $g(h,\rho_1,...,\rho_d)$

subsequent calls to the same procedure. These calls form a tree $\mathcal{T}$. Equipped with the sequence $h_1, h_2, ..., h_w$, we can describe $\mathcal{T}$ in a more specific manner. Given a call JOIN$(h, \rho_1, ..., \rho_d)$, let us refer to the value of h as the call's *axis*. The initial call JOIN$(1, r_1, ..., r_d)$ has axis $h_1 = 1$. In general, an axis-h_i ($i \in [1, w-1]$) call generates axis-h_{i+1} calls, and hence, parents those calls in $\mathcal{T}$. Finally, all axis-h_w calls are leaf nodes in $\mathcal{T}$ (recall that an axis-h_w call simply invokes the small-join algorithm of Lemma 3). In other words, $\mathcal{T}$ has w *levels*; and all the calls at level $\ell \in [1, w]$ have an identical axis h_ℓ.

Given a level $\ell \in [1, w]$, define function $cost(\ell, \rho_1, ..., \rho_d)$ to be the number of I/Os performed by JOIN$(h_\ell, \rho_1, ..., \rho_d)$. Our goal is to prove that $cost(1, r_1, ..., r_d)$ is as claimed in Theorem 2.

Case $\ell = w$. Lemma 3 immediately shows:

$$cost(w,\rho_1,...,\rho_d) = O\Big(d + sort\Big(d\sum_{i=1}^{d}|\rho_i|\Big)\Big). \quad (5)$$

Case $\ell < w$. Define for $\ell \in [1, w-1]$:

$$\mu_\ell = 2\tau_{h_\ell}/\tau_{h_{\ell+1}}.$$

Consider the set Φ defined in (4). Recall that for every $a \in \Phi$, $freq(a) > \tau_{h_{\ell+1}}/2$. Hence:

$$|\Phi| < 2|\rho_1|/\tau_{h_{\ell+1}} \le 2\tau_{h_\ell}/\tau_{h_{\ell+1}} = \mu_\ell.$$

where the second inequality is due to (3).

For emitting red tuples, the cost is dominated by that of the point-join algorithm whose total I/O cost, by Lemma 4, is bounded by:

$$O\Big(\sum_{a\in\Phi}\Big(d + sort\Big(d^2|\rho_{h_{\ell+1}}| + d\sum_{i\in[1,d]\setminus\{h_{\ell+1}\}}\big|\rho_i^{red}[a]\big|\Big)\Big)\Big)$$

$$= O\Big(d|\Phi| + sort\Big(d^2|\Phi||\rho_{h_{\ell+1}}| + d\sum_{i=1}^{d}|\rho_i|\Big)\Big)$$

$$= O\Big(d\cdot\mu_\ell + sort\Big(d^2\mu_\ell|\rho_{h_{\ell+1}}| + d\sum_{i=1}^{d}|\rho_i|\Big)\Big). \quad (6)$$

The cost of emitting blue tuples comes from recursion. Therefore, we can establish a recurrence:

$$cost(\ell,\rho_1,...,\rho_d)$$

$$= (6) + \sum_{j=1}^{q} cost\Big(\ell+1, \rho_1^{blue}[I_j], ..., \rho_{h_{\ell+1}-1}^{blue}[I_j], \rho_{h_{\ell+1}}, \rho_{h_{\ell+1}+1}^{blue}[I_j], ..., \rho_d^{blue}[I_j]\Big). \quad (7)$$

Recall that q is the number of disjoint intervals that JOIN$(h_\ell, \rho_1, ..., \rho_d)$ uses to divide $dom(A_\ell)$ for blue tuple emission (see Section 3.2).

The rest of the subsection is devoted to solving this non-conventional recurrence. Let functions $f(\ell, \rho_1, ..., \rho_d)$ and $g(\ell, \rho_1, ..., \rho_d)$ be as defined in Figure 1. The following proposition is fundamental:

PROPOSITION 1. $cost(\ell, \rho_1, ..., \rho_d) = f(\ell, \rho_1, ..., \rho_d) + O(sort(g(\ell, \rho_1, ..., \rho_d)))$.

PROOF. By the convexity of function $sort(x)$. □

To prove Theorem 2, our target is to give an upper bound on $cost(1, r_1, ..., r_d) = f(1, r_1, ..., r_d) + O(sort(g(1, r_1, ..., r_d)))$.

3.3.1 Bounding $f(1, r_1, ..., r_d)$

Define m_ℓ as the total number of level-ℓ calls in $\mathcal{T}$. Each level-ℓ call contributes $O(d\cdot\mu_\ell)$ I/Os to $f(1, r_1, ..., r_d)$ (see Figure 1).[3] Hence:

$$f(1,r_1,...,r_d) = \sum_{\ell=1}^{w} O(m_\ell\cdot d\cdot\mu_\ell). \quad (8)$$

We say that a level-ℓ call JOIN$(h_\ell, \rho_1, ..., \rho_d)$ *underflows* if $|\rho_1| < \tau_{h_\ell}/2$; otherwise, we say that it is *ordinary*. Consider all the calls JOIN$(h_\ell, \rho_1, ..., \rho_d)$ at level ℓ. The sets ρ_1 in the first parameters of those calls are disjoint. Hence, there can be at most $O(n_1/\tau_{h_\ell})$ ordinary calls at level ℓ. Moreover, if $\ell < w$, then a level-ℓ call creates at most one underflowing call at level $\ell + 1$. These facts indicate that, for each $\ell \in [2, w]$:

$$m_\ell = O\left(m_{\ell-1} + \frac{n_1}{\tau_{h_\ell}}\right) = O\left(\sum_{i=1}^{\ell}\frac{n_1}{\tau_{h_i}}\right) = O\left(\frac{n_1}{\tau_{h_\ell}}\right), \quad (9)$$

where the second equality used $m_1 = 1 = n_1/\tau_{h_1}$, and the last equality used the fact that $\tau_{h_i} > 2\tau_{h_{i+1}}$ for every $i \in [1, w-1]$.

Applying $\tau_{h_w} = M/d$, we get from (9):

$$m_w = O(dn_1/M).$$

Moreover, for each $\ell \in [1, w-1]$:

$$m_\ell\mu_\ell = O\left(\frac{n_1}{\tau_{h_\ell}}\right)\frac{2\tau_{h_\ell}}{\tau_{h_{\ell+1}}} = O\left(\frac{n_1}{\tau_{h_{\ell+1}}}\right).$$

[3] Here define a boundary dummy $\mu_w = 1$.

We can now derive from (8):

$$f(1, r_1, ..., r_d) = O\left(\frac{d^2 n_1}{M} + \sum_{\ell=1}^{w-1} \frac{d \cdot n_1}{\tau_{h_{\ell+1}}}\right) = O\left(\frac{d^2 n_1}{M} + \frac{d n_1}{\tau_{h_w}}\right) = O\left(\frac{d^2 n_1}{M}\right). \quad (10)$$

3.3.2 Bounding $g(1, r_1, ..., r_d)$

Figure 1 shows that, in $\mathcal{T}$, each level-ℓ ($\ell < w$) call $\text{JOIN}(h_\ell, \rho_1, ..., \rho_d)$ contributes $d^2\mu_\ell|\rho_{h_{\ell+1}}| + d\sum_{i=1}^{d}|\rho_i|$ to $g(1, r_1, ..., r_d)$. We can amortize the contribution onto the tuples in $\rho_1, ..., \rho_d$, such that:

- Each tuple in $\rho_{h_{\ell+1}}$ contributes $d^2\mu_\ell$ to $g(1, r_1, ..., r_d)$;
- Each tuple in any other relation ρ_i ($i \neq h_{\ell+1}$) contributes d to $g(1, r_1, ..., r_d)$.

Similarly, for every level-w call $\text{JOIN}(h_w, \rho_1, ..., \rho_d)$, each tuple in ρ_1, ..., ρ_d contributes d to $g(1, r_1, ..., r_d)$.

Our strategy for bounding $g(1, r_1, ..., r_d)$ is to sum up the largest possible contribution made by *each* individual tuple in the input relations $r_1, ..., r_d$. For this purpose, given a value $i \in [1, d]$, we define L_i as follows:

- $L_1 = 0$;
- If $i \geq 2$ but no call in the entire $\mathcal{T}$ has axis i, then $L_i = 0$;
- Otherwise, suppose that the level-ℓ calls of T have axis $h_\ell = i$; then we define $L_i = \ell - 1$.

Now, let us concentrate on a single tuple t in an arbitrary input relation r_i (for any $i \in [1, d]$). Consider a level-ℓ call ($1 \leq \ell \leq w$) $\text{JOIN}(h_\ell, \rho_1, ..., \rho_d)$ in $\mathcal{T}$. We say that t *participates in* the call if $t \in \rho_i$. If t does not participate in the call, then t contributes nothing to $g(1, r_1, ..., r_d)$. Otherwise, the contribution of t depends on whether $h_{\ell+1}$ happens to be i. As explained earlier, if $h_{\ell+1} = i$, t contributes $d^2\mu_\ell$, or else t contributes d.

Denote by $\gamma_\ell(t)$ the number of level-ℓ calls that t participates in; specially, define $\gamma_0(t) = 0$. Then, the sequence $L_1, L_2, ..., L_d$ defined earlier allows us to represent concisely the total contribution of t as

$$\gamma_{L_i}(t) \cdot d^2\mu_{L_i} + \sum_{\ell \in [1,w] \setminus L_i} \gamma_\ell(t) \cdot d \quad (11)$$

defining a boundary dummy value $\mu_0 = 1$.

LEMMA 5. *If $L_i = 0$, then $\gamma_\ell(t) \leq 1$ for all $\ell \in [1, w]$. If $L_i \neq 0$, then*

$$\gamma_\ell(t) = \begin{cases} O(1) & \text{if } \ell \in [1, L_i] \\ O(\mu_{L_i}) & \text{if } \ell \in [L_i + 1, w] \end{cases} \quad (12)$$

PROOF. See appendix. □

By applying the lemma to (11), we know that, in total, t contributes to $g(1, r_1, ..., r_d)$

$$O(d^2\mu_{L_i} + w \cdot \mu_{L_i} \cdot d) = O(d^2\mu_{L_i}).$$

By summing up the contribution of all the tuples, we get:

$$g(1, r_1, ..., r_d)$$
$$= O\Big(\sum_{i \in [1,d] \text{ s.t. } L_i \neq 0} \sum_{t \in r_i} d^2\mu_{L_i} + \sum_{t \in [1,d] \text{ s.t. } L_i = 0} \sum_{t \in r_i} d^2\Big)$$
$$= O\Big(\sum_{i \in [1,d] \text{ s.t. } L_i \neq 0} d^2\mu_{L_i} n_i + \sum_{i=1}^{d} d^2 n_i\Big)$$
$$= O\Big(\sum_{\ell=2}^{w} d^2\mu_{\ell-1} n_{h_\ell} + d^2 \sum_{i=1}^{d} n_i\Big)$$

where the last equality is due to the definition of L_i.

It remains to bound $\mu_{\ell-1} n_{h_\ell}$ for each $\ell \in [2, w]$. For this purpose, we prove:

LEMMA 6. $\mu_{\ell-1} = O(Ud^{\frac{1}{d-1}}/n_{h_\ell})$ *for each* $\ell \in [2, w]$.

PROOF. See appendix. □

The lemma indicates that

$$g(1, r_1, ..., r_d) = O\Big(\sum_{\ell=2}^{w} Ud^{2+\frac{1}{d-1}} + d^2 \sum_{i=1}^{d} n_i\Big) = O\Big(d^{3+\frac{1}{d-1}}U + d^2 \sum_{i=1}^{d} n_i\Big).$$

Combining the above equation with (1), (10), and Proposition 1, we now complete the whole proof of Theorem 2.

4. A FASTER ALGORITHM FOR ARITY 3

The algorithm developed in the previous section solves the LW enumeration problem for any $d \leq M/2$. In this section, we focus on $d = 3$, and leverage intrinsic properties of this special instance to design a faster algorithm, which will establish Theorem 3 (and hence, also Corollaries 1 and 2). Specifically, the input consists of three relations: $r_1(A_2, A_3)$, $r_2(A_1, A_3)$, and $r_3(A_1, A_2)$; and the goal is to emit all the tuples in the result of $r_1 \bowtie r_2 \bowtie r_3$.

As before, for each $i \in [1, 3]$, set $n_i = |r_i|$, and denote by $dom(A_i)$ the domain of A_i. Without loss of generality, we assume that $n_1 \geq n_2 \geq n_3$.

4.1 Basic Algorithms

Let us start with:

LEMMA 7. *If $r_1(A_2, A_3)$ and $r_2(A_1, A_3)$ have been sorted by A_3, the 3-arity LW enumeration problem can be solved in $O(1 + \frac{(n_1+n_2)n_3}{MB} + \frac{1}{B}\sum_{i=1}^{3} n_i)$ I/Os.*

PROOF. If $n_3 \leq M$, we can achieve the purpose stated in the lemma using the small-join algorithm of Lemma 3 with straightforward modifications (e.g., apparently sorting is not required). When $n_3 > M$, we simply chop r_3 into subsets of size M, and then repeat the above small-join algorithm $\lceil n_3/M \rceil$ times. □

We call $r_1 \bowtie r_2 \bowtie r_3$ an A_1*-point join* if both conditions below are fulfilled:

- all the A_1 values in $r_2(A_1, A_3)$ are the same;
- $r_1(A_2, A_3)$ and $r_2(A_1, A_3)$ are sorted by A_3.

LEMMA 8. *Given an A_1-point join, we can emit all its result tuples in $O(1 + \frac{n_1 n_3}{MB} + \frac{1}{B}\sum_{i=1}^{3} n_i)$ I/Os.*

PROOF. We first obtain $r'(A_1, A_2, A_3) = r_1 \bowtie r_2$, and store all the tuples of r' into the disk. Since all the tuples in r_2 have the same A_1-value, their A_3-values must be distinct. Hence, each tuple in r_1 can be joined with at most one tuple in r_2, implying that $|r'| \leq n_1$. Utilizing the fact that r_1 and r_2 are both sorted on A_3, r' can be produced by a synchronous scan over r_1 and r_2 in $O(1 + (n_1 + n_2)/B)$ I/Os.

Then, we use the classic *blocked nested loop* (BNL) algorithm to perform the join $r' \bowtie r_3$ (which equals $r_1 \bowtie r_2 \bowtie r_3$). The only difference is that, whenever BNL wants to write a block of $O(B)$ result tuples to the disk, we skip the write but simply emit those tuples. The BNL performs $O(1 + \frac{|r'|n_3}{MB} + \frac{r'+n_3}{B})$ I/Os. The lemma thus follows. □

Symmetrically, we call $r_1 \bowtie r_2 \bowtie r_3$ an *A_2-point join* if

- all the A_2 values in $r_1(A_2, A_3)$ are the same.
- $r_1(A_2, A_3)$ and $r_2(A_1, A_3)$ are sorted by A_3.

LEMMA 9. *Given an A_2-point join, we can emit all its result tuples in $O(1 + \frac{n_2 n_3}{MB} + \frac{1}{B}\sum_{i=1}^{3} n_i)$ I/Os.*

PROOF. Symmetric to Lemma 8. □

4.2 3-Arity LW Enumeration Algorithm

Next, we give our general algorithm for LW enumeration with $d = 3$. We will focus on $n_1 \geq n_2 \geq n_3 \geq M$; otherwise, the algorithm in Lemma 7 already solves the problem in linear I/Os after sorting.

Set:

$$\theta_1 = \sqrt{\frac{n_1 n_3 M}{n_2}}, \text{ and } \theta_2 = \sqrt{\frac{n_2 n_3 M}{n_1}}. \quad (13)$$

For values $a_1 \in dom(A_1)$ and $a_2 \in dom(A_2)$, define:

$$\begin{aligned} freq(a_1, r_3) &= \text{number of tuples } t \text{ in } r_3 \text{ with } t[A_1] = a_1 \\ freq(a_2, r_3) &= \text{number of tuples } t \text{ in } r_3 \text{ with } t[A_2] = a_2. \end{aligned}$$

Now we introduce:

$$\begin{aligned} \Phi_1 &= \{a_1 \in dom(A_1) \mid freq(a_1, r_3) > \theta_1\} \\ \Phi_2 &= \{a_2 \in dom(A_2) \mid freq(a_2, r_3) > \theta_2\}. \end{aligned}$$

Let t^* be a result tuple of $r_1 \bowtie r_2 \bowtie r_3$. We can classify t^* into one of the following categories:

1. *Red-red*: $t^*[A_1] \in \Phi_1$ and $t^*[A_2] \in \Phi_2$
2. *Red-blue*: $t^*[A_1] \in \Phi_1$ and $t^*[A_2] \notin \Phi_2$
3. *Blue-red*: $t^*[A_1] \notin \Phi_1$ and $t^*[A_2] \in \Phi_2$
4. *Blue-blue*: $t^*[A_1] \notin \Phi_1$ and $t^*[A_2] \notin \Phi_2$.

We will emit each type of tuples separately, after a partitioning phase, as explained in the sequel.

Partitioning r_3. Define:

$$\begin{aligned} r_3^{red,red} &= \text{set of tuples } t \text{ in } r_3 \text{ s.t. } t[A_1] \in \Phi_1, t[A_2] \in \Phi_2 \\ r_3^{red,blue} &= \text{set of tuples } t \text{ in } r_3 \text{ s.t. } t[A_1] \in \Phi_1, t[A_2] \notin \Phi_2 \\ r_3^{blue,red} &= \text{set of tuples } t \text{ in } r_3 \text{ s.t. } t[A_1] \notin \Phi_1, t[A_2] \in \Phi_2 \\ r_3^{blue,blue} &= \text{set of tuples } t \text{ in } r_3 \text{ s.t. } t[A_1] \notin \Phi_1, t[A_2] \notin \Phi_2 \end{aligned}$$

$$\begin{aligned} r_3^{blue,-} &= r_3^{blue,red} \cup r_3^{blue,blue} \\ r_3^{-,blue} &= r_3^{red,blue} \cup r_3^{blue,blue}. \end{aligned}$$

Divide $dom(A_1)$ into $q_1 = O(1 + n_3/\theta_1)$ disjoint intervals I_1^1, I_2^1, ..., $I_{q_1}^1$ with the following properties:

- $I_1^1, I_2^1, ..., I_{q_1}^1$ are in ascending order.
- For each $j \in [1, q_1]$, $r_3^{blue,-}$ has at most $2\theta_1$ tuples whose A_1-values fall in I_j^1.

Similarly, we divide $dom(A_2)$ into $q_2 = O(1 + n_3/\theta_2)$ disjoint intervals $I_1^2, I_2^2, ..., I_{q_2}^2$ with the following properties:

- $I_1^2, I_2^2, ..., I_{q_2}^2$ are in ascending order.
- For each $j \in [1, q_2]$, $r_3^{-,blue}$ has at most $2\theta_2$ tuples whose A_2-values fall in I_j^2.

We now define several partitions of r_3:

1. For each $a_1 \in \Phi_1$ and $a_2 \in \Phi_2$:
$$r_3^{red,red}[a_1, a_2] = \text{the (only) tuple } t \text{ in } r_3^{red,red} \text{ with } t[A_1] = a_1 \text{ and } t[A_2] = a_2.$$
2. For each $a_1 \in \Phi_1$ and $j \in [1, q_2]$:
$$r_3^{red,blue}[a_1, I_j^2] = \text{set of tuples } t \text{ in } r_3^{red,blue} \text{ with } t[A_1] = a_1 \text{ and } t[A_2] \text{ in } I_j^2.$$
3. For each $j \in [1, q_1]$ and $a_2 \in \Phi_2$:
$$r_3^{blue,red}[I_j^1, a_2] = \text{set of tuples } t \text{ in } r_3^{blue,red} \text{ with } t[A_1] \text{ in } I_j^1 \text{ and } t[A_2] = a_2.$$
4. For each $j_1 \in [1, q_1]$ and $j_2 \in [1, q_2]$:
$$r_3^{blue,blue}[I_{j_1}^1, I_{j_2}^2] = \text{set of tuples } t \text{ in } r_3^{blue,blue} \text{ with } t[A_1] \text{ in } I_j^1 \text{ and } t[A_2] \text{ in } I_j^2.$$

It is fundamental to produce all the above partitions with $O(sort(n_3))$ I/Os in total.

Partitioning r_1 and r_2. Let:

$$\begin{aligned} r_1^{red} &= \text{set of tuples } t \text{ in } r_1 \text{ s.t. } t[A_2] \in \Phi_2 \\ r_1^{blue} &= \text{set of tuples } t \text{ in } r_1 \text{ s.t. } t[A_2] \notin \Phi_2 \\ r_2^{red} &= \text{set of tuples } t \text{ in } r_2 \text{ s.t. } t[A_1] \in \Phi_1 \\ r_2^{blue} &= \text{set of tuples } t \text{ in } r_2 \text{ s.t. } t[A_1] \notin \Phi_1 \end{aligned}$$

We now define several partitions of r_1:

1. For each $a_2 \in \Phi_2$:
$$r_1^{red}[a_2] = \text{set of tuples } t \text{ in } r_1^{red} \text{ with } t[A_2] = a_2.$$
2. For each $j \in [1, q_2]$:
$$r_1^{blue}[I_j^2] = \text{set of tuples } t \text{ in } r_1^{blue} \text{ with } t[A_2] \text{ in } I_j^2.$$

Similarly, we define several partitions of r_2:

1. For each $a_1 \in \Phi_1$:
$$r_2^{red}[a_1] = \text{set of tuples } t \text{ in } r_2^{red} \text{ with } t[A_1] = a_1.$$
2. For each $j \in [1, q_1]$:
$$r_2^{blue}[I_j^1] = \text{set of tuples } t \text{ in } r_2^{blue} \text{ with } t[A_1] \text{ in } I_j^1.$$

It is also fundamental to produce the above partitions using $O(sort(n_1+n_2+n_3))$ I/Os in total. With the same cost, we make sure that all these partitions are sorted by A_3.

Emitting Red-Red Tuples. For each $a_1 \in \Phi_1$ and each $a_2 \in \Phi_2$, apply Lemma 7 to emit the result of $r_1^{red}[a_2] \bowtie r_2^{red}[a_1] \bowtie r_3^{red,red}[a_1,a_2]$.

Emitting Red-Blue Tuples. For each $a_1 \in \Phi_1$ and each $j \in [1,q_2]$, apply Lemma 8 to emit the result of the A_1-point join $r_1^{blue}[I_j^2] \bowtie r_2^{red}[a_1] \bowtie r_3^{red,blue}[a_1,I_j^2]$.

Emitting Blue-Red Tuples. For each $j \in [1,q_1]$ and each $a_2 \in \Phi_2$, apply Lemma 9 to emit the result of the A_2-point join $r_1^{red}[a_2] \bowtie r_2^{blue}[I_j^1] \bowtie r_3^{blue,red}[I_j^1,a_2]$.

Emitting Blue-Blue Tuples. For each $j_1 \in [1,q_1]$ and each $j_2 \in [1,q_2]$, apply Lemma 7 to emit the result of $r_1^{blue}[I_{j_2}^2] \bowtie r_2^{blue}[I_{j_1}^1] \bowtie r_3^{blue,blue}[I_{j_1}^1,I_{j_2}^2]$.

4.3 Analysis

We now analyze the algorithm of Section 4.2, assuming $n_1 \geq n_2 \geq n_3 \geq M$. First, it should be clear that

$$\begin{aligned}
|\Phi_1| &\leq \frac{n_3}{\theta_1} = \sqrt{\frac{n_2 n_3}{n_1 M}} \\
|\Phi_2| &\leq \frac{n_3}{\theta_2} = \sqrt{\frac{n_1 n_3}{n_2 M}} \\
q_1 &= O\Big(1+\frac{n_3}{\theta_1}\Big) = O\Big(1+\sqrt{\frac{n_2 n_3}{n_1 M}}\Big) \\
q_2 &= O\Big(1+\frac{n_3}{\theta_2}\Big) = O\Big(\sqrt{\frac{n_1 n_3}{n_2 M}}\Big).
\end{aligned}$$

By Lemma 7, the cost of red-red emission is bounded by (remember that $r_3^{red,red}[a_1,a_2]$ has only 1 tuple):

$$\begin{aligned}
&\sum_{a_1,a_2} O\Big(1+\frac{|r_1^{red}[a_2]|+|r_2^{red}[a_1]|}{B}\Big). \\
=\;& O\Big(|\Phi_1||\Phi_2| + \sum_{a_2}\frac{|r_1^{red}[a_2]||\Phi_1|}{B} + \sum_{a_1}\frac{|r_2^{red}[a_1]||\Phi_2|}{B}\Big) \\
=\;& O\Big(\frac{n_3}{M}+\frac{n_1|\Phi_1|}{B}+\frac{n_2|\Phi_2|}{B}\Big) = O\Big(\frac{\sqrt{n_1 n_2 n_3}}{B\sqrt{M}}\Big).
\end{aligned}$$

By Lemma 8, the cost of red-blue emission is bounded by:

$$\begin{aligned}
&\sum_{a_1,j} O\Big(1+\frac{|r_1^{blue}[I_j^2]||r_3^{red,blue}[a_1,I_j^2]|}{MB} \\
&+\frac{|r_1^{blue}[I_j^2]|+|r_2^{red}[a_1]|+|r_3^{red,blue}[a_1,I_j^2]|}{B}\Big). \\
&= O\Big(|\Phi_1|q_2 + \sum_j \frac{|r_1^{blue}[I_j^2]|\sum_{a_1}|r_3^{red,blue}[a_1,I_j^2]|}{MB} \\
&+\frac{|\Phi_1|\sum_j |r_1^{blue}[I_j^2]|}{B} + \frac{q_2\sum_{a_1}|r_2^{red}[a_1]|}{B} + \frac{n_3}{B}\Big). \qquad (14)
\end{aligned}$$

Observe that $\sum_{a_1}|r_3^{red,blue}[a_1,I_j^2]|$ is the total number of tuples in $r_3^{red,blue}$ whose A_2-values fall in I_j^2. By the way $I_1^2,\dots,I_{q_2}^2$ are constructed, we know:

$$\sum_{a_1}|r_3^{red,blue}[a_1,I_j^2]| \leq 2\theta_2.$$

(14) is thus bounded by:

$$\begin{aligned}
&O\Big(\frac{n_3}{M}+\sum_j\frac{|r_1^{blue}[I_j^2]|\theta_2}{MB}+\frac{|\Phi_1|n_1}{B}+\frac{q_2 n_2}{B}+\frac{n_3}{B}\Big) \\
=\;& O\Big(\frac{n_1\theta_2}{MB}+\frac{|\Phi_1|n_1}{B}+\frac{q_2 n_2}{B}+\frac{n_3}{B}\Big) = O\Big(\frac{\sqrt{n_1 n_2 n_3}}{B\sqrt{M}}\Big).
\end{aligned}$$

A similar argument shows that the cost of blue-red emission is bounded by $O(\frac{\sqrt{n_1 n_2 n_3}}{B\sqrt{M}}+\frac{n_1}{B})$. Finally, by Lemma 7, the cost of blue-blue emission is bounded by:

$$\begin{aligned}
&\sum_{j_1,j_2} O\Big(1+\frac{\big(|r_1^{blue}[I_{j_2}^2]|+|r_2^{blue}[I_{j_1}^1]|\big)|r_3^{blue,blue}[I_{j_1}^1,I_{j_2}^2]|}{MB} \\
&+\frac{|r_1^{blue}[I_{j_2}^2]|+|r_2^{blue}[I_{j_1}^1]|+|r_3^{blue,blue}[I_{j_1}^1,I_{j_2}^2]|}{B}\Big). \qquad (15)
\end{aligned}$$

Let us analyze each term of (15) in turn. First:

$$\begin{aligned}
&\sum_{j_1,j_2}|r_1^{blue}[I_{j_2}^2]||r_3^{blue,blue}[I_{j_1}^1,I_{j_2}^2]| \\
&= \sum_{j_2}|r_1^{blue}[I_{j_2}^2]|\sum_{j_1}|r_3^{blue,blue}[I_{j_1}^1,I_{j_2}^2]| \qquad (16)
\end{aligned}$$

$\sum_{j_1}|r_3^{blue,blue}[I_{j_1}^1,I_{j_2}^2]|$ gives the number of tuples in $r_3^{blue,blue}$ whose A_2-values fall in I_j^2. By the way $I_1^2,\dots,I_{q_2}^2$ are constructed, we know:

$$\sum_{j_1}|r_3^{blue,blue}[I_{j_1}^1,I_{j_2}^2]| \leq 2\theta_2.$$

Therefore:

$$(16) = O\Big(\theta_2\sum_{j_2}|r_1^{blue}[I_{j_2}^2]|\Big) = O(n_1\theta_2).$$

Symmetrically, we have:

$$\sum_{j_1,j_2}|r_2^{blue}[I_{j_1}^1]||r_3^{blue,blue}[I_{j_1}^1,I_{j_2}^2]| = O(n_2\theta_1).$$

Thus, (15) is bounded by:

$$\begin{aligned}
&O\Big(q_1 q_2 + \frac{n_1\theta_2+n_2\theta_1}{MB} \\
&+\frac{q_1\sum_{j_2}|r_1^{blue}[I_{j_2}^2]|}{B}+\frac{q_2\sum_{j_1}|r_2^{blue}[I_{j_1}^1]|}{B}+\frac{n_3}{B}\Big) \\
=\;& O\Big(q_1 q_2+\frac{n_1\theta_2+n_2\theta_1}{MB}+\frac{q_1 n_1}{B}+\frac{q_2 n_2}{B}+\frac{n_3}{B}\Big) \\
=\;& O\Big(\frac{\sqrt{n_1 n_2 n_3}}{B\sqrt{M}}+\frac{n_1}{B}\Big).
\end{aligned}$$

As already mentioned in Section 4.2, the partitioning phase requires $O(sort(\sum_{i=1}^{3} n_i))$ I/Os. We now complete the proof of Theorem 3.

ACKNOWLEDGEMENTS

This work was supported in part by Grants GRF 4168/13 and GRF 142072/14 from HKRGC.

5. REFERENCES

[1] S. Abiteboul, R. Hull, and V. Vianu. *Foundations of Databases*. Addison-Wesley Publishing Company, 1995.

[2] A. Aggarwal and J. S. Vitter. The input/output complexity of sorting and related problems. *CACM*, 31(9):1116–1127, 1988.

[3] L. Arge, P. Ferragina, R. Grossi, and J. S. Vitter. On sorting strings in external memory (extended abstract). In *STOC*, pages 540–548, 1997.

[4] A. Atserias, M. Grohe, and D. Marx. Size bounds and query plans for relational joins. *SIAM J. of Comp.*, 42(4):1737–1767, 2013.

[5] C. Beeri and M. Vardi. On the complexity of testing implications of data dependencies. *Computer Science Report, Hebrew Univ*, 1980.

[6] P. C. Fischer and D. Tsou. Whether a set of multivalued dependencies implies a join dependency is NP-hard. *SIAM J. of Comp.*, 12(2):259–266, 1983.

[7] M. R. Garey and D. S. Johnson. *Computers and Intractability: A Guide to the Theory of NP-Completeness*. W. H. Freeman, 1979.

[8] X. Hu, Y. Tao, and C.-W. Chung. I/O-efficient algorithms on triangle listing and counting. *To appear in ACM TODS*, 2014.

[9] P. C. Kanellakis. On the computational complexity of cardinality constraints in relational databases. *IPL*, 11(2):98–101, 1980.

[10] D. Maier. *The Theory of Relational Databases*. Available Online at http://web.cecs.pdx.edu/~maier/TheoryBook/TRD.html, 1983.

[11] D. Maier, Y. Sagiv, and M. Yannakakis. On the complexity of testing implications of functional and join dependencies. *JACM*, 28(4):680–695, 1981.

[12] H. Q. Ngo, E. Porat, C. Ré, and A. Rudra. Worst-case optimal join algorithms: [extended abstract]. In *PODS*, pages 37–48, 2012.

[13] J. Nicolas. Mutual dependencies and some results on undecomposable relations. In *VLDB*, pages 360–367, 1978.

[14] R. Pagh and F. Silvestri. The input/output complexity of triangle enumeration. In *PODS*, pages 224–233, 2014.

APPENDIX

Proof of Lemma 3

Without loss of generality, suppose that r_1 has the smallest cardinality among all the input relations. Let us first assume that $n_1 \le cM/d$ where c is a sufficiently small constant so that r_1 can be kept in memory throughout the entire algorithm. With r_1 already in memory, we merge all the tuples of $r_2, ..., r_d$ into a set L, sorted by attribute A_1. For each $a \in dom(A_1)$, let $L[a]$ be the set of tuples in L whose A_1-values equal a.

Next, for each $a \in dom(A_1)$, we use the procedure below to emit all the tuples t^* in the result of $r_1 \bowtie r_2 \bowtie ... \bowtie r_d$ such that $t^*[A_1] = a$. First, initialize empty sets $S_2, ..., S_d$ in memory. Then, we process each tuple $t \in L[a]$ as follows. Suppose that t originates from r_i for some $i \in [2, d]$. Check whether r_1 has a tuple t' satisfying

$$t'[A_j] = t[A_j], \qquad \forall j \in [2, d] \setminus \{i\}. \tag{17}$$

If the answer is no, t is discarded; otherwise, we add it to S_i. Note that the checking happens in memory, and thus, entails no I/O. Having processed all the tuples of $L[a]$ this way, we emit all the tuples in the result of $r_1 \bowtie S_2 \bowtie S_3 \bowtie ... \bowtie S_d$ (these are exactly the tuples in $r_1 \bowtie r_2 \bowtie ... \bowtie r_d$ whose A_1-values equal a). The above tuple emission incurs no I/Os due to the following lemma.

LEMMA 10. *$r_1, S_2, ..., S_d$ fit in memory.*

PROOF. It is easy to show that $|S_i| \le n_1 \le cM/d$ for each $i \in [2, d]$. A naive way to store S_i takes $d|S_i|$ words, in which case we would need $\Omega(dM)$ words to store $r_1, S_2, ..., S_d$, exceeding the memory capacity M.

To remedy this issue, we store S_i using only $|S_i|$ words as follows. Given a tuple $t \in S_i$, we store a single integer that is the memory address[4] of the tuple t' in (17). This does not lose any information because we can recover t by resorting to (17) and the fact that $t[A_1] = a$.

Therefore, $r_1, S_2, ..., S_d$ can be represented in $O(d \cdot n_1)$ words, which is smaller than M when the constant c is sufficiently small. □

The overall cost of the algorithm is dominated by the cost of (i) merging $r_2, ..., r_d$ into L, which takes $O(d+(d/B)\sum_{i=2}^{d} n_i)$ I/Os, and (ii) sorting L, which takes $O(sort(d\sum_{i=2}^{d} n_i))$ I/Os, using a algorithm of [3] for string sorting in EM. Hence, the overall I/O complexity is as claimed in Theorem 2.

It remains to consider the case where $n_1 > cM/d$. We simply divide r_1 arbitrarily into $O(1)$ subsets each with cM/d tuples, and then apply the above algorithm to emit all the result tuples produced from each of the subsets.

Proof of Lemma 4

For each $i \in [1, d] \setminus \{H\}$, define $X_i = R_i \cap R_H$ (i.e., X_i includes all the attributes in R except A_i and A_H).

In ascending order of $i \in [1, d] \setminus \{H\}$, we invoke the procedure below to process r_i and r_H, which continuously removes some tuples from r_H. First, sort r_i and r_H by X_i, respectively. Then, synchronously scan r_i and r_H according to the sorted order. For each tuple t in r_H, we check during the scan whether r_i has a tuple t' that has the same values as t on *all* the attributes in X_i. The sorted order ensures that if t' exists, then t and t' must appear consecutively during the synchronous scan[5]. If t' exists, t is kept in r_H; otherwise, we discard t from r_H (t cannot produce any tuple in $r_1 \bowtie r_2 \bowtie ... \bowtie r_d$).

After the above procedure has finished through all $i \in [1, d] \setminus \{H\}$, we know that every tuple t remaining in r_H *must* produce exactly one result tuple t' in $r_1 \bowtie r_2 \bowtie ... \bowtie r_d$. Clearly, $t'[A_i] = t[A_i]$ for all $i \in [1, d] \setminus \{H\}$, and (by definition of point join) $t'[A_H] = a$. Therefore, we can emit all such t' with one more scan of the (current) r_H.

The claimed I/O cost follows from the fact that r_H is sorted $d-1$ times in total, while r_i is sorted once for each $i \in [1, d] \setminus \{H\}$.

Proof of Lemma 5

Let us first understand how t is passed from a call to its descendants in $\mathcal{T}$. Let JOIN($h_\ell, \rho_1, ..., \rho_d$) be a level-$\ell$ call that t participates in. If $h_{\ell+1} \neq i$, then t participates in *at most one* of the call's child nodes in $\mathcal{T}$. Otherwise, t may participate in *all* of the call's child nodes in $\mathcal{T}$.

We first consider the case $L_i = 0$, under which there are two possible scenarios: (i) $i = 1$, or (ii) i is not the axis of any call in $\mathcal{T}$. In neither case will we have a call JOIN($h_\ell, \rho_1, ..., \rho_d$) with $h_{\ell+1} = i$. This implies that $\gamma_\ell(t) \le 1$ for all $\ell \in [1, w]$.

Now consider that $L_i \in [1, w-1]$. Let JOIN($h_\ell, \rho_1, ..., \rho_d$) be a level-$\ell$ call that t participates in. If $\ell \neq L_i$, then the call passes t to at most one of its child nodes. If $\ell = L_i$, then by definition of

[4]This address requires only $\lg_2 n_1$ bits by storing an offset.

[5]Note that r_i can have at most one tuple t' that has the same values as t on all attributes in X_i (recall that $t'[A_H]$ is fixed to a by definition of point join).

L_i, we have $i = h_{1+L_i}$. In this scenario, the call may pass t to all its q child nodes where

$$\begin{aligned} q &= O(1 + |\rho_1|/\tau_i) \\ \text{(by (3))} \quad &= O(1 + \tau_{h_{L_i}}/\tau_i) \\ &= O(1 + \tau_{h_{L_i}}/\tau_{h_{1+L_i}}) \\ &= O(\mu_{L_i}). \end{aligned}$$

This implies the equation of $\gamma_\ell(t)$ given in (12).

Proof of Lemma 6

By the definition of $\mu_{\ell-1}$, it suffices to show that $\tau_{h_{\ell-1}}/\tau_{h_\ell} = O(Ud^{\frac{1}{d-1}}/n_{h_\ell})$. (2) implies that

$$\frac{\tau_{h_{\ell-1}}}{\tau_{h_\ell}} = \frac{(Ud^{\frac{1}{d-1}})^{h_\ell - h_{\ell-1}}}{\prod_{j=1+h_{\ell-1}}^{h_\ell} n_j}. \tag{18}$$

If $h_\ell = 1 + h_{\ell-1}$, then

$$(18) = \frac{Ud^{\frac{1}{d-1}}}{n_{h_\ell}}.$$

For the case where $h_\ell > 1 + h_{\ell-1}$, the definition of h_ℓ indicates that

$$\frac{\tau_{h_{\ell-1}}}{\tau_{h_\ell - 1}} = \frac{(Ud^{\frac{1}{d-1}})^{h_\ell - 1 - h_{\ell-1}}}{\prod_{j=1+h_{\ell-1}}^{h_\ell - 1} n_j} \le 2;$$

otherwise, h_ℓ would not be the smallest integer in $[1 + h_{\ell-1}, d]$ satisfying $\tau_{h_\ell} < \tau_{h_{\ell-1}}/2$. Hence,

$$(18) \le 2 \cdot \frac{Ud^{\frac{1}{d-1}}}{n_{h_\ell}},$$

which completes the proof.

Private Multiplicative Weights Beyond Linear Queries

Jonathan Ullman*
Columbia University
New York, NY
jullman@cs.columbia.edu

ABSTRACT

A wide variety of fundamental data analyses in machine learning, such as linear and logistic regression, require minimizing a convex function defined by the data. Since the data may contain sensitive information about individuals, and these analyses can leak that sensitive information, it is important to be able to solve convex minimization in a privacy-preserving way.

A series of recent results show how to accurately solve a single convex minimization problem in a differentially private manner. However, the same data is often analyzed repeatedly, and little is known about solving multiple convex minimization problems with differential privacy. For simpler data analyses, such as linear queries, there are remarkable differentially private algorithms such as the private multiplicative weights mechanism (Hardt and Rothblum, FOCS 2010) that accurately answer exponentially many distinct queries. In this work, we extend these results to the case of convex minimization and show how to give accurate and differentially private solutions to *exponentially many* convex minimization problems on a sensitive dataset.

Categories and Subject Descriptors

F.0 [**Theory of Computation**]: General

General Terms

Theory

Keywords

Differential Privacy; Convex Optimization; Statistical Estimation

*The majority of this work was done while the author was at the Center for Research on Computation and Society at Harvard University. Supported by NSF grant CNS-1237235.

PODS'15, May 31–June 4, 2015, Melbourne, Victoria, Australia.

http://dx.doi.org/10.1145/2745754.2745755.

1. INTRODUCTION

Consider a dataset $D = (x_1, \ldots, x_n) \in \mathcal{X}^n$ in which each of the n rows corresponds to an individual's record, and each record consists of an element of some data universe $\mathcal{X}$. The goal of privacy-preserving data analysis is to enable rich statistical analyses on such a dataset while protecting the privacy of the individuals. It is especially desirable to achieve *differential privacy* [11], which guarantees that no individual's data has a significant influence on the information released about the dataset.

In this work we consider differentially private algorithms that answer *convex minimization (CM) queries* on the sensitive dataset. A CM query is specified by a convex *loss function* $\ell : \Theta \times \mathcal{X} \to \mathbb{R}$, where Θ is a convex set, and the corresponding *query* $q_\ell : \mathcal{X}^* \to \Theta$ selects the point $\theta \in \Theta$ that minimizes the average loss on the rows of D. That is,

$$q_\ell(D) = \operatorname*{argmin}_{\theta \in \Theta} \frac{1}{n} \sum_{i=1}^{n} \ell(\theta; x_i).$$

These queries capture fundamental data analyses such as linear and logistic regression and support vector machines. For example, we may have a dataset consisting of n labeled examples $(x_1, y_1), \ldots, (x_n, y_n)$ from the data universe $\mathcal{X} = \mathbb{R}^d \times \mathbb{R}$ (corresponding to d attributes and a single label per individual), and wish to compute the linear regression

$$\theta^* = \operatorname*{argmin}_{\theta \in \mathbb{R}^d} \frac{1}{n} \sum_{i=1}^{n} (\langle \theta, x_i \rangle - y_i)^2$$

Starting with the results of Dwork and Lei [10] and Chaudhuri, Monteleone, and Sarwate [8], there has been a long line of work [24, 27, 22, 3] showing how to compute an accurate and differentially private answer to a single CM query. However, in practice the same sensitive dataset will be analyzed by many different analysts, and together these analysts will need answers to a large number of distinct CM queries on the dataset. Any algorithm for solving a single CM query can be applied repeatedly to answer multiple CM queries using the well known composition properties of differential privacy. However, this straightforward approach incurs a significant loss of accuracy, and renders the answers meaningless after a small number of queries (roughly n^2 in most natural settings).

Fortunately, for many interesting types of queries, there are remarkable differentially private algorithms [5, 12, 15, 26, 19, 17, 18] that are capable of giving accurate answers to *exponentially many* different queries—far greater than what can be achieved using straightforward composition. The most extensively studied case is *linear queries*, which are specified by a property p and ask "What fraction of rows in D satisfy p?" It is also known how to answer exponentially many arbitrary Lipschitz, real-valued queries [15], which generalize linear queries. There are, however, no known non trivial algorithms for privately and accurately answering large sets of CM queries.

In this work we show for the first time that it is possible to give accurate and differentially private answers to exponentially many convex minimization queries. We do so via an extension of the simple and elegant private multiplicative-weights framework of Hardt and Rothblum [19], which is known to achieve asymptotically optimal worst-case accuracy [6] and worst-case running time [29] for answering large families of linear queries. Moreover, private multiplicative weights was shown to have a number of practical advantages [18], including good accuracy and running time in practice on low-dimensional datasets, parallelism, and simple implementation, all of which are preserved by our extension. We believe that our technique for adapting the private multiplicative weights framework beyond linear queries may be useful in the future design of differentially private algorithms for other types of non linear queries.

1.1 Our Results

We can now state our results for answering large numbers of CM queries. In order to answer even a single CM query, we need to place some sort of restrictions on the loss function ℓ. In particular, we consider the following types of restrictions on ℓ:

- Lipschitz. $\|\nabla\ell(\theta;x)\|_2 \leq 1$ for every $\theta \in \Theta, x \in \mathcal{X}$ (where the gradient is taken with respect to θ for fixed x).
- d-Bounded. $\Theta \subseteq \{\theta \in \mathbb{R}^d \mid \|\theta\|_2 \leq 1\}$.
- σ-Strongly Convex. $\ell(\theta';x) \geq \ell(\theta;x) + \langle\nabla\ell(\theta;x), \theta' - \theta\rangle + \frac{\sigma}{2}\|\theta' - \theta\|_2^2$ for every $\theta, \theta' \in \Theta, x \in \mathcal{X}$ (where, again, the gradient is taken with respect to θ for fixed x).
- Unconstrained Generalized Linear Models (UGLM). $\Theta = \mathbb{R}^d$, $\mathcal{X} \subseteq \mathbb{R}^d$ and $\ell(\theta;x) = \ell'(\langle\theta, x\rangle)$ for a convex function $\ell' : \mathbb{R} \to \mathbb{R}$.

The constant 1 in the the Lipschitz and boundedness conditions is arbitrary. One can obtain more general statements in terms of these parameters by rescaling. For simplicity, we will assume throughout that all loss functions ℓ are differentiable, and thus will freely use the gradient operator. However, for all our algorithms and theorems, the assumption that ℓ is differentiable is unnecessary and $\nabla\ell$ can be replaced with an arbitrary subgradient of ℓ.

Table 1 summarizes our results for these different restrictions on the loss functions. In all cases our algorithms are interactive. They take a dataset $D \in \mathcal{X}^n$ as input, interact with a data analyst who chooses a sequence of loss functions $\ell^1, \ldots, \ell^k$, and return answers $\hat{\theta}^1, \ldots, \hat{\theta}^k \in \Theta$ such that for every $j = 1, \ldots, k$

$$\frac{1}{n}\sum_{i=1}^{n} \ell^j(\hat{\theta}^j; x_i) \leq \left(\min_{\theta\in\Theta} \frac{1}{n}\sum_{i=1}^{n} \ell^j(\theta; x_i)\right) + \alpha$$

for some error parameter α. We note that the data analyst may be *adaptive*, meaning the choice of ℓ_j can depend on the previous losses and answers $\ell^1, \hat{\theta}^1, \ldots, \ell^{j-1}, \hat{\theta}^{j-1}$. Differential privacy becomes easier to achieve as n becomes larger. Thus, we ask how big n has to be to achieve a given level of accuracy α for answering k queries from a family of loss functions $\mathcal{L}$.

Our results are summarized in the following table. We emphasize that if one were to use an algorithm for answering a single CM query repeatedly via composition, then required database size n would depend polynomially on k, whereas the error depends only polylogarithmically on k in each of our results.

Restrictions	n needed for one query	n needed for k queries
Linear Queries	$O\left(\frac{1}{\alpha}\right)$ [11]	$\tilde{O}\left(\frac{\sqrt{\log\lvert\mathcal{X}\rvert}\cdot\log k}{\alpha^2}\right)$ [19]
Lipschitz, d-Bounded	$\tilde{O}\left(\frac{\sqrt{d}}{\alpha}\right)$ [3]	$\tilde{O}\left(\max\left\{\frac{\sqrt{d\cdot\log\lvert\mathcal{X}\rvert}}{\alpha^2}, \frac{\log k\cdot\sqrt{\log\lvert\mathcal{X}\rvert}}{\alpha^2}\right\}\right)$
Lipschitz, d-Bounded, UGLM	$\tilde{O}\left(\frac{1}{\alpha^2}\right)$ [22]	$\tilde{O}\left(\max\left\{\frac{\sqrt{\log\lvert\mathcal{X}\rvert}}{\alpha^3}, \frac{\log k\cdot\sqrt{\log\lvert\mathcal{X}\rvert}}{\alpha^2}\right\}\right)$
Lipschitz, d-Bounded, σ-Strongly Convex	$\tilde{O}\left(\sqrt{\frac{d}{\sigma\alpha}}\right)$ [3]	$\tilde{O}\left(\max\left\{\sqrt{\frac{d\cdot\log\lvert\mathcal{X}\rvert}{\sigma\alpha^3}}, \frac{\log k\cdot\sqrt{\log\lvert\mathcal{X}\rvert}}{\alpha^2}\right\}\right)$

Table 1: Accuracy guarantees for answering various families of CM queries under differential privacy. New results are shown in green. Error bounds for linear queries, which are a special case of Lipschitz, 1-bounded CM queries are shown for comparison. Error bounds for answering a single CM query under each restriction is also shown for comparison. All results are stated for (ε, δ)-differential privacy for ε constant and δ a negligible function of n.

Our algorithms have running time poly$(n, |\mathcal{X}|, k)$ assuming oracle access to ℓ and its gradient for every ℓ. Thus, our algorithms are not generally efficient, as $|\mathcal{X}|$ will often be exponential in the dimensionality of the data. For example, if $\mathcal{X} = \{0,1\}^d$, then the dataset consists of nd bits yet our algorithms run in time 2^d, even when k is polynomial and every loss function and its gradient can be efficiently computed. Unfortunately this exponential running time is inherent, under widely believed cryptographic assumptions. Even answering $n^{2+o(1)}$ linear queries, which are a special case of Lipschitz, 1-Bounded CM queries, requires exponential time [29].

Additionally, our algorithms require significantly more error than answering a single CM query. For example, in the case of Lipschitz, d-Bounded CM queries, a single query can be answered with a dataset of size $n = \tilde{O}(\sqrt{d}/\alpha)$, whereas answering poly$(n)$ queries with our algorithm requires a dataset of size $n = \tilde{O}(\sqrt{\log|\mathcal{X}|} \cdot \log k/\alpha^2)$. By the results of Kasiviswanathan, Rudelson, and Smith [23], a database of size at least $n = \Omega(1/\alpha^2)$ is necessary when answering $\gg 1/\alpha^2$ queries. See Section 4.3 for a more detailed discussion of the lower bounds and computational complexity issues that arise.

Since the error bounds and running time of our algorithm both depend on $|\mathcal{X}|$, our error guarantees may appear vacuous when $\mathcal{X}$ is infinite. For example, in many common applications $\mathcal{X} = \{\theta \in \mathbb{R}^d \mid \|\theta\|_2 \leq 1\}$ is the d-dimensional unit ball. However, in many settings it is essentially without loss of generality (up to, say, a factor of 2 in the error) to round the data points to some finite, data universe. Typically if the data points lie in a d-dimensional space, the size of such a data universe will be $(d/\alpha)^{O(d)}$. We leave it for future work to find algorithms that apply to continuous data universes in a more natural way.

1.2 Techniques

In order to describe our algorithms, it will be helpful to start by sketching the private multiplicative weights framework of Hardt and Rothblum [19] for answering linear queries. Here, we focus on the "offline" variant from [16, 17, 18], in which the k loss functions $\mathcal{L} = \{\ell^1, \ldots, \ell^k\}$ are specified in advance by the analyst. The offline variant contains the main novel ideas, although we will present our algorithm for the online case.

The algorithm receives as input a dataset $D \in \mathcal{X}^n$ and a set of queries $\mathcal{Q}$. It will be useful to represent D as a "histogram" over $\mathcal{X}$, which is a vector indexed by $\mathcal{X}$ where the x-th entry is the probability that a random row of D has type x. In this representation, a linear query q can be written as $\langle q, D\rangle$.

The algorithm begins with a hypothesis dataset D^1, which represents an uneducated guess about D. It then produces a sequence of T differentially private hypotheses $D^1, \ldots, D^T$ that are increasingly good approximations to D. In each round $t = 1, \ldots, T$, the algorithm will privately find the query $q^t \in \mathcal{Q}$ such that D^t gives a maximally inaccurate answer. That is, $|\langle q^t, D^t\rangle - \langle q^t, D\rangle|$ is as large as possible. Finding this query can be done privately using a standard application of the exponential mechanism [25]. The algorithm then generates D^{t+1} using D^t and q^t via the multiplicative weights update rule.

One can show that after a small number of rounds T, the hypothesis D^T answers every query accurately. The key to the analysis is the following standard fact about the multiplicative-weights update rule: if one can find a vector u^t such that $|\langle u^t, D^t\rangle - \langle u^t, D\rangle|$ is large, then the distance between D^{t+1} and D decreases significantly. Notice that this condition on u^t is precisely that u^t is a linear query for which D^t is inaccurate. Thus, when answering linear queries, we can simply take u^t to be q^t.

In the case of CM queries, we can still use the exponential mechanism to find a loss function $\ell^t \in \mathcal{L}$ such that the minimizer of ℓ^t on D^t is not a good minimizer of the loss on the true dataset D. However, since CM queries are non linear, this information does not immediately give us a suitable vector u^t for the multiplicative-weights update. The key new step in our algorithm is a differentially private way to find a suitable vector u^t. Specifically, we show how to take a query q_ℓ such that $q_\ell(D^t)$ is inaccurate for the true dataset D, and a differentially private approximation to the correct answer $q_\ell(D)$, and use it to find a differentially private vector u^t such that the error $|\langle u^t, D^t\rangle - \langle u^t, D\rangle|$ is large. As with linear queries, having such vectors is sufficient to argue accuracy of the algorithm.

Our approach is inspired by the work of Kasiviswanathan, Rudelson, and Smith [23] who prove lower bounds on the error required for answering certain CM queries. Specifically, they use sufficiently accurate answers to non linear CM queries to extract linear constraints on the dataset, and these linear constraints can then be combined with linear reconstruction attacks to violate privacy. For our results, we use the information that D^t gives an inaccurate answer to a non linear CM query to find a linear query that D^t also answers inaccurately. To do so, we make use of the "dual certificate" style of argument from convex optimization. That is, we derive and analyze the linear query using the first-order optimality conditions on the gradient of ℓ.

1.3 Connection to Generalization Error in Adaptive Data Analysis

Very recently, Dwork et al. [9] and Hardt and Ullman [21] showed a connection between differential privacy and *generalization error* in adaptive data analysis, in which the analyst asks an adaptively chosen sequence of queries. By generalization error, we mean the difference between the answers to the queries on the dataset D and the answers to the queries on the unknown population from which D was drawn. Dwork et al. showed that differentially private algorithms that have low error with respect to the dataset D also have low generalization error. Surprisingly, using known differentially private algorithms for answer linear queries yields state-of-the-art bounds on the generalization error required to answer an interactive sequence of linear queries. Bassily et al. [2] extended the connection between differential privacy and generalization error to the more general family of CM queries. Plugging the results of this paper into their theorem yields state-of-the-art bounds on the generalization error required to answer adaptively chosen CM queries.

2. PRELIMINARIES

2.1 Datasets and Differential Privacy

We define a *dataset* $\mathcal{D} \in \mathcal{X}^n$ to be a vector of n rows $\mathcal{D} = (x_1, \ldots, x_n) \in \mathcal{X}^n$ from a *data universe* $\mathcal{X}$. We say that two datasets $\mathcal{D}, \mathcal{D}' \in \mathcal{X}^n$ are *adjacent* if they differ on only a single row, and we denote this by $\mathcal{D} \sim \mathcal{D}'$. We now define *differential privacy* [11].

Definition 1. An algorithm $\mathcal{A} : \mathcal{X}^n \to \mathcal{R}$ satisfies (ε, δ)-*differentially private* if for every two adjacent datasets $\mathcal{D} \sim \mathcal{D}'$ and every subset $S \subseteq \mathcal{R}$,

$$\Pr(\mathcal{A}(\mathcal{D}) \in S) \leq e^{\varepsilon} \cdot \Pr(\mathcal{A}(\mathcal{D}') \in S) + \delta.$$

In our algorithm and analysis it will be useful to represent a dataset by its *histogram*. In the histogram representation, the dataset $\mathcal{D}$ is viewed as a probability distribution over $\mathcal{X}$. We represent this probability distribution as a vector in $D \in \mathbb{R}^{\mathcal{X}}$ where for every $x \in \mathcal{X}$, $D(x) = \Pr_{x' \leftarrow_{\mathrm{R}} \mathcal{D}}(x' = x)$. The condition that $\mathcal{D} \sim \mathcal{D}'$ implies that their histograms satisfy $\|D - D'\|_1 \leq 1/n$. In the technical sections of this work we will assume all datasets are represented as histograms.

2.2 Convex Minimization (CM) Queries and Accuracy

In this work we are interested in algorithms that answer *convex minimization (CM) queries* on the dataset. A CM query is defined by a convex *loss function* $\ell : \Theta \times \mathcal{X} \to \mathbb{R}$, where $\Theta \subseteq \mathbb{R}^d$ is a convex set. The associated query q_ℓ :

$\mathcal{X}^* \to \Theta$ seeks to find $\theta \in \Theta$ that minimizes the expected loss. Formally,

$$q_\ell(D) = \operatorname*{argmin}_{\theta \in \Theta} \mathop{\mathbb{E}}_{x \leftarrow_R D} (\ell(\theta; x)) = \operatorname*{argmin}_{\theta \in \Theta} \sum_{x \in \mathcal{X}} D(x) \cdot \ell(\theta; x)$$

We will use $\mathcal{L} = \{\ell_1, \ell_2, \dots\}$ to denote a set of convex loss functions and $\mathcal{Q}_\mathcal{L} = \{q_{\ell_1}, q_{\ell_2}, \dots\}$ to denote the associated set of convex minimization queries. We will often want to think of ℓ as a function of θ, with x fixed. To this end, we will write $\ell_x(\theta) = \ell(\theta; x)$. We will also abuse notation and write $\ell(\theta; D) = \sum_{x \in \mathcal{X}} D(x) \cdot \ell(\theta; x)$ and $\ell_D(\theta) = \ell(\theta; D)$.

In order to define what it means to answer a CM query accurately, we define the following notion of *error*, also known as "excess empirical risk".

Definition 2. For a loss function $\ell : \Theta \times \mathcal{X} \to \mathbb{R}$, database $D \in \mathcal{X}^*$, and answer $\hat{\theta} \in \Theta$, we define *the error of $\hat{\theta}$ on ℓ with respect to D* to be

$$\mathrm{err}_\ell(D, \hat{\theta}) = \ell(\hat{\theta}; D) - \min_{\theta \in \Theta} \ell(\theta; D).$$

It will also be useful in describing an analyzing out algorithm to define the notion of *error of a database* as follows.

Definition 3. For a loss function $\ell : \Theta \times \mathcal{X} \to \mathbb{R}$, database $D \in \mathcal{X}^*$, and another database $D' \in \mathcal{X}^*$, we define *the error of D' on ℓ with respect to D* to be

$$\mathrm{err}_\ell(D, D') = \ell_D \left(\operatorname*{argmin}_{\theta' \in \Theta} \ell_{D'}(\theta') \right) - \min_{\theta \in \Theta} \ell_D(\theta).$$

We now define what it means for an algorithm $\mathcal{A}$ to be *accurate* for answering a sequence of CM queries from a family $\mathcal{L}$. We do so by means of a game between $\mathcal{A}$ and an adversary $\mathcal{B}$, defined in Figure 1.

> $\mathcal{B}$ chooses $D \in \mathcal{X}^n$.
> For $j = 1, \dots, |\mathcal{L}|$
> $\mathcal{B}$ outputs a loss function $\ell^j \in \mathcal{L}$.
> $\mathcal{A}(D, \ell^j)$ outputs $\hat{\theta}^j$.
> (As $\mathcal{B}$ and $\mathcal{A}$ are stateful, ℓ^j and $\hat{\theta}^j$ may depend on the history $\ell^1, \hat{\theta}^1, \dots, \ell^{j-1}, \hat{\theta}^{j-1}$.)

Figure 1: The Sample Accuracy Game $\mathsf{Acc}_{n,k,\mathcal{L}}[\mathcal{A}, \mathcal{B}]$

Definition 4. Let $\mathcal{L}$ be a set of convex loss functions and $\mathcal{Q}_\mathcal{L}$ be the associated set of CM queries. Let $0 < \alpha, \beta \le 1$ and $k, n \in \mathbb{N}$ be parameters. We say that an algorithm $\mathcal{A}$ is *(α, β)-accurate for answering k CM queries from $\mathcal{Q}_\mathcal{L}$ given a database of size n* if for every adversary $\mathcal{B}$,

$$\Pr_{\mathsf{Acc}_{n,k,\mathcal{L}}} \left(\max_{j=1,\dots,k} \mathrm{err}_{\ell^j}(D, \hat{\theta}^j) \le \alpha \right) \ge 1 - \beta.$$

3. ONLINE PRIVATE MULTIPLICATIVE WEIGHTS FOR CM QUERIES

In this section we present and analyze a differentially private algorithm that answers any family of CM queries provided black-box access to a differentially private algorithm that answers any single CM query from the family.

3.1 The Online Sparse Vector Algorithm

Just like when using private multiplicative weights to answer linear queries, a key ingredient in our algorithm is the *online sparse vector algorithm.* At a high level, the online sparse vector algorithm takes a database $D \in \mathcal{X}^n$ and a sequence of queries $q_1, \dots, q_k$, but it provides only a very weak accuracy guarantee. Each query is answered with a single bit in $\{\top, \bot\}$. For a given query q and some threshold α, if $q(D) \ge \alpha$ then the algorithm answering $\top$ and if $q(D) \le \alpha/2$ it answers $\bot$. If the answer is in $(\alpha/2, \alpha)$ any answer is allowed. The key feature of the online sparse vector algorithm is that the size of the dataset n only needs to be proportional to $\sqrt{T} \cdot \log k$, where T is the number of queries whose answer is above the threshold. Whereas, approximately answering every query requires n to grow like $\sqrt{k}$.

To maintain brevity, and since the algorithm is standard (see [14] for a textbook treatment), we will not specify the algorithm. Instead we will define its properties as a black box. We define the guarantees of the sparse vector algorithm via the following game between the online sparse vector algorithm $\mathcal{SV}$ and an adversary $\mathcal{B}$.

> $\mathcal{B}$ chooses a dataset $D \in \mathcal{X}^n$.
> For $j = 1, \dots, k$:
> $\mathcal{B}$ outputs a $(3S/n)$-sensitive query q^j
> (The query q^j may depend on the previous queries and answers $q^1, a^1, \dots, q^{j-1}, a^{j-1}$.)
> $\mathcal{SV}$ returns an answer $a^j \in \{\top, \bot\}$.

Figure 2: $\mathsf{ThresholdGame}_{n,T,k,\alpha}[\mathcal{SV}, \mathcal{B}]$

The requirement that $\mathcal{B}$ outputs a $(3/n)$-sensitive query means that q satisfies $|q(D) - q(D')| \le 3S/n$ for every pair of neighboring databases $D \sim D' \in \mathcal{X}^n$. The choice of $(3S/n)$ can be replaced with any parameter Δ, but we fix it to $3S/n$ to cut down on notation, since we'll use that choice in the next section.

THEOREM 1. *There is an algorithm $\mathcal{SV} = \mathcal{SV}(T, k, \alpha, \varepsilon, \delta)$ such that for every $T, k \in \mathbb{N}$ and $\alpha, \varepsilon, \delta > 0$, the following three conditions hold.*

1. *$\mathcal{SV}$ is (ε, δ)-differentially private.*
2. *$\mathcal{SV}$ halts when T queries are answered with $\top$.*
3. *If*

$$n \ge \frac{256 \cdot S \cdot \sqrt{T \cdot \log(2/\delta)} \cdot \log(4k/\beta)}{\varepsilon \alpha},$$

then

$$\Pr_{\mathsf{ThresholdGame}_{n,T,k,\tau}[\mathcal{SV}, \mathcal{B}]} (ACC) \ge 1 - \beta,$$

where

$$ACC = \left\{ \forall j \in [k], \begin{array}{c} q^j(D) \ge \alpha \Longrightarrow a^j = \top \\ q^j(D) \le \alpha/2 \Longrightarrow a^j = \bot \end{array} \right\}$$

3.2 The Algorithm

We are now ready to describe our algorithm for answering exponentially many convex minimization queries from some family $\mathcal{L} = \{\ell : \Theta \times \mathcal{X} \to \mathbb{R}\}$. Assume every $\ell \in \mathcal{L}$ satisfies the scaling condition

$$\max_{x \in \mathcal{X}, \theta, \theta' \in \Theta} |\langle \theta - \theta', \nabla \ell_x(\theta) \rangle| \le S.$$

The algorithm is defined in Figure 3. Note that in the algorithm there are two sequences of queries that it will be useful to distinguish. The first is the set of queries actually issued by the analyst, which are index by the letter j and are $\ell^1, \dots, \ell^k$. There is also the *subsequence* of queries such that $a^j = \top$ and lead to updates. We use the letter t to index these queries, which are $\ell^1, \dots, \ell^T$ (there cannot be more than T such queries, since $\mathcal{SV}$ would halt, though there may be fewer). Sometimes it will be useful to consider only the subsequence of queries that are used for updates, which is why we use a separate index for this sequence.

3.3 Accuracy Analysis

In this section, we prove that our algorithm is accurate for any family of CM queries $\mathcal{L}$, provided that the oracle $\mathcal{A}'$ is accurate for any single CM query from $\mathcal{L}$. As with previous variants of private multiplicative weights [19, 16, 17, 18], we will derive the accuracy guarantee using the well known "bounded regret" property of the multiplicative weights update rule, combined with the utility guarantees of the online sparse vector algorithm.

To start the analysis we will assume that two conditions are satisfied. First, we assume that $\mathcal{SV}$ answered accurately—formally, we assume that

$$\forall j \in [k], \quad \begin{array}{l} \mathrm{err}_{\ell^j}(D; \hat{D}^t) \ge \alpha \Longrightarrow a^j = \top \\ \mathrm{err}_{\ell^j}(D; \hat{D}^t) \le \alpha/2 \Longrightarrow a^j = \bot \end{array} \tag{1}$$

where $\hat{D}^t$ is the current dataset $\hat{D}^t$ that is in use at the time the loss function ℓ^j is considered. By the accuracy of the online sparse vector algorithm $\mathcal{SV}$ (Theorem 1), the event (1) holds with probability at least $1 - \beta/2$ as long as n is sufficiently large.

Second, we will assume that every time $a^j = \top$ and $\mathcal{A}'(D, \ell^j)$ is called, it returns an accurate answer—formally,

$$\forall j \text{ such that } a^j = \top, \ \mathrm{err}_{\ell^j}(D, \theta^t) \le \alpha_0. \tag{2}$$

Since $\mathcal{A}'$ is assumed to be (α_0, β_0) accurate for one query provided that $n \ge n'$, and $\mathcal{A}'$ is called at most T times, we can conclude that the event (2) holds with probability at least $1 - \beta/2$. The following claim is immediate.

CLAIM 1. *If*

$$n \ge \max\left\{ n', \frac{512 \cdot \sqrt{T \cdot \log(4/\delta)} \cdot \log(8k/\beta)}{\varepsilon\alpha} \right\},$$

then with probability at least $1 - \beta$, *the events* (1) *and* (2) *both hold.*

Thus, we are justified proving that the online private multiplicative weights algorithm is accurate conditioned on (1) and (2). We start by observing that the algorithm can only fail to be accurate if it halts before the entire sequence of k queries has been asked (because $t = T$ updates have been performed and $\mathcal{SV}$ halted).

CLAIM 2. *Assume that the algorithm does not terminate before answering k queries, and that* (1) *and* (2) *both hold. Then the algorithm answers every query with error at most* α. *That is, for every* $j \in [k]$, $\mathrm{err}_{\ell^j}(D, \hat{\theta}^j) \le \alpha$.

Input and parameters: A dataset $D \in \mathcal{X}^n$, parameters $\varepsilon, \delta, \alpha, \beta, S, k > 0$, and oracle access to $\mathcal{A}'$, an $(\varepsilon_0, \delta_0)$-differentially private algorithm that is (α_0, β_0)-accurate for one convex minimization query in $\mathcal{L}$ on datasets of size n', for parameters $\varepsilon_0, \delta_0, \alpha_0, \beta_0$.

$$T = \frac{64 S^2 \log |\mathcal{X}|}{\alpha^2} \qquad \eta = \sqrt{\frac{\log |\mathcal{X}|}{T}}$$

$$\varepsilon_0 = \frac{\varepsilon}{\sqrt{8T \log(4/\delta)}} \qquad \delta_0 = \frac{\delta}{4T}$$

$$\alpha_0 = \frac{\alpha}{4} \qquad \beta_0 = \frac{\beta}{2T}$$

Let $\mathcal{SV} = \mathcal{SV}(T, k, \alpha, \varepsilon/2, \delta/2)$ be the online sparse vector algorithm (Section 3.1).
Let $t = 1$. Let $\hat{D}^t \in \mathbb{R}^{\mathcal{X}}$ be the uniform histogram over $\mathcal{X}$.
For $j = 1, \dots, k$:
  Receive loss function $\ell = \ell^j \in \mathcal{L}$.
  Let q^j be the $(3/n)$-sensitive query

$$q^j(D) = \mathrm{err}_\ell(D, \hat{D}^t).$$

  Run $\mathcal{SV}$ on q^j, to obtain an answer $a^j \in \{\top, \bot\}$.
  (If $\mathcal{SV}$ halts, then halt.)
  If $a^j = \bot$:
    Output the answer $\hat{\theta}^j = \mathrm{argmin}_{\theta \in \Theta}\, \ell(\theta; \hat{D}^t)$.
  Else if $a^j = \top$:
    Let $\ell^t = \ell$.
    Let $\theta^t \leftarrow_{\mathrm{R}} \mathcal{A}'(D, \ell^t)$ be a private estimate of the minimizer of ℓ^t on D.
    Output the answer $\hat{\theta}^j = \theta^t$.
    Update $\hat{D}^t$:
      Let $\hat{\theta}^t = \mathrm{argmin}_{\theta \in \Theta}\, \ell(\theta; \hat{D}^t)$
      and let $u^t \in [-S, S]^{\mathcal{X}}$ be the vector

$$u^t(x) = \left\langle \theta^t - \hat{\theta}^t, \nabla \ell_x^t(\hat{\theta}^t) \right\rangle$$

      Let $\hat{D}^{t+1}(x) \propto \exp(\eta \cdot u^t(x)) \cdot \hat{D}^t(x)$
      Let $t = t + 1$.
      (Note that $t \le T$, or $\mathcal{SV}$ would have halted.)

Figure 3: Online Private Multiplicative Weights for CM Queries

---

PROOF. If the algorithm has not terminated, then each query ℓ^j is answered in one of two ways. If $a^j = \bot$, then we answer with $\hat{\theta}^j = \mathrm{argmin}_{\theta \in \Theta}\, \ell(\theta; \hat{D}^t)$. In this case, since (1) holds, and $a^j = \bot$, we have $\mathrm{err}_{\ell^j}(D, \hat{\theta}^j) \le \alpha$. But, by definition, $\mathrm{err}_{\ell^j}(D, \hat{D}^t) = \mathrm{err}_{\ell^j}(D, \hat{\theta}^j)$. So the algorithm answers accurately when $a^j = \bot$. $\mathrm{err}_{\ell^j}(D, \hat{\theta}^j) \le \alpha$

If $a^j = \top$, then we answer with $\hat{\theta}^j = \theta^j = \mathcal{A}'(D, \ell^j)$. Since (2) holds, we have

$$\mathrm{err}_{\ell^j}(D, \hat{\theta}^j) = \mathrm{err}_{\ell^j}(D, \theta^t) \le \alpha_0 \le \alpha,$$

as desired. □

To complete the proof, it suffices to show that the algorithm does not terminate early. Here is where we rely on the "bounded regret" property of the multiplicative weights update rule.

LEMMA 1. *[See e.g. [1]] For every sequence* $u^1, \dots, u^T \in [-S, S]^{\mathcal{X}}$,

$$\frac{1}{T}\sum_{t=1}^{T}\left\langle u^t, \hat{D}^t - D\right\rangle \le 2S\sqrt{\frac{\log|\mathcal{X}|}{T}}$$

Recall that the algorithm only terminates early if there are T queries ℓ^j such that $a^j = \top$, and by (1), $a^j = \top$ only if the error of $\hat{D}^t$ on ℓ^j is at least $\alpha/2$. Thus, in light of the preceding lemma, we would like to show that if $\hat{D}^t$ has error $\alpha/2$ for a query ℓ, then $\langle u^t, \hat{D}^t - D\rangle$ is also large, say $\alpha/4$. If we can show such a statement, then by our choice of T, it will be impossible to perform a sequence of T updates, and thus the algorithm will not terminate early.

The key lemma, and the main novelty in our analysis, is to relate $\langle u^t, \hat{D}^t - D\rangle$ to the error of $\hat{D}^t$ on a query ℓ^j. We show that $\langle u^t, \hat{D}^t - D\rangle$ is at least the additional loss incurred by $\hat{\theta}^t$ over that of θ^t.

CLAIM 3. *For every* $t = 1, \dots, T$,

$$\left\langle u^t, \hat{D}^t - D\right\rangle \ge \ell^t_D(\hat{\theta}^t) - \ell^t_D(\theta^t)$$

Recall that θ^t is an approximation to the optimal solution for ℓ^t_D, whereas $\hat{\theta}^t$ has large error with respect to D. Thus we expect the right hand side of the expression to be positive and large.

PROOF. Recall that we chose

$$\hat{\theta}^t = \operatorname*{argmin}_{\theta\in\Theta} \ell^t_{\hat{D}^t}(\theta).$$

By the first-order optimality condition, and the fact that $\theta^t, \hat{\theta}^t \in \Theta$ for a convex set Θ, the directional derivative of $\ell^t_{\hat{D}^t}$ at $\hat{\theta}^t$ in the direction of $\theta^t - \hat{\theta}^t$ will be positive. So we have

$$\begin{aligned} 0 \le \left\langle \theta^t - \hat{\theta}^t, \nabla\ell^t_{\hat{D}^t}(\hat{\theta}^t)\right\rangle &= \sum_{x\in\mathcal{X}} \hat{D}^t(x)\cdot\left\langle \theta^t - \hat{\theta}^t, \nabla\ell^t_x(\hat{\theta}^t)\right\rangle \\ &= \left\langle u^t, \hat{D}^t\right\rangle. \end{aligned} \tag{3}$$

The first equality uses linearity of the gradient and the definition $\ell^t_{\hat{D}^t}(\cdot) = \sum_{x\in\mathcal{X}} \hat{D}^t(x)\cdot\ell^t_x(\cdot)$

Similarly, we can look at the directional derivative of ℓ^t_D again taken at $\hat{\theta}^t$ and in the direction of $\theta^t - \hat{\theta}^t$.

$$\begin{aligned} \left\langle \theta^t - \hat{\theta}^t, \nabla\ell^t_D(\hat{\theta}^t)\right\rangle &= \sum_{x\in\mathcal{X}} D(x)\cdot\left\langle \theta^t - \hat{\theta}^t, \nabla\ell^t_x(\hat{\theta}^t)\right\rangle \\ &= \langle u^t, D\rangle. \end{aligned} \tag{4}$$

If $\hat{\theta}^t$ is far from optimal for the input dataset D, then moving in the direction of $\theta^t - \hat{\theta}^t$ should significantly decrease the loss. Thus, since ℓ is convex, this directional derivative must be significantly negative. Specifically, since ℓ^t_D is convex, ℓ^t_D lies above all of its tangent lines. Thus,

$$\ell^t_D(\theta^t) \ge \ell^t_D(\hat{\theta}^t) + \left\langle \theta^t - \hat{\theta}^t, \nabla\ell^t_D(\hat{\theta}^t)\right\rangle = \ell^t_D(\hat{\theta}^t) + \langle u^t, D\rangle.$$

where the equality is from (4) Rearranging terms, we have

$$-\langle u^t, D\rangle \ge \ell^t_D(\hat{\theta}^t) - \ell^t_D(\theta^t). \tag{5}$$

Combining (3) and (5), we have

$$\left\langle u^t, \hat{D}^t - D\right\rangle \ge \ell^t_D(\hat{\theta}^t) - \ell^t_D(\theta^t),$$

which completes the proof. □

Using Claim 3, and the guarantees (1) and (2), we can now lower bound $\langle u^t, \hat{D}^t - D\rangle$.

CLAIM 4. *For every* $t = 1, \dots, T$, *if the algorithm has not terminated, and* (1) *and* (2) *both hold, then*

$$\langle u^t, \hat{D}^t - D\rangle > \alpha/4.$$

PROOF. Our goal is to lower bound $\langle u^t, \hat{D}^t - D\rangle$ by the quantity $\mathrm{err}_{\ell^t}(D, \hat{D}^t) = \ell^t_D(\hat{\theta}^t) - \min_{\theta\in\Theta}\ell^t_D(\theta)$. This condition is almost implied by Claim 3, except with $\ell^t_D(\theta^t)$ in place of the minimum. In the next claim, we extend the previous claim to handle an approximate minimizer.

However, by (2), $\theta^t = \mathcal{A}'(D, \ell^t)$ is an approximate minimizer. That is,

$$\ell^t_D(\theta^t) \le \min_{\theta\in\Theta}\ell^t_D(\theta) + \alpha_0. \tag{6}$$

Combining Claim 3 with (6) we conclude that if $n \ge n'$, then for every $t = 1, \dots, T$, with probability at least $1 - \beta_0$,

$$\begin{aligned} \left\langle u^t, \hat{D}^t - D\right\rangle &\ge \ell^t_D(\hat{\theta}^t) - \left(\min_{\theta\in\Theta}\ell^t_D(\theta) + \alpha_0\right) \\ &= \mathrm{err}_{\ell^t}(D, \hat{D}^t) - \alpha_0 \end{aligned} \tag{7}$$

Given (7) we would like to show that $\mathrm{err}_{\ell^t}(D, \hat{D}^t)$ is large. But, by (1), we would only do an update if $\mathrm{err}_{\ell^t}(D, \hat{D}^t) > \alpha/2$. Therefore we must have

$$\begin{aligned} \left\langle u^t, \hat{D}^t - D\right\rangle \ge \ell^t_D(\hat{\theta}^t) - \left(\min_{\theta\in\Theta}\ell^t_D(\theta) + \alpha_0\right) &> \alpha/2 - \alpha_0 \\ &= \alpha/4, \end{aligned}$$

as desired. □

We are now ready to show that the online private multiplicative weights algorithm does not terminate early.

CLAIM 5. *If* (1) *and* (2) *both hold, then the algorithm does not terminate before answering* k *queries.*

PROOF. Assume for the sake of contradiction that the algorithm does terminate early because of the condition $t = T$. Then, by Claim 4, there is a sequence of T queries such that for every query

$$\langle u^t, \hat{D}^t - D\rangle \ge \alpha/4.$$

Then, using the bounded-regret property of multiplicative weights (Lemma 1), we must have

$$\begin{aligned} \alpha/4 &< \frac{1}{T}\sum_{t=1}^{T}\left\langle u^t, \hat{D}^t - D\right\rangle \\ &\le 2S\sqrt{\frac{\log|\mathcal{X}|}{T}} && \text{(Lemma 1)} \\ &\le \alpha/4, \end{aligned}$$

which is a contradiction. □

The analysis of this section immediately implies the following theorem

THEOREM 2. *The online private multiplicative weights algorithm is (α, β)-accurate for answering k CM queries from $\mathcal{Q}_{\mathcal{L}}$ given a dataset of size n for*

$$n = \max\left\{n', \frac{4096 \cdot S^2 \cdot \sqrt{\log|\mathcal{X}| \cdot \log(4/\delta)} \cdot \log(8k/\beta)}{\varepsilon\alpha^2}\right\}.$$

3.4 Privacy Analysis

In this section we show that our algorithm (Figure 3) is differentially private. Privacy will follow rather easily from privacy of the online sparse vector algorithm, privacy of $\mathcal{A}'$, and well known composition properties of differential privacy.

THEOREM 3. *If $\mathcal{A}'$ is $(\varepsilon_0, \delta_0)$-differentially private, for ε_0, δ_0 as stated, then the algorithm in Figure 3 is (ε, δ)-differentially private.*

3.4.1 Composition of Differential Privacy

Before proceeding to the privacy analysis of our algorithm, we recall the composition properties of differential privacy.

A well-known fact about differential privacy is that the parameters ε, δ degrade gracefully under composition. Specifically, we will make use of the strong composition theorem due to Dwork, Rothblum, and Vadhan [15]. Formally, we say that an algorithm $\mathcal{A}$ is a T-fold adaptive composition of $(\varepsilon_0, \delta_0)$-differentially private algorithms if $\mathcal{A}$ can be expressed as an instance of the following game for some adversary $\mathcal{B}$:

> Let D be a database, let $\mathcal{B}$ be an adversary, T be a parameter
> For $t = 1, \ldots, T$
> $\mathcal{B}(z_1, \ldots, z_{t-1})$ outputs an $(\varepsilon_0, \delta_0)$-DP $\mathcal{A}_t$
>   Let $z_t = \mathcal{A}_t(D)$
> Output $z_1, \ldots, z_T$

Figure 4: T-Fold Adaptive Composition

THEOREM 4 ([15]). *For every $T \in \mathbb{N}$ and $0 \le \varepsilon_0, \delta_0, \delta' \le 1/2$, if $\mathcal{A}$ is a T-fold adaptive composition of algorithms that are $(\varepsilon_0, \delta_0)$-differentially private, then $\mathcal{A}$ is $(\varepsilon, \delta' + T\delta_0)$-differentially private for*

$$\varepsilon = \sqrt{2T\log(1/\delta')} \cdot \varepsilon_0 + 2T \cdot \varepsilon_0^2.$$

In particular, if $\mathcal{A}$ is a T-fold adaptive composition of $(\varepsilon_0, \delta_0)$-differentially private algorithms, where

$$\varepsilon_0 = \frac{\varepsilon}{\sqrt{8T\log(2/\delta)}} \qquad \delta_0 = \frac{\delta}{2T},$$

then $\mathcal{A}$ is (ε, δ)-differentially private.

3.4.2 Proof of Theorem 3

There are only two places where the algorithm uses the private dataset D: (1) when using the online sparse vector algorithm to answer the queries $q^j = \mathrm{err}_{\ell^j}(D, \hat{D}^t)$, and (2) when using $\mathcal{A}'$ to obtain a private approximation to the minimizer of some loss function ℓ^t. First, we will show that the online sparse vector algorithm is $(\varepsilon/2, \delta/2)$-differentially private. This claim will follow immediately from Theorem 1 provided that the queries q^j are indeed $(3S/n)$-sensitive. To show this, first, observe that if $\ell : \Theta \times \mathcal{X} \to \mathbb{R}$ satisfies

$$\max_{x\in\mathcal{X},\theta,\theta'\in\Theta} |\langle\theta - \theta', \nabla\ell_x(\theta)\rangle| \le S,$$

then for every $x \in \mathcal{X}$, there exists $b_x \in \mathbb{R}$ such that for every $\theta \in \Theta$, $\ell(\theta, x) \in [b_x, S]$. That is, for every x, there is some interval of width S that bounds the loss $\ell(\theta, x)$. With this information we can bound the sensitivity of the error function in the following way: Fix any $\ell \in \mathcal{L}$. Let $\bar{\ell}(\theta, x) = \ell(\theta, x) - b_x$. Let $\bar{\theta} = \mathrm{argmin}_{\theta\in\Theta}\, \ell_{\hat{D}^t}(\theta)$.

$$\begin{aligned}
&\max_{D,D'\in\mathcal{X}^n} \left|\mathrm{err}_\ell(D, \hat{D}^t) - \mathrm{err}_\ell(D', \hat{D}^t)\right| \\
&= \max_{D,D'\in\mathcal{X}^n} \left|\left(\ell_D(\bar{\theta}) - \min_{\theta\in\Theta}\ell_D(\theta)\right) - \left(\ell_{D'}(\bar{\theta}) - \min_{\theta\in\Theta}\ell_{D'}(\theta)\right)\right| \\
&= \max_{D,D'\in\mathcal{X}^n} \left|\left(\bar{\ell}_D(\bar{\theta}) - \min_{\theta\in\Theta}\bar{\ell}_D(\theta)\right) - \left(\bar{\ell}_{D'}(\bar{\theta}) - \min_{\theta\in\Theta}\bar{\ell}_{D'}(\theta)\right)\right| \\
&= \max_{D,D'\in\mathcal{X}^n} |(\bar{\ell}_D(\bar{\theta}) - \ell_{D'}(\bar{\theta}))| + \left|\left(\min_{\theta\in\Theta}\bar{\ell}_D(\theta) - \min_{\theta\in\Theta}\bar{\ell}_{D'}(\theta)\right)\right| \\
&\le \frac{S}{n} + \frac{2S}{n} = \frac{3S}{n}.
\end{aligned}$$

Since this bound holds for every $\ell \in \mathcal{L}$, we have

$$\max_{\ell\in\mathcal{L}} \max_{D,D'\in\mathcal{X}^n} \left|\mathrm{err}_\ell(D, \hat{D}^t) - \mathrm{err}_\ell(D', \hat{D}^t)\right| \le \frac{3S}{n}.$$

Thus, the queries given to $\mathcal{SV}$ are indeed $(3S/n)$-sensitive and we are justified in assuming that $\mathcal{SV}$ is an $(\varepsilon/2, \delta/2)$-differentially private algorithm.

Now, we return to analyzing the privacy loss of $\mathcal{A}'$. By assumption, for every fixed ℓ^t, the choice of $\theta^t = \mathcal{A}'(D, \ell^t)$ is $(\varepsilon_0, \delta_0)$-differentially private with respect to the input D. Moreover, the choice of ℓ^t depends only on the output of $\mathcal{SV}$, which we have already argued is $(\varepsilon/2, \delta/2)$-differentially private. Therefore, we can view all of the calls to $\mathcal{A}'$ as a single T-fold adaptive composition of $(\varepsilon_0, \delta_0)$-differentially private algorithms. For ε_0, δ_0 as specified in the online private multiplicative weights algorithm, the result will be $(\varepsilon/2, \delta/2)$-differentially private. Since these are the only two ways in which the private dataset D is used, we have proven that the entire algorithm is (ε, δ)-differentially private.

4. APPLICATIONS OF THEOREM 2

In this section we give some interpretation of Theorem 2 and show how it can be applied to specific interesting cases that have been considered in the literature on differentially private convex minimization in order to obtain the results stated in the introduction.

4.1 Interpreting Theorem 2

In Theorem 2, we have assumed that there exists an $(\varepsilon_0, \delta_0)$-differentially private algorithm $\mathcal{A}'$ that is (α_0, β_0)-accurate for any one ℓ from $\mathcal{L}$ given n' samples. By a standard argument, if there exists a $(1, \delta_0)$-differentially private algorithm $\mathcal{A}''$ that is (α_0, β_0)-accurate for ℓ given n'' samples, then there exists an $(\varepsilon_0, \delta_0)$-differentially private algorithm with the same accuracy given $O(n''/\varepsilon_0)$ samples. Applying this observation, simplifying, and dropping the dependence on

$\beta, \varepsilon, \delta$, we can write the requirement in Theorem 2 as

$$n \gtrsim \max\left\{\frac{n''}{\varepsilon_0}, \frac{S^2 \cdot \log k}{\alpha^2}\right\}$$
$$\lesssim \frac{S \cdot \sqrt{\log |\mathcal{X}|} \cdot \log k}{\alpha} \cdot \max\left\{n'', \frac{S}{\alpha}\right\}$$

The first term in the max is just the size of dataset required to answer a single convex minimization query in $\mathcal{L}$ with $\varepsilon = 1$. The second term in the max can be either larger or smaller than n''. However, for the most basic setting of a single, Lipschitz loss function over a bounded domain, $n'' \gg S/\alpha$, so the second term will be dominated by the first term.

Thus, in some cases, Theorem 2 can be interpreted as saying that the amount of data required to answer k queries from $\mathcal{L}$ is only a factor of $\approx (S \cdot \sqrt{\log |\mathcal{X}|} \cdot \log k)/\alpha$ larger than the amount of data required to both answer a single query in $\mathcal{L}$. Using the simple composition approach where each of the k queries is answered independently would require a factor of $\approx \sqrt{k}$ more data than answering a single query. Thus our algorithm is a substantial improvement when $\sqrt{k} \gg (S \cdot \sqrt{\log |\mathcal{X}|} \cdot \log k)/\alpha$.

4.2 Applications

We now show how to instantiate Theorem 2 with various differentially private algorithms for answering convex minimization queries to obtain the results in the Introduction.

4.2.1 *Lipschitz and Bounded Loss Functions.*

In much of the work on differentially private convex minimization, the queries are normalized so that the parameter θ lies in a unit L_2 ball, and the loss function ℓ satisfies a Lipschitz condition. Bassily, Smith, and Thakurta [3] recently showed optimal upper and lower bounds for answering a single query from this family. Formally,

THEOREM 5 ([3]). *Let $\ell : \Theta \times \mathcal{X} \to \mathbb{R}$ be a convex loss function where $\Theta \subseteq \{\theta \in \mathbb{R}^d \mid \|\theta\|_2 \le 1\}$ and for every $\theta \in \Theta$, $x \in \mathcal{X}$, $\|\nabla \ell_x(\theta)\|_2 \le 1$. Let q_ℓ be the associated CM query. There is a $(\varepsilon_0, \delta_0)$-differentially private algorithm that is (α_0, β_0)-accurate for q_ℓ on datasets of size n for*

$$n = O\left(\frac{\sqrt{d}}{\alpha_0 \varepsilon_0}\right) \cdot \mathrm{polylog}\left(\frac{1}{\delta_0}, \frac{1}{\beta_0}\right).$$

Note that if Θ is contained in a unit L_2 ball and ℓ is 1-Lipschitz, then the scaling parameter S is at most 2. Combining Theorem 2 and Theorem 5 yields the following result.

THEOREM 6. *Let $\mathcal{L}$ be the set of convex loss functions $\ell : \Theta \times \mathcal{X} \to \mathbb{R}$ for $\Theta \subseteq \{\theta \in \mathbb{R}^d \mid \|\theta\|_2 \le 1\}$ such that for every $\ell \in \mathcal{L}$, $\theta \in \Theta$, $x \in \mathcal{X}$, $\|\nabla \ell_x(\theta)\|_2 \le 1$. Let $\mathcal{Q}_{\mathcal{L}}$ be the associated family of CM queries. There is an (ε, δ)-differentially private algorithm that is (α, β)-accurate for k CM queries from $\mathcal{Q}_{\mathcal{L}}$ on datasets of size n for*

$$n = \tilde{O}\left(\frac{\sqrt{\log |\mathcal{X}|}}{\alpha^2 \varepsilon} \cdot \max\left\{\sqrt{d}, \log k\right\}\right) \cdot \mathrm{polylog}\left(\frac{1}{\delta}, \frac{1}{\beta}\right).$$

4.2.2 *Generalized Linear Models.*

Using the algorithm of Theorem 5, n must grow polynomially with d to solve even a single CM query in dimension d, and this was shown to be inherent by Bassily et al. [3] (building on [6]). However, the work of Jain and Thakurta [22] shows that dependence on d can be avoided for the important class of *unconstrained generalized linear models*. For example, logistic regression and linear regression are generalized linear models. A convex loss function $\ell : \Theta \times \mathcal{X} \to \mathbb{R}$ is a generalized linear model if $\Theta \subseteq \mathbb{R}^d$, $\mathcal{X} \subseteq \mathbb{R}^d$, and $\ell(\theta, x)$ depends only on the inner product of θ and x. That is, there exists a convex function $\ell' : \mathbb{R} \to \mathbb{R}$ such that $\ell(\theta, x) = \ell'(\langle \theta, x \rangle)$. We say that the generalized linear model is unconstrained if there are no constraints other than boundedness. That is, $\Theta = \{\theta \in \mathbb{R}^d \mid \|\theta\|_2 \le 1\}$.

THEOREM 7 ([22]). *Let $\ell : \Theta \times \mathcal{X} \to \mathbb{R}$ be an unconstrained generalized linear model with the domain $\Theta = \{\theta \in \mathbb{R}^d \mid \|\theta\|_2 \le 1\}$ and for every $\theta \in \Theta$, $x \in \mathcal{X}$, $\|\nabla \ell_x(\theta)\|_2 \le 1$. Let q_ℓ be the associated CM query. There is a $(\varepsilon_0, \delta_0)$-differentially private algorithm that is (α_0, β_0)-accurate for q_ℓ on datasets of size n for*

$$n = O\left(\frac{1}{\alpha_0^2 \varepsilon_0}\right) \cdot \mathrm{polylog}\left(\frac{1}{\delta_0}, \frac{1}{\beta_0}\right).$$

Combining Theorem 2 and Theorem 7 yields the following result.

THEOREM 8. *Let $\mathcal{L}$ be the set of unconstrained generalized linear models $\ell : \Theta \times \mathcal{X} \to \mathbb{R}$ with the domain $\Theta \subseteq \{\theta \in \mathbb{R}^d \mid \|\theta\|_2 \le 1\}$ such that for every $\ell \in \mathcal{L}$, $\theta \in \Theta$, $x \in \mathcal{X}$, $\|\nabla \ell_x(\theta)\|_2 \le 1$. Let $\mathcal{Q}_{\mathcal{L}}$ be the associated family of CM queries. There is an (ε, δ)-differentially private algorithm that is (α, β)-accurate for k CM queries from $\mathcal{Q}_{\mathcal{L}}$ given n records for*

$$n = \tilde{O}\left(\frac{\sqrt{\log |\mathcal{X}|}}{\alpha^2 \varepsilon} \cdot \max\left\{\frac{1}{\alpha}, \log k\right\}\right) \cdot \mathrm{polylog}\left(\frac{1}{\delta}, \frac{1}{\beta}\right).$$

4.2.3 *Strongly Convex Loss Functions.*

Stronger accuracy guarantees for answering a single CM query are also achievable in the common special case where ℓ is strongly convex. Informally, ℓ is strongly convex if it can be lower bounded by a quadratic function. Specifically, for a parameter $\sigma \ge 0$, the function $\ell : \Theta \times \mathcal{X} \to \mathbb{R}$ is 2σ-strongly convex if for every $\theta, \theta' \in \Theta$ and $x \in \mathcal{X}$, $\ell(\theta'; x) \ge \ell(\theta; x) + \langle \theta' - \theta, \nabla \ell(\theta; x) \rangle + \sigma \|\theta' - \theta\|_2^2$. In the previous statement, the gradient is with respect to θ.

THEOREM 9 ([3]). *Let $\ell : \Theta \times \mathcal{X} \to \mathbb{R}$ be a σ-strongly convex loss function where $\Theta \subseteq \{\theta \in \mathbb{R}^d \mid \|\theta\|_2 \le 1\}$ and for every $\theta \in \Theta$, $x \in \mathcal{X}$, $\|\nabla \ell_x(\theta)\|_2 \le 1$. Let q_ℓ be the associated CM query. There is a $(\varepsilon_0, \delta_0)$-differentially private algorithm that is (α_0, β_0)-accurate for q_ℓ on datasets of size n for*

$$n = O\left(\frac{\sqrt{d}}{\sqrt{\sigma \alpha_0} \varepsilon_0}\right) \cdot \mathrm{polylog}\left(\frac{1}{\delta_0}, \frac{1}{\beta_0}\right).$$

Combining Theorem 2 and Theorem 9 yields the following result.

THEOREM 10. *Let $\mathcal{L}$ be the set of σ-strongly convex loss functions $\ell : \Theta \times \mathcal{X} \to \mathbb{R}$ for $\Theta \subseteq \{\theta \in \mathbb{R}^d \mid \|\theta\|_2 \le 1\}$ such that for every $\ell \in \mathcal{L}$, $\theta \in \Theta$, $x \in \mathcal{X}$, $\|\nabla \ell_x(\theta)\|_2 \le 1$. Let $\mathcal{Q}_{\mathcal{L}}$ be the associated family of CM queries. There is an (ε, δ)-differentially private algorithm that is (α, β)-accurate for k CM queries from $\mathcal{Q}_{\mathcal{L}}$ on datasets of size n for*

$$n = \tilde{O}\left(\frac{\sqrt{\log |\mathcal{X}|}}{\varepsilon} \max\left\{\frac{\sqrt{d}}{\sqrt{\sigma}\alpha^{3/2}}, \frac{\log k}{\alpha^2}\right\}\right) \cdot \mathrm{polylog}\left(\frac{1}{\delta}, \frac{1}{\beta}\right)$$

4.3 Running Time and Discussion of Computational Complexity

In this section we discuss the computational complexity of the algorithm. To do so, we assume $\Theta \subseteq \mathbb{R}^d$, and for simplicity and concreteness we consider a natural choice of data universe $\mathcal{X} = \{0,1\}^d$ or $\mathcal{X} = \left\{\frac{\pm 1}{\sqrt{d}}\right\}^d$. Since our algorithm uses the ability to solve a single CM query in $\mathcal{L}$ as a blackbox, we assume that this step can be done in $\text{poly}(n,d)$ time both privately and non-privately. For this informal discussion, we also ignore the dependence in running time on $S, \alpha, \beta, \varepsilon, \delta$, which will not substantially affect the conclusions.

There are three main steps that dominate the running time of each of the k iterations:

1. Running the online sparse vector algorithm $\mathcal{SV}$ on q^j. This step can be done in time $\text{poly}(n,d)$.
2. If $a^j = \top$, finding a private approximate minimizer of ℓ^j. By assumption, this step can be done in time $\text{poly}(n,d)$.
3. If $a^j = \top$, computing the new histogram $\hat{D}^{t+1}$. This step requires time $\tilde{O}(2^d)$.

Since each of these steps is carried out for k steps, the overall running time is $\text{poly}(n, 2^d, k)$. Even tough it was useful to think of the database as a histogram, which is a vector of length 2^d, the input database D would more naturally be represented as a collection of records $D \in (\{0,1\}^d)^n$. Thus it is natural to look for an algorithm with running time $\text{poly}(n,d,k)$. In summary, even when the individual loss functions can be privately minimized in $\text{poly}(n,d)$ time, our algorithm requires time $\text{poly}(n, 2^d, k)$, which is exponential in the dimension of the data. More generally, there is a polynomial dependence on $|\mathcal{X}|$, where one would hope for a polylogarithmic dependence.

Unfortunately, this exponential running time is inherent. Since CM queries generalize the well studied class of linear queries, we can carry over the hardness results of Ullman [29] to this setting. Specifically, assuming the existence of one-way functions, there is no $\text{poly}(n,d)$-time algorithm that takes as input a set of k arbitrary differentiable convex loss functions, and a database $D \in (\{0,1\}^d)^n$ for $n \le k^{1/2-o(1)}$, and and outputs answers that are even $1/100$-accurate for each query in $\mathcal{L}$.

Although the hardness result rules out an efficient mechanism for answering an arbitrary large set of CM queries, more efficient algorithms may be possible for specific families $\mathcal{L}$. In the setting of counting queries, such algorithms are known for special cases such as *interval queries* [4] and *marginal queries* [16, 20, 28, 7, 13]. It would be interesting to see if techniques from those works can be applied to give more efficient algorithms for natural families of CM queries. We remark that Ullman and Vadhan [30] show that efficient algorithms that output synthetic data cannot be accurate even for very simple families of counting queries, and thus also for certain very simple families of CM queries. Our algorithm indeed can be modified to output a synthetic dataset (namely, the final histogram $\hat{D}^t$ used in the execution of the algorithm), and thus substantially different techniques would be required to answer interesting classes of CM queries more efficiently. We leave it as an interesting direction for future work to improve the running time of our algorithm for interesting restricted families of CM queries.

Acknowledgements

We would like to thank Adam Smith and Salil Vadhan for helpful discussions.

5. REFERENCES

[1] S. Arora, E. Hazan, and S. Kale. The multiplicative weights update method: a meta-algorithm and applications. *Theory of Computing*, 8(1):121–164, 2012.

[2] R. Bassily, A. Smith, T. Steinke, and J. Ullman. More general queries with better generalization error in adaptive data analysis. Manuscript, 2015.

[3] R. Bassily, A. Smith, and A. Thakurta. Private empirical risk minimization, revisited. *CoRR*, abs/1405.7085, 2014.

[4] A. Beimel, K. Nissim, and U. Stemmer. Private learning and sanitization: Pure vs. approximate differential privacy. In *APPROX-RANDOM*, pages 363–378. Springer, 21-23 August 2013.

[5] A. Blum, K. Ligett, and A. Roth. A learning theory approach to non-interactive database privacy. In *ACM Symposium on Theory of Computing (STOC '08)*, pages 609–618. ACM, 17-20 May 2008.

[6] M. Bun, J. Ullman, and S. P. Vadhan. Fingerprinting codes and the price of approximate differential privacy. In *ACM Symposium on Theory of Computing (STOC '14)*. ACM, 1–3 June 2014.

[7] K. Chandrasekaran, J. Thaler, J. Ullman, and A. Wan. Faster private release of marginals on small databases. In *Innovations in Theoretical Computer Science (ITCS '14)*, pages 387–402. ACM, 12-14 January 2014.

[8] K. Chaudhuri, C. Monteleoni, and A. D. Sarwate. Differentially private empirical risk minimization. *Journal of Machine Learning Research*, 12:1069–1109, 2011.

[9] C. Dwork, V. Feldman, M. Hardt, T. Pitassi, O. Reingold, and A. Roth. Preserving statistical validity in adaptive data analysis. In *STOC*. ACM, June 14–17 2015.

[10] C. Dwork and J. Lei. Differential privacy and robust statistics. In *ACM Symposium on Theory of Computing (STOC '09)*, pages 371–380. ACM, 31 May - 2 June 2009.

[11] C. Dwork, F. McSherry, K. Nissim, and A. Smith. Calibrating noise to sensitivity in private data analysis. In *Theory of Cryptography (TCC '06)*, pages 265–284. Springer, 4–7 March 2006.

[12] C. Dwork, M. Naor, O. Reingold, G. N. Rothblum, and S. P. Vadhan. On the complexity of differentially private data release: efficient algorithms and hardness results. In *ACM Symposium on Theory of Computing (STOC '09)*, pages 381–390. ACM, 31 May - 2 June 2009.

[13] C. Dwork, A. Nikolov, and K. Talwar. Efficient algorithms for privately releasing marginals via convex relaxations. *CoRR*, abs/1308.1385, 2013.

[14] C. Dwork and A. Roth. The algorithmic foundations of differential privacy. *Foundations and Trends in Theoretical Computer Science*, 9(3-4):211–407, 2014.

[15] C. Dwork, G. N. Rothblum, and S. P. Vadhan. Boosting and differential privacy. In *IEEE Symposium*

on Foundations of Computer Science (FOCS '10), pages 51–60. IEEE Computer Society, 23-26 October 2010.

[16] A. Gupta, M. Hardt, A. Roth, and J. Ullman. Privately releasing conjunctions and the statistical query barrier. In *ACM Symposium on Theory of Computing (STOC '11)*, pages 803–812. ACM, 6-8 June 2011.

[17] A. Gupta, A. Roth, and J. Ullman. Iterative constructions and private data release. In *Theory of Cryptography (TCC '12)*, pages 339–356. Springer, 19-21 March 2012.

[18] M. Hardt, K. Ligett, and F. McSherry. A simple and practical algorithm for differentially private data release. In *Neural Information Processing Systems (NIPS '12)*, pages 2348–2356, 3-6 December 2012.

[19] M. Hardt and G. N. Rothblum. A multiplicative weights mechanism for privacy-preserving data analysis. In *IEEE Symposium on Foundations of Computer Science (FOCS '10)*, pages 61–70. IEEE Computer Society, 23-26 October 2010.

[20] M. Hardt, G. N. Rothblum, and R. A. Servedio. Private data release via learning thresholds. In *ACM-SIAM Symposium on Discrete Algorithms (SODA '12)*, pages 168–187. SIAM, 17-19 January 2012.

[21] M. Hardt and J. Ullman. Preventing false discovery in interactive data analysis is hard. In *FOCS*. IEEE, October 19-21 2014.

[22] P. Jain and A. G. Thakurta. (near) dimension independent risk bounds for differentially private learning. In *ICML*, pages 476–484. JMLR.org, 21-26 June 2014.

[23] S. P. Kasiviswanathan, M. Rudelson, and A. Smith. The power of linear reconstruction attacks. In *SODA*, pages 1415–1433. SIAM, 6-8 Jan 2013.

[24] D. Kifer, A. D. Smith, and A. Thakurta. Private convex optimization for empirical risk minimization with applications to high-dimensional regression. In *Conference on Learning Theory (COLT '12)*, pages 25.1–25.40. JMLR.org, 25-27 June 2012.

[25] F. McSherry and K. Talwar. Mechanism design via differential privacy. In *FOCS*, pages 94–103. IEEE Computer Society, 20-23 October 2007.

[26] A. Roth and T. Roughgarden. Interactive privacy via the median mechanism. In *ACM Symposium on Theory of Computing (STOC '10)*, pages 765–774. ACM, 5-8 June 2010.

[27] A. Thakurta and A. Smith. Differentially private feature selection via stability arguments, and the robustness of the lasso. In *Conference on Learning Theory (COLT '13)*, pages 819–850. JMLR.org, 12-14 June 2013.

[28] J. Thaler, J. Ullman, and S. P. Vadhan. Faster algorithms for privately releasing marginals. In *International Colloquium on Automata, Languages, and Programming (ICALP '12)*, pages 810–821. Springer, 9-13 July 2012.

[29] J. Ullman. Answering $n^{2+o(1)}$ counting queries with differential privacy is hard. In *ACM Symposium on Theory of Computing (STOC '13)*, pages 361–370. ACM, 1-4 June 2013.

[30] J. Ullman and S. P. Vadhan. PCPs and the hardness of generating private synthetic data. In *Theory of Cryptography (TCC '11)*, pages 400–416. Springer, 28-30 March 2011.

Symmetric Weighted First-Order Model Counting

Paul Beame
University of Washington
beame@cs.washington.edu

Guy Van den Broeck
KU Leuven
guy.vandenbroeck@cs.kuleuven.be

Eric Gribkoff
University of Washington
eagribko@cs.washington.edu

Dan Suciu
University of Washington
suciu@cs.washington.edu

ABSTRACT

The FO Model Counting problem (FOMC) is the following: given a sentence Φ in FO and a number n, compute the number of models of Φ over a domain of size n; the Weighted variant (WFOMC) generalizes the problem by associating a weight to each tuple and defining the weight of a model to be the product of weights of its tuples. In this paper we study the complexity of the symmetric WFOMC, where all tuples of a given relation have the same weight. Our motivation comes from an important application, inference in Knowledge Bases with soft constraints, like Markov Logic Networks, but the problem is also of independent theoretical interest. We study both the data complexity, and the combined complexity of FOMC and WFOMC. For the data complexity we prove the existence of an FO^3 formula for which FOMC is $\#P_1$-complete, and the existence of a Conjunctive Query for which WFOMC is $\#P_1$-complete. We also prove that all γ-acyclic queries have polynomial time data complexity. For the combined complexity, we prove that, for every fragment FO^k, $k \geq 2$, the combined complexity of FOMC (or WFOMC) is #P-complete.

1. INTRODUCTION

Probabilistic inference is becoming a central data management problem. Large knowledge bases, such as Yago [19], Nell [2], DeepDive [6], Reverb [11], Microsoft's Probase [43] or Google's Knowledge Vault [8], have millions to billions of uncertain tuples. These systems scan large corpora of text, such as the Web or complete collections of journal articles, and extract automatically billions of structured facts, representing large collections of knowledge. For an illustration, Google's Knowledge Vault [8] contains 1.6B triples of the form (subject, predicate, object), for example, `</m/02mjmr, /people/person/place_of_birth /m/02hrh0_>` where `/m/02mjmr` is the Freebase id for Barack Obama, and `/m/02hrh0_` is the id for Honolulu [8]. The triples are extracted automatically from the Web, and each triple is annotated with a probability p representing the confidence in the extraction.

A central and difficult problem in such systems is probabilistic inference, or, equivalently weighted model counting. The classical FO Model Counting problem (FOMC) is: given a sentence Φ in First-Order Logic (FO) and a number n, compute the number of structures over a domain of size n that satisfy the sentence Φ; in this paper we consider only *labeled structures*, i.e. isomorphic structures are counted as distinct. We denote the number of models by $\text{FOMC}(\Phi, n)$, for example $\text{FOMC}(\forall x \exists y R(x,y), n) = (2^n - 1)^n$.[1] In the Weighted FO Model Counting (WFOMC) variant, one further associates a real number $w(t)$ called *weight* to each tuple t over the domain of size n, and defines the weight of a structure as the product of the weights of all tuples in that structure. The Weighted Model Count $\text{WFOMC}(\Phi, n, \mathbf{w})$ is defined as the sum of the weights of all structures over a domain of size n that satisfy the sentence Φ. Weights map immediately to probabilities, in the following way: if each tuple t is included in the database independently with probability $w(t)/(1+w(t))$, then the probability that a formula Φ is true is $\Pr(\Phi) = \text{WFOMC}(\Phi, n, \mathbf{w}) / \text{WFOMC}(\text{true}, n, \mathbf{w})$, where $\text{WFOMC}(\text{true}, n, \mathbf{w}) = \prod_t (1 + w(t))$ is the sum of weights of all structures.

In this paper we study the *symmetric* WFMOC problem, where all tuples from the same relation have the same weight, which we denote w_i. For example, a random graph $G(n,p)$ is a symmetric structure, since every edge is present with the same probability p (equivalently: has weight $p/(1-p)$), and FOMC is another special case where all weights are set to 1. The symmetric WFMOC problem occurs naturally in Knowledge Bases with soft constraints, as we illustrate next.

Example 1.1. *A Markov Logic Network (MLN) [7] is a finite set of soft or hard constraints. Each constraint is a pair (w, φ), where φ is a formula, possibly with free variables $\mathbf{x}$, and $w \in [0, \infty]$ is a weight*[2]*. For example,*

[1]For a fixed x, there are 2^n assignments to $R(x,y)$, which all satisfy $\exists y R(x,y)$, except the one where all atoms are false. Moreover, the models for the n values of x can be counted independently and multiplied.

[2]In typical MLN systems, users specify the log of the weight rather than the weight. The pair $(1.098, \varphi)$ means that the weight of φ is $w = \exp(1.098) \approx 3$. Using logs simplifies the learning task. We do not address learning and will omit logs; (w, φ) means that φ has weight w.

PODS'15, May 31–June 4, 2015, Melbourne, Victoria, Australia.

http://dx.doi.org/10.1145/2745754.2745760.

the soft constraint

$$(3, Spouse(x, y) \wedge Female(x) \Rightarrow Male(y)) \qquad (1)$$

specifies that, typically, a female's spouse is male, and associates the weight $w = 3$ to this constraint. If $w = \infty$ then we call (w, φ) a hard constraint.

The semantics of MLNs naturally extend the Weighted Model Counting setting. Given a finite domain (set of constants), an MLN defines a probability distribution over all structures for that domain (also called possible worlds*). Every structure D has a weight*

$$W(D) = \prod_{(w,\varphi(\mathbf{x}))\in MLN, \mathbf{a}\in D^{|\mathbf{x}|}: w<\infty \wedge D\models\varphi[\mathbf{a}/\mathbf{x}]} w$$

In other words, for each soft constraint (W, φ), and for every tuple of constants **a** *such that $\varphi(\mathbf{a})$ holds in D, we multiply D's weight by w. For example, given the MLN that consists only of the soft constraint (1), the weight of a world D is 3^N, where N is the number of pairs of constants a, b for which $Spouse(a, b), Female(a) \Rightarrow Male(b)$ holds in D. The weight $W(\Phi)$ of a sentence Φ is defined as the sum of weights of all worlds D that satisfy both Φ and all hard constraints in the MLN; its probability is obtained by normalizing $\Pr_{MLN}(\Phi) = W(\Phi)/W(true)$. Notice that the symmetric WFOMC problem corresponds to the special case of an MLN consisting of one soft constraint $(w_i, R_i(\mathbf{x}_i))$ for each relation R_i, where $|\mathbf{x}_i| = arity(R_i)$.*

Today's MLN systems (Alchemy [26], Tuffy [30, 44]) use an MCMC algorithm called MC-SAT [31] for probabilistic inference. The theoretical convergence guarantees of MC-SAT require access to a uniform sampler over satisfying assignments to a set of constraints. In practice, MC-SAT implementations rely on SampleSAT [42], which provides no guarantees on the uniformity of solutions. Several complex examples are known in the literature where model counting based on SampleSAT leads to highly inaccurate estimates [16].

A totally different approach to computing $\Pr_{MLN}(\Phi)$ is to reduce it to a symmetric WFOMC [39, 15, 37, 22], and this motivates our current paper. We review here briefly one such reduction, adapting from [22, 37].

Example 1.2. *Given an MLN, replace every soft constraint $(w, \varphi(\mathbf{x}))$ by two new constraints: $(\infty, \forall\mathbf{x}(R(\mathbf{x}) \vee \varphi(\mathbf{x})))$ and $(1/(w-1), R(\mathbf{x}))$. Here R is a new relational symbol with the same arity as the number of free variables in φ, and the constraint $(1/(w-1), R(\mathbf{x}))$ defines R as a relation where all tuples have weight $1/(w-1)$. Therefore, the probability of a formula Φ in the MLN can be computed as a conditional probability over a symmetric, tuple-independent database: $\Pr_{MLN}(\Phi) = \Pr(\Phi|\Gamma)$, where Γ is the conjunction of all hard constraints[3]. Note that this reduction to WFOMC is independent of the finite domain under consideration.*

For example, the soft constraint in (1) is translated into the hard constraint:

$$\forall x, y(R(x, y) \vee \neg Spouse(x, y) \vee \neg Female(x) \vee Male(y))$$

and a tuple-independent probabilistic relation R where all tuples have weight $1/(3-1) = 1/2$, or, equivalently, have probability $(1/2)/(1 + (1/2)) = 1/3$.

Thus, our main motivation for studying the symmetric WFOMC is very practical, as symmetric models have been extensively researched in the AI community recently, for inference in MLNs and beyond [24, 39, 29, 41]. Some tasks on MLNs, such as parameter learning [38], naturally exhibit symmetries. For others, such as computing conditional probabilities given a large "evidence" database, the symmetric WFOMC model is applicable when the database has bounded Boolean rank [36]. Moreover, the problem is of independent theoretical interest as we explain below. We study both the data complexity, and the combined complexity. In both settings we assume that the vocabulary $\sigma = (R_1, \ldots, R_m)$ is fixed, and so are the weights $\mathbf{w} = (w_1, \ldots, w_m)$ associated with the relations. In *data complexity*, the formula Φ is fixed, and the only input is the number n representing the size of the domain. In this case WFOMC is a counting problem over a unary alphabet: *given an input 1^n, compute* WFOMC$(\Phi, n, \mathbf{w})$. It is immediate that this problem belongs to the class $\#P_1$, which is the set of #P problems over a unary input alphabet [34]. In the *combined complexity*, both n and the formula Φ are input.

In this paper we present results on the data complexity and the combined complexity of the FOMC and WFOMC problem, and also some results on the associated decision problem.

Results on Data Complexity

In a surprising result [37] has proven that for FO^2 the data complexity of symmetric WFOMC is in PTIME (reviewed in Appendix C).[4] This is surprising because FO^2 (the class of FO formulas restricted to two logical variables) contains many formulas for which the asymmetric problem was known to be #P-hard. An example is $\Phi = \exists x \exists y(R(x) \wedge S(x, y) \wedge T(y))$, which is #P-hard over asymmetric structures, but the number of models is[5] $2^{2n+n^2} - \sum_{k,m} \binom{n}{k}\binom{n}{m} 2^{n^2-km}$, which is a number computable in time polynomial in n.[6] More generally, the symmetric WFOMC problem for Φ is in PTIME.

This begs the question: could it be the case that *every* FO formula is in PTIME? The answer was shown to be negative by Jaeger and Van den Broeck [21, 20], using the following argument. Recall that the *spectrum*, $\mathsf{Spec}(\Phi)$, of a formula Φ is the set of numbers n for which Φ has a model over a domain of size n [9]. Jaeger and Van den Broeck observed that the spectrum membership problem, "*is $n \in \mathsf{Spec}(\Phi)$?*", can be reduced to WFOMC, by checking whether FOMC$(\Phi, n) > 0$.

[3]The reason why this works is the following: in original MLN, each tuple **a** contributes to $W(D)$ a factor of 1 or w, depending on whether $\varphi(\mathbf{a})$ is false or true in D; after the rewriting, the contribution of **a** is $1/(w-1)$ when $\varphi(\mathbf{a})$ is false, because in that case $R(\mathbf{a})$ must be true, or $1 + 1/(w-1) = w/(w-1)$ when $\varphi(\mathbf{a})$ is true, because $R(\mathbf{a})$ can be either false or true. The ratio is the same $1 : w = [1/(w-1)] : [w/(w-1)]$.

[4]PTIME data complexity for symmetric WFOMC is called *domain-liftability* in the AI and lifted inference literature [35].

[5]Fix the relations R, T, and let their cardinalities be $|R| = k$ and $|T| = m$. Then the structure does *not* satisfy Φ iff S contains none of the km tuples in $R \times T$, proving the formula.

[6]Tractability of Φ was noted before in, for example [32, 35].

Then, using a result in [23], if $\texttt{ETIME} \neq \texttt{NETIME}$, then there exists a formula Φ for which computing WFOMC is not in polynomial time[7]. However, no hardness results for the symmetric WFOMC were known to date.

What makes the data complexity of the symmetric WFOMC difficult to analyze is the fact that the input is a single number n. Valiant already observed in [34] that such problems are probably not candidates for being #P-complete. Instead, he defined the complexity class $\#P_1$, to be the set of counting problems for NP computations over a single-letter input alphabet. Very few hardness results are known for this class: we are aware only of a graph matching problem that was proven by Valiant, and of a language-theoretic problem by Bertoni and Goldwurm [1].

Our data complexity results are the following. First, we establish the existence of an FO sentence Θ_1 for which the data complexity of the FOMC problem is $\#P_1$-hard; and we also establish the existence of a conjunctive query Υ_1 for which the data complexity of the WFOMC problem is $\#P_1$-hard. Second, we prove that every γ-acyclic conjunctive query without self-joins is in polynomial time, extending the result in [37] from FO^2 to γ-acyclic conjunctive queries. We give now more details about our results, and explain their significance.

The tractability for FO^2 [37] raises a natural question: do other restrictions of FO, like FO^k for $k \geq 3$, also have polynomial data complexity? By carefully analyzing the details of the construction of Θ_1 we prove that it is actually in FO^3. This implies a sharp boundary in the FO^k hierarchy where symmetric WFOMC transitions from tractable to intractable: for k between 2 and 3. The tractability of γ-acyclic queries raises another question: could all conjunctive queries be tractable for symmetric WFOMC? We answer this also in the negative: we prove that there exists a conjunctive query Υ_1 for which the symmetric WFOMC problem is $\#P_1$-hard. It is interesting to note that the decision problem associated to WFOMC, namely *given n, does $n \in \mathbf{Spec}(\Phi)$?* is trivial for conjunctive queries, since every conjunctive query has a model over any domain of size $n \geq 1$. Therefore, our $\#P_1$-hardness result for Υ_1 is an instance where the decision problem is easy while the corresponding weighted counting problem is hard. We note that, unlike WFOMC, we do not know the exact complexity of the unweighted, FOMC problem for conjunctive queries.

0-1 Laws. Our data complexity hardness result sheds some interesting light on 0-1 laws. Recall that, if C is a class of finite structures and P is a property over these structures, then $\mu_n(P)$ denotes the fraction of labeled[8] structures in C over a domain of size n that satisfy the property P [27]. A logic has a 0-1 law over the class of structures C, if for any property P expressible in that logic, $\mu(P) \stackrel{\text{def}}{=} \lim_{n\to\infty} \mu_n(P)$ is either 0 or 1. Fagin [13] proved a 0-1 law for First-Order logic and all structures, by using an elegant transfer theorem: there exists a unique, countable structure $\mathbf{R}$, which is characterized by an infinite set of *extension axioms*, τ. He proved that, for every extension axiom, $\lim \mu_n(\tau) = 1$, and this implies $\lim \mu_n(\Phi) = 1$ if Φ is true in $\mathbf{R}$, and $\lim \mu_n(\Phi) = 0$ if Φ is false in $\mathbf{R}$. Compton [3] proved 0-1 laws for several classes of structures C. A natural question to ask is the following: does there exists an elementary proof of the 0-1 laws, by computing a closed formula $\text{FOMC}(\Phi, n)$ for every Φ, then using elementary calculus to prove that that $\mu_n(\Phi)$ converges to 0 or 1? For example, if $\Phi = \forall x \exists y R(x, y)$, then $\text{FOMC}(\Phi, n) = (2^n - 1)^n$ and $\mu_n(\Phi) = (2^n - 1)^n / 2^{n^2} \to 0$; can we repeat this argument for every Φ? On a historical note, Fagin confirms in personal communication that he originally tried to prove the 0-1 law by trying to find such a closed formula, which failed as an approach. Our $\#P_1$-result for FO proves that no such elementary proof is possible, because no closed formula for $\text{FOMC}(\Phi, n)$ can be computed in general (unless $\#P_1$ is in PTIME).

Results on the Combined Complexity

Our main result on the combined complexity is the following. We show that, for any $k \geq 2$, the combined complexity of FOMC for FO^k is #P-complete; membership is a standard application of Scott's reduction, while hardness is by reduction from the model counting problem for Boolean formulas. Recall that the vocabulary σ is always assumed to be fixed: if it were allowed to be part of the input, then every Boolean formula is a special case of an FO^0 formula, by creating a new relational symbol of arity zero for each Boolean variable, and all hardness results for Boolean formulas carry over immediately to FO^0.

The Associated Decision Problem

We also discuss and present some new results on the decision problem associated with (W)FOMC: "*given Φ, n, does Φ have a model over a domain of size n?*". The data complexity variant is, of course, the spectrum membership problem, which has been completely solved by Jones and Selman [23], by proving that the class of spectra coincides with NETIME, that is, $\{\mathtt{Spec}(\Phi) \mid \Phi \in FO\} = \mathtt{NETIME}$. Their result assumes that the input n is represented in binary, thus the input size is $\log n$. In this paper we are interested in the unary representation of n, as 1^n, which is also called the *tally notation*, in which case case NETIME naturally identifies with NP_1. Fagin proved that, in the tally notation, $\{\mathtt{Spec}(\Phi) \mid \Phi \in FO\} = NP_1$ [12, Theorem 6, Part 2].

For the decision problem, our result is for the combined complexity: given both Φ, n, does $n \in \mathtt{Spec}(\Phi)$? We prove that this problem is NP-complete for FO^2, and PSPACE-complete for FO. The first of these results has an interesting connection to the finite satisfiability problem for FO^2, which we discuss here. Recall the classical satisfiability problem in finite model theory: "*given a formula Φ does it have a finite model?*", which is equivalent to checking $\mathtt{Spec}(\Phi) \neq \emptyset$. Grädel, Kolaitis and Vardi [17] have proven the following two

[7] Recall that $\mathtt{ETIME} = \bigcup_{c\geq 1} \mathtt{DTIME}(2^{cn})$ and $\mathtt{NETIME} = \bigcup_{c\geq 1} \mathtt{NTIME}(2^{cn})$, and are not to be confused with the more familiar classes EXPTIME and NEXPTIME, which are $\bigcup_{c\geq 1} \mathtt{DTIME}(2^{n^c})$ and $\bigcup_{c\geq 1} \mathtt{NTIME}(2^{n^c})$ respectively.

[8] The attribute *labeled* means that isomorphic structures are counted as distinct; 0-1 laws for unlabeled structures also exist. In this paper, we discuss labeled structures only.

results for FO^2: if a formula Φ is satisfiable then it has a finite model of size at most exponential in the size of the sentence Φ, and deciding whether Φ is satisfiable is NEXPTIME-complete in the size of Φ. These two results already prove that the combined complexity for deciding $n \in \texttt{Spec}(\Phi)$ cannot be in polynomial time: otherwise, we could check satisfiability in EXPTIME by iterating n from 1 to exponential in the size of Φ, and checking $n \in \texttt{Spec}(\Phi)$. Our result settles the combined complexity, proving that it is NP-complete.

The paper is organized as follows: we introduce the basic definitions in Section 2, present our results for the data complexity of the FOMC and WFOMC problems in Section 3, present all results on the combined complexity in Section 4, then conclude in Section 5.

2. BACKGROUND

We review here briefly the main concepts, some already introduced in Section 1.

Weighted Model Counting (WMC). The *Model Counting* problem is: given a Boolean formula F, compute the number of satisfying assignments $\#F$. In *Weighted Model Counting* we are given two real functions $w, \bar{w} : \text{Vars}(F) \rightarrow \mathbf{R}$ associating two weights $w(X), \bar{w}(X)$ to each variable in $\text{Vars}(F) = \{X_1, \ldots, X_n\}$. The weighted model count $\text{WMC}(F, w, \bar{w})$ is defined as:

$$\text{WMC}(F, w, \bar{w}) \stackrel{\text{def}}{=} \sum_{\theta:\theta(F)=1} W(\theta) \tag{2}$$

where, $\forall\theta : \text{Vars}(F) \rightarrow \{0, 1\}$:

$$W(\theta) \stackrel{\text{def}}{=} \prod_{i:\theta(X_i)=0} \bar{w}(X_i) \times \prod_{i:\theta(X_i)=1} w(X_i) \tag{3}$$

The model count is a special case $\#F = \text{WMC}(F, 1, 1)$.

The standard definition of WMC in the literature does not mention $\bar{w}$, instead sets $\bar{w} = 1$; as we will see, our extension is non-essential. When $\bar{w} = 1$, then we simply drop $\bar{w}$ from the notation, and write $\text{WMC}(F, w)$ instead of $\text{WMC}(F, w, 1)$. In the *probability computation problem*, each variable X_i is set to true with some known probability $p(X_i) \in [0, 1]$, and we want to compute $\Pr(F, p) \stackrel{\text{def}}{=} \text{WMC}(F, p, 1 - p)$, the probability that F is true. All these variations are equivalent, because of the following identities:

$$\text{WMC}(F, w, \bar{w}) = \text{WMC}(F, w/\bar{w}, 1) \times \prod_i \bar{w}(X_i) \tag{4}$$

$$\text{WMC}(F, w, \bar{w}) = \Pr(F, w/(w + \bar{w})) \times \prod_i (w(X_i) + \bar{w}(X_i))$$

Throughout the paper we write 1 for the constant function with value 1, and $w_1 + w_2$, and w_1/w_2 for functions $X \mapsto w_1(X) + w_2(X)$ and $X \mapsto w_1(X)/w_2(X)$ resp.

Weighted First-Order Model Counting (WFOMC). Consider FO formulas over a fixed relational vocabulary $\sigma = (R_1, \ldots, R_m)$ and equality $=$. Given a domain size n, denote $\text{Tup}(n)$ the set of ground tuples (i.e., ground atoms without equality) over the domain, thus $|\text{Tup}(n)| = \sum_i n^{\text{arity}(R_i)}$. The *lineage* of an FO sentence Φ refers to a Boolean function $F_{\Phi,n}$ over $\text{Tup}(n)$ (a ground FO sentence), as well as the corresponding Boolean function over propositional variables referring to ground tuples (a propositional sentence). It is defined inductively by $F_{t,n} = t$ for ground tuples t, $F_{\neg\Phi,n} = \neg F_{\Phi,n}$, $F_{(\Phi_1 \text{ op } \Phi_2),n} = F_{\Phi_1,n} \text{ op } F_{\Phi_2,n}$ for $\text{op} \in \{\wedge, \vee\}$, $F_{a=b,n} = \texttt{false}$, $F_{a=a,n} = \texttt{true}$ and $F_{\exists x\Phi,n} = \bigvee_{a\in[n]} F_{\Phi[a/x],n}$, $F_{\forall x\Phi,n} = \bigwedge_{a\in[n]} F_{\Phi[a/x],n}$. For any fixed sentence Φ, the size of its lineage is polynomial in n. Given a domain size n and weight functions $w, \bar{w} : \text{Tup}(n) \rightarrow \mathbf{R}$, the Weighted First-Order Model Count of Φ is $\text{WFOMC}(\Phi, n, w, \bar{w}) \stackrel{\text{def}}{=} \text{WMC}(F_{\Phi,n}, w, \bar{w})$.

Symmetric WFOMC. In the *symmetric* WFOMC, the weight of a tuple depends only on the relation name and not on the domain constants. We call a *weighted vocabulary* a triple $(\sigma, \mathbf{w}, \bar{\mathbf{w}})$ where $\sigma = (R_1, \ldots, R_m)$ is a relational vocabulary and $\mathbf{w} = (w_1, \ldots, w_m)$, $\bar{\mathbf{w}} = (\bar{w}_1, \ldots, \bar{w}_m)$ represent the weights (real numbers) for the relational symbols. For any domain size n, we extend these weights to $\text{Tup}(n)$ by setting $w'(R_i(a_1, \ldots, a_k)) = w_i$ and $\bar{w}'(R_i(a_1, \ldots, a_k)) = \bar{w}_i$, and we define $\text{WFOMC}(\Phi, n, \mathbf{w}, \bar{\mathbf{w}}) \stackrel{\text{def}}{=} \text{WFOMC}(\Phi, n, w', \bar{w}')$. Throughout this paper we assume that WFOMC refers to the symmetric variant, unless otherwise stated.

For a simple illustration, consider the sentence $\varphi = \exists y S(y)$. Then $\text{WFOMC}(\varphi, n, w_S, \bar{w}_S) = (\bar{w}_S + w_S)^n - (\bar{w}_S)^n$, because the sum of the weights of all possible worlds is $(\bar{w}_S + w_S)^n$, and we have to subtract the weight of the world where $S = \emptyset$. For another example, consider $\Phi = \forall x \exists y R(x, y)$. The reader may check that $\text{WFOMC}(\Phi, n, w_R, \bar{w}_R) = ((w_R + \bar{w}_R)^n - \bar{w}_R^n)^n$. In particular, over a domain of size n, the formula Φ has $(2^n - 1)^n$ models (by setting $w_R = \bar{w}_R = 1$).

Data Complexity and Combined Complexity. We consider the weighted vocabulary $(\sigma, \mathbf{w}, \bar{\mathbf{w}})$ fixed. In the *data complexity*, we fix Φ and study the complexity of the problem: *given* n, *compute* $\text{WFOMC}(\Phi, n, \mathbf{w}, \bar{\mathbf{w}})$. In the combined complexity, we study the complexity of the problem: *given* Φ, n, *compute* $\text{WFOMC}(\Phi, n, \mathbf{w}, \bar{\mathbf{w}})$. All our upper bounds continue to hold if the weights $\mathbf{w}, \bar{\mathbf{w}}$ are part of the input. We also consider the data- and combined-complexity of the associated decision problem (where we ignore the weights) *given* n, *does* Φ *have a model over a domain of size* n*?*

Weights and Probabilities. While in practical applications the weights are positive real numbers, and the probabilities are numbers in $[0, 1]$, in this paper we impose no restrictions on the values of the weights and probabilities. The definition (2) of $\text{WMC}(F, w)$ applies equally well to negative weights, and, in fact, to any semiring structure for the weights [25]. There is, in fact, at least one application of negative probabilities [22], namely the particular reduction from MLNs to WFOMC described in Example 1.2: a newly introduced relation has weight $1/(w - 1)$, which is negative when

Problem	Weights for R, S, and T tuples	Solution for $\Phi = \forall x \forall y (R(x) \vee S(x, y) \vee T(y))$
Symmetric FOMC	$w = \bar{w} = 1$	$\text{FOMC}(\Phi, n) = \sum_{k,m=0,n} \binom{n}{k}\binom{n}{m} 2^{n^2-km}$
Symmetric WFOMC	$w_R, w_S, w_T,$ $\bar{w}_R, \bar{w}_S, \bar{w}_T$	$\text{WFOMC}(\Phi, n, \mathbf{w}, \bar{\mathbf{w}}) = \sum_{k,m=0,n} \binom{n}{k}\binom{n}{m} W_{k,m}$ where $W_{k,m} = w_R^{n-k} \cdot \bar{w}_R^k \cdot w_S^{km} \cdot (w_S + \bar{w}_S)^{n^2-km} \cdot w_T^{n-m} \cdot \bar{w}_T^m$
Asymmetric WFOMC	$w(R(i)), w(S(i,j)), w(T(j))$ $\bar{w}(R(i)), \bar{w}(S(i,j)), \bar{w}(T(j))$ depend on i, j	#P-hard for Φ [4]

Table 1: Three variants of WFOMC, of increasing generality, illustrated on the sentence $\Phi = \forall x \forall y (R(x) \vee S(x, y) \vee T(y))$. This paper discusses the symmetric cases only.

$w < 1$. Then, the associated probability $p = w/(1 + w)$ belongs to $(-\infty, 0) \cup (1, \infty)$.

As a final comment on negative weights, we note that the complexity of the symmetric WFOMC problem is the same for arbitrary weights as for positive weights. Indeed, the expression $\text{WFOMC}(\Phi, n, \mathbf{w})$ is a multivariate polynomial in m variables $w_1, \ldots, w_m$, where each variable has degree n. The polynomial has $(n+1)^m = n^{O(1)}$ real coefficients. Given access to an oracle computing this polynomial for arbitrary positive values for w, we can compute in polynomial time all $n^{O(1)}$ coefficients with as many calls to the oracle; once we know the coefficients we can compute the polynomial at any values $w_1, \ldots, w_m$, positive or negative.

For all upper bounds in this paper we assume that the weights $w, \bar{w}$, or probabilities p, are given as rational numbers represented as fractions of two integers of n bits each. We assume w.l.o.g. that all fractions have the same denominator: this can be enforced by replacing the denominators by their least common multiplier, at the cost of increasing the number of bits of all integers to at most n^2. It follows that the weight of a world $W(\theta)$ (Eq.(3)) and $\text{WMC}(F, w, \bar{w})$ can be represented as ratios of two integers, each with $n^{O(1)}$ bits.

Summary. Table 1 summarizes the taxonomy and illustrates the various weighted model counting problems considered in this paper. Throughout the rest of the paper, FOMC and WFOMC refer to the symmetric variant, unless otherwise mentioned.

3. DATA COMPLEXITY

Recall that the language FO^k consists of FO formulas with at most k distinct logical variables.

3.1 Lower Bounds

Our first lower bound is for an FO^3 sentence:

Theorem 3.1. *There exists an FO^3 sentence, denoted Θ_1, s.t. the FOMC problem for Θ_1 is $\#P_1$-complete.*

Van den Broeck et al. [37] have shown that the Symmetric WFOMC problem for every FO^2 formula has polynomial time data complexity (the proof is reviewed in Appendix C); Theorem 3.1 shows that, unless $\#\text{P}_1$ is in PTIME, the result cannot extend to FO^k for $k > 2$.

Our second lower bound is for a conjunctive query, or, dually, a positive clause without equality. Recall that a *clause* is a universally quantified disjunction of literals, for example $\forall x \forall y (R(x) \vee \neg S(x, y))$. A *positive clause* is a clause where all relational atoms are positive. A *conjunctive query* (CQ) is an existentially quantified conjunction of positive literals, e.g. $\exists x \exists y (R(x) \wedge S(x, y))$. Positive clauses without the equality predicate are the duals of CQs, and therefore the WFOMC problem is essentially the same for positive clauses without equality as for CQs. Note that the dual of a clause with the equality predicate is a CQ with $\neq$, *e.g.* the dual of $\forall x \forall y (R(x, y) \vee x = y)$ is $\exists x \exists y (R(x, y) \wedge x \neq y)$.

Corollary 3.2. *There exists a positive clause Ξ_1 without equality s.t. the Symmetric WFOMC problem for Ξ_1 is $\#P_1$-hard. Dually, there exists a CQ Υ_1 s.t. the Symmetric WFOMC problem for Υ_1 is $\#P_1$-hard.*

Corollary 3.2 shows that the tractability result for γ-acyclic conjunctive queries (discussed below in Theorem 3.6) cannot be extended to all CQs. The proof of the Corollary follows easily from three lemmas, which are of independent interest, and which we present here; the proofs of the lemmas are in the appendix. We say that a vocabulary σ' *extends* σ if $\sigma \subseteq \sigma'$, and that a weighted vocabulary $(\sigma', \mathbf{w}', \bar{\mathbf{w}}')$ *extends* $(\sigma, \mathbf{w}, \bar{\mathbf{w}})$ if $\sigma \subseteq \sigma'$ and the tuples $\mathbf{w}', \bar{\mathbf{w}}'$ extend $\mathbf{w}, \bar{\mathbf{w}}$.

Lemma 3.3. *Let $(\sigma, \mathbf{w}, \bar{\mathbf{w}})$ be a weighted vocabulary and Φ an FO sentence over σ. There exists an extended weighted vocabulary $(\sigma', \mathbf{w}', \bar{\mathbf{w}}')$ and sentence Φ' over σ', such that Φ' is in prenex-normal form with a quantifier prefix $\forall^*$, and* $\text{WFOMC}(\Phi, n, \mathbf{w}, \bar{\mathbf{w}}) = \text{WFOMC}(\Phi', n, \mathbf{w}', \bar{\mathbf{w}}')$ *for all n.*

This lemma was proven by [37], and says that all existential quantifiers can be eliminated. The main idea is to replace a sentence of the form $\forall \mathbf{x} \exists y \psi(\mathbf{x}, y)$ by $\forall \mathbf{x} \forall y (\neg \psi(\mathbf{x}, y) \vee A(\mathbf{x}))$, where A is a new relational symbol of arity $|\mathbf{x}|$ and with weights $w_A = 1, \bar{w}_A = -1$. For every value $\mathbf{x} = \mathbf{v}$, in a world where $\exists y \psi(\mathbf{v}, y)$ holds, $A(\mathbf{v})$ holds too and the new symbol contributes a factor $+1$ to the weight; in a world where $\exists y \psi(\mathbf{v}, y)$ does not hold, then $A(\mathbf{v})$ may be true or false, and the weights of the two worlds cancel each other out.

Note that the lemma tells us nothing about the model count of Φ and Φ', since in Φ' we are forced to set some negative weights. If we had $\text{FOMC}(\Phi, n) = \text{FOMC}(\Phi', n)$, then we could reduce the satisfiability problem for an arbitrary FO sentence Φ to that for a sentence with a $\forall^*$ quantifier prefix, which is impossible, since the former is undecidable while the latter is decidable.

The next lemma, also following the proof in [37], says that all negations can be eliminated.

Lemma 3.4. *Let $(\sigma, \mathbf{w}, \bar{\mathbf{w}})$ be a weighted vocabulary and Φ a sentence over σ in prenex-normal form with quantifier prefix $\forall^*$. Then there exists an extended weighted vocabulary $(\sigma', \mathbf{w}', \bar{\mathbf{w}}')$ and a positive FO sentence Φ' over σ', also in prenex-normal form with quantifier prefix $\forall^*$, s.t.* $\text{WFOMC}(\Phi, n, \mathbf{w}, \bar{\mathbf{w}}) = \text{WFOMC}(\Phi', n, \mathbf{w}', \bar{\mathbf{w}}')$ *for all n.*

The idea is to create two new relational symbols A, B for every negated subformula $\neg\psi(\mathbf{x})$, replace the formula by $A(\mathbf{x})$, and add the sentence $\forall \mathbf{x}(\psi(\mathbf{x}) \vee A(\mathbf{x})) \wedge (A(\mathbf{x}) \vee B(\mathbf{x})) \wedge (\psi(\mathbf{x}) \vee B(\mathbf{x}))$. By setting the weights $w_A = \bar{w}_A = w_B = 1$, $\bar{w}_B = -1$ we ensure that, for every constant $\mathbf{x} = \mathbf{v}$, either $\neg\psi(\mathbf{v}) \equiv A(\mathbf{v})$, in which case $B(\mathbf{v})$ is forced to be true and the two new symbols contribute a factor $+1$ to the weight, or $\psi(\mathbf{v}) \equiv A(\mathbf{v}) \equiv \texttt{true}$, in which case $B(\mathbf{v})$ can be either true or false, and the weights cancel out.

Finally, we remove the $=$ predicate.

Lemma 3.5. *Let $(\sigma, \mathbf{w}, \bar{\mathbf{w}})$ be a weighted vocabulary and Φ a sentence over σ. Then there exists an extended vocabulary σ' and sentence Φ' without the equality predicate $=$, such that, for all n,* $\text{WFOMC}(\Phi, n, \mathbf{w}, \bar{\mathbf{w}})$ *can be computed in polynomial time using $n + 1$ calls to an oracle for* $\text{WFOMC}(\Phi', n, \mathbf{w}', \bar{\mathbf{w}}')$, *where $(\sigma', \mathbf{w}', \bar{\mathbf{w}}')$ is an extension of $(\sigma, \mathbf{w}, \bar{\mathbf{w}})$.*

The idea is to introduce a new relational symbol E, replace every atom $x = y$ with $E(x, y)$, and add the sentence $\forall x\ E(x, x)$. Let $\mathbf{w}', \bar{\mathbf{w}}'$ be the extension of $\mathbf{w}, \bar{\mathbf{w}}$ with $w'_E = z$, $\bar{w}'_E = 1$. Then $\text{WFOMC}(\Phi', n, \mathbf{w}', \bar{\mathbf{w}}')$ is a polynomial of degree n^2 in z where each monomial has degree $\geq n$ in z, because the hard constraint $\forall x\ E(x, x)$ forces $|E| \geq n$. Moreover, the coefficient of z^n is precisely $\text{WFOMC}(\Phi, n, \mathbf{w}, \bar{\mathbf{w}})$, because that corresponds to the worlds where $|E| = n$, hence it coincides with $=$. We compute this coefficient using $n + 1$ calls to an oracle for $\text{WFOMC}(\Phi', n, \mathbf{w}', \bar{\mathbf{w}}')$.

Now we give the proof of Corollary 3.2. Starting with the $\#\text{P}_1$-complete sentence Θ_1, we apply the three lemmas and obtain a positive sentence Φ, with quantifier prefix $\forall^*$ and without the equality predicate, that is $\#\text{P}_1$-hard. We write it as a conjunction of clauses, $\Phi = C_1 \wedge C_2 \wedge \cdots \wedge C_k$ (recall that a clause is universally quantified), and then apply the inclusion-exclusion formula: $\Pr(\Phi) = \sum_{s \subseteq [k], s \neq \emptyset} (-1)^{|s|+1} \Pr(\bigvee_{i \in s} C_i)$. Since any disjunction of clauses is equivalent to a single clause, we have reduced the computation problem $\Pr(\Phi)$ to computing the probabilities of $2^k - 1$ clauses. By duality, this reduces to computing the probabilities of $2^k - 1$ conjunctive queries, $\Pr(Q_1), \Pr(Q_2), \ldots, \Pr(Q_{2^k-1})$. We can reduce this problem to that of computing the probability of a single conjunctive query Υ_1, by the following argument. Create $2^k - 1$ copies of the relational symbols in the FO vocabulary, and take the conjunction of all queries, where each query uses a fresh copy of the vocabulary. Then $\Pr(Q_1 \wedge \cdots \wedge Q_{2^k-1}) = \Pr(Q_1) \cdots \Pr(Q_{2^k-1})$, because now every two distinct queries Q_i, Q_j have distinct relational symbols. Using an oracle to compute the probability of $\Upsilon_1 \stackrel{\text{def}}{=} \bigwedge_i Q_i$, we can compute any $\Pr(Q_i)$ by setting to 1 the probabilities of all relations occurring in Q_j, for $j \neq i$: in other words, the only possible world for a relation R in Q_j is one where R is the cartesian product of the domain; assuming $n \geq 1$, Q_j is true, $\Pr(Q_j) = 1$, and hence $\Pr(\Upsilon_1) = \Pr(Q_i)$. We repeat this for every i and compute $\Pr(Q_1), \ldots, \Pr(Q_{2^k-1})$. This proves that the CQ Υ_1 is $\#\text{P}_1$-hard. Its dual, Ξ_1, is a $\#\text{P}_1$-hard positive clause without equality. This proves Corollary 3.2.

3.2 Upper Bounds

A CQ is *without self-joins* if all atoms refer to distinct relational symbols. It is standard to associate a hypergraph with CQs, where the variables are nodes, and the atoms are hyper-edges. We define a γ-acyclic conjunctive query to be a conjunctive query w/o self-joins whose associated hypergraph is γ-acyclic. We prove:

Theorem 3.6. *The data complexity of Symmetric WFOMC for γ-acyclic CQs is in PTIME.*

Fagin's definition of γ-acyclic hypergraphs [14] is reviewed in the proof of Theorem 3.6.

An open problem is to characterize the conjunctive queries without self-joins that are in polynomial time. While no such query has yet been proven to be hard (Υ_1 in Corollary 3.2 has self-joins), it is widely believed that, for any $k \geq 3$, the symmetric WFOMC problem for a *typed cycle* of length k, $C_k = \exists x_1 \cdots x_k(R_1(x_1, x_2), R_2(x_2, x_3), \ldots, R_k(x_k, x_1))$, is hard. We discuss here several insights into finding the tractability border for conjunctive queries, summarized in Figure 1.

This boundary does not lie at γ-acyclicity: the query $c_\gamma = R(x, z), S(x, y, z), T(y, z)$ is γ-cyclic (with cycle $RxSyTzR$; see Fagin [14]), yet it still has PTIME data complexity. The key observation is that γ-cycles allow the last variable z to appear in all predicates, turning it into a *separator variable* [5], hence $\Pr(Q) = \prod_{a \in [n]} \Pr(Q[a/z])$, which is $[\Pr(Q[a/z])]^n$ by symmetry; $Q[a/z]$ is isomorphic to the query in Table 1 and can be computed in polynomial time. A weaker notion of acyclicity, called *jtdb* (for join tree with disjoint branches), can be found in [10]. It also does not characterize the tractability boundary: *jtdb* contains the γ-cyclic query above, but it does not contain the PTIME query $c_{jtdb} = R(x, y, z, u), S(x, y), T(x, z), V(x, u)$.

Fagin [14] defines two increasingly weaker notions of acyclicity: β- and α-acyclic. α-Acyclic queries are as hard as any conjunctive query without self-joins. Indeed, if $Q = \exists \mathbf{x}\varphi(\mathbf{x})$ is a conjunctive query w/o self-joins, then the query $Q' = \exists \mathbf{x}(A(\mathbf{x}) \wedge \varphi(\mathbf{x}))$ is α-acyclic, where A is a new relational symbol, containing all variables of Q. By setting the probability of A to 1, we have $\Pr(Q) = \Pr(Q')$. Thus, if all α-acyclic queries have PTIME data complexity, then all conjunctive queries w/o self-joins have PTIME data complexity.

For all we know, β-acyclic queries could well coincide with the class of tractable conjunctive queries w/o self joins. We present here some evidence that all β-cyclic queries are hard, by reduction from typed cycles, C_k. For that, we need to consider a slight generalization of WFOMC for conjunctive queries w/o self-joins, were each existential variable x_i ranges over a distinct domain, of size n_i: the standard semantics corresponds to the special case where all domains sizes n_i are equal. We prove that for any β-cyclic query Q, there exists k such that $\text{WFOMC}(C_k, \mathbf{n}, \mathbf{w}, \bar{\mathbf{w}})$ can be reduced to

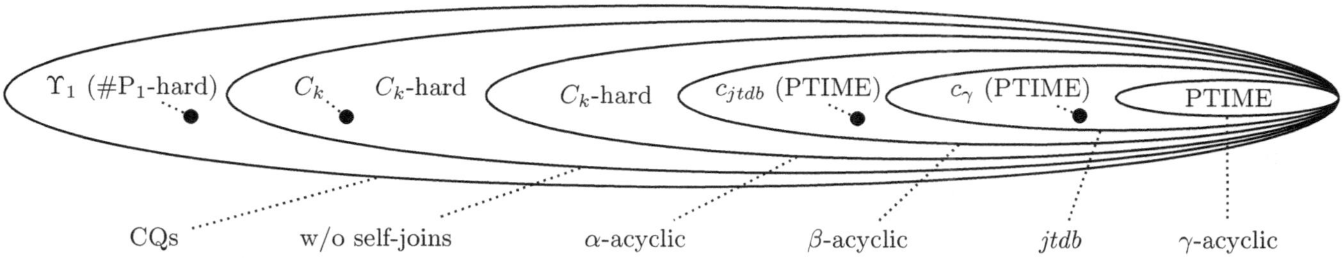

Figure 1: A summary of data complexity results for conjunctive queries (or positive clauses). C_k-hardness is an informal concept described in the main text.

WFOMC($Q, \mathbf{n}', \mathbf{w}', \bar{\mathbf{w}}'$). Hence, the existence of a β-cyclic query with PTIME data complexity would imply PTIME data complexity for at least one C_k (informally called C_k-hardness in Fig. 1). The reduction is as follows. By definition, a β-cyclic query Q contains a weak β-cycle [14] of the form $R_1 x_1 R_2 x_2 \ldots x_{k-1} R_k x_k R_{k+1}$, where $k \geq 3$, all x_i and R_i are distinct, each x_i occurs in both R_i and R_{i+1}, but in no other R_j, and $R_{k+1} = R_1$. Then, we reduce the WFOMC for C_k to that of Q. First, for each relational symbol R_j in Q, if R_j appears in the cycle then we define $w'_j = w_j$ and $\bar{w}'_j = \bar{w}_j$, otherwise $w'_j = \bar{w}'_j = 1$. Second, for all variables x_i that appear in the cycle we set their domain size n_i to be the same as that of the corresponding variable in C_k, otherwise we set $n_i = 1$. Then Q and C_k have the same WFOMC.

Finally, we discuss a peculiar sentence, whose complexity we left open in [18]:

Theorem 3.7. *The data complexity of the symmetric WFOMC problem is in PTIME for the query*

$$Q_{S4} = \forall x_1 \forall x_2 \forall y_1 \forall y_2 (S(x_1, y_1) \vee \neg S(x_2, y_1) \vee S(x_2, y_2) \vee \neg S(x_1, y_2))$$

In [18] we showed that Q_{S4} is in PTIME under the modified semantics, where S is a bipartite graph. This implies that the range of the variables x_1, x_2 is disjoint from the range of the variables y_1, y_2. Now we extended the proof to the standard semantics used in this paper. What makes this query interesting is that the algorithm used to compute it requires a subtle use of dynamic programming, and none of the existing lifted inference rules in the literature are sufficient to compute this query. This suggests that we do not yet have a candidate for a complete set of lifted inference rules for the symmetric WFOMC.

3.3 Proofs

Proof of Theorem 3.1. We briefly recall the basic notions from Valiant's original papers [33, 34]. A *counting Turing machine* is a nondeterministic TM with a read-only input tape and a work tape, that (magically) prints in binary, on a special output tape, the number of its accepting computations. The class #P$_1$ consists of all functions computed by some counting TM with polynomial (non-deterministic) running time and a unary input alphabet. A function f is #P$_1$-hard if, for any function g in #P$_1$ there exists a polynomial time, deterministic TM T_{det} with access to an oracle for f that computes g. Notice that T_{det}'s input alphabet is unary. As usual, f is called #P$_1$-complete if it is both hard, and in #P$_1$.

Our proof of Theorem 3.1 consists of two steps. First we construct a #P$_1$-complete function f, which is computable by a linear time counting TM U_1, which we call a *universal* #P$_1$ machine; in fact, we will define f by describing U_1. A similar construction in [34] is sketched too briefly to see how the particular pairing function can work; we use a different pairing function and give full details. To prove FO^3 membership, we also need to ensure U_1 runs in (nondeterministic) linear time, which requires some care given that the input is given in unary. Once we have defined U_1, the second step of the proof is a standard construction of an FO formula to simulate U_1: we follow Libkin [28, p. 167], but make several changes to ensure that the formula is in FO^3. The two steps are:

Lemma 3.8. *There exists a counting TM, U_1, with a unary input alphabet, such that (i) U_1 runs in linear time, and (ii) the function f that it computes is #P$_1$-hard.*

It follows immediately that f is #P$_1$-complete.

Lemma 3.9. *Let T be any counting TM with a unary input alphabet computing some function f. Suppose T runs in time $O(n^a)$. Then there exists an FO^k formula Φ over some relational vocabulary σ, s.t. $f(n) =$ FOMC$(\Phi, n)/(n!)$, where $k = 3a$ for $a \geq 1$.*

Theorem 3.1 follows by applying this lemma to U_1, hence $a = 1$ and the formula is in FO^3. By allowing runtimes $O(n^a)$ with $a > 1$, the lemma implies: $\#\text{P}_1 = \{f \mid \exists \Phi \in FO, \forall n : f(n) = \lfloor \text{FOMC}(\Phi, n)/n! \rfloor\}$; this is an extension of the classic result by Jones and Selman [23], which, restated for the tally notation says $\text{NP}_1 = \{\texttt{Spec}(\Phi) \mid \Phi \in FO\}$ (see [12], [9, Sec.5]). By considering FOMC over unlabeled structures, denoted UFOMC, the correspondence becomes even stronger. In UFOMC, all models that are identical up to a permutation of the constants are counted once, and $\#\text{P}_1 = \{\text{UFOMC}(\Phi, n) \mid \Phi \in FO\}$.

Proof of Lemma 3.8. The idea for U_1 is simple: its input n is represented in unary and encodes two numbers i, j: $n = e(i, j)$, for some encoding function e to be defined below. U_1 first computes i, j from n, then simulates the ith #P$_1$ counting TM on input j. The difficult part is to ensure that U_1 runs in linear time:

every TM i that it simulates runs in time $O(j^{k_i})$ for some exponent k_i that depends on i, and thus if we construct U_1 naively to simply simulate machine i on input j, then its runtime is no longer polynomial.

We start by describing an enumeration of counting TMs in $\#\mathrm{P}_1$, $M_1, M_2, \ldots, M_i, \ldots$ with the property that M_i runs in time $\leq (i \cdot j^i + i)^2$ on an input j. We start by listing all counting TMs over a unary input alphabet in standard order $M'_1, M'_2, \ldots$. Then we dovetail pairs of the form $M_i = (M'_r, s)$ where r is an index in the standard TM order and s is a number. M_i represents the counting TM that simulates M'_r on input j with a timer for $s \cdot j^s + s$ steps. The machine M_i can be constructed with at most quadratic slowdown over M'_r (due to the need to increment the counter). We further ensure that dovetailing $M_i = (M'_r, s)$ is done such that $i \geq s$; for that, it suffices to advance r in such a way that i advances at least as fast as s, that is, $M_1 = (M'_1, 1), M_2 = (M'_2, 1), M_3 = (M'_1, 2), M_4 = (M'_2, 2), M_5 = (M'_1, 3), \ldots$. It follows that, for every i, the runtime of M_i on input j is $\leq (i \cdot j^i + i)^2$. It remains to show that the list $M_1, M_2, \ldots, M_i, \ldots$ enumerates precisely all $\#\mathrm{P}_1$ functions. Indeed, each function in this list is in $\#\mathrm{P}_1$, because the runtime of M_i is polynomial in the input j. Conversely, every function in $\#\mathrm{P}_1$ is computed by some M_i in our list, because it is computed by some M'_r whose runtime on input j is $\leq a_r \cdot j^{k_r} + b_r$ and this is $\leq s \cdot j^s + s$ if we choose $s \stackrel{\text{def}}{=} \max(a_r, b_r, k_r)$. This completes the construction of the enumeration $M_1, M_2, \ldots$.

We describe now the counting machine U_1. Its input is a number n in unary, which represents an encoding $n = e(i,j)$ of two integers i, j. We will choose the encoding function e below such that it satisfies three properties: (a) U_1 can compute i, j from $n = e(i,j)$ in linear time (with auxiliary tapes), (b) $e(i,j) \geq (i \cdot j^i + i)^2$, and (c) for every fixed i, the function $j \mapsto e(i,j)$ can be computed in PTIME. We first prove the lemma, assuming that e satisfies these three properties.

The counting machine U_1 starts by computing a binary representation of its unary input n on its work tape: this step takes linear time in n. Next, it extracts i, j in linear time in n (by property (a)), then it simulates M_i on input j. The runtime of the last step is $\leq (i \cdot j^i + i)^2 \leq e(i,j)$ (by property (b)), hence U_1 runs in linear time in the input $n = e(i,j)$. It remains to prove that the function f computed by U_1 is $\#\mathrm{P}_1$-hard. Consider any function g in $\#\mathrm{P}_1$: we will describe a polynomial-time, deterministic Turing machine T_{det} with an oracle for f that computes g. Since g is in $\#\mathrm{P}_1$ there exists i such that g is computed by M_i. On input j, T_{det} computes $n = e(i,j)$ in PTIME (by property (c)), stores it on the oracle tape, then invokes U_1 and obtains the result $g(j) = f(n)$.

It remains to describe the encoding function e. We take $e(i,j) = 2^i 3^{4i \cdot \lceil \log_3 j \rceil}(6j+1)$. To prove (a), note that i is obtained by counting the trailing zeroes in the binary representation of n, j is obtained by first computing a ternary representation of $3^{4i \cdot \lceil \log_3 j \rceil}(6j+1)$, ignoring trailing zeros and deriving j from $6j+1$. (b) $2^i 3^{4i \cdot \lceil \log_3 j \rceil}(6j+1) \geq (i \cdot j^i + i)^2$ follows through direct calculations, using the fact that $3^{4i \cdot \lceil \log_3 j \rceil} \geq j^{4i}$. (c) is straightforward. □

Proof of Lemma 3.9. We describe here the most important steps of the proof, and delegate the details to Appendix B. We will consider only the case $k = 1$, i.e. the counting TM runs in linear time: the case when $k > 1$ is handled using a standard technique that encodes n^k time stamps using a relation of arity k. We briefly review Trakhtenbrot's proof from Libkin [28, p. 167]: for every deterministic TM, there is a procedure that generates a formula Θ_1 such that TM has an accepting computation starting with an empty input tape iff Θ_1 is satisfiable. The signature for Θ_1 is (this is a minor variation over Libkin's):

$$\sigma = \{<, Min, T_0, T_1, H, (S_q)_{q \in \text{States}(T)}\}$$

Then Θ_1 states that (1) $x < y$ is a total order on the domain and $Min(x)$ is its minimum element, (2) $T_0(t,p)$ (or $T_1(t,p)$) is true iff at time t the tape has a 0 (or a 1) on position p, (3) $H(t,p)$ is true iff at time t the head is on position p, and $S_q(t)$ is true iff at time t the machine is in state q. Libkin [28] describes the sentence Θ_1 that states that all these constraints are satisfied.

We adapt this to a more general construction that is sufficient to prove Lemma 3.9. We address five changes: (1) Our TM is non-deterministic, (2) has k tapes instead of 1, (3) its runtime is $c \cdot n$ instead of n, for some $c > 1$, (4) the input tape initially contains n symbols 1, and (5) Θ_1 needs to be in FO^3.

Support for non-deterministic transitions requires only a slight modification to the sentences. It is also easy to represent multiple tapes, by using k different relations $T_{0\tau_i}, T_{1\tau_i}$, and similarly k head relations H_{τ_i}, for $i = 1, k$. To encode transitions in FO^3, we will assume that the multi-tape TM always reads or writes only one tape at each time. This is without loss of generality: a state that reads and writes all tapes can be converted into a sequence of $2k$ states that first read one by one each tape and "remember" their symbols, then write one by one each tape and move their heads.

Next, we show how to encode running times (and space) up to $c \cdot n$ for some integer constant $c > 1$, with only a domain of size n available. The standard way is to increase the arity of the relations, e.g. with arity a we can represent n^a time steps, but this is not possible within FO^3. Instead, we partition the computation into c *epochs*, each having exactly n time steps, and similarly we partition the tapes into c regions, each with n cells. We denote $T_{0\tau er}(t,p)$, $T_{1\tau er}(t,p)$ the relations T_0, T_1 specialized to tape τ, epoch e, and region r, and similarly define $H_{\tau er}$ and S_{qe}. Furthermore, we modify the sentences that encode the TM transition relation to move the heads across epochs and regions, using only 3 variables. The fourth item is easy: we write a formula stating that initially (at time 1 of epoch 1), region 1 of (input) tape τ_1 is full of 1's, and all other regions and tapes are full of 0's. Moreover, Appendix B shows that Θ_1 can be written in FO^3.

Finally, $\mathrm{FOMC}(\Theta_1, n)$ is precisely the number of accepting computations of the TM on input n, times $n!$, coming from the $n!$ ways of ordering the domain. □

Proof of Theorem 3.6. We show how to compute $\Pr(Q)$ rather than WFOMC(Q, n): we have seen in Sec. 2 that these two are equivalent. We actually prove the theorem for a more general form of query, where each variable x_i range over a domain of size n_i, thus, $Q = \exists x_1 \in [n_1], \ldots, \exists x_m \in [n_m]\varphi$, where φ is quantifier-free. The probability of a query under the standard semantics (when all variables range over the same domain $[n]$) is obtained by simply setting $n_1 = \cdots = n_m = n$.

To prove the theorem, we use an equivalent definition of γ-acyclicity given by Fagin [14], which we give here together with our algorithm for computing $\Pr(Q)$. The graph is γ-acyclic if it can be reduced to an empty graph by applying the following rules, in any order.

(a) If a node x is isolated (i.e., it belongs to precisely one edge, say $R(x, y, z)$), then delete x. In this case we replace the relation $R(x, y, z)$ by a new relation $R'(y, z)$, where each tuple has probability $1 - (1 - p)^{n_x}$, where p is the probability of tuples in R.

(b) If an edge $R(x)$ is a singleton (i.e., if it contains exactly one node), then delete that edge (but do not delete the node from other edges that might contain it). Here, we condition on the size $k = |R|$. For each k, let p_k be the probability of the *residual query* obtained by removing $R(x)$ and restricting the range of x to $[k]$. By symmetry, this probability depends only on $k = |R|$, and does not depend on the choice of the k elements in the domain. Then $\Pr(Q) = \sum_k \binom{n_x}{k} p_R^k (1 - p_R)^{n_x - k} p_k$, where p_R denotes the probability of a tuple $\Pr(R(i))$, and is the same for all constants i (by symmetry).

(c) If an edge is empty, $R()$, then delete it. We multiply the probability of the residual query by p_R.

(d) If two edges (say $R(x, y, z)$, $S(x, y, z)$) contain precisely the same nodes, then delete one of these edges. Here we replace the two atoms by a new atom $R'(x, y, z)$ whose probability is $p_R \cdot p_S$.

(e) If two nodes x, y are edge-equivalent, then delete one of them from every edge that contains it. (Recall that two nodes are edge-equivalent if they are in precisely the same edges.) Here we replace the two variables x, y by a new variable z, whose range has size $n_z \stackrel{\text{def}}{=} n_x \cdot n_y$.

Each operation above is in polynomial time in the size of the binary representation of the inputs, and there are only polynomially many operations. Therefore the entire computation is in polynomial time, because each intermediate result can be represented using polynomially many bits. This follows from the fact that the number of models is $2^{O(n^a)}$, where a is the maximum arity of any relation in Q, hence the number of models can be represented using $O(n^a) = n^{O(1)}$ bits.

Example 3.10. *Consider the following linear chain query:*

$$Q = \exists x_0 \exists x_1 \cdots \exists x_m R_1(x_0, x_1) \wedge \cdots R_m(x_{m-1}, x_m)$$

where the probabilities of the m relations are $p_1, \ldots, p_m$. Denote $P_{n_0,\ldots,n_m}$ the probability of Q when the domains of $x_0, x_1, \ldots, x_m$ are sets of sizes $n_0, n_1, \ldots, n_m$ (thus, initially $n_0 = n_1 = \cdots = n_m = n$). Then the variable x_m is isolated (item a), hence we can eliminate it and update the probability of R_m to $1-(1-p_m)^{n_m}$. Now R_m is a singleton relation, hence we can remove it (item b), and restrict the domain of x_{m-1} to have size k_{m-1}, for $k_{m-1} = 1, n_{m-1}$. Therefore:

$$P_{n_0,\ldots,n_{m-1},n_m} = \sum_{k_{m-1}=1,n_{m-1}} P_{n_0,\ldots,n_{m-2},k_{m-1}} \cdot \binom{n_m}{k_m} \cdot [1 - (1 - p_m)^{k_m}]^{k_{m-1}} \cdot [(1 - p_m)^{k_m}]^{n_{m-1} - k_{m-1}}$$

Repeating this process we arrive at an expression that is computable in polynomial time in n (for a fixed m). Notice that this formula does not appear to be computable in polynomial time in both n and m. We leave open the combined complexity of acyclic queries.

Proof of Theorem 3.7. First note that, by using resolution, the query implies the following statement, for every $k \geq 2$:

$$\forall x_1, y_1, \ldots, x_k, y_k (S(x_1, y_1) \vee \neg S(x_2, y_1) \vee S(x_2, y_2) \vee \neg S(x_2, y_3) \vee \ldots \vee \neg S(x_1, y_k)) \tag{5}$$

For any two numbers n_1, n_2, denote $Q_{n_1 n_2} = \forall x_1 \in [n_1], \forall x_2 \in [n_1], \forall y_1 \in [n_2], \forall y_2 \in [n_2], (S(x_1, y_1) \vee \neg S(x_2, y_1) \vee S(x_2, y_2) \vee \neg S(x_1, y_2))$, in other words we restrict the range of the variables to some domains $[n_1], [n_2]$. These domains are not required to be disjoint, instead we use the standard assumption $n_1 \leq n_2$ implies $[n_1] \subseteq [n_2]$. When $n_1 = n_2 = n$ then $Q_{n_1 n_2}$ is equivalent to Q_{S4}. We claim the following. If D is a model of $Q_{n_1 n_2}$, then either property P_a or P_b holds in D:

$$P_a \equiv \exists x \in [n_1], \forall y \in [n_2], S(x, y)$$
$$P_b \equiv \exists y \in [n_2], \forall x \in [n_1], \neg S(x, y)$$

Suppose not. Consider any model of $Q_{n_1 n_2}$ that does not satisfy P_a, P_b. Pick any element $x_1 \in [n_1]$. As P_a does not hold, $\exists y_1 \in [n_2] \neg S(x_1, y_1)$. As P_b does not hold, $\exists x_2 \in [n_1], S(x_2, y_1)$. Continuing, $\exists y_2 \in [n_2]$, $\neg S(x_2, y_2)$, $\exists x_3 \in [n_1], S(x_3, y_2)$ and $\exists y_3 \in [n_2]$, $\neg S(x_3, y_3)$. Continuing, we obtain an arbitrarily long sequence of values $x_1, y_1, x_2, \ldots$ such that: $\neg S(x_1, y_1)$, $S(x_2, y_1)$, $\neg S(x_2, y_2)$, $\ldots$, $S(x_{n_1}, y_{n_1 - 1})$, $\neg S(x_{n_1}, y_{n_1})$. Note that we can never have $x_i = x_j$ or $y_i = y_j$, for $i \neq j$, because that would violate Eq.(5) for $k = j - i$. Since the domain is finite, this is a contradiction.

Therefore, either P_a or P_b holds. Clearly, both statements cannot hold, as they are exclusive events. Denote f and g the weighted model count for $Q_{n_1 n_2}$ in these two cases:

$$f(n_1, n_2) = \text{WFOMC}(Q_{n_1 n_2} \wedge P_a, n, w, \bar{w})$$
$$g(n_1, n_2) = \text{WFOMC}(Q_{n_1 n_2} \wedge P_b, n, w, \bar{w})$$

Then we have WFOMC$(Q_{n_1 n_2}, n, w, \bar{w}) = f(n_1, n_2) + g(n_1, n_2)$. It remains to show how to compute f, g.

Consider a model that satisfies P_a, hence the set $X = \{x \mid \forall y \in [n_2], S(x, y)\}$ is non-empty, hence $k = |X| \geq 1$.

Remove the elements X from the domain $[n_1]$ (and rename the elements such that $[n_1] - X = [n_1 - k]$) and call D' the resulting substructure. Then D' still satisfies the query $Q_{(n_1-k),n_2}$, and, by the removal of all elements X, cannot satisfy P_a, hence it must satisfy P_b. This justifies the following recurrence, completing the proof of Theorem 3.7:

$$f(n_1, 0) = 1 \quad f(n_1, n_2) = \sum_{k=1}^{n_1} \binom{n_1}{k} w^{kn_2} g(n_1 - k, n_2)$$

$$g(0, n_2) = 1 \quad g(n_1, n_2) = \sum_{\ell=1}^{n_2} \binom{n_2}{\ell} \bar{w}^{n_1 \ell} f(n_1, n_2 - \ell)$$

4. COMBINED COMPLEXITY

In the combined complexity we consider a fixed vocabulary $\sigma = (R_1, \ldots, R_m)$, and assume that both Φ and n are given as part of the input. As before, n is given in unary (tally) notation. We consider both the FOMC problem, "*compute* FOMC(Φ, n)", and the associated decision problem "*is* $n \in$ **Spec**(Φ)*?*". Our upper bound for FOMC also holds for WFOMC. Recall that the spectrum $\texttt{Spec}(\Phi)$ of a formula Φ is the set of numbers n for which Φ has a model over a domain of size n.

Vardi [40] proved that the model checking problem, "*given* Φ *and a structure* D*, is* Φ *true in* D*?*" is PSPACE-complete. This implies that the above decision problem is also in PSPACE: to check $n \in \texttt{Spec}(\Phi)$ enumerate over all structures D of a domain of size n, and check if Φ is true in D. By the same argument, FOMC is also in PSPACE. We prove:

Theorem 4.1. *(1) For every $k \geq 2$, the combined complexity for FOMC for FO^k is #P-complete. (2) The combined complexity for the decision problem $n \in$ **Spec**(Φ) is NP-complete for FO^2, and is PSPACE-complete for FO.*

The #P-membership in (1) also holds for the WFOMC problem. Recall that the vocabulary σ is fixed. If σ were allowed to be part of the input, then the lower bound in (1) follows immediately from the #P-hardness result for #SAT, because any Boolean formula is trivially encoded as an FO^0 formula, by introducing a new, zero-ary relational symbol for every Boolean variable.

Proof of Theorem 4.1. We start by proving item (1) of Theorem 4.1. To prove membership in #P, it suffices to show that the lineage of a sentence φ of size s over a domain of size n is polynomial in s and n, then use the fact that WMC for Boolean functions is in #P. However, FO^k formulas have, in general, exponentially large lineage, e.g. the formula checking for the existence of a path of length n, $\exists x \exists y (R(x, y) \wedge \exists x (R(y, x) \wedge \exists y (R(y, x) \wedge \ldots)))$, over a domain of size n has lineage of size $\Omega(n^n)$. Instead, we first transform the formula by removing all nested variables. For that, we apply Scott's reduction, which we give below, following the presentation by Grädel, Kolaitis, and Vardi [17, Prop.3.1]; while Scott's reduction was described for FO^2, it carries over unchanged to FO^k. More precisely, the reduction converts a sentence φ of size s into a new sentence φ^* over an extended vocabulary, satisfying the following properties:

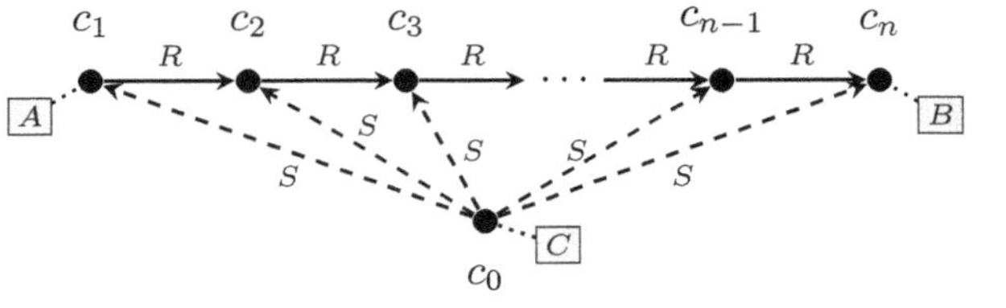

Figure 2: All models of φ_F represent graphs of the depicted form. There is a linear graph of R-edges between the distinguished nodes A and B. The S-edges go from a distinguished node C to all others. They are optional, and are in one-to-one correspondence with the variables X_i in F.

1. The finite models of φ and φ^* are in one-to-one correspondence, and the corresponding models have the same weight.
2. φ^* has size $O(s)$.
3. φ^* is a conjunction of sentences in prenex normal form, i.e. $Q_1 x_1 Q_2 x_2 \cdots Q_k x_k \psi$ where each Q_i is either $\forall$ or $\exists$, and ψ is quantifier-free.

The new formula has a lineage of size $O(n^k s)$, because its quantifier depth is bounded by $k = O(1)$, which implies WFOMC is in #P. It remains to describe Scott's reduction, which we review here briefly, for completeness. Introduce a new relational symbol S_ψ for every subformula ψ of φ, where the arity of S_ψ equals the number of free variables in ψ, and define the sentence $\theta_\psi \equiv \forall x_1 \cdots \forall x_\ell (S_\psi(x_1, \ldots, x_\ell) \Leftrightarrow \theta'_\psi)$, where θ'_ψ depends on the structure of ψ as follows: if ψ is an atomic formula, then $\theta'_\psi = \psi$, if $\psi = \psi_1 \wedge \psi_2$ then $\theta'_\psi = S_{\psi_1} \wedge S_{\psi_2}$, if $\psi = \neg\psi_1$ then $\theta'_\psi = \neg S_{\psi_1}$ and if $\psi = \forall x \psi_1$ then $\theta'_\psi = \forall x S_{\psi_1}$. The new formula φ^* is defined as $S_\varphi \wedge \bigwedge_\psi \theta_\psi$. By setting $w(S_\psi) = \bar{w}(S_\psi) = 1$ for all new symbols, we ensure that the models of φ and φ^* are not just in one-to-one correspondence; they have the same weights.

Next we prove #P-hardness for FO^2 (this implies hardness for FO^k for every $k \geq 2$). We use reduction from #SAT: given a Boolean formula F over n variables $X_1, \ldots, X_n$, compute $\#F$. This problem is #P-hard [33].

Define the vocabulary σ consisting of 3 unary symbols A, B, C, and 2 binary symbols R, S. Given a Boolean formula F, we construct an FO^2 sentence φ_F such that, over a domain of size $n+1$, the number of models of φ_F is FOMC($\varphi_F, n+1$) $= (n+1)! \cdot \#F$. The sentence φ_F enforces a particular graph structure, as illustrated in Figure 2, by asserting the following:

- There exists three unique, distinct elements x, y, z such that $A(x), B(y), C(z)$ are true: $\exists x A(x) \wedge \forall x, \forall y (A(x) \wedge A(y)) \Rightarrow x = y$, and similarly for B and C; $\neg \exists x (A(x) \wedge B(x))$ and similarly for A, C, and B, C.
- There exist n elements $x_1, \ldots, x_n$ such that the following holds: $A(x_1), R(x_1, x_2), R(x_2, x_3), \ldots, R(x_{n-1}, x_n), B(x_n)$. This is expressible in FO^2, by reusing variables.

Untyped triangles	$\exists x, y, z(R(x, y), R(y, z), R(z, x))$
Typed triangles (3-cycle)	$\exists x, y, z(R(x, y), S(y, z), T(z, x))$
k-cycle, for $k \geq 3$	$\exists x_1, \ldots, x_k(R_1(x_1, x_2), R_2(x_2, x_3), \ldots, R_k(x_k, x_1)$
Transitivity	$\forall x, y, z(E(x, y) \wedge E(y, z) \Rightarrow E(x, z))$
Homophily	$\forall x, y, z(R(x, y) \wedge S(x, z) \Rightarrow R(z, y))$
Extension Axiom (Simplified)	$\forall x_1, x_2, x_3(x_1 \neq x_2 \wedge x_1 \neq x_3 \wedge x_2 \neq x_3 \Rightarrow \exists y E(x_1, y) \wedge E(x_2, y) \wedge E(x_3, y))$

Table 2: A list of open problems: for each formula it is conjectured that FOMC is hard.

- For every number $m \in [2n] - \{n\}$, it is not the case that there exists m elements $x_1, \ldots, x_m$ such that: $A(x_1), R(x_1, x_2), R(x_2, x_3), \ldots, R(x_{m-1}, x_m), B(x_m)$.
- For all x, y, if $R(x, y)$ then neither $C(x)$ nor $C(y)$.
- For all x, y, if $S(x, y)$ then $C(x)$.
- Finally, φ_F contains a statement obtained from F by replacing each Boolean variable X_i by the sentence $\gamma_i \stackrel{\text{def}}{=} \exists x, \exists z(S(z, x) \wedge \alpha_i(x))$, where $\alpha_i(x)$ is the following formula with free variable x: there exists a path $A(x_1), R(x_1, x_2), \ldots, R(x_{i-1}, x)$ (if $i = 1$ then $\alpha_1(x) \equiv A(x)$).

The reader may check that, for any database instance D over a domain of size $n+1$ that satisfies φ_F there exists a unique permutation $c_0, c_1, \ldots, c_n$ over its domain such that the relations A, B, C and R contain precisely the following tuples: $C(c_0), A(c_1), B(c_n), R(c_1, c_2), \ldots, R(c_{n-1}, c_n)$. Indeed, if it contained some $R(c_i, c_j)$ with $j \neq i+1$, then $c_1, \ldots, c_i, c_j, c_{j+1}, \ldots, c_n$ forms a path from A to B of some length $m \leq 2n$ and $m \neq n$, which contradicts the sentence φ_F; notice also that $\alpha_i(x)$ is true iff $x = c_i$. Therefore the only relation that is left unspecified in D is S, which may contain an arbitrary number of tuples of the form $S(c_0, c_i)$. These tuples are in one-to-one correspondence with the Boolean variables X_i, proving our claim.

Now we prove item (2) of Theorem 4.1. The claim for FO^2 follows immediately from the proof above. It remains to prove that the combined complexity for FO is PSPACE, for which we use a reduction from the Quantified Boolean Formula (QBF) problem, which is known to be PSPACE complete. A *Quantified Boolean Formula* is a formula of the form $Q_1X_1Q_2X_2 \ldots Q_nX_nF$ where each Q_i is a quantifier $\forall$ or $\exists$, and F is a Boolean formula over the variables $X_1, \ldots, X_n$. We make the following change to the construction above. Recall that a Boolean variable X_i in F was represented by $S(c_0, c_i)$. Now we extend S to a ternary relation $S(x, y, u)$, restrict u to two constants (we choose c_1 and c_n arbitrarily) and represent X_i by $S(c_0, c_i, c_1)$ and $\neg X_i$ by $S(c_0, c_i, c_n)$. Then, we replace the quantifiers $\forall X_i$ or $\exists X_i$ with $\forall u$ or $\exists u$. More precisely, the new formula φ_F contains the following statements:

- If $S(x, y, u)$ is true, then u is either the distinguished A or the distinguished B element: $\forall x, y, u(S(x, y, u) \Rightarrow A(u) \vee B(u))$.
- If u, v are the distinguished A and B elements, then $S(x, y, u)$ is the negation of $S(x, y, v)$: $\forall u, v, x, y(A(u) \wedge B(v) \Rightarrow (S(x, y, u) \texttt{ xor } S(x, y, v)))$.

Finally, we rewrite a QBF $\forall X_i(\ldots)$ into $\forall u(A(u) \vee B(u) \Rightarrow \ldots)$ and a QBF $\exists X_i(\ldots)$ into $\exists u((A(u) \vee B(u)) \wedge \ldots)$. We omit the straightforward details.

5. CONCLUSIONS

In this paper we discuss the symmetric Weighted FO Model Counting Problem. Our motivation comes from probabilistic inference in Markov Logic Networks, with applications to modern, large knowledge bases, but the problem is also of independent theoretical interest. We studied both the data complexity, and the combined complexity. For the data complexity we established for the first time the existence of an FO sentence for which the Symmetric Model Counting problem is $\#P_1$-hard, and also the existence of a Conjunctive Query for which the Symmetric Weighted Model Counting problem is $\#P_1$-hard. We also showed that for all γ-acyclic conjunctive queries WFOMC can be computed in polynomial time. For the combined complexity, we proved a tight bound of #P-completeness for FO^2. We also discussed the associate decisions problem.

We end this paper with a list of open problems, listed in Table 2: for each query in the table, the complexity of the FOMC or the WFOMC problem is open.

Acknowledgments. We thank Ronald Fagin, Phokion Kolaitis and Lidia Tendera for discussions on topics related to this paper. This work was partially supported by NSF IIS-1115188, IIS-0911036, CCF-1217099, and the Research Foundation-Flanders (FWO-Vlaanderen).

6. REFERENCES

[1] Alberto Bertoni and Massimiliano Goldwurm. On ranking 1-way finitely ambiguous NL languages and $\#P_1$-complete census functions. *ITA*, 27(2):135–148, 1993.

[2] Andrew Carlson, Justin Betteridge, Bryan Kisiel, Burr Settles, Estevam R. Hruschka Jr., and Tom M. Mitchell. Toward an architecture for never-ending language learning. In *AAAI*, 2010.

[3] Kevin J. Compton. The computational complexity of asymptotic problems i: Partial orders. *Inf. Comput.*, 78(2):108–123, 1988.

[4] Nilesh N. Dalvi and Dan Suciu. Efficient query evaluation on probabilistic databases. *VLDB J.*, 16(4):523–544, 2007.

[5] Nilesh N. Dalvi and Dan Suciu. The dichotomy of probabilistic inference for unions of conjunctive queries. *J. ACM*, 59(6):30, 2012.

[6] http://deepdive.stanford.edu/.

[7] Pedro Domingos and Daniel Lowd. *Markov Logic: An Interface Layer for Artificial Intelligence.* Morgan & Claypool Publishers, 2009.

[8] X. Dong, E. Gabrilovich, G. Heitz, W. Horn, N. Lao, K. Murphy, T. Strohmann, S. Sun, and W. Zhang. Knowledge vault: A web-scale approach to probabilistic knowledge fusion. In *KDD*, 2014.

[9] Arnaud Durand, Neil D. Jones, Johann A. Makowsky, and Malika More. Fifty years of the spectrum problem: survey and new results. *Bulletin of Symbolic Logic*, 18(4):505–553, 2012.

[10] David Duris. Some characterizations of γ and β-acyclicity of hypergraphs. *Information Processing Letters*, 112(16):617–620, 2012.

[11] Anthony Fader, Stephen Soderland, and Oren Etzioni. Identifying relations for open information extraction. In *EMNLP*, pages 1535–1545, 2011.

[12] Ronald Fagin. Generalized first-order spectra and polynomial-time recognizable sets. In *SIAM-AMS Proceedings 7*, pages 43–73, 1974.

[13] Ronald Fagin. Probabilities on finite models. *J. Symb. Log.*, 41(1):50–58, 1976.

[14] Ronald Fagin. Degrees of acyclicity for hypergraphs and relational database schemes. *J. ACM*, 30(3):514–550, 1983.

[15] Vibhav Gogate and Pedro Domingos. Probabilistic theorem proving. In *UAI*, pages 256–265, 2011.

[16] Carla P Gomes, Joerg Hoffmann, Ashish Sabharwal, and Bart Selman. From sampling to model counting. In *IJCAI*, pages 2293–2299, 2007.

[17] Erich Grädel, Phokion G. Kolaitis, and Moshe Y. Vardi. On the decision problem for two-variable first-order logic. *Bulletin of Symbolic Logic*, 3(1):53–69, 1997.

[18] Eric Gribkoff, Guy Van den Broeck, and Dan Suciu. Understanding the complexity of lifted inference and asymmetric weighted model counting. In *UAI*, pages 280–289, 2014.

[19] Johannes Hoffart, Fabian M. Suchanek, Klaus Berberich, and Gerhard Weikum. Yago2: A spatially and temporally enhanced knowledge base from wikipedia. *AIJ*, 194:28–61, 2013.

[20] Manfred Jaeger. Lower complexity bounds for lifted inference. *TPLP*, 2012.

[21] Manfred Jaeger and Guy Van den Broeck. Liftability of probabilistic inference: Upper and lower bounds. In *StarAI*, 2012.

[22] Abhay Kumar Jha and Dan Suciu. Probabilistic databases with MarkoViews. *VLDB*, 5(11):1160–1171, 2012.

[23] Neil Jones and Alan Selman. Turing machines and the spectra of first-order formulas with equality. In *STOC*, pages 157–167, 1972.

[24] Kristian Kersting, Babak Ahmadi, and Sriraam Natarajan. Counting belief propagation. In *UAI*, pages 277–284, 2009.

[25] Angelika Kimmig, Guy Van den Broeck, and Luc De Raedt. Algebraic model counting. *arXiv preprint arXiv:1211.4475*, 2012.

[26] S. Kok, P. Singla, M. Richardson, and P. Domingos. The alchemy system for statistical relational AI, 2005.

[27] Phokion G. Kolaitis and Moshe Y. Vardi. 0-1 laws for fragments of existential second-order logic: A survey. In *MFCS*, pages 84–98, 2000.

[28] Leonid Libkin. *Elements of Finite Model Theory*. Springer, 2004.

[29] Mathias Niepert. Symmetry-aware marginal density estimation. In *AAAI*, 2013.

[30] Feng Niu, Christopher Ré, AnHai Doan, and Jude W. Shavlik. Tuffy: Scaling up statistical inference in Markov logic networks using an RDBMS. *VLDB*, 4(6):373–384, 2011.

[31] Hoifung Poon and Pedro Domingos. Sound and efficient inference with probabilistic and deterministic dependencies. In *AAAI*, pages 458–463, 2006.

[32] Dan Suciu, Dan Olteanu, Christopher Ré, and Christoph Koch. *Probabilistic Databases*. Morgan & Claypool Publishers, 2011.

[33] Leslie G. Valiant. The complexity of computing the permanent. *Theor. Comput. Sci.*, 8:189–201, 1979.

[34] Leslie G. Valiant. The complexity of enumeration and reliability problems. *SIAM J. Comput.*, 1979.

[35] Guy Van den Broeck. On the completeness of first-order knowledge compilation for lifted probabilistic inference. In *NIPS*, pages 1386–1394, 2011.

[36] Guy Van den Broeck and Adnan Darwiche. On the complexity and approximation of binary evidence in lifted inference. In *NIPS*, 2013.

[37] Guy Van den Broeck, Wannes Meert, and Adnan Darwiche. Skolemization for weighted first-order model counting. In *KR*, 2014.

[38] Guy Van den Broeck, Wannes Meert, and Jesse Davis. Lifted generative parameter learning. In *StaRAI*, 2013.

[39] Guy Van den Broeck, Nima Taghipour, Wannes Meert, Jesse Davis, and Luc De Raedt. Lifted probabilistic inference by first-order knowledge compilation. In *IJCAI*, pages 2178–2185. AAAI Press, 2011.

[40] Moshe Y. Vardi. The complexity of relational query languages (extended abstract). In *STOC*, pages 137–146, 1982.

[41] Deepak Venugopal and Vibhav Gogate. Scaling-up importance sampling for markov logic networks. In *NIPS*, 2014.

[42] Wei Wei, Jordan Erenrich, and Bart Selman. Towards efficient sampling: Exploiting random walk strategies. In *AAAI*, pages 670–676, 2004.

[43] Wentao Wu, Hongsong Li, Haixun Wang, and Kenny Qili Zhu. Probase: a probabilistic taxonomy for text understanding. In *SIGMOD*, pages 481–492, 2012.

[44] Ce Zhang and Christopher Ré. Towards high-throughput gibbs sampling at scale: a study across storage managers. In *SIGMOD*, pages 397–408, 2013.

APPENDIX

A. THE THREE LEMMAS

A.1 Proof of Lemma 3.3: Removing Exists

Following the proof of [37], we show how to eliminate existential quantifiers from a WFOMC problem (a form of Skolemization). Assume that Φ is in prenex normal form: $\Phi = Q_1x_1Q_2x_2 \ldots Q_kx_k\Psi$, where each Q_i is either $\forall$ or $\exists$, and Ψ is quantifier-free. Let i be the first position of an $\exists$, and denote $\varphi(\mathbf{x}, x_i) = Q_{i+1}x_{i+1} \ldots Q_kx_k\Psi$; note that φ is a formula with free variables $\mathbf{x} = (x_1, \ldots, x_{i-1})$. We have:

$$\Phi = \forall \mathbf{x} \exists x_i \varphi(\mathbf{x}, x_i)$$

Let A be a fresh relational symbol of arity i. The new formula Φ' is:

$$\Phi' = \forall \mathbf{x}((\exists x_i \varphi(\mathbf{x}, x_i)) \Rightarrow A(\mathbf{x})) \quad (6)$$

Let $w', \bar{w}'$ denote the weights of Φ's vocabulary extended with $w(A) = 1$ and $\bar{w}(A) = -1$. We claim that $\text{WFOMC}(\Phi, n, w, \bar{w}) = \text{WFOMC}(\Phi', n, w', \bar{w}')$. Consider a possible world $D \subseteq \text{Tup}(n)$ that satisfies Φ'. Call D "good" if it also satisfies Φ. In a good world D, for any constants $\mathbf{x} = \mathbf{a}$, the sentence $\exists x_i \varphi(\mathbf{a}, x_i)$ is true, hence $A(\mathbf{a})$ is also true (because Φ' is true), and therefore the weight of D is the same as the weight of $D - \{A\}$, the world obtained from D by removing all tuples referring to the relational symbol A: $W(D, w', \bar{w}') = W(D - \{A\}, w, \bar{w})$. Thus, the sum of the weights of the good worlds (see Eq.(3)) is precisely $\text{WFOMC}(\Phi, n, w, \bar{w})$. We prove that the sum of the weights of the bad worlds is zero. Let D be a bad world: it satisfies Φ' but not Φ. Thus, there exists some constants $\mathbf{a}$ s.t. the sentence $\exists x_i \varphi(\mathbf{a}, x_i)$ is false; choose $\mathbf{a}$ to be the first such constants, in some lexicographic order. Let D' be the world obtained from D by flipping the status of $A(\mathbf{a})$: thus D, D' are identical, but one sets $A(\mathbf{a})$ to true and the other to false. Both satisfy Φ', and $W(D, w', \bar{w}') = -W(D', w', \bar{w}')$, therefore they cancel out in the sum of Eq.(3). This proves that $\text{WFOMC}(\Phi, n, w, \bar{w}) = \text{WFOMC}(\Phi', n, w', \bar{w}')$.

We note that Φ' can be written equivalently as:

$$\Phi' = \forall \mathbf{x} \forall x_i (\neg \varphi(\mathbf{x}, x_i) \vee A(\mathbf{x}))$$

In other words, we have replaced the first existential quantifier in Φ by a universal quantifier (and may have increased the number of $\exists$ on positions $i+1, i+2, \ldots$). Lemma 3.3 follows by applying this procedure inductively.

A.2 Proof of Lemma 3.4: Removing Negation

Let $\neg\psi(\mathbf{x})$ be a negated subformula of Φ, with k free variables $\mathbf{x}$. Let A, B be two new relational symbols of arity k. Let Φ_p denote the sentence obtained from Φ by replacing the subformula $\neg\psi(\mathbf{x})$ with $A(\mathbf{x})$. Denote:

$$\Delta = \forall \mathbf{x}[(\psi(\mathbf{x}) \vee A(\mathbf{x})) \wedge (A(\mathbf{x}) \vee B(\mathbf{x})) \wedge (\psi(\mathbf{x}) \vee B(\mathbf{x}))] \quad (7)$$

Extend the weight functions $w, \bar{w}$ to $w', \bar{w}'$ by setting $w(A) = \bar{w}(A) = w(B) = 1$, $\bar{w}(B) = -1$. Define $\Phi' = \Phi_p \wedge \Delta$. We claim that $\text{WFOMC}(\Phi, n, w, \bar{w}) = \text{WFOMC}(\Phi', n, w', \bar{w}')$. To prove this, consider a world $D \subseteq \text{Tup}(n)$ over the vocabulary of Φ', and assume that D satisfies Φ'. Call D "good", if the statement $\forall \mathbf{x}(\psi(\mathbf{x}) \text{ xor } A(\mathbf{x}))$ holds. It is easy to see that in any good world, $\forall \mathbf{x} B(\mathbf{x})$ holds too, hence the good world has the same weight as the world obtained by stripping it of the additional relations A, B, and, furthermore, their contributions to $\text{WFOMC}(\Phi', n, w', \bar{w}')$ is precisely $\text{WFOMC}(\Phi, n, w, \bar{w})$. Consider a bad world: it satisfies Φ', but there exists $\mathbf{a}$ such both $\psi(\mathbf{a})$ and $A(\mathbf{a})$ are true. In that case $B(\mathbf{a})$ can be set arbitrarily to true or false and still satisfy the formula Φ', hence the contributions of these two pairing worlds cancel out. This proves that $\text{WFOMC}(\Phi, n, w, \bar{w}) = \text{WFOMC}(\Phi', n, w', \bar{w}')$.

Lemma 3.4 follows by apply this process repeatedly.

A.3 Proof of Lemma 3.5: Removing Equality

Let $E(x, y)$ be a new predicate symbol, with weights $w(E) = z$ and $\bar{w}(E) = 1$, where z is a real value to be determined below. Define Φ_E to be obtained from Φ by replacing every equality predicate $x = y$ with $E(x, y)$, and define:

$$\Phi' = \Phi_E \wedge \forall x E(x, x)$$

Consider the count $f(z) = \text{WFOMC}(\Phi', n, w', \bar{w}')$ as a function of z, where $w', \bar{w}'$ extend $w, \bar{w}$ with $w(E) = z, \bar{w}(E) = 1$. This is a polynomial of degree n^2 in z. Since Φ' asserts $\forall x E(x, x)$, all monomials in f have a degree $\geq n$. Let $c \cdot z^n$ be the monomial of degree n. Then we claim that its coefficient $c = \text{WFOMC}(\Phi, n, w, \bar{w})$. Indeed, every world D where E has exactly n tuples is a world where E is interpreted as the equality predicate. We can compute c using $n+1$ calls to an oracle for $f(z)$ as follows. Fix $\delta > 0$, and denote $\Delta^0 f = f$, $\Delta^{k+1} f(z) = (\Delta^k f)(z + \delta) - (\Delta^k f)(z)$. Then $\Delta^n f(0) = c \cdot n! = \binom{n}{0} f(0) - \binom{n}{1} f(\delta) + \binom{n}{2} f(2\delta) - \cdots (-1)^n \binom{n}{n} f(n\delta)$.

B. A #P$_1$-HARD SENTENCE Θ_1

We prove here Lemma 3.9: shows how to reduce a linear-time, multi-tape counting TM with a unary input alphabet (such as the #P$_1$-complete TM) to the FOMC problem on a first-order sentence. The sentence that encodes the #P$_1$-complete TM is referred to as Θ_1. This proof is based on the standard encoding of a deterministic Turing machine into first-order logic, as used to prove Trakhtenbrot's theorem [28, p. 167]. We extend this construction in several ways: (1) towards non-deterministic counting Turing machines, (2) with multiple tapes, (3) with a run time of $c \cdot n$ for some fixed c, instead of n, (4) to have n symbols 1 on the input tape, followed by symbols 0, and finally (5) to obtain a sentence in FO^3.

As discussed in Section 3.3, we need to encode run times and space with lengths up to $c \cdot n$, yet we only have a domain size of exactly n available. This is solved by partitioning the run time into c *epochs* of n steps, and the space into c *regions* of n cells. Moreover, we assume w.l.o.g. that there are two symbols: $\{0, 1\}$.

B.1 Signature

The signature of Θ_1 consists of the following predicates P/a, where a is the arity of P:

- $</2$, denoting a *strict linear order* on the domain,

- *Succ*/2, denoting the *successor* relation w.r.t. the order on the domain,
- *Min*/1 and *Max*/1, denoting the *smallest* and *largest* domain element
- *state* predicates $S_{qe}/1$, where $S_{qe}(t)$ is true precisely when the machine is in state q at time t in epoch e,
- *head* predicates $H_{\tau er}/2$, where $H_{\tau er}(t,p)$ is true precisely when at time t in epoch e, the head for tape τ is at position p in region r, and
- *tape* predicates $T_{s\tau er}/2$, where $T_{s\tau er}(t,p)$ is true precisely when at time t in epoch e, tape τ contains symbol $s \in \{0,1\}$ at position p in region r,
- *movement* predicates $\mathit{Left}_{\tau er}/2$ and $\mathit{Right}_{\tau er}/2$, where $\mathit{Left}_{\tau er}(t,p)$ is true precisely when the head on tape τ at time t in epoch e is to the left of p in region r (or when p, r is the first cell on its tape and the head is there), and *Right* is defined similarly, and
- *frame* predicate $\mathit{Unchanged}_{\tau er}/2$, where we have that $\mathit{Unchanged}_{\tau er}(t,p)$ is true precisely when position p in region r of tape τ did not change going from time t in epoch e to the next time step.

B.2 Sentences

To encode the Turing machine, we let Θ_1 consist of the following sentences.

1. $<$ is an arbitrary strict linear order (total, antisymmetric, irreflexive, and transitive):

$$\forall x, \forall y,\ \neg(x = y) \Rightarrow (x < y) \vee (y < x)$$
$$\forall x, \forall y,\ \neg(x < y) \vee \neg(y < x)$$
$$\forall x, \forall y, \forall z,\ (x < y) \wedge (y < z) \Rightarrow (x < z)$$

2. *Min* is the smallest element, and *Max* is the largest element:

$$\forall x,\ \mathit{Min}(x) \Leftrightarrow \neg\exists y, (y < x)$$
$$\forall x,\ \mathit{Max}(x) \Leftrightarrow \neg\exists y, (x < y)$$

3. *Succ* is the successor relation:

$$\forall x, \forall y,\ \mathit{Succ}(x,y) \Leftrightarrow (x < y) \wedge \neg\exists z, (x < z) \wedge (z < y)$$

4. At any time, the machine is in exactly one state:

$$\bigwedge_{q,q',e:q\neq q'} \forall t,\ \neg S_{qe}(t) \vee \neg S_{q'e}(t)$$
$$\bigwedge_{e} \forall t,\ \bigvee_{q} S_{qe}(t)$$

5. At any time, the head is in exactly one position per tape:

   (a) The head is in at least one position:

$$\bigwedge_{\tau,e} \forall t, \exists p, \bigvee_{r} H_{\tau er}(t,p)$$

   (b) The head is in at most one region:

$$\bigwedge_{\tau,e,r} \forall t, \forall p,\ H_{\tau er}(t,p) \Rightarrow \bigwedge_{r':r'\neq r} \forall p', \neg H_{\tau er'}(t,p')$$

   (c) The head is in at most one position per region:

$$\bigwedge_{\tau,e,r} \forall t, \forall p,\ H_{\tau er}(t,p) \Rightarrow \neg\exists p', \neg(p = p') \wedge H_{\tau er}(t,p')$$

6. At any time, each tape position has exactly one symbol:

$$\bigwedge_{\tau,e,r} \forall t, \forall p,\ T_{0\tau er}(t,p) \Leftrightarrow \neg T_{1\tau er}(t,p)$$

7. In the initial configuration of the TM (first time step),

   (a) it is in state q_1, and its heads are in the first position:

$$\forall x, \mathit{Min}(x) \Rightarrow S_{q_1 e_1}(x) \wedge \bigwedge_{\tau} H_{\tau e_1 r_1}(x,x)$$

   (b) the first (input) tape τ_1 contains n symbols 1 in the first region, followed by symbol 0 in all other regions (starting with cell $n+1$), and all other tapes τ_i contain symbol 0:

$$\forall t, \mathit{Min}(t) \Rightarrow \forall p, T_{1\tau_1 e_1 r_1}(t,p) \wedge \bigwedge_{i:i>1} T_{0\tau_1 e_1 r_i}(t,p) \wedge \bigwedge_{i,r:i>1} T_{0\tau_i e_1 r}(t,p)$$

8. An encoding of the transition relation δ. For example, that state q_a operates on tape τ_a, and that $\delta(q_a, 0) = \{(q_b, 1, L), (q_c, 0, R)\}$ is encoded into the following sentences.

   (a) What changed when t is before the end of an epoch (i.e., has a successor in the epoch):

$$\bigwedge_{e,r} \forall t, t', \forall p, \begin{bmatrix} S_{q_a e}(t) \\ \wedge H_{\tau_a er}(t,p) \\ \wedge T_{0\tau_a er}(t,p) \\ \wedge \mathit{Succ}(t,t') \end{bmatrix} \Rightarrow \begin{bmatrix} S_{q_b e}(t') \\ \wedge \mathit{Left}_{\tau_a er}(t',p) \\ \wedge T_{1\tau_a er}(t',p) \end{bmatrix} \vee \begin{bmatrix} S_{q_c e}(t') \\ \wedge \mathit{Right}_{\tau_a er}(t',p) \\ \wedge T_{0\tau_a er}(t',p) \end{bmatrix}$$

   (b) What changed when t is at the end of an epoch:

$$\bigwedge_{i,r:1\leq i<c} \forall t, t', \forall p, \begin{bmatrix} S_{q_a e_i}(t) \\ \wedge H_{\tau_a e_i r}(t,p) \\ \wedge T_{0\tau_a e_i r}(t,p) \\ \wedge \mathit{Max}(t) \\ \wedge \mathit{Min}(t') \end{bmatrix} \Rightarrow \begin{bmatrix} S_{q_b e_{i+1}}(t') \\ \wedge \mathit{Left}_{\tau_a e_{i+1} r}(t',p) \\ \wedge T_{1\tau_a e_{i+1} r}(t',p) \end{bmatrix} \vee \begin{bmatrix} S_{q_c e_{i+1}}(t') \\ \wedge \mathit{Right}_{\tau_a e_{i+1} r}(t',p) \\ \wedge T_{0\tau_a e_{i+1} r}(t',p) \end{bmatrix}$$

   (c) What does not change on the tapes: other cells in the region of τ_a where the head is, regions with no head, and tapes other than τ_a.

$$\bigwedge_{e,r} \forall t, \forall p, \left[\begin{array}{r} S_{q_a e}(t) \\ \wedge H_{\tau_a e r}(t,p) \end{array} \right]$$

$$\Rightarrow \forall p', (p = p') \vee \mathit{Unchanged}_{\tau_a e r}(t, p')$$

$$\bigwedge_{\tau,e,r} \forall t, \forall p, H_{\tau e r}(t,p)$$

$$\Rightarrow \bigwedge_{r':r' \neq r} \forall p, \mathit{Unchanged}_{\tau e r'}(t,p)$$

$$\bigwedge_{e} \forall t, S_{q_a e}(t)$$

$$\Rightarrow \bigwedge_{\tau,r:\tau \neq \tau_a} \forall p, \mathit{Unchanged}_{\tau e r}(t,p)$$

(d) The positions of the heads on tapes other than τ_a do not change:

$$\bigwedge_{\tau,e,r:\tau \neq \tau_a} \forall t, t', \forall p, \left[\begin{array}{r} S_{q_a e}(t) \\ \wedge H_{\tau e r}(t,p) \\ \wedge Succ(t,t') \end{array} \right]$$

$$\Rightarrow H_{\tau e r}(t', p)$$

$$\bigwedge_{\tau,i,r:\tau \neq \tau_a, 1 \leq i < c} \forall t, t', \forall p, \left[\begin{array}{r} S_{q_a e_i}(t) \\ \wedge H_{\tau e_i r}(t,p) \\ \wedge Max(t) \\ \wedge Min(t') \end{array} \right]$$

$$\Rightarrow H_{\tau e_{i+1} r}(t', p)$$

9. The movement predicates are defined as

$$\bigwedge_{\tau,e,r} \forall t, \forall p, p', \left[\begin{array}{r} \mathit{Left}_{\tau e r}(t,p) \\ \wedge Succ(p',p) \end{array} \right] \Leftrightarrow H_{\tau e r}(t,p')$$

$$\bigwedge_{\tau,e,i:1 \leq i < c} \forall t, \forall p, p', \left[\begin{array}{r} \mathit{Left}_{\tau e r_{i+1}}(t,p) \\ \wedge Min(p) \\ \wedge Max(p') \end{array} \right] \Leftrightarrow H_{\tau e r_i}(t,p')$$

$$\bigwedge_{\tau,e} \forall t, \forall p, \left[\begin{array}{r} \mathit{Left}_{\tau e r_1}(t,p) \\ \wedge Min(p) \end{array} \right] \Leftrightarrow H_{\tau e r_1}(t,p)$$

$$\bigwedge_{\tau,e,r} \forall t, \forall p, p', \left[\begin{array}{r} \mathit{Right}_{\tau e r}(t,p) \\ \wedge Succ(p,p') \end{array} \right] \Leftrightarrow H_{\tau e r}(t,p')$$

$$\bigwedge_{\tau,e,i:1 \leq i < c} \forall t, \forall p, p', \left[\begin{array}{r} \mathit{Right}_{\tau e r_i}(t,p) \\ \wedge Max(p) \\ \wedge Min(p') \end{array} \right] \Leftrightarrow H_{\tau e r_{i+1}}(t,p')$$

$$\bigwedge_{\tau,e} \forall t, \forall p, \left[\begin{array}{r} \mathit{Right}_{\tau e r_c}(t,p) \\ \wedge Max(p) \end{array} \right] \Leftrightarrow H_{\tau e r_c}(t,p)$$

10. The frame predicates are defined as

$$\bigwedge_{s,\tau,e,r} \forall t, t', \forall p, \left[\begin{array}{r} T_{s \tau e r}(t,p) \\ \wedge \mathit{Unchanged}_{\tau e r}(t,p) \\ \wedge Succ(t,t') \end{array} \right]$$

$$\Leftrightarrow T_{s \tau e r}(t', p)$$

$$\bigwedge_{s,\tau,i,r:1 \leq i < c} \forall t, t', \forall p, \left[\begin{array}{r} T_{s \tau e_i r}(t,p) \\ \wedge \mathit{Unchanged}_{\tau e_i r}(t,p) \\ \wedge Max(t) \\ \wedge Min(t') \end{array} \right]$$

$$\Leftrightarrow T_{s \tau e_{i+1} r}(t', p)$$

11. The machine terminates in an accepting state (e.g., q_1, q_5, q_{42}, etc.) :

$$\forall t, Max(t) \Rightarrow S_{q_1 e_c}(t) \vee S_{q_5 e_c}(t) \vee S_{q_{42} e_c}(t) \vee \ldots$$

It is easy to verify that Θ_1 uses at most three logical variables per sentence, and that Θ_1 is therefore in FO^3. Note that FO^3 permits variables to be reused within the same sentence.

For a fixed model of $</2$, that is, a fixed order on the domain, the models of Θ_1 for domain size n correspond one-to-one to the accepting computations of the TM on input n. Since there are exactly $(n!)$ models of $</2$, we can compute the number of accepting computations from the FOMC efficiently.

C. PTIME DATA COMPLEXITY FOR FO^2

The proof of the fact that the data complexity for FO^2 is in PTIME is spread over two references, [35] and [37]. We include here a brief proof, for completeness.

Given an FO^2 formula φ of size s, we start by applying the reduction in [17], which converts φ into a formula φ^* with the following properties:

- Every relational symbol occurring in φ^* has arity at most 2.
- Items 1 and 3 of Scott's reduction hold. (Item 2 becomes: φ^* has size $O(s \log s)$. In our case φ is fixed, so it suffices to note that the size of φ^* is $O(1)$.)

The reduction consists of Scott's reduction described above, plus the following transformation that ensures that all relational symbols have arity ≤ 2. Replace each relational atom of arity > 2 by a new unary or binary symbol, for example, replace the atoms $R(x, y, x)$, $R(y, y, y)$, $R(x, x, y)$ by $R_1(x, y)$, $R_2(x)$, $R_3(x, y)$. Then append to φ^* conjuncts asserting how the new relational symbols relate, for example $\forall x (R_1(x, x) \leftrightarrow R_2(x))$; we refer the reader to [17] for details.

We perform one more transformation: remove all existential quantifiers by using Lemma 3.3, thus transforming φ^* into a universally quantified sentences:

$$\varphi^* = \forall x \forall y \, \psi(x, y)$$

where $\psi(x, y)$ is a quantifier-free formula.

If φ^* contains any relational symbol R of arity zero then we perform a Shannon expansion and compute $P(\varphi^*) = \Pr(\varphi^*[R = \texttt{false}]) \cdot (1 - p(R)) + \Pr(\varphi^*[R = \texttt{true}]) \cdot p(R)$. Thus, we can assume w.l.o.g. that all relational symbols in φ^* have arity 1 or 2.

Assume first that all relational symbols in φ^* have arity 2. Then we write its lineage as:

$$F = \bigwedge_{a,b \in [n]:a<b} \psi(a, b) \wedge \bigwedge_{c \in [n]} \psi(c, c)$$

Since all atoms are binary, for any two distinct sets $\{a, b\} \neq \{a', b'\}$, the formulas $\psi(a, b)$ and $\psi(a', b')$ are independent probabilistic events, because they depend on disjoint sets of ground tuples: one depends on tuples of the form $R(a,b)$ or $R(b,a)$, the other on tuples of the form $R(a',b')$ or $R(b',a')$, and they are disjoint. (This would fail if ψ contained a unary atom, say $U(x)$, because we may have $a = a'$, $b \neq b'$, and in that case both formulas depend on the tuple $U(a)$.) Therefore:

$$\Pr(F) = \prod_{a,b\in[n]:a<b} \Pr(\psi(a,b)) \cdot \prod_{c\in[n]} \Pr(\psi(c,c))$$

Because the probabilities are symmetric, the quantity $p_1 = \Pr(\psi(a,b))$ is independent of a,b, while $p_2 = \Pr(\psi(c,c))$ is independent of c, and both can be computed in time $O(1)$. Therefore, $\Pr(\varphi) = \Pr(\varphi^*) = p(F) = p_1^{n(n-1)/2} p_2^n$. For a simple illustration, consider $\varphi^* = \forall x \forall y (R(x,y) \vee T(x,y)) \wedge (R(x,y) \vee T(y,x))$. Then:

$$\begin{aligned} F = & \bigwedge_{a,b\in[n]:a<b} (R(a,b) \vee T(a,b)) \wedge (R(a,b) \vee T(b,a)) \\ & \wedge (R(b,a) \vee T(b,a)) \wedge (R(b,a) \vee T(a,b)) \\ & \wedge \bigwedge_{c\in[n]} (R(c,c) \vee T(c,c)) \end{aligned}$$

and the probability is given by $p_1^{n(n-1)/2} p_2^n$ where $p_1 = \Pr((R(a,b) \vee T(a,b)) \wedge (R(a,b) \vee T(b,a)) \wedge (R(b,a) \vee T(b,a)) \wedge (R(b,a) \vee T(a,b)))$ and $p_2 = \Pr(R(c,c) \vee T(c,c))$, both quantities that can be computed using brute force.

Next consider the case when φ^* has both unary and binary relational symbols. Let $R_1, \ldots, R_m$ be all unary symbols. Consider the 2^m cells defined by conjunctions of these atoms or their negation, denote them $C_1, \ldots, C_{2^m}$; that is $C_1(x) \equiv \neg R_1(x) \wedge \cdots \wedge \neg R_m(x)$, ..., $C_{2^m}(x) \equiv R_1(x) \wedge \cdots \wedge R_m(x)$. Let P denote any partition of $[n]$ into 2^m disjoint sets, i.e. $P = (S_1, \ldots, S_{2^m})$ such that $S_1 \cup \cdots \cup S_{2^m} = [n]$. Denote $(C_1, \ldots, C_{2^m}) = P$ the event that the 2^m cells define precisely the partition P. Then, summing over all partitions P gives us:

$$\Pr(\varphi^*) = \sum_P \Pr(\varphi^* \wedge (C_1, \cdots, C_{2^m}) = P) \qquad (8)$$

Next, we split φ^* into a conjunction of several formulas, each x ranging over some cell S_i and y over some cell S_j:

$$\begin{aligned} \varphi^* = & \bigwedge_{i,j\in[2^m]:i<j} \forall x : S_i, \forall y : S_j, (\psi(x,y) \wedge \psi(y,x)) \\ & \wedge \bigwedge_{\ell\in[2^m]} \forall x : S_\ell, \forall y : S_\ell, \psi(x,y) \end{aligned}$$

When x ranges over S_i, then every unary predicate $R(x)$ containing the variable x is either true or false. Similarly, when y ranges over S_j, a predicate $R(y)$ is either true or false. Let $\psi_{ij}(x,y)$ (or $\psi_\ell(x,y)$) denote the formula $\psi(x,y) \wedge \psi(y,x)$ (or $\psi(x,y)$) where all the unary predicates have been replaced by true or false, according to the cells S_i, S_j (or S_ℓ respectively). Therefore:

$$\begin{aligned} \varphi^* = & \bigwedge_{i,j\in[2^m]:i<j} \forall x : S_i, \forall y : S_j, \psi_{ij}(x,y) \\ & \wedge \bigwedge_{\ell\in[2^m]} \forall x : S_\ell, \forall y : S_\ell, \psi_\ell(x,y) \end{aligned}$$

Notice that ψ_{ij} and ψ_ℓ have only binary predicates. All conjuncts in the expression above are independent probabilistic events: if $\{i_1, j_1\} \neq \{i_2, j_2\}$ then $\forall x : S_{i_1}, \forall y : S_{j_1}, \psi_{i_1 j_1}(x,y)$ and $\forall x : S_{i_2}, \forall y : S_{j_2}, \psi_{i_2 j_2}(x,y)$ are independent. Therefore, denoting $n_i = |S_i|$ for $i = 1, 2^m$, we have: $\Pr(\varphi^* \wedge (C_1, \cdots, C_{2^m}) = P) = \prod_{i,j\in[2^m]:i<j} q_{ij} \cdot \prod_{\ell\in[2^m} r_\ell$, where:

$$\begin{aligned} q_{ij} = & \Pr(\forall x : S_i, \forall y : S_j, \psi_{ij}(x,y)) \\ = & \prod_{a\in S_i, b\in S_j} \Pr(\psi_{ij}(a,b)) = r_{ij}^{n_i n_j} \\ r_\ell = & \Pr(\forall x : S_\ell, \forall y : S_\ell, \psi_\ell(x,y)) \\ = & \prod_{a,b\in S_\ell:a<b} \Pr(\psi_\ell(a,b) \wedge \psi_\ell(b,a)) \cdot \prod_{c\in S_\ell} \Pr(\psi_\ell(c,c)) \\ = & s_\ell^{n_\ell*(n_\ell-1)/2} \cdot t_\ell^{n_\ell} \end{aligned}$$

where $r_{ij} = \Pr(\psi_{ij}(a,b))$, $s_\ell = \Pr(\psi_\ell(a,b) \wedge \psi_\ell(b,a))$, and $t_\ell = \Pr(\psi_\ell(c,c))$ are independent of the choices of a,b,c respectively, and can be computed by brute force in time $O(1)$. Finally, we use the fact that the probabilities are symmetric, which implies that the expression in Eq. (8) depends only on the cell cardinalities $n_1, \ldots, n_{2^m}$, and not on the actual cells $S_1, \ldots, S_{2^m}$. Therefore:

$$\begin{aligned} \Pr(\varphi^*) = & \sum_{n_1,\ldots,n_{2^m}:n_1+\cdots+n_{2^m}=1} \frac{n!}{n_1! \cdots n_{2^m}!} \\ & \cdot r_{ij}^{n_i n_j} s_\ell^{n_\ell*(n_\ell-1)/2} \cdot t_\ell^{n_\ell} \end{aligned}$$

For a simple illustration, consider $\varphi^* = \forall x \forall y (R(x) \vee U(x,y) \vee T(y)) \wedge (\neg R(x) \vee \neg U(x,y) \vee \neg T(y))$. Denoting the four cells $\neg R \wedge \neg T$, $\neg R \wedge T$, $R \wedge \neg T$, $R \wedge T$ by $C_1, \ldots C_4$ respectively, we split φ into a conjunct of $6 + 4$ expressions, such that in each expression x and y are restricted to the domains C_i and C_j respectively, for $i \leq j$. Denoting $n_1, \ldots, n_4$ the sizes of these cells, we have:

$$\Pr(\varphi^*) = \sum_{n_1+\cdots+n_4=n} \frac{n!}{n_1! n_2! n_3! n_4!} r_{ij}^{n_i n_j} s_\ell^{n_\ell*(n_\ell-1)/2} \cdot t_\ell^{n_\ell}$$

where $r_{12} = \Pr(U(a,b))$ (because $\forall x : S_1, \forall y : S_2, (R(x) \vee U(x,y) \vee T(y)) \wedge (\neg R(x) \vee \neg U(x,y) \vee \neg T(y)) \equiv \forall x : S_1, \forall y : S_2, T(x,y))$, and similarly for the others.

Smooth Tradeoffs between Insert and Query Complexity in Nearest Neighbor Search

Michael Kapralov
IBM Watson
Yorktown Heights, NY, USA
michael.kapralov@gmail.com

ABSTRACT

Locality Sensitive Hashing (LSH) has emerged as the method of choice for high dimensional similarity search, a classical problem of interest in numerous applications. LSH-based solutions require that each data point be inserted into a number A of hash tables, after which a query can be answered by performing B lookups. The original LSH solution of [IM98] showed for the first time that both A and B can be made sublinear in the number of data points. Unfortunately, the classical LSH solution does not provide any tradeoff between insert and query complexity, whereas for data (respectively, query) intensive applications one would like to minimize insert time by choosing a smaller A (respectively, minimize query time by choosing a smaller B). A partial remedy for this is provided by Entropy LSH [Pan06], which allows to make either inserts or queries essentially constant time at the expense of a loss in the other parameter, but no algorithm that achieves a smooth tradeoff is known.

In this paper, we present an algorithm for performing similarity search under the Euclidean metric that resolves the problem above. Our solution is inspired by Entropy LSH, but uses a very different analysis to achieve a smooth tradeoff between insert and query complexity. Our results improve upon or match, up to lower order terms in the exponent, best known data-oblivious algorithms for the Euclidean metric.

1. INTRODUCTION

Similarity search is a classical problem of interest to numerous applications in data-mining such as duplicate detection, content-based search [KG09, LJW+07], collaborative filtering [DDGR07], pattern classification [CH67], clustering [Ber02]. In the similarity search problem the algorithm is given a database of objects to preprocess and is then required to find, for each query object q, the object in the database that is closest to q in some metric. In these applications, objects in the database are usually represented by high dimensional feature vectors, resulting in a nearest neighbor search problem in $\mathbb{R}^d$ under an appropriate metric. In this paper, we consider the Euclidean metric, or ℓ_2.

PODS'15, May 31–June 4, 2015, Melbourne, Victoria, Australia.

http://dx.doi.org/10.1145/2745754.2745761.

For the exact nearest neighbor problem a family of tree-based approaches have been developed such as K-D trees [Ben75], cover trees [BKL06], navigating nets [KL04], R-trees [Gut84], and SR-trees [KS97]. However, the performance of these techniques degrades very fast with the dimensionality of the problem (known as the 'curse of dimensionality') and in fact degrades to a linear scan of the data quite quickly [WSB98]. Since the exact version of the nearest neighbor problem suffers from the 'curse of dimensionality', substantial attention has been devoted to the *Approximate Nearest Neighbor Problem.* In this problem, instead of reporting the closest point to the query q, the algorithm only needs to return a point that is at most a factor $c > 1$ further away from q than its nearest neighbor in the database. Specifically, let $D = \{p_1, \dots, p_N\}$ denote a database of points, where $p_i \in \mathbb{R}^d, i = 1, \dots, N$. In the Euclidean *c-Approximate Nearest Neighbor* problem one is required to report, for each query q, a point $\hat{p} \in D$ such that

$$||q - \hat{p}||_2 \leq c \cdot \min_{p \in D} ||q - p||_2.$$

One can see [IM98, KOR98] that this problem reduces, with a slight overhead in space and time, to the so-called (c, r)-*Near Neighbor* problem ((c, r)-NN for short). In the (c, r)-NN problem the goal is to return a data point within distance cr of the query point q if a data point within distance r of q exists. The simple reduction from the c-Approximate Near Neighbor problem to the (c, r)-NN problem can be obtained by considering a sequence of geometrically increasing radii r, which increases the space and time requirement only by a logarithmic factor.

Locality Sensitive Hashing (LSH) has emerged as the method of choice for the (c, r)-NN problem [IM98]. LSH is based on a special hashing scheme such that similar points have a higher chance of getting mapped to the same buckets than distant points. Then for each query, the nearest neighbor among the data points mapped to the same bucket as the query point is returned as the search result. We now describe the LSH approach formally. We start with the definition of a *locality sensitive family* of hash functions:

DEFINITION 1. *Let the space $\mathbb{R}^d$ be equipped with a norm $||\cdot||$, let $r \geq 0$ be a distance threshold, let $c > 1$. A family of hash functions $\mathcal{H} = \{h : \mathbb{R}^d \to \mathcal{U}\}$ is said to be a (r, cr, p_1, p_2)-LSH family if for all $x, y \in \mathbb{R}^d$,* **(1)** *if $||x - y|| \leq r$, then $\mathbf{Pr}_{h\in\mathcal{H}}[h(x) = h(y)] \geq p_1$; and* **(2)** *if $||x - y|| \geq cr$, then $\mathbf{Pr}_{h\in\mathcal{H}}[h(x) = h(y)] \leq p_2$.*

Points $x, y \in \mathbb{R}^d$ are called *near* points in the former case and *far* points in the latter. An LSH family can be used to obtain the following solution to the (c, r)-NN problem:

THEOREM 2 ([IM98]). *Let $\mathcal{H}$ denote a (r, cr, p_1, p_2)-LSH family for a norm $||\cdot||$ on $\mathbb{R}^d$. Then $\mathcal{H}$ can be used to solve the (c, r)-NN problem with norm $||\cdot||$ on a database D on N points using space $dN^{1+\rho+o(1)}$ and query time $dN^{\rho+o(1)}$ as long as $p_1 \geq N^{-o(1)}$, where $\rho = \frac{\log(1/p_1)}{\log(1/p_2)}$.*

The algorithm that yields Theorem 2 hashes the points in the database into N^ρ/p_1 hash tables, resulting in space usage $dN^\rho/p_1 = dN^{\rho+o(1)}$. Then for each query lookups are performed in N^ρ/p_1 tables, resulting in the stated query time. As seen from Theorem 2, the ratio $\rho = \frac{\log(1/p_1)}{\log(1/p_2)}$ governs the quality of the solution provided by LSH, so constructing LSH families with the smallest possible ρ is crucial. The original paper [IM98] exhibited an LSH familty for the Hamming cube with $\rho \leq 1/c$. For the Euclidean metric, which we consider in this paper, a simple and practical LSH familty achieving $\rho \leq \frac{1}{c}$ was constructed in [DIIM04]. An LSH familty achieving $\rho = \frac{1}{c^2} + o(1)$ was constructed in [AI, And09]. This dependence of ρ on c is optimal [MNP06, OWZ11]. The LSH scheme of [AI] implements the *ball-carving* approach. First, the points of the database are projected to a smaller *reduced space* $\mathbb{R}^n$, where $n \ll \log N$. Then the reduced space $\mathbb{R}^n$ is covered by randomly shifted grids of Euclidean balls, and each point in the reduced space is hashed to the lexicographically first ball that covers it. We will use a similar approach as our basic hashing scheme in this paper (see Algorithm 1 in section 3).

The main disadvantage of the conventional LSH indexing scheme is the relatively large number (in practice, up to hundreds [GIM99]) of hash tables required for good search quality. This imposes large space requirements and insert time. To mitigate the space inefficiency, Panigrahy [Pan] introduced the Entropy LSH scheme, which uses only $\tilde{O}(1)$ hash tables as opposed to $N^{1/c}$:

THEOREM 3 ([PAN]). *There exists a data structure for solving the (c, r)-NN problem under the ℓ_2 metric in $\mathbb{R}^d$ that uses $\tilde{O}(N)$ space and $\tilde{O}(N^{2.06/c})$ query time for sufficiently large $c > 1$.*

This result guarantees extremely small space (or, insert time) at the expense of an increase of query time from $N^{1/c}$ of [IM98] to $N^{2.06/c}$. Alternatively, [Pan] also showed that the query time can be made very efficient (constant time) at the expense of larger space requirements:

THEOREM 4 ([PAN]). *There exists a data structure for solving the (c, r)-NN problem under the ℓ_2 metric in $\mathbb{R}^d$ that uses $\tilde{O}(N^{1/(1-2.06/c)})$ space and polylogarithmic query time.*

In [And09] an algorithm inspired by Entropy LSH is given that achieves $\tilde{O}(n)$ space and query time $N^{O(1/c^2)}$ for the same setting.

As seen from the above, despite its efficiency, the classical LSH solution does not provide any tradeoff between the insert and query complexity. However, for data (respectively, query) intensive workloads one would like to minimize one parameter, even if it entails an increase in the other. Entropy LSH provides a partial remedy for this, allowing to make either inserts or queries extremely efficient ($N^{o(1)}$ time per point) at the expense of a loss in the other parameter, but no algorithm that achieves a *smooth tradeoff* is known. In this paper we provide the first algorithm for nearest neighbor search that achieves a smooth tradeoff between insert and query complexity, improving upon or matching known results for parameter settings that algorithms were known for before.

Our results.

As before, we denote the database of points by $D = \{p_1, \ldots, p_N\}$. Our main result is

THEOREM 5. *Let $\alpha \in [0, 1]$ be a constant. Let $c \geq 1$ be the desired approximation ratio, and assume that $c^2 \geq 3(1-\alpha)^2 - \alpha^2 + \delta$ for a small constant $\delta > 0$. Then there exists a data structure for the (c, r)-NN problem under ℓ_2 with $dN^{\alpha^2\rho_\alpha+o(1)}$ insert time[1], $dN^{(1-\alpha)^2\rho_\alpha+o(1)}$ query time and space $dN^{1+\alpha^2\rho_\alpha(1+o(1))}$, where $\rho_\alpha = \frac{4}{c^2+(1-\alpha)^2-3\alpha^2}$. Furthermore, setting $\alpha = 0$ results in a data structure with space dN, and $\alpha = 1$ results in a single probe data structure. The success probability is $1 - o(1)$ for any fixed query.*

We note that the constraint on the approximation ratio c is only nontrivial when one is interested in very low query complexity, i.e. α is close to 1. When $\alpha = 1$, our condition constrains c to be strictly larger than $\sqrt{3}$. This constraint is inherent to the approach, and is also inherent in Entropy LSH (see Theorem 4 above, where c is required to be larger than a constant).

Note that setting $\alpha = 0$, we get a data structure with space dN, $dN^{o(1)}$ insert time and $dN^{\frac{4}{c^2+1}}$ query time. Prior to our work, the best known scheme with linear space and $O(1/c^2)$ dependence of the exponent was due to [And09], where $dN^{O(1/c^2)}$ dependence was achieved with unspecified constant in the $O(\cdot)$ notation. Setting $\alpha = 1/2$, we obtain a data structure with $dN^{1/c^2+o(1/c^2)}$ insert and query time, as well as $dN^{1+1/(c^2-1/2)+o(1)}$ space, matching, up to lower order terms, the best known exponent of $1/c^2$ obtained in [AI, And09]. Setting $\alpha = 1$, we obtain a single probe data structure with $dN^{4/(c^2-3)+o(1)}$ insert time that succeeds with probability $1 - o(1)$. The query time is $dN^{o(1)}$ and the space is $dN^{1+4/(c^2-3)+o(1)}$.

It is interesting to note that, unlike Entropy LSH, which requires knowledge of the distance between near points up to $1 \pm o(1)$ factor, our scheme only needs an *upper bound* on the distance between near points, similarly to the classical construction of [IM98]. Also, interestingly, our approach yields success probability $1 - o(1)$ even in the linear space or single probe regime, as opposed to $\Omega(1/\log N)$ success probability provided by Entropy LSH [Pan].

Our techniques.

At a high level, our algorithm is a natural interpolation between two extremes of Entropy LSH (Theorem 3 and Theorem 4). The algorithm is parameterized by a $\alpha \in [0, 1]$,

[1] Note that our expressions for runtime have a extra *additive* $o(1)$ term in the exponent. This term is due to the time needed to evaluate our hash function. On the other hand, the space complexity only suffers from a *multiplicative* $1 + o(1)$ loss in the exponent. The latter loss is zero at the extreme points, where $\alpha = 0$ or $\alpha = 1$, yielding strictly linear space ($\alpha = 0$) and single probe ($\alpha = 1$) data structures with success probability $1 - o(1)$ respectively.

which governs the tradeoff between the insert and query complexity. Our data structure uses exactly one random hash function, which is selected at initialization. In order to insert a data point p into the data structure, we project p to a reduced space $\mathbb{R}^n$ using a dimensionality reduction matrix S, generate $A = N^{\alpha^2 \rho_\alpha (1+o(1))}$ perturbations $Sp + u^i, i = 1, \ldots, A$ of p, and insert p into buckets that these perturbations $Sp + u^i$ hash to. The magnitude of the perturbation u^i is proportional to α. Similarly, given a query q, we generate $B = N^{(1-\alpha)^2 \rho_\alpha (1+o(1))}$ perturbations $Sq + v^j, j = 1, \ldots, B$ of q, examine buckets that these perturbations $Sq + v^j$ hash to, and return the closest point found (see Fig. 2) . The magnitude of the perturbation v^j is proportional to $1 - \alpha$.

While our algorithm is inspired by [Pan], our analysis is fundamentally different. In [Pan] correctness of hashing schemes is argued using an entropy based approach. One shows that for a random hash function and two near points p, q the conditional entropy I of $\mathbf{h}(p)$ given $\mathbf{h}$ and q is small, and then generates about 2^I samples from this conditional distribution. This many samples are sufficient to ensure a collision with nontrivial probability. In [And09] Andoni achieves the nearly optimal $O(1/c^2)$ dependence of the exponent on the approximation parameter c at the expense of introducing a more complex framework that still relies on entropy considerations.

In this paper, we take a more direct approach to analyzing our algorithm, avoiding entropy-based arguments altogether. In order to achieve correctness, we need to prove two statements: lower bounds on collision probability for (perturbations of)near points, and upper bounds on collision probability for (perturbations of)far points. For the first claim, we need to prove that for a given pair of near points p, q, with high probability over the choice of the hash function $\mathbf{h}$ and the perturbations $u^i, i = 1, \ldots, A, v^j, j = 1, \ldots, B$ (see Fig. 2) at least one of $Sp + u^i$ collides with at least one of $Sq + v^j$ under our hash function. This claim turns out to be rather delicate: we cannot prove that a fixed perturbation $Sp + u^i$ is likely to collide with at least one of the perturbations $Sq + v^j$ since this is simply not true. One can prove, for example, that a given perturbation $Sp + u^i$ collides with at least one of the $Sq + v^j$'s with nontrivial probability, but that does not lead to the result since such events for different u^i's are dependent (via the q^j's). Instead, we define a point $z := (1 - \alpha)p + \alpha q$ lying on the line segment between p and q, and show that **(a)** at least one of $Sp + u^i$'s collides with Sz under $\mathbf{h}$ with probability $1 - o(1)$ and **(b)** at least one of $Sq + v^j$'s collides with z with probability $1 - o(1)$. A union bound over the failure events for these two claims yields the result.

The proof of the upper bound on the collision probability is also somewhat subtle, and requires a careful setting of parameters. The main issue is that we need to argue about the probability that the pair of points $Sp + u^i, Sq + v^j$ collide under hashing. This probability depends on the distribution of the vector $(Sp + u^i) - (Sq + v^j)$, which is not particularly simple, for example, when u^i and v^j are sampled uniformly from a ball of fixed radius (the most convenient setting for the first claim). To remedy this, we sample the perturbations u^i, v^j from balls whose radii are sampled from an appropriate distribution, so that u^i, v^j are vectors of independent Guassians. Since $S(p - q)$ is Gaussian, this ensures that the vector $(Sp + u^i) - (Sq + v^j) = S(p - q) + u^i - v^j$ is a vector of independent Gaussians, making analysis a manageable task.

Related work.

The problem of proving lower bounds for nearest neighbor search has received a lot of attention in the literature. The results of [MNP06, OWZ11] Euclidean metric show that $\rho = 1/c^2 + o(1)$ achieved by LSH functions of [AI] is best possible up to lower order terms. The results of [PTW08, PTW] show that that single-probe algorithms for (c, r)-NN under the Euclidean metric must use $N^{1+\Omega(1/c^2)}$ space (these lower bounds hold for the cell probe model). In a recent paper [AINR14] showed how to use LSH functions in a more efficient way than Theorem 2 to obtain better space and query time, namely $N^{1+(7/8)/c^2}$ space and $N^{(7/8)/c^2}$ query time for large c. Unlike previous works, their approach is *data-dependent*: the family of LSH functions is chosen carefully as a function of the database as opposed to sampled uniformly at random from a fixed distribution. It would be very interesting to see if similar analysis can be used to improve our tradeoffs.

Organization.

We give some definitions and relevant results from probability and high dimensional geometry in section 2. The algorithm is presented in section 3. The analysis is presented in section 4. An outline of the analysis is given in section 4.1, some technical lemmas are presented in section 4.2. Upper and lower bounds on collision probability of far and near points respectively are given in sections 4.3 and 4.4 respectively, and are put together in section 4.5 to obtain a proof of Theorem 5. Proofs of main technical lemmas are given in section 5.

2. PRELIMINARIES

DEFINITION 6. *The Gamma distribution with shape parameter $k > 0$ and scale $\theta > 0$, denoted by $\Gamma(k, \theta)$, has the pdf $\frac{1}{\Gamma(k)\theta^k} x^{k-1} e^{-x/\theta}$.*

CLAIM 7. *[BGMN05] Let $X \sim \frac{1}{\sqrt{\pi}} e^{-|x_i|^2}$. Then $|X|^2 \sim \Gamma(1/2, 1)$.*

We will define the distribution $\mathcal{D} \sim 2\Gamma(n/2 + 1, 1)$, where n is the dimension of our reduced space (see section 3 below). This distribution will be used extensively throughout the algorithm. For any real t we write $t \cdot \mathcal{D}$ to denote the distribution of $t \cdot X$, where $X \sim \mathcal{D}$. We write $\mathcal{N}(0, I_n)$ to denote the Gaussian distibution on $\mathbb{R}^n$ with covariance matrix I_n.

CLAIM 8. *Let $X \geq 0$ be a random variable. For any event $\mathcal{E}$ one has $\mathbf{E}[X|\mathcal{E}] \leq \frac{1}{\mathbf{Pr}[\mathcal{E}]} \mathbf{E}[X]$.*

In what follows for a vector x we write $||x||$ or $||x||_2$ to denote the ℓ_2-norm of x. We write $\mathbb{B}_R(x)$ to denote the ℓ_2 ball of radius R around x, and write $|\mathbb{B}_R(x)|$ to denote the volume of $\mathbb{B}_R(x)$. Let $C(u, r)$ denote the volume of the spherical cap at distance u from the center of a ball $\mathbb{B}_r(0)$. Let $I(u, r) = \frac{C(u,r)}{|\mathbb{B}_r(0)|}$ be the relative cap volume.

LEMMA 9. *Let $a, w \in \mathbb{R}^n$. Let $r, R \in \mathbb{R}^+$ be parameters, and suppose that $R > r$. Let $d = ||a - w||_2$. Let $x = \frac{r^2+d^2-R^2}{2d}$. If $x > 0$, then*

$$I(x) \leq \frac{|\mathbb{B}_r(a) \cap \mathbb{B}_R(w)|}{|\mathbb{B}_r(a)|} \leq 2I(x).$$

We will use

LEMMA 10. *[[AI], Lemma 2.1] For any $n \geq 2$ and $0 \leq u \leq r$ one has $\frac{C'}{\sqrt{n}}\left(1 - \left(\frac{u}{r}\right)^2\right)^{n/2} \leq I(u, r) \leq \left(1 - \left(\frac{u}{r}\right)^2\right)^{n/2}$, where C' is an absolute constant.*

3. THE ALGORITHM

In this section we describe our algorithm. We denote data points by $p \in \mathbb{R}^d$, and query points by $q \in \mathbb{R}^d$. The number of points in the database is denoted by N, as before. In the preprocessing stage for each point p we perform the following operation K times independently (we index the independent repetitions by $l = 1, \ldots, K$). First, we project p down to dimension $n \ll \log N$ using a dimensionality reduction matrix S_l. Then we perturb $S_l p$ by an appropriately chosen vector of independent Gaussians (the magnitude of the perturbation is proportional α). Finally, we hash the perturbed points using a ball-carving approach described below (see BASICHASH). Thus, for each perturbation of p and for each l we obtain a hash value. We concatenate these values and hash point p into the corresponding bucket. The query phase is analogous, the only difference is the magnitude of the perturbations (specified below). We now describe these steps in details.

Dimensionality reduction.

Let $S \in \mathbb{R}^{(K \cdot n) \times d}$ denote a matrix of independent Gaussians of unit variance. We partition the rows of S into K blocks, corresponding to K hash functions. Thus $S_l \in \mathbb{R}^{n \times d}$ is the dimensionality reduction matrix for the l-th hash function. Since entries of S are chosen as Gaussians with unit variance, for any $p, q \in \mathbb{R}^d$ we have $S_l(p - q) \sim ||p - q||_2 \cdot \mathcal{N}(0, I_n)$. We will also write $Sp \in R^{K \cdot n}$ for $p \in \mathbb{R}^d$ to denote the concatenation of $S_l p$'s.

Perturbation..

Let d_{near} denote the distance between near points in the original space $\mathbb{R}^d$ (this corresponds to the radius r in the (c, r)-NN problem). For each l the perturbations of a projected data point p are of the form $S_l p + u_l^i$, $i = 1, \ldots, A$, where $u_l^i \sim \alpha d_{near} \cdot \mathcal{N}(0, I_n)$. Note that by Lemma 14 this is the same as first sampling a radius $r_{p,l}$ so that $r_{p,l}^2 \sim (\alpha d_{near})^2 \cdot \mathcal{D}$, and then sampling u_l^i uniformly from the ball $\mathbb{B}_{r_{p,l}}(0)$ (see Algorithm 2). The perturbation for query points is analogous: for each l the perturbations of a projected query point q are obtained as $S_l q + v_l^j$, $j = 1, \ldots, B$, where $v_l^j \sim (1 - \alpha) d_{near} \cdot \mathcal{N}(0, I_n)$ (see Algorithm 3).

Ball-carving.

We use the ball-carving approach of [AI] as the basic scheme, i.e. we first project point in $\mathbb{R}^d$ down to smaller dimension $n = o(\log N)$, and then perform ball-carving in the reduced space $\mathbb{R}^n$. We will use ball-carving with ℓ_2 balls as the basic scheme. The (expected) distance between near points after dimensionality reduction will be at most $d_{near}\sqrt{n}$ for $d_{near} = n^{-1/4}$, the distance between far points will be at least $c \cdot d_{near}\sqrt{n}$. We will be carving with Euclidean balls of radius R_l, for $l = 1, \ldots, K$. The radii R_l are sampled independently from the distribution $R_l^2 \sim \mathcal{D}$ at the beginning of the algorithm and passed as a parameters to all functions (see Algorithms 1, 2 and 3).

We now describe how the reduced space $\mathbb{R}^n$ is covered by Euclidean balls. For each $l = 1, \ldots, K$ let $\mathcal{U}_l$ denote a subset of $[0, \sqrt{\pi} n R_l]^n$ of size

$$\begin{aligned} T &= (C \log N) \cdot \frac{(\sqrt{\pi} n R_l)^n}{\text{vol}(\mathbb{B}_{R_l}(0))} \\ &= (C \log N) \cdot \frac{(\sqrt{\pi} n R_l)^n}{\pi^{n/2}\Gamma(n/2+1)R_l^n} \\ &= (C \log N) \cdot \frac{n^n}{(n/2)!} \end{aligned} \tag{1}$$

sampled uniformly at random. Here $C > 0$ is an appropriately large constant, and N is the number of points in the database. Note that T is integer as long as n is even and $(C \log N) \geq 1$ is an integer, which we assume from now on. Let $\mathcal{G} := (\sqrt{\pi} n R) \cdot \mathbb{Z}^n$ denote an infinite grid of scaled integer points. Our basic hashing function BASICHASH, for each l, will map the input point to one of the balls of radius R_l centered at shifts $u + \mathcal{G}$ of the grid, for $u \in \mathcal{U}_l$ (note that the balls centered at different grid points do not overlap) . More precisely, for each $l \in [1 : K]$ the centers of the balls are given by

$$\mathcal{W}_l := \mathcal{U}_l + \mathcal{G},$$

where we use the notation $S_1 + S_2 = \{a + b : a \in S_1, b \in S_2\}$ for $S_1, S_2 \subset \mathbb{R}^n$. We refer to points in $\mathcal{W}_l$ as *centers*. First note that for any l a ball of radius R_l around any point $x \in \mathbb{R}^d$ contains exactly $C \log N$ centers in $\mathcal{W}_l$ in expectation by choice of parameters. We will need the fact that with high probability over the choice of $\mathcal{U}_l$ all perturbed points below have about $C \log N$ centers in the ball of radius R_l around them. We now make this precise. Fix a constant $\alpha \in [0, 1]$. Let p, q denote a query and its near point. Define the event

$$\begin{aligned} \mathcal{E}^*(p, q) := \Big\{ &\mathbb{B}_{R_l}(S_l p + u_l^i) \cap \mathcal{W}_l \leq 2C \log N \\ &\text{and} \\ &\mathbb{B}_{R_l}(S_l q + v_l^j) \cap \mathcal{W}_l \leq 2C \log N \text{ for all } i, j, l \Big\}. \end{aligned} \tag{2}$$

One has

CLAIM 11. *Let $\alpha \in [0, 1]$ be a constant. Let $c \geq 1$ be the desired approximation ratio, and assume that $c^2 \geq 3(1 - \alpha)^2 - \alpha^2 + \delta$ for an arbitrarily small constant $\delta > 0$, as in Theorem 5. Suppose that the constant C in (1) is sufficienlty large. Then for any pair of points p, q one has $\mathbf{Pr}[\mathcal{E}^*(p, q)] \geq 1 - 1/N$.*

PROOF. Recall that by assumption of Theorem 5 one has $c^2 \geq 3(1 - \alpha)^2 - \alpha^2 + \delta$ for a constant $\delta > 0$, so the number of perturbations is always bounded by $N^{8/\delta}$, say.

Fix l. Then by standard concentration inequalities on has

$$\mathbf{Pr}[|\mathbb{B}_{R_l}(S_l p + u_l^i) \cap \mathcal{W}_l| > 2C \log N] < N^{-8/\delta - 2}$$

for any i, and

$$\mathbf{Pr}[|\mathbb{B}_{R_l}(S_l q + v_l^i) \cap \mathcal{W}_l| > 2C \log N] < N^{-8/\delta - 2}$$

for any j as long as the constant C is sufficiently large. Now the claim follows by a union bound over all $l = 1, \ldots, K$ and at most $2N^{8/\delta}$ perturbations of p and q. $\square$

The basic hash function simply returns such a center if it is unique, and a uniformly random element of a large universe otherwise:

Algorithm 1 ℓ_2-ball carving LSH for ℓ_2: hashing data points

```
procedure BasicHash(x, R, n, W)
    If |W* ∩ B_R(x)| ≠ 1 return UNIF([0,1]^n)    ▷ If no center falls into B_R(x), return a random element of a large universe
    return a uniformly random element of W* ∩ B_R(x)
end procedure
```

The function BasicHash can be evaluated in time $n^{O(n)}$, which we will ensure to be $N^{o(1)}$ below (see Claim 24 in Appendix A for the runtime bound).

Algorithm 2 ℓ_2-ball carving LSH for ℓ_2: hashing data points

```
procedure HashData(p, α, S, K, {R_l}_{l=1}^K, B, n, , {U_l}_{l=1}^K, d_near)
    ▷ We have d_near = n^{-1/4} and R_l ≈ √n
    for l = 1, ..., K do
        Sample r_{p,l}^2 ~ (α d_near)^2 · D.
    end for
    for j = 1, ..., A do ▷ Generating A points around p
        for l = 1, ..., K do
            u_l^i ← UNIF(B_{r_{p,l}}(0))
                            ▷ So that u_l^i ~ (α d_near)^2 · N(0, I_n)
            h_l ← BasicHash(S_l p + u_l^i, R_l, n, U_l)
        end for
        Put(h, p)                ▷ Insert ⟨h, p⟩ into hash table
    end for
end procedure
```

Queries are performed as follows:

Algorithm 3 ℓ_2-ball carving LSH for ℓ_2: query

```
procedure Query(q, α, S, K, {R_l}_{l=1}^K, A, n, {U_l}_{l=1}^K, d_near)
    ▷ We have d_near = n^{-1/4} and R_l ≈ √n
    T ← ∅                                   ▷ Candidate points
    for l = 1, ..., K do
        Sample r_{q,l}^2 ~ ((1 − α) d_near)^2 · D.
    end for
    for i = 1, ..., B do ▷ Generating B points around q
        for l = 1, ..., K do
            v_l^i ← UNIF(B_{r_{q,l}}(0))
                     ▷ So that v_l^j ~ ((1 − α) d_near)^2 · N(0, I_n)
            h_l ← BasicHash(S_l q + v_l^i, R_l, n, U_l)
        end for
        If |T| > N^{(1−α)^2 ρ_α + o(1)} then break
        T ← T ∪ Get(h)
                  ▷ Retrieve at most N^{(1−α)^2 ρ_α + o(1)} points
    end for
    return closest point to q in T
end procedure
```

Note that the main difference between Algorithms 2 and 3 is the magnitude of the perturbations to projected points (see Fig. 1). We gather useful properties of random variables used in Algorithms 2 and 3 below.

Claim 12. *Let p be a data point, let q be a query point such that $p - q = \lambda d_{near}$. Let $i \in [A], j \in [B], l \in [K]$. Then the vector $(S_l p + u_l^i) - ((S_l q + v_l^j)$ is uniformly random in the ball $\mathbb{B}_{r'}(0)$, where*

$$(r')^2 \sim (\lambda^2 + \alpha^2 + (1-\alpha)^2) d_{near}^2 \cdot \mathcal{D}.$$

and $(S_l p + u_l^i) - (S_l q + v_l^j) \sim \sqrt{\lambda^2 + \alpha^2 + (1-\alpha)^2} d_{near} \cdot \mathcal{N}(0, I_n)$.

Proof. Recall that u_l^i is sampled uniformly at random from $\mathbb{B}_{r_{p,l}}(0)$, where $r_{p,l}^2 \sim (\alpha d_{near})^2 \cdot \mathcal{D}$. By Corollary 15 we thus have that $u_l^i \sim \alpha d_{near} \cdot \mathcal{N}(0, I_n)$. Similarly, $v_l^j \sim (1-\alpha) d_{near} \cdot \mathcal{N}(0, I_n)$. Also, $S_l p - S_l q \sim \gamma d_{near} \cdot \mathcal{N}(0, I_n)$ by the choice of S and 2-stability of the Gaussian disrtibution. Thus, we have

$$(S_l p + u_l^i) - (S_l q + v_l^j) \sim$$
$$\sqrt{||p-q||_2^2 + \alpha^2 d_{near}^2 + (1-\alpha)^2 d_{near}^2} \cdot \mathcal{N}(0, I_n).$$

The distribution of $(r')^2$ follows by Corollary 15. $\square$

Claim 13. *Let $x \in \mathbb{R}^d$. Let $w_l :=$ BasicHash$(S_l x, R_l, n, \mathcal{U}_l)$, and condition on $\mathcal{E}^*$. Then w_l is a uniformly random point in $\mathbb{B}_{R_l}(x)$. In particular, $w_l - x \sim \mathcal{N}(0, I_n)$.*

Proof. By conditioning on $\mathcal{E}^*$ the output of BasicHash is a center in $\mathcal{W}_l$. Since BasicHash outputs a uniformly random center that falls into $\mathbb{B}_{R_l}(x)$, the first claim follows. Further, since $R_l^2 \sim \mathcal{D}$ by definition of R_l, we have that $w_l - x \sim \mathcal{N}(0, I_n)$ by Corollary 15. $\square$

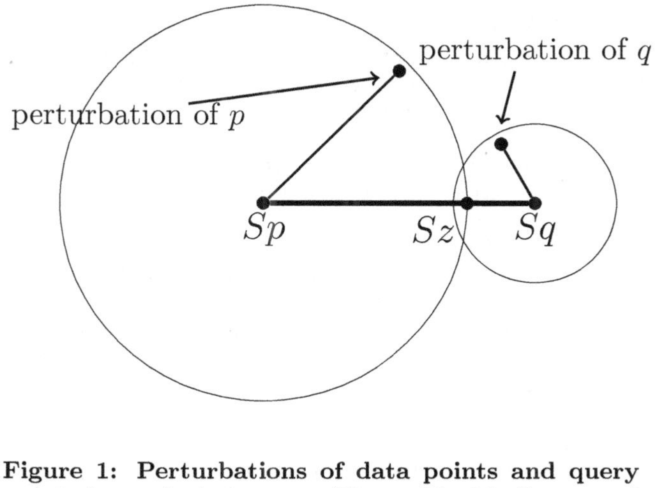

Figure 1: Perturbations of data points and query points in projected space. The radii of balls around projected points Sp and Sq are about $\alpha||Sp - Sq||$ and $(1-\alpha)||Sp - Sq||$ respectively. The radii are sampled from a distribution independently, so they do not add up to $||Sp - Sq||$ in general.

In the next section we give the analysis of our algorithms, resulting in a proof of Theorem 5. We give a glossary of main parameters here for convenience of the reader.

Glossary of parameters.

- α – parameter governing balance between insert and query complexity. $\alpha \in [0, 1]$ is assumed to be an absolute constant.
- N – number of points in the database
- d – dimension of the original space
- d_{near} – distance between near points in the original space (the r in (c, r)-NN problem)
- n – dimension of the reduced space, i.e. the space in which BASICHASH performs ball-carving
- K – number of hash functions to concatenate
- R_l – radius of balls used for carving in the reduced space for the l-th hash function, $l = 1, \ldots, K$. R_l is sampled from the distribution $R_l^2 \sim \mathcal{D}$.
- $\mathcal{W} = \bigcup_{l=1}^{K} \mathcal{W}_l$ – set of centers in reduced space that points are hashed to. The sets $\mathcal{W}_l$ are inifiinite, since $\mathcal{W}_l = \mathcal{U}_l + \mathcal{G}$ ($\mathcal{U}_l$ are the shifts), and they are represented implicitly by $\mathcal{U}_l$.
- $S_l \in \mathbb{R}^{n \times d}, l = 1, \ldots, K$ – dimensionality reduction matrices for the l independent hash functions (each S_l is a matrix of independent unit variance Gaussians).
- r_l – radius of the small balls around projected points $S_l p, S_l q$ that we sample perturbed points from (see Fig. 1).
- $C \log N$ – expected number of centers $w \in \mathcal{W}$ that belong to the ball $\mathbb{B}_R(a)$ for a typical point $a \in \mathbb{R}^n$ in the reduced space.

4. ANALYSIS

In this section we give the formal analysis of our algorithm. We start with an outline in section 4.1, then present some technical lemmas in section 4.2. Upper and lower bounds on collision probability of far and near points respectively are given in sections 4.3 and 4.4 respectively, and are put together in section 4.5 to obtain a proof of Theorem 5.

4.1 Proof outline

We now give intuition for the analysis. Recall that algorithm first projects a pair of points $p, q \in \mathbb{R}^d$ to $\mathbb{R}^n$ for a slowly growing parameter n. Then at prepreccesing time $A \approx N^{\alpha^2/c^2}$ random points in a ball of radius proportional to α around data point p are generated. Similarly, at query time $B \approx N^{(1-\alpha)^2/c^2}$ random points in a ball of radius proportional to $1-\alpha$ around q are generated (see Algorithm 2 and 3 respectively).These points are then hashed using BASICHASH: the reduced space $\mathbb{R}^n$ is covered with a sufficient number of Euclidean balls, and a point is hashed to a uniformly random ball in our collection that contains it. This is repeated K times independently, and the outputs are concatenated to obtain the final hash function.

In order to establish our result, we need to prove lower bounds on collision probability for (perturbations of) near points, and upper bounds on collision probability for (perturbations of) far points.

Near points.

Given a pair of points p, q such that $||p - q|| \leq d_{near}$, we need to argue that with probability at least $1 - o(1)$ over the choice of the hash function $\mathbf{h}$ and perturbations u^i, v^j (see Fig. 1) one has $\mathbf{h}(Sp + u^i) = \mathbf{h}(Sq + v^j)$ for at least one pair i, j. This claim turns out to be rather delicate: we cannot prove that a fixed perturbation $p + u^i$ is likely to collide with at least one of the perturbations $q + v^j$ since this is simply not true. One can prove, for example, that a given perturbation $p + u^i$ collides with at least one of the $q + v^j$'s with nontrivial probability, but that does not lead to the result since such events for different u^i's are dependent (via the q^j's). Instead, we define the point $z = (1 - \alpha)p + \alpha q$ on the line segment joining p and q, and argue that **(1)** $\mathbf{h}(Sq + v^j) = \mathbf{h}(Sz)$ for at least one j and **(2)** $\mathbf{h}(Sp + u^i) = \mathbf{h}(Sz)$ for at least one i with probability $1 - o(1)$ over the choice of $\mathbf{h}$ and $\{u^i\}, \{v^j\}$. Steps **(1)** and **(2)** are similar, so we outline the proof of **(1)** only.

We first note that $\mathbf{h}(Sq + v^j) = \mathbf{h}(Sz)$ if and only if $\mathbf{h}_l(Sq + v^j) = \mathbf{h}_l(Sz)$ for all l, i.e. the collision should happen in every independent repetition. Now fix l, and let $w_l \in \mathcal{W}_l$ denote the center that $S_l z$ hashes to under BASICHASH. By definition of BASICHASH our point $S_l q + v_l^j$ collides with $S_l z$ if and only if two conditions are satisified: **(a)** $w_l \in \mathbb{B}_{R_l}(S_l q + v_l^j)$ and **(b)** w_l is chosen as the center to be hashed to in line 3 of BASICHASH. Condition **(b)** is easy to handle, so we describe our approach to ensuring **(a)**.

Note that for a fixed hash function $\mathbf{h}$ and fixed $i = 1, \ldots, B$ we have

$$\mathbf{Pr}_{v^j}\left[w_l \in \mathbb{B}_{R_l}(S_l q + v_l^j) \text{ for all } l = 1, \ldots, K\right]$$
$$= \prod_{l=1}^{K} \mathbf{Pr}_{v^j}\left[w_l \in \mathbb{B}_{R_l}(S_l q + v_l^j)\right]$$

by independence of perturbations v^j across different repetitions. On the other hand, since the perturbed query point $S_l q + v_l^j$ is uniformly random in the ball $\mathbb{B}_{r_{q,l}}(S_l q)$, we have

$$\mathbf{Pr}_{v^j}\left[w_l \in \mathbb{B}_{R_l}(S_l q + v_l^j)\right] = \frac{|\mathbb{B}_{r_{q,l}}(S_l q) \cap \mathbb{B}_{R_l}(w_l)|}{|\mathbb{B}_{r_{q,l}}(S_l q)|}. \quad (3)$$

Denote the rhs by ξ_l, and note that ξ_l is a random variable that depends on the projection matrix S_l, random shifts $\mathcal{U}_l$ and radius R_l used in repetition l. In section 4.4 below we prove a concentration result for $\prod_{l=1}^{K} \xi_l$, implying that the lhs of (3) is quite tightly concentrated. More precisely, we prove that $\sum_{l=1}^{K} \ln \xi_l$ is within a $1 + o(1)$ factor of its expectation with probability $1 - o(1)$, which is sufficient for our purposes. Note that concentration is not immediate, since the rhs of (3) may in general take arbitrarily small values. However, a careful choice of parameters allows to control the variance and prove concentration.

The details of this argument are presented in section 4.4. The argument requires a good estimate for

$$\mathbf{E}[\ln \xi_l] = \mathbf{E}\left[\frac{|\mathbb{B}_{r_{q,l}}(S_l q) \cap \mathbb{B}_{R_l}(w_l)|}{|\mathbb{B}_{r_{q,l}}(S_l q)|}\right].$$

Such an estimate is provided by Lemma 16 below, one of our two main technical lemmas.

Far points.

Consider a pair of far points $p, q \in \mathbb{R}^d$, i.e. $||p - q|| \geq c \cdot d_{near}$. We need to prove that the perturbations of p

and q in projected space, i.e. $S_l p + u_l^i$ and $S_l q + v_l^j$, are unlikely to collide under all K hash functions. Fix l and let $w_l \in \mathcal{W}_l$ denote the center that $S_l q + v_l^j$ hashes to. We need to upper bound the probability that $S_l p + u_l^i$ belongs to the ball $\mathbb{B}_{R_l}(w_l)$. This quantity depends on the distribution of

$$(S_l p + u_l^i) - (S_l q + v_l^j), \tag{4}$$

which is in general quite complicated if radii $r_{p,l}, r_{q,l}$ of the small balls that perturbations are sampled from are fixed. This is the reason why we sample these radii from the (scaled) distribution $\mathcal{D}$ – this sampling ensures that u_l^i, v_l^j are simply vectors of independent Gaussians. But $S_l(p-q)$ also is a vector of independent Gaussians by the choice of S. Thus, (4) is just a vector of independent Gaussians. Finally, again by Lemma 14, (4) is a uniformly random vector in a ball of radius r that satisfies $r^2 \sim \gamma^2\mathcal{D}$ for some $\gamma > 0$. Thus, all we are interested in is the expectation of

$$\frac{|\mathbb{B}_r(a) \cap \mathbb{B}_R(w_l)|}{|\mathbb{B}_r(a)|},$$

where $r^2 \sim \gamma^2 \cdot \mathcal{D}$, $a = S_l q + v_l^j$, $w_l - a \sim \mathcal{N}(0, I_n)$, and $R^2 = ||w-a||^2 + Y, Y \sim 2\Gamma(1,1)$. A bound on this quantity is provided by Lemma 17. The details of the analysis outlined above are provided in section 4.3.

In the rest of this section we state our main technical lemmas in section 4.2, prove the upper bound on collision probability in section 4.3 and prove the lower bound in section 4.4. We then put these results together in section 4.5 to obtain a proof of Theorem 5.

4.2 Technical lemmas

The follows lemma will be very useful for our analysis:

LEMMA 14. *Let $X_i \sim \frac{1}{\sqrt{\pi}}e^{-x^2}$, $i = 1, \ldots, n$. Let Y be exponential with mean 1. Let $R = (X_1^2 + \ldots + X_n^2 + Y)^{1/2}$. Then $(X_1, \ldots, X_n)$ is uniformly distributed in the ball $R \cdot \mathbb{B}(0)$.*

The proof of Lemma 14 is given in Appendix B. Note that the random variables X_i for $p = 2$ in Lemma 14 are Gaussian with variance 1/2. Since we work with unit norm Gaussians, we need to introduce appropriate scaling:

COROLLARY 15. *Let $X_i \sim N(0,1)$, $i = 1, \ldots, n$. Let $Y \sim 2\Gamma(1,1)$. Let $R = (X_1^2 + \ldots + X_n^2 + Y)^{1/2}$, so that $R^2 \sim \mathcal{D}$. Then $(X_1, \ldots, X_n)$ is uniformly distributed in the ball $R \cdot \mathbb{B}(0)$.*

The following two lemmas will be our main tool in bounding collision probability for near and far points in section 4.3 and 4.4 below.

LEMMA 16. *Let $a, b \in \mathbb{R}^n$ such that $a - b \sim \gamma' \cdot \mathcal{N}(0, I_n)$. Let $r^2 \sim \gamma^2 \cdot \mathcal{D}$, where $\gamma = o_n(1)$, $\gamma' \le \gamma$. Let $w - a \sim \mathcal{N}(0, I_n)$, and let $R^2 = ||w-a||^2 + Y, Y \sim 2\Gamma(1,1)$ (see Fig. 2(a) for an illustration). Let*

$$\xi := \frac{|\mathbb{B}_r(b) \cap \mathbb{B}_R(w)|}{|\mathbb{B}_r(b)|}.$$

Then there exists an event $\mathcal{E}$ with $\mathbf{Pr}[\bar{\mathcal{E}}] \le e^{-\gamma^2 n}$ such that $\mathbf{E}[\ln \xi | \mathcal{E}] \ge -\frac{1}{2}\gamma^2 n(1 + o(1))$. Furthermore, one has $\ln \xi > -n$ conditional on $\mathcal{E}$.

The proof of this lemma is given in Section 5. The next lemma will be useful for upper bounding collision probability:

LEMMA 17. *Let $a \in \mathbb{R}^n$. Let $r^2 \sim \gamma^2 \cdot \mathcal{D}$, where γ is such that $\gamma^2 n = \omega(1)$. Let $w - a \sim \mathcal{N}(0, I_n)$, and let $R^2 = ||w-a||^2 + Y, Y \sim 2\Gamma(1,1)$ (see Fig. 2(b) for an illustration). Let*

$$\xi := \frac{|\mathbb{B}_r(a) \cap \mathbb{B}_R(w)|}{|\mathbb{B}_r(a)|}.$$

Then $\mathbf{E}[\xi] \le 2exp\left(-\frac{1}{8}\gamma^2 n(1 - O(\gamma))\right)$.

The proof of this lemma is given in Section 5. We note this is quite similar to the upper bound on the probability p_2 that two points at distance $2r$ from each other collide under hashing proved in [AI] (see equation (2) in [AI]). Indeed, since b is uniformly random in a ball of radius r as above, $a - b$ can be viewed as the Gaussian projection of a fixed length vector $x - y$ in $\mathbb{R}^d$. We are thus intrested in the probability that w, the point that a hashes to, is within distance R of b. This is up to a factor of 2 the quantity studied in [AI], with the minor difference that the radius R of the balls that we are carving with is sampled from a distribution rather than fixed.

4.3 Upper bound on collision probability for far points

In this and the next section we state the main lemmas of our analysis (the proofs of the lemmas are given in Section 5), and then put them together to obtain a proof of Theorem 5 in section 4.5.

We gather some of the random variables used in Algorithms 2 and 3 here for convenience of the reader. Recall that $S \in \mathbb{R}^{(K \cdot n) \times d}$ is a matrix of independent Gaussians of unit variance used for dimensionality reduction. For each $l = 1, \ldots, K$ we have

1. $r_{p,l}^2 \sim (\alpha d_{near})^2 \cdot \mathcal{D}$, $r_{q,l}^2 \sim ((1-\alpha)d_{near})^2 \cdot \mathcal{D}$.
2. $u^i = (u_1^i, \ldots, u_K^i) \in \mathbb{R}^{K \cdot n}, i = 1, \ldots, A$, $v^j = (v_1^j, \ldots, v_K^j) \in \mathbb{R}^{K \cdot n}, j = 1, \ldots, B$ be sampled by choosing u_l^i independent uniformly random in $\mathbb{B}_{r_{p,l}}(0)$, and v_l^j uniformly at random in $\mathbb{B}_{r_{q,l}}(0)$.

Also, $R_l, l = 1, \ldots, K, R_l^2 \sim \mathcal{D}$ are the radii of the balls that BASICHASH uses for carving. $\mathcal{U}_l, l = 1, \ldots, K$ are the shifts of the grids $\mathcal{G}$, and $\mathcal{W}_l = \mathcal{U}_l + \mathcal{G}$ is the set of centers of balls used for carving.

LEMMA 18. *Let $\alpha \in [0,1]$ be a constant. Let $c > 1$ denote the desired approximation ratio, and suppose that $K = n^{\Theta(1)}$. Let $d_{near} = n^{-1/4}$. Let $p, q \in \mathbb{R}^d$ be a pair of far points, i.e. $||p - q||_2 \ge c d_{near}$.*
Consider an invocation of
HASHDATA$(p, \alpha, S, K, \{R_l\}_{l=1}^K, B, n, \{\mathcal{U}_l\}_{l=1}^K, d_{near})$ *and* QUERY$(q, \alpha, S, K, \{R_l\}_{l=1}^K, A, n, \{\mathcal{U}_l\}_{l=1}^K, d_{near})$.
Then for each $i \in [1:A], j \in [1:B]$ one has

$$\mathbf{Pr}[\mathbf{h}(Sp + u^i) = \mathbf{h}(Sq + v^j)] \le e^{-(c^2 + \alpha^2 + (1-\alpha)^2) \cdot d_{near}^2 (1 - o(1)) nK/8}.$$

The proof of the Lemma is given in Section 5.

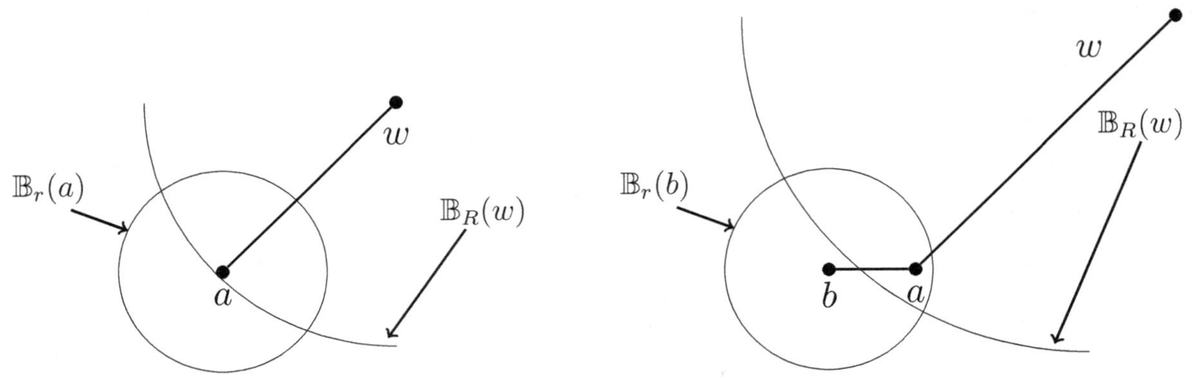

(a) Illustration for Lemma 16. The boundary of the ball $\mathbb{B}_R(w)$ is shown.

(b) Illustration for Lemma 17. The boundary of the ball $\mathbb{B}_R(w)$ is shown.

4.4 Lower bound for near points

LEMMA 19. *Let $\alpha \in [0,1]$ be a constant. Let $c > 1$ denote the desired approximation ratio, and suppose that $K = n^{\Theta(1)}$, $Kd^2_{near} = n^{\Omega(1)}, d^2_{near}n = n^{\Omega(1)}, n = \omega(1), n = o(\log N)$. Let $p, q \in \mathbb{R}^d$ be a pair of near points, i.e. $||p - q||_2 \leq d_{near}$. Consider an invocation of* HASHDATA$(p, \alpha, S, K, \{R_l\}_{l=1}^K, B, n, \{\mathcal{U}_l\}_{l=1}^K, d_{near})$ *and* QUERY$(q, \alpha, S, K, \{R_l\}_{l=1}^K, A, n, \{\mathcal{U}_l\}_{l=1}^K, d_{near})$. *Then*

$$\mathbf{Pr}[\exists i \in [1:A], j \in [1:B] \text{ s.t. } \mathbf{h}(Sp+u^i) = \mathbf{h}(Sq+v^j)] = 1-o(1)$$

as long as

$$A \geq (C \log N)^{2K} e^{(1+o(1))\alpha^2 d^2_{near} nK/2},$$

and

$$B \geq (C \log N)^{2K} e^{(1+o(1))(1-\alpha)^2 d^2_{near} nK/2}.$$

If $\alpha = 0$ then setting $A = 1$ and B as above is sufficient. Similarly, if $\alpha = 1$, setting A as above and $B = 1$ is sufficient.

The proof of the Lemma is given in Section 5.

4.5 Putting it together

We can now give the proof of our main theorem:

Proof of Theorem 5:

Let $K' = d^2_{near}nK/2$, and recall that $d_{near} = n^{-1/4}$. We choose the scaling so that $||p - q||_2 \leq d_{near}$ for near points and $||p - q||_2 \geq cd_{near}$ for far points. We choose

$$K' := \frac{4}{c^2 + \alpha^2 - 3(1-\alpha)^2} \ln N,$$

and set K, n as follows. Recal that $K' = d^2_{near}nK/2 = n^{1/2}K/2$, i.e. $n^{1/2}K = 2K'$. We let $K = (2K')^{3/4}$ and $n = (2K')^{1/2}$. Note that we have $K = n^{\Theta(1)}$, as required by Lemma 18. Furtheremore, we have $Kd^2_{near} = Kn^{-1/2} = (2K')^{3/4-1/4} = (2K')^{1/2} = \omega(1)$ and $d_{near}n = n^{1/2} = n^{\Omega(1)}$, as required by Lemma 19. We now verify that the factor $(2C \log N)^{2K}$ that arises in Lemma 19 is $N^{o(1)}$, and that the BASICHASH function can be computed in time $N^{o(1)}$ for our choice of parameters.

For the first claim, note that we have $K = O(\log^{3/4} N)$, and hence

$$(2C \log N)^K = e^{O(\log^{3/4} N \log \log N)} = N^{o(1)}. \quad (5)$$

Also, we have

$$n^{O(n)} = (\log N)^{O(\log^{1/2} N)} = N^{o(1)}, \quad (6)$$

implying that BASICHASH can be computed in time $N^{o(1)}$ by Claim 24.

Let

$$A = (2C \log N)^{2K} e^{K'\alpha^2(1+\epsilon)} = N^{\alpha^2 \rho_\alpha (1+o(1))}$$
$$B = (2C \log N)^{2K} e^{K'(1-\alpha)^2(1+\epsilon)} = N^{(1-\alpha)^2 \rho_\alpha (1+o(1))},$$

where $\epsilon = o(1)$ as in Lemma 19. When $\alpha = 0$, we set $A = 1$ and B as above, and when $\alpha = 1$, we set $B = 1$ and A as above, in accordance with Lemma 19. The space and insert and query complexity are immediate. Correctness is guaranteed by Lemma 19 if pruning were not done in lines 11 and 12 of Algorithm 3. We now argue correctness formally.

Consider a query q. We now show that the number of collisions of perturbations $q + v^j$ of q with perturbations $p' + u^{j'}$ of points p' that are **far** from q is bounded by $N^{(1-\alpha)^2\rho_\alpha + o(1)}$. By Lemma 18 the expected number of such collisions is bounded by

$$ABNe^{-\frac{1}{4}(c^2+\alpha^2+(1-\alpha)^2)K'(1-o(1))}. \quad (7)$$

Indeed, this is because there are N points in the database, each of which is inserted into the hash table A times, and the near neighbor query for point q performs B lookups. The expected query time is bounded by B plus (7). The latter term equals

$$\begin{aligned}
&ABNe^{-\frac{1}{4}(c^2+\alpha^2+(1-\alpha)^2)K'(1-o(1))} \\
&= (2C \log N)^{4K} \cdot Ne^{(\alpha^2+(1-\alpha)^2-\frac{1}{4}(c^2+\alpha^2+(1-\alpha)^2))K'(1-o(1))} \\
&= N^{1+o(1)} e^{-\frac{1}{4}(c^2-3\alpha^2-3(1-\alpha)^2)K'} \\
&= N^{o(1)} \cdot e^{\frac{1}{4}(c^2+(1-\alpha)^2-3\alpha^2)K'} \cdot e^{-\frac{1}{4}(c^2-3\alpha^2-3(1-\alpha)^2)K'} \\
&= N^{o(1)} \cdot e^{(1-\alpha)^2 K'} = N^{(1-\alpha)^2\rho_\alpha + o(1)}.
\end{aligned}$$

Thus, by Markov's inequality the number of collisions of perturbations $q + v^j$ of q with perturbations $p' + u^{j'}$ of points p' that are far from q is bounded by $N^{(1-\alpha)^2\rho_\alpha + o(1)}$ with probability $1 - o(1)$, so the pruning step does not prune away a near point if it exists, and correctness follows. $\square$

5. PROOFS OF MAIN TECHNICAL LEMMAS

We will need

CLAIM 20. *Let $X \sim \Gamma(k,1)$ for some $k \geq 1$. Then for any $\delta \in (0,1)$ one has*

$$\mathbf{Pr}[X \notin (1 \pm \delta)\mathbf{E}[X]] < e^{-\Omega(\delta^2 k)}.$$

Proof of Lemma 9: Note that $\mathbb{B}_r(a) \cap \mathbb{B}_R(w)$ is the union of a spherical cap of $\mathbb{B}_r(a)$ and a spherical cap of $\mathbb{B}_R(w)$. Since $R > r$, the volume of the first spherical cap is at least the volume of the second one, so we concentrate on bounding this volume. Let x be the distance from p to the plane that defines the smaller cap. Then $r^2 - x^2 = R^2 - (d-x)^2$. Since $R^2 - (d-x)^2 = R^2 - d^2 + 2dx - x^2$, this implies $x = \frac{r^2+d^2-R^2}{2d}$ as required.

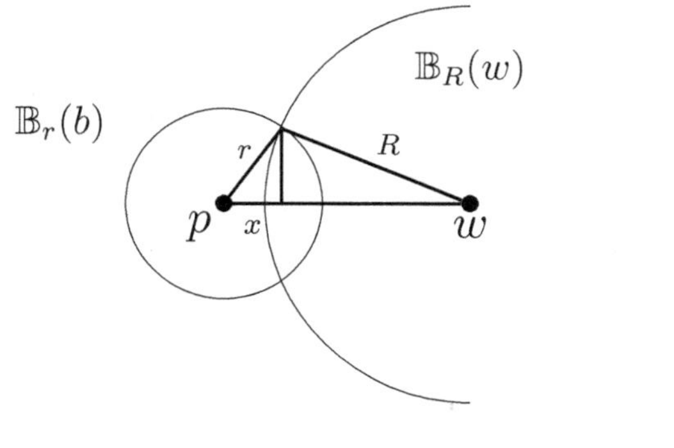

Figure 2: Intersection of $\mathbb{B}_r(a)$ and $\mathbb{B}_R(w)$.

□

Proof of Lemma 16: By Lemma 9

$$\xi \geq I\left(\frac{||c-b||^2 + r^2 - R^2}{2||c-b||}, r\right).$$

First note that

$$\begin{aligned}||c-b||^2 - R^2 &= ||c-a||^2 + ||a-b||^2 + 2\langle c-a, a-b\rangle - R^2\\ &= (||c-a||^2 - R^2) + ||a-b||^2\\ &\quad + 2||a-b|| \cdot \langle c-a, \frac{a-b}{||a-b||}\rangle\\ &= -Y + ||a-b||^2 + 2||a-b|| \cdot Z,\end{aligned}$$

where $Z = \langle c-a, \frac{a-b}{||a-b||}\rangle \sim N(0,1)$ is Gaussian. Thus, by Lemma 10

$$\xi \geq \frac{C'}{\sqrt{n}}\left(1 - \left(\frac{-Y + r^2 + ||a-b||^2 + 2||a-b|| \cdot Z}{2||c-b||r}\right)^2\right)^{n/2} \tag{8}$$

for a constant $C' > 0$.

We now show that all quantities involved in (8) are tightly concentrated, and use this fact to prove the claimed result. By Claim 20 with $\delta = \Theta(\gamma)^2$ one has

1. $\mathbf{Pr}[r \notin (1 + O(\gamma))\gamma\sqrt{n}] < e^{-\gamma^2 n}$
2. $\mathbf{Pr}[||a-b|| \notin (1 + O(\gamma))\gamma'\sqrt{n}] < e^{-\gamma^2 n}$
3. $\mathbf{Pr}[||c-b|| \notin (1 + O(\gamma))\sqrt{1+\gamma^2}\sqrt{n}] < e^{-\gamma^2 n}$

Before we prove the claim of the lemma, we show that

$$\frac{-Y + r^2 + ||a-b||^2 + 2||a-b|| \cdot Z}{2||c-b||r} \leq 100\gamma \tag{9}$$

with high probability. Let $\mathcal{E} = \{|-Y + r^2 + ||a-b||^2 + 2||a-b|| \cdot Z| < 100\gamma||c-b||r\}$.

By concentration results 1, 2, 3 above, we have

$$\begin{aligned}\mathbf{Pr}[\bar{\mathcal{E}}] &\leq e^{-\gamma^2 n} + \mathbf{Pr}[|-Y + 2\gamma^2 n + 4\gamma\sqrt{n} \cdot Z| < 50\gamma^2 n]\\ &\leq e^{-\gamma^2 n} + \mathbf{Pr}[|-Y + 4\gamma\sqrt{n} \cdot Z| < 40\gamma^2 n]\\ &\leq e^{-\gamma^2 n} + \mathbf{Pr}[Y > 20\gamma^2 n] + \mathbf{Pr}[4\gamma\sqrt{n} \cdot |Z| > 20\gamma^2 n]\\ &\leq e^{-\gamma^2 n} + e^{-\Omega(\gamma^2 n)} + e^{-\Omega(\gamma^2 n)} = e^{-\Omega(\gamma^2 n)}.\end{aligned} \tag{10}$$

We now get a proof of the last claim of the lemma by noting that

$$\ln \xi \geq (n/2)\ln\left(1 - \left(\frac{-Y + r^2 + ||a-b||^2 + 2||a-b|| \cdot Z}{2||c-b||r}\right)^2\right) - O(\ln n) \geq -O(\gamma)n,$$

where we used the bound $\ln(1-x) \geq -(1+O(\gamma))x$ for $x = O(\gamma)$.

We condition on $\mathcal{E}$ in what follows, so we have

$$\xi \geq \frac{C'}{\sqrt{n}}\left(1 - W^2\right)^{n/2} \geq \frac{C'}{\sqrt{n}}\exp\left(-(1+O(\gamma))(n/2)W^2\right),$$

where $W = \frac{-Y+r^2+||a-b||^2+2||a-b|| \cdot Z}{2||c-b||r}$. Taking logarithms of both sides, we get

$$\begin{aligned}\ln \xi &\geq -(1+O(\gamma))\frac{n}{2}\left(\frac{-Y + r^2 + ||a-b||^2 + 2||a-b|| \cdot Z}{2||c-b||r}\right)^2\\ &\quad - O(\ln n)\\ &\geq -\frac{1+O(\gamma)}{8(1+\gamma^2)\gamma^2 n}\left(-Y + r^2 + ||a-b||^2 + 2||a-b|| \cdot Z\right)^2\\ &\quad - O(\ln n).\end{aligned} \tag{11}$$

By (11) we now have

$$\begin{aligned}&\mathbf{E}[\ln \xi|\mathcal{E}] \geq\\ &-\frac{1+O(\gamma)}{8(1+\gamma^2)\gamma^2 n}\mathbf{E}[(-Y + r^2 + ||a-b||^2 + 2||a-b|| \cdot Z)^2|\mathcal{E}]\\ &- O(\ln n),\end{aligned} \tag{12}$$

and thus it is sufficient to upper bound

$$\begin{aligned}&\mathbf{E}[(-Y + r^2 + ||a-b||^2 + 2||a-b|| \cdot Z)^2|\mathcal{E}] \leq\\ &\leq \frac{1}{\mathbf{Pr}[\mathcal{E}]}\mathbf{E}[(-Y + r^2 + ||a-b||^2 + 2||a-b|| \cdot Z)^2].\end{aligned} \tag{13}$$

[2]This choice of δ is not unique in that any choice of $\delta = \Omega(\gamma)$ would have been sufficient to obtain the claimed result, with this choice affecting the precise form of the $o(1)$ term in the result of the lemma. We choose $\delta = \Theta(\gamma)$ to minimize the amount of notation.

For the latter quantity we have using independence of $Y, Z, a-b, r$

$$\begin{aligned}&\mathbf{E}_{Y,Z,a-b,r}[(-Y+r^2+||a-b||^2+2||a-b||\cdot Z)^2]\\&\leq \mathbf{E}[r^4+||a-b||^4+2r^2||a-b||^2]+o(r^4)\\&\leq 4r^4+o(r^4),\end{aligned}$$

where we used that $\gamma' \leq \gamma$. Substituting this into (12), using (13) and (10), we get

$$\mathbf{E}[\ln \xi|\mathcal{E}] \geq -\frac{1}{2}\gamma^2 n(1+o(1))$$

and $\mathbf{Pr}[\mathcal{E}] \geq 1-e^{-\gamma^2 n}$, as desired. □

Proof of Lemma 17: By Lemma 9 and Lemma 10 one has

$$\begin{aligned}\xi &\leq 2I\left(\frac{r^2+||a-c||^2-R^2}{2||a-c||}, r\right) = 2I\left(\frac{r^2-Y}{2||a-c||}, r\right) \leq\\&\leq 2\exp\left(-(n/2)\left(\frac{r^2-Y}{2r||a-c||}\right)^2\right)\end{aligned}$$

as long as $Y < r^2$. If $Y > r^2$, we upper bound the probability of collision by 1. This corresponds to a negligible $e^{-r^2/2}$ term.

By Claim 20 one has $||a-c|| \in (1 \pm O(\gamma))n$ with probability at least $1-e^{-\gamma^2 n}$. Also, by Claim 20 one has $r \in (1 \pm O(\gamma))\gamma n > 8$ with probability at least $1-e^{-\gamma^2 n}$. We condition on this event (call it $\mathcal{E}$) in what follows. We get

$$\begin{aligned}&\frac{1}{2}\int_0^{r^2} \exp\left(-\frac{n}{8r^2||a-c||^2}(r^2-y)^2\right)e^{-y/2}dy\\&\leq \frac{1}{2}\int_0^{r^2} \exp\left(-\frac{(1-O(\gamma))}{8r^2}(r^2-y)^2\right)e^{-y/2}dy\\&\leq \frac{1}{2}\int_0^{r^2} \exp\left(-\frac{(1-O(\gamma))}{8r^2}(r^2-y)^2\right)e^{-(1-\delta)y/2}dy\\&= \frac{1}{2}\int_0^{\infty} \exp\left(-\frac{1-O(\gamma)}{8r^2}(r^4+2r^2y+y^2)\right)dy\\&= \frac{1}{2}\int_0^{\infty} \exp\left(-\frac{1-O(\gamma)}{8r^2}(r^2+y)^2\right)dy\end{aligned}$$

We now show that the value of this integral is essentially upper bounded by the value of the integrand at the left endpoint, i.e. when $y=0$:

$$\begin{aligned}&\int_0^{\infty} \exp\left(-\frac{1-O(\gamma)}{8r^2}(r^2+y)^2\right)dy\\&= \exp\left(-\frac{(1-O(\gamma))r^2}{8}\right)\cdot\\&\cdot\int_0^{\infty} \exp\left(-\frac{1-O(\gamma)}{8r^2}\left[(r^2+y)^2-r^4\right]\right)dy\\&= \exp\left(-\frac{(1-O(\gamma))r^2}{8}\right)\cdot\\&\cdot\int_0^{\infty} \exp\left(-\frac{1-O(\gamma)}{8r^2}\left[2yr^2+y^2\right]\right)dy\end{aligned}$$

We now show that the integral in the last line is bounded by a constant. First note that $r \geq 8$ by our conditioning. We have

$$\int_0^{\infty} \exp\left(-\frac{1-O(\gamma)}{8r^2}\left[2yr^2+y^2\right]\right)dy \leq \int_0^{\infty} \exp(-y)\,dy \leq 1$$

Since we conditioned on an event of probability $1-e^{-\gamma^2 n} < 9/10$ for sufficiently large $\gamma^2 n$, the result follows. □

We now give a proof of Lemma 18. We restate the lemma here for convenience of the reader.

Lemma 18 *Let $\alpha \in [0,1]$ be a constant. Let $c > 1$ denote the desired approximation ratio, and suppose that $K = n^{\Theta(1)}$. Let $d_{near} = n^{-1/4}$. Let $p, q \in \mathbb{R}^d$ be a pair of far points, i.e. $||p-q||_2 \geq cd_{near}$. Consider an invocation of* HashData$(p, \alpha, S, K, \{R_l\}_{l=1}^K, B, n, \{\mathcal{U}_l\}_{l=1}^K, d_{near})$ *and* Query$(q, \alpha, S, K, \{R_l\}_{l=1}^K, A, n, \{\mathcal{U}_l\}_{l=1}^K, d_{near})$.

Then for each $i \in [1:A], j \in [1:B]$ one has

$$\begin{aligned}&\mathbf{Pr}[\mathbf{h}(Sp+u^i) = \mathbf{h}(Sq+v^j)] \leq\\&\leq e^{-(c^2+\alpha^2+(1-\alpha)^2)\cdot d_{near}^2(1-o(1))nK/8}.\end{aligned}$$

PROOF. Recall that $\mathbf{h}$ is a concatenation of K independent hash functions. Fix $l \in [1:K]$ and consider the l-th hash function. We will prove that for each $i \in [1:A], j \in [1:B]$ and each $l \in [1:K]$ one has

$$\mathbf{Pr}[\mathbf{h}_l(Sp+u^i) = \mathbf{h}_l(Sq+v^j)] \leq e^{-(c^2+\alpha^2+(1-\alpha)^2)(1-o(1))d_{near}^2 n/8} \tag{14}$$

where $\mathbf{h}_l$ stands for the l-th component of l. The result will then follow by independence of $\mathbf{h}_l$ for different l. Let $a = S_l p + u_l^i, b = S_l q + v_l^j$. By Claim 12 we have

$$a - b \sim \gamma \cdot \mathcal{N}(0, I_n),$$

where $\gamma = \sqrt{||p-q||_2^2 + \alpha^2 d_{near}^2 + (1-\alpha)^2 d_{near}^2}$. We also have by Claim 12 that b is a uniformly random point in the ball $\mathbb{B}_r(a)$, where $r^2 \sim \gamma^2 \cdot \mathcal{D}$.

Let $\mathbb{B}_{R_l}(a) \cap \mathcal{W}_l = \{w_1, \ldots, w_Q\}$. Each w_q is uniformly random in $\mathbb{B}_{R_l}(a)$. Let w_q be the uniformly random element of $\mathbb{B}_{R_l}(a) \cap \mathcal{W}_l$ that a hashes to (by line 3 of BasicHash). By Claim 13 $w_q - a \sim \mathcal{N}(0, I_n)$, so we are in the setting of Lemma 17, i.e. we are interested in upper bounding

$$\xi = \frac{|\mathbb{B}_r(a) \cap \mathbb{B}_{R_l}(w)|}{|\mathbb{B}_r(a)|}.$$

By Lemma 17 we have

$$\mathbf{E}[\xi] \leq 2\exp\left(-\frac{1}{8}\gamma^2 n(1+O(\gamma))\right),$$

where the expectation is over the choice of centers $\mathcal{W}_l$, dimensionality reduction matrix S_l and perturbations u_l^i, v_l^j. Let $q \in [1:Q]$ denote the (uniformly random) center that a hashes to (by line 3 of BasicHash). We have

$$\begin{aligned}&\mathbf{Pr}[w_q \in \mathbb{B}_{R_l}(b)|w_q \in \mathbb{B}_{R_l}(a)]\\&\leq 2\exp\left(-\frac{1}{8}\gamma^2 n(1+O(\gamma))\right)\\&\leq 2\exp\left(-\frac{1}{8}(c^2+\alpha^2+(1-\alpha)^2)d_{near}^2 n(1-o(1))\right)\end{aligned} \tag{15}$$

where the probability is over $\mathcal{W}_l, S_l, u_l^i, v_l^j$. This yields the required bound when $Q \neq 0$. It remains to note that if $\mathbb{B}_{R_l}(a) \cap \mathcal{W}_l = \emptyset$, then a is hashed to a uniformly random element from an arbitrarily large universe, so the collision probability can easily be made polynomially small in the number of input points by choosing the universe to be poly(N) size. Since $n = o(\log N)$ by assumption of the lemma, a $1/\text{poly}(N)$ term is smaller than the rhs of (15), and (14) follows by a union bound over these two cases. The result of the lemma now follows by independence of the hashing process for different $l = 1, \ldots, K$. $\square$

We now give a proof of Lemma 19. We restate the lemma here for convenience of the reader.

Lemma 19 *Let $\alpha \in [0,1]$ be a constant. Let $c > 1$ denote the desired approximation ratio, and suppose that $K = n^{\Theta(1)}$, $Kd_{near}^2 = n^{\Omega(1)}, d_{near}^2 n = n^{\Omega(1)}, n = \omega(1), n = o(\log N)$. Let $p, q \in \mathbb{R}^d$ be a pair of near points, i.e. $||p-q||_2 \le d_{near}$. Consider an invocation of*
$\text{HASHDATA}(p, \alpha, S, K, \{R_l\}_{l=1}^K, B, n, \{\mathcal{U}_l\}_{l=1}^K, d_{near})$
and $\text{QUERY}(q, \alpha, S, K, \{R_l\}_{l=1}^K, A, n, \{\mathcal{U}_l\}_{l=1}^K, d_{near})$. *Then*

$$\mathbf{Pr}[\exists i \in [1:A], j \in [1:B] \text{ s.t. } \mathbf{h}(Sp + u^i) = \mathbf{h}(Sq + v^j)] = 1 - o(1)$$

as long as

$$A \ge (C \log N)^{2K} e^{(1+o(1))\alpha^2 d_{near}^2 nK/2},$$

and

$$B \ge (C \log N)^{2K} e^{(1+o(1))(1-\alpha)^2 d_{near}^2 nK/2}.$$

If $\alpha = 0$ then setting $A = 1$ and B as above is sufficient. Similarly, if $\alpha = 1$, setting A as above and $B = 1$ is sufficient.

We prove Lemma 19 in a sequence of steps. We start by giving an outline of the proof, then prove every step formally and put them together below. We need to prove that if a sufficiently large number of perturbations $u^i, v^j, i = 1, \ldots, A, j = 1, \ldots, B$ are used, then at least one pair of perturbed points collides under $\mathbf{h}$, i.e.

$$\mathbf{Pr}[\exists i \in [1:A], j \in [1:B] \text{ s.t. } \mathbf{h}(Sp + u^i) = \mathbf{h}(Sq + v^j)] = 1 - o(1)$$

as long as A, B are sufficiently large. Here the probability is over the choice of the hash function $\mathbf{h}$ (which consists of dimensionality reduction matrices S_l and centers $\mathcal{W}_l$, $l = 1, \ldots, K$) as well as the choice of perturbations u^i, v^j. Also, each perturbed point choose a center in $\mathcal{W}$ to hash to in line 3 of BASICHASH independently uniformly at random. Our argument proceeds as follows. First, we define the point (see Fig. 1)

$$z = (1-\alpha)p + \alpha q.$$

We then follow these three steps:

(1) Prove that if the number of perturbations B of the *query point* q is sufficiently large, then at least one of them will collide with z under $\mathbf{h}$:

$$\mathbf{Pr}[\exists j \in [1:B] \text{ s.t. } \mathbf{h}(Sq + v^i) = \mathbf{h}(Sz)] = 1 - o(1).$$

(2) Prove that if the number of perturbations A of the *data point* p is sufficiently large, then at least one of them will collide with the z under $\mathbf{h}$:

$$\mathbf{Pr}[\exists i \in [1:A] \text{ s.t. } \mathbf{h}(Sp + u^i) = \mathbf{h}(Sz)] = 1 - o(1).$$

(3) Conclude, using the union bound, that at least one perturbation of p is very likely to collide with at least one perturbation of q, obtaining the result.

In what follows we give the argument for **Step 1.** and **Step 2** (which are symmetric, so we will only give the details for **Step 1**). Thus, we are now interested in proving that

$$\mathbf{Pr}[\exists j \in [1:B] \text{ s.t. } \mathbf{h}(Sq + v^j) = \mathbf{h}(Sz)] = 1 - o(1), \quad (16)$$

where the probability is over the choice of the hash function $\mathbf{h}$ (i.e. matrices S_l and centers $\mathcal{W}_l$, $l = 1, \ldots, K$), and the choice of perturbations v^j. Let $w_l \in \mathcal{W}_l$ denote the element that $S_l z$ hashes to, i.e. $\text{BASICHASH}(S_l z, R_l, n, \mathcal{W}_l)$ (this is well-defined if the ball of radius R_l around $S_l z$ contains a center in $\mathcal{W}_l$ – see below).

Our argument now proceeds in three steps:

Step 1a. Prove that with probability $1-o(1)$ over the choice of the dimensionality reduction matrix S and centers $\mathcal{W}$ one has

$$\mathbf{Pr}_{v^j}[w_l \in \mathbb{B}_{R_l}(S_l q + v_l^j) \text{ for all } l = 1, \ldots, K] \ge$$
$$\ge e^{-K\frac{1}{2}(1-\alpha)^2 d_{near}^2 n(1+o(1))}.$$

Denote this event by $\mathcal{E}^a$. Note that this is by itself not sufficient for (16), since for each $l = 1, \ldots, K$ BASICHASH chooses a uniformly random center from $\mathcal{W}_l \cap \mathbb{B}_{R_l}(x)$ to output. However, for any fixed pair of points p, q if the event $\mathcal{E}^*(p,q)$ occurs (see (2)), then all balls $\mathbb{B}_{R_l}(S_l q + v^j)$ around perturbations of q and p contain at most $2C \log N$ centers. Thus, conditional on the high probability event $\mathcal{E}^*(p,q)$, a given perturbation $S_l q + v^j$ is reasonably likely (probability at least $1/(2C\log N)$) to get hashed to w_l after all. By independence of these perturbations, we should be able to argue that at least one of them will get hashed to w_l with overwhelming probability, as long as the number of trials is sufficiently large. In **Step 1b** below we argue that the number of independent trials is large, and in **Step 1c** below show that this number of trials is sufficient.

Step 1b. Prove that, conditional on $\mathcal{E}^a$, with probability $1-o(1)$ over the choice of perturbations $v^j, j = 1, \ldots, B$ there exists a set $J \subseteq [B]$ of size at least $(2C \log N)^{2K}/2$ such that

$$w_l \in \mathbb{B}_{R_l}(S_l q + v_l^j) \text{ for all } l = 1, \ldots, K$$

and all $j \in J$. Call this event $\mathcal{E}^b$.

Step 1c. Prove that conditional on $\mathcal{E}^*(p,q) \wedge \mathcal{E}^a \wedge \mathcal{E}^b$, with probability $1 - o(1)$ over the choices of centers to hash to in BASICHASH there exists $j \in J$ such that $\mathbf{h}(Sq + v^j) = \mathbf{h}(Sz)$.

We now give the details of **Steps 1a-1c**.

Step 1a. is given by

LEMMA 21. *Let $\alpha \in [0,1]$ be a constant. Let $c > 1$ denote the desired approximation ratio, and suppose that $K = n^{\Theta(1)}$, $Kd_{near}^2 = n^{\Omega(1)}, d_{near}^2 n = n^{\Omega(1)}, n = \omega(1), n = o(\log N)$. Let $p, q \in \mathbb{R}^d$ be a pair of near points, i.e. $||p - q||_2 \le d_{near}$. Let $z = (1-\alpha)p + \alpha q$.*

Let $w_l \in \mathcal{W}_l$ denote the element that $S_l z$ hashes to, i.e. $\text{BASICHASH}(S_l z, R_l, n, \mathcal{W}_l)$. *Then with probability $1 - o(1)$ over the choice of the dimensionality reduction matrix S and centers $\mathcal{W}$ one has for all j*

$$\mathbf{Pr}_{v^j}[w_l \in \mathbb{B}_{R_l}(S_l q + v_l^j) \text{ for all } l = 1, \ldots, K]$$
$$\ge e^{-K\frac{1}{2}(1-\alpha)^2 d_{near}^2 n(1+o(1))}.$$

Similarly, for all i

$$\mathbf{Pr}_{u^i}[w_l \in \mathbb{B}_{R_l}(S_l p + u_l^i) \text{ for all } l = 1, \ldots, K]$$
$$\ge e^{-K\frac{1}{2}\alpha^2 d_{near}^2 n(1+o(1))}.$$

PROOF. We prove the first claim (the proof of the second is analogous).

If $\alpha = 1$, then the claim is obvious, since $v_l^j = 0$ for all j and l. Thus, we assume that $\alpha \neq 1$ in what follows, i.e. α is bounded away from 1 since α is a constant. Fix $j \in [1 : B]$, and let $v := v^j$ to simplify notation. First note that for any fixed S and $\mathcal{W}$ one has by independence of perturbations in different coordinates

$$\begin{aligned}&\mathbf{Pr}_v[w_l \in \mathbb{B}_{R_l}(S_l q + v_l) \text{ for all } l = 1, \ldots, K] \\ &= \prod_{l=1}^{K} \mathbf{Pr}_{v_l}[w_l \in \mathbb{B}_{R_l}(S_l q + v_l)].\end{aligned}$$

Recall that for each $l = 1, \ldots, K$ w_l is the center that $S_l z$ is hashed to. By Claim 13 we have $S_l z - w_l \sim \mathcal{N}(0, I_n)$. Also,

$$S_l z - S_l q \sim (1-\alpha)||p-q||_2 \mathcal{N}(0, I_n) \tag{17}$$

by 2-stability of the Gaussian distribution. Recall that $S_l q + v_l$ is a uniformly random point in $\mathbb{B}_{r_{q,l}}(S_l q)$, so the probability that w_l is at distance at most R from it is given by

$$\xi_l = \frac{|\mathbb{B}_{r_{p,l}}(S_l q) \cap \mathbb{B}_{R_l}(w_l)|}{|\mathbb{B}_{r_{p,l}}(S_l q)|}. \tag{18}$$

We are in the setting of Lemma 16, where we have $\gamma' = (1-\alpha)||p-q||_2$ by (17) and $\gamma = (1-\alpha)d_{near}$ by definition of $r_{p,l}$. Note that $\gamma' \leq \gamma$ as required by Lemma 16 since p and q are near points by assumption. Thus for each l there exists an event $\mathcal{E}_l^1$ with $\mathbf{Pr}[\mathcal{E}_l^1] \geq 1 - e^{-\Omega((1-\alpha)^2 d_{near}^2 n)}$ such that

$$\mathbf{E}[\ln \xi_l | \mathcal{E}_l^1] \geq -\frac{1}{2}(1-\alpha)^2 d_{near}^2 n(1+o(1))$$

and $|\ln \xi| \leq n$ conditional on $\mathcal{E}_l^1$. Let $\mathcal{E}^1 := \bigwedge_{l=1}^K \mathcal{E}_l^1$. Note that $\mathbf{Pr}[\bar{\mathcal{E}}_1] \leq Ke^{-\Omega(\gamma^2 n)} = n^{O(1)} e^{-n^{\Omega(1)}} = o(1)$ (we used that $K = n^{\Theta(1)}$ and $d_{near}^2 n = n^{\Omega(1)}$ by the assumptions of the lemma). By Chernoff bounds we have for any $\epsilon > 0$

$$\begin{aligned}&\mathbf{Pr}\left[\sum_{l=1}^{K} \ln \xi_l \in -(1 \pm \epsilon)K\frac{1}{2}(1-\alpha)^2 d_{near}^2 n(1+o(1)) \middle| \mathcal{E}^1\right] \\ &< e^{-\Omega(\epsilon^2 K \frac{1}{2}(1-\alpha)^2 d_{near}^2)} \\ &\leq e^{-\Omega(\epsilon^2 K (1-\alpha)^2 d_{near}^2)}.\end{aligned} \tag{19}$$

We have

$$K(1-\alpha)^2 d_{near}^2 = \omega(1) \tag{20}$$

by assumption of the lemma, so the rhs of (19) is $o(1)$. Now note that by (19) and (20) there exists a setting of $\epsilon = o(1)$ such that with probability $1 - o(1)$ over $\mathcal{W}, S$, conditional on $\mathcal{E}^1$

$$\sum_{l=1}^{K} \ln \xi_l \in -(1 \pm \epsilon)K\frac{1}{2}(1-\alpha)^2 d_{near}^2 n(1+o(1)),$$

implying that with probability at least $1 - o(1)$ over the choice of the centers $\mathcal{W}$ and the dimensionality reduction matrix S one has for each j

$$\begin{aligned}&\mathbf{Pr}_v[w_l \in \mathbb{B}_{R_l}(S_l q + v_l) \text{ for all } l = 1, \ldots, K | \mathcal{E}^1] \\ &= \prod_{l=1}^{K} \frac{|\mathbb{B}_{r_{p,l}}(S_l q) \cap \mathbb{B}_{R_l}(w_l)|}{|\mathbb{B}_{r_{p,l}}(S_l q)|} \geq e^{-K\frac{1}{2}(1-\alpha)^2 d_{near}^2 n(1+\epsilon)}\end{aligned}$$

for some $\epsilon = o(1)$. Since $\mathbf{Pr}[\mathcal{E}^1] \geq 1 - o(1)$, this gives the claimed result. □

We now give the formal argument for **Step 1b.**

LEMMA 22. *Let $\alpha \in [0,1]$ be a constant. Let $c > 1$ denote the desired approximation ratio, and suppose that $K = n^{\Theta(1)}$, $Kd_{near}^2 = n^{\Omega(1)} = \omega(1), d_{near} n = n^{\Omega(1)}$. Let $p, q \in \mathbb{R}^d$ be a pair of near points, i.e. $||p-q||_2 \leq d_{near}$. Let $z = (1-\alpha)p + \alpha q$.*

Let $w_l \in \mathcal{W}_l$ denote the element that $S_l z$ hashes to, i.e. BASICHASH$(S_l z, R_l, n, \mathcal{W}_l)$. Suppose that $B \geq (C \log N)^{2K} e^{(1+o(1))(1-\alpha)^2 d_{near}^2 nK/2}$ and $S, \{\mathcal{U}_l\}$ are such that

$$\begin{aligned}&\mathbf{Pr}_{v^j}[w_l \in \mathbb{B}_{R_l}(S_l q + v_l^j) \text{ for all } l = 1, \ldots, K] \\ &\geq e^{-K\frac{1}{2}(1-\alpha)^2 d_{near}^2 n(1+o(1))}.\end{aligned}$$

Then with probability $1 - o(1)$ over the choice of perturbations $v^j, j = 1, \ldots, B$ there exists a set $J \subseteq [B]$ of size at least $(2C \log N)^{2K}/2$ such that

$$w_l \in \mathbb{B}_{R_l}(S_l q + v_l^j) \text{ for all } l = 1, \ldots, K$$

and all $j \in J$. An analogous statement holds for perturbations of data points.

PROOF. For each $j = 1, \ldots, B$ let $Y_j = 1$ if $w_l \in \mathbb{B}_{R_l}(S_l q + v_l^j)$ for all $l = 1, \ldots, K$ and 0 otherwise. Since the choices of v^j are independent for different j, we get that $\sum_{j=1}^B Y_j$ is a sum of independent Bernoulli 0/1 rv's with $\mathbf{E}[Y_j] \geq e^{-K\frac{1}{2}(1-\alpha)^2 d_{near}^2 n(1+\epsilon)}$ for some $\epsilon = o(1)$. Thus, $\mathbf{E}[\sum_{j=1}^B Y_j] \geq (2C \log N)^{2K}$, and by standard concentration inequalities

$$\mathbf{Pr}\left[\sum_{j=1}^{B} Y_j < (2C \log N)^{2K}/2\right] = o(1)$$

as required, where the probability is over the choice of perturbations v^j. □

Step 1c. is provided by

LEMMA 23. *Let $\alpha \in [0,1]$ be a constant. Let $c > 1$ denote the desired approximation ratio, and suppose that $K = n^{\Theta(1)}$, $Kd_{near}^2 = n^{\Omega(1)}, d_{near}^2 n = n^{\Omega(1)}, n = \omega(1), n = o(\log N)$. Let $p, q \in \mathbb{R}^d$ be a pair of near points, i.e. $||p - q||_2 \leq d_{near}$. Let $z = (1-\alpha)p + \alpha q$. Suppose that there exists a set $J \subseteq [B]$ of size at least $(2C \log N)^{2K}/2$ such that*

$$w_l \in \mathbb{B}_{R_l}(S_l q + v_l^j) \text{ for all } l = 1, \ldots, K$$

and all $j \in J$. Then with probability $1 - o(1)$ over the choice of center to hash to in line 3 of BASICHASH *there exists $j \in J$ such that $\mathbf{h}(Sq + v^j) = \mathbf{h}(Sz)$.*

PROOF. Recall that if the event $\mathcal{E}^*(p,q)$ occurrs (see (2) and Claim 11), then for every perturbed point $S_l q + v_l^j$ one has

$$\left|\mathbb{B}_{R_l}(S_l q + v_l^j) \cap \mathcal{W}_l\right| \leq 2C \log N.$$

Thus, each perturbation $j \in J$ chooses w_l independently with probability at least $1/(2C \log N)$ for each $l = 1, \ldots, K$. By independence of these choices for different v_l^j's, at least one perturbation v^j, $j \in J$ is hashed to $\mathbf{h}(Sz)$ with probability at least

$$\begin{aligned}&1 - (1 - (2C \log N)^{-K})^{(2C \log N)^{2K}} \\ &\geq 1 - e^{-\Omega((2C \log N)^K)} = 1 - o(1).\end{aligned}$$

Since by Claim 11 one has $\mathbf{Pr}[\mathcal{E}^*(p, q)] \geq 1 - 1/N$, the result follows. □

We can now get

Proof of Lemma 19: Follows by putting together Lemma 21, Lemma 22 and Lemma 23. □

Acknowledgements

This research was supported by NSF award CCF-1065125, MADALGO center and Simons Foundation. We also acknowledge financial support from grant #FA9550-12-1-0411 from the U.S. Air Force Office of Scientific Research (AFOSR) and the Defense Advanced Research Projects Agency (DARPA).

6. REFERENCES

[AI] A. Andoni and P. Indyk. Near-optimal hashing algorithms for approximate nearest neighbor in high dimensions. In *FOCS'06*.

[AINR14] Alexandr Andoni, Piotr Indyk, Huy L. Nguyen, and Ilya Razenshteyn. Beyond locality-sensitive hashing. *SODA*, 2014.

[And09] Alexandr Andoni. *Nearest Neighbor Search: the Old, the New, and the Impossible.* Ph.D. Thesis, MIT, 2009.

[Ben75] J. Bentley. Multidimensional binary search trees used for associative searching. In *Comm. ACM*, 1975.

[Ber02] P. Berkhin. A survey of clustering data mining techniques. Springer, 2002.

[BGMN05] Franck Barthe, Olivier Guédon, Shahar Mendelson, and Assaf Naor. A probabilistic approach to the geometry of the l_p^n-ball. *The Annals of Probability*, 33:480–513, 2005.

[BKL06] A. Beygelzimer, S. Kakade, and J. Langford. Cover trees for nearest neighbors. In *ICML*, 2006.

[CH67] T. Cover and P. Hart. Nearest neighbour pattern classification. In *IEEE Trans. on Inf. Theory*, 1967.

[DDGR07] A. Das, M. Datar, A. Garg, and S. Rajaram. Google news personalization: Scalable online collaborative filtering. In *WWW*, 2007.

[DIIM04] Mayur Datar, Nicole Immorlica, Piotr Indyk, and Vahab S. Mirrokni. Locality-sensitive hashing scheme based on p-stable distributions. In *Symposium on Computational Geometry*, pages 253–262, 2004.

[GIM99] A. Gionis, P. Indyk, and R. Motwani. Similarity search in high dimensions via hashing. In *VLDB*, 1999.

[Gut84] A. Guttman. R-trees: a dynamic index structure for spatial searching. In *SIGMOD*, 1984.

[IM98] P. Indyk and R. Motwani. Approximate nearest neighbors: Towards removing the curse of dimensionality. In *STOC*, 1998.

[KG09] B. Kulis and K. Grauman. Kernelized locality-sensitive hashing for scalable image search. In *ICCV*, 2009.

[KL04] R. Krauthgamer and J. Lee. Navigating nets:simple algorithms for proximity search. In *SODA*, 2004.

[KOR98] E. Kushilevitz, R. Ostrovsky, and Y. Rabani. Efficient search of approximate nearest neighbor in high dimensional spaces. In *STOC*, 1998.

[KS97] N. Katayama and S. Satoh. The sr-tree: an index structure for high-dimensional nearest neighbor queries. In *SIGMOD*, 1997.

[LJW+07] Q. Lv, W. Josephson, Z. Wang, M. Charikar, and K. Li. Multi-probe lsh: Efficient indexing for high-dimensional similarity search. In *VLDB*, 2007.

[MNP06] R. Motwani, A. Naor, and R. Panigrahy. Lower bounds on locality sensitive hashing. In *SCG '06: Proceedings of the twenty-second annual symposium on Computational geometry*, pages 154–157, 2006.

[OWZ11] Ryan O'Donnell, Yi Wu, and Yuan Zhou. Optimal lower bounds for locality sensitive hashing (except when q is tiny). *ITCS*, 2011.

[Pan] Rina Panigrahy. Entropy based nearest neighbor search in high dimensions. In *SODA'06*.

[PTW] R. Panigrahy, K. Talwar, and U. Wieder. Lower bounds on near neighbor search via metric expansion. *FOCS'10*.

[PTW08] Rina Panigrahy, Kunal Talwar, and Udi Wieder. A geometric approach to lower bounds for approximate near-neighbor search and partial match. *FOCS*, pages 414–423, 2008.

[RR91] S. T. Rachev and L. Ruschendorf. Approximate independence of distributions on spheres and their stability properties. *The Annals of Probability*, 19(3):1311–1337, 07 1991.

[SZ90] G. Schechtman and J. Zinn. On the volume of intersection of two l_p balls. *Proc. Amer. Math. Soc.*, 110:217–224, 1990.

[WSB98] R. Weber, H. Schek, and S. Blott. A quantititative analysis and performance study for similarity search methods in high dimensional spaces. In *VLDB*, 1998.

APPENDIX

A. OMITTED PROOFS FROM SECTION 3

CLAIM 24. BASICHASH *can be implemented to run in expected time* $(C \log n) n^{O(n)}$.

PROOF. In order to implement BASICHASH it is sufficient, given input point x, to form a list $\{w_1, \ldots, w_Q\}$ of centers in $\mathcal{W}_l$ that belong to $\mathbb{B}_{R_l}(x)$, and output a uniformly random such center. To form the list, we consider the $T = (C \log N) n^{O(n)}$ shifted grids $u + \mathcal{G}$, $u \in \mathcal{U}_l$. For a fixed shift u, it is sufficient to round $x - u$ to the closest grid point (this can be done in $O(n)$ time), and check if this grid point is within Euclidean distance R_l of x. Thus, BASICHASH can be implemented in stated time. □

B. PROOF OF LEMMA 14

In this section we give a proof of Lemma 14. We use the notation $\mathbb{B}(0)$ for the unit ball in ℓ_2 norm. To estimate the intersection we will use the following results of [BGMN05].

THEOREM 25. *[BGMN05] Let* $X_i \sim \frac{1}{\sqrt{\pi}} e^{-x_i^2}$, *and let* $Y \sim e^{-y}$. *Then*

$$\left(\frac{X_1}{(|X_1|^2 + \ldots + |X_n|^2 + Y)^{1/2}}, \ldots, \right.$$
$$\left. , \ldots, \frac{X_n}{(|X_1|^2 + \ldots + |X_n|^2 + Y)^{1/2}} \right)$$

is uniformly distributed in $\mathbb{B}(0)$.

THEOREM 26. *([RR91, SZ90]; see also [BGMN05], Theorem 2) Let* $X_i \sim \frac{1}{\sqrt{\pi}} e^{-|x_i|^2}$. *Then the random vector*

$$\left(\frac{X_1}{(|X_1|^2 + \ldots + |X_n|^2)^{1/2}}, \ldots, \frac{X_n}{(|X_1|^2 + \ldots + |X_n|^2)^{1/2}} \right)$$

is independent of $(|X_1|^2 + \ldots + |X_n|^2)^{1/2}$.

In this section we derive an expression for a uniformly random point in $R \cdot \mathbb{B}(0)$, where $R^2 \sim \Gamma(n/2 + 1)$. By Theorem 25 sampling a uniformly random point from $R \cdot \mathbb{B}$ can be done as follows. Sample $X_1, \ldots, X_n \sim \frac{1}{\sqrt{\pi}} e^{-x^2}$, $Y \sim e^{-y}$ and $R^2 \sim \Gamma(n/2 + 1, 1)$ independently. Then

$$R \cdot \left(\frac{X_1}{(X_1^2 + \ldots + X_n^2 + Y)^{1/2}}, \ldots, \frac{X_n}{(X_1^2 + \ldots + X_n^2 + Y)^{1/2}} \right). \tag{21}$$

is a uniformly random point in $R \cdot \mathbb{B}_\epsilon(0)$. We now rewrite (21) as

$$\begin{aligned} R \cdot & \left(\frac{X_i}{(X_1^2 + \ldots + X_n^2 + Y)^{1/2}} \right)_{i=1}^n \\ &= \left(\frac{X_i}{(X_1^2 + \ldots + X_n^2)^{1/2}} \right)_{i=1}^n \cdot \frac{(X_1^2 + \ldots + X_n^2)^{1/2}}{(X_1^2 + \ldots + X_n^2 + Y)^{1/2}} \cdot R \\ &= \left(\frac{X_i}{(X_1^2 + \ldots + X_n^2)^{1/2}} \right)_{i=1}^n \cdot \frac{1}{(1 + Y/(X_1^2 + \ldots + X_n^2))^{1/2}} \cdot R \\ &= V \cdot \frac{1}{(1 + Q)^{1/2}} \cdot R, \end{aligned} \tag{22}$$

where

$$V = \left(\frac{X_i}{(X_1^2 + \ldots + X_n^2)^{1/2}} \right)_{i=1}^n \in \mathbb{R}^n,$$

and

$$Q = Y/(X_1^2 + \ldots + X_n^2).$$

By Theorem 26 V is independent of $X_1^2 + \ldots + X_n^2$. In particular, since R is sampled independently of (V, Q), this implies that V, Q, R are independent. Let μ denote the distribution of Q.

We now prove

LEMMA 27. *Let* $X_i \sim \frac{1}{\sqrt{\pi}} e^{-x^2}$, $i = 1, \ldots, n$. *Let* Y *be exponential with mean* 1. *Let* $R = (X_1^2 + \ldots + X_n^2 + Y)^{1/2}$. *Then*

$$(X_1, \ldots, X_n)$$

is uniformly distributed in the ball $R \cdot \mathbb{B}(0)$.

PROOF. We have

$$\begin{aligned} (X_i)_{i=1}^n &= \left(\frac{X_i}{(X_1^2 + \ldots + X_n^2)^{1/2}} \right)_{i=1}^n \cdot \left(\frac{X_1^2 + \ldots + X_n^2}{X_1^2 + \ldots + X_n^2 + Y} \right)^{1} \\ & \cdot (X_1^2 + \ldots + X_n^2 + Y)^{1/2} \\ &= \left(\frac{X_i}{X_1^2 + \ldots + X_n^2} \right)_{i=1}^n \cdot \left(\frac{1}{1 + Y/(X_1^2 + \ldots + X_n^2)} \right)^{1/} \\ & \cdot (X_1^2 + \ldots + X_n^2 + Y)^{1/2} \\ &= V \cdot \left(\frac{1}{1 + Q'} \right)^{1/2} \cdot R. \end{aligned} \tag{23}$$

Note that $Q' \sim \mu$ if we do not condition on R. Furthermore, $R^2 \sim \Gamma(n/2+1, 1)$ by Claim 7 and the additivity property of the Γ distribution, so R has the correct distribution as well. Hence, it is sufficient to show that V, Q', R are independent. First, V is independent of $X_1^2 + \ldots + X_n^2$ by Theorem 26, and independent of Y by definition. Thus, since Q' is a function of $X_1^2 + \ldots + X_n^2$ and Y, V is independent of (Q', R). It remains to show that Q' is independent of R.

Let $Z^2 = X_1^2 + \ldots + X_n^2$. Note that $Z^2 \sim \Gamma(n/2, 1)$ and $Y \sim \Gamma(1, 1)$. We now compute the distribution of Y/Z^2 conditional on $Y + Z^2 = R^2$:

$$\begin{aligned} & \mathbf{Pr}[Y/Z^2 \geq \alpha | Y + Z^2 = R^2] \\ &= \frac{\int_{R^2\alpha/(1+\alpha)}^{R^2} e^{-y}(R^2 - y)^{n/2-1} e^{-(R^2-y)} dy}{\int_0^{R^2} e^{-y}(R^2 - y)^{n/2-1} e^{-(R^2-y)} dy} \\ &= \frac{\int_{R^2\alpha/(1+\alpha)}^{R^2} (R^2 - y)^{n/2-1} dy}{\int_0^{R^2} (R^2 - y)^{n/2-1} dy} \\ &= \frac{(R^2 - R^2\alpha/(1+\alpha))^{n/2}}{(R^2)^{n/2}} = (1+\alpha)^{-n/2}, \end{aligned} \tag{24}$$

which is independent of R. Thus, V, Q', R are independent, which completes the proof.

□

Proof of Lemma 14: Follows by Lemma 27 and Claim 7.
□

Erratum for: Approximating and Testing k-Histogram Distributions in Sub-linear Time

Piotr Indyk
CSAIL, MIT, Cambridge MA 02139.
indyk@theory.lcs.mit.edu

Reut Levi
Ècole Normale Supèrieure and Universitè Paris Diderot, France
reuti.levi@gmail.com

Ronitt Rubinfeld
CSAIL, MIT, Cambridge MA 02139 and the Blavatnik School of Computer Science, Tel Aviv University.
ronitt@csail.mit.edu

This is an erratum for our PODS 2012 paper "Approximating and Testing k-Histogram Distributions in Sub-linear Time" [ILR12]. We made a mistake in the final accounting of the running time in Theorem 2 in Subsection 3.1. The running time is $\tilde{O}((k^5/\epsilon^4)\ln^2 n)$ and not $\tilde{O}((k/\epsilon)^2 \ln n)$ as stated in the theorem. As noted in the proof of the theorem we decrease the number of iterations in Step (7) from $\binom{n}{2}$ to at most $\binom{3\ell+1}{2}$ which is $\tilde{O}((k/\epsilon)^4 \ln^2 n)$. Since the number of iterations of the outer loop is $O(k\ln(1/\epsilon))$, we obtain that the total running time is $\tilde{O}((k^5/\epsilon^4)\ln^2 n)$. The sample complexity remains $\tilde{O}((k/\epsilon)^2 \ln n)$ as stated in the theorem.

The corrected version of the paper has been posted as an ECCC Technical Report TR11-171, Revision 1 [ILR11].

Acknowledgments

We would like to thank Jerry Li who brought this issue to our attention.

The original paper appeared in the Proceedings of the 31st Symposium on Principles of Database Systems. DOI link: http://doi.acm.org/10.1145/2213556.2213561.

SIGMOD'15, May 31–June 4, 2015, Melbourne, Victoria, Australia.

ACM 978-1-4503-2758-9/15/05 ...$15.00.
http://dx.doi.org/10.1145/2745754.2745784.

1. REFERENCES

[ILR11] Piotr Indyk, Reut Levi, and Ronitt Rubinfeld. Approximating and testing k-histogram distributions in sub-linear time. *Electronic Colloquium on Computational Complexity (ECCC)*, 18:171, 2011.

[ILR12] Piotr Indyk, Reut Levi, and Ronitt Rubinfeld. Approximating and testing k-histogram distributions in sub-linear time. In *Proceedings of the 31st ACM SIGMOD-SIGACT-SIGART Symposium on Principles of Database Systems, PODS 2012, Scottsdale, AZ, USA, May 20-24, 2012*, pages 15–22, 2012.

Author Index

www.ingramcontent.com/pod-product-compliance
Lightning Source LLC
Chambersburg PA
CBHW080907220326
41598CB00034B/5505
* 9 7 8 1 4 5 0 3 3 8 6 5 3 *